The World Book Encyclopedia

L Volume 12

World Book, Inc.

a Scott Fetzer company

Chicago London Sydney Toronto

The World Book Encyclopedia

Copyright © 1987, U.S.A.
by
World Book, Inc.

Ll

L is the 12th letter of our alphabet. It was also a letter in the alphabet used by the Semites, who once lived in Syria and Palestine. They named it *lamed*, their word for *goad*, or *crooked staff*. They adapted an Egyptian hieroglyphic, or picture symbol, for goad, to represent the letter. The ancient Greeks took the letter into their alphabet and called it *lambda*. Later, the Romans borrowed it from the Greek alphabet and gave the letter its present capital L form. See ALPHABET.

Uses. L or l is the 11th most frequently used letter in books, newspapers, and other printed material in English. L is the Roman numeral for *50*. When it is written with the crossbar, as £, it is the sign for pound in English money, and comes from the Latin word *libra*, or *pound*. In physics, L stands for *length*, as it does in most measurement formulas. In geography, L indicates *longitude*, and l stands for *latitude*. The l also stands for *lira* in Italian money; for *leaf* in describing books, and for *left* as in *l.f.*, or *left field;* and for *lower* as in *l.c.*, or *lower case*, a term used in typography and journalism.

Pronunciation. In English, l is pronounced by placing the tongue on the edge of the lower front teeth and with its sides free. The velum, or soft palate, is closed, and the vocal cords are vibrated with the breath.

L is silent in words such as *would*, *salmon*, or *half*. In Mexican and other American Spanish dialects, ll is pronounced as *y* is pronounced in English. See PRONUNCIATION.　　　　　　　　　　　MARIANNE COOLEY

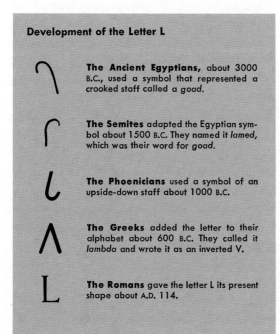

Development of the Letter L

The Ancient Egyptians, about 3000 B.C., used a symbol that represented a crooked staff called a *goad*.

The Semites adapted the Egyptian symbol about 1500 B.C. They named it *lamed*, which was their word for *goad*.

The Phoenicians used a symbol of an upside-down staff about 1000 B.C.

The Greeks added the letter to their alphabet about 600 B.C. They called it *lambda* and wrote it as an inverted V.

The Romans gave the letter L its present shape about A.D. 114.

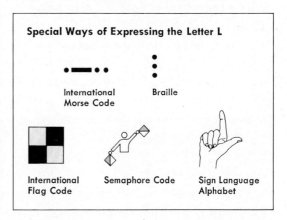

The Small Letter l appeared during the A.D. 500's. Writers gradually dropped the horizontal stroke, and, by the 800's, the letter had developed its present shape.

A.D. 500　　　800　　　Today

Special Ways of Expressing the Letter L

International Morse Code

Braille

International Flag Code

Semaphore Code

Sign Language Alphabet

Common Forms of the Letter L

Handwritten Letters vary from person to person. *Manuscript* (printed) letters, *left*, have simple curves and straight lines. Cursive letters, *right*, have flowing lines.

Roman Letters have small finishing strokes called *serifs* that extend from the main strokes. The type face shown above is Baskerville. The italic form appears at the right.

Sans-Serif Letters are also called *gothic letters*. They have no serifs. The type face shown above is called Futura. The italic form of Futura appears at the right.

Computer Letters have special shapes. Computers can "read" these letters either optically or by means of the magnetic ink with which the letters may be printed.

1

LABELING

LABELING. See Bar Coding; Consumerism; Pure Food and Drug Laws; Union Label.

LABIUM, *LAY bee uhm,* is the lower lip of an insect. A pair of *maxillae* (membrane bones or appendages), joined in the middle, form the labium. The labium closes the insect's mouth and helps it to retain food. It also helps the insect move its food around in its mouth while chewing. See also Insect (Mouth Parts).

LABOR, in birth. See Childbirth.

LABOR, in economics. See Labor Movement.

LABOR, DEPARTMENT OF, is an executive department of the United States government. The secretary of labor, a member of the President's Cabinet, heads the department. The Department of Labor administers and enforces laws that seek to promote the welfare of U.S. wage earners, to improve their working conditions, and to advance their opportunities for employment.

Functions. The Department of Labor administers federal laws on child labor, agricultural labor, minimum wages, overtime, and public contracts. It develops standards and policies for promoting the welfare of workers. It carries out federal laws on workers' compensation programs, and handles appeals from federal workers regarding compensation. It develops apprenticeship standards for the training of skilled workers. The department administers laws dealing with the election of labor union officers and with union financial reports. It also regulates private pension and welfare plans. In addition, the department enforces federal regulations requiring businesses doing government work to take affirmative action and to ensure nondiscriminatory hiring and employment practices. These regulations are designed to promote equal employment opportunity for minorities, women, handicapped people, and disabled and Vietnam War veterans.

The department serves as the government's chief fact-finding agency in labor economics. It collects, analyzes, and publishes information on employment and unemployment, wages and industrial relations, occupational safety and health, price trends, productivity and technology, and economic growth and employment projections. It protects the safety and health of workers by enforcing standards that it develops. It also administers the

Secretaries of Labor

Name	Took Office	Under President
William B. Wilson	1913	Wilson
James J. Davis	1921	Harding, Coolidge, Hoover
William N. Doak	1930	Hoover
*Frances Perkins	1933	F. D. Roosevelt, Truman
Lewis B. Schwellenbach	1945	Truman
Maurice J. Tobin	1948	Truman
Martin P. Durkin	1953	Eisenhower
James P. Mitchell	1953	Eisenhower
*Arthur J. Goldberg	1961	Kennedy
W. Willard Wirtz	1962	Kennedy, L. B. Johnson
*George P. Shultz	1969	Nixon
James D. Hodgson	1970	Nixon
Peter J. Brennan	1973	Nixon, Ford
John T. Dunlop	1975	Ford
W. J. Usery, Jr.	1976	Ford
Ray Marshall	1977	Carter
Raymond J. Donovan	1981	Reagan
William E. Brock III	1985	Reagan

*Has a separate biography in WORLD BOOK.

public employment service and the unemployment insurance programs and promotes the interests of U.S. workers in international affairs. The Department of Labor also administers the Job Training Partnership Act of 1982. Under this act, local governments receive federal funds to establish training programs that provide the disadvantaged and unemployed with job skills.

The Secretary of Labor is appointed by the President subject to the approval of the Senate. The secretary establishes policies for the department and is the President's chief adviser on labor matters.

The undersecretary of labor is the secretary's chief assistant. The undersecretary directs the department in the secretary's absence. Other leading members of the staff include eight assistant secretaries, a commissioner of labor statistics, and a *solicitor* (chief legal officer).

Organization. The Department of Labor has headquarters in Washington, D.C. The department consists of various administrations and bureaus.

The assistant secretary for employment and training directs the Employment and Training Administration, which includes the U.S. Employment Service, Un-

Department of Labor

Department of Labor Headquarters are at 200 Constitution Avenue NW, Washington, DC 20210.

Department of Labor

The Department of Labor works to promote the welfare of American workers. The department seal includes an anvil, pulley, lever, inclined plane, and plow. The anvil represents manufacturing industries, and the plow stands for agricultural industries. The pulley, lever, and inclined plane symbolize the use of inventions to make work easier. All machinery, no matter how complex, is based on the principles employed by these simple devices.

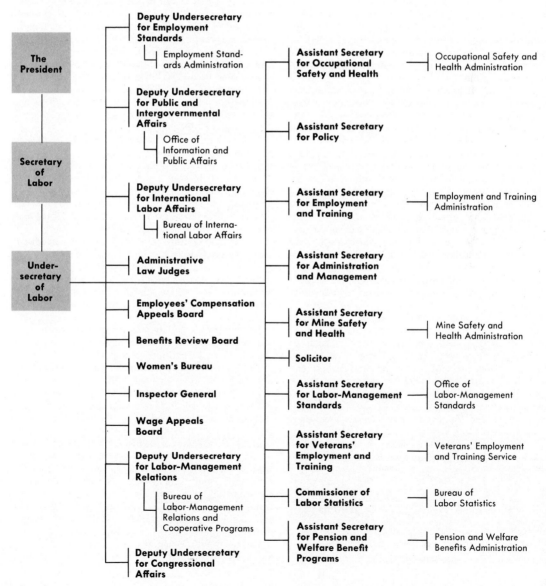

employment Insurance Service, Bureau of Apprenticeship and Training, and the Work Incentive (WIN) program. It also includes job training and employment programs authorized by the Job Training Partnership Act. The deputy undersecretary for employment standards directs the Employment Standards Administration, which includes the Office of Federal Contract Compliance Programs, the Office of Workers' Compensation Programs, and the Wage and Hour Division.

The assistant secretary for labor-management standards supervises the Office of Labor-Management Standards, which administers laws affecting certain union activities. The Pension and Welfare Benefits Administration, headed by an assistant secretary, oversees pension and welfare benefit programs under the Employee Retirement Income Security Act of 1974. This act, often called ERISA, sets minimum standards for the funding and operation of private pension and welfare plans. The assistant secretary for occupational safety and health directs the Occupational Safety and Health Administration, which develops and enforces job safety and health standards for most industries. The assistant secretary for mine safety and health administers programs to reduce health hazards and the frequency and severity of accidents in the mining industry.

The Women's Bureau promotes employment opportunities for women in the labor force. The inspector general conducts investigations to determine whether department programs use public money efficiently and effectively. The department also has an assistant secretary for administration and management, an assistant secretary for policy, an assistant secretary for veterans' employment and training, a deputy undersecretary for labor-management relations, a deputy undersecretary for public and intergovernmental affairs, and a deputy undersecretary for congressional affairs.

The commissioner of labor statistics directs the Bureau of Labor Statistics. The deputy undersecretary for international affairs directs the Bureau of International Labor Affairs. The bureau helps plan U.S. foreign economic policy and participates in trade negotiations. It also provides technical assistance to developing countries.

History. On June 27, 1884, Congress established a Bureau of Labor in the Department of the Interior. In 1888, Congress gave the bureau independent status as the Department of Labor. In 1903, Congress established the new Department of Commerce and Labor, and made the Department of Labor a bureau in it.

On March 4, 1913, the President signed a law creating an independent Department of Labor. The department was the first Cabinet office to have a woman as its head, when Frances Perkins became secretary of labor in 1933. Critically reviewed by the DEPARTMENT OF LABOR

Related Articles in WORLD BOOK include:

Employment Service, United States	Labor Statistics, Bureau of
Fair Labor Standards Act	Occupational Safety and Health Administration
Flag (picture: Flags of the United States Government)	Unemployment Insurance
	Wages and Hours
Job Corps	Women's Bureau

LABOR, DIVISION OF. See MASS PRODUCTION; TRADE (Trade and Specialization).

LABOR, KNIGHTS OF. See KNIGHTS OF LABOR.

LABOR DAY is a holiday honoring working people. It is observed as a legal holiday on the first Monday in September throughout the United States, Puerto Rico, and Canada. Labor organizations sponsor various celebrations, but for most persons it is a day of rest and recreation. It also has become a symbol of the end of summer. In Australia, Labor Day is called *Eight Hour Day*, and commemorates the successful struggle for a shorter working day. In Europe, Labor Day is observed on May 1.

Two men have been credited with suggesting a holiday to honor working people in the United States— Matthew Maguire, a machinist from Paterson, N.J., and Peter J. McGuire, a New York City carpenter who helped found the United Brotherhood of Carpenters and Joiners. Both men played an important part in staging the first Labor Day parade in New York City in September 1882. In 1887, Oregon became the first state to make Labor Day a legal holiday. President Grover Cleveland signed a bill in 1894 making Labor Day a national holiday. ELIZABETH HOUGH SECHRIST

LABOR FORCE is the segment of a nation's population that works for pay or is actively seeking work. This group produces most of the nation's goods and services, and its size and productivity determine the nation's economic growth. The labor force of the United States expanded from about 2 million in 1800 to about 115 million in the mid-1980's. This growth helped transform the United States from a largely agricultural country to an advanced industrial nation.

The United States government uses the term *labor force* for people at least 16 years old who have civilian jobs or are actively looking for jobs, or who are in the armed forces. Groups not in the labor force include disabled persons, full-time homemakers, retired people, and students. The labor force also does not include discouraged jobseekers who have stopped looking for work because they think none is available.

The United Nations (UN) uses the term *economically active population* instead of *labor force*. The economically active population consists of people of all ages who are employed or looking for jobs. The percentages of teenagers and old people in this group are much higher in many developing countries than they are in industrial nations.

Economists use the term *human resources* for the total number of men and women available to work if needed. During a war, for example, many people not normally in the labor force take jobs in war plants and other industries.

Changes in the Labor Force since 1900 include differences in sex, age, and occupational makeup. In 1900, the labor force included only about 20 per cent of American women, compared with over 50 per cent in the mid-1980's. Most of the increase was among married women. Many women joined the labor force because of changing social attitudes, rising divorce rates, declining birth rates, and higher wages. Another cause of increased female employment was an increase in the number of *white-collar jobs*. These jobs include business, clerical, and professional positions, which many women choose.

During the same period, the percentage of men 65 and older who were in the labor force fell from about 65

Occupation Groups in the United States

Occupation Groups	Number of Employed Persons
White-collar workers	**57,933,000**
Clerical (bookkeepers, secretaries, typists, etc.)	16,908,000
Professional and technical (accountants, engineers, nurses, teachers, etc.)	16,616,000
Sales (brokers, insurance agents, salesclerks, etc.)	12,388,000
Managers, officials, and proprietors (private and government workers)	12,021,000
Blue-collar workers	**29,182,000**
Operatives (assemblers, butchers, riveters, truckdrivers, welders, etc.)	16,412,000
Craftworkers (carpenters, machinists, automobile mechanics, painters, etc.)	12,770,000
Service workers	**14,276,000**
Other than private household (barbers, cooks, hairdressers, janitors, police, etc.)	13,243,000
Private household workers (housekeepers, maids, etc.)	1,033,000
Farm, Forestry, and Fishing Workers	**2,953,000**
Other farm, forestry, and fishing workers (paid laborers, unpaid family workers, etc.)	1,614,000
Farmers and farm managers (full and part owners, tenants, etc.)	1,339,000
Total workers	**104,344,000**

Source: *Employment and Earnings*, February 1985, U.S. Bureau of Labor Statistics.

LABOR-MANAGEMENT REPORTING ACT

per cent to about 15 per cent. A major cause of this decline in the number of older men in the work force was the introduction of social security, which enabled many older men to retire. Compulsory retirement rules, plus job discrimination against the elderly, also pushed older men out of the labor force.

In 1900, white-collar workers made up about 20 per cent of the labor force, compared with about 55 per cent in the 1980's. The percentage of farmworkers dropped from about 40 per cent to less than 5 per cent during the same period. These changes resulted largely from increased technology, which boosted the demand for white-collar employees and reduced the need for agricultural workers.

The Government and the Labor Force. The U.S. government, through the Department of Labor, has various agencies and programs that promote full employment of the nation's labor force. For example, an agency called the United States Employment Service matches jobseekers with available positions. The Job Corps program provides work training for disadvantaged youths.

The main job program of the U.S. government is a revenue-sharing plan authorized by the Job Training Partnership Act of 1982. Under this law, state and local governments receive federal funds to provide job training for unskilled, disadvantaged youths and for needy adults. GERALD G. SOMERS

See also CAREERS (table: Annual Income in the United States by Amount of Education); UNEMPLOYMENT.

LABOR LEGISLATION. See LABOR MOVEMENT; CHILD LABOR; STRIKE; WORKERS' COMPENSATION.

LABOR-MANAGEMENT RELATIONS. See INDUSTRIAL RELATIONS.

LABOR-MANAGEMENT REPORTING AND DISCLOSURE ACT. See LABOR MOVEMENT (Charges of Corruption).

Men and Women in the United States Labor Force

Total labor force (including armed forces)*

Year	Men in Labor Force	Male Percentage of Labor Force	Women in Labor Force	Female Percentage of Labor Force
1890	18,129,000	83%	3,704,000	17%
1900	22,641,000	82%	4,999,000	18%
1910	†	†	†	†
1920	32,053,000	80%	8,229,000	20%
1930	37,008,000	78%	10,396,000	22%
1940	42,020,000	75%	14,160,000	25%
1950	45,446,000	71%	18,412,000	29%
1960	48,870,000	68%	23,272,000	32%
1970	54,343,000	63%	31,560,000	37%
1980	62,088,000	58%	44,733,000	42%
1984	65,386,000	57%	49,855,000	43%

*1890-1946, persons 14 years old and over; since 1947, persons 16 years old and over.
†Not available.

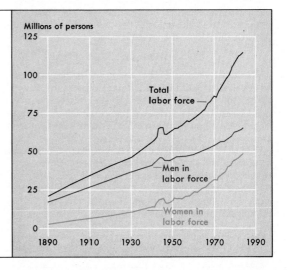

Source: U.S. Bureau of Labor Statistics.

LABOR MOVEMENT

LABOR MOVEMENT is a term that refers to the efforts of workers as a group to improve their economic position. The movement consists chiefly of attempts by labor unions to promote the welfare of wage earners. But political parties and other groups have also played a part in the labor movement.

Before the development of unions, individual laborers had almost no voice in determining their wages, hours, or working conditions. There was a plentiful supply of labor, and employers could easily replace anyone who threatened to quit. The competition for jobs forced poor people to work under almost any conditions.

Workers formed unions because their bargaining power as a group was greater than that of individuals. If all the employees in a factory or other business stopped work, it would be difficult to replace them. But early unions faced strong opposition. Courts regarded the first attempts at group bargaining as illegal, and employers refused to recognize unions as the representatives of workers.

In the United States, the labor movement began to be more widely accepted during the 1930's. The National Labor Relations Act of 1935 and other laws required employers to bargain with unions. Today, organized labor is one of the most powerful economic forces in the world. About a fourth of the nonagricultural workers in the United States are represented by unions. The highest percentage of union members are in construction, manufacturing, mining, and transportation industries. During the 1960's and 1970's, the union movement began to spread to new groups of workers, including government employees and farm laborers.

The labor movement has given workers a higher standard of living than ever before. Compared to past laborers, modern workers earn higher wages, work shorter hours, are better protected against accidents, and receive more fringe benefits. However, some people believe that unions have become too large and too powerful.

In the United States and Canada, union goals and activities are much alike. The labor movement in most other countries differs greatly from that in these two nations. Most of the sections of this article deal with the labor movement in the United States.

What Labor Unions Do

The chief aims of a labor union are to improve the wages, hours, working conditions, and job security of its members. Usually, the first step for any union is to get workers to join it. After a union has become established in a plant or industry, its major functions are arranging labor contracts and handling job disputes. Labor groups help provide apprenticeship programs and other benefits for their members. Unions are also concerned with political activities and public relations.

Organizing Workers is the process of bringing wage earners together into a union. In some cases, the workers themselves form a union to increase their bargaining

power. But in most cases, an existing union decides to organize the employees of a particular plant or industry. The union sends men and women called *organizers* to persuade workers to join.

Most unions insist on being the sole representative of a particular group of employees. They do not want to share the privilege of representing the workers with any other group. This practice is called the *principle of exclusive jurisdiction*. The National Labor Relations Board conducts secret-ballot elections at firms engaged in *interstate commerce* (trade across state lines) to determine which union workers want, if any.

A union tries to get all the workers in a plant or industry to join the union. In some establishments, the union and the employer agree to set up a *union shop*. In a union shop, the employer can hire anyone. But new employees must join the union within a certain period or pay the equivalent of union dues. This arrangement spreads the cost of union representation evenly among the employees, who also share any benefits the union wins. But individuals who oppose the union must contribute to it against their wishes. Twenty-one states, most of them in the South, have laws banning union shops. Such laws are called *right-to-work laws* because they guarantee a person's right to obtain employment without joining or supporting a union.

A business that employs both union and nonunion workers is called an *open shop*. Union dues are higher in most open shops than in union shops because fewer people share the cost of union representation. In a *closed shop*, which is now generally illegal, the employer could hire only union members.

During the 1800's and early 1900's, many employers insisted that their workers sign a promise not to join a union. Such an agreement was called a *yellow-dog contract*. The Norris-La Guardia Act of 1932 said that an employee could not be sued in federal court for breaking a yellow-dog contract. As a result, such agreements became unenforceable and gradually disappeared.

Arranging Contracts. Labor's goals are often different from those of management. Higher wages and most other benefits increase costs, and management usually wants to reduce costs in order to earn a larger profit. The two sides settle their differences and establish conditions that are acceptable to both through a process called *collective bargaining*.

In a typical bargaining session, union representatives make demands and management then makes a counteroffer that meets some, but not all, of the union's demands. The two sides then try to work out a compromise. The bargainers may call in outside experts to help, including lawyers, economists, and industrial engineers. Many meetings also include state or federal government representatives to help settle disagreements. The results of the bargaining go into a written contract.

Usually, contract talks begin several months before the existing agreement comes to an end. Some unions have a *no contract-no work* rule and stop work if their contract expires before a new one is signed.

A labor contract describes in detail the arrangements concerning wages, hours, and other terms of employment. Some of the most important matters covered are (1) union security, (2) wages and hours, (3) fringe benefits, (4) seniority, (5) safety measures, and (6) the handling of grievances.

Mark Perlman, the contributor of this article, is University Professor of Economics at the University of Pittsburgh.

At the Bargaining Table, representatives of management, *left,* and labor, *right,* meet to establish conditions of employment that are acceptable to both sides. This process is called *collective bargaining.*

Union Security is a term for the part of a labor contract that provides for the position and rights of the union. Most agreements begin by stating that management recognizes the union as sole bargaining agent for a specific group of employees. In some cases, the employer agrees to deduct union dues from the pay of members. This arrangement, called a *checkoff,* is easier for the union than collecting from individual members. Most contracts also include rules about whether union officials can meet with employees during working hours. Other union security agreements cover whether the plant is a union or open shop and what kinds of union business can be conducted on company time.

Wages and Hours. Nearly all labor contracts specify wage rates either by the hour or by the number of goods produced. Some agreements also guarantee employees a minimum number of hours of work.

Contracts also cover overtime pay. Federal law requires that firms engaged in interstate commerce pay overtime for any work that exceeds 40 hours per week. The overtime rate must be at least one and a half times the usual pay. Some companies pay overtime for work over 30 or 35 hours a week. Under certain circum-stances, the overtime rate may be as much as three times the normal rate.

Many labor contracts last for two or three years. A general rise in prices during this period will cause the workers' purchasing power to drop. To make up for this loss of buying power, many agreements include a provision called an *escalator clause.* Such a clause provides for automatic wage increases as prices rise. The changes are often tied to the Consumer Price Index, a figure reported by the federal government (see Cost of Living).

Fringe Benefits developed during World War II (1939-1945), when the federal government prohibited nearly all wage increases. War industries attracted workers by offering benefits in addition to wages. For example, many employers paid part of the cost of food served in their cafeterias. Later, companies also furnished medical insurance, life insurance, accident and disability insurance, and college tuition for workers and their families.

Since then, fringe benefits have grown in importance. Employers have introduced new benefits, including free dental care and company stock purchase plans. Unions often accept fringe benefits instead of higher pay be-

The Settlement of Labor Disputes

These drawings show some of the steps that labor and management take as they attempt to settle disputes over wages, hours, and other issues.

Union bargainers make demands, and management makes an offer that meets some, but not all, of the demands.

If the two sides cannot agree, they call in a neutral third party called a *mediator* to suggest solutions to the dispute.

If mediation fails, a specialist called an *arbitrator* hears the case and delivers a decision that is binding on both sides.

cause most benefits are not subject to income tax.

Seniority refers to employees' rights based on length of service. To most workers, the provision defining and protecting seniority is one of the most important parts of a contract. Detailed rules specify how seniority is acquired. It may be based on how long a worker has served in a particular job, department, or plant. If the company must lay off any workers, it first dismisses employees with the least seniority.

Safety Measures. Some labor contracts include minimum safety standards for factories and other workplaces. The rules deal with fire prevention, protective clothing and railings, and other safety matters.

The Handling of Grievances. Most work agreements specify a series of steps that can be used to handle a worker *grievance* (complaint). An employee with a grievance discusses the matter with his or her supervisor. In most cases, a union representative accompanies the worker. Nearly all problems end at this level. If the matter is not resolved, the worker may file a complaint with a higher level of management. If the employee is still not satisfied, he or she may request a neutral third party to deliver a decision.

Handling Labor Disputes. Most disputes between unions and management involve wages, hours, or other conditions of employment. If labor and management cannot settle their differences, they may receive outside help called *mediation*. If the two sides still cannot agree, they may submit to a process called *arbitration*. A person called an arbitrator hears the evidence and hands down a decision that is binding on both sides. Unless it has a no-strike agreement, the union may call a strike to press its demands at any time during the dispute.

Unions—or the workers themselves, against union advice—may use several methods other than a strike to press their demands. For example, they may order a *slowdown*—that is, a deliberate reduction in the rate of production. A union may refuse to deal with a firm and urge the public not to buy its products. This action is called a *boycott*. Large numbers of workers may call in sick. Government employees sometimes use this tactic in states where the law forbids them to strike. For example, police officers may threaten an outbreak of "blue flu" to protest job conditions.

Mediation and Arbitration. In mediation, a neutral third party called a *mediator* suggests solutions to the dispute. Neither side is required to accept the recom-

AFL-CIO

A Picket Line patrols the entrance of a factory, office, or store where workers are on strike. A strike or the threat of a strike is a main bargaining weapon of organized labor.

mendations, however. Sometimes, labor and management ask for help from a local citizen whom both sides respect and trust. However, most disputes that require mediation go to a government agency called the Federal Mediation and Conciliation Service or to a similar state agency. If mediation fails, the two sides may enter into binding arbitration (see ARBITRATION).

A special agency called the National Mediation Board settles disputes in the railway and airline industries. Congress established the agency in 1934, when railway unions were strong and railroad strikes could cripple the economy. The board later received authority to deal with airline disputes as well.

The National Labor Relations Board also helps settle some labor disputes. If an individual, employer, or union files charges of unfair labor practices, the board investigates and corrects the situation if necessary.

Strikes occur when workers feel such action is the best way to pressure their employer into granting their demands. Before a union calls a strike, it must put the question to a vote by its members. In most unions, a

The Handling of Grievances

Most labor contracts specify a series of steps that can be used to handle a worker *grievance* (complaint). These drawings show one common grievance procedure.

WORLD BOOK illustrations by David Cunningham

An employee with a grievance explains the problem to the union representative in his or her department.

Together, the worker and the union representative discuss the matter with the employee's supervisor.

Nearly all problems end at this stage. An employee who is still not satisfied may appeal to a higher level of management.

strike cannot be called unless a majority of those voting support such action.

There are several kinds of strikes. In the most common type, called a *strike* or *walkout*, the employees as a group leave work or refuse to come to work. The union organizes small groups of strikers, called *pickets*, to patrol the entrances to the factory, office, or store. The pickets form a *picket line* and carry signs announcing the strike. Members of nonstriking unions usually refuse to cross a picket line. The pickets try to prevent other employees from working and the public from doing business with the company. Strikers call individuals who work during a strike *scabs* or *blacklegs*.

Another type of dispute is a *sit-down strike*, in which the strikers stop work but continue to occupy the facilities. Their action prevents management from bringing in replacements called *strikebreakers*. A *sympathy strike* is a work stoppage by employees who are not directly involved in a dispute. They strike to show support of another group of workers. A similar action is a *secondary boycott*, in which nonstriking workers refuse to handle goods produced by a company whose employees are on strike. A work stoppage by all the laborers in a community, region, or country is called a *general strike*. A *wildcat strike* is one started by a group of workers or by local union officials without authorization from the national union. Such actions are also called *outlaw strikes* or *quickie strikes*. A *jurisdictional strike* is a struggle between two rival unions for the right to represent a group of workers or to handle a job.

Many strikes succeed during periods of low unemployment and prosperous economic conditions. During periods of high unemployment and less prosperity, more strikes fail. Workers can no longer afford the loss of income, and they may return to work without winning any of their demands. Many unions maintain a strike fund to provide small payments to striking members. *Lockouts* are management's own version of a strike. In a lockout, the company refuses to let employees work until they accept its terms.

Wide World

A Union Hiring Hall is a facility where members report for job openings. Such employment services are common in shipping and other industries where workers are hired by the day or the week.

Conducting Apprenticeship Programs. Apprenticeship is a formal system of training young people for skilled trades, such as bricklaying and printing. Unions in these trades conduct apprenticeship programs in cooperation with employers and vocational high schools. The training combines on-the-job experience with individual or classroom instruction.

Other Union Activities. Some unions provide facilities called *hiring halls* where members report for job openings. Such hiring is common in the building trades, shipping, and other industries where workers are employed by the day or week.

A number of labor organizations operate vacation resorts or other recreational centers for members and their families at low cost. Some groups have credit unions, which lend money at low interest rates to members. A few labor unions form purchasing cooperatives to buy goods in large quantities at low prices.

Many labor organizations provide educational programs dealing with economics, the history of the labor movement, or other subjects. A number of groups offer college scholarships for members and their children.

Labor unions spend large sums of money on education and advertising to convince people of the importance of their goals. Many organizations employ public relations experts to help win favorable public opinion. Unions also do community service. For example, they may conduct blood donation or fund-raising drives.

Political activities are also an important part of the labor movement. Union officials urge workers and their families to vote for candidates they consider sympathetic to union goals. Because of the ability of union leaders to influence votes, most elected officials listen carefully to what labor leaders want. In this way, organized labor influences the city, state, and federal government.

Types of Unions

People often divide labor unions into two chief types: (1) craft unions and (2) industrial unions. A craft union is made up of skilled workers in a particular craft or trade, such as carpentry or plumbing. The members of the union may work in many different industries. An industrial union is made up of both skilled and unskilled workers in the same industry, such as the automobile or steel industry. When a craft union bargains with an employer, it speaks for only part of the firm's workers—for example, the electricians or the bricklayers. When an industrial union bargains, it speaks for all the workers in the company except management personnel.

The members of craft unions tend to be better educated and more highly trained than members of industrial unions. Most craft unions are unified because the members share common training and interests.

Industrial unions tend to have larger memberships than craft unions. Most also have greater bargaining power, because all the workers in a plant will respond if the union calls a strike. But the large membership may cause problems if different groups of workers within the union develop conflicting interests.

Most labor experts think it is misleading to divide unions into craft and industrial unions because few groups are purely one or the other. The same union

Important United States Labor Unions*

Name	Membership
†Amalgamated Clothing and Textile Workers Union	380,000
†American Federation of State, County and Municipal Employees	1,200,000
†American Federation of Teachers	580,000
Bakery, Confectionery and Tobacco Workers' International Union	155,000
Boilermakers, Iron Shipbuilders, Blacksmiths, Forgers and Helpers, International Brotherhood of	145,000
Bricklayers and Allied Craftsmen, International Union of	135,000
Bridge, Structural and Ornamental Iron Workers, International Association of	183,000
†Carpenters and Joiners of America, United Brotherhood of	800,000
Communications Workers of America	650,000
Electrical, Radio, and Machine Workers of America, United (Ind.)	163,000
†Electrical Workers, International Brotherhood of	1,000,000
Electronic, Electrical, Technical, Salaried, and Machine Workers, International Union of	190,000
†Engineers, International Union of Operating	420,000
Fire Fighters, International Association of	170,000
†Garment Workers' Union, International Ladies'	283,000
Government Employees, American Federation of	300,000
Government Employees, National Association of (Ind.)	195,000
Graphic Communications International Union	200,000
†Hotel Employees and Restaurant Employees International Union	370,000
†Laborers' International Union of North America	560,000
Letter Carriers of the United States of America, National Association of	250,000
†Machinists and Aerospace Workers, International Association of	837,900

Name	Membership
Maintenance of Way Employees, Brotherhood of	100,000
†Musicians, American Federation of	300,000
Office and Professional Employees International Union	135,000
Oil, Chemical and Atomic Workers International Union	125,000
Painters and Allied Trades, International Brotherhood of	193,000
Paperworkers International Union, United	400,000
Plumbing and Pipe Fitting Industry of the U.S. and Canada, United Association of Journeymen and Apprentices of the	350,000
Postal Workers Union, American	300,000
Railway, Airline, and Steamship Clerks, Freight Handlers, Express and Station Employees, Brotherhood of	200,000
Retail, Wholesale and Department Store Union	225,000
Rubber, Cork, Linoleum and Plastic Workers of America, United	130,000
Service Employees International Union	650,000
Sheet Metal Workers' International Association	160,000
†Steelworkers of America, United	1,000,000
†Teamsters, Chauffeurs, Warehousemen and Helpers of America, International Brotherhood of (Ind.)	1,900,000
Transit Union, Amalgamated	160,000
Transport Workers Union of America	150,000
Transportation Union, United	246,000
Typographical Union, International	80,000
†United Automobile, Aerospace and Agricultural Implement Workers of America, International Union	1,100,000
†United Farm Workers of America	100,000
†United Food and Commercial Workers International Union	1,300,000
†United Mine Workers of America (Ind.)	245,000
Woodworkers of America, International	115,000

*Union is AFL-CIO affiliate unless indicated as Independent (Ind.).
†Has a separate article in THE WORLD BOOK ENCYCLOPEDIA.

Source: Encyclopedia of Associations: 1985, © 1984 by Gale Research Company; reprinted by permission of the publisher.

may function as a craft union in some branches of an industry and as an industrial union in others. For example, the United Food and Commercial Workers International Union serves as a craft union for skilled butchers in stores. But it is an industrial union in the meat packing industry, where it represents all workers regardless of the work they do.

The Levels of Union Organization

In most unions, there are three levels of union organization: (1) local unions, (2) national unions, and (3) the American Federation of Labor and Congress of Industrial Organizations (AFL-CIO).

Local Unions, often called locals, are the smallest unit of labor organization. A local represents the workers in a particular plant, neighborhood, city, or other area. It is usually the local union that bargains with an employer, though the national union may assist.

Many local unions employ one or more people called business representatives or business agents. These employees work full-time to administer the union's contract and to handle grievances.

The union members in each division of a company elect one of the members to serve as *shop steward*. The steward helps workers deal with management and en-

sures that union rules are followed in the department. Most local unions also elect an executive board that includes a president, a secretary, and a treasurer.

National Unions are made up of local unions throughout the United States. Many national unions are called *international* because they include Canadian locals. National unions promote legislation favorable to their members. They also organize new workers, especially in industries or geographical areas with little union representation. A few national unions, including those in the clothing and steel industries, carry on industry-wide bargaining. The bargaining sets wages and hours for the entire industry, regardless of local conditions.

National unions are governed by conventions, to which each local sends representatives. The conventions meet every one to five years. A president, a secretary-treasurer, and an executive council manage union affairs between gatherings. In addition to these officers, most groups have a staff that includes lawyers, public relations experts, and editors. National unions are supported by dues, initiation fees, and other charges paid by members. Many groups collect dues from each worker equal to two hours' wages a month.

The AFL-CIO is a *federation* (league) of national unions. About 80 per cent of the union members in the

Union Membership in the United States

Year	Total Workers (Nonagricultural)	Union Members	Per Cent in Unions
1930	29,424,000	3,401,000	12%
1935	27,053,000	3,584,000	13%
1940	32,376,000	8,717,000	27%
1945	40,394,000	14,322,000	36%
1950	45,222,000	14,267,000	32%
1955	50,675,000	16,802,000	33%
1960	54,234,000	17,049,000	31%
1965	60,815,000	17,299,000	28%
1970	70,920,000	19,381,000	27%
1975	76,945,000	19,564,000	25%
1980	87,480,000	20,095,000	23%
1984	91,331,000	17,417,000	19%

Source: U.S. Bureau of Labor Statistics.

WORLD BOOK graph

United States belong to groups that are members of the federation. The president of the AFL-CIO is probably the most powerful American labor leader, but the organization itself does little collective bargaining. Its major activities include promoting legislation favorable to labor, educating the public about the labor movement, and settling conflicts between member unions. For more information, see AMERICAN FEDERATION OF LABOR AND CONGRESS OF INDUSTRIAL ORGANIZATIONS.

Origins of the Labor Movement

Various scholars trace the beginnings of the labor movement to different sources. Some historians have compared labor unions with medieval *craft guilds*. The guilds were associations of skilled workers in Europe during the Middle Ages, which lasted from the A.D. 400's to the 1500's. Other scholars have different theories about the origins of the labor movement.

Craft Guilds, like labor unions, worked to establish reasonable wages and hours and to increase job security. But there are important differences between guilds and unions. A guild consisted of ranks of members. The highest-ranking guild members were the *masters*, who had their own shops. They employed less experienced workers called *journeymen* and beginners called *appren-*

tices. Apprentices and journeymen eventually became masters themselves and had their own employees. Modern labor unions do not include employers, and few union members ever start a business or employ others. Because of these differences, many labor historians think the two institutions have little in common.

Other Possible Origins. One theory is that workers organized to protect themselves against the effects of price competition on the labor market. Competition among products tends to reduce prices because consumers try to buy at the lowest possible price. As prices fall, manufacturers must reduce costs. The easiest way to do so is to pay workers less, to get more production from them, or a combination of the two. Many scholars believe that workers banded together to keep employers from reducing wages.

Other scholars think workers formed unions because the Industrial Revolution, which began during the 1700's, gave employers too much power. Before the revolution, workers needed only a few tools to go into business for themselves. Many worked in their own homes. Afterward, most people worked in factories and only wealthy employers or corporations could afford the expensive machinery used to produce goods. Employees may have banded together to equalize bargaining power between themselves and their bosses, who controlled the means of production.

Gains by the Labor Movement

This chart shows how average working hours and other conditions have changed in the United States since the 1880's, largely as the result of the labor movement.

	1880	Today
Length of Workday	10 hours	8 hours or less
Length of Workweek	6 or 7 days	5 days
Overtime Pay	Almost none	At least one and a half times normal
Paid Vacations	Almost none	2 to 4 weeks a year
Paid Holidays	Almost none	10 a year
Hospital Insurance	Paid for by individuals or unions	Provided by most employers

Development of the American Labor Movement

Most historians trace the American labor movement to the early 1800's. During the 1820's and 1830's, carpenters, masons, printers, and other skilled workers established city wide organizations to obtain better pay.

The First Nationwide Labor Organizations developed during the mid-1800's. Workers in many different trades established national unions. William H. Sylvis, a Philadelphia ironworker, founded the National Union of Iron Molders in 1859. In 1867, boot and shoe workers formed a national organization called the Knights of St. Crispin. Blacksmiths, machinists, printers, and other skilled workers also established national unions during this period, though most groups lasted only a few years.

LABOR MOVEMENT

In 1866, Sylvis united a number of national labor unions into a federation called the National Labor Union. But the federation became involved in an ambitious program of social reform and gave little attention to its members' specific needs. It dissolved in 1872.

The first national federation to remain active for more than a few years was the Noble Order of the Knights of Labor. It was established in 1869 by a group of Philadelphia garment workers. The Knights of Labor differed from other labor organizations by including farmers and merchants as well as wage earners. The group's goals included equal pay for equal work, the abolition of child labor, and an 8-hour workday. At that time, most laborers worked about 10 hours a day.

The Knights of Labor reached the height of its power during the 1880's under the leadership of Terence V. Powderly. The group won a strike against railroads owned by the American millionaire Jay Gould in 1885. By 1886, the organization had about 700,000 members. But the Knights lost a second strike against the Gould railroads that year, and membership declined rapidly. By 1900, the group had almost disappeared.

In 1881, Samuel Gompers and other leaders organized a federation that, unlike the Knights of Labor, included only wage earners. It was called the Federation of Organized Trades and Labor Unions of the United States and Canada.

In 1886, the federation was reorganized and changed its name to the American Federation of Labor (AFL). Gompers became the AFL's first president. He served as its president for 37 years—from 1886 to 1894 and from 1896 until his death in 1924.

Under Gompers' leadership, the AFL stressed wage increases and other job demands instead of political issues. The group's chief means of achieving its goals was collective bargaining. Another AFL tactic was the use of marks called *union labels* to identify goods manufactured by its members. The federation urged shoppers to "look for the union label" and buy union-made products.

Opposition to Unions increased during the late 1800's. Employers exchanged *blacklists*—lists of workers suspected of union membership—to prevent such workers from getting jobs. Factory owners hired strikebreakers and armed guards to crush strikes. Sometimes, the state or federal government sent troops to end a labor dispute. Many states passed laws to restrict union activity. The Sherman Antitrust Act of 1890, which was designed to prohibit trusts that hindered trade, was used mostly against labor. Union leaders were found guilty of violating that law by interfering with commerce. On this basis, judges issued court orders called *injunctions* forbidding strikes.

In 1886, a disaster called the Haymarket Riot increased antilabor feeling throughout the country. A meeting of workers was held in Haymarket Square in Chicago to protest police actions against strikers at an industrial plant. Near the end of the meeting, an unknown person threw a bomb, and a riot broke out. Eight police officers and two other persons were killed. Many Americans blamed the labor movement for the violence. The police charged eight labor leaders, none of whom was present at the bomb throwing, with aiding the unknown person to commit murder. Although no evidence linked the leaders with the incident, seven of them were sentenced to death and four were hanged. The remaining leaders were pardoned by Illinois Governor John P. Altgeld in 1893.

Several violent strikes during the 1890's hurt the labor movement even more. One of the most bitter was the Homestead Strike of 1892, which involved the Carnegie Steel Company and the Amalgamated Association of Iron, Steel, and Tin Workers. The union called a strike after the company reduced wages at its Homestead, Pa., plant. The company hired guards from the Pinkerton Detective Agency to protect the steelworks. Violence broke out between the strikers and the guards, and several persons were killed. The strike failed after most workers quit the union and returned to work.

Another violent dispute was the Pullman Strike of 1894. Employees of the Pullman Palace Car Company, which manufactured railroad cars, struck to protest

The Knights of Labor, established in 1869, was one of the first national labor organizations in the United States. Its members included farmers and merchants as well as workers from many trades.

The Pullman Strike, a railroad strike in 1894, ended after the United States government sent federal troops to keep the mail trains running.

a wage cut. Members of the American Railway Union, a group of railroad workers headed by Eugene V. Debs, declared a sympathy strike. They supported the Pullman strikers by refusing to handle the company's cars. The U.S. government sent troops to end the strike, declaring that it interfered with mail trains. Debs and other leaders were sent to prison, and Debs's union was so weakened that it dissolved three years later.

The Early 1900's. The labor movement suffered a number of failures in the early 1900's. One major setback was the case of *Lochner v. New York,* a 1905 ruling of the Supreme Court of the United States. The court held that minimum-wage laws were unconstitutional because they restricted the right of an individual to contract for employment. It based the decision on the principle that individuals had "liberty of contract" derived from the 14th Amendment to the Constitution. After this ruling, employers used the "liberty of contract" principle to defeat union wage demands.

The AFL also suffered a major defeat in 1919, when

it tried to organize workers in the steel industry. The federation called a strike for higher wages and other benefits. But the steel companies brought in enough strikebreakers to continue production, and the AFL was forced to cancel the strike. After this failure, AFL membership dropped from about 4 million in 1920 to about 3 million in 1929.

The Industrial Workers of the World. The setbacks of the early 1900's made many labor leaders and workers dissatisfied with the AFL, which accepted the capitalist system and sought benefits within it. To oppose the AFL's conservative policies, radicals founded the Industrial Workers of the World (IWW) in 1905. This group, also known as the Wobblies, sought to overthrow the capitalist system and replace it with socialism. Wobbly composers wrote many songs about the labor movement and the poor that became popular folk songs. These songs included "Dump the Bosses off Your Back" and "Hallelujah, I'm a Bum."

In 1912, the IWW led a strike by textile workers in

The Industrial Workers of the World (IWW) was a radical labor organization of the early 1900's. It staged many demonstrations like this one in New York City and led a number of violent strikes.

Lawrence, Mass., to protest a pay cut. The strikers' food and money soon ran low. To help them hold out, strike leaders sent the workers' children to stay with labor sympathizers in other cities. The strike succeeded, and workers actually won a wage increase.

The IWW was also involved in a strike by silk workers in Paterson, N.J., in 1913. But the Wobblies lost that strike and a series of others and had nearly disappeared by 1920.

Unions Gain Strength. Despite the setbacks of the early 1900's, developments near the end of the period led to a later revival. A number of unions abandoned their aims of sweeping social reform. They concentrated instead on higher wages and other job goals, which were easier to achieve and more important to their members. Another development that strengthened unions was the Immigration Act of 1924, which limited the number of immigrants admitted to the United States. The restriction on immigration reduced the number of new arrivals competing for jobs and increased the bargaining power of American workers.

The Great Depression, which began in 1929, left millions of workers jobless. But it also changed the attitude of many Americans toward the labor movement. Before 1929, most people regarded business executives as the nation's leaders and union members as dangerous radicals. But people lost faith in business leaders after business could not relieve the depression. Many Americans began to believe the way to fight the slump was to increase the purchasing power of wage earners. The political climate changed from one favoring management to one favoring labor.

In 1932, Congress passed one of the first prolabor laws. It was called the Norris-La Guardia Act after its sponsors, Senator George W. Norris of Nebraska and Representative Fiorello H. La Guardia of New York. The act made yellow-dog contracts unenforceable and limited the power of federal courts to issue injunctions in labor disputes.

The New Deal, President Franklin D. Roosevelt's program to end the depression, included several laws that benefited labor. One of the most important was the National Industrial Recovery Act of 1933. The act guaranteed workers a minimum wage, reasonable hours, collective bargaining, and the right to join unions. But in the 1935 case of *Schechter v. United States*, the Supreme Court declared the law unconstitutional.

To replace the overturned law, the federal government enacted the National Labor Relations Act of 1935. The act was also called the Wagner Act, after Senator Robert F. Wagner of New York, who led the fight for its passage. Like the earlier law, the Wagner Act sought to protect labor's right to organize and to bargain collectively. It also established the National Labor Relations Board to administer its provisions. The board was given the power to punish unfair labor practices and to determine which union should represent workers. Many employers believed the Wagner Act was unconstitutional. But the Supreme Court upheld it in a 1937 landmark case known as *National Labor Relations Board v. Jones and Laughlin Steel Corporation*.

Formation of the CIO. The automobile and steel industries and other industries that used mass-production

Public Affairs Press

A Sit-Down Strike is one in which the strikers stop work but refuse to leave the factory. The strikers shown in the window above took over a General Motors plant at Flint, Mich., in 1937.

techniques had expanded rapidly during the early 1900's. As a result, the number of workers in those industries also increased. Most of them lacked union representation. The craft unions that controlled the AFL opposed efforts to unionize these workers, most of whom were unskilled or semiskilled. Many AFL leaders feared that attempts to organize these factory workers would fail, as had attempts to organize steelworkers in 1919.

Nevertheless, several AFL unions established the Committee for Industrial Organization (CIO) to conduct an organizing drive in the mass-production industries. The CIO quickly gained millions of members and unionized workers in many plants that previously had no unions. Its greatest successes were in the automobile, rubber, and steel industries.

But the dispute over industrial organization continued. In 1938, the AFL expelled the unions that formed the CIO. The CIO then established its own federation, changing its name to the Congress of Industrial Organizations. John L. Lewis of the United Mine Workers became the federation's first president.

World War II and the Postwar Period. The United States entered World War II in 1941. Shortly afterward, President Roosevelt called a conference of the nation's most important labor leaders. The leaders promised to avoid strikes for the duration of the war so that the nation's defense production would not be interrupted.

Union membership soared during the war. By 1945, more than a third of all nonagricultural workers belonged to a union. The government prohibited general wage increases during the war, but unions won many important fringe benefits. These gains included company-financed hospital insurance, paid vacations and holidays, and retirement pensions.

After the war ended in 1945, the United States entered the greatest period of economic growth in its history. Prosperity spread to more Americans than ever before, and unions took steps to enable their members to share in the new wealth. A wave of strikes began, and the number of work stoppages reached an all-time high in 1946. Unions scored some of their most impressive victories, including large wage hikes and the first escalator clauses.

The Taft-Hartley Act. Many Americans began to believe that the unions had become too powerful. They resented the inconvenience caused by strikes and blamed soaring prices on union demands. Many people believed that individual workers were bullied by "strike-happy" union leaders. They demanded a new law to curb the power of organized labor. The result was the Labor-Management Relations Act of 1947, usually called the Taft-Hartley Act. Its sponsors were Senator Robert A. Taft of Ohio and Representative Fred A. Hartley, Jr., of New Jersey.

The Taft-Hartley Act, which Congress passed over the veto of President Harry S. Truman, introduced new government controls over unions. Labor leaders bitterly opposed the legislation, which they called a "slave labor law." It prohibited use of the secondary boycott, sympathy strike, and jurisdictional strike. The act outlawed the closed shop and banned union political contributions in national elections. It increased the amount of support a union needed to establish a union shop. A union needed a majority of the workers eligible to vote instead of a majority of those voting. Finally, the act established cooling-off periods and other special rules for handling strikes that endangered the nation's health or safety.

Reunification of the AFL and the CIO. Faced with growing opposition to labor, the AFL and the CIO be-

gan to consider joining forces. One of the major differences between the two groups was their attitude toward Communism. The AFL was strongly anti-Communist, but many officials of the CIO either were Communists or supported Communist ideals. These Communist leanings became a problem after World War II, when intense anti-Communist feeling swept through the nation. Many CIO unions overthrew leaders thought to be Communist sympathizers. For example, Walter P. Reuther opposed Communist influence in the United Automobile Workers and became president of that union in 1946. In 1949 and 1950, the CIO expelled 11 unions that it claimed were dominated by Communists or Communist sympathizers.

Ridding the CIO of Communist influence removed one of the chief barriers to reunification. Another obstacle disappeared when Philip Murray, the president of the CIO, and William Green, head of the AFL, died in 1952. Both men had played major roles in the split between the two organizations.

George Meany became president of the AFL, and Reuther headed the CIO. The new leaders then began discussion of reunification. In 1955, the two groups merged into a single organization called the American Federation of Labor and Congress of Industrial Organizations (AFL-CIO). Meany became its first president.

Charges of Corruption. In 1957, the U.S. Senate formed a committee headed by Senator John L. McClellan of Arkansas to investigate charges of corruption among labor leaders. The investigation revealed that officials of the Teamsters Union and other groups took union funds for their own use and had links with organized crime. As a result of the investigation, the AFL-CIO expelled the Teamsters and two other unions.

In 1959, Congress passed the Labor-Management Reporting and Disclosure Act to guard against corrupt union leadership. The act was also called the Landrum-Griffin Act after its sponsors, Representatives Phillip M. Landrum of Georgia and Robert P. Griffin of Michigan. It gave the government greater control over union affairs by providing for federal supervision of union elections and financial accounts. Individuals who had been in prison could not run for union office until five years after their release. At the insistence of Senator John F. Kennedy of Massachusetts, the act also included a "Bill of Rights" for union members. It guaranteed them freedom of speech, control over union dues, and other rights.

The Challenge of Automation. Beginning in the late 1950's, many factories introduced automatic machinery to perform tasks formerly done by workers. Such automation caused many labor disputes when new machines and methods threatened to eliminate jobs.

Unions called for a variety of measures to protect the jobs and incomes of workers affected by automation. The demands included free retraining and shorter workweeks to spread the available work among more employees. In 1962, the United Steelworkers of America and the Kaiser Steel Corporation agreed to a landmark plan for dealing with automation. The plan called for the money saved by automation to be shared with workers through higher wages. Laborers replaced by machines would go into an employment pool. There, they

AFL-CIO

The Merger of the AFL and CIO in 1955 united the two leading U.S. labor federations. AFL president George Meany, *left*, and CIO president Walter P. Reuther, *right*, join hands in celebration of the merger of their groups to form the AFL-CIO.

LABOR MOVEMENT

Wide World

Migrant Workers and other farm laborers joined the U.S. labor movement during the 1960's. Cesar E. Chavez, a Mexican-American labor leader, *front left,* founded what is now the United Farm Workers of America (UFW).

would draw full pay until they were retrained or assigned to a new job. See AUTOMATION (Automation and Jobs).

New Groups Become Unionized. Several groups of workers became unionized for the first time during the 1960's and 1970's. Two of the most important were farmworkers and public employees.

Cesar E. Chavez, a Mexican-American labor leader, began to organize agricultural workers in California during the 1960's. Chavez established what is now the United Farm Workers of America (UFW), a union of migrant workers and other farm laborers.

In 1962, President John F. Kennedy issued an executive order that gave federal employees the right to organize and to bargain collectively but not to strike. Many states passed similar legislation, and a few even allowed government workers to strike. These laws encouraged the rapid growth of unionism among public employees. Strikes by police, teachers, and other government employees affected many cities and states during the 1970's. The American Federation of State, County and Municipal Employees, a union of public workers, became the fastest-growing U.S. labor group.

Union membership among blacks, Mexican Americans, and women also increased during this period. Unions helped these workers obtain equal pay and other rights. Labor leaders convinced their members that any group deprived of equal pay would form a cheap source of labor that would compete with union members for jobs.

Labor Unions Today face the twin challenges of a declining industrial base and increasing automation. Lower labor costs have helped foreign companies in the automobile, electronics, and other industries gain larger shares of the American market. Many large U.S. facto-ries in these industries have closed, and large numbers of union members have lost their jobs. The rapidly increasing use of robots and other advanced technology also continues to hurt the labor movement.

Another problem for labor is a decline in the percentage of workers who belong to unions. In 1945, about 36 per cent of all laborers in nonagricultural jobs were members of unions. Only about 19 per cent are members today.

Critics of organized labor charge that many unions are too big, inefficient, and corrupt. They also complain that many unions put the interests of their members above those of the nation. But other people point out that the same criticisms apply to many other groups.

Labor Around the World

The labor movement is strongest in the industrial nations, including Canada, Japan, the United States, and most countries of Western Europe. The developing countries of Africa, Asia, and Latin America have far fewer labor organizations because most of the people work in agriculture.

In Canada, labor unions are usually called *trade unions.* The history of labor in Canada has been similar to that in the United States, and unions in both countries are very much alike.

Most Canadian trade unions belong to a federation called the Canadian Labour Congress (CLC). The federation includes the Canadian locals of many international unions that in the United States belong to the AFL-CIO. A smaller federation called the Confederation of National Trade Unions (CNTU) is made up mostly of French-speaking unions from Quebec.

In Other Countries, the labor movement differs from that in the United States. American unions have concentrated on job issues, such as wages and hours. They seek to obtain benefits within the existing free enterprise system. The chief goals of labor groups in most other countries are political and social reform. Unions in France, Great Britain, Italy, and many other countries have socialist aims. They seek to reorganize the political and economic system to achieve public ownership of industry. This goal is called *nationalization.*

Labor unions in the United States achieve most of their gains by collective bargaining, but those in most other countries rely more on legislation. In many nations, labor groups have founded their own political party. The unions have little influence if their party loses an election. In the United States, unions have much influence with both major parties.

The labor movement in Great Britain has close ties with the Labour Party, a political party that represents trade unions and socialist groups. The party has socialist aims, including nationalization of basic industries and programs to aid the needy. The party came to power twice during the 1920's. But it was not able to put its socialist ideals into effect until 1945, when it won a landslide victory. Since then, control of the government has alternated between the Labour Party and its rival, the Conservative Party. During the Labour Party's years in power, it nationalized the coal mines, the iron and steel industry, shipbuilding, and other industries. It also established an extensive program of pensions, free medical care, and other benefits.

In Japan, most of the unions are *enterprise unions.*

Such unions consist of the employees of a particular firm. This type of union developed because most Japanese workers are employed by the same company all their careers. A firm almost never fires anyone, and few workers move from one firm to another. However, the tradition of life employment has begun to fade.

In Russia and the other Communist countries of Eastern Europe, the role of labor unions differs from that of unions elsewhere. Unions exist mainly to support the aims of government planners and to help meet production goals. Labor groups also sponsor social and cultural activities and administer such worker benefits as social insurance and vacations. But the power of unions to bargain on behalf of their members is severely limited. The government determines wages and hours, and strikes are forbidden.

International Organizations. Representatives of labor groups from about 55 nations, including the American CIO, founded the World Federation of Trade Unions (WFTU) in 1945. But the CIO withdrew in 1949, after organizations from Communist countries gained control of the federation.

That same year, representatives of the AFL, the CIO, and other labor groups from non-Communist countries established a new federation. This organization, created to oppose the Communist policies of the WFTU, was called the International Confederation of Free Trade Unions (ICFTU). Its goals originally included the promotion of free unions and better working conditions throughout the world.   MARK PERLMAN

Related Articles in WORLD BOOK include:

AMERICAN LABOR LEADERS

Bridges, Harry	Jones, Mary Harris
Chavez, Cesar E.	Lewis, John L.
Debs, Eugene V.	McBride, Lloyd
Dubinsky, David	Meany, George
Fitzsimmons, Frank E.	Murray, Philip
Flynn, Elizabeth G.	O'Reilly, Leonora
Fraser, Douglas A.	Owen (Robert Dale Owen)
Galarza, Ernesto	Petrillo, James C.
Gompers, Samuel	Randolph, A. Philip
Green, William	Reuther, Walter P.
Haywood, William D.	Shanker, Albert
Hillman, Sidney	Woodcock, Leonard
Hoffa, James R.	

LABOR DISPUTES

Arbitration	Homestead Strike	Sabotage
Boycott	Lockout	Strike
Haymarket Riot	Pullman Strike	

LABOR LEGISLATION

Norris-La Guardia Act	Right-to-Work Law
Railway Labor Act	Taft-Hartley Act

LABOR ORGANIZATIONS

See the articles on labor unions listed in the table with this article. See also:
American Federation of Government Employees
American Federation of Labor and Congress
  of Industrial Organizations (AFL-CIO)
Congress of Industrial Organizations (CIO)
Industrial Workers of the World
International Confederation of Free Trade Unions
International Labor Organization
Knights of Labor
Molly Maguires
Newspaper Guild
Railway Brotherhoods

GOVERNMENT AGENCIES

Federal Mediation and	National Labor
Conciliation Service	Relations Board
Labor, Department of	National Mediation Board

OTHER RELATED ARTICLES

Apprentice	Industrial	Pension
Automation	Revolution (The	Piecework
Blacklist	Working Class)	Profit Sharing
Bonus	Industry (Labor)	Railroad
Child Labor	Labor Day	(Rail Unions)
Closed Shop	Labor Force	Sweatshop
Coal (Labor	Labour Party	Union Label
Unions)	Lochner v.	Union Shop
Guild	New York	Wages and Hours
Industrial	Migrant Labor	Walesa, Lech
Relations	Minimum Wage	Yellow-Dog
	Open Shop	Contracts

Outline

I. What Labor Unions Do
  A. Organizing Workers   D. Conducting Apprenticeship
  B. Arranging Contracts   Programs
  C. Handling Labor   E. Other Union Activities
    Disputes
II. Types of Unions
III. The Levels of Union Organization
  A. Local Unions   C. The AFL-CIO
  B. National Unions
IV. Origins of the Labor Movement
  A. Craft Guilds   B. Other Possible Origins
V. Development of the American Labor Movement
VI. Labor Around the World
  A. In Canada   C. International Organizations
  B. In Other Countries

Questions

When did fringe benefits develop?
What is the difference between a *closed shop*, an *open shop*, and a *union shop?*
Who was Samuel Gompers?
What are the three levels of union organization?
Why did the AFL expel unions that set up the CIO?
What is the difference between *mediation* and *arbitration?*
Why is there a special agency to settle labor disputes in the railway and airline industries?
How have the goals and methods of the labor movement in most other countries differed from those in the United States?
What is the difference between *craft unions* and *industrial unions?*
What tactics other than a strike can a union use to press its demands?

Reading and Study Guide

See *Labor Movement* in the RESEARCH GUIDE/INDEX, Volume 22, for a *Reading and Study Guide.*

Additional Resources

BROOKS, THOMAS R. *Toil and Trouble: A History of American Labor.* 2nd ed. Delacorte, 1971.
DULLES, FOSTER R., AND DUBOFSKY, MELVYN. *Labor in America: A History.* 4th ed. Harlan Davidson, 1984.
FONER, PHILIP S. *Women and the American Labor Movement: From Colonial Times to the Eve of World War I.* Macmillan, 1979. *Women and the American Labor Movement: From World War I to the Present.* 1980.
MORTON, DESMOND, and COPP, TERRY. *Working People: An Illustrated History of the Canadian Labour Movement.* Deneau (Ottawa), 1980.
STURMTHAL, ADOLF F., and SCOVILLE, J. G., eds. *The International Labor Movement in Transition: Essays on Africa, Asia, Europe, and South America.* Univ. of Illinois Press, 1973.

LABOR PARTY

LABOR PARTY. See Labour Party.

LABOR RELATIONS. See Personnel Management.

LABOR STATISTICS, BUREAU OF (BLS), is an agency of the United States Department of Labor. It collects and interprets information about the labor force and the performance of the economy.

The bureau conducts research on employment and unemployment, productivity and technological developments, wages, industrial relations, work injuries, prices and living conditions, and foreign labor and trade. This information is used by labor, industry, other government agencies, and the public. It appears in the official BLS publication, the *Monthly Labor Review,* and in bulletins, reports, and special periodicals.

The agency was established in 1884 as the Federal Bureau of Labor. It received its present name in 1913.   Critically reviewed by the Bureau of Labor Statistics

LABOR UNION. See Labor Movement.

LABORATORY is a place equipped with apparatus for conducting scientific experiments, investigations, and tests. Many devices and products used in everyday life resulted from laboratory work. They include automobile engines, plastics, radios, synthetic fabrics, telephones, television sets, and transistors. Laboratories may be found in schools, in research institutes and industrial organizations, and in government departments. They serve as a training ground for scientists and a means for discovering new knowledge.   George J. Pallrand

See also Chemistry (Tools of the Chemist; pictures); Language (picture: A Language Laboratory).

LABORATORY SCHOOL is a school used for the observation and study of children, and for the evaluation of teaching methods. It is sometimes called a *campus school,* because it is usually located on the campus of a college or a university. It may be an elementary school, a high school, or a combination of the two.

The laboratory school carries on all the functions of a regular public school. It also provides opportunity for one or more of the following activities: (1) College students in education can observe children and teaching methods. (2) Students can practice teaching under the supervision of experienced teachers. (3) College staff members and students can do research and experimentation in teaching methods.   Donald H. Eichhorn

LABORERS' INTERNATIONAL UNION OF NORTH AMERICA, formerly called the Hod Carriers' Union, is a trade union affiliated with the American Federation of Labor and Congress of Industrial Organizations. The union has more than 900 locals in the United States and Canada. It consists primarily of building and construction workers who perform helpers' tasks for other crafts. For example, membership is open to tenders for carpenters, plasterers, and masons; to workers who mix or handle construction materials; and to general laborers.

The union was organized in 1903. It has headquarters at 905 16th Street NW, Washington, D.C. 20006. For membership, see Labor Movement (table: Important United States Labor Unions).   Jack Barbash

LABOUR PARTY is one of the two main political parties in Great Britain. The Conservative Party is the other one. The Labour Party receives much support from working class voters, especially members of trade unions. It promotes socialistic policies, and has brought about many changes in the British economic system. If the party wins a majority in Parliament, its leader becomes prime minister. Many other countries also have a Labour (or Labor) Party.

Early History. The number of voters in the working classes in Great Britain was increased by the Reform Bill of 1867. But, unlike the socialist workers on the European continent, the British workers did not at first favor independent political action. Not until later in the 1800's did the Labour Party begin to take shape. This occurred under the leadership of several groups, particularly the Fabian Society and the Independent Labour Party. After years of discussion, the first really effective steps were taken in 1900, with the formation of a Labour Representation Committee. It included representatives of trade unions and socialist groups. The Labour Party elected 29 candidates in 1906, but its growth was uneven. During World War I, some of its leaders alarmed the country by their pacifism.

After the war, the party openly declared itself in favor of socialism. Its membership grew, and, in 1924, James Ramsay MacDonald formed the first Labour government. But the Labour Party still depended on Liberal votes for its majority in the House of Commons, so it had little chance to follow an independent policy. In 1931, MacDonald and other Labourites left the party to join a coalition government which was formed to combat the depression. However, the Labour Party offered stiff opposition throughout the 1930's.

Later Development. During World War II, Labour joined with Winston Churchill's government to carry the nation to victory. After Germany's defeat in 1945, cooperation ended, and an election was held. Labour won by a large margin, and Clement Attlee became prime minister. Clement Attlee led the party from 1935 to 1955. From 1945 to 1951, a Labour government with Attlee as prime minister carried out much of the party's program. It passed laws *nationalizing* (placing under government control) about one-fifth of the country's industry. It also provided more social services. New and revised programs extended insurance and pension coverage. The National Health Service Act provided for free medical and dental care for the entire population.

The Conservatives regained control of Parliament in 1951, and held it until 1964. Hugh Gaitskell was Labour Party leader from 1955 until his death in 1963. Harold Wilson became party leader in 1963 and prime minister in 1964. The Labour Party was defeated by the Conservatives in 1970, but returned to power in 1974, still headed by Wilson. Wilson retired in 1976. James Callaghan replaced him as Labour leader and prime minister. In 1979, the Conservatives regained control of Parliament, and Callaghan's term as prime minister ended. Callaghan resigned as party leader in 1980. Michael Foot, leader of the party's left wing, succeeded him. A number of moderate Labourite members of Parliament quit the party in protest to Foot's left wing policies. They formed the Social Democratic Party. Foot resigned as party leader in 1983. Neil Kinnock, also a member of the party's left wing, succeeded Foot.

In Other Countries. Other countries that have a Labour (or Labor) Party include Australia, Ireland, Israel, the Netherlands, New Zealand, and Norway. Canada has a farmer-labor party called the Cooperative Commonwealth Federation. Labour (or labor) parties have never been powerful in the United States. But a few, such as the American Labor Party, the Farmer-Labor Party, and the Socialist Labor Party, have had some influence in certain localities. The American Labor Party was most active in New York City during the 1930's. The Farmer-Labor Party of Minnesota was most active during the 1920's and 1930's. The Socialist Labor Party, founded in 1877, continues to support its own presidential candidate.   JAMES L. GODFREY

Related Articles in WORLD BOOK include:

Attlee, Clement R.	MacDonald, James Ramsay
Fabian Society	Webb, Sidney and Beatrice
Kinnock, Neil G.	Wilson, Lord
Laski, Harold J.	

LABRADOR is a large peninsula in northeastern Canada. It covers about 500,000 square miles (1,300,000 square kilometers) between the Atlantic Ocean and Hudson Bay. The western part of Labrador belongs to Quebec. Labrador's so-called eastern "coast" forms part of Newfoundland. Since 1927, the term "coast" has meant the coast as well as an inland area extending as much as 450 miles (724 kilometers) west from the Atlantic. This article discusses the Newfoundland part of Labrador, which covers 112,826 square miles (292,218 square kilometers).

Labrador extends farther east than any other part of the North American mainland. The Strait of Belle Isle in the southeast separates Labrador from the island of Newfoundland. Quebec forms Newfoundland's southern and western boundaries in Labrador.

The abundance of fur-bearing animals and the rich coastal fisheries brought French settlers to Labrador in the early 1700's. Fishing still provides a living for many people of Labrador. The fur industry is no longer of primary importance. Rich iron ore deposits in the west support a mining industry that began to develop in the 1950's.

Labrador is a land with long, severe winters. In the interior, snow covers the ground from September to

June. The average July temperature ranges from 45° to 60° F. (7° to 16° C). The climate makes agriculture difficult, except for some vegetable growing. The people depend on supplies brought from other parts of Canada for nearly all their food except fish and game meat. As part of Newfoundland, Labrador sends three representatives to the provincial legislature.

The Land and Its Resources

Labrador lies on a rough plateau of ancient rock formations. Valleys and rapid rivers draining into the Atlantic have deeply cut the coastal edge of the plateau. The 600-mile (970-kilometer) Churchill River is the largest river of Labrador. Churchill Falls on the Churchill represents the chief source of hydroelectric energy. Lakes cover much of southwestern Labrador. The *physical map* with the NEWFOUNDLAND article shows that Labrador's highest mountains rise in the northeastern coastal region. Mont d'Iberville, the highest point in Newfoundland, rises 5,400 feet (1,646 meters) in the Torngat Mountains in northern Labrador.

Labrador may be divided into two distinct parts, each with a different economy. The economy of *Coastal Labrador* depends on rich fisheries and fur trapping. White settlers came to this area in the 1700's. *Western Labrador* has great iron ore wealth, discovered in 1895. The resources of this area remained unexplored and undeveloped for many years, because of the severe climate and rugged terrain, and the lack of settlers willing to live in the region.

Labrador has about 21,000 square miles (54,400 square kilometers) of valuable timber. The main forest trees are spruce, balsam fir, and birch. Wild animals include caribou, bears, beavers, foxes, hares, lynxes, martens, minks, moose, otters, porcupines, squirrels, weasels, and wolves. Atlantic salmon, cod, herring, seals, and trout are caught in the coastal waters. Ducks and

Barry Matthews

The Eskimo Fishing Village of Nain lies on Nain Bay along the east coast of Labrador. The village is the most northern permanent settlement in Labrador.

LABRADOR

The Labrador Peninsula lies in northeastern Canada. Most of the peninsula is in Quebec. The eastern part, which belongs to Newfoundland, is often referred to as Labrador.

WORLD BOOK map

geese and other migratory water birds visit Labrador each year.

Climate. Weather reports come mainly from the coastal area, because few people live in the interior. Temperatures in Labrador fall below freezing almost every month of the year. Temperatures on the coast sometimes fall as low as $-40°$ F. ($-40°$ C) in winter, and occasionally rise to more than 80° F. (27° C) in summer. The interior and the northern coast have especially severe winters. In summer, drifting ice from the Arctic may chill the coast while the interior remains warm. Labrador has an annual average precipitation (including melted snow) of 30 inches (76 centimeters). The average annual snowfall (unmelted) measures 150 inches (381 centimeters). The coast has frequent storms, especially during the autumn and winter months, when gales often blow.

The People and Their Work

Labrador's population, based on the 1981 Canadian census, is 31,318. Most white settlers live in western mining communities, small fishing villages, and places such as Happy Valley-Goose Bay, which grew in connection with defense bases. Mining and fishing are the chief sources of income in Labrador. Eskimos and Indians make up about a tenth of the population.

Labrador has valuable Arctic char, Atlantic salmon, trout, and seal fisheries. Cod, the most plentiful fish, provides the greatest income. The fishing season usually begins in early June and ends in late September or early October. Fur trapping was a major occupation for many years, but it declined greatly in the mid-1900's, with less demand for long-haired furs. Fox, lynx, and marten furs lead in value. Some people around Happy Valley-Goose Bay and along the Strait of Belle Isle raise potatoes, cabbage, beets, and turnips.

The Labrador Trough, a narrow belt of land rich in iron ore, stretches along the western edge of Labrador. The Trough is not more than 45 miles (72 kilometers) wide at any point, but it extends 1,700 miles (2,740 kilometers) in a vast horseshoe through central Quebec, Labrador, and the Hudson Bay region. The Labrador

part of the Trough alone has iron ore deposits estimated at more than 8 billion short tons (7 billion metric tons).

During the 1940's, exploration of the Knob Lake area on the Labrador-Quebec frontier uncovered about 400 million short tons (360 million metric tons) of high-grade iron ore. The 357-mile (575-kilometer) Quebec, North Shore, and Labrador Railway brings this ore to markets. The railway runs between Knob Lake and Sept-Îles, a Quebec port on the Gulf of St. Lawrence. A branch of the railway runs to iron ore deposits near Carol and Wabush lakes. Ships carry the ore to steel mills in the United States. Labrador has five highways. Labrador also has three airports. They are at Churchill Falls, Happy Valley-Goose Bay, and Wabush.

During the months that the coast is ice-free, from June to November, the Canadian government maintains a steamer and motorboat coastal service. It provides passenger service and brings mail and supplies to the people. Airplanes with special landing gear serve the coastal communities during the harsh winters, as well as at other times of the year. In northern Labrador, the people—mainly Indians and Eskimos—can buy supplies at trading posts operated by the provincial government.

Labrador City, Happy Valley-Goose Bay, Wabush, North West River, and Churchill Falls, in that order, are Labrador's largest populated places. Labrador City and Wabush are iron ore mining communities in southwestern Labrador. Happy Valley-Goose Bay and North West River lie near Lake Melville, about 150 miles (241 kilometers) from the Atlantic coast.

History

Viking explorers probably visited Labrador between A.D. 950 and A.D. 1050. John Cabot, an Italian explorer in the service of England, probably sailed to Labrador shortly before 1500. The origin of the word *Labrador* may be linked to Cabot's voyages. According to tradition, a farmer from the Azores (Portuguese islands) sailed with Cabot. The Portuguese word for farmer is *llavrador*. This may account for the name *Labrador*, but no one is sure of its origin. Many other European explorers visited Labrador after Cabot.

Until the 1700's, only Eskimos and the Naskapi and Montagnais Indians of Algonquian origin lived in Labrador. The earliest white settlers were French fur traders and seal hunters. They established trading posts along the coast before Britain seized Labrador from France in 1759, during the French and Indian War. English-speaking settlers also built homes there, mostly in the 1800's. Explorers of the Hudson's Bay Company ventured into Labrador's interior in the 1840's.

The white settlers, Eskimos, and Indians were leading lives of extreme hardship when Wilfred T. Grenfell, an English medical missionary, first visited them in 1892. Grenfell made their suffering known and obtained money to build hospitals, schools, and church missions in Labrador.

Newfoundland and Quebec disputed the ownership and boundaries of the Labrador interior as interest grew in the area's resources. In 1927, the British Privy Council finally settled this question by defining the present boundaries in favor of Newfoundland. It interpreted the term "coast" as "watershed." Thus, the Newfoundland part of Labrador includes the area drained by rivers

20

flowing into the Atlantic Ocean along the east coast.

During World War II, the U.S. Army arranged with Great Britain to station American troops in Labrador to keep Nazi submarine raiders from using the coastal waters as a base. Newfoundland became a province of Canada in 1949. Industrial companies then began to develop the rich natural resources of Labrador.

In 1967, construction on the largest hydroelectric development in the Western Hemisphere started at Churchill Falls. The plant's first generators began operating in 1971. The facility has a generating capacity of 5,225,000 kilowatts.   FRED W. ROWE

Critically reviewed by GORDON OLIVER ROTHNEY

See also CHURCHILL RIVER; GOOSE BAY; GRENFELL, SIR WILFRED T.; LABRADOR CURRENT; NEWFOUNDLAND.

LABRADOR CURRENT is a cold ocean current that rises in the Arctic Ocean. It flows along the shores of Labrador to a point near the island of Newfoundland, where it meets the Gulf Stream. The influence of the Labrador Current is felt as far south as New England. The harbors of Labrador are blocked with ice for about half the year, partly because of this cold current. But

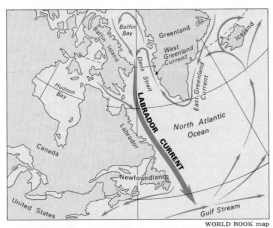

WORLD BOOK map

The Labrador Current flows along the eastern shore of Labrador and the island of Newfoundland. It is formed in the Davis Strait by converging cold currents.

the ports of the British Isles, which have the same latitude as Labrador, remain open to shipping throughout the year. These ports are ice-free partly because of the warm Gulf Stream. When cold air above the Labrador Current meets the warm, moist winds above the Gulf Stream, heavy fogs form off the coast.   HENRY STOMMEL

See also FOG; OCEAN (How the Ocean Moves).

LABRADOR DUCK. See BIRD (Extinct Birds).

LABRADOR RETRIEVER is a very popular breed of dog trained to bring back game that has been shot. The dog originally came from Newfoundland, not Labrador. It was developed in England. The Labrador has two outstanding characteristics, its coat and its tail. The coat is thick and water-resistant. It is usually black, but may be yellow or chocolate. The dog's tail is short and unusually thick at the base.   MAXWELL RIDDLE

See also DOG (color picture: Sporting Dogs).

LABRADOR TEA is the name of six kinds of small evergreen plants in the heath family. They grow in the swamps of Greenland, Northern Europe, and in northern and subarctic North America. The leaves have a mild narcotic substance and have been used for tea and as a substitute for hops in making beer. Tannin, used in tanning animal hides, also comes from the leaves.

Scientific Classification. Labrador tea plants are members of the heath family, *Ericaceae*. These plants make up the genus *Ledum*.   HAROLD NORMAN MOLDENKE

LABRADORITE. See FELDSPAR.

LA BREA PITS, *luh BRAY uh*, are one of the world's richest known sources of Ice Age fossils. They lie in Hancock Park in Los Angeles. Beginning in 1906, when the remains of a giant prehistoric bear were found, about a million well-preserved skeletons of saber-toothed tigers, giant wolves, llamas, camels, horses, giant ground sloths, and other ancient animals have been dug from the various layers of oil and tar. These animals became trapped when they came to drink from the shallow pool that covered the sticky asphalt bog. Some of the Indians in this area used the pitch to cover their baskets and canoes. Early Spanish settlers waterproofed their adobe houses with it. Exposition Park in Los Angeles displays a number of plants and animals which were taken from the La Brea pits.   GEORGE SHAFTEL

LA BRUYÈRE, *la bryoo YAIR*, **JEAN DE** (1645-1696), was a French satirist. He is best known for *The Characters of Theophrastus, Translated from the Greek, with the Characters and Mores of This Age*. The book appeared in 1688 as an appendix to his translation of a work by Theophrastus, a Greek philosopher of the 200's B.C. In each of the nine editions published during his lifetime, La Bruyère increased his own contribution so that the *Characters* stands as an original work. La Bruyère ridiculed the injustice and hypocrisy he saw in French life. He grouped his observations under 16 chapter titles, including "The City," "The Court," "Fashion," and "Personal Merit."

La Bruyère was born in Paris. He spent much of his life tutoring the children of noble families. In 1693, he was admitted to the French Academy.   JULES BRODY

LABURNUM, *luh BUR num*, is a small tree with bright yellow blossoms. Its glossy leaves remain green until late in the autumn. The seeds grow in pods. The *common laburnum*, native to Asia, is sometimes called *golden chain* because of its long clusters of yellow flowers. It is also called *bean tree* and *bean trefoil*. This kind of laburnum is somewhat sensitive to cold. The *Scotch laburnum* is native to southern Europe. It is hardier than the common laburnum, and has longer flower clusters. Laburnums have hard, fine-grained wood. The seeds, roots, and other parts of the laburnum contain a poisonous substance called *cytisine*.

Scientific Classification. Laburnums belong to the pea family, *Leguminosae*. The common laburnum is genus *Laburnum*, species *L. anagyroides*.   T. EWALD MAKI

LABYRINTH, in anatomy. See EAR (The Inner Ear).

LABYRINTH was a building with many confusing paths and passageways. According to legend, Daedalus built it for King Minos of Crete. Minos wanted it as a prison for the monster called the Minotaur. He sacrificed seven Greek youths and seven maidens to the Minotaur every year.

Theseus, the son of a Greek king, went into the

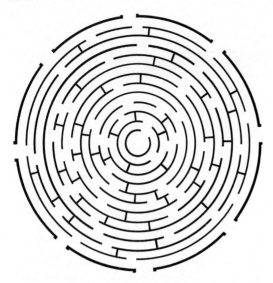

The Labyrinth, or Maze, was first designed as a prison. The ancient Egyptians built a labyrinth similar to the one shown here.

labyrinth, killed the Minotaur, and found his way out of the twisting passages. Ariadne, Minos' daughter, had given him a ball of thread to unwind as he went in. He followed the thread and escaped.

Archaeologists have discovered a palace which may have been the Cretan labyrinth. It is full of winding passages, and stands on a mountainside near Knossos in Crete. Traces of another great labyrinth were found in Egypt. Herodotus says that the Egyptian labyrinth was more marvelous than the Pyramids. It was probably built in imitation of the older Cretan labyrinth.

Buildings with confusing and seemingly endless networks of passages are found in many amusement parks. A modern labyrinth of this nature is sometimes called a *maze*, and is used for testing skill in escape. Many toys and games are based on the pattern of the labyrinth. Psychologists use mazes in experiments to test the reactions of animals (see LEARNING [Multiple-Response Learning]). PADRAIC COLUM

See also MINOTAUR; NEW HARMONY (picture).

LAC is a sticky substance given off by scale insects. They gather by the hundreds of thousands on the twigs and branches of the soapberry and acacia trees of India and Burma. The sticky substance these insects secrete is called *lac*. It comes from the Persian word *lak* and the Hindu word *lakh*, both of which mean *hundred thousand*. The shellac that protects furniture and floors is made from lac (see SHELLAC).

Lac insects are tiny and scaly, with wings that fold back along their bodies. They pierce the bark of trees with their long beaks and feed on the sap. As they do so, they discharge a quantity of lac to protect themselves from their enemies. The female insect lays several hundred eggs before she dies. The young insects hatch out as wormlike *larvae*. When the larvae grow into insects, they look for new, fresh twigs to feed on. This period in their life cycle is called *swarming*.

Lac is usually harvested by cutting almost all the twigs before the larvae mature. Workers leave some larvae to provide future generations of insects. When the larvae are ready to swarm, the twigs are fastened onto trees where the workers want the insects to feed.

The crude substance gathered from the twigs is called *stick lac*. Workers grind it between stones and wash it in water to remove the coloring matter. In this stage, the substance is called *seed lac*. Workers melt seed lac in long, narrow cloth bags and squeeze it through the cloth to filter out impurities. Then they take the warm lac between their teeth, toes, and fingers and stretch it into thin sheets. When these sheets cool, they are broken into flakes. The orange-colored shellac we buy is made from these flakes by dissolving them in alcohol. Lac may also be bleached and sold as white shellac. It is often formed into cakes called *button lac*.

Shellac can be molded into electric insulators and other articles. It is also used in abrasives, sealing wax, and some phonograph records. CHARLES L. MANTELL

LAC LÉMAN. See LAKE GENEVA.

LACCADIVE ISLANDS, *LAK uh dive*, are a group of tiny coral islands off the southwestern coast of India. They occupy about 7 square miles (18 square kilometers) in the Arabian Sea and are part of the Union Territory of Lakshadweep, formerly known as Laccadive, Minicoy, and Amindivi Islands Territory (see INDIA [physical map]). The territory covers about 12 square miles (32 square kilometers) and has a population of about 32,000. Most of the people in the territory live on the Laccadive Islands. The rest inhabit the Amindivi Islands.

Most of the islanders speak the Malayalam language, but they belong to various Arabian tribes. The women make an elastic fiber called *coir* from coconut husks. Coir is used in the manufacture of matting. The men build boats and trade on the mainland. They exchange their copra and coconut fiber chiefly for rice, their principal food. ROBERT I. CRANE

LACE is an open fabric made with threads of linen, cotton, silk, silver, or gold. It may also be made from nylon and, to a limited extent, from wool. Handmade lace is usually made from linen thread, because of the thread's softness and strength. Most lace consists of two elements: the pattern, called the *toilé*, and the ground that holds the pattern together, called the *réseau*. The word *lace* comes from the Latin word *laqueus*, which means *noose* or *snare*.

The two main types of lace are *bobbin* and *needlepoint*. Other types of lace are *crocheting*, made with a needle, and *tatting*, made by knotting threads.

Bobbin Lace is associated with the Flemish people of Belgium and The Netherlands. But it is also made in Italy, France, and England. Bobbin lace is sometimes called *pillow lace*, because the design is drawn on a pillow or on parchment fastened to a pillow. The lacemaker sticks small pegs into the pillow along the lines of the design, and works many small bobbins of thread around the pegs to produce the lace. As the lace is completed, the lacemaker pulls the pins out and removes the lace from the pillow. Some of the best-known bobbin laces include Mechlin, Binche, Maltese, Valenciennes, Lille, Chantilly, Honiton, and Cluny.

Needlepoint Lace. The ground for needlepoint lace may be either net or connecting threads called *brides*. In making this type of lace, the lacemaker first draws the design on parchment and stitches it to a backing

Some Types of Bobbin Lace

Bobbin lace, also called *pillow lace*, is made by drawing a design on a pillow or on parchment fastened to a pillow. Pegs are stuck into the pillow along the lines of the design, and bobbins of thread are pulled around the pegs to produce the lace.

Chantilly

Irish, Limerick

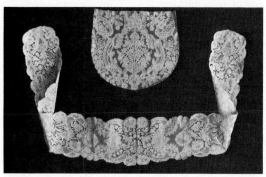

Point d'Angleterre

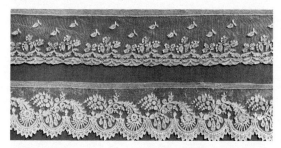

Valenciennes

Some Types of Needlepoint Lace

When making needlepoint lace, the lacemaker first draws a design on a piece of parchment. The parchment is then stitched to a stiff linen backing. Next, the lacemaker fills in the design with a needle and thread.

Spanish

Alençon

Argentan

Venetian, Gros

LACEDAEMON

Fine Bobbin Lace, long associated with the Flemish people, is still made by hand in Bruges, a city in Belgium.

of stout linen. Lace is then made by filling in the pattern with buttonhole stitches. The pattern may be made separately and the ground added later. Or the lacemaker may create the two together by carrying several threads along to make stitches for the pattern and ground at the same time.

Needlepoint lace is called *point* in France and *punto* in Italy. Both words mean *stitch*. This type of lace should not be confused with a kind of embroidery that is also called needlepoint (see NEEDLEPOINT). Examples of needlepoint lace include Venetian, Alençon, Argentan, and Brussels.

Development. The first lacelike decorations, called *passementerie*, consisted of narrow braids or edgings known as *passements*. Lace, as we know it, developed in Italy in the 1400's. It grew out of the cutwork, or open pattern, in embroidery. The beautiful lace of the Renaissance was glorified in art by such painters as Raphael, Frans Hals, and Velázquez. It was a mark of prosperity. Catherine de Médicis introduced lace into France in 1533. Lafayette first brought it to America.

Most lace is now made by machine. Machines can copy accurately almost every kind of lace made by hand. The lace machine was developed in England. By 1780, net machines were used in France. In 1809, John Heathcoat of England patented a "bobbin net" machine, which John Leavers improved in 1813. This machine became the basis for lace machines used today. Rhode Island produces about 70 per cent of all Leavers lace made in the United States.

Comparison of machine-made and handmade laces indicates that the latter can be raveled, and have more irregularities in pattern. The threads are interwoven so that they will not slide back and forth. Machine-made lace has a flat, dull appearance.   HELEN MARLEY CALAWAY

See also CROCHETING; BELGIUM (picture: Beautiful Lace); TEXTILE (Other Fabrics).

LACEDAEMON. See SPARTA.

LA CEIBA, *lah SAY bah* (pop. 38,582), a chief Caribbean port of Honduras, lies 115 miles (185 kilometers) north of Tegucigalpa. La Ceiba is a distribution center for the products of north and northeast Honduras. Industries in La Ceiba produce footwear, cigars, soap, and coconut oil. The area's exports include abacá fiber, coconuts, and oranges. For the location of La Ceiba, see HONDURAS (map).

LACERATION. See BRUISE.

LACEWING is a frail insect with two pairs of pretty lacy wings for which it is named. Lacewings lay their eggs on the tips of small threadlike stems attached to a leaf. Only one egg is laid on a stem. This prevents the hungry newly hatched larva from eating its neighbors. The larvae are yellow or grayish. They have large sickle-shaped jaws to capture and suck the juices of aphids, scales, mites, leafhoppers, and thrips. The larvae are sometimes called *aphis lions*. The full-grown larva spins a silk cocoon. After two weeks, an adult lacewing emerges.

Scientific Classification. Lacewings belong to the order Neuroptera. They make up the green lacewing family, Chrysopidae, and the brown lacewing family, Hemerobiidae.   E. GORTON LINSLEY

See also INSECT (picture: Familiar Insects of North America); LARVA (picture).

The Lacewing Deserves Its Name. The four graceful wings are so thin and delicate that they look like spun glass.

LACHESIS. See FATES.

LACHINE, *luh SHEEN*, Que. (pop. 37,521), is an industrial center and port on the island of Montreal. The island is at the eastern end of Lake St. Louis at the head of the Lachine Rapids (see QUEBEC [political map]). The 9-mile (14-kilometer) Lachine Canal, which permitted ships on the St. Lawrence River to by-pass the rapids, was closed in 1970. A causeway was built over the canal for the 1967 Montreal World's Fair. Factories in Lachine make cement, electrical apparatus, steel products, rubber, and wire. Lachine was settled in the late 1600's.   MURRAY G. BALLANTYNE

LACHRYMAL GLAND. See TEARS.

LACKAWANNA RIVER, *LACK uh WAHN uh,* is a small stream in Pennsylvania. Its valley holds the largest *anthracite* (hard coal) fields in the United States. The Lackawanna rises in the northeastern part of the state near Union Dale and flows southwest for about 50 miles (80 kilometers) through a narrow pass between the Shawnee and Moosic mountains. The river empties into the Susquehanna River at Pittston. Scranton is the industrial center of the valley.   S. K. STEVENS

LACKLAND. See JOHN of England.

LACLÈDE LIGUEST, PIERRE. See SAINT LOUIS.

LACOMBE, ALBERT. See ALBERTA (The Missionaries).

LACONIA. See SPARTA.

LACQUER, *LACK er,* is a shiny, protective film used on metals, woods, and porcelain. Lacquer is made from compounds of cellulose, resin, or lac.

Lacquer made with resin is called a true "spirit" varnish. The resin is usually mixed with turpentine. The turpentine evaporates when it is exposed to air, leaving only the coating of resin on the material. When a cellulose compound is used to make lacquer, the compound is usually dissolved in butyl alcohol or butyl acetate. The butyl compounds also evaporate when exposed to air. When lac is used to make lacquer, the evaporating solution used is ethyl alcohol. These lacquers are made in all colors that are commonly found in paints.

In the Orient, a natural lacquer is obtained from the sap of the lacquer, or varnish, tree. The Japanese and Chinese tap the tree and collect the sap. Then they strain the sap, and dry it by heat. This makes a dark-brown liquid as thick as syrup. The liquid is diluted and sometimes colored before it is used as lacquer.

Modern lacquers are used to finish thousands of materials, including metals, paper, wood, and fabrics. The paper industry uses both clear and colored lacquers to finish packages, labels, and book covers. In the furniture industry, lacquers are especially useful in retaining the color of blond furniture. They also give a waterproof finish to furniture. In the automobile industry, lacquers are used to give a high gloss to automobile finishes. Acrylic-resin lacquers make an excellent coating for polished metals such as brass and chromium.   WILLIAM M. MILLIKEN

See also CELLULOSE; LAC; RESIN; VARNISH.

LACQUER WARE is a beautiful Oriental product made by applying many coats of a certain varnish to

Field Museum of Natural History

Buddhist Head was carved from hardened lacquer. This head probably dates from the Sung dynasty in China.

The Art Institute of Chicago

A Carved Chinese Plate of Red Lacquer Ware, made about 1300, has a design of peony flowers, buds, and leaves.

such articles as trays, boxes, dishes, vases, and furniture. The true lacquer of China and Japan comes from the sap of the lacquer tree (*Rhus verniciflua*), which grows in China. But the shellac and nitrocellulose compositions made in Europe and North America are also called lacquer.

The Japanese learned the process of lacquering from China, probably in the A.D. 500's. The treasure of the Shoshoin in Nara, Japan, found in 756, has early examples of Chinese lacquer.

A piece of Japanese lacquer ware has a foundation of wood, sometimes as thin as paper, with perhaps 35 thin coats of black lacquer. Each coat is dried and highly polished before the next one is put on. The pictures are drawn with powders of various colors. They are protected with a coat of transparent lacquer.

Good lacquer wares are works of art. They are so durable that they show no wear for hundreds of years. A collection of lacquer ware recovered from a sunken ship was exhibited in Vienna in 1878. Eighteen months of exposure in sea water had failed to damage the lacquer.   WILLIAM M. MILLIKEN

See also LACQUER.

LA CROSSE, Wis. (pop. 48,347; met. area pop. 91,-056), is a manufacturing and trading center at the junction of the La Crosse and Mississippi rivers in the southern part of the state. For location, see WISCONSIN (political map). It ranks as Wisconsin's largest city on the Mississippi. The city is named after the Indian game of lacrosse. Founded in 1842, and chartered as a city in 1856, La Crosse early became an important sawmill center and manufacturing point for agricultural machinery. Today, the city makes aircraft instruments, automobile parts, air-conditioning equipment, farm tools, and rubber boots and shoes.

Viterbo College and a campus of the University of Wisconsin are in La Crosse. The city also has about 30 primary and secondary schools. La Crosse has a mayor-council form of government, and is the county seat of La Crosse County.   JAMES I. CLARK

Lacrosse is a fast team sport. Players use a stick with a net pocket at one end to move the ball down the field. A team tries to score by putting the ball into the opponent's goal.

Jerry Wachter, Focus on Sports

LACROSSE, *luh KRAWS,* is a fast game adopted from the North American Indians. It is popular in Australia, Canada, England, and the United States. The object of lacrosse is to score a goal by throwing, scooping, or kicking a solid rubber ball into the opposing team's goal. Players move the ball with a stick that has a net pocket at one end. The word *lacrosse* comes from the French words *la crosse,* meaning *the crook.* The stick is formally called a *crosse.*

Men's Lacrosse is played on a field 110 yards (101 meters) long and 53⅓ to 60 yards (49 to 55 meters) wide. The net goals are centered between the sidelines with 15 yards (14 meters) of playing area behind each goal. The goals are 6 feet (1.8 meters) high and 6 feet wide. A circle with an 18-foot (5.5-meter) diameter, called the *goal crease,* surrounds each goal. The field is divided in half by the center line.

A team consists of a goalkeeper, three defensemen, three midfielders, and three attackmen. Each player uses his stick to throw, catch, or carry the ball. Sticks have two parts, a handle and a head. Most handles are made of aluminum or wood. The head consists of a leather and

string pocket attached to a plastic frame. Sticks range from 40 inches to 6 feet (102 to 180 centimeters) long, and the heads from 6½ to 10 inches (16.5 to 25.4 centimeters) wide. Attacking players use shorter sticks with smaller heads than defensive players. The goalie's stick is 10 to 12 inches (25.4 to 30.5 centimeters) wide. The ball is slightly smaller than a baseball. When thrown, it can travel up to 100 miles (160.9 kilometers) per hour. Players wear shorts, cleated shoes, plastic helmets, arm pads, and padded gloves.

A game consists of four 15-minute quarters. A *face-off* in the center of the field starts play at the beginning of each quarter, and after a goal is scored. In a face-off, two midfielders crouch down with their sticks on the ground. The referee places the ball between the two sticks, and the players try to gain possession of it at the referee's signal. The other midfielders can move when play begins, but the defensemen, attackmen, and goalkeepers must remain in their own areas until possession is indicated by the referee. The ball is carried in the stick and passed or kicked by the players to get it in the opponent's goal.

Each team must always have at least three players on the offensive end of the field and four players on the defensive end. Violation of this rule is called *offsides.* Only the goalkeepers may touch or bat the ball with their hands. A referee, an umpire, and a field judge serve as officials.

Opposing players may *check* (block) each other with the stick or the body. Body checking above the knees and from the front is legal. Illegal body checks are *personal fouls,* requiring the player to leave the game for 1 to 3 minutes, depending on how serious the official considers the foul. In most cases, players must leave for 30 seconds for such *technical fouls* as offsides. A team must play short-handed during this time.

Women's Lacrosse is usually played on a field 120 yards (110 meters) long and 70 yards (64 meters) wide. But rules do not list specific field dimensions. A team consists of 12 players. The game is 50 minutes long, divided into 25-minute halves with a 10-minute intermission between halves. Women's rules do not allow body contact.

History. Lacrosse developed from a game played by Canadian Indians. The Indian game was a rough, often brutal sport, with as many as a thousand warriors taking

Lacrosse Field Diagram and Players' Positions

This diagram shows a men's lacrosse field and the positions players take at the start of a game. The game begins with a face-off between two midfielders at the cross mark in the center of the field. Women's games are played with 12 players on each side instead of 10. The women's field has no official boundaries but is usually somewhat longer and wider than a men's field.

Key to Positions

D = Defenseman
A = Attackman
M = Midfielder
G = Goalkeeper

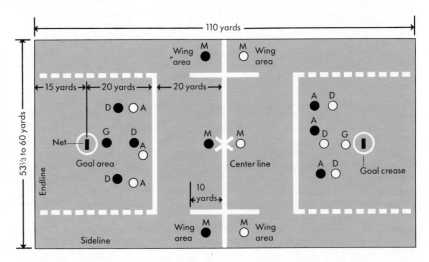

part. Canadians adopted the Indian game, forming the Montreal Lacrosse Club in 1856. In 1868, the game was brought to the United States. The first intercollegiate lacrosse association was formed in 1882. Don Zimmerman

Additional Resources

Brackenridge, Celia. *Women's Lacrosse.* Barron's, 1978.

James, Stuart. *Lacrosse for Beginners.* Messner, 1981. For younger readers.

Scott, Bob. *Lacrosse: Techniques and Tradition.* Johns Hopkins, 1978.

Walker, Jay R. *How to Play Winning Lacrosse.* Cornerstone, 1980. For younger readers.

LACTATION, *lak TAY shuhn,* is the giving of milk by mammals. Before pregnant mammals give birth to their young, milk begins to form in the mother's *mammary glands* (see MAMMARY GLANDS). Certain chemicals called *hormones* stimulate cells in the mammary glands to produce milk. Lactation begins as soon as the infant is born. Young mammals feed on milk until they are able to get food by themselves. Milk contains substances necessary for growth, such as carbohydrates, fats, and proteins. After a while, other hormones stop the milk production.

The lactation period varies in different *species* (kinds) of mammals. For example, the lactation period lasts about 10 months in cows, and about 2 years in walruses. When the mammal becomes pregnant again, the lactation period begins once more.

See also MAMMAL.

LACTIC ACID, *LAK tihk,* is the common organic acid found in milk and other dairy foods that have turned "sour." It also occurs in sauerkraut, pickles, and beer. One form, called *sarcolactic acid,* is found in blood and muscles. It has been called the "acid of fatigue," because the amount of sarcolactic acid in the muscles increases when a person is tired.

Lactic acid is formed naturally by the fermentation of *lactose* (milk sugar). Its name comes from the Latin word *lac,* which means *milk.* Carl Scheele, a Swedish chemist, first isolated the acid from sour milk in 1780.

Commercially, the acid is prepared by fermentation of cornstarch, glucose, molasses, or *whey* (the watery part of milk). It is widely used in foods and beverages to bring out flavor. The tanning industry uses crude lactic acid to remove lime from hides. The textile industry uses it in dyeing wool. It combines with alcohols to form *lactate esters,* used as lacquer solvents.

Lactic acid is a colorless or yellowish syrupy liquid that mixes readily with water. Its chemical formula is $C_2H_4(OH)COOH$. It has several forms that differ only in the arrangement of the atoms. John E. Leffler

See also ACID; SCHEELE, CARL WILHELM.

LACTOSE. See CARBOHYDRATE.

LADIES' GARMENT WORKERS' UNION, INTERNATIONAL. See GARMENT WORKERS' UNION, INTERNATIONAL LADIES'.

LADIES PROFESSIONAL GOLF ASSOCIATION. See GOLF (Major Tournaments; Women's Golf).

LADING, BILL OF. See BILL OF LADING.

LADOGA, LAKE. See LAKE LADOGA.

LADRONE. See PIRATE.

LADY is a member of the nobility or the wife of a nobleman. In Great Britain, a woman who holds a title in her own right, including *marchioness, countess, viscountess,* or *baroness,* ranks as a lady. The daughter of a

duke, marquess, or earl is also called a lady. The wife of a knight or baronet carries the title *lady,* but loses it if her husband dies and she marries a commoner. A lady of the royal household is a *lady in waiting,* and a lord mayor's wife is a *lady mayoress.* The first ladies gained seats in the House of Lords in 1958. See also NOBILITY (Privileges of the Peerage). I. J. Sanders

LADY GODIVA. See GODIVA, LADY.

LADY OF THE LAKE. See SCOTT, SIR WALTER (HIS LIFE).

LADYBUG, also called *ladybird,* is a small beetle with a round body shaped like half a pea. It is often bright red or yellow, with black, red, white, or yellow spots. Ladybugs feed chiefly on plant lice and scale insects. For this reason, fruitgrowers find ladybugs helpful. During the early 1900's, plant lice almost destroyed the fruit crop of California, and ladybugs were brought in to destroy the plant lice and save the crop. There are two kinds of ladybugs that harm beans, melons, squashes, and other garden plants. But the work of the beneficial kinds of ladybugs far outweighs the damage done by the few harmful ones.

USDA

Ladybug

Scientific Classification. Ladybugs are in the order Coleoptera and make up the family Coccinellidae. There are about 150 species in the United States. R. E. Blackwelder

See also APHID; BEETLE (color picture); INSECT (Insect Control; pictures: Insect Predators; A Swarm of Ladybugs).

LADY'S-SLIPPER, also called *moccasin flower,* is any one of several showy wild flowers of the orchid family. The plants grow in moist woodlands of many parts of Europe, Asia, and America. Certain petals of the blossoms are large and lip-shaped so that they resemble a slipper or moccasin.

The *showy lady's-slipper,* or *pink and white lady's-slipper,* is the state flower of Minnesota. Its large flowers are white, but its lip is tinged with brilliant pinkish purple. The *yellow lady's-slipper* has beautiful, waxy, yellow flowers. Its petals twist in a spiral. The *pink lady's-slipper* is the provincial flower of Prince Edward Island. The blossoms have a velvety pink or white lip with reddish veins and greenish brown sepals. The *small white lady's-slipper* grows in such damp places as bogs and marshy meadows.

Some tropical orchids with slipper-shaped petals are also called lady's-slippers. They grow in North and South America and in Asia.

Scientific Classification. Lady's-slippers belong to the orchid family, Orchidaceae. There are four genera of lady's-slippers: *Cypripedium, Paphiopedilum, Phragmipedium,* and *Selenipedium.* Robert W. Hoshaw

See also ORCHID.

LADY'S-THUMB. See SMARTWEED.

LAËNNEC, *lay NEHK,* **RENÉ THÉOPHILE HYACINTHE,** *ruh NAY tay aw FEEL ya SANT* (1781-1826),

LAETRILE

a French physician, invented the stethoscope in 1816. Doctors use this instrument to listen to the sounds of the heart and other organs. Laënnec investigated diseases of the heart and the lungs, and published his conclusions in *A Treatise on Mediate Auscultation* (1819). He died from tuberculosis, a disease on which he had become an expert. Laënnec was born in Quimper, France, and studied with Jean Nicolas Corvisart, Napoleon's favorite physician. See also STETHOSCOPE.   GEORGE ROSEN

LAETRILE, *LAY uh trihl,* is a controversial drug used to treat cancer. Most cancer specialists oppose the use of laetrile because it has not been proved effective as a cancer treatment. But supporters of laetrile claim that it has halted or even cured cancer in many patients.

Laetrile is extracted from apricot pits. Certain enzymes in many foods break down laetrile. During this process, a poisonous substance called *cyanide* is released. Many supporters of laetrile claim that the enzymes are also present in cancer cells. They believe that after laetrile is injected into the bloodstream of a patient, cyanide is released in the cancer cells and kills them. According to this theory, healthy body cells are not affected because they do not contain the enzymes that break down laetrile.

Laetrile is usually administered by injecting it into the bloodstream. However, some cancer victims take laetrile pills, which are broken down in the stomach by certain enzymes contained in many foods. Cyanide poisoning, which can be fatal, may result.

In the United States, 18 states have legalized the manufacture, sale, and use of laetrile. But the U.S. Food and Drug Administration (FDA) has banned the transportation of laetrile—and of substances used to make it—across state borders. As a result, laetrile is generally not available in the United States, even in states that have legalized it. Many Americans receive laetrile treatment in Mexico, where the drug is legal and readily available.

Some people in the United States favor nationwide legalization of laetrile. They insist that cancer patients have the right to choose any form of treatment that they may desire. Opponents argue that if laetrile were available, many cancer victims would choose it mainly because it has fewer side effects than other forms of therapy. As a result, the patients who chose laetrile would lose any chance of being helped by traditional forms of treatment.

In an effort to settle the controversy over laetrile's effectiveness, the National Cancer Institute began a study of the drug in 1980. The results from this study, released in 1981, showed that laetrile had been ineffective in treating cancer in human patients and that the drug could be dangerous.   THOMAS H. MAUGH II

LA FARGE, *luh FAHRZH,* **JOHN** (1835-1910), was an American painter. In the 1860's, La Farge painted many landscapes and still lifes of flowers that reveal a sensitivity to delicate shadings of light and atmosphere. During the 1880's and 1890's, he painted a number of murals in a style derived from Italian Renaissance art. La Farge visited Japan in 1886 and Polynesia in 1890 and 1891. These trips inspired a series of fresh, bright water colors. La Farge made an important contribution to stained-glass design by inventing new techniques for

Maua, Our Boatman, an oil painting on canvas; Addison Gallery of American Art, Phillips Academy, Andover, Mass.

A John La Farge Portrait of a Tahitian man was painted in 1891, while the artist was visiting Polynesia. La Farge was one of the first American artists to travel to the Pacific Islands. He painted many pictures of the scenery and people he saw there.

producing colors of remarkable brilliance. He designed richly colored stained-glass windows for the mansions of wealthy clients and for churches.

La Farge was born in New York City. He traveled widely and was part of an intellectual circle that included the writers Henry Adams and Henry James. La Farge also lectured and wrote on art theory.   SARAH BURNS

LA FARGE, *luh FAHRZH,* **OLIVER** (1901-1963), was an American author and anthropologist. La Farge was best known for his novels and short stories about Indian life in the American Southwest and in Central America. He also wrote studies of Indian ceremonies, customs, and languages. La Farge became a leading spokesman for the rights of Indians in the United States.

La Farge received the 1930 Pulitzer prize for fiction for his first novel, *Laughing Boy* (1929). The book describes a Navajo Indian's problems adapting to white society. La Farge's other fiction about Indians includes the novels *Sparks Fly Upward* (1931), *The Enemy Gods* (1937), and the stories collected in *All the Young Men* (1935). One of his major anthropological works is *Tribes and Temples* (1927), written with the American anthropologist Frans Blom. The book describes the Maya Indian language.

Oliver Hazard Perry La Farge was born in New York City. During the 1920's, he made several archaeological expeditions to Arizona, Mexico, and Guatemala to study Indian culture. La Farge was also active in a number of organizations devoted to improving the life of American Indians. La Farge settled in Santa Fe, N. Mex., about 1940.   SAMUEL CHASE COALE

LA FAYETTE, MADAME DE (1634-1693), was a French novelist. *The Princess of Cleves* (1678), her masterpiece, has been called the first French psychological novel. The book is noted for its sober style and simple structure. Set in the 1500's, it is the story of a princess who is secretly in love with the Duke of Nemours, a dashing nobleman at the court of Henry II. The princess confides her secret to her adoring husband, who dies of a broken heart. But the princess refuses to marry Nemours because she believes he is incapable of remaining faithful to her. She retires to a convent and dies a lonely death. Madame de La Fayette wrote two lesser works, *The Princess of Montpensier* (1662), a novelette; and *Zayde* (1670), a rambling romantic tale.

Madame de La Fayette was born Marie Madelaine Pioche de La Vergne in Paris, and married François, Comte de La Fayette.   JULES BRODY

LAFAYETTE, MARQUIS DE (1757-1834), was a French soldier and statesman. He fought for American independence and was a prominent leader in the French Revolution. Lafayette's liberal beliefs cost him his fortune, his social position, and even his freedom, but his actions won the respect of Americans and Frenchmen alike.

Lafayette was born at Chavaniac, in Haute Loire, on Sept. 6, 1757. His full name was Marie Joseph Paul Yves Roch Gilbert du Motier. His father died in battle when the boy was 2 years old. When his mother and grandfather died 11 years later, he inherited a great fortune. Lafayette came from a long line of soldiers and studied at the Military Academy in Versailles. At the age of 16, he married Adrienne de Noailles, a daughter of one of the most influential families in France. Shortly afterward, Lafayette became a captain in the cavalry.

Service to the United States. Lafayette disliked court life. He welcomed the American Revolution as an opportunity to win military glory by fighting against England for France. He purchased a ship and landed in America in 1777 with a party of soldier-adventurers. The 20-year-old marquis impressed the Continental Congress. He was made a major general without pay, and joined George Washington's staff.

Lafayette was wounded at the battle of Brandywine. At Gloucester, he defeated a small party of Hessians. This earned him the command of a division. He served at Valley Forge during part of the terrible winter of 1777-1778. Early in 1778, at Albany, N.Y., he was given command of a proposed invasion of Canada. The plan was abandoned because of the mismanagement of others. He led troops in the battles of Barren Hill and Monmouth, and in the campaign of Rhode Island.

In 1779, after France declared war on England, Lafayette returned home as a hero. He hoped to join an invasion of England, but it never took place. Instead, he persuaded his government to send aid to the American colonists.

In April, 1780, Lafayette returned to his post as major general in the American Army. Later that year, he served in the court-martial that condemned Major John André to be hanged as a spy for plotting with Benedict Arnold to surrender West Point (see ANDRÉ, JOHN).

In 1781, Lafayette led a small American force in Virginia that evaded and then stopped the British under General Charles Cornwallis. After the French fleet bot-

Oil portrait on canvas (1799) by Charles Willson Peale; courtesy of Washington and Lee University, Lexington, Va.

Marquis de Lafayette helped the colonists during the Revolutionary War in America. He became a major general in the American Army, persuaded France to aid the colonists, and assisted in the negotiations that won American independence.

tled up the English at Yorktown, Lafayette cooperated with the Comte de Rochambeau and Washington in forcing Cornwallis to surrender.

Lafayette had become a "hero to two worlds" when he reached France in 1782. He assisted in the negotiations that won American independence, and, at the age of 24, was raised to the rank of *marechal-de-camp* (brigadier general) in the French Army by King Louis XVI. He was now influential in both America and in France. At home in France, he cooperated closely with Benjamin Franklin, and later with Thomas Jefferson, in behalf of American interests.

Later Visits to America. Lafayette revisited America in 1784 and stayed at Mount Vernon with Washington. He came again in 1824. Both times, a grateful nation received him with enthusiasm. American appreciation also took the form, in 1803, of a huge land grant to Lafayette in Louisiana. During his last visit, Congress voted that $200,000 and a township in Florida be given to him. Lafayette had by that time lost nearly all his French properties. He sold most of his American land.

Reforms at Home. After 1782, Lafayette became absorbed in the questions of free trade, tax reform, emancipation of slaves, and religious freedom for Protestants. In the events leading to the French Revolution in 1789, he did not hesitate to sacrifice court favor and position in behalf of his liberal ideas. Lafayette was one of the first persons to advocate a National Assembly, and he worked to make France a constitutional monarchy.

As commander of the new National Guard, Lafayette was one of the most powerful men in France from 1789 to 1791. But he did not believe in seizing power for himself. He was unwilling to work with the corrupt but able Comte de Mirabeau. Queen Marie Antoinette and her court resented Lafayette. She said: "It would be better to perish than be saved by M. de Lafayette." As radicalism spread, Lafayette found it necessary to suppress mob violence. By the summer of 1791, his popularity had gone. He found himself hated by the people, the former nobles, and the court.

After the Constitution of 1791 went into effect, Lafayette temporarily retired from active politics. When war against England broke out early in 1792, he took charge of troops in what is now Belgium. As the military front collapsed, he unsuccessfully tried to suppress the rising tide of Jacobin radicalism at home (see JACOBINS). But the king and queen would not accept his help, and the troops he tried to turn on the Paris mob would not follow his orders. Lafayette, denounced as a traitor, fled abroad. The Austrians imprisoned him in 1792 until Napoleon's victories won his release in 1797.

The impoverished Lafayette returned to France when Napoleon became first consul in 1799. He refused to help Napoleon's dictatorship, rejecting a seat in the senate and a diplomatic post in the United States. In 1815, after his first abdication, Napoleon returned from Elba and gave France a liberal constitution. Lafayette was elected to the Chamber of Deputies. As one of the vice-presidents of the chamber, Lafayette worked for Napoleon's second abdication after the Battle of Waterloo.

Except for the reactionary periods of 1815 to 1817 and 1824 to 1827, Lafayette continued to serve in the Chamber of Deputies. He became a center of liberal resistance to the Bourbon kings. He upheld American interests, and fought for the cause of independence and reform in Greece, Spain, Portugal, Italy, Poland, and the South American republics.

Last Years. Once more, in 1830, Lafayette became the leader of a revolution that dethroned the Bourbons. Again in command of the National Guard, he refused a popular demand that he become president of the new republic. Instead, he used his influence to make Louis Philippe the constitutional monarch of France. But Lafayette came to regret this decision and, before his death in 1834, he began to hope for a pure republic in France.   RAYMOND O. ROCKWOOD

See also MORSE, SAMUEL F. B. (picture); WASHINGTON, GEORGE (picture: Lafayette and Washington).

Additional Resources

BUCKMAN, PETER. *Lafayette: A Biography*. Paddington, 1977.
GOTTSCHALK, LOUIS R. *Lafayette Comes to America*. Univ. of Chicago Press. First of 6 vols. about Lafayette by this author and publisher, 1935-1973.
LAFAYETTE, MARQUIS DE. *Lafayette in the Age of the American Revolution: Selected Letters and Papers, 1776-1790*. 4 vols. Cornell Univ. Press, 1977-1981.

LAFFITE, *lah FEET,* **JEAN** (1780?-1826?), also spelled LAFITTE, was a New Orleans smuggler, pirate, and patriot. In 1810, he became chief of a band of outlaws with headquarters on Grande Terre Island in Barataria Bay in the Gulf of Mexico. With his brother Pierre, he commanded a fleet of ships and raided both Spanish and neutral vessels in the Gulf. His ships flew the flags of the Central and South American nations revolting against Spain.

In 1813, Governor William Claiborne of Louisiana offered $500 for Laffite's capture. Laffite, then at the height of his power, boldly offered $1,500 for the governor's head. All efforts to take and prosecute Laffite under the law failed.

In 1814, the British were at war with the United States. They offered Laffite $30,000, a pardon, and a naval captaincy if he would aid them in attacking New Orleans. He refused, informed the United States government of the plans, and offered the services of the Barataria smugglers to the United States. Laffite fought for General Andrew Jackson in the Battle of New Orleans on Jan. 8, 1815, and received a pardon from President James Madison.

American forces had destroyed the community at Barataria, so Laffite moved to Galveston Island. There, he established a town called Campeachy, and returned

Culver

Lafayette and George Washington began their lifelong friendship in 1777, when Lafayette volunteered to serve the American colonists during the Revolutionary War. The Frenchman spent much time and money helping the colonists.

to piracy. He made himself "governor" of the island. After he raided the Louisiana coast and scuttled an American ship, the United States sent an expedition in 1821 to destroy the Galveston pirate colony. Laffite, who in spite of his swagger could be a gallant gentleman, quietly yielded, set fire to his town, and sailed away. Most historians believe that he died either in exile in Yucatán or in battle. Jean Laffite was born in France. WILLARD H. BONNER

See also LOUISIANA (Places to Visit [Grand Isle]).

Additional Resources

GONZALEZ, CATHERINE. *Lafitte: The Terror of the Gulf.* Eakin Pub., 1981.
STOCKTON, FRANK R. *Buccaneers and Pirates of Our Coasts.* Macmillan, 1967.
TALLANT, ROBERT. *The Pirate Lafitte and the Battle of New Orleans.* Random House, 1951. Also suitable for younger readers.

LA FOLLETTE, *luh FAHL iht,* is the name of an American family that was prominent in politics and social reform.

Robert Marion La Follette, Sr. (1855-1925), sometimes called "Battling Bob," was an American political leader and reformer. For 25 years, he was the most important figure in Wisconsin politics.

La Follette became a lawyer in 1880, and a United States congressman in 1885. Following his defeat in the election of 1890, he practiced law in Madison, Wis. He became the

Culver Service

Robert M. La Follette, Sr.

leader of a group within the Republican Party that opposed the conservative state leadership. Elected governor in 1900, La Follette made Wisconsin progressive. At his urging, the legislature provided for direct primary elections, equalization of taxation, conservation of forests, and control of railroad rates.

From 1906 to 1925, La Follette served as a United States senator. He advocated strict railroad regulation, lower tariffs, conservation, and better conditions for American sailors. He opposed U.S. entry into World War I and U.S. membership in the League of Nations.

La Follette broke with the Republicans in 1924 when Calvin Coolidge was nominated for President. La Follette accepted the presidential nomination of a new Progressive Party, backed by independents and many labor groups. He received almost 5 million votes but carried only Wisconsin. La Follette was born in Primrose, Wis., near Mount Vernon. He represents Wisconsin in Statuary Hall in the U.S. Capitol. See PROGRESSIVE PARTY.

Belle Case La Follette (1859-1931), the wife of Robert M. La Follette, Sr., was a noted journalist, speaker, and social reformer. She promoted many progressive causes and strongly supported women's rights.

In 1885, Belle La Follette became the first woman to graduate from the University of Wisconsin Law School. She did not practice law but used her legal training extensively in assisting her husband throughout his political career. In 1909, she and her husband established *La Follette's Magazine.* She edited its "Home and Educa-

tion" department. Belle La Follette strongly opposed war, and she worked with the Woman's Peace Party during World War I. After the war, she helped found the Women's Committee for World Disarmament.

Many Wisconsin leaders urged Belle La Follette to run for her husband's seat in the U.S. Senate after he died in 1925. She refused to do so but helped her son Robert win election to the office. She was born in Summit, Wis., near Mauston.

Robert Marion La Follette, Jr. (1895-1953), was elected United States senator from Wisconsin after his father's death. He supported the rights of organized labor and led a movement to increase the efficiency of Congress. The Wisconsin Progressives, under La Follette's leadership, continued as an independent party until 1946, when they rejoined the Republicans. La Follette was defeated in a try for renomination to the Senate in the 1946 Republican primary. He was born in Madison.

Philip Fox La Follette (1897-1965), the second son of Robert La Follette, Sr., and Belle La Follette, served as governor of Wisconsin from 1931 to 1933, and again from 1935 to 1939. During his terms, legislation was passed to aid labor, farmers, and homeowners. La Follette was born in Madison. DAVID P. THELEN

Additional Resources

MANEY, PATRICK J. *Young Bob La Follette: A Biography of Robert M. La Follette, Jr., 1895-1953.* Univ. of Missouri Press, 1978.
THELEN, DAVID P. *Robert M. La Follette and the Insurgent Spirit.* Little, Brown, 1976.

LA FONTAINE, *lah fawn TEHN,* **JEAN DE,** *zhahn duh* (1621-1695), a French poet, is famous for his *Fables* (1668-1694). Modeled on *Aesop's Fables,* La Fontaine's fables portray human behavior through animal characters. But La Fontaine suggests more forcefully than Aesop that life is a jungle. La Fontaine treated such serious subjects as power, greed, and violence with an amused, philosophical acceptance. He wrote his fables in light, natural verse. Despite their pessimism and sophistication, the *Fables* still play a large role in the education of French children. La Fontaine also wrote a collection of racy stories called *Contes* (*Tales*) (1664-1666).

La Fontaine was born in Château-Thierry. His friends described him as childlike, absent-minded, and ill-at-ease in society. A series of wealthy, cultured patrons supported him. JULES BRODY

LAFONTAINE, *lah fawn TEHN,* **SIR LOUIS HIPPOLYTE,** *lwee ee paw LEET* (1807-1864), a champion of self-government for Canada, served with Robert Baldwin as joint head of the government from 1842 to 1843 and 1848 to 1851. He became chief justice of Lower Canada in 1853. He had supported the French-Canadian reformer Louis Papineau, but he opposed force and broke with Papineau before the rebellion of 1837 (see REBELLION OF 1837-1838). Lafontaine was born in Boucherville, Que. JEAN BRUCHÉSI

LAG BA'OMER, *lahg BOH muhr,* is a minor Jewish festival that falls on the 18th day of the Hebrew month of Iyar. It is the 33d day of the *omer,* the days separating the festivals of Passover and Shabuot (see PASSOVER; SHABUOT). Lag Ba'Omer is called *The Scholar's Festival* because it celebrates the end of a violent epidemic that raged among the students of Rabbi Akiba in Palestine during the A.D. 100's. LEONARD C. MISHKIN

LAGAN. See FLOTSAM, JETSAM, AND LAGAN.

LAGERKVIST, *LAH guhr KVIHST,* **PÄR FABIAN,** *pair* (1891-1974), a Swedish novelist, playwright, and poet, won the Nobel Prize for literature in 1951. He is known for such plays as *The Hangman* (1933), *Midsummer Night in the Workhouse* (1941), and *Let Man Live* (1949), and such novels as *The Dwarf* (1944), *Barabbas* (1951), and *Pilgrim at Sea* (1964). His lyrical poetry has deep philosophical content. He wrote about the cruelty of his time, and urged people to show more humanity and tolerance. He was born in Växjö, Sweden. EINAR HAUGEN

LAGERLÖF, *LAH gehr LUHF,* **SELMA** (1858-1940), a Swedish writer, won the 1909 Nobel Prize for literature. She is best remembered for the meaning and depth she gave to materials of folk origin. *Gösta Berling's Saga* (1891), her first novel, is her most admired book. It is a fantastic romance in loosely related episodes that deal with a swashbuckling defrocked minister and his fellow adventurers. Like much of Lagerlöf's fiction, the book is set in Värmland, the province in west-central Sweden where Lagerlöf was born.

Selma Lagerlöf

Religion plays an important part in Lagerlöf's writing. In her two-volume novel *Jerusalem* (1901-1902), she tells the story of a Swedish religious group awaiting the second coming of Christ. In *Christ Legends* (1904), she elaborates on Christian mythology.

The Wonderful Adventures of Nils (1906-1907) is a geography textbook in fairy tale form. It describes Sweden through the eyes of a boy traveling over the country on the back of a wild goose. The book is both factually sound and full of charm. Lagerlöf also used fairy tale elements in *Liljecrona's Home* (1911), a story based on her own family in the early 1800's. The trilogy *The Ring of the Löwenskölds* (1925-1928) combines mystery, romance, and family history. It includes *The General's Ring, Charlotte Löwensköld,* and *Anna Svärd.*

Selma Ottiliana Lovisa Lagerlöf was born in Mårbacka, her simple family home in Värmland. She was a teacher from 1885 to 1895. Her home is now a Swedish national shrine. RICHARD B. VOWLES

LAGOON is a shallow body of water separated from the open sea. The land that separates a lagoon from the sea may be a coral reef, a sandy ridge called a *spit,* or a narrow expanse of sand called a *barrier island.* Lagoons formed by barrier islands are found along the east coast of the United States and along the Gulf of Mexico.

Sand and other sediments carried in by ocean tides build up in a lagoon because it is protected from the pounding action of waves. These deposits eventually fill in the lagoon and connect the two stretches of land that it separates. See also ATOLL. ANTHONY J. LEWIS

LAGOS, *LAH gohs* or *LAY gahs* (pop. 1,149,200), is the capital and largest city of Nigeria. Located in south-

Pictorial Parade

Lagos is Nigeria's capital and chief port. Automobiles and other motor vehicles crowd the streets of this busy commercial center.

western Nigeria, Lagos lies partly on the African mainland and partly on four islands in the Gulf of Guinea. For location, see NIGERIA (political map).

Lagos is Nigeria's chief port and commercial center. The city's harbor handles about 2 million short tons (1.8 million metric tons) of cargo yearly. Lagos serves as the chief outlet for Nigeria's animal hides and skins, cacao, palm tree products, peanuts, and timber. The city's air, railway, road, and water transportation facilities provide links with other parts of Nigeria. An international airport operates at nearby Ikeja.

Lagos is Nigeria's main manufacturing city. Its industries include the assembly of motor vehicles and radios, brewing, food processing, oil storage, steel processing, tire retreading, and the production of textiles, soap, and candles.

Yoruba people lived in what is now Lagos before Portuguese explorers arrived in the late 1400's. Lagos was a major slave market until 1851, when it became a British protectorate. Britain annexed Lagos in 1861 and made it the capital of Nigeria in 1914.

In 1979, the Nigerian government began building a new city called Abuja near the center of the country to replace Lagos as the capital. But by the mid-1980's, little progress had been made in the construction of Abuja, and Lagos remained the capital. J. F. ADE AJAYI

LAGRANGE, *luh GRAYNJ* or *lah GRAHNZH,* **JOSEPH LOUIS** (1736-1813), was a French mathematician. His most famous work, *Analytical Mechanics* (1788), is an algebraic study of the forces and motion involved in orbits of planets, the flow of liquids, and vibrating strings. Lagrange also wrote on interpolation, probability, and number theory, and helped set up the French metric system. Lagrange was born in Turin, Italy. At the age of 16, he became a professor of mathematics in the royal artillery school in Turin. PHILLIP S. JONES

See also NUMBER THEORY.

LA GUAIRA, *lah GWY rah* (pop. 20,344), is a Venezuelan port. It handles most of the trade of the country's central highlands, and also serves as a port for Caracas, 10 miles (16 kilometers) inland. For location, see VENEZUELA (political map).

LA GUARDIA, *luh GWAHR dee uh,* **FIORELLO HENRY,** *FEE uh REHL oh* (1882-1947), gained national fame as the mayor of New York City from 1934 to 1945. He became known as an efficient reformer. His program included park and street development and slum clearance. La Guardia kept in touch with the people, and was admired by members of all political parties.

La Guardia's political career began in the United States House of Representatives, where he served from 1917 to 1921 and from 1923 to 1933. A liberal Republican, he cosponsored the Norris-La Guardia Anti-Injunction Act of 1932, which protected the rights of striking workers. La Guardia was born in New York City, and was graduated from the New York University law school. JOHN A. GARRATY

United Press Int.
Fiorello La Guardia

LA GUARDIA AIRPORT, *luh GWAHR dee uh,* on Flushing Bay in Queens County, N.Y., serves the New York City metropolitan area. About 300,000 planes a year land or take off at the airport. The airport's more than 20 scheduled airlines carry about 20 million passengers a year. The 650-acre (263-hectare) airport opened in 1939. It was leased to The Port of New York Authority (now The Port Authority of New York and New Jersey) in 1947. A redevelopment program was completed in 1967. The project included a new passenger terminal and runways on piles over Flushing Bay.

Critically reviewed by THE PORT AUTHORITY OF NEW YORK AND NEW JERSEY

LAHORE, *luh HOHR* (pop. 2,952,689), is the capital of Punjab Province in Pakistan. The town lies in a rich farming area (see PAKISTAN [political map]). It is a center of weaving, milling, and other industries. Lahore is also an educational center. It has a museum and several schools, including the Punjab University.

The oldest part of the town is at least a thousand years old. It has many landmarks that recall the glories of the Mogul period in India's history. Lahore was the capital of the Sikh Empire before the British took it over, and has many historic Sikh shrines. Under British rule, it was the capital of the entire Punjab. A brick wall 15 feet (5 meters) high surrounds the old section of Lahore. Many of the houses have balconies and lattice windows ornamented with carved woodwork. Lahore has a magnificent Muslim mosque, a mausoleum, and a royal palace. The European quarter was founded in 1849 outside the city walls. ROBERT I. CRANE

LAIRD, MELVIN ROBERT (1922-   ), served as secretary of defense under President Richard M. Nixon from January 1969 to January 1973. In June 1973, he became counselor to the President for domestic affairs. Laird left this post in January 1974 to become a senior counselor of the Reader's Digest Association. Laird had previously spent 16 years in the United States

House of Representatives, where he became an influential Republican Party leader.

Laird was elected to the U.S. House in 1952 after six years in the Wisconsin state Senate. As a member of the appropriations committee, he specialized in defense and health programs. Laird was chairman of the platform committee at the 1964 Republican convention. He was chairman of the House Republican Conference from 1965 through 1968.

As secretary of defense, Laird became noted for his support of U.S. military superiority in order to negotiate from strength with the Soviet Union. He also supported the establishment of a volunteer army.

Laird was born in Omaha, Nebr., and grew up in Marshfield, Wis. He graduated from Carleton College. Laird served in the United States Navy during World War II (1939-1945). DAVID S. BRODER

LAISSEZ FAIRE, *LEHS ay FAIR,* is a theory of economic policy which states that government generally should not interfere with decisions made in an open, competitive market. These decisions include setting prices and wages and making other choices that affect the sale of goods and services. According to laissez faire, workers are most productive and a nation's economy functions most efficiently when people can pursue their private economic interest in relative freedom.

Laissez faire is a French phrase meaning *allow to do.* It was first made popular by a group of French writers called *physiocrats* between the 1750's and 1780's. At that time, the governments of many European countries practiced a set of policies known as *mercantilism.* Mercantilism involved strict regulation of agriculture, industry, and trade. Its chief goal was to ensure that exports exceeded imports. The physiocrats insisted that such restrictions actually hindered the growth of trade.

A group of thinkers called the *British classical school,* led by the Scottish economist Adam Smith, gave the laissez-faire principle its fullest explanation and defense between the 1770's and the 1840's. Their support came at a time when laissez faire suited the needs of a rapidly developing industrial economy. The classical economists started from the assumption that individuals are motivated by self-interest. They maintained that people serve their own interests best when they provide the goods and services most wanted by others. Individuals who are free to operate in an open, competitive market automatically promote prosperity for all. Thus, the government should have little to do with the economy.

The theory of laissez faire greatly influenced economic thought and action during the early and mid-1800's. Later, however, critics charged that laissez faire failed to solve many economic and social problems that had arisen. Gradually, the governments of industrialized nations started to regulate economic activities more closely. They also began to pass laws aimed at relieving such social problems as poverty and unemployment.

Some modern economists call for a return to laissez-faire policies. The American economist Milton Friedman ranks as one of the leading supporters of such policies. WILLIAM D. G. HUNTER

See also CAPITALISM; ECONOMICS (Capitalism; Early Theories); FREEDOM (Economic Freedom); PHYSIOCRATS; SMITH, ADAM.

Mike Roberts Studios

Different Kinds of Lakes include artificial lakes, glacial lakes, and volcanic lakes. Artificial lakes are created by blocking streams to store up water for irrigation, electric power, and recreation. Shasta Lake, *above,* was formed when Shasta Dam was built on the Sacramento River in California.

LAKE is a body of water surrounded by land. Lakes may be found in all parts of the world. Some large bodies of water commonly known as seas are really lakes. These include the Dead Sea, the Sea of Galilee, and the Caspian Sea. Some lakes lie near the highest regions of the earth, and others are far below sea level. Lake Titicaca, in South America, is 12,507 feet (3,812 meters) above sea level. The Dead Sea, between Israel and Jordan, lies about 1,310 feet (399 meters) below sea level. The word *lake* comes from the Greek word *lakkos,* meaning *hole* or *pond.*

The Life of a Lake

How Lakes Are Formed. The greatest number of lakes lie in regions that were once covered by glaciers. Glaciers cut deep valleys as they travel, and glacial deposits act as a dam. When a glacier begins to melt, its waters often collect in these valleys to form lakes. This action of glaciers explains why there are more lakes in the northern part of the United States than in the southern part. Minnesota has about 11,000 lakes formed by the action of glaciers. The Great Lakes were formed partly by glacial action.

Other areas that abound in lakes are regions lying on bedrocks of limestone, such as the Florida peninsula. More than 1,400 lakes and ponds lie in Lake County,

Florida. In a limestone region, the underlying lime rock dissolves slowly in rainwater, which is slightly acid. This action eventually forms a pattern of underground streams to carry off the rainfall. When the tops of these subterranean passages collapse, a depression called a *sinkhole* appears on the surface. The sinkhole may then fill with water and become a lake or a pond.

Sinkholes may be 60 feet (18 meters) or more deep. They sometimes lie in the course of a fast-flowing underground stream. In such cases, the sinkhole fills quickly, forming a beautiful pool of crystal-clear water. The uplands region of northern Florida has many of these "springs," as they are known locally. The largest and best known is Silver Springs.

Lakes may also form in a number of other ways. The natural collection of rainwater in the craters of extinct volcanoes can create lakes. Crater Lake in Oregon was formed in this manner. Lakes may appear when rivers deposit silt until the natural outlet to the sea is closed, and the water backs up. Dam construction creates great artificial lakes called *reservoirs.* The lake behind the dam in Kariba Gorge, on Africa's Zambezi River, is more than 175 miles (282 kilometers) long.

How Lakes Are Fed. Rivers and mountain streams feed some lakes. Other lakes do not appear to have any water coming into them. They are actually fed by

Thomas Hollyman, Photo Researchers

Volcanic Lakes form when water collects in the craters of extinct volcanoes. Poás Volcano in Costa Rica, *above,* contains a volcanic lake in one of its craters.

Glacial Lakes form in areas where glaciers have cut deep gashes in the earth's surface. The beautiful lakes, *right,* near Bergen, Norway, are glacial lakes.

J. L. Stage, Photo Researchers

underground springs or streams. Still other lakes have inlets but no outlets. The Great Salt Lake in Utah is an example of a lake which has no streams running out of it.

How Lakes Disappear. The lakes that now exist will probably disappear in time. Lakes dry up because of a change in climate or a change in the course of the waters that feed them. A bursting volcano or earthquake sometimes changes the surface of the surrounding region and causes lakes to disappear. Lakes may also drain into other bodies of water and vanish.

Ground water fills the sinkholes in limestone areas. A long drought in such areas can completely dry up lakes and ponds in sinkholes. A seepage outlet in a sinkhole may also dry up a lake by draining the water into an underground cavern. Many low-lying regions on the earth's surface are the basins of lakes that have disappeared. The dried-out beds of former lakes may form excellent soils.

The Lake Habitat. Lakes create little worlds of their own. Water plants of all shapes and sizes live under the surface. Some of the plants are attached to the lake bottom, and other float free. This vegetation provides food for water creatures such as bugs, snails, and fish. Lakes are also the favorite haunts of waterfowl such as ducks, geese, swans, flamingos, egrets, cranes, and others.

Land animals use lakes for drinking water. They also get food from lakes in the form of fish, birds, and plant life.

The Importance of Lakes

Climate. The presence of large lakes in a region greatly influences the lives of the people living nearby. Lakes affect weather conditions over a large area. In summer, a lake never gets as warm as the surrounding land. As a result, breezes blowing over the water are cooled. In winter, a lake does not cool off as fast as the land, and may cause the climate to be warmer.

Warm winds blowing off a lake in autumn make it possible for certain crops to grow especially well. The warming influence of Lake Ontario in autumn extends the growing season of southern Ontario, making it possible to raise fruits and corn. The great fruit belt of Michigan, along the east shore of Lake Michigan, depends partly on winds off the lake. Cool spring winds delay the blossoming of the fruit trees until the danger of a killing frost has passed. Warm winds in autumn allow the fruit crops to be harvested before the frost strikes. The thousands of lakes in central Florida have an important effect on the location of the state's citrus-fruit industry. Careful studies have shown that these lakes help reduce the damaging effects of cold spells which might cause great loss to fruitgrowers.

World's Largest Natural Lakes

Lake	Location	Area In sq. mi.	Area In km²	Length In mi.	Length In km	Maximum width In mi.	Maximum width In km	Maximum depth In ft.	Maximum depth In m
Caspian Sea*	Iran-Russia	143,630	372,000	746	1,201	300	483	3,264	995
Lake Superior	Canada-United States	31,700	82,103	350	563	160	257	1,333	406
Lake Victoria	Kenya-Tanzania-Uganda	26,828	69,484	260	418	150	241	270	82
Aral Sea*	Russia	25,660	66,459	270	435	175	282	223	68
Lake Huron	Canada-United States	23,050	59,699	206	332	183	295	750	229
Lake Michigan	United States	22,300	57,757	307	494	118	190	923	281
Lake Tanganyika	Burundi-Tanzania-Zaire-Zambia	12,700	32,893	420	676	30	48	4,708	1,435
Great Bear Lake	Canada	12,275	31,792	211	340	110	177	1,350	411
Lake Baikal	Russia	12,162	31,499	395	636	49	79	5,315	1,620
Lake Nyasa	Malawi-Mozambique-Tanzania	11,100	28,749	350	563	50	80	2,300	701

*Salt-water

Travel and Trade Routes. The growth of travel and commerce on the Great Lakes provides a typical example of people's use of lakes. The early explorers of North America used lakes and their connecting rivers as their chief travel routes. Some of these explorers paddled canoes up the St. Lawrence River to the Great Lakes.

Steamboats took the place of canoes as the civilization of white people expanded. Today, freighters, tugboats, and barges work their way along inland navigation routes on the Great Lakes, carrying raw materials to the industrial cities along the lakes. Products carried on the Great Lakes include coal, iron, and grain.

Irrigation. Lakes provide an important source of water for irrigation. Water may be fed from the lakes to farmers' fields by ditches or canals, or it may be pumped into an overhead system of sprinklers. People have built huge dams on rivers in desert areas to create reservoirs of water for irrigation. The Egyptians built the Aswan High Dam on the Nile River partly for this purpose. The dams on the Indus River provide water to irrigate $36\frac{1}{2}$ million acres (14.8 million hectares) of desert land. These irrigated regions, which lie mainly in Pakistan, supply food for millions of persons.

Water Supply has been a serious problem ever since people started to live in towns and cities. Lakes offered a natural reservoir of water for early communities. But most cities today have outgrown such natural supplies, and people have built huge storage dams to provide additional water. The reservoirs formed by these dams sometimes lie far away from the city. For example, New York City uses water from the Catskill Mountains more than 100 miles (160 kilometers) away.

Recreation. People use lakes for a variety of recreational activities. They flock to lakes to enjoy fishing, boating, swimming, water-skiing, hunting, ice skating, and ice boating. In states such as Florida, the freshwater recreational industry provides millions of dollars of income every year. SIGISMOND deR. DIETTRICH

Related Articles in WORLD BOOK include:

AFRICA

Lake Albert
Lake Bangweulu
Lake Chad
Lake Edward
Lake Nasser
Lake Nyasa

Lake Tana
Lake Tanganyika
Lake Turkana
Lake Victoria
Lake Volta

ASIA AND AUSTRALIA

Aral Sea
Caspian Sea
Dead Sea
Lake Baikal

Lake Balkhash
Lake Eyre
Lake Torrens
Sea of Galilee

CANADA

Great Bear Lake
Great Lakes
Great Slave Lake
Lake Agassiz
Lake Athabasca
Lake Champlain
Lake Erie
Lake Huron
Lake Louise
Lake Manitoba
Lake Memphremagog

Lake of the Woods
Lake Ontario
Lake Saint Clair
Lake Saint Lawrence
Lake Superior
Lake Winnipeg
Lake Winnipegosis
Muskoka Lakes
Rainy Lake
Reindeer Lake

CENTRAL AMERICA AND SOUTH AMERICA

Gatun Lake
Lake Maracaibo

Lake Nicaragua
Lake Titicaca

EUROPE

Caspian Sea
Lake Como
Lake Constance
Lake Geneva
Lake Ilmen
Lake Ladoga
Lake Maggiore

Lake of Lucerne
Lake Onega
Lake Peipus
Lakes of Killarney
Loch Lomond
Lough Neagh
Windermere

UNITED STATES

Crater Lake
Finger Lakes
Great Lakes
Great Salt Lake
Kentucky Lake
Lake Champlain
Lake Erie
Lake George
Lake Huron
Lake Mead
Lake Memphremagog
Lake Michigan
Lake O' The Cherokees
Lake of the Ozarks
Lake of the Woods
Lake Okeechobee

Lake Ontario
Lake Ouachita
Lake Placid
Lake Pontchartrain
Lake Powell
Lake Saint Clair
Lake Saint Lawrence
Lake Superior
Lake Tahoe
Lake Texoma
Lake Winnebago
Lake Winnipesaukee
Oneida Lake
Rainy Lake
Reelfoot Lake
Salton Sea

OTHER RELATED ARTICLES

Lagoon
Lake Xochimilco
Limnology

Oxbow Lake
Pond

LAKE is a coloring substance that will not wash out. It is formed by combining *mordants* with dyestuffs. Mordants are usually metallic salts which change to metallic hydroxides. These react chemically with soluble dyes to form the insoluble, colored lakes.

There are two kinds of lakes. One is produced from natural dyes. The other is made from coal-tar dyes. Natural lakes include carmine, madder, and the Vienna dyes fixed with aluminum or tin. Carmine lake is prepared from the coloring matter of cochineal insects. Carmine lake is a beautiful scarlet color. Madder lake is red. It comes from the root of the madder plant. Vienna lake is a violet color and comes from brazilwood.

Coal-tar dyes can give a much wider range of color. These dyes are produced at a much lower cost. They have almost entirely replaced the natural lakes. Lakes are used in calico-printing, silk-dyeing, for decorative work, color-printing, and also as color pigments in paints and lacquers. HOWARD L. NEEDLES

See also MORDANT.

LAKE AGASSIZ, *AG uh SEE,* was a large body of water which once existed in North America. It covered much of the area of present-day Manitoba, and portions of neighboring states and provinces. The lake came into existence late in the Ice Age (see ICE AGE). As the ice sheet which covered the area moved northeastward, it left a large, shallow basin behind it. Melting ice and river water filled the basin to form Lake Agassiz. When the ice continued to melt at the lake's north and east shores, the waters drained away toward Hudson Bay. Several smaller lakes, including Winnipeg, Winnipegosis, and Manitoba, were left in the deeper part of the area. The shorelines of the ancient lake are visible. The plain of Canada's Red River of the North, one of the world's most fertile wheat-growing regions, is the former lake bed. Its rich soil was deposited by Lake Agassiz. JOHN BRIAN BIRD

See also RED RIVER OF THE NORTH.

LAKE ALBANO, *al BAHN oh,* lies in the crater of an extinct volcano in west-central Italy. For location, see ITALY (physical map). Ancient Romans vacationed at this lake, then called *Albanus Lacus.* According to legend, the city of Alba Longa was founded here by Ascanius, son of the Trojan warrior Aeneas.

LAKE ALBERT, also called Albert Nyanza, one of the sources of the Nile River, lies between Uganda and Zaire. It covers about 1,640 square miles (4,248 square kilometers). It is about 100 miles (160 kilometers) long and about 20 miles (32 kilometers) wide. For location, see NILE RIVER (map). The waters of Lake Albert come from Lake Edward to the south through the Semliki River, and drain out to the north by way of the Albert Nile. Lake Albert was named for the husband of Queen Victoria of Great Britain. HARRY R. RUDIN

LAKE ATHABASCA, *ATH uh BAS kuh,* is the fourth largest lake entirely within the borders of Canada. It has an area of 3,120 square miles (8,081 square kilometers). About a third of the lake lies in the northeastern part of the province of Alberta, and the rest in Saskatchewan. The Athabasca River flows into the southwestern tip of the lake. The Slave River discharges from this tip of Lake Athabasca. During the breeding season, many Canadian geese nest along the low, sandy shores of Lake Athabasca. Wood Buffalo National Park borders the western end of the lake. JOHN BRIAN BIRD

LAKE BAIKAL, *by KAHL,* also spelled *Lake Baykal,* is the deepest lake in the world. It also contains more water than any other freshwater lake. Lake Baikal lies in southeastern Siberia, a part of the Soviet Union. It is 5,315 feet (1,620 meters) deep at its deepest point and consists of more than 20 per cent of the world's unfrozen fresh water. Lake Baikal covers an area of 12,162 square miles (31,499 square kilometers). It measures about 395 miles (636 kilometers) long and about 49 miles (79 kilometers) wide at its widest point. The Soviet Union's first national park, consisting of Lake Baikal and the surrounding area, was established in 1967.

Lake Athabasca

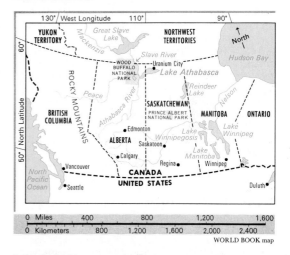

WORLD BOOK map

Lake Baikal

Area: 12,162 sq. mi. (31,499 km²)
Elevation: 1,493 ft. (455 m) above sea level
Deepest Point: • 5,315 ft. (1,620 m)

— Road +— Railroad

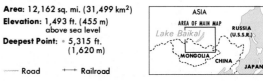

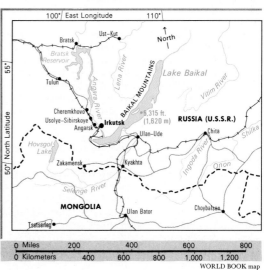

WORLD BOOK map

LAKE BALKHASH

Lake Baikal is one of the world's oldest lakes. It was formed about 25 million years ago by movements of the earth's crust. Many kinds of wildlife 'live only in Lake Baikal or the nearby area. They include the golomyanka and other kinds of fish. The Baikal seal—found only in the lake—is one of the few kinds of seals that live in bodies of fresh water.

The large volume of water in Lake Baikal affects the weather in the surrounding area. For example, the area nearest the lake has temperatures several degrees warmer in winter, and cooler in summer, than places farther inland. The lake's surface is frozen from January to May. Although 336 rivers flow into Lake Baikal, only one, the Angara, empties out of it.

The chief products of the Lake Baikal region include cellulose, paper, timber, and fish. Hydroelectric dams on the Angara River supply power to the city of Irkutsk and other nearby communities.   GEORGE J. DEMKO

LAKE BALKHASH, *bahl KAHSH,* is a large lake in southeastern Kazakhstan in Russia. The lake lies 1,122 feet (342 meters) above sea level and has an area of 6,670 square miles (17,275 square kilometers). It is only 6 miles (10 kilometers) wide in the eastern part, and 54 miles (87 kilometers) wide at the western end. The water in the western part of the lake is fresh because of the inflow of the Ili River, but there is salt water at the eastern end. Several rivers empty into Lake Balkhash, but the lake has no outlet. Ice covers the lake from November to April. For location of Lake Balkhash, see RUSSIA (physical map).   THEODORE SHABAD

LAKE BANGWEULU, *BANG wee OO loo,* is a shallow depression about 50 miles (80 kilometers) long and 30 miles (48 kilometers) wide in northern Zambia (formerly Northern Rhodesia). For location, see ZAMBIA (map). Much of the area to the south and southeast is swamp, which floods in the rainy season. The normal size of the lake is about 1,900 square miles (4,920 square kilometers), but the flood waters increase it to about 4,500 square miles (11,700 square kilometers).

The Luapula River, which flows out of the southern end of Lake Bangweulu, is one of the headstreams of the Congo River. David Livingstone, the British explorer, reached Lake Bangweulu in 1868. Livingstone died near the lake in 1873.   KENNETH ROBINSON

See also STANLEY AND LIVINGSTONE.

LAKE BAYKAL. See LAKE BAIKAL.

LAKE CHAD is a large lake in north-central Africa. Most of it lies within Chad, and the rest lies in Nigeria, Cameroon, and Niger. For location, see CHAD (map). Scientists think its average size expands and contracts in 10-year cycles, but its overall size has shrunk for many years. It now has an area of about 6,300 square miles (16,300 square kilometers). Its shoreline changes in relation to the quantity of water that rivers emptying into it pour into the lake, and the rate of water evaporation. It is much larger in rainy seasons than in dry seasons. Lake Chad is seldom deeper than 22 feet (7 meters) because its basin is so shallow that water overflows into the countryside. Many islands rise from the surface, which is covered by a tangle of grasses and weeds. This matted surface has caused many people to refer to the lake as "a drowned prairie." The lake's name in French is *Lac Tchad.*   ALAN P. MERRIAM

Lake Champlain

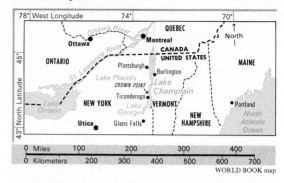

WORLD BOOK map

LAKE CHAMPLAIN, *sham PLAYN,* is a long, narrow lake lying on the border between New York and Vermont, with its northern end extending into the province of Quebec, Canada. The lake is 125 miles (201 kilometers) long and from $\frac{1}{2}$ to 14 miles (0.8 to 23 kilometers) wide. Its greatest depth is 400 feet (122 meters). The lake was named for the French explorer Samuel de Champlain, who in 1609 became the first European to reach it. Summer homes and resorts lie on many islands in the lake. During the Revolutionary War and the War of 1812, the lake was the scene of several naval battles.   WILLIAM E. YOUNG

See also CHAMPLAIN, SAMUEL DE.

LAKE CHAMPLAIN, BATTLE OF. See WAR OF 1812 (Chief Battles of the War).

LAKE CHARLES (pop. 75,226; met. area pop. 167,223) is an industrial and shipping center in southwestern Louisiana. Lake Charles lies on a lake of the same name and on the Calcasieu River. A channel links the city and the Gulf of Mexico, which lies about 34 miles (55 kilometers) to the south (see LOUISIANA [political map]).

The center of Lake Charles, which includes City Hall and a civic center, lies along the lake. The Arcade Theater, built in 1910, is one of the city's landmarks. In the early 1900's, road shows traveling west from New Orleans performed at the theater. McNeese State University is in Lake Charles.

In the early 1780's, Charles Sallier became the first white person to settle within the present city limits of Lake Charles. The settlement around the lake came to be known as Charlestown (or Charleston), and was renamed Lake Charles in 1867. Oil and natural gas were discovered in the area in the late 1800's, and the channel to the Gulf of Mexico was opened in 1926. Petroleum, chemical, and shipping industries were developed. The city's products now include chemicals, refined petroleum, plastics, and synthetic rubber. Lake Charles is the *parish* (county) seat of Calcasieu Parish and has a mayor-council form of government.   JAMES C. "JIM" BEAM

LAKE CLARK NATIONAL PARK is in southern Alaska, across Cook Inlet from Anchorage. For location, see ALASKA (political map). The park's features include lakes, rivers, valleys, and mountains—including two active volcanoes. Lake Clark, in the park, provides an important breeding ground for red salmon. Wildlife includes bears, caribou, Dall sheep, foxes, minks, otters, and wolves. The park attracts several thousand visitors a year, but much of it is unexplored.

Lake Como

Area: 56 sq. mi. (145 km²)
Elevation: 653 ft. (199 m) above sea level
Deepest Point: • 1,345 ft. (410 m)

—— Road

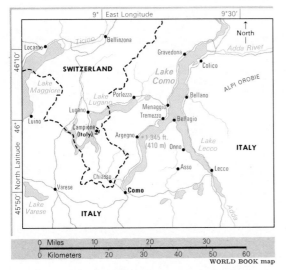

WORLD BOOK map

The area was established as a national monument in 1978 and became a national park in 1980. For its area, see NATIONAL PARK SYSTEM (table: National Parks).

Critically reviewed by the NATIONAL PARK SERVICE

LAKE COMO, *KOH moh*, is a famous beauty spot of northern Italy. Lake Como is called *Lago di Como* in Italian. It lies in the province of Lombardy at the foot of the Alps. The lake covers an area of 56 square miles (145 square kilometers). Its shores are lined with handsome summer homes, fine gardens, and fertile vineyards. The Adda River runs through Lake Como. Thousands of tourists visit Como, the chief town on the lake, each year.   W. R. McCONNELL

LAKE CONSTANCE, or BODENSEE in German, lies at the eastern end of the Swiss Plateau, at the border of Germany, Switzerland, and Austria. The lake covers 208 square miles (539 square kilometers). It is about 45 miles (72 kilometers) long and 10 miles (16 kilometers) wide. Of glacial origin, Lake Constance occupies a basin in the Rhine River. The level of the lake rises and falls with the melting of ice and snow in the neighboring Alps. Many towns and villages line the shore of the lake, including Constance and Romanshorn. Old castles, monasteries, and churches dot the countryside. Vineyards and orchards grow near the shore of Lake Constance.   FRANKLIN CARL ERICKSON

LAKE DWELLING. Early peoples in Europe sometimes built dwelling places in lakes or at the edges of lakes or creeks. Scientists have come to call these houses lake dwellings. The people placed their houses on wooden platforms which stood on *piles*, or posts. They drove the foundations deep into the mud, and often held them steady by stones stacked around their bases. Some houses were clustered in villages.

The Greek historian Herodotus, who lived in the 400's B.C., made the first known mention of lake dwell-

ings. He wrote of a lake-dwelling community in Macedonia. Archaeologists first found the remains of prehistoric lake houses in 1853, in a lake near Zurich, Switzerland. The relics had been preserved by the waters of the lake, and by the mud of the lake bottom. Since 1853, scientists have found the ruins of lake dwellings in various parts of Switzerland and also beside the lakes and streams of other countries in Europe. They have found weapons of bone, stone, and metal, as well as crude pottery bowls and dishes, near the sites of the lake dwellings. Some of the pottery vessels still contained cereal grains and fruit. Scientists believe the pottery and weapons belonged to the owners of the lake dwellings.

Archaeologists have used the ruins of lake dwellings to learn about the early people who built the wooden houses. The scientists believe that there was a sequence, or series, of lake dwellings built in Europe. The first, and finest, were put up about 5,000 years ago, during the Neolithic period, or New Stone Age. Later peoples built lake dwellings during the Bronze and Iron ages.

The early people of Scotland and Ireland built primitive dwellings called *crannogs* in lakes and bogs. The name comes from the Celtic word *crann*, which means *tree*. These rude houses were artificial islands of wood, stones, and earth. Wooden stakes driven deep into the mud held the islands in place.

People in some parts of the world still live in wooden houses built on piles over the waters of a lake or bay. Some of the people of New Guinea, the Malay Archipelago, and Venezuela build lake dwellings which serve as protection against their enemies, and against floods.   BRIAN M. FAGAN

LAKE EDWARD is one of the sources of the Nile River. It lies in the Rift valley of central Africa between Uganda and Zaire. Most of the lake is in Zairian territory. For location, see NILE RIVER (map).

Lake Edward is about 40 miles (64 kilometers) long and 32 miles (51 kilometers) wide, and covers 830 square miles (2,150 square kilometers). Fish life is abundant in the lake. The Semliki River flows north from Lake Edward into Lake Albert in a valley west of the Ruwenzori Range (see LAKE ALBERT).

Henry M. Stanley reached the lake in 1889. The explorer named it for the Prince of Wales, later King Edward VII. Its original name was Albert Edward Nyanza. *Nyanza* means *lake* in the Bantu language.   HARRY R. RUDIN

LAKE ERIE, lying on the international border between the United States and Canada, is the farthest south of the five Great Lakes of North America (see GREAT LAKES). It is bordered by the states of New York, Pennsylvania, Ohio, and Michigan, and the province of Ontario.

Lake Erie is about 240 miles (386 kilometers) long, and ranges from 38 to 57 miles (61 to 92 kilometers) in width. With an area of 9,910 square miles (25,667 square kilometers), it is the fourth largest of the five Great Lakes. It is a shallow lake, only 210 feet (64 meters) deep at its deepest point. For this reason, the lake is quickly stirred by storms and often has violent waves. French explorers called Lake Erie *Lac du Chat* (Lake of the Cat) because the Iroquois Indians called the tribe of Indians living near the lake *Erieehronons*. This Indian word probably meant *the people of the panther*.

Lake Erie lies between Lake Ontario and Lake Huron,

and is one of the links in the St. Lawrence system. It receives the waters of Lake Huron through the St. Clair River, Lake St. Clair, and the Detroit River. It drains through the Niagara River into Lake Ontario. It is also connected to Lake Ontario, which lies 325 feet (99 meters) below Erie's level of 570 feet (174 meters) above sea level, by the Welland Canal. Eastward from Buffalo, N.Y., the New York State Barge Canal System joins Lake Erie with the Hudson River and the Atlantic Ocean. Much of the heavy lake traffic terminates on Erie's southern shore. Iron ore and taconite from Minnesota and limestone from Michigan are shipped to Ohio ports for use in Ohio steel mills and for mills in Pittsburgh, Pa. Buffalo is the most important grain-shipping port on the lake, and Toledo, Ohio, is a busy coal-shipping port. The principal Lake Erie ports are Toledo, Sandusky, Cleveland, Ashtabula, and Conneaut, all in Ohio; Erie, Pa.; and Buffalo.

Industries and cities have polluted Lake Erie by dumping waste chemicals and sewage into it. Pollution has greatly reduced the lake's once-abundant fish supply and its recreational value. JOHN H. GARLAND

See also WELLAND SHIP CANAL.

LAKE ERIE, BATTLE OF. See WAR OF 1812.

LAKE ERIE COLLEGE. See UNIVERSITIES AND COLLEGES (table).

LAKE EYRE, *air,* is the largest lake in Australia. It is shallow and salty, and lies 52 feet (16 meters) below sea level. Eyre is nearly divided into two lakes. The northern part is 90 miles (145 kilometers) long and 40 miles (64 kilometers) wide, and the southern part 38 miles (61 kilometers) long and 16 miles (26 kilometers) wide. The lake covers 3,700 square miles (9,583 square kilometers). C. M. H. CLARK

LAKE FOREST COLLEGE is a coeducational liberal arts and sciences college at Lake Forest, Ill. It is a private college affiliated with the United Presbyterian Church. The school was founded in 1857 as Lind University. In 1865, it became Lake Forest University. The school received its present name in 1965. For enrollment, see UNIVERSITIES AND COLLEGES (table).

LAKE GARDA is the largest lake in Italy. It is about 35 miles (56 kilometers) long and covers an area of 143 square miles (370 square kilometers). Lake Garda lies in beautiful Alpine country about midway between Milan and Venice. For the location of Lake Garda, see ITALY (physical map).

LAKE GENEVA is one of the largest lakes in central Europe. It is formed by a natural damming of the Rhône River. The lake has an area of 224 square miles (580 square kilometers), 141 square miles (365 square kilometers) of which lie in Switzerland and the rest in France. Lake Geneva is crescent-shaped, and 43 miles (69 kilometers) long. Its name in French is LAC DE GENÈVE. It is also called LAC LÉMAN in French. German-speaking Swiss call it the GENFER SEE.

Lake Geneva is noted for its clear blue waters. Its greatest depth is 1,017 feet (310 meters). A mountain region of great beauty, including the Bernese Alps and the Jura Mountains, surrounds the lake. The city of Geneva is at the western end of the lake. On an island near the eastern shore stands the historic castle of Chillon that was made famous by Lord Byron's poem,

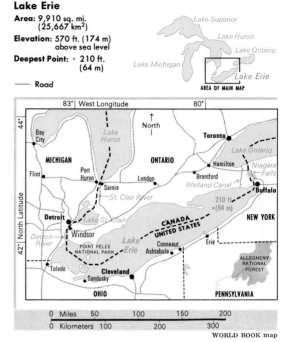

Lake Erie
Area: 9,910 sq. mi. (25,667 km²)
Elevation: 570 ft. (174 m) above sea level
Deepest Point: • 210 ft. (64 m)
—— Road

WORLD BOOK map

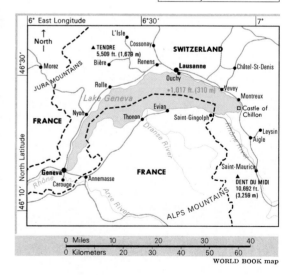

Lake Geneva
Area: 224 sq. mi. (580 km²)
Elevation: 1,220 ft. (372 m) above sea level
Deepest Point: • 1,017 ft. (310 m)
—— Road

WORLD BOOK map

"The Prisoner of Chillon." FRANKLIN CARL ERICKSON

LAKE GEORGE, in eastern New York, is a popular summer resort. This lake had a part in early American history. Battles were fought along its shores in both the French and Indian War and the Revolutionary War. The French, English, and Americans controlled it in

Lake Huron

Area: 23,050 sq. mi.
    (59,699 km²)
Elevation: 579 ft. (176 m)
    above sea level
Deepest Point: 750 ft. (229 m).

——— Road

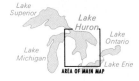

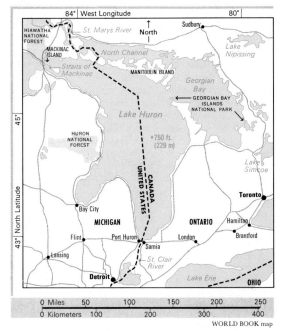

WORLD BOOK map

Lake Louise

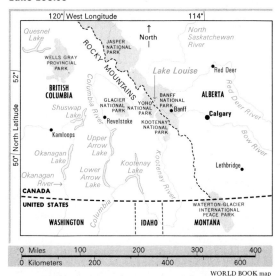

WORLD BOOK map

turn. Early settlers called the lake *Horicon*. In 1755, General William Johnson named it for the British king, George II. Lake George is 36 miles (58 kilometers) long and from 1 to 3 miles (1.6 to 5 kilometers) wide. It empties into Lake Champlain to the north. For location, see NEW YORK (physical map).　　WILLIAM E. YOUNG

LAKE GUANOCO. See ASPHALT.

LAKE HURON, *HYUR uhn,* is one of the five Great Lakes of North America. It was named for the Huron Indians who lived on its shores. Lake Huron lies between Lake Michigan and Lake Erie, and forms part of the boundary between the United States and Canada. The lake is about 206 miles (332 kilometers) long, and its greatest width is about 183 miles (295 kilometers). Its area, including the North Channel and Georgian Bay, is 23,050 square miles (59,699 square kilometers).

Huron lies at the same level as Lake Michigan, 579 feet (176 meters) above sea level. The deepest part of Lake Huron is 750 feet (229 meters) below the surface. The lake drains an area of about 51,700 square miles (133,902 square kilometers).

The St. Marys River connects Lake Huron with Lake Superior, and the Straits of Mackinac connect it with Lake Michigan. The waters of Lake Huron flow into Lake Erie by way of the St. Clair River, Lake St. Clair, and the Detroit River.

The clear waters of Lake Huron have many kinds of fish. Small islands dot the northern surface of the lake. The two most important islands are Mackinac Island, in Michigan, and Manitoulin Island, in Ontario, Canada. Violent storms that frequently occur between December and May make Lake Huron dangerous for shipping during the winter. The shores of the lake are low except on the southeastern coast, where rough cliffs rise 150 feet (46 meters).　　JOHN H. GARLAND

See also GEORGIAN BAY; GREAT LAKES.

LAKE ILMEN, *IHL muhn,* is a freshwater lake in the Soviet Union, just south of Novgorod. It is about 26 miles (42 kilometers) long and 21 miles (34 kilometers) wide. Rivers entering the lake include the Msta, Lovat', and Shelon'. Lake Ilmen empties north through the Volkhov River into Lake Ladoga. The Msta and Volkhov rivers are linked by two canals, parts of the waterway extending from the Baltic Sea to the Black Sea. For location, see RUSSIA (terrain map).　　ROBERT O. REID

LAKE ITASCA, *eye TAS kuh,* is the source of the Mississippi River. See MISSISSIPPI RIVER (The Course of the Mississippi; picture; map); MINNESOTA (Lakes, Rivers, and Waterfalls; picture).

LAKE LADOGA, *LAD uh guh* or *LAH dah gah,* in the Soviet Union, is the largest lake that lies entirely in Europe. It forms part of a canal system that links the Baltic and White seas. The lake lies 40 miles (64 kilometers) northeast of Leningrad. It covers 6,835 square miles (17,703 square kilometers).

A portion of Lake Ladoga belonged to Finland until 1940, when the entire waterway became part of the Soviet Union. Several canals have been built along the shores of Lake Ladoga. For location, see RUSSIA (terrain map).　　THEODORE SHABAD

LAKE LOUISE, *loo EEZ,* located in Banff National Park in southern Alberta, is called *Pearl of the Canadian Rockies.* The lake is quiet and peaceful because it is so shut off by the Rockies that winds do not stir its surface. The changeable blue waters of the lake mirror the colors and shapes of the sky, clouds, dark forests, cliffs, and snowy mountains. More people visit Lake Louise and Banff National Park than any other places in the Canadian Rockies. Banff was established as a national

Lake Manitoba

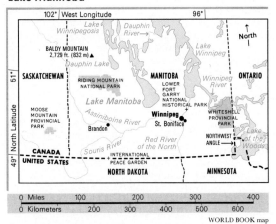

| 0 Miles | 100 | 200 | 300 | 400 |
| 0 Kilometers | 200 | 300 | 400 | 500 | 600 |

WORLD BOOK map

Lake Maracaibo

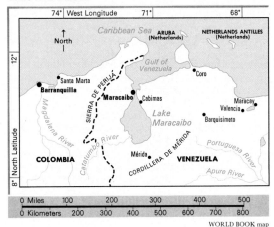

| 0 Miles | 100 | 200 | 300 | 400 | 500 |
| 0 Kilometers | 200 | 300 | 400 | 500 | 600 | 700 | 800 |

WORLD BOOK map

Lake Mead

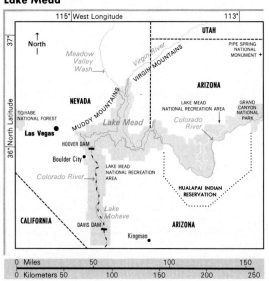

| 0 Miles | 50 | 100 | 150 |
| 0 Kilometers 50 | 100 | 150 | 200 | 250 |

WORLD BOOK map

park in 1885. The well-known Chateau Lake Louise, on the shore of Lake Louise, accommodates many of the tourists. Lake Louise is about 1½ miles (2.4 kilometers) long. See also ALBERTA (color picture).   D. F. PUTNAM

LAKE LUGANO, loo GAH noh, lies at the southern foot of the Alps between Lakes Maggiore and Como. For location, see SWITZERLAND (color map). The River Tresa connects Lugano and Maggiore. Lake Lugano extends from northern Italy into southern Switzerland. It is 20 miles (32 kilometers) long and 2 miles (3 kilometers) wide. Italians call the lake *Lago di Lugano* or *Lago Ceresio*.

LAKE MAGGIORE, muh JOHR ee, is one of the best-known lakes in Italy. Most of it lies in Italy, but a small part in the north extends into Switzerland. The Italians call this lake *Lago Maggiore*, which means *greater lake*. Lake Maggiore is 40 miles (64 kilometers) long and covers 82 square miles (212 square kilometers). In some places the lake is more than 1,200 feet (366 meters) deep. High mountains rise to the north and west of the lake. On the south are hills covered with vineyards. The most important cities on the lake are Locarno, Palanza, and Streza. For location, see SWITZERLAND (color map).   SHEPARD B. CLOUGH

LAKE MANITOBA, MAN ih TOH buh, lies in the south-central part of Manitoba. It and lakes Winnipeg and Winnipegosis are the remains of glacial Lake Agassiz, which once occupied southern Manitoba (see LAKE AGASSIZ). Lake Manitoba, the smallest of the three lakes, covers 1,817 square miles (4,706 square kilometers). It is 135 miles (217 kilometers) long and 25 miles (40 kilometers) wide, and is unusually shallow. It drains through the Dauphin River into Lake Winnipeg. An important waterfowl research station lies at the south end of the lake, at Delta, Man.   JOHN BRIAN BIRD

LAKE MARACAIBO, MAR uh KY boh, is the trade waterway of the farming and rich petroleum region of northwestern Venezuela. Lake Maracaibo is the largest lake in South America. It covers 5,217 square miles (13,512 square kilometers). It is connected with the Caribbean Sea by a short channel and the Gulf of Venezuela. A bridge 5½ miles (8.9 kilometers) long crosses the channel. The bridge is high enough to allow ocean-going ships to move under it. There are many oil wells in the lake and along its shores.   W. DONALD BEATTY

LAKE MEAD is the reservoir behind Hoover (Boulder) Dam, and the largest artificial lake in the United States. It lies about 15 miles (24 kilometers) east of Las Vegas, Nev. Lake Mead is 115 miles (185 kilometers) long and stores about 29,755,000 acre-feet (36,702 million cubic meters) of water. It covers about 250 square miles (650 square kilometers). The lake is the center of a playground region. The National Park Service administers Lake Mead. See also HOOVER DAM.

LAKE MEMPHREMAGOG, MEHM free MAY gahg, lies on the boundary between the United States and Canada. About a third of the lake is in Vermont and the rest is in the province of Quebec. Lake Memphremagog is about 30 miles (48 kilometers) long and from 2 to 5 miles (3 to 8 kilometers) wide. It empties into the St. Lawrence River through the Magog and St. Francis rivers. The shores of Memphremagog are known for their beautiful scenery. Summer cottages and estates surround the lake. For location, see VERMONT (physical map).   MURRAY G. BALLANTYNE

LAKE MICHIGAN is the largest body of fresh water in the United States. It is the third largest of the Great Lakes and the only one of the group that lies entirely inside the United States. Lake Michigan forms an important link in the great waterway system that reaches east to the Atlantic Ocean and south, through the Mississippi River, to the Gulf of Mexico.

Indians who lived on the shores of the lake called it *Michi-guma*, which means *big water. Michi-guma* became *Michigan* through popular use.

General Description

Location. Lake Michigan extends southward into Michigan, dividing that state into two peninsulas. Wisconsin and Illinois form its western border. A small part of Indiana touches the southern end of the lake.

Size. Lake Michigan is 307 miles (494 kilometers) long and its greatest width is 118 miles (190 kilometers). It covers 22,300 square miles (57,757 square kilometers).

Surface Features. Lake Michigan is 923 feet (281 meters) deep at some points. Its surface is 579 feet (176 meters) above sea level.

Green Bay is the largest arm of Lake Michigan. It lies at the northwestern corner of the lake. Grand Traverse and Little Traverse bays are on the east. Among the large rivers that enter Lake Michigan are the St. Joseph, the Fox, the Kalamazoo, the Grand, and the Menominee. The Chicago River flows out of Lake Michigan. It once flowed into the lake, but its course was reversed (see CHICAGO SANITARY AND SHIP CANAL).

Commerce

Routes. Lake Michigan empties into Lake Huron through the Straits of Mackinac. The St. Lawrence Seaway connects it with the Atlantic Ocean. Lumber, grain, and mineral products from this region are shipped to all parts of the world. The Chicago Sanitary and Ship Canal and the Chicago and Illinois rivers connect the lake with the Mississippi River.

Ports. Among the important Michigan ports on the lake are Escanaba, Frankfort, Grand Haven, Ludington, Manistee, Menominee, Muskegon, Port Dolomite, Port Inland, and Stoneport. Important Wisconsin ports are Green Bay, Kewaunee, Manitowoc, Milwaukee, Oak Creek, Port Washington, Racine, and Sheboygan. Gary and Indiana Harbor are important Indiana ports. Chicago and Waukegan are the busiest Illinois ports on the lake.   JOHN H. GARLAND

See also CHICAGO; GREAT LAKES; GREEN BAY; MICHIGAN (Climate).

LAKE MINNETONKA. See MINNESOTA (Lakes, Rivers, and Waterfalls).

LAKE NASSER was formed when waters of the Nile River were blocked by the Aswan High Dam in Egypt. It was named for the president of Egypt, Gamal Abdel Nasser. The dam, which began operating in 1968, is 425 miles (684 kilometers) south of Cairo. The lake completely filled in 1981. It covers about 1,550 square miles (4,014 square kilometers). Water from the lake will be used to irrigate land and generate hydroelectric power. The *Abu Simbel* temples, built by the pharaoh Ramses II, were cut out of cliffs along the Nile and moved to higher ground to escape the rising waters (see ABU SIMBEL, TEMPLES OF).   JAMES MATTHAI

See also ASWAN HIGH DAM.

LAKE NASSER

Lake Michigan

Area: 22,300 sq. mi. (57,757 km²)

Elevation: 579 ft. (176 m) above sea level

Deepest Point: • 923 ft. (281 m)

—— Road

AREA OF MAIN MAP

WORLD BOOK map

Lake Nasser

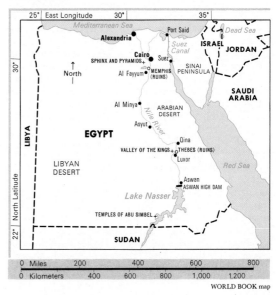

WORLD BOOK map

41

LAKE NEAGH

LAKE NEAGH. See Lough Neagh.

LAKE NEMI, *NAY mee*, lies about 15 miles (24 kilometers) southeast of Rome, Italy. For location, see Italy (physical map). It covers less than 1 square mile (2.6 square kilometers). Draining of the lake in the 1930's revealed remains of Roman pleasure boats.

LAKE NICARAGUA, *NIHK uh RAH gwuh*, lies in western Nicaragua, about 12 miles (19 kilometers) east of the Pacific Ocean and 70 miles (113 kilometers) west of the Caribbean Sea. For location, see Nicaragua (color map). The lake covers 3,060 square miles (7,925 square kilometers) and is 96 miles (154 kilometers) long and 39 miles (63 kilometers) wide. Several large islands lie in the lake. Ometepe, the biggest, has two volcanoes. The Tipitapa River connects Lake Nicaragua with Lake Managua on the north. Gary Brana-Shute

LAKE NYASA, *ny AS uh*, is the southernmost of a chain of large fresh-water lakes in the Great Rift Valley of eastern Africa. It lies about 400 miles (640 kilometers) inland from the Indian Ocean. Lake Nyasa, also called Lake Malawi, flows into the Indian Ocean by way of the Shire and Zambezi rivers (see Malawi). The lake is 350 miles (563 kilometers) long, and it has an area of 11,100 square miles (28,749 square kilometers). The waters of Lake Nyasa are 2,300 feet (701 meters) deep. Hibberd V. B. Kline, Jr.

LAKE OF LUCERNE, *loo SURN*, is the scene of some of the adventures of the legendary Swiss patriot, William Tell (see Tell, William). It lies in central Switzerland. For location, see Switzerland (color map). The lake's German name is *Vierwaldstätter See*, or *Lake of Four Forest Cantons*. Four wooded *cantons* (states)—Lucerne, Schwyz, Uri, and Unterwalden—surround it. The lake covers 44 square miles (114 square kilometers). It has the form of a rough cross, 24 miles (39 kilometers) long and 2 miles (3 kilometers) wide. Franklin C. Erickson

LAKE O' THE CHEROKEES, *CHEHR uh keez*, is an artificially created lake in northeastern Oklahoma. The lake is formed by Pensacola Dam on the Neosho or Grand River. It was created in 1940. The lake is 66 miles (106 kilometers) long and has about 1,300 miles (2,090 kilometers) of shoreline. It is the center of a leading resort area. The dam supplies electric power and flood control for the surrounding area. James Matthai

LAKE OF THE OZARKS, *OH zahrks*, was formed by the completion of the Bagnell Dam on the Osage River in 1931. The lake and its environs have become a popular resort and recreation center. The lake winds for about 130 miles (209 kilometers) among the Ozark Mountains of central Missouri. Dale Robert Martin

See also Missouri (picture).

LAKE OF THE WOODS lies on the boundary between the United States and Canada. Some of the first trading posts in the West were located on the shores of this lake. Today, the lake is best known as a summer resort. It was named for the forests that cover its hilly shores and islands. The lake covers about 1,485 square miles (3,846 square kilometers), most of which lie in Ontario. Two small bays are in Manitoba. The rest of the lake borders Minnesota. The northwest shore is the northernmost part of the continental United States, excluding Alaska. The lake is 65 miles (105 kilometers) long, and from 10 to 50 miles (16 to 80 kilometers) wide.

Lake Nyasa

Area: 11,100 sq. mi.
  (28,749 km²)
Elevation: 1,550 ft. (472 m)
  above sea level
Deepest Point: 2,300 ft.
  (701 m)

—— Road

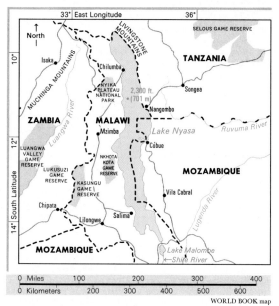

WORLD BOOK map

Lake O' The Cherokees

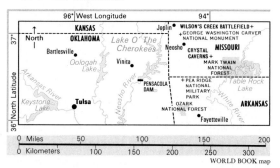

WORLD BOOK map

Lake of the Ozarks

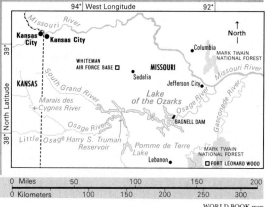

WORLD BOOK map

Lumbering is the chief occupation of the region. Fishing is important both as an industry and as a sport. Railways run along the northern and southern shores. In summer, tourist steamers sail up the lake.

The Lake of the Woods was an important factor in several boundary disputes between the United States and Great Britain. According to the treaty that ended the Revolutionary War, the boundary was to run from the northwest angle of the lake "on a due course west to the river Mississippi." The source of the Mississippi was later found to be 100 miles (160 kilometers) farther south. The Convention of London fixed the present boundary in 1818.   HAROLD T. HAGG

LAKE OF THUN, *toon,* lies 1,830 feet (558 meters) above sea level in the Bernese Alps, a popular tourist region in west-central Switzerland. Interlaken is nearby. For location, see SWITZERLAND (color map). The lake

Lake of the Woods

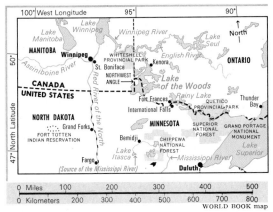

0 Miles 100 200 300 400 500
0 Kilometers 200 300 400 500 600 700 800
WORLD BOOK map

Lake Ontario

Area: 7,550 sq. mi.
(19,554 km²)
Elevation: 245 ft. (75 m)
above sea level
Deepest Point: ● 802 ft.
(244 m)
—— Road

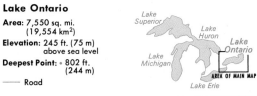

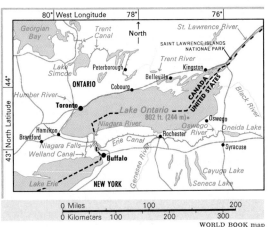

0 Miles 100 200
0 Kilometers 100 200 300
WORLD BOOK map

LAKE ONTARIO

is formed by the Aare River, and receives the waters of the Simme River at its western end. The Lake of Thun is 10 miles (16 kilometers) long and averages about 2 miles (3 kilometers) in width. It covers 18 square miles (47 square kilometers).

LAKE OHRID. See ALBANIA (Land).

LAKE OKEECHOBEE, *OH kee CHO bee,* is the largest lake in the Southern United States. Okeechobee is a Seminole Indian word that means *plenty big water.* The lake lies in the Everglades of Florida, about 35 miles (56 kilometers) west of the Atlantic Coast (see EVERGLADES). It covers about 700 square miles (1,800 square kilometers), and has an average depth of 7 feet (2.1 meters). Marshy jungles and cypress swamps line the shores of Okeechobee. A system of canals provides outlets to the Atlantic Ocean on the east and the Gulf of Mexico on the west.   KATHRYN ABBEY HANNA

See also FLORIDA (physical map).

LAKE ONEGA, *oh NEHG uh,* is one of the largest lakes in Europe. Lake Onega lies near the northwest corner of Russia. For location, see RUSSIA (physical map). The lake is part of the canal system that connects the White and Baltic seas. Lake Onega has an area of 3,820 square miles (9,894 square kilometers). Lake Onega empties into Lake Ladoga, about 70 miles (110 kilometers) to the southwest, through the Svir River. It joins the Volga and northern Dvina rivers by a series of rivers and canals.   THEODORE SHABAD

LAKE ONTARIO is the smallest and most eastern of the five Great Lakes. It forms an important link in the St. Lawrence Seaway system. Although Lake Ontario is open to large ships throughout the year, it has less traffic than the other Great Lakes.

Lake Ontario lies between the province of Ontario and the northwestern part of New York. The lake is about 193 miles (311 kilometers) long and 53 miles (85 kilometers) wide. It covers an area of 7,550 square miles (19,554 square kilometers). The shore of the lake is about 480 miles (772 kilometers) around. Offshore, the lake is very deep, ranging from 500 to 802 feet (150 to 244 meters). Its surface lies 245 feet (75 meters) above sea level. The great depth of the lake, together with its low-lying surface, means that two-thirds of its waters lie below sea level and are not touched by surface winds and currents. A steady top current moves across the lake from west to east at a rate of about $\frac{1}{3}$ mile (0.5 kilometer) per hour.

Lake Ontario does not freeze in winter, except along the shore, where the water is more shallow. The depth of its waters makes its surface cooler than the air above in summer, and warmer than the air in winter. So the lake has a moderating effect on the climate of the area. The eastern outlet of the lake never has a really hot day, and the temperature of the southern shore is so moderate that fruit trees grow throughout this region on both sides of the United States-Canada border.

Lake Ontario empties into the Atlantic Ocean through the St. Lawrence River. The Niagara River and the Welland Canal connect it to Lake Erie on the southwest. It is connected with the Hudson River and New York City by the Erie Canal, the Genesee River, and the Oswego Canal. The rivers that empty into Lake Ontario include the Black, Genesee, Oswego, Trent,

43

LAKE OUACHITA

Lake Ouachita

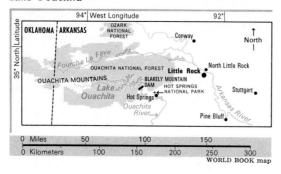

WORLD BOOK map

Lake Pontchartrain

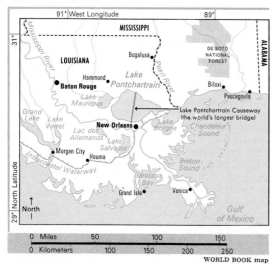

WORLD BOOK map

Lake Powell

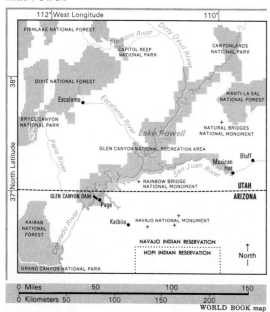

WORLD BOOK map

and Humber. The lake has many good harbors. The chief lake ports include Rochester and Oswego, N.Y. Important Canadian ports are Cobourg, Toronto, Hamilton, and Kingston.   JOHN H. GARLAND

See also GREAT LAKES; WELLAND SHIP CANAL.

LAKE OUACHITA, *WASH ih taw,* is an artificially created lake near Hot Springs, Ark. The lake covers about 63 square miles (163 square kilometers) and is about 20 miles (32 kilometers) long, and about 5 miles (8 kilometers) wide at its widest point. It has 690 miles (1,110 kilometers) of shoreline. Lake Ouachita is formed by the Blakely Mountain Dam on the Ouachita River. Created in 1955, it provides flood control and hydroelectric power. Lake Ouachita is located in the Ouachita National Forest. Ouachita State Park lies along the lake.   JAMES MATTHAI

LAKE PEIPUS, *PIE poos,* is a body of water on the border between Estonia and Russia. For location, see RUSSIA (physical map). It is 93 miles (150 kilometers) long and covers 1,400 square miles (3,626 square kilometers). During World War II, the lake played an important part in the fighting during the siege of Leningrad. Both the Russians and the Germans crossed its frozen surface in winter.   THEODORE SHABAD

LAKE PLACID is one of the small, beautiful lakes in the Adirondack Mountains of Essex County, New York. Among the other lakes nearby are the Saranac Lakes. Glaciers formed the lakes in this area during the Ice Age. Lake Placid is about 4 miles (6 kilometers) long and $\frac{1}{2}$ mile (0.8 kilometer) wide.

The village of Lake Placid, a summer and winter resort, is near the lake's southern end. It surrounds tiny Mirror Lake. Summer activities of the area include boating, swimming, and other water sports; golf; hiking; mountain climbing; and tennis. In the winter, visitors to the village enjoy bobsledding, hockey, ice skating, and skiing. The winter Olympics took place at Lake Placid in 1932 and in 1980. Abolitionist John Brown is buried there.   WILLIAM E. YOUNG

LAKE POETS were William Wordsworth, Samuel Taylor Coleridge, and Robert Southey. They were so named by the *Edinburgh Review* because they lived in the Lake District of northwestern England. Their only characteristic in common was a dislike of the stiff classicism which prevailed in the early 1800's. They worked to cultivate a simple and natural style of poetry. For some years the term *Lake Poets* was used scornfully, but it is now one of praise.

Wordsworth was a lover of nature and a pantheist. He wrote many poems about common people and familiar subjects, trying to write in simple language. Coleridge was more dreamy and visionary, but he also had a keen, critical mind and produced much excellent Shakespearean criticism. Southey was the least talented of the three, and wrote long romantic tales in verse. The three men are sometimes spoken of as the "first generation" of romantic poets.   KNOX WILSON

See also the separate articles on each of the Lake Poets.

LAKE PONTCHARTRAIN, *PAHN cher TRAIN,* is a beautiful lake of brackish water in southeastern Louisiana. It is 40 miles (64 kilometers) long and 25 miles (40 kilometers) wide, and covers 625 square miles (1,619 square kilometers). It is a major recreational center. The Inner Harbor Navigation Canal connects the lake with

44

the Mississippi River to the south. New Orleans lies between the lake and the river. The Lake Pontchartrain Causeway, which spans the lake, is the world's longest over-water highway. It is 29.2 miles (47 kilometers) long, with 23.9 miles (38.5 kilometers) over water. French colonists in Louisiana named Lake Pontchartrain for the Comte de Pontchartrain, minister of marine under Louis XIV. FRED B. KNIFFEN

LAKE POWELL is one of the largest man-made lakes in the world. It lies on the Utah-Arizona border. Glen Canyon Dam, built across Glen Canyon to generate hydroelectric power, created Lake Powell. The lake was named after Major John Wesley Powell, who discovered and named Glen Canyon. The dam blocks the Colorado River to form a lake that is 186 miles (299 kilometers) long and about 500 feet (150 meters) deep at its deepest point. Most of the lake lies in Utah. The town of Page, Ariz., was built alongside the dam to house construction workers. Lake Powell is a popular recreation area. See NATIONAL PARK SYSTEM (picture: Glen Canyon). JAMES MATTHAI

LAKE RUDOLF. See Lake Turkana.

LAKE SAINT CLAIR, together with the St. Clair River on the north and the Detroit River on the south, forms a waterway connecting Lakes Huron and Erie. For location, see ONTARIO (physical map). Lake St. Clair has been dredged so that large ships can cross it. Roughly circular in shape, the lake is 25 miles (40 kilometers) across at the center and covers an area of 460 square miles (1,191 square kilometers). It forms part of the boundary between the state of Michigan and the province of Ontario. JOHN BRIAN BIRD

LAKE SAINT LAWRENCE is the wide portion of the St. Lawrence River between Ogdensburg and Massena, N.Y. The lake is 28 miles (45 kilometers) long and from 1 to 4 miles (1.6 to 6.4 kilometers) wide. It is 84 feet (26 meters) deep. Lake St. Lawrence was created in 1958 to drown out the rapids of the St. Lawrence River as an aid to navigation and to form a pool for the development of electricity. WILLIAM R. WILLOUGHBY

See also SAINT LAWRENCE SEAWAY (maps).

LAKE SCUTARI. See ALBANIA (Land); YUGOSLAVIA (Rivers and Lakes).

LAKE SUPERIOR, one of the five Great Lakes of North America, is the largest body of fresh water in the world. Among the Great Lakes, it is the deepest, the highest above sea level, and the farthest north and west (see GREAT LAKES). Lake Superior forms part of the interior waterway system of the United States and Canada. This system extends from the Atlantic Ocean through the St. Lawrence Seaway, the Great Lakes, and the Mississippi River to the Gulf of Mexico (see SAINT LAWRENCE SEAWAY). Early French fur traders gave the name *Lac Supérieur*, French for *Upper Lake*, to the lake.

Location and Size. Lake Superior lies across the international border between the United States and Canada. The Canadian province of Ontario is to the north and east of the lake. Michigan and Wisconsin lie to the south of the lake, and Minnesota to the west.

Lake Superior covers 31,700 square miles (82,103 square kilometers). Its greatest length from east to west is 350 miles (563 kilometers), and its greatest width is 160 miles (257 kilometers). The lake lies about 600 feet (183 meters) above sea level, and is 1,333 feet (406 meters) deep at its deepest point.

Description. The coastline of Lake Superior is bold and rocky. In some places, especially along the northern shore of the lake, cliffs rise from the water's edge. Colorful sandstone walls, known as the Pictured Rocks, rise along some areas of the lake's shore in Michigan. The highway that follows the rocky Minnesota shore is lined with summer resorts, fishing villages, and state parks. Split Rock Lighthouse, a famous landmark, warns lake shipping from reefs in Beaver Bay along the Minnesota shore.

Forests cover much of the land that borders the lake. About 200 rivers, most of them short, empty into Lake Superior. Many of these rivers form waterfalls that plunge over the high, rocky headlands. The largest river emptying into the lake is the St. Louis River, the extreme headwater of the St. Lawrence River. It drains into Lake Superior's western end. The Keweenaw Peninsula, famous for its copper deposits, juts into the lake in Upper Michigan.

Lake Superior

AREA OF MAIN MAP

Area: 31,700 sq. mi. (82,103 km²)

Elevation: 600 ft. (183 m) above sea level

Deepest Point: 1,333 ft. (406 m)

—— Road

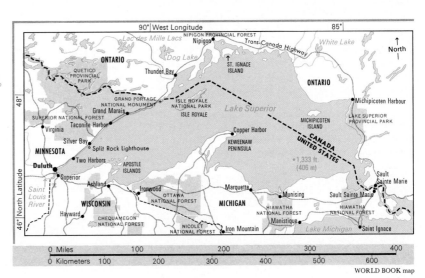

WORLD BOOK map

LAKE SUPERIOR STATE COLLEGE

Many islands dot the surface of the lake. The largest of these islands are Michigan's Isle Royale and Ontario's St. Ignace and Michipicoten. Many small islands, named the Apostle Islands, lie off the northern Wisconsin shore.

Commerce. The lake does not freeze over in winter, but frozen harbors restrict shipping. The shipping season extends from about mid-April to December. Boats carry iron ore, taconite, wheat, lumber, copper, and other minerals to ports along the Great Lakes and farther east. The locks of the Soo Canals in Sault Ste. Marie carry ships around the rapids of the St. Marys River (see Soo Canals). This river connects Lake Superior and Lake Huron. The chief ports on Lake Superior are Duluth, Two Harbors, Taconite Harbor, Silver Bay, and Grand Marais, all in Minnesota; Superior and Ashland, Wis.; Marquette, Mich.; and Thunder Bay and Michipicoten Harbour, Ont.   JOHN H. GARLAND

LAKE SUPERIOR STATE COLLEGE. See UNIVERSITIES AND COLLEGES (table).

LAKE TAHOE, *TAH hoh,* is a beautiful, oval-shaped, glacial lake that lies in a valley of the Sierra Nevada on the California-Nevada border. The lake is 23 miles (37 kilometers) long and 12 miles (19 kilometers) wide. It lies 6,228 feet (1,898 meters) above sea level. Lake Tahoe is 1,640 feet (500 meters) deep at its deepest point, and is one of the deepest lakes in the continental United States. Camps, homes, and resorts line its shores. The lake and the mountain streams that feed it attract fishermen. Boating, water-skiing, and hunting are also popular. In 1844, the American explorer John C. Frémont became the first white man to see the lake. It empties through the Truckee River into Pyramid Lake.   GEORGE SHAFTEL

See also NEVADA (picture).

LAKE TANA, *TAH nah,* or *Tsana,* *TSAH nah,* lies in northern Ethiopia. For location, see ETHIOPIA (map). It serves as the main source of the Blue Nile, or Abbai River. The Blue Nile receives its color from the silt-free water of Lake Tana. Lying 6,000 feet (1,829 meters) above sea level, Lake Tana is 47 miles (76 kilometers) long and 44 miles (71 kilometers) wide.

LAKE TANGANYIKA, *TANG guhn YEE kuh,* in east-central Africa, is the world's longest fresh-water lake and the second deepest. Only Lake Baikal, in Russia, is deeper. The lake is bordered by Burundi and Tanzania on the east and by Zaire and Zambia on the west. Lake Tanganyika is 420 miles (680 kilometers) long, and its greatest depth is 4,708 feet (1,435 meters). The lake covers about 12,700 square miles (32,893 square kilometers). Its shores are mountainous. Only one major river, the Rusizi, drains into the lake. It flows from Lake Kivu in the north. Lake Tanganyika's outlet is the Lukuga River.

The first Europeans to see Lake Tanganyika were Sir Richard Burton and John Hanning Speke who reached Ujiji on the eastern shore in 1858. Henry M. Stanley found the missing missionary-explorer, Dr. David Livingstone, at the same point in 1871 (see STANLEY AND LIVINGSTONE).   HARTMUT WALTER

LAKE TEXOMA is one of the largest man-made lakes in the United States. It covers about 140 square miles (363 square kilometers) on the Texas and Oklahoma

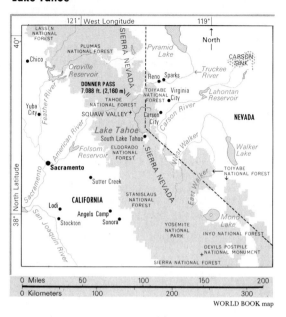

WORLD BOOK map

Lake Tanganyika

Area: 12,700 sq. mi. (32,893 km²)
Elevation: 2,534 ft. (772 m) above sea level
Deepest Point: 4,708 ft. (1,435 m)

— Road

WORLD BOOK map

Lake Texoma

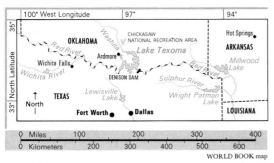

Lake Titicaca

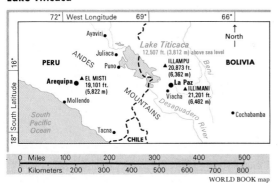

Lake Victoria

Area: 26,828 sq. mi.
(69,484 km²)

Elevation: 3,723 ft. (1,135 m)
above sea level

Deepest Point: 270 ft. (82 m)

—— Road   ‖ Waterfall

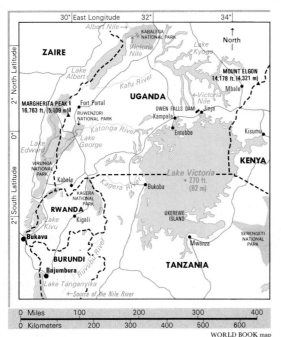

border, about 80 miles (130 kilometers) south of Oklahoma City. The lake was formed in 1944 by Denison Dam, which was built on the Red River to produce hydroelectric power, control floods, and allow navigation. Lake Texoma has become popular for fishing, hunting, and water sports.   JAMES MATTHAI

LAKE TIBERIAS. See SEA OF GALILEE.

LAKE TITICACA, *TEE tee KAH kah*, is the highest navigable lake in the world. Located on the border between Peru and Bolivia, it lies 12,507 feet (3,812 meters) above sea level. The lake is 110 miles (180 kilometers) long and about 45 miles (72 kilometers) wide. It covers about 3,200 square miles (8,300 square kilometers), and is more than 900 feet (270 meters) deep in places. The Desaguadero River flows out of its southern end, and empties into Lake Poopó in Bolivia.

Many islands lie in the lake. Some have ruins of Indian civilizations that existed before the Spanish conquest of South America in the 1500's. Numerous Indian villages lie near Lake Titicaca's shore. Many villagers make boats from reeds called *totoras*, which grow on the shores of the lake. These boats provide transportation for local Indian commerce (see BOLIVIA [picture: Lake Titicaca]; SOUTH AMERICA [picture]). Many trout are found in Lake Titicaca. Some of these fish are about 3 feet (1 meter) long.   ROBERT C. EIDT

LAKE TORRENS, *TAWR uhnz*, is a shallow body of salt water in South Australia. The lake is 120 miles (193 kilometers) long and 40 miles (64 kilometers) wide. Lake Torrens has an area of 2,230 square miles (5,776 square kilometers). For location, see AUSTRALIA (terrain map).

LAKE TROUT. See TROUT.

LAKE TURKANA, *TUHR KAN uh*, is a long, narrow lake in east-central Africa. Most of it lies in northern Kenya. Its northern tip extends into southern Ethiopia. For location, see KENYA (map). The lake covers 2,473 square miles (6,405 square kilometers).

Lake Turkana is known for its plentiful supply of large fish, especially huge Nile perch. Turkana people inhabit the shore and fish and raise livestock for a living. Many Nile crocodiles breed in the Lake Turkana area. Koobi Fora National Park, on the lake's east shore, contains fossils of early forms of human beings and wildlife. Lake Turkana receives fresh water from rivers of the Ethiopian highlands. However, the lake has no outlet, and the region's hot, dry climate causes a high rate of evaporation of the fresh water. As a result, the lake's water is slightly salty.

Lake Turkana first became known to Europeans after an expedition from Austria-Hungary reached it in 1888. The African people of the area then called the lake Basso Narok (Dark Water). The European expedition was led by Samuel Teleki, a Hungarian count. Teleki named the body of water Lake Rudolf in honor of Rudolf, the crown prince of Austria-Hungary. The lake is still sometimes called Lake Rudolf.   HARTMUT WALTER

LAKE UNION. See SEATTLE (The City).

LAKE VICTORIA, or, in Bantu, VICTORIA NYANZA, is the largest lake in Africa and the second largest freshwater lake in the world. Its area of 26,828 square miles (69,484 square kilometers) is exceeded only by that of Lake Superior. Lake Victoria lies in east-central Africa, partly in Kenya, partly in Tanzania, and partly in Uganda. The equator crosses the lake.

Lake Victoria is the largest source of the Nile River. Owen Falls Dam, which was built across the Nile between 1949 and 1954, has raised Lake Victoria's level about 3 feet (91 centimeters) to an elevation of 3,723 feet (1,135 meters) above sea level. Its greatest depth is 270 feet (82 meters).

In 1858, the English explorer John Hanning Speke became the first European to reach Lake Victoria. He named the lake in honor of Queen Victoria of Great Britain.   HARTMUT WALTER

LAKE VOLTA, in central Ghana, is one of the world's largest man-made lakes. It is the reservoir behind Akosombo Dam on the Volta River. Lake Volta extends 250 miles (402 kilometers) north of the dam and was formed by the completion of the dam in 1965. The lake covers an area of 3,275 square miles (8,482 square kilometers). The power station at Akosombo Dam uses water from Lake Volta to generate electric power for the area.   JAMES MATTHAI

LAKE WASHINGTON. See SEATTLE (The City).

LAKE WINDERMERE. See WINDERMERE.

LAKE WINNEBAGO, the largest lake in Wisconsin, covers 215 square miles (557 square kilometers) in the east-central part of the state. It is about 30 miles (48 kilometers) long, and 5 to 10 miles (8 to 16 kilometers) wide. The Fox River enters the lake on the west at Oshkosh, and leaves at the northwest end at Neenah and Menasha. Fond du Lac lies along the southern shore. For the location of Lake Winnebago, see WISCONSIN (physical map).

LAKE WINNIPEG, in south-central Manitoba, is the third largest lake lying entirely within Canada. Only Great Bear Lake and Great Slave Lake in the Northwest Territories are larger. Lake Winnipeg lies about 35 miles (56 kilometers) north of the city of Winnipeg. It covers an area of 9,398 square miles (24,341 square kilometers), and is known as one of the "Great Lakes of Manitoba" (see MANITOBA [Rivers and Lakes]). The lake is 260 miles (418 kilometers) long, and from 20 to 60 miles (32 to 97 kilometers) wide. It does not exceed 70 feet (21 meters) in depth. In ancient times, Lake Winnipeg and its two large neighbors—Lakes Winnipegosis and Manitoba—formed parts of large, shallow Lake Agassiz, created by glaciers during the Ice Age (see LAKE AGASSIZ). Large islands in Lake Winnipeg include Reindeer Island and Hecla Island. The lake's fisheries are the most important in Manitoba. Lake Winnipeg is a storage reservoir for the Saskatchewan-Nelson river system.   W. L. MORTON

LAKE WINNIPEGOSIS, *WIN ih peg OH sis*, lies in the lowlands of southern Manitoba. It covers 2,013 square miles (5,214 square kilometers), and is about 120 miles (193 kilometers) long, 20 miles (32 kilometers) wide, and 38 feet (12 meters) deep. The lake drains into Lake Manitoba by way of the Waterhen River. For the location of Lake Winnipegosis, see MANITOBA (physical map). Lake Winnipegosis formed part of Lake Agassiz during the Ice Age.   D. F. PUTNAM

See also LAKE AGASSIZ.

LAKE WINNIPESAUKEE, *WIN uh puh SAW kee*, in east-central New Hampshire attracts many summer

Lake Volta

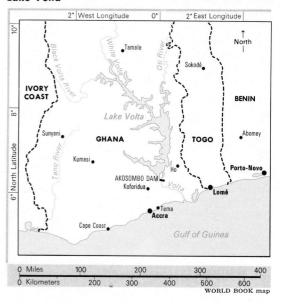

WORLD BOOK map

Lake Winnipeg

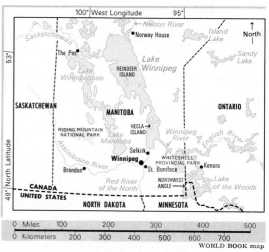

WORLD BOOK map

Lake Winnipesaukee

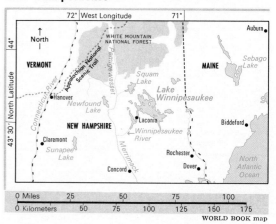

WORLD BOOK map

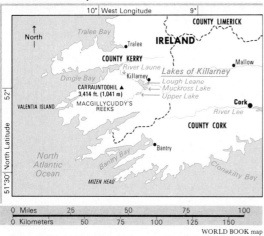

0 Miles	25	50	75	100
0 Kilometers	50	75	100	125	150

WORLD BOOK map

visitors. The lake is about 22 miles (35 kilometers) long and from 1 to 10 miles (1.6 to 16 kilometers) wide. It has 365 islands.

See also NEW HAMPSHIRE (picture: Lake Winnipesaukee at Center Harbor).

LAKE XOCHIMILCO, *SOH chee MEEL koh,* a swamplike lake in Mexico City, Mexico, is noted for its so-called "floating gardens." By the time the Spaniards conquered the region in 1521, the Indians had created five shallow lakes out of a larger one by building dikes. They heaped soft mud onto interwoven twigs, and made seed beds for flowers and vegetables. These "floating gardens" gradually increased in size and became anchored by the interlacing plant roots. Many tourists travel through the canals that separate these artificially created islands.   JOHN A. CROW

LAKELAND TERRIER is one of the bravest dogs that ever dug a fox out of the ground. It comes from the Lake District of northern England. It was first raised to hunt marauding foxes and to protect sheep. It has a narrow body and a long head, with a beard around its chin. It may be black or blue with tan markings, red, or mustard color. The lakeland terrier weighs from 15 to 17 pounds (7 to 8 kilograms).   JOSEPHINE Z. RINE

WORLD BOOK photo by E. F. Hoppe

The Lakeland Terrier Comes from Northern England.

LAKES OF KILLARNEY, *kih LAHR nee,* are three famous lakes of great beauty in County Kerry, Ireland. They lie among mountains in southwestern Ireland, about 2 miles (3 kilometers) south of the town of Killarney. A winding stream connects the three lakes. They drain through the River Laune into Dingle Bay. Lough Leane, or Lower Lake, covers 8 square miles (21 square kilometers). Muckross Lake (also called Lough Torc or Middle Lake) covers about 1 square mile (2.6 square kilometers). The ruins of Muckross Abbey, built in the 1400's, stand on a peninsula that separates Muckross Lake from Lough Leane. Upper Lake, the most scenic of the three, lies in a deep valley and covers 430 acres (174 hectares).

The lakes and the surrounding area attract large numbers of tourists. The area around the lakes is preserved as a national park.   T. W. FREEMAN

LA LECHE LEAGUE INTERNATIONAL, *lah LAY chay,* is an organization of women who offer information and encouragement to mothers who want to breast-feed their babies. The Spanish words *la leche* mean *the milk.* The league works through local discussion groups and publishes a book called *The Womanly Art of Breastfeeding.* It also distributes brochures on childbirth, child care, and related subjects.

La Leche members believe breast-feeding contributes to a child's well-being and promotes good mother-child relationships. A group of mothers founded the organization in 1956. It had been their experience that many physicians knew little about breast-feeding and so could not advise their patients.

The league has about 2,600 local groups in the United States and about 40 other countries. Headquarters are located at 9616 Minneapolis Avenue, Franklin Park, Ill. 60131.   Critically reviewed by
LA LECHE LEAGUE INTERNATIONAL

LALO, *la LOH,* **ÉDOUARD,** *ay DWAR* (1823-1892), a French composer of Spanish descent, gained fame for his violin concerto, *Symphonie Espagnole* (1873). His other works include the opera, *The King of Ys* (1888) and the ballet, *Namouna* (1882), which he later arranged into two orchestral suites. Lalo's music is considered characteristic of French culture at its best. He was born at Lille, France. His full name was Victor Antoine Édouard Lalo. In 1839, he entered the Paris Conservatory, where he studied violin.   THEODORE M. FINNEY

LAMAISM, *LAH muh ihz uhm,* is a form of Buddhism practiced in Tibet and Mongolia. It is sometimes called *Tibetan Buddhism.* Lamaism is named for the Buddhist *Lamas* (monks), who teach the faith. Many Lamaists follow a branch of Buddhism called *tantrism,* which stresses meditation and secret rituals.

Shortly before A.D. 650, monks from India introduced Buddhism into Tibet. Through the years, Buddhism was combined with traditional Tibetan religious beliefs to form Lamaism. The Lamaists built monasteries called *Lamaseries,* which became political and educational centers in Tibet. Between 900 and 1400, several Lamaist sects developed in Tibet. The most powerful one was called the Yellow Hat sect because its monks wore yellow uniforms. The sect leader became known as the *Dalai Lama.* From the mid-1600's until 1950, the Dalai Lama was the supreme political and spiritual ruler

49

of Tibet. The Chinese invaded Tibet in 1950 and eventually removed the Buddhists from power. The Dalai Lama went into exile in India in 1959. KENDALL W. FOLKERT

See also ASIA (Way of Life in Central Asia); BUDDHISM; DALAI LAMA; TIBET; PAINTING (Indian Painting).

LAMAR, *luh MAHR,* **LUCIUS QUINTUS CINCINNATUS,** *LOO shuhs KWIHN tuhs SIHN suh NAT uhs* (1825-1893), a Mississippi statesman and politician, worked for good feeling between the North and the South after the Civil War. In 1861, he had urged the South to withdraw from the Union. He held Confederate diplomatic and military posts during the war. But, in 1874, Lamar attracted national attention with his tribute to the late Senator Charles Sumner of Massachusetts. Southerners had hated Sumner for his harsh policy toward them.

Lamar served in the U.S. House of Representatives from 1873 to 1877, and in the U.S. Senate from 1877 to 1885. He served as secretary of the interior from 1885 to 1888, and then was appointed associate justice of the U.S. Supreme Court. Lamar was born in Putnam County, Georgia. RICHARD N. CURRENT

LAMARCK, *luh MAHRK,* **CHEVALIER DE,** *SHEHV uh LIHR duh* (1744-1829), was a French biologist and botanist. He became one of the first to propose a theory of biological evolution. Lamarck was a founder of *invertebrate paleontology* (the study of fossils of animals without backbones).

From his work in botany, Lamarck concluded that plants and animals change their forms to adapt to their environment, and that these changes are passed along to their offspring. His studies of plant and animal life greatly aided Charles R. Darwin in his development of the theory of evolution.

In 1788, Lamarck became conservator of the royal herbarium. He transferred his interest from the study of plants to that of animals. In 1793 he was appointed a professor of zoology at the Museum of Natural History in Paris. While teaching, he developed a system for classifying invertebrate animals.

Lamarck was the first scientist to try to forecast the weather. He published an annual meteorological report from 1799 to 1810. It is said that he was responsible for the names of the various cloud types: *cirrus, stratus, cumulus,* and *nimbus.*

Lamarck was born in Bazentin, Picardy. His given and family name was Jean Baptiste Pierre Antoine de Monet. He inherited the title Chevalier de Lamarck from his father. He studied briefly for the priesthood, then served as an army officer during the Seven Years' War. He started the study of medicine in 1768, but at the age of 24 began studying under the noted botanist Bernard de Jussieu. His views on evolution influenced thought in the 1800's. In his later years Lamarck was completely blind, but he continued his work with the assistance of others. ROGERS McVAUGH

See also DARWIN, CHARLES R.; EVOLUTION (Early Theories); HEREDITY (Early Ideas About Heredity).

LAMARTINE, *la mar TEEN,* **ALPHONSE DE,** *al FAWNS duh* (1790-1869), was a French writer and statesman. The death of the woman he loved inspired some of his greatest poems. *Poetic Meditations* (1820), his first published collection, was a key work in the development of French romantic literature and won Lamartine

fame. In this work, he expressed sadness and a yearning for the past, and told of the consolation he found in religious faith, the hope of immortality, and the memory of his ideal love. He began a vast work symbolically describing humanity's struggle to reach God by suffering and atonement. Only two episodes, *Jocelyn* (1836) and *The Fall of an Angel* (1838), were finished.

Alphonse Marie Louis de Prat de Lamartine was born in Mâcon. He served briefly as provisional chief of state after the Revolution of 1848. He lost his popularity, and he died heavily in debt. IRVING PUTTER

LAMB is meat obtained from sheep that are less than 1 year old. Lamb is a red, tender meat with a delicate flavor. It is high in food value. It provides a good source of protein and B vitamins and is rich in the minerals phosphorus and iron. Lamb is a popular food in Australia, Great Britain, Greece, New Zealand, and many other countries. In the United States, however, less than 2 pounds (0.9 kilogram) of lamb per person is eaten annually. The meat obtained from sheep more than 1 year old is called *mutton.*

In the United States, the U.S. Department of Agriculture (USDA) grades lamb for quality based on the age, shape, and fatness of the *carcass.* The carcass is the part of the butchered animal that remains after the skin, head, feet, and internal organs have been removed. The grade is stamped on the carcass. USDA grades for lamb are, from the highest to the lowest, prime, choice, good, utility, and cull. Supermarkets generally sell only prime and choice grades of lamb.

The lamb carcass is divided into seven wholesale cuts: leg, loin, flank, rack, breast, shoulder, and foreshank. Grocers may divide these wholesale cuts into smaller pieces for sale to consumers. Roasts, chops, and steaks are cut from the leg, loin, and rack. These tender cuts should be roasted or broiled. Small chops, however, may be pan fried. Many other lamb cuts are less tender and should be *braised* (cooked by moist heat in a covered pan) or cooked in liquid. DONALD H. BEERMANN

See also EASTER (The Lamb); MEAT; MUTTON; SHEEP.

LAMB, CHARLES (1775-1834), was an English author. He became famous for his informal, personal essays and his literary criticism. Lamb used the pen name *Elia* for many of his essays.

His Life. Lamb was born in London and had a simple, outwardly uneventful life. His only formal education was at a London school called Christ's Hospital. The poet Samuel Taylor Coleridge was also a student there, and he and Lamb became close friends. In 1792, Lamb went to work as a clerk for the East India Company. He worked for the firm until his retirement on a pension at the age of 50. Lamb never married. He lived with his sister Mary, and took loving care of her even during periods when she was mentally unbalanced. Lamb's quiet devotion to his sister led the author William Makepeace Thackeray to call him "Saint Charles."

His Essays. Lamb's reputation rests on his essays

Lithograph by Robert Hancock; National Portrait Gallery, London

Charles Lamb

and his literary criticism. But he also wrote a few undistinguished poems and two unsuccessful plays. His farce *Mr. H.* failed miserably at its first performance in 1806, and Lamb joined the audience in hissing his own play. Lamb's best and most popular essays appeared from 1820 to 1825 in *The London Magazine*. They were collected in two volumes known as *Essays of Elia* (1823) and *The Last Essays of Elia* (1833). Lamb's literary and dramatic criticism appears in his essays and in his notes to a collection of excerpts from Elizabethan plays. The notes and excerpts were published as *Specimens of English Dramatic Poets Who Lived about the Time of Shakespeare* (1808).

Lamb's writing reveals much about him—his gentle and whimsical nature, his great capacity for friendship, and his warm humanity. Some of his essays recall his youth. Others are character sketches of eccentric people in whom Lamb found something to like. Many essays discuss books and the theater, both of which he loved.

The titles of some of Lamb's essays show the range of his interests—"Poor Relations," "Mrs. Battle's Opinions on Whist," "My First Play," "Dream Children," "A Bachelor's Complaint of the Behaviour of Married People," and "A Dissertation Upon Roast Pig." Even subjects that seemed ordinary came to life through his original, sympathetic point of view. In his essays, Lamb stayed close to common realities—"sun, and sky, and breeze, and solitary walks, and summer holidays, and the greenness of fields and the delicious juices of meats and fishes, and society, and the cheerful glass, and candlelight, and fireside conversations."

Behind Lamb's warmth and humor lay robust common sense. He scorned what he called "the namby-pamby." His literary criticism is highly individual and penetrating. Close friendships with such writers as Coleridge, William Wordsworth, Robert Southey, and William Hazlitt made him part of the romantic movement of the early 1800's. Yet Lamb could make fun of the solemnity of much of Wordsworth's poetry. When he called Coleridge "an archangel, a little damaged," and said that "he had a hunger for eternity," Lamb expressed what other critics might have taken a page to say. In his criticism of William Shakespeare and other dramatists, Lamb always tried to get at the deepest realities of life and art.

Mary Ann Lamb (1764-1847), Charles' sister, fatally stabbed their mother in 1796 during a fit of temporary insanity. She was placed under Charles' guardianship, even though he was only 21. When normal, Mary was affectionate and intelligent. She worked with Charles in writing three books for children. The most famous is *Tales from Shakespeare* (1807). In retelling the stories of Shakespeare's plays, Charles wrote the tragedies and Mary wrote the comedies. Their other books for children are a collection of stories called *Mrs. Leicester's School* (1807) and *Poetry for Children* (1809). After Charles died, Mary lived on his pension and savings. She was born in London.   JOHN W. DODDS

Additional Resources

COURTNEY, WINIFRED F. *Young Charles Lamb, 1775-1802.* New York Univ. Press, 1982.
LUCAS, EDWARD V. *The Life of Charles Lamb.* Richard West, 1978. Reprint of 1905 edition. Standard biography.
Portable Charles Lamb. Ed. by John M. Brown. Greenwood, 1975. Reprint of 1949 edition.

LAMB, WILLIS EUGENE, JR. (1913-   ), an American nuclear physicist, shared the 1955 Nobel Prize with Polykarp Kusch. Working independently, they discovered slight deviations from the Dirac theory on the behavior of the hydrogen atom (see DIRAC, PAUL ADRIEN MAURICE). Lamb was cited for his discoveries of the hyperfine structure of the hydrogen spectrum. Lamb was born in Los Angeles. He has taught at the University of California, and Harvard, Stanford, and Oxford universities.   R. T. ELLICKSON

LAMBERT PROJECTION. See MAP (Conic Projections).

LAMB'S-QUARTERS is a tall weed related to beets and spinach. It grows in fields and gardens and along roads in most of North America, Europe, and Asia. The plants range in size from 1 foot (30 centimeters) to 10 feet (3 meters). Clusters of tiny greenish flowers hang from the stem. Lamb's-quarters is also called *pigweed* or *goosefoot*. It is a nuisance to farmers because the seeds become mixed with grain seeds. The tasty leaves are sometimes cooked and eaten as greens.

Scientific Classification. Lamb's-quarters belongs to the goosefoot family, Chenopodiaceae. It is genus *Chenopodium*, species *C. album*.   ARTHUR CRONQUIST

LAME DUCK AMENDMENT is a popular name for Amendment 20 to the United States Constitution. It was passed in 1933. This amendment provides that the President's term of office begins on January 20 instead of March 4. It also provides that the terms of Senators and Representatives begin on January 3 following their election in November, and that a new session of Congress would open on this day. This moved the date an elected official takes office closer to the date of his election. Under the old law, newly elected members of Congress began to attend regular sessions 13 months after their elections. *Lame ducks* (Congressmen who were not reelected) attended the short session of Congress which began the month after their defeat and lasted until the following March.

See also CONSTITUTION OF THE UNITED STATES (Amendment 20).

LAMENTATIONS, *LAM uhn TAY shuhnz,* is one of the poetical books of the Old Testament, or Hebrew Bible. According to tradition, the prophet Jeremiah wrote it. Four of the book's five chapters contain *elegies* (songs of mourning) on the destruction of Jerusalem in 587 B.C. (see JEWS [Invasions and Conquests]). Jeremiah had foretold the event and lived to witness it himself. The fifth chapter is a plea to the Lord for forgiveness and restoration.

The songs, called *kinot*, describe the corruption of the leaders and the people, and their sufferings after the conquest. They also contain moving prayers to God. The first four kinot are written in an alphabetical acrostic. Each stanza begins with a letter of the Hebrew alphabet in its proper order.   ROBERT GORDIS

LAMINATED GLASS. See GLASS (Specialty Glasses).

LAMINATING, *LAM uh NAY tihng,* is a process of permanently bonding together two or more pieces of wood with glues, pressure, and sometimes heat. In laminating, alternate layers of wood are placed with their grains running at right angles to each other. This gives the wood added strength. Lamination may also be used to im-

LAMMERGEIER

prove the appearance of wood products. A thin veneer of costly beautiful wood can be bonded on top of a piece of cheap, unattractive wood. Plywood is the most common type of laminated wood (see PLYWOOD). Paper, metal, and plastics are other materials that may be bonded to wood by lamination.   PETER E. TERZICK

See also PLASTICS (Making Plastics Products).

LAMMERGEIER, *LAM uhr GY uhr*, is one of the largest vultures of the mountain regions of Africa, Asia, and Europe. Its body is from 42 to 46 inches (107 to 117 centimeters) long and its wingspread is between 9 and 10 feet (2.7 and 3 meters). It feeds on dead animals. But it is also said to capture and kill live animals, especially helpless young ones. The lammergeier has dark wings

New York Zoological Society

The Lammergeier is also called the "bearded vulture," because it has a tuft of bristly black feathers that hangs down like a beard from the base of its bill.

with white streaks. Its black "beard" contrasts with its orange neck and breast.

Scientific Classification. The lammergeier is in the Old World vulture family, Accipitridae. It is genus *Gypaëtus,* species *G. barbatus aureus*.   OLIN SEWALL PETTINGILL, JR.

LAMOORE, LOUIS DEARBORN. See L'AMOUR, LOUIS.

L'AMOUR, *luh MOOR,* **LOUIS,** *LOO ee* (1908-   ), is a popular American author known for his exciting novels about Western frontier life in America. L'Amour's stories have been praised for their historical accuracy and detailed descriptions of Western wildlife and geography. He is also known for his sensitive portrayals of American Indians and Mexicans. A number of L'Amour's novels place a high value on family ties. Many of these stories feature three fictional pioneer families named Sackett, Talon, and Chantry.

Louis Dearborn L'Amour (originally spelled LaMoore) was born in Jamestown, N.D. He left home as a teen-ager and wandered for many years throughout the West, working at a variety of jobs. Encouraged by friends, he began to write down stories he had heard from his grandfather about Indian fighting and the Civil War. L'Amour's first novel, *Westward the Tide* (1950),

was followed by the popular *Hondo* in 1953. Since that time, L'Amour has written an average of three books a year. His other novels include *The Daybreakers* (1960), which introduced the Sackett family; *Bendigo Shafter* (1979); and *The Lonesome Gods* (1983). Many of L'Amour's stories have been made into motion pictures and television dramas.   ARTHUR R. HUSEBOE

LAMP is any device made to produce light. It ranks as one of the most important inventions. Since the invention of the lamp thousands of years ago, people have not had to depend entirely on the sun for light. Lamps enable people to work and to take part in countless other activities by artificial light.

Through the centuries, people have made many kinds of lamps. But all of them have been one of three basic types: (1) fat or oil, (2) gas, or (3) electric. Today, people use electric lamps almost entirely. Some people keep other kinds of lamps for emergency use in case electricity is not available.

Fat or Oil Lamps produce light by burning fat, grease, oil, or wax as fuel. These lamps have a wick that performs two functions. The wick serves as a place for the flame to form, and it draws the fuel up to the flame by *capillary* action (see CAPILLARITY).

The first lamps were fat lamps, which prehistoric people made from sea shells or hollowed-out stones. They used pieces of grasslike plants called *rushes* as wicks and burned animal fat as fuel in these lamps.

The ancient Egyptians also made stone lamps. But the Egyptian lamps burned oil and had cotton wicks. The ancient Greeks and Romans made lamps from bronze or pottery. Early Greek lamps looked like saucers and burned olive oil or the oil of other plants. The wick simply floated on the oil. Later Greek lamps had a groove at the edge of the saucer to hold the wick. Some Roman lamps resembled a teakettle. The body of the "kettle" held the oil, and the "spout" held the wick.

Candles are a type of fat lamp. The earliest candles were made by coating a wick with wax and pitch. Later, candlemakers used *tallow,* a waxy substance obtained from animal fat. The best candles consisted of beeswax or *paraffin,* a wax obtained from petroleum. Most candles cost more than other types of lamps. Cheap lamps called *rushlights* burned like candles. They were made by dipping dried rushes into animal fat. See CANDLE.

A type of oil lamp called a *cruise* appeared in Scotland during the Middle Ages. This lamp consisted of an iron pan that had a trough sticking out from it. The trough held the wick. Many cruises had a second trough beneath the first to catch any dripping oil. The American colonists made cruises called *Betty lamps*. The colonists usually burned fish oil or whale oil in these lamps.

Through the years, people added reflectors to lamps to *diffuse* (spread out) or concentrate the light. Otherwise, few improvements occurred in lamps until the late 1700's. In the 1780's, a Swiss chemist named Aimé Argand invented a lamp with the wick bent into the shape of a hollow cylinder. Such a wick allowed air to reach the center of the flame. As a result, the Argand lamp produced a brighter light than other lamps did. Later, one of Argand's assistants made another improvement after discovering that a flame burns better inside a glass tube. His discovery led to the invention of the *lamp chimney,* a clear glass tube that surrounds the flame. During this period, whale oil and *colza oil,* an oil from the rape plant, became important fuels for lamps. The birth of the oil industry in the mid-1800's led to the widespread use of kerosene, a petroleum product, as lamp fuel.

Gas Lamps produce light by means of one or more small gas flames. These lamps need no wick. The gas flows from the lamp through a small opening and then burns after mixing with air. Gas lamps burn many kinds of gas, including acetylene, butane, coal gas, natural gas, producer gas, and water gas.

William Murdock, a Scottish engineer, developed the first commercially important gas lamps. In 1792, Murdock lit his home with gas lamps that burned coal gas. By the early 1800's, gas lamps had come into use as

street lamps in London and other cities. Gas lamps served as important sources of light until the late 1800's, when electric lamps began to replace them.

The gas lamp had one chief problem, the open gas flame. The flame often flickered and produced uneven light. Some gas lamps had a glass chimney, like that of an Argand lamp, to help control the flickering. In the late 1800's, a device called a *mantle* solved the problem. A mantle is a loosely woven cloth bag soaked with a chemical substance. The cloth quickly burns away in the lamp, and the chemical glows steadily as the gas burns around it. Most modern gas lamps, including the

Lamps Through the Ages Throughout history, people have used many kinds of lamps. Until electric lights were developed in the late 1800's, all lamps produced light by burning fuels, such as fat, gas, or oil. The most important types of fuel-burning lamps are shown below.

British Crown Copyright. Science Museum, London

A Hollowed-Out Stone was one of the first lamps. Ancient peoples used plant fibers as a wick to burn fat placed in the hollow.

Wadsworth Atheneum, Hartford, Conn.
Gift of J. P. Morgan

A Roman Lamp made of bronze, *above,* burned oil in its spout. This lamp could stand on a table or be hung by a chain.

A Candle, *right,* is an improved type of fat lamp. Candles once cost so much that only wealthy people could afford to use them.

British Crown Copyright.
Science Museum, London

WORLD BOOK photo

The Kerosene Lamp became popular during the mid-1800's. The lamp shown above has a reflector to provide as much light as possible.

Museum of Fine Arts, Boston,
M. & M. Karolik Collection

The Argand Lamp was invented in the 1780's. It had a hollow wick so that more air reached the flame, making a brighter light.

British Crown Copyright.
Science Museum, London

The Gas Lamp lit streets and homes. The above lamp has a glass shade that softens its light.

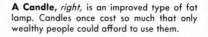

LAMP

53

The Coleman Company

A Gasoline Lantern gives campers a bright, portable light. Such fuel-burning lamps provide light in places that have no electricity, or during periods of electric power failure.

portable gas and liquid fuel lamps used by campers, have mantles.

Electric Lamps produce light by means of electric energy. The American inventor Thomas A. Edison developed the first practical electric lamp in 1879. Electric lamps came into widespread use during the early 1900's and have replaced other types of fat, gas, or oil lamps for almost every purpose. Electric lamps produce more and better light than the earlier lamps. They are also less expensive and easier to use. For information on electric lamps, see the WORLD BOOK articles on ELECTRIC LIGHT and LIGHTING. RONALD N. HELMS

See also GALILEO (picture); INVENTION (Inventions That Give People Light); LIGHTING (Lighting Problems; Lighting Devices).

LAMP SHADE. See LIGHTING (Quantity of Light).

LAMPANG, *LAHM pahng* (pop. 43,112), is a city in Thailand, about 45 miles (72 kilometers) southeast of Chiang Mai. See THAILAND (color map). It is a lumber center in a heavily forested area where many teak trees grow. Lampang's industries include cotton mills and tanneries. Copper, iron, and lead come from nearby mines.

LAMPBLACK. See CARBON.

LAMPER EEL. See LAMPREY (Destructiveness).

LAMPMAN, ARCHIBALD (1861-1899), one of Canada's leading poets, published three volumes of poetry: *Among the Millet* (1888), *Lyrics of Earth* (1893), and *Alcyone* (1899). Lampman felt that there is a universal harmony in nature which human society has failed to achieve. His work is noted for the accuracy of its nature descriptions and the skill of its craftsmanship. Lampman was born in Morpeth, Ont., and studied at Trinity College, Toronto. DESMOND PACEY

See also CANADIAN LITERATURE (After Confederation).

LAMPREY, *LAM pree*, is a fish with a long eellike body. Scientists consider the lamprey one of the least developed *vertebrates* (animals with backbones). Unlike most other fishes, the lamprey has no bony skeleton. It has a backbonelike *notochord* made of rubbery tissue called *cartilage*. The lamprey has fins on its back but not on its sides. Its round mouth has no jaws but can create strong suction. Adults of some species develop horny teeth. Such an adult attaches itself to other fishes by sucking with its mouth and clamping with its teeth. It feeds on its victims' blood and other body fluids.

Body. The lamprey's skin is smooth, shiny, and scaleless. *Brook lampreys*, which live in small streams throughout temperate parts of Europe, Asia, and North America, grow about 8 inches (20 centimeters) long. Larger *species* (kinds) live in rivers and lakes.

Sea lampreys, which may grow as much as 3 feet (91 centimeters) long, live in the North Atlantic and North Pacific oceans. All lampreys are dull colored, ranging from light-tan to mottled-brown or bluish-black. They do not have true bony teeth. The lamprey's teeth are horny developments that grow from the inner surface of the mouth.

Government of Canada Sea Lamprey Control Centre

The Lamprey attaches itself to a fish, such as a lake trout, *above*, and sucks out blood and other body fluids. Lampreys may greatly reduce the number of large fish in a body of water.

Woodrow Jarvis; American Museum of Natural History

The Lamprey's Mouth, *above,* is especially suited for sucking fluids from the bodies of other fish. Horny teeth on the inside of the mouth help the lamprey attach itself to a victim. Similar teeth on the lamprey's tongue rip open the skin of its victim.

Habits. Lampreys spawn in clear, freshwater streams. The male and female dig a shallow nest in the gravel or pebbles of the stream bottom. The female deposits the eggs in the nest. The adults die after spawning. *Larval* (young) lampreys are called *ammocoetes.* They are blind and toothless, and look like worms. The ammocoetes live in the sand and mud of the stream bottom for several years. Then they change into adults, with eyes and teeth.

Parasitic lampreys feed by attaching themselves to fishes, scraping a hole through the skin, and sucking out blood and other body fluids. The adults of the *nonparasitic* lampreys do not eat. Their digestive organs degenerate, and they live only until the spawning season. Then they spawn and die.

Destructiveness. Large sea lampreys rank as the most destructive to fishes. As adults, they descend to the sea and prey on large fishes. But some sea lampreys that spawned in streams flowing into Lake Ontario once entered the upper Great Lakes through the Welland Canal. Later generations of these lampreys no longer descend to the sea, but prey on lake trout, whitefish, and other large lake fishes. By the late 1950's, they had killed most of the lake trout in the Great Lakes. Scientists tried to control the lampreys by putting electric *weirs* (fences) across streams to prevent the lampreys from spawning. But the weirs were costly and difficult to maintain. Researchers discovered that a chemical called TFM would kill lampreys but would not harm other fish in the rivers. The treatment of streams with this chemical caused a sharp decline in the number of lampreys by the mid-1960's. Wildlife officials then stocked the lakes with *coho* salmon, lake trout, and other fishes.

At one time lampreys were used for food in New England, and smoked "lamper eels" were considered a delicacy.

Scientific Classification. Lampreys belong to the lamprey family, Petromyzontidae. The lamprey found in the Great Lakes is *Petromyzon marinus.*   HENRY W. ROBISON

See also HAGFISH.

LANAI. See HAWAII (The Islands).

LANCASTER was the name of the branch of the Plantagenet royal family that ruled England from 1399 to 1461. The House of Lancaster also ruled for a short time in 1470 and 1471.

John of Gaunt, 4th son of Edward III, founded the dynasty when he became Duke of Lancaster through his marriage to Blanche of Lancaster. The House of York stemmed from Gaunt's brother Edmund.

Gaunt's son became Henry IV in 1399, taking the throne away from his childless cousin, Richard II. This act led to the Wars of the Roses between the House of Lancaster and the House of York, which broke out more than 50 years later.

Henry IV's eldest son succeeded him as Henry V. Through his conquests in France, Henry V became one of the most famous warrior kings of England. In William Shakespeare's play *Henry IV,* he is identified as Prince Hal. Henry V died in 1422, leaving the throne to his baby son, Henry VI. All that his father won, the kindly but weak-minded Henry VI lost. The House of York defeated him in battle in 1461 and put Edward IV on the throne.

Henry regained the throne for a few months in 1470-1471, but lost it when he was imprisoned in the Tower of London. He was murdered a few days later, and the direct line of the House of Lancaster came to an end.   PAUL M. KENDALL

See also HENRY (IV) of England; JOHN OF GAUNT; WARS OF THE ROSES.

LANCASTER, Pa. (pop. 54,725; met. area pop. 362,346), is the commercial center of Lancaster County, one of the richest farming regions in the United States. It is also an important manufacturing city. It lies along the Conestoga River in southeastern Pennsylvania. For the location of Lancaster, see PENNSYLVANIA (political map).

Lancaster's chief products include aluminum, ammunition, building materials, industrial power tubes, steel, and watches. The city is the trading center for the region's farm products, which include cattle, poultry, tobacco, and corn.

Lancaster has many historical buildings. The city's Fulton Opera House was built in 1852 and is one of the oldest continuously used theaters in the United States. Wheatland, the estate of President James Buchanan, is in Lancaster. Lancaster is the home of Franklin and Marshall College and Lancaster Theological Seminary.

Amish and Mennonite settlers left Germany and—with members of other religious groups—founded Lancaster County in the early 1700's. These and other peoples became known as the *Pennsylvania Dutch* (see PENNSYLVANIA DUTCH). The settlers were skilled farmers and developed the area's rich farmland. They also invented the Conestoga Wagon. Lancaster was chartered as a borough in 1742 and incorporated as a city in 1818. During the Revolutionary War in America (1775-1783), the city provided food and guns for the Continental Army. It was the capital of the United States for one day, Sept. 27, 1777, when Congress moved from Philadelphia to York. Lancaster served as the capital of Pennsylvania from 1799 to 1812. The Lancaster Turnpike, the nation's first hard-surfaced road, was built between Lancaster and Philadelphia in 1794. Lancaster has a mayor-council form of government and is the seat of Lancaster County. JOHN H. BRUBAKER III

LANCE. See FIREWORKS (How Fireworks Work).

LANCE. See SPEAR.

LANCELET. See AMPHIOXUS.

LANCELOT, *LAN suh laht*, **SIR,** was a great British knight in medieval legends of King Arthur's Round Table. Lancelot won fame for his bravery and skill in combat, and he became Arthur's favorite knight. But Lancelot had a love affair with Queen Guenevere, Arthur's wife, that led to his downfall. The scandal that resulted from their affair contributed to the breakup of the Round Table. See ROUND TABLE.

Lancelot was the son of Ban, the king of Brittany. The Lady of the Lake, a woman with magic powers, took Lancelot as an infant to her castle at the bottom of a lake. After he reached manhood, the Lady of the Lake brought him to Arthur's court. Lancelot had a brief affair with Elaine of Astolat, a British princess. They had an illegitimate son, Galahad, who became a famous knight of the Round Table.

Along with many other knights, Lancelot went on the search for the *Holy Grail*, the cup or dish that Jesus Christ used at the Last Supper. Because he was morally imperfect, Lancelot did not find the Holy Grail. But his son, Sir Galahad, did find it.

Lancelot and Guenevere had fallen in love at Arthur's court. After Arthur discovered their affair, the lovers fled to Lancelot's castle, Joyous Garde. Lancelot killed several of his fellow knights after they found him with the queen. Later, Lancelot returned Guenevere to Arthur and left Britain. Arthur pursued Lancelot to France but went back to Britain after learning that Modred had seized his kingdom. According to various accounts, Modred was either Arthur's nephew or his son. Lancelot returned to Britain after Arthur's death and learned that Guenevere had become a nun. He became a priest and died shortly after Guenevere did.

Lancelot first appeared as an important character in a French story written about A.D. 1180 by Chrétien de Troyes. Sir Thomas Malory, an English writer, gave the fullest account of Lancelot in English in *Le Morte Darthur* (about 1469). Lancelot was also a chief character in *Idylls of the King*, a series of poems by the English poet Lord Tennyson. ROBERT W. ACKERMAN

LANCEWOOD is a tough wood used for archery bows, fishing rods, tool handles, and objects made on a lathe. It comes from two types of trees that grow in tropical America. Scientists call these trees *Oxandra lanceolata* and *Calycophyllum candidissimum*. Lancewood is yellowish brown, finely textured, and quite heavy. HARRY E. TROXELL

LAN-CHOU, *lahn joh* (pop. 1,364,480), also spelled *Lanzhou*, is the capital of Kansu Province in China. It was known as the *Gateway to China* in the Middle Ages. At that time, the city was the eastern end of the Silk Road, a caravan path to the west. It was also called *Kao-*

lan. Marco Polo and other traders traveled the Silk Road, carrying Chinese products to Europe and western Asia. As a Chinese frontier town, Lan-chou had a varied population. Chinese officials and merchants in silk robes rubbed shoulders with coolies in blue cotton suits. Tibetans in woolen ear-muff hats met Mongols carrying rifles and riding ponies. For the location of Lan-chou, see CHINA (political map).

After the Communists took over China in 1949, Lan-chou became an important center for the industrial development of China's northwest. The city now has factories that produce chemicals, machinery, and petroleum and lubricants. Railroads link Lan-chou with cities to the north, east, and south. THEODORE H. E. CHEN

LAND. See EARTH (The Earth's Surface); REAL ESTATE; SOIL.

LAND, EDWIN HERBERT (1909-   ), an American inventor, scientist, and business executive, invented the Polaroid Land camera, the first instant camera. Instant cameras produce a photograph seconds after the photographer takes a picture.

Land holds more than 500 patents. In 1934, he patented *polarized light filters*, which help eliminate glare and reflections on glass and other surfaces. In 1937, Land founded the Polaroid Corporation to manufacture the filters. He became its president and chairman of the board. Land developed light filters for use in automobile headlights, sunglasses, and cameras.

In 1947, Land demonstrated the first instant cameras. These cameras took only black-and-white pictures, which developed in about a minute. In 1963, Land introduced a color film that developed into photographs inside the camera within 50 seconds. By 1972, Land had improved this system to take color pictures that developed outside the camera, allowing the photographer to take another picture immediately.

Land was born in Bridgeport, Conn. He attended Harvard University, though he never graduated. He retired as president of Polaroid in 1975 and as chairman of the board in 1982. ROBERT A. SOBIESZEK

See also PHOTOGRAPHY (Instant Processing); POLARIZED LIGHT (Polarizing Materials).

LAND BANK, FEDERAL. See FARM CREDIT.

LAND-GRANT COLLEGE OR UNIVERSITY is a school endowed under the Morrill, or Land-Grant, Act of 1862. Congress granted every state 30,000 acres (12,141 hectares) of land for each senator and representative it had in Congress. The land was to be sold, the proceeds invested, and the income used to create and maintain a college for agriculture and the mechanical arts.

For several years, people had clamored for colleges to teach the finer points of farming and manufacturing. Finally the Land-Grant Act, sponsored by Representative Justin S. Morrill of Vermont, was passed. The act added military science and tactics to the proposed curriculum. Altogether, the states and territories received 11,367,832 acres (4,600,398 hectares) of land. Congress added money to its gifts through the Second Morrill Act of 1890 and an amendment in 1907. Today, all states and Puerto Rico receive federal grants to help support land-grant colleges and universities.

Not all the states used the land-grant money as planned by the act. Thirty states, mainly in the Middle West and South, set up new agricultural and mechanical colleges. Eighteen gave the money to state universities to finance new agricultural and mechanical departments. Three gave the money to private colleges. Also, most of the states were unable to sell all the lands given them. The land they did sell was sold at a price so low that the states made almost no money.

But the educational value of the land-grant idea has been priceless. As a result of this program, old colleges have been able to expand, and new colleges have been created. Land-grant schools include such well-known institutions as the University of California and the University of Illinois.   ALAN GRIFFIN

LAND MANAGEMENT, BUREAU OF, is a United States government agency that administers about 475 million acres (192 million hectares) of public land. Most of this land lies in the Western States and Alaska and has never been privately owned. The land provides food for livestock, supplies forest products and minerals, furnishes recreation facilities, and serves as a natural home for wildlife.

The bureau has classified the land according to its best use and manages it in the public interest. The bureau sells pieces of land at public auction when such sales are in the national interest.

The Bureau of Land Management was established in 1946 as part of the Department of the Interior. It took over the functions of two previous agencies, the General Land Office and the Grazing Service. The bureau has headquarters in Washington, D.C., and offices in the Western States and Alaska.

Critically reviewed by the BUREAU OF LAND MANAGEMENT

LAND REFORM aims at improving the social and economic conditions of farmers. In the past, it fought remnants of feudal laws that prevented peasants from buying land. It also tried to modify the law of *primogeniture*, which allowed only the eldest son to inherit, thus concentrating land holdings. Advanced technology and political interference in buying and selling land have increased the tendency of a small number of persons to own a large part of the world's farmland.

One phase of land reform involves *redistribution* of land, or dividing large holdings among the landless. Laws that redistribute farmland are called *agrarian laws*. But more equal land distribution is not a sure cure for the ills of farming societies. Land reformers must consider that farm plots should not be too small to support a family, and that modern technology tends to reduce the size of the farming population.

Many countries have provided greater opportunity for farmers to own their land by passing laws to assure clearer land titles, credit on reasonable terms, fair taxes, and better distribution of their products. Other laws have helped tenant farmers by protecting their rights, prohibiting unfair rentals, and improving the wages paid for farm labor.

Land reform may be a revolutionary slogan or program, and has often been exploited in political conflicts, especially between peasants and landholders. Communists promise land reform to attract followers of revolutionary movements.   STEFAN T. POSSONY

See also SOUTH AMERICA (Agriculture); MEXICO (Agriculture).

LANDERS, ANN (1918-   ), writes a popular newspaper column that gives advice and information to readers. She is considered one of the most influential people in the United States. The column is published

in about 1,000 newspapers in the United States and other countries. About 70 million people read it daily.

People write to Landers about such matters as family life, health, marriage, and social issues. She consults attorneys, physicians, psychologists, members of the clergy, and experts in other fields to help answer questions. In her replies, many of which are humorous and light-hearted, Landers also uses common sense and personal experience.

Landers, whose real name is Esther Pauline "Eppie" Friedman Lederer, was born in Sioux City, Iowa, and attended Morningside College. She began her career in 1955, when she took over the advice column of the *Chicago Sun-Times*. Landers has written several books, including *Ann Landers Talks to Teenagers About Sex* (1963) and

Dave Cooper, *Toronto Star*
Ann Landers

The Ann Landers Encyclopedia From A To Z (1978). Her twin sister, Pauline Friedman Phillips, writes a popular advice column called *Dear Abby* under the name Abigail Van Buren.   JANICE DALE

LANDES, BERTHA KNIGHT (1868-1943), was the first woman to serve as mayor of a major United States city. A Republican, she was mayor of Seattle, Wash., from 1926 to 1928. She served on the city council there from 1922 to 1926.

Landes was born in Ware, Mass., and attended Indiana University. After public service, she became a lecturer and writer.   C. BREWSTER COULTER

LANDING CRAFT. See AMPHIBIOUS SHIP.

LANDING GEAR. See AIRPLANE (Landing Gear).

LANDIS, KENESAW MOUNTAIN, *KEHN ih SAW* (1866-1944), an American judge, served as the first commissioner of professional baseball. During many years as judge of the United States District Court of Northern Illinois, Landis earned a reputation for fairness. In 1907, he won national attention by fining the Standard Oil Company of Indiana $29,240,000 for accepting freight rebates.

In 1919, the Chicago White Sox allowed the Cincinnati Reds to "win" the World Series. To protect baseball from further dishonesty and scandal, the club owners appointed Landis commissioner of baseball in 1920. Landis ruled baseball with an iron hand, and the game acquired an unquestionable reputation for honesty. He was elected to the National Baseball Hall of Fame in 1944. Landis was born in Millville, Ohio.   ED FITZGERALD

See also BASEBALL (The Black Sox Scandal).

LANDLORD. See TENANT; LEASE.

LANDON, ALFRED MOSSMAN (1887-   ), was the Republican candidate for President in 1936. He and his running mate, Frank Knox, lost the election to Franklin D. Roosevelt and John Nance Garner.

Landon served two terms as governor of Kansas. He won the 1932 and 1934 elections despite the Democratic national landslide. Landon's ability to balance the

LANDOWSKA, WANDA

state budget helped bring him the presidential nomination in 1936.

Landon was born in West Middlesex, Pa., and graduated from the University of Kansas. In 1912, he and three partners established a company to develop oil wells. Landon became a leader in the petroleum industry. In 1928, he served as chairman of the Republican State Central Committee.

Alfred M. Landon

Landon's daughter Nancy Landon Kassebaum was elected to the United States Senate from Kansas in 1978. GEORGE M. WALLER

LANDOWSKA, *lan DAWF skuh,* **WANDA,** *WAHN duh* (1879-1959), a Polish harpsichordist, pianist, and composer, revived an interest in music and musical instruments of the past. Beginning in 1906, she made concert tours throughout Europe and Africa, playing both the piano and the harpsichord. Gradually the harpsichord became her specialty. She made her North American debut in 1923, as soloist with the Philadelphia Symphony Orchestra. In 1925, Landowska founded a school near Paris dedicated to the study of early music. She moved to the United States in 1941 after the German invasion of France. Her books include *The Music of the Past* (1923), which she wrote with her husband. She was born in Warsaw, Poland. ROBERT U. NELSON

LANDRUM-GRIFFIN ACT. See LABOR MOVEMENT (Charges of Corruption).

LAND'S END, a cape in Cornwall, is the westernmost point of land in England. It juts into the English Channel where the channel opens into the Atlantic Ocean. For location, see GREAT BRITAIN (color map). Land's End is a granite promontory with cliffs from 60 to 100 feet (18 to 30 meters) high that have been carved into strange shapes by the waves. It is the last part of England seen from ships sailing west to the Americas. Longships Lighthouse, on a small island about 1 mile (1.6 kilometers) from Land's End, marks dangerous reefs. JOHN W. WEBB

LANDSCAPE ARCHITECTURE is the art of developing or redesigning land and the objects on it for greater human use and enjoyment. People professionally trained to do such work are called *landscape architects.*

Landscape architects plan outdoor spaces much as building architects organize indoor spaces. They create plans for land developments. These developments may range from large national parks to small city squares, or from huge housing developments to single houses. Landscape architects locate outdoor facilities so the facilities function smoothly and blend with the surroundings.

Landscape architects plan ways to organize living, working, and recreation space. For example, landscape architects plan trees and grassy areas in downtown areas to serve as walkways and shield pedestrians from automobile noises and fumes. Roofs of city parking garages have been converted into tree-lined shopping *malls*

(walks). Abandoned sand and gravel pits have been converted into attractive home and recreation sites.

Land Planning. Landscape architects help decide what land is best suited for residential, industrial, transportation, recreation, and conservation purposes. In making these decisions, they study such area features as climate, water supply, vegetation, the composition of the soil, and the slope of the land. They attempt to preserve attractive views and landmarks, and to avoid erosion, flooding, and the pollution of air and water. In developing land use plans, landscape architects work with traffic engineers, economists, city planners, and public officials.

Site Design. After land use has been determined, landscape architects prepare site development plans and supervise construction contractors. They work with building architects to fit structures to land forms, arranging them to make best use of breezes, sunlight, and views. In designing roads, parks, and other sites, landscape architects keep mature trees for immediate shade and arrange for proper grading and drainage. They design walls, fences, steps, pavements, and planting arrangements where needed.

Landscape architects work on various types of projects. A state park might need cabins, campsites, and roads located without destroying natural scenery. Or a city square might call for the design of elaborate pavement patterns, fountains, and ornamental plants. Landscape architects may be asked to create imagina-

Ezra Stoller

Landscaped Grounds blend natural and artificially created objects to beautify the home. Mature trees are kept for shade, and steps, walks, and plants are placed where needed.

tive equipment for a playground, or propose a master plan for university expansion. Or they might plan the layout of a shopping center, golf course, apartment building grounds, zoo, hospital grounds, or trailer park.

History. Landscape architecture as a profession dates from the mid-1800's. But the art of landscape architecture has been practiced for thousands of years. For example, many Roman homes built between the 400's B.C. and the A.D. 400's had elaborate courtyards (see ROME, ANCIENT (Food, Clothing, and Shelter; picture). Other early examples include the gardens of ancient Persia (A.D. 200's to 600's) and Japan (A.D. 500's). The Italians designed and built beautiful hillside estates and civic plazas during the 1400's and 1500's. In the 1600's and 1700's, France became noted for its magnificent palaces and city gardens (see VERSAILLES [picture]). English designers planned natural-appearing country estates in the 1800's.

Many of these early projects were gardens and country estates. Thus, the designers were often called *landscape gardeners.* Frederick Law Olmsted, an American, was the first person to call himself a landscape architect. In the 1850's, Olmsted and Calvert Vaux designed New York City's Central Park. When Olmsted signed these plans, he placed the words *landscape architect* under his name. He saw his job as creating outdoor environments much as architects plan buildings. In 1899, his followers formed the American Society of Landscape Architects, the profession's national organization.

Today, landscape architects are employed as private consultants, teachers, or staff members of government agencies. To qualify, they must have a degree in landscape architecture from an accredited college or university.   WILLIAM G. CARNES

Related Articles in WORLD BOOK include:

Botanical Garden	New Harmony (picture)
City Planning	Olmsted (family)
Le Nôtre, André	Saskatchewan (color picture)

LANDSCAPE PAINTING. See PAINTING (What Do Painters Paint?).

LANDSLIDE occurs when a mass of earth or rocks slides down a slope. Water seepage, cracks in rocks, and earthquakes are common causes of landslides. The action of waves on a coastline also may cause a landslide. In politics, the term *landslide* means one political party has received an overwhelming majority of votes.

See also AVALANCHE; EARTH (Mass Movement).

LANDSTEINER, *LAND* STY *nuhr* or *LAHNT* SHTY *nuhr,* **KARL** (1868-1943), won the 1930 Nobel Prize for physiology or medicine for his discovery of the main types of human blood—A, B, AB, and O. His discovery made safe blood transfusions possible for the first time. In 1940, he and A. S. Wiener discovered the Rh blood factor, an important cause of stillbirths. Landsteiner also contributed information on how the body becomes immune to certain disease bacteria. In addition, Landsteiner proved that a virus causes poliomyelitis.

Landsteiner was born in Vienna, Austria. He moved to the United States in 1922, and was a member of the Rockefeller Institute for Medical Research (now Rockefeller University) from 1922 to 1939.   MORDECAI L. GABRIEL

See also BLOOD (Blood Types); RH FACTOR.

LANFRANC, *LAN frangk* (1005?-1089), was an important medieval teacher and scholar. He was an adviser to William the Conqueror, the first Norman king of England, and served under him as archbishop of Canterbury.

Lanfranc was born in Pavia, Italy. He became a monk in the Benedictine order at Bec, in Normandy, about 1042. Lanfranc was head of the monastery school for about 18 years, and achieved distinction as a teacher of theology. Under his leadership, the school became one of the most famous in Europe. Saint Anselm and the future Pope Alexander II were among Lanfranc's students. Lanfranc also wrote several influential books on monastic life and the sacrament of Communion.

In 1070, William appointed Lanfranc archbishop of Canterbury. As archbishop, Lanfranc reformed the

Johnson, Johnson, & Roy, Inc.

City Landscaping Projects develop outdoor facilities that are useful and pleasing to the eye. This treelined plaza in Canton, Ohio, is converted into an ice skating rink during the winter months.

guidelines for the marriage of priests, and established the church's court system in England.   WILLIAM J. COURTENAY

LANG, ANDREW (1844-1912), was a Scottish scholar and author. Lang wrote a large number of works on a wide variety of subjects. He published poetry, fiction, literary criticism, anthropological studies, translations, children's books, histories, and biographies.

Lang's studies of folklore are probably the most enduring of his works. His book *Myth, Ritual, and Religion* (1887) is an important statement of Lang's theories about the relationship between folklore and mythology. Lang worked with other scholars on translations of the Greek epics the *Iliad* and the *Odyssey*. His translations and critical works on ancient Greek writers made a significant contribution to contemporary interpretations of classical literature.   AVROM FLEISHMAN

See also LITERATURE FOR CHILDREN (Books to Read [Folk Literature/Fairy Tales, Folk Tales, and Myths]).

LANG, FRITZ (1890?-1976), was a motion-picture director who made classic horror and suspense films in both Germany and the United States. Lang first gained recognition in Germany for his silent films about the corruption of society by criminals and mad scientists. The most important of these movies were *Dr. Mabuse, the Gambler* (1922), *Metropolis* (1926), and *Spies* (1928). Lang's first sound film, *M* (1931), describes the search for an insane killer of children.

Lang fled Germany in 1933 rather than direct motion pictures for the Nazis, and he settled in the United States. His best American films all concern a man being pursued by an evil force that drives him to desperation. For example, *Fury* (1936), Lang's first American film, deals with a man threatened by a lynch mob. *The Big Heat* (1953) portrays a man's battle against gangsters. Lang's other American movies include *You Only Live Once* (1937), *The Return of Frank James* (1940), *Man Hunt* (1941), *The Ministry of Fear* (1944), *The Woman in the Window* (1945), and *Rancho Notorious* (1952).

Lang was born in Vienna. He directed his first motion picture in 1919.   JOHN F. MARIANI

LANGDON, JOHN (1741-1819), was a New Hampshire signer of the Constitution of the United States. He actively represented his state at the 1787 Constitutional Convention in Philadelphia and spoke in favor of a strong national government on numerous occasions. Langdon later helped win *ratification* (approval) of the Constitution by New Hampshire.

Langdon was born near Portsmouth, N.H. Before the Revolutionary War in America (1775-1783), he was a successful ship captain and merchant. During the war, Langdon represented New Hampshire in the Second Continental Congress and was speaker of the New Hampshire legislature. He also built ships for the Continental Navy. Langdon served as chief executive of New Hampshire in 1785, 1786, 1788, and 1789. From 1789 to 1801, Langdon served as a U.S. senator. He then returned to state politics and led New Hampshire's Democratic-Republican Party. Langdon acted as speaker of the state legislature from 1803 to 1805. He was governor of New Hampshire from 1805 to 1809 and from 1810 to 1812.   JERE DANIELL

LANGE, *LAWNG ee,* **DAVID RUSSELL** (1942-   ), became prime minister of New Zealand in 1984. He

New Zealand Embassy
David R. Lange

took office after the Labour Party, which he heads, defeated the governing National Party in the July 1984 elections. A moderate socialist, Lange favors some government and some private ownership of industries. In foreign policy matters, he supports greater independence from Great Britain and the United States. Under Lange, the government established a policy that excluded from New Zealand ports and territorial waters all ships powered by nuclear fuel or armed with nuclear weapons. These ships include military vessels belonging to the United States. In 1985, a U.S. destroyer was denied access to a New Zealand port after U.S. officials refused to announce whether or not the ship carried nuclear weapons.

Lange was born in Auckland, New Zealand. He earned law degrees from the University of Auckland in 1966 and 1970. For several years, he worked as a lawyer, often taking the cases of people who could not afford to pay him. He first won election to Parliament in 1977. He represents Mangere, a working-class suburb of Auckland. Lange became the leader of the Labour Party in 1983.   RUSSELL HILL

LANGE, DOROTHEA, *DAWR oh THEE uh* (1895-1965), was an American photographer known for her pictures of migratory farm workers of the 1930's.

Library of Congress
A Photograph by Dorothea Lange taken in 1936 captures the despair of a migrant family during the Great Depression.

Lange's photographs honestly and sympathetically portray families who were victims of drought and the Great Depression. Her pictures, which appeared in several newspapers and magazines, helped create support for government relief programs for migrant workers. Many of Lange's photographs were published in her book *An American Exodus: A Record of Human Erosion* (1939).

Lange was born in Hoboken, N.J., and studied photography at Columbia University. She traveled to San Francisco in 1918 and opened a portrait studio there the next year. During World War II (1939-1945), Lange photographed many Japanese-Americans whom the government moved to relocation camps from their homes on the West Coast. After the war, she photographed Mormon towns, life in California, and other subjects. She also took photographs in Asia, Egypt, Ireland, and South America. CHARLES HAGEN

See also PHOTOGRAPHY (picture: Documentary Photographs).

LANGLAND, WILLIAM (1330?-1400?), wrote *Piers Plowman*, a great English poem of the Middle Ages. Scholars know little about Langland's life, but they believe he was born in Shropshire in western England and was educated in monasteries. During the late 1300's, he wrote three versions of *Piers Plowman*. All use alliteration instead of rhyme and are written in Middle English, the chief literary language of England during Langland's time.

The main theme of *Piers Plowman* is the need to reform England spiritually through Christian faith and love. The poem is a complex religious allegory in which each character represents an abstract quality or a type of person. The main character, Will, represents the will of every person who wants salvation. Piers, another character, symbolizes all true ministers of God. The action consists of Will's quest for Truth, or God. Will has nine dreams, in which most of the action occurs. The poem alternates between vivid scenes and long speeches and has much wit and power. DAVID S. CHAMBERLAIN

See also ENGLISH LITERATURE (picture: *The Vision of Piers Plowman*).

LANGLEY, SAMUEL PIERPONT (1834-1906), was an American astronomer, physicist, and pioneer in aeronautics. His interest in *aerodynamics* (the theory of flight) led him to experiment with heavier-than-air flying machines. His power-driven models made a few successful flights of about ½ mile (0.8 kilometer) in 1896. The U.S. government later gave Langley $50,000 to build a passenger-carrying "aerodrome." This machine twice was launched from a houseboat on the Potomac River in 1903. Both tests failed, but one using a smaller model succeeded. The second full-size model test was made in December 1903, shortly before the Wright brothers' epoch-making flight at Kitty Hawk, N.C.

In 1914, eight years after Langley's death, several changes were made in his "aerodrome" machine, and it was flown at Hammondsport, N.Y., by Glenn H. Curtiss. The United States Navy honored Langley by naming its first aircraft carrier after him. It was sunk in the Java Sea early in 1942. A second carrier named *Langley* served later in World War II. The Langley Air Force Base in Virginia is also named after him.

Langley was born in Roxbury, Mass., and attended Boston Latin School. He spent several years studying architecture and engineering before turning to astronomy, in which he had been interested since boyhood. His several inventions included an instrument called the *bolometer*, which measures the sun's radiation (see BOLOMETER).

From 1867 to 1887, Langley was professor of physics and astronomy, and director of the Allegheny Observatory, at the Western University of Pennsylvania in Pittsburgh. He served as secretary of the Smithsonian Institution from 1887 until his death. While in this office, he established the National Zoological Park and the Astrophysical Observatory. His writings include *Experiments in Aerodynamics* (1891) and *The Internal Work of the Wind* (1893). PAUL EDWARD GARBER

See also AIRPLANE (Powered Flight).

LANGLEY AIR FORCE BASE, Va., is the headquarters of the U.S. Air Force Tactical Air Command. This command provides a fast reacting air combat force. The 3,200-acre (1,290-hectare) base lies 3 miles (5 kilometers) from Hampton. Troop carrier aircraft, fighter-interceptors, and air defense missiles are based there. A National Aeronautics and Space Administration research center is located there. The base was established in 1916 as an experimental station. It was named for Samuel P. Langley, an American air pioneer (see LANGLEY, SAMUEL PIERPONT). RICHARD M. SKINNER

LANGMUIR, *LANG myoor*, **IRVING** (1881-1957), won the 1932 Nobel prize in chemistry for his work in surface chemistry and in the electron theory of matter. His investigations of surface films led to important advances in the study of microorganisms. Langmuir also did research in physics and engineering. He helped develop the gas-filled incandescent bulb, the vacuum tube, and an atomic hydrogen welding process. He also developed a way to produce rain and snow by seeding clouds with dry ice. Langmuir was born in Brooklyn, N.Y., and studied at Columbia University and in Göttingen, Germany. He conducted research at the General Electric laboratory from 1909 to 1950. HERBERT S. RHINESMITH

LANGTON, STEPHEN CARDINAL (1165?-1228), one of England's greatest archbishops of Canterbury, was a famous theologian, Biblical scholar, and statesman. In the late 1100's, he became known as the greatest commentator on the Bible.

When King John wished to choose his own candidate as archbishop of Canterbury, Pope Innocent III objected and appointed Langton in 1207. The king refused to accept him, and Langton had to remain in exile in France. The pope placed England under an interdict, and excommunicated the king in order to force him to accept Langton. John finally accepted Langton in 1213. As archbishop, Langton defended the freedom of the church and promoted peace between John and his barons. Also, he helped bring about the Magna Carta (see MAGNA CARTA). WILLIAM J. COURTENAY

LANGTRY, *LANG tree*, **LILLIE** (1852-1929), a British actress known as "Jersey Lily," became a stage favorite in England and the United States. The town of Langtry, Tex., was named for her. Langtry's most famous role was that of Rosalind in William Shakespeare's *As You Like It*. Oscar Wilde wrote *Lady Windermere's Fan* (1892) especially for her. Langtry was born Emily Charlotte le Breton at St. Helier, Jersey. Jersey is one of the Channel Islands. RICHARD MOODY

LANGUAGE

LANGUAGE is human speech, either spoken or written. Language is the most common system of communication. It allows people to talk to each other and to write their thoughts and ideas. The word *language* may be loosely used to mean any system of communication, such as traffic lights or Indian smoke signals. But the origin of the word shows its basic use. It comes from the Latin word *lingua*, meaning *tongue*. And a language still is often called a *tongue*.

Wherever there is human society, there is language. Most forms of human activity depend on the cooperation of two or more persons. A common language enables human beings to work together in an infinite variety of ways. Language has made possible the development of advanced, technological civilization. Without language for communication, there would be little or no science, religion, commerce, government, art, literature, and philosophy.

Scholars have determined that there are about 3,000 languages spoken in the world today. This number does not include *dialects* (local forms of a language). Many languages are spoken only by small groups of a few hundred or a few thousand persons. There are more than a hundred languages with a million or more speakers. Of these languages, 19 have over 50 million speakers each: Arabic, Bengali, Chinese, English, French, German, Hindi, Italian, Japanese, Korean, Malay-Indonesian, Marathi, Portuguese, Punjabi, Russian, Spanish, Tamil, Telugu, and Urdu. Hindi and Urdu are sometimes grouped together as Hindustani. People in many countries use some of these major languages, including English, French, Spanish, Portuguese, and Arabic. Other major languages have little use outside their own areas.

Most people learn their own language without fully realizing what is taking place. Young children feel a need to communicate their particular needs and they begin listening to older persons and imitating them. They gradually learn to select and to make the sounds used in the language spoken around them. They also learn to disregard other possible sounds that their voices could make. At the same time, children learn to connect individual words with objects, ideas, and actions. Their responses become automatic. For example, upon seeing a dog, an English-speaking child automatically calls it a "dog." Youngsters also learn, largely by imitation, to arrange words in certain ways. By the age of 5 or 6, most children have learned the patterns of their language fairly well. They can then communicate well enough for most of their own practical purposes. In school, the language-learning process becomes conscious and deliberate. Children become aware of how the sounds and words of their language are arranged in systems. They can then learn to speak or write precisely about more complex matters.

Learning a Foreign Language

There are many important reasons for learning a foreign language. Among them are the following:

(1) Learning a foreign language increases your range of communication. For example, if you speak only English, you can communicate with over 400 million other persons. If you also learn Spanish, you could speak to any of the 297 million Spanish-speaking people in Latin America, Spain, and other parts of the world.

(2) By learning another language, you gain knowledge of the customs and ways of life of other nations. While learning French, you find out how French people live, behave, and think.

(3) A foreign language can help add to your knowledge of your own language. For example, by studying Latin, you can improve your understanding of many of the thousands of English words that have their roots in Latin.

(4) Learning a foreign language helps you add to your general stock of information. It can be a key that unlocks new fields of knowledge. If you learn German you will be able to read books written in German on almost any subject you may wish to study.

(5) Knowledge of a foreign language can help you gain a spirit of broad human tolerance. You will find that other peoples may think, speak, and act in ways different from yours. But these ways are not necessarily less desirable than yours.

Learning any language involves four different skills: (1) speaking, (2) understanding, (3) reading, and (4) writing. If you understand a foreign language, and can make yourself understood in speech and writing, you have mastered it.

Methods of Study. No language is easy or difficult in itself. The ease or difficulty of any language depends on the age of the person learning it. Before the age of 10, all languages are equally easy when learned by the *natural speaking* method (listening and imitating). After 10, our language habits are set in our own tongue. From then on, another language is easy insofar as it resembles our own. It is difficult insofar as it differs from our own. Therefore, it is desirable to learn foreign languages as early as possible. Some schools start foreign language instruction in kindergarten or in the primary grades.

After the age of 10, students can learn foreign languages by either, or both, of two methods: (1) the grammar method, and (2) the spoken language method.

In the *grammar* method, students learn general rules of grammar and apply them to specific situations. A French grammar lesson may stress the correct use of *gender* (masculine or feminine). Students learn that *le livre* (the book) is masculine and *la chaise* (the chair) is feminine. In this way, they learn grammar while they increase their vocabularies.

In the *spoken language* method, students try to duplicate the process by which young children learn language. They listen to the teacher, then imitate the sounds, words, and sentences.

Both the grammar method and the natural speaking method are effective. The ideal method for older children and adults seems to be a combination of the two.

Study Aids. For hundreds of years, language students have used grammar books, exercise books, and dictionaries. Modern study aids—especially for spoken language—include (1) voice recordings with accompanying booklets; (2) tape recorders, which permit students to listen, repeat, erase their own repetition, then try again; (3) videotapes and closed-circuit TV's, which let students watch their mouth movements and compare them with those of a speaker; and (4) computers, which correct student translations of words and phrases on a video

A Language Laboratory has tape recorders, earphones, and special desks. The recorders allow students to record their own voices as they learn a foreign language. They use the earphones to listen to their pronunciation, or to the pronunciation of the teacher, *rear.* The walls at the sides of the desks help keep out noise.

International Language Communications, Chicago

display screen. These language study aids provide not only instruction and practice, but also self-instruction, because they can be used without a teacher.

The Makeup of Language

All languages have certain things in common. These include (1) a sound-pattern, (2) words, and (3) grammatical structure.

A Sound-Pattern is a group of sounds that the human speech organs can utter. Most languages have from 20 to 60 of these sounds.

Words are sounds or sound-patterns that have a meaning. Words may stand for objects, actions, or ideas.

Grammatical Structure is the manner in which words are combined to form larger, meaningful units such as sentences. Grammatical structure may take either or both of two forms. One form, called *syntax,* is the arrangement of words in a particular order. The order of words makes their meaning clear. In English, when we say *John sees Mark,* we show that *John* is the doer of the action and *Mark* the receiver. We do this by putting *John* before *sees* and *Mark* after *sees.* Other languages use quite different orders. However, as long as the meaning depends on word order, the languages are using syntax.

The other form of grammatical structure is called *morphology.* It uses a variation in the form of a word to show the function of the word in a group. In Latin, both *Johannes videt Marcum* and *Videt Marcum Johannes* mean *John sees Mark.* In this case, we know that *Johannes* (*John*) is the doer of the action, no matter where the word occurs, because it ends in *-s* (not *-m*). Similarly, we know that *Marcum* (*Mark*) is the receiver because it ends in *-m* (not *-s*).

Some languages, such as Chinese, use syntax only. In other languages, such as Latin, the order of the words has little importance because word endings tell the story. Old English, or Anglo-Saxon (the form of English spoken until about A.D. 1100), resembled Latin in this way.

Modern English uses a blend of syntax and morphology. When we say *I see him,* we give two indications that *I* is the doer and *him* is the receiver. One indication is the position of *I* before *see* and *him* after *see.* The other is the fact that we use *I* (not *me*) for the doer, and *him* (not *he*) for the receiver.

Development of Language

The makeup of a language does not remain the same over long periods of time. Grammar, vocabulary, and sound-patterns all change with usage.

Linguistic Terms

*Accent is the emphasis placed on a certain syllable of a word. We accent the syllable *lang* in the word *language.*

Agreement occurs when one part of speech changes its form to conform with another part. For example, the word *come* changes to *comes* when used with a third person singular subject, as in *he comes.*

Blend is a word made up of parts of two or more other words. *Brunch* (breakfast and lunch) is a blend.

Cognates are words in different languages that have the same original source. The English word *water* and the German word *Wasser* are cognates.

Coinage is an invented word. Manufacturers coined the words *kodak* and *zipper* to advertise their products.

Colloquialism is an informal, but not slang, expression such as *I've got it.* Colloquialisms are out of place in formal speech, but are widely used in daily speech.

*Diacritical Mark is a written sign used to show changes in sounds and pronunciation. The Spanish *tilde* (˜) gives an *n* an *ny* sound.

*Etymology is a branch of linguistics that studies the origin and development of words.

Hybrid Word is composed of parts from two or more languages. In the word *automobile, auto* comes from Greek and *mobile* from Latin.

*Idiom is an expression in one language that cannot be accurately translated into another. The meaning of an idiom cannot be seen from the individual words in it. For example, *Look out!* means *Be careful!*

*Illiteracy is the inability to read and write.

Jargon is a vocabulary and set of expressions used by a particular group of persons. Doctors, for example, use many words and expressions not used by the general public.

Loan Word, such as *spaghetti,* is borrowed from another language, either in its original form or modified.

*Linguistics is the scientific study of language in the broadest sense. *Philology* is an older term for the scientific study of language.

Neologism is a newly coined word that has not been generally accepted. *Grismal,* a combination of *grim* and *dismal,* is a neologism. The term also refers to the use of a word in a new meaning. For example, *contact* was once only a noun. Today, it is also a verb, as in *We will contact you,* and an adjective, as in *Football is a contact sport.*

*Semantics is the study of the meaning of words.

*Slang consists of words and phrases that are used in unconventional ways. An example is the word *grub* (food). The slang expression *klutz* means a *clumsy person.*

Vernacular is the spoken language of any area.

*Has a separate article in WORLD BOOK.

LANGUAGE

How Language Began. No one knows how language began. Because all people who are not handicapped have the ability to speak, language has probably existed at least as long as the modern human species. Most scholars believe that language developed very slowly from sounds, such as grunts, barks, and hoots, made by prehuman creatures. According to this view, a simple system of vocal communication became more and more complex as the human brain and speech organs evolved. But no one knows when or how this process took place. In fact, there is no record of language for most of its existence. The first real evidence of language is writing. But scholars believe that writing did not appear until thousands of years after the origin of spoken language. The earliest known written records are Sumerian word-pictures made about 3500 B.C. and Egyptian hieroglyphics that date from about 3000 B.C. (see HIEROGLYPHICS). Written Chinese dates from perhaps 1500 B.C., Greek from about 1400 B.C., and Latin from about 500 B.C.

How Language Changes. No one knows all the reasons why languages change, but they continue to do so as long as people speak them. In a few cases, the changes can be explained. For example, words are added to a vocabulary to refer to new ideas or objects. Contacts between speakers of different languages may cause words from one language to enter another language.

Most language changes occur for unknown reasons. Languages do not become better or worse, only different. The change is very slow. People who speak English do not notice that their own language is changing from one year to the next. But if present-day speakers of English try to read Old English, they find that it is as unlike modern English as are French or German. In modern industrial societies, language changes take place even more slowly. Educational systems and such centralized communication systems as radio and television promote the use of a standard form of a language. Under these conditions, a language is likely to remain more stable. However, language will probably never stop changing entirely.

Only when a language loses all its speakers does it stop changing completely. A language that is no longer spoken is called a *dead language*. Such languages include Sumerian, ancient Egyptian, Akkadian, Hittite, Etruscan, and Gothic.

Language Families

Scholars classify languages into families. Language families are groups of languages that are related because they all developed slowly from a single earlier language called a *parent language*. When speakers of a language become divided into groups that are out of contact with each other, the language of each group continues to change in its own way. After several centuries, the individual groups speak so differently that they cannot understand each other. But the languages in each family are still related because all of them came from the same parent language.

Indo-European is the most important language family. Some 2,238,000,000 persons, or about half the world's population, speak languages in this family. Most of the nations that gave rise to Western civilization speak Indo-European languages. Speakers of these

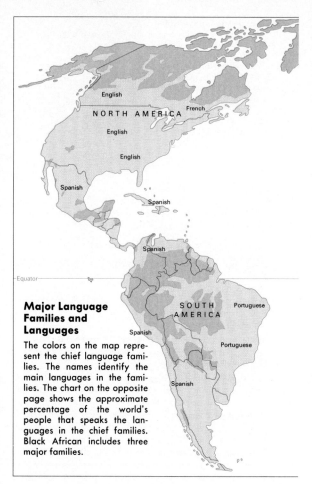

Major Language Families and Languages

The colors on the map represent the chief language families. The names identify the main languages in the families. The chart on the opposite page shows the approximate percentage of the world's people that speaks the languages in the chief families. Black African includes three major families.

languages originally lived in an area extending from northern India to western Europe. They now live in other parts of the world as well. Indo-European languages have become the most important tongues in most European countries, in Australia and New Zealand, and in the countries of North, Central, and South America.

The Indo-European family has eight living branches. They are: (1) *Germanic*, or *Teutonic*, which includes English, German, Dutch, and the Scandinavian tongues—Danish, Icelandic, Norwegian, and Swedish; (2) *Romance*, or *Latin-Romance*, including French, Spanish, Portuguese, Italian, and Romanian; (3) *Balto-Slavic*, including Russian, Ukrainian, Polish, Czech, Slovak, Serbo-Croatian, Slovenian, Bulgarian, Lithuanian, and Latvian; (4) *Indo-Iranian*, which includes Hindi, Urdu, Bengali, Farsi, and Pashto; (5) *Greek;* (6) *Celtic*, including Irish (Gaelic), Scots Gaelic, Welsh, and Breton; (7) *Albanian;* and (8) *Armenian*.

All languages in the Indo-European family have the same original structure, based on *inflections* (see INFLECTION). They all have clearly defined parts of speech. These include nouns, adjectives, pronouns, and verbs, which take certain endings to show gender, number, case, person, tense, mood, or voice. Many simple, basic words are similar in Indo-European languages. For example, the English word *mother* is *mata* in San-

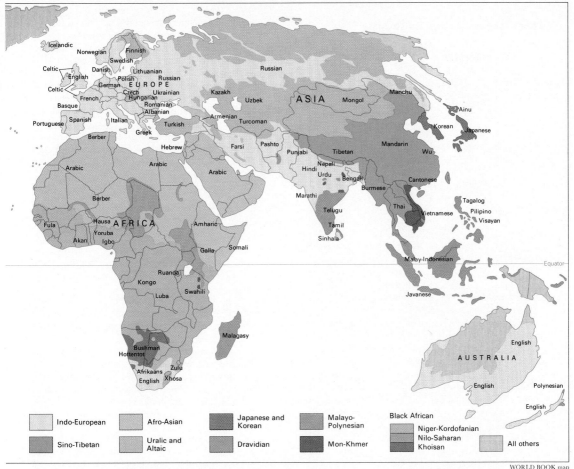

skrit, *meter* in Greek, *mater* in Latin, *madre* in Spanish, *Mutter* in German, and *mat'* in Russian.

Speakers of the parent Indo-European language probably lived in the area north of the Black Sea. From there, they likely migrated in every direction, changing the language along the way. The earliest Indo-European language of which we have a record is Hittite, followed by Greek and Sanskrit.

Other Language Families. Besides Indo-European, scholars have discovered many other language families.

The Sino-Tibetan family is second in numerical importance, with over a billion speakers. This family includes Chinese with its many dialects, Thai, Burmese, and Tibetan. These languages are the leading languages of East Asia. The Sino-Tibetan languages consist of one-syllable words. Speakers show the different meanings of otherwise identical words by changing their tone of voice.

The Afro-Asian family includes Arabic and Hebrew, the Berber tongues of North Africa, and the Amharic of Ethiopia. About 187 million persons speak languages in this family, which is concentrated in North Africa, the Near East, and northeast Africa.

The Uralic and Altaic family includes Finnish, Hungarian (or Magyar), Turkish, Mongol, Manchu, and most of the languages spoken in the Asian part of Russia. About 110 million persons speak the languages

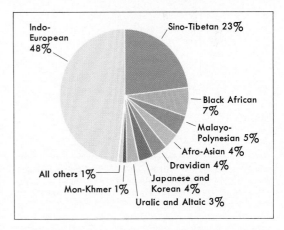

in this family, which is found in Finland, Hungary, Turkey, Mongolia, and Manchuria, as well as Russia.

Japanese and Korean form a family with about 181 million speakers. They are largely limited to Japan, North Korea, and South Korea.

The Dravidian family is located in southern India and parts of Sri Lanka. It consists of Tamil, Telugu, and other languages. These languages have about 192 million speakers. See Dravidians.

65

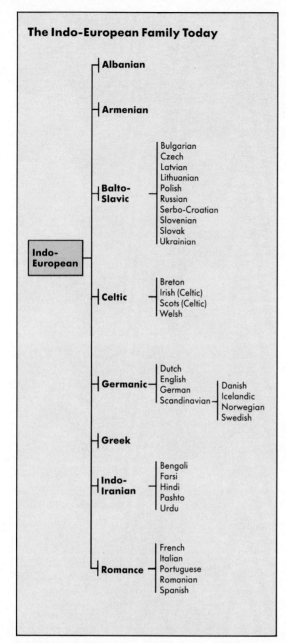

The Indo-European Family Today

Indo-European

- **Albanian**
- **Armenian**
- **Balto-Slavic**
  - Bulgarian
  - Czech
  - Latvian
  - Lithuanian
  - Polish
  - Russian
  - Serbo-Croatian
  - Slovenian
  - Slovak
  - Ukrainian
- **Celtic**
  - Breton
  - Irish (Celtic)
  - Scots (Celtic)
  - Welsh
- **Germanic**
  - Dutch
  - English
  - German
  - Scandinavian
    - Danish
    - Icelandic
    - Norwegian
    - Swedish
- **Greek**
- **Indo-Iranian**
  - Bengali
  - Farsi
  - Hindi
  - Pashto
  - Urdu
- **Romance**
  - French
  - Italian
  - Portuguese
  - Romanian
  - Spanish

Indo-European is the most important language family today. About half the people in the world speak a language that belongs to this family. Scholars divide the Indo-European languages into several groups, such as Balto-Slavic, Germanic, and Romance.

The Malayo-Polynesian family includes the languages of Indonesia, the Philippines, Hawaii, New Zealand, Madagascar, and most other islands of the Pacific and Indian oceans. This language family has about 233 million speakers.

The Mon-Khmer family has about 70 million speakers in Southeast Asia and parts of India. This family is sometimes called Austro-Asiatic.

Black African languages are spoken in areas south of the Sahara and west of the Sudan, Ethiopia, and Somalia. The three main families of these African languages are Nilo-Saharan, Niger-Kordofanian, and Khoisan. These three groups have about 330 million speakers.

American Indian languages number over 1,000. But they are difficult to classify because of the great differences among them. Their total number of speakers does not exceed 20 million. These languages appear in isolated areas of North, Central, and South America.

Unusual Languages and dialects include the pidgin and Creole tongues spoken in many parts of the world. They make communication possible between two or more groups that speak different languages. Examples include the colorful Melanesian pidgin English of the Solomon Islands and New Guinea, and the French Creole of Haiti. See CREOLE; PIDGIN ENGLISH.

Universal Languages

People have long been interested in having one language that could be spoken throughout the world. Such a language would help promote understanding and better feeling among nations. A universal language also would increase cultural and economic ties among various countries.

Through the years, at least 600 universal languages have been proposed. *Esperanto* is the most successful universal tongue. About 10 million people have learned Esperanto since its creation in 1887.

Some persons suggest that an existing language, such as English, French, or Russian, be adopted as a universal language. The adoption of any language, artificial or natural, would greatly simplify communication among nations. The real problem, however, lies in the choice of such a language, because there are so many possibilities.

Many persons oppose artificial languages. They believe that an artificial tongue does not reflect a true culture as existing languages do. Others oppose the use of any existing language as a world language. They claim that the culture of one or a few nations would be forced on all nations. As long as these arguments continue, the possibility of adoption of one world language appears dim. See UNIVERSAL LANGUAGE.

The Science of Language

The ancient Greeks and Romans studied the nature and origin of language. But their studies lacked a systematic, scientific basis. During the Middle Ages, from the A.D. 400's to the 1500's, many people thought all languages came from Biblical Hebrew. The scientific study of language did not start until the late 1700's. At first, scholars such as Friedrich Schlegel, Jakob Grimm, and Franz Bopp, all of Germany, studied languages by the *comparative* method. They compared the world's languages and noted relationships among them. Their findings led to a classification of languages into families. During the early 1900's, Ferdinand de Saussure, a Swiss scholar, led a new movement. He studied languages by the *general* method. He established laws that apply to all languages.

Today, the science of language (called *linguistics* or *philology*) is divided into two areas: (1) comparative or historical and (2) descriptive. The comparative method studies language through thousands of years. It seeks to determine the history and development of individual languages and language groups. The descriptive method concentrates mainly on present-day languages. See Linguistics.   PAUL W. BROSMAN, JR.

Related Articles. Many WORLD BOOK articles on countries have sections on language. For example, see CANADA (Languages). Other related articles include:

LANGUAGES OF THE WORLD

Afrikaans Language	Japanese Language
Arabic Language	Latin Language
Aramaic Language	Portuguese Language
Chinese Language	Russian Language
English Language	Sanskrit Language
French Language	and Literature
Gaelic Language	Semitic Languages
German Language	Spanish Language
Greek Language	Yiddish Language
Hebrew Language and Literature	and Literature
Italian Language	

SPOKEN LANGUAGE

Dialect	Pronunciation	Vocabulary
Oratory	Speech	Voice
Phonetics		

WRITTEN LANGUAGE

Composition	Hieroglyphics	Rune
Cuneiform	Punctuation	Writing

OTHER RELATED ARTICLES

Accent	Indian, American (Language;
Alphabet	Table of Tribes)
Anthropology	Interlingua
(Linguistic	Language Arts
Anthropology)	Linguistics
Basic English	Literature
Celts	Pacific Islands (Languages)
Communication	Pidgin English
Consonant	Reading
Creole	Semantics
Dictionary	Sentence
Eskimo (Language)	Sign Language
Esperanto	Slang
Etymology	Spelling
Figure of Speech	Teutons
Grammar	Universal Language
Idiom	Volapük
Illiteracy	Vowel

Outline

I. Learning a Foreign Language
   A. Methods of Study   B. Study Aids
II. The Makeup of Language
III. The Development of Language
   A. How Language Began
   B. How Language Changes
IV. Language Families
   A. Indo-European   C. Unusual Languages
   B. Other Language Families
V. Universal Languages
VI. The Science of Language

Questions

How can learning a foreign language help you?
What three things do all languages have in common?
What is the chief language family?
What are the earliest written records of language?
What is the difference between *syntax* and *morphology*?
Why do some people oppose a universal language?
What is a *parent language*?
When does a language become a *dead language*?
How many languages are spoken in the world?
What are some reasons why languages change?

Additional Resources

BALDI, PHILIP. *An Introduction to the Indo-European Languages.* Southern Illinois Univ. Press, 1983.

CHOMSKY, NOAM. *Language and Mind.* Rev. ed. Harcourt, 1972. Study of language structure and human intelligence.
HAYAKAWA, S. I. *Language in Thought and Action.* 3rd ed. Harcourt, 1972.
PEI, MARIO. *The Story of Language.* Rev. ed. Lippincott, 1965.
Words: The Evolution of Western Languages. Ed. by Victor Stevenson. Van Nostrand, 1984.

LANGUAGE ARTS is a term used in American elementary and secondary education to refer to training in reading, writing, and speaking, as distinguished from training in literary appreciation and scholarship. The term is also used in many colleges and universities. Language arts, also referred to as "programs in communication," freely utilizes all knowledge, especially the social sciences and psychology, in the study of language and literature.

Beyond the elementary stages of reading, writing, and speaking, language arts includes a variety of topics: phonetics (for the improvement of pronunciation), remedial reading, linguistics, semantics (for the improvement of comprehension), creative writing, and bibliotherapy (the study of the kinds of reading that promote emotional growth and health). Language arts also includes the following studies: literature as a source of psychological and social insights (rather than exclusively as an art), the effects of mass communication (motion pictures, newspapers, radio, and television), and the relations between language and culture.

The difference between the traditional approach to literature and the language-arts approach may be roughly described as that between the consumer viewpoint (learning to enjoy literature) and that of the producer (learning to perform language skills and understand their operation).   S. I. HAYAKAWA

See also LANGUAGE and its list of *Related Articles.*

LANIER, *luh NEER,* **SIDNEY** (1842-1881), was an American poet. He became famous for his poems about the beauty of the South. Lanier's works also include children's poems and books on English literature.

Lanier's best-known poem, "The Marshes of Glynn" (1878), describes a wild, swampy, heavily wooded area near the coast of Georgia. His other major poems include "Corn" (1875) and "The Symphony" (1875). In "Corn," Lanier contrasted the abundance of Southern agriculture with what he considered the false, sterile values of Northern commerce. In "The Symphony," he experimented with the use of musical concepts, such as tone and rhythm. Throughout this poem, Lanier attempted to imitate the sounds of the various instruments of an orchestra. "The Symphony" became popular during the 1800's, but later critics do not rank it among Lanier's best works.

Lanier was born in Macon, Ga., and graduated from Oglethorpe College (now Oglethorpe University) in 1860. He served in the Confederate Army during the Civil War (1861-1865) and spent four months in a Union prison camp. Lanier returned to Macon after the war, penniless and in poor health. He suffered from tuberculosis for the rest of his life. In 1867, he published his only novel, *Tiger-Lilies,* an account of his war experiences. Later, Lanier studied law and then entered his father's law firm because he could not earn enough money as a writer.

In 1873, Lanier resumed his writing career. He moved to Baltimore, where he helped support his family by playing flute in the Peabody Orchestra. He soon gained a reputation as a poet and, in 1879, became a lecturer in English literature at Johns Hopkins University. At Johns Hopkins, Lanier wrote such works as *The Science of English Verse* (1880) and *The English Novel* (1883). In his book about English poetry, Lanier declared that a poem's sound is its most important and exciting quality.

During his last years, Lanier edited children's books. He wrote "The Revenge of Hamish" (1878), which became one of his most popular poems for children. Lanier also retold the legends of King Arthur's court in *The Boy's King Arthur* (1880).   CLARK GRIFFITH

See also AMERICAN LITERATURE (Individualists).

LANKESTER, *LANG kih stuhr*, **SIR EDWIN RAY** (1847-1929), a British zoologist, did extensive research in comparative anatomy and embryology. His work helped support the theory of evolution (see EVOLUTION). Lankester served as director of the British Museum's natural history department from 1898 until his retirement. From 1869 to 1920 he edited *The Quarterly Journal of Microscopical Science*.

Lankester was born in London. He studied at Cambridge and Oxford universities.   MORDECAI L. GABRIEL

LANOLIN, *LAN uh lihn*, is a common name for *wool wax*, which is made from a greasy coating found on sheep's wool. The name is used especially when the wax is purified and mixed with water. Lanolin is a yellowish, sticky substance, as thick as ordinary wax. It does not react readily with acids or alkalies. It will absorb from 25 to 30 per cent of its own mass in water. When lanolin is mixed with water, it breaks up easily into tiny droplets. This forms an emulsion known as *hydrous lanolin*, or *lanolin USP* (see EMULSION). Hydrous lanolin is widely used in medicines such as salves and ointments, and in cosmetics, because it is easily absorbed by the skin. Lanolin is also used as a dressing for leather goods, as a protective coating for metals, and as a base in grease paints and shoe polishes.   GEORGE L. BUSH

LANSDOWNE, *LANZ down*, **MARQUESS OF** (1845-1927), served as governor general of Canada from 1883 to 1888. During his administration, the Canadian Pacific Railway (now CP Rail) was completed. The problems of his term included the Saskatchewan, or Riel, Rebellion (see RIEL, LOUIS). Later, Lansdowne served as Viceroy of India and held posts in the British Cabinet. As secretary of state for foreign affairs, he helped negotiate agreements with Japan in 1902 and with France in 1904. His full name was Henry Charles Keith Petty-Fitzmaurice. He was born in London.   LUCIEN BRAULT

LANSING, Mich. (pop. 130,414), is the state capital and an automobile-manufacturing city. It lies at the meeting place of the Grand and Red Cedar

Brown Bros.
Lord Lansdowne

Leavenworth
Downtown Lansing, Mich., includes the domed State Capitol, *background,* and many office and government buildings.

rivers in south-central Michigan. The 34-square-mile (88-square-kilometer) city is about 85 miles (137 kilometers) northwest of Detroit. For the location of Lansing, see MICHIGAN (political map). Lansing and East Lansing form a metropolitan area of 419,750 people.

Over 150 industries operate in Lansing. The chief products include automobiles, trucks, farm tools, and gas engines. Lansing also acts as a trading center for the surrounding rich farmlands. Freight railroads, buses, trucks, and airlines serve the city. Four radio stations and two television stations broadcast from Lansing. The city publishes one daily newspaper.

Students may attend over 30 public schools and several private ones in Lansing. The Michigan School for the Blind also is there. East Lansing serves as the home of Michigan State University, the first state school to offer agricultural courses for credit. The State Library and the Michigan Historical Museum are located in Lansing.

Settlers first came to the site of Lansing in 1837. The legislature chose Lansing to succeed Detroit as the state capital in 1847. It received its city charter 12 years later, in 1859. Workers completed the white sandstone capitol in 1878. It covers an area of four city blocks near the city's business section. Lansing has a mayor-council form of government.   WILLIS F. DUNBAR

LANSING, ROBERT (1864-1928), served as secretary of state under President Woodrow Wilson from 1915 to 1920. He dealt with the difficult problems resulting from World War I, and attended the Peace Conference held at Versailles, France, as one of the five American delegates in 1919 (see VERSAILLES, TREATY OF).

As a specialist in international law, Lansing served as American counsel in disputes concerning the Alaskan boundary and the North Atlantic fisheries. He wrote several books on international law and on the Versailles peace negotiations.

Lansing was born in Watertown, N.Y., and studied

at Amherst College. He began his legal practice in 1889 in Watertown, N.Y. NELSON M. BLAKE

LANTERN is any light enclosed in a casing that protects it from wind and rain. The light is provided by electric batteries, carbide gas, gasoline, or kerosene. Some lanterns can be carried from place to place. Lanterns are used on ships and trains, as warning signals at railroad crossings, and for ornamental purposes.

LANTERN FISH has organs or glands that give off light. The organs look like little pearls. Some lantern fish live in the deep sea. Others come to the surface at night. They have several series of the lighted organs on the sides of the head and body.

The *deep-sea anglers* also have a *luminous* (light-giving) gland. They are not close relatives of the lantern fish. An angler has a strange appearance, with an enormous head and a huge mouth armed with long sharp teeth. The luminous gland is at the tip of a stalk that rises from the end of the snout.

None of these fish has any value for commerce, but zoologists find them of scientific interest.

Scientific Classification. The lantern fish is a member of the lantern fish family, *Myctophidae*. It is genus *Diaphus*, species *D. theta*. The deep-sea anglers are in the angler fish family, *Ceratidae*. LEONARD P. SCHULTZ

See also BIOLUMINESCENCE.

The Curious Lantern Fish Creates Its Own Light as it swims about the dark depths of the ocean.

LANTHANIDE. See RARE EARTH; ELEMENT, CHEMICAL (Periodic Table of the Elements).

LANTHANUM, *LAN thuh nuhm* (chemical symbol, La), is a soft, silvery-white metal and one of the chemical elements. It has an atomic number of 57 and an atomic weight of 138.906. The name comes from the Greek word *lanthano*, meaning *to be hidden* or *concealed*. The Swedish chemist Carl Mosander discovered lanthanum in 1839. It is found with rare earths in monazite, bastnasite, and other minerals. It is always found among the fission products of uranium, thorium, and plutonium. It is separated from the rare earths by fractional crystallization. This metal melts at about 920° C (1688° F.), and boils at about 3469° C (6276° F.). It is used in misch metal to make important alloys. The oxide is used in camera lenses. See also ELEMENT, CHEMICAL (table); RARE EARTH. FRANK H. SPEDDING

LAO TZU, according to legends, wrote the *Lao Tzu*, one of the basic books of the Chinese philosophy called *Taoism*. This book is often called the *Tao Te Ching* (*The Classic of the Way and the Virtue*).

Unreliable accounts say that Lao Tzu lived during the 500's B.C. However, the *Tao Te Ching*, made up of 81 brief sections, was probably compiled and revised during the 200's and 100's B.C. More than half its sections are in rhyme. The remainder of the *Tao Te Ching*

Restored marble sculpture by Agesander, Polydorus, and Athenodorus of Greece, about A.D. 100; Vatican Museums, Rome (Art Reference Bureau)

Laocoön was a Trojan priest in Greek mythology. Two huge sea serpents killed Laocoön and his two sons during the Trojan War.

includes popular sayings and Taoist teachings in prose.

The *Tao Te Ching* describes the *Tao* (Way), the unity of nature that makes each thing in the universe what it is and determines its behavior. This unity can be understood only by mystical intuition. The book teaches that, because yielding eventually overcomes force, a wise man desires nothing. He never interferes with what happens naturally in the world or in himself. One passage says: "The highest good is like water. Water excels in giving benefit to all creatures, but never competes. It abides in places that most men despise, and so comes closest to the Tao." The *Tao Te Ching* also teaches that simplicity and moving with the flow of events are the keys to wise government. N. SIVIN

See also TAOISM; CHUANG TZU.

LAOCOÖN, *lay AHK oh ahn*, a Trojan priest, warned his people against the Greeks at Troy. The Trojans and the Greeks had been at war for 10 years. Pretending to give up the siege, the Greeks left a huge wooden horse outside the gates of Troy. Laocoön suspected treachery, and told the Trojans not to take the horse inside the city walls. "I fear the Greeks, even when bringing gifts," he said.

Later, as Laocoön worshiped, two sea serpents attacked him and his sons and crushed them to death. Believing this to be a punishment from the gods, the Trojans rejected Laocoön's warning and took the wooden horse into the city. Laocoön had been right. The horse concealed Greek soldiers who came out of the horse during the night, and captured the city. Virgil describes the death of Laocoön in the second book of the *Aeneid*. JOSEPH FONTENROSE

See also TROJAN WAR.

LAOMEDON. See PRIAM.

Laos

★ Capital
• Other City or Town
—— Road
+—+ Rail Line
▲ MOUNTAIN
〜 River

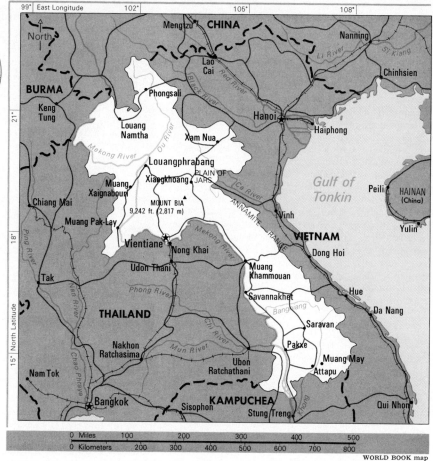

WORLD BOOK map

LAOS, *LAH ohs,* is a country in Southeast Asia. It is a tropical land of mountains and thick forests drenched by heavy rains. Laos has rich soil and valuable mineral deposits, but its economy has never been developed. Vientiane is its capital and largest city.

France ruled Laos as part of French Indochina for more than 50 years. In 1954, an international agreement recognized Laos as an independent, neutral nation. But civil war broke out in 1960 between Laotian government troops and the Communist-led *Pathet Lao* (Lao Country) forces. Another international agreement in 1962 failed to settle the differences between the two sides, and fighting continued throughout the 1960's and early 1970's. In 1975, the Pathet Lao won the war and took control of Laos.

Government. Laos was a constitutional monarchy before the Pathet Lao victory in 1975. A king was officially the head of state, but he actually had little power. A coalition government made up of Communists and non-Communists ruled the country.

The Pathet Lao abolished the coalition government and the monarchy after they gained control of Laos.

David P. Chandler, the contributor of this article, is Senior Lecturer in History at Monash University in Australia, and coauthor of In Search of Southeast Asia.

They set up a Communist government called the Provisional Government of the National Union. A 42-member National Political Council advises the government. The Pathet Lao held elections for village, district, and provincial governments in 1975.

People of Laos belong to two language groups, the Sino-Tibetan from China, and the Mon-Khmer from southern Asia. The Sino-Tibetan group includes the *Lao, Meo,* and *Thai* peoples. The Mon-Khmer group includes the *Kha* peoples. Laos' official language is Lao, which is similar to the language of Thailand.

The Lao, who make up about half of the population, are the political and social leaders of the country. The Kha, the original inhabitants of Laos, have traditionally been treated as little more than slaves by the Lao. The Pathet Lao said they would improve the status of the Kha after they took over the country.

Most of the Thai live in northern mountain valleys. The Meo live on the mountain slopes. They raise most of Laos' opium, an illegal but profitable export.

Almost all the people of Laos are farmers. Most of them raise rice along the Mekong River and its tributaries. Laotians who live in the highlands grow corn, cotton, rice, and tobacco. The people live in houses perched on wooden posts 6 to 8 feet (1.8 to 2.4 meters) above ground. The houses have covered porches, bamboo floors and walls, and thatched roofs.

Capital: Vientiane.

Official Language: Lao.

Form of Government: Socialist republic (Communist).

Area: 91,431 sq. mi. (236,804 km²). *Greatest Distances*— northwest-southeast, 650 mi. (1,046 km); northeast-southwest, 315 mi. (510 km).

Population: *Estimated 1987 Population*—4,644,000; distribution, 84 per cent rural, 16 per cent urban; density, 51 persons per sq. mi. (20 per km²). *Estimated 1992 Population*—5,220,000.

Chief Products: Benzoin, cardamom, cattle, cinchona, citrus fruits, coffee, corn, cotton, leather goods, opium, pottery, rice, silk, silverwork, tea, teak, tin, tobacco.

Flag: The flag has a red horizontal stripe at the top and the bottom, and a blue horizontal stripe in the center. A white circle appears in the center of the flag. The red symbolizes the blood and soul of the Laotian people. The blue stands for prosperity. The white circle represents the promise of a bright future. Adopted in 1975. See FLAG (picture: Flags of Asia and the Pacific).

National Anthem: "Pheng Sat" ("National Music").

Money: *Basic Unit*—kip. See MONEY (table).

Most of the Laotian village dwellers are poor. Their lives are a continual round of planting and harvesting crops. The songs of traveling ballad singers are often the only source of news. Almost half of the people 15 years of age or older can read and write. Many villages do not have schools. Most Laotians are Buddhists, and much of the country's social life centers around Buddhist festivals and holidays.

Land. Laos lies in the Mekong Basin, between the Mekong River and the Annamite Range, a chain of mountains. Rugged plateaus and mountains in the north and along the eastern border range from 500 to 4,000 feet (150 to 1,200 meters) high. Mount Bia (9,242 feet, or 2,817 meters) in central Laos is the highest point.

The most productive farmland is the fertile lowland beside the Mekong and its tributaries. Laos has rich gold, gypsum, lead, silver, tin, and zinc deposits. Its forests have teak and other valuable woods.

From May to September, monsoons from the southwest bring up to 10 inches (25 centimeters) of rain a month. Temperatures average about 82° F. (28° C) during that period. From November to March, rainfall

Almasy

Farmers in Laos still use many of the tools and methods their ancestors used. For example, oxen pull wooden plows through the soggy rice fields. Rice is the country's most important crop.

in Laos averages less than 1 inch (2.5 centimeters) a month, and temperatures average about 70° F.(21° C).

Economy. Laos has an underdeveloped economy. Its mineral resources have not been developed, and the country has few manufacturing industries. Agriculture is the chief economic activity. But old-fashioned farming equipment and methods hold down the country's agricultural output. Rice is the chief product of Laos. Other farm products include coffee, corn, cotton, tobacco, and livestock. Some Laotians grow and export opium even though these activities are illegal.

The Mekong River and its tributaries are the chief means of transportation in Laos. Most roads are passable only in the dry season. In many areas airplanes are the only means of moving supplies. Laos has no railroads, but a railroad line links Nong Khai—across the Mekong River from Vientiane—with Bangkok, Thailand.

History. Ancestors of the Lao and Thai probably moved into Laos in the A.D. 800's. They set up small states ruled by princes. In 1353, the ruler of Muong Swa (now Louangphrabang) united most of what is now Laos in the kingdom of *Lan Xang* (land of a million elephants). About 1700, three separate kingdoms—Louangphrabang, Vientiane, and Champasak—were formed. In the late 1800's, France made Laos a protectorate and ruled it as part of Indochina. See INDOCHINA.

A Free Laos committee, headed by brother princes Phetsarat, Souvanna Phouma, and Souphanouvong, negotiated Laos' first constitution in 1947 with France. Independence within the French Union came in 1949. The princes then split into rival factions, and Souphanouvong moved to northeastern Laos. There he made contact with Ho Chi Minh, the North Vietnamese Communist leader, and set up the Communist-inspired Pathet Lao movement.

Ho Chi Minh's forces defeated the French at Dien Bien Phu in Vietnam in 1954. A peace conference at Geneva, Switzerland, then established Laos as a neutral country, a "buffer" between Communist North Vietnam and non-Communist Thailand (see GENEVA ACCORDS). Laos became a member of the United Nations in 1955. A series of governments ruled Laos from 1954 to 1960.

In 1960, Captain Kong Le, a Laotian army officer, overthrew the pro-Western government and demanded a neutralist government. Civil war soon broke out. Kong Le and the Pathet Lao seized control of most of northern Laos before a cease-fire was declared in 1961.

But fighting continued, and in 1962, a 14-nation conference at Geneva set up a coalition government in Laos. Prince Souvanna Phouma, a neutralist, became prime minister. Prince Boun Oum, an anti-Communist, and Prince Souphanouvong, a pro-Communist, were made cabinet ministers. The Geneva agreement guaranteed Laos' neutrality under the supervision of an International Control Commission. The agreement also ordered all foreign troops to leave Laos.

In 1963, Souphanouvong withdrew from the government. Fighting broke out again between the Pathet Lao and government forces. The Pathet Lao received support from Chinese and Russian military advisers and thousands of North Vietnamese troops. The Laotian government was backed by troops from Thailand and South Vietnam, and military advisers from the United States.

Lyn, APF

Shoppers in Vientiane buy meat and vegetables at the city's central market. Their skirts are woven at home.

By 1970, Souvanna Phouma's government troops controlled only western Laos. Pathet Lao forces, led by Souphanouvong, held eastern Laos.

During the Vietnam War, North Vietnam used the Ho Chi Minh Trail in Laos and Kampuchea to move troops and supplies into South Vietnam. United States planes bombed the trail and other areas in Laos. In 1971, South Vietnamese troops, supported by U.S. bombers and helicopters, entered Laos to attack Communist supply routes.

In 1973, the Laotian government and the Pathet Lao agreed to a cease-fire and to the formation of a coalition government. A new government was set up in 1974, with Souvanna Phouma as prime minister and Souphanouvong as head of an advisory body. In 1975, pro-Communist demonstrations occurred, and many non-Communist government officials resigned and were replaced by Communists. The government came under Communist domination. At the same time, the Pathet Lao took over large amounts of land.

The Vietnam War ended in April 1975, when South Vietnam fell to the Communists. Communists also won control of Kampuchea that month. Later in the year, the Pathet Lao took over Laos, and the country became a Communist state. Since the Communist take-over, thousands of Laotians have fled the country. Since shortly after the take-over, large numbers of Vietnamese troops have been stationed in Laos. The Vietnamese have much influence over the Laotian government.   DAVID P. CHANDLER

See also LOUANGPHRABANG; VIENTIANE; SOUTHEAST ASIA; COLOMBO PLAN; MEKONG RIVER; VIETNAM WAR.

LA PAZ, *lah PAHS* or *luh PAZ* (pop. 881,404), is the largest city and chief commercial center of Bolivia. It also serves as the country's actual capital. The official capital is Sucre, but almost all government agencies are in La Paz. La Paz is the highest capital in the world. It

lies 12,795 feet (3,900 meters) above sea level. The city covers the slopes, and part of the bottom, of a canyon in the *altiplano* (high plateau) region of western Bolivia. Snow-capped peaks of the Andes Mountains overlook the city. For location, see BOLIVIA (map).

Aymara Indians make up about half the population of La Paz. Many of them live on the upper terraces of the canyon in adobe huts with corrugated iron or red tile roofs. Farther down both sides of the canyon are modern skyscrapers and government buildings. The center of city life is the Plaza Murillo, a garden square. The Legislative Palace, a cathedral, and other large buildings face the plaza. At the bottom of the canyon is a residential section of modern houses. There, many of the city's whites and *mestizos* (people of mixed European and Indian ancestry) live.

La Paz has a large market where Indians sell flowers, fruits, meats, vegetables, and such handmade products as *serapes* (shawls) and blankets. Institutions of higher learning in the city include the Higher University of San Andres and the Bolivian Catholic University.

La Paz has a high unemployment rate. The Bolivian government employs about half the people who have a job. Importing and exporting companies are the city's most important businesses. La Paz has few large factories. The chief manufactured products include beer, canned food, cement, glass, and textiles.

Spanish settlers led by Alonso de Mendoza founded La Paz in 1548 on the site of an Aymaran Indian village. The town grew steadily because it lay on the route used to transport silver from rich mines in southeastern Bolivia to the Pacific coast. In 1898, most of Bolivia's government agencies moved from Sucre to La Paz. Since then, La Paz has been both the governmental and commercial center of Bolivia. The city has grown especially rapidly since the early 1950's. Its population has about tripled since that time.   NATHAN A. HAVERSTOCK

LAPIDARY is the cutting and polishing of gems. The word *lapidary* also refers to a person who does this type of work. Professional lapidaries flourished in Assyria,

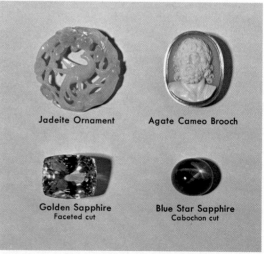

Jadeite Ornament   Agate Cameo Brooch

Golden Sapphire   Blue Star Sapphire
Faceted cut   Cabochon cut

Lizzadro Museum of Lapidary Art (WORLD BOOK photo)

Examples of Lapidary Art show how gems can be cut and polished in different styles. Lapidaries carved the ornament and brooch and used electrically powered tools to shape the sapphires.

Lizzadro Museum of Lapidary Art (WORLD BOOK photos)

A Stone is polished on a lapidary wheel, *right*. The picture on the left shows how a piece of dolomite looks before and after it has been shaped and polished. The lapidary cuts the stone into an oval shape with a saw and then grinds and polishes it.

Babylonia, and Egypt more than 6,000 years ago.

Gems may be cut in several ways. Different machines and techniques are used, depending on the type of stone being cut. For example, lapidaries cut some stones in a style called *cabochon*, with a rounded top and a flat bottom. Many gems, such as diamonds, are cut so they have numerous flat, polished *facets* (surfaces). Lapidary also includes the carving and engraving of gems.

Professional lapidaries have traditionally kept their methods secret. During the 1920's in the United States, several men who collected gems as a hobby decided to learn how to cut and polish their own stones. They built equipment and developed techniques by trial and error. Amateur lapidary soon became a popular hobby. Today, there are many amateur lapidary clubs, some of which have groups for teen-agers. But most diamond cutting is done by professionals because of the special machines and methods involved.   PANSY D. KRAUS

See also DIAMOND; GEM.

LAPIS LAZULI, *LAP is LAZ yu lye*, is a beautiful azure-blue mineral whose color makes it valuable as an ornament. The mineral is sometimes called *lazurite*. Lapis lazuli consists chiefly of aluminum, sodium, silica, and sulfur. The mineral occurs in masses of fine grains and in crystals. Most of these deposits are in beds of limestone. Lapis lazuli sometimes is flecked with brilliant, shining spots. These spots are pyrite, an iron sulfide, and they help to identify genuine lapis lazuli.

The Egyptians used this mineral in their jewelry. So did the Romans, who called it "sapphire," a name now confused with a more valuable jewel. Lapis lazuli was once the only source of ultramarine, a blue pigment used in artists' paints (see ULTRAMARINE). This pigment is now made chiefly by chemical methods.

Ancient peoples believed that this mineral had medicinal value. They ground lapis lazuli stones to a powder, which they mixed with milk. The mixture was used as a dressing for boils and ulcers. The best specimens of lapis lazuli come from Afghanistan.   FREDERICK H. POUGH

See also GEM (color picture).

LAPLACE, *lah PLAHS,* **MARQUIS DE** (1749-1827), PIERRE SIMON DE LAPLACE, a French astronomer and mathematician, became famous for his theory regarding the origin of the solar system. In his *Exposition of the System of the Universe* (1796), he started with a theoretical primitive nebula. He believed that this huge, lens-shaped cloud of gas rotated, cooled, contracted, and threw off planets and satellites. The remaining matter formed the sun. Laplace's nebular hypothesis was accepted for a long time, but has now been replaced by other theories. However, scientists still have not solved the problem. See EARTH (How the Earth Began).

Laplace also contributed studies in mathematical astronomy. Sir Isaac Newton had satisfactorily explained movements of the solar system in general. But certain problems were not solved because no one in Newton's time had devised the necessary mathematical tools. Laplace accounted for the intricacies in the movements of the heavenly bodies. In *Celestial Mechanics* (1798-1825), he summed up the achievements in theoretical astronomy from the time of Newton.

Laplace was born at Beaumont-en-Auge, France, the son of a farmer. He became a professor of mathematics in Paris at the age of 20.   EDWARD ROSEN

LAPLAND, *LAP land,* lies in the extreme northern part of Europe, above the Arctic Circle. The region is called Lapland because it is the home of a small, sturdy people known as the Lapps. But it does not form a separate country. The region that makes up Lapland belongs to Norway, Sweden, Finland, and Russia.

Lapland has a cold climate. Winter lasts nine months every year. The other three months resemble spring in areas that have mild climates. Because Lapland lies so far north, it has a period of two months in summer when the sky never darkens. The sun never rises above the horizon for two months each winter.

Location and Size. Lapland covers about 150,000 square miles (388,000 square kilometers). It stretches across the northern parts of Norway, Sweden, Finland, and Russia. The region includes all of northern Norway, the Swedish province of Norrbotten and part of Norrland, all of northern Finland, and the Kola Peninsula of Russia (see EUROPE [color map]). Lapland has no

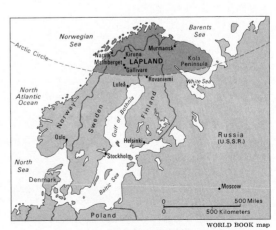

WORLD BOOK map

Location of Lapland

Burton Holmes, Ewing Galloway

Reindeer Are the Cattle of Lapland. From them, this Lapp gets his tent, his blankets, part of his clothing, and his food.

They average only about 5 feet (150 centimeters) in height, but are strong and muscular. Lapps look somewhat like Chinese or Japanese. They have low foreheads, high cheekbones, straight black hair, and slightly yellowish skin. Their noses are often broad and flat, and their lips are straight and thin. Some Lapps live outside Lapland, in central Sweden and Finland and in Norway. Many have married Swedes, Finns, or Norwegians, and their physical type is changing.

The Lapps are mostly a nomadic people who follow reindeer herds. But many have settled in fishing or farming villages. They dress in clothes made of wool and reindeer skins. Their everyday garments are so colorful that they resemble holiday costumes. The Lapps are healthy and happy, although they must work hard to live in their bleak land.

Language and Religion. The language of Lapland is related to that spoken in Finland. The people in various sections speak sharply different dialects. Many Lapps have no formal education, because there are few schools.

All Lapps once believed in a form of magic called *shamanism*. The *shaman* (medicine man) beats drums to foretell the future (see SHAMAN). Today, most Lapps belong to the Lutheran or Eastern Orthodox churches. The people often have trouble attending church because they live so far away. But they will cross vast distances to attend church when they are to be married or wish to bury their dead.

Work of the People. The Lapps may be grouped according to their primary means of livelihood. These groups are: (1) the Mountain Lapps, (2) the Sea Lapps, and (3) the River Lapps.

Mountain Lapps live a wandering life. They move from one place to another with their herds of reindeer. These nomads pitch their tents where there is enough vegetation to feed the herds. An entire family lives in a single cone-shaped tent, shared by the family dogs. The Mountain Lapps live chiefly on reindeer meat, milk, and cheese.

Sea Lapps live along the coast in huts made of wood and covered with sod. They earn their livelihood primarily by fishing. The Sea Lapps are more civilized than the Mountain Lapps. The Sea Lapps often build their huts in groups to form fishing communities.

River Lapps live in settlements along the river banks. They are the most progressive people in Lapland. They

definite boundary to the south. The Norwegian, Barents, and White seas lie to the north.

The Land and Its Resources. Lapland is a bleak, barren region with few trees and thin, stunted vegetation. Of the trees, only birches, pines, and firs manage to survive. But they are only midget trees, kept small by the cold climate. Plant life consists primarily of mosses and lichens. Many reindeer feed on the scanty vegetation. Some wander wild, but the people herd many reindeer like cattle. The reindeer are an important source of food and serve as draft and pack animals.

Iron and nickel provide the most valuable mineral resources. Beds of iron lie deep under the soil of southern Swedish Lapland. The nickel deposits are in the Russian part of the region. Lapland's iron deposits rank among the largest in the world. The iron mines at Gällivare, Kiruna, and Malmberget are some of the world's richest. A railroad links the iron fields with Luleå, on the Gulf of Bothnia, and another connects with Narvik, Norway. The railroads carry iron ore to these ports for export to other countries.

The People. Lapland has a population of about 34,000. About 2,500 of the people live in Finland, 10,000 in Sweden, 20,000 in Norway, and 1,500 in Russia. The Lapps are among the smallest peoples of Europe.

Vagn Hansen, Black Star

Lapp School Children live in these wooden pyramid huts near the school. Many students come from far away to attend school.

Alan Band Associates

Rovaniemi is one of the largest towns of Finnish Lapland. The community was almost destroyed in 1944, during World War II. Some of Finland's top architects designed the buildings erected in Rovaniemi after the war.

Pix

Lapps in Their Holiday Costumes greet the pastor as they leave a church service during the winter market festival.

have a kind of community life, and occasionally do a little farming. The River Lapps fish and hunt, and keep herds of reindeer, cattle, and sheep.

History. Anthropologists believe that the Lapps moved to Lapland from central Asia thousands of years ago. Finnish merchants began to trade with the Lapps in the 1300's. Swedish kings held the title "King of the Lapps" in the 1500's and 1600's. But the people have always lived about the same way as they do today, with only loose community organization and little government control.   JOHN H. WUORINEN

See also SWEDEN (People); CLOTHING (picture: Lapp Family); EUROPE (picture: Reindeer).

LA PLATA, *lah PLAH tah* (pop. 506,287), is a city 35 miles (56 kilometers) southeast of Buenos Aires, Argentina, on the estuary called the Río de la Plata. For location, see ARGENTINA (map).

La Plata is the capital of the province of Buenos Aires. It is also an important cattle and grain port, with meat-packing, cold-storage, and oil-refining plants. In 1951, the city was named Eva Perón in honor of the wife of President Juan D. Perón. When the Perón government fell in 1955, the name again became La Plata.   GEORGE I. BLANKSTEN

LA PLATA, RÍO DE. See RÍO DE LA PLATA.

LAPPING. See MACHINE TOOL (Grinding).

LAPPS. See LAPLAND.

LAPWING is a crested plover that lives in Western Europe and the British Isles. The lapwing's name comes from the awkward way it flaps its wings as it flies. The bird is also called a *peewit* because of its shrill, wailing cry. The lapwing has a bronze-green back, and blue-black throat and breast. When the lapwing's nest is threatened, it limps and pretends to be hurt, and lures its enemies away.

Scientific Classification. The lapwing belongs to the plover and lapwing family, *Charadriidae*. It is classified as genus *Vanellus*, species *V. vanellus*.   ALFRED M. BAILEY

The Lapwing's Crest Rises to a Pointed Peak above its head. The bird is not a graceful flier, but it cleverly lures enemies away from its nest by pretending to be injured. ▶

LARACHE, *lah RAHSH* (pop. 45,710), is a seaport on the northern Atlantic coast of Morocco (see MOROCCO [color map]). The city serves as an important fishing and agricultural center. Larache is well known for its oranges, which it exports along with other fruits, cereals, hides, and wool. The city was founded in the 800's near the ancient ruins of Lixus, a Phoenician and Roman colony. It served as a haven for pirates between the 1300's and the 1800's. Spain ruled Larache during most of the 1600's. It then came under a sultan. Spain reoccupied Larache in 1912, and ruled it until Morocco became free in 1956.   KEITH G. MATHER

LARAMIE, *LAR uh mih* (pop. 24,410), the third largest city of Wyoming, lies on the Laramie Plains about 50 miles (80 kilometers) west of Cheyenne (see WYOMING [political map]). The Laramie River flows past the city.

Laramie, the county seat of Albany County, has a council-manager government. Tourists enjoy sightseeing and trout fishing in the Medicine Bow Mountains 30 miles (48 kilometers) west of the city. The University of Wyoming provides Laramie residents with their chief source of income. The Union Pacific Railroad is the second largest employer in Laramie.

The city serves as a transportation center for a large cattle- and sheep-raising region. Manufactures include cement, lumbering, and bricks and tiles. Municipal Airport is near the city.

Laramie, named for Jacques Laramie, an American trapper, was founded in 1868, when the tracks of the Union Pacific reached the city.   T. A. LARSON

LARAMIE, JACQUES (? -1821), was an American fur trapper who explored southeastern Wyoming. He became the first white man to visit certain sections of that area.

While trapping in the Colorado region about 1818, Laramie entered southeastern Wyoming. In 1820, he built a cabin on the river which he explored and which

John Markham

75

was named for him. Although little is known of him, many geographical features and places in Wyoming bear his name. Among these are the Laramie Mountains, Laramie Park, Laramie County, and the city of Laramie. Laramie was probably born in Canada of French parentage or descent. His name may have been spelled *Lorimier* or *La Ramée*.   WILLIAM P. BRANDON

LARCENY, *LAHR suh nee,* is the crime of stealing a person's money or other property. Larceny is a nonviolent crime. It thus differs from robbery, in which a thief uses violence or the threat of violence to take another's property. Examples of larceny include bicycle theft, pickpocketing, and shoplifting.

The laws of most states of the United States divide larceny into two classes, *grand* and *petty* (sometimes spelled *petit*). In many states, a thief who steals money or goods worth $50 or more has committed grand larceny. A theft of property worth less than $50 is petty larceny. The dividing line between grand and petty larceny in different states varies from $10 to $200. The laws of some states classify as grand larceny the theft of automobiles, firearms, livestock, or certain other property, regardless of value.

Grand larceny, a type of crime called a *felony*, is punishable by imprisonment for a year or more. The penalty in most cases of petty larceny, a less serious type of offense called a *misdemeanor*, is a jail sentence of less than a year.   RONALD R. DAVENPORT

See also BURGLARY; CRIME (tables); ROBBERY.

LARCH is a tree that belongs to the pine family. Unlike most trees that have needlelike leaves, larches shed their needles every fall and go through the winter "naked." Such trees are called *deciduous*. Most other trees of the pine family are *evergreens* (see TREE [Needleleaf Trees]).

Larches grow throughout the Northern Hemisphere. Three species are native to the United States. It is easy to recognize larches by their needles, which grow in clusters on spurlike branches. Cones grow from some of the buds. Ripe cones are about 1 inch (2.5 centimeters) long. At first, they are a bright red. Then they turn dark red. When ripe, they become chestnut-brown. The cone remains on the trees after the needles have fallen off. Larches are commonly planted as ornamental trees because of their attractive shape and their open, yellow-green crowns.

Eastern larch, often called *tamarack* or *hackmatack,* is a medium-sized tree, reaching heights up to 60 feet (18 meters). Its branches form a narrow pyramid. It grows from Canada through the eastern United

U.S. Forest Service
The Tall, Slender Larch is easy to recognize. It produces a durable timber.

States, as far south as Pennsylvania and west to Illinois. It is not important commercially, but its wood is sometimes used as poles. The American Indians used its tough roots to bind their canoes.

Western larch is a large tree, growing up to 150 feet (46 meters) tall. It grows extensively in Oregon, Washington, Idaho, Montana, and British Columbia, and is commercially

Rutherford Platt
Larch Needles and Cones

important for its lumber. Its wood closely resembles that of the Douglas fir. It has an orange-red, scaly bark, and open crowns of light green foliage.

European larch, another important timber species, has been widely planted in the eastern United States. The *subalpine larch* is a rare, small, timberline tree. It thrives in the western United States and Canada.

Scientific Classification. Larches are in the pine family, *Pinaceae.* They make up the genus *Larix.* The eastern larch is genus *Larix,* species *laricina.* The western larch is *L. occidentalis.*   RICHARD PRESTON, JR.

See also CONE-BEARING PLANT; DECIDUOUS TREE; EVERGREEN; PINE.

LARD is obtained by refining the fat of hogs. The fat is *rendered,* or melted, and strained to remove any bits of flesh or tissue. The lard is then cooled in containers, or in firm white blocks later cut into squares, or bricks, and packaged to be sold in grocery stores.

The finest lard comes from the fat around the kidneys of the hog. This *leaf* lard is the best lard to use for cooking. When it is fresh, good lard has a mild flavor and a pleasant odor. It is light and almost crumbly in texture when first rendered. Modern developments have produced a lard of bland flavor and odor that does not become rancid or sour at ordinary room temperatures.

Lard from other parts of the hog is usually broken up into three glycerin compounds: *olein, palmitin,* and *stearin.* Most lard contains 62 parts of olein to 38 parts of the other two compounds.

Olein is an oily substance used as a lubricant. Palmitin is used to make soap and candles. Stearin is used in the manufacture of soap, ointments, and some kinds of margarine.   LEONE RUTLEDGE CARROLL

LARDNER, RING (1885-1933), an American writer, was a master of the short story. He began his career by working as a reporter for the *South Bend* (Ind.) *Times* in 1906 and 1907. Lardner then moved to Chicago, where he earned a reputation as an excellent sportswriter. He specialized in baseball writing, and this interest resulted in a collection of humorous short stories, *You Know Me, Al* (1916). In these stories, Lardner described the career of Jack Keefe, a pitcher who fails in the major leagues.

Lardner proved his mastery of the short story with three later collections, *How to Write Short Stories* (1924), *The Love Nest* (1926), and *Round Up* (1929). These stories reflect Lardner's great ability to reproduce American slang and everyday speech in written form. He also displayed a keen sense of irony and deep insight into the character of ordinary Americans.

One of Lardner's best-known tales is "Haircut," in which a small-town barber tells an ironic story of cruelty and revenge. The barber, however, does not understand the bitter ironies that he reveals. In this and other stories, Lardner showed a cynical attitude toward people. But he also created some characters who represent human decency.

Lardner helped write two successful plays, *Elmer the Great* (1928), with George M. Cohan, and *June Moon* (1929), with George S. Kaufman. Lardner also wrote a humorous novel, *The Big Town* (1921), and a mock autobiography, *The Story of a Wonder Man* (1927). His poetry appears in collections called *Bib Ballads* (1915) and *Regular Fellows I Have Met* (1919). Ringgold Wilmer Lardner was born in Niles, Mich.   EUGENE K. GARBER

LAREDO, *luh RAY doh*, Tex. (pop. 91,449; met. area 99,258), on the Pan American Highway, is the chief port of entry on the U.S.-Mexico border. A bridge links it with its sister city, Nuevo Laredo, in Mexico. Laredo lies on the Rio Grande along the southern edge of the state (see TEXAS [political map]). It ranks as an important center of natural gas production and serves as a market for the fruits and vegetables raised on nearby farms. It also ships cattle, and manufactures machine tools, hats, children's dresses, and other products. Laredo is the home of Laredo State University of the University System of South Texas.

Founded by a group of Spaniards in 1755, Laredo boasts of being the oldest independent city in the state of Texas. Laredo has a mayor-council government. It is the seat of Webb County.   H. BAILEY CARROLL

LARES AND PENATES, *LAY reez, pee NAY teez,* were gods and spirits of the home and hearth in Roman mythology. To the Romans, the words *Lares* and *Penates* came to mean the same as *house* or *home.* In each Roman household, the family worshiped its own Lar, to protect the home from outside damage. In later times, households included two Lares. Each family also worshiped its own two Penates, to protect the interior of the home, its storehouse, and the family table. At every meal, the family offered part of its food to these gods. Safety and success, the family believed, depended upon their faithfulness to these family gods and spirits.

Ancient Roman cities also had Lares and Penates, as if each city was a big family. Vesta, the goddess of the hearth in home, city, and state, was associated with the Lares and Penates (see VESTA).   O. M. PEARL

LARGO. See MUSIC (Terms).

LARIAT. See COWBOY (His Rope).

LARK is any one of a group of birds found chiefly in the Eastern Hemisphere. Perhaps the best known of the larks is the *skylark*, which nests throughout Europe and in temperate regions of Asia. It grows about 7 inches (18 centimeters) long. Its sandy brown coat has dark brown streaks. All larks have a long, straight claw on each hind toe.

The skylark usually builds its nest on the ground in the open field. It may use grass, hair, bits of cloth, rags, or sticks as building material. The female lays four or five dull-gray eggs marked with olive brown. Larks may raise two broods a season. Skylarks have been introduced into North America, but have survived only on Vancouver Island, British Columbia.

The skylark is famous for its flight song. People often hear the song when the bird is out of sight in the sky.

The English poet, Percy Bysshe Shelley, wrote one of his finest poems, "Ode to a Skylark," about this song. One of William Shakespeare's famous songs begins "Hark! Hark! the lark at Heaven's gate sings." A famous painting by Jules Adolphe Breton shows a farm woman who stopped her work to listen to the skylark's song (see BRETON, JULES ADOLPHE [picture]).

The *horned lark* lives in the Northern Hemisphere. It breeds throughout most of Canada and the United States. This lark grows about 7½ inches (19 centimeters) long. It has pinkish or grayish-brown plumage. Dark feathers grow in small tufts that look like horns above and behind the bird's eyes. During the breeding season, the males soar high and sing, like skylarks. At other times, they sing while they are on the ground. The

Allan D. Cruickshank, NAS

The Horned Lark of North America has two tufts of dark feathers sticking out from the top of its head that look like horns.

meadow lark is not a true lark but is related to blackbirds and orioles.

Scientific Classification. Larks make up the family *Alaudidae.* The skylark is genus *Alauda,* species *A. arvensis.* The horned lark is *Eremophila alpestris.*   GEORGE J. WALLACE

See also BIRD (picture: Birds of Europe and Asia); MEADOW LARK.

LARK BUNTING. See BIRD (table: State Birds; picture: Birds of Grasslands); BUNTING.

LARKSPUR is a popular name for the *delphinium,* a group of flowers that belong to the crowfoot family. Gardeners usually give the name *larkspur* to the annual flowers in this group or the wild woodland species. The perennial garden flowers are called *delphinium.* Larkspur grows in the cool regions of both hemispheres. The name comes from a curved, spurlike growth on the upper sepal of each flower. The leaves are finely divided, the lobes spreading like fingers on a hand.

There are hundreds of larkspurs. The smallest grow about 1 foot (30 centimeters) high. Some of the larger may grow 7 feet (2.1 meters) tall. Colors range from blue or white to pink or reddish purple. Some larkspurs can poison cattle. Cases of larkspur poisoning have occurred on Western ranges. Sheep are almost immune to the poison, and horses are only slightly affected. A European larkspur has been used in medicine.

J. Horace McFarland
Larkspur

Many kinds of larkspur are cultivated as ornamental plants. Most grow easily because they do not require any special care. They do best in the open, on rich soil. Most larkspurs are planted from seed in the autumn or early spring, and bloom in summer. Some grow from root divisions, or from cuttings made from young shoots in the spring. The stately flower spikes are also suitable for cutting. Larkspurs look especially attractive as clusters of single colors in flower beds.

Larkspurs may become infected with a fungus disease called *sclerotium rot*. This disease yellows the leaves and wilts the plant. It can be checked by removing the infected plant and replacing the earth within a 1½-foot (46-centimeter) radius from the plant. Larkspurs may also be troubled by mildew.

Scientific Classification. Larkspurs belong to the crowfoot family, Ranunculaceae. They make up the genus *Delphinium*.   ROBERT W. SCHERY

See also FLOWER (picture: Garden Annuals).

L'ARLÉSIENNE. See BIZET, GEORGES.

LA ROCHEFOUCAULD, *la rawsh foo KOH*, **DUC DE** (1613-1680), was a French writer famous for his *Maxims* (1665). This work is a collection of about 500 sayings written to expose the vanity and hypocrisy the author saw underlying behavior. For example, La Rochefoucauld wrote, "We always love those who admire us, but we do not always love those whom we admire," and "True love, however rare, is still more common than true friendship." The *Maxims* have been called pessimistic, but they really state in nonreligious terms a traditional Christian view of vice and weakness.

François de La Rochefoucauld was born into a noble family in Paris. He was seriously wounded in 1652 while fighting with the nobles against the French king Louis XIV in an unsuccessful revolt called the *Fronde*. La Rochefoucauld lived quietly after that, devoting himself to literature.   JULES BRODY

LA ROCHELLE, *lah roh SHEHL* (pop. 75,840), is a city on the west coast of France that is famous for its historical religious importance. It lies along the Bay of Biscay, an arm of the Atlantic Ocean (see FRANCE [political map]). La Rochelle is France's leading Atlantic fishing port. Its other economic activities include automobile assembly, ship construction, and the manufacture of railroad equipment. The city serves as the capital of the Charente-Maritime *department* (administrative district). It is the site of a theater festival that is held each spring. The city's landmarks include a scenic harbor, a town hall built in the 1500's, and the Cathedral of St. Louis, which dates from the 1700's.

A fishing port since ancient times, La Rochelle was chartered as a city in the 1100's. In the 1500's, French Protestants—called Huguenots—were discriminated against by the country's Roman Catholic majority. But in 1598, the Edict of Nantes established 100 French communities, including La Rochelle, as areas of Protestant security. French Protestants were guaranteed self-rule and religious freedom in the communities. In 1627, the French government demanded the return of the communities to its control. The city withstood a siege by the French Army for 14 months, but its people were finally starved into obedience.   MARK KESSELMAN

LARVA, *LAHR vuh*, is an active, immature stage of an animal. It differs noticeably from the adult stage in such characteristics as structure, behavior, food habits, and environment. The development of an animal through egg, larval, and sometimes pupal stages to the adult is called *metamorphosis*.

Larvae occur in the metamorphoses of many groups of animals. They are especially common in the insects and in animals that live in the water. The larva of the sponge is a tiny, oval creature that swims about by means of short, hairlike *cilia*. Eventually, it attaches itself to a solid object, and then develops into an almost immobile, adult sponge. Flukes, tapeworms, and roundworms usually have one or two parasitic larval stages.

Marine annelid worms have larvae called *trochophores* that swim about by means of cilia. Many mollusks, including clams, oysters, scallops, snails, and periwinkles, have a free swimming larva called a *veliger*. Some of them also have another larval stage, a trochophore similar to that of the annelids. The larvae of fresh-water mussels, called *glochidia*, fasten themselves to the gills or skin of fishes and ride about on them. Then they drop off, settle down, and burrow in the bottom. Many crustaceans, including lobsters and crabs, have active, free-swimming, large-eyed larvae. Barnacles have two distinct larval stages, called *nauplii* and *cyprids*. These larvae swim and drift great distances before fastening themselves to solid objects and becoming adults. The larvae of many water animals are important food for fishes. They float about as part of the *plankton*, or mass of small, drifting animal and plant life (see PLANKTON).

Most insects have larvae more or less distinct from the adults. Larvae that change directly to the adult stage are often called *naiads* if they belong to water insects. If they belong to land insects, they are called *nymphs*. The *caterpillar* of a moth or butterfly, the *grub* of a beetle, and the *maggot* of a fly are all examples of larvae.

Among the vertebrates, or animals with backbones, many fishes have distinct larvae. For example, eels have ribbon-shaped transparent larvae. Frogs and toads, which are amphibians, have larvae called *tadpoles* or *polliwogs*.   ALEXANDER B. KLOTS

Related Articles in WORLD BOOK include:

Bee	Frog	Leaf Miner
Caterpillar	Grub	Metamorphosis
Fly	Hellgrammite	Moth

LARYNGITIS, *LAR uhn JY tihs*, is an inflammation of the tissues of the larynx, or voice box. It may be caused by various conditions. Sometimes germs invade the tissues and cause them to become inflamed. Doctors believe that laryngitis may result from the use of irritating materials, such as tobacco and alcohol. Breathing irritating substances may also cause inflammation of the

USDA, Bureau of Entomology and Plant Quarantine; L. W. Brownell

The Larva of the Mosquito looks transparent.

The Larva of the Blowfly is like a small worm.

The Tadpole of the Bullfrog is a well-known larva. It is often called a *polliwog*. The legs have started to grow on this little animal.

USDA, Bureau of Entomology and Plant Quarantine; Cornelia Clarke

The Larva of the Silkworm is usually called a caterpillar. Silk is made from the fibers of its cocoon. Unlike many larvae, it is useful to human beings.

The Larva of the Lacewing has hairy spines, and large jaws with which it captures and eats insects.

larynx. Improper use of the voice, which puts extra strain on the larynx and the vocal cords, may frequently cause laryngitis.

When the inflammation begins, the tissues of the larynx swell. Soon the patient becomes hoarse. If the condition continues, use of the voice may be lost temporarily because the vocal cords become thick and cannot vibrate to produce sound. Most cases of laryngitis should be treated by a physician.   ALBERT P. SELTZER

See also LARYNX.

LARYNGOSCOPE. See GARCÍA (Manuel).

LARYNX, *LAR ihngks,* is a section of the air passage in the throat. It is located between the back of the tongue and the *trachea* (windpipe). The larynx is sometimes called the *voice box,* because it contains the vocal cords. Every breath that passes in and out of the lungs passes through the larynx.

The larynx is shaped like a box, and it has a supporting structure made up of nine sections of cartilage. The thyroid cartilage, in front, and the cricoid cartilage, in back, are the most important. The *thyroid cartilage* consists of two wing-shaped plates that meet to form the projection called the *Adam's apple.* These plates make up the side walls of the larynx. The ring-shaped *cricoid cartilage* forms the back wall of the larynx.

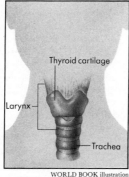

Thyroid cartilage

Larynx

Trachea

WORLD BOOK illustration by Charles Wellek

The Larynx has a framework of cartilage. The thyroid cartilage forms much of the front and side walls of the larynx.

Voice production occurs in the space inside the larynx called the *glottis.* The *vocal cords,* two bands of elastic tissue, lie along the sides of the glottis. Small muscles in the vocal cords are attached to the glottis wall. These muscles can stretch the vocal cords, change their shape, or bring them close together. When the cords are close together, air rushing between them produces sound. The shape and stretch in the cords determines the *pitch* (highness or lowness) of the voice. The shape of the throat, nose, and mouth determines the *quality* of a person's voice.   A. C. GUYTON

See also the Trans-Vision three-dimensional picture with HUMAN BODY; also LARYNGITIS; VOICE.

LA SALLE, JEAN. See JEAN BAPTISTE DE LA SALLE, SAINT.

LA SALLE, *luh SAL,* **SIEUR DE** (1643-1687), RENÉ-ROBERT CAVELIER, was a French explorer. He led the first European expedition to track the Mississippi River to the Gulf of Mexico. La Salle claimed the entire Mississippi Valley for France. His many explorations strengthened France's hopes for a great empire in the New World.

Early Life. La Salle was born in Rouen, France. His real name was René-Robert Cavelier. He took the name La Salle from the name of his family's estate. As a youth, La Salle went to schools run by Jesuit priests and studied to be a Jesuit. However, he left the religious training in 1665 to seek adventure. The following year, La Salle sailed to Canada, where France had established a colony.

La Salle obtained some land near Montreal and became a prosperous fur trader. He did much of his trading with Indians, who told him of two great rivers to the southwest, the Mississippi and the Ohio. The Indians believed these rivers flowed into the sea. La Salle

79

LA SALLE, SIEUR DE

thought one or both of the rivers might be a route through North America to the Pacific Ocean. In 1669, he sold his land and set out in search of the rivers.

Archives Nationales du Québec
Sieur de La Salle

First Explorations. From 1669 to 1673, La Salle wandered through the vast interior of North America. Historians believe he traveled as far as what is now Ohio. By the end of his journey, he was convinced the Mississippi emptied into the Gulf of Mexico.

La Salle returned to France in 1674, and King Louis XIV gave him land that included Fort Frontenac, on the site of the present city of Kingston, Ont. La Salle established a fur trading post at the fort and soon became one of the most powerful persons in Canada. In 1677, he again sailed to France, where he obtained permission from King Louis to explore the Mississippi River.

In 1679, after returning to Canada, La Salle launched an expedition to give France control of the Great Lakes region. The following year, he founded the first European settlement in what is now Illinois. It stood on the Illinois River, near present-day Peoria, and was named Fort Crèvecoeur (Fort Heartbreak). After La Salle built this fort, he went back to Canada for supplies.

Expeditions to the Gulf of Mexico. La Salle returned to the Illinois region in late 1681. Indians had destroyed Fort Crèvecoeur, but La Salle pushed on. He led a party of about 20 Frenchmen and about 30 Indians down the Illinois River in canoes to the Mississippi.

The expedition started down the Mississippi River on Feb. 13, 1682, and reached the Gulf of Mexico on April 9. Near the mouth of the Mississippi, La Salle erected a cross and a column bearing the French coat of arms. He claimed all the land drained by the Mississippi and its tributaries for France. This region extended from the Appalachian Mountains on the east to the Rocky Mountains on the west, and from the Great Lakes on the north to the Gulf of Mexico on the south. La Salle named the region Louisiana in honor of King Louis.

Later in 1682, La Salle built Fort Saint Louis on a bluff along the Illinois River. This bluff is now in Starved Rock State Park. La Salle wanted to establish a colony at the mouth of the Mississippi. In late 1683, he left for France to pick up supplies and settlers for such a colony.

In 1684, La Salle sailed from France for the Gulf of Mexico with 4 ships and more than 300 colonists. But this expedition never reached the Mississippi because La Salle sailed past the river by mistake. In 1685, he set up a colony, also called Fort Saint Louis, west of the Mississippi. This site was near Matagorda Bay, or about 80 miles (130 kilometers) east of the present site of Corpus Christi, Tex.

Indians threatened the new settlement, and many colonists died from disease. By 1687, the colony desperately needed help. La Salle and several men began an overland march to find the Mississippi, which they planned to follow to Canada. But they could not find the river. Some of the men rebelled and killed La Salle's nephew and then murdered La Salle.   WILLIAM JAY JACOBS

See also HENNEPIN, LOUIS; TONTI, HENRI DE.

Additional Resources

DELANGLEZ, JEAN. *Some La Salle Journeys*. Loyola Univ. Institute of Jesuit History, 1938.

PARKMAN, FRANCIS. *La Salle and the Discovery of the Great West*. Corner House, 1968. Reprint of 1897 ed.

TERRELL, J. UPTON. *La Salle: The Life and Times of an Explorer*. Weybright & Talley, 1968.

LAS CAMPANAS OBSERVATORY. See MOUNT WILSON OBSERVATORY.

LAS CASAS, *lahs KAH sahs,* **BARTOLOMÉ DE** (1474-1566), was an early Spanish missionary to America. He arrived in 1502 with the newly appointed Spanish governor of the island of Hispaniola. Las Casas became a Roman Catholic priest in 1510, and later joined the Dominican order. He was the first priest ordained in America. He protested vigorously against the enslavement of the Indians on Hispaniola, and worked to help them. In 1547, Las Casas returned to Spain. He was born in Seville.   JAMES A. CORBETT and FULTON J. SHEEN

LASCAUX CAVE. See CAVE (table: Interesting Caves of the World); PAINTING (color picture).

LAS CRUCES, *lahs KROO ses,* N. Mex. (pop. 45,086; met. area pop. 96,340), is the trading center for the rich farmlands of the Mesilla Valley. The city lies on the Rio Grande in south-central New Mexico (see NEW MEXICO [political map]). The name *Las Cruces* is Spanish for *the crosses.* Las Cruces is the home of New Mexico State University. The Organ Mountains rise east of the city, and the White Sands National Monument stands to the northeast. Military proving grounds lie north and south of the monument. *El Camino Real*, the old Spanish road from Chihuahua to Santa Fe, N. Mex., ran through this region. Las Cruces was settled in 1849. It has a council-manager form of government.   FRANK D. REEVE

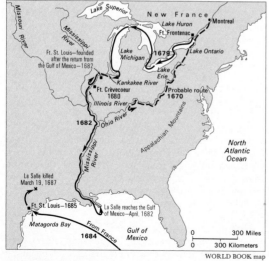

The Explorations of Sieur de La Salle through North America strengthened France's hopes for a great empire in the New World. La Salle claimed the entire Mississippi River Valley for France.

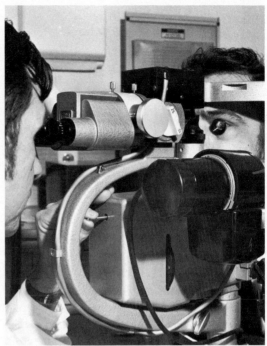

Korad

Coherent Radiation

Lasers Produce Thin Beams of Light of varying intensity. The beam of a solid laser, *left*, is used to cut through a sheet of hard metal in a fraction of a second. In eye surgery, *right*, the physician uses a precisely focused beam from a gas laser to repair damaged tissue.

LASER is a device that *amplifies* (strengthens) light. A laser produces a thin beam of light that can burn a hole in a diamond or carry the signals of many different television pictures at the same time. The word *laser* stands for *light amplification by stimulated emission of radiation*.

The light from a laser differs from the light produced by other sources, such as electric bulbs, fluorescent lamps, and the sun. The light from these other sources travels in all directions. The light from a laser is highly directional. In other words, it travels in only one direction. It travels in a narrow beam, and the sides of the beam stay almost parallel. For example, a beam $\frac{1}{2}$ inch (13 millimeters) wide may spread to only about 3 inches (7.6 centimeters) after traveling a distance of a mile (1.6 kilometers).

Laser light also differs from other light in terms of *frequency*, the number of vibrations of a light wave per second. The light from a laser consists of one or, at most, a few frequencies. The light from other sources consists of many frequencies. Because laser light has so few frequencies, a laser beam has a narrow frequency range on the *electromagnetic spectrum*, an arrangement of frequencies from lowest to highest.

The frequencies of a laser beam may be in only the visible region of the electromagnetic spectrum. Or they may be in only the infrared or ultraviolet regions, both of which are invisible. The frequencies of light produced by most other sources are in the visible and invisible regions of the electromagnetic spectrum at the

same time. See ELECTROMAGNETIC WAVES (The Electromagnetic Spectrum).

How Lasers Are Used

The unusual characteristics of laser light make lasers a valuable tool in (1) communications, (2) industry, (3) medicine, (4) military operations, and (5) scientific research.

In Communications, a laser can transmit voice messages and television signals. It has great advantages over ordinary electronic transmitters, such as those used to produce radio and television signals. For example, a laser operates at a much higher frequency than do electronic transmitters. The high frequency of laser light enables a laser beam to carry much more information than radio waves can. Therefore, one of these beams can transmit many telephone calls and television programs at the same time.

A laser can transmit information with little interference because it produces a highly directional beam. A laser beam can be directed to fall solely on the desired laser-receiving equipment. Because the equipment receives only the laser beam directed at it, most interference is eliminated.

A laser also may serve as an efficient long-distance transmitter because of its highly directional beam. Laser beams, unlike radio waves, spread only slightly as they travel. For this reason, scientists believe a laser beam may provide an excellent communications link with spacecraft. On the earth, a laser beam may be sent

Lasers Provide Accurate Measurements. The laser shown above is sending a beam toward the construction worker in the background. The worker uses the beam to measure the tilt of the wall.

Micro-Grade Laser Systems, Inc.

from one relay station to another through a long glass fiber. The beam is reflected through the fiber and can travel great distances with little loss of energy (see FIBER OPTICS).

In Industry, the laser has a variety of uses. For example, it may be used as a source of intense heat. The sides of a laser beam are nearly parallel, and so a lens can focus the beam to a point only $\frac{1}{10,000}$ inch (0.0025 millimeter) wide. When the beam is concentrated on such a small area, it may produce temperatures higher than 10,000° F. (5538° C). In this way, a laser beam can be used to melt extremely hard materials.

Manufacturers use short bursts of laser light to weld miniature metal parts together in electronic equipment. For example, a laser can be used to connect wires sealed inside a glass tube. In heavy industry, high-power lasers are used to weld large metal parts together. Surveyors use a laser range finder to measure distances in making maps.

In Medicine, surgeons use the heating action of a laser beam to remove diseased body tissue. The beam burns away the unhealthy tissue in a fraction of a second with little damage to the surrounding healthy area. Eye specialists use the laser to correct a condition called *retinal detachment* (see EYE [Diseases]). They aim a laser beam into the patient's eye and focus it on the retina. The heat of the beam "welds" the loose retina into place.

In Military Operations, a laser beam can be bounced off a target, such as an enemy airplane or ship, to determine its distance and speed. Laser *gyroscopes* (guidance devices) are being developed to direct bombs and artillery shells to their target. Laser range finders and gyroscopes may be used in commercial navigation as well as by military forces.

In Scientific Research, a laser has many uses. For example, it may be used to create hot gases called *plasmas.* The study of plasmas may help scientists learn to control *nuclear fusion,* the process by which lightweight atoms combine into heavier ones to produce energy. The control of this process and the use of lasers in similar research could help solve the energy needs of mankind. See NUCLEAR ENERGY (Nuclear Fusion).

How a Laser Works

Light is a form of energy that is released from individual atoms or molecules in a substance. To understand how a laser works, it is necessary to know something about the nature of atoms and how they interact with light and other forms of energy.

Every atom is a storehouse of energy. The amount of energy in an atom depends on the motion of the electrons that orbit the atom's nucleus. When an atom absorbs energy, its energy level increases, and the atom is said to be *excited.* The atoms of a substance become excited when they absorb heat, light, or other forms of energy that pass through the substance. An excited atom can return to its normal energy level by releasing its excess energy in the form of light. This release of energy is called *spontaneous emission.*

In spontaneous emission, excited atoms release light irregularly. As a result, the light has different frequencies and travels in different directions. Light released in this way is called *incoherent light.* Such light is produced by the sun and by ordinary electric bulbs.

Excited atoms also may release light systematically. This kind of release, called *stimulated emission,* is the main process that takes place in a laser. Stimulated emission occurs when the energy released from one atom interacts with another atom that is still excited. The interaction triggers the excited atom into releasing its own extra energy as light. Most of the light produced by stimulated emission has the same frequency as the triggering light. It also travels in the same direction,

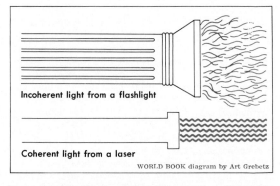

Incoherent light from a flashlight

Coherent light from a laser

WORLD BOOK diagram by Art Grebetz

Lasers Produce Coherent Light. Waves of coherent light, unlike waves of incoherent light, move "in step" with one another. As a result, they spread only slightly—even over great distances.

and so it combines with and amplifies the triggering light. Such light is called *coherent light*.

The basic parts of a laser include a power source and a light-amplifying substance. Stimulated emission results when energy from the power source interacts with excited atoms in the substance. The total energy produced by a laser is always less than the energy produced by the power source. But the laser produces a much more intense light.

Kinds of Lasers

There are three major kinds of lasers, based on their light-amplifying substance: (1) solid lasers, (2) gas lasers, and (3) liquid lasers.

Solid Lasers are the most widely used type of laser. Their light-amplifying substance may be a crystal, glass, or a *semiconductor*. A semiconductor conducts electricity, but not so well as true conductors, such as copper or iron.

Crystal Lasers have a fluorescent crystal, such as that of a ruby, as their light-amplifying substance. The power for a ruby laser comes from a flash tube, which may be coiled around the crystal. The flash tube

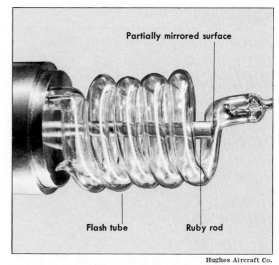

Partially mirrored surface

Flash tube   Ruby rod

Hughes Aircraft Co.

A Ruby Crystal Laser, *above,* produces powerful bursts of light. The flash tube generates laser light inside the ruby. The light shoots out through the partially mirrored surface.

How a Ruby Laser Works

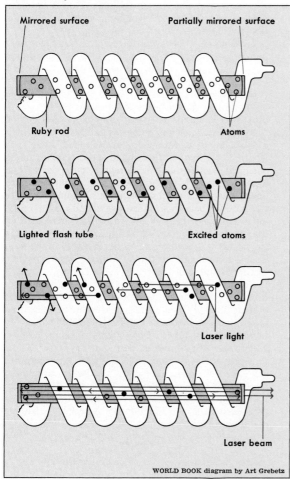

Mirrored surface   Partially mirrored surface

Ruby rod   Atoms

Lighted flash tube   Excited atoms

Laser light

Laser beam

WORLD BOOK diagram by Art Grebetz

The diagrams at the left represent the light-amplifying material in a ruby laser. Each atom in the ruby has a certain amount of energy, depending on the motion of its electrons. This orbiting motion is shown in the diagrams at the right.

Orbiting electrons

Atom

A powerful flash tube sends intense light through the ruby. The light excites some of the ruby's atoms. These atoms are shown by the solid circles. An atom becomes excited when absorbed light energy changes the orbit of one of its electrons.

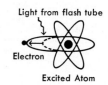

Light from flash tube

Electron

Excited Atom

Excited atoms radiate light as their electrons drop back to low-energy orbits. Some of this light passes out the sides of the ruby. But part travels along the axis of the ruby as laser light.

Laser light

Radiating Atom

The laser light is reflected back and forth by mirrors and stimulates other excited atoms into releasing their energy. This amplifies the laser light many times. Part of the amplified light passes through the partial mirror as an intense laser beam.

Reflected laser light   Amplified laser light

Stimulated Atom

Kinds of Lasers

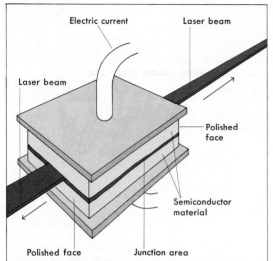

Electric current

Laser beam

Laser beam

Polished face

Semiconductor material

Polished face   Junction area

A Semiconductor Laser consists of two layers of material that differ electrically. Electric current passing through the layers produces laser light in the area of their junction. The light shoots out through the polished faces.

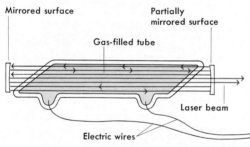

Mirrored surface

Partially mirrored surface

Gas-filled tube

Laser beam

Electric wires

A Gas Laser has a tube filled with gas as its light-amplifying substance. Electric current excites atoms of gas inside the tube. The atoms then generate a beam of laser light, which shoots out the partially mirrored surface.

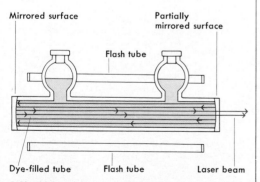

Mirrored surface

Partially mirrored surface

Flash tube

Dye-filled tube   Flash tube   Laser beam

A Liquid Laser has a tube filled with a dye as its light-amplifying substance. Flash tubes cause atoms of the dye to produce laser light. The frequency of the light can be adjusted by circulating different dyes through the tube.

WORLD BOOK diagram by Art Grebetz

produces a brilliant flash of light. The flash excites a large number of chromium *ions* (electrically charged atoms) in the ruby. This process of using a flash to excite the atoms is called *optical pumping*.

A ruby laser may be used to melt hard materials. It produces powerful bursts of light that can burn a hole through $\frac{1}{16}$ of an inch (1.6 millimeters) of steel with one burst. The ruby laser can normally produce light only in bursts because the flash tube generates intense heat in the ruby. Another type of crystal laser, the Nd:YAG (neodymium yttrium aluminum garnet) laser, produces a continuous beam of light. It can do so because it requires less power to operate than does a ruby laser, and it can be cooled by water. Such a laser may be used as a drill or as a range finder.

Glass Lasers resemble ruby lasers and operate in much the same way. They use glass instead of a crystal as their light-amplifying substance. Most glass lasers have a flash tube as their power source and produce light in bursts. Scientists use these lasers in experiments with plasmas.

Semiconductor Lasers, also called *injection lasers*, have a tiny cube of a semiconductor as their light-amplifying substance. A common material used is gallium arsenide. The semiconductor consists of two layers that differ in their electric charge. Current passing through the semiconductor produces coherent light along the junction between the two layers.

Semiconductor lasers convert electricity into coherent light very efficiently. The small size of semiconductor lasers makes them useful for carrying radio and television signals through a glass fiber.

Gas Lasers use a gas or a mixture of gases as their light-amplifying substance. In most cases, the gas is contained in a glass or quartz tube from 1 to 3 feet (30 to 91 centimeters) long. Some gas lasers have been built in glass tubes measuring up to 30 feet (9 meters) in length. Gas lasers have several power sources, including chemical reactions, electric current, electron beams, and ultraviolet rays. Most gas lasers, unlike ruby and glass lasers, produce a continuous beam of light. They also can produce beams of higher average power than solid lasers can. They can do so because they are cooled by the gas as it flows through the tube. The light from a gas laser has a narrower frequency range than the light from a solid laser. For this reason, a gas laser is more useful in communications and in measuring.

Liquid Lasers produce both bursts of light and continuous light. The light-amplifying substance of most of these lasers is a dye, such as rhodamine 6G, dissolved in methanol or a similar liquid. The substance is contained in a glass tube. Liquid lasers that produce bursts of light use a flash tube as their source of power. Those that produce continuous light get their power from a gas laser. They are cooled by the liquid circulating through the tube. A liquid laser is the only kind of laser that can have the frequency of its light adjusted. Scientists use such a laser to study the properties of atomic and molecular systems.

History

Scientists developed the laser during the late 1950's and early 1960's. Laser research grew out of earlier studies of microwave amplifying devices called *masers* (see MASER). As a result, early lasers were also called *optical masers* because they amplified light in much the same way that masers amplified microwaves.

Two United States physicists, Arthur L. Schawlow and C. H. Townes, first proposed the idea of the laser in 1958. Similar ideas were developed at that time by the Russian physicists N. G. Basov and A. M. Prokhorov. Theodore H. Maiman of the United States built the first laser, a ruby laser, and operated it for the first time in 1960. In 1961, Ali Javan, another U.S. physicist, operated the first continuous laser. Semiconductor lasers were first operated in 1962 by three separate teams of United States scientists. The first liquid laser was operated in 1966 by Peter Sorokin of the United States.

In 1969, astronauts on the Apollo 11 space flight placed a mirrored device called a *laser reflector* on the moon. Scientists use this device to measure precisely the distance between the earth and the moon. They do so by measuring the time required for the laser beam to travel to the reflector and back.   ANTHONY J. DE MARIA

See also HOLOGRAM.

Additional Resources

HECHT, JEFF, and TERESI, DICK. *Laser: Supertool of the 1980s.* Ticknor & Fields, 1982.
KETTELKAMP, LARRY. *Lasers, the Miracle Light.* Morrow, 1979. For younger readers.
MAURER, ALLAN. *Lasers: Light Wave of the Future.* Arco, 1982.
McKIE, ROBIN. *Lasers.* Watts, 1983. For younger readers.

LASHLEY, KARL SPENCER (1890-1958), was an American psychologist known for his research on the function of the brain in relation to behavior. Lashley developed two main principles as a result of his research. The first, the *principle of mass action*, states that in many types of learning the cerebral cortex of the brain acts as a whole. The second principle, the *principle of equipotentiality*, states that certain small areas of the brain can take on the function of larger, related areas that have been destroyed.

Lashley was born in Davis, W.Va. He received his Ph.D. in zoology from Johns Hopkins University in 1914. Lashley taught at the universities of Minnesota and Chicago and at Harvard University. From 1942 to 1955, he served as director of the Yerkes Laboratories of Primate Biology in Orange Park, Fla. ROBERT G. WEYANT

LASKI, HAROLD JOSEPH (1893-1950), a British political scientist, achieved fame as an educator and as a leader of the Labour Party. From 1914 to 1920, Laski lectured at universities in Canada and in the United States. He taught at the University of London between 1926 and 1950. Laski served on the executive committee of the Labour Party from 1936 to 1949, and was chairman for one year. His books include *The American Presidency* (1940) and *The American Democracy* (1948). Laski was born in Manchester, and attended Oxford.   ALFRED F. HAVIGHURST

LASSEN PEAK (10,457 feet, or 3,187 meters) is a volcano in northeastern California, near the southern end of the Cascade Mountains. Lassen Volcanic National Park lies around the volcano. The peak was named for Peter Lassen, who blazed one of the early trails of California across its slopes. The volcano was inactive for many years after its discovery. On May 30, 1914, it erupted and sent up a shower of mud, dust, stones, and fine sand. Several other eruptions occurred afterwards, the last in February, 1921.   PAUL R. HANNA

LASSEN VOLCANIC NATIONAL PARK is located in northeastern California. The park includes 10,457-foot (3,187-meter) Lassen Peak. The park was established in 1916.

In the park's Chaos region, hundreds of steep domes of lava that were pushed up from below the earth's surface form odd-looking formations. These formations are called Chaos Crags and Chaos Jumbles. More than 40 glacier-made lakes are in the park. Reflection Lake mirrors Lassen Peak. Three large lakes called the Chain-of-Lakes lie in the eastern part of the park. Hot springs bubble on the surface of Boiling Spring Lake. The park is a preserve for many wild animals. For the area of the park, see NATIONAL PARK SYSTEM (table: National Parks).   PAUL R. HANNA

See also LASSEN PEAK.

LASSO, ORLANDO DI (1532?-1594), is considered the greatest of the early Netherlands composers. His work represents the high point in the development of Dutch *polyphony* (many-voiced music). Lasso produced more than 2,000 compositions, most of which are vocal music. His compositions include secular madrigals and chansons, as well as religious masses and motets. The madrigal, the most refined form of secular music, influenced the motet and the mass. The style of Lasso is less melodious and more harmonic than most music of his day, and his work is considered more dramatic than that of his contemporary, Giovanni Palestrina.

As a boy, Lasso had a beautiful soprano voice. He received much of his early musical training as a choirboy. Later, he studied music in such Italian cities as Milan and Naples. In 1556, Lasso went to Munich, Germany, where he served as a court musician and gained favor with the nobility. He was born Roland de Lassus in Mons, Belgium, and was also known by the name Orlandus Lassus.   WARREN S. FREEMAN

Lassen Peak in Lassen Volcanic National Park erupted intermittently from 1914 to 1921. Hardened lava from these eruptions covers the slopes. Hot springs flow from the south side.

Shasta-Cascade Wonderland Association

LAST SUPPER. See Jesus Christ (The Passion); Da Vinci, Leonardo; Holy Grail.

LAS VEGAS, *lahs VAY guhs* (pop. 164,674; met. area pop. 463,087), the largest city in Nevada, is famous for its gambling casinos and nightclubs. The city attracts about 10 million visitors annually and ranks as a major tourist center of the United States. Las Vegas lies in the southeastern corner of the state. For location, see Nevada (political map).

Las Vegas was founded as a station on what is now the Union Pacific Railroad route. The site consisted of fertile grassland, and the name of the city comes from two Spanish words meaning *the meadows*.

Description. Las Vegas, the county seat of Clark County, covers 60 square miles (155 square kilometers). Most of the city's casinos and nightclubs line downtown Fremont Street. Many other casinos lie along the Strip, a highway located just outside the city. Every year, about 400 organizations from various parts of the country hold conventions in the Las Vegas Convention Center.

A campus of the University of Nevada is in Las Vegas. The University Museum there exhibits Indian and pioneer relics. Every spring, a festival called Helldorado Days takes place in the city. Las Vegas citizens and visitors wear Old West costumes for this event, which features parades, rodeos, and street dances. Near Las Vegas are Hoover Dam, one of the largest dams in the world; and Lake Mead, which ranks as one of the world's largest artificially created lakes.

The tourist industry ranks as the city's largest employer, with about 50,000 workers. Two nearby facilities of the government, Nellis Air Force Base and the Energy Research and Development Administration's Nevada Test Site, employ another 18,000 Las Vegas residents. The city serves as a shipping center for a large mining and ranching area.

Government and History. Las Vegas has a council-manager form of government. The voters elect a mayor and four commissioners to four-year terms. The mayor and the commissioners are responsible for appointing a city manager, whose actions are subject to the commission's approval.

Paiute Indians lived in what is now the Las Vegas area before white people arrived. Las Vegas was founded in 1905 and received a city charter in 1911. The city grew rapidly during the 1930's. In 1931, the state legalized gambling, and small casinos began to appear in Las Vegas. That same year, hundreds of workers arrived to begin the construction of Boulder (now Hoover) Dam on the Colorado River.

Nellis Air Force Base was established during World War II (1939-1945). The city's first big gambling casino opened in 1946. By the mid-1950's, gambling in Las Vegas had become one of the nation's leading tourist attractions. The expanding tourist industry created many new jobs in the 1960's, and the city continued to grow.

In 1980, a fire destroyed the MGM Grand Hotel in Las Vegas. It killed 85 people. Another fire damaged the Las Vegas Hilton Hotel in 1981, killing eight people. A major sports and recreation facility, Cashman Field Center, was completed by the city in 1983. The center includes a stadium and a building with convention facilities and a theater. Neil Lever

For the monthly weather in Las Vegas, see Nevada (Climate). See also Nevada (pictures).

LATAKIA, *LAT uh KEE uh* (pop. 234,000), is Syria's main seaport. It lies about 110 miles (177 kilometers) north of Beirut, Lebanon (see Syria [map]). In the 1950's, Syria improved the port to make it useful to large ships. The city has given its name to the famous tobacco it exports.

LA TÈNE STYLE. See Celts.

LATERAN is the common name for the Basilica of St. John Lateran in Rome. It is the cathedral church of the pope in his role as bishop of Rome. The name Lateran comes from Lateranus, the name of an ancient noble Roman family. The family's house stood on the site of the present church.

The original basilica was built on land donated by Emperor Constantine the Great in 313. The church was destroyed and rebuilt several times in the next 1,300 years. In the 1640's, architect Francesco Borromini remodeled the building in the baroque style, adding much of its elaborate interior decoration. The building owes much of its present appearance to Borromini's work. A new *facade* (front) was added in 1735. The church was extensively restored in the late 1800's.

Next to the basilica is the octagonal baptistery of St. John, a building in which baptisms were performed. The structure dates back to the time of Constantine. Also near the church is the Lateran Palace, which was the home of the popes from the 300's until 1305. The

David G. Wacker, Tom Stack & Assoc.

Downtown Las Vegas has many gambling casinos and nightclubs. These entertainment spots have made the city a major vacation center.

palace burned down in 1308 and was not rebuilt until the 1580's. It now houses church administrative offices. In 1929, the Lateran Treaty between Italy and the Roman Catholic Church made the three Lateran buildings part of the Vatican state.   WILLIAM J. HENNESSEY

LATERAN TREATY. See PAPAL STATES.

LATEX, *LAY tehks,* is the milky juice given off by plants and trees of the sapodilla family. It differs from sap because it flows between the bark layers rather than in the wood. Certain gums and rubbers, used in many manufacturing processes, are made from latex.

The hevea tree and the guayule and milkweed plants produce *rubber latex,* used to make articles ranging from rubber balls to *Lastex,* a vulcanized-rubber yarn. The balata and the gutta-percha tree give off latex that is used to make balata and gutta-percha gums. The naseberry, or sapodilla tree, produces *chicle latex.* Manufacturers use the tough, fragrant chicle in making chewing gum.

Fresh latex is not stable. Preservatives must be added within three or four hours after collection to prevent bacterial decomposition or coagulation. From 0.6 to 1 per cent of ammonia is used. The preserved latex contains 38 to 40 per cent of solids.   CHARLES L. MANTELL

See also RUBBER (First Uses; Natural Rubber); CHICLE; GUAYULE.

LATHAM, *LAY thuhm,* **JEAN LEE** (1902-   ), an American writer for young people, received the Newbery medal in 1956 for her book *Carry On, Mr. Bowditch* (1955). Her other books include *Story of Eli Whitney* (1953); *Medals for Morse* (1954); *Trail Blazer of the Seas* (1956); *This Dear Bought Land* (1957); *On Stage, Mr. Jefferson!* (1958); and *David Glasgow Farragut* (1967). During World War II, Latham trained signal-corps inspectors for the U.S. Army. She was born in Buckhannon, W.Va.   CHARLEMAE ROLLINS

LATHE. See MACHINE TOOL (Turning); ENGINE TURNING.

LATHROP, *LAY thruhp,* **DOROTHY P.** (1891-1980), an American artist and writer for children, won the first Caldecott medal for *Animals of the Bible* in 1938. In creating her drawings of animals, Lathrop worked from live models, and her household included many animal pets. Her other books include *The Fairy Circus* (1931), *Little White Goat* (1933), *Lost Merry-Go-Round* (1934), *Who Goes There?* (1935), *The Colt from Moon Mountain* (1941), *Let Them Live* (1951), and *Bouncing Betsy* (1964).

Lathrop was born in Albany, N.Y., and studied at Teachers College of Columbia University, the Pennsylvania Academy of the Fine Arts, and the Art Students League in New York City.   RUTH HILL VIGUERS

LATHROP, *LAY thruhp,* **JULIA CLIFFORD** (1858-1932), was the first chief of the Children's Bureau of the United States Department of Labor. She became the first woman to head an important government bureau in the United States. A college friend of Jane Addams, she worked at Hull House almost from its beginning, first as a county visitor and then as a member of the Illinois State Board of Charities (see HULL HOUSE). She resigned from the board in 1901, in protest against a political appointment, but was reappointed by a new governor. She served 11 years, and took a leading part in the establishment of the first Juvenile Court.

President William Howard Taft called her to the Children's Bureau when it was formed in 1912, and she

Julia Clifford Lathrop

served as its chief until 1921. The bureau owes its emphasis on research and on qualified child-welfare workers to her. She encouraged states to improve birth registration and to provide aid for mothers to prevent unnecessary removal of their children. She was born in Rockford, Ill.   ALAN KEITH-LUCAS

LATHROP, *LAY thruhp,* **ROSE HAWTHORNE** (1851-1926), was the main founder of a Roman Catholic nursing order of nuns. She set up the order in New York City to aid poor cancer patients and also established two nursing homes for cancer victims.

Rose Hawthorne, the daughter of the famous author Nathaniel Hawthorne, was born in Lenox, Mass. She married George Parsons Lathrop, a writer, in 1871 and became a Catholic in 1891. She began working with cancer patients after taking a nursing course in 1896. That same year, she opened a small infirmary for cancer patients in a New York City slum.

Lathrop's husband died in 1898. That year, she and Alice Huber, an associate, formed a nursing society, the Servants of Relief for Incurable Cancer. They also opened a home in New York City for cancer patients. Lathrop took her first vows as a nun in 1900 and her final vows in 1909. Also in 1900, she and Huber founded the nursing order, the Dominican Congregation of St. Rose of Lima. Lathrop became known as Mother Mary Alphonsa. She opened a second nursing home in 1901. Lathrop wrote a book about her father called *Memories of Hawthorne* (1897). NANCY SPELMAN WOLOCH

LATIMER, *LAT uh muhr,* **HUGH** (1485?-1555), was a martyr of the Protestant Reformation in England. Born in Thurcaston, England, he studied at Cambridge University and became a Roman Catholic priest. His refusal to condemn the views of Martin Luther concerning the church caused him to be called before Thomas Cardinal Wolsey in 1525 for investigation. But later he was named one of the clergymen who were to examine the legality of King Henry VIII's marriage with Catherine of Aragon. His support of Henry made him a favorite of the king, who named Latimer one of his chaplains. In 1535, after Henry had broken away from the Roman Catholic Church, Latimer became Protestant bishop of Worcester. But he resigned because he opposed the Six Articles, which he thought favored Roman Catholicism.

Later, the Roman Catholic Queen Mary had him arrested along with other Protestant churchmen. He was called before a church court and was condemned to be burned at the stake. On Oct. 16, 1555, Latimer and Nicholas Ridley were brought to their place of execution opposite Balliol College, Oxford University. It is said that Latimer exclaimed to his companion, "We shall this day light such a candle, by God's grace, in England, as I trust shall never be put out." Latimer's martyrdom caused widespread sympathy for all persecuted Protestants.   GEORGE L. MOSSE

Copacabana Beach in Rio de Janeiro, Brazil

Loren McIntyre

Nicholas Devore III, Bruce Coleman Inc.

Coffee Berry Pickers in Costa Rica

Andrew Rakoczy, Bruce Coleman Inc.

A Modern Shopping Mall near Mexico City

Odyssey Productions

Farmland Alongside Guatemala's Lake Atitlán

City and Country Life in Latin America contrast sharply. Many city dwellers live and work in sleek, modern buildings. Peasants in the countryside rent or own small plots of land or work on huge plantations. Many poor peasants have flocked to the cities looking for better jobs.

LATIN AMERICA

LATIN AMERICA is a large region that covers all the territory in the Western Hemisphere south of the United States. It consists of Mexico, Central America, South America, and the islands of the West Indies. The region is divided into 33 independent countries and 13 other political units. Brazil is by far the largest country in Latin America both in area and in population. It occupies more than 40 per cent of the region's land area and has about a third of its people.

During the late 1400's, people from southern Europe, especially Spain and Portugal, began to settle in Latin America. These people brought their own languages, religious beliefs, and customs with them. Today, the majority of Latin Americans speak Spanish, Portuguese, or French, each of which developed from Latin. For this reason, the region is called *Latin America*. English or Dutch is the official language in several areas of the region that were colonized by England or the Netherlands. Scholars disagree about whether such areas should be considered part of Latin America. This article includes these areas in its discussion of the region (see the table *Political Units in Latin America*).

Before the first Europeans settled in Latin America, the region had long been inhabited by American Indians. Soon after the Europeans arrived, they began to bring in many black Africans as slaves, especially to the West Indies and some mainland coastal areas. Over the centuries, numerous whites, Indians, and blacks intermarried. Today, most Latin Americans are of mixed ancestry. They are chiefly of Indian and white descent or of black and white descent. Most other Latin Americans are of unmixed Indian, black, or white ancestry.

The people of Latin America share many traditions and values that spring from their common colonial heritage. However, there are great local differences in the way of life throughout Latin America. Such differences largely reflect various combinations of the region's African, American Indian, and European cultural heritage. Differences in the way of life also arise from differences in geography and in economic development from one part of Latin America to another.

Nathan A. Haverstock, the contributor of this article, is director of The Latin American Service *in Washington, D.C., and the author of* The Organization of American States: The Challenge of the Americas *and other books on Latin America.*

Christopher Columbus, an Italian navigator in the service of Spain, reached Latin America in 1492. By that time, Indians had been living in the region for thousands of years. Such Indian groups as the Aztec, Inca, and Maya had developed highly advanced civilizations. The Europeans who followed Columbus to Latin America quickly conquered most of the Indians and established colonies. European rule of Latin America lasted about 300 years.

During the early 1800's, many Latin-American colonies gained their independence and became republics. However, the leaders of the new republics lacked the experience necessary to deal with serious social and economic problems. As a result, the new republics did not work as well as many people had hoped. In some Latin-American countries, military dictators seized control of the government. Other nations were ruled by a few powerful families who used their positions to increase their personal wealth. Antigovernment protests and violent revolutions occurred frequently throughout Latin America. During the 1900's, civilian and military leaders have tried to bring political stability to the region. But in the process, many of these leaders have restricted the people's civil rights.

Until the mid-1900's, the majority of Latin Americans lived in rural areas. Today, most of the people live in urban areas. The difficulty of raising enough food from the poor soil has led millions of rural people to seek work in the cities. However, many of these people are uneducated and unskilled. As a result, they cannot find jobs and so continue to live in wretched poverty. The widespread poverty, overpopulation, and violations of human rights all help create political and social unrest in much of Latin America today.

This article discusses the people, way of life, arts, and history of Latin America. To understand the region more thoroughly, see the WORLD BOOK articles on each of the independent countries and other political units in Latin America. See also NORTH AMERICA, CENTRAL AMERICA, SOUTH AMERICA, and WEST INDIES.

LATIN AMERICA/*People*

Population. Latin America has a population of about 422 million. The population is increasing about 2.4 per cent a year, making Latin America one of the fastest-growing regions in the world.

Latin America's population has more than tripled since 1940. The increase is due to a high birth rate and improvements in health care, which have led to a decline in the region's death rate. About 40 per cent of all Latin Americans are under 15 years old.

Latin America covers about 8 million square miles (21 million square kilometers). If the population were evenly distributed throughout the region, there would be only about 53 people per square mile (20 per square kilometer). But the population is far from evenly distributed. Vast areas of the interior of South and Central America have few or no people. Much of the interior is covered by tropical rain forests. Some dry grasslands, desert areas, and high mountain regions of Latin America

are also thinly settled. Most of the people live near seacoasts or rivers or in highland areas that have good farmland. Some parts of Latin America are extremely crowded. Barbados, Puerto Rico, and certain other West Indian islands rank among the most densely populated places in the world. Other heavily populated areas in

People of Latin America

Latin Americans include people of American Indian, European, and African ancestry. Those of mixed Indian and white descent are called *mestizos*. Those of mixed black and white descent are called *mulattoes*.

Owen Franken, Stock, Boston
Bolivian Indian Woman

Don Cowan, FPG
Ecuadorean Indian Man

Porterfield-Chickering, Photo Researchers
West Indies Black Man

Claus C. Meyer, Black Star
Brazilian White Woman

Odyssey Productions
Mexican Mestizo Man

Claus C. Meyer, Black Star
Brazilian Mulatto Man

Latin America include the coasts of Argentina and Brazil; central Mexico; and northern Colombia and Venezuela.

Ancestry. Latin America has a varied population in terms of ancestry. The main population groups are (1) Indians, (2) whites, (3) blacks, and (4) people of mixed ancestry.

Most Latin-American countries have a class system based largely on ancestry. The relatively small upper class consists chiefly of whites. People of mixed ancestry make up most of the middle class. The large lower class consists mainly of Indians or blacks. However, social position is not decided only on the basis of ancestry. Being of Indian, black, or mixed descent does not necessarily restrict a person to low social status. In Brazil and the West Indies, for example, many black people have become prominent in the arts, business, politics, or science. In Mexico, having Indian ancestry is a point of pride for people of all walks of life. On the other hand, being

white does not guarantee high social position. White people can be found in all classes. However, there are higher percentages of white people among the lower classes in countries that have small Indian or black populations.

Indians lived in Latin America long before the first white settlers arrived in the late 1400's. The Indians descended from people who migrated to North America from Asia thousands of years ago. Such groups as the Aztec, Inca, and Maya developed highly advanced civilizations. The whites soon conquered most of the Indians and forced them to work in mines or on plantations. Millions of Indians died of harsh treatment, in warfare, or of diseases brought by the whites. In some areas of Latin America, the Indian population almost completely disappeared. To survive, many Indians moved to highland areas or remote forest regions. Today, Indians make up a large percentage of the population in Bolivia, Ecuador, Guatemala, and Peru.

Political Units in Latin America

Independent Countries

Map Key	Name	Capital	Official Language
C5	Antigua and Barbuda	St. John's	English
H4	Argentina	Buenos Aires	Spanish
B4	Bahamas	Nassau	English
C5	Barbados	Bridgetown	English
C3	Belize	Belmopan	English
F5	Bolivia	La Paz; Sucre	Spanish
E6	Brazil	Brasília	Portuguese
G4	Chile	Santiago	Spanish
D4	Colombia	Bogotá	Spanish
C3	Costa Rica	San José	Spanish
B3	Cuba	Havana	Spanish
C5	Dominica	Roseau	English
C4	Dominican Republic	Santo Domingo	Spanish
D3	Ecuador	Quito	Spanish
C3	El Salvador	San Salvador	Spanish
C5	Grenada	St. George's	English
C2	Guatemala	Guatemala City	Spanish
D5	Guyana	Georgetown	English
C4	Haiti	Port-au-Prince	French
C3	Honduras	Tegucigalpa	Spanish
C4	Jamaica	Kingston	English
B2	Mexico	Mexico City	Spanish
C3	Nicaragua	Managua	Spanish
D3	Panama	Panama City	Spanish
G5	Paraguay	Asunción	Spanish
E4	Peru	Lima	Spanish; Quechua
C5	St. Christopher and Nevis	Basseterre	English
C5	St. Lucia	Castries	English
C5	St. Vincent and the Grenadines	Kingstown	English
D6	Suriname	Paramaribo	Dutch
C5	Trinidad and Tobago	Port-of-Spain	English
H6	Uruguay	Montevideo	Spanish
D5	Venezuela	Caracas	Spanish

Other Political Units

Map Key	Name	Capital	Status
B5	Anguilla	The Valley*	British dependency; some self-government
C4	Aruba	Oranjestad	Self-governing part of the Netherlands
B3	Cayman Islands	Georgetown	British dependency
I5	Falkland Islands	Stanley	British dependency
D6	French Guiana	Cayenne	Overseas department of France
C5	Guadeloupe	Basse-Terre	Overseas department of France
C5	Martinique	Fort-de-France	Overseas department of France
C5	Montserrat	Plymouth	British dependency
C4	Netherlands Antilles	Willemstad	Self-governing part of the Netherlands
C5	Puerto Rico	San Juan	United States commonwealth
B4	Turks and Caicos Islands	Grand Turk	British dependency
C5	Virgin Islands, British	Road Town	British dependency; some self-government
C5	Virgin Islands, United States	Charlotte Amalie	U.S. organized unincorporated territory

Each independent country and major dependency has a separate article in WORLD BOOK.

*Unofficial

Latin America
Political Map

⊛ Capital

• Other city or town

▲ Mountain

〜 River

Abbreviations on map
(Fr.)............France   (Neth.) Netherlands
(G.B.) Great Britain   (U.S.) United States

WORLD BOOK map

The area of Latin America is about two and a half times larger than the area of the United States, excluding Alaska and Hawaii.

Distance Scale

| 0 Miles | | 1000 | | 2000 | | 3000 | | 4000 | | 5000 |

| 0 Kilometers 1000 | 2000 | 3000 | 4000 | 5000 | 6000 | 7000 | 8000 |

Whites. Most white Latin Americans are of European descent. At first, nearly all the region's white settlers came from Spain or Portugal. But since the early 1800's, Latin America has attracted numerous immigrants from other European nations. Large numbers of people from France, Germany, Great Britain, Italy, the Netherlands, and Poland have settled in Latin America. Today, most of the people of Argentina, Costa Rica, and Uruguay are whites. Brazil and Chile also have large white populations.

Blacks were brought from Africa to Latin America as slaves from the 1500's to the 1800's. Europeans brought millions of black people to work on plantations in the West Indies and in coastal areas on the mainland of Central and South America. Today, most of the people of Barbados, Haiti, and Jamaica are blacks. Many other parts of the West Indies—as well as some tropical lowland areas of Central and South America—also have large numbers of blacks.

People of Mixed Ancestry. Through the centuries, many whites, blacks, and Indians in Latin America have intermarried. As a result, most Latin Americans are of mixed ancestry. The largest groups are *mestizos* (people of mixed Indian and white descent) and *mulattoes* (people of mixed black and white descent). Mestizos make up a majority of the population in El Salvador, Honduras, Nicaragua, Colombia, Mexico, Paraguay, and Venezuela. Mulattoes are numerous in Brazil, Panama, and the West Indies.

Languages. Most Latin Americans speak the language of the European nation that colonized their counry. Nearly two-thirds of the people speak Spanish. It is the official language of Cuba, the Dominican Republic, Mexico, and most countries in Central and South America. About a third of all Latin Americans speak Portuguese, the official language of Brazil. French is the official language of Haiti, and Dutch is the official language of Suriname. English is the official language of Belize, Guyana, and other West Indian nations formerly ruled by Great Britain. Many Latin Americans speak a dialect of their country's official language or a mixture of languages.

Many Indians in Latin America speak their traditional languages. In Paraguay, an Indian tongue called Guaraní is as widely used as Spanish, the nation's official language. Peru has two official languages. That country's chief Indian tongue, Quechua, is an official language along with Spanish.

Where the People of Latin America Live

The population of Latin America is distributed very unevenly. This map shows that most of the people live near the coasts and in the highland regions of Mexico and the Andes Mountains of western South America. Heavily populated areas are shown in darker colors. The map also shows the location of Latin America's largest cities.

Major Urban Centers

● More than 5 million inhabitants

● 2 to 5 million inhabitants

○ 1 to 2 million inhabitants

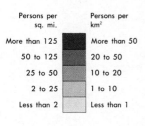

Persons per sq. mi.	Persons per km²
More than 125	More than 50
50 to 125	20 to 50
25 to 50	10 to 20
2 to 25	1 to 10
Less than 2	Less than 1

WORLD BOOK map

Life styles in urban areas of Latin America contrast sharply with those in rural areas. City life moves at a fast pace. Large cities are the centers of political, economic, and intellectual life. They offer a variety of exciting cultural and recreational activities. Although a great many urban dwellers are poor, a growing number of city people enjoy a good standard of living. Life in Latin America's rural areas has changed little over the centuries. In most countries, a relatively few wealthy people or large corporations own much of the land. Most rural people work long hours on huge plantations for low wages. Many of them live in miserable poverty.

City Life. In 1940, about 65 per cent of the people of Latin America lived in rural areas. Today, about 70 per cent live in urban areas. Latin America has more than 20 metropolitan areas with populations of over a million. Mexico City and its suburbs make up the world's largest metropolitan area. It has more than 14 million people. Three other metropolitan areas in Latin America also rank among the world's biggest, with more than 9 million people each. They are São Paulo, Brazil; Buenos Aires, Argentina; and Rio de Janeiro, Brazil.

In many ways, large cities in Latin America resemble those in the United States and Canada. Steel and glass skyscrapers rise in busy commercial and financial districts. Tall apartment buildings line broad boulevards. Elegant shops, restaurants, bars, and nightclubs attract large numbers of customers. Cars and trucks jam wide expressways at rush hours. Modern bus and subway systems carry millions of people to and from work.

In the old sections of many Latin-American cities, Spanish-style buildings stand crowded together along narrow cobblestone streets. The buildings are made of stone or adobe, and many have iron grillwork over the windows. Government agencies have purchased many such buildings and restored them for use as museums.

Wealthy city dwellers in Latin America include bankers, industrialists, military and political leaders, and owners of large agricultural enterprises who prefer to live in the city. These people make up only a small percentage of the population, but they largely control the economic and political systems in most countries. The rich live in luxurious city apartments or in suburban mansions with swimming pools. Many wealthy people travel widely and send their children to universities in the United States.

All large Latin-American cities have a growing middle class. It consists of professional people, government employees, skilled office and factory workers, and owners of small businesses. Most middle-class families live in comfortable apartments or small single-family houses in the suburbs. They can afford a car, nice clothes, and regular vacations.

Latin America's big cities, like large cities in many other parts of the world, face such serious problems as air and water pollution, overcrowding, housing shortages, and high crime rates. Poverty and unemployment are widespread in Latin-American cities. Millions of poor rural people have moved to the cities to look for jobs. Many of these people cannot find work because they lack the necessary skills and education. Most of those who have jobs earn a low income.

Most poor city dwellers live in the slums that surround many of Latin America's large cities. In some cities, more than a fourth of the people live in slums. Families live crowded together in shacks made of cardboard, wood, and tin on land they do not own. Most slums lack electricity, running water, and sewers. Millions of slum children have been abandoned by their parents because they cannot feed or clothe them. These homeless children wander the streets and must beg, steal, or take odd jobs to survive.

A number of Latin-American governments have torn down slums and replaced them with low-cost public housing. But in many cities, the construction cannot keep up with the rapidly increasing urban population.

Jeffrey Sylvester, Alpha

Middle-Class Housing in Latin America consists of modern apartment buildings and comfortable single-family homes. Latin-American cities have a growing middle class. The small and large apartment buildings at the left are in a middle-class neighborhood in La Paz, Bolivia.

Many governments are trying to encourage industrial growth in smaller cities to ease the pressure on large urban areas. Public youth centers have taken in many abandoned children. But slums, overcrowding, and poverty remain serious problems.

Rural Life. About 30 per cent of all Latin Americans live in rural areas. The majority of them are poor farmers, often called *campesinos* in Spanish. Most campesinos earn a bare living on huge plantations owned by wealthy people or private corporations. These plantations are called *haciendas* in Spanish-speaking countries and *fazendas* in Portuguese-speaking Brazil.

Most campesinos in the West Indies and tropical coastal areas of the mainland are blacks. They work on plantations that grow bananas, sugar cane, or cotton. Most campesinos who live inland on the mainland are mestizos. Some work on coffee plantations. Others rent or own small plots on which they raise crops and livestock to feed their families. Most of them cannot afford machinery and so use hand tools to work their land.

Many campesinos live in small villages. Early each morning, they walk or ride buses or trucks from their village homes to the fields. Some villages consist of only a few houses crowded together. Larger settlements have a church, a few shops, and government buildings around a public square called a *plaza*. People gather in the plaza for socializing, entertainment, and ceremonies. Many villages also have an open-air market, where people gather on the weekend to buy or sell food or handmade goods and to exchange news.

Most rural houses in Latin America have one or two rooms. In tropical areas, the houses may have walls of wood or dried mud and sticks, dirt floors, and thatch or tin roofs. In mountain villages, most houses are built of stone or adobe and have red tile roofs. On their estates, wealthy landowners live in luxurious mansions. However, many landowners hire managers to run their farms and spend most of their time in cities.

In general, rural people have a much lower standard of living than do city people. Many rural families do not have such conveniences as electricity, indoor plumbing, or a telephone. In addition, many villages lack adequate schools and medical facilities.

The uneven distribution of wealth in Latin America's rural areas has led to serious social and economic problems. In a majority of countries, a small number of wealthy people own nearly all the choice farmland. Most of this land was originally held by the owners' colonial ancestors and is used to grow bananas, coffee, corn, sugar cane, and other export crops. Most campesinos own no land. Those who own or can rent small plots scratch out a living from the poor soil. Despairing of getting ahead in the country, many campesinos have flocked to the cities to seek jobs.

Since the mid-1900's, many Latin-American governments have tried to improve rural life so that people will not move to already crowded cities. Some governments have established land reform programs that buy large estates and divide them into small plots for distribution to poor farmers. Many governments have built roads and extended electricity and other modern conveniences to thousands of towns and villages. The improved roads have opened up uninhabited areas to settlers. Since the 1960's, many families have moved from economically depressed rural areas to new settlements. However, a number of the settlements failed because of the high cost of making the poor soil more productive.

Family Life has always been extremely important in Latin-American culture. Strong feelings of loyalty and cooperation bind together not only parents and children but also grandparents, aunts, uncles, and cousins. Such feelings are often shared with friends and business associates. This *extended family* provides its members with financial help, security, and social life.

The typical Latin-American household consists of parents, children, and grandparents. Some households

David Mangurian

Sprawling Slums surround many large Latin-American cities. Such areas have grown as millions of poor rural people have moved to the cities to seek a better life. At the left, many poor families live crowded together in crude wooden shacks in a slum in São Paulo, Brazil.

Odyssey Productions

Chip and Rosa Maria Peterson

Preparing Tortillas (pancakes made from corn flour) is a daily task for these Mexican women. Many people in Mexico and Central America eat tortillas at every meal. Most Latin Americans cannot afford meat often, and grain is their chief food.

Outdoor Markets like this one in Riobamba, Ecuador, can be found throughout Latin America.

also include other family members. Generally, the man who contributes most to the family's economic support acts as head of the household. However, women make most household decisions. Children learn obedience toward their parents, and both children and adults are expected to show respect for their elders.

Traditionally, only Latin-American men were expected to have jobs outside the home. Women remained at home to care for their families. Many women, especially in rural areas, still follow this tradition. Since the mid-1900's, however, increasing educational and career opportunities have become available to women. As a result, a growing number of women, particularly in urban areas, now work outside the home. By the early 1960's, women in all Latin-American countries had gained the right to vote. Some women take an active role in politics, and women have held high government posts in several Latin-American countries.

Among Indians and blacks in Latin America, feelings of loyalty and kinship typically extend beyond the family to the community. Most Indians and blacks are fiercely proud of their ethnic heritage. Many live in small communities and work for common goals instead of personal enrichment. Many Indians and blacks take more pride in being a member of their ethnic group or tribe than in being a citizen of their country.

Clothing. Clothing styles in Latin America vary from region to region, depending on climate and custom. Many city people wear clothing like that worn in the United States and Canada. But many villagers prefer traditional clothing styles. On holidays and other special occasions, many Latin Americans wear traditional costumes, which commonly feature bright colors and bold patterns. For pictures of these traditional costumes, see the article CLOTHING.

Rural Latin Americans who live in tropical climates prefer lightweight cotton clothing. Men usually wear loose-fitting shirts. Most women dress in long skirts and blouses. People in mountain villages need heavier clothing for protection against the cold. Both men and women wear *ponchos* (blankets with a slit in the middle for the head). Women also dress in full skirts and long-sleeved blouses. They commonly drape brightly colored shawls around their shoulders. In the highlands, men wear coarse handwoven shirts and baggy pants. Farmers wear straw or felt hats for protection against the sun while working in the fields. Rural people generally go barefoot or wear sandals, many of which have soles made from old automobile tires.

Clothing styles in some parts of Latin America are highly distinctive. For example, Indian women who live in the highlands of Bolivia wear black derbies. The *gauchos* (cowboys) of Argentina and Uruguay dress in ponchos, baggy trousers tucked into low boots, and wide-brimmed hats. Many Indian groups wear brightly colored clothing with traditional patterns. Among such groups, each village has its own special colors and designs, which have been used for hundreds of years. Numerous Indian women wear braided belts around their waists. They often use the belts as headbands to hold in place bundles that they carry on their heads.

Food and Drink. Grain is the chief food of most Latin Americans. Many people in Mexico and Central America serve *tortillas* (pancakes made from corn flour) at most meals. Beans and rice form a major part of the diet of most West Indians. People who live in the mountainous areas of South America commonly eat potatoes. People in tropical areas eat a starchy root called *cassava*. In Argentina and Uruguay, people eat many foods made from wheat.

Most Latin Americans eat little meat because they cannot afford it. However, people eat a great deal of beef in the cattle-raising countries of Argentina and Uruguay. People who live along rivers or near the oceans commonly eat fish and shellfish. Many Latin-American dishes are highly seasoned with onions and hot peppers.

91

In tropical areas, the people enjoy such fruits as bananas, mangoes, oranges, and pineapples. Latin Americans drink coffee, a variety of fruit juices, and a kind of tea called *maté*. Favorite alcoholic beverages include beer, rum, wine, and *aguardiente*, a brandylike drink made from sugar cane.

Middle- and upper-class Latin Americans enjoy a much wider choice of food than poor people can afford. They regularly eat a variety of meats as well as other fresh and processed foods. The diet of most poor Latin Americans consists mainly of starchy foods and lacks important nutritional elements. Many poor people in rural areas and urban slums suffer from malnutrition.

Recreation. Latin Americans enjoy a wide variety of outdoor activities. Soccer is the region's most popular sport. Many boys and girls begin playing soccer as soon as they can walk. Hundreds of thousands of spectators jam huge stadiums throughout Latin America to watch professional soccer games. Soccer stars have become national heroes. The Brazilian star Pelé won fame as the world's greatest soccer player in the 1960's.

Baseball is especially popular in parts of the West Indies and in mainland countries that border the Caribbean Sea. A number of Latin Americans have become stars on professional baseball teams in the United States and Canada. Cricket is popular in the Bahamas, Jamaica, and Trinidad and Tobago. Bullfights draw large crowds in Colombia, Mexico, Peru, and Venezuela. Other popular sports include automobile racing, basketball, horse racing, and volleyball.

In coastal areas, large crowds regularly flock to beaches on weekends. Favorite activities include boating, fishing, swimming, surfing, and water-skiing. Many families take overnight camping trips to national forests. During the winter months, well-to-do people enjoy skiing at beautiful mountain resorts.

Latin Americans take part in a number of other leisure activities. Visiting with family and friends is a major pastime. Many people enjoy listening to the radio or watching television. In cities, popular pastimes include visiting parks and museums and attending plays, concerts, and motion pictures. Large numbers of Latin Americans take part in colorful *fiestas* (festivals), which are held on national or religious holidays. Many fiestas feature colorful parades with richly decorated floats, costumed street dancers, lively musical performances, games, and fireworks.

Religion. Most Latin Americans are Christians. The great majority are Roman Catholics, but a growing number belong to Protestant churches. The laws of all Latin-American countries guarantee freedom of worship, though some countries officially support the Roman Catholic Church. Other religious groups in Latin America include Buddhists, Hindus, and Jews. Some Indian and black peoples worship the gods of their own cultures.

Roman Catholicism. The early Spanish and Portuguese explorers brought the Roman Catholic religion to much of Latin America and converted many Indians to Catholicism. Today, about 80 per cent of the people belong to the Roman Catholic Church. However, the number of Catholics who actively practice their religion

Robert Frerk

Soccer is the favorite sport in Latin America. Many of the region's large cities have huge stadiums, like this one in Mexico City, which draw overflow crowds for championship matches.

varies from country to country. Many people of Indian or black African ancestry combine Catholic religious practices with spiritual beliefs of their own traditions.

In some Latin-American countries, the Roman Catholic Church greatly influences the daily lives of the people. Church officials represent a wide range of political opinion and participate in all levels of government. They take an active role on zoning and planning boards and in human welfare agencies. In addition to performing their religious duties, many neighborhood and village priests work for social reforms on behalf of the poor in their districts.

During European rule, the Roman Catholic Church exercised great political power throughout Latin America. The Catholic Church also dominated education and owned huge estates and other property. During the early 1800's, many Latin-American colonies won their freedom. Some members of the clergy supported the independence movement. However, many others opposed it. After independence, many Latin-American governments took steps to decrease the Catholic Church's power. They seized much of its property and limited or took away its control of education, hospitals, cemeteries, and public charities.

During the early 1900's, the Catholic Church became closely linked to military leaders and wealthy landowners who controlled many Latin-American governments. Since the late 1960's, however, the church has become increasingly active in the fight for civil and human rights and social justice. Many Catholic officials have sharply criticized Latin-American governments for failing to provide adequate services for the poor. This criticism has led to serious clashes between religious and political leaders in a number of countries. See ROMAN CATHOLIC CHURCH (In Latin America).

Protestantism. Protestants make up about 5 per cent of Latin America's population. They include Baptists, Episcopalians, Lutherans, and Methodists. Many Protestants live on West Indian islands formerly ruled by Great Britain and in the Netherlands Antilles.

Since the late 1960's, millions of Latin Americans have joined a variety of churches based on *Pentecostalism*. Pentecostalism is an emotional form of worship that emphasizes prayer (see PENTECOSTAL CHURCHES). Most new members of Pentecostal churches are former Catholics who had quit practicing that religion. Many of them disagreed with the Catholic Church's active involvement in social reform movements. The Church of Jesus Christ of Latter-day Saints has also won many converts. It and the Pentecostal churches are the fastest-growing religious groups in Latin America.

Education in Latin America has improved greatly since 1960. Larger percentages of Latin Americans than ever are attending elementary schools, high schools, and colleges. In many countries, the *literacy rate* (percentage of people aged 15 or older who can read and write) has increased enormously. In such nations as Argentina, Chile, Cuba, and Uruguay, the literacy rate is more than 90 per cent. Many governments have set up programs to teach uneducated adults to read and write. In spite of the progress in education, serious problems remain. In such countries as Guatemala and Haiti, the literacy rate is less than 50 per cent. Throughout Latin America, educational levels are generally lower in rural areas than they are in the cities.

Nearly all Latin-American nations require children to complete elementary school. But many students, particularly in rural areas and urban slums, cannot fulfill this requirement because of a shortage of schools, educational materials, and qualified teachers. Numerous other

Milt and Joan Mann

Public Education has become increasingly available to Latin Americans since 1960. The high school students above are attending a chemistry class in Oruro, Bolivia.

students must leave school after a few years to look for work and help support their families. All Latin-American governments have built schools and sponsored programs to extend education to more people. However, the population is growing faster than schools can be built or teachers trained. In addition, the costs of education are constantly increasing.

In many Latin-American countries, students can receive a free public education from kindergarten through college. However, large numbers of students, especially from middle- and upper-class families, go to private schools, which charge tuition. The private schools also receive government funds. The Catholic Church operates many private schools in Latin America. For many years, private schools provided a better education than did public schools. But increased financial support has enabled many public schools to offer an education at least equal to that of private schools.

Latin America has a number of excellent public and private colleges and universities. Four of the universities date from the 1500's. Santo Domingo University in the Dominican Republic was founded in 1538. It is the oldest institution of higher learning in the Western Hemisphere. The National University of San Marcos in Lima, Peru, and the National Autonomous University of Mexico in Mexico City date from 1551. Saint Thomas University in Bogotá, Colombia, dates from 1580.

Enrollment in Latin America's colleges and universities has increased greatly since the 1960's. In several nations, the number of qualified high school graduates who want to attend public universities exceeds the number that these schools can enroll. Many Latin-American countries have a shortage of skilled workers, scientists, teachers, and other professionals. To meet the need for such workers, many nations have built technical schools that prepare young people for careers in agriculture, business, and engineering.

Latin America has some fine public and school libraries. For information about libraries in Latin America, see LIBRARY (Latin America).

George Holton, Photo Researchers

Religious Festivals, called *fiestas,* are an important part of Latin-American life. These Guatemalans, wearing colorful traditional costumes, are celebrating the fiesta of Saint Thomas.

93

The artistic traditions of Latin America date back thousands of years to the region's ancient Indian cultures. The ruins of magnificent temples and other structures built by advanced Indian civilizations still stand in such countries as Mexico, Peru, and Guatemala. The Indians also produced beautiful textiles, jewelry, pottery, and other handicraft items. When Spanish and Portuguese colonists began arriving in Latin America during the late 1400's, they brought their European artistic traditions with them. European styles dominated the region's arts for hundreds of years. After the colonists imported black slaves, African traditions influenced such arts as popular music and dancing. During the 1800's and 1900's, various Latin-American arts began to develop a strong national character, rather than reflect European styles.

Architecture. Highly developed Indian civilizations constructed enormous buildings and impressive cities before the first Europeans reached Latin America. The greatest Indian architects were the Aztec and Toltec in Mexico, the Maya in Mexico and Central America, and the Inca in the Andes Mountains of western South America. The outstanding Aztec, Maya, and Toltec structures were huge stone pyramids topped by temples. Inca architects designed cities that clung to mountainsides. The stones for Inca buildings were cut so precisely that they fit together without cement. See ARCHITECTURE (Pre-Columbian Architecture).

Tom Hollyman, Photo Researchers

Magnificent Religious Art of the Spanish colonial period can still be found in many Latin-American churches. The elaborate altar above is in La Compañía, a cathedral in Quito, Ecuador.

The first major buildings constructed by Europeans in Latin America had a religious or governmental purpose. Some of the finest structures were huge cathedrals and sprawling monasteries that included a church, chapels, living quarters, and a courtyard surrounded by high, thick stone walls. Beginning in the late 1600's, many cathedrals, palaces, and mansions were built in the *baroque* style of architecture. This style featured elaborately carved columns, ornate sculptures, and lavish use of colored tile, gold, and silver.

Modern Latin-American architecture combines simple geometric forms with bold decorations and curving shapes inspired by the region's Indian and baroque heritage. Many architects cover all or part of their buildings with stunning paintings or *mosaics* (designs or pictures made of pieces of stone or other material). Such buildings can be found at the National Autonomous University of Mexico in Mexico City and at the Central University of Venezuela in Caracas. The great Brazilian architect Oscar Niemeyer created strikingly modern designs for buildings in Brasília, the capital of Brazil.

Literature. Latin-American literature includes works by writers from the Spanish-speaking countries and Puerto Rico and from Portuguese-speaking Brazil. For a discussion of the region's rich literary tradition, see LATIN-AMERICAN LITERATURE.

Painting. Precolonial Latin-American painting includes brilliantly colored murals by Indian artists. Some

Fred Fehl

Spectacular Folk Dances are performed by the Ballet Folklórico of Mexico. The company preserves the traditional dances of the Indians of Mexico and the settlers from Spain.

of these murals decorate temples and feature lifelike figures taking part in battles and ceremonies. Some Indian groups also painted pottery and sculptures.

During colonial times, many Latin-American painters imitated European styles. Most artists painted pictures with religious themes for churches and cathedrals. The leading centers of painting during the colonial period included Mexico City; Quito, Ecuador; and Cusco, Peru.

About 1900, Latin-American artists began to develop painting styles that were distinctly Latin American. Many of them adopted the vivid colors and bold designs that stemmed from the region's Indian heritage. Such Mexican artists as José Clemente Orozco, Diego Rivera, and David Siqueiros became famous for their gigantic murals. The murals portray scenes from Mexican history, especially the struggle for independence and Mexico's 1910 revolution. The Brazilian painter Cândido Portinari used modern abstract styles to create powerful pictures of everyday life in Brazil. In Haiti, an outstanding group of self-taught artists, including Hector Hyppolite and Philomé Obin, has produced imaginative scenes of local life and folklore.

Sculpture. Before the Europeans arrived, Latin-American Indians created many beautiful sculptures, ranging from masks and statuettes to huge, elaborately carved panels and monuments. Indian sculptors carved a large number of their works from stone, but they also used clay, jade, gold, and wood. Many of their sculptures depicted gods and religious symbols and were used to decorate temples and religious centers. See SCULPTURE (American Indian).

Early colonial sculpture consisted mainly of architectural decoration on churches. Much of the carving was in the *plateresque* style, a form of stone design that resembled the delicate work of *plateros* (silversmiths). The Brazilian sculptor Antônio Francisco Lisbôa, also known as Aleijadinho, created some of the finest works

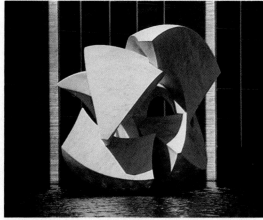

Loren McIntyre

Modern Latin-American Sculpture differs greatly from the ornate style of colonial times. This marble work, titled *Meteor,* was made in the 1960's by Bruno Giorgi, a Brazilian sculptor.

of the late 1700's and early 1800's. He carved magnificent religious figures from wood and stone for churches in the Brazilian state of Minas Gerais.

Since the mid-1800's, much Latin-American sculpture has reflected a strong national pride and a growing interest in the region's Indian heritage. Many sculptors have produced impressive monuments to heroes of Latin America's revolutions and wars of independence.

Music. Latin Americans enjoy many kinds of music. Street performances of live music are common in the region. Performances of traditional Indian and black music and Western classical music draw large and enthusiastic crowds. Rock music is also popular among young Latin Americans.

Indian music of Latin America dates from precolonial times. It played a major part in most Indian ceremonies

The People Go to the University—the University Goes to the People (1956); Carter, Black Star

Colorful Mexican Murals became internationally famous during the 1900's. This mural by David Siqueiros decorates the Administration Building of the National Autonomous University of Mexico in Mexico City.

Coumbite (1971), an oil painting on masonite by Gerard Valcin; Flagg Tanning Corporation

Latin-American Painting by Self-Taught Artists in Haiti draws upon themes from local life and folklore. The painting above shows workers on a Haitian plantation.

and remains important in areas that have a large Indian population. European settlers introduced Western musical forms and instruments into Latin America. *Mestizo music* combines Indian tunes with lively Spanish strains. Music in the West Indies and coastal mainland areas reflects African traditions introduced by black plantation slaves. Complicated African rhythms can be heard in the *calypso* music of Trinidad and in the *samba* and *bossa nova* styles of Brazil.

In playing traditional Latin-American music, musicians use various special instruments. These instruments include wooden and steel drums; the *cuatro* (a four-stringed guitar); the *marimba* (an instrument similar to the xylophone); and *maracas* (rattles made from gourds). Much traditional music also features flutes, harps, horns, violins, and tambourines.

Many large cities in Latin America have symphony orchestras, chamber groups, and opera companies. These organizations perform the works of the great European classical composers. European styles strongly influenced the region's classical music until the 1800's. A number of Latin-American composers then began to express their national heritage in their music. During the 1900's, such internationally known composers as Heitor Villa-Lobos of Brazil and Carlos Chávez of Mexico used folk melodies and rhythms as well as traditional instruments in their works.

Dancing has long been important in the lives of Latin Americans. Indians and blacks developed dances to accompany religious worship, to celebrate such events as birth and marriage, and to mourn the dead. European immigrants introduced the folk dances of their native countries into Latin America. Dancing continues to play a major role in the religious ceremonies and community celebrations of many Latin Americans. It is also a highly popular form of recreation. In many countries,

national dance companies stage colorful productions of traditional folk dances. One of the most famous companies is the Ballet Folklórico of Mexico, which has performed in many parts of the world.

Most Latin-American countries have their own traditional dances. Many of these dances include steps from Spanish or Portuguese folk dances. For example, the Spanish *zapateado* (heel-beating steps) are part of the *cueca* of Bolivia and Chile; the *joropo* of Venezuela; and the *jarabe tapatío*, or *Mexican hat dance*, of Mexico. In the West Indies, African and Spanish influences were combined in such ballroom dances as the *rumba* and *cha-cha*. The rumba, cha-cha, and some other Latin-American dances, including the Argentine *tango*, Brazilian *samba*, and Cuban *conga*, are popular outside Latin America.

Handicrafts. Many handcrafted items made by Latin Americans combine artistic beauty with practical use. This type of art is called *artes populares* (popular arts) and is part of daily life in much of Latin America. Superb craftwork can be found in tools and household items as well as in ornaments and religious objects. Latin Americans have long been famous for their excellent glassware, metalwork, pottery, and textiles.

Most handicrafts are inexpensive. Many craftworkers produce these items in their homes using local materials. For example, Indians of the Andes Mountains weave wool from such animals as alpacas and llamas into beautifully designed ponchos and sweaters. In the West Indies, people make dishes for baking seafood from sea shells and carve coconut shells into serving dishes. In the tropical lowlands of Central America, people make lightweight chairs from sturdy plant fibers.

Many handcrafted items are decorated with such folk art figures as chickens, dogs, and frogs or with Indian religious symbols. The *eye of god*, an Indian religious symbol, is a popular wall decoration. It consists of colored threads woven in a special pattern around crossed sticks.

Odyssey Productions

Handicrafts are practiced widely in Latin America. The Indians are especially famous for their metalwork, pottery, and textiles. This Zapotec Indian of Mexico is weaving brightly colored cloth.

This section traces the broad outlines of Latin-American history. For the history of a particular country, see the WORLD BOOK article on that country. See also the articles listed under "Biographies" and "History" in the *Related Articles* at the end of this article.

The First Inhabitants of Latin America were American Indians. Scientists believe that the ancestors of these Indians came to North America from Asia more than 20,000 years ago. At that time, a land bridge connected Asia and North America where the Bering Strait now separates Siberia and Alaska. The people from Asia probably crossed the land bridge, following the animals they hunted. The descendants of these people became known as Indians. By about 6000 B.C., the Indians had spread throughout much of the Americas to the southern tip of South America.

For thousands of years, the Indians lived in small groups. They traveled continuously in search of animals and wild plants for food. Eventually, some Indians began to farm the land. The Indians were the first people to grow cacao, corn, kidney and Lima beans, peanuts, potatoes, squash, tobacco, and tomatoes. Indians who farmed could remain in one place and produce enough food for many others. They built permanent houses and settled in small villages. As the Indian population increased, some villages grew into towns and cities, and several advanced civilizations developed.

One of the earliest known Indian civilizations was

Odyssey Productions

Maya Ruins include the Temple of the Giant Jaguar, *above,* in Guatemala. The Maya civilization reached its height in Mexico and Guatemala between about A.D. 250 and 900.

Important Dates in Latin America

c. 6000 B.C. Indians had spread throughout much of the Americas to the southern tip of South America.

A.D. 250-900 The civilization of the Maya Indians, located in southern Mexico and northern Central America, reached its peak.

1400's-early 1500's The Aztec in Mexico and the Inca in western South America controlled large empires.

1492 Christopher Columbus became the first European to reach Latin America.

1494 Spain and Portugal agreed to the Line of Demarcation, which fixed their areas of rule in Latin America.

Early 1500's Spanish troops conquered most of Latin America's Indian civilizations.

Early 1800's Most Latin-American colonies gained independence.

Late 1800's Cooperation between Latin-American countries and the United States, called *Pan-Americanism*, began to grow.

Mid-1900's Violence erupted in many Latin-American countries as rival political groups struggled for power.

1959 Fidel Castro established a Communist state in Cuba.

1960's-1980's Military governments controlled several Latin-American countries.

that of the Olmec. The Olmec civilization thrived in what is now eastern Mexico from about 1200 to 100 B.C. The Maya civilization of southern Mexico and northern Central America reached its peak between about A.D. 250 and 900. The Maya produced magnificent architecture, painting, pottery, and sculpture. They developed a calendar and an advanced system of writing. The Maya also had great knowledge of astronomy, which helped them accurately predict growing seasons for their crops. They also constructed a vast system of underground irrigation canals.

The Toltec controlled central Mexico from about 900 to 1200, when they were conquered by the Aztec. The Aztec civilization flourished until the early 1500's. Both the Toltec and the Aztec constructed gigantic pyramids and other structures, many of which still survive. The Inca ruled a huge empire along the west coast of South America during the 1400's and early 1500's. The Inca were superb architects and farmers. They built an extensive system of roads through the Andes Mountains to connect the distant cities of their empire. Inca farmers cut terraces into steep hillsides and brought water to these plots through irrigation canals.

European Discovery and Exploration. In 1492, Christopher Columbus, an Italian navigator in the service of Spain, became the first European to reach Latin America. Columbus sailed west from Spain in hope of finding a short sea route to eastern Asia. He landed on the island of San Salvador in the West Indies and believed that he had reached Asia.

After Columbus returned to Spain, news of his discovery created great excitement in Europe. To prevent disputes between Portugal and Spain over which country could claim the newly discovered lands, Pope Alexander VI drew the Line of Demarcation in 1493. This imaginary north-south line lay about 350 miles (563 kilometers) west of two island groups in the North Atlantic

Ocean—the Azores and the Cape Verde Islands. All lands west of the line belonged to Spain, and all lands to the east belonged to Portugal. However, the Portuguese soon became dissatisfied because they thought the line gave Spain too much territory. In 1494, Portugal and Spain signed the Treaty of Tordesillas, which moved the line about 1,295 miles (2,084 kilometers) west. As a result, Portugal gained the right to settle the eastern section of what is now Brazil. Portugal took possession of this area in 1500, when a Portuguese navigator named Pedro Álvares Cabral landed on the east coast of Brazil.

Columbus made four voyages to Latin America between 1492 and 1502. During these voyages, he explored many islands in the West Indies and the coasts of what are now Honduras, Costa Rica, Nicaragua, Panama, and Venezuela. Other explorers soon followed Columbus to Latin America. The Europeans quickly realized that the region was not Asia but a new land. Mapmakers named the land *America* in honor of the Italian-born explorer Amerigo Vespucci. Vespucci made several voyages to Latin America in the late 1490's and early 1500's for Spain and Portugal. He was

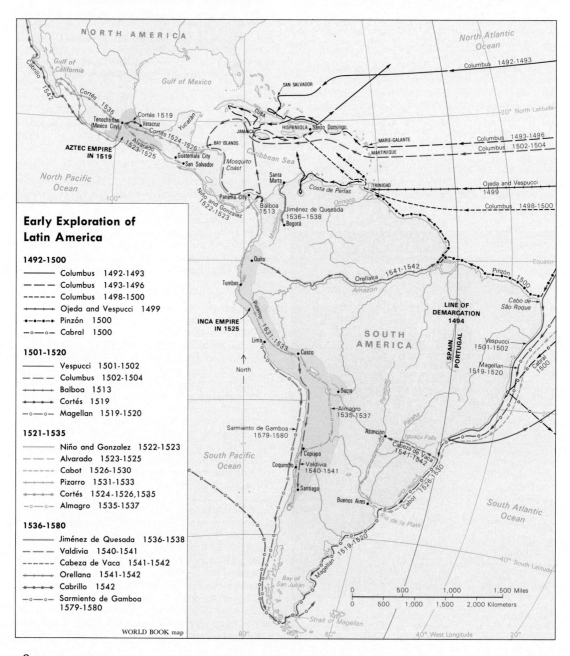

Early Exploration of Latin America

1492-1500

——— Columbus 1492-1493
– – – Columbus 1493-1496
- - - - Columbus 1498-1500
+—+—+ Ojeda and Vespucci 1499
•–•–•– Pinzón 1500
–o–o– Cabral 1500

1501-1520

——— Vespucci 1501-1502
– – – Columbus 1502-1504
+—+—+ Balboa 1513
•–•–• Cortés 1519
–o–o– Magellan 1519-1520

1521-1535

——— Niño and Gonzalez 1522-1523
– – – Alvarado 1523-1525
- - - - Cabot 1526-1530
+—+—+ Pizarro 1531-1533
•–•–• Cortés 1524-1526,1535
–o–o– Almagro 1535-1537

1536-1580

——— Jiménez de Quesada 1536-1538
– – – Valdivia 1540-1541
- - - - Cabeza de Vaca 1541-1542
+—+—+ Orellana 1541-1542
•–•–• Cabrillo 1542
–o–o– Sarmiento de Gamboa 1579-1580

WORLD BOOK map

one of the first explorers to state that the region was a "New World."

In 1513, the Spanish adventurer Vasco Núñez de Balboa crossed Panama and became the first European to see the eastern shore of the Pacific Ocean. His discovery provided additional proof that America was a separate continent between Europe and Asia. In 1520, the Portuguese navigator Ferdinand Magellan became the first European to discover the waterway that connects the Atlantic and Pacific oceans at the southern tip of South America. He sailed down the east coast of South America and through the strait that now bears his name.

The Conquest of the Indians began soon after the Europeans arrived in Latin America. By the mid-1500's, a small group of Spanish adventurers known as *conquistadors* (conquerors) had defeated the great Indian civilizations and given Spain a firm hold on most of Latin America. The conquistadors led relatively small but well-equipped forces. They easily defeated large armies of Indians, who had never seen guns or horses.

The first major conquests of the Indians occurred in Mexico and Central America. The conquistador Hernando Cortés landed in Mexico in 1519. By 1521, he had conquered the great Aztec empire. The following year, another conquistador, known as Pedrarias, conquered the Indians of what are now Costa Rica and Nicaragua. In 1523, Pedro de Alvarado, one of Cortés' officers, conquered what are now El Salvador and Guatemala. These conquistadors, together with Balboa in Panama, secured Central America for Spain.

In 1531, the conquistador Francisco Pizarro sailed south from Panama to what is now Peru. During the next three years, his army marched about 3,000 miles (4,800 kilometers) through the Andes Mountains and conquered the huge Inca empire. Pizarro founded Lima in 1535. The city became Peru's capital and the center of Spanish government in South America. One of the few areas the Spanish failed to conquer was southern Chile, where the Araucanian Indians resisted for more than 300 years.

Colonial Rule. Even before the military conquest of Latin America was complete, Spanish and Portuguese settlers began pouring into the region. Many of them came in search of adventure and mineral wealth. Others established plantations to grow sugar cane, tobacco, and other crops to export to Europe. Much of Latin America was colonized by the time the first European settlers arrived on the Atlantic coast of North America in the mid-1500's. During the 1600's, the Dutch, English, and French established small colonies in Latin America, chiefly in the West Indies.

Large numbers of Latin-American Indians died of diseases brought by Europeans or were killed in warfare. During the early 1500's, Spain established the *encomienda* system in Latin America. Under this system, colonists were granted large tracts of land plus the Indians who lived on the land. The colonists collected tribute in the form of slave labor from the Indians, making them farm the land or work in the mines. In return, the colonists were supposed to protect the Indians and convert them to Christianity. However, many colonists treated the Indians cruelly. Several outstanding Roman Catho-

Granger Collection

The Spanish Conquest of the Aztec Indians of Mexico was completed in 1521. With their horses and superior weapons, the Spanish easily conquered the Aztec. This drawing by an Aztec artist shows the Spanish and their Indian allies battling Aztec warriors.

lic missionaries, especially Bartolomé de Las Casas, pleaded for more humane treatment of the Indians. But millions of Indians died from overwork and harsh treatment. As the Indian population declined, Europeans began to import black Africans as slaves (see SLAVERY).

Power in colonial Latin America rested with three groups. One group consisted of government officials appointed by European rulers. In each colony, these officials controlled a highly centralized government. This type of administration, in which a few individuals held power, enabled the Europeans to govern the colonies for one main purpose—to exploit their natural resources to the fullest.

The Roman Catholic clergy was another power group. The clergy controlled education in the colonies and was charged with converting the Indians and blacks to Christianity.

The third power group in colonial Latin America consisted of landowners and mine operators. Many settlements in Latin America sprang up near choice farmland or important mineral resources. As a result, numerous communities lay far from the centers of colonial government. In many such cases, the local landowners or mine operators held economic and political control. Some owners and operators used their power justly, but others were ruthless dictators.

Europe profited tremendously from Latin America's mineral wealth and agricultural products. Ships filled with silver and gold regularly departed from Latin-American ports for Europe. Agricultural exports included coffee, cotton, sugar cane, and tobacco. Over the years, Spain's economy became increasingly dependent on Latin America. The country suffered hardship if vessels from the colonies carrying valuable cargo were sunk in Atlantic storms or raided by pirates.

The Beginnings of Colonial Unrest. Colonial rule of Latin America lasted about 300 years. During that time, discontent among the colonists gradually grew. Many Latin Americans wanted greater control over their economic and political affairs. But the European powers ignored the demands for more self-government until the movement for independence was unstoppable.

The desire for independence among Latin Americans arose for several reasons. The *criollos* (people of Spanish ancestry born in Latin America) resented the fact that officials from Spain held all the top posts in colonial government. These officials looked down on the criollos because they had not been born in Europe.

Dissatisfaction was even greater among Latin Americans of mixed European and Indian ancestry. Many of these *mestizos* had gained wealth and property and wanted to take an active role in colonial government. However, mestizos had little social or political standing among the Europeans who controlled Latin America.

The continual flow of the region's resources to Europe also angered many Latin Americans. Spain and Portugal permitted the colonies to trade only with their mother countries. The colonies could not even trade among themselves. In addition, Spain and Portugal hampered Latin America's economic growth by discouraging the development of manufacturing. The colonial rulers wanted Latin Americans to buy European-made products rather than manufacture products for themselves.

The political and economic injustices suffered by the colonists led to a growing desire for independence in Latin America. Although Spain and Portugal introduced a number of reforms in the colonies before 1800, many Latin Americans still wanted freedom.

The Wars of Independence in Latin America were finally triggered by events in North America and Europe. The success of the Revolutionary War in America (1775-1783) and the ideals of freedom and equality promised by the French Revolution (1789-1799) inspired the unhappy colonists. At the same time, Spain and Portugal were losing their importance as world powers. In 1807, the forces of Napoleon Bonaparte of France invaded and conquered Portugal. The next year, Napoleon drove Ferdinand VII from the Spanish throne and replaced him with his own brother, Joseph Bonaparte. Spain's control over its colonies was thereby weakened, and many Latin Americans took the opportunity to fight for independence.

Mexico began its revolt against Spain in 1810. The struggle was first led by two Roman Catholic priests, Miguel Hidalgo y Costilla and José Mariá Morelos y Pavón. The initial revolt failed, however, and Spanish troops executed both Hidalgo and Morelos. Mexico did not win its independence until 1821.

Central America also gained its freedom from Spain in 1821. Central America had little economic importance, and so Spain largely ignored the area. As a result, Central Americans won their independence without bloodshed. In 1822, Costa Rica, El Salvador, Guatemala,

WORLD BOOK map

In 1790, after about 300 years of colonial rule, five European countries controlled all of Latin America. From then on, revolutions in Latin America weakened European power in the region.

Battle of Junín (1900), an oil painting on canvas by Martin Tovar y Tovar (Angelo Hurtado, Museum of Modern Art of Latin America)

Honduras, and Nicaragua became part of Mexico. In 1823, however, they broke away from Mexico and formed a political union called the United Provinces of Central America. Bitter regional rivalries caused this union to begin to collapse in 1838, and each of the states had become an independent republic by 1841. The territory of Panama was a Colombian province from 1821 until 1903, when it rebelled against Colombia with help from the United States and became an independent country. Belize was a British colony from 1862 to 1981, when it gained independence.

Spanish South America. The two greatest heroes in the fight for independence in Spanish South America were the Venezuelan general Simón Bolívar and the Argentine general José de San Martín. Bolívar helped win freedom for Bolivia, Colombia, Ecuador, Peru, and Venezuela. San Martín fought for the independence of Argentina, Chile, and Peru.

The Venezuelan revolutionist Francisco de Miranda led an unsuccessful revolt against the Spanish in 1806. Bolívar, who had been a follower of Miranda's, launched a new campaign in 1813. His armies fought against the Spanish forces for about 10 years before winning a final, great victory at Ayacucho, Peru, in 1824. The victory assured independence for the Spanish colonies in northern South America.

In the south, landowners in Chile declared their country's freedom in 1810. However, Spanish forces overcame them. Lasting independence was won for Chile in 1818 by armies led by San Martín and the Chilean hero Bernardo O'Higgins. Earlier, in 1816, San Martín had freed Argentina from Spanish rule. His armies later fought for Peru's independence.

Brazil won its freedom from Portugal without firing a shot. When Napoleon invaded Portugal in 1807, the Portuguese ruler, Prince John, fled to Brazil. John returned to Portugal 14 years later, after Napoleon's defeat. He left his son Pedro to govern Brazil. But the Bra-

zilians no longer wanted to be ruled by Europeans. They demanded freedom from Portugal. In 1822, Pedro declared Brazil an independent empire and took the throne as Emperor Pedro I.

The West Indies. In 1791, Toussaint L'Ouverture led black African slaves in Haiti in a revolt against their French rulers. Haiti won its freedom in 1804 and became the first independent nation in Latin America. The Dominican Republic declared its independence in 1844. A revolt broke out against Spanish rule in Cuba in 1895. The United States sided with the Cuban rebels, which led to the Spanish-American War (1898) between Spain and the United States. The United States won the war, and Cuba became a republic in 1902. Under the terms of the peace treaty, Spain also gave up its colony of Puerto Rico to the United States. Most small West Indian islands remained under British, Dutch, or French control until the mid-1900's. Since then, most of these islands have become independent. Many of the others have gained more control over their affairs.

The Problems of Independence. During colonial times, Latin Americans were governed by the laws of distant monarchs and had almost no voice in their own affairs. When they rebelled and established their own countries, they thus had little experience in government. For that reason, some leaders thought it unwise to establish republics in Latin America. But eager patriots, inspired by the French Revolution and the Revolutionary War in America, demanded republican government.

After achieving independence, Latin Americans soon found that it was easier to set up a republican government than to make it work. The inexperience of the new leaders led to violent struggles throughout Latin America. Ambitious dictators seized power in a number of countries. Armies that had fought for independence often helped keep dictators in power. In other countries, wealthy landowners controlled the government.

Immediately upon gaining independence, many

Border Wars broke out between some Latin-American nations after independence. In the War of the Triple Alliance (1865-1870), Argentina, Brazil, and Uruguay defeated Paraguay. Many fierce battles were fought on the Paraguay River, *above*.

Historical Pictures Service

Latin-American republics abolished slavery. By the late 1800's, all the slaves in the region had been freed. However, independence brought little improvement in the lives of most Latin Americans. Wealthy criollos and mestizos took over the established economic, political, and social institutions. Poor mestizos, Indians, and blacks had little, if any, power. For many of these people, life became even harder than it had been under colonial rule.

Border Disputes. Since independence, relations between a number of Latin-American countries have been severely damaged by disagreements over national boundaries. War broke out in 1825 between Argentina and Brazil over disputed territory bordering both countries. A treaty signed three years later established the area as the independent nation of Uruguay. In the War of the Triple Alliance (1865-1870), Argentina, Brazil, and Uruguay defeated Paraguay. The war firmly established the common borders of those countries. About half of Paraguay's population was killed in the conflict. In the War of the Pacific (1879-1883), Chile fought Bolivia and Peru over a nitrate-rich area along the Pacific Ocean. Chile won the war and took possession of the territory, leaving Bolivia without a seacoast. Bolivia has remained landlocked ever since.

From 1932 to 1935, Bolivia and Paraguay fought for control of the Gran Chaco, a lowland region bordering both countries. Most of the area was eventually awarded to Paraguay. Fighting broke out several times during the early 1900's between Peru and Ecuador over a wild, uncharted area of the Amazon River Basin between Ecuador and Brazil. Peru annexed the area in the 1940's, but Ecuador still claims it. In other continuing disputes, Guatemala claims land controlled by Belize, and Venezuela claims about two-thirds of Guyana.

Trade Relations and Economic Developments. Since colonial times, the economies of most Latin-American countries have depended heavily on the export of a few agricultural and mineral products. The exports of some nations consist chiefly of one product—for example, bananas in Honduras; coffee in Colombia; copper in Chile; petroleum in Ecuador, Mexico, and Venezuela; sugar in Cuba and the Dominican Republic; and tin in Bolivia. A drop in the market price for these exports causes severe economic hardships. Since the mid-1900's, many countries have spent large sums of money to develop other industries and so lessen their dependence on agricultural and mineral exports. Many of these countries have received loans from regional and international economic organizations for this purpose. They have also been given direct economic aid from other nations.

In the past, most Latin-American nations imported many manufactured goods from Europe and the United States. Latin-American countries traded relatively little with one another because they produced similar products. With the growth of manufacturing, however, several economic unions have been formed to encourage regional trade. They include the Latin American Integration Association, the Central American Common Market, the Caribbean Community and Common Market, and the Andean Pact. These organizations work to lower trade barriers among the member countries and to promote economic growth in the region.

Before the 1960's, most major industries in Latin America were owned by United States and European companies. Many Latin Americans believed that these foreign businesses were only interested in making huge profits and cared little for the welfare of the region's people. Since the late 1960's, some countries have passed laws prohibiting foreign ownership of certain key industries. The governments of such nations as Bolivia, Guyana, Peru, and Venezuela took control of industries previously owned by U.S. and European companies. However, most countries also encourage foreign investment in industries that require modernization.

In 1975, most of the region's independent nations joined the Latin American Economic System. The major goals of this organization include the promotion of regional economic interests and the establishment of locally owned companies to offset the influence of European, Japanese, and U.S. businesses.

The Movement to Establish Unity among the nations of North and South America, called *Pan-Americanism*, dates from the early 1800's. In 1826, the great Venezuelan general Simón Bolívar called the first in a series of conferences of the newly independent Latin-American countries. Bolívar believed that the republics needed to work together to solve common problems. But for more than 60 years, national jealousies kept the republics from achieving regional cooperation.

In 1890, the United States and 18 Latin-American nations formed the International Union of American Republics. The central office of this organization, called the Commercial Bureau of the American Republics, was renamed the Pan American Union in 1910. The purpose of the Pan American Union was to establish closer economic, cultural, and political cooperation among member nations. The Organization of American States (OAS) was established in 1948, and the Pan American Union became its permanent governing body. The membership of the OAS consists of the United States and all the independent countries of Latin America except Belize and Guyana. The OAS seeks to provide for collective self-defense, regional cooperation, and the peaceful settlement of disputes.

In 1947, the United States and nearly all the Latin-American republics signed the Inter-American Treaty of Reciprocal Assistance. The treaty was drawn up in Rio de Janeiro, Brazil, and is commonly called the Rio Treaty. It states that an armed attack against any country that signed the treaty would be considered an attack against all the other countries.

Latin America and the United States have often had a difficult relationship. The United States supported the Latin-American colonies in their wars of independence. In 1823, U.S. President James Monroe issued the Monroe Doctrine, which warned European powers not to meddle in the affairs of the Western Hemisphere. But the doctrine caused much resentment among Latin Americans. Many of them felt that the United States was assuming its superiority over Latin America by making itself the region's protector.

Numerous Latin Americans distrust the United States because of its great wealth and power. At times, they have suspected it of trying to control the entire hemisphere. Such suspicions arose when the United States fought the Mexican War (1846-1848) after annexing Texas in 1845. Latin Americans were also concerned when the United States won control of Puerto Rico in 1898 as a result of the Spanish-American War.

The presence of U.S. military forces in Latin America increased during the early 1900's. In 1903, U.S. troops helped Panama win its independence from Colombia. In return, Panama gave the United States permanent control of the zone where the Panama Canal was later built. Latin Americans were especially upset when the United States stationed marines in Nicaragua from 1912 to 1933, in Haiti from 1915 to 1934, and in the Dominican Republic from 1916 to 1924. The marines were sent to these countries to protect U.S. interests during times of political unrest. Several Latin-American countries sided with the United States against Germany during World War I (1914-1918), but most remained neutral.

Latin-American distrust of the United States decreased somewhat after a Pan-American conference in 1933. All the nations pledged themselves to the Good Neighbor Policy outlined by U.S. President Franklin D. Roosevelt. The policy provided that no nation would interfere in the affairs of any other nation. During World War II (1939-1945), all the Latin-American nations supported the Allies, though only Brazil and Mexico provided troops.

Since the mid-1900's, the United States has sent billions of dollars and many technical experts to help Latin-American countries solve their social and economic problems. Such aid programs as the Alliance for Progress and the Peace Corps have helped improve Latin-American agriculture, industry, educational systems, and health services.

Relations between Latin America and the United States showed signs of strain during the 1970's and early 1980's. The United States cut back its aid to some Latin-American governments that had violated the civil rights of their citizens. For their part, many Latin Americans saw hidden motives in U.S. actions, even aid programs. They opposed U.S. influence in their affairs and demanded greater independence from the United States. On the other hand, the rulers of some nations have asked the United States for additional economic and military aid because of the rise in violence among their citizens demanding reforms.

The United States has taken several steps to relieve tensions in the area. In 1977, for example, the United

Theodore Roosevelt Collection, Harvard College Library

U.S. President Theodore Roosevelt, *center,* visited the construction site of the Panama Canal in 1906. Panama had given the United States control of the Canal Zone in 1903.

Karl Schumacher, The White House

U.S. President Jimmy Carter, *left,* at a 1977 ceremony, signed a treaty that will give Panama complete control of the Panama Canal beginning on Dec. 31, 1999.

States and Panama signed a treaty that will give Panama total control of the Panama Canal beginning on Dec. 31, 1999.

Political Unrest. During the early and mid-1900's, widespread protests broke out in many Latin-American countries as the people demanded major economic and political reforms. Revolutions overthrew a number of dictators. However, the end of dictatorship did not bring about stability or more representative government in many of the countries. During the mid-1900's, violence frequently erupted as rival political groups struggled for power. Bombings, kidnappings, and assassinations occurred in numerous countries.

Since the 1960's, military leaders have taken control of several Latin-American governments. These leaders have often violated the people's civil rights, claiming it was necessary in order to achieve stability and reforms. They have closed universities, shut down newspapers, established strict censorship laws, and jailed thousands of people without trial as suspected terrorists.

One of the most significant political developments in Latin America occurred in 1959. That year, Fidel Castro led a revolution in Cuba that overthrew the military dictatorship of Fulgencio Batista. Castro established a Communist dictatorship and became closely allied with the Soviet Union. He pledged to help Communist rebels in other Latin-American countries gain power.

Since the Castro revolution, activity by Communist and other leftist organizations has increased greatly in Latin America. In 1979, a revolution led by members of the Sandinista National Liberation Front, a Communist group supported by Cuba, overthrew Nicaragua's dictator, Anastasio Somoza. In response to such Communist activity, the United States has increased the amount of military and economic aid that it provides to several Latin-American countries.

Since the early 1980's, protests against military governments have grown in several Latin-American countries. As a result, civilian governments elected by the people have replaced military governments in such countries as Argentina and El Salvador.

Latin America Today faces many serious social, economic, and political problems. The gap between the

J. Pavlovsky, Sygma

Civil War and Protest shatter the peace in several Latin-American countries. Armored vehicles rumble down a street in El Salvador, *above,* where government troops fight leftist rebels.

rich and the poor continues to widen. Millions of Latin Americans live in miserable poverty. The region's rapidly increasing population makes it difficult for countries to provide enough jobs, housing, and vital services for their people. Growing demands for social and economic reforms continue to explode into violent protests and civil wars.

Latin America's economy grew during the 1960's and early 1970's. By the late 1970's, however, several factors slowed that growth. Prices rose sharply for such needed imports as petroleum, chemical fertilizers, and industrial machinery. At the same time, the prices that Latin-American nations received for their agricultural and mineral exports dropped. Many countries had to borrow huge sums of money at high interest rates to finance their development. By the early 1980's, some of these nations had trouble raising the money they needed to repay their loans.   NATHAN A. HAVERSTOCK

LATIN AMERICA/*Study Aids*

Related Articles in WORLD BOOK include:

BIOGRAPHIES

<table>
<tr><td>Alvarado, Pedro de</td><td>Miranda, Francisco de</td></tr>
<tr><td>Balboa, Vasco Núñez de</td><td>O'Higgins (family)</td></tr>
<tr><td>Bolívar, Simón</td><td>Pedro (emperors)</td></tr>
<tr><td>Cabral, Pedro Álvarez</td><td>Pizarro, Francisco</td></tr>
<tr><td>Columbus, Christopher</td><td>San Martín, José de</td></tr>
<tr><td>Cortés, Hernando</td><td>Toussaint L'Ouverture</td></tr>
<tr><td>Hidalgo y Costilla, Miguel</td><td>Vespucci, Amerigo</td></tr>
<tr><td>Magellan, Ferdinand</td><td></td></tr>
</table>

COUNTRIES AND OTHER POLITICAL UNITS

See the separate articles on Latin-American countries and other political units listed in the *table* with this article. See also the following articles:

<table>
<tr><td>Central America</td><td>South America</td></tr>
<tr><td>North America</td><td>West Indies</td></tr>
</table>

United Press Int.

Fidel Castro waves to crowds in Havana, Cuba, in 1959 after leading a successful revolution against the dictator Fulgencio Batista. Under Castro, Cuba became a Communist dictatorship.

Questions

How do city and country life differ in Latin America?
What are *mestizos? Mulattoes?*
How does the Roman Catholic Church influence the daily lives of Latin Americans in some countries?
What was the Line of Demarcation?
Why do many Latin-American children fail to complete elementary school?
Why did the Indian population decline after European colonists arrived in Latin America?
What are *artes populares?*
Why have millions of rural Latin Americans moved to urban areas?
What were the main reasons Latin-American colonists wanted independence from their European rulers?
Why do numerous Latin Americans distrust the United States?

Additional Resources

Level I

AGUILAR, LUIS E. *Latin America.* Stryker-Post. Revised annually. Profiles of each country.
CARTER, WILLIAM E. *South America.* Rev. ed. Watts, 1983. An introduction to 13 countries.
COMINS, JEREMY. *Latin American Crafts and Their Cultural Backgrounds.* Lothrop, 1974.
JENNESS, AYLETTE, and KROEBER, L. W. *A Life of Their Own: An Indian Family in Latin America.* Crowell, 1975.
MANGURIAN, DAVID. *Children of the Incas.* Four Winds, 1979.
WALTON, RICHARD J. *The United States and Latin America.* Seabury, 1972.

Level II

ALBA, VICTOR. *The Latin Americans.* Praeger, 1969.
ARIAS, ESTHER and MORTIMER. *The Cry of My People: Out of Captivity in Latin America.* Friendship, 1980. Deals with religion as an aspect of the culture.
ATKINS, G. POPE. *Latin America in the International Political System.* Free Press, 1977.
BANNON, JOHN F., and DUNNE, P. M. *Latin America: An Historical Survey.* 4th ed. Bruce, 1977.
BÉHAGUE, GERARD. *Music in Latin America: An Introduction.* Prentice-Hall, 1979.
BURNS, E. BRADFORD. *Latin America: A Concise Interpretive History.* Prentice-Hall, 1972.
Encyclopedia of Latin America. Ed. by Helen Delpar. McGraw, 1974.
GÓNGORA, MARIO. *Studies in the Colonial History of Spanish America.* Cambridge, 1975.
Human Rights and Basic Needs in the Americas. Ed. by Margaret E. Crahan. Georgetown, 1982. Discusses economic issues of Latin-American countries and includes a discussion of U.S.-Latin-American relations.
Latin American Foreign Policies: An Analysis. Ed. by Harold Eugene Davis and L. C. Wilson. Johns Hopkins, 1975.
LOTHROP, SAMUEL K. *Treasures of Ancient America: Pre-Columbian Art from Mexico to Peru.* Rizzoli, 1979.
SKIDMORE, THOMAS E., and SMITH, P. H. *Modern Latin America.* Oxford, 1984.
URBANSKI, EDMUND STEPHEN. *Hispanic America and Its Civilizations: Spanish Americans and Anglo-Americans.* Univ. of Oklahoma Press, 1979.
VELIZ, CLAUDIO. *The Centralist Tradition of Latin America.* Princeton, 1980.

LATIN-AMERICAN LITERATURE consists of the literature of the Spanish-speaking countries of the Western Hemisphere, of Puerto Rico, and of Portuguese-speaking Brazil. For the historical background of the literature, see LATIN AMERICA.

Colonial Literature

The colonial period began with the first Spanish and Portuguese explorations of the New World in the late 1400's. It ended with the colonial wars for independence more than 300 years later. The earliest colonial literature consisted mostly of chronicles and narratives written by soldiers and missionaries who described their amazing encounters with new landscapes and civilizations. The authors mixed fantasy with realism in describing their adventures and contacts with unfamiliar peoples, customs, animals, and plants.

Hernando Cortés, the Spanish conqueror of the Aztec empire, wrote a series of five reports for King Charles I of Spain. These accounts, known as the *Five Letters* (1519-1526), are a gripping and detailed presentation of his campaign. Bernal Díaz del Castillo, who served in Cortés' Aztec campaigns, wrote a lively chronicle, *The True History of the Conquest of New Spain* (1522).

Many works dealt with the period of conquest. In *In Defense of the Indian* (1552), the Dominican missionary Bartolomé de Las Casas criticized the brutal treatment of the Indians by the Europeans. Garcilaso de la Vega's *Royal Commentaries* (1609) dramatized the history of the Inca empire. The greatest poem of the time was *La Araucana* (1569-1589) by Alonso de Ercilla y Zúñiga. It recounted the bravery of the Chilean Indians who resisted the Spanish invaders. The first colonial poet to write in Portuguese was Bento Texeira Pinto. In his epic *Prosopopéia* (1601), he dealt with the individual and nature in the American environment.

A new literary style called the *baroque* emerged during the second half of the 1600's. Baroque authors wrote in an ornate and artificial style and used cutting wit and intricate wordplay. The complex baroque style produced works that were often difficult to understand.

The leading writer of the baroque period was the Mexican nun Sor Juana Ines de la Cruz, who is generally considered the finest writer in colonial Latin-American literature. She wrote plays, satires, philosophical works, and various types of poetry.

Juan del Valle y Caviedes of Peru composed satirical poetry that criticized the corruption he saw in colonial society. Gregório de Matos of Brazil also wrote satirical poetry. The Brazilian poet Tomás Antônio Gonzaga wrote some of the finest lyric poetry in the Portuguese language, notably his love poem *Marília de Dirceu* (1792). The Brazilian writers José Basílio da Gama and José de Santa Rita de Durão continued the tradition of epic poetry. Da Gama's *Uruguay* (1769) describes the war between the European conquerors and the Paraguayan Indians. De Durao's *Caramurú* (1781) narrates the discovery and settlement of Brazil.

The 1800's

Most of the Latin-American colonies began fighting for their independence from Spain and Portugal in the early 1800's. Hostility toward the colonial powers led to the so-called Wars of Independence, which began in 1810 and lasted for about 16 years. The wars inspired writers to compose patriotic poetry and fiction that satirized the colonial powers. José Joaquín Fernández de Lizardi wrote perhaps the first Latin-American novel, *The Itching Parrot* (1816), a satirical story about the corrupt colonial society of Mexico City. José Joaquín Olmedo of Ecuador wrote the famous patriotic poem "Song to Bolívar" (1825).

Romanticism was a cultural movement that began in Europe in the late 1700's and spread to Latin America. Romanticism emphasized individualism and nationalism. It also stressed artistic freedom to pursue new subject matter and fresh literary forms.

José María Heredia of Cuba was one of Latin America's earliest romantic writers. He wrote the melancholy nature poem "On the Pyramid of Cholula" (1820). Some of the poetry of Andrés Bello of Venezuela has subtle romantic elements, especially "Ode to the Agriculture of the Torrid Zone" (1826).

A type of romanticism called *nativism* developed in the 1800's. Nativist writers dealt with the distinctive regional characteristics of their countries. Esteban Echeverría of Argentina expressed his love of the vast Argentine *Pampas* (plains) in his lyric poetry. Gaucho literature became especially popular. Gauchos were nomadic cowboys who were depicted as romantic outlaws. José Hernández of Argentina wrote the best-known example of gaucho literature, the epic poem *Martín Fierro* (1872). This work recounts the gaucho hero's lonely life, his encounters with Indians, and the harsh treatment he receives from an insensitive government.

The novel flourished during the romantic period. Jorge Isaacs of Colombia wrote *María* (1867), a sentimental love story that remains one of the most popular works in Latin-American literature. José Marmol of Argentina and Ignacio Manuel Altamirano of Mexico were liberal writers who wrote novels that opposed political injustice. Another political writer, Domingo

Faustino Sarmiento of Argentina, mixed essays and fiction in *Civilization and Barbarism: Life of Juan Facundo Quiroga* (1845).

The romantic concept of the *noble savage* became a popular theme during the 1800's. To the romantics, non-Europeans such as the Indians were superior because they were not corrupted by European civilization. In Brazil, the poetry of Antônio Gonçalves Dias won praise for its glorified portrayal of the Indians. Indians were the heroes of the novels *O Guarani* (1857) by José de Alencar of Brazil and *Cumandá* (1879) by Juan León Mera of Ecuador and of the epic poem *Tabaré* (1888) by Juan Zorrilla de San Martín of Uruguay.

The Peruvian writer Ricardo Palma created a unique literary form called *tradición*. The form consisted of prose sketches that combined history, legend, gossip, stories, and humor. Palma's sketches were collected in *Peruvian Traditions*, published from 1872 to 1910.

Realism was a literary movement that developed in the late 1800's. Writers tried to capture external reality in a detailed and objective way. Their works showed how human beings are influenced by their social environment. Some writers wrote in a more severe and pessimistic form of realism called *naturalism*.

The leading Latin-American realists included the novelists Alberto Blest Gana and Baldomero Lillo of Chile, Clorinda Matto de Turner of Peru, Eugenio Cambaceres of Argentina, and Federico Gamboa of Mexico. Probably the most important realist was the Brazilian novelist Joaquim Maria Machado de Assis. His best-known novels, *Epitaph of a Small Winner* (1881) and *Dom Casmurro* (1900), show a mastery of characterization and narrative technique.

A number of writers emphasized the local customs, habits, and speech of Spanish America's regions in sketches, short stories, and novels. Their works became known as *costumbrismo*. The leading costumbrista authors included Javier de Viana of Uruguay, Roberto J. Payró of Argentina, and Tomás Carrasquilla of Colombia. All these writers emphasized descriptions of local rural landscapes and types in their stories. The best-known realist playwright was Florencio Sánchez of Argentina, who wrote plays dealing with human conflict in rural Argentina.

Modernismo, which lasted from about 1888 to 1910, was one of the most significant literary periods in Latin-American literature. The most important writers were poets. The Nicaraguan poet Rubén Darío gave modernismo its form. Darío believed that poetry should avoid messages. Instead, poetry should strive to attain beauty in its purest form while liberating verse from traditional styles. In their search for the unusual, poets turned to such exotic sources as Greek, Oriental, and Nordic mythology. Darío's book of poems called *Azul* (1888) marked the beginning of modernismo. Leopoldo Lugones of Argentina was another leading poet of the period.

José Enrique Rodó, a Uruguayan essayist, exerted almost as much influence as Darío. Rodó's essay *Ariel* (1900) became a landmark of Latin-American thought. Rodó appealed to the young people of Latin America to strive for idealism and high spiritual goals, both of which were being threatened by modern materialism. José Martí of Cuba was another influential Latin-American intellectual. He was a celebrated journalist, essayist, and poet who was honored as a patriot after he died fighting for Cuban independence.

The 1900's

The Early 1900's. A group of women poets won praise during the early 1900's. Many of their poems dealt with love and womanhood in a society dominated by men. One of the poets, Gabriela Mistral of Chile, won the 1945 Nobel Prize for literature. She became the first Latin-American writer to receive the prize. Other leading woman poets included Delmira Agustini and Juana de Ibarbourou of Uruguay and Alfonsina Storni of Argentina.

Novelists took a fresh interest in regional themes. José Eustasio Rivera of Colombia portrayed the Amazon rain forest as a place of beauty and terror in *The Vortex* (1924). Rómulo Gallegos wrote about the tropical plains of Venezuela in *Doña Bárbara* (1929). Ricardo Güiraldes of Argentina told the adventures of a boy who receives spiritual guidance from a gaucho in *Don Segundo Sombra* (1926). José Lins do Rego's "sugarcane cycle" of novels (1932-1943) recaptures the author's childhood on a sugar plantation in Brazil.

Many regional novels explored social and political problems. *Rebellion in the Backlands* (1902) by Euclides da Cunha gives a dramatic picture of a military conflict between poverty-stricken peasants and government forces. The Mexican revolution of 1910 inspired Mariano Azuela's novel *The Underdogs* (1916). Graciliano Ramos' *Barren Lives* (1938) and Jorge Amado's *The Violent Land* (1942) criticized social conditions in Brazil. The mistreatment of Indians is portrayed in *Huasipungo* (1934) by Jorge Icaza of Ecuador, *El indio* (1935) by Gregorio López y Fuentes of Mexico, and *Yawar Fiesta* (1940) by José María Arguedas of Peru.

Several Latin-American poets of the 1920's experimented with form and technique. The most important of these poets were Vicente Huidobro and Pablo Neruda of Chile, César Vallejo of Peru, Mario de Andrade of Brazil, and Jorge Luis Borges of Argentina. They rejected traditional forms to create poetry with unusual imagery. Such poems were intended to reveal the subconscious mind. Andrade's *Hallucinated City* (1922) is an example of the experimental poetry of the time.

The Mid-1900's. A variety of themes dominated the literature of the mid-1900's. A sense of isolation and lack of human communication was expressed by Eduardo Mallea of Argentina in his novels *Bay of Silence* (1940) and *All Green Shall Perish* (1941). Ciro Alegría of Peru wrote a novel of social protest about the abuses of Peruvian Indians in *Broad and Alien Is the World* (1941). Jorge Luis Borges wrote philosophical short stories of fantasy in *Ficciones* (1944).

During the mid-1940's, writers combined authentic subject matter, varied themes, and experiments in language to produce the "new novel." Novelists became more aware of their cultural identity, but they avoided extreme expressions of nationalism. The best-known examples of the "new novel" included *El señor presidente* (1946) by Miguel Angel Asturias of Guatemala, *The Edge of the Storm* (1947) by Augustín Yáñez of Mexico, *Adán Buenosayres* (1948) by Leopoldo Marechal of Argentina, *Born Guilty* (1951) by Manuel Rojas of Chile, *The Lost Steps* (1953) by Alejo Carpentier of Cuba, and *Pedro Páramo* (1955) by Juan Rulfo of Mexico.

The leading Latin-American poet at midcentury was the Mexican Octavio Paz. Much of his verse deals with Mexican identity and history. He also wrote essays on literary criticism, art, and politics.

Recent Developments. The most important development in Latin-American literature since the 1950's has been the sudden and unprecedented international attention enjoyed by novelists. The large number of important novels produced by these writers has been called the "boom." The original boom novelists were Carlos Fuentes of Mexico, Julio Cortázar of Argentina, Mario Vargas Llosa of Peru, and Gabriel García Márquez of Colombia. All four use literary invention in their narratives to express their cultural heritage. They experimented with language and structure, often injecting fantasy and fragmenting time and space. The boom produced a style known as "magical realism," which blended dreams and magic with everyday reality.

Carlos Fuentes' major novels provide a panorama of life in modern Mexico. His major works include *Where the Air Is Clear* (1958) and *The Death of Artemio Cruz* (1962). Cortázar's most influential novel is *Hopscotch* (1963), which experiments with narrative technique and revolts against traditional uses of language. Many critics consider Cortázar's short stories to be even better than his novels. Fantasy, allegory, and philosophy characterize such story collections as *A Change of Light* (1974). Vargas Llosa writes about modern Peruvian society. His most ambitious work, *The War of the End of the World* (1981), is a historical novel of high adventure based on Euclides da Cunha's *Rebellion in the Backlands*.

The most famous boom novelist is Gabriel García Márquez, who won the 1982 Nobel Prize for literature. His novel *One Hundred Years of Solitude* (1967) ranks as a landmark of Latin-American fiction. The novel contains much historical fact, but the author also includes fantasy, extraordinary characters, bizarre events, suspense, and unusual humor. García Márquez maintained his international reputation with such works as *The Autumn of the Patriarch* (1975) and *Chronicle of a Death Foretold* (1981).   DICK GERDES

Related Articles in WORLD BOOK include:

Amado, Jorge	Gaucho
Asturias, Miguel Angel	Machado de Assis,
Borges, Jorge Luis	Joaquim Maria
Cunha, Euclides da	Martí, José Julián
Darío, Rubén	Mistral, Gabriela
Fuentes, Carlos	Neruda, Pablo
García Márquez,	Paz, Octavio
Gabriel José	Rodó, José Enrique

Additional Resources

ANDERSON-IMBERT, ENRIQUE. *Spanish American Literature: A History.* Wayne State Univ. Press, 1963.

The Borzoi Anthology of Latin American Literature. Ed. by Emir Rodriguez Monegal. 2 vols. Random House, 1977.

A Dictionary of Contemporary Latin American Authors. Ed. by David W. Foster. Arizona State Univ. Center for Latin American Studies, 1975.

Modern Latin American Literature. Ed. by David W. Foster and V. R. Foster. 2 vols. Ungar, 1975.

The Oxford Companion to Spanish Literature. Ed. by Philip Ward. Oxford, 1978. This work covers important authors and trends in Latin-American literature.

LATIN GRAMMAR SCHOOL. See SCHOOL (Colonial Schools).

LATIN LANGUAGE

LATIN LANGUAGE was the principal language of western Europe for hundreds of years. It was the language of the Roman Empire, and Roman soldiers and traders took it wherever they went. Latin, because of its precise expression, was a perfect language for law and government. As used by the Roman poet Virgil and other literary masters, Latin achieved a dignity and tone rarely equaled by any other language.

Latin has not been a spoken language since the end of the Middle Ages in the early 1500's. However, many Latin words helped shape modern scientific and legal terms. For example, the word *gravity* comes from the Latin word *gravis*, meaning *heavy*. The word *verdict* comes from the Latin words *verus*, meaning *truth*, and *dicere*, meaning *to speak*. The Roman Catholic Church still considers Latin its official language, though Mass is celebrated in the tongue of the local community.

Structure

Alphabet. The Latin alphabet was borrowed from the Greeks, probably through the Etruscans, an ancient people who lived in Italy. In classical times, Latin had 23 letters, but it lacked the *j*, *u*, and *w* of the English language. The Roman alphabet became the basis of most modern alphabets. See the WORLD BOOK articles on ALPHABET and on each letter of the English alphabet.

Grammar. Latin belongs to the Indo-European family of languages and is therefore closely related to the Celtic, Germanic, Greek, Sanskrit, and Slavic languages. Like Greek, Latin is highly *inflected*—that is, changes in meaning are often indicated by changes in word endings. For an example of the inflections of a Latin noun, see CASE (Cases in Latin).

Development

Latin was one of several related languages of ancient Italy. Others, such as Oscan and Umbrian, died out as the influence of Latin spread.

In Ancient Times. Examples of the earliest Latin, which is sometimes called *preliterary Latin*, were preserved in inscriptions and religious texts. During the 200's and 100's B.C., Latin changed from a spoken language to a highly developed literary tongue. It reached its highest level of development in the Golden Age of Latin literature, from 106 B.C. to A.D. 14. Works of prose by Julius Caesar and Cicero, and the poetry of Virgil and Horace, set standards of excellence for future writers. See LATIN LITERATURE (The Golden Age).

A *vernacular* (common) form of Latin developed at the same time as literary Latin. It underwent many changes after the Golden Age. Inflections were simplified, and word order became more regular. The spread of Christianity, plus invasions by Germanic tribes, contributed to the fall of the West Roman Empire in the 300's and 400's. The Christians and the invaders changed Latin further by adding new words and meanings to the language.

During the Middle Ages, the spoken Latin of the late Roman Empire developed into the Romance languages, including French, Italian, Portuguese, Romanian, and Spanish (see ROMANCE LANGUAGE). At this time, a form of literary Latin called *Medieval Latin* was the language of the Christian church and of education. It ranked as an international tongue and was used by scholars in universities and religious schools throughout western Europe.

Latin Today

In Schools. Latin has been taught in schools since the Middle Ages, though its popularity has declined during the 1900's. American college students of the 1700's and 1800's were required not only to read Latin fluently, but also to write original essays and poems in Latin. During the 1900's, most colleges and universities in the United States have relaxed or eliminated these requirements. However, many universities in Great Britain and other European countries still require Latin.

Many educators believe the study of Latin trains a student to think precisely and to understand grammatical relationships. For example, students of Latin can derive the meanings of difficult English words based on their knowledge of Latin roots. They also learn to appreciate the ancient Roman civilization as a source of modern culture. In addition, a knowledge of Latin aids students in learning modern languages, especially the Romance languages.

Latin and English. Scholars estimate that about half of all English words in current use are of Latin origin. Most of them were borrowed from Old French, and reflect forms and meanings that Latin words had acquired in that language. But scholars also borrowed many words directly from Latin. Consequently, we have such words as *loyal* and *legal*, both from the Latin *legalis*, meaning *legal*. The form *loyal* was borrowed from the French, with its new feudal meaning.

The vast majority of English abstract words are Latin in origin. When we speak of the "power of liberty," the "spirit of independence," or the "virtue of charity," the two important words in each phrase are Latin. Many English scientific terms come from Latin. The title of every rank in the army, from *private* to *general*, has a Latin origin. Some common Latin idioms remain unchanged in English, including such phrases as *persona non grata*, *ad infinitum*, and *P.S.* (*post scriptum*). The richness and variety of the English language owe much to the contributions of Latin.   DAVID H. KELLY

LATIN LITERATURE includes the essays, histories, poems, plays, and other writings of the ancient Romans. In many ways, it seems to be a continuation of Greek literature, using many of the same forms. But it also mirrored the life and history of ancient Rome.

Characteristics of Latin Literature

Much Latin writing reflects the great interest the Romans had in *rhetoric*, the art of speaking and persuading. Public speaking had great importance for educated

Some Unusual Latin Derivations

antler, from *antocularis*, before the eye	**shambles,** from *scamellum,* bench
bugle, from *buculus*, young bull	**soldier,** from *solidus,* gold coin
chapel, from *cappella*, cloak	**sullen,** from *solus*, alone
hoosegow, from *judicare*, to judge (through the Spanish *juzgado*)	**travel,** from *trepalium*, instrument of torture (through the French *travailler*)
pay, from *pacare*, to make peace	**villain,** from *villanus*, farm hand

Romans, because most of them hoped for successful political careers. When Rome was a republic, effective speaking often determined who would be elected or what bills would be passed. After Rome became an empire, the ability to impress and persuade people by the spoken word lost much of its importance. But training in rhetoric continued to flourish and to affect styles of writing. A large part of rhetoric consists of the ability to present a familiar idea in a striking new manner that attracts attention. Latin authors became masters of this art of variety.

Language and Form. Latin is a highly *inflected* language, with many grammatical forms for various words. As a result, it can be used with a pithiness and brevity unknown in English (see INFLECTION). It also lends itself to elaboration, because its tight syntax holds even the longest and most complex sentence together as a logical unit. Latin can be used with striking conciseness, as in the works of Sallust and Tacitus. Or it can have wide, sweeping phrases, as in the works of Livy and the speeches of Cicero.

Latin lacks the rich poetic vocabulary that marks Greek poetry. Some earlier Latin poets tried to make up for this deficiency by creating new compound words, as the Greeks had done. But Roman writers seldom invented words. Except in epic poetry, they tended to use a familiar vocabulary, giving it poetic value by imaginative combinations of words and by rich sound effects. Rome's leading poets had great technical skill in the choice and arrangement of language. They also had an intimate knowledge of the Greek poets, whose themes appear in almost all Roman literature.

Latin moves with impressive dignity in the writings of Lucretius, Cicero, or Virgil. It reflects the seriousness and sense of responsibility that characterized the ruling class of Rome during the great years of the republic. But the Romans could also relax and allow what Horace called the "Italian vinegar" in their systems to pour forth in wit and satire.

Latin in Translation. The best Latin literature has been translated into most major languages. Until the 1900's, the majority of educated people in the West knew at least some Latin. Today, fewer people are familiar with the language, but an increasing number enjoy Latin literature through translations.

Some translators *paraphrase*—that is, they try to keep the beauty and spirit of the original work without providing the exact meaning of each phrase. During the 1600's and 1700's, a number of English poets translated much Latin poetry by paraphrasing. Perhaps the outstanding example was John Dryden's English version of the poems of Virgil, published in 1697.

Other translators provide literal translations, trying to imitate exactly the writings of Latin authors. However, these translations lose much of the beauty and style that made the originals such works of art. The chief value of literal translations lies in helping students read Latin more easily.

Early Latin Literature

Formal Latin literature began in 240 B.C., when a Roman audience saw a Latin version of a Greek play. The adaptor was Livius Andronicus, a Greek who had been brought to Rome as a prisoner of war in 272 B.C. Andronicus also translated Homer's Greek epic the *Od-*

yssey into an old type of Latin verse called *Saturnian*. The first Latin poet to write on a Roman theme was Gnaeus Naevius during the 200's B.C. He composed an epic poem about the first Punic War, in which he had fought. Naevius' dramas were mainly reworkings of Greek originals, but he also created tragedies based on Roman myths and history.

Other epic poets followed Naevius. Quintus Ennius wrote a historical epic, the *Annals* (soon after 200 B.C.), describing Roman history from the founding of Rome to his own time. He adopted Greek dactylic hexameter, which became the standard verse form for Roman epics. He also became famous for his tragic dramas. In this field his most distinguished successors were Marcus Pacuvius and Lucius Accius. These three writers rarely used episodes from Roman history. Instead, they wrote Latin versions of tragic themes that the Greeks had already handled. But even when they copied the Greeks, they did not translate slavishly. Only fragments of their plays have survived.

We know much more about early Latin comedy, because we have 20 complete plays by Plautus and 6 by Terence. These men modeled their comedies on Greek plays known as New Comedy. But they treated the plots and wording of the originals freely. Plautus scattered songs through his plays and increased the humor with puns and wisecracks, plus comic actions by the actors. Terence's plays were more polite in tone, dealing with domestic situations. His works provided the chief inspiration for French and English comedies of the 1600's, and even for modern American comedy.

The prose of the period is best known through *On Agriculture* (160 B.C.) by Cato the Elder. Cato also wrote the first Latin history of Rome and of other Italian cities. In addition, he was the first Roman to put his political speeches in writing as a means of influencing public opinion.

Early Latin literature ended with Gaius Lucilius, who created a new kind of poetry in his 30 books of *Satires* (100's B.C.). He wrote in an easy, conversational tone about books, food, friends, and current events. In the early A.D. 100's, Juvenal perfected the biting form of satire that has served as a model for many later writers. See SATIRE.

The Golden Age

Latin literature was at its height from 81 B.C. to A.D. 17. This period began with the first known speech of Cicero and ended with the death of Ovid.

The Age of Cicero. Cicero was the greatest master of Latin prose. He dominated Latin literature from about 80 B.C. until his death in 43 B.C. Cicero's many writings can be divided into four groups: (1) letters, (2) rhetorical treatises, (3) philosophical works, and (4) orations. His letters provide detailed information about an important period in Roman history and offer a vivid picture of the public and private life among the Roman governing class. Cicero's works on oratory are our most valuable Latin sources for ancient theories on education and rhetoric. His philosophical works were the basis of moral philosophy during the Middle Ages. His speeches inspired many European political leaders and the founders of the United States.

LATIN LITERATURE

Julius Caesar and Sallust were outstanding historical writers of Cicero's time. Caesar wrote commentaries on the Gallic and civil wars in a straightforward style to justify his actions as a general. Sallust adopted an abrupt, pointed style in his historical works. He wrote brilliant descriptions of people and their motives.

The birth of lyric poetry in Latin occurred during the same period. The short love lyrics of Catullus have never been surpassed in emotional intensity. Catullus also wrote masterful poems that attacked his enemies. In his longer poems, he suggested beautiful images in rich, delicate language.

In contrast, the poet Lucretius undertook to interpret the ideas of the Greek philosopher Epicurus. Lucretius' work *De rerum natura* (55 B.C.) contains many majestic passages. It is a triumph of poetic genius over unpoetic matter.

The most learned writer of the period was Varro. He wrote about a remarkable variety of subjects, from religion to poetry. Unfortunately, only his writings on agriculture and the Latin language survive in their complete form.

The Age of Augustus. The emperor Augustus took a personal interest in the literary works produced during his years of power from 27 B.C. to A.D. 14. This period is sometimes called the *Golden Age of Latin Literature*. Virgil published his pastoral *Eclogues;* the *Georgics*, perhaps the most beautiful poem ever written about country life; and the *Aeneid*, an epic poem describing the events that led to the creation of Rome. Virgil told how the Trojan hero Aeneas became the ancestor of the Roman people. Virgil also provided divine justification for Roman rule over the world. Although Virgil died before he could put the finishing touches on his poem, it was soon recognized as the greatest work of Latin literature. Critics still agree on this judgment.

Virgil's friend Horace wrote *Epodes, Odes, Satires* and *Epistles*. The perfection of the *Odes* in content, form, and style has charmed readers for hundreds of years. The *Satires* and *Epistles* discuss ethical and literary problems in an urbane, witty manner. Horace's *Art of Poetry*, probably published as a separate work, greatly influenced later poetic theories. It stated the basic rules of classical writing as the Romans understood and used them. After Virgil died, Horace was Rome's leading poet.

The Latin elegy reached its highest development in the works of Tibullus, Propertius, and Ovid. Most of this poetry is concerned with love (see ELEGY). Ovid also wrote the *Fasti*, which describes Roman festivals and their legendary origins. Ovid's greatest work, the *Metamorphoses* weaves various myths into a fast-paced, fascinating story. Ovid was a witty writer who excelled in creating lively and passionate characters. The *Metamorphoses* was the best-known source of Roman mythology throughout the Middle Ages and the Renaissance. It inspired many poets, painters, and composers.

In prose, Livy produced a history of the Roman people in 142 books. Only 35 survive, but they are a major source of information on Rome.

Later Latin Literature

The Imperial Period. From the death of Augustus in A.D. 14 until about 200, Roman authors emphasized style and tried new and startling ways of expression. During the reign of Nero from 55 to 68, the Stoic philosopher Seneca wrote a number of dialogues and letters on such moral themes as mercy and generosity. In his *Natural Questions*, Seneca analyzed earthquakes, floods, and storms. Seneca's tragedies greatly influenced the growth of tragic drama in Europe. His nephew Lucan wrote the *Pharsalia* (about 60), an epic poem describing the civil war between Caesar and Pompey. The *Satyricon* (about 60) by Petronius was the first Latin novel. Only fragments of the complete work survive. It describes the adventures of various low-class characters in absurd, extravagant, and dangerous situations, often in the world of petty crime.

Epic poems included the *Argonautica* of Valerius Flaccus, the *Thebaid* of Statius, and the *Punica* of Silius Italicus. At the hands of Martial, the epigram achieved the stinging quality still associated with it. Juvenal brilliantly satirized vice.

Among prose writers, the historian Tacitus probably deserves first place. He painted an unforgettably dark picture of the early empire in his *Histories* and *Annals*, both written in the early 100's. His contemporary Suetonius wrote biographies of the 12 Roman rulers from Julius Caesar through Domitian. The letters of Pliny the Younger described Roman life of the period. Quintilian composed the most complete work on ancient education that we possess. Important works from the 100's include the *Attic Nights* of Aulus Gellius, a collection of anecdotes and reports of literary discussions among his friends; and the letters of the orator Fronto to Marcus Aurelius. The most famous work of the period was *Metamorphoses*, also called *The Golden Ass*, by Lucius Apuleius. This novel concerns a young man who is accidentally changed into a donkey. The story is filled with colorful tales of love and witchcraft.

Later Periods. Pagan Latin literature showed a final burst of vitality in the late 200's and 400's. Ammianus Marcellinus in history, Symmachus in oratory, and Ausonius and Rutilius in poetry all wrote with great talent. The *Mosella* by Ausonius had a modernism of feeling that indicates the end of classical literature as such.

At the same time, other men laid the foundations of Christian Latin literature during the 300's and 400's. They included the church fathers Augustine, Jerome, and Ambrose, and the first great Christian poet, Prudentius.   ELAINE FANTHAM

Related Articles in WORLD BOOK include:

Ambrose, Saint	Jerome, Saint	Pliny
Apuleius, Lucius	Juvenal	Quintilian
Augustine, Saint	Livy	Sallust
Caesar, Julius	Lucretius	Seneca
Cato	Marcus Aurelius	Suetonius
Catullus	Martial	Tacitus
Cicero	Ovid	Terence
Classicism (Rome)	Petronius	Virgil
Horace	Plautus	

Additional Resources

DAVENPORT, BASIL, ed. *A Portable Latin Reader*. Penguin, 1979.

FRANK, TENNEY. *Life and Literature in the Roman Republic*. Univ. of California Press, 1930.

KENNEY, E. J., and CLAUSEN, W. V., eds. *Latin Literature*. Cambridge, 1982.

LATINOS are Americans of Latin-American descent. About 16 million Latinos live in the United States.

They include approximately 10½ million Mexican Americans, who make up the nation's second largest minority group. The largest minority group consists of the more than 28 million black Americans. Latinos make up the fastest-growing groups of U.S. minorities.

The largest Latino groups, after the Mexican Americans, are Puerto Ricans and Cuban Americans. Many Latinos are descendants of Latin-American immigrants or are immigrants themselves. Others are descendants of people who lived in Puerto Rico, the present-day Southwest, and other regions that the United States annexed during the 1800's. Latinos also have a wide variety of racial ancestries (see LATIN AMERICA [People]).

Latinos are sometimes called *Hispanic Americans*. Most Latinos speak both Spanish and English, though the native language of some is French or Portuguese. The majority of Latinos are Roman Catholics, and most are also young. The median age of Latinos is 24, compared with a median age of 31 for the national population. More than a third of all Latinos are under 18 years old.

The various Latino groups live throughout the United States. About 80 per cent of these people live and work in cities. Most Latinos have close *extended families*, which include grandparents, aunts, uncles, and cousins as well as parents and children. Partly because of this family attachment, Latinos form strong communities and prefer to work in or near their communities.

Latinos face major problems in education, employment, and political representation. As a group, Latinos have less education, hold fewer jobs in the professions and management, and earn less money than most other Americans. In addition, despite the large Latino population, few Latinos serve in high levels of government. Discrimination and language barriers are among the factors that have slowed their progress in all these areas. The problems are especially severe for the millions of Latino *undocumented aliens*, who do not have immigration papers and therefore are in the United States illegally.

Latinos are making major efforts to increase their educational and employment opportunities, to challenge discrimination, to increase their voter registration, and to become stronger in politics. They also are striving for greater unity among Latino groups of different origins, especially through the establishment of national Latino organizations. Two such organizations are the American G. I. Forum and the League of United Latin American Citizens (see AMERICAN G. I. FORUM; LEAGUE OF UNITED LATIN AMERICAN CITIZENS).   CARLOS E. CORTÉS

See also MEXICAN AMERICANS.

LATINUS. See AENEID.

LATITUDE, *LAT uh tood*, describes the position of a point on the earth's surface in relation to the equator. Latitude is one of the two *coordinates* that locate any point on the earth. The other coordinate is longitude.

The latitude of a point is measured along the *meridian*, or imaginary north-south line, that runs through it (see MERIDIAN). Latitude is measured in degrees. A point on the equator has a latitude of zero degrees (written 0°). The North Pole has a latitude of 90° *north* and the South Pole has a latitude of 90° *south*. These are sometimes written +90° and −90°. Degrees of latitude are divided into 60 *minutes* ('), and the minutes consist of 60 *seconds* (").

All points on the earth's surface that have the same latitude lie on an imaginary circle called a *parallel of latitude*. The distance between two parallels that are 1° apart is about 60 *nautical* (sea or air) miles, or 69 *statute* (land) miles or 111 kilometers. This length of 1° of latitude varies from 59.7 nautical miles near the equator to 60.3 nautical miles near the poles. The variation results because the earth is not a perfect sphere. A difference in latitude of 1 minute equals about 1 nautical mile.   WILLIAM MARKOWITZ

See also LONGITUDE; EQUATOR; MAP; CLIMATE (Differences in Latitude); STAR (Measuring Direction and Position).

Latitude

Imagine a series of lines running around the earth parallel to the equator, *left below*. These are lines of *latitude*. Every point on the earth's surface can be located on such a line. It shows the position of that spot in relation to the equator.

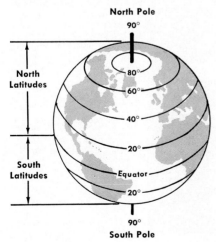

North Pole
90°
80°
60°
40°
20°
Equator
20°
90°
South Pole

North Latitudes

South Latitudes

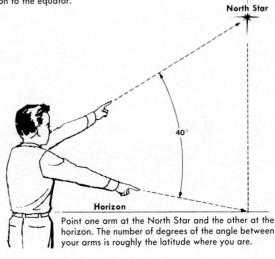

North Star

40°

Horizon

Point one arm at the North Star and the other at the horizon. The number of degrees of the angle between your arms is roughly the latitude where you are.

LATIUM

LATIUM, *LAY shee uhm,* was an area in the central part of ancient Italy. It was located in the same general area as the present province of Latium (see ITALY [physical map]). Its chief cities fought the Romans from 340 to 338 B.C. The Romans won, and Latium became part of the Roman territory. The people were given partial Roman citizenship. The Latin language was named for Latium. HERBERT M. HOWE

LATROBE, *luh TROHB,* **BENJAMIN HENRY** (1764-1820), was the first important professionally trained architect to practice in the United States. Latrobe established the Roman-Renaissance classical style for the new federal government buildings in Washington, D.C. He also introduced the Greek Revival style in the United States. Latrobe's design for the Bank of Pennsylvania (1798-1801) in Philadelphia was based on the form of the Ionic Temple. The Bank of Pennsylvania became the first pure Greek Revival building in the United States.

Latrobe was born in Yorkshire, England, and came to the United States in 1796. In 1803, he was appointed Surveyor of Public Buildings by President Thomas Jefferson. His most famous work still standing in Washington is his completion of the south wing of the United States Capitol. From 1814 to 1817, Latrobe directed much of the reconstruction of Washington, D.C., after the city's partial destruction during the War of 1812. DAVID GEBHARD

See also ADAMS, JOHN (picture: John Adams Was the First).

LATTER DAY SAINTS, REORGANIZED CHURCH OF JESUS CHRIST OF, is a religious denomination formed by members of the original Church of Jesus Christ of Latter Day Saints. It rejects the doctrine of polygamy and maintains that Joseph Smith, Jr., founder of the church, did not teach or practice polygamy (see POLYGAMY).

The Reorganized Church bases its teachings on the Bible, as the source of moral and spiritual law; the *Book of Mormon,* a history of the early peoples of the Western Hemisphere; and modern revelation, as published in the *Book of Doctrine and Covenants.* It stresses the ideals of Christian community life and stewardship. It also maintains *tithing,* whereby members annually contribute one-tenth of their income after deducting living and personal expenses.

The church claims succession from the original church founded by Joseph Smith, Jr., in 1830. The church reorganization began in the 1850's, and Joseph Smith III, son of the founder, served as president from 1860 to 1914. His sons succeeded him in office in the following order: Frederick M. Smith, 1915-1945; Israel A. Smith, 1946-1958; and W. Wallace Smith, 1958-1978. Wallace B. Smith, the son of W. Wallace Smith, became president in 1978. The church has a world membership of more than 200,000. The Reorganized Church has congregations in North and South America, Europe, Africa, Asia, and the Pacific Islands. Its headquarters are in Independence, Mo. W. WALLACE SMITH

See also MORMONS; SMITH, JOSEPH; YOUNG, BRIGHAM.

LATTER-DAY SAINTS, THE CHURCH OF JESUS CHRIST OF. See MORMONS.

LATVIA, *LAT vee uh,* a land on the eastern shore of the Baltic Sea, is one of the 15 republics of the Soviet Union. Its official name is the Latvian Soviet Socialist Republic. Latvia covers approximately 24,600 square miles (63,700 square kilometers) and has a population of about 2,587,000. Riga is Latvia's capital and largest city.

Latvia was an independent nation from 1918 to 1940. Before that period, it was ruled by various peoples, including the Germans, Poles, Russians, and Swedes.

Sovfoto

Riga, Latvia, lies on the Western Dvina River, south of the Gulf of Riga. It is the capital and largest city of Latvia. Riga is also an important shipping and industrial center. It has a blend of old and modern buildings.

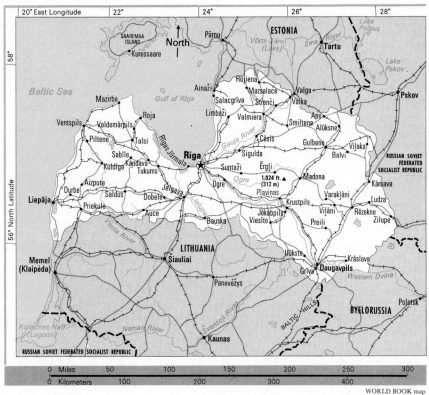

Capital ★

Other City or Town ●

Road

Rail Line

▲ Highest Known Elevation

River

WORLD BOOK map

Soviet troops occupied Latvia in 1940. Later that year, the Soviet government forcibly made it part of the Soviet Union. The United States and some other countries refused to recognize this action and still consider Latvia a separate nation.

Russia has a great influence on the social, economic, and political way of life in Latvia. But many Latvians strive nevertheless to maintain their own culture, language, and historical traditions.

The People. About 54 per cent of the people of Latvia are Latvians, also called *Letts*. They are ethnically related to the Lithuanians and have their own culture and language. Russians, who speak the Russian language, make up about 33 per cent of the population of Latvia. Byelorussians make up about 5 per cent of Latvia's population, Poles and Ukranians each account for about 3 per cent, and Lithuanians account for approximately 2 per cent.

The influence of the Latvians in their own country has declined rapidly since 1940. Previously, Latvians had made up about 75 per cent of the population. But many thousands were killed or driven from Latvia during World War II (1939-1945) or sent to Siberia after the war. Others escaped to the West. Many Latvians do not want to live under Soviet control, and others have been kept out of Latvia by the Russians. Thousands of Russians have migrated into Latvia since World War II, and many of them have replaced Latvians in important positions in the government and in business.

The Latvian language is one of the oldest in Europe. It is related to Sanskrit, a language of ancient India.

Today, all Latvians must learn Russian, which the Soviets made the official language of the republic. Russian has replaced the Latvian language in many government offices and in a number of schools. It is used in about a third of the newspapers and two-thirds of the TV programs.

Tass from Sovfoto

Latvians generally dress in Western-style clothes. But they may wear gaily decorated costumes for special events. The young people shown above are preparing materials for a student exhibit.

109

LATVIA

About two-thirds of the Latvian people live in urban areas. Many of the city dwellers have apartments in modern buildings constructed after World War II. Thousands of the city people moved from rural areas to the cities to work in various industries. Most of Latvia's rural people work on collective or state farms, which were established by the Soviet Union to replace private farms.

Latvians generally wear Western-style clothing, but many wear colorful national costumes during holiday festivals. Latvians have a rich tradition of folklore, especially folk songs. Choral singing is highly popular, and the people take part in a number of annual song festivals. Latvians enjoy ballet, drama, and opera and participate in a variety of sports, including basketball and soccer.

The Soviet government has restricted religion in Latvia by permitting religious services but no religious teaching. The government also discourages the people from going to church. For example, church attendance may bar persons from good educational and job opportunities. Before the Soviet take-over, about 70 per cent of the Latvians were members of the Lutheran Church. About 25 per cent were Roman Catholics. The rest were Jews or belonged to one of the Eastern Orthodox Churches.

Almost all the people of Latvia can read and write. Soviet law requires children to attend school from the age of 7 to 17. About 41,000 students attend Latvia's 10 universities, the largest of which is the Latvian P. Stuchka State University in Riga.

Land and Climate. Latvia, Estonia, and Lithuania are often called the Baltic States. They make up a region that forms part of the large coastal plain of northern Europe. Latvia consists chiefly of low hills and shallow valleys. It has many small lakes and swamps. Forests cover about 40 per cent of the land. The highest point is a hill in central Latvia that rises 1,024 feet (312 meters) above sea level.

Latvia's chief river is the Western Dvina (Daugava in Latvian). It flows northwest from Byelorussia through central Latvia and empties into the Gulf of Riga. Latvia has about 293 miles (472 kilometers) of coastline. Many of its beaches are popular resort areas.

Temperatures in Latvia range from about 19° to 27° F. (−7° to −3° C) in January to 61° to 64° F. (16° to 18° C) in July. Latvia receives from 20 to 31 inches (51 to 80 centimeters) of rain annually.

Economy. Manufacturing makes up about three-fourths of the value of production in Latvia. The Soviet government owns all the industries. Latvia's chief industries produce electronic equipment, household appliances, machinery, and processed foods and metals. The republic also produces some buses, railroad cars, and steel, which is used in manufacturing agricultural machinery.

Latvian workers have the highest average productivity in the Soviet Union. Latvians rank second to the Estonians in average income. Riga is Latvia's main industrial center. Other centers of manufacturing in Latvia include Daugavpils, Kuldīga, Liepāja, Limbaži, and Rēzekne.

Agriculture accounts for less than a fifth of the value of production in Latvia. Farm products include barley, flax, oats, potatoes, and rye. Many of the farmers work on dairy and cattle farms. The Soviet government owns Latvia's farms, which are organized as collective farms. Each collective farm unit consists of more than 400 farm families. The farmers receive a share of the farm production.

History. People lived in what is now Latvia as early as 7000 or 8000 B.C. They were forced out about the time of Christ by invaders who became the ancestors of the Latvians. In time, these people established trade with various groups, including Arabs, Estonians, Lithuanians, and Romans. They gradually developed their own language and culture.

The Vikings raided Latvia during the A.D. 800's, and Russian forces attacked Latvia several times in the 900's. The Teutonic Knights, an organization of German crusaders, invaded Latvia during the 1200's. War between the Latvians and the Knights lasted until the late 1200's, when the Latvians surrendered. See TEUTONIC KNIGHTS.

For more than 200 years, the Teutonic Knights governed Latvia as part of a larger state called Livonia. But by 1562, most of Latvia had come under the rule of Poland and Lithuania. A German-ruled duchy was also established there. Sweden conquered northern Latvia in 1621, and Russia took control of this area in 1710. By 1800, Russia ruled all of Latvia. But German merchants and landowners in Latvia continued to hold much political power.

During the late 1800's, the Latvians began to organize an independence movement. This movement became stronger in the early 1900's as Russian and German authority declined in Latvia. On Nov. 18, 1918, just after the end of World War I, Latvia proclaimed itself independent. Russia and Germany tried to keep control of the new nation, but they finally recognized Latvia's independence in 1920.

In 1922, Latvia adopted a constitution that established a democratic form of government. The new democratic government passed land reform laws that broke up the large estates owned by a few wealthy persons. The government divided this land into small farms and distributed the farms among the people. In 1936, during the Great Depression, Latvian democracy suffered a setback. The president seized power and reduced the role of parliament and the rights of the nation's political parties.

In 1939, shortly before World War II began, Russia and Germany agreed secretly to divide much of eastern Europe between themselves. Russia then forced Latvia to sign a treaty under which the Soviets built military bases in Latvia. Soviet troops occupied Latvia in June 1940, and Latvian Communists took over the government. In August, Russia made Latvia part of the Soviet Union.

German forces invaded Latvia in 1941. They occupied Latvia until 1944, when Soviet troops recaptured it. Many Latvians tried to prevent the Russians from taking over their country again. But the Soviets killed or deported those who opposed them.

Life in Latvia has changed greatly under the Russians. The Soviet Union established a powerful Communist government and took control of all industry and land. In addition, a growing number of Russian immigrants has reduced the influence of the Latvian culture and language. Despite such changes, however, many Latvians continue to express their national spirit and to oppose Russian rule. V. STANLEY VARDYS

See also BALTIC STATES; RIGA.

LAUBACH, *LAW bahk,* **FRANK CHARLES** (1884-1970), an American missionary, preacher, and educator, won world fame for teaching illiterate peoples to read. His system used symbols to represent phonetic sounds. Laubach first used the system while serving as a missionary in the Philippines from 1915 to 1936. Governments of many countries later sponsored his program. Laubach was co-author of more than 200 primers for illiterate adults in over 165 languages. "Each one teach one" became one of his principles. He was born in Benton, Pa. GALEN SAYLOR

LAUD, *lawd,* **WILLIAM** (1573-1645), was the dominating figure in the Church of England during the struggle between King Charles I and the Puritan-controlled Parliament. Charles became king in 1625, and in 1633 he appointed Laud as archbishop of Canterbury.

Laud believed that, since the Church of England was the national church, all Englishmen should belong to it. He directed his efforts to enforce uniformity in religion mainly against the Puritans. Laud believed in the importance of formal religious worship and the "beauty of holiness." Laud was too impatient to try persuasion. Instead, he gathered together all the legal machinery of church and state and used it against the Puritans. His stand aroused anger against both Laud and King Charles, which eventually contributed to the Civil War.

In 1640 Laud was arrested on charges of treason. In early 1645, Parliament passed a bill of attainder condemning Laud to death, even though there was no evidence to support the charges against him. Laud was beheaded soon afterward.

Laud was born in Reading, England, and attended St. John's College, Oxford University. He became a clergyman and rapidly rose to prominence under the rule of King Charles I. GEORGE L. MOSSE

LAUDANUM. See OPIUM (History).

LAUE, *LOW uh,* **MAX THEODOR FELIX VON,** *mahks TAY oh DOHR FAY lihks fuhn* (1879-1960), a German physicist, received the 1914 Nobel Prize in physics for his research in X-ray diffraction. Von Laue discovered that X rays might be *diffracted* (bent) by certain crystals such as rock salt. This made it possible to measure wave lengths of X rays and to study the relative position of atoms within a crystal. He also contributed to the theory of relativity. He was born in Pfaffendorf, near Koblenz, Germany. RALPH E. LAPP

LAUGHING GAS. See NITROUS OXIDE.

LAUGHING JACKASS. See KOOKABURRA.

LAUGHTON, *LAW tuhn,* **CHARLES** (1899-1962), an American actor, gained fame for his character portrayals on the stage and in films. Laughton succeeded almost from the beginning of his career. He won an Academy Award in 1933 for his performance in *The Private Life of Henry VIII.* He was born in Scarborough, England. He became a U.S. citizen in 1950. HARRIET VAN HORNE

LAULAU. See HAWAII (Food).

LAUNCH VEHICLE. See ROCKET (Launching Probes and Satellites; Space Travel); SPACE TRAVEL (Launch Vehicles; Launching a Spacecraft).

LAUNCHING. See GUIDED MISSILE (Launching Equipment); ROCKET; SHIP (Launching and Outfitting a Ship); SPACE TRAVEL (Launching a Spacecraft).

LAUNFAL, *LAWN fuhl,* **SIR,** was a knight of King Arthur's Round Table in medieval British legend. Launfal was the hero of several literary works. The earliest-known one, *Lai de Lanval,* was written in the late 1100's by the French poet Marie de France. In this story, Launfal falls in love with a beautiful fairy. She gives him wealth and happiness but makes him promise not to reveal their source.

The American poet James Russell Lowell wrote the best-known modern story of Launfal, *The Vision of Sir Launfal* (1848). In this tale, Launfal dreams of searching for the Holy Grail, the cup or dish that Jesus Christ used at the Last Supper. Launfal does not find the Grail, but he learns its meaning when he helps a starving leper. The leper teaches him that the Grail symbolizes charity and mercy. ROBERT W. ACKERMAN

LAURA INGALLS WILDER AWARD is presented to an author or illustrator who has made "a lasting and substantial contribution" to children's literature. The Association for Library Service to Children, a division of the American Library Association, selects the winner. The award was established in 1954 to honor Laura Ingalls Wilder, an American author best known for her "Little House" series. The award, a bronze medal, depicts Wilder as a child holding a doll. The award was given every five years from 1960 to 1980. Since 1980, it has been given every three years. MARILYN FAIN APSELOFF

Laura Ingalls Wilder Award Winners

Year	Winner	Year	Winner
1954	*Laura Ingalls Wilder	1980	*Theodor Geisel
1960	Clara Ingram Judson		(Dr. Seuss)
1965	*Ruth Sawyer	1983	*Maurice Sendak
1970	*E. B. White	1986	Jean Fritz
1975	*Beverly Cleary		

*Has a separate biography in WORLD BOOK.

LAUREATE. See POET LAUREATE.

LAUREL is a family of trees and shrubs that grow mostly in tropical and subtropical areas and are known for their spicy odor. The family includes avocado, camphor, cinnamon, and sassafras. *True laurel,* or *sweet bay,* grows near the Mediterranean Sea. Ancient Greeks used its leaves to crown victorious athletes. The *California,*

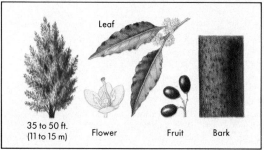

Leaf

35 to 50 ft.
(11 to 15 m)   Flower   Fruit   Bark

WORLD BOOK illustration by Christabel King

The True Laurel is found in the Mediterranean region. It has smooth, shiny leaves and bears yellow flowers and dark-colored berries. Laurels grow mainly in areas with hot or warm climates.

LAUREL

or *Oregon*, laurel is called *myrtlewood*. It grows along the Pacific Coast. Its rich, light-brown wood is valued for furniture and decorations. Plants of other families are called laurels. *Cherry*, or *English*, laurel is a group of evergreen cherry trees in the rose family. The *mountain laurel* is in the heath family.

Scientific Classification. True laurels belong to the laurel family, Lauraceae. They are *Laurus nobilis*. California laurels also belong to the laurel family. They are *Umbellularia californica.* ELBERT L. LITTLE, JR.

Related Articles in WORLD BOOK include:

Avocado	Cinnamon	Sassafras
Camphor	Mountain Laurel	

LAUREL, Miss. (pop. 21,897), founded as a sawmill town in 1882, is one of the state's leading industrial centers. It is on the edge of the vast yellow pine forest of southern Mississippi (see MISSISSIPPI [political map]). It produces lumber and wood products, tools for oil fields, refrigeration equipment, canned foods, and garments. Oil fields opened near Laurel in 1944, and a refinery was built nearby in 1945. Laurel has a commission form of government. CHARLOTTE CAPERS

LAUREL AND HARDY were the most popular comedy team in American motion-picture history. Stan Laurel (1890-1965) played a timid little dimwit. He continually exasperated his partner, Oliver (Ollie) Hardy (1892-1957), who played a fat, bullying know-it-all. The team starred in more than 60 short films and 27 feature movies from 1926 to 1952. Unlike most stars of the silent film era, Laurel and Hardy also made successful sound films. One of these movies, *The Music Box* (1932), won an Academy Award.

Laurel, whose real name was Arthur Stanley Jefferson, was born in Ulverson, England, and began his career in vaudeville. He came to the United States in 1910 and made his first film in 1917. Oliver Norvell Hardy was born in Harlem, Ga. He made his first short comedies in 1913 and moved to Hollywood in 1918.

Laurel and Hardy teamed up for the first time in 1926 in *Putting Pants on Philip*, which was released in 1927. Their later films included *Babes in Toyland* (1934), *Sons of the Desert* (1934), *Way Out West* (1937), and *Blockheads* (1938). CHARLES CHAMPLIN

Scene from *Helpmates* (1931); the Granger Collection

Laurel and Hardy formed a famous film comedy team. Hardy, *left,* played a blustery character. Laurel was his dumb partner.

In the Park (1924), an oil painting on canvas; National Gallery of Art, Washington, D.C., the Chester Dale Collection

A Laurencin Painting portrays a group of young women in casual poses. The pale colors are typical of the artist's style.

LAURENCIN, *law rahn SAN,* **MARIE** (1885-1956), was a French painter and designer. Her best-known paintings portray young upper-class women, often during moments of leisure. In the 1920's, Laurencin created a slender, long-waisted female type that contributed to the *flapper* fashions of that period. Laurencin painted in a decorative style she easily adapted to commercial art. She became a successful designer of book illustrations, stage sets, wallpaper, textiles, and women's clothing.

Laurencin was born in Paris. In the early 1900's, she became part of a circle of modern artists that included Pablo Picasso and Henri Matisse. Laurencin was an illegitimate child and never learned her father's identity. Some scholars believe that her paintings of single figures of women and women in small groups indicate a sense of isolation and an antimale attitude. ALBERT BOIME

LAURENTIAN PLATEAU. See CANADIAN SHIELD.

LAURENTIAN UNIVERSITY, *law REHN shuhn,* is a coeducational university in Sudbury, Ont. It is supported mainly by the province. It has courses in arts, commerce, engineering, nursing, physical education, science, social work, and translation. It grants bachelor's degrees, and master's degrees in science. Classes are taught in French and English. Huntington, Sudbury, and Thorneloe universities in Sudbury, Algoma College in Sault Sainte Marie, Nipissing College in North Bay, and Le Collège de Hearst in Hearst are part of Laurentian University. It was founded in 1960. For enrollment, see CANADA (table: Universities and Colleges).

Critically reviewed by LAURENTIAN UNIVERSITY

SIR WILFRID LAURIER

Prime Minister of Canada
1896-1911

TUPPER	LAURIER	BORDEN
1896	1896-1911	1911-1920

Detail of a portrait by John Russell;
House of Commons, Ottawa (John Evans)

LAURIER, *LAW rih ay,* **SIR WILFRID** (1841-1919), was the first French-Canadian to become Prime Minister of Canada. He held the office from 1896 to 1911. Laurier served in Parliament for 45 years and was leader of the Liberal Party for 32 years.

Throughout his long public service, Laurier worked to unite French-speaking and English-speaking Canadians for the good of Canada. He also laid the foundation for Canadian independence by opposing strong ties with the British Empire. During Laurier's term as Prime Minister, Canada enjoyed great prosperity. The settlement of western Canada led to the establishment in 1905 of two new western prairie provinces—Alberta and Saskatchewan.

The "Old Chief," as many called Laurier, looked like a model of an aristocrat. He wore a black frock coat with a vest. His coat lapels were lined with a white frill. His collar rose high and straight, and his tie was so wide that it hid his shirt.

Laurier spoke English and French equally well. He became one of the outstanding orators in Canadian history. He used few gestures as he spoke, but the rich tones of his voice often held audiences spellbound.

Early Life

Boyhood and Education. Wilfrid Laurier was born on Nov. 20, 1841, in Quebec in the village of St. Lin (now Laurentides), near L'Épiphanie. His ancestors had come to Canada from Normandy, France. One of them was a soldier under Paul de Chomedey, Sieur de Maisonneuve, who founded Montreal in 1642.

Wilfrid's mother, Marie Marcelle Martineau Laurier,

died when he was 6 years old. His father, Carolus Laurier, later married Adelaine Ethier. Wilfrid had three half brothers and a half sister.

Carolus Laurier was a farmer and surveyor. A man of strong liberal beliefs, he did not want Wilfrid to grow up knowing only the French culture. When Wilfrid was about 11, his father sent him to live for two years with a Scots-Canadian family in a neighboring village. There the boy learned the English language and became familiar with English ways of life.

Laurier attended L'Assomption College, a French-Canadian school in L'Assomption, Que. He liked public speaking and helped form a debating society there.

In 1861, Laurier began to study law at McGill University in Montreal. His father had little money at this time, and Wilfrid took a part-time job with the Montreal law firm of Laflamme and Laflamme. Rodolphe Laflamme, the head of the firm, was an active Liberal. Laurier received his law degree in 1864.

Young Lawyer. Laurier practiced law in Montreal for two years after his graduation. In 1866, he developed a serious lung ailment. At the suggestion of a friend, Laurier moved to Arthabaskaville, a new settlement in Arthabaska County, Quebec. He hoped the country air would restore his health. In Arthabaskaville, he became a popular and successful lawyer. He also edited the newspaper *Le Defricheur* for about six months. Laurier wrote editorials that Roman Catholic leaders considered too radical. The newspaper went out of business, chiefly because of lack of funds.

Laurier married Zoe Lafontaine (1841-1921) of Montreal on May 13, 1868. The couple lived in Arthabaskaville until Laurier became Prime Minister. They often returned there for rest during the busy years that followed. The Lauriers had no children.

Early Public Career

In 1871, at the age of 29, Laurier was elected to the Quebec legislature as a Liberal. Three years later, in 1874, he was elected to parliament from Drummond-Arthabaska, Quebec.

The poet Louis Honoré Fréchette described reaction to Laurier's first speech in the house of commons: "... Who could be this young politician ... who thus, in a maiden speech, handled the deepest public questions with such boldness and authority? ... On the following day, the name of Laurier was on every lip. ... It seemed as if every one realized that a future chieftain had just proclaimed himself ..."

In 1877, Laurier accepted the invitation of Prime Minister Alexander Mackenzie to join his cabinet as minister of inland revenue. He held the office for less than a year because the Liberals were defeated in the 1878 election. For the next 18 years, until he became Prime Minister, Laurier sat on the opposition side of the house of commons.

During the late 1800's, the Liberals in Quebec met strong opposition from the Roman Catholic Church. In 1877, Laurier made a speech on liberalism that became a classic in Canadian political history. In this speech, he distinguished between liberalism in politics and liberalism in religion. Laurier declared that French-Canadian Catholics had the right to form their own political opinions without interference from the church. But he warned against the possible creation of a French-Canadian Catholic political party. Such a party, Laurier said, would inevitably be met by an English-Canadian Protestant party that would oppose the French-Canadians. And, he pointed out, most Canadians were English-Canadians.

In 1880, Edward Blake succeeded Alexander Mackenzie as leader of the Liberal party. Laurier became Blake's aide and leader of the party's Quebec wing.

The Execution of Louis Riel in 1885 brought Laurier back into the spotlight. Riel had led French-Canadian *métis* (persons of mixed European and Indian descent) in the rebellion in Saskatchewan against the government. They revolted in fear of being thrown off their lands. Riel was captured and sentenced to death. French-Canadians considered Riel a hero, and demanded that he be pardoned. English-Canadians demanded his death for treason. Prime Minister Sir John A. Macdonald let the sentence stand, and Riel was hanged. See RIEL, LOUIS; SASKATCHEWAN REBELLION.

French-Canadians in Montreal staged a demonstration in protest against Riel's execution. Laurier joined in the demonstration. He declared that if he lived along the Saskatchewan River, where the revolt started, he would have shouldered his musket along with the métis. Blake joined Laurier in protesting Riel's execution. But most Liberals outside Quebec refused to follow them. The Conservatives won the 1887 election.

The Liberals had now lost three successive elections—in 1878, 1882, and 1887. In despair, Blake resigned as Liberal party leader. He advised the party to elect

Laurier his successor. On June 7, 1887, Laurier became leader of the Liberal party—the first French-Canadian to head one of Canada's major political parties. Most English-Canadian Liberals, as well as Laurier himself, felt that because he was a French-Canadian he could

IMPORTANT DATES IN LAURIER'S LIFE

1841 (Nov. 20) Born in St. Lin, Que.
1871 Elected to the Quebec legislature.
1874 Elected to parliament.
1877 Appointed minister of inland revenue.
1887 (June 7) Elected leader of the Liberal party.
1896 (July 11) Became Prime Minister of Canada.
1897 Knighted by Queen Victoria.
1899 Sent Canadian troops to aid Britain in the Boer War.
1905 Alberta and Saskatchewan became provinces.
1910 Proposed building a Canadian navy.
1911 (Sept. 1) Resigned as Prime Minister after the Liberals lost the election.
1917 Refused to join the coalition Union government in support of conscription.
1919 (Feb. 17) Died in Ottawa.

Marge and Philip Shackleton

Homesteaders, lured by rich prairie lands, rapidly settled western Canada during the late 1800's and the early 1900's.

Laurier Sent Troops to aid Britain in the Boer War (1899-1902) although French-Canadians hotly opposed the move.

never win the support of English-speaking Canadians.

Laurier wanted to distract attention from the bitter English-French quarrel over Riel. Partly in an effort to do so, he proposed an unrestricted reciprocal trade agreement with the United States (see RECIPROCAL TRADE AGREEMENT). Prime Minister Macdonald opposed such a pact. He declared that completely free trade would lead to eventual political union with the United States. In the election of early 1891, Macdonald and the Conservatives defeated Laurier and the Liberals on the issue of trade with the United States.

Macdonald died in June, 1891. During the next five years, the Conservative party slowly lost popularity under the leadership of four Conservative Prime Ministers—Sir John J.C. Abbott (1891-1892), Sir John S.D. Thompson (1892-1894), Sir Mackenzie Bowell (1894-1896), and Sir Charles Tupper (1896).

The Manitoba School Issue brought Laurier and the Liberals to power. In 1890, the Manitoba legislature had abolished tax support for Roman Catholic, French-

language schools in the province. It felt that one school system for all children would be more efficient than separate public and Roman Catholic schools. Catholics in Manitoba charged that they were being deprived of their constitutional rights. In 1895, the Canadian government ordered Manitoba to restore tax funds to the Catholic schools. Manitoba refused. In 1896, the Conservative government introduced a bill providing for separate schools in Manitoba. The issue was hotly debated in the election of that year. Laurier declared that a compromise could be reached by "sunny ways" rather than by force. Although Roman Catholic leaders opposed Laurier, French-Canadians supported him. The Liberals won the election.

Prime Minister (1896-1911)

At the age of 54, Wilfrid Laurier took office as Prime Minister of Canada on July 11, 1896. He succeeded

IMPORTANT EVENTS DURING LAURIER'S ADMINISTRATION

Alaska Boundary Dispute between Canada and the United States was settled in 1903 by a special commission.

Railways, built with the aid of Laurier's government, speeded development of the prairies in the early 1900's.

Manitoba School Issue involved religious instruction and the use of French. Laurier won a compromise in 1896.

Laurier House was the home of two Canadian Prime Ministers—Sir Wilfrid Laurier and Mackenzie King. The home in Ottawa, Ont., is now a public museum.

National Film Board

Conservative Sir Charles Tupper. Laurier soon worked out a compromise solution in the Manitoba school problem. The province agreed to permit religious teaching and the use of French during certain periods of the school day. The amount of such instruction was based on the number of pupils who desired it.

When Laurier came to power, a long period of falling prices was ending. Europe had grown prosperous and had become a booming market for Canadian wheat and other food products. Laurier acted to take advantage of the favorable economic situation. During his administration, the government helped about 2,000,000 immigrants enter Canada. Most of the newcomers settled on the western prairies. The government also helped build the Canadian Northern and the Grand Trunk Pacific railways to carry out the wheat that the settlers grew. The country enjoyed its greatest prosperity since 1867. The Liberals won re-election in 1900, 1904, and 1908. Queen Victoria knighted Laurier in 1897.

Prosperity helped soften the conflict between French- and English-Canadians. But in 1905, the government established two new provinces—Saskatchewan and Alberta—in the area between Manitoba and British Columbia. Laurier allowed each of these provinces to have a separate Roman Catholic school system. Another storm over religion and education arose, but it died down fairly quickly.

Relations With Great Britain caused further hostility between English- and French-Canadians. The chief question was what action Canada would take if Great Britain should go to war.

In 1897, the British colonial secretary, Joseph Chamberlain, suggested closer economic ties between members of the British Empire. Laurier's government agreed that year to decrease tariffs on British goods. But Laurier opposed any system that would bind Great Britain and the British colonies in one economic unit. Laurier maintained his opposition to the empire as a close-knit unit at the four Imperial Conferences that he attended in 1897, 1902, 1907, and 1911.

In 1899, Great Britain went to war against the Boers in South Africa (see BOER WAR). English-Canadians demanded that Canada send troops to support Britain. French-Canadians, who made up less than half the population, opposed any aid. Laurier decided that the majority should rule. He sent troops to Africa. French-Canadians protested strongly. Even Henri Bourassa, Laurier's most promising young lieutenant in Quebec, rebelled against the policy. From then on, French-Canadians and English-Canadians became more divided on Canada's role in the British Empire.

By 1910, Great Britain faced the threat of war with Germany. Laurier decided to build a Canadian navy to support Britain if war began. Parliament approved his Naval Service Bill, but many Canadians opposed it. Some French-Canadians thought Laurier "too British" because he had supported Britain. Some English-Canadians considered him "too French" because of his background and opposition to closer ties with Britain.

Defeat. In 1911, the United States offered Canada a limited reciprocal trade treaty. Laurier accepted, and the two governments drew up an agreement that seemed to give equal benefits to each. But a number of Canadians still feared domination by the United States. Many resented the settlement in 1903 of the Alaska border dispute between the two countries (see ALASKA [The Early 1900's]).

The Liberals lost the election of September, 1911, chiefly because of the public's opposition to the naval bill and the trade agreement with the United States. In Quebec, Bourassa helped defeat Laurier by forming an alliance with the Conservatives. Robert L. Borden, a Conservative, became Prime Minister.

Later Years

The Conscription Crisis. For the rest of his life, Sir Wilfrid Laurier continued to serve as leader of the Liberal party. When World War I began in 1914, Laurier supported the Conservative government in joining the war to aid Great Britain.

As the war dragged on, it became clear that far fewer French-Canadians than English-Canadians were enlisting for military service. By 1917, the Canadian forces fighting in Europe needed replacements. Until then, all Canadian servicemen had enlisted voluntarily. Prime Minister Borden decided that *conscription* (drafting of men for military service) had become necessary.

Borden wanted both parties to approve conscription so that unity could be kept among all Canadians. To carry out the policy, Borden asked Laurier to join a Union Government made up of both Liberals and Conservatives. Laurier refused. He felt he would lose control of the Liberals in Quebec if he joined the proposed government. Bourassa and his followers also firmly opposed conscription. They felt they had no direct responsibility in the war.

Most of Laurier's English-Canadian followers broke away from him and helped Borden form the Union Government. They felt that Laurier was too concerned with keeping his hold on Quebec and that he did not consider the national interests of Canada as a whole. But Laurier felt it would be dangerous if Bourassa's radical nationalism replaced his moderate leadership.

In the election of December, 1917, English-Canadians voted overwhelmingly for the Union Government. Borden stayed in power. But most French-Canadians voted against the Union Government and conscription.

The split between English- and French-Canadians saddened Laurier. Ever since entering parliament more than 40 years before, he had worked to unite the two groups. But later events proved that his efforts had not been in vain. After Laurier died in 1919, W. L. Mackenzie King succeeded in reuniting French- and English-Canadian Liberals.

Death. Sir Wilfrid Laurier died on Feb. 17, 1919, at the age of 77. He was buried in Ottawa. Lady Laurier died in 1921. In her will, she left Laurier House, their home in Ottawa, to Mackenzie King. After King died in 1951, the Canadian government made Laurier House a museum. Laurier's birthplace at St. Lin is a national historic site. FRANK H. UNDERHILL

Related Articles in WORLD BOOK include:

Lausanne, Switzerland, is a famous tourist center. The city is built on hills nestled along the northern shore of beautiful Lake Geneva. Behind the city are the towering peaks of the Alps.

Beringer and Pampalucchi, from Conzett and Huber

Additional Resources

CLIPPINGDALE, RICHARD. *Laurier: His Life and World.* McGraw (Scarborough, Ont.), 1979.

DAFOE, JOHN W. *Laurier: A Study in Canadian Politics.* Macmillan (Toronto), 1963. Reprint of 1922 ed.

SCHULL, JOSEPH. *Laurier: The First Canadian.* St. Martin's, 1965. A biography.

LAUSANNE, *loh ZAN* or *loh ZAHN* (pop. 132,400; met. area pop. 227,200), is a city in western Switzerland, on the north shore of Lake Geneva (see SWITZERLAND [map]). Lausanne is a major center of tourism and the commercial and industrial center of its region. It also serves as the capital of the *canton* (state) of Vaud.

Lausanne is a hilly city with steep roads. Huge bridges connect some of the hills. Lausanne's landmarks include a medieval castle and a medieval Gothic cathedral with beautiful stained glass windows. Its many industries include printing, woodworking, and the manufacture of chemicals, metal products, and radios.

Roman soldiers established a colony on the site of what is now Lausanne in about 50 B.C. The Swiss city of Bern conquered Lausanne and the rest of Vaud in 1536.

Vaud gained independence in the late 1700's. In 1803, it joined the union of Swiss cantons called the Swiss Confederation. HEINZ K. MEIER

LAUSANNE, TREATY OF. See GREECE (World War I).

LAUSANNE CONFERENCE. See WAR DEBT (The Lausanne Conference).

LAUSSEDAT, AIMÉ. See PHOTOGRAMMETRY.

LAVA is molten rock that pours out of volcanoes or from cracks in the earth. It comes from deep in the earth where the heat is great. When lava first comes to the surface it is red hot, reaching temperatures from seven to ten times hotter than boiling water.

Properties of Lava. Lava is a solution of silicate minerals (see SILICA). It is similar to the hot liquid that would result if granite or basalt were melted. When lava cools quite rapidly, only a few crystals can form. The lava hardens into a rock that contains large amounts of natural glass.

The volcanoes or earth *fissures* (cracks) that contain the lava are sometimes explosive. From time to time they blow out large quantities of dust and rock fragments that form layers between lava flows. Some types

© G. D. Plage, Bruce Coleman Inc.

Red-Hot, Fiery Lava may reach temperatures from 7 to 10 times as hot as boiling water. The photograph above shows lava flowing from Nyiragongo, a volcano in eastern Zaire.

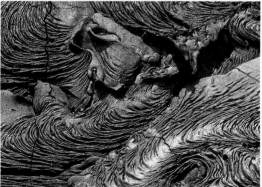

© Gerald A. Corsi, Tom Stack & Assoc.

Cooling Lava hardens into various formations. Highly fluid lava forms smooth, folded sheets of rock, such as those found in the Galapagos Islands, *above.* Stickier lava produces jagged sheets.

113

LAVA BEDS NATIONAL MONUMENT

of lava contain large amounts of dissolved gases. As the gases expand, they are trapped in the lava, and form many bubbles. *Pumice* is a type of lava that contains many bubbles (see PUMICE).

Lands that were once covered with lava often become quite fertile after weathering has broken the lava into

Grant Heilman

Spongelike Rock forms from lava with a high gas content. As such lava cools, it traps the gases and creates bubbles.

Glassy Rock results from lava that cools and hardens so quickly that only a few crystals can form.

fine soil. Some lavas, such as a glassy lava called *perlite*, are heated in furnaces. They expand into a frothy material used to manufacture lightweight concrete.

Kinds of Lava. There are two kinds of lava. One kind is *viscous* (sticky) and moves slowly like thick molasses. The other kind is so fluid that when it first erupts it flows down the side of a volcano faster than a person can run. Both the viscous and the fluid types of lava form a crust of rock.

Sometimes the liquid lava inside the crust cracks the hardened lava surface into many rough blocks that drag and tumble along as the lava creeps down the side of the volcano. At other times, the lava breaks a hole through the rocky crust and flows through, leaving a huge lava cave or tunnel. In Idaho, in the area of the Craters of the Moon, a person can walk into many lava caves that were formed only a few thousand years ago. The surface of such lava is covered with many wrinkles.

Location of Lava Beds. Many regions of the earth consist of piled-up sheets of lava. In the northwestern United States, the Columbia lava plateau is made up of a great lava pile more than 5,000 feet (1,500 meters) thick in places. The islands of Hawaii are a chain of volcanoes built mostly of lava. The mountain belt of southern Mexico, with its hundreds of volcanoes, also has a great lava pile.   ERNEST E. WAHLSTROM

See also IGNEOUS ROCK; ROCK (Igneous); VOLCANO.

LAVA BEDS NATIONAL MONUMENT is in northern California. It includes exhibits of volcanic action and lava flows. The monument, established in 1925, was the main battleground of the Modoc Indian War of 1873. For its area, see NATIONAL PARK SYSTEM (table: National Monuments).

LAVAL, *luh VAL*, Que. (pop. 268,335), is the second largest city in Quebec. A part of the Montreal metropolitan area, it lies on Jésus Island, which lies just north of Montreal where the Ottawa and St. Lawrence rivers meet. Four bridges link Laval with Montreal, Canada's largest city. For location, see QUEBEC (political map).

Laval factories manufacture furniture, industrial machinery, iron and steel, paper products, and pharmaceutical products. In 1681, four French families settled on the island. Eventually, 14 small towns were formed there. In 1965, these towns were combined to form Laval. The city has a council-manager government.

LAVAL, *luh VAL,* **PIERRE** (1883-1945), was a French politician who collaborated with the Germans during World War II. After the Germans invaded France in May, 1940, Laval urged surrender. He held office in the Vichy government and succeeded Henri Pétain as premier of Vichy France in April, 1942 (see PÉTAIN, HENRI PHILIPPE; VICHY). After Germany surrendered in 1945, Laval was handed over to the new French government and was convicted of treason. He swallowed poison in a suicide attempt on the day of his execution, but was revived and shot by a firing squad.

United Press Int.

Pierre Laval

Laval was born in Auvergne province in southern France. He studied at the universities of Lyon and Paris. In 1914 he was elected to the French Chamber of Deputies, and after World War I began to rise in politics. He held several cabinet posts and was premier twice. In 1935, as premier, he shared in the Hoare-Laval Agreement, proposing that France and Britain negotiate peace between Italy and Ethiopia. In 1938 he supported the Munich Agreement, giving Germany part of Czechoslovakia.   ERNEST JOHN KNAPTON

LAVAL DE MONTMORENCY, *luh VAL duh mawn maw rahn SEE,* **FRANÇOIS XAVIER DE,** *frahn SWAH gzah VYAY duh* (1623-1708), was the first Roman Catholic bishop of the city of Quebec. Quebec was then the capital of New France, a French colony that included much of Canada and part of what is now the United States.

Laval was a major figure in the religious and civil affairs of the colony from 1659 to 1688. He founded the Seminary of Quebec (now Laval University) in 1663 to train priests for work in New France. Laval tried to end practices that he considered evil. His efforts caused many conflicts between him and government officials. For example, he tried to prevent traders from selling liquor to Indians. But some government officials who wanted to protect the traders opposed him.

Laval was born in Montigny-sur-Avre, near Paris, France. He became a Jesuit priest in 1647 and a bishop in 1658. He was sent to Quebec in 1659. Poor health forced him to retire in 1688.   P. B. WAITE

LAVAL UNIVERSITY is the oldest institution of higher learning in Canada. It is a coeducational Roman Catholic school in Ste.-Foy, Que. Founded in 1663 as the Seminary of Quebec, the school was granted a royal charter as Laval University in 1852. It received a new charter from the provincial government in 1970. Laval University offers courses in all major fields and grants bachelor's, master's, and doctor's degrees. Instruction is in French. For the enrollment of Laval University, see CANADA (table: Universities and Colleges).

Critically reviewed by LAVAL UNIVERSITY

LAVENDER is a small bush that bears fragrant flowers and leaves. It belongs to the mint family. It grows wild in Mediterranean countries, and occasionally is cultivated.

Lavender grows from 3 to 4 feet (91 to 120 centimeters) high. It has long, narrow, pale green leaves and pale purple flowers. This shade of purple is called *lavender* after the flowers. The flowers grow in whorls around a single stalk. When dried, they keep their fragrance for a long time.

Lavender comes from the Latin word *lavo*, meaning *to wash*. This name was used because the Romans put the leaves and flowers in the water when they bathed. In tradition, lavender represents purity. Ladies once stored their linens and clothing with dried lavender and leaves. The expression "lavender and old lace" is often used to mean someone with gentle manners. The lavender plant is used in making some perfumes.

J. Horace McFarland

The Long Slender Leaves of the lavender grow on the same single stalk from which the fragrant flowers extend.

Scientific Classification. Lavender belongs to the mint family, *Labiatae*. The plant is classified as genus *Lavandula*, species *L. officinalis*. GEORGE A. BEACH

See also MINT; PERFUME.

LAVENDER PIT, one of the world's largest open-pit copper mines, is located at Bisbee, Ariz. It is owned by the Phelps Dodge Corporation. The mine is named after Harrison M. Lavender, a company officer who carried out the plan to produce valuable copper ore from low-grade copper-bearing rock. Production of the ore began in 1954. ALICE B. GOOD

LAVER, ROD (1938-), is one of the leading tennis players of all time. He was born the year that Don Budge became the first man to win the Australian, British, French, and United States championships. In 1962, Laver became the only man to equal Budge's feat. In 1969, Laver again won the "grand slam" of tennis. He was the first player to do so twice.

Rodney George Laver was born in Rockhampton, Australia, and played on four winning Australian Davis Cup teams. He lost two Davis Cup matches in 1959 but won all six of his singles events in the 1960, 1961, and 1962 Davis Cup finals. Laver became a professional player in 1963. HERMAN WEISKOPF

LAVERAN, *lah VRAHN,* **CHARLES LOUIS AL-PHONSE** (1845-1922), a French Army surgeon, discovered the parasite that causes malaria. He also made other contributions to the knowledge of tropical diseases. He received the 1907 Nobel prize in medicine.

In Algeria, in 1880, Laveran recognized the malaria parasite in the blood of soldiers suffering from the disease. As early as 1884, he became convinced that mosquitoes played an important part in spreading the disease. In 1892, he described several species of *trypanosomes*, the parasites that cause sleeping sickness.

Laveran was born in Paris and served as a military physician for 29 years. He retired from the army in 1907 and became director of the Honorary Service of the Pasteur Institute in Paris. HENRY J. L. MARRIOTT

LA VÉRENDRYE, *lah vay RAHN dree,* **SIEUR DE** (1685-1749), PIERRE GAULTIER DE VARENNES, was a French-Canadian fur trader and explorer. In 1731, La Vérendrye, three of his sons, and a nephew set out from Montreal to find an overland route to the Pacific Ocean. They got as far west as what are now Saskatchewan and the Dakotas by 1738. Two of the sons may have reached the Rocky Mountains in 1742. Along the way, La Vérendrye established outposts that served as forts and fur-trading stations, and he claimed much land for the French king. His reports added to the knowledge of the geography of the area. His fur-trading business was unprofitable, and he returned to Montreal in 1743.

La Vérendrye was born in Trois-Rivières, Que. He served in the French Army in Canada and France before he began exploring. P. B. WAITE

See also MANITOBA (History); NORTH DAKOTA (History); SOUTH DAKOTA (History).

LA VERNE COLLEGE. See UNIVERSITIES AND COLLEGES (table).

LA VILLITA. See SAN ANTONIO (The City).

LAVOISIER, *lah vwah ZYAY,* **ANTOINE LAURENT** (1743-1794), was a French chemist. He gave the first accurate, scientific explanation of the mysteries of fire. In 1777, after a series of careful experiments with fire, he stated that burning is the result of the rapid union of the burning material with oxygen.

Lavoisier also proved the law of conservation of matter. This law states that matter can be neither created nor destroyed, but can only be changed from one form into another. When a candle burns, it appears to have been destroyed. Lavoisier showed that there is as much mass or weight present after the candle burns as before. The substances have only changed their forms. He applied his ideas to combustion in the body, and showed that the source of energy is the slow burning of food.

These ideas led him to write the first chemical equation. In such an equation, the mass of materials before any chemical change must equal the mass of products after it. Lavoisier and other French chemists worked out the present-day system of chemical names. He wrote *Elements of Chemistry* (1789), the first modern textbook of chemistry.

Lavoisier was born in Paris of well-to-do parents, and attended the Collège Mazarin. He became especially interested in physical sciences and mathematics while in school. In 1766, the French Academy of Sciences awarded him a gold medal for a plan of lighting city streets. Two years later he became a member of the academy. He established agricultural experiment stations and tried to improve farming methods in France. For most of his life, Lavoisier was a member of the financial company that collected taxes for the government. The leaders of the French Revolution regarded this group as aristocrats. Lavoisier and the other members of the financial company were put to death on the guillotine by the revolutionists. HENRY M. LEICESTER

See also OXYGEN; CHEMISTRY (The Beginning of Modern Chemistry).

LAW

LAW is the set of enforced rules under which a society is governed. Law is one of the most basic social institutions—and one of the most necessary. No society could exist if all people did just as they pleased, without regard for the rights of others. Nor could a society exist if its members did not recognize that they also have certain obligations toward one another. The law thus establishes the rules that define a person's rights and obligations. The law also sets penalties for people who violate these rules, and it states how government shall enforce the rules and penalties. However, the laws enforced by government can be changed. In fact, laws frequently are changed to reflect changes in a society's needs and attitudes.

In most societies, various government bodies, especially police agencies and courts, see that the laws are obeyed. Because a person can be penalized for disobeying the law, most people agree that laws should be just. Justice is a moral standard that applies to all human conduct. The laws enforced by government have usually had a strong moral element, and so justice has generally been one of the law's guiding principles. But governments can, and sometimes do, enforce laws that many people believe to be unjust. If this belief becomes widespread, people may lose respect for the law and may even disobey it. In democratic societies, however, the law itself provides ways to amend or abolish unjust laws.

This article discusses the main branches of the law, the world's major legal systems, and the methods that democracies use to change laws. The article also traces the development of law, examines current issues in U.S. law, and discusses law as a career. Many separate WORLD BOOK articles provide detailed information on topics related to law. For a list of these articles, see the *Related Articles* at the end of this article.

Branches of the Law

Law can be divided into two main branches: (1) private law and (2) public law. Private law deals with the rights and obligations people have in their relations with one another. Public law concerns the rights and obligations people have as members of society and as citizens. Both private law and public law can be subdivided into several branches. However, the various branches of public and private law are closely related, and in many cases they overlap.

Private Law is also called *civil law*. It determines a person's legal rights and obligations in many kinds of activities that involve other people. Such activities include everything from borrowing or lending money to buying a home or signing a job contract.

The great majority of lawyers and judges spend most of their time dealing with private-law matters. Lawyers handle most of these matters out of court. But numerous situations arise in which a judge or jury must decide if a person's private-law rights have been violated.

Bernard Schwartz, the contributor of this article, is Edwin D. Webb Professor of Law at the New York University School of Law. He is also the author of the American Heritage History of the Law in America *and many other books on law and the history of law.*

More than a million such cases, called *lawsuits* or *civil suits*, are tried in U.S. courts each year.

Private law can be divided into six major branches according to the kinds of legal rights and obligations involved. These branches are (1) contract and commercial law, (2) tort law, (3) property law, (4) inheritance law, (5) family law, and (6) corporation law. The dividing line between the various branches is not always clear, however. For example, many cases of property law also involve contract law.

Contract and Commercial Law deals with the rights and obligations of people who make contracts. A contract is an agreement between two or more persons that can be enforced by law. A wide variety of business activities depend on the use of contracts. A business firm makes contracts both with other firms, such as suppliers and transporters, and with private persons, such as customers and employees.

Tort Law. A tort is a wrong or injury that a person suffers because of someone else's action. The action may cause bodily harm; damage a person's property, business, or reputation; or make unauthorized use of a person's property. The victim may sue the person or persons responsible. Tort law deals with the rights and obligations of the persons involved in such cases. Many torts are unintentional, such as damages in traffic accidents. But if a tort is deliberate and involves serious harm, it may be treated as a crime.

Property Law governs the ownership and use of property. Property may be *real*, such as land and buildings, or *personal*, such as an automobile and clothing. The law ensures a person's right to own property. However, the owner must use the property lawfully. People also have the right to sell or lease their property and to buy or rent the property of others. Property law determines the rights and obligations involved in such dealings.

Inheritance Law, or *succession law*, concerns the transfer of property upon the death of the owner. Nearly every country has basic inheritance laws, which list the relatives or other persons who have first rights of inheritance. But in most Western nations, people may *will* their property to persons other than those specified by law. In such cases, inheritance law also sets the rules for the making of wills.

Family Law determines the legal rights and obligations of husbands and wives and of parents and children. It covers such matters as marriage, divorce, adoption, and child support.

Corporation Law governs the formation and operation of business corporations. It deals mainly with the powers and obligations of management and the rights of stockholders. Corporation law is often classed together with contract and commercial law as *business law*.

Public Law involves government directly. It defines a person's rights and obligations in relation to government. Public law also describes the various divisions of government and their powers.

Public law can be divided into four branches: (1) criminal law, (2) constitutional law, (3) administrative law, and (4) international law. In many cases, the branches of public law, like those of private law, overlap. For example, a violation of administrative law may also be a violation of criminal law.

Criminal Law deals with crimes—that is, actions considered harmful to society. Crimes range in seriousness from disorderly conduct to murder. Criminal law defines these offenses and sets the rules for the arrest, the possible trial, and the punishment of offenders. Some crimes are also classed as torts because the victim may sue for damages under private law.

In the majority of countries, the central government makes most of the criminal laws. In the United States, each state, as well as the federal government, has its own set of criminal laws. However, the criminal laws of each state must protect the rights and freedoms guaranteed by federal constitutional law.

Constitutional Law. A constitution is a set of rules and principles that define the powers of a government and the rights of the people. The principles outlined in a constitution form the basis of constitutional law. The law also includes official rulings on how a constitution's principles are to be interpreted and carried out.

Most nations have a written constitution. A major exception is Great Britain. The British constitution is unwritten. It consists of all the documents and traditions that have contributed to Britain's form of government. In most democracies, the national constitution takes first place over all other laws. In the United States, the federal Constitution has force over all state constitutions as well as over all other national and state laws.

Conflicts between a constitution and other laws are settled by constitutional law. In the United States, the courts have the power of *judicial review*, under which they may overturn any laws judged to be *unconstitutional*. A law is declared unconstitutional if the court determines that it violates the U.S. Constitution or a state constitution. The U.S. Supreme Court is a nation's highest court of judicial review.

Administrative Law centers on the operations of government agencies. It is one of the fastest-growing and most complicated branches of the law.

National, state or provincial, and local governments set up many *administrative agencies* to do the work of government. Some of these agencies regulate such activities as banking, communications, trade, and transportation. Others deal with such matters as education, public health, and taxation. Still other agencies administer social welfare programs, such as old-age and unemployment insurance. In most cases, the agencies are established in the executive branch of government under powers granted by the legislature. Administrative law consists chiefly of (1) the legal powers granted to administrative agencies by the legislature and (2) the rules that the agencies make to carry out their powers. Administrative law also includes court rulings in cases between the agencies and private citizens.

International Law deals with the relationships among nations both in war and in peace. It concerns trade, communications, boundary disputes, methods of warfare, the uses of the ocean, and many other matters. Laws to regulate international relations have been developed over the centuries by customs and treaties. But international law, unlike other branches of the law, is difficult to enforce.

Systems of Law

Every independent country has its own legal system. The systems vary according to each country's social traditions and form of government. But most systems can be classed as either (1) a common-law system or (2) a civil-law system. The United States, Canada, Great Britain, and other English-speaking countries have a common-law system. Most other countries have a civil-law system. Many countries combine features of both systems.

The Branches of Law This table lists the major branches of private and public law and some of the legal matters they cover. A matter governed by one branch may also involve one or more other branches. For example, many cases of property law also concern contract law.

Private Law

Contract and Commercial Law
Credit purchases
Employment
  contracts
Guarantees
Insurance policies
Patents
Promissory notes
Sales contracts
Subscriptions

Tort Law
Invasion of privacy
Personal injury
Product liability
Professional
  malpractice
Slander and libel
Traffic accidents
Trespass
Unfair
  competition

Property Law
Landlord and
  tenant
  relations
Mortgages
Transfers of
  ownership
Unclaimed
  property

Inheritance Law
Estates
Probate
Trusts
Wills

Family Law
Adoption
Annulment
Divorce
Marriage

Corporation Law
Corporate
  finance
Documents of
  incorporation
Mergers and
  acquisitions

Public Law

Criminal Law
Arson
Bribery
Burglary
Extortion
Forgery
Kidnapping
Larceny
Manslaughter
Murder
Perjury
Rape
Robbery

Constitutional Law
Civil rights
Federal and
  state powers
Relations between
  the states
Separation of
  executive, judicial,
  and legislative
  powers

Administrative Law
Consumer protection
Currency
Environmental
  protection
Interstate commerce
Public safety
Social welfare
Taxation
Workers' wages
  and hours

International Law
Arms control
Extradition
Hijacking and
  piracy
Human rights
Territorial waters
Uses of outer
  space
Uses of the
  ocean
War crimes

LAW

Common-Law Systems are based largely on *case law* —that is, on court decisions. The common-law system began in England many hundreds of years ago. The English called their system *the common law* because it applied throughout the land.

English common law developed from the rules and principles that judges traditionally followed in deciding court cases. Judges based their decisions on legal *precedents*—that is, on earlier court rulings in similar cases. But judges could expand precedents to make them suit particular cases. They could also *overrule* (reject) any precedents that they considered to be in error or outdated. In this way, judges changed many laws over the years. The common law thus came to be law made by judges.

However, some common-law principles proved too precious to change. For example, a long line of hard-won precedents defended the rights and liberties of citizens against the unjust use of government power. England—and the other common-law countries—have kept these principles almost unchanged.

The United States, Canada, and other countries that were colonized by England based their national legal systems on the common law. In addition, every state in the United States except Louisiana and every Canadian province except Quebec adopted a common-law system. Louisiana and Quebec were colonized by France, and their legal systems are patterned after the French civil-law system.

Case law is still important in common-law countries. However, the lawmaking role of legislatures in these countries has increased greatly during the 1900's. For example, the U.S. Congress has made major changes in American contract and property law. The changes have dealt with such matters as labor-management relations, workers' wages and hours, and environmental protection. Nevertheless, common-law countries have kept the basic feature of the English legal system, which is the power of judges to make laws. In addition, constitutional law in these countries continues the common-law tradition of defending the people's rights and liberties.

Civil-Law Systems are based mainly on *statutes* (legislative acts). The majority of civil-law countries have assembled their statutes into one or more carefully organized collections called *codes*. Most modern law codes can be traced back to the famous code commissioned by the Roman emperor Justinian I in the A.D. 500's. Justinian's code updated and summarized the whole of Roman law. It was called the *Corpus Juris Civilis*, meaning *Body of Civil Law*. For this reason, legal systems that are based on the Roman system of statute and code law are known as *civil-law* systems. This use of the term *civil law* should not be confused with its use as an alternate term for private law. Civil-law systems include both private law and public law.

In civil-law countries, such as France and West Germany, the statutes, not the courts, provide the final answer to any question of law. Judges may refer to precedents in making their decisions. But they must base every decision on a particular statute and not on precedent alone.

Other Systems. Many countries have patterned their legal system after both civil law and common law. For example, Japan and most Latin-American nations have assembled all their private law into a code. But public law in these countries has been greatly influenced by common-law principles, especially those that guarantee the rights and liberties of the people.

Most Communist governments have overturned the legal systems that existed when they came to power. The majority of these were civil-law systems. But the new Communist governments then set up legal systems also based on statutes and codes. The Soviet Union, for example, has a private-law code patterned after earlier Western European and Russian models. But unlike the earlier codes, the Soviet code allows for direct government interference in private-law matters. Public law in the Communist countries heavily restricts the rights of the people in relation to their government.

How Laws Are Changed

Social conditions continually change, and so the law must also change or become outdated. Every nation changes its laws in the manner that its political system prescribes. In a dictatorship, only the top government leaders can change the law. Democracies, however, have developed four main methods of changing the law: (1) by court decision, (2) by legislation, (3) by administrative action, and (4) by direct action of the people.

By Court Decision. Judges in common-law countries change many laws by expanding or overruling precedents. Especially in the United States, judges often overrule precedents to bring the law into line with changing social conditions. In 1896, for example, the U.S. Supreme Court upheld a law that provided for "separate but equal" public facilities for blacks and whites. But in 1954, the Supreme Court ruled that racial segregation in public schools is unconstitutional.

By Legislation. Legislatures may change laws as well as make them. A legislature can change a statute by amending it; by *repealing* (canceling) it; or by passing a new law on the same subject. In most countries with a written constitution, some form of legislative action is required to amend the constitution.

By Administrative Action. Government agencies may be authorized to amend, repeal, or replace the regulations they make. They may also be authorized to interpret an old regulation to meet changing conditions.

By Direct Action of the People. Some national and many local governments give the people direct power to change the law by *referendum* and by *initiative*. In a referendum, a law or a proposed law is submitted to the voters for their approval or rejection. In an initiative, a group of citizens proposes a law, which is then approved or rejected by the legislature or by referendum. Many countries—and most states in the United States—have repealed their constitution one or more times and replaced it with a new one. In most such cases, the new constitution cannot take effect until it has been approved by referendum.

The Development of Law

Civilized societies are so complex that they could not exist without a well-developed system of law. Scholars therefore conclude that people began to formulate laws in prehistoric times, before the first civilizations arose. Prehistoric people had no system of writing, and so they left no record of their laws. The earliest laws were *cus-*

tomary laws—that is, laws established by custom and handed down orally from one generation to the next.

The first civilizations and first systems of writing appeared between about 3500 and 3000 B.C. The invention of writing enabled people to assemble law codes. The development of written codes made the law a matter of public knowledge and so helped advance the rule of law in society. The first law codes were produced by ancient civilizations in the Middle East.

Early Developments in the East. The first known law codes appeared in the ancient Middle Eastern land of Babylonia. A Babylonian king named Ur-Nammu assembled the earliest known code about 2100 B.C. Other Babylonian rulers produced codes during the following centuries. A king named Hammurabi drew up the most complete and best known of these codes during the 1700's B.C. Hammurabi's code, like the earlier ones, consisted mainly of a long list of rules to settle specific types of cases. The code laid down the law for such matters as the unfaithfulness of a wife, the theft of a farm animal, and the faulty work of a housebuilder. Many of the punishments were harsh by today's standards. For example, a son found guilty of striking his father had his hand cut off.

From about 1000 to 400 B.C., the Hebrew people of the Middle East assembled their religious and social laws into a code. The code reflected the teachings of Moses, a great Hebrew leader of the 1200's B.C., and so it is often called the *Mosaic Code* or the *Law of Moses*. The Mosaic Code stressed moral principles. It became a key part of the first books of the Hebrew Bible and later of the Christian Bible. According to the Bible, the part of the code known as the *Ten Commandments* was given to Moses by God. The commandments therefore have had enormous influence on the moral content of the law in Western civilization.

By about 500 B.C., the civilizations of India and China had also produced codes of law. The codes in both countries stressed the moral obligations of the law. However, except for the religious laws of the Hebrew people, the legal traditions of Eastern civilizations have had little direct influence on today's major systems of law. Many Eastern peoples, even those influenced by Western traditions, still stress the moral obligations of the law. Accused persons have little opportunity to defend themselves. Concern for the rights of an accused person—and for the rights of all citizens—developed mainly in Western civilization. But this development occurred slowly over many hundreds of years. Most scholars regard the ancient Greeks as the founders of both Western law and Western civilization.

The Influence of Ancient Greece. Unlike earlier civilizations, the civilization of ancient Greece made the law a clearly human institution. Before the Greeks, most people believed that only gods and goddesses had the power to make laws. The gods and goddesses gave the laws to certain chosen leaders, who passed them on to the people. Like earlier peoples, the Greeks believed that gods and goddesses required human beings to obey the law. But the Greeks also believed that human beings have the power to make laws—and to change them as the need arises. The Greek city-state of Athens became the chief center of this development.

A politician named Draco drew up Athens' first law code in 621 B.C. It became famous mainly for its harsh penalties for lawbreakers. In the early 590's B.C., the ruling council of Athens authorized a high-ranking official named Solon to reform the city's legal and political system. Solon repealed most of Draco's stern laws and drew up a much fairer code in their place. Solon also made the Athenian assembly more representative and increased its lawmaking powers. In time, elected assemblies of citizens gained more and more legislative power in Athens. The Greeks thus began another key development of Western civilization—the founding of democratic government. However, as many as a third of the people of Athens were slaves. The Athenians, like other ancient peoples, denied slaves the legal rights of citizens.

The Greeks believed strongly in the importance of law. They considered respect for the law to be the mark of the good citizen. The great Athenian philosopher and teacher Socrates became the supreme example of this belief. The court sentenced Socrates to death in 399 B.C. for teaching Athenian youths to disrespect the law. Socrates knew that he was innocent. But he accepted his sentence to show his respect for the law.

Ancient Roman Law. Ancient law reached its peak under the Romans. Roman law included all the main branches of public and private law that exist today. In fact, the scientific classification of the law began with the Romans. The Romans designed their laws not only to govern the people of Rome but also to build and hold together a vast empire. By the early A.D. 100's, the Roman Empire included much of Europe and the Middle East and most of northern Africa.

Early Roman Times. The first known Roman law code, called the Laws of the Twelve Tables, was written about 450 B.C. It set down the chief customary laws of the Roman people in a form that was easy to remember. For hundreds of years, Roman boys had to memorize the code as part of their schoolwork.

The principles expressed in the Twelve Tables long remained the basis of Roman law. But the Romans gradually amended these principles to meet changing social conditions. After 367 B.C., a high public official called a *praetor* made the chief amendments. Each year, the praetor issued an *edict* (public order) that made any necessary changes. After 27 B.C., the Roman emperor could make or change laws as he wished. Eventually, the whole body of Roman law became extremely complex. The task of interpreting this great mass of laws fell to a group of highly skilled lawyers called *juris prudentes*, a Latin term for *experts in law*. Since that time, the science of law has been known as *jurisprudence*.

For many years, Romans and non-Romans within the empire were governed under different sets of laws. Roman citizens were governed under the *jus civile* (civil law). The Romans developed a special set of laws, called the *jus gentium* (law of the nations), to rule the peoples they conquered. They based these laws on principles of justice that they believed applied to all people. Such principles are known as *natural law*.

However, neither the jus civile nor the jus gentium granted any legal rights to slaves. Under Roman law, only Roman citizens could own property, make contracts and wills, and sue for damages. Slaves were not citizens, and so they had none of these rights. As the

LAW

Romans developed the idea of natural law, however, they recognized that slaves had human rights that should be respected. Roman law thus began to require that slaves be treated fairly and decently.

Late Roman Times. The belief in natural law also led to the idea that non-Romans within the empire should have the same rights as citizens. In A.D. 212, the Romans granted Roman citizenship to most of the peoples they had conquered, except slaves. The jus civile then became the law of the entire empire.

However, the principles of natural law set down in the jus gentium remained part of Roman law. These principles were important to future generations because they led to the belief in equal rights for all citizens. But hundreds of years passed before people fully developed· the principles of equality that were outlined by the Romans. Once the principles had been developed, they contributed to the building of democratic governments in the United States, France, and many other countries.

Beginning with Julius Caesar, a long line of Roman rulers had tried to organize all the empire's laws into an orderly code. Emperor Justinian I finally completed this task. Justinian's code, the famous *Corpus Juris Civilis* (Body of Civil Law), went into effect in 533 and 534. It covered the whole field of law so completely and so skillfully that it later became the model for the first modern law codes. Even today, the codes of most civil-law countries are based on Roman law.

The Middle Ages. In 395, the Roman Empire split into two parts—the West Roman Empire and the East Roman, or Byzantine, Empire. The West Roman Empire, which had its capital in Rome, fell to invading Germanic tribes in the late 400's. The empire's fall marked the start of the 1,000-year period known as the Middle Ages. The East Roman Empire, which had its capital in Constantinople (now Istanbul), escaped the invasions and continued to function. In 527, Justinian I became the ruler of the eastern empire, and his great code of Roman law was mainly enforced there. In Western Europe, most of the legal and cultural institutions developed by the Romans gradually died out.

However, Roman law survived in the West as the basis for *canon law*—the legal system developed by the Roman Catholic Church. Most Europeans during the Middle Ages were Catholics, and so canon law had a powerful influence on their lives.

The Germanic tribes that overthrew the West Roman Empire had their own law codes, which they introduced into the regions they conquered. But these codes were undeveloped compared with Roman law. They consisted chiefly of long lists of fines for specific offenses, such as stealing a neighbor's ox or dog.

By the 800's, Europeans had developed a political and military system known as *feudalism*. Under feudalism, people owed allegiance to individual lords rather

How Laws Have Varied Through the Ages

Over the years, many identical matters of law have been treated differently. This table shows how several such matters have been treated (1) in the code of Roman law issued by Justinian I in A.D. 533-534; (2) in England in the late Middle Ages; and (3) in the United States today.

Legal Matter	Code of Justinian	English Law in the Late Middle Ages	Modern U.S. Law
Actions Punished by Death	Rape, treason, and certain cases of embezzlement, forgery, and kidnapping. Murder was punished by banishment.	Any action classed as a serious crime, including arson, burglary, counterfeiting, murder, rape, robbery, and treason.	Many states have banned the death penalty. The states that have the penalty use it mainly to punish murder.
Theft	Not treated as a crime. The victim could sue the thief and receive up to four times the value of the stolen property.	A crime punished by fine, imprisonment, branding, whipping, or death.	A crime punished by a fine or a jail or prison sentence—or by both a fine and a sentence.
Failure to Pay a Debt	Early Roman law allowed a creditor to sell a debtor into slavery. The Code of Justinian required a creditor to sue to recover a debt.	A creditor could seize a debtor's property and have the person imprisoned.	A creditor must sue to recover a debt.
Inheritance	Estate divided equally among the children. Wives could not inherit, unless provided by will.	Estate went automatically to the oldest son. Wives could not inherit the estate, but they received a share of its income.	Estate divided in varying proportions between surviving husband or wife and surviving children, unless otherwise directed by will.
Rights of Women	Both married and unmarried women could own property, make contracts and wills, and sue for damages.	Unmarried women had most of the same legal rights as men. Married women needed their husband's consent to own property, to make contracts and wills, and to sue or be sued. They could not be accused of a crime. A woman's husband was normally held responsible for any crimes she committed.	Both married and unmarried women have nearly the same legal rights as men.

than to a central government. A lord enforced the law in his territory and granted protection to the people who served in his armies and who lived and worked on his land. The legal system of the Middle Ages was largely based on this relationship between lords and the people who depended on them.

In particular, feudal law spelled out the duties that people owed to their lord. But a lord could not demand more than the law allowed. The people thus had a right to refuse any demands by their lord that went beyond the limits of the law. Europeans later used this principle to resist monarchs who claimed too much power. The principle thus played an important role in the struggle for democracy in Europe.

Feudal law remained the basic law in Western Europe until about 1300. By then, Western Europeans had begun to establish improved legal systems. However, this development differed greatly between the countries of mainland Europe and the island country of England.

Developments in Mainland Europe. The economy of Western Europe began to grow rapidly during the 1000's. As commerce and industry increased, they created a need for a set of laws that was more complex and varied than feudal law. Scholars believed that ancient Roman law could meet this need. During the 1100's, the University of Bologna in northern Italy began to train law students from many parts of Europe in the principles of the Corpus Juris Civilis. Interest in the code soon spread to other European universities. Roman law thus gradually began to replace feudal law throughout mainland Europe.

Developments in England. England already had a strong, unified legal system by the 1200's, when Roman law was beginning to spread across Europe. As a result, England did not adopt the Roman system.

England's legal system had grown out of the country's courts. English courts had long based their decisions on the customs of the English people. But customs varied from district to district. As a result, similar cases were often judged differently in different districts. In the early 1100's, however, strong English kings began to set up a nationwide system of royal courts. Judges in these courts applied the same rulings in all similar cases. In this way, the courts soon established a body of *common law*—that is, law which applied equally anywhere in England. Judges could change the law as the nation's needs and customs changed, but any change applied in all common-law courts.

As English common law developed over the years, it established many precedents that limited the powers of government and protected the rights of the people. These precedents made even the monarch subject to the law. The common law thus assisted the growth of democracy in England. The right known as *habeas corpus* was one of the chief common-law safeguards of personal freedom. *Habeas corpus* is a Latin term meaning *you are ordered to have the body*. As developed in English common law, habeas corpus means that a person cannot be held in prison without the consent of the courts. The Founding Fathers of the United States considered this right so essential to human liberty that they wrote it into the Constitution (Article I, Section 9).

The First Modern Law Codes. Roman law had been adopted throughout most of Europe by the end of the 1500's. But only England had a monarchy strong

enough to establish a unified legal system. In other countries, law codes were drawn up and enforced mainly by local governments. These local codes differed greatly from one part of a country to another. Beginning in the 1500's, many European monarchs set out to form strong central governments. To help achieve this goal, they began to assemble the assorted local codes of their countries into national codes—a development called the *codification movement*.

The codification movement reached its peak under the French ruler Napoleon Bonaparte. In 1800, Napoleon appointed a committee of legal scholars to turn the whole of French private law into a compact, well-reasoned code. The new code, called the *Code Civil* or *Code Napoléon*, was a skillful blend of Roman law, French customs, and democratic philosophy. It went into effect in 1804 and has remained France's basic

Illuminated manuscript (about 1450) by an unknown English artist;
The Masters of the Bench of the Inner Temple

The King's Bench was England's chief criminal court during the late Middle Ages. It helped establish the nation's *common law*—that is, a uniform body of law that applied throughout England. In this picture, chained prisoners, *bottom*, await their turn to be tried before the judges, *top*.

code of private law ever since. It has also been a model for the private-law codes of most civil-law countries. Thus, Roman law, as contained in the Code Napoléon, still influences people's lives.

Beginnings of U.S. Law. When the American colonists declared their independence from England in 1776, they based their claims partly on the ancient Greek and Roman ideas of natural law. These ideas had been developed in detail by various French philosophers of the 1700's, such as Claude Helvétius and Jean Jacques Rousseau. The French had especially promoted the idea that the natural law gives all people equal rights. The U.S. Declaration of Independence echoed this idea in the famous phrase ". . . all men are created equal [and] are endowed by their Creator with certain unalienable Rights."

However, the American colonists based their claims for independence chiefly on common-law principles. The English settlers who established the American Colonies had brought these principles with them. Moreover, many of the leaders in the colonies' struggle for independence were lawyers who had been trained in the common law. These men were especially dedicated to the common-law principles that put the rights of the people above the will of a monarch. The common law thus became a driving force behind the writing of the Declaration of Independence. Common-law principles also influenced the development of the U.S. Constitution and the Bill of Rights.

Constitutional Law. American courts had the same power to make laws that English courts had. A series of U.S. Supreme Court decisions in the early 1800's strengthened this power. The court's decision in 1803 in the case of *Marbury v. Madison* was especially important. In this decision, the court declared a federal law unconstitutional for the first time. The principle of judicial review was thus firmly established, enabling U.S. courts to overturn any law they judged to be unconstitutional.

Other Branches of the Law. The U.S. legal system adopted the basic ideas, not the whole body, of English common law. Many parts of the common law were impractical for the new, rapidly expanding nation of the United States. English property law was particularly unsuited. Land was scarce in England, and so the law heavily restricted the transfer of land from one owner to another. But much of the land in the United States was unsettled, and the nation was constantly expanding its frontiers. To ensure the nation's growth, people had to be free to buy and sell land. American property law therefore began to stress the rights and obligations involved in land transfers. The English laws that restricted such transfers were discarded.

Contract law became more important in the new nation than it had been in England. By the early 1800's, Americans had begun to develop a flourishing economy based almost entirely on free enterprise. In a free enterprise system, business people regulate their dealings largely by contract. The rapid growth of the U.S. economy during the 1800's therefore brought an enormous increase in contract law. The law especially emphasized freedom of contract, with no government interference. This emphasis lasted into the 1900's. In 1905, in the case of *Lochner v. New York*, the Supreme Court upheld the right of employers to decide the terms of employment contracts free from government control.

The Development of Canadian Law. Canada's legal history dates from the legal system established by the first French settlers in the 1600's. The French set up a civil-law system in the areas they colonized, including what is now the province of Quebec. They based their system on one of the major local law codes in France— a code known as the *Custom of Paris*.

Great Britain gained control of France's Canadian possessions in 1763 and introduced a common-law system. But French Canadians objected to giving up their legal traditions. In 1774, the British Parliament passed the Quebec Act, which allowed French Canadians to follow their traditional system in private-law matters. The common law, however, remained the basis of all other law in Canada. In 1866, Quebec adopted a private-law code based on the Code Napoléon.

The British North America Act, passed by the British Parliament in 1867, created the Dominion of Canada. The act gave Canada limited self-government and provided a constitutional framework for the new Canadian federal government. The federal legal system was based on the common law. Each province could keep its traditional legal system except in matters of public law. All the provinces except Quebec based their legal system on the common law. Quebec kept its civil-law system in matters of private law. Canada's Parliament was authorized to set up the nation's criminal-law system.

Law in the 1900's. During the 1800's, Western systems of law spread throughout the world. Many countries, for example, adopted private-law codes patterned after the Code Napoléon. The U.S. Constitution influenced the making of written constitutions in many countries. The main systems of law—that is, the civil- and common-law systems—have remained basically unchanged during the 1900's. However, the role of the law has undergone dramatic changes in nearly every country. This section discusses how these changes have affected private law and public law in the United States. But the changes have had a similar effect in many other countries.

Developments in Private Law. By 1900, U.S. private law dealt mainly with protecting the rights of property owners and businesses. Freedom of contract remained the law's key doctrine. Contracts were regarded strictly as private agreements. Judges paid little attention to their social effects.

Complete freedom of contract had served the needs of America's rapidly expanding economy during the 1800's. But by 1900, many businesses in the United States were using this freedom to increase their profits at the expense of their employees, stockholders, and customers. For example, factory owners claimed that efforts to protect the rights of workers interfered with the owners' rights to contract freely with their employees. Employees often had to accept unfavorable contracts or lose their jobs.

During the 1800's, most Americans accepted the idea that the law should interfere with private business as little as possible. But the public's attitude toward the law has changed greatly during the 1900's. Today, most people believe that the private interests of some members of society should not deprive other members of their rights. Legislation and court decisions during the

1900's have reflected this belief, especially by stressing the social aspects of contract law. For example, Congress and the state legislatures have passed many laws to help ensure the fairness of employment contracts. Some of these laws regulate working conditions and workers' wages and hours. Other laws guarantee the right of workers to organize and to strike.

Legislation and court decisions have also changed many features of property, tort, and family law during the 1900's. The social obligations of property owners have been enforced by zoning laws and by laws prohibiting environmental pollution. During the 1800's, tort law held that a person could collect for an injury only if another person could be proved at fault. But the development of private and public insurance programs during the 1900's helped establish that a person should be paid for accidental injuries regardless of who was at fault. This "no fault" principle has made it unnecessary to sue for damages in certain cases. Changes in family law during the 1900's reduced the legal controls of husbands over their wives and of fathers over their children. The law thus placed increased emphasis on women's and children's rights.

Developments in Public Law. Since the early 1900's, the executive branch of government has gained more and more lawmaking power in the United States. In addition, hundreds of agencies have been formed in the executive branch. The rules and regulations issued by these agencies have brought about a huge increase in administrative law.

During the mid-1900's, the U.S. Supreme Court also became more active than it had ever been before. The court acted particularly in matters that it believed legislators had neglected. The great majority of these matters were in the field of civil rights. During the 1950's and 1960's, the court used the power of judicial review to strike down a variety of state and local laws that supported racial segregation. The court based these decisions on the 14th Amendment to the Constitution, which guarantees equal protection under the law. The court has also used this amendment to help ensure fair

and equal treatment for women, aliens, poor people, and persons accused of crime.

Current Issues in U.S. Law

The Problem of Too Many Laws. Congress and the state legislatures pass thousands of laws each year. These laws are added to the hundreds of volumes of federal and state statutes already in force. The regulations issued by federal and state agencies also accumulate at a rapid rate. By the mid-1970's, the federal regulations alone filled more than 57,000 pages.

As the number of laws has grown, the whole body of law has become more and more difficult to administer. In addition, the law has become so complex that people cannot possibly know how it affects them in every case. A nation can make its laws simpler by organizing them into a uniform code. But common-law traditions are so strong in the United States that all efforts to codify the nation's private laws have failed.

The enormous number of laws issued each year raises the question of whether society expects too much of the law. Many people believe that nearly every need and want of society can be met simply by "passing a law." This belief has led legislatures and the courts to make more and more laws to satisfy not only society's demands but also the demands of small, special-interest groups. However, there are limits to what the law can do. If the law tries to satisfy every demand, it can easily fail. People may then begin to doubt that the law can do anything at all. In addition, people tend to resent laws that interfere in their private affairs. But as the number of laws grows, more and more aspects of life become regulated.

The Question of Who Should Make Laws. The common law as developed in England enables the courts to make laws. However, American courts have expanded their powers far beyond the English idea to bring about revolutionary social changes, especially in the field of civil rights. Some of these changes have been extremely

Milt and Joan Mann

Legal Clinics, such as this one in a middle-income neighborhood, help meet the growing demand for low-cost legal assistance. A clinic provides routine legal services at reduced rates. It thus makes the services available to many people who could not otherwise afford them.

A Law School Competition called a *moot court* tests the ability of law students to argue court cases. In a moot court session, two teams of students take opposing sides in an imaginary case. A panel of lawyers or student lawyers decides which contestants have presented the most convincing arguments.

Bill Benoit

unpopular with many Americans. But through the power of judicial review, the courts can overrule the wishes of even the vast majority of the people.

Many experts believe that questions of great social importance should be settled by legislation, not by court decisions. These experts point out that democratic government depends on the freedom of the legislature to reflect the will of the people. If the courts block this freedom, democracy is seriously weakened. Other experts believe that the courts must defend the constitutional rights of every American, regardless of popular support.

The Right to Legal Assistance. As the law has grown more complex, the demand for professional legal services has increased. As a result, even the most routine services, such as drawing up contracts and wills, have become more and more costly. Large corporations and wealthy people generally can afford all the legal help they need. Since the early 1960's, court decisions and legislation have ensured legal help for criminal defendants too poor to hire a lawyer. In addition, public and private legal aid services provide poor people with free counsel in private-law cases. However, many poor people do not know they have a right to these services, and so they do not benefit from them.

Millions of middle-income Americans have great difficulty getting professional legal help when they need it. These people cannot afford to hire a lawyer. Yet they do not qualify for the free legal services available to the poor. To help remedy this problem, some lawyers in large cities have set up *legal clinics*. The clinics provide middle-income families with routine legal services at reduced rates.

Social Obligations and Individual Rights. As we have seen, court decisions and legislation have increasingly stressed the social aspects of the law in the United States. More and more laws have thus been made to ensure equality for all Americans and to protect the economic and environmental interests of society. To achieve these goals, the law has had to limit many of the rights traditionally granted to individuals under private law. Property rights and freedom of contract, in particular, have been heavily restricted—a matter of deep concern to many Americans.

Most experts believe, however, that the social trend of the law will continue. In that case, the rights and freedoms of individuals under private law will become even more restricted. Legislatures and courts therefore face an enormous challenge. On the one hand, they must formulate laws to meet the needs of a complex and rapidly changing society. But they must also be careful that these laws do not so restrict property rights and freedom of contract as to make free enterprise impossible.

A Career as a Lawyer

In most countries today, a person must be trained and licensed to practice law. However, the training and licensing of lawyers vary greatly from country to country. This section deals with law as a career in the United States.

Law Education. To practice law in most states of the United States, a person must first have a degree from a law school. The majority of law schools are a part of large universities. A few are independent institutions. Most major U.S. law schools admit only four-year college graduates. During their college training, *prelaw* students do not have to take any particular courses. But the majority of students planning to go to law school specialize in the social sciences.

Most law school programs require three years of study. During this time, students take courses in all the major branches of public and private law. Upon completing the required program, a student receives a J.D. (Doctor of Jurisprudence) degree. Some law schools admit students without a college degree. These students receive an LL.B. (Bachelor of Laws) degree rather than a J.D. degree upon completing their law studies. In general, law schools at state universities in the United States have the lowest tuition fees, and private institutions require the highest.

The first U.S. institution devoted entirely to the teaching of law operated in Litchfield, Conn., from 1774 to 1833. Harvard University established the first university law school in the United States in 1817. Between 1830 and 1860, law schools were founded at other U.S. universities. They included Columbia University, the University of Michigan, New York University, Northwestern University, the University of Pennsylvania, and Yale University.

All the early law schools used traditional teaching methods. Students attended lectures and studied standard textbooks. During the 1870's, a new method of teaching law, the *case method,* was developed at Harvard University. This method trained students in precise legal reasoning through the reading, analysis, and discussion of actual court cases. Today, almost all U.S. law schools use the case method.

Law school standards have been steadily raised in the United States since the mid-1800's, largely through the work of the American Bar Association (ABA) and the Association of American Law Schools (AALS). The ABA is a private, nationwide organization of lawyers that was founded in 1878. The AALS was founded in 1900 by 35 of the about 100 U.S. law schools that were then in existence. Both organizations have continually raised the minimum educational standards that a law school must meet to gain their approval. Today, the United States has about 220 law schools. About 175 of them are approved by either the ABA or the AALS or by both organizations.

In the past, nearly all law students—and nearly all lawyers—were men. But the number of women law students has been steadily increasing. Today, women make up more than two-fifths of the total enrollment in the major U.S. law schools.

Licensing of Lawyers. Each state has its own bar—that is, the body of lawyers who have a license to practice in the state. The word *bar* originally referred to the railing or partition that traditionally separates spectators from the proceedings in a courtroom. Lawyers represent their clients *before the bar* rather than from the spectator area in the back of the courtroom. Because of the lawyer's position in the courtroom, the whole body of lawyers became known as the *bar.*

Most states issue a license to law school graduates who pass the state's *bar examination.* A few states automatically license graduates of approved law schools in the state, without a bar examination. The United States has about 630,000 licensed lawyers.

The highest court or the legislature in each state sets rules of conduct for lawyers. The court has the power to *disbar* (suspend from practice) any member of the state bar who violates these rules.

The Practice of Law. The majority of U.S. lawyers conduct most of their business out of court. But some lawyers, particularly those who specialize in criminal cases, do much trial work.

Many American lawyers have a general practice. They provide every kind of legal service, from drawing up wills and other legal papers to handling court cases. Many other lawyers—especially in big cities—concentrate on a particular branch of the law, such as corporation law or administrative law. Some of these lawyers work for large law firms. Such firms provide clients with specialized services in one or more branches of the law. Most large business corporations employ experts in corporation law.

Because of the greatly increased demand for legal services, many lawyers have more work than they can handle. Some large law firms have therefore begun to employ specially trained persons called *lawyer's assistants.* A lawyer's assistant does *paralegal* work—that is, routine legal tasks under a lawyer's supervision. Lawyers who employ such assistants can devote more time to complex legal cases.

The law has long been one of the most common roads to public office. Congress, the state legislatures, and the administrative agencies have attracted more people from the law than from any other profession. Almost all judges have been lawyers, and such public officials as district attorneys and prosecutors must be lawyers. About two-thirds of all of the Presidents of the United States were lawyers. Further information on careers in the law can be obtained by contacting the American Bar Association, 750 N. Lake Shore Drive, Chicago, Ill. 60611. BERNARD SCHWARTZ

Related Articles. See the *Government* section of the various state, province, and country articles, such as ALABAMA (Government); ALBERTA (Government); ARGENTINA (Government). See also the following articles:

BRANCHES OF PRIVATE LAW

BUSINESS LAW

Agent	Credit	Negotiable
Attachment	Debt	Instrument
Bankruptcy	Draft	Note
Bill	Garnishment	Partnership
Bill of Exchange	Guaranty	Patent
Bill of Lading	Interest	Pawnbroker
Blue-Sky Laws	I.O.U.	Power of
Bond	Joint-Stock	Attorney
Business Law	Company	Rebate
Check	Legal Tender	Receiver
Common Carrier	Limited	Stock, Capital
Conglomerate	Company	Trademark
Contract	Loan Company	Trust
Copyright	Money Order	Usury
Corporation	Moratorium	

TORT LAW

Assault and Battery	Slander
Damages	Tort
Libel	Trespass
Negligence	

PROPERTY LAW

Abandonment	Escrow	Occupancy
Abstract	Eviction	Personal
Air Rights	Fee	Property
Appraisal	Fixture	Property
Assignment	Joint	Real Estate
Bill of Sale	Tenancy	Riparian Rights
Deed	Lease	Squatter
Easement	Lien	Tenant
Eminent	Mechanic's	Title
Domain	Lien	Torrens System
Encumbrance	Mortgage	

INHERITANCE LAW

Administrator	Heir
Dower	Legacy
Entail	Next of Kin
Escheat	Probate
Estate	Will
Executor	

FAMILY LAW

Abandonment	Adoption	Alienation of Affections

LAW

Alimony
Breach of Promise
Community Property
Desertion
Divorce
Dower
Guardian
Marriage
Ward

BRANCHES OF PUBLIC LAW

CRIMINAL LAW

Abandonment
Accessory
Arson
Assassination
Assault and
  Battery
Bigamy
Blackmail
Breach of the Peace
Bribery
Burglary
Conspiracy
Contempt
Counterfeiting
Crime

Embezzlement
Euthanasia
Extortion
False Imprisonment
Felony
Forgery
Fraud
Homicide
Juvenile
  Delinquency
Kidnapping
Larceny
Libel
Lynching
Manslaughter

Mayhem
Misdemeanor
Murder
Perjury
Polygamy
Riot
Robbery
Sabotage
Slander
Smuggling
Treason
Trespass
Vagrancy
Vandalism

CONSTITUTIONAL LAW

Articles of Confederation
Bill of Rights
British North America Act
Canada, Government of
  (The Constitution)
Citizenship
Civil Rights
Constitution
Constitution of the
  United States
Due Process of Law
Enabling Act

Freedom of Religion
Freedom of Speech
Freedom of the Press
Great Britain (The
  Constitution)
Magna Carta
Petition of Right
States' Rights
Supreme Court of the
  United States
  (Landmark Decisions)

ADMINISTRATIVE LAW

See the following articles and their lists of *Related Articles:*
LOCAL GOVERNMENT; STATE GOVERNMENT; UNITED STATES,
GOVERNMENT OF THE; CANADA, GOVERNMENT OF; and TAXA-
TION.

INTERNATIONAL LAW

See INTERNATIONAL LAW and its list of *Related Articles.*

LAWMAKING

Amendment
Canada, Government of
  (How a Bill Becomes Law)
Cloture
Code
Common Law
Congress of the
  United States
Diet
Duma
Filibustering
House of Burgesses

House of Commons
House of Lords
House of Representatives
Legislature
Lobbying
Parliament
Repeal
Senate
United States, Govern-
  ment of the (How a Bill
  Becomes Law)
Veto

LEGAL PROCEDURES AND TERMS

Affidavit
Alias
Alibi
Appeal
Arraignment
Attainder
Autopsy
Bail
Bona Fide
Brief
Confession

Deposition
Equity
Evidence
Grand Jury
Habeas Corpus
Incompetence
Indictment
Injunction
Inquest
Judgment
Jury

Mandamus
Minor
Oath
Petition
Plea
  Bargaining
Statute of
  Limitations
Subpoena
Suit

Summons
Trial
Witness
Writ
Writ of Assistance

LAW ENFORCEMENT

See the following articles and their lists of *Related Articles:*
COURT; CRIME; LAW ENFORCEMENT; and POLICE.

HISTORY

Code Napoléon
Draco
Feudalism
Hammurabi
Inns of Court
Justinian Code
Lycurgus

Moses
Plato
Solon
Star Chamber
Ten Commandments
Trial by Combat
Twelve Tables, Laws of the

OTHER RELATED ARTICLES

American Bar Association
Case Method
Civil Disobedience
Civil Law
Class Action
Criminal Justice System
Franchise
Impeachment
Justice, Department of

Law Day U.S.A.
Lawyer
Legal Aid
License
Maritime Law
Martial Law
Parliamentary Procedure
Public Opinion

Outline

I. Branches of the Law
  A. Private Law   B. Public Law
II. Systems of Law
  A. Common-Law Systems   C. Other Systems
  B. Civil-Law Systems
III. How Laws Are Changed
  A. By Court Decision C. By Administrative Action
  B. By Legislation   D. By Direct Action of the People
IV. The Development of Law
V. Current Issues in U.S. Law
  A. The Problem of Too Many Laws
  B. The Question of Who Should Make Laws
  C. The Right to Legal Assistance
  D. Social Obligations and Individual Rights
VI. A Career as a Lawyer
  A. Law Education   C. The Practice of Law
  B. Licensing of Lawyers

Questions

What kind of legal system do English-speaking countries have? How did it develop?

How did the ancient Greeks make the law a clearly
human institution?

What method do almost all U.S. law schools use in
teaching law?

What are the two main branches of the law?

How did the common law become a driving force behind the writing of the Declaration of Independence?

How have legislation and court decisions during the
1900's changed contract law in the United States?

What is *judicial review*? What part has it played in the
field of civil rights in the United States?

What are the four main methods of changing the law
in democratic countries?

Additional Resources

BATTEN, JACK. *Lawyers*. Macmillan, 1980. An overview of the
  Canadian legal system and profession.
BLACK, DONALD. *The Behavior of Law*. Academic Press, 1976.
DAVID, RENÉ, and BRIERLEY, J. E. C. *Major Legal Systems in the
  World Today: An Introduction to the Comparative Study
  of Law*. 2nd ed. Macmillan, 1978.
*Family Legal Guide: A Complete Encyclopedia of Law for the Lay-
  man*. Reader's Digest, 1981.
ROSS, MARTIN J. and JEFFREY S. *Handbook of Everyday Law*.
  4th ed. Harper, 1981.
SCHWARTZ, BERNARD. *The Law in America: A History*. McGraw,
  1974.

LAW, ANDREW BONAR (1858-1923), a British statesman, served as prime minister from 1922 to 1923. He entered Parliament in 1900, and became leader of the Conservative Party in 1911. In December 1916, he refused the king's offer to try to form a new cabinet, and served under Prime Minister David Lloyd George, as Chancellor of the Exchequer. In 1922, Law and other Conservatives forced Lloyd George's resignation. Law was born in New Brunswick, Canada, but moved to Scotland when he was 12.   ALFRED F. HAVIGHURST

LAW, BERNARD FRANCIS CARDINAL (1931-   ), was appointed a cardinal of the Roman Catholic Church by Pope John Paul II in 1985. The pope had named Law archbishop of Boston in 1984. Law had previously served as bishop of the diocese of Springfield-Cape Giradeau, Mo.

Law was born in Torreón, Mexico, to American parents. He was ordained a priest in 1961. He served as a parish priest in Vicksburg, Miss., from 1961 until 1963, when he became editor of the diocesan newspaper of Jackson, Miss. In 1968, Law became executive director of the Committee on Ecumenical and Interreligious Affairs, a group sponsored by the National Conference of Catholic Bishops. He was appointed vicar-general of the Natchez-Jackson, Miss., diocese (now the Jackson diocese) in 1971, and bishop of the Springfield-Cape Girardeau diocese in 1973.   KENNETH GUENTERT

LAW, JOHN (1671-1729), a Scottish financier and gambler, tried to revive the French economy by opening a bank in 1716 to issue paper money. His plans also included land speculation and trade in Louisiana, which became famous as the *Mississippi Scheme.*

Law was born in Edinburgh. In 1694, he killed a man in a duel, and was arrested and sentenced to death. He escaped from prison and fled to Amsterdam, where he studied the operations of the Bank of Amsterdam. He then accumulated a large fortune through gambling.

Law opened a bank in France in 1716. The paper money issued by the bank soon became readily acceptable. In 1717, Law established a company which soon monopolized trade with nearly all French possessions. In 1718, the bank became the Royal Bank.

Law's bank issued excessive quantities of paper money. Much of it was used to speculate in stock issued by his trading company. Speculators soon demanded gold for their paper money. The whole project collapsed, leaving thousands bankrupt in the panic that followed (see MISSISSIPPI SCHEME).   JOHN B. MCFERRIN

LAW DAY U.S.A. is celebrated throughout the United States on May 1 to emphasize the importance of law in American life. The American Bar Association and state and local bar associations sponsor Law Day U.S.A. Many schools, courts, churches, and organizations hold special programs on Law Day U.S.A. These programs include naturalization ceremonies for new citizens, mock trials, and courthouse tours. President Dwight D. Eisenhower proclaimed the first Law Day in 1958.

Critically reviewed by the AMERICAN BAR ASSOCIATION

LAW ENFORCEMENT is the means by which a community, state, or country keeps order. The enforcement of civil and criminal law by government agencies helps the members of a society to live together peaceably.

Civil law regulates many conflicts between people. Disputes about such matters as contracts, ownership of property, and payment for personal injury are settled in court through lawsuits. The enforcement of civil law takes up most of the time of most lawyers and courts, but it does not involve the police.

Criminal law covers actions harmful to society. Such crimes as murder, rape, and robbery threaten the order of a society. This article discusses the enforcement of criminal law. People who violate criminal law may be (1) arrested by the police and (2) put on trial by the local, state, or national government. If found guilty, they may be (3) imprisoned.

Arrest. Police enforce criminal law by arresting anyone they reasonably believe has committed a crime. In some cases, a police officer must have a court order called a *warrant* before making an arrest. But an officer does not need a warrant to arrest a person he or she observes violating the law. Most people who go on trial were arrested without a warrant shortly after the crime of which they were accused.

Trial. The evidence that a person committed a crime is given by the police to a government attorney called a *prosecutor.* At a *preliminary hearing* held before a judge, the prosecutor must show "probable cause" to justify holding the defendant for trial. The judge appoints a defense attorney to handle the person's case if the accused cannot afford to hire one. The judge sets bail if he or she believes the defendant should go on trial. A defendant who does not have enough money to put up bail must stay in jail until the trial.

Formal charges against the defendant may be made in the form of an *information* by the prosecutor or as an *indictment* by a grand jury. In many cases, the accused agrees to plead guilty in exchange for being charged with a less serious crime or being promised a shorter prison sentence. This process is called *plea bargaining.* The judge takes the plea at a hearing called an *arraignment.* About 90 per cent of all defendants plead guilty, most of them as a result of plea bargaining.

Defendants who plead not guilty may have a trial by jury, or the judge alone may decide the facts of the case. If the defendant is found guilty, the judge then sentences the individual.

Imprisonment. Most criminal laws specify the longest and shortest prison term to which an offender may be sentenced. The judge decides the exact length of the sentence, depending on what he or she feels will best serve both the offender and society. Prison terms are meant to punish offenders, reform criminals, remove dangerous offenders from society, and show possible future lawbreakers the penalties for crime.

If the judge believes a prison term would not help an offender, the individual may be sentenced to a period of probation. A lawbreaker who is on probation remains free, but a probation officer assigned by the court may check on the individual's activities. An offender who violates the rules of the probation may be imprisoned.   GEORGE T. FELKENES

Related Articles in WORLD BOOK include:

Arraignment	Court	Jury	Prison
Arrest	Crime	Law	Sentence
Bail	Indictment	Parole	Trial
Civil Law	Interpol	Police	Warrant

See also *Crime and Law Enforcement* in the RESEARCH GUIDE/INDEX, Volume 22, for a *Reading and Study Guide.*

LAW OF THE LAND. See Due Process of Law.

LAWLESS, THEODORE KENNETH (1892-1971), a black American physician, became known for his work in the field of *dermatology* (the study of skin diseases). He helped develop cures for several rare and baffling skin diseases. He also worked actively for many civic organizations. Lawless won the 1954 Spingarn medal. He was born in Thibodaux, La., and received his medical degree from Northwestern University. He taught dermatology at Northwestern from 1924 to 1941, and also did research there.　　　Noah D. Fabricant

LAWMAKING. See Legislature; United States, Government of the (How a Bill Becomes Law); Canada, Government of (How a Bill Becomes Law in Canada); Congress of the United States.

LAWN is an area or plot of ground that has a thick covering of closely cut grass. A lawn may surround a home or apartment building, or it may form part of the landscape around a public building. Lawns also serve as recreation areas in parks and playgrounds.

People grow lawns for several reasons. Lawns beautify the surroundings and help prevent soil erosion. In hot weather, they cool the air near the earth's surface. They also reduce noise pollution by absorbing sound.

Growing a Lawn

A successful lawn should grow evenly, and its color and texture should both be uniform throughout. Before starting a lawn, be sure the site is well drained and fairly smooth. It may be uneven but should have no steep slopes. Next, follow certain steps in preparing the soil and planting the grass.

Preparing the Soil. Plan to prepare the soil at least a week before planting the grass. First, grade the site by removing all topsoil. A small tractor with a special blade attached may be used for a large area. Such a tractor can be rented from a garden supply center. Or, you may use a hoe, a rake, a shovel, a spade, or some other gardening tool. Be sure to pile up the topsoil as it is removed. It will later be used to cover the subsoil that is exposed during the grading process. Also, be sure to remove any debris, such as rocks, sticks, and clods of dirt.

After grading the lawn site, test the quality of the subsoil with a soil-testing kit. Add lime to the subsoil if it is too acid. Turn the subsoil over with a shovel or a spade to a depth of 3 to 6 inches (8 to 15 centimeters). Then, if fertilizer is required, add 2 to 3 pounds (0.9 to 1.4 kilograms) to each 100 square feet (9 square meters) of land.

After fertilizing the subsoil, cover it with the topsoil, which provides the chemical elements that grass needs to grow. To make sure the topsoil has these elements, add lime and an organic fertilizer, such as manure or peat moss. You should also add 2 to 4 pounds (0.9 to 1.8 kilograms) of mineral fertilizer to each 100 square feet (9 square meters) of land. See Fertilizer (Kinds of Fertilizers).

Mix the fertilizer and lime thoroughly into the soil by dragging a steel-toothed rake over the site. For a large area, you may use a small tractor with an attachment called a *harrow*, which breaks up soil. Smooth the soil with a bamboo rake and then roll the soil with a power or push-type roller. Rolling the soil provides a compact surface, which grass needs to grow well.

Planting the Grass. Be sure to use a variety of grass that is suitable for the climate. The most widely grown lawn grass is *Kentucky bluegrass*, which thrives in most climates. *Bent grass*, another common lawn grass, can

O. M. Scott & Sons

Warren's Turf Nurseries

O. M. Scott & Sons

Most Lawns are planted in one of three ways. In sodding, *left*, sections of soil covered with grass are laid on the ground. Sprigging, *center*, starts a lawn with plugs of grass that spread to cover the entire lawn area. Seeding, *right*, can be done with a mechanical seed spreader.

LAWN ENEMIES

Weeds

The plants shown below are among the most common lawn weeds. They may be removed by hand or with tools, or they can be controlled with chemicals. Manufacturers make a variety of substances that kill weeds or prevent their growth. Such products may be spread or sprayed onto the lawn. Some of them affect only weeds, but others also include a fertilizer that nourishes the grass.

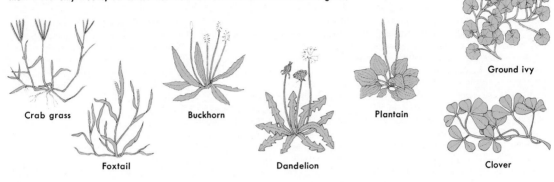

Crab grass

Foxtail

Buckhorn

Dandelion

Plantain

Ground ivy

Clover

Insects

Common lawn pests include grubs, sod webworms, and chinch bugs. Grubs feed on the roots of grass. Sod webworms eat plant leaves and stems. Chinch bugs damage leaves by sucking the juice from them. If not controlled, some insects can ruin a large section of lawn in a short time. Insects, like weeds, can be controlled with a variety of chemical products.

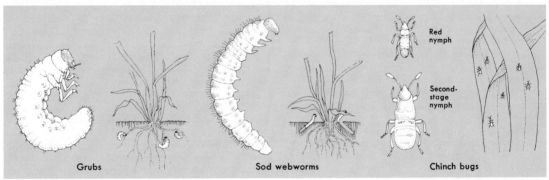

Grubs

Sod webworms

Red nymph

Second-stage nymph

Chinch bugs

WORLD BOOK illustrations by Margaret Ann Moran

Diseases

Most lawn diseases are caused by some kind of fungus. A fungus attack results in discolored or damaged leaves and may kill an entire lawn. Various diseases affect different kinds of grass and thrive in different climates. Most diseases may be controlled with chemicals, but some, such as stripe smut fungus, can be controlled only by planting disease-resistant grass.

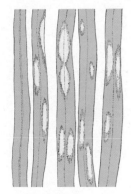

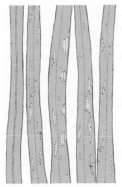

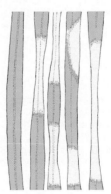

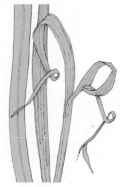

Leaf spot fungus

Rust fungus

Dollar spot fungus

Stripe smut fungus

grow in acid soil that has poor drainage. Bent grass also may be cut more closely than most other lawn grasses.

Lawn grasses that grow well in cool, humid areas include *bluegrasses, fescues,* and *bent grass.* White clover may be planted with these grasses to improve the fertility of the soil. Many commercial seed mixtures for cool, humid regions contain some ryegrass seed. Such seed grows quickly and produces a lawn rapidly. But ryegrass lives only a short time before it disappears, leaving room for the longer-lasting grass in the mixture. Ryegrass is sometimes called *nurse grass.*

Common lawn grasses in warm, humid regions include *Bermuda grass, St. Augustine grass,* and *zoysia grass. Carpet grass* and *centipede grass* are also grown in such locations. *Grama grass* and *buffalo grass* do well as lawn grasses in dry regions. See GRASS.

Grass can be planted in three ways: (1) seeding, (2) sodding, or (3) sprigging.

Seeding is the commonest and cheapest method of planting grass. The seeds can be distributed by hand on most lawn sites. For large areas, you should use a push-type seeder, which can also be used to spread grain-type fertilizers and pesticides.

The best time to sow seed is in early fall or early spring. First, divide the seed into two equal amounts. Sow half the seed by walking back and forth over the soil. Sow the other half by walking at right angles to the first direction. Cover the seed by raking the soil lightly, but be sure not to bunch the seed. Roll the soil lightly to provide a compact surface. You may cover the soil with a light layer of clean straw. This cover, called *mulch,* helps conserve moisture, prevent erosion, and protect the seedlings from drying out. Water the soil lightly and frequently until the lawn has developed fairly well.

Sodding is the most expensive way to plant grass. Sections of soil already covered with grass are dug up, carried to the lawn site, and laid over the soil. This method is used mostly on small areas where grass is needed quickly, or on slopes that would otherwise erode. Sod may be obtained from a garden supply center or a professional landscaper. Most sodding is done by professionals.

Sprigging involves the use of *sprigs* (small chunks or cuttings of grass). Sprigs are planted at various intervals, depending on the variety of grass. As the sprigs grow, their low-lying stems creep along the ground and root in the soil, thus filling in the lawn site. Sprigging is used chiefly in regions where grass cannot be grown from seed.

Caring for a Lawn

The care of a lawn involves such tasks as (1) mowing; (2) watering; (3) fertilizing; and (4) controlling diseases, pests, and weeds.

Mowing. The height to which grass should be cut depends chiefly on the kind grown. For example, bent grass may be mowed to a height of 1 inch (2.5 centimeters) or less. Other varieties, including bluegrass and St. Augustine grass, should be mowed to a height of $1\frac{1}{2}$ inches (4 centimeters) or more.

A manual or push-type mower is well suited for a lawn smaller than 500 square feet (46 square meters). Power mowers are easy to use on any size lawn. A riding mower or a small tractor with a mower attachment works best on lawns larger than $\frac{1}{2}$ acre (0.2 hectare).

A power mower may have a battery, an electric, or a gasoline motor and a reel-type or rotary blade. A reel mower resembles a manual mower but is powered by a motor or pulled by a tractor. It is best used on lawns that require close cutting. A rotary mower has a propellerlike blade that spins rapidly. It costs less than a reel mower and is easier to operate and maintain.

Watering of lawns is unnecessary in most climates because of the normal rainfall. Even during dry periods, a lawn should not be watered more than once a week. Light daily watering may cause weeds or weedy grasses to grow more rapidly than the lawn grass itself.

Fertilizing. Most lawns must be fertilized twice a year. Early each spring and fall, spread from 15 to 25 pounds (7 to 11 kilograms) of mineral fertilizer on every 1,000 square feet (93 square meters) of lawn. Be sure to distribute the fertilizer evenly, which can best be done with a push-type spreader. Fertilizer should be applied much as grass seed is sown. When the spreader is stopped or turned around, it should be turned off so that too much fertilizer does not fall on one area.

Controlling Diseases, Pests, and Weeds. Common lawn diseases include *brown patch, dollar spot,* and *leaf spot.* Like most lawn diseases, they are caused by a type of fungus. Such diseases may be controlled by fungicides. Pests that may infest lawns include *ants, army worms, chinch bugs, cutworms, grubs, mole crickets,* and *webworms.* They can be kept under control with insecticides. The most common lawn weeds include *chickweed, clover, crab grass, dandelions, plantains,* and *thistles.* They probably cannot be prevented from growing. But they can be kept from spreading by applying chemical weedkillers or by digging out their roots with a V-pointed knife.   ELVIN McDONALD

LAWN BOWLING is a game in which the players roll wooden or plastic balls at a smaller target ball. Lawn bowling traditionally is played outdoors on a smooth, level, grass plot called a *green.* But the game may also be played indoors on an artificial surface.

A standard bowling green measures about 120 feet (36.6 meters) square. It consists of six to eight *rinks* (alleys), each 14 to 19 feet (4.3 to 5.8 meters) wide by 120 feet long. Up to eight matches can be played at the same time.

The *bowls* (balls) vary in size from $4\frac{11}{16}$ to $5\frac{1}{8}$ inches (11.9 to 13 centimeters) in diameter and weigh no more than $3\frac{1}{2}$ pounds (1.6 kilograms). They are not round. One side of a bowl is larger than the other, and this shape causes the bowl to roll in a curving line. The players control the amount of curve by the manner and speed of their delivery of the bowl. They bowl from a rubber or plastic mat at each end of the rink. The target ball, called the *jack,* is round and has a diameter of about $2\frac{1}{2}$ inches (6.35 centimeters). The jack weighs about 10 ounces (283 grams).

The game may be played by *singles, pairs, triples,* or *fours* (teams of one to four players). The players try to roll their bowls as close as possible to the jack. Players also try to knock an opponent's bowl away from the jack or to knock the jack away from an opponent's

Annan Photo Features

Lawn Bowling is a game in which players roll balls at a white target ball. The game is played on grass or artificial turf.

Grove Press

D. H. Lawrence

there. This novel, like most of Lawrence's other works, criticizes social attitudes that he believed were filled with hypocrisy and self-deception. It urges men and women to follow their instincts and is highly critical of industrial society. Lawrence thought such a society separates people from their individual feelings.

Lawrence used experimental techniques and unconventional themes that made him one of the most controversial authors of his time. For example, his frank discussion of sexual passion shocked many readers, and some of his novels were considered obscene. Lawrence's most famous novel, *Lady Chatterley's Lover* (1928), was banned from publication in the United States until 1944, when a shortened version appeared. The complete novel was not published in the United States until 1959.

Lawrence's other novels include *The Rainbow* (1915), *Women in Love* (1920), and *The Plumed Serpent* (1926). A collection of his essays called *Studies in Classic American Literature* (1923) ranks as a classic of literary criticism. Lawrence wrote many short stories, including "The Captain's Doll," "The Fox," "St. Mawr," "The Man Who Died," "The Rocking Horse Winner," "The Virgin and the Gypsy," and "Odour of Chrysanthemums." He also wrote several poems and plays.

Lawrence suffered from tuberculosis and traveled widely in an effort to improve his health. He made several trips to Australia, Italy, and Mexico, and these journeys supplied the background for many of his works.   HELENE MOGLEN

Additional Resources

BURGESS, ANTHONY. *Flame into Being: The Life and Work of D. H. Lawrence*. Arbor House, 1985.

MOORE, HARRY T. *The Priest of Love: A Life of D. H. Lawrence*. Southern Illinois Univ. Press, 1977. Reprint of 1974 revised edition.

SAGAR, KEITH. *D. H. Lawrence: Life into Art*. Univ. of Georgia Press, 1985. Focuses on Lawrence's writings.

LAWRENCE, ERNEST ORLANDO (1901-1958), an American physicist, helped develop the *cyclotron*, a machine for accelerating atomic particles. He received the Nobel Prize in physics in 1939 and the 1957 Enrico Fermi award of the Atomic Energy Commission.

Lawrence started construction of a huge cyclotron before World War II (1939-1945), and converted it during the war to separate the isotopes of uranium. In 1946, he completed this *synchro-cyclotron*, which speeds particles to an energy of 400 million electron volts. In 1948, it produced the first artificially created *mesons* (see MESON). In 1954, he and other scientists completed the *bevatron*, a particle accelerator that produces energy up to 7 billion electron volts. Lawrence was born in Canton, S. Dak.   RALPH E. LAPP

See also CYCLOTRON; SYNCHRO-CYCLOTRON; LAWRENCE BERKELEY LABORATORY; LAWRENCE LIVERMORE NATIONAL LABORATORY.

bowl. In addition, players may try to guard a bowl thrown by a teammate. Each side faces the challenge of the jack's position, the course of the bowls, and the need to counter the other team's strategy.

The first bowler, called the *lead*, rolls the jack to the far end of the rink. The lead then delivers the first bowl as directed by the team's *skip* (captain). Then the lead of the other team bowls. Opposing players alternate turns until each player has delivered the permitted number of bowls. The skip bowls last. Each player uses four bowls in singles and pairs, three in triples, and two in fours. A team scores one point for each bowl lying closer to the jack than the nearest bowl of the opponent.

After both sides have delivered all bowls from one end of the rink, they have completed an *end* (inning). They play the next end from the other end of the rink. Games of pairs, triples, and fours consist of a certain number of ends, usually 12 or 14. A singles game is usually played until one player has scored 18 or 21 points. Tournament games may be longer.

Lawn bowling dates back to ancient Egypt, Greece, and Rome. It has flourished in England since the 1100's. Today, about 20 nations, including the United States and Canada, have lawn bowling associations. These organizations sponsor annual tournaments.

Critically reviewed by the AMERICAN LAWN BOWLS ASSOCIATION

LAWN TENNIS. See TENNIS (The Court).

LAWRENCE, D. H. (1885-1930), was an English writer known chiefly for his novels. His fiction shows deep concern for the relationships between men and women and the complications of these relationships. Many of his works deal with people torn by the need for both love and independence.

David Herbert Lawrence was born in Eastwood, a coal-mining town in Nottinghamshire. His first major novel, *Sons and Lovers* (1913), describes his early life

LAWRENCE, GERTRUDE (1901-1952), an English actress, achieved stardom in both England and the United States. She was admired for her sparkling performances in *Private Lives*, *Lady in the Dark*, and *The King and I*. She also played leading roles in *Susan and God*, *Pygmalion*, *Skylark*, and *Tonight at 8:30*. During World War II, she entertained soldier audiences in England, France, and the Pacific areas. She was born in London and started her stage career as a child. She came to the United States in 1924.   RICHARD MOODY

LAWRENCE, JAMES (1781-1813), a United States naval officer, commanded the *Chesapeake* in an attack on the British ship *Shannon*, during the War of 1812. The *Shannon* easily captured the *Chesapeake*, and Lawrence was fatally wounded. His dying command, "Don't give up the ship," became a watchword of the United States Navy. Lawrence was born in Burlington, N.J., and joined the Navy in 1798. In 1812, Lawrence took command of the *Hornet*, which captured two British ships.   RICHARD S. WEST, JR.

LAWRENCE, SAINT. See ESCORIAL.

LAWRENCE, T. E. (1888-1935), a British soldier and writer, became world famous as *Lawrence of Arabia*. He was one of the most adventurous personalities of World War I (1914-1918). In *The Seven Pillars of Wisdom* (1926), Lawrence described his exploits in Arabia. A shortened version appeared in 1927 as *Revolt in the Desert*.

Thomas Edward Lawrence was born in Tremadoc, Wales. He attended Oxford University, where he studied archaeology and the Near East. When World War I started, Lawrence was working as an archaeologist for the British government. He was sent to Egypt to head the military intelligence department. Later, as a colonel, he helped organize the Arab revolt against Turkey, and became passionately devoted to the Arab cause. He won success as a leader of daring guerrilla raids. His military and diplomatic genius led to the defeat of the Turks and the entry of the Arabs into Damascus, the capital of Syria.

Lawrence refused all honors and decorations. But the Arabs hailed him as a hero, and he was called "the uncrowned King of Arabia." At the Versailles Conference in 1919, he unsuccessfully pleaded the cause of Arabian independence.

In 1921, Lawrence became adviser on Arab affairs to the British Colonial Office, but he was disappointed in the treatment of the Arabs. Feeling that his failure had betrayed his friends, he resigned the next year and enlisted in the Royal Air Force under the name of J. H. Ross. His identity was discovered, and he transferred to the tank corps under the name of T. E. Shaw. In 1925, he returned to the R.A.F. He legally adopted the name of T. E. Shaw. Lawrence was killed in a motorcycle accident in England.   G. E. BENTLEY

Additional Resources

MACK, JOHN E. *A Prince of Our Disorder: The Life of T. E. Lawrence*. Little, Brown, 1978. First published in 1976.
YARDLEY, MICHAEL. *Backing into the Limelight: A Biography of T. E. Lawrence*. Harrap, 1985.

LAWRENCE BERKELEY LABORATORY, in Berkeley, Calif., is one of the world's leading centers of research in nuclear physics. Scientists at the laboratory study elementary particles and have created several new elements. They investigate new sources of energy and energy conservation methods, attempt to find ways of reducing environmental hazards, and seek medical uses for radioactive materials. Research at the laboratory also involves such areas as engineering, mathematics, materials science, and computer science.

The laboratory was established in 1932 by Ernest O. Lawrence, an American physicist. In 1952, a laboratory in Livermore, Calif., joined with the Berkeley laboratory to form the Lawrence Radiation Laboratories. The two facilities were formally separated and given their present names—Lawrence Berkeley Laboratory and Lawrence Livermore National Laboratory—in 1971. Lawrence Berkeley Laboratory is operated by the University of California under contract with the United States Department of Energy.   ALVIN W. TRIVELPIECE

See also NATIONAL LABORATORY.

LAWRENCE LIVERMORE NATIONAL LABORATORY, in Livermore, Calif., is a research facility involved primarily in designing nuclear weapons for the United States. The laboratory has produced nuclear warheads for land and air strategic missiles, and it is involved in research efforts directed toward the development of a defensive shield against nuclear attack.

Scientists at the laboratory also conduct research in other areas, such as biology and environmental science. They have developed a laser isotope separation process for enriching uranium and other nuclear fuels. In addition, they are working to produce new forms of energy technology, particularly ones involving the control of fusion for the generation of electricity (see FUSION).

Lawrence Livermore National Laboratory is operated by the University of California under contract with the United States Department of Energy. It was named after the American physicist Ernest O. Lawrence. The laboratory opened in 1952.   ALVIN W. TRIVELPIECE

See also LAWRENCE BERKELEY LABORATORY; NATIONAL LABORATORY.

LAWRENCE OF ARABIA. See LAWRENCE, T. E.

LAWRENCE RADIATION LABORATORIES. See LAWRENCE BERKELEY LABORATORY; LAWRENCE LIVERMORE NATIONAL LABORATORY.

Detail of painting, reproduced by courtesy of the Trustees of the Tate Gallery, London

T. E. Lawrence became famous as *Lawrence of Arabia*. British portrait artist Augustus John painted him in this role.

LAWRENCIUM (chemical symbol, Lr) is an artificially created radioactive element. It has an atomic number of 103. Lawrencium was discovered in 1961 by four American scientists, Albert Ghiorso, Torbjørn Sikkeland, Almon E. Larsh, and Robert M. Latimer, at the Lawrence Radiation Laboratory (now the Lawrence Berkeley Laboratory) of the University of California. They produced the element by bombarding californium, element 98, with boron ions from a heavy-ion linear accelerator. The half-life of the isotope they obtained was eight seconds, but its mass number is not known for certain. Isotopes with mass numbers of 256 and 257 have since been produced. They have half-lives of about 40 seconds. Lawrencium belongs to the *actinide series* of the periodic table. TORBJØRN SIKKELAND

LAWSON, ERNEST (1873-1939), was an American painter. His style was strongly influenced by his contact with the American impressionist painters John H. Twachtman and J. Alden Weir. But unlike Twachtman and Weir, Lawson used the impressionist style as a vehicle to express his own feelings. He portrayed city landscapes through rugged, simple forms.

Lawson's sense of independent expression typified artist Robert Henri's own conception of art. Lawson joined a group of realistic painters headed by Henri, and called *The Eight* (later the *Ashcan School*). The group exhibited together in 1908. For more information on the group, see ASHCAN SCHOOL. Lawson was born in San Francisco. E. MAURICE BLOCH

Collection Whitney Museum of American Art, New York City

Ernest Lawson's *High Bridge* was painted in 1934. It shows the influence of impressionism on this American realistic painter.

LAWSON, ROBERT (1892-1957), was an American illustrator and writer of children's books. He became prominent as an illustrator in 1936, with his pictures for *The Story of Ferdinand* by Munro Leaf. In 1941 he won the Caldecott Medal for his picture book *They Were Strong and Good*. Lawson received the Newbery Medal in 1945 for *Rabbit Hill*. The first book he wrote and illustrated was *Ben and Me* (1939). Lawson was born in New York City. He studied art at the New York School of Fine and Applied Art. RUTH HILL VIGUERS

LAWYER is a man or a woman who represents members of the public in a court of law. He or she is also called an *attorney*, a *counselor*, or a *solicitor*. A person who seeks a lawyer's services is called a *client*. In Great Britain, a lawyer who has the right to argue cases in higher courts is called a *barrister*. A barrister appointed to represent the king is called a *king's counsel*. The lawyer's duty is to see that all the points of law and any facts that favor the client's case are brought to the attention of the court, and that justice is done.

A lawyer's duty to his client usually covers all legal matters, including contracts, wills, and business matters. A lawyer tries to avoid lawsuits by giving legal advice that will keep the client out of trouble. Legally, anyone may act as his or her own lawyer in any court. But authorities say that it is not wise for an untrained person to do so.

Learning to become a lawyer requires several years of study. Some law schools admit only students who have college degrees. In the United States, law school usually takes three years to complete. Graduates receive a Bachelor of Laws (LL.B.) or a Juris Doctor (J.D.) degree. Most states require lawyers to pass a state bar examination before they practice. THOMAS A. COWAN

See also LAW (A Career as a Lawyer).

LAXATIVE is a medicine that speeds the emptying of the *bowels* (intestines). *Mineral oil* is a laxative that helps empty the bowels by lubricating the bowel contents. *Phenolphthalein*, the active ingredient in chewable and chocolate laxatives, has a direct effect on the intestine, but how it works is not clear. Some laxatives, including *Epsom salt*, provide bulk in the form of retained water. The water increases the bowel contents and forces the bowels to empty. Other laxatives, including *castor oil*, act by irritating the walls of the bowels. Laxatives should not be taken continually over a long period of time because the bowels may become lazy and fail to function on their own. Laxatives may also cause harmful side-effects in other parts of the body. They should never be taken by people who have abdominal pain. *Constipation* (infrequent bowel movements) can often be relieved by eating more bulk foods, such as cereals, whole fruits, and leafy vegetables. SOLOMON GARB

Related Articles in WORLD BOOK include:

Cascara Sagrada	Epsom Salt	Mineral Oil
Castor Oil	Glauber's Salt	Phenolphthalein
Constipation	Magnesia	

LAYTON, IRVING (1912-), is a Canadian poet. He writes forceful poems that praise creativity and energy. Much of his verse expresses the idea that human beings and nature are identical. Layton's love poems, in which he attacks accepted standards of respectability, have a frank, unrestrained quality.

Layton's first collection of poems, *Here and Now*, was published in 1945. Two of his several later volumes, *The Improved Binoculars* (1956) and *A Red Carpet for the Sun* (1959), together provide a survey of Layton's work. *A Red Carpet for the Sun* won the 1959 Governor General's Award for the best book of Canadian poetry.

Layton was born in Tîrgu Neamţ, Romania, and came to Montreal as a child. He has influenced Canadian verse as a critic, poet, and teacher. In 1969, Layton joined the English faculty of York University in Toronto. CLAUDE T. BISSELL

LAZARUS was the brother of Mary and Martha of Bethany. He was the youngest member of a family that

Jesus loved (John 11: 1-44). Lazarus became ill and died while Jesus was preaching beyond the River Jordan. Jesus came to his tomb four days later and said, "Lazarus, come forth." The Bible says that Lazarus came out of the tomb alive. Lord Tennyson and Robert Browning used this story in poems, and Eugene O'Neill wrote a play about it. The name also belongs to a beggar in the parable of the rich man and Lazarus (Luke 16: 19-31). See also NEW TESTAMENT (picture).　FREDERICK C. GRANT

LAZARUS, EMMA (1849-1887), an American poet and essayist, wrote the sonnet inscribed on the pedestal of the Statue of Liberty. A full text of the sonnet appears in the article STATUE OF LIBERTY. Lazarus was born in New York City. She worked as a philanthropist, and organized relief for persecuted Jews immigrating to the United States from Russia.　PETER VIERECK

LAZEAR, JESSE WILLIAM (1866-1900), an American physician, became known for his work in controlling yellow fever. In 1900, an outbreak of yellow fever occurred in Havana, Cuba. Lazear was appointed a member of the Yellow Fever Commission, along with Walter Reed, James Carroll, and Aristides Agramonte, to study the disease. The four men proved that the bite of a mosquito transmitted yellow fever. During the course of their experiments in Cuba, Carroll submitted to the bite of an infected mosquito, developed yellow fever, and recovered. Lazear was bitten accidentally by an infected mosquito and died of yellow fever. Shortly after his death, the disease came under control. Lazear was born in Baltimore, Md., and graduated in medicine from Columbia College.　NOAH D. FABRICANT

LAZURITE. See LAPIS LAZULI.

L-DOPA. See PARKINSON'S DISEASE.

LEACHING. See METALLURGY (Leaching).

LEACOCK, STEPHEN BUTLER (1869-1944), ranks as the most popular humorist in Canadian literature. He also wrote serious works and was a distinguished professor of political science.

The majority of Leacock's humorous works poke fun good-naturedly at everyday people and events by treating them with mock seriousness. In addition, he wrote many *parodies*, which are humorous imitations of other authors' styles of writing.

Most of Leacock's humorous writings first appeared as essays and short stories in magazines and newspapers. The first of the many collections of his humorous works, *Literary Lapses*, was published in 1910. Other well-known collections include *Nonsense Novels* (1911), *Sunshine Sketches of a Little Town* (1912), and *Arcadian Adventures with the Idle Rich* (1914). About 35 of Leacock's more than 60 books were humorous, but he also wrote biographies and works on political science, economics, history, and literary criticism.

Leacock was born in Swanmore, England, near Southampton. His family moved to a farm near Lake Simcoe, Ont., when he was 6 years old. Leacock taught political science at McGill University from 1901 until he retired in 1936. His unfinished autobiography, *The Boy I Left Behind Me*, was published in 1946 after his death.　ROSEMARY SULLIVAN

LEAD, a heavy, bluish-gray element, is one of the world's oldest known metals. People have used lead for thousands of years as a building material and to make

WORLD BOOK photo

Lead, *foreground,* is refined mainly from *galena,* a gray metallic ore, *background.* Much lead is also obtained by removing it from scrap products and recycling it.

pottery and other objects. Today, lead is important to many industries, especially to those that produce chemicals, nuclear energy, and petroleum.

In spite of its usefulness, lead can be harmful. If too much lead builds up in the body, a condition called *lead poisoning* can result. This condition occurs chiefly among persons who work in certain chemical plants or other factories or refineries where there are large quantities of lead fumes or dust in the air.

The amount of lead used is significantly greater than the quantity of lead mined. Annual lead use worldwide exceeds $4\frac{3}{4}$ million short tons (4.3 million metric tons), but yearly lead production from mines is only about $3\frac{3}{4}$ million short tons (3.4 million metric tons). The rest is obtained by removing lead from scrap products and recycling it. The United States is the leading lead-mining country. However, recycled lead makes up about 60 per cent of the lead used in the nation yearly.

Properties. Pure lead is soft and has little strength. As a result, lead producers often *alloy* (mix) it with small amounts of other metals to form *lead alloys*. The added metals, such as antimony and tin, increase the strength of lead and give it other desirable properties. Lead also combines chemically with chlorine, oxygen, and many other elements to form various compounds. For example, it combines with sulfur to produce lead sulfide, also known as *galena*.

Lead is highly *malleable*—that is, it can be hammered or pressed into thin sheets. Lead also possesses great *ductility*, the ability to be permanently stretched without breaking. It resists corrosion by water and by sulfuric acid and other powerful chemicals. Lead is a poor conductor of electricity.

Lead has an atomic weight of 207.19, and its atomic number is 82. Its chemical symbol, *Pb*, comes from the Latin word for lead, *plumbum*. Lead melts at 327.5° C and boils at 1740° C. At 20° C, it has a density of 11.35 grams per cubic centimeter (see DENSITY).

Uses. The largest single use of lead is in the manufacture of lead-acid storage batteries. These batteries contain pure lead and lead compounds, and certain parts of them are made of a lead-antimony alloy. Storage batteries provide power for the electrical sys-

Lead-Acid Storage Batteries make up the largest single use of lead. The worker above is making and installing lead terminal posts for the batteries.

Laboratory Technicians wear protective aprons and gloves lined with lead when using an X-ray machine, above. Lead's high density makes it a good shield against radiation.

tems of airplanes, automobiles, and many other vehicles. See BATTERY (Lead-Acid Storage Batteries).

The second largest use of lead is in the production of *tetraethyl lead*, an ingredient added to gasoline to improve the performance of certain automobile engines. However, the burning of tetraethyl lead in engines also produces chemicals that contribute to air pollution. See TETRAETHYL LEAD.

Several lead compounds are important to the manufacture of some paints and dyes. For example, paints made with the lead compounds called red lead and white lead are used on bridges and other steel structures to prevent corrosion. Manufacturers also use lead compounds in explosives, insecticides, and rubber products.

Lead alloys have a wide variety of uses. Cable coverings made with lead alloys protect telephone and power lines from moisture and corrosion. Manufacturers of automobiles and electronic products use a lead-tin alloy called *solder* to join metal surfaces. Producers of heavy machinery use a lead alloy called *babbitt metal* in the manufacture of bearings, which reduce friction between moving parts (see BABBITT METALS).

Lead's strong resistance to corrosion makes it especially important to the chemical industry. Chemical manufacturers use pipes, storage tanks, and other equipment made of lead alloys for shipping and storing certain chemicals.

The high density of lead makes it a good shield against radiation. Sheets of lead alloys line the walls of hospital X-ray rooms, nuclear reactors, and other facilities in which radioactive materials are present. In addition, radioactive wastes are placed in lead containers for shipment and disposal.

Hazards of Lead. People take lead into their bodies through the *inhalation* (breathing in) or *ingestion* (swallowing) of lead particles, or through the absorption of these particles through the skin. The danger of lead poisoning is greater when an individual is exposed to lead over a long period of time.

Lead interferes with the production of red blood cells and may damage the brain, kidneys, liver, and other organs. Many victims of lead poisoning suffer fatigue, headaches, stomach cramps, and other symptoms. Severe cases of overexposure to lead may be fatal,

but such reported cases of this condition are rare.

Major sources of lead pollution include the exhaust from automobiles that burn leaded gasoline and the dust and fumes released by industrial plants that use lead. Many children who eat chips of dried paint with a high lead content develop lead poisoning. Such paint is found in many older buildings. The United States government now restricts the amount of lead in paint and gasoline, as well as the amount of lead that can be released into the air.

How Lead Is Obtained. Nearly all lead ores are produced from underground mines. Many minerals contain lead, but the principal source of the element is galena, a gray metallic ore. In its pure form, galena consists of only lead and sulfur. However, it rarely occurs in such a form in nature. Instead, most deposits of galena, like those of most other lead ores, contain some copper, gold, silver, and zinc.

After galena is mined, dirt, rocks, and other substances are *concentrated* (separated) from the ore. Most lead refiners concentrate ore by a process called *flotation*. In this process, the ore is crushed and then placed in a tank that contains a flotation chemical, such as copper sulfate or oil. The chemical causes the ore to rise to the top of the tank and particles of dirt and rock to sink to the bottom. Workers then skim off the concentrated ore.

Next, the concentrated ore is roasted in a smelter. During the roasting process, the sulfur in the ore combines with oxygen and escapes as sulfur dioxide gas. In addition, the lead in the ore combines with oxygen to form particles of lead oxide. Additional heat is applied to the lead oxide, causing the particles to *sinter* (join together) into hard lumps.

Workers mix the sintered lead oxide with lumps of coke and feed the mixture into the top of a blast furnace. Inside the furnace, the burning coke reacts with the lead oxide to produce liquid lead. Waste products, called *slag*, are separated from the metal before it reaches the bottom of the furnace.

The crude lead that comes from the blast furnace contains such metals as copper, gold, and silver. Refiners use several methods to purify the lead. Copper normally collects on the surface of liquid lead that has

LEAD

Leading Lead-Mining Countries

United States	464,800 short tons (512,400 metric tons)
Australia	421,500 short tons (464,600 metric tons)
Soviet Union	390,000 short tons (430,000 metric tons)
Canada	309,300 short tons (341,000 metric tons)
Peru	186,000 short tons (205,000 metric tons)
China	140,600 short tons (155,000 metric tons)
Mexico	132,300 short tons (145,800 metric tons)
Yugoslavia	104,300 short tons (115,000 metric tons)
Morocco	99,800 short tons (110,000 metric tons)
Bulgaria	90,700 short tons (100,000 metric tons)

Source: U.S. Bureau of Mines. Figures are for 1982.

Leading Lead-Mining States, Provinces, and Territories

Missouri	523,000 short tons (474,460 metric tons)
British Columbia	92,300 short tons (83,660 metric tons)
New Brunswick	89,800 short tons (81,480 metric tons)
Northwest Ter.	70,500 short tons (63,960 metric tons)
Yukon Ter.	39,100 short tons (35,500 metric tons)

Sources: U.S. Bureau of Mines; Statistics Canada. Figures are for 1982.

cooled slightly. Workers simply skim off the top to remove the copper. Gold and silver are removed by reheating the lead and adding zinc. The precious metals dissolve more easily in zinc than in lead. When the lead cools, workers remove the zinc crust, which contains most of the gold and silver.   A. L. PONIKVAR

See also GALENA; LEAD POISONING.

LEAD, leed, S. Dak. (pop. 4,330), is the site of the Homestake mine, the largest gold mine in the United States. The town stands in the Black Hills of western South Dakota. For location, see SOUTH DAKOTA (political map).

Lead was founded in 1876. It has a commission form of government.   EVERETT W. STERLING

LEAD, lehd, **SOUNDING,** is an instrument that sailors once used to measure the depth of water in harbors and near shores. The sounding lead is a tapered lead cylinder attached to a line of rope or wire. The ship is stopped and the lead is dropped until it touches bottom. Then the line is marked, pulled in, and measured. The *hand lead,* used in waters less than 20 fathoms, or 120 feet (37 meters), deep, weighs from 5 to 14 pounds (2 to 6 kilograms). The lead's underside is hollow and contains tallow which brings up mud or ooze to prove the lead has touched bottom. The sounding lead is still used in exploring shallow waters. See also FATHOMETER; PLUMB LINE; SONAR.   E. G. STRAUS

LEAD MONOXIDE. See LITHARGE.

LEAD PENCIL. See GRAPHITE; PENCIL.

LEAD POISONING is an illness caused by excess lead in the body. It may result from swallowing objects that contain lead or from inhaling lead dust or fumes. Some forms of lead can be absorbed through the skin.

Lead poisoning afflicts many children who eat chips of dried paint that has a high lead content. Such paint is found in many older homes. Lead poisoning also strikes adults who work in smelting, battery manufacturing, and other industries that use lead. Such industries may pollute the environment with lead dust and fumes, which may cause poisoning in people who live near the plants. Another source of lead pollution is the exhaust from automobiles that use leaded gasoline.

Lead interferes with the production of red blood cells and may damage the brain, liver, and other organs. Symptoms of lead poisoning include anemia, headaches, irritability, and weakness. Many victims also experience abdominal pain, vomiting, and constipation, a group of symptoms sometimes called *painter's colic* or *lead colic.* In severe cases, victims may have convulsions, enter a coma, and become paralyzed. Such cases may be fatal.

In the late 1970's, researchers found that even small amounts of lead absorbed by the body over a long period can harm a child. Although such absorption does not cause physical illness, it can damage a child's brain and result in learning difficulties.

Physicians can detect lead poisoning by testing samples of a person's urine or blood and by taking X rays of the bones. If the illness is detected early, permanent damage may be prevented. Doctors recommend that children between 1 and 6 years old be tested for lead poisoning at least once a year.

Physicians treat lead poisoning with drugs that help the body discharge lead through the urine. Treatment may last several months. Many cases of lead poisoning can be prevented by reducing the amount of lead in the environment. The United States government restricts the lead content of paint and certain other products and regulates industrial uses of lead. The government also sets air quality standards that limit the amount of lead that can be released into the air.   HERBERT L. NEEDLEMAN

LEADER. See FISHING (Leaders).

LEADVILLE, Colo. (pop. 3,879), is often called *Cloud City* because it is the highest incorporated city in the United States. This mining center lies 10,200 feet (3,110 meters) above sea level, about 80 miles (130 kilometers) southwest of Denver. For location, see COLORADO (political map). It was named Leadville because of the large quantities of lead ore in the area. Silver, gold, iron, copper, bismuth, manganese, tungsten, and zinc are also mined in the region. The largest molybdenum mine in the world lies 13 miles (21 kilometers) northeast of the city.

The discovery of rich silver-lead mines brought thousands of fortune seekers to Leadville after 1878. The city was incorporated in 1878. Leadville has a mayor-council form of government and is the seat of Lake County.   HAROLD H. DUNHAM

LEADWORT. See PLUMBAGO.

Leaves, the Chief Food-Making Parts of Plants, vary greatly in appearance. Most plants have broad, flat leaves, such as those of a maple tree, *left.* But oats, *center,* and other grasses have long, narrow leaves. Pines, *right,* and most other cone-bearing plants have needle leaves.

LEAF

LEAF is the main food-making part of almost all plants. Garden flowers, grasses, shrubs, and trees depend on their leaves to make food for the rest of the plant. So do ferns, vegetables, vines, weeds, and many other kinds of plants.

Leaves work like tiny food factories. They capture energy from sunlight and use it to make food out of water from the soil and *carbon dioxide,* a gas in the air. This food provides plants with energy to grow, to produce flowers and seeds, and to carry on all their other activities. Plants store the food made by leaves in their fruits, roots, seeds, and stems and even in the leaves themselves. Without this food, plants could not live. In addition, all the food that people and animals eat comes either from plants or from animals that eat plants.

Leaves vary tremendously in appearance. Some are round, and others oval. Still others are shaped like arrowheads, feathers, hands, hearts, or any number of other objects. However, most leaves can be divided into three groups according to their basic shape. (1) *Broad leaves* are the type of leaf that most plants have. These leaves are fairly wide and flat. Plants that have such leaves include maple and oak trees, pea plants, and rosebushes. (2) *Narrow leaves* are long and slender. Such leaves grow on grasses. Grasses include not only lawn grasses but also corn, oats, wheat, and other cereal grasses. Lilies, onions, and certain other plants also have narrow leaves. (3) *Needle leaves* grow on firs, pines, spruces, and most other cone-bearing trees and shrubs. Such leaves resemble short, thick sewing needles. A few

Nels R. Lersten, the contributor of this article, is Professor of Botany at Iowa State University. The drawings were prepared for World Book *by James Teason, unless otherwise credited.*

other kinds of cone-bearing plants, including certain cedars and junipers, have scalelike leaves.

Most leaves grow 1 to 12 inches (2.5 to 30 centimeters) long. Some plants, however, have huge leaves. The largest leaves grow on the African raffia palm. The leaves of this tree measure up to 65 feet (20 meters) long. The giant water lily of South America has round, floating leaves up to 6 feet (1.8 meters) across. In contrast, some plants have extremely small leaves. The true leaves of asparagus plants, for example, are so tiny that they are hard to see without a magnifying glass. In these plants, the stems, not the leaves, produce food.

The number of leaves on plants ranges from several to thousands. Most soft-stemmed plants have few leaves. For instance, a barley or wheat plant produces only 8 to 10 leaves each season. But trees may have an enormous number of leaves. A fully grown elm or pine tree may produce thousands of leaves.

Some plants do not have leaves. Such plants as molds and mushrooms do not make their own food. Instead, they feed on living plants or animals or on decaying matter. These plants, called *fungi,* do not need leaves. Even some simple plants that manufacture their own food do not have leaves. For example, algae, liverworts, and mosses are simple food-making plants that lack true leaves. In some of these simple plants, however, the green food-making tissues look like tiny leaves.

The Importance of Leaves

The chief job of leaves is to make food for plants. This food-making activity, called *photosynthesis,* occurs in fully grown leaves. But young leaves also are important. They wrap tightly around the tips of growing stems. They thus keep the delicate tips moist and help protect them from insects, cold, and other dangers.

Leaves are also vital to animals. Animals cannot make their own food. They depend on plants for their basic supply of food. Many animals eat leaves. For example, antelope, sheep, and other grazing animals eat grass leaves. People also eat leaves, such as those of cabbage, lettuce, and spinach plants. But even when people and animals eat the fruits, roots, seeds, and stems of plants, they are obtaining food made by leaves. In the same way, eggs, meat, milk, and all other animal foods can be traced back to food made by photosynthesis.

Leaves help make the air breathable. They release oxygen during photosynthesis. People and animals must have oxygen to live. Without the activities of leaves, the earth's supply of breathable oxygen would probably soon be used up.

People obtain many products from leaves in addition to food. For instance, we use the leaves of the tea plant to make tea. Peppermint and spearmint leaves contain oils used to flavor candy and chewing gum. Such leaves as bay, sage, and thyme are used in cooking to flavor foods. Some drugs come from leaves. For example, the drug digitalis, which is used to treat certain heart diseases, comes from the leaves of the purple foxglove, a common garden flower. Leaves of abacá and sisalana plants provide fiber used in making rope. Finally, the leaves of the tobacco plant are used to make cigarettes, cigars, and other tobacco products.

The Life Story of a Leaf

A Leaf Begins Its Life in a bud. Buds are the growing areas of a stem. They form along the sides of the stem, at the point just above where a fully grown leaf is attached. A bud also grows at the tip of the stem. A leaf bud contains undeveloped leaf and stem tissues. Within the bud is a mound slightly larger than the head of a pin. Each leaf starts out as a tiny bump on the side of this mound. The mature bud contains a tightly packed group of tiny leaves.

In most soft-stemmed plants, the buds are hard to see. A new leaf becomes noticeable only after it begins to unfold. Most soft-stemmed plants continue to form new leaves until the plants flower or until cold weather sets in. In *temperate regions*, which have warm summers and cold winters, the aboveground parts of many soft-stemmed plants die after the first hard frost, but the roots live through the winter. Other soft-stemmed plants die completely after the cold weather arrives.

Woody plants, on the other hand, may live many

years. They grow several sets of leaves during their lifetime. Most needleleaf trees and shrubs shed old leaves and grow new ones continuously throughout the year. So do most broadleaf trees in the tropics. But in temperate regions, the majority of broadleaf trees and shrubs are *deciduous*. Deciduous plants of temperate regions shed all their leaves each autumn and grow a new set each spring.

Deciduous trees and shrubs start growing the next year's leaves even before the present year's leaves have fallen. The new leaves are enclosed in *winter buds*. The leaves in the winter buds stop growing during the summer and remain *dormant* (inactive) throughout the winter. During the winter months, the buds are protected from drying out by special outer leaves called *bud scales*. In spring, warmth and moisture cause the dormant leaves to become active. The bud scales drop off, and the leaves unfold.

The Leaf Becomes Fully Grown. Leaves complete their growth within one week to several weeks, depending on the kinds of plants that produce them. At first, the unfolding leaf must get all its food from older leaves or from food stored by the plant. Soon, however, the young leaf turns a deeper green and begins to make its own food. Gradually, the leaf produces extra food, which is sent to the rest of the plant.

During the growing season, the color of the leaf changes from bright green to a duller green. The leaf also becomes tougher because its cells develop thicker walls. During this time, a special change occurs in the leaves of deciduous trees and shrubs. A corky layer of cells known as the *abscission zone* develops where the stalk of the leaf joins the stem. This zone breaks down in autumn, causing the leaf to separate from the stem.

The Leaf Changes Color. The leaf is green because it contains a green *pigment* (coloring matter) called *chlorophyll*. This pigment plays a major role in photosynthesis. The leaf also has other colors, but they are hidden by the chlorophyll. As autumn approaches, however, the shorter days and cooler nights cause the chlorophyll in deciduous broad leaves to break down.

The hidden colors of the deciduous broad leaf appear as the chlorophyll breaks down. The leaf may then show the yellow color of the pigment *xanthophyll* or the orange-red tones of the *carotene* pigments. In addition, a group of red and purple pigments called *anthocyanins* forms in the dying leaf. The color of the autumn leaf de-

How Leaves Develop on a Lilac Bush

Leaves Form Inside a Bud. The *winter bud* above protects the tiny leaves during winter.

The Bud Opens in spring as warmth and moisture cause the bud scales to fall off.

The Young Leaves Unfold. As they turn a darker green, they begin to make food.

A Twig Develops with many young leaves several weeks after the bud opened.

Leaf Edges

The blades of broadleaf plants have three chief types of edges: (1) smooth, (2) toothed, and (3) lobed. Smooth-edged leaves are most common on plants native to warm climates. Many temperate broadleaf plants have jagged, toothed blades. Other temperate species have lobed blades, which look as if large bites were taken out of them.

Smooth-Edged Leaf Blade
(Rubber Plant)

Toothed Leaf Blade
(White Birch)

Lobed Leaf Blade
(White Oak)

pends on which of the three pigments is most plentiful in the leaf.

The Leaf Dies. After the chlorophyll breaks down, the leaf can no longer make food. The tiny pipelines between the leaf and the stem become plugged. These pipelines carried water to the leaf and food from it. The cells in the abscission zone separate or dissolve, and the dying leaf hangs from the stem by only a few strands. These strands dry and twist in the wind. When the strands break, the dead leaf floats to the ground.

After the leaf falls, a mark remains on the twig where the leafstalk had been attached. This mark is called a *leaf scar*. The broken ends of the water and food pipelines can be seen within the leaf scar.

On the ground, the dead leaf becomes food for bacteria and fungi. They break the leaf down into simple substances, which then sink into the soil. There, these substances will be absorbed by plant roots and provide nourishment for new plant growth.

The Parts of a Leaf

Most leaves have two main parts: (1) the blade and (2) the petiole, or leafstalk. The leaves of some kinds of plants also have a third part, called the *stipules*.

The Blade, or *lamina*, is the broad, flat part of the leaf. Photosynthesis occurs in the blade, which has many green food-making cells. Leaf blades differ from one another in several ways. The chief differences are in: (1) the types of edges, (2) the patterns of the veins, and (3) the number of blades per leaf.

The Types of Edges. Almost all narrow, grasslike leaves and needle leaves have a blade with a smooth edge. But the edge of broadleaf blades varies greatly among the different types of plants.

Many broadleaf plants, particularly those that are native to warm climates, have smooth-edged leaf blades. The rubber plant, a common house plant, is a good example of such a plant.

The leaves of many temperate broadleaf plants have small, jagged points called *teeth* along the blade edge. Birch and elm trees have such leaves. In many plants, the teeth contain *hydathodes*, tiny valvelike structures that can release excess water from the leaf. The teeth of young leaves on many plants, including cottonwood and pin cherry trees, bear tiny glands. These glands produce liquids that protect the young leaf from plant-eating insects.

Some temperate broadleaf plants—including sassafras trees and certain mulberry and oak trees—have *lobed* leaves. The edge of such a leaf looks as if large bites have been taken out of it. The lobing helps heat escape from the leaf.

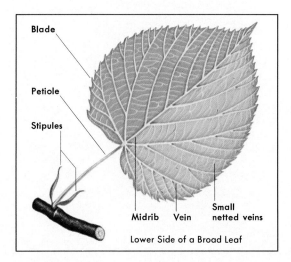

Blade

Petiole

Stipules

Midrib   Vein   Small netted veins

Lower Side of a Broad Leaf

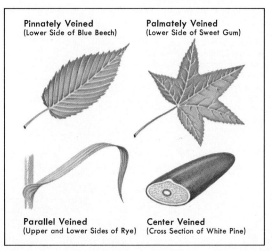

Pinnately Veined
(Lower Side of Blue Beech)

Palmately Veined
(Lower Side of Sweet Gum)

Parallel Veined
(Upper and Lower Sides of Rye)

Center Veined
(Cross Section of White Pine)

The Parts of a Leaf. Most leaves have two main parts: (1) a flat *blade* and (2) a stemlike *petiole*. The leaves of many plants also have a third main part, two small flaps called the *stipules.*

Vein Patterns differ among leaves. Most broad leaves have a *pinnate* (featherlike) or *palmate* (palmlike) vein pattern. Grasses have parallel veins. Needle leaves have one or two center veins.

LEAF

The Patterns of the Veins. Veins are pipelines that carry food and water in a leaf. If you hold a leaf blade up to light, you can see the pattern of its veins.

In most broad leaves, the veins form a netlike pattern, with several large veins connected by many smaller ones. The smallest veins supply every part of the blade with water. They also collect the food made by the green cells.

There are two main types of net-vein patterns—*pinnate* (featherlike) and *palmate* (palmlike or handlike). Pinnately net-veined leaves have one large central vein, called the *midrib*, which extends from the base of the blade to its tip. Other large veins branch off on each side of the midrib. The leaves of beech, birch, and elm trees have such a vein pattern. A palmately net-veined leaf has several main veins of about equal size, all of which extend from a common point at the base of the blade. The vein patterns of maple, sweet gum, and sycamore leaves are palmate.

Narrow leaves and needle leaves are not net-veined. Narrow leaves have a parallel-vein pattern. Several large veins run alongside one another from the base of the blade to the tip. Small crossveins connect the large veins. Needle leaves are so small that they have only one or two veins. These veins run through the center of the blade.

Leaf veins do more than carry water and food. They also support the blade, much as the metal ribs support the fabric of an open umbrella. The veins are tougher and stronger than the green tissue around them. They help the leaf keep its shape and prevent it from collapsing or tearing.

The Number of Blades per Leaf. A leaf may have one or more blades. A leaf with only one blade is called a *simple leaf*. Apple and oak trees, grasses, and many other plants have simple leaves. A leaf with more than one blade is known as a *compound leaf*. The blades of a compound leaf are called *leaflets*.

The leaflets in a compound leaf may be arranged in a pinnate or palmate pattern. In pinnately compound leaves, the leaflets grow in two rows, one on each side of a central stalk, called the *rachis*. Plants with pinnately compound leaves include ash and walnut trees and garden peas. The leaflets in a palmately compound leaf all grow from the tip of the leafstalk. Clover, horse chestnut trees, and many other plants have palmately compound leaves.

A few plants—including carrots, honey locust trees, and Kentucky coffeetrees—have *double compound leaves*. In double compound leaves, each leaflet is divided into a number of still smaller leaflets. One double compound leaf looks more like a group of twigs and leaves than like a single leaf.

The Petiole is the stemlike part of the leaf. It joins the blade to the stem. Within a petiole are tiny tubes, bound together tightly like a bundle of drinking straws. These tubes connect with the veins in the blade. Some of the tubes carry water into the leaf. Others carry away food that the leaf has made.

The leaves of many plants have petioles that grow extra long if the blades are shaded. For example, white clover plants growing among unmowed grass may have petioles up to 6 inches (15 centimeters) long. These long petioles lift the clover leaflets into the sunlight. In a lawn where the grass is kept short, the clover petioles may measure less than 1 inch (2.5 centimeters) long.

In many trees and shrubs, the petioles bend in such a way that the blades receive the most sunlight. As a result of this bending, few of the leaves are shaded by other leaves. The petiole also provides a flexible "handle" that enables the blade to twist in the wind and so avoid damage.

In some plants, the petioles are much larger than the stems to which they are attached. For example, the

Simple and Compound Leaves

A leaf may have one or more blades. If a leaf has only one blade, it is called a *simple leaf*. A leaf with more than one blade is known as a *compound leaf*. The blades of a compound leaf are called *leaflets*. They may be arranged in a palmate or pinnate pattern. A few plants have *double compound leaves*, in which each leaflet is further divided into still smaller leaflets.

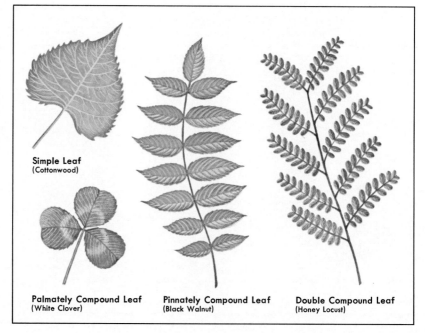

Simple Leaf
(Cottonwood)

Palmately Compound Leaf
(White Clover)

Pinnately Compound Leaf
(Black Walnut)

Double Compound Leaf
(Honey Locust)

parts we eat of celery and rhubarb plants are petioles. In contrast, the leaves of some soft-stemmed plants, particularly grasses, have no petioles.

The Stipules are two small flaps that grow at the base of the petiole of some plants. Many stipules look like tiny green leaf blades. In some plants, the stipules grow quickly, enclosing and protecting the young blade as it develops. Some stipules, such as those of willows and certain cherry trees, produce substances that prevent insects from attacking the developing leaf.

In many plants, the stipules drop off after the blade has developed. But garden peas and a few other kinds of plants have large stipules that serve as an extra food-producing part of the leaf.

How a Leaf Makes Food

A green leaf is a marvelous food-making factory. Using only the energy of the sun, it takes simple materials and turns them into energy-rich food. This section describes how a leaf obtains the raw materials needed to make food. It then provides a simple explanation of how the leaf produces food through photosynthesis. Finally, this section discusses *transpiration*, a process of water loss that plays a key role in the operation of the leaf food factory.

Obtaining the Raw Materials. A leaf needs three things to make food. They are (1) carbon dioxide, (2) water, and (3) light. The carbon dioxide and water serve as the raw materials of photosynthesis. The light, which is normally sunlight, provides the energy that powers photosynthesis.

Carbon Dioxide enters a leaf from the air. The *epidermis* (outer surface) of the leaf has many tiny pores. These openings, called *stomata*, enable carbon dioxide to enter the leaf. Each pore is surrounded by two curved, bean-shaped *guard cells* that can swell and relax. When they swell, the pore is opened wide, and carbon dioxide enters the leaf. When the guard cells relax, the pore closes. In most plants, the stomata open during the day and close at night.

A leaf has many stomata. For example, a cottonwood leaf may have 1 million stomata, and a sunflower leaf nearly 2 million. However, the pores are so small that they make up less than 1 per cent of the leaf's surface. In most plants that grow in full sun, the majority of the stomata are in the shaded lower epidermis of the leaves. In many other plants, the stomata are about equally divided between the upper and lower epidermis.

Water. A leaf obtains water that has been absorbed by the plant's roots. This water travels up the stem and enters the leaf through the petiole. The leaf's veins carry the water throughout the blade. The smallest veins carry the water to nearly every cell in the blade.

Normally, the inside of the blade is very humid. The epidermis is covered by a waxy coating called the *cuticle*. The cuticle helps keep the leaf from drying out. Nevertheless, a leaf does lose much water. Most of this water escapes as vapor through the stomata by the process of transpiration.

Light. Leaves cannot make food without light. But most leaves work best when the sunlight is at a certain level of brightness. If the light is too dim, the leaf will not make enough food. But if the light is too bright, it can damage the food-making cells.

The leaves of many plants that grow in bright sunlight have an extremely thick cuticle, which helps filter out strong light and guards against excess water loss. The leaves may also have many hairs growing out of the epidermis. The hairs further reduce the intensity of bright light. The leaves of such plants as geraniums and white poplar trees have so many epidermal hairs that they feel fuzzy.

Some plants, including the herbs, ferns, and shrubs of the forest floor, thrive in shade. The leaves of most of these plants have a thin cuticle and few epidermal hairs. These features allow as much of the dim light as possible to enter the leaves.

Photosynthesis occurs inside the leaf blade in two kinds of food-making cells—*palisade cells* and *spongy cells*. The tall, slender palisade cells are the chief food producers. They form one to three layers beneath the upper epidermis. The broad, irregularly shaped spongy cells lie between the palisade cells and the lower epidermis. Floating within both kinds of cells are numerous small green bodies known as *chloroplasts*. Each chloroplast contains many molecules of the green pigment chlorophyll.

Water enters the food-making cells from the tiny veins of the blade. Partly surrounding each palisade and spongy cell is an air space filled with carbon dioxide and other gases. The cells absorb carbon dioxide from this air space. When light strikes the chloroplasts, photosynthesis begins. The chlorophyll absorbs energy from the light. This energy splits the water molecules

WORLD BOOK diagram by Larry Miller, Graphic Direction, Inc.

Photosynthesis

Green leaves make food through *photosynthesis*. This process begins when sunlight strikes *chloroplasts*, small bodies that contain a green substance called *chlorophyll*. The chlorophyll absorbs energy from the sunlight. This energy splits water molecules into hydrogen and oxygen. The hydrogen combines with carbon dioxide, forming a simple sugar. Oxygen is released as a by-product.

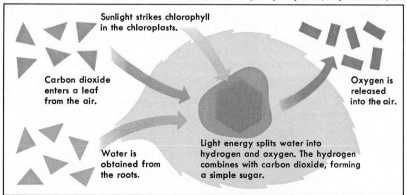

Sunlight strikes chlorophyll in the chloroplasts.

Carbon dioxide enters a leaf from the air.

Oxygen is released into the air.

Water is obtained from the roots.

Light energy splits water into hydrogen and oxygen. The hydrogen combines with carbon dioxide, forming a simple sugar.

Inside a Green Leaf

This cross section shows the many structures of a leaf blade. Palisade and spongy cells serve as food producers. In the veins, xylem tissue distributes water, and phloem tissue carries away food. *Stomata* (pores) on the underside of the blade enable gases to enter and leave the leaf.

Upper epidermis   Palisade cell   Phloem tissue   Xylem tissue   Chloroplasts

Lower epidermis   Stoma   Supporting fibers   Vein   Spongy cell

Section of the Leaf Enlarged at the Left

Pore closed   Pore open

Guard Cells

Guard cells regulate the amount of carbon dioxide and water vapor that pass through a stoma. The stomata are usually open while the leaf is making food.

---

into molecules of hydrogen and oxygen. The hydrogen then combines with carbon dioxide, which results in a simple sugar. This process is extremely complicated and involves many steps. The oxygen that is left over from the splitting of the water molecules enters the air through the stomata.

The sugar produced by photosynthesis is carried through the petiole to the stem and all other parts of the plant. In the plant cells, the sugar may be burned and thus release energy for growth or other activities. Or the sugar may be chemically altered and form fats and starches. In addition, the sugar may be combined with various minerals, and so produce proteins, vitamins, and other vital substances. The minerals enter the plant dissolved in the water absorbed by the roots.

Transpiration occurs as the sun warms the water inside the blade. The warming changes much of the water into water vapor. This gas can then escape through the stomata. Transpiration helps cool the inside of the leaf because the escaping vapor has absorbed heat.

Transpiration also helps keep water flowing up from the roots. Water forms a continuous column as it flows through the roots, up the stem, and into the leaves. The molecules of water in this column stick to one another. Scientists believe that as molecules at the top of the column are lost through transpiration, the entire column of water is pulled upward. This pulling force is strong enough to draw water to the tops of the tallest trees. In addition, transpiration ensures a steady supply of dissolved minerals from the soil.

A plant may lose much water through transpiration. A single corn plant, for example, may lose about 4 quarts (3.8 liters) of water on a hot day. If the roots of the plant cannot replace this water, the leaves wilt and photosynthesis stops.

Specialized Leaves

Some leaves have special functions along with or instead of food making. Such specialized leaves in-clude (1) protective leaves, (2) storage leaves, (3) tendrils, (4) bracts, and (5) insect-capturing leaves.

Protective Leaves include bud scales, prickles, and spines. As described earlier, bud scales are specialized leaves that protect the young, undeveloped tissues of the bud. Bud scales are short and broad, and they overlap like roof shingles. In many plants, the bud scales have an outer layer of waterproof cells.

Prickles and spines are sharp leaf structures that protect the plant from being eaten. For instance, sharp prickles cover the leaves of the Canada thistle, protecting the plant from grazing animals. Many cactus plants have clusters of spines. In many species of cactuses, the pointed spines replace the leaves on the mature plants. In these plants, the green stem has taken over the job of photosynthesis.

Storage Leaves. Most plants store food in their roots or stems. But some plants have special leaves that hold extra food. Onion and tulip bulbs, for example, consist mainly of short, fat storage leaves called *bulb scales.* These leaves cannot make food. Their job is to store food underground during the winter. See BULB.

Many plants that grow in dry places have thick leaves that store water. The mosslike stonecrop plants that grow on rocky cliffs in the Southwestern United States have such leaves. The traveler's-tree, which grows in Madagascar, has enormous leaves that hold much water in their hollow petioles. Thirsty travelers can obtain a drink by punching a hole in the base of a petiole.

Tendrils are slender, whiplike structures that help hold climbing plants in place. They wrap around twigs, wires, and other solid objects. Among many climbing plants, specialized leaves serve as tendrils. For example, climbing garden peas have compound leaves in which the upper leaflets are threadlike tendrils. In one kind of sweet pea, a garden flower, the entire leaf blade becomes a tendril. The plant's stipules enlarge and take over the food-making job. In the greenbrier vine, the stipules form long, curving tendrils.

Bracts grow just below the blossoms of certain plants. Most bracts are smaller and simpler in shape than a plant's regular leaves. Many members of the daisy family—including daisies, goldenrods, marigolds, and sunflowers—have bracts. These bracts form a cup beneath the plant's cluster of flowers.

A few kinds of plants, such as the flowering dogwood and poinsettia, have large, showy bracts. These bracts look like part of the flower, but they are not.

Insect-Capturing Leaves. *Carnivorous* (meat-eating) plants, such as the butterwort, pitcher plant, sundew, and Venus's-flytrap, have leaves that capture insects. These leaves, like other leaves, can make food using sunlight. But they also have features that attract, trap, and then digest insects. Plants with insect-capturing

leaves grow in wetlands, where the soil contains little nitrogen. They obtain this necessary nutrient from the captured insects. For a description of these plants and their leaves, see the article CARNIVOROUS PLANT.

How to Collect Leaves

Collecting leaves or leaf rubbings and prints can be an enjoyable hobby. You can find plants with interesting leaves in fields, forests, and gardens and even along city streets. But before you remove any leaves from a plant, be sure to obtain permission from the owner of the land. In many parks and other public lands, it is illegal to take leaves.

Specialized Leaves Some leaves perform special tasks in addition to or instead of food making. Such specialized leaves include protective leaves, storage leaves, tendrils, bracts, and insect-capturing leaves. Some specialized leaves, such as the spines of a cactus plant, do not even look like leaves. Botanists identify these structures as leaves because of their growth patterns.

Ray Hunold

Protective Leaves include spines like those on the hedgehog cactus above. They prevent animals from eating the plant.

WORLD BOOK photo

Food Storage Leaves include the bulb scales of a tulip, *above*. These fat leaves store food underground in winter.

Dick Keen

Water Storage Leaves are common on plants that grow in dry regions. Such plants include the stonecrop, *above*.

Edward S. Ross

Tendrils hold climbing plants in place. The tendrils of the garden pea plant above are wrapped around wires.

Robert H. Glaze, Artstreet

Bright Red Bracts surround the flowers of the poinsettia above. These leaves help attract pollinating insects to the flowers.

L. West, Bruce Coleman Inc.

Insect-Capturing Leaves attract, trap, and digest insects. Butterwort leaves, *above*, trap their prey in a sticky film.

LEAF

When you collect large leaves, remove only a few. Always pick a complete leaf, including the petiole. In most leaves, the petiole will separate easily from the stem. If you are collecting compound leaves, remember to keep all the leaflets attached to the long petiole. When you collect small leaves, you may need to cut off part of a twig. Keep the leaves attached to the twig, and treat the cutting as if it were a single leaf. Always collect the small needle leaves of firs, pines, and spruces this way.

How to Preserve Leaves. Freshly cut leaves will curl and crack unless you press them. To press leaves, arrange them between several sheets of newspaper. Then place a weight on the newspapers. A piece of plywood with books stacked on it makes a good weight. After a week of pressing, the leaves should remain flat. You can then mount them on stiff paper by placing a strip of tape across the petiole.

How to Make Leaf Rubbings and Prints. To make a leaf rubbing, lay the leaf lower-side up on a tabletop. Cover the leaf with a sheet of tracing paper or thin typing paper. Then rub the paper lightly and rapidly with the side of a sharpened soft pencil, a piece of charcoal, or a wax crayon. The outline of the leaf and the larger veins will gradually appear on the paper.

To make a leaf print, you need printer's or etcher's ink and a roller. These materials can be obtained at an art supply store. Use the roller to spread a thin layer of ink on a glass plate or a smooth piece of cardboard. Next lay the leaf lower-side down on the ink. Then place a piece of paper over the leaf and rub the entire leaf with your fingers. After rubbing, remove the paper and carefully pick up the leaf. Place the leaf's inky surface on a sheet of plain paper. Now cover the leaf with another sheet of paper and rub. Be careful not to move the leaf as you rub. After rubbing the leaf, remove the top sheet of paper and the leaf. A print of the leaf will appear on the lower sheet. NELS R. LERSTEN

Related Articles. Many WORLD BOOK articles on individual plants contain information about leaves. For example, see IVY; MAPLE; PALM; POINSETTIA. For illustrations of the leaves of many common North American trees, see TREE (Familiar Broadleaf and Needleleaf Trees of North America). Other related articles include:

Bud
Chlorophyll

Photosynthesis
Plant

Outline

I. **The Importance of Leaves**
II. **The Life Story of a Leaf**
  A. A Leaf Begins Its Life
  B. The Leaf Becomes Fully Grown
  C. The Leaf Changes Color
  D. The Leaf Dies
III. **The Parts of a Leaf**
  A. The Blade
  B. The Petiole
  C. The Stipules
IV. **How a Leaf Makes Food**
  A. Obtaining the Raw Materials
  B. Photosynthesis
  C. Transpiration
V. **Specialized Leaves**
  A. Protective Leaves
  B. Storage Leaves
  C. Tendrils
  D. Bracts
  E. Insect-Capturing Leaves

VI. **How to Collect Leaves**
  A. How to Preserve Leaves
  B. How to Make Leaf Rubbings and Prints

Questions

Why do deciduous broad leaves change color as autumn approaches?
What is *transpiration?*
Why are leaves vital to plants and animals?
How do carnivorous plants obtain nitrogen?
How do simple and compound leaves differ?
What are some products that come from leaves?
How does a leaf obtain carbon dioxide?
What is the *abscission zone?* A *leaf scar?*
How do you make a leaf rubbing?
What is a *petiole?* Do all leaves have one?

Additional Resources

Level I

CAULFIELD, PEGGY. *Leaves.* Coward, 1962.
DAVIS, BURKE. *Biography of a Leaf.* Putnam, 1972.
HUTCHINS, ROSS E. *This is a Leaf.* Dodd, 1962.

Level II

ASIMOV, ISAAC. *Photosynthesis.* Basic Books, 1969.
POLING, JAMES. *Leaves: Their Amazing Lives and Strange Behavior.* Holt, 1971.
WOHLRABE, RAYMOND A. *Exploring the World of Leaves.* Crowell, 1976.

LEAF-CUTTER ANT. See ANT (Fungus Growers).

LEAF INSECT is an insect that looks much like a green leaf or a twig. It is sometimes called a *walking leaf* because of this similarity. It is found in Africa, southeastern Asia, and northern Australia, and on the many islands of the South Pacific. Several related species called *walking sticks* live in America.

The best-known leaf insect is an East Indian species. It is bright green in color and grows about 3 inches (8 centimeters) long. It looks much like a leaf because of its broad ribbed wings, which fold over its back in the shape of a leaf. It also has leaflike growths on the joints of the legs. The eggs look like the seeds of plants. Leaf insects live among the leaves of trees and shrubs, where they are hard to find because of their shape and color. They feed on leaves at night and usually stay quiet during the day.

USDA

A Leaf Insect of the Philippines is more than 3 inches (8 centimeters) long. Its greenish color helps the insect hide among the leaves.

Scientific Classification. The East Indian leaf insect belongs to the walking stick family, Phasmidae. Some scientists classify leaf insects in the order Orthoptera. Others put them in the order Phasmida. URL LANHAM

See also WALKING STICK.

LEAF MINER is a tiny fly, moth, or beetle which, in the larval stage, lives between the upper and lower skins of leaves. Leaf miners eat the inside of the leaf, leaving white winding tunnels or broad whitish blotches. The larvae of some species mine under the skin of fruits, stems, or branches of shrubs and trees. These larvae can be highly destructive. See LARVA.

The lives of leaf miners begin when the females lay small eggs on the undersides of plant leaves. From the eggs are hatched larvae that begin to eat tunnels, or mines, in the leaf. There may be one or more larvae in a leaf, and some migrate from leaf to leaf. They may become full grown in one to three weeks, and then

Hugh Spencer
Leaf Miner Larvae eat tunnels through leaves.

they enter the pupal stage of their lives (see INSECT [The Life Cycle of Insects]). Some drop to the ground and make cocoons. Others stay on or inside the leaf until they develop into adults. Three or four generations of leaf miners may appear in one season. Leaf miners are found throughout the world. There are many species.

Scientific Classification. Leaf miners belong to the orders Diptera, Lepidoptera, and Coleoptera.

LEAFHOPPER is one of a large group of insects that feed on plants. These insects are found throughout the world. All species have piercing-sucking mouth parts. They rob plants of their juices, causing them to dry up and wilt. They run sideways, and the winged species fly easily. Many carry plant diseases. The leafhopper has a small, slender body of many colors. It is usually only $\frac{1}{20}$ to $\frac{1}{4}$ inch (1.3 to 6.4 millimeters) long.

Scientific Classification. Leafhoppers belong to the leafhopper family, Cicadellidae. The apple leafhopper is genus *Empoasca*, species *E. mali*.

USDA
The Apple Leafhopper spreads fire blight in apple orchards, and also feeds on potatoes and other crops.

LEAGUE is a measure of length. A *statute league* equals 3 statute, or land, miles. It also equals 15,840 feet, or 4.828 kilometers. A *nautical league* equals 3 nautical or sea miles. It also equals 18,228.346 feet, or 5.555963 kilometers. The word *league* is sometimes used by British and American sailors. The league has been used since ancient times. The Gauls made it equal to 1,500 Roman paces, or what would be 1.376 modern English miles (2.2 kilometers). The Normans brought the league to England. At that time it equaled 2 English miles, or 2.9 modern statute miles (4.7 kilometers).　E. G. STRAUS

See also MILE.

LEAGUE OF NATIONS was an international association of countries created to maintain peace among the

nations of the world. The victors of World War I—including France, Great Britain, Italy, Japan, and the United States—drew up a *covenant* (constitution) for the League in 1919. The League was established in January, 1920, with headquarters in Geneva, Switzerland. President Woodrow Wilson of the United States was the chief planner of the League, but he could not persuade the U.S. to join it. The League was dissolved in April, 1946, and the United Nations took its place.

Wilson believed that world wars would continue to occur as long as each nation had to be responsible for its own defense. Under this condition, nations would form competing groups, each arming against the other. Wilson wanted the nations of the world to join together in the League of Nations, and pledge to defend the territory and independence of any member attacked by another nation. He believed that even a powerful nation, knowing it would face the united opposition of all other powerful nations, would not go to war.

Wilson got other countries to agree to his plans for the League, but he and members of the U.S. Senate differed over the terms on which the United States would join. In March, 1920, the U.S. Senate rejected the treaty which would have made the United States a member (see WILSON, WOODROW [Opposition to the League; Wilson's Collapse]). Within a few years, most Americans decided there was no need to concern themselves with conflicts overseas, and the United States never did join the League of Nations.

Powers and Organization

The League Covenant contained articles pledging member nations to preserve the independence and territory of all members against attack. Members agreed to submit any disputes that might lead to war either to *arbitration* (decision by a third party) or to an investigation by the League Council. They promised not to go to war with any member that agreed to the recommendations of a court of arbitration or the League Council. If any member went to war in violation of these articles, member nations agreed they would apply economic *sanctions* (penalties), such as stopping trade with the offending nation. At the League Council's request, they would also use military force against that nation.

The Council was the principal peacekeeping agency. Its size varied from 8 to 14 members during the League's history. The most powerful members of the League had permanent seats on the Council. France, Germany, Great Britain, Italy, Japan, and the Soviet Union held permanent seats during the years they were members of the League. The remaining seats were rotated among the small nations of the League. Peacekeeping recommendations of the Council had to be decided by unanimous vote.

The Assembly was composed of all member nations, and each member had one vote. The Assembly controlled the League budget, admitted new members, elected the temporary Council members, and made amendments to the Covenant. On these matters, the Assembly could decide by a two-thirds or a majority vote. The Assembly also could discuss threats to the peace. It needed a majority vote plus the votes of all Council members to recommend on such a matter.

United Press Int.

The Palace of Nations in Geneva, Switzerland, served as headquarters of the League of Nations. When the League was dissolved in 1946, the building was given to the United Nations.

The Secretariat provided the administrative staff of the League. A secretary-general, who was nominated by the Council and approved by the Assembly, headed a staff of about 600 officials. These officials assisted the peacekeeping work of the League and provided personnel for special study commissions on disarmament and colonial affairs. The Secretariat also staffed the various international organizations set up by the League to promote cooperation in international trade, finance, transportation, communication, health, and science.

The League in Action

Wilson and the other statesmen who designed the League hoped it would lead nations to stop seeking protection through special alliances. Instead, they favored a system of *collective security*, in which the security of each member would be guaranteed by the protection of all. For collective security to work, it was essential that all League members—especially the most powerful ones—come to the aid of any member attacked.

Neither the Council nor the Assembly could force members to help an attacked nation. This action had to be voluntary. Each member nation had to believe that a threat to the peace of any nation—even a small, distant nation—was a threat to its own peace.

Disagreement Among Members. The most powerful nations did not agree that collective security was the main purpose of the League. France saw the League mainly as an instrument to maintain the territorial settlement imposed on Germany after World War I. The Germans resented the League because it seemed to them, too, that this was the League's real purpose. British leaders considered it a meeting place for powerful nations to consult in event of a threat to peace. But they did not want to commit themselves in advance to do anything as a result of such talks. The Soviet Union be-

The League of Nations

The following nations were the original members of the League. Many other nations joined later, and many withdrew from the League before it was disbanded.

Argentina	Great Britain	Panama
Australia	Greece	Paraguay
Belgium	Guatemala	Peru
Bolivia	Haiti	Poland
Brazil	Honduras	Portugal
Canada	India	Romania
Chile	Iran	South Africa
China	Italy	Spain
Colombia	Japan	Sweden
Cuba	Liberia	Switzerland
Czechoslovakia	Netherlands	Thailand
Denmark	New Zealand	Uruguay
El Salvador	Nicaragua	Venezuela
France	Norway	Yugoslavia

lieved the League was an imperialist fraud, because Communism taught that war was inevitable among capitalist nations. Japan and Italy showed their disregard for collective security by attacking member nations.

Japan withdrew from the League in 1933 because the League refused to recognize its conquest of Manchuria. Germany, admitted to the League in 1926, withdrew in 1933 because the League would not change the arms limitations imposed on Germany after World War I. Italy withdrew from the League in 1937 to join Japan and Germany in an alliance against the Soviet Union. The Soviet Union, which joined the League in 1934, was expelled in 1939 for attacking Finland.

The League achieved some success in ending armed conflicts between small nations. For example, it ended fighting between Greece and Bulgaria in 1925, and between Poland and Lithuania in 1927. But when a powerful nation was involved, the League was ineffective.

Why the League Failed was most dramatically illustrated when Italy attacked Ethiopia in October 1935. The Council declared that Italy had violated the Covenant. This action obligated League members to apply economic sanctions and to consider the use of force against Italy. Members agreed to stop all imports from Italy and to send no money or war material to Italy.

But the United States, Japan, and Germany were not League members. Therefore, the overwhelming "community of power" that Wilson had in mind for use against an aggressor was reduced to three nations—France, Great Britain, and the Soviet Union. The other League members did not have enough power to affect Italian policy. Even so, France, Great Britain, and the Soviet Union would have been able to stop the Italian attack, if they had been united and determined to do so.

However, Britain and France were not willing to use force or to employ measures that might risk war. They even failed to use such economic measures as an oil embargo, which would have seriously hurt the Italian war effort. By May 1936, Italy had conquered Ethiopia. The League canceled its sanctions in July.

French policy was the main reason for the failure of the League. Great Britain and the Soviet Union might have taken stronger actions against Italy if France had supported them. But France feared another war with Germany, and wanted Italy as an ally. It made no sense to French leaders to lose the friendship of Italy just to protect the independence of Ethiopia. The Ethiopian case completely discredited the League as an instrument to keep the peace.   WARNER R. SCHILLING

See also UNITED NATIONS; INTERNATIONAL RELATIONS; MANDATED TERRITORY; WILSON, WOODROW; WORLD WAR II (Problems Left by World War I).

Additional Resources

JOYCE, JAMES AVERY. *Broken Star: The Story of the League of Nations (1919-1939)*. Humanities, 1978.
WALTERS, F. P. *A History of the League of Nations*. Oxford, 1960. Reprint of 1952 edition.

LEAGUE OF UNITED LATIN AMERICAN CITIZENS

is an organization of Spanish-speaking peoples in the United States. The group, known as LULAC, encourages patriotism among its members and works to protect their economic, political, and social rights.

LULAC has a number of educational centers that offer counseling on admission and financial aid to young people who want to attend college. The league endorses political candidates and organizes voter registration drives. Local councils sponsor holiday parades and fiestas to preserve Latin-American culture.

The league provides legal assistance to fight discrimination through court action. During the 1940's, the organization helped file suits that ended segregation of Mexican-American students in several school districts in California and Texas. In New Mexico, the league's campaign against job discrimination led to passage of a state fair employment practices law in 1949.

LULAC was founded in 1929 in Corpus Christi, Tex. It has about 500,000 members in more than 30 states. Headquarters are at 3033 N. Central Avenue, Phoenix, AZ 85012.   FELICIANO RIVERA

LEAGUE OF WOMEN VOTERS

is a nonpartisan organization that promotes informed, active public participation in government. Both men and women may belong to the league. It has about 1,300 local groups in the United States, Puerto Rico, and the Virgin Islands.

The league believes that political education helps create a sense of responsibility in Americans for democratic government. It encourages all eligible Americans to register and vote, and it provides nonpartisan information on candidates and issues before elections. It does not endorse candidates or political parties.

The League of Women Voters selects certain local, state, and national issues for study and action. It has supported the United Nations; water conservation; and such programs as equal opportunity in education, employment, and housing. Local and state leagues have worked for changes in city charters and state constitutions, court reforms, and improved state and local services in education, health, and welfare.

The League of Women Voters was organized in 1920 as an outgrowth of the woman suffrage movement in the United States. National headquarters are at 1730 M Street NW, Washington, DC 20036.

Critically reviewed by the LEAGUE OF WOMEN VOTERS

See also CATT, CARRIE CHAPMAN; WOMAN SUFFRAGE.

LEAHY, *LAY hee,* **WILLIAM DANIEL** (1875-1959), served as chief of staff to President Franklin D. Roosevelt during World War II. His long career in naval affairs and diplomacy greatly aided him in advising the President on military affairs. Leahy served in the Philippines during the Spanish-American War, in Nicaragua

during the American occupation, and in World War I. From 1927 to 1931, he was chief of the Navy Bureau of Ordnance. He later became chief of naval operations. He retired in 1939 with the rank of admiral.

Leahy was ambassador to France from 1940 to 1942, when he returned to naval duty. He became fleet admiral in 1944. Leahy was chief of staff from 1942 to 1949. He was born in Hampton, Iowa.   DONALD W. MITCHELL

LEAKEY FAMILY includes three noted anthropologists—a husband and wife and their son—who made important discoveries in eastern Africa concerning the origins of human beings. They are Louis S. B. Leakey, Mary D. Leakey, and Richard E. F. Leakey.

Louis Seymour Bazett Leakey (1903-1972) was largely responsible for convincing scientists that Africa was the most significant area to search for evidence of human origins. Most anthropologists had looked for such evidence in Asia because of the discovery of human fossils in Java (now part of Indonesia) and in China.

Leakey began leading fossil-hunting expeditions to eastern Africa during the 1920's. He married Mary D. Nicol in 1936, and the couple discovered many important fossils together. In 1962, an expedition led by the Leakeys found species of an apelike jaw and teeth about 14 million years old in Kenya. Louis Leakey named the creature *Kenyapithecus*. Also during the early 1960's, Leakey found fossils at Olduvai Gorge in Tanzania that he considered remains of an early human being. Leakey and other scientists named the species *Homo habilis* and identified it as the earliest member in the genus of human beings (see HOMO HABILIS).

Leakey was born in Kabete, Kenya, near Nairobi. His parents were British missionaries. He wrote a two-volume autobiography, *White African* (1937) and *By the Evidence* (1974).

Mary Douglas Leakey (1913-   ) has also worked chiefly in Kenya and Tanzania. In 1948, she found the skull of a creature that lived about 20 million years ago in Kenya. This creature, named *Proconsul africanus*, is regarded by some scientists as close to the common ancestor of human beings and apes. In 1959, Mary Leakey found the skull of a humanlike creature at Olduvai Gorge. This creature, named *Zinjanthropus*, lived about 1,750,000 years ago. This discovery was one of the first indications that humanlike creatures once lived in eastern Africa. See ZINJANTHROPUS.

In 1978, a team led by Mary Leakey found a trail of footprints preserved in volcanic ash at Laetoli, Tanzania. Most scientists believe these fossils belonged to a humanlike creature who lived about 3,700,000 years ago. The specimens are among the oldest known fossils of a humanlike ancestor. See AUSTRALOPITHECUS.

Mary Nicol was born in London. Her books include *Africa's Vanishing Art: The Rock Paintings of Tanzania* (1983) and an autobiography, *Disclosing the Past* (1984).

Richard Erskine Frere Leakey (1944-   ) became director of the National Museums of Kenya in 1968. He has found many important fossils at Lake Turkana in Kenya. There, in 1972, Leakey discovered part of the skull of a prehistoric human who lived about 1,900,000 years ago. Most scientists believe the skull belonged to *Homo habilis*. It is the oldest known *Homo habilis* fossil.

In 1975, Leakey uncovered the skull of a more advanced type of prehistoric human being known as *Homo erectus*. This skull, also found at Lake Turkana, was about 1,600,000 years old. In 1984, Leakey and British paleontologist Alan Walker discovered an almost complete *Homo erectus* skeleton at Lake Turkana. See HOMO ERECTUS.

Leakey was born in Nairobi, Kenya. Among his books are *The Making of Mankind* (1981) and an autobiography, *One Life* (1983). ANDREW HILL

LEAN, SIR DAVID (1908-) is a highly acclaimed English motion-picture director. He won Academy Awards as best director for *The Bridge on the River Kwai* (1957) and *Lawrence of Arabia* (1962).

Lean was born in Croydon. He began his motion-picture career in London at the age of 19. He performed a variety of duties before becoming a successful film editor in the mid-1930's. Lean made his debut as a director in *In Which We Serve* (1942), which he co-directed with English playwright Sir Noel Coward. The movie won praise for its portrayal of the heroism of British sailors during World War II (1939-1945).

Lean directed two popular movies adapted from the novels of English author Charles Dickens, *Great Expectations* (1946) and *Oliver Twist* (1948). He also directed the comedy fantasy *Blithe Spirit* (1945), the love stories *Brief Encounter* (1945) and *Summertime* (1955), the Russian historical epic *Dr. Zhivago* (1965), and the Asian drama *A Passage to India* (1984). Lean produced and directed *The Sound Barrier* (1952), an exciting aviation drama. He was knighted by Queen Elizabeth II in 1984. JOHN F. MARIANI

LEANDER. See HERO AND LEANDER.

LEANING TOWER OF PISA is a famous bell tower at Pisa, Italy. It is often considered one of the seven wonders of the modern world. The tower tips so far to one side that it looks as though it will fall. But it has stood for hundreds of years. It was begun in 1173 and completed in 1372. The ground beneath the tower started to sink after the first three stories were built. The tower began to lean. Today, the tower is about 17 feet (5.2 meters) out of line. Measurements began in 1911. Since then, the tower has increased its lean by an average of 1.25 millimeters a year.

It is said that Galileo made his famous experiments with falling weights in 1589 from the top of the tower. But many scholars no longer believe this story.

The tower, or *campanile*, built entirely of marble, is a fine example of Romanesque architecture. The tower, the cathedral, and the baptistery form one of the most famous building groups in the world.

The leaning tower is 177 feet (54 meters) tall. The walls are 13 feet (4 meters) thick at the base and from 6 to 7 feet (1.8 to 2.1 meters) thick at the top. A row of arches, resting on 15 columns, surrounds the first story. Each of the next 6 stories is surrounded by 30 columns. The top story has 12 columns. This top story houses the bells. An inner staircase of nearly 300 steps leads to the top of the tower. G. HOLMES PERKINS

LEAP YEAR has 366 days, or one more day than an ordinary year. A leap year occurs in every year that can be divided evenly by four, except the years that mark the even hundreds, as 1500. The only century years that are leap years are those that can be divided evenly by

H. Armstrong Roberts

The Leaning Tower of Pisa has been one of the world's most famous architectural wonders since it was completed in 1372. Many consider it one of the seven wonders of the modern world. Tourists can climb its winding stairs for a view of Pisa.

400, such as 1600 and 2000. Leap years were added to the calendar to make the calendar year nearly the same as the solar year, which is the time it takes for the sun to pass the vernal equinox twice. The extra day is added to the end of February and occurs as February 29 once every four years. See also YEAR. PAUL SOLLENBERGER

LEAR, EDWARD (1812-1888), an English writer and artist, became famous for his humorous poems for children. Lear's first book of poems, *A Book of Nonsense* (1846), ranks as a masterpiece of children's literature. His best-known poem, "The Owl and the Pussy-Cat" (1871), also became a classic. Lear became especially noted for his short rhymed verses called *limericks*. One of these appears in the WORLD BOOK article on LIMERICK.

Lear was born in London. He began to earn his living at the age of 15 by drawing birds and doing other art work. Lear established a reputation as a natural-history artist with his first book of drawings of parrots, published in 1832. He also became known for his detailed landscape paintings. During the mid-1830's, while drawing and painting for a living, Lear began to write nonsense verse for children. However, none of his verses was published until 1846. Lear also drew many illustrations for his books.   JAMES DOUGLAS MERRITT

LEAR, KING. See SHAKESPEARE, WILLIAM (Shakespeare's Plays).

LEARNING is an important field of study in psychology. Psychologists define learning as the process by which changes in behavior result from experience or practice. By *behavior*, psychologists mean any response that an organism makes to its environment. Thus, behavior includes actions, emotions, thoughts, and the responses of muscles and glands. Learning can produce changes in any of these forms of behavior.

Not all changes in behavior are the result of learning. Some changes result from *maturation* (physical growth). Other behavior changes, including those caused by illness or fatigue, are only temporary and cannot be called learning.

How We Learn

We can see learning taking place all the time, but there is no simple explanation of the process. Psychologists have examined four kinds of learning in detail: (1) classical conditioning or respondent learning, (2) instrumental conditioning or operant learning, (3) multiple-response learning, and (4) insight learning.

Classical Conditioning is perhaps the simplest kind of learning. This learning process is based on stimulus-response relationships. A *stimulus* is an object or a situation that excites one of our sense organs. A light is a stimulus because it excites the retina of the eye, allowing us to see. Often a stimulus makes a person *respond* in a certain way, as when a flash of light makes us blink. Psychologists say that in this instance the stimulus *elicits* (draws forth) the response.

In classical conditioning, learning occurs when a new stimulus elicits behavior similar to that originally produced by an old stimulus. Suppose a person tastes some lemon juice, which makes the person salivate. While the person is tasting it, a tone is sounded. Suppose these two stimuli—the lemon juice and the tone—occur together many times. Eventually, the tone by itself will make the person salivate. Classical conditioning has occurred because the new stimulus (the tone) elicits the response of salivation in much the same way as the lemon juice did.

Any condition that makes learning occur is said to *reinforce* the learning. When a person learns to salivate to a tone, the reinforcement is the lemon juice that the tone is paired with. Without the lemon juice, the person would not learn to salivate to the tone.

The classical conditioning process is particularly important in understanding how we learn emotional behavior. When we develop a new fear, for example, we learn to fear a stimulus that has been combined with some other frightening stimulus.

Studies of classical conditioning are based on experiments performed in the early 1900's by the Russian physiologist Ivan P. Pavlov. He trained dogs to salivate to such signals as lights, tones, or buzzers by using the signals when he gave food to the dog (see REFLEX ACTION). Pavlov called the learned response a *conditioned response* because it depended on the conditions of the stimulus. To emphasize the fact that a stimulus

produces a response in this kind of learning, classical conditioning is often called *respondent learning*.

Instrumental Conditioning. Often a person learns to perform a response as a result of what happens after the response is made. A child may learn to beg for candy. There is no one stimulus that elicits the response of begging. The child begs because such behavior occasionally results in receiving candy. Every time the child receives candy, the tendency to beg becomes greater. Candy, therefore, is the reinforcer. Instrumental conditioning is also called *operant conditioning* because the learned response *operates* on the environment to produce some effect.

The American psychologist B. F. Skinner performed important experiments with instrumental conditioning in the 1930's. He trained rats to press levers to get food. In one experiment, a hungry rat was placed in a special box containing a lever attached to some concealed food. At first, the rat ran around restlessly. Eventually, it happened to press the lever, and the food dropped into the box. The food reinforced the response of pressing the lever. After repeating the process many times, the rat learned to press the lever for food.

Skinner's experiments were based on those performed earlier in the 1900's by the American psychologist E. L. Thorndike. In Thorndike's experiments, an animal inside a puzzle box had to pull a string, press a pedal, or make some other response that would open the box and expose some food. Thorndike noted that the animal learned gradually. It improved on a puzzle in time, but the entire learning process was slow and gradual. Thorndike called this type of learning *trial-and-error behavior*.

Multiple-Response Learning. When we learn skills, we first learn a sequence of simple movement-patterns. We combine these movement-patterns to form a more complicated behavior pattern. In most cases, various stimuli guide the process. For example, operating a typewriter requires putting together many skilled finger movements. These movements are guided by the letters or words that we want to type. At first, a person has to type letter by letter. With practice, the person learns to type word by word or phrase by phrase. In verbal learning, such as memorizing a poem or learning a new language, we learn sequences of words. We then combine these sequences of responses into a complex organization. Learning that involves many responses requires much practice to smooth out the rough spots.

To examine this kind of learning, psychologists have observed animals learning to run through a maze. Starting at the beginning, the animal wanders through the maze until it finds food at the end. The animal periodically comes to a choice-point, where it must turn right or left. Only one choice is correct. Eventually the animal learns the correct sequence of turns. Psychologists have found that the two ends of the maze are learned more easily than the parts near the middle. In the same way, when we learn a list of things, we usually find the beginning and end easier than the middle.

Insight Learning. The term *insight* refers to solving a problem through understanding the relationships of various parts of the problem. Insight often occurs suddenly, as when a person looks at a certain problem for

LEARNING

some time and then suddenly grasps the solution to it.

The psychologist Wolfgang Köhler performed important insight experiments in the early 1900's. He showed that chimpanzees sometimes use insight instead of trial-and-error responses to solve problems. When a banana was placed high out of reach, the animals stacked boxes on top of each other to reach it. They also put two sticks together to reach an object that was too far away to reach with one stick. The chimpanzees appeared both to see and to use the relationships involved in reaching their goals.

Theories of Learning are based on facts obtained from experiments such as those on classical and instrumental conditioning. Psychologists differ in their interpretation of these facts. As a result, there are a number of learning theories. These theories can be divided into three groups.

One group of psychologists emphasizes stimulus-response relationships and the experiments with classical and instrumental conditioning. They say all learning is the forming of habits. When we learn, we connect a stimulus and a response that did not exist before, thus forming a habit (see HABIT). Habits can range from the simplest ones to complex ones that are involved in learning skills. These psychologists believe that when we meet a new problem, we use appropriate responses learned from past experience to solve it. If this procedure does not lead to the solution, we use a trial-and-error approach. We use one response after another until we solve the problem. Sometimes we cannot find a response that proves successful. In such a case, certain types of stimulus-response methods called *behavior modification* may help change habits.

A second group of psychologists stresses *cognition* (the act of knowing) above the importance of habit. These experts feel that experiments with classical and instrumental conditioning are too limited to explain such complex learning as understanding concepts and ideas. This approach emphasizes the importance of the learner's discovering and perceiving new relationships and achieving insight and understanding.

A third group of psychologists has developed *humanistic* theories. According to these theories, much human learning results from the need to express creativity. Creativity may be expressed through almost any activity. For example, athletics, business dealings, and homemaking all serve as creative outlets. The psychologists in this group believe that each person must become involved in challenging activities—and must do reasonably well at them—to have a satisfying life. The individual gains a sense of control, growth, and knowledge from such activities. For learning to occur, people must feel free to make their own decisions. They also must feel worthy, relatively free from anxiety, self-respecting, and respected by others. Under these conditions, their own inner drives will lead them to learn. Some kinds of group therapy try to provide an accepting, supporting environment. Such an environment is intended to increase people's awareness of their own thoughts and of the world around them.

Learning involves changes in the nervous system. Through research, scientists are trying to discover the processes that take place in the brain to produce learning. Such experiments may lead to a physiological theory of learning.

Efficient Learning

Readiness to Learn. Learning occurs more efficiently if a person is ready to learn. This readiness results from a combination of growth and experience. Children cannot learn to read until their eyes and nervous systems are mature enough. They also must have a sufficient background of spoken words and prereading experience with letters and pictures.

Motivation. Psychologists and educators also recognize that learning is best when the learner is motivated to learn (see MOTIVATION). Rewards are often used to increase motivation to learn. Punishment, particularly the threat of punishment, is also used to control learning. Experiments have shown that reward serves as a more effective aid to learning than punishment. This is due largely to two factors: (1) learners can recognize the direct effects of reward more easily than they can the effects of punishment; and (2) the by-products of reward are more favorable. For example, reward leads to liking the rewarded task, but punishment leads to dislike of the punished deed.

Psychologists also look at the motivation of learning from the point of view of the learner. They tend to talk about success and failure, rather than reward and punishment. Success consists of reaching a goal that learners set for themselves. Failure consists of not reaching the goal. An ideal learning situation is one in which learners set progressively more difficult goals for themselves, and keep at the task until they succeed.

Skill Learning and Verbal Learning. Through research, psychologists have discovered some general rules designed to help a person learn.

The following rules apply particularly to learning skills. (1) Within a given amount of practice time, you can usually learn a task more easily if you work in short practice sessions spaced widely apart, instead of longer sessions held closer together. (2) You can learn many tasks best by imitating experts. (3) You should perform a new activity yourself, rather than merely watch or listen to someone. (4) You learn better if you know immediately how good your performance was. (5) You should practice difficult parts of a task separately and then try to incorporate them into the task as a whole.

Two additional rules apply mainly to verbal learning. (1) The more meaningful the task, the more easily it is learned. You will find a task easier to learn if you can relate it to other things you have learned. (2) A part of a task is learned faster when it is distinctive. When studying a book, for example, underlining a difficult passage in red makes the passage distinctive and easier to learn.

Transfer of Training. Psychologists and educators recognize that new learning can profit from old learning because learning one thing helps in learning something else. This process is called *transfer of training*.

Transfer of training can be either positive or negative. Suppose a person learns two tasks. After learning Task 1, the person might find Task 2 easier or harder. If Task 2 is easier, then the old learning has been a help and positive transfer of training has occurred. If Task 2 is harder, the old learning is a hindrance and negative transfer has occurred.

Whether transfer is positive or negative depends on the relationship between the two tasks. Positive transfer occurs when the two tasks have similar stimuli and both stimuli elicit the same response. For example, if we know the German word *gross*, it is easier to learn the French word *gros* because both words mean *large*. In this case, similar stimuli (*gross* and *gros*) elicit the same response (*large*).

Negative transfer occurs when the two tasks have similar stimuli, which elicit different responses. After you learn the German word *Gras* (grass), it is harder to learn the French word *gras* (fat). The words are similar, but they have different meanings. In this case, similar stimuli (*Gras* and *gras*) elicit different responses.

Psychologists believe new learning can profit from old learning because of three factors: (1) positive transfer of training, (2) general principles that we learn in one task and apply to another task, and (3) good study habits that we learn in one task which help us learn another task.   LEONARD M. HOROWITZ

Related Articles in WORLD BOOK include:

Animal (Behavior; Intelligence of Animals)	Motivation
	Pavlov, Ivan P.
Association	Perception
Behavior	Personality
Comparative Psychology	Piaget, Jean
Developmental Psychology	Psychology (History)
Educational Psychology	Skinner, B. F.
Instinct	Teaching Machine
Köhler, Wolfgang	Testing
Learning Disabilities	Thorndike, Edward L.
Memory	Tolman, Edward C.

Additional Resources

BORGER, ROBERT, and SEABORNE, A. E. *The Psychology of Learning.* 2nd ed. Penguin, 1982.
BOWER, GORDON H., and HILGARD, E. R. *Theories of Learning.* 5th ed. Prentice-Hall, 1981.
EDSON, LEE. *How We Learn.* Time Inc., 1975.

LEARNING DISABILITIES are disorders that damage a child's ability to learn. Children with learning disabilities may have average or above-average intelligence, and they also have normal hearing and vision. But they apparently cannot use information transmitted by the senses to the brain as accurately as most other children can. Therefore, they do poorly in school, or not as well as they might.

Learning disabilities can interfere with the development of such basic skills as concentration, coordination, language, and memory. Some children with learning disabilities have more than the usual difficulty speaking, understanding spoken language, or paying attention in class. Others have difficulty learning to read, spell, or solve arithmetic problems.

In the United States, from 5 to 10 per cent of all children between the ages of 5 and 17 have one or more learning disabilities. Early diagnosis and treatment are important because specialized teaching techniques can help many of these students overcome their handicaps and succeed in school. Learning problems may continue into adulthood unless a child receives help.

Causes. Physicians cannot always discover the specific cause of a child's learning disability. But scientists believe that most learning disabilities result from minor damage to the brain or to major nerves leading to the brain. For example, illness or poor nutrition in a pregnant woman can injure the brain tissue and nerv-

ous system of her unborn child. Brain damage can occur at birth if the baby's brain does not receive enough oxygen. Such damage can take place during a long, difficult birth or if the mother receives an overdose of a pain-killing drug. A child also may inherit a learning disability from his or her parents.

Many other factors may increase a child's chances of developing a learning disability. An imbalance of certain chemicals in the body or a lack of nutritious foods can delay or permanently damage the development of the nervous system. Medical research suggests that certain chemicals, especially lead used in paint, may trigger learning disabilities in some children.

Even a child with no physical problem may develop a learning disability. Disabilities can result from a lack of the early learning experiences that stimulate mental growth and development. These experiences include hearing language, manipulating objects, and exploring the environment.

Types. There are many types of learning disabilities. For example, *perceptual disorders* hinder the brain's ability to organize and interpret sights and sounds. Children with a perceptual disorder may be unable to pinpoint where one word ends and another begins on a page. Or such children may not be able to distinguish between words that sound somewhat alike. Perceptual disorders make learning to speak and read difficult.

Another type of learning disability affects memory. Children with this problem cannot easily recall what familiar objects look like or what sounds the objects make. They may not be able to remember a series of instructions or learn a sequence, such as the alphabet or a telephone number.

Other learning disabilities interfere with the ability to behave properly and concentrate. *Distractible* children daydream almost constantly. They cannot direct their attention to any topic for more than a few minutes. In contrast, children with a disability called *perseveration* cannot easily shift their attention from one activity to another. They may continue working at a task long after it has been finished. *Hyperactive*, or *hyperkinetic*, children cannot sit still. They speak and act on impulse and tend to become impatient and boisterous in the classroom (see HYPERACTIVE CHILD). A child with *emotional lability* has unexpected changes in mood for no apparent reason.

An *orientation-related disability* damages a child's sense of direction, distance, and space. Individuals with this problem may be unaware of where they are and feel lost even in familiar surroundings. They cannot distinguish left from right or up from down. They become poor readers because they cannot remember to read from left to right. They also may not recognize the difference between letters that resemble each other, such as *b* and *d*.

Other types of learning disabilities interfere with effective muscle control and can cause clumsiness and loss of balance. Some of these disabilities prevent specific movements necessary for certain activities. For example, *dyspraxia* is the inability to properly move the lips, tongue, and other parts of the body in speech. *Dysgraphia* affects the brain's control of the small finger muscles used in writing.

LEASE

Learning disabilities that block the development of language skills are called *psycholinguistic disabilities*. One such condition, called *dysphasia*, interferes with the ability to produce or understand human speech. *Dyslexia* damages a child's capacity to understand printed or written words. Learning problems that hinder a child's progress in particular subjects, such as arithmetic or spelling, are *specific learning disabilities*.

Diagnosis and Treatment. Not all learning and behavioral problems are caused by learning disabilities. Parents who suspect that their son or daughter may have a learning disability should have the child examined by a team of specialists. Many school districts provide such testing free or at a reasonable cost. Tests by a *pediatrician* (children's doctor), eye and ear specialists, a psychiatrist, and a social worker may find other possible causes of the problem. Such causes include emotional disturbances, mental retardation, and poor hearing and vision. If the test results are normal, a physician called a *neurologist* should examine the child for evidence of damage to the brain or nervous system. Then a psychologist should test each of the child's learning processes to determine which ones have been affected. Finally, a special-education teacher must measure the child's school achievement to learn in which subjects he or she needs special help.

The method of treatment suggested by the teacher depends on the type and extent of the disability. Some learning-disabled children learn best in special classes with others who have similar problems. But many youngsters can do exercises to improve their weak skills in classes with nonhandicapped children. Some learning experts suggest more controversial treatments, including drugs called *amphetamines*, special diets, and exercises. Scientists are studying the effectiveness and safety of many of these methods.   DIANNE SHIELDS

Additional Resources

OSMAN, BETTY B. *Learning Disabilities: A Family Affair*. Random House, 1979. *No One to Play With: The Social Side of Learning Disabilities*. 1982.
STEVENS, SUZANNE H. *The Learning-Disabled Child: Ways That Parents Can Help*. Blair, 1980.

LEASE is a contract between a person who owns land or other property and a person who rents it from the owner. The person who grants the lease is called the *lessor*. The person to whom the lease is granted is called the *lessee*, or *tenant*. The compensation which the tenant agrees to pay the lessor is called the *rent*.

A lease for life ends when the tenant dies. A lease for a term of years begins and ends at dates set in the lease. The lease does not end when the tenant or lessor dies, but is binding on the heirs of both parties. Some leases are for a long period, such as 99 years. Such leases usually give the lessee greater privileges than those granted a short-term tenant.

Rents are generally paid in money, although occasionally they are paid in goods. For example, a person who rents a farm may agree to pay with crops.

A lease must include certain items of information to be a legal contract. These include the names of the lessor and tenant, the dates of the beginning and end of the lease, the amount of rent, a complete description of the property, and a complete statement of the rights and duties of each party. Most state laws provide that leases that cover a period of less than a year need not be written, but leases for a longer period must be in writing. Sometimes leases are prepared by the lessor's lawyer and the lessee's lawyer.   WILLIAM TUCKER DEAN

See also CONTRACT; FIXTURE; TENANT.

LEASE, MARY ELIZABETH (1850-1933), was an American orator and reformer. She helped establish the Populist Party, a national political party (see POPULISM).

Lease was born in Ridgway, Pa. She moved to Kansas in 1870 and became active in the Farmers' Alliance movement there. Debt-ridden Midwestern farmers established the movement to protest against bank and railroad monopolies, and Lease forcefully voiced their complaints. In 1891, she worked with the Farmers' Alliance, the Knights of Labor, and other groups to form the Populist Party. Lease seconded the nomination of James B. Weaver for President at the party's nominating convention in 1892, and he became the Populist presidential candidate that year. She urged such Populist programs as government ownership of railroads and free coinage of silver (see FREE SILVER).

Brown Brothers

Mary Elizabeth Lease

Lease left the Populist Party in 1896 because it supported William Jennings Bryan, the Democratic candidate for President. She continued to work for women's right to vote and other reforms. Lease discussed her views on politics and reform in her book *The Problem of Civilization Solved* (1895).   NANCY SPELMAN WOLOCH

LEATHER is a tough, flexible material made from the skin of animals. Cattle hides provide the source of most leathers, but deer, goat, pig, and sheep skins are also widely used. Specialty leathers are made from alligator, shark, and snake hides. The process of turning the animal skin into a leather product that can be made into useful objects is called *tanning*.

Leather is used to make shoes, boots, belts, gloves, jackets, hats, shirts, trousers, skirts, purses, and many other objects. Baseballs, basketballs, and footballs have leather covers. Industries use drive belts made from leather, and automobiles, trucks, and buses run on bearings protected by leather seals.

Leather is strong and long-lasting. It can be made as flexible as cloth or as stiff as wood. Some kinds of leather are thick and heavy, but others are thin. Leather can be dyed, polished to a glossy finish, or *embossed* (decorated with raised figures).

People have known how to make leather since prehistoric times. Some tanning methods that were developed by the ancient Greeks and Romans are still in use. Today, the United States is one of the world's largest producers of leather. New York, Massachusetts, California, and Wisconsin are the nation's leading leather-producing states.

Kinds of Leather

The chief kinds of leather are *shoe sole leather, shoe upper leather, chamois*, and *suede*. Shoe sole leather is pro-

Leather Is Used to Make a Wide Variety of Products. The type of leather used depends on the product. This photo shows a purse made of *chrome-tanned leather,* shoes made of highly polished, glossy *patent leather,* a hat made of soft leather called *suede,* and a polishing cloth made of clothlike *chamois.*

duced from the thick skins of cattle and other large animals. Shoe upper leather is obtained from the thinner skins of calves, goats, and other smaller animals or by splitting heavy hides into thin layers. About 80 per cent of all tanned leather is made into shoes.

Chamois leather was originally made from the chamois, an animal that lives in Europe and Asia and resembles the antelope. But today, most chamois leather is made from split sheepskin. Properly tanned chamois leather is as soft as cloth and will hold water like cloth. Chamois leather is often used as a washing and polishing cloth.

Suede leather is often made from the inside flesh layer of a cowhide that has been split. In the past, goatskins or sheepskins were used for this leather. Suede is soft, flexible, warm, and water-resistant. It is used to make jackets, coats, dresses, pants, and shoe uppers.

How Leather Is Made

Preparing the Hides. Before animal hides can be tanned, they must undergo certain preparations. These preparations include (1) curing, (2) fleshing, (3) unhairing, and (4) bating.

Curing. Most animal hides used to make leather come from a meat packer or slaughterhouse. Most tanneries are located some distance from the hide source. In fact, many of the skins used in the United States are imported.

The skins are cured before they start the trip to the tannery to keep them from rotting. Hides are cured by applying salt to the flesh side of the skin, by soaking them in *brine* (salty water), by partially drying and salting them, or by just drying them. After they are cured, the skins are stacked in revolving drums filled with water. The water removes dirt and blood, washes out most of the salt, and replaces the moisture lost during the curing process.

Fleshing. After the skins are washed and remoisturized, they are fleshed. Workers run the hides across a fleshing machine equipped with sharp knives, removing all fat and meat on the flesh side of the skin. More and more hides are being fleshed at the packing house, thereby eliminating the fleshing step at the tannery.

Unhairing. Workers put the fleshed hides in vats containing a lime and water solution that has a small amount of the chemical sodium sulfide. The solution weakens the hair roots by chemical action, and in a few days the hair is loose. The hides are then run through an unhairing machine that scrapes the hair away. The hair is kept for use in making felt and other products. After unhairing, the hides are refleshed to remove bits of fat loosened by the unhairing process. Then, they are washed in clean water.

Bating. After unhairing, the skins are bated—that is, they are placed in a mild acid bath to neutralize the unhairing solutions left in them. This process is necessary because the solutions used for tanning are acidic. If the alkaline solutions used for unhairing were not neutralized in this way, they could prevent the tanning solutions from penetrating the skin. Enzymes are also added to the bath to digest soluble proteins in the hide that could interfere with the tanning process.

Tanning. After the hides have been cured, fleshed, unhaired, and bated, they are ready for tanning. There are four chief methods of tanning hides: (1) vegetable tanning, (2) chrome tanning, (3) combination tanning, and (4) oil tanning.

Vegetable Tanning is generally carried out in large vats filled with tanning solutions, which are made from water and *tannin.* Tannin is a bitter substance that is obtained from such plants as the chestnut, hemlock, mangrove, oak, and quebracho trees.

Workers increase the strength of the tanning solution in proportion to the amount of time the hide is left in the solution. Tanning solutions commonly start at about 0.5 per cent tannin and are increased to as much as 25 per cent tannin by the completion of the tanning process. Vegetable-tanning processes usually take from one to three months, but thick skins are sometimes tanned for as long as a year.

Vegetable-tanned leather is firmer and more water-resistant than chrome-tanned leather. Vegetable-tanned leather may be *stuffed*—that is, materials such as fats and oils may be worked into it. Stuffing makes the leather water-repellant and more resistant to wear. Vegetable-tanned leather is made into bookbindings and heavy belts for machinery. Pure vegetable tanning is also used for such specialty leathers as *basil,* made from sheepskin; some pigskin; and buffalo, ostrich, rhinoceros, and walrus hides.

Chrome Tanning is the most widely used mineral tanning process. It is performed with a tanning solution of *chrome salts* (compounds of chromium). Before skins are chrome tanned, they are *pickled* (soaked in a solution of sulfuric acid and salt). The skins are soaked until their acidic content reaches a predetermined level. Then they are removed and washed.

After washing the skins, workers place them in tanning drums that are filled with water and chromium sulfate. The chromium sulfate solution tans the skins and gives them a light blue color as well. The skins are usually completely tanned in a few hours.

Chrome-tanned leather can be made much faster than vegetable-tanned leather. It is also more resistant to heat and scratching, more flexible, and easier to soften. Leather for shoe uppers, gloves, wallets, luggage, and

LEATHER

upholstery is generally chrome tanned. However, some of these leathers are retanned with *syntans* (synthetic tanning materials), vegetable-tanning solutions, or substances containing formaldehyde, to give them special characteristics.

Combination Tanning involves the use of both the chrome-tanning and vegetable-tanning methods. Combination tanning is used for leathers with special qualities, such as extremely soft garment, glove, or shoe upper leathers. In today's tanneries, most leather is chrome tanned, either as the complete tanning process, or as a *pretan* for vegetable tanning. Pretanning speeds up the vegetable-tanning process and also gives vegetable-tanned leather more flexibility. Some shoe soles are vegetable tanned, but usually they are pretanned with a chrome tan.

Oil Tanning is used for the chamois leather that is made from sheepskin. First the wool is removed from the sheepskin and the skin is split into layers. The flesh *split* (side) is used for chamois, and workers begin by shaving the split to remove the fat cells. Next, they put the shaved split into a machine that hammers cod-liver oil into the skin. After the oil has penetrated it, the skin is removed from the machine and dried. It is then buffed to soften it and to give it a *nap* (soft, woolly surface). Saddle leather and leather seals used on some machinery are also oil tanned. However, they are pretanned with chrome before being oil tanned.

Final Processing that is carried out after the skins are tanned includes (1) splitting, (2) dyeing, (3) staking, and (4) finishing.

Splitting. The tanned skins are removed from the tanning materials and dried. Some are then split by a machine that cuts the skins into two layers. The top layer is called *top grain*. The bottom, or flesh, layer is often called *suede leather*. The skin is further divided into four sections. The *bend* section is the skin on either side of the backbone from the rump to the shoulder. The bend section provides the finest leather. The *shoulder* section is also fine leather, but it often is wrinkled. The *head* section is good leather, but the pieces are small and uneven. The *belly* section is poorest in quality because it is uneven and tends to stretch.

Dyeing. Almost all leather is dyed after tanning. Dyeing is often done in large drums similar to those used in the chrome tanning operation. Leather can be dyed with a number of aniline dyes, natural wood dyes, acid dyes, and even some tanning agents. The dyeing takes place while the skin is being tumbled with a mixture of warm water and the dyeing material. Oil is usually added to further soften the skin. This process is called *fat-liquoring* the skin. After the hide is dyed and fat-liquored, it is dried in drying vats, by pasting the hide onto a glass plate or a metal sheet. The hide may also be dried by *toggling* (pinning) it to a large wooden sheet with holes in it.

Staking. Some leather must be made softer after it is dyed. The dried skin is partially remoisturized by putting it in a room with a highly humid atmosphere, or by covering it with damp sawdust or a similar material. Then it is placed on a staking machine, where steel pegs stretch and work the leather to soften it. If extremely soft leather is desired, it is tumbled in wooden drums. Glove leather is often softened in this way.

How Leather Is Made

Tanning Begins as workers place the animal hides in a solution of certain chemicals and water. The solution loosens the hair on the hides.

Leather Is Dried following the tanning process. In one drying method, the leather is stretched on large wooden *toggling frames* that have holes in them.

Some Leather Is Split into layers by a splitting machine. Workers measure the thickness of the layers with a special gauge.

Dry Milling is one of several methods used to soften leather. In this method, workers place the leather in large drums and then tumble it for hours.

A Seasoning Machine smooths the surface of the leather. The rollers apply such seasoning materials as pigments, shellacs, and waxes.

Cromwell Leather Company, Inc.

The Finishing Process includes spraying the leather with such substances as proteins, waxes, and oils. The spraying machine above is activated by a computer.

Leather from the Past has often survived in good condition because of its durable quality. The leather sandals from ancient Egypt, *far left*, are about 2,000 years old. The Spanish leather gameboard and box, *left*, was probably made in the 1700's.

Finishing. After staking, the leather is ready for the final finishing process. *Casein* (a protein found in milk), other substances obtained from blood and milk, waxes, and oils are some of the materials used for a final finish on leather. The finish is sprayed on in layers. Between applications, a cylindrical piece of glass or steel is rolled over the leather to smooth and glaze it. The most highly polished leather is called *patent leather*. It is produced by applying successive coats of heavy oil varnish at the end of the finishing process. This varnish gives patent leather a high, durable gloss.

History

People have tanned animal skins since prehistoric times. The ancient Egyptians made such durable leather that specimens over 3,000 years old have been discovered in almost perfect condition. Evidence of oil tanning has been found in leather from Egyptian tombs. The early Greeks and Romans also made contributions to the science of leathermaking. Some of their methods are still in use today.

Many ancient peoples tanned their leather by placing layers of bark, leaves, and fruit over hides and adding water. This process took months, and in the case of thick skins, even years. As early as 800 B.C., people discovered the mineral salt alum and began using it as a tanning agent. The Assyrians, Babylonians, Greeks, and Sumerians used this mineral method of tanning because it was much faster than previous techniques.

The American Indians used deerskins to make leather for their moccasins, cloaks, and tents. Colonial settlers refined the leathermaking process, and leather became one of the most widely used materials in the U.S. territories.

In 1809, Samuel Parker, an American inventor, patented the leather splitting machine. This machine allowed workers to make two skins out of one, thereby doubling production. Fleshing and unhairing machines were invented shortly after the splitting machine.

Manufacturers did not begin producing leather for a large market until the 1800's. In the United States, leather became more widely available as the standard of living rose. As more cattle began to be consumed for meat, more hides became available for tanning. Augustus Schultz, an American dye salesman, perfected a chrome-tanning process in 1884. The method was perfected about 10 years later by Martin Dennis. Chrome tanning allowed more attractive and flexible leathers to be produced at a much faster rate.

Because of the increasing demand for leather, researchers have developed synthetic leather. Synthetic leather closely resembles natural leather and has many uses. However, it does not have natural leather's ability to *breathe*—that is, to allow perspiration to escape without letting in water from the outside.   JAMES E. CHURCHILL

Related Articles in WORLD BOOK include:

Buckskin	Crocodile	Shoe
Chamois	Leathercraft	Suede

LEATHERCRAFT is the art of making useful and decorative objects out of leather. Suede and fur can also be used. The most popular leather-crafted objects include belts, moccasins, hats, purses, saddles, and shoes. Leatherworkers also use leather to create furniture, jewelry, sculptures, and wallhangings.

Leather can be cut, carved, glued, sewn, dyed, and painted. It can also be combined with other materials, such as fabrics and wood, and with other craft techniques, including weaving and macramé.

Basic leatherworking consists of four procedures: (1) designing, (2) cutting and assembling, (3) coloring, and (4) finishing.

Designing involves drawing the desired pattern onto the leather. The leatherworker may use chalk or pencil.

Cutting and Assembling. Sharp instruments must be used for cutting. These instruments range from knives and household scissors to special leather-cutting shears. The choice of cutting tool depends on the thickness of the material. For example, thick shoe leather requires sharp knives while suede, which is thinner, can be cut with a pair of scissors. Most cuts within the leather are made with special punches. These are sharp steel tools with points in a variety of shapes, such as ovals, diamonds, or stars. The leatherworker places the sharp end of the punch on the leather and drives it into the surface by hitting the blunt end with a rawhide mallet. Designs can be added by *tooling* the surface with chrome-plated carving and stamping instruments. See EMBOSSING.

The leatherworker can assemble the leather parts in several ways. For example, he or she can make a series of evenly spaced holes or slits with a leather punch or a pronged chisel. The parts are then assembled by lacing or stitching. Pieces can also be attached by gluing or by nailing one to another with special brads. Leather can be shaped by wetting the material and then folding it or tacking it onto a wooden form. The leather retains the shape of the fold or the form after it dries.

Coloring. Dyes in liquid or powder form are the most reliable for coloring leather. To produce deep tones, the

LEATHERNECKS

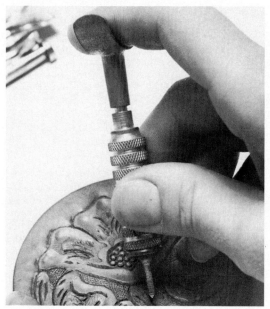

Bett's Leathers (WORLD BOOK photo by Steve Hale)

A Leathercrafter needs special tools to decorate leather. A swivel knife, *above,* is used to carve designs into the leather.

leatherworker dampens the leather, thus allowing the dye to penetrate the pores of the material. Softer tones can be created by applying dyes to dry leather. Special coloring effects can be achieved by using household fabric dyes, acrylic paints, or wood stains. The surface may be polished or buffed after the coloring has dried.

Finishing involves trimming, smoothing, and beveling the edges. Then the surface of the object is polished and buffed. DONA Z. MEILACH

LEATHERNECKS. See MARINE CORPS, UNITED STATES.

LEAVEN, *LEHV uhn,* is a substance that causes fermentation of dough in breadmaking. A leaven acts by causing the formation of carbon dioxide gas which bubbles through and lightens and expands the batter or dough while it is baking. Yeast, sour milk and soda, and baking powder are common leavens. KAY L. FRANZEN

See also BREAD (Kinds of Bread; History); YEAST (How Yeast Is Used).

LEAVENWORTH, *LEHV uhn wurth,* Kans. (pop. 33,656), the oldest city in the state, is a distributing and manufacturing center. The city lies on the Missouri River about 30 miles (48 kilometers) northwest of Kansas City (see KANSAS [political map]). Its factories make furniture, batteries, cotton gloves, flour, mill machinery, and foundry and steel products.

Fort Leavenworth was established near the site of the city in 1827. For many years it was the most important army post on the western frontier. The U.S. Army Command and General Staff College is at Fort Leavenworth. Leavenworth Prison is also in the fort. The city is the home of St. Mary College. Leavenworth has a commission government. WILLIAM F. ZORNOW

LEAVENWORTH PRISON, *LEHV uhn wurth,* is one of the six federal penitentiaries in the United States. Its official name is United States Penitentiary, Leavenworth,

Kans. It is on the Fort Leavenworth reservation on the Missouri River north of Leavenworth. Besides the buildings of the civil prison, a federal military prison also stands on the grounds. Leavenworth Prison was established in 1895. It has about 1,000 prisoners.

Critically reviewed by the BUREAU OF PRISONS

LEAVES. See LEAF.

LEBANON, *LEHB uh nuhn,* is a small country at the eastern end of the Mediterranean Sea and the western end of Asia. It has long been a world center of transportation, trade, and finance. Lebanon is slightly smaller than the state of Connecticut. Sandy beaches lie along its coast, and rugged mountains rise in the interior.

Lebanon has a population of about 2,762,000. Beirut, on the coast, is the nation's capital and largest city. About a fourth of the country's people live in the Beirut area. Most of Lebanon's people are Arabs. Almost all the people are either Christians or Muslims. Political differences between Lebanese Christians, and Lebanese Muslims and their Palestinian Liberation Organization (PLO) allies have erupted into bloody battles. A civil war that took place in Lebanon during the mid-1970's, and has continued off and on since then, has caused much destruction and death, and damage to the country's economy.

Government

Lebanon is a republic. A president heads the government. The country's National Assembly (parliament) elects the president to a six-year term. The president appoints a prime minister. The prime minister has less power than the president, but traditionally the prime minister and president have worked as a team. The prime minister, with the president's approval, chooses a Council of Ministers (cabinet), which carries out the operations of the government. The National Assembly makes the country's laws. Its members are elected by the people to four-year terms.

To maintain a political balance between Christians

Siegfried E. Wilheim, Bruce Coleman, Inc.

The Snow-Covered Lebanon Mountains rise above the town of Hammana in central Lebanon.

Lebanon

▬▬▬	International boundary
▬▬▬	Road
▬▬▬	Railroad
⊛	National capital
•	Other city or town
+	Elevation above sea level

0   20   40   60   80 Miles
0 20 40 60 80 100 Kilometers

WORLD BOOK map

and Muslims in Lebanon, the government has traditionally been composed of members of both of these groups on a proportional basis. A Maronite Christian serves as president of Lebanon, and a Sunni Muslim serves as prime minister.

Lebanon is divided into five provinces, each of which is headed by a governor. Most of the provinces are divided into districts, which are governed by district heads. Lebanon's main courts are, from highest to lowest, the Court of Cassation, the Courts of Appeal, and the Courts of First Instance.

People

Ethnic Groups and Religion. About 90 per cent of Lebanon's people are Arabs. The Arab population includes more than 400,000 Palestinian Arabs, who are refugees from the Arab-Israeli wars. The Palestinians had lived on land that is now part of Israel, Lebanon's neighbor to the south. Other ethnic groups in Lebanon include Armenians, Assyrians, and Kurds. Almost all Lebanese speak Arabic, the official language.

Approximately half of the Lebanese people are Muslims, and about half are Christians. But Muslims probably slightly outnumber Christians in the country. Among all the world's Arab countries, Lebanon has the highest percentage of Christians. Most of Lebanon's Muslims belong to either the Sunni or Shi'ah sect of the Muslim faith. A religious group in Lebanon called the *Druse* practices a secret religion related to Islam. The majority of Lebanese Christians are members of the Maronite Church, which is part of the Roman Catholic Church.

Way of Life. About four-fifths of Lebanon's people live in urban areas, and about one-fifth live in rural areas. Most wealthy and middle-class Lebanese live in cities, and most are either Christians or Sunni Muslims. The country's poor people—mainly Shi'ah Muslims

Facts in Brief

Capital: Beirut.

Official Language: Arabic.

Form of Government: Republic.

Area: 4,015 sq. mi. (10,400 km²). *Greatest Distances—* north-south, 120 mi. (193 km); east-west, 50 mi. (80 km). *Coastline—*130 mi. (209 km).

Elevation: *Highest—*Qurnat as Sawda, 10,115 ft. (3,083 m) above sea level. *Lowest—*sea level.

Population: *Estimated 1987 Population—*2,762,000; distribution, 80 per cent urban, 20 per cent rural; density, 688 persons per sq. mi. (266 per km²). *1970 Census—*2,126,325. *Estimated 1992 Population—*3,095,000.

Chief Products: *Agriculture—*apples, cherries, cucumbers, grapes, lemons, oranges, peaches, tomatoes. *Manufacturing—*cement, chemicals, electric appliances, furniture, processed foods, textiles.

Flag: The flag has three horizontal stripes—red, white, and red. A cedar tree on the white stripe symbolizes holiness, eternity, and peace. Adopted in 1943. See FLAG (color picture: Flags of Asia and the Pacific).

National Anthem: "Kulluna lil watan lil ula lil alam" ("All of Us for the Country, Glory, and Flag").

Money: *Basic Unit—*pound. See MONEY (table).

Lebanon Tourist & Information Office

Beirut Harbor is Lebanon's chief port facility. Shipping at the port declined after the outbreak of the civil war.

I 49

A Majestic Temple stands among the ruins of the ancient city of Baalbek in Lebanon's Bekaa region. Baalbek was built by the Romans, who took control of Lebanon in 64 B.C.

and Palestinian refugees—live in rural areas or in rundown sections of cities. Large numbers of the Palestinians live in crowded refugee camps.

Traditional Lebanese houses have thick limestone walls and roofs made of orange tiles or earth. This type of house is being rapidly replaced in the cities by modern Western-style concrete houses and high-rise apartment buildings.

Most Lebanese wear the same styles of clothing as do people in Western nations. But many rural people still wear traditional Lebanese clothes. Some peasant women, for example, wear colorful long dresses with ankle-length trousers underneath. Some elderly Druse religious men wear tightly woven multicolored jackets and white brimless hats.

Bread, fruits, grains, meat, vegetables, and yogurt are the chief foods of most Lebanese. The people combine these foods with herbs and spices to create a variety of tasty dishes. Popular beverages in Lebanon include soft drinks, Arabic coffee, wine, beer, and a strong liquor called *arak*, also spelled *arrack*.

Many Lebanese enjoy the literature, music, and art of both Western and Arabic cultures. Lebanese artists are noted for the beautiful silverware, brassware, jewelry, needlework, and colorful glassware they produce. Popular sports in Lebanon include soccer, skiing, and volleyball. The beaches south of Beirut are a favorite recreation area.

Education. Lebanese law does not require children to attend school. However, most parents send their children to both elementary and secondary school. More than half the schoolchildren go to private schools, which charge tuition, and the rest attend free public schools. School attendance has been disrupted by the fighting in the country since the mid-1970's.

Universities and colleges in Lebanon include the Lebanese University, the Beirut Arab University, Beirut University College, Haigazian College, the American University of Beirut, and St. Joseph University. The American University of Beirut and St. Joseph University

were founded by foreign missionaries in the mid-1800's. The American University of Beirut is a private school that is controlled by a board of trustees in the United States. St. Joseph University is a Roman Catholic school of the Jesuit religious order.

Land and Climate

Lebanon covers 4,015 square miles (10,400 square kilometers). Its coast extends about 130 miles (209 kilometers) along the Mediterranean Sea. A narrow plain runs along the coast. Farmers raise a variety of fruits on the plain, and most of Lebanon's main cities are located there.

The rugged Lebanon Mountains rise east of the coastal plain. They extend, from north to south, down most of the length of the country—a distance of about 100 miles (160 kilometers). The country's highest peak, Qurnat as Sawda, is in the Lebanon Mountains. It rises 10,115 feet (3,083 meters) above sea level. Farmers raise fruit on irrigated terraces built on the slopes of the mountains. The upper slopes of the Lebanon Mountains once were covered with the majestic cedars of Lebanon, few of which remain today. Most of the trees were cut down in past centuries. Another range, the Anti-Lebanon Mountains, runs parallel to the Lebanon Mountains along the country's eastern border.

A fertile valley called the *Bekaa* lies between the Lebanon and Anti-Lebanon mountains. The Bekaa ranges from 5 to 10 miles (8 to 16 kilometers) in width. It is the site of the ruins of several ancient cities. Much of the Bekaa is used for vegetable farming.

Lebanon's main rivers are the Litani, Nahr Ibrahim, and Orontes. Temperatures in the country's coastal area average about 55°F. (13°C) in January and about 84°F. (29°C) in June. Most of the area is very humid during the summer. Lebanon's inland areas have generally lower average temperatures and less humidity than the coast. About 35 inches (89 centimeters) of rain falls annually along the coast. The mountains receive from 50 to 60 inches (130 to 150 centimeters) of rain yearly and much snow during the winter. The Bekaa receives less rain than the mountains.

Economy

The civil war of the mid-1970's and numerous battles that have followed have seriously damaged Lebanon's economy. The fighting closed many businesses and left many people unemployed. Since the late 1970's, Lebanon has made some progress in rebuilding its economy.

Trade and service industries, including finance and tourism, rank as Lebanon's chief sources of income. For hundreds of years, Lebanon served as a major import and export center of the Middle East. It was also a major financial center. About 100 banks, including many branches of foreign banks, operated there. In addition, the country attracted large numbers of tourists, whose spending contributed greatly to the economy. Since the war, trade and finance have decreased in Lebanon, but they remain important to the economy. The fighting all but ended the flow of tourists into the country.

Manufacturing and agriculture are also important economic activities in Lebanon. The chief manufactured products include cement, chemicals, electric appliances, furniture, processed foods, and textiles. Fruits—including apples, cherries, grapes, lemons, oranges, and peaches—rank as Lebanon's chief farm products. Potatoes, sugar beets, and other vegetables are also important. Lebanon has had to rebuild many factories and farms that were destroyed during the fighting.

Beirut is Lebanon's chief port. The country has more than 3,000 miles (4,800 kilometers) of surfaced roads and 259 miles (417 kilometers) of railroad track. One radio station and three television stations serve Lebanon. About 40 daily newspapers are published in the country.

History

Ancient Times. Lebanon has been inhabited since prehistoric times. Phoenicians were the first well-known group of people to live there. They probably moved to the region from the south about 3000 B.C. The Phoenicians were sailors, traders, and explorers. They established powerful independent city-states along the coast.

Beginning about 1800 B.C., other foreign powers controlled the Phoenician city-states at different times. They included, in order of rule, Egyptians, Hittites, Assyrians, Babylonians, and Persians. In 332 B.C., the famous Macedonian general Alexander the Great conquered Lebanon. The region came under the control of the Roman Empire in 64 B.C. Ruins of Roman structures still stand. They include huge temples at Baalbek, in the Bekaa; and the town at Bayt Miri, near Beirut. Christianity was introduced into Lebanon about A.D. 325, during the Byzantine Empire—a continuation of the Roman Empire. Many Lebanese became Christians.

Muslim Rule. In the early A.D. 600's, Muslims from the Arabian Peninsula occupied Lebanon. Islam gradually replaced Christianity along Lebanon's coast. However, Christianity remained strong in the mountains.

Crusaders from Europe invaded Lebanon about 1100. The Crusaders were Christians who hoped to regain the nearby Holy Land (Palestine) from the Muslims (see CRUSADES). Christians in the mountains of Lebanon developed friendly relations with the Crusaders. In about 1300, the Mameluke dynasty of Egypt drove the last of the Crusaders out of Lebanon.

Ottoman Rule and Independence. Ottoman Turks conquered Lebanon in 1516 and made it part of the Ottoman Empire, which had its capital at Istanbul, in what is now Turkey. But Mount Lebanon, the central part of the country, retained limited self-government under local rulers. The Ottoman Empire ruled Lebanon until World War I (1914-1918), when Great Britain and France occupied the country.

In 1922, France took over Lebanon's political affairs and started to prepare Lebanon for independence. The French united the Christians in Mount Lebanon and the Muslims along the coast under one government. They also helped write Lebanon's Constitution. Lebanon became completely independent in 1943. Christian and Muslim leaders agreed to share power in the government. Following independence, Lebanon prospered more than ever as a center of trade and finance.

Internal Conflicts. Lebanon retained strong ties with the West after it became independent. The country remained peaceful until 1958, when some Lebanese, largely Muslims, rebelled against the government. The rebels opposed government plans for political and military alliances with the West. In July 1958, the United States sent thousands of marines to Lebanon at the request of the country's president. This American intervention helped restore peace, and the marines left in October.

In 1969, the activities of the Palestine Liberation Organization (PLO) led to fighting in Lebanon. The PLO—whose chief goal is to establish a Palestinian state for the Arab people of Palestine—raided targets in Israel from bases in southern Lebanon. The Israelis, in turn, attacked PLO forces in Lebanon.

In the 1970's, conflict between Lebanese Christian and Muslim groups flared up. The Christians opposed, and the Muslims supported, the presence of armed PLO

A. Dejean, Sygma

Lebanon's Civil War of the mid-1970's caused great damage in many cities. The scene above shows a damaged area in Beirut.

members in the country. Also, the country's Muslim population had grown, and the Muslims demanded more power in the government. The PLO supported the Muslims. The Christians opposed Muslim demands for increased power in the government and resented the alliance between the Muslims and the PLO.

In 1975, a bloody civil war broke out between Christians and the Muslim-PLO alliance. The fighting killed tens of thousands of people and caused widespread property damage. In the spring of 1976, Syria—which borders Lebanon on the north and east—sent thousands of troops to the country to help the government restore order.

Recent Developments. Full-scale fighting in Lebanon ended in late 1976. However, tension has continued between Christians and the Muslim-PLO alliance. Also, both Christian groups and Muslim groups began fighting among themselves. In addition, battles have broken out between Christians and Syrian troops in Lebanon.

Conflicts between Israel and the PLO have also continued. Because of the continual conflict, the United Nations (UN) sent a peacekeeping force to Lebanon in 1978. But fighting continued to break out.

In June 1982, a large Israeli force invaded Lebanon and drove the PLO forces out of the southern part of the country. The Israelis laid siege to western Beirut, an area where many PLO leaders and troops were stationed. The Israelis demanded that the PLO leave the city and the rest of Lebanon. The invasion resulted in many deaths—both military and civilian—and much damage. In late August and early September, the PLO forces left Beirut. Some PLO troops remained in northern Lebanon.

In mid-September, members of the Lebanese Christian militia killed hundreds of unarmed Palestinian men, women, and children in refugee camps in western Beirut. Israeli forces were aware of what was going on, but chose not to intervene. Many people criticized the Israelis for their inaction.

The United States, France, and Italy had sent troops to Lebanon to help ensure that the PLO forces could leave the country safely. The troops left Lebanon after the PLO withdrawal. But about two weeks later—following the massacre—the Lebanese government requested that the foreign troops return to help keep order. The United States, France, Italy, and Great Britain then sent troops to Lebanon. Also, the UN peacekeeping force and the Israeli and Syrian troops, who had entered the country earlier, remained in Lebanon.

In late 1983, foreign troops in Lebanon became victims of terrorist bombings. On October 23, a suicide terrorist crashed a truck loaded with explosives into U.S. Marine headquarters at the Beirut airport. The resulting explosion killed 241 U.S. troops. At about the same time, a similar attack killed 54 French troops in a nearby building. On November 4, an attack at the Israeli military headquarters in Tyre killed 28 Israelis.

In early February 1984, Druse forces and Shiite Muslims—members of the Shi'ah sect—took control of part of Beirut from the Lebanese government. The United States, Great Britain, France, and Italy removed their troops from Lebanon following this takeover. In 1985, Israel withdrew all its combat forces from

Lebanon. But about 1,000 Israeli troops remained in a buffer zone located at the Israeli-Lebanon border.

ELSA MARSTON HARIK and ILIYA HARIK

Related Articles in WORLD BOOK include:

Arab League	Druses	Tripoli
Beirut	Lebanon Mountains	Tyre
Cedar	Phoenicia	

Additional Resources

GORDON, DAVID C. *The Republic of Lebanon: Nation in Jeopardy.* Westview, 1983

HITTI, PHILIP K. *A Short History of Lebanon.* St. Martin's, 1965.

KHALIDI, WALID. *Conflict and Violence in Lebanon: Confrontation in the Middle East.* Harvard, 1980.

NEWMAN, GERALD. *Lebanon.* Watts, 1978. For younger readers.

LEBANON MOUNTAINS, in Lebanon, extend for about 100 miles (160 kilometers) along the eastern shore of the Mediterranean Sea. The mountains are part of a longer range extending from Turkey through Israel. See LEBANON (Land and Climate).

LEBBAEUS. See JUDE, SAINT.

LE CARRÉ, *leh kuh RAY,* **JOHN** (1931-), is the pen name of David John Moore Cornwell, an English novelist. He is known chiefly for his realistic, unromantic spy stories. Le Carré avoids both high adventure and dashing heroes. Most of his spies are lower-level British civil servants who are involved with the routine affairs and rivalries of a government bureaucracy as well as with cloak-and-dagger intrigue.

In *The Spy Who Came in from the Cold* (1963) and *The Looking Glass War* (1965), le Carré created central characters who are uncertain of themselves. They are manipulated by their superiors and partially fail in their assignments. Le Carré wrote three novels about British secret service agent George Smiley—*Tinker, Tailor, Soldier, Spy* (1974), *The Honourable Schoolboy* (1977), and *Smiley's People* (1979). Le Carré's other novels include *Call for the Dead* (1961), *A Murder of Quality* (1962), *A Small Town in Germany* (1963), *The Little Drummer Girl* (1983), and *A Perfect Spy* (1986).

Le Carré was born in Poole. He served briefly as a British intelligence officer in Austria shortly after World War II. From 1961 to 1964, he was an officer in the British Foreign Service. MARCUS KLEIN

LECITHIN. See SOYBEAN (Soy Oil).

LE CORBUSIER, *luh kawr byoo ZYAY,* (1887-1965), was the professional name of Charles Édouard Jeanneret-Gris, often considered the most important architect of the 1900's. He demonstrated his mastery of design in a series of residences during the 1920's. They included the villa "Les Terraces" (1926-1927) near Paris and the Villa Savoye (1929-1931) in Poissy, France. These houses are examples of what came to be known as the *International Style* of architecture.

The International Style was identified by white cubic shapes and the avoidance of ornament. Such characteristics, however, are not central to Le Corbusier's work. In his "Five Points" (1926), a series of diagrams, he made an apparently simple but imaginative connection between theory and practice. He used certain characteristics of reinforced concrete construction to enclose and use space in new ways.

Le Corbusier's five points called for the use of (1) *pilotis* (columns that raise a building above the ground); (2) flat roofs with gardens; (3) the *free plan* (independence of the structural frame from the walls); (4) the *free façade* (no structural limitation on window placement); and (5) a continuous horizontal window (one aspect of the free façade).

Le Corbusier's new approach to a structure's form and use was part of what he called the New Spirit that humanity sets free for humanity's own full development. This spirit—especially as it appeared in the arts—was discussed in a magazine called *l'Esprit Nouveau* (1920-1925), edited by Le Corbusier and the French painter Amédée Ozenfant. Le Corbusier's essays on architecture were collected in his major book, *Towards a New Architecture* (1923).

During the 1930's and 1940's, Le Corbusier built few buildings. His interest in city planning became dominant. He proposed the demolition of urban areas and their rebuilding according to his ideas on planning and architecture. His major achievement in city planning was his plan and design for the principal buildings of the new city of Chandigarh, India, in the 1950's.

In his final buildings, Le Corbusier continued to demonstrate his understanding for architectural form interacting with functional and social conditions. These works include the Unité d'Habitation apartment building in Marseille, France (1947-1952); the pilgrimage chapel in Ronchamp, France (1950-1955); the Convent of La Tourette near Lyon, France (1955-1960); and the Carpenter Center for the Visual Arts at Harvard University in Cambridge, Mass. (1961-1963).

Le Corbusier was born in La Chaux-de-Fonds, Switzerland, and settled in Paris in 1917. He received most of his architectural training by traveling in Europe and by working under the architects Auguste Perret in Paris and Peter Behrens in Berlin.

For examples of Le Corbusier's work, see the pictures with ARCHITECTURE (Modern Architecture); and FRANCE (Arts).   STANFORD ANDERSON

LEDERBERG, JOSHUA (1925-   ), an American geneticist, shared the 1958 Nobel Prize for physiology or medicine. He received the award "for his discoveries concerning genetic recombination and the organization of the genetic material of bacteria." Lederberg was born in Montclair, N.J.   HENRY H. FERTIG

LEDGER. See BOOKKEEPING (Ledgers).

LEE, CHARLES (1731-1782), was an officer in the American Army during the Revolutionary War. Although he fought bravely, he was not always obedient, and some historians regard him as a traitor.

Lee was born in Chester, England, and joined the British Army. He served in the Seven Years' War, taking part in the capture of Montreal in 1760. Returning to America in 1773, Lee joined the patriots against the British. He became a major general in 1775. The next year, he served in New York and commanded the American Army in the South.

The British captured Lee in 1776 at Basking Ridge, N.J., and held him in New York for a year. They released him in 1778, and Lee returned to fight with the patriot forces. At the Battle of Monmouth in 1778, he advanced with the American forces against the British Army, then retreated. Lee asked for a court-martial, and he was found guilty of misconduct.   JOHN R. ALDEN

LEE, DORIS EMRICK (1905-1983), was an American artist. Her paintings portray the American scene in a lively, sometimes humorous, and always colorful manner. Her painting *Thanksgiving* won the Logan Medal

at the 1935 annual exhibition of contemporary American painting at the Art Institute of Chicago. She painted a mural for the Post Office Department building in Washington, D.C.

Doris Lee was born in Aledo, Ill. She studied at the Kansas City Art Institute, at the California School of Fine Arts, and in Paris.   EDWIN L. FULWIDER

See also THANKSGIVING DAY (color picture).

LEE, FRANCIS LIGHTFOOT (1734-1797), a signer of the Declaration of Independence, was active in the American Revolutionary movement. As a member of the Virginia House of Burgesses, he helped lead the protest against the Stamp Act and other British measures that were unpopular with the colonies. He helped form the Virginia Committee of Correspondence (see COMMITTEES OF CORRESPONDENCE). In 1775, Lee was elected as a delegate to the Continental Congress, where he ably served the colonial cause. He resigned in 1779 to return to his plantation. Lee was a brother of the Revolutionary leader Richard Henry Lee and a relative of Confederate General Robert E. Lee. He was born in Westmoreland County, Virginia.   CLARENCE L. VER STEEG

LEE, HARPER (1926-   ), is an American author who became famous with her only novel, *To Kill a Mockingbird* (1960). The book won the 1961 Pulitzer Prize for fiction.

The plot centers on a small-town lawyer in Alabama who defends a young black falsely accused of raping a white woman. The story is told by the lawyer's young daughter. The appeal of the novel lies in the author's ability to weave together the vivid eccentric characters of a small Southern town, the observations of a sensitive child, and a plea for social justice.

Nelle Harper Lee was born in Monroeville, Ala., and grew up in the state.   EUGENE K. GARBER

LEE, HENRY (1756-1818), was an American soldier and statesman of the Revolutionary period. His success as a scout and in making lightning raids won him the nickname of "Light-Horse Harry." He was the father of Confederate General Robert E. Lee.

Lee became a captain in the Virginia cavalry in 1776,

Chicago Historical Society

"Light-Horse Harry" Lee was a brave and daring cavalry leader in the American Army during the Revolutionary War.

and the next year his company joined George Washington's army. In 1778, Lee became a major in charge of a cavalry troop called "Lee's Legion," which he led in a daring raid on the British post at Paulus Hook, N.Y. (now Jersey City, N.J.). As a lieutenant colonel in 1780, he fought under General Nathanael Greene.

After the war, Lee entered the Virginia House of Delegates. He served in the Congress of the Confederation from 1785 until 1788. He was also a member of the Virginia convention that ratified the United States Constitution. Lee served as governor of Virginia from 1791 to 1794, and commanded the troops that President Washington sent in 1794 to end the Whiskey Rebellion (see WHISKEY REBELLION). Lee was a member of the Federalist Party. From 1799 to 1801, he was a member of Congress. He wrote the famous epitaph of George Washington, "First in war, first in peace, and first in the hearts of his countrymen."

Lee fell deeply into debt in later years, and was imprisoned in 1808 and 1809. During this time, he wrote his *Memoirs of the War in the Southern Department of the United States*. In 1812, he was injured while trying to protect a friend from rioters in Baltimore. He never recovered from this injury.

Lee was born on Jan. 29, 1756, at "Leesylvania," Prince William County, Virginia. He was graduated from the College of New Jersey (now Princeton University) in 1773.   JOHN R. ALDEN

See also LEE, ROBERT EDWARD.

LEE, JASON (1803-1845), was a Methodist missionary. He is remembered for his missionary expeditions to the Oregon region, for his support of popular education, and for his work in helping to form the Oregon territorial government. Lee was born in Stanstead, Que., and attended Wesleyan Academy, Wilbraham, Mass. In 1830 he was licensed to preach, and in 1833 was sent to Oregon. He traveled with the explorer Nathaniel Wyeth to Fort Vancouver, and established several schools in the Pacific Northwest.

A statue of Jason Lee represents the state of Oregon in Statuary Hall.   L. J. TRINTERUD

LEE, MANFRED B. See QUEEN, ELLERY.

LEE, RICHARD HENRY (1732-1794), was a signer of the Declaration of Independence. With Patrick Henry and Thomas Jefferson, he helped lead the patriot cause in Virginia.

Lee was born at Stratford, Va., and was educated in England. In 1758, he was elected to the Virginia legislature, where he served until the outbreak of the Revolutionary War. He became especially active in Virginia's campaign of resistance to the Stamp Act and Townshend Acts.

In 1774, Virginia sent Lee as a delegate to the First Continental Congress in Philadelphia. At first, he favored a policy of economic pressure on the British government. But, by late 1775, he began to

Richard Henry Lee

think and plan in terms of independence. On June 7, 1776, Lee introduced a resolution that "these united colonies are, and of right ought to be, free and independent states; that they are absolved from all allegiance to the British Crown; and that all political connection between them and the State of Great Britain is, and ought to be, totally dissolved." The adoption of this resolution by the Congress on July 2 was the signal for American independence.

Lee was elected president of the Congress in 1784. He helped lead the opposition to the ratification of the United States Constitution, but served as a U.S. Senator from Virginia after it was adopted. Lee's last great service was the enthusiastic support he gave to the successful movement to add the Bill of Rights to the Constitution.   CLINTON ROSSITER

LEE, ROBERT EDWARD (1807-1870), was a great general who commanded the Confederate Army in the Civil War. He is one of the most beloved figures in American history. Lee's fame rests on his military achievements as Confederate commander in the face of overwhelming odds, and on his outstanding personal character. He won the admiration and respect of Northerners as well as Southerners. Lee fought for one section of the young nation, but the struggle did not make him intolerant. He fought, not for personal gain, but to prove himself worthy of a cause. Union General Ulysses S. Grant, to whom Lee was finally forced to surrender, said about Lee: "There was not a man in the Confederacy whose influence with the whole people was as great as his."

Unlike President Abraham Lincoln, who led the North in the Civil War, Lee was not a self-made man. Lee's family was the leading family of Virginia, and one of the most distinguished in the United States. A kinsman, Thomas Lee, had served as royal governor of the colony. Lee was also related to Francis Lightfoot Lee and Richard Henry Lee, who had been statesmen and soldiers in Revolutionary War days. His father, Henry Lee, known as "Light-Horse Harry," was a brilliant cavalry commander in the Revolutionary War. When the Lee mansion, Matholic, burned in the early 1700's, Queen Caroline of England gave Thomas Lee money to help rebuild it. Lee called the new building Stratford Hall.

Robert E. Lee was a handsome man, 5 feet 10½ inches (179 centimeters) tall and weighing about 170 pounds (77 kilograms). He presented a commanding appearance—straight, alert, and intelligent. He was never known to smoke, drink alcoholic beverages, or use profane language. Lee was a moralist, and once said that *duty* is the sublimest word in the English language.

Early Years

Robert E. Lee was born in Stratford Hall, near Montross, Va., on Jan. 19, 1807. He grew up with a deep devotion to country life and to his native state, which continued throughout his life. He was a serious boy, and spent many hours in his father's library. In 1825 he entered the United States Military Academy at West Point, where his classmates admired him for his brilliance, leadership, and devotion to duty. He graduated from the academy with high honors in 1829, and he was commissioned as a second lieutenant in the Corps of Engineers.

In the Corps of Engineers. Lee served for 17 months at Fort Pulaski on Cockspur Island, Georgia. In 1831, the army transferred him to Fort Monroe, Virginia, as assistant engineer. While stationed there, he married Mary Anna Randolph Custis (1808-1873), Martha Washington's great-granddaughter. They lived in her family home, Arlington, which still stands on a Virginia hill overlooking Washington, D.C. Their seven children —George Washington Custis, Mary, William H. Fitzhugh, Agnes, Annie, Robert Edward, and Mildred— were reared chiefly at Arlington. All three sons served as Confederate officers under Lee during the Civil War.

Lee served as an assistant in the chief engineer's office in Washington from 1834 to 1837, but spent the summer of 1835 helping to lay out the boundary line between Ohio and Michigan. His first important independent job came in 1837 when, as a first lieutenant of engineers, he supervised the engineering work for St. Louis harbor and for the upper Mississippi and Missouri rivers. His work there earned him a promotion to captain. In 1841 he was transferred to Fort Hamilton in New York harbor, where he took charge of building fortifications.

The Mexican War. When war broke out between the United States and Mexico in 1846, the army sent Lee to Texas to serve as assistant engineer under General John E. Wool. All his superior officers, especially General Winfield Scott, were impressed with the brave young Virginian.

Early in the war, Lee supervised the construction of bridges for Wool's march toward the Mexican border. He then did excellent work on scouting trips. He was shortly transferred to General Winfield Scott's command and took part in the capture of Veracruz. Lee's engineering skill made it possible for American troops to cross the difficult mountain passes on the way to the capital. During the march to Mexico City, Lee was promoted to brevet major, then to brevet lieutenant colonel. He

Oil painting on canvas (1904) by Theodore Pine; Lee Chapel, Washington and Lee University, Lexington, Va.

General Robert E. Lee commanded the Confederate Army during the Civil War. He ranks among the nation's greatest heroes.

was promoted to brevet colonel before the war ended.

The official reports praised Lee highly. Scott declared that his "success in Mexico was largely due to the skill, valor, and undaunted courage of Robert E. Lee . . . the greatest military genius in America."

Superintendent of West Point. After three years at Fort Carroll in Baltimore harbor, Lee became superin-

Brown Bros.

Lee posed astride his famous horse, Traveller, which he rode throughout the Civil War. The famous Southern general was known for his dignity and calm, even in times of stress.

tendent of West Point in 1852. He would have preferred duty in the field, instead of at a desk, but assumed his post without complaint. During his three years at West Point, he improved the buildings and the courses, and spent much time with the cadets. One cadet, "Jeb" Stuart, later served as one of Lee's best cavalry officers. Lee won a reputation during his service there as a fair and kind superintendent.

Other Duties. In 1855, Lee became a lieutenant colonel of cavalry and was assigned to duty on the Texas frontier. There he helped protect settlers from attacks by the Apache and Comanche Indians. Once again he proved to be an excellent soldier and organizer. But these were not happy years for Lee. He did not

Bettmann Archive

Colonel Lee served as superintendent of the United States Military Academy in West Point, N.Y., from 1852 to 1855. He became known as a kind and just administrator.

like to be away from his family for long periods of time, particularly because of Mrs. Lee, who was becoming an invalid. Lee came home to see her as often as possible. He happened to be in Washington at the time of John Brown's raid on Harpers Ferry in 1859, and was sent there to arrest Brown and restore order. He accomplished this task quickly and with little loss of life, then returned to his regiment in Texas. When Texas seceded from the Union in 1861, Lee was recalled to Washington, D.C., to wait for further orders.

The Civil War

Unlike many Southerners, Lee did not believe in slavery and did not favor secession. He felt that slavery had an evil effect on masters as well as slaves. Long before the war, he had freed the few slaves whom he

had inherited. Lee greatly admired George Washington, and hated the thought of a divided nation. But he came to feel that his state was protecting the very liberty, freedom, and legal principles for which Washington had fought. He was willing to leave the Union, as Washington had left the British Empire, to fight what the South regarded as a second war of independence.

Lee had great difficulty in deciding whether to stand by his native state or remain with the Union, even though Lincoln offered him the field command of the United States Army. He wrote his sister: ". . . in my own person I had to meet the question whether I should take part against my native state. With all my devotion to the Union, and the feeling of loyalty and duty of an American citizen, I have not been able to make up my mind to raise my hand against my relatives, my children, my home. I have therefore resigned my commission in the army, and, save in defense of my native state—with the sincere hope that my poor services may never be needed—I hope I may never be called upon to draw my sword."

Lee grieved at parting from the companions with whom he had served in other wars. He had always felt that the "cordiality and friendship in the army was the great attraction of the service." The break with General Scott, his commander in chief, was especially difficult because the two men were close friends.

Opening Campaigns. For a time after Lee joined the Confederate Army, he had no troops under his command. He served in Richmond, Va., as military adviser to Confederate President Jefferson Davis, and in May, 1861, was appointed a full general. In the fall, he succeeded in halting a threatened invasion from western Virginia. Later, he took charge of fortifying the coast of South Carolina against invasion.

When Lee returned to Richmond in 1862, he helped draw up plans for the Confederate forces in Virginia, then under the command of General Joseph E. Johnston. Johnston was wounded on May 31, 1862, in the Battle of Fair Oaks (Seven Pines). The next day, Lee took command of Johnston's army, which he called the Army of Northern Virginia.

From his first day of command, Lee faced what looked like an impossible task. Union General George B. McClellan had approached within 7 miles (11 kilometers) of Richmond with 100,000 men. Three forces were closing in on the Confederate troops of General "Stonewall" Jackson in the Shenandoah Valley of Virginia. A fourth Union force was camped on the Rappahannock River, ready to aid McClellan. In a series of engagements known as the Battles of the Seven Days, Lee forced McClellan to retreat. This campaign taught Lee the need for simpler methods and organization. Jackson had earlier conducted a brilliant campaign in the Shenandoah Valley, and became Lee's most trusted subordinate. Jackson was so devoted to Lee that he said he would follow him into battle blindfolded.

With Jackson's help, Lee won a major victory over General John Pope in the second Battle of Bull Run (Manassas), in August, 1862. He was then free to invade Maryland. Unfortunately, McClellan intercepted a battle order which a Confederate staff officer had carelessly lost. Knowing Lee's plans in advance, McClellan halted him in the Battle of Antietam (Sharpsburg). Lee returned to Virginia to reorganize his army.

Later Battles. General Ambrose E. Burnside led an attack against Lee in December, 1862, at Fredericksburg, Va. It was on this occasion that Lee made a statement that has since become famous. Fog covered the battlefield early in the morning before the battle began. As it lifted and the Confederate command surveyed the panorama of thousands of troops in full array, Lee remarked: "It is well that war is so terrible—we would grow too fond of it."

Lee's troops badly defeated the Union forces. But Lee could not take advantage of his victory. The Northern troops had been too cleverly placed, and could fall back without breaking their lines of communication. The Confederates had few reserves of men and supplies. Lee felt that his army could not win the war by fighting defensively, and that it was too costly simply to hold the enemy without destroying it. But first he had to fight another defensive battle.

General Joseph Hooker, who had taken over from Burnside, attacked Lee at Chancellorsville in the spring of 1863. The Confederate forces won a spectacular victory, but they paid a terrible price for it—the death of Jackson, who was accidentally shot by his own men when he went ahead of his line of battle to scout.

Determined to take the offensive, Lee moved into Pennsylvania and encountered the Northern army now under General George G. Meade, at Gettysburg. Bitter fighting continued for three days, from July 1 to 3, 1863. Some of Lee's corps commanders failed to act quickly, and many historians have criticized General James Longstreet's delay in carrying out Lee's orders to attack. The Confederates met defeat in what proved to be a turning point of the war. Always generous to those under him, Lee insisted on taking the blame for the failure of the campaign.

Final Engagements. In the spring of 1864, Lee first faced General Ulysses S. Grant. In a series of fierce and bloody battles called the Wilderness campaign, Grant pounded the Confederate Army to pieces with his larger forces and guns. During one of these battles, Lee's men vividly demonstrated the affectionate regard they all felt for "Marse Robert." As a division of Texans marched past Lee on their way to the front, he left his post to join them. But the soldiers insisted that he return to the rear, saying "We won't go unless you go back!"

Lee held out for nine months in the siege of Petersburg, but his tired, hungry men finally had to retreat. Early in 1865, Lee was made general in chief of all the Confederate armies. Richmond fell in April, 1865, and Lee's ragged army retreated westward. Northern forces cut off and surrounded the Confederate Army at Appomattox Court House, Va., where Lee surrendered to Grant on April 9, 1865. Grant tried to make the surrender as easy as possible, and allowed the Confederate troops to take their horses home for spring plowing. As Lee made his last ride down the lines on his famous horse Traveller, he told his army: "Men, we have fought through the war together. I have done my best for you; my heart is too full to say more."

Last Years

Lee now became a private citizen for the first time in 40 years. The Proclamation of Amnesty and Reconstruction of 1865 barred him from taking public office. But he applied for a complete individual pardon as

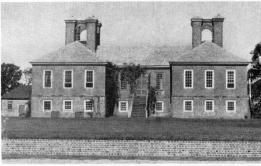

H. Armstrong Roberts

Lee's Birthplace, Stratford Hall, *above,* in Westmoreland County, Virginia, is now a museum. His later home, Arlington, *below,* was begun in 1802 by a step-grandson of George Washington. Made into a memorial to Lee in 1955, it is now called Arlington House. It overlooks the Potomac in Arlington National Cemetery.

Brown Bros.

provided by the proclamation, hoping to set an example for other Southern leaders to follow. However, the application lacked a required oath of allegiance to the United States. Lee then signed an oath and sent it to Washington. But the oath became lost, and Lee was not pardoned before his death. A general amnesty of 1868 restored his right to vote. However, Lee still lacked the right to hold public office. In 1970, an employee of the National Archives found Lee's oath. In 1975, Congress restored Lee's full citizenship.

Lee could have had many positions of wealth and prestige, but he chose to spend his last years as president of Washington College in Lexington, Va. He soon raised the small college to high levels of scholarship, and established schools of commerce and journalism. Young men from all parts of the South flocked to "General Lee's school," which was named Washington and Lee University after his death.

Lee urged his students and friends to keep the peace and accept the outcome of the war. His attitude was extremely important at a time when bitterness and hatred swept both North and South. Instead of increasing this feeling, Lee opposed it, doing everything in his power to restore the political, economic, and social life of the South. "Make your sons Americans," he urged.

His health began to fail in 1870, and, after a brief illness, he died on Oct. 12, 1870. People throughout the country felt his death as a personal loss. Viscount Garnet Wolseley, a distinguished British soldier, spoke eloquently of Lee: "I have met many of the great men of my time, but Lee alone impressed me with the feeling that I was in the presence of a man who was cast in a grander mold and made of different and finer metal than

157

all other men. He is stamped upon my memory as a being apart and superior to all others in every way—a man with whom none I ever knew, and very few of whom I have read, were worthy to be classed."

Lee is buried in the chapel he built on the campus in Lexington, along with other members of the Lee family. This chapel is sometimes called "The Shrine of the South," and is visited by thousands every year. Lee's home has been preserved in Arlington National Cemetery, near Washington, D.C. January 19, Lee's birthday anniversary, is a legal holiday in most Southern states. Lee represents Virginia in Statuary Hall in the Capitol in Washington. MARSHALL W. FISHWICK

See also CIVIL WAR; LEE, HENRY. *For a Reading and Study Guide*, see *Lee, Robert E.*, in the RESEARCH GUIDE/INDEX, Volume 22.

Additional Resources

CONNELLY, THOMAS L. *The Marble Man: Robert E. Lee and His Image in American Society.* Knopf, 1977.
FLOOD, CHARLES BRACELEN. *Lee: The Last Years.* Houghton, 1981.
FREEMAN, DOUGLAS S. *R. E. Lee: A Biography.* 4 vols. Scribner, 1934-1935. The standard biography.

LEE, TSUNG DAO (1926-   ), shared the 1957 Nobel Prize in physics with Chen Ning Yang. They proposed that the "conservation of parity," a basic principle of nuclear physics, did not hold true in some cases (see PARITY [in physics]). Lee has also concentrated on field theory, astrophysics, and hydrodynamics.

Lee was born in Shanghai, China. He was educated at Chinese universities and the University of Chicago, where he received a Doctor of Philosophy degree in 1950. RALPH E. LAPP

LEECH, also called *bloodsucker*, is a worm that has a disklike sucker at each end. It has a mouth centered in the front sucker, and may also have small teeth. Some leeches live as parasites, sucking on the blood and tissue of other animals for nourishment. Others feed on decaying animal and plant material. Parasitic leeches attach to their victim with the front sucker, make a wound, and then suck out blood. Bloodsucking leeches give out a liquid containing a chemical substance called *hirudin*. Hirudin prevents the blood from thickening and makes it easier for the leech to suck the blood. Doctors once used what they called *medicinal* (health-giving) leeches to remove blood from patients. The leeches were used to help heal bruises and cure diseases. Doctors seldom recommend the use of medicinal leeches today.

A leech's body is made up of a series of ringlike *segments* (parts). Leeches may be from $\frac{3}{4}$ to 8 inches (2 to 20 centimeters) long and can stretch or shorten their bodies.

Cornelia Clarke
The Leech was once used by doctors to remove blood from their patients.

They are black, red, or brown and may have stripes or spots. They have clusters of light-sensitive cells called "eyes" near the front end. They are also sensitive to touch, temperature, and drying. A leech contains both male and female reproductive organs.

Leeches live in damp places such as jungles, or in the shallow water of streams, lakes or oceans.

Scientific Classification. Leeches make up the class *Hirudinea* of the phylum *Annelida*. Members of the genus *Haemadipsa* are the troublesome land leeches of the jungle. The medicinal leech is genus *Hirudo*, species *H. medicinalis*. JAMES A. McLEOD

See also WORM (Segmented Worms).

LEECHEE. See LITCHI.

LEEDS (pop. 696,714; met. area pop. 2,021,707) is the center of the wool-manufacturing district of England. It lies in the north-central part of the country on the River Aire (see GREAT BRITAIN [political map]). The nearby great coal fields of Yorkshire furnish cheap power for the industries of Leeds. The town is connected with the east coast by the River Aire. Canals furnish a water connection with the west coast. Leeds also has railroad connections with other English cities. With its modern transportation systems, Leeds developed into an important industrial center. The Leeds and Liverpool Canal connects the city with Liverpool.

Leeds is the largest of a cluster of towns where the spinning and weaving of wool have been important industries since the Middle Ages. About four-fifths of the woolworkers in England live in this region. Leeds is the wholesale clothing center of the country, and is also noted for its leather, iron, and steel products. The town is a cultural and intellectual center of northern England.

Leeds is the home of the University of Leeds, which was founded in 1904. The school has grown to be one of England's largest and best-known universities.

The site of Leeds was inhabited as early as the 600's. Its organization was rural, and no town existed until after the Norman Conquest in 1066. Leeds received its first charter in 1207. FREDERICK G. MARCHAM

LEEK is a vegetable that resembles the onion but has a mild flavor. Unlike an onion it grows thick along the entire stem. It is related to onions, garlic, shallots, and chives. Leeks are not grown much in home gardens, and have little commercial value. The blanched stems and leaves are used as a flavoring for soups and stews, or are boiled and served like asparagus.

The Welsh like to eat them. The leek is also the national flower of Wales. Many Welsh people wear a sprig of leek on St. David's Day, March 1. Leeks are grown from seeds just as onions are. Earth is often packed around the shoots to blanch them. The crop needs a full season before it is ready for harvest.

J. Horace McFarland
Leek

Scientific Classification. Botanists consider the leek a member of either the amaryllis family, Amaryllidaceae, or the lily family, Liliaceae. The plant's scientific name is *Allium porrum*.   Arthur J. Pratt

LEEUWENHOEK, *LAY vuhn* hook, **ANTON VAN** (1632-1723), a Dutch amateur scientist, revealed a new world of microscopic life through his observations, drawings, and writings. He is called the father of microbiology because he was the first in the field to leave written records of his findings.

Through tedious hand-grinding techniques, Leeuwenhoek prepared hundreds of lenses with magnifying powers up to 270 diameters (see Microscope). With these lenses, he studied such diverse materials as stagnant water, teeth scrapings, blood cells, muscle fibers, and spermatozoa. His *animalcules* (tiny animals) were described as being 1,000 times smaller than the eye of a louse, which he used as a standard measurement because its size is remarkably constant.

While Leeuwenhoek is considered more of an observer than a theoretician, he opposed the popular notion that living things can arise from dead matter. He was born in Delft, the Netherlands.   Stanley E. Wedberg

LEEWARD ISLANDS, *LEE wuhrd* or *LOO uhrd*, lie in the West Indies. They stretch from Puerto Rico to the Windward Islands, and form part of the Lesser Antilles. For the location of the Leeward Islands, see West Indies (map). The islands were named *Leeward* because they are sheltered from the trade winds. The word *lee* is a sailing term referring to the side of a boat that is sheltered from the wind.

The Leeward Islands include about 15 islands and many islets. They have an area of 1,542 square miles (3,994 square kilometers) and a population of 678,000. The Leeward group includes three independent countries: Antigua and Barbuda, Dominica, and St. Christopher and Nevis. The Leeward group also includes Anguilla, the British Virgin Islands, and Montserrat, which are British dependencies; St. Eustatius, Saba, and St. Martin, Dutch territories; Guadeloupe, a French overseas department; and the Virgin Islands of the United States, a United States territory.

The climate varies, but it is generally dry and healthful. Most of the people are farmers or fruitgrowers. The main products raised in the islands include tobacco, cotton, onions, coconuts, tomatoes, limes, molasses, sugar, and dairy products.   W. L. Burn

See also British West Indies; Guadeloupe; Virgin Islands; West Indies; Windward Islands.

LEFT WING is a term which means a liberal or radical party or branch of a political group. The term originated in the first French legislature after the French Revolution. The conservative representatives were seated to the right of the speaker, and the more radical deputies were seated to the left. Later, people throughout the world used the terms *left* and *right* to denote the two opposing political beliefs, liberalism and conservatism. Today, the left wing is often identified with socialism or Communism.   William Ebenstein

LEG is the limb that supports the body of a human being or animal. Properly, it is only that section of the lower limb between the ankle and the knee. The part of the limb between the knee and hip is called the *thigh*. In human beings, the thigh contains the *femur*, the longest, strongest bone of the body. The femur meets the hipbone at the hip joint. This is a ball-and-socket joint that allows a person to move the limb freely, but

also provides the stability needed to bear the weight of the body. See Hip.

The Thigh. Muscles attached to the bones by *tendons* (strong cords of tissue) make it possible for people to move their limbs. The front of the thigh consists of a four-parted muscle, the *quadriceps femoris*. This muscle allows a person to straighten the limb at the knee, and to bend the thigh at the hips. Three long muscles, called the *hamstring muscles*, allow a person to bend the knee and straighten the thigh. The tendons of these muscles connect with the leg bones and can easily be felt on either side of the leg behind the knee. The quadriceps femoris and hamstring muscles are chiefly used for walking, kicking, and climbing.

The Leg, or lower part of the limb, contains two bones. These are the *tibia* (shinbone) which can be felt close to the middle front section of the leg, and the *fibula* in the muscles of the side of the leg.

Seven muscles make up the *calf* (fleshy part of the back of the leg). The *gastrocnemius* is the most prominent. These muscles allow a person to bend the toes and to raise the body on the balls of the feet. The *tendo calcaneus*, or *Achilles' tendon*, connects three of the calf muscles with the heel bone. This tendon forms the prominent ridge on the back of the leg, extending upward from the heel to the lower calf. Four muscles on the front of the leg bend the foot upward and straighten the

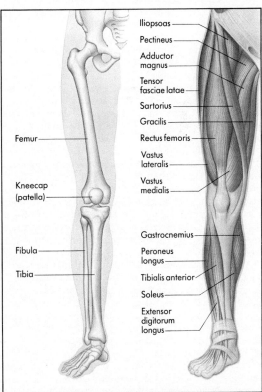

Iliopsoas
Pectineus
Adductor magnus
Tensor fasciae latae
Sartorius
Gracilis
Rectus femoris
Vastus lateralis
Vastus medialis
Gastrocnemius
Peroneus longus
Tibialis anterior
Soleus
Extensor digitorum longus

Femur
Kneecap (patella)
Fibula
Tibia

WORLD BOOK illustrations by Robert Demarest

The Leg contains large, strong bones, *left,* which support the weight of the body. Powerful leg muscles, *right,* permit such movements as walking, jumping, climbing, and kicking.

toes. Two additional muscles near the fibula bend the foot sideways.

The Knee Joint, between the femur and tibia, acts like a hinge. It also allows a little movement from side to side. The *patella* (kneecap) is a shield-shaped bone in front of the knee joint. It acts as a pulley for the tendon of the quadriceps femoris muscle. Only human beings, other mammals, and birds have kneecaps.

Blood and Nerve Supply. The *femoral artery* is the main artery that carries blood to the lower leg. It runs down the front of the thigh, then travels behind the knee, where it becomes the *popliteal artery*. Finally, it branches to form the arteries of the leg. The largest nerve of the entire body, the *sciatic nerve*, extends down the back of the thigh to the leg and foot. It supplies the nerves for the skin of the foot and most of the leg, for all of the foot and leg muscles, and for the muscles on the back of the thigh.　WILLIAM V. MAYER

Related Articles in WORLD BOOK include:

Achilles' Tendon	Joint
Ankle	Knee
Foot	Ligament
Human Body	Muscle
(Trans-Vision)	Tendon

LEGACY, *LEHG uh see,* is a disposition of personal property made by the terms of a will. *Specific legacies* are gifts of particular pieces of property, such as jewelry, books, or clothing. *General legacies* are usually sums of money. *Residual legacies* are what remains of a person's estate after the specific and general legacies have been paid. For instance, a man leaves bequests to his friends and servants, and states that the rest of his estate is to be divided between his wife and son (see WILL).

Before any legacies are given out, the debts of the dead person must be paid. Next, the specific legacies are paid out, and then the general legacies. The residual legatees divide what remains. If a person dies leaving less property or more debts than when his or her will was made, those who were to inherit the bulk of the estate may receive nothing.　WILLIAM TUCKER DEAN

LEGAL AGE. See MINOR.

LEGAL AID is the name of any of several programs that provide legal service for people who cannot afford an attorney. In the United States, legal aid agencies are sponsored by charitable organizations; law schools; lawyers' associations; and the federal, state, and local governments. The federal government provides funds to help support some government and private legal aid organizations.

Agencies furnishing legal aid handle chiefly *civil cases*. Such cases involve such matters as adoptions, bankruptcies, divorces, and job and rent disputes. Congress has prohibited legal aid agencies from using federal funds in *criminal cases*. These cases involve actions considered harmful to society. Many states employ lawyers who serve as *public defenders* in criminal cases (see PUBLIC DEFENDER).

The first legal aid agency in the United States was established in 1876 by the German Society, an organization in New York City. The society set up the agency to help German immigrants with legal problems. Lawyers' associations in many cities have set up legal aid programs during the 1900's. In 1911, an organization was founded to furnish legal aid to the needy. This group is now called the National Legal Aid and Defender Association. It publishes information and holds conferences for workers in the legal aid field.

In 1964, Congress set up the Office of Legal Services as part of the War on Poverty program of President Lyndon B. Johnson. This agency helped organize legal aid programs in many states. The government cut back a number of these programs in the early 1970's, and many needy people could not obtain legal help. In 1974, Congress dissolved the Office of Legal Services and transferred its functions to a private, nonprofit corporation, the Legal Services Corporation. This agency provides funds, information, and training programs for legal aid agencies. The United States has about 1,600 of these agencies.　RONALD R. DAVENPORT

LEGAL BLINDNESS. See BLINDNESS.

LEGAL HOLIDAY. See HOLIDAY.

LEGAL TENDER is any type of money that must, by law, be accepted in payment of a debt. The Legal Tender Act of 1933 gave unlimited legal-tender power to all United States currency in circulation.

Before 1933, gold coins and certificates had unlimited legal-tender power. Standard silver dollars had full legal-tender power, unless they were specifically declared unacceptable by contract. United States notes (greenbacks) were legal tender for all purposes except payment of customs duties and interest on the public debt. All other forms of paper money—whether issued by the U.S. Treasury, the Federal Reserve Banks, or private commercial banks—had legal-tender status for payment of taxes, but not for the settlement of private debts. Half dollars, quarters, and dimes were legal tender for amounts not more than $10. Nickels and pennies were legal tender only for amounts not more than 25 cents.

Most other nations restrict the legal-tender power of coins in fractional denominations of the monetary unit. For example, the Canadian Currency Act makes coins of 10 cents or more legal tender for amounts not exceeding $10; 5-cent coins legal tender for amounts not exceeding $5; and 1-cent coins legal tender only for amounts of 25 cents or less.　ARTHUR A. WICHMANN

LE GALLIENNE, *luh GAL yuhn,* is the family name of a poet and an actress, father and daughter.

Richard Le Gallienne (1866-1947) was an English poet of French descent. After working several years as an accountant, he took an interest in literature and became a leading member of the London literary group in the 1890's. He wrote many volumes of verse, including *English Poems* (1892) and *October Vagabonds* (1910). Among his most lasting works are a novel, *The Quest of the Golden Girl* (1896), and his memoir, *The Romantic Nineties* (1926). Richard Le Gallienne was born and educated in Liverpool.　HARRY T. MOORE

Eva Le Gallienne (1899-　) founded and directed the Civic Repertory Theatre in New York City. From 1926 to 1932, this theater group performed outstanding plays at low admission prices. As an actress, Miss Le Gallienne gained her first major success in *Liliom* in 1921. She also had leading parts in *The Inheritors* and *Thérèse*. Her later theatrical triumphs included roles in *Camille, The Master Builder, Uncle Harry,* and *Mary Stuart.* Miss Le Gallienne was born in London.　MARY VIRGINIA HEINLEIN

LEGATION is a diplomatic mission from one nation to another that is headed by a minister. Ministers rank below ambassadors. Before World War II (1939-1945), most nations maintained legations abroad rather than embassies. Since then, many countries have replaced their legations with embassies. The United States has not had a legation since 1966. See also AMBASSADOR; MINISTER.

LEGEND. See MAP (Symbols).

LEGEND is a popular type of folk story. In some ways, legends resemble *myths*, another type of folk story. But myths, most of which describe events of long ago, deal with such religious subjects as the birth and death of gods and goddesses. Most legends tell about recognizable people, places, and events of more recent times. Some legends are based on real persons or events, but many are entirely fictional and concern imaginary characters, such as Paul Bunyan and Pecos Bill. A number of these characters have superhuman powers.

Every society has some legends, and most of them reflect the attitudes and ideals of the group that created them. The heroes of legends have qualities that their society considered admirable. For example, many legends tell about George Washington or Abraham Lincoln. Such legends emphasize the courage and fairness of these great Presidents of the United States. On the other hand, evil characters in legends have such qualities as cowardice or greed, which society regards as undesirable.

The majority of societies have both local and national legends. Local legends tell about heroes of a particular ethnic group, occupation, or region. For example, John Henry is a legendary hero of black Americans, and Casey Jones has the same rank among railroad engineers. National legends are shared by an entire people. Many British men, women, and children take pride in the achievements described in the tales of King Arthur and his knights of the Round Table. C. SCOTT LITTLETON

See also FOLKLORE with its list of *Related Articles;* LITERATURE FOR CHILDREN (Books to Read [Folk Literature]).

LEGENDRE, *luh ZHAHN dr'*, **ADRIEN MARIE** (1752-1833), a French mathematician, influenced the teaching of geometry in America. He wrote *Elements of Geometry* (1794), which was published in the United States in 1819. It made considerable use of numbers and of algebra, unlike the traditional geometry book. He also helped set up the metric system, and worked on the theory of numbers, elliptic functions, differential equations, and trigonometric tables (see METRIC SYSTEM). Legendre was born in Toulouse, France. PHILLIP S. JONES

LÉGER, ALEXIS. See PERSE, SAINT-JOHN.

LÉGER, *lay ZHAY,* **FERNAND** (1881-1955), was a French artist who developed a distinctive style that reflects modern technology. Léger's works feature cylindrical and tubular shapes that have a machinelike quality. Some of his paintings are more abstract than others, but objects and figures can be identified in most of them. Léger's subjects include such mechanical devices as machine cogs and railway wheels and such human subjects as construction workers and mechanics. His painting *Three Women* is reproduced in the PAINTING article.

Léger was born in Argentan, near Alençon. His early paintings show the influence of the French artist Paul

Oil painting on canvas (1919); Philadelphia Museum of Art, Louise and Walter Arensberg Collection

Fernand Léger's *The City* shows how the artist used cylindrical forms to express his fascination with modern machines.

Cézanne and of the cubist movement. Beginning in the early 1940's, Léger enclosed his forms with heavy black lines that gave his pictures a posterlike simplicity. In some later pictures, he painted outlined figures and objects over abstract color patterns. WILLARD E. MISFELDT

LÉGER, JULES (1913-1980), was governor general of Canada from 1974 to 1979. The governor general serves as the representative of Queen Elizabeth II of Great Britain, who is also queen of Canada. Léger succeeded Roland Michener in the office.

Léger was born in St.-Anicet, Que., near Huntingdon. He graduated from the University of Montreal and the University of Paris. During the late 1930's, he worked as a newspaper editor in Ottawa and taught diplomatic history at the University of Ottawa. Léger joined the Canadian foreign service in 1940. He became Canada's ambassador to Italy in 1962 and ambassador to France in 1964. Léger served as undersecretary of state from 1968 until 1973, when he became ambassador to Belgium and Luxembourg. D. M. L. FARR

LÉGER, PAUL-ÉMILE CARDINAL (1904-), became archbishop of Montreal, Can., in 1950. He was raised to the rank of cardinal in 1953. In 1967, Cardinal Léger resigned from his diocese to devote himself to working with lepers.

Cardinal Léger was born in Valleyfield, Que. He served as vicar-general of that diocese from 1940 to 1947. Cardinal Léger was rector of the Canadian College in Rome, Italy, from 1947 to 1950. THOMAS P. NEILL

161

LEGERDEMAIN. See MAGICIAN (Sleight of Hand).

LEGHORN (pop. 175,371) is a major Italian seaport. Its Italian name is Livorno (pronounced *lee VAWR NOH*). Leghorn lies on the shore of the Ligurian Sea, about 62 miles (100 kilometers) southwest of Florence (see ITALY [political map]). It is an important industrial city, with steelworks, glass factories, and automobile plants. Leghorn hats, made from wheat straw, and coral ornaments are exported. Other exports include marble, olive oil, boric acid, silk, and wine. Leghorn has many canals.

The most interesting of its public buildings include the cathedral, a Jewish synagogue, the Academy of Sciences, and the naval academy. The *Tower of the Sculptured Lion*, a leading landmark, is a relic of the days when the city was a free port.

Leghorn was a little fishing village when the Florentines took it in 1421. It has grown steadily in importance and prosperity. The sulfur springs and sea bathing attract many visitors. SHEPARD B. CLOUGH

LEGION was a division of the Roman army. Its size varied from about 4,000 to 6,000 men during different periods of Roman history. After Rome became an empire, a general chosen by the emperor commanded each legion. Six young commissioned officers called *military tribunes* served under him. But the 60 veteran noncommissioned officers called *centurions* were the most effective and important leaders. Each centurion led a *century* (a unit of about 100 men).

Before the late 100's B.C., legions were divided into *maniples* of 120 men each. On the battlefield, a legion formed into three rows of maniples, with the maniples positioned like the black squares on a checkerboard. Spaces as wide as a maniple were left between the maniples. This arrangement proved effective against masses of invading warriors and against enemy forces advancing in tight ranks. The men in the front row of maniples hurled their spears at the enemy, then attacked with drawn swords. The second row charged into the empty spaces to relieve their comrades. Finally, the third row advanced with thrusting spears to secure the victory.

In 107 B.C., a general named Gaius Marius rearranged the legions into *cohorts* of about 400 men each. He also opened the legions to men of the lower classes, and an army of loyal, professional soldiers soon developed (see MARIUS, GAIUS). In the early days of the Roman Empire, the army had nearly 30 legions. These formed the backbone of the Roman army. FRANK C. BOURNE

See also ROME, ANCIENT (The Army).

LEGION, AMERICAN. See AMERICAN LEGION.

LEGION, FOREIGN. See FOREIGN LEGION.

LEGION OF HONOR. See DECORATIONS AND MEDALS (Other Countries); KNIGHTHOOD, ORDERS OF.

LEGION OF MERIT. See DECORATIONS AND MEDALS (Military Awards).

LEGIONNAIRES' DISEASE is an infectious respiratory illness that, in its most severe form, causes pneumonia and can be fatal. It afflicts people of any age but occurs most frequently among elderly persons who have a *chronic* (long-term) illness.

Legionnaires' disease was first identified in 1976. That year, 182 persons became ill, and 29 of them died, after being in or near the Bellevue-Stratford Hotel in Philadelphia. The American Legion was holding a convention at the hotel when these victims were afflicted. All the victims had the same illness, and most of them developed pneumonia. Physicians did not know what caused the illness, which they named Legionnaires' disease.

In January 1977, scientists identified the bacterium that causes the disease. They later reported that this bacterium had caused several outbreaks of the illness before the American Legion convention. The earliest known case of Legionnaires' disease occurred in 1965 in Washington, D.C. Since January 1977, the disease has occurred in many parts of the United States and in Europe.

The disease can strike the year around, but it most commonly occurs in late summer and fall. Symptoms appear from 2 to 10 days after a person becomes infected. Medical researchers have identified two forms of the disease. One form causes only fever, headache, and muscle ache, and is not fatal. A second form causes chills; high fever; a hard, dry cough; and severe pneumonia. An attack of this more serious form may last more than a week and can be fatal. Physicians use such drugs as erythromycin and rifampin to treat Legionnaires' disease. CHARLES ALAN PHILLIPS

LEGISLATIVE ASSEMBLY. See CANADA, GOVERNMENT OF (Provincial and Territorial Governments); FRENCH REVOLUTION (The Legislative Assembly).

LEGISLATIVE COUNCIL. See STATE GOVERNMENT (Organization).

LEGISLATIVE DEPARTMENT OF THE UNITED STATES GOVERNMENT. See CONGRESS OF THE UNITED STATES; HOUSE OF REPRESENTATIVES; SENATE; CONSTITUTION OF THE UNITED STATES (Article I).

LEGISLATURE is the lawmaking branch of a government. In the United States, the national legislature is called the *Congress*. In Great Britain and Canada, it is the *Parliament*. In Russia, it is the *Supreme Soviet of the Union of Soviet Socialist Republics*. Most legislatures have the power to pass laws (sometimes called *statutes*), which all citizens must obey. Sometimes legislatures have more authority than a government's executive head, and can supervise and regulate the leader's activities.

In parliamentary forms of government, as in Great Britain and Canada, the legislature determines the appointment of the prime minister and the cabinet. The ministry can remain in office only so long as it has the support of a majority in the legislature. In presidential systems, as in the United States, the chief executive is elected for a definite number of years. The chief executive holds office for that length of time even without the support of a majority in the legislature.

Most legislatures today are divided into two separate groups, called houses or chambers. A legislature of two chambers is called a *bicameral* legislature. In the United States, these two chambers are the *Senate* and the *House of Representatives*. In Great Britain, they are the *House of Lords* and the *House of Commons*. In Canada, they are the *Senate* and the *House of Commons*. In most two-house legislatures, both houses must approve a bill before it becomes a law. But in Great Britain, only the approval of the House of Commons is necessary to pass any law relating to money matters.

In the U.S. Senate, each state, regardless of population, is equally represented. But members of the U.S.

House of Representatives are divided among the states according to their population. Most state legislatures resemble the national legislature in organization and method of operating. But Nebraska has a one-house legislature chosen on the basis of population. A one-house body is known as a *unicameral* legislature. In 1964, the Supreme Court of the United States ruled that representation in both houses of state legislatures must be based on population.

Most national legislatures hold a regular session each year. Special sessions may be called to meet problems that come up between the regular sessions. In the United States, over four-fifths of the state legislatures hold yearly sessions. The other states meet every two years. But any of these state legislatures may be called into special session when the need arises.

The members of legislatures are elected to office for a varying number of years. Members of the U.S. Senate are elected for six years, and members of the House of Representatives for two years. For information on the terms of state legislators, see the *Legislature* sections of the state articles, such as ALABAMA (Legislature).

In cities, the legislature is usually called the *board of aldermen*, *common council*, or *city council*. Sometimes it is called the *commission*. Laws passed by city legislatures are usually called *ordinances*.   PAYSON S. WILD

Related Articles in WORLD BOOK include:

Address, Forms of	Law
Amendment	Lobbying
Apportionment	Local Government
Bill	Local Option
City Government	Mace
Cloture	Omnibus Bill
Committee of the Whole	Parliament
Congress of the United States	Parliamentary
Congressman	Procedure
Constitution of the United	Pork Barrel
States (Article I)	Proportional
Diet	Representation
Duma	Quorum
Enabling Act	Repeal
House of Burgesses	Senate
House of Commons	Sergeant at Arms
House of Lords	Speaker
House of Representatives	State Government
Initiative and Referendum	Veto

LE GUIN, *leh GWIHN,* **URSULA,** *UR suh luh* (1929-   ), is an American author of science fiction for adults and children. Many of Le Guin's novels and short stories for adults involve conflicts between individuals and society. Two of her finest adult novels are *The Left Hand of Darkness* (1969) and *The Dispossessed* (1974). Both works feature highly imaginative descriptions of civilizations on distant planets. Her other adult novels include *The Lathe of Heaven* (1971) and *The Word for World Is Forest* (1976). Many of her short stories were collected in *The Wind's Twelve Quarters* (1975) and *Orsinian Tales* (1976). Her essays on science fiction and fantasy were published in *Language of the Night* (1979).

Le Guin's most popular work for children is the *Earthsea trilogy.* It consists of—*A Wizard of Earthsea* (1968), *The Tombs of Atuan* (1971), and *The Farthest Shore* (1972). The three books describe the adventures of God, who, as a boy and adult, struggles against the forces of evil in the imaginary Land of Earthsea. Ursula Kroeber Le Guin was born in Berkeley, Calif. MARILYN FAIN APSELOFF

LEGUME, *LEHG yoom* or *lih GYOOM,* is any of the plants that belong to the pea family. They make up the

second largest family of flowering plants. The composite family is the largest (see COMPOSITE FAMILY). Botanists recognize between 14,000 and 17,000 *species* (kinds) of legumes. The group gets its name from the *legumes* (seed pods) that most of the plants bear.

Many legumes are of great economic importance throughout the world. Such legumes as peas, beans, and peanuts are valuable foods. Alfalfa, clover, and vetch are important forage and pasture plants. Other legumes yield medicines, dyes, oils, and timber.

Legumes grow in most parts of the world. They vary widely and may be trees, shrubs, or herbs. Many are climbing plants. The flowers of one large subfamily of legumes look like butterflies. Botanists call this group *Papilionoideae,* from the Latin word for *butterfly.* The common sweet pea belongs to this group. The flowers of other legumes may be small and regular. The flowers of still others may be irregular, with spreading petals.

Legumes take nitrogen into their roots from the air. Certain bacteria, called *rhizobia,* live in *nodules* (knotlike growths) that form along the roots of the plants. These bacteria take nitrogen from the air and change it into forms that can be used by plants. This characteristic makes leguminous plants valuable in agriculture. Farmers often use them as green manure and as cover crops to improve poor soil (see NITROGEN).

Each plant mentioned in this article has a separate article in WORLD BOOK.

Scientific Classification. Legumes make up the pea family, Leguminosae.   WAYNE W. HUFFINE

LEHÁR, *LAY hahr* or *LEH hahr,* **FRANZ,** *frahnts* (1870-1948), was a Hungarian composer of light operas. He began his career by following in his father's footsteps as a violinist, bandsman, and conductor. The composer Antonín Dvořák encouraged him to write music. Lehár's most successful operetta was *The Merry Widow* (1905), with its "Merry Widow Waltz." He also wrote the operettas *The Count of Luxembourg* (1909), *Eva* (1911), *The Land of Smiles* (1923), and *Cloclo* (1924). He was born in Komárom, Hungary.   JOYCE MICHELL

LE HAVRE, *luh HAH vruh* (pop. 199,388; met. area pop. 254,595), is the second busiest seaport city in France—after Marseille—and a major industrial center. It lies along the English Channel, in northern France, at the mouth of the Seine River. For location, see FRANCE (political map).

Le Havre's port and downtown area were badly damaged during World War II (1939-1945). After the war, they were rebuilt according to a master plan. The port was equipped with excellent facilities that can accommodate very large vessels. Many modern buildings were constructed in the downtown area. Much of France's crude petroleum is imported at Le Havre. The city's many industries include shipbuilding, automobile assembling, and the production of chemicals, petrochemicals, and electrical goods.

Le Havre was founded as a seaport in the 1500's. It soon became a major French center of international trade and industry. It has kept its key role in the country's economy ever since.   MARK KESSELMAN

LEHMAN CAVES NATIONAL MONUMENT, in eastern Nevada, has limestone caverns of great beauty and scientific interest. The monument was established in 1922. For area, see NATIONAL PARK SYSTEM (table: National Monuments). See also NEVADA (picture).

LEHMANN, *LAY muhn,* **LILLI,** *LIHL ee* (1848-1929), was a German soprano. She made her debut in 1865, and later became a leading member of the Berlin Royal Opera. In 1876, she sang in the first production of Richard Wagner's *Nibelungen Ring* in Bayreuth, Germany. She joined the Metropolitan Opera Company of New York City in 1885, and appeared in a variety of coloratura and dramatic roles. She became famous as a singer of German art songs and as a teacher. She was born in Würzburg, Germany.   SCOTT GOLDTHWAITE

LEHMANN, *LAY muhn,* **LOTTE,** *LOHT uh* (1888-1976), a German soprano, won fame as a concert and opera singer. Early in her career, she became known as an outstanding interpreter of the music of Richard Wagner and Richard Strauss. One of her finest creations was that of the Marschallin in Strauss's *Der Rosenkavalier.* She is also well remembered for her singing of the German art songs called *lieder.* After her retirement, she wrote several books on the interpretation of songs. She was born in Perleberg, Germany.   MARTIAL SINGHER

LEHMBRUCK, *LAYM bruk,* **WILHELM,** *VIHL hehlm* (1881-1919), was a German sculptor. His early work shows the strong influence of the French sculptor Aristide Maillol. Lehmbruck gave his early figures Maillol's solid forms and broad proportions. Lehmbruck added a mournful quality of expression to these early works.

About 1911, Lehmbruck's style changed. Largely under the influence of Gothic sculpture, he gave his figures exaggerated proportions that were elongated and slender. These features increased their effect of delicacy and melancholy. Lehmbruck's later works have increasingly slender forms and attitudes of despair reflecting the inner turmoil that led to his suicide. He was born in what is now Duisburg.   MARCEL FRANCISCONO

LEI. See HAWAII (Clothing; pictures).

LEIBNIZ, *LYP nihts,* **GOTTFRIED WILHELM,** *GOHT freet VIHL hehlm* (1646-1716), was a German scholar, mathematician, and philosopher. His name is sometimes spelled *Leibnitz.* Leibniz shares with Sir Isaac Newton the distinction of developing the theory of the differential and integral calculus (see CALCULUS). His other work in mathematics included combinatorial problems and a start in the development of symbolic logic. He also invented a calculating machine.

Leibniz also wrote a number of works on his philosophy, which has been named *monadology* or *leibnizianism.* In his philosophy, each person and thing is a *monad* (a completely separate being) whose existence is in harmony with God and is separate from outer experience. He believed that people should accept their lot in life and not try to change it, because this was the "best of all possible worlds." Voltaire, the French satirist, made fun of this theory in his book *Candide.*

Leibniz was born in Leipzig, Germany. He had mastered Latin, Greek, and philosophy before entering the University of Leipzig at the age of 15. He later studied at the universities of Jena and Altdorf. He helped found the Berlin Society of Sciences, and planned the Academy of St. Petersburg for Peter the Great of Russia. In 1712, Leibniz was appointed a baron and imperial privy councilor.   PHILLIP S. JONES

LEICESTER, *LEHS tuhr,* is an industrial and historic city in central England. It is the largest city in the district of Leicester, which has a population of 276,245. For location, see ENGLAND (political map).

The center of Leicester includes a modern shopping and business district, a bustling marketplace, and the University of Leicester. Nearby, Jewry Wall—part of public baths built by Romans in the A.D. 100's—stands next to a modern hotel. Among the other landmarks in the city are churches and the remains of a castle that date from the 1100's. Factories in Leicester produce a variety of goods, including hosiery, shoes, and engineering products.

Roman soldiers built a fort on the site of what is now Leicester shortly after they began the conquest of Britain in the A.D. 40's. During the Middle Ages, Leicester gained importance as a center of the wool trade. It became a prosperous industrial city in the 1800's, and has remained so to the present day.   PETER R. MOUNFIELD

LEICESTER, *LEHS tuhr,* **EARL OF** (1532?-1588), was an English nobleman who led a life of intrigue at the court of Queen Elizabeth I. He was the fifth son of the Duke of Northumberland.

The earl was a favorite of Queen Elizabeth. When his wife was found dead, Leicester was said to have killed her in order to marry the queen. But Elizabeth's advisers opposed the marriage. Leicester's marriage to the Countess of Essex in 1578 is believed to have angered Elizabeth. Two years later, she had Leicester arrested on a charge of plotting against her, but later released him. He headed an English army against Spain in 1585. Leicester was born in Cornbury, Oxfordshire, England. His given and family name was Robert Dudley.   ANDRÉ MAUROIS

LEIDEN, *LYD uhn,* also spelled *Leyden* (pop. 103,819; met. area pop. 174,501), lies 22 miles (35 kilometers) southwest of Amsterdam on the Rhine River (see NETHERLANDS [map]). It lies 3.8 feet (116 centimeters) below sea level. Products manufactured in the city include chemicals, cloth, cotton, and twine.

The painters Rembrandt van Rijn, Jan Steen, and Gerard Dou were born in Leiden. William of Orange founded a university there in 1575 to reward the citizens for their heroic defense against a siege by the Spaniards in 1573-1574. During the early 1600's, Leiden was the home of about 40 of the Pilgrims who sailed to America on the *Mayflower* in 1620.   BENJAMIN HUNNINGHER

LEIF ERICSON. See ERICSON, LEIF.

LEILA ARBORETUM. See MICHIGAN (Places to Visit).

LEIPZIG, *LYP sihg* (pop. 563,980), a city in East Germany, is a trade, industrial, and cultural center. Leipzig is also the name of the surrounding administrative district. The city developed into a prosperous trading center during the Middle Ages because it lay at the intersection of several European trade routes. Leipzig later became world famous for its great trade fairs, and gained a reputation as one of the greatest literary and musical centers of Europe. About a fourth of the city's buildings were destroyed during World War II. After the war, Leipzig became a part of Russian-controlled East Germany. In 1952, the district of Leipzig was created from parts of Saxony, Saxon-Anhalt, and Thuringia.

Location and Description. Leipzig lies in east-central Germany, in the northwest corner of the former Ger-

Leipzig's Old City Hall is one of many landmarks in this historic East German city. The building served as the city hall from 1556 to 1907. It now houses the Museum of the History of the City of Leipzig.

man state of Saxony. It is about 74 miles (119 kilometers) northwest of Dresden and 111 miles (179 kilometers) southwest of Berlin. For location, see GERMANY (political map). The inner part of the city has crowded, narrow streets and quaint houses with high-pitched roofs. Many of the churches and other buildings date from the Middle Ages. The famous trade fairs are held in the center of the city and on the fair grounds just outside the city. Leipzig's suburbs include Mockau, Gohlis, Eutritzsch, Möckern, Lindenau, Plagwitz, Connewitz, Stötteritz, Reudnitz, Volkmarsdorf, Schönefeld, and Wahren.

Industry. Leipzig became a center of fur-trading early in its history. Later, it grew into a great manufacturing city. Its industries include wood carving, papermaking, and the manufacture of many kinds of scientific instruments. The city is a center of textile manufacturing, and also makes steel products, plastics, and processed food products. Before World War II, Leipzig was the center of German book and music publishing. At one time more than 270 newspapers and magazines were published in the city. Only about 35 of the 400 publishing houses that thrived there before the war are still in operation.

Transportation. Leipzig's location at the junction of the Elster, Pleisse, and Parthe rivers makes it a great port. A canal connects the city with the Elbe and Saale rivers. Leipzig has two large airports, and is an important railroad and highway hub.

Cultural Life. There are many schools, art galleries, and museums in Leipzig. The University of Leipzig (renamed Karl Marx University by the communists after World War II) was founded in 1409. One of its most famous graduates was the great German poet Johann Wolfgang von Goethe. Other Leipzig schools include a conservatory founded by the composer Felix Mendelssohn in 1843, an art college, and an academy of graphic and book arts. Leipzig has played a great part in the history of German music. Johann Sebastian Bach, Robert Schumann, Mendelssohn, and other musical figures lived in the city. The composer Richard Wagner and the philosopher Gottfried Leibniz were born there. The city enjoyed its greatest period as a center of music and literature during the 1800's.

History. Leipzig was chartered in 1174, and became a trade center. Its printing industry dates from around 1480. The city became a battleground during the religious wars of the 1600's. The first Battle of Leipzig was fought near the city in 1631. Swedish forces led by Gustavus Adolphus won a great victory over the German army. The second Battle of Leipzig, fought between the Germans and the Swedes in 1642, also was won by the Swedes. They occupied Leipzig until 1650. In 1813, in the third Battle of Leipzig, Prussia, Russia, Austria, and Sweden defeated Napoleon.

The first major German railroad began operating between Leipzig and Dresden in 1839. After World War II, the Russians took over Leipzig and revived its two great annual industrial fairs.   JAMES K. POLLOCK

LEISLER, *LYS lur,* **JACOB** (1640-1691), served as governor of the English colony of New York from 1689 to 1691. The people of the middle class chose him as their protector against attacks from the French in Canada. They regarded him as their champion against the wealthy merchants and landowners. He ruled without authority from the king, and, when William and Mary became rulers of England, they sent Henry Sloughter to replace him. Leisler yielded to Sloughter, but the merchants and landowners accused him of treason. Leisler was tried and executed. He was born in Frankfurt, Germany.   IAN C. C. GRAHAM

LELAND, HENRY M. See AUTOMOBILE (Mass Production).

LE MANS, *luh MAHN* (pop. 147,697; met. area pop. 200,000), is a city in western France. It lies along the Sarthe River (see FRANCE [political map]).

Le Mans is famous as the site of an annual 24-hour sports car race. The Cathedral of St. Julien stands in the old central section of Le Mans. Built between the 1000's and 1200's, it is noted for its Gothic architecture and large stained-glass windows. The outskirts of the city have much industry and modern housing.

Le Mans serves as the capital of the Sarthe *department* (administrative district). It is an important grain market and the commercial and railroad center of its region. The city's factories produce agricultural machinery, automobiles, electrical equipment, motors, paper, plastics, textiles, and tobacco products.

Le Mans dates from ancient times. Julius Caesar conquered the area about 50 B.C. A major battle of the French Revolution took place in Le Mans in 1793. In 1871, Prussian armies defeated the French at Le Mans during the Franco-Prussian War.   MARK KESSELMAN

LEMAY, CURTIS EMERSON (1906-   ), commanded the Strategic Air Command of the United States Air Force from 1948 to 1957. During a period in which American foreign policy depended heavily upon the striking power of the Strategic Air Command's long-range bombers, LeMay became one of America's most famous airmen.

In 1957, LeMay became Vice Chief of Staff of the Air Force. He served as Air Force Chief of Staff from 1961 until January 1965, when he retired as a four-star general. In 1968, LeMay was the American Independent Party candidate for Vice President of the United States. George C. Wallace was the presidential candidate (see WALLACE, GEORGE C.).

LeMay was born in Columbus, Ohio, and was graduated from Ohio State University. He enlisted as a flying cadet in the Army Air Corps in 1928. During World War II, he won attention as a bomber commander in Europe. In 1943, he commanded the Third Bombardment Division of the Eighth Air Force. In September 1944, LeMay took command of the 20th Bomber Command in India.

When the Pacific islands of Guam and Saipan became the main bases for the growing B-29 offensive against Japan, LeMay took charge as the commander of the 21st Bomber Command. From January 1945 until the end of the war, he directed an air assault of mounting intensity against Japan.   ALFRED GOLDBERG

LEMELIN, ROGER (1919-   ), a Canadian novelist, became famous for his witty but accurate and sympathetic stories of French-Canadian family life. In 1936, he was injured in a ski-jumping accident. During his recovery, he wrote his first novel, published in English translation as *The Town Below* (1945). The book enjoyed immediate success. *The Plouffe Family* (1948) formed the basis of a Canadian television series. In 1952, Lemelin published *In Quest of Splendor*. He was born in the city of Quebec.   DESMOND PACEY

LEMMING, *LEHM ihng,* is a plump little animal related to the mouse. Lemmings live in the cold, northern parts of the world. The best-known kind lives in Scandinavia. Every few years, according to legend, great numbers of lemmings march to the sea and drown themselves. However, scientists no longer believe this. The animals do move away from their mountain homes because of crowding caused by increases in the number of lemmings. But few ever get as far as the sea. Most of them die of starvation or are killed by other animals.

Lemmings are from 4 to 5 inches (10 to 13 centimeters) long, including their stubby tails. Most kinds are gray or brown. Lemmings eat plants. They dig soil to build their nests, which they line with grass and moss.

Scientific Classification. Lemmings are in the New World rat and mouse family, *Cricetidae*. Lemmings make up the genus *Lemmus*.   DANIEL BRANT

See also ANIMAL (picture: Animals of the Polar Regions).

LEMON is a small, oval citrus fruit. People in many parts of the world enjoy lemon-flavored foods and beverages. Lemons have a pleasing scent, and most varieties have a tart taste. Lemons are rich in vitamin C and contain several B vitamins.

The lemon is a type of berry called a *hesperidium*. A lemon measures about 3 inches (7.6 centimeters) in length and about 2 inches (5 centimeters) in diameter. It has a nipplelike bulge at one end. The interior of the fruit consists of 8 to 10 segments, which contain the pulp, juice, and seeds. The leathery yellow rind has many tiny glands, which produce a spicy oil.

People rarely eat fresh lemons because of the fruit's sour taste. However, lemon juice and oil are used in a wide variety of food products. For example, lemonade, several soft drinks, and many other beverages are made with lemon juice. Such foods as candy, cakes, cookies, and salads, as well as various fish and meat dishes, are flavored with lemon juice and oil.

Lemon oil is also used as a scent in various non-food items. For example, it is used in household cleaning products, in soap, and in shampoo, perfume, and other cosmetics.

More than $3\frac{1}{2}$ million short tons (3.2 million metric tons) of lemons are grown throughout the world annually. Italy leads the world in lemon production, followed by the United States and Spain. Growers in the United States raise more than 800,000 short tons (730,000 metric tons) of the fruit yearly. California harvests about four-fifths of the nation's lemons. Arizona also produces the fruit. About half the U.S. lemon crop is processed into juice and oil. The other half is sold as fresh fruit.

Raising Lemons. Lemon trees can grow from 22 to 25 feet (6.7 to 7.6 meters) tall. They are covered with thorns and have long, pointed, pale green leaves. The trees produce large, white, fragrant flowers throughout the year, except for the winter. Lemons develop from the ovaries of the blossoms and ripen about 7 or 8 months after the flowers bloom. Lemon trees may carry blossoms and fruit at the same time.

Lemon trees are grown from buds cut from trees that produce the type of lemon desired. The buds are grafted to seedling lemon trees called *rootstocks* (see GRAFTING [Other Kinds of Grafting]). Rootstock varieties are chosen for their resistance to disease and for various other reasons. Lemon trees start to produce fruit about 4 years after grafting, and some continue to bear fruit for 50 years.

Lemon trees may be severely damaged by frost and freezing temperatures, and growers use a variety of methods to protect the trees from cold weather. For example, some growers prevent frost by warming the cold air near the ground with oil-burning heaters. Other lemon growers use large fans called wind machines to mix the cold surface air with the warmer air above it.

Lemon trees may also be attacked by such insect pests as mites, scale insects, and thrips. Mites and scale insects feed on the leaves, fruit, and twigs of the trees. Thrips attack the buds and the fruit. Growers combat the insects by growing varieties of trees that resist the pests and by spraying the trees with insecticides. In addition, they spray orchards with fungicides to fight fungal diseases, which attack the leaves, fruit, and roots of the trees.

Leading Lemon-Growing Countries

Italy	942,000 short tons (855,000 metric tons)
United States	807,000 short tons (732,000 metric tons)
Spain	577,000 short tons (523,000 metric tons)
Argentina	353,000 short tons (320,000 metric tons)
Turkey	254,000 short tons (230,000 metric tons)

Source: U.S. Department of Agriculture. Figures are for 1984.

Harvesting and Processing. Lemon trees bear fruit throughout the year, and growers harvest the fruit 2 to 10 times a year. The largest harvests occur in the autumn and winter. However, lemons are commonly stored for several months for sale in the spring and summer.

Lemons that are to be sold as fresh fruit are picked before they grow to their full size and maturity. Then they are cured and stored under special conditions. These lemons are less likely to be damaged during shipment and are more attractive than those that mature on the tree. Bruised lemons and lemons that are too mature when they are harvested are sent directly to factories where they are processed.

History. Lemons probably originated in northeastern India, near the Himalaya. Lemons were taken from India to Italy by the Arabs in the A.D. 100's, and to Spain in the A.D. 1100's.

In 1493, the Italian navigator Christopher Columbus planted the first lemon trees in America. By the late 1700's, lemon trees had been taken to California by Spanish missionaries. The first commercial lemon orchards in the United States were planted during the late 1800's.

Scientific Classification. Lemons are members of the rue family, Rutaceae. Commercial lemons belong to the species *Citrus limon*. WILLIAM J. WILTBANK

See also CITRIC ACID; CITRUS; FRUIT (table).

LE MOYNE, *luh MWAN*, **CHARLES,** *shahrl* (1626-1685), a Canadian colonist, founded the city of Longueuil. He was the first of a large family of French-Canadian heroes. Le Moyne left France in 1641. In Canada, he lived first at a Jesuit mission to the Huron Indians, where he learned several Indian dialects. Later, he became a fur trader, farmer, and soldier.

The French government honored Le Moyne with many titles, including that of *Sieur de Longueuil*, and gave him large grants of land. Le Moyne encouraged many French settlers to live on these lands and helped them during their pioneer years. He was born in Dieppe, France. He married Catherine Thierry-Primot.

Seven of Le Moyne's sons won fame fighting for France. Two of his sons, Sieur d'Iberville and Sieur de Bienville, explored the gulf regions of the Mississippi River and the river mouth. They claimed the land for France. Sieur d'Iberville served as governor general of the region and, upon his death, Sieur de Bienville succeeded him. Sieur de Bienville founded the city of New Orleans in 1718. See also BIENVILLE, SIEUR DE; IBERVILLE, SIEUR D'. HOWARD R. LAMAR

Historical Pictures Service

Charles Le Moyne

LE MOYNE, JEAN BAPTISTE. See BIENVILLE, SIEUR DE.

LE MOYNE, PIERRE. See IBERVILLE, SIEUR D'.

LEMUR, *LEE muhr*, is a long-tailed mammal with fluffy fur. Some kinds of lemurs resemble monkeys.

WORLD BOOK illustration by Kate Lloyd-Jones, Linden Artists Ltd.

Grant Heilman

Lemon, *left,* is a popular citrus fruit that is raised mainly for its tart juice and fragrant oil. Lemons are rarely eaten as fresh fruit. Lemon trees, *above,* bear fruit throughout the year, and so growers harvest the fruit up to 10 times annually.

LEMUR

Others look more like mice or squirrels. Scientists classify lemurs, along with human beings, apes, and monkeys, as *primates*. Lemurs live only in Madagascar and Comoros, island countries off the southeast coast of the African mainland.

Most lemurs live in trees most of the time. They eat fruit, leaves, birds and their eggs, and insects and other small animals. Some kinds of lemurs move about chiefly during the day, and others are active at night.

Lemurs vary greatly in size, color, and appearance. The *lesser mouse lemur*, one of the world's smallest primates, weighs 2 ounces (57 grams) and grows 5 inches (13 centimeters) long, not including the tail. These brownish or grayish animals look like furry mice. *Ring-tailed lemurs* and *ruffed lemurs* resemble monkeys, except that they have a long pointed snout. The ring-tailed lemur grows 15 inches (38 centimeters) long. It has a gray back, white underparts, and rings of black and white on its tail. The ruffed lemur grows 24 inches (61 centimeters) long and has especially fluffy fur. Most ruffed lemurs have a black-and-white coat with a fluffy white *ruff* (collar). Some have red-brown fur instead of white. Another kind of lemur, the raccoonlike *aye-aye*, does not resemble any other lemurs (see AYE-AYE).

Two monkeylike lemurs, the *indri* and the *sifaka*, have long, powerful hind legs. In the trees, these lemurs spring from trunk to trunk. Most animals that live in trees jump from branch to branch. The indri, the largest kind of lemur, grows about 28 inches (71 centimeters) long. It has a black back and white or red-brown fur on its undersides. The sifaka grows about 20 inches (51 centimeters) long.

Lemurs have few enemies because there are few large *predators* (animals that eat other animals) in the region where they live. But many species of lemurs have become endangered. People have cut down many trees in the forests in which these animals lived.

Scientific Classification. The lesser mouse lemur, the ring-tailed lemur, and the ruffed lemur belong to the family *Lemuridae*. The lesser mouse lemur is genus *Microcebus*, species *M. murinus*. The ring-tailed lemur is genus *Lemur*, species *L. catta*. The ruffed lemur is genus *Lemur*, species *L. variegatus*. The indri and the sifaka belong to the family *Indriidae*. The indri is genus *Indri*, species *I. indri*. Sifakas form the genus *Propithecus*. A common species is *P. verreauxi*. CLYDE A. HILL

LEMUR, FLYING. See FLYING LEMUR.

LENA RIVER, *LEE nuh*, is the chief waterway of a large district of eastern Siberia. The river rises on the slopes of the Baikal Mountains and flows northeast for 2,734 miles (4,400 kilometers). It empties into the Arctic Ocean through the Laptev Sea. The river's delta is about 250 miles (402 kilometers) wide. Ships can sail up the river for about 2,000 miles (3,200 kilometers).

The Lena River drains an area of about 1 million square miles (2.6 million square kilometers), which is nearly one-third the size of Canada. For the location of the river, see RUSSIA (physical map). Its chief branches are the Vitim, Olekma, Aldan, and Vilyuy rivers. Gold is mined along the Vitim and the Aldan.

Along its middle course, the Lena River flows through a region that is inhabited by the Yakuts, a Turkish people. The Yakuts make their living by fishing, farming, and raising livestock. The largest city on the river is Yakutsk. THEODORE SHABAD

LE NAIN, *luh NAN*, **LOUIS,** *lwee* (1593-1648), painted realistic scenes of peasant life in France. His paintings are thoughtful descriptions of peasant faces and costumes of the time. The lighting of the outdoor scenes suggests that he painted the people in his studio and then painted in the landscape background. Le Nain's two brothers, Antoine (1588-1648) and Mathieu (1607-1677?), also painted peasant scenes. All three brothers were born in Laon, France. JOSEPH C. SLOANE

LENAPE. See DELAWARE INDIANS.

LEND-LEASE was a plan developed by the United States early in World War II to aid the countries which were then fighting the Axis powers. The Lend-Lease Act became law on March 11, 1941. It provided that the President of the United States could transfer weapons, food, or equipment to any nation whose fight against the Axis aided U.S. defense. Under Lend-Lease, billions of dollars worth of American supplies were transferred to Great Britain, China, and Russia. President Franklin D. Roosevelt described the Lend-Lease Act as helping to put out the fire in your neighbor's house *before* your own house caught fire and burned down.

After World War II, no terms were decided upon for the return of goods by countries that received United States equipment under the Lend-Lease Act. Some countries, especially Great Britain, had already balanced part of the account by furnishing goods and services to United States troops.

Kenneth W. Fink, NAS

The Ring-Tailed Lemur, one of the most common species, lives in the southwest part of Madagascar. Unlike other lemurs, it usually dwells on the ground rather than in trees.

Many people felt that to accept a return of the goods that had been lent would injure American producers. Some authorities pointed out that all nations fighting the Axis powers contributed everything they could to the final defeat of the enemy. They argued that American Lend-Lease contributions were balanced by the sacrifices of the other Allies.   ROBERT D. PATTON

L'ENFANT, *lahn FAHN,* **PIERRE CHARLES,** *pyair shahrl* (1754-1825), a French engineer and architect, became the first modern city planner. In 1791, he was commissioned to prepare a plan for the new U.S. capital city in the District of Columbia. His plan envisioned a city of parks, public buildings, and wide, radiating streets. His headstrong temperament led him into a disagreement with President George Washington, and L'Enfant was dismissed as engineer-in-charge in 1792. But his plan was retained and formed the basis for the development of Washington, D.C. See WASHINGTON, D.C.

L'Enfant was born and educated in Paris. He came to America in 1777, and served as an engineering officer in the Revolutionary War. He designed Federal Hall in New York City (see FEDERAL HALL). He spent the later years of his life trying to obtain greater compensation for his work at Washington, D.C. In 1909, Congress erected a monument to him in Arlington National Cemetery, where he is buried.   ROBERT W. ABBETT

L'ENGLE, MADELEINE (1918-   ), an American author, won the Newbery medal in 1963 for *A Wrinkle in Time* (1962). She also wrote *Ilsa* (1946), *And Both Were Young* (1949), *Meet the Austins* (1959), and *The Moon by Night* (1963). She was born in New York City, and graduated from Smith College. See also LITERATURE FOR CHILDREN (Fiction).

LENGTH. See MEASUREMENT; METRIC SYSTEM; WEIGHTS AND MEASURES.

LENIN, *LEHN ihn,* **V. I.** (1870-1924), founded the Communist Party in Russia and set up the world's first Communist Party dictatorship. He led the October Revolution of 1917 in which the Communists seized power in Russia. He then ruled Russia until his death in 1924.

Lenin's goals were the destruction of *free enterprise* (privately owned and controlled business) and the creation of a *classless society* (a society without groups of rich or poor people). His ideas were based largely on the theories of Karl Marx, a German social philosopher. According to Marx, free enterprise would someday destroy itself. At first, industry and business would grow and the owners would get rich. The workers would grow poorer and finally revolt and take over the industries. The means of production would then be owned by all the people. The country would be controlled by the workers and would have no social classes. Marx believed that these revolutions would occur in the highly industrial Western nations.

In the early 1900's, during Lenin's rise to power, Russia was politically backward and largely agricultural. Lenin believed that the nation's social and political system could be destroyed only by the use of force. In time, he said, *revolutionaries* (persons who work to overthrow a government) would organize in all countries. They would take over their governments by violent revolution. The workers and peasants could not carry out revolutions by themselves, but would have to be led by a small political party of professional revolutionaries. After the revolution, the party would control

Sovfoto

Lenin Set Up the World's First Communist Dictatorship

the government and build a classless Communist society. The party would be a tight-knit organization operated like an army, and would allow no one to oppose it. Lenin also believed that the Communist states and the *capitalistic states* (nations based on free enterprise) could never live peacefully together. He declared that the two groups would struggle until one destroyed the other.

Lenin set a pattern for Communist revolution. He used force and terror to work toward his goals. After Lenin seized power, he ruled as a dictator, and did not permit other political parties or any anti-Communist speech or publication.

During the last years of his life, Lenin tried to make changes in the Communist movement that were based upon his experiences. For example, he wanted to limit

Important Dates in Lenin's Life

1870 (April 22) Born in Simbirsk, Russia.
1891 Graduated from St. Petersburg University.
1897 Exiled to Siberia for political activities.
1898 (July 22) Married Nadezhda Krupskaya.
1900 Returned from exile and went to Western Europe.
1903 Became leader of the Bolsheviks.
1905 Returned to Russia and engaged in revolutionary activity.
1908-1917 Conducted revolutionary activities abroad.
1917 Returned to Russia and led the October Revolution.
1917 (Nov. 8) Became ruler of Soviet Russia.
1918 Shot by Dora Kaplan.
1918-1921 Led the Bolsheviks in the Russian civil war.
1921 Introduced the New Economic Policy.
1924 (Jan. 21) Died in Gorki, near Moscow.

LENIN, V. I.

the use of violence in revolution and government. He also introduced a new economic policy and aimed to improve industrial skills and education.

Today, more than a billion persons live in countries ruled by Communist party dictatorships. The Communist world considers Lenin and Marx its greatest heroes. Communists quote Lenin's words as a basis for their actions. His works are also studied in the Free World, to provide an understanding of the Communist threat. Lenin is often thought of only as a man of action. Some of his ideas, however, rank among the most powerful forces of modern times.

For a discussion of Communism and conditions in Russia during Lenin's time, see the articles COMMUNISM and RUSSIA (History).

Early Life

Boyhood. Lenin was born on April 22, 1870, in Simbirsk (now Ul'yanovsk), a quiet little town on the Volga River. His real name was VLADIMIR ILYICH ULYANOV. He adopted the name *Lenin* in 1901. The name may refer to the Lena River of Siberia.

Lenin's father, Ilya Nikolayevich Ulyanov (1841-1886), was a teacher who became director of schools in Simbirsk province. Lenin inherited his father's dark complexion, high cheekbones, and dark brown eyes. His mother, Maria Aleksandrovna Blank (1835-1916), was the daughter of a doctor. She was an educated woman and was highly devoted to her children. Lenin had two brothers and three sisters. All the children, except one sister who died at the age of 20, became revolutionists.

Lenin had a pleasant childhood. He often imitated his brother Alexander, who was four years older. Lenin swam, hiked, fished, hunted, and played chess. His sister Anna recalled that he had no close friends.

Education. Lenin learned to read when he was 5 years old. He was taught by a teacher who came to the Ulyanov home. Lenin entered school in 1879, at the age of 9, and became a brilliant student.

During Lenin's youth, Russia was generally quiet and peaceful. The Russian government was an *autocracy*, a system in which one man holds supreme power. Czar Alexander III had come to power in 1881 after the murder of his father, Alexander II. Alexander III kept some of the improvements his father had introduced, but added few of his own. Russia was rapidly becoming an industrial country, though living standards remained low and persons in many areas were starving.

In 1886, Lenin's father died. The next year, Lenin's brother Alexander was hanged for taking part in an unsuccessful plot to kill the czar. The tragedy deeply influenced Lenin. At his trial, Alexander said he had wanted to kill the czar to gain "political freedom" for the Russian people.

In 1887, the year his brother was hanged, the 17-year-old Lenin finished school. He won a gold medal for excellence in studies. In the fall of 1887, Lenin enrolled in the law school at Kazan University in Kazan. He was expelled three months later for taking part in a student meeting protesting the lack of freedom in the school. Lenin unsuccessfully applied several times for permission to re-enter. In 1890, St. Petersburg

University admitted Lenin as a student, but he was not permitted to attend classes. However, he was allowed to study on his own and to take examinations.

Lenin received a law degree from St. Petersburg University in 1891, and joined a law firm in Samara (now Kuybyshev). By this time, he was absorbed in the study of Marxism. In 1893, Lenin joined a Social Democratic group, a Marxist organization. Later that year, he moved to St. Petersburg (now Leningrad), and became an active revolutionary.

Young Revolutionist. In St. Petersburg, Lenin soon became a leader of a Marxist, or Social Democratic, revolutionary group. Lenin had the qualifications for leadership. He was highly intelligent and well educated. His writing was accurate, detailed, and clear.

Czar Alexander III died in 1894, and his son, Nicholas II, became czar. Between April and September, 1895, Lenin traveled to France, Germany, and Switzerland to contact other Marxists. In December, Lenin was arrested in St. Petersburg by the czar's police while preparing a revolutionary newspaper, *The Workers' Cause*. After being held for questioning for more than a year, Lenin was *exiled* (expelled) to Siberia in 1897.

Exile in Siberia did not mean imprisonment. The government paid Lenin a small allowance, and he rented quarters in Shushenskoye near Abakan. Lenin enjoyed much freedom and continued his revolutionary writings. On July 22, 1898, Lenin married

Sovfoto

Lenin's Birthplace was a large house in Simbirsk. His father, a schoolteacher, rented a wing of the home from another family.

Sovfoto

Lenin and His Wife, Nadezhda Krupskaya, met at a meeting of revolutionaries in 1894. They later were married in Siberia.

Nadezhda Konstantinovna Krupskaya (1869-1939), another exiled revolutionary. The couple had no children. While in Siberia, Lenin wrote one of his leading works, *The Development of Capitalism in Russia* (1899).

Revolutionist Leader

Beginnings of Revolution. In 1898, while Lenin was in exile, a number of secret Marxist groups in Russia joined and formed the Russian Social Democratic Labor party. After Lenin's exile ended in January, 1900, he got permission from the government to leave Russia. He went to Germany to help found the party newspaper, *Iskra* (Spark). *Iskra* was an illegal paper that had to be smuggled into Russia. The editors of *Iskra* also published *Zarya* (Dawn), which dealt with Marxist theory. It was in *Zarya* in 1901 that Vladimir Ulyanov began using the name *Lenin*. Many revolutionaries changed their names to confuse the police.

In 1902, Lenin wrote *What Is to Be Done?* This pamphlet described his ideas on party organization. In 1903, the Russian Social Democratic Labor party split into two groups, apparently over a dispute about membership. Lenin became the leader of the *bolshinstvo* (majority), or, as this group came to be known, the *Bolsheviks*. The other group became known as the *menshinstvo* (minority), or *Mensheviks*. The Bolsheviks wanted party membership limited to a small number of full-time revolutionaries. They believed that for the revolution to succeed, trained professionals should lead the party, and the party should organize the *proletariat* (workers). The Mensheviks wanted fewer restrictions on party membership and preferred democratic practices to secret plotting.

Revolt. By the early 1900's, a spirit of revolt against the czar had developed in Russia. The citizens wanted more political freedom, land for the peasants, social legislation and higher wages for the workers, and greater representation in the government. They also wanted an end to the war going on between Russia and Japan.

On Sunday, Jan. 22, 1905, Father George Gapon, a Russian Orthodox priest, organized about 200,000 persons for a peaceful march on the Winter Palace in St. Petersburg. The unarmed marchers planned to present their requests to the czar. Troops fired on the crowd and killed or wounded hundreds of persons. This *Bloody Sunday* caused more revolutionary unrest. By autumn, strikes had paralyzed the country. On Oct. 30, 1905, the czar granted freedom of speech, some voting rights, and a parliament. He also pardoned all political exiles. Lenin returned to Russia in November and called for a general revolt. A mass strike began in Moscow on December 20, and was followed by strikes in other cities. Soon the strike developed into a full-fledged revolution. By the end of December, the revolution was crushed. Years later, Lenin declared that "without the general rehearsal of 1905, the victory of the October Revolution of 1917 would have been impossible."

Outcast. From 1906 to 1908, Lenin spent most of his time writing revolutionary pamphlets, and attending party congresses in England, Germany, and Sweden. Lenin found it too difficult to carry on revolutionary activities in Russia. After two years in Finland, he went to Switzerland and then to France. His main purpose was to keep the Bolshevik organization together.

In April, 1912, in St. Petersburg, several Bolsheviks

established *Pravda* (Truth), a revolutionary newspaper that was sold openly. To be closer to Russia, Lenin moved to Kraków, then in Austria-Hungary but now in Poland, and became *Pravda's* chief contributor.

World War I began two years later. Germany declared war on Russia on Aug. 1, 1914. The Austrian government arranged for Lenin to go to Switzerland, which did not take part in the war. The Russian revolutionaries split into two groups. One group favored a Russian victory. The group headed by Lenin worked for Russia's defeat. Through these opposite policies, both aimed for the goal of world revolution.

After the war began, Germany supplied money to some revolutionaries, including Lenin. The Germans hoped the revolutionaries would weaken the Russian war effort. In 1915, Lenin promised the Germans that if he came to power, he would sign a peace treaty.

The Road to Power

The February Revolution. By 1917, Russia was losing the war. Unrest mounted, and food shortages were unchecked. The value of money went down. Early in March (February on the old Russian calendar), bread supplies ran short in Petrograd (formerly St. Petersburg, now Leningrad). Long lines of women appeared before the bread shops. Russian workers went on strike. By March 9, about 200,000 strikers were demonstrating in the capital. The soldiers refused to maintain order. *Soviets* (councils) of workers and soldiers had sprung up in Russia during the revolution of 1905. On March 12, 1917, a group called the Soviet of Workers' and Soldiers' Deputies was established in Petrograd.

Czar Nicholas II gave up the throne on March 15, and a democratic government was established. Prince George Lvov, a Russian political leader, became prime minister. For a time, the Petrograd soviet shared control of Russia with the government. But the Bolsheviks soon demanded "all power to the soviets."

Return from Exile. Nothing about the February revolution had followed the pattern expected by the revolutionaries. The Bolsheviks were disorganized and only a few of them had taken part in it. Lenin was in Switzerland and most of the other top leaders were in Siberia. The exiles rushed back from Siberia. Lenin and a group of Bolsheviks returned from Switzerland through Germany. While in Germany, which was at war with Russia, Lenin and his followers were not allowed to get off the train. For this reason, it is often said that Lenin traveled in a "sealed car." Lenin arrived in Petrograd on April 16, 1917, and received a hero's welcome.

Lenin called for an end to the war, for government ownership of all land, and for the overthrow of the government. The Bolsheviks regarded these proposals as too extreme. They had been prepared to accept Lvov's government. Lenin quickly regained party leadership, but he was not able to seize the government. In July, 1917, following an unsuccessful Bolshevik uprising, the government was reorganized under Alexander Kerensky. On July 19, the government ordered Lenin's arrest as a German agent. Lenin fled to Finland.

While in Finland, Lenin wrote *The State and Revolution* (1917), one of his most important works. He told in

LENIN, V. I.

Keystone

Lenin's Powerful Speeches persuaded the Russian people to follow his leadership. Leon Trotsky stands on the platform steps.

this pamphlet how to organize a revolution and what kind of government to establish after the power had been seized. In September, 1917, Lenin wrote the Central Committee of the Bolshevik party and declared that the time for speechmaking was over. It was time for action. "History will not forgive us if we do not assume power now," Lenin said.

The October Revolution. In October, 1917, Lenin returned to Petrograd. He urged the Central Committee to begin a revolt immediately. Kerensky's government and leadership were weak. Leon Trotsky, the Bolshevik president of the Petrograd soviet, got control over some government troops. Some naval crews also agreed to support the revolt. The Bolsheviks decided to act.

With little violence, the Bolsheviks seized Petrograd on November 7 (October 25 on the old Russian calendar). Kerensky fled. The struggle for Moscow was more violent than in Petrograd, but by November 15, the Bolsheviks also held that city. Henceforth, the Bolsheviks controlled the Russian government. They had come to power with the help of a simple slogan: "Bread, peace, land." This slogan had little to do with the theories of Marx. But it had real meaning to starving housewives and their families, soldiers sick of war, and peasants hungry for land.

Lenin the Dictator

The Second All-Russian Congress of Soviets opened on Nov. 8, 1917, with delegates from most parts of the country. The congress, controlled by the Bolsheviks, appointed a Council of People's Commissars. Lenin was made chairman of the council and thus became head of the new Soviet state. At Lenin's first appearance before the congress, he requested permission to ask Germany for a three-month halt in the war. He also asked for the abolition of private landownership. The congress approved both requests. The Bolsheviks started peace talks with Germany, and *nationalized* (put

under government control) all privately owned land.

Lenin hardly had time to begin nationalizing industry, banks, and private business, when he found himself battling to stay in power. The Russian army had fallen apart, the Germans were advancing into Russia, and forces that opposed the Bolsheviks were gathering in many parts of the country.

Lenin forced Russia to withdraw from the war. On March 3, 1918, Russia signed the peace treaty of Brest-Litovsk. Russia gave Germany large territories, including the Baltic region, Bessarabia, Finland, Russian Poland, and the Ukraine. Russia also promised raw materials to Germany. On their part, the Germans helped keep Lenin in power.

In 1918, at Lenin's suggestion, the Bolsheviks changed the name of the Russian Social Democratic Labor party to the Russian Communist party (Bolsheviks).

Rule by Terror. In December, 1917, Lenin established the *Cheka*, a political police force, and set up rule by terror. Persons opposed to the Bolshevik government were imprisoned or murdered. In July, 1918, the Bolsheviks killed Czar Nicholas II and his family. Lenin described his own dictatorship as "power, based directly upon force, and unrestricted by any laws."

On Aug. 30, 1918, after speaking to the workers at a Moscow factory, Lenin was shot by Dora Kaplan, a member of the Social Revolutionary party. Lenin was hit by two bullets, but recovered in several weeks. Dora Kaplan was executed. To discourage other attempts, the Bolsheviks executed hundreds of so-called "hostages."

Civil War. The revolution had spread quickly in the large cities of central Russia. But resistance in distant regions developed into civil war. In January, 1918, Lenin formed the Red army. It was named for the color of the flag of the world Communist movement. The forces opposing the Reds became known as the Whites. The Whites included revolutionaries, democrats, Russian nationalists, and those who preferred the old government and opposed any change. The Whites lacked unity of purpose, and were unable to organize effectively. By 1920, the Bolsheviks had won the deciding battles, and by 1922 the war ended.

The Russian economy had collapsed. Industrial output was at the vanishing point. Agricultural production had fallen disastrously. People in the cities were starving. Millions of Russians had died or had fled abroad. But the Communist government survived.

Even during the civil war, Lenin did not lose sight of his goal of Communist world revolution. In 1919, he had organized the *Comintern* (Communist International). The Comintern ran parties in all parts of the world and helped gain international support for the Bolsheviks during the civil war. In 1920, Lenin tried to export the revolution by military means by way of Poland to Central Europe. Lenin did not expect the Russian revolution to survive unless Communism was gaining ground in Western Europe.

After the civil war, Lenin took extreme measures to keep control of his weakened country. In March, 1921, he introduced a program called the New Economic Policy (NEP). This program replaced many of the socialist measures started at the beginning of his rule. Small businesses were permitted to resume limited operations. Free retail trade was allowed again. Foreign

Lenin's Tomb in Red Square in Moscow attracts thousands of visitors each day. A glass-covered casket containing Lenin's embalmed body lies inside the huge memorial.

Sovfoto

"capitalists" were invited to invest in Russia. Peasants were allowed to sell food to private customers. Food supplies sent by the United States Commission for Relief saved hundreds of thousands of starving Russians. The commission was headed by Herbert Hoover, who later became President of the United States.

Lenin asked England, France, Germany, and the United States for credit, trade, and diplomatic recognition. But these nations were unwilling to deal with the Bolshevik government which had refused to pay Russia's debts and which favored a world revolution. By 1919, no major country maintained diplomatic relations with the Soviet government. But after the New Economic Policy was begun, most European states resumed diplomatic relations.

Death. Lenin's health had been shattered by the strain of revolution and war. He was ill by November 1921. In May 1922, Lenin suffered a stroke. He worked on against his doctor's advice.

Lenin was concerned over the direction the revolution was taking. He began to challenge some basic ideas of the Bolshevik government. Lenin opposed the concentration of power in government bureaus. He also feared the Bolshevik enthusiasm for military glory and Russian nationalism. Shortly before Lenin's stroke, he had appointed Joseph Stalin general secretary of the party. Now, Lenin had serious doubts about Stalin, who was reaching out for purely personal power.

In December 1922, Lenin suffered a second stroke. In January 1923, Lenin warned that Stalin was "too rude" and lacked the talents necessary for party leadership. Lenin wrote that he planned to remove Stalin as party secretary. On March 9, 1923, he had a third stroke and lost his power to speak clearly. From this time on, he required constant care. His illness kept him from appointing a new party secretary. On Jan. 21, 1924, Lenin died of a brain hemorrhage. The government preserved his body by a special process. Lenin's tomb, in Red Square in Moscow, is one of the country's most honored monuments.   Critically reviewed by STEFAN T. POSSONY

Related Articles in WORLD BOOK include:

Alexander (family)	Krupskaya,	Politburo
Bolsheviks	Nadezhda K.	Russia
Communism	Marx, Karl	(History)
International, The	Mensheviks	Stalin, Joseph
Kerensky,	Moscow	Trotsky, Leon
Alexander F.	Nicholas (family)	World War I

Reading and Study Guide

See *Lenin, V. I.*, in the RESEARCH GUIDE/INDEX, Volume 22, for a *Reading and Study Guide*.

Additional Resources

FISCHER, LOUIS. *The Life of Lenin.* Harper, 1964.
HILL, CHRISTOPHER. *Lenin and the Russian Revolution.* Penguin, 1978.
WEBER, GERDA, and HERMAN. *Lenin: Life and Works.* Facts on File, 1981.

LENINGRAD, *LEHN ihn GRAD* (pop. 4,295,000; met. area pop. 4,827,000), is the second largest city in the Soviet Union. Only Moscow, the capital, has more people. Leningrad is a major port of the Soviet Union and one of the world's leading industrial and cultural centers. The city lies in the northwestern part of the country, at the eastern end of the Gulf of Finland, an arm of the Baltic Sea. For location, see RUSSIA (political map).

Leningrad was the first Russian city built in imitation of Western European cities. Its magnificent palaces, handsome public buildings, and wide public squares resemble those of such cities as London, Paris and Vienna. In the early 1800's, a planning commission that included the noted Italian architect Carlo Rossi established a design for the center of the city that includes a series of squares.

The city has had three names. Czar Peter I (the Great) founded it in 1703 as St. Petersburg. After Russia went to war against Germany in 1914, at the start of World War I, the name was changed to Petrograd. The country's officials chose this name, which means *Peter's City* in Russian, to get rid of the German ending *burg*. In 1924, the Communist government renamed the city in honor of V. I. Lenin, the founder of the Soviet Communist Party.

The City lies on a marshy lowland where the Neva River empties into the Gulf of Finland, at about 60° north latitude. Because of its far northern location, Leningrad has very short periods of daylight in winter. For about three weeks in June, it has "white nights," during which the sky is never completely dark.

The center of Leningrad is on the southern bank of the Neva. This area includes the main business district and most of Leningrad's famous buildings. Many fine examples of baroque and neoclassical architecture have been preserved in the area, and few modern structures have been built there.

Tom Tracy, Black Star

Huge Crowds jam Leningrad's main street, Nevsky Prospekt. Many fine restaurants and shops line the street.

Vance Henry, Taurus

A Luxurious Palace built during the 1700's still stands in Petrodvorets, a suburb of Leningrad. Hundreds of fountains beautify the grounds of the palace, which was the summer residence of several Russian czars.

The historic Winter Palace (now the Hermitage Museum), completed in 1762, stands in the center of the city. The palace was the winter home of the czars. The General Staff Building, designed by Rossi and completed in 1829, stands across Palace Square from the Winter Palace. Several blocks away is the Cathedral of St. Isaac of Dalmatia, whose massive golden dome dominates Leningrad's skyline.

The center of Leningrad is surrounded by old residential areas that have stone or brick apartment buildings. Near the outskirts of the city are thousands of modern concrete apartment buildings. The western section of Leningrad is the chief industrial district.

Several luxurious palaces built in the 1700's still stand in three suburbs of Leningrad—Pavlovsk, Petrodvorets, and Pushkin. These palaces, which are famed for their architectural excellence, were summer homes of the czars. Today, they are popular resorts and tourist attractions.

Education and Cultural Life. More than 40 institutions of higher learning are in Leningrad. The University of Leningrad, with about 20,000 students, is one of the Soviet Union's largest universities. The Conservatory of Music, established in 1862, is the nation's oldest music school. Its graduates include such famous composers as Sergei Prokofiev, Dimitri Shostakovich, and

Vance Henry, Taurus

The Neva River flows through the heart of Leningrad. The massive golden dome of the Cathedral of St. Isaac of Dalmatia rises in the background of this view of the city.

172

Peter Ilich Tchaikovsky. The Choreographic School has trained such famous ballet dancers as Vaslav Nijinsky, Rudolf Nureyev, and Anna Pavlova. The city's two largest libraries are the M. E. Saltykov-Shchedrin State Public Library and the Library of the Academy of Sciences of the U.S.S.R.

Leningrad is the home of many fine museums and theaters. The Hermitage is known throughout the world for its masterpieces. It exhibits outstanding collections of ancient Greek and Roman sculpture; Islamic art; and Baroque, Renaissance, and French impressionist paintings. The Russian Museum has a large collection of Russian art. The Kirov Theater presents ballet and opera. Dramatic productions are offered by several theaters, including the Gorki Academic Theater, the Pushkin Theater, and the Young Spectators' Theater.

The city has an important place in Russian literature. A number of famous Russian authors have used Leningrad as a background for many of their works. These writers include Alexander Pushkin, Fyodor Dostoevsky, and Andrey Bely.

The People. Most of Leningrad's people are members of the Russian nationality, or ethnic, group. Jews and Ukrainians are the city's largest minority groups.

Many Leningraders live in old apartment buildings in the mid-city area. Most of the apartment buildings on the outskirts of Leningrad are less crowded than those of the inner city. But many people prefer to live in the center of the city because of its shops, museums, theaters, and other attractions.

Few Leningraders own automobiles, but the city has an efficient public transportation system of buses, streetcars, and subway and commuter trains. Like other large cities, Leningrad has such problems as air pollution and overcrowding. However, Leningrad has far less crime than most cities of similar size outside the Soviet Union.

Economy. Leningrad accounts for about 3 per cent of the Soviet Union's industrial production. The city has been a major shipbuilding center since the early 1700's. During the 1800's, it became an important manufacturer of machine tools. Today, the production of machinery makes up about 40 per cent of the city's industry. Other important products include chemicals, electrical equipment, textiles, and timber.

Leningrad's industry and location make it an important trade and distribution center. The city has an excellent port and is served by 12 railroads.

History. Peter the Great founded the city as St. Petersburg in 1703. Peter had visited Western Europe and wanted to bring Western culture and technology to Russia. He made St. Petersburg his "window to the West," a showcase for his efforts to westernize Russian life. Western architects played an important role in the city's construction. In 1712, Peter moved the nation's capital from Moscow to St. Petersburg. The new capital soon became the intellectual and social center of the Russian Empire. By 1800, more than 220,000 people lived in St. Petersburg.

The city played an important part in many major events in Russian history. In 1825, an unsuccessful uprising against Czar Nicholas I took place there. In 1881, a group of Russian revolutionaries assassinated Czar Alexander II in St. Petersburg. Early in 1905, troops of Czar Nicholas II killed or wounded hundreds

of unarmed demonstrators in front of the Winter Palace. This *Bloody Sunday* slaughter led to the Revolution of 1905.

The city's name was changed to Petrograd in 1914. Riots and strikes occurred there during the Revolution of 1917, which ended czarist rule in the country. Late that year, Bolshevik (Communist) forces seized the city and formed a new government, headed by Lenin. The Bolsheviks moved the capital back to Moscow in 1918. Petrograd was renamed Leningrad upon Lenin's death in 1924.

In 1934, a Communist Party leader named Sergey Kirov was assassinated in Leningrad. His murder touched off the *Great Purge*, during which the government's secret police killed or imprisoned millions of people. During World War II (1939-1945), Leningrad was a major target of Germany's attack on the Soviet Union. The Germans laid siege to the city from August 1941 to January 1944. About a million Leningraders died during the siege, most of them from starvation. The city was badly damaged by German bombers and artillery but it did not fall.

A large number of Leningrad's historic structures were rebuilt after World War II. The city also carried out construction projects to overcome a severe housing shortage. More than 600,000 apartments were provided in buildings that went up from 1961 to 1973, and housing construction has continued in an attempt to meet the needs of the city's growing population. In 1966, Leningrad adopted a long-range program aimed at achieving a more satisfactory distribution of housing, office buildings, and parks in the city.   ROBERT A. LEWIS

See also RUSSIA (pictures).

LENNI-LENAPE. See DELAWARE INDIANS.

LENNON, JOHN. See BEATLES.

LENOIR, *luh NWAHR*, **JEAN JOSEPH ÉTIENNE,** *zhahn zhoh ZEHF ay TYEHN* (1822-1900), a French citizen born in Luxembourg, was one of the first to build a practical internal-combustion engine. By 1860, he was producing a reliable engine equipped with an electric ignition system and using illuminating gas as a fuel. Many hundreds of these engines were constructed. They were used throughout Paris. About 1863, Lenoir built one of the first automobiles to use a gas engine. This engine was a one-cylinder unit of his own design. See also AUTOMOBILE (The Gasoline Car); GASOLINE ENGINE (Development).   SMITH HEMPSTONE OLIVER

LENOIR RHYNE COLLEGE is a coeducational liberal arts school at Hickory, N.C. It was founded in 1891 by the Lutheran Synod in North Carolina. Courses offered lead to the B.A. and B.S. degrees. For enrollment, see UNIVERSITIES AND COLLEGES (table).

LENORMAND, SEBASTIEN. See PARACHUTE.

LE NÔTRE, *luh NAW truh,* **ANDRÉ,** *ahn DRAY* (1630-1700), a French landscape designer, created most of the famous gardens of his day. These included Kensington Gardens and St. James's Park in London; Versailles, Saint-Cloud, Fontainebleau, Vaux, and Chantilly gardens in France; and the Quirinal and the Vatican gardens in Rome. He used sculpture to create effects of grandeur. Le Nôtre considered the Chantilly garden his finest work. He was born in Paris. See also VERSAILLES.   ROBERT E. EVERLY

LENS

LENS is a piece of transparent material that has at least one curved surface. Lenses *refract* (bend) light rays and in doing so can form images of an object. The images may be larger, smaller, or the same size as the object itself. Scientists sometimes use lenses to concentrate or spread a beam of light.

Lenses are an important part of eyes. They make it possible for the eyes to form sharp images of both near and distant objects. Lenses in the form of glasses and contact lenses are used to correct various imperfections in eyesight. Lenses are also an essential part of binoculars, cameras, microscopes, projectors, telescopes, and many other devices.

Artificial lenses are made of glass, plastic, or a transparent crystal such as *quartz*. Quartz is used to refract *ultraviolet rays*, an invisible form of light.

There are two kinds of simple lenses, *converging lenses* and *diverging lenses*. They differ in the way they are curved and therefore in the manner in which they refract light. *Compound lenses* consist of two or more simple lenses fitted together.

A Plano-Convex Lens has one plane surface and one convex surface. It is used in certain types of slide projectors.

A Plano-Concave Lens has one plane surface and one concave surface. It is combined with other lenses for cameras.

A Double-Convex Lens has two convex surfaces. It is used in various magnifying glasses.

A Double-Concave Lens has two concave surfaces. It is used in reducing glasses.

 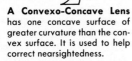

A Concavo-Convex Lens has one convex surface of greater curvature than the concave surface. It is used to help correct farsightedness.

A Convexo-Concave Lens has one concave surface of greater curvature than the convex surface. It is used to help correct nearsightedness.

Converging Lenses, also called *positive lenses* or *convex lenses*, are thicker in the middle than at the edges. When parallel rays of light pass through this type of lens, they are bent inward and meet at a point called the *focus*. The distance from the center of the lens to the focus is known as the *focal length*.

The size, position, and type of image produced by a converging lens vary according to the distance of the object from the lens. If an object is more than one focal length from the lens, an inverted *real image* of it is formed on the opposite side of the lens. A real image is one through which light rays from an object actually pass

and which can be focused on a screen. When an object is located a distance of two focal lengths from a converging lens, the image is the same size as the object and is located a distance of two focal lengths on the opposite

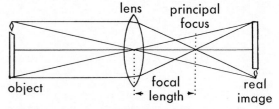

A Real Image can be formed by a convex lens if the object is more than one focal length from the lens. A real image is always upside down and on the opposite side of the lens. It is the same size as the object if the object is twice the focal length away.

side of the lens. A smaller image of the object can be obtained by moving the object more than two focal lengths from the lens. A larger image can be produced by placing the object between one and two focal lengths from the lens.

If an object is less than one focal length from the lens, a magnified *virtual image* is formed behind the object and is right side up. Light rays from an object do not actually pass through a virtual image, and such an image cannot be focused on a screen.

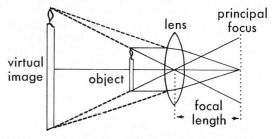

A Virtual Image can be formed by a convex lens, *above,* if the object is less than one focal length from the lens. A virtual image is always right side up and on the same side of the lens as the object. With convex lenses, it is always larger than the object. A concave lens can form only a virtual image, *below.* With concave lenses, the virtual image is always smaller than the object.

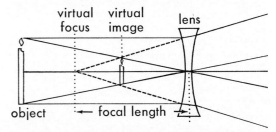

Diverging Lenses are also called *negative lenses* or *concave lenses*. Diverging lenses are thicker at the edges than they are at the center. Light rays passing through a diverging lens are bent outward. Diverging lenses form only virtual images. The images are always right side up and reduced in size.

Compound Lenses. Simple lenses generally produce *aberrated* (imperfect) images. These imperfections in image formation can be reduced through the use of compound lenses. For example, diverging lenses are often used to correct aberrations produced by converging lenses. See ABERRATION.   BRIAN J. THOMPSON

Related Articles in WORLD BOOK include:

Astigmatism	Glasses
Binoculars	Magnifying Glass
Camera	Microscope
Contact Lens	Refraction
Eye	Telescope

LENS, CONTACT. See CONTACT LENS.

LENSKI, LOIS (1893-1974), was an American writer and illustrator of children's books. She received the Newbery Medal in 1946 for *Strawberry Girl*. She won the Regina Medal in 1969. She wrote and illustrated many picture books, historical stories, and modern regional stories of American life. Her works include *The Little Auto* (1934), *Phebe Fairchild* (1936), *Ocean-Born Mary* (1939), *Blueberry Corners* (1940), *Indian Captive* (1941), *Bayou Suzette* (1943), *Judy's Journey* (1947), *Prairie School* (1951), *San Francisco Boy* (1955), *Policeman Small* (1962), and *Deer Valley Girl* (1968).

Lois Lenski was born in Springfield, Ohio. She attended Ohio State University and the Westminster School of Art in London.   GEORGE E. BUTLER

LENT is a religious season observed in the spring by Christian churches. It begins on Ash Wednesday, 40 days before Easter, excluding Sundays, and ends on Easter Sunday. The term *Lent* comes from the Old English word *lencten*, which meant springtime. The word used in church liturgy is *Quadragesima*. Lent is part of the regular church year in the Eastern Orthodox, Lutheran, and Roman Catholic churches, and churches that belong to the Anglican Communion. Many other churches hold religious services, meetings, or preaching missions to honor the Lenten season. Some churches prescribe a special book of devotions for Lent. In the Roman Catholic Church, each day of Lent has its special mass.

Many Christians observe Lent by fasting, performing penance, giving alms, abstaining from amusements, or not solemnizing marriages. The season originated as one of spiritual preparation for Easter in remembrance of the suffering, death, and Resurrection of Jesus Christ. It also symbolized the mourning of the Church, the bride, for the departure of Christ, the bridegroom. The length of time for observing Lent varied through the ages. For many years, it was considered a 36-day period of fast. By the reign of Charlemagne, about A.D. 800, four days were added, making it 40. This may have been done as a reminder of the 40 days that Jesus Christ fasted in the wilderness.   BERNARD RAMM

See also ASH WEDNESDAY; EASTER; PALM SUNDAY.

LENT, BLAIR (1930-   ), an American book illustrator, won the 1973 Caldecott Medal for his illustrations for *The Funny Little Woman*. This story is an adaptation by Arlene Mosel of a Japanese folk tale written by Lafcadio Hearn, an American author.

Lent was born in Boston and studied art at the Boston Museum School. His illustrations for three books were runners-up for the Caldecott Medal. These books were *The Wave* (1964), *Why the Sun and the Moon Live in the Sky* (1968), and *The Angry Moon* (1970).   ZENA SUTHERLAND

LENTICEL, *LEHN tuh SEHL,* is a round or long swelling on the bark of woody stems and roots that functions as a breathing pore. Lenticels are formed when growth areas

develop beneath the *cork* (outer layers of the bark). Each growth area produces a mass of new growing cells. As these cells enlarge, they press against and finally break the outer layer of the bark to form a lenticel. The cells of the lenticel are separated by spaces through which air reaches the inner parts of the stem. The rounded marks on horse chestnut stems and the long marks on cherry bark are lenticels.   JAMES D. MAUSETH

See also BARK.

LENTIL, *LEHN tuhl,* is an ancient food plant. It belongs to the leguminous family of plants, and grows in Egypt, southern Europe, the United States, and western Asia. Its long fruits, or pods, look like those of the pea and bean. The seeds of the lentil are the part used as food. They are red-brown, gray, or black, and never grow more than $\frac{1}{2}$ inch (13 millimeters) in diameter. The seeds are shaped like a lens. The lens itself was so named because it looked like a lentil seed.

Lentil seeds have a distinct flavor, and are among the most nutritious legumes. They are rich in protein and carbohydrates and are usually used to make casseroles, salads, and soups. As a table food, lentil seeds are not as common in the United States as they are in many other parts of the world.

The lentil plant grows best in light, dry soil. Plants grown in too rich a soil do not bear many pods. The plant can be used as fodder for sheep, horses, and cattle. The lentil, one of the earliest cultivated food plants, was first grown about 2200 B.C. According to Genesis 25:34, Esau sold his birthright for a "pottage of lentils."

The New York Botanical Garden

The Lentil is a food plant that grows in Egypt, the United States, western Asia, and southern Europe. The plant was first grown about 2200 B.C.

Scientific Classification. The lentil belongs to the pea family, *Leguminosae.* This plant is classified as genus *Lens,* species *L. culinaris.*   S. H. WITTWER

LENZ'S LAW, *LEHN zuhz,* is a principle of physics important in the design of electric generators. It was developed by Heinrich F. E. Lenz, a German-born scientist who was working in Russia. Lenz's law says that in an electric generator, the current produced creates a magnetic field that opposes the action of the force that produces the current. In other words, work must be done to generate electricity. Powerful turbines are needed to run generators that supply large amounts of current. According to Lenz's law, the magnetic field can be used as a "brake" to slow down the electric generating mechanism.   IRA M. FREEMAN

See also ELECTRIC GENERATOR (Electromagnetism).

LEO

LEO is the name of 13 popes of the Roman Catholic Church. Five of the popes were *canonized* (made saints) in the church. Leo XIII was an especially important pope. Their reigns were:

Leo I, Saint	(440-461)	Leo VIII	(963-965)
Leo II, Saint	(682-683)	Leo IX, Saint	(1049-1054)
Leo III, Saint	(795-816)	Leo X	(1513-1521)
Leo IV, Saint	(847-855)	Leo XI	(1605)
Leo V	(903)	Leo XII	(1823-1829)
Leo VI	(928)	Leo XIII	(1878-1903)
Leo VII	(936-939)		

Saint Leo I (? -461), one of two popes commonly given the title *The Great*, brought the qualities of energy, perseverance, and human understanding to the papal office. Conscious of his rights as pope, he successfully enforced his authority in both the West and the East. In the western provinces, Leo regulated discipline and attacked heresy. He persuaded Attila the Hun to spare Italy in 452. Three years later, Leo persuaded the Vandal leader Genseric (Gaiseric) not to subject Rome to fire and slaughter (see ATTILA).

Leo's greatest triumph was over the Eastern bishops. When he sent a formal statement of the church's teaching to settle authoritatively an Eastern theological dispute, the Eastern bishops accepted it with the famous statement: "Peter has spoken through Leo."

Saint Leo III (? -816) crowned Charlemagne Emperor of the Romans in 800. This appointment cemented a close relationship between the church and the state. Charlemagne guaranteed the pope's temporal authority in the Papal States, and the pope gave his blessing to Charlemagne's imperial rule (see CHARLEMAGNE).

Leo X (1475-1521) helped Rome become the center of the artistic and literary world. He was an ardent scholar and patron of the arts. Through his efforts, scholars obtained high positions in the papal court.

Leo encouraged the preaching of indulgences in Germany to raise money for the rebuilding of Saint Peter's Church. The preaching of indulgences helped cause Martin Luther's break from the Roman Catholic Church and the beginning of the Reformation. Up to the time of his death in 1521, Leo never took the movement started by Luther seriously (see LUTHER, MARTIN).

Leo was born in Florence, Italy, the son of Lorenzo the Magnificent of the Medici family (see MEDICI).

Leo XIII (1810-1903) enjoyed one of the longest reigns in papal history. He is best known for his *encyclicals* (papal letters to bishops) on social and religious subjects. His most famous encyclical, *Rerum Novarum*, is often called "the Magna Carta of labor" because it upheld the rights of the working classes.

Leo, a brilliant diplomat, helped make the Roman Catholic Church acceptable to the non-Catholic world. His diplomatic successes included mediating a dispute between Spain and Germany over the Caroline Islands and directing French Catholics to support loyally their republican government.

Born Gioacchino Vincenzo Raffaello Luigi Pecci, in Carpineto, he studied in Viterbo and in Rome. He was ordained a priest in 1837, and served for over 20 years as archbishop of Perugia. He became a cardinal in 1853.   THOMAS P. NEILL and FULTON J. SHEEN

See also POPE (picture: Leo XIII).

LEO, a constellation. See ASTRONOMY (map: The Stars and Constellations of the Northern Hemisphere).

LEO is the fifth sign of the zodiac. It is symbolized by a lion. Astrologers believe that Leo is ruled by the sun. Leo is a fire sign.

Astrologers regard people born under the sign of Leo, from July 23 to August 22, as energetic, generous, and strong-willed. Both the lion and the sun are traditionally linked with kings, and Leos have kingly characteristics. They are good leaders and enjoy being

Leo—The Lion

Birth dates: July 23–August 22.
Group: Fire.
Characteristics: Cheerful, colorful, generous, kind, powerful, proud.

Symbol

Signs of the Zodiac

Aries
Mar. 21–Apr. 19
Taurus
Apr. 20–May 20
Gemini
May 21–June 20
Cancer
June 21–July 22
Leo
July 23–Aug. 22
Virgo
Aug. 23–Sept. 22
Libra
Sept. 23–Oct. 22
Scorpio
Oct. 23–Nov. 21
Sagittarius
Nov. 22–Dec. 21
Capricorn
Dec. 22–Jan. 19
Aquarius
Jan. 20–Feb. 18
Pisces
Feb. 19–Mar. 20

WORLD BOOK illustration by Robert Keys

the center of attention and importance. However, Leos can sometimes be too proud.

Leos like colorful, showy things. They are attracted to occupations in such fields as the jewelry business and the theater.   CHRISTOPHER MCINTOSH

See also ASTROLOGY; HOROSCOPE; ZODIAC.

LEÓN (pop. 83,693) is the chief intellectual center and an important farm produce market in Nicaragua. It lies in a farming district in western Nicaragua, about 50 miles (80 kilometers) northwest of Managua. For location, see NICARAGUA (color map).

León is the home of the National University of Nicaragua, as well as a national institute and two religious colleges. The city's many fine buildings include the largest cathedral in Central America.

Spanish explorers founded León in 1525 on the shores of Lake Managua. It was moved to its present location in 1610 after the old town was destroyed by an earthquake. León served as the provincial capital of Nicaragua for many years, and then as the capital of the republic until 1855.   ROLLIN S. ATWOOD

LEÓN, LUIS. See SPANISH LITERATURE (The Golden Age [Poetry]).

LEÓN, PONCE DE. See PONCE DE LEÓN, JUAN.

LEONARD, BENNY. See BOXING (table: Lightweights; picture).

LEONARDO DA VINCI. See DA VINCI, LEONARDO.

LEONCAVALLO, *lay ohn kah VAHL loh,* **RUGGIERO** (1858-1919), was an Italian opera composer. He is best known for his two-act *Pagliacci* (1892). This opera is a violent tragedy about a group of traveling players in Italy. It is an example of a melodramatic form of realism called *verismo*. Leoncavallo was inspired to write the opera by the success of Pietro Mascagni's one-act verismo opera, *Cavalleria Rusticana* (1890). The two works are usually performed together.

Leoncavallo was born in Naples, and studied music there. He met Richard Wagner in 1876, and decided to imitate the German composer by becoming an opera composer and writing his own texts. Leoncavallo wrote many operas, but none of his other works matched the success of *Pagliacci*.   Miloš Velimirović

See also OPERA (Verismo Opera; The Opera Repertoire [*Pagliacci*, I]).

LEONE, *lee OH nay*, **GIOVANNI** (1908-   ), served as president of Italy from 1971 to 1978. He had been elected to the office by Parliament after bitter disagreement among Italy's various political parties. He succeeded Giuseppe Saragat. Leone, a Christian Democrat, had served as premier in 1963 and from 1968 to 1969.

Leone was born in Pomigliano d'Arco, near Naples, and received a law degree from the University of Naples in 1929. He joined the Christian Democratic Party in 1944. In 1946, Leone took part in writing a new constitution for Italy. He won election to the Chamber of Deputies in 1948 and became deputy speaker of the Chamber in 1950. Leone served as speaker of the Chamber from 1955 to 1963. He ran for president in 1964 but lost. In 1967, Saragat appointed Leone to the Senate for life.   Norman Kogan

LEONIDAS I, *lee AHN ih duhs* (? -480 b.c.), was a king of ancient Sparta. Little is known about his life, but his heroic death at Thermopylae is one of the most famous episodes in history (see THERMOPYLAE).

Leonidas became king of Sparta about 488 b.c. The Persian king, Xerxes, invaded Greece in 480 b.c., with a large army. Leonidas, with an army of about 6,000 Greeks, tried to stop the Persians at Thermopylae, a narrow pass between mountains and sea. The Greeks held the pass for two days. Then the Persians found a new path over the mountains and threatened the Greeks from the rear. Leonidas sent most of the Greeks to safety in southern Greece, and tried to hold off the Persians with about 300 Spartans and 1,100 other Greeks. Leonidas and most of these soldiers were killed. Thomas W. Africa

LEONIDS are meteors that seem to come from the constellation Leo. The *meteoroids* (chunks of matter in space) that cause the Leonids travel around the sun in an orbit that brings them near the earth about November 17 each year. They become visible when they enter the earth's atmosphere. Heavy meteor showers occurred in 1799, 1833, 1866, and 1966, when the earth passed through the thickest part of the meteoroid swarm. In most years, few Leonids are seen.   Joseph Ashbrook

LEONTIEF, *lyih AWNT' yuhf*, **WASSILY** (1906-   ), an American economist, won the 1973 Nobel prize in economics for the development of *input-output analysis*. Input-output analysis is a method used to forecast the effect of a change in one segment of a nation's economy on another.

Leontief developed a table that breaks the economy down into various groups of industries. The table shows each industry's total *output* (production) and the amount of its *inputs*, such as fuel, labor, machinery, and raw materials. The output of one industry may be an input of another. For example, a decrease in production by the steel industry could result in a shortage of raw materials in the automobile industry. Economists in many countries use input-output analysis to recommend national policy (see INPUT-OUTPUT ANALYSIS).

Leontief was born in Saint Petersburg (now Leningrad), Russia. He received a Ph.D. degree from the University of Berlin in 1928. Leontief taught at Harvard University from 1931 to 1975, when he joined the faculty of New York University. He became a United States citizen in 1939.   William H. Miernyk

LEOPARD, *LEHP uhrd*, is a large member of the cat family. It is the third largest cat of the Eastern Hem-

Giuseppe Mazza

The Powerful and Graceful Leopard lives both on the ground and in trees. On the ground, this skillful hunter blends in with the surroundings, *left*, as it stalks its prey. After making a kill, a leopard may drag the animal up a tree, *right*, and store the prey there until it is hungry.

isphere. Only the lion and tiger are larger. Leopards live in Africa as far north as the Sahara, and in Asia from Israel to Korea, Malaysia, and Java.

Leopards are graceful, alert, and cunning. They average 2 feet 4 inches (71 centimeters) high at the shoulder and 7 feet 6 inches (2.3 meters) long. But a big male may measure almost 9 feet (2.7 meters) from nose to tail and weigh from 100 to 160 pounds (45 to 73 kilograms). A big female may weight about 75 pounds (34 kilograms). Leopards bear two, three, or four young in a litter.

The usual coat of leopards is light tan, with many black spots close together. The tail has dark rings around it. All leopards are much alike, but those that live in forests are darker than those that live on open plains and desert scrub. The black leopard is so dark that the spots are hard to see. The whole animal looks black. Albinos are much rarer than the black variety, which is found in Malaysia and in southwestern China.

These fierce animals eat meat and hunt their prey. They feed on such animals as monkeys, antelope, muntjacs, jackals, peacocks, snakes, sheep, goats, and dogs. In Africa, they even kill the big porcupines that have quills 1 foot (30 centimeters) or more in length.

Leopards seldom attack human beings. But once they discover that people are easy victims, they may become more dangerous than tigers or lions. Leopards are good climbers and spend part of their time in trees. They are unbelievably strong. Carcasses of prey weighing 80 to 150 pounds (36 to 68 kilograms) have been found in trees 12 to 20 feet (4 to 6 meters) above the ground where a leopard had carried them.

The handsome markings of the leopard make its fur valuable for coats. So many leopards have been killed for their fur that the animals have become rare in many places, and several subspecies face possible extinction. For this reason, the United States government forbids the importation of leopard skins for coats.

Scientific Classification. The leopard belongs to the cat family, *Felidae*. It is classified as genus *Panthera*, species *P. pardus*. ERNEST S. BOOTH

See also CAT; FUR (Trapping); SNOW LEOPARD.

LEOPARD CAT. See OCELOT.

LEOPARD FROG. See FROG (Kinds of Frogs; picture).

LEOPARD SEAL. See ANTARCTICA (Seals).

LEOPARDI, *lay oh PAHR dee*, **GIACOMO** (1798-1837), was an Italian lyric poet. He was sickly and physically deformed, and felt lonely and unloved despite the brilliance of his career. His poems are sensitive expressions of the despair he found in living. However, the hopeless tone in his poetry is always softened by hope in the future and an underlying love of life.

Leopardi's verse collections include *Idyls* (1825) and *Songs* (1836). His other important work is *Le operette morali* (*Moral Essays*, 1824-1832). In this series of essays, he reinterpreted historical figures and ancient myths and legends to show their timeless meaning.

Leopardi was born in Recanati. By the age of 16, he had mastered several languages and was writing scholarly essays as well as poetry. SERGIO PACIFICI

See also ITALIAN LITERATURE (In the 1800's).

LEOPOLD is the name of three kings of Belgium.

Leopold I (1790-1865), son of Francis, Duke of Saxe-Coburg, was elected by the Belgians as their king in 1831. He was the uncle of Queen Victoria of Great Britain, and became noted as a wise statesman. He was born in Coburg, Germany.

Leopold II (1835-1909) was the son of Leopold I. He became particularly interested in the exploration and colonization of Africa. He founded the Congo Free State, which he gave to Belgium in 1908. He was born in Brussels.

Leopold III (1901-1983), the grandnephew of Leopold II, became king in 1934 after the death of his father, King Albert. He was very popular at first. But he lost much of this popularity in 1940 when he surrendered his army to the Germans after a gallant resistance. Instead of escaping to England, he remained a prisoner in Belgium. When the war ended, many Belgians refused to have him as their ruler. After some trouble, Leopold agreed to withdraw in favor of his son. He formally abdicated in 1951, and his eldest son, Baudouin, became king. Leopold was born in Brussels. JANE K. MILLER

See also BAUDOUIN.

LEOPOLD, ALDO (1886-1948), an American naturalist, won international fame as an authority on wildlife conservation. He pioneered in applying the principles of ecology to wildlife management. Leopold, an enthusiastic outdoorsman, believed that people should enjoy wilderness areas as places for recreation. But he declared that the wild characteristics of such areas should be preserved as much as possible.

Leopold wrote a number of books and articles about conservation. His textbook *Game Management* (1933) is considered a classic. *A Sand County Almanac* (1949) and *Round River* (1953) include many of Leopold's philosophic essays on conservation. These essays stress the need for wilderness areas.

Leopold was born in Burlington, Iowa. He graduated from Yale University in 1908 and earned a Master of Forestry degree there the next year. Leopold worked for the U.S. Forest Service from 1909 to 1927. In 1933, he accepted a professorship at the University of Wisconsin. Leopold remained on the faculty there until his death in 1948. LORUS J. MILNE and MARGERY MILNE

LÉOPOLDVILLE. See KINSHASA.

LEPANTO, BATTLE OF. See NAVY (Famous Sea Battles); TURKEY (The Start of the Ottoman Decline); CERVANTES, MIGUEL DE.

LEPCHAS. See SIKKIM (People).

LEPIDOLITE. See MICA.

LEPIDOPTERA, *LEHP ih DAHP tuh ruh*, is a large order of insects that includes the butterflies and moths. The name comes from Greek words for *scale* and *wing*. The wings of these insects are covered with tiny scales or flat hairs. The mouth parts form a long tube called a *proboscis*, which is used for sucking. See also BUTTERFLY; INSECT (table); LEAF MINER; METAMORPHOSIS; MOTH (with its list of Related Articles).

LEPIDUS, MARCUS AEMILIUS. See ANTONY, MARK; AUGUSTUS; TRIUMVIRATE.

LEPRECHAUN. See FAIRY.

LEPROSY, or HANSEN'S DISEASE, attacks the skin and nerves and causes the skin to swell and become lumpy and discolored. Leprosy is one of the most feared diseases because it damages the patient's appearance. But leprosy seldom causes death. It may weaken victims, however, and make them more likely to contract other diseases. Leprosy usually affects the *peripheral* (end) nerves near the surface of the face, arms, and legs. Nerve damage causes a loss of feeling in the skin. Leprosy patients may injure or burn themselves without realizing it. Severe nerve damage may cause paralysis.

The Cause of leprosy is a *bacillus* (rod-shaped bacterium) about $\frac{1}{4,000}$ inch (0.0064 millimeter) long. The germ's scientific name is *Mycobacterium leprae*. It is also called *Hansen's bacillus*, because it was discovered by Norwegian physician G. Armauer Hansen in 1874. Scientists believe the germ escapes from infected persons in discharges from nose and skin sores. It is possible that the germs enter the bodies of healthy persons through small breaks or cuts in the skin.

Leprosy is contagious, but the danger of catching it from another person has been greatly exaggerated. Relatively few persons exposed to the disease develop it. To get leprosy, a person must have low resistance and live in contact with a person whose body contains large numbers of the germ. Leprosy develops in only about 5 per cent of those persons married to leprosy patients. It is rare among doctors and nurses who care for leprosy patients. Scientists believe children are more likely to get leprosy than adults. A mild form of leprosy may develop in about 30 per cent of the children whose parents have severe leprosy. However, the disease of leprosy persists in only about 6 per cent of these children.

Types of Leprosy. There are two main kinds of leprosy. They are *tuberculoid* and *lepromatous*.

Tuberculoid Leprosy produces *macules* (patchy spots) on the body of the patient. Few bacilli grow in the patient's body, but they cause inflamed nerves. Patients with tuberculoid leprosy seldom spread the disease to other persons.

Lepromatous Leprosy causes a general thickening of the skin over most of the body, especially on the face and ear lobes. Facial lines deepen and the eyebrows fall out. *Nodules* (lumps) may appear in the skin. When germs enter the eyes they cause a painful inflammation called *iritis*. In severe cases, these germs may cause blindness. In late stages of the disease, nerve damage becomes as severe as in tuberculoid leprosy. Lepromatous leprosy spreads much more easily than tuberculoid leprosy, because many bacilli are present in the skin and nose.

Treatment and Control. Many persons fail to realize that leprosy is often a mild disease that may be *arrested* (stopped) without treatment. Skin discolorations may disappear or leave only faint traces. If the disease is not checked, however, severe nerve damage can cause muscles in the hands and feet to become weak. As a result, the fingers and toes may curl inward. Early treatment of leprosy is important in preventing deformities and other physical handicaps. Proper treatment can help handicapped persons lead an almost normal life. Bone and tendon surgery often helps to restore the use of disabled hands and feet. Such a treatment as simple massage may prevent deformities.

Since 1941, the most widely used drug to treat leprosy has been *DDS* (di-amino-diphenyl sulfone). It causes improvement in most patients within a year. During the early 1980's, however, DDS proved ineffective in a growing number of cases. For this reason, physicians began using combinations of DDS and the drugs *rifampin* or *clofazamine*.

Leprosy becomes inactive in most patients who undergo treatment for from three to five years or more. But the cure is not always permanent. To prevent the disease from returning, patients must consult their doctors at least twice a year and continue taking drugs. These persons can be safely employed without fear of their passing the disease on to others.

In regions where leprosy is common, the best control measure is to find persons with the disease and treat them promptly. At one time, most victims were isolated in special hospitals called *leprosariums*. But experience has shown that persons with leprosy will hide their symptoms if the official policy is to isolate patients.

Today, leprosariums serve mainly as research centers. Most leprosy victims are now treated as hospital outpatients. Outpatient clinics also examine persons who associate closely with leprosy patients.

History. Leprosy is an ancient disease. Historians believe it existed in China, Egypt, and India over 2,500 years ago. As used in the Bible, the word *leprosy* may refer to a number of different skin diseases.

Roman soldiers may have brought leprosy to Greece from Egypt, and to Italy from eastern Asia Minor. The disease spread through Europe from A.D. 400 to 1400. It began to decline in most parts of Europe during the

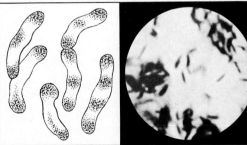

WORLD BOOK photo by W. R. Wilson

The Germ That Causes Leprosy is *Mycobacterium leprae,* a sausage-shaped bacterium. The drawing, *above left,* shows its shape. The bacteria are shown in microscopic view, *above right.*

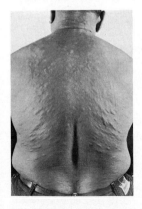 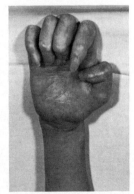

WORLD BOOK photos by W. R. Wilson

The Symptoms of Leprosy depend on the type of attack. Lepromatous leprosy causes lumps on the skin, *above left.* Tuberculoid leprosy often causes "claw hands," *above right.* Victims cannot use their fingers in a coordinated manner because the muscles have wasted away.

1500's. But cases were still reported in Norway and in northern Europe as late as the 1900's.

Some historians believe slaves from Africa brought leprosy to North and South America. People from China spread leprosy throughout the Pacific area during the early 1800's.

Leprosy occurs chiefly among people living in warm climates. But some countries with mild climates, such as Japan and South Korea, have many cases of leprosy. Even Iceland had some leprosy patients until recent years.

Estimates on the total number of leprosy cases in the world range from 10 million to 15 million. The majority of these cases are found in Africa, India, South America, and Southeast Asia. There are about 4,000 cases in the United States, but about three-fourths of these patients were born in other countries where they may have contracted the disease. In the United States, the disease occurs chiefly in California, Florida, Louisiana, and Texas. JOHN H. HANKS

See also DAMIEN DE VEUSTER, JOSEPH; SCHWEITZER, ALBERT.

LEPTON, *LEHP tahn,* is one of the three major families of elementary particles. The other families are *quarks* and *bosons.* Most physicists believe leptons are fundamental units of matter—that is, the particles do not consist of smaller units.

Physicists have identified six types of leptons—*electrons, muons, taus,* and three kinds of *neutrinos.* Electrons, muons, and taus have a negative electric charge. Muons and taus have a much larger mass than that of electrons. A muon is 207 times as heavy as an electron, and a tau is 3,490 times as heavy. No difference has been found between muons and electrons other than their mass. Although scientists have not yet determined the precise properties of the tau, which was discovered in 1975, they believe it also differs from an electron only in mass.

The three kinds of neutrinos have no electric charge. They are called *electron-, mu-,* and *tau-neutrinos* because each is associated with one type of charged lepton. Their mass has so far proved too small to measure.

All leptons have antimatter counterparts called *antileptons.* Antileptons have the same mass as leptons, but all other properties are reversed. Because neutrinos have no charge, their antiparticles also are neutral.

Muons and taus are unstable particles, and so they *decay* (break down) into lighter particles. A muon decays into an electron, a mu-neutrino, and an electron-antineutrino in about 2 millionths of a second. The lifetime of a tau is less than 2 trillionths of a second. A tau, because of its large mass, can decay into several different combinations of lighter particles. ROBERT H. MARCH

See also ANTIMATTER; NEUTRINO.

LESAGE, *luh SAZH,* **ALAIN RENÉ,** *a LAN ruh NAY* (1668-1747), was a French novelist and dramatist. He first practiced law, but left this career to become a writer. He was among the first to earn his living by writing. Lesage's most famous work, the novel *Gil Blas* (1715-1735), is a witty satire set in Spain. The story is told in the first person by Gil Blas, who learns to his sorrow that life can be harsh when one has to make one's own way without help. His innocence and vanity make him an easy victim. Lesage was born in Sarzeau, France.

LESLIE, FRANK (1821-1880), was a publisher of periodicals. His most popular publication was *Frank Leslie's Illustrated Newspaper,* later *Leslie's Weekly,* which was issued from 1855 to 1922. His paper was a forerunner of today's picture magazines. It grew out of his work as a wood engraver. Leslie was born Henry Carter in Ipswich, England. But he signed his engravings Frank Leslie, and adopted that name. Leslie came to New York City in 1848. JOHN ELDRIDGE DREWRY

LESOTHO, *luh SOH toh,* is a rugged, mountainous country surrounded by the Republic of South Africa. It lies about 200 miles (320 kilometers) inland from the South African coastline on the Indian Ocean. Lesotho is about the same size as the state of Maryland.

Lesotho is called the *Switzerland of Southern Africa* because of its beautiful mountain scenery. But it is a poor country. It has no manufacturing industries and no minerals, except for a few diamond deposits. Many young people of Lesotho go to South Africa to find jobs.

Lesotho was formerly the British colony of Basutoland. It became independent in 1966 as the KINGDOM OF LESOTHO. Maseru, which has a population of about 45,000, is the capital of Lesotho and its largest town (see MASERU).

Government. The king, who is also Paramount Chief of Lesotho, has some limited powers. But the government is actually directed by a military council and a cabinet made up of military and civilian members. See the *History* section of this article for details on the country's political process since independence.

Lesotho

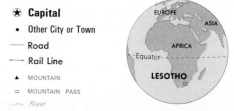

★ **Capital**
• Other City or Town
— Road
←— Rail Line
▲ MOUNTAIN
= MOUNTAIN PASS
River

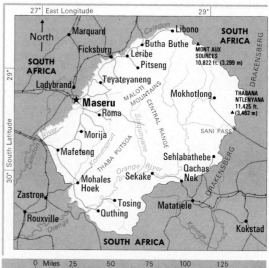

WORLD BOOK map

Capital: Maseru.

Official Languages: English and Sesotho.

Official Name: Kingdom of Lesotho.

Area: 11,720 sq. mi. (30,355 km²).

Population: *Estimated 1987 Population*—1,600,000; distribution, 94 per cent rural, 6 per cent urban; density, 137 persons per sq. mi. (53 per km²). *1976 Census*—1,216,815. *Estimated 1992 Population*—1,823,000.

Chief Products: *Agriculture*—beans, corn, hides and skins, livestock, millet, mohair, oats, peas, wheat, wool.

Flag: The flag has narrow vertical stripes of green and red near the hoist. A white straw hat lies on a blue field in the center. The colors are those of the Lesotho National Party; the hat is common Lesotho dress. See FLAG (color picture: Flags of Africa).

Money: *Basic Unit*—loti.

National Anthem: "Lesotho Fatse La Bo-Ntata Rona" ("Lesotho Our Fatherland").

People. Most of Lesotho's 1,600,000 people are black Africans called *Basotho* or *Basuto*. They are strong, independent people who raise livestock and food crops. The wealth of a family is usually measured by the number of cattle it owns, and cattle are often used instead of money. In the courts, many offenders pay their fines in cattle. When a man marries, he usually gives his bride's family at least 15 head of cattle.

Most Basotho live in villages of fewer than 250 people. Family groups build their huts around a cattle *kraal* (pen) with open space separating each group. The huts have mud or sod walls with thatched roofs. The Basotho often paint designs in gay colors on the doors and walls of their huts. Each village has a *khotla* (meeting place) where men discuss village business.

The Basotho raise crops on the land surrounding the villages. All land is owned in common by all the people, and local chiefs assign the land to the people.

The women do most of the heavy work on the farms and in the homes. They hoe and weed the land, harvest the crops, and build the houses. The men plow the land and look after the sheep, cattle, and goats. From the time they are 5 or 6 years old, boys herd livestock. On farms in the western plains, they return home with their herds every night. In the eastern highland areas, boys often spend months away from home, moving about with their flocks and herds in search of pasture.

Corn, millet, milk, and vegetables are the chief foods of the people. The women brew millet beer. The Basotho once wore clothes made from animal skins. Most of them now wear Western clothes, but they often wrap themselves in multi-colored blankets to keep warm.

English and Sesotho, a Bantu language, are the country's two official languages. The traditional religions of the people are based on ancestor worship (see ANCESTOR WORSHIP). But over half of Lesotho's people now are Christians.

Lesotho has a better developed educational system than most African countries. About 75 per cent of the children attend elementary school, and about 70 per cent of the people can read and write. About two-thirds of all schoolchildren are girls, because many boys spend their youth herding livestock. Missionaries run most of the schools. Lesotho's university is in Roma.

Land. Most of Lesotho is mountainous. The Drakensberg, a mountain range, rises to over 11,000 feet (3,350 meters) above sea level in the east. The Maloti Mountains, a part of the Drakensberg, cover much of central Lesotho. The only plains lie in the west. The Orange River, longest river in southern Africa, rises in northeastern Lesotho (see ORANGE RIVER).

Most of Lesotho has a mild, moist climate, because most of the country lies more than 5,000 feet (1,500 meters) above sea level. The rainfall varies from year to year and place to place. Annual rainfall averages 28 inches (71 centimeters) and most of it falls between October and April. Temperatures in the western plains range from 90° F. (32° C) in summer to 20° F. (−7° C) in winter. In the highlands, temperatures often fall below freezing in the winter.

Economy. The most important industry is raising livestock. Exports include wool, mohair, hides and skins, and cattle. Most Basotho raise crops such as corn and millet to feed their families. Some raise beans, peas, and

Lesotho's Capital, Maseru, lies near the northwestern border of the country. The national coat of arms is displayed on a pole, *upper right corner,* on the main street of the city. Only about 6 per cent of Lesotho's people live in cities.

LESOTHO

wheat for export. Most of Lesotho's trade is with South Africa. The best farming land lies in the western plains, where about two-thirds of the people live. Over-cultivation and over-grazing have damaged Lesotho's soil.

There are few jobs in Lesotho. At any one time, about half of all the men are working under 6- or 9-month contracts in the mines and industries of South Africa. These workers receive part of their pay while they are in South Africa and the balance in Lesotho when their contract ends. Many Basotho send money home to their families, and the money Basotho men earn in South Africa is important to the economy of Lesotho.

Most of the country's 1,200 miles (1,930 kilometers) of roads lie in the western plains. In the highland areas, the Basotho travel on hardy ponies and horses along winding trails.

History. Tribal wars swept over southern Africa in the late 1700's and early 1800's. Tribes were almost completely wiped out and their homes were destroyed. Some of the victims of this fighting fled into the highlands of Lesotho. There they were given protection by an African chief named Moshesh. He built a stronghold on a hill called *Thaba Bosiu* (Mountain of Night), about 15 miles (24 kilometers) from where Maseru now stands. By 1824, Moshesh had about 21,000 followers. He united them into the Basotho nation.

Later, British and Boer settlers tried unsuccessfully to defeat the Basotho (see BOERS). From 1856 to 1868, the Basotho were at war with Boer settlers. In 1868, Moshesh asked Britain for protection, and he and his people became British subjects. Moshesh died in 1870, and in 1871 the territory was placed under the rule of the British Cape Colony, which is now part of South Africa.

The government of the British Cape Colony tried to disarm the Basotho, but the Basotho fought off the Cape's soldiers. In 1884, Basutoland was reestablished as a British colony.

In 1910, the Basutoland Council was established. It consisted of chiefs and elected members. The council was the national legislative council until the country became independent. District councils, set up in 1943, administer local government.

The constitution, drawn up in 1960 and revised in 1964, was a major step toward self-government. The first general election under this constitution was held in 1965. The Basutoland National Party (BNP) won 31 of the then 60 seats in the National Assembly, and Chief Leabua Jonathan, the BNP leader, became prime minister. Paramount Chief Motlotlehi Moshoeshoe II, great-grandson of Moshesh, became king.

During a general election in 1970, early vote returns showed that the BNP would not keep its majority in the National Assembly. Chief Jonathan then suspended the constitution and elections. He continued to rule Lesotho as prime minister. In 1973, a temporary National Assembly was formed to serve as a legislature until a new election was held. But in 1984, Chief Jonathan dissolved the temporary National Assembly, and no election was held. In 1986, military leaders overthrew Chief Jonathan and took control of the government.

Critically reviewed by LORD RADCLIFFE-MAUD

LESPEDEZA, *LEHS puh DEE zuh,* is the name of a group of herbs and shrublike plants. It grows in Asia, Australia, and North America. Lespedeza shrubs are called *bush clover.* The leaves have smooth edges and three leaflets. The plant's small pea-shaped flowers grow in clusters. The fruit is a short pod with one seed. A lespedeza called *Japan clover* has been grown chiefly in the

Wide World

A Small Lesotho Village nestles under a rocky cliff near the capital, Maseru. Most of the people of Lesotho live in small villages like this. Their houses have mud or sod walls and thatched roofs.

M. S. Offutt, University of Arkansas
Lespedeza Is Any of a Group of Shrublike Plants.

southern United States as forage and as a fertilizer.

Scientific Classification. Lespedeza belongs to the pea family, Leguminosae. Japan clover is genus *Lespedeza*, species *L. striata.*   WAYNE W. HUFFINE

LESSEPS, FERDINAND MARIE DE. See DE LESSEPS, FERDINAND MARIE.

LESSING, DORIS (1919-   ), is an English writer noted mainly for her novels. Her fiction shows a deep concern for moral, political, and psychological attitudes and for woman's role in modern society. Most of her works emphasize the complexity of life and deal with humanity's struggle to understand the world.

Lessing was born in Kermanshah, Persia (now Kermanshah, Iran) and grew up in southern Rhodesia. She moved to England in 1949. While in Africa, she experienced many personal problems that she later described in her works. Her first highly praised novel, *The Grass Is Singing* (1950), and her series of semiautobiographical novels, *The Children of Violence* (1952-1969), describe the difficulties of white women living in Africa.

Lessing repeated many of the themes of her previous works in her novel *The Golden Notebook* (1962). This book describes the anxiety and confusion that a woman encounters in the modern world. In *The Summer Before the Dark* (1973), Lessing explored the subject of middle age. She has written a series of philosophical science fiction novels called *Canopus in Argos: Archives*. The series began with *Shikasta* (1979). She has also written many plays, poems, and short stories.   THOMAS A. ERHARD

LESSING, GOTTHOLD EPHRAIM, *GOHT hohlt AY frah ihm* (1729-1781), was a German playwright, critic, and philosopher. He is often considered the father of modern German literature. Lessing helped free German writing from neoclassical French influences. He turned the attention of German writers to English literature, especially the works of Shakespeare. Lessing introduced English middle-class tragedy into Germany with his dramas *Miss Sara Sampson* (1755) and *Emilia Galotti* (1772). His play *Minna von Barnhelm* (1767) is one of the greatest German comedies. It was the first German play with a German background of that time. Its sentimental but realistic style influenced German popular theater throughout the 1800's.

While serving as a theater critic in Hamburg, Lessing wrote *The Hamburg Dramaturgy* (1767-1769). The work began as reviews of performances. It later became a series of essays in which Lessing discussed the drama of his time in relation to Aristotle's principles for tragedy. In his essay *Laokoön* (1766), Lessing discussed the relationship between poetry and painting. The essay is basic to classical German ideas of beauty.

Lessing's last works dealt with religious tolerance. He pleaded for tolerance in his drama *Nathan the Wise*

(1779) and his essay *The Education of the Human Race* (1780). Lessing was born in Saxony.   CORA LEE NOLLENDORFS

See also GERMAN LITERATURE (The Enlightenment).

LE SUEUR, *luh SOOR*, **PIERRE** (1657?-1705?), a French explorer and trader, helped open up the upper Mississippi River Valley. He came to Canada about 1679 and became an Indian trader. He persuaded the Sioux and Chippewa tribes to keep peace, and in 1695 took chiefs from these tribes to Montreal on a peace mission. During this period, he built Fort Le Sueur in what is now Minnesota. Later, he explored the Mississippi. He built Fort l'Huillier in 1700. Le Sueur was born in Artois, France.   THOMAS D. CLARK

LETHBRIDGE, Alberta (pop. 54,072), is an industrial and distributing center for grain, livestock, coal, lumber, and natural gas in southern Alberta. It lies on the Oldman River, about 145 miles (233 kilometers) southeast of Calgary (see ALBERTA [political map]).

Lethbridge has a brewery, stockyards, and factories that make food products, housing units, metal products, mobile homes, and recreational vehicles.

The city began as a coal-mining village in 1870, and was once known as Coalbanks. It was incorporated as a town in 1891, and became a city in 1906. Lethbridge has a council-manager government.   W. D. McDOUGALL

LETHBRIDGE, UNIVERSITY OF, is a coeducational provincially funded university in Lethbridge, Alta. It offers courses leading to degrees in arts and science, education, fine arts, management arts, and music. It grants bachelor's degrees and a professional diploma in education. The school was founded in 1967. For enrollment, see CANADA (table: Universities and Colleges).

Critically reviewed by the UNIVERSITY OF LETHBRIDGE

LETHE, *LEE thee*, was one of the five rivers of the Lower World, or Hades, in Greek and Roman mythology. In Greek legend, a drink of its waters made people forget everything that had happened before. The spirits of the dead drank from it before they entered Hades and so forgot their worries on earth. The spirits that left Hades to live again in the Upper World drank so they would not remember their joys in the Lower World. A branch of Lethe flowed by the cave of Hypnos, god of sleep. *Lethe* comes from a Greek word that means *forgetfulness*. See also HADES.   PADRAIC COLUM

LETO. See ARTEMIS; NIOBE.

LETTER. See ALPHABET; LETTER WRITING.

LETTER OF CREDIT is issued by a bank, permitting an individual or a business firm to draw up to a stated amount of money on that bank. A letter of credit often is used by companies to finance the movement of goods between countries. It is also used by travelers.

A person or business firm may obtain a letter of credit by depositing funds with a bank. The bank issues the letter, which states the terms under which money can be withdrawn. The letter holder can obtain money by presenting the letter to another bank and making out a *draft* (order to pay). The letter may be addressed to one bank, or it may be a *circular* letter, which is good almost anywhere in the world. If the bank is in another country, the holder receives the money in the currency of that country. Any money not withdrawn is refunded to the depositor.   JAMES B. LUDTKE

See also TRAVELER'S CHECK.

LETTER WRITING

WORLD BOOK photo

Exchanging Letters is one of the oldest forms of long-distance communication between people. This girl writes to her grandfather to share news of the family.

LETTER WRITING is a way of communicating a message in written words. People write letters for both business and personal reasons. Business letters are generally more formal than personal letters. Business letters include those used to apply for jobs, complaint letters, sales letters, and collection letters. Personal letters include correspondence between family members or friends, invitations, and thank-you notes.

Studies show that people who write well are more likely to have successful careers. Skill in writing business and personal letters can make a difference in your life. For example, a well-written letter applying for a job may lead to a fine position. A good personal letter can help build or keep a valuable friendship.

Characteristics of a Good Letter

A well-written letter should be clear, accurate, complete, concise, and courteous. The first step in preparing a good letter is deciding what to say. Make a brief list of the ideas you want to cover, and then plan the arrangement of these ideas. Next, decide how best to put your thoughts into words. It may help to write a rough copy of your letter simply to get the words on paper. Finally, go back and fix the sentence structure, grammar, and wording. Use simple, direct statements rather than long, involved sentences. Make each phrase easy for the reader to understand.

Be sure every statement in the letter is accurate. Business firms write letters every day just to clear up mistakes they made in previous letters. These follow-up letters would not be necessary if writers would take the time to give the facts correctly in their first letters.

Think carefully about your reader's familiarity with your topic. Have you included everything the reader needs to know? Forgetting even one necessary item can create confusion. If the letter discusses an appointment, be sure you mention the location, date, and time.

Say what you have to say and then stop. Too often,

letters become cluttered with wordy phrases, stuffy expressions, and unnecessary details that dilute your message. Use plain, natural language and get to the point.

The tone of the letter is as important as its language. In general, make the tone friendly and polite. Stress points that will interest the reader.

The Parts of a Letter

A letter has six standard parts. They are (1) the heading, (2) the inside address, (3) the salutation, (4) the body, (5) the complimentary close, and (6) the signature.

The Heading in a business letter includes the writer's address and the date. It is located on the top of the page, and it usually has three lines. The first line gives the writer's street address, and the second gives the city, state, and ZIP Code. The third tells the date the letter was written. Most of the heading may be omitted in a personal letter, but always include the date.

Business firms have printed or engraved letterheads that provide their name, address, and telephone number. Some also add the name or title of the writer, or the writer's department or section.

The Inside Address shows the name and address of the *recipient*—that is, the person or firm to whom the letter is written. In many business letters, the inside

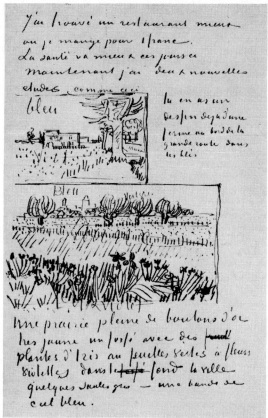

Courtesy New York Graphic Society

Vincent van Gogh Wrote to his brother Theo, including sketches as parts of many letters. "Just now I have done two new studies like these: you have a drawing of one of them already." He marked blue, green, yellow, and violet on them.

address can be written in three lines. The name of the recipient appears on the first line; the street address on the second; and the city, state, and ZIP Code on the third. The inside address of a letter directed to an individual in an office should include the person's business title and the name of the firm. Most names and titles should be written out in full. However, some abbreviations of titles are commonly used, especially *Dr.*, *Mr.*, *Mrs.*, and *Ms.* See ADDRESS, FORMS OF.

The first line of the inside address should be placed at least two lines lower than the date. An inside address should appear in all business letters, but it is optional in personal letters.

The Salutation is also called the greeting. It should begin two lines below the last line of the inside address. In business letters, the most common salutation combines a title and the person's last name, such as *Dear Ms. Dobson* or *Dear Dr. Davis*. Use *Dear Sir or Madam* when the recipient's name is unknown or when writing to a company. Call friends by their first name or a nickname, such as *Dear David* or *Dear Cindy*. Use a colon after the salutation in a business letter, but use a comma in a personal letter.

The Body contains the writer's actual message. In a typewritten letter, the body should begin two lines below the salutation. All paragraphs within the body should be separated by a space of one extra line.

The Complimentary Close. Just as the salutation greets the reader at the beginning of a letter, the complimentary close says good-bye at the end. These two parts of the letter should be consistent in their degree of formality.

In a letter that opens with *Dear Mr. Caldwell* or *Dear Sir or Madam*, the complimentary close could be *Sincerely*, *Sincerely yours*, or *Very truly yours*. For an informal closing, *Cordially* or *Best regards* is appropriate. If the salutation is *Dear Bill*, proper closings include *Sincerely*, *Cordially*, and *With warmest regards*. The complimentary close should end with a comma. The close should be placed two lines below the body of the letter.

The Signature is the writer's name. It should be handwritten in ink below the complimentary close. In typewritten letters, the writer's name should be typed four or five lines below the complimentary close, with the handwritten signature placed between the closing and the typewritten signature. The writer may add his or her title in parentheses to the left of the typewritten name, as in *(Dr.) Jackson Baty* or *(Ms.) Leigh Rigby*. The abbreviation *Ms.* has now largely replaced *Miss* or *Mrs.* Many women prefer this title because it does not reveal their marital status. However, a married woman might add her married name in parentheses beneath her legal name, as in *Annie Peters* with *(Mrs. Kevin Peters)* written beneath it. In some companies, the writer's business title or department is placed on the line beneath the typed signature. The company's name may also be included with the signature, though most firms omit it.

The Form

The form of a letter depends on the way the six parts of the letter are arranged on the page. The most common forms are *full block* and *semiblock*. Each may be used for both business and personal letters.

The Full Block Form is the most commonly used form, probably because it is the easiest and quickest to type. All parts of a letter in the full block form begin at the left margin. New paragraphs are not indented. An extra line of space separates the paragraphs.

The Semiblock Form is less formal than the full block form. The heading is placed in the upper right-hand corner. Both the complimentary close and the typed signature line up vertically with the heading. All other parts of the letter begin at the left margin. New paragraphs are not indented. Like the full block form, the semiblock form separates the paragraphs with an extra line of space.

The Envelope Address usually is the same as the inside address of the letter. It is most commonly centered

Parts of a Letter

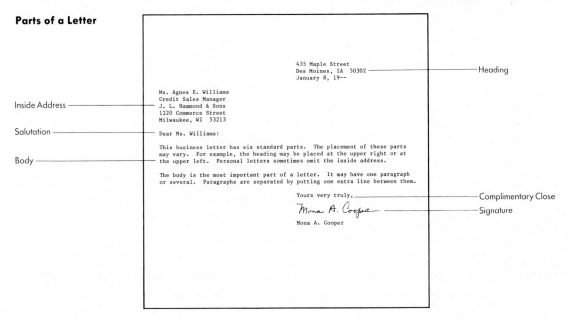

LETTER WRITING

on the envelope. The address should be at least three lines long. Use the capitalized, two-letter post office abbreviation for the state or province. For a list of state abbreviations, see POST OFFICE (table: Postal Service Abbreviations). The writer's return address goes in the upper left-hand corner of the envelope. Always single-space addresses.

Business Letters

There are many kinds of business letters. However, the same principles of good writing apply to each kind. This section describes the following typical business letters: (1) letters of application, (2) complaint letters, (3) sales letters, and (4) collection letters. This section also offers several suggestions that are helpful in most business letters.

Letters of Application are written by people seeking a job. This type of letter normally consists of two parts,

the *cover letter* and the *résumé*. A cover letter introduces the applicant to the employer. It accompanies a résumé, which is a biographical summary listing the applicant's education and work experience. For more information about résumés, see CAREERS (Writing a Résumé).

The first paragraph of the cover letter tells what job the writer is applying for and how the applicant found out about the position. In the next one or two paragraphs, the writer should briefly emphasize the parts of his or her background that relate most closely to the job. United States law prohibits employers from asking applicants their sex, race, religion, nationality, or marital status. Thus, including such information is optional. A cover letter should be no more than three or four paragraphs long. In the final paragraph, the applicant should politely ask the employer to reply and to schedule a job interview.

A letter of application can also combine the information that appears in a cover letter and résumé. It is usually two or three pages long. Like a cover letter, it

Full Block Form

Semiblock Form

An Envelope Address should be at least three lines long, *left,* but it may be longer, *right.* It usually is the same as the inside address of the letter. Addresses should always be single-spaced.

A Cover Letter and a Résumé make up a typical job application. The cover letter, *left,* introduces the applicant to the employer. The résumé, *right,* describes the applicant's background.

should say what job the writer is applying for and point out parts of the applicant's education and experience that best fit the requirements of the job. Most employers prefer a résumé with a cover letter rather than a combined letter of application because the résumé and cover letter are more concise and easier to read.

After a job interview, applicants should send a *follow-up letter,* which is a short letter thanking the employer for the interview. This letter should be written and sent to the employer within two days of the interview. A follow-up letter shows the applicant's continued interest in the job.

Complaint Letters are written to call attention to a problem and to persuade the reader to take corrective action. Although it is proper to express disappointment or dissatisfaction, such strong emotions as anger and sarcasm are appropriate only as a last resort after several letters. The tone of the letter may be cool and firm, but it should also be courteous. State the complaint clearly at the beginning of the letter. Include everything the reader needs to know to take action, such as account numbers, relevant dates, and photocopies of bills or canceled checks. Make a specific request for action, and politely ask for a reply telling exactly what will be done and when.

The reply to a complaint letter should also be courteous. It should open with a polite acknowledgment of the complaint letter. If the complaint is justified, apologize for the problem and explain what action will be taken to correct it. If the complaint is not justified, tactfully explain why the requested action will not be taken. The reply should always end with a positive statement about future dealings and a friendly close.

A Follow-Up Letter should be sent within two days after a job interview. This short letter thanks the employer for the interview and expresses continued interest in the job.

LETTER WRITING

Sales Letters are intended to convince the reader to buy something. Firms sometimes send sales letters in series. They begin with an *opening* letter, then send several follow-up letters.

Whatever the purpose of the series, all good sales letters include certain elements. The opening paragraph must get the reader's attention and arouse interest. It may do this by asking a challenging question or by presenting a startling statement of fact. The following paragraphs should describe the article or service for sale, and how it would benefit the reader. The letter also should give the reader information about the quality and reliability of the product or service. The last paragraph of the letter should be especially persuasive and should ask for a specific response from the reader.

Collection Letters. No business can succeed unless it receives payment for the goods and services it sells. Firms write collection letters to get money from customers who have fallen behind in paying their bills. A collection letter should be designed to get the money as quickly as possible, without offending the customer. It should be courteous and understanding in tone, yet specific in its request for payment. It should mention the exact amount of the bill and the length of time that payment has been past due.

Some companies send collection letters, like sales letters, in series. They usually make the first letter mild in tone. It simply reminds the customer of the past-due account and asks for cooperation in paying it. Each succeeding letter becomes firmer in tone. The company may point out that paying this bill will help maintain the customer's sound credit standing. The company may finally demand the payment and spell out actions to be taken if the account is not settled, such as turning it over to a collection agency or to a lawyer.

Improving Your Letters. It is usually best to deal with only one subject in a business letter. This makes it easier for the reader to file the letter after responding to it. If you need to discuss two or more subjects with the same person, consider writing more than one letter.

When writing to business people, you may want to use a *reference headline*. A reference headline consists of the abbreviation *Re* and a short phrase describing the topic of the letter. Place it at the beginning of the letter just beneath the inside address and before the salutation. By opening with such words as "Re: a design flaw in your new product," you are helping the reader understand your topic at first glance.

Consider putting topic labels, called *headlines*, on different sections or paragraphs of a letter to help clarify for the reader the points you wish to make. For example, copies of your letter may be going to two or more readers who have different levels of familiarity with your subject. In this case, you may want to put a section labeled "Background" towards the end of your letter. People who need this extra information can skim to the back, while those more familiar with the subject will find important facts such as "Results of a Survey" in a section at the start of the letter.

Personal Letters

People generally use a more casual tone and style in personal letters than in business letters. As a result, there

```
                                          1226 Sierra Drive
                                          Chandler, AZ  85224
                                          June 5, 19--
Widget Toy Company
307 14th Street
New York, NY  10003

Dear Sir or Madam:

On May 7, I mailed your company an order for two Hyper-Space Blasters.  I
enclosed 50 cents cash plus four Sugar Sprocket candy wrappers.  When I
opened your package today, I discovered that you had sent me only one
Blaster.

Please send me another Hyper-Space Blaster as soon as possible.  I'll be
watching the mail every day.  Thank you.

                              Sincerely,

                              Ronnie Johnson

                              Ronnie Johnson
```

A Complaint Letter calls attention to a problem and requests corrective action. The letter should be firm but polite.

are fewer rules governing the form of personal letters than there are for business letters. However, some rules should be followed, especially in sending or receiving invitations. This section describes some of the guidelines for writing both formal and informal invitations, as well as thank-you notes and general personal correspondence.

Formal Invitations are written in the third person. For example, a wedding invitation might begin, "Mr. and Mrs. Howard Jones request your presence at the marriage of their daughter, Delia Pauline, to . . . ." Most formal invitations are either engraved or handwritten. Some business invitations are typed on executive letterheads.

The invitation should begin with the name of the person or people doing the inviting. Next comes the event. Identify what the event is—such as a dinner, wedding, or party—and its date, time, and location. The heading of a formal invitation should be placed below the body of the invitation. The date should appear on the first line and the address should appear on the second line. The date should be spelled out. No signature is used in a formal invitation.

The letters *R.S.V.P.* may appear on the invitation. The letters are an abbreviation for the French phrase *Répondez, s'il vous plaît*, which means *Please reply*. An invitation may also say *Please reply* or *The favor of a reply is requested* instead of R.S.V.P. Any request for a reply should appear in the lower left-hand corner of an invitation.

Informal Invitations are usually handwritten and friendlier in tone than formal invitations. The heading of an informal invitation remains at the top, with the date, unabbreviated, first and the writer's address next. A salutation comes next, ending with a comma. The body of an informal invitation contains the same kind of information that appears on a formal invitation. Some

> *Mr. and Mrs. James Clark request the pleasure of Miss Abbott's company at dinner on the evening of April fifth, at half-past seven o'clock.*
>
> *March twenty-eighth*
> *15 Astor Place*

Formal Invitation

> *Miss Abbott accepts with pleasure Mr. and Mrs. Clark's kind invitation for April fifth at half-past seven o'clock.*
>
> *March thirtieth*
> *157 St. James Street*

Acceptance

> *Miss Abbott regrets that absence from the city prevents her acceptance of the kind invitation of Mr. and Mrs. Clark for April fifth.*
>
> *Philadelphia, April second.*

Declining

writers list the location, date, and time above each other. For example:

Location: 23 Dumas Avenue
           Hampton, NH 03842
Date: June 29, 19--
Time: 6:00 p.m. to 10:00 p.m.
Telephone: (613)934-6089

The informal invitation concludes with a complimentary close and signature. An R.S.V.P. may appear in the lower left-hand corner.

> *35 South 33rd Street*
> *April the fourth*
>
> *Dear Mrs. James;*
> *Will you and Mr. James dine with us on Tuesday, the fifteenth of April, at eight o'clock?*
>
> *We shall be very glad if you are able to come.*
>
> *Very sincerely,*
> *Alice Jones*

Informal Invitation

Thank-You Notes are simply brief letters of thanks for a gift, a dinner, or some other kind of hospitality. Writing a thank-you note shows gratitude and good manners. Make the note sound as if you were talking to your host or hostess in person. Thank-you notes are usually handwritten on a card or personal stationery.

Other Personal Letters include pen pal letters and correspondence between family members or friends. These letters follow no particular rules. Their primary purpose is to share news and thoughts with other people.

Young people can make friends with others their age in another state, province, or country through pen pal letters. Many organizations and some magazines exist to provide names and addresses of people seeking pen pals. These people exchange letters, become friends, and eventually may meet in person. Girl Scout and Boy Scout groups have pen pal services, or your local library may be able to help. DEBORAH DUMAINE

Related Articles in WORLD BOOK include:

Address, Forms of	Post Office (table:
Careers (Writing a Résumé)	Postal Service
Etiquette	Abbreviations)
Grammar	Punctuation
Handwriting	Spelling

Outline

I. Characteristics of a Good Letter
II. The Parts of a Letter
    A. The Heading   D. The Body
    B. The Inside Address   E. The Complimentary Close
    C. The Salutation   F. The Signature
III. The Form
    A. The Full Block Form
    B. The Semiblock Form
    C. The Envelope Address
IV. Business Letters
    A. Letters of   C. Sales Letters
       Application   D. Collection Letters
    B. Complaint Letters   E. Improving Your Letters
V. Personal Letters
    A. Formal Invitations   C. Thank-You Notes
    B. Informal Invitations   D. Other Personal Letters

Questions

What are the characteristics of a good letter?

How should a salutation be punctuated in (1) a business letter? (2) a personal letter?

What are the six parts of a letter?

Where is the heading of a letter placed?

What does *R. S. V. P.* mean?

When are the following complimentary closes proper: (1) Very truly yours? (2) Cordially? (3) Sincerely yours?

How should the inside address of a business letter be arranged?

Why do people write complaint letters?

What purposes do sales letters serve?

How should writers organize a cover letter?

Additional Resources

DUMAINE, DEBORAH. *Write to the Top: Writing for Corporate Success*. Random House, 1983.

FREEMAN, JOANNA A. *Basic Technical and Business Writing*. Iowa State Univ. Press, 1979.

FRUEHLING, ROSEMARY T., and BOUCHARD, SHARON. *The Art of Writing Effective Letters*. McGraw, 1972.

VENOLIA, JAN. *Better Letters: A Handbook of Business and Personal Correspondence*. Rev. ed. Periwinkle Press, 1982.

LETTERS OF THE ALPHABET. See ALPHABET; and the separate articles on each letter.

LETTS. See LATVIA (The People).

Lettuce Harvesting, *left,* begins after the heads become firm. Workers cut the heads, *above,* and pack them in boxes. A truck takes the boxes to a cooling tunnel. There, the heads are cooled before being shipped to market in precooled vehicles.

LETTUCE is a popular vegetable used chiefly in salads. People usually eat it fresh and uncooked. Lettuce forms a part of many weight-control diets because it contains few calories and provides calcium, iron, and vitamin A. Most kinds of lettuce have large, green leaves and grow close to the ground on extremely short stems. Lettuce ranks as an important farm crop in many areas of the United States, and home gardeners raise several varieties of the plant. Lettuce farming probably began in Persia as early as 550 B.C.

Kinds of Lettuce. There are three main kinds of lettuce: (1) *head;* (2) *leaf;* and (3) *cos,* or *romaine.*

Head Lettuce has leaves that curl around the center of the plant, forming a ball-shaped head. *Crisp head lettuce,* or *iceberg lettuce,* has a tight head and brittle, juicy leaves. It is the major type of lettuce grown commercially in the United States. Widely grown varieties of crisp head lettuce include Great Lakes and Imperial. *Butterhead lettuce* has a looser, more open head and soft, oily leaves. Butterhead spoils easily, and so it is not so popular as crisp head. Varieties of butterhead lettuce include Bibb and Boston.

Leaf Lettuce forms dense, leafy clumps instead of heads. Gardeners grow more of it than of any other kind. Most leaf lettuce has light green leaves, but a few red varieties have been developed. The waxy, crinkled leaves vary in shape among various types of leaf lettuce. Popular varieties include Black-Seeded Simpson and Grand Rapids.

Cos, or Romaine, Lettuce grows long and upright and its leaves curl inward. The leaves are tender and can be easily damaged in shipment. For this reason, cos is the least widely grown kind of lettuce.

Other Kinds of Lettuce include *celtuce* and *wild lettuce.* Celtuce looks and tastes like a combination of celery and lettuce. Wild lettuce, from which all present-day varieties of the plant were developed, grows in mild climates throughout the world.

Growing Lettuce. Most kinds of commercial lettuce grow well in temperatures between 70° F. (21° C) and 75° F. (24° C). Some varieties that were developed for gardeners thrive at just below 80° F. (27° C). In the Northeastern United States, commercial growers plant lettuce in spring for harvest during the summer. Growers in the Southern and Southwestern states plant in fall or winter for harvest during the spring.

California leads the United States in lettuce production, with about 70 per cent of the country's commercial crop. Crisp head lettuce grows nearly the year around in the cool Salinas Valley of California. The other top lettuce-growing states are, in order of importance, Arizona, Florida, Colorado, and New York.

Planting and Cultivating. Most commercial lettuce growers plant their crop directly in the field. Some growers in the Northeastern United States plant seedlings that have been raised in greenhouses. Many gardeners also plant seedlings. In some areas, winter lettuce crops may be grown entirely in greenhouses.

Weeding and fertilizing should take place at or just below the surface of the ground, or the plant's shallow root system may be injured. Lettuce requires a steady supply of water and fertilizer.

Harvesting. Workers harvest lettuce by cutting off the heads just above the soil. Then they remove any dead or damaged leaves. Head and cos lettuce are harvested when the leaves are firmest, about 60 to 120 days after seeding, depending on the variety. Leaf lettuce can be harvested whenever the leaves reach the desired size.

Packing and Shipping. Lettuce spoils quickly and must be packed, cooled, and shipped immediately after being cut. On most commercial lettuce farms, workers pack and cool the lettuce in the field. They pack the lettuce in cardboard cartons and put the cartons into a special refrigerated truck. In this truck, the temperature of the lettuce drops to just above freezing. On some farms, the lettuce is packed between layers of crushed

Leading Lettuce-Growing States

Lettuce grown each year

California	2,223,000 short tons (2,017,000 metric tons)
Arizona	613,000 short tons (556,000 metric tons)
Florida	115,000 short tons (104,000 metric tons)
Colorado	38,300 short tons (34,700 metric tons)
New York	38,000 short tons (34,000 metric tons)

Figures are for 1985. Source: *Vegetables*, Dec. 30, 1985, U.S. Department of Agriculture.

Kinds of Lettuce

Crisp lettuce is the basic ingredient of most salads. Many people also use lettuce in sandwiches. The various kinds of lettuce differ in shape, taste, and texture. Several of the most popular kinds are pictured below.

Boston Lettuce is a butter-head variety that forms loose, partially folded heads.

Iceberg Lettuce, a type of crisp head lettuce, can be bought throughout the year.

Romaine Lettuce. Leaves of romaine curl inside one another, forming long rolls.

Leaf Lettuce. Home gardeners find this type of lettuce the easiest kind to grow.

Bibb Lettuce has dark green leaves that grow in small, loose clusters.

The Kroger Co.

Celtuce Lettuce. This leafy vegetable combines the flavors of celery and lettuce.

ice in wooden crates. The cartons or crates are then put into refrigerated trucks or railroad cars for shipment to market.

Diseases and Insect Pests. The chief diseases of lettuce include *bottom rot, downy mildew,* and *lettuce drop.* Crop rotation and chemical treatment of the soil help prevent these diseases. Another disease, *tipburn,* may be caused by too much heat or humidity. Scientists have developed types of lettuce that resist tipburn. These types include Minetto and Fulton. Such insect pests as aphids, cabbage loopers, and cutworms destroy lettuce leaves and stems, but most of these pests can be controlled with insecticides.

Scientific Classification. Lettuce belongs to the composite family, *Compositae.* It is genus *Lactuca,* species *L. sativa.* Head lettuce is *L. sativa,* variety *capitata.* Leaf lettuce is variety *crispa,* and cos lettuce is variety *longifolia.* H. T. ERICKSON

LEU, *LEH oo,* is a standard coin of Romania. The plural is *lei.* The coin is made of nickel-clad steel. It was formerly a silver coin. The leu equals 100 bani. For the price of the leu, see MONEY (table: Exchange Rates).

LEUCIPPUS. See MATERIALISM.

LEUCOCYTE. See BLOOD (White Blood Cells).

LEUCOCYTOSIS, *LOO koh sy TOH sihs,* is an increase in the number of *leucocytes* (white blood cells). This condition normally occurs during digestion and in pregnancy. It may also occur because of inflammation or fevers.

LEUCTRA, BATTLE OF. See THEBES.

LEUKEMIA, *loo KEE mee uh,* is a kind of cancer in which certain of the *leucocytes* (white blood cells) grow in an uncontrolled manner. The white cells defend the body against germs, viruses, and foreign materials of all kinds (see BLOOD [White Blood Cells]).

The uncontrolled growth of the white blood cells harms the body in many ways. Useless white cells flood the tissues and blood. The *bone marrow* (center part of the bones) loses its ability to produce red blood cells and blood production is affected. This leads to *anemia* (see ANEMIA). People with leukemia may have an enlarged spleen and enlarged *lymph* (body fluid) glands. They also may bleed easily.

There are at least three kinds of white blood cells in the body: granulocytes, lymphocytes, and monocytes. Leukemia may affect any of the three kinds. Doctors classify leukemia according to the type of white blood cell affected. All kinds of leukemia can be either *acute* or *chronic.* Without treatment, acute leukemia progresses rapidly and the patient may die within a few months. Chronic leukemia develops more slowly and may continue for years.

Scientists do not know the exact cause of leukemia in human beings. They believe that certain chemicals, large doses of radiation, and genetic disorders may contribute to the development of the disease. Viruses can cause leukemia in laboratory animals, and many researchers suspect that leukemia in humans may also be due to a virus. However, medical research has not yet demonstrated that a virus causes the disease in people.

Modern treatment using chemicals, blood transfusions, and radiation therapy can relieve the symptoms of leukemia and, in some instances, may even cure the

A Mural by Emanuel Leutze in the United States Capitol honors the pioneers who settled the Far West during the 1800's. The painter called the mural *Westward the Course of Empire Takes Its Way.*

disease. In many cases, however, the abnormal growth of white blood cells returns after treatment and causes the death of the patient. JOSEPH V. SIMONE

See also CANCER.

Additional Resources

GLUCKSBERG, HAROLD, and SINGER, J. W. *Cancer Care: A Personal Guide.* Rev. ed. Scribner, 1982. Main groups of cancers, including the leukemias, are reviewed.

MARGOLIES, CYNTHIA P., and McCREDIE, K. B. *Understanding Leukemia.* Scribner, 1983.

TUCKER, JONATHAN B. *Ellie: A Child's Fight Against Leukemia.* CBS Publishing, 1982.

LEUTZE, *LOYT suh,* **EMANUEL GOTTLIEB** (1816-1868), gained fame as a painter of American historical subjects. His best-known painting is *Washington Crossing the Delaware* (1851). He painted his masterpiece in Germany, using the Rhine as a model for the Delaware. This painting is reproduced in the WASHINGTON, GEORGE article. In 1860, Congress commissioned him to paint a mural for the U. S. Capitol, *Westward the Course of Empire Takes Its Way.* Leutze was born at Gmünd, Germany, and studied art in Philadelphia and Düsseldorf, Germany. In 1859, he settled in New York City. SARAH BURNS

LEV, *lehf,* is the gold monetary unit of Bulgaria. For the price of a lev, see MONEY (table: Exchange Rates).

LEVANT, *luh VANT,* is the land at the eastern end of the Mediterranean Sea. It includes the coast region and islands of Asia Minor and Syria. The Levant is sometimes considered as extending east to the Euphrates River and through the Nile Valley, and including Greece and Egypt. The name *Levant* is a French word that means *rising,* and which originally meant *the place where the sun rises. Levant morocco* is a fine quality of leather that is made from the skins of goats raised throughout the Levant. SYDNEY N. FISHER

LEVASSOR, ÉMILE. See AUTOMOBILE (The Gasoline Car; picture).

LEVEE, *LEHV ee,* is a wide wall built along the banks of rivers to keep them from flooding over the land. Levees are made mostly of sandbags and banked-up earth. The name comes from the French word *lever,* which means *to raise.* In the United States, the term is used especially to describe walls, or dikes, built along the southern part of the Mississippi River. Irrigation engineers use the term *levee* to describe a small dike or ridge of earth which confines areas of land that are to be flooded for agricultural purposes.

The first Mississippi River levee was only 3 feet (91 centimeters) high. It was built at New Orleans in 1718 to keep the river from flooding a strip of fertile land. Gradually a few more levees were built. Many years later the seven states that lie south of where the Mississippi meets the Ohio asked the federal government for help to check floods. In 1882, the year of a great Mississippi flood, the government set aside $1,300,000 for the improvement of the river. Part of the money was to be used for making levees. Since then the federal and state governments have spent millions of dollars for the building and repairing of levees.

The earth embankments on the Mississippi are 15 to 30 feet (4.6 to 9.1 meters) high. They are 8 feet (2.4 meters) wide on top and over 100 feet (30 meters) wide at the base. More than 2,000 miles (3,200 kilometers) of levees have been built along the Mississippi, but they still do not fully control the overflow. The completed

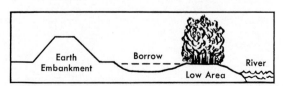

Levees Help Control Floodwaters. Earth embankments, *above,* rise above ground level to keep river water from flooding the surrounding land.

program will have an additional 2,500 miles (4,020 kilometers) of levees. About 1,500 miles (2,410 kilometers) of the total planned length of the levees have been built since 1905. Some authorities object to the building of levees that enclose a river so much that the water is high above the surrounding countryside. This makes floods even more dangerous when they occur. If a levee were to break under these circumstances, a wall of water would rush across the countryside, smashing everything in its way. Experts who oppose high levees believe regulating floods by headwater control is better than attempting to regulate them with levees.   T. W. MERMEL

See also FLOOD; JETTY; MISSISSIPPI RIVER.

LEVEL is an instrument used by carpenters, plumbers, and other construction workers to determine if a surface is perfectly horizontal. Most levels consist of a small, arched glass tube set in a bar of wood or metal. The tube is marked at its center, which is its highest point. It contains alcohol or another liquid and a bubble of air. When a level is placed lengthwise on a perfectly horizontal surface, the bubble rests at the center of the tube. If the surface being checked is tilted, the bubble rises to the high end of the tube. Some levels have additional tubes that are set at right angles to the length of the tool. These tubes enable workers to tell if a surface is *plumb* (vertical).

Levels generally derive their names from their use. For example, *mason's levels* are used by masons in building walls of brick or stone. These levels measure 4 feet (1.2 meters) long and are the longest levels. A *carpenter's level* is similar to a mason's level, but is commonly about 2 feet (60 centimeters) long. *Line levels*, sometimes called *string levels*, are hung along a tight line or string. Builders use them in laying foundations and in performing other work that involves leveling long spans. Line levels,

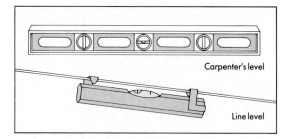

Carpenter's level

Line level

Kinds of Levels include the *carpenter's level,* which checks horizontal or vertical surfaces, and the *line level,* which is hung along a tight string for leveling long spans.

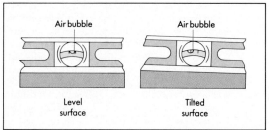

Air bubble

Air bubble

Level surface

Tilted surface

WORLD BOOK illustrations by Zorica Dabich

How a Level Works is shown above. If the surface is level, the air bubble comes to rest at the center of the tube. If the surface is tilted, the bubble is off center.

which are about 3 inches (8 centimeters) long, are the shortest levels. An *engineer's level*, also called a *surveyor's level*, is attached to a telescope and mounted on a *tripod* (three-legged stand). It provides engineers and surveyors with a perfectly horizontal line of sight.   ALVA H. JARED

LEVELLERS were political radicals in England during the mid-1600's who believed that all persons deserved a voice in government. They declared that "The poorest that lives hath as true a right to give a vote as well as the richest and greatest." They voiced many democratic ideas that developed in England and America during the 1700's and 1800's.

The Levellers had strong support among small farmers, artisans, and craftworkers, and they threatened the political power of the aristocratic landowners. Many soldiers who fought in the parliamentary army during the English Civil War in the 1640's were Levellers. But the Levellers found the new parliamentary government almost as aristocratic as the monarchy it had replaced. Leveller influence declined after an army mutiny was crushed in 1649.   LACEY BALDWIN SMITH

LEVER, *LEHV uhr* or *LEE vuhr*, is one of the six simple machines for performing work. It consists of a rod or plank that is free at both ends, and some steady object on which the plank can rest. The braced, or fixed, part is called the *fulcrum.* The distance from the load to the fulcrum is the *load arm.* The distance between the fulcrum and the lifting force is the *effort arm.* A lever helps lift weights with less effort. Prying something loose with a crowbar or a board is using a lever.

Classes of Levers

First-Class Levers have the fulcrum placed between the load and the effort, as in the seesaw, crowbar, and balance scale. If the two arms of the lever are of equal length, the effort must be equal to the load. To lift 10 pounds, an effort of 10 pounds must be used. If the effort arm is longer than the load arm, as in the crowbar, the effort travels farther than the load and is less than the load. A pair of scissors is a *double lever* of the first class.

Second-Class Levers have the load between the effort and the fulcrum. A wheelbarrow is a second-class lever. The wheel is the fulcrum, the handles take the effort, and the load is placed between them. The effort always travels a greater distance and is less than the load. A nutcracker is a double lever of this class.

Third-Class Levers have the effort placed between the load and the fulcrum. The effort always travels a shorter distance and must be greater than the load. The forearm is a third-class lever. The hand holding the weight is lifted by the biceps muscle of the upper arm which is attached to the forearm near the elbow. The elbow joint is the fulcrum.

Compound Levers combine two or more levers, usually to decrease the effort. By applying the principle of the compound lever, a person could use the weight of one hand to balance a load weighing a ton.

Law of Equilibrium

A lever is in equilibrium when the effort and the load balance each other. The law of equilibrium is:

The effort multiplied by the length of the effort arm equals the load multiplied by the length of the load arm.

Classes of Levers

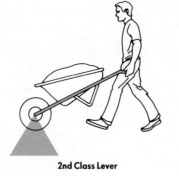
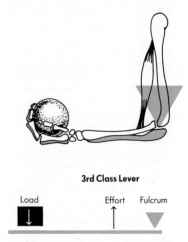

1st Class Lever	2nd Class Lever	3rd Class Lever
Effort — Load	Load — Effort	Load — Effort — Fulcrum
Fulcrum	Fulcrum	

WORLD BOOK illustrations by Bill and Judie Anderson

In a 1st Class Lever, the fulcrum is between the effort and the load.

In a 2nd Class Lever, the load is between the fulcrum and the effort.

In a 3rd Class Lever, the effort is between the load and the fulcrum.

For example, suppose you have a first-class lever with the load 1 foot from the fulcrum. If the effort is applied 2 feet from the fulcrum on the other side, an effort of 1 pound would balance a load of 2 pounds.

This law of equilibrium is true for all classes of levers. An effort multiplied by its lever arm is called the *moment of the effort*, or *torque* (see MOMENT). The law of levers may be stated simply by saying that the moments of all the efforts on one side of the fulcrum must equal the moments of all on the other side.

Let L be the load, E the effort, e the effort arm, and w the load arm. The law of equilibrium may be stated in the following mathematical formula: L is to e as E is to w, or $E \times e$ equals $L \times w$.

To see how the formula works, imagine two children sitting on a seesaw. One child weighs 40 kilograms and sits 1.5 meters from the fulcrum. Where must the other child sit to balance the seesaw if the other child weighs 30 kilograms? Let the first child equal the load, L, and the second child the effort, E.

$$30 \text{ kilograms} \times e = 40 \text{ kilograms} \times 1.5 \text{ meters}$$
$$e = \frac{60 \text{ kilogram-meters}}{30 \text{ kilograms}}$$
$$e = 2 \text{ meters}$$

Another example of a first-class lever is that of a person lifting a 300-pound stone with a 6-foot crowbar. The stone is 1 foot from the fulcrum. The person then pushes down on the crowbar 5 feet from the fulcrum. So, $E \times 5$ feet $= 300$ pounds $\times 1$ foot; or $E = 60$ pounds, the force needed to balance the stone.

The *mechanical advantage* of a lever tells how many pounds of load can be moved by each pound of effort. It can be calculated by dividing the load by the effort or the length of the effort arm by the length of the load arm. In the crowbar example above, the mechanical advantage is 5, that is, 300 pounds divided by 60 pounds, or 5 feet divided by 1 foot.   ROBERT F. PATON

See also ARCHIMEDES; TORQUE; WHEEL AND AXLE.

LEVERHULME, *LEE vuhr HYOOM,* **VISCOUNT** (1851-1925), founded Lever Bros., one of the world's largest soap manufacturers. He helped develop mass-produc-tion methods. He also developed plans for short hours, good wages, and profit-sharing by employees. Port Sunlight, his model factory town, encouraged town planning. Leverhulme was born William Hesketh Lever in Bolton, England. From 1906 to 1909, he served in Parliament. He received his title in 1922.   LOUIS FILLER

LÉVESQUE, *lay VEHK,* **RENÉ,** *reh NAY* (1922-   ), served as prime minister of the Canadian province of Quebec from 1976 to 1985. He was once a leader of the Quebec separatist movement, which aims to make Quebec an independent French-speaking nation. But in 1985, Lévesque's government made economic development, instead of separatism, its main goal for Quebec.

Lévesque was born in New Carlisle, Que. From 1956 to 1959, he hosted *"Point de Mire"* (Point of View), a public affairs television program. From 1960 to 1970, Lévesque served in Quebec's legislature and held several cabinet posts. He founded a separatist group in 1967 and merged with a similar group in 1968 to form the *Parti Québécois* (Quebec Party), a political party. At that time, Lévesque believed that only independence could give Quebec control of its economy and end what he considered job and wage discrimination against French-speaking Quebecers. English-speaking Canadians and Americans exercised great control over Quebec's economy, and nearly all the province's best-paying jobs required a knowledge of English.

In 1976, the Parti Québécois won control of Quebec's legislature. Lévesque became prime minister and announced that he would seek independence for the province. In 1980, however, the province's voters rejected a proposal that would have given Lévesque the authority to negotiate with the Canadian government for independence. Lévesque's emphasis on economic development in 1985 divided the Parti Québécois, and he resigned as party chief later that year.   LAURIER L. LAPIERRE

LEVI, *LEE vee,* **EDWARD HIRSCH** (1911-   ), served as attorney general of the United States from 1975 to 1977 under President Gerald R. Ford. One of Levi's chief goals in office was to restore public confidence in the Department of Justice. Trust in the department had

194

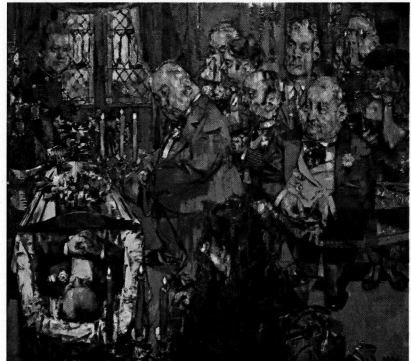

Jack Levine's *Gangster Funeral* shows the distorted forms and rich color typical of the artist's style. Levine has been compared to the French artist Honoré Daumier in the satirical treatment of his subjects.

Oil painting on canvas (1953); collection of the Whitney Museum of American Art, New York City

declined because of the Watergate scandal (see WATER-GATE). Another of Levi's main concerns as attorney general was enforcement of antitrust laws, which prohibit monopolies and conspiracies to curb competition. He was known as an expert on these laws.

During most of the period since 1936, Levi has served on the staff of the University of Chicago. He was a professor of law, dean of the law school, and provost of the university. From 1968 to 1975, he served as president of the university. He returned to the faculty in 1977 as a professor of law.

Levi was born in Chicago. He graduated from the University of Chicago in 1932 and earned a law degree there in 1935. In 1938, Levi received a doctor's degree in law from Yale University. From 1940 to 1945, he served as a special assistant to the United States attorney general. WILLIAM J. EATON

LÉVI-STRAUSS, *LAY vee strohs,* **CLAUDE** (1908-   ), a French anthropologist, developed *structuralism* in the study of human culture. Structuralism is a method of analysis that examines the structure of relationships between things, rather than simply the things themselves.

Lévi-Strauss derived the structural approach from *structural linguistics,* a science that studies languages through the structure of their sounds and words. He used structuralism to study family relationships, the myths of North and South American Indians, and even cooking methods.

According to Lévi-Strauss, myths throughout the world are transformations of one another. The myths of different cultures may appear to be different. But if the myths have the same structure, they may actually be saying the same thing.

Lévi-Strauss was born in Brussels, Belgium, and studied at the University of Paris. His books include *The Elementary Structures of Kinship* (1949), *The Savage Mind* (1962), and a four-volume study of myth, *Mythologiques* (1964-1971). IGOR KOPYTOFF

LEVIATHAN. See HOBBES, THOMAS.

LEVINE, *luh VEEN,* **JACK** (1915-   ), is an American artist who has won fame as a critic of life in the United States. Many of his paintings portray cruelty and political corruption. He has also painted realistic street scenes that show workers or the life of the poor. Levine has painted several works on Jewish themes.

Levine was born in Boston, Mass. In 1935, he joined the Federal Art Project, a government program under the Works Progress Administration. ALLEN S. WELLER

LEVINE, *leh VYN,* **JAMES** (1943-   ), is an American conductor and pianist. He became principal conductor of the Metropolitan Opera in New York City in 1973 and the company's music director in 1976. He was scheduled to become artistic director in 1986.

Levine was born in Cincinnati and began piano lessons at the age of 4. He made his debut as a soloist at the age of 10, performing with the Cincinnati Symphony Orchestra. From 1964 to 1970, he was apprentice conductor and then assistant conductor of the Cleveland Orchestra. Levine made his Metropolitan Opera debut in 1971. Since 1973, he has been music director of the sum-

Siegfried Lauterwasser, Metropolitan Opera
James Levine

mer Ravinia Festival near Chicago. He also conducts at the annual Bayreuth Festival in West Germany and the Salzburg Festival in Austria. Levine has been a guest conductor of the Berlin Philharmonic and the London Symphony Orchestra. LEONARD W. VAN CAMP

LEVITES, *LEE vyts,* were a tribe in ancient Israel. According to the Bible, all Levites were descendants of Jacob's son Levi. Each family of Levites had special duties in caring for the Tabernacle (see TABERNACLE). When Canaan was divided among the tribes, no section was given to the Levites. But they received 48 scattered towns and were supported by a tithe from the other tribes. WILLIAM WILSON SLOAN

LEVITICUS, *leh VIHT uh kuhs,* is the third book of the Bible. It is the only one made up entirely of religious and ethical laws. Its name comes from the tribe of *Levi,* from which the priests were descended. The book includes priestly regulations, and laws concerning marriage, sacrifices, and religious festivals. Chapter 11 gives the basic dietary laws that traditional Jews still observe (see KOSHER). Chapter 16 describes the ritual of *Yom Kippur* (the Day of Atonement).

Chapters 19 to 25 are often called the *Holiness Code.* They contain fundamental principles of human conduct, such as the command "thou shalt love thy neighbor as thyself" (19:18). The verse inscribed on the Liberty Bell in Philadelphia—"Proclaim liberty throughout all the land unto all the inhabitants thereof" —also comes from this section (25:10). ROBERT GORDIS

See also PENTATEUCH; YOM KIPPUR.

LEVITT, WILLIAM JAIRD (1907-), brought mass production to the housing industry and became the biggest builder of houses in the United States. Between 1946 and 1951, he changed 1,200 acres (486 hectares) of farmland at Levittown, Long Island, N.Y., into a community of 17,450 homes with a population of over 35,000. He also built a community at Levittown, Pa. Levitt was born in Brooklyn, N.Y. WILLIAM T. ARNETT

LEVITTOWN, N.Y. (pop. 57,045), is a community on Long Island. It developed from a housing project begun in 1946 for veterans of World War II. The firm of Levitt & Sons, Inc., began the housing project in an area that consisted of potato fields. Levittown grew from a population of about 450 in 1946 to 60,000 by the late 1950's. The homes were mass-produced and look very much alike except for their color.

Careful planning of the area has resulted in many advantages. Levittown has no slums or dangerous traffic intersections. It has central shopping districts and modern schools and recreation areas. For location, see NEW YORK (political map). WILLIAM E. YOUNG

See also LEVITT, WILLIAM JAIRD.

LEVULOSE. See FRUCTOSE.

LEWIN, KURT (1890-1947), became a leading child and social psychologist. He studied the effect of authoritarian and democratic behavior on groups, and the forces that change social groups. Lewin was a professor at Stanford, Cornell, and Iowa universities, and directed the Research Center for group dynamics at the Massachusetts Institute of Technology. Lewin was born in Mogilno, Germany (now in Poland). He came to the United States in 1932. CLAUDE A. EGGERTSEN

See also SENSITIVITY TRAINING.

LEWIS, ANDREW. See VIRGINIA (Westward Expansion).

LEWIS, C. S. (1898-1963), a British author, wrote more than 30 books, including children's stories, science fiction, and literary and religious works. Most of his writings teach moral lessons. After years of experiencing religious doubt, Lewis converted to Christianity in the 1930's. Lewis then became a leading defender of Christianity.

Lewis taught medieval literature at Oxford University from 1925 to 1954 and at Cambridge University from 1954 to 1963. In his first important work of literary criticism, *The Allegory of Love* (1936), Lewis examined the theme of love in medieval literature. His first science fiction novel, *Out of the Silent Planet* (1938), tells of three scientists who travel to Mars and find strange creatures living there.

Lewis' most popular religious work, *The Screwtape Letters* (1942), is a witty satire in which an old devil advises a young devil. His other books on religion include *The Problem of Pain* (1940), *The Abolition of Man* (1943), and *Mere Christianity* (1952).

Between 1950 and 1956, Lewis wrote a series of seven children's books called *The Chronicles of Narnia.* These books combine myth and fantasy with moral principles.

Clive Staples Lewis was born in Belfast, Northern Ireland. In an autobiography of his early life, *Surprised by Joy* (1955), Lewis discussed the development of his religious beliefs. THOMAS A. ERHARD

Additional Resources

GIBSON, EVAN K. *C. S. Lewis, Spinner of Tales: A Guide to His Fiction.* Eerdmans, 1980.
GILBERT, DOUGLAS, and KILBY, C. S. *C. S. Lewis: Images of His World.* Eerdmans, 1973.
GREEN, ROGER L., and HOOPER, W. C. *C. S. Lewis: A Biography.* Harcourt, 1974.
SMITH, ROBERT H. *Patches of Godlight: The Pattern of Thought of C. S. Lewis.* Univ. of Georgia Press, 1981.

LEWIS, FRANCIS (1713-1802), a New York signer of the Declaration of Independence, spent most of his fortune in support of the patriot cause during the American Revolutionary War. From 1775 to 1779, he served as a delegate to the Continental Congress. He distinguished himself by his committee work, especially on the problem of army supply. Lewis was born in Llandaff, Wales. He came to America in 1738, and became a wealthy merchant. CLARENCE L. VER STEEG

LEWIS, GILBERT NEWTON (1875-1946), an American chemist, helped develop the modern electron theory of valence, a theory that explains the forces that hold atoms together in molecules. In 1916, he proposed that a pair of electrons, held jointly by two atoms, constitutes a chemical bond. He further suggested that a shell of eight electrons arranged in pairs about the atom resulted in increased stability for the atom. These ideas were expanded into an electron theory by such chemists as Irving Langmuir and Linus Pauling.

Lewis was born in Weymouth, Mass., and received his doctor's degree from Harvard in 1899. In 1912, he became professor of chemistry and dean at the University of California. Here he introduced thermodynamics into the chemistry curriculum. HERBERT S. RHINESMITH

LEWIS, JOHN AARON (1920-), is an American composer and pianist who became successful in both classical music and jazz. As a composer, he pioneered in the development of *third stream music*, a blend of jazz and classical music. Lewis formed the Modern Jazz Quartet in 1952 and serves as its music director and pianist.

Lewis was born in La Grange, Ill., and studied anthropology and music at the University of New Mexico. He went to New York City in 1945 and worked in the big band of Dizzy Gillespie. During the 1950's and 1960's, Lewis composed music for a ballet, a Broadway play, and motion pictures. He occasionally led "Orchestra U.S.A.," a large group that gave concerts of jazz, classical, and third stream music.   LEONARD FEATHER

LEWIS, JOHN L. (1880-1969), was a powerful American labor leader. He became acting president of the United Mine Workers of America (UMW) in 1919. He was elected president in 1920 and held that post until he retired in 1960.

Lewis' career was marked by bitter strikes and sharp conflicts with union opponents. He challenged the craft organization of the American Federation of Labor (AFL) by forming the Committee for Industrial Organization (CIO) in 1935. Unions that joined the CIO were suspended by the AFL Executive Council in 1936 and ousted in 1938. In 1938, the CIO formed its own federation, and changed its name to the Congress of Industrial Organizations. Under Lewis' leadership, the CIO organized strong industrial unions in the mass-production industries.

Lewis took the UMW out of the CIO in 1942. The UMW rejoined the AFL in 1946, but it has been an unaffiliated union since 1947. Lewis' last great achievement for the UMW was the adoption of

United Press Int.
John L. Lewis

the union's health and retirement programs. John Llewellyn Lewis was born in Lucas, Iowa.   JACK BARBASH

Additional Resources

ALINSKY, SAUL D. *John L. Lewis: An Unauthorized Biography*. Random House, 1970. Reprint of 1949 edition. A favorable account.

DUBOFSKY, MELVYN, and VAN TINE, WARREN. *John L. Lewis: A Biography*. Harper, 1983. Reprint of 1977 edition.

WECHSLER, JAMES A. *Labor Baron: A Portrait of John L. Lewis*. Greenwood, 1972. Reprint of 1944 edition. Presents an unfavorable view.

LEWIS, MERIWETHER (1774-1809), commanded the first exploration by white people of the Missouri and Columbia rivers and the area between them. He also served as governor of the Louisiana Territory.

In 1801, Lewis became private secretary to President Thomas Jefferson. Both of them were interested in exploring a land route to the Pacific Ocean. The completion of the Louisiana Purchase in 1803 made exploration urgent (see LOUISIANA PURCHASE).

In 1804, an expedition led by Lewis and William Clark started from a camp near St. Louis. By late fall, the explorers had reached the Mandan Indian villages, where they spent the winter. The following spring, Sacagawea, an Indian woman, accompanied the expedition

up the Missouri River and across the Rocky Mountains. When the explorers reached the Columbia River, they traveled down to the Pacific Ocean in canoes. On the return trip, Lewis followed the Marias River and Clark went down the Yellowstone River. They reached St. Louis in September 1806, and found they had been given up for lost.

Brown Bros.
Meriwether Lewis

In 1807, Lewis became governor of the Louisiana Territory. In 1809, he started for Washington, D.C., from St. Louis. He stopped for a night at an inn in Tennessee and was found fatally wounded the next day. It has never been determined whether he committed suicide or was murdered.

Lewis was born in Albemarle County, Virginia. At age 20, he helped put down the Whiskey Rebellion.

The Lewis and Clark Centennial Exposition was held in Portland, Ore., in 1905.   WILLIAM P. BRANDON

See also CLARK, WILLIAM; LEWIS AND CLARK EXPEDITION; SACAGAWEA; WHISKEY REBELLION.

LEWIS, SINCLAIR (1885-1951), gained international fame for his novels attacking the weaknesses he saw in American society. In 1930, Lewis became the first American author to win the Nobel Prize for literature.

Harry Sinclair Lewis was born on Feb. 7, 1885, in Sauk Centre, Minn. At the age of 21, he lived briefly at Helicon Hall, a socialist community in New Jersey founded by writer Upton Sinclair. Lewis was graduated from Yale University in 1908. In 1914, while working as a newspaperman, he published his first novel, *Our Mr. Wrenn*. The book is a gently satiric account of a meek New York clerk traveling in Europe.

Lewis wrote four more novels and achieved only modest success. But *Main Street* (1920) caused a sensation and brought him immediate fame. The book is a withering satire on the dullness and lack of culture of a "typical" American small town, and the narrow-mindedness and self-satisfaction of its inhabitants. Written in minute detail, *Main Street* chronicles the fruitless efforts of the heroine Carol Kennicott to awaken and improve her town. Lewis based the novel on Sauk Centre, renaming the town "Gopher Prairie."

Babbitt (1922) focuses even more effectively Lewis' idea of a "typical" small city businessman, George F. Babbitt. The novel describes the futile attempt of its central character to break loose from the confining life of a "solid American citizen" —a middle-class, middle-aged realtor, civic booster, and club joiner. Possibly no two works of literature did more to make Ameri-

Eric Schaal, Pix
Sinclair Lewis

cans aware of the limitations of their national life and culture than did *Main Street* and *Babbitt.*

With a sharp, satiric eye, Lewis continued to examine other aspects of what he considered national inadequacy. *Arrowsmith* (1925) describes the frustrations of an idealistic young doctor in conflict with corruption, jealousy, meanness, and prejudice. The novel won the 1926 Pulitzer Prize, which Lewis declined, perhaps because he felt he should have received a prize sooner. *Elmer Gantry* (1927) satirizes religious hypocrisy and bigotry in the Midwest.

In 1928, Lewis married Dorothy Thompson (1894-1961), a famous foreign correspondent and newspaper columnist. The marriage ended in divorce in 1942.

Dodsworth (1929) was perhaps the last of Lewis' best works. The novel contrasts American with European life while relating the marriage difficulties of a prosperous American businessman on a European tour.

Lewis' later novels were primarily shallow photographic realism. Critics now consider Lewis less a truly creative artist than an extraordinarily accomplished observer with a vivid reportorial style. Lewis died lonely and unhappy in Italy in 1951.   JOSEPH N. RIDDEL

Additional Resources

LUNDQUIST, JAMES. *Sinclair Lewis.* Ungar, 1973. Criticism and interpretation of Lewis' novels.
O'CONNOR, RICHARD. *Sinclair Lewis.* McGraw, 1971. This biography is suitable for younger readers.
SCHORER, MARK. *Sinclair Lewis: An American Life.* McGraw, 1961.

LEWIS AND CLARK EXPEDITION was the first exploration by the United States government of the country's vast northwestern wilderness. The expedition, led by Meriwether Lewis and William Clark, began in 1804 and lasted more than two years.

Lewis and Clark started up the Missouri River from

Detail of an oil portrait (1807) by Charles Willson Peale; Independence National Historical Park Collection, Philadelphia
Meriwether Lewis

Detail of an oil portrait (1810) by Charles Willson Peale; Independence National Historical Park Collection, Philadelphia
William Clark

St. Louis and traveled almost 7,700 miles (12,400 kilometers) to the Pacific Coast. They returned with maps of the frontier and information about the region's natural resources and the Indian tribes who lived there. The success of the expedition enabled the United States to claim the Oregon region. This claim, in turn, helped make possible the great pioneer movement that settled the West during the 1800's.

Jefferson's Plans. Soon after Thomas Jefferson became President in 1801, he began to plan an expedition to chart a route through the Northwest. Jefferson wanted the expedition to travel up the Missouri River, cross the Rocky Mountains, and then go down the Columbia River to the Pacific Coast. He believed this route could be part of a passage by land and rivers to transport goods between the Atlantic and Pacific oceans. Jefferson's plan included gathering information about animals, plants, and minerals of the Northwest. He also wanted to establish communication with the Indians of the region.

The route planned by Jefferson ran through the Louisiana Territory and the Oregon region. The United

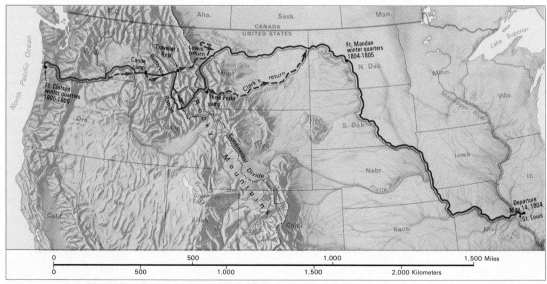

WORLD BOOK map

The Lewis and Clark Expedition left a camp near St. Louis in 1804, journeyed up the Missouri River, and crossed the Rocky Mountains. The explorers reached the Pacific Coast in 1805. They returned to St. Louis in 1806 with valuable information about the new frontier.

States bought the Louisiana Territory from France in 1803 (see LOUISIANA PURCHASE). However, no nation had claimed the Oregon region.

Jefferson chose Lewis, an Army captain, to lead the expedition. Jefferson and Lewis selected Clark, a former Army officer, to be second in command. Lewis and Clark had known each other in the Army, and they agreed privately to be co-leaders of the expedition. Both men had lived in the wilderness, and Clark knew how to draw maps of the unexplored land for which they were headed.

Preparation. Lewis and Clark recruited men for the expedition from Army posts, and they also chose some woodsmen and hunters. The selected men had such qualities as strength, knowledge of the wilderness, and the ability to speak Indian languages. The expedition consisted of about 45 persons. John Colter, who later became a famous American trapper, was in the group.

In December 1803, the men of the expedition built Camp Dubois across the Mississippi River from St. Louis. They stayed at the camp during the winter. A large flat-bottomed boat called a *keelboat* was built for the trip. It measured about 55 feet (18 meters) long and could be rowed or sailed, or poled like a raft. Lewis and Clark stored many tons of supplies, including flour, meal, medicine, salt, and weapons. The men also acquired a large supply of colored beads and other small gifts for the Indians they expected to meet.

Up the Missouri. On May 14, 1804, the expedition set out in the keelboat and two dugouts. As the men traveled up the Missouri River, Lewis went ashore occasionally and was amazed by the large number of animals he saw. He wrote in his journal: "I do not think I exaggerate when I estimate the number of buffalo which could be comprehended [seen] at one view to amount to 3,000."

In September, the explorers had their first encounter with Indians. Some of them went ashore to talk to a

group of Sioux Indians and offer them gifts. However, the Indians demanded more gifts and would not allow Clark to return to the boat. The Sioux let him go when Clark's men showed they were ready to fight.

In October, the expedition reached a village of friendly Mandan Indians in what is now North Dakota. The explorers built Fort Mandan near the village and spent the winter there. During the winter, a French-Canadian trader named Toussaint Charbonneau and his wife, Sacagawea, a Shoshoni Indian, joined the expedition.

West to the Rockies. The journey resumed on April 7, 1805. The explorers were now traveling in the two dugouts, plus six canoes that they had built with the help of the Mandan. Lewis and Clark sent the keelboat back to St. Louis with several men because the river had become too narrow for it.

As the explorers traveled farther west, they saw many grizzly bears. Lewis described one of the bears the men had shot: "Captain Clark thought he [the bear] would weigh 500 pounds. For my own part, I think the estimate too small by 100 pounds." The huge bears threatened the expedition continually. An attacking grizzly had to be shot several times before it died.

On May 26, Lewis climbed to the top of a hill and saw the snow-capped Rocky Mountains for the first time. He wrote that he "felt a secret pleasure" at being near the headwaters of the Missouri River.

The explorers hoped an Indian tribe would provide the horses and information they needed to cross the Rockies. By coincidence, they met the band of Shoshoni Indians to which Sacagawea had belonged at birth. Her brother was now the chief of the band. Sacagawea helped the explorers trade gifts to the Indians for horses and supplies. The Shoshoni also advised the men how to travel through the mountains.

Detail of a mural (1938) by Barry Faulkner and F. H. Schwarz in the State Capitol, Salem, Ore.; Oregon State Highway Department

The Explorers reached the Columbia River in 1805 after crossing the Rockies. Lewis and Clark, *center,* led the group down the river to the Pacific Coast. A Shoshoni Indian woman, Sacagawea, *right,* helped the explorers trade with Indians for supplies and horses.

LEWIS AND CLARK EXPEDITION

Crossing the Mountains was the most difficult part of the journey. The explorers had to get off their horses and lead them along rocky, narrow mountain paths. Some of the horses lost their footing and fell to their death. As the expedition traveled farther into the Rockies, there were fewer and fewer animals to hunt for food. The explorers killed some of their horses and ate them.

The group crossed the Rockies in about a month. After reaching the Clearwater River in what is now Idaho, they built new canoes and paddled toward the Columbia River. The expedition reached the Columbia in October and traveled as fast as possible so they could reach the Pacific Coast before winter. They arrived at the coast in November 1805 and built Fort Clatsop near the mouth of the Columbia River. They spent the winter at the fort.

The Homeward Journey began in March 1806. Lewis and Clark had spent the winter studying the information collected on the journey. They concluded that the route they had followed through the mountains was not the shortest one because it had taken them too far south. They decided to split the return expedition into two groups in order to possibly discover a shorter route.

The explorers crossed the first range of the Rocky Mountains in June. Lewis then led one group along a new route, directly east to the Missouri River. Clark led the other party back by way of the original route of the expedition.

After Lewis and his group reached the Missouri River, he decided to explore one of the river's branches before meeting Clark downstream. During this trip, the explorers had a brief fight with a group of Blackfeet Indians who tried to steal their guns. The explorers escaped unharmed, but one Indian was killed. Clark's group also had trouble with Indians when a group of Crow warriors stole most of their horses. Clark and his party completed their journey by canoe. The two groups reunited in August and returned to St. Louis with no further difficulty. They arrived on Sept. 23, 1806, and were welcomed by the cheers of the city's people.

Results of the Expedition. The most important result of the Lewis and Clark expedition was that it enabled the United States to claim the Oregon region. This claim, plus the purchase of the Louisiana Territory, played an important part in the settlement of the West. However, Jefferson's proposed route to the Northwest was too rugged to be used for commercial transportation.

The explorers established peaceful contact with most of the Indian tribes that they met—the Blackfeet, Mandan, Nez Percé, Shoshoni, and Sioux. The United States government hoped to begin a fur trade with these Indians. The expedition also collected a variety of Indian objects and brought back knowledge of the tribal languages.

The journals of Lewis and Clark contain many of their observations. For example, the men noted that the vast prairies along the Missouri River would be suitable for farming. They reported the dense forests and the giant trees around Fort Clatsop. The journals

were published in 1814 and quickly became popular in the United States.   JOHN L. ALLEN

See also CLARK, WILLIAM; LEWIS, MERIWETHER; SACAGAWEA; COLTER, JOHN.

Additional Resources

Atlas of the Lewis and Clark Expedition. Ed. by Gary E. Moulton. Univ. of Nebraska, 1983.

EIDE, INGVARD H., comp. *American Odyssey: The Journey of Lewis and Clark.* Rand McNally, 1969.

HAWKE, DAVID FREEMAN. *Those Tremendous Mountains: The Story of the Lewis and Clark Expedition.* Norton, 1980.

LEWISTON, Ida. (pop. 27,986), lies on the western border of Idaho. It is often called the *Seaport of Idaho.* River boats travel 480 miles (772 kilometers) to the city from the Pacific Ocean by way of the Columbia and Snake rivers. For location, see IDAHO (political map). See also IDAHO (Climate).

The city is a trading center for a large mining, lumbering, and farming region. It has the world's largest white-pine sawmill, a pulp and paper mill, a plywood and veneer plant, frozen-food plants, and factories that make gun cartridges. Farmers in the area raise fruit, wheat, and cattle.

Meriwether Lewis and William Clark camped near the site of Lewiston in 1805. The city was founded in 1861 and named after Lewis. It served as the first capital of the Idaho Territory from 1863 to 1864, and in 1863 became the territory's first incorporated town. Lewiston is the home of Lewis-Clark State College. The seat of Nez Perce County, Lewiston has a mayor-council government.   WILLIAM S. GREEVER and JANET GROFF GREEVER

LEWISTON (pop. 40,481) is the second largest city of Maine. Only Portland has more people. Lewiston lies on the east bank of the Androscoggin River, across from Auburn (see MAINE [political map]). Lewiston and Auburn form a metropolitan area with about 84,690 people. The area is southwestern Maine's major industrial center.

Textile manufacturing has been an important industry in Lewiston since the mid-1800's. Other major industries produce footwear, electrical equipment, fabricated metals, and plastic and rubber products. A canal fed by the Androscoggin River runs through downtown Lewiston and provides water power for many industries. Several large brick buildings along the canal house industries. Lewiston's downtown commercial area has undergone major urban renewal since 1980. But the area still has a number of office buildings that date from the 1800's. The city is the home of Bates College.

Lewiston was first settled in 1770. It became a city in 1861. Many French Canadians settled there after the Civil War ended in 1865 to work in its mills. Lewiston has a mayor-council government.   MARK A. LESLIE

LEXICOGRAPHER, *LEHK suh KAHG ruh fuhr,* is a person who compiles a dictionary. The word *lexicon,* another word for dictionary, comes from a Greek expression that means *word book.* In 1755, Samuel Johnson compiled the first English dictionary that included examples taken from English writers. Johnson extracted quotations from the books of these writers to illustrate the actual use of words. Today, lexicographers base their dictionaries on the research of language scholars who have studied the pronunciation, grammar, history, and usage of a language.   ROBERT K. BARNHART

See also JOHNSON, SAMUEL; WEBSTER, NOAH.

LEXINGTON, Ky. (pop. 204,165; met. area pop. 317,629), is one of the nation's chief trading centers for tobacco. The Lexington area also is a leading market for race horses. Lexington ranks as Kentucky's second largest city. Only Louisville is bigger. For Lexington's location, see KENTUCKY (political map).

Lexington was founded in 1775. Some pioneers were building the first cabin on the site when they heard about the opening battle of the Revolutionary War in America. They named the settlement for the battle, which was fought in Lexington, Mass.

Description. Lexington is the county seat of Fayette County. Its economy depends heavily on race horses and burley tobacco, both of which are raised nearby. The grass and water of the area are rich in minerals that give horses strong bones and muscles. Auction markets in the Lexington area handle hundreds of Standardbred and Thoroughbred horses annually and sell millions of pounds or kilograms of tobacco.

The Lexington metropolitan area has about 125 industrial plants. Their products include fabricated metal goods, printed materials, and processed foods.

Lexington is the home of the University of Kentucky and Transylvania University. Transylvania, chartered in 1780, was the first college west of the Allegheny Mountains. Lexington's museums include Ashland, the home of the famous American statesman Henry Clay; and the International Museum of the Horse.

History. Shawnee Indians hunted in what is now the Lexington area when whites first settled there in 1775. The pioneers abandoned Lexington in 1776 but settled there permanently in 1779. Lexington served as the state capital in 1792 and 1793. By the early 1800's, horse farms had spread across the rolling meadows of the Lexington area. Lexington was incorporated as a city in 1832. Tobacco became important in the area after the 1860's, when growers developed a variety of the plant especially suited to the soil and climate there.

The Lexington area began to grow rapidly as a manufacturing center during the 1950's. In 1974, the city combined its government with that of Fayette County. The area became known as Lexington-Fayette Urban County. Lexington Center, a downtown civic center, opened in 1976. It includes a sports arena, a convention hall, a hotel, and stores. ANDREW ECKDAHL

For the monthly weather in Lexington, see KENTUCKY (Climate). See also KENTUCKY.

LEXINGTON, BATTLE OF. See REVOLUTIONARY WAR IN AMERICA (Lexington and Concord).

LEYDEN. See LEIDEN.

LEYDEN JAR, *LY duhn*, was one of the first devices used to store an electric charge. It was invented in Leiden (sometimes spelled Leyden), the Netherlands, in 1746. A Leyden jar is a glass jar sealed with a cork. Sheets of metal foil cover about half of the inside and outside of the jar. The foil conducts electricity, but the glass does not. A brass rod is inserted through the cork and brought in contact with the foil inside the jar.

When the brass rod is connected to a source of electricity, current travels through the rod and charges the inner foil. Current cannot pass through the glass, but the foil on the outside becomes charged by *induction* if it is properly grounded (see INDUCTION, ELECTRIC). The outer foil has a charge opposite to the charge inside the jar. When the flow of current into the jar stops, a charge remains stored in the jar. If the inner and outer layers of foil are then connected by a conductor, their opposite charges will cause a spark that discharges the jar. GREGORY BENFORD

Sargent-Welch Scientific Company

The Leyden Jar is an old type of electric capacitor.

LEYTE. See PHILIPPINES (The Main Islands).

LEYTE GULF, BATTLE FOR. See NAVY (Famous Sea Battles); WORLD WAR II (The War in Asia and the Pacific).

LHASA, *LAH suh* (pop. 83,540), is the capital and holy city of Tibet. The Dalai Lama, a spiritual leader and exiled ruler of Tibet, lived in Lhasa until the Chinese Communists forced him to leave in 1959. Lhasa was also the home of another spiritual leader, the Panchen Lama. Tibetans consider the city's temples sacred. Lhasa is sometimes called *The Forbidden City*, because Europeans are distrusted there. Until 1904, Europeans were banned from the city.

Lhasa lies 11,800 feet (3,597 meters) above sea level in the Himalaya Mountains of southeastern Tibet. It is the second highest capital in the world after La Paz, Bolivia, which lies about 12,700 feet (3,871 meters) above sea level. Lhasa serves as a center for caravan trade to and from India, Burma, and China.

Lhasa is a closely packed city of stone and brick houses and shops. Many monasteries and temples stand

Keeneland Association

Race Horse Buyers gather to bid for Thoroughbred horses at an auction in Keeneland, Ky., near Lexington. The Lexington area is one of the nation's leading markets for race horses.

among the other buildings. Most of the houses have low, flat roofs and no chimneys. Oiled paper, instead of glass, is used in the windows. At night, the city glows with light from torches and from crude lamps that burn vegetable oil.   THEODORE H. E. CHEN

See also TIBET (Cities; map).

LHASA APSO, *LAH suh AP soh,* is a dog that came originally from Lhasa, the capital of Tibet. It was once known as a terrier, but is now classed as a nonsporting dog. This dog has a long, heavy coat that looks like a mop. Its hair falls thickly over its face, covering its eyes and ears. It also has whiskers and a beard. The dog has

WORLD BOOK photo by E. F. Hoppe
The Lhasa Apso Originally Came from Tibet.

a long, low body, and carries its tail curled tightly over its back. In Lhasa, it was used as a watchdog, even though it is only about 10 inches (25 centimeters) high. A large dog guarded the door outside, while the little Lhasa apso stayed inside to warn of danger. See also SHIH TZU.   JOSEPHINE Z. RINE

LI HSIEN-NIEN. See LI XIANNIAN.

LI PO, *lee bwoh* (701-762), was one of China's greatest poets. He was also known as Li T'ai-po (pronounced *lee ty bwoh*) and his name is spelled several other ways. Li Po's poetry is admired for its eloquence, wit, humor, and romantic descriptions of nature. Li Po also wrote many poems praising the virtues of wine. He composed many poems at banquets and special occasions to entertain his friends and patrons. He believed his most important works were his poems on ethics and morality.

Li Po was probably born in what is now the Kirgiz republic of the Soviet Union. His family came from China, and they returned to the country when Li Po was 5 years old. From 725 until his death, Li Po traveled throughout China, supporting himself by writing poems and documents for wealthy people.   DAVID R. KNECHTGES

See also CHINESE LITERATURE (Poetry).

LI T'AI-PO. See LI PO.

LI XIANNIAN, *lee shee ehn nee ehn* (1907?-), also spelled *Li Hsien-nien,* is a leading Chinese official. He has been a member of the Politburo—the ruling body of China's Communist Party—since 1956. In 1983, he was named president of China, a largely ceremonial govern-

ment position. Li was a vice-premier of the government from 1978 to 1983 and has also served as an economic advisor to the premier of China. He was China's minister of finance from 1954 to 1966.

Li, the son of poor peasants, was born in Hubei (or Hupeh) province. He received almost no education, and worked as a carpenter in his youth. In 1927, he joined a Communist-led peasant uprising. For the next 10 years, he led Communist guerrillas in central China against the Chinese Nationalist forces. Li commanded Communist troops during the war between China and Japan (1937-1945). After the Communists conquered China in 1949, he became a party and government administrator in the industrial city of Wuhan.   DONALD W. KLEIN

LI YUAN, *LEE yoo AHN* (A.D. 566-635), a Chinese emperor, founded the T'ang dynasty (A.D. 618-907). Historians consider this dynasty one of the greatest periods in Chinese history. Li Yuan reigned from 618 to 627. He established T'ang control over rebellious sections of central and south China and defeated the Turks who were invading from the north.

Li Yuan was born in Ch'ang-an (now Sian) of a noble family. He became a general and served from 615 to 617 as military commander in Shansi province in north China. Li was loyal to the emperor until 617, when his son Li Shih-min persuaded him to rebel. Li Yuan's forces captured Ch'ang-an, the western capital of the ruling Sui dynasty. In 618, the Sui ruler was murdered in a rebellion and Li became emperor. In 627, Li Shih-min forced his father from the throne and became the second emperor of the T'ang dynasty.   EUGENE BOARDMAN

See also CHINA; T'ANG DYNASTY.

LIABILITY INSURANCE. See INSURANCE (Property and Liability Insurance).

LIBBY, WILLARD FRANK (1908-1980), an American chemist, received the Nobel Prize in chemistry in 1960. He earned the award for discovering carbon 14, or radiocarbon, in 1947, and finding a way to use it to determine the age of prehistoric plant and animal remains (see RADIOCARBON).

Libby was born in Grand Valley, Colo. He was graduated from the University of California, and taught there from 1933 to 1945. He then taught at the Institute for Nuclear Studies at the University of Chicago. In 1950, he became a consultant to the Atomic Energy Commission. After serving as a member of the commission from 1954 to 1959, he rejoined the faculty of the University of California.   HERBERT S. RHINESMITH

LIBEL is a written or printed statement that harms a person's reputation. Pictures, signs, and information broadcast on either radio or television may also be libelous. Individuals are most often the subjects of libel, but businesses and groups may be libeled as well. *Slander* is similar to libel. However, slander involves spoken words that damage a person's reputation.

The offense of libel does not consist of writing or developing the harmful material, but in showing it. If the writer of such harmful information shows it to another person, the writer has *published* the libel.

In the United States, a person who believes he or she has been libeled can file a lawsuit in civil court. The *plaintiff* (person filing the charges) must prove three things. First, the plaintiff must prove that something was published by the defendant. Second, the plaintiff must prove that the published material was about him or her. Third, the plaintiff must prove that the material was *defamatory* (damaging) to his or her reputation. Some possible examples of libel include reporting that a person committed a crime or was repeatedly fired from jobs.

However, a defendant who proves that the published material is true—even if it is defamatory—cannot lose a libel suit. In addition, the legal doctrine of "fair comment" protects printed matter that is presented as opinion rather than as fact. Thus, a negative opinion in a review of a book or a movie cannot be libelous.

Libel first became a constitutional issue in 1964. That year, the Supreme Court of the United States decided the landmark case of *New York Times Co. v. Sullivan.* The case arose when the *Times* printed an advertisement that accused officials in Montgomery, Ala., of harassing civil rights leader Martin Luther King, Jr. Five government officials sued the *Times.* The court ruled that the First Amendment to the Constitution of the United States prevents public officials from winning a libel suit against the press unless the press is guilty of *actual malice.* The court defined actual malice as knowledge of a falsehood or reckless disregard of the truth.

In the 1974 case of *Gertz v. Robert Welch, Inc.*, the Supreme Court ruled that public figures must also prove actual malice when suing the media. The court defined a public figure as a person outside the government who voluntarily enters the public spotlight to influence the outcome of public issues. The court also ruled that private persons do not have to prove actual malice to win a libel suit against the media. But the court said private persons must prove at least that the media acted negligently in its reporting.

Libel laws have come under heavy criticism. Some journalists have complained that libel suits often cost a great deal in legal fees and take years to settle. Other people say that the "actual malice" rule makes it too hard for public officials and public figures to win libel suits. But some attorneys and media researchers believe that the courts often rule in favor of plaintiffs without requiring enough proof that their reputation has been damaged. Studies have also indicated that the complexity of libel laws sometimes confuses juries.   JEREMY COHEN

LIBERAL ARTS are the learned habits of thought and speech considered essential for a free human being. Historically, the liberal arts included two groups of studies. The first group was the correct use of language (grammar), thinking clearly (logic), and expressing one's ideas persuasively (rhetoric). The second group included the various branches of mathematics. Originally, these were arithmetic, geometry, astronomy, and harmony.

Out of these traditional groups of studies have come the groupings into natural sciences, social sciences, and humanities. American colleges that concentrate on these studies are usually referred to as liberal arts colleges.   MERLE L. BORROWMAN

LIBERAL PARTY is one of the two major political parties of Canada. The other is the Progressive Conservative Party, which is often called the Conservative Party. The Liberals have governed Canada during most of the 1900's.

In general, the Liberal Party has favored the expansion of social welfare programs. It strongly supports national unity. Much of the Liberal Party's success in the 1900's has resulted from support by French-speaking Canadians.

The Liberal Party developed in the 1850's. It originally consisted of several reform groups, including the Clear Grit Party of Upper Canada (now Ontario) and the Rouge Party of Lower Canada (now Quebec). Today, members of the Liberal Party are sometimes called "Grits." In the 1860's, the Liberals split over the issue of confederation for the British colonies in North America. The party began to gain strength after the birth of the Dominion of Canada in 1867.

The Conservatives dominated Canadian politics during the nation's first 30 years. The Liberals ruled only from 1873 to 1878, when Alexander Mackenzie served as the first Liberal prime minister. In 1896, the Liberals returned to power under Wilfrid Laurier, the first French-Canadian prime minister. Laurier was popular among both English- and French-speaking Canadians, and he worked to settle disputes between the two groups. Canada prospered under Laurier, and the Liberals remained in power until 1911.

The Liberal Party was out of power until 1921, when W. L. Mackenzie King became prime minister. King served as prime minister three times between 1921 and 1948 and held the office for a total of more than 21 years. Under his leadership, Canada gained independence within the British Commonwealth. King's government also introduced important social legislation and led the nation through World War II (1939-1945).

King resigned in 1948, but the Liberals remained in power and have governed Canada almost continuously since then. Despite French-Canadian support, Liberal governments of the 1960's and 1970's faced growing dissatisfaction among French-speaking Canadians. In the 1970's and early 1980's, Liberal Prime Minister Pierre E. Trudeau worked to block efforts of Quebec's government to make the province a separate nation. In 1984, the Liberals lost control of the federal government to the Progressive Conservative Party.   J. L. GRANATSTEIN

See also CANADA, HISTORY OF.

LIBERAL PARTY is a political organization in Great Britain. From the mid-1800's until the 1920's, the Liberal Party and the Conservative Party were Britain's two largest political organizations. Today, however, the Liberal Party is much smaller than either the Conservative Party or the Labour Party. The Liberals generally favor policies that fall between those of the Conservatives on the right and Labour on the left.

Beginnings. During the early 1800's, some members of Britain's Whig Party formed an alliance with reformers called Radicals. This alliance came to be called the Liberal Party. The early Liberals led a movement in Parliament that resulted in political reforms, including child labor laws and an act that increased the representation in Parliament of areas with large populations.

A Major Party. By the 1850's, the Liberal and Conservative parties had replaced the Whig and Tory parties as Britain's two largest political organizations. During the second half of the 1800's, control of the British government passed back and forth between the Liberals and Conservatives. The most famous Liberal leader of the period was William E. Gladstone. He served as prime minister of Britain from 1868 to 1874, from

LIBERAL REPUBLICAN PARTY

1880 to 1885, in 1886, and from 1892 to 1894. Under Gladstone, the Liberals led a movement for additional reforms. These reforms included the extension of voting rights to the lower classes and a system of free elementary schools open to all children.

The strength of the Liberal Party continued into the early 1900's. Its leading members of the period included the Earl of Rosebery, prime minister from 1894 to 1895; Sir Henry Campbell-Bannerman, prime minister from 1905 to 1908; Herbert H. Asquith, prime minister from 1908 to 1916; and David Lloyd George, prime minister from 1916 to 1922. Liberal reforms between 1906 and 1914 included the Workmen's Compensation Act, the Old Age Pension Act, and measures to aid the unemployed. Such reforms laid the foundation for the establishment of Britain's welfare state.

Party Split and Decline. When Lloyd George became prime minister in 1916, the Liberals and Conservatives set up a coalition to govern the country. The coalition led to a split between Liberal followers of Asquith—who opposed the coalition—and those of Lloyd George. The split helped the Labour Party, which had been formed in 1906, replace the Liberal Party as the main opposition to the Conservative Party. The Liberal Party became much smaller than the Conservative and Labour parties.

Alliance with the Social Democrats. In 1981, a number of members of Parliament who belonged to the moderate wing of the Labour Party quit that party and formed the Social Democratic Party. In general, the Social Democrats and Liberals have similar policies. The two parties formed an alliance in 1981. They agreed that they would not oppose each other in elections for seats in the House of Commons. They also agreed to act as a coalition in the government. David Steel, the head of the Liberal Party, was a major leader in the formation of the alliance.   RICHARD ROSE

Related Articles in WORLD BOOK include:

LIBERAL REPUBLICAN PARTY was a U.S. political party formed in 1872 to oppose the re-election of President Ulysses S. Grant. It was made up of members of the Republican Party who suspected Grant's administration of corruption. They also disliked Grant's policies on civil service, tariff reform, and the South. Liberals and reformers started the Liberal Republican Party, but it soon attracted a mixed group of politicians. The members found it difficult to agree on a candidate or a platform at the party convention, which was held in Cincinnati.

In the end, the party nominated newspaper editor Horace Greeley for the presidency on a platform of "universal amnesty and universal enfranchisement." This meant the immediate establishment of civil governments in each of the former Confederate states, and the removal of all restrictions on the political rights of their citizens. The Liberal Republican Party, even with Democratic support, was badly defeated in the election of 1872, and quickly disappeared.   DONALD R. McCOY

See also GRANT, ULYSSES S. (Election of 1872).

LIBERALISM is a political and economic philosophy that emphasizes freedom, equality, and opportunity. The philosophy called *conservatism*, on the other hand, emphasizes order, tradition, and ownership of private property. Liberals have generally favored more rapid social change than have conservatives. But liberalism is a confusing term, because its meaning and emphasis have changed considerably over the years.

Early Liberalism. The right to rebel against a government that severely restricts personal freedom was one of the principal doctrines of early liberalism. Liberal ideas inspired the English revolution of 1688, the American revolution of 1775, and the French revolution of 1789. Liberal revolutions led to the establishment of many governments based on rule by law and by the consent of the governed. Many such constitutional governments had detailed bills of rights that proclaimed the individual's right to freedom of speech, the press, assembly, and religion. The bills of rights also attempted to provide safeguards against the abuse of police and judicial power. The liberal philosophy is clearly stated in the Declaration of Independence and in the writings of Thomas Jefferson. Jefferson, in turn, was influenced by the ideas of the English philosopher John Locke.

Early liberals favored constitutional government, but they usually distrusted democracy. They tried to restrict the exercise of political power to members of the property-owning middle class. But as the industrial working class grew larger, it adopted the liberal principle that government should rest on the consent of the governed. By the late 1800's, a liberal was a person who favored democracy and voting rights for adult citizens.

Political and economic liberalism were closely connected until the 1900's. Early liberals believed that the government which governs least governs best. They argued that all people benefit most when each individual is allowed to follow his or her own self-interest. They believed that the economy is self-regulating if left alone to operate according to its own rules. Therefore, they concluded, government regulation of the economy is unnecessary. The ideas of economic liberalism were arranged into a system by the Scottish economist Adam Smith, and discussed in his book *The Wealth of Nations* (1776). This system was called *capitalism*, or *free enterprise*. See CAPITALISM.

Liberalism Today. Liberalism has undergone a significant change of emphasis in the 1900's. In the late 1800's, many liberals began to think of freedom less in terms of freedom from this or that restriction, and more in terms of freedom of opportunity. They became convinced that government action is frequently necessary to provide the conditions under which individuals can realize their potentials as human beings.

Today, liberals favor an active role for the government in regulating the economy in the public interest. They support government programs to provide economic security and ease human suffering. Such programs include unemployment insurance, minimum-wage laws, old-age pensions, health insurance, civil rights legislation, and various antipoverty measures. Modern liberals claim a kinship with early liberalism by saying that they, too, believe in the primary importance of individual freedom. But they maintain that government must actively remove obstacles to the enjoyment of that freedom. Persons who support the earlier ideas of economic liberalism are now frequently described as *conservative* or *reactionary*.　JOHN H. HALLOWELL

See also CONSERVATISM; POLITICAL SCIENCE (Liberalism); AMERICANS FOR DEMOCRATIC ACTION.

Additional Resources

GERBER, WILLIAM. *American Liberalism: Laudable End, Controversial Means.* Twayne, 1975.
KRONENWETTER, MICHAEL. *Are You a Liberal? Are You a Conservative?* Watts, 1984. Suitable for younger readers.
TSONGAS, PAUL. *The Road from Here: Liberalism and Realities in the 1980's.* Knopf, 1981.

LIBERIA, *ly BEER ee uh,* is the oldest independent black nation in Africa and the second oldest in the world. Only Haiti is older. Liberia became independent more than 110 years before any other country in tropical Africa. It was founded in 1822 by an American charitable society to provide a home for freed black slaves from America. Aid from the United States helped these settlers resist both European colonial powers and opposition from Africans. Liberian settlers issued their Declaration of Independence in 1847.

Liberia lies just north of the equator where the west coast of Africa bulges out into the Atlantic Ocean. The country is about as big as the state of Tennessee, but has less than half as many people. Liberia is hot and rainy. Swamps lie along its coast and thick, green rain forests cover much of the interior. Hunters have killed most of the big game in Liberia. But big herds of gazelle and deer, and many leopards, otters, monkeys, and snakes are found there. Liberia is also the home of the rare pygmy hippopotamus.

The country's official name is Republic of Liberia. The name *Liberia* comes from the Latin word *liber,* which means *free.* Monrovia, which has a population of about 200,000, is the capital and largest city.

Government

Liberia is a republic. A president heads the government. The people elect the president to a 6-year term. The Legislature of Liberia, consisting of a Senate and a House of Representatives, passes the nation's laws. The people elect members of the Senate to 9-year terms and members of the House to 6-year terms. The president appoints a Cabinet to carry out the functions of the government.

The court system is headed by a Supreme Court. For purposes of local government, Liberia is divided into 13 counties. The president appoints a superintendent to head each county.

The People

About 90 per cent of the people of Liberia are descendants of black Africans who came to the area in the 1400's. They belong to about 20 ethnic groups that practice different customs, and speak different languages.

Only about 5 per cent of the people are *Americo-Liberians,* the descendants of blacks from the United States who settled there in the early 1800's. In general, the Americo-Liberians have been far better off economically than the Africans. Before a group of Africans revolted in 1980, Americo-Liberians held most of the top offices in the government and controlled the country's political system. The revolt brought the Africans to power.

The majority of the Americo-Liberians are English-

Liberia

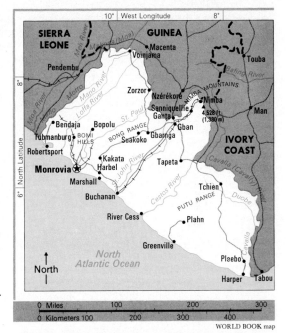

WORLD BOOK map

speaking Protestants who live in coastal cities. Many work in shops or business offices, and some own businesses. Some Lebanese shopkeepers, Swiss mechanics, and American missionaries live in Liberia. But only people who have black ancestry may become citizens.

Facts in Brief

Capital: Monrovia.

Official Language: English.

Form of Government: Republic.

Area: 43,000 sq. mi. (111,370 km²). *Greatest Distances*—east-west, 230 mi. (370 km); north-south, 210 mi. (338 km). *Coastline*—315 mi. (507 km).

Elevation: *Highest*—Nimba Mountains, 4,528 ft. (1,380 m) above sea level. *Lowest*—sea level along the coast.

Population: *Estimated 1987 Population*—2,334,000; distribution, 60 per cent rural, 40 per cent urban; density, 54 persons per sq. mi. (21 per km²). *1974 Census*—1,503,368. *Estimated 1992 Population*—2,741,000.

Chief Products: *Agriculture*—bananas, cassava, coffee, rice, rubber. *Forest Products*—kola nuts, palm oil, piassava. *Mining*—diamonds, gold, iron ore.

Flag: The flag has 6 red and 5 white horizontal stripes that represent the 11 signers of the Liberian Declaration of Independence. A white star appears on a dark blue canton in the upper left corner. Adopted in 1847. See FLAG (color picture: Flags of Africa).

Money: *Basic Unit*—United States dollar.

Monrovia is the capital and largest city of Liberia. The Temple of Justice, *left,* where the country's supreme court hears cases, is one of the city's most modern buildings.

Brent Jones

Life in the Cities is somewhat like life in the United States. Most of the Americo-Liberians dress like Americans and live in brick, wood, or concrete block houses. They like tennis and soccer, and like to go to motion pictures and night clubs. The YMCA and informal clubs are popular. Many cities have sections in which the poor people live in roughly built houses of wood, concrete, and corrugated iron.

Life in Rural Areas. Members of the Bassa and Kru ethnic groups live along the coast, and work on cargo ships or catch fish for a living. Most of the other ethnic groups, such as the Kpelles and the Lomas, are made up of farmers who live in rural villages scattered through the inland forests.

Most of the farmers live in round huts that have mud walls and thatched roofs. Many of the people wear blouses or shirts with a long piece of cloth called a *lappa* wrapped around the waist like a skirt. Family ties are strong in all the ethnic groups. Some people practice Christianity or Islam. Most still practice traditional religions based on a deep respect for ancestors and a belief that trees, rocks, and other objects have "spirits." Some people still practice magic and witchcraft.

Farm families work together to raise their crops. The men clear the fields and prepare them for planting. The women and children plant cassava, rice, taro, and yams. Cassava has an edible root and taro (also called *eddo*) has an edible underground stem. Young boys guard the crops, chasing away birds and baboons. The women harvest the crops, and the girls *winnow* the rice (separate the grains from the worthless husks).

Until the government began a road-building program in the 1960's, many rural people were isolated. Each village produced only those things it needed. Farmers made their own crude tools, and the people used rough iron sticks as money. Roads brought greater contact with the cities, and traders brought in hoes, cloth, and other goods. Many farmers are abandoning their old ways. Some now plant only crops they can sell for cash. Many others are moving away to work in cities, the mines, or on rubber plantations.

Education. About a fourth of all Liberians can read and write. Because there are few classrooms and books, only about two out of ten children can go to school. The government and missionaries operate most primary and secondary schools, but there are a few private schools. Liberia has Cuttington University College at Suakoko, Our Lady of Fatima College at Harper, and the University of Liberia at Monrovia.

The Land

Liberia has a flat coastal plain that extends about 50 miles (80 kilometers) inland. Thick forests once covered the plain, but the people have cleared most of the land for farm and rubber plantations. Monrovia and several other cities lie along the coast. Inland from the plain, the land rises to a forest-covered plateau that is about 800 feet (240 meters) above sea level. The Bomi Hills and the Bong Range tower above the plateau. Further inland, the Nimba Mountains rise 4,528 feet (1,380 meters) above sea level.

Liberia has a warm, humid climate. Temperatures average about 80° F. (27° C), and coastal areas get as much as 200 inches (500 centimeters) of rain during the rainy season (from April to October). The dry season lasts from November to March. In January, the *harmattan* (a dry, cool wind that forms over the Sahara) blows great clouds of red dust across Liberia toward the coast. It sends temperatures as low as 50° F. (10° C).

Economy

Most Liberians are farmers. The country's chief crops are rice and cassava. Most farm families also raise some goats and chickens. The farm people usually can raise only enough food for their village. As a result, people in the cities have to import much of their food.

Liberia has one of the world's richest deposits of iron ore. Iron ore is the country's leading export, and makes up about half the nation's income. United States and European firms operate the iron ore mines. Some diamonds and gold are also mined. Liberia also has deposits of lead, manganese, zinc, and *bauxite* (the ore used in making aluminum). Its vast forests contain ebony, mahogany, and other valuable trees. But these natural resources have not yet been developed.

Rubber is the chief cash crop and one of Liberia's leading exports. About 40 per cent of the nation's income comes from the rubber industry. The Firestone Plantations Company, a United States firm, operates the largest rubber plantation in Liberia.

Liberia exports some bananas, coffee, and citrus fruits. Liberia has little industry, and must import all the heavy machinery and petroleum products it needs.

The largest merchant fleet in the world is registered

under the Liberian flag. But only a few ships are owned by Liberians. The rest are owned by people from other countries who register their ships in Liberia because taxes are lower there. Liberia collects about $11 million a year from ship registration fees.

Liberia's transportation system was greatly improved in the 1950's and 1960's. The government began building roads to connect isolated areas in the forests with Monrovia. Mining companies built railroads to link their mines with the ports in Monrovia and Buchanan. Monrovia has two airports.

History

Scientists have discovered mysterious stone circles and other ancient handcrafted objects in Liberia. But they know little about the early people who lived in the region. Local legends suggest, however, that the ancestors of the present-day ethnic groups fled from the mighty Muslim warriors in northeastern Africa and settled in the region in the 1400's and 1500's.

In the early 1800's, the American Colonization Society was formed in the United States to take freed blacks back to Africa. The society bought land from the Africans living in what is now Liberia. They started a settlement in 1822 and named it *Monrovia* in honor of U.S. President James Monroe. See BLACK AMERICANS (Free Blacks).

American blacks settled in Liberia throughout the 1800's. The colonization society let them manage some of their own affairs, and in 1838 the blacks elected their own legislative council. In the 1840's, disputes arose between the settlers and the society. The settlers declared their independence in 1847. They elected Joseph Jenkins Roberts, an Americo-Liberian who had been governor of Liberia since 1841, as the first president.

Early Expansion. At first, most of Liberia's land was along the coast. But gradually it expanded its territory by signing treaties with local chiefs, by buying land,

Firestone Tire & Rubber Co.

Workers Tap Rubber Trees and collect latex on large plantations. Rubber has been a chief source of income since the 1930's.

and by exploring and claiming other areas. Liberia had trouble with Great Britain and France, which were building colonies in West Africa. Along the coasts, the Kru and Grebo ethnic groups fought against the Liberian government and raided Liberian settlements. The Kru continued their rebellion until the early 1900's.

Liberia sent troops to fight in France in World War I. During World War II, the United States built Robertsfield air base (now called Roberts International Airport) near Monrovia. The air base was a vital link in the Allied supply lines to Europe and the Middle East. After the war, Liberia joined the United Nations.

Recent Developments. William V. S. Tubman, who served as president from 1944 until his death in 1971, encouraged social and economic reforms. He started a "unification policy" to end discrimination by Americo-Liberians against the country's ethnic groups. His "open door policy" encouraged U.S. and European companies to develop Liberia's natural resources. Under Tubman, Liberia played a leading part in seeking economic and cultural cooperation among African nations. Vice President William R. Tolbert, Jr., succeeded Tubman and generally continued his policies.

Until 1980, most of Liberia's top government leaders, including Tubman and Tolbert, were Americo-Liberians. In 1980, a small group of military men, who were descendants of Liberia's original ethnic groups, staged a revolt. They assassinated Tolbert, overthrew his government, and established a military government. They later executed several other former government leaders. Samuel K. Doe, an army sergeant, led the revolt. He became head of state in the new government. In October 1985, elections were held to choose a president and a Legislature. The people elected Doe president, and his party won a majority of seats in the Legislature. The new government took office in January 1986.   J. GUS LIEBENOW

See also MONROVIA; RUSSWURM, JOHN B.; TUBMAN, WILLIAM V. S.

Additional Resources

SHICK, TOM W. *Behold the Promised Land: A History of Afro-American Settler Society in Nineteenth-Century Liberia.* Johns Hopkins, 1980.

WILSON, CHARLES M. *Liberia: Black Africa in Microcosm.* Harper, 1971.

LIBERTARIAN PARTY is an American political party that favors increasing individual liberties by limiting government activities. The party's platform combines liberal and conservative beliefs.

Libertarians believe that government is the main threat to individual liberties. For this reason, the party supports the repeal of laws that limit freedom of personal behavior. Libertarians also feel that some services presently provided by the government should be available instead from private companies. Citizens who want such services could hire companies to provide them and thus reduce taxes. The Libertarian Party opposes government aid to and regulation of business. It favors a neutral foreign policy for the United States, including withdrawal from the United Nations (UN) and an end to any U.S. military role abroad. The Libertarian Party was founded in 1971. It enters candidates in races for federal, state, and local offices.   HUBERT MARSHALL

LIBERTY. See FREEDOM.

LIBERTY, STATUE OF. See STATUE OF LIBERTY.

LIBERTY BELL is a treasured relic of the early days of American independence. It was rùng July 8, 1776, with other church bells, to announce the adoption of the Declaration of Independence. Its inscription, "Proclaim Liberty throughout all the land unto all the inhabitants thereof," is from the Bible (Leviticus 25:10).

The Liberty Bell weighs over 2,080 pounds (943 kilograms). The province of Pennsylvania paid about $300 for it in 1752. It now hangs in Liberty Bell Pavilion, just north of Independence Hall in Philadelphia.

The Liberty Bell was first cast in England. It broke in ringing after its arrival and was recast in Philadelphia from the same metal, with the same inscription, in 1753. The Liberty Bell rang at each successive anniversary of the adoption of the Declaration until 1835. The bell broke on July 8 that year, while being rung during the funeral of John Marshall, chief justice of the United States. The bell became known as the Liberty Bell about 1839, when abolitionists began to refer to it that way. Previously, the bell had been called the Old State House Bell, the Bell of the Revolution, or Old Independence.

The Liberty Bell is no longer rung, but it has been struck on special occasions. On June 6, 1944, when Allied forces landed in France, Philadelphia officials struck the bell. Sound equipment broadcast the tone to all parts of the nation. Independence Hall was the permanent residence of the bell from 1753 until Jan. 1, 1976, when it was moved to the pavilion. JOHN R. ALDEN

LIBERTY CAP is a famous symbol of freedom. In modern times, the liberty cap has appeared on certain American coins and on the seals of several Central and South American republics.

The modern liberty cap is copied from the cone-shaped Phrygian headdress that was given to a freed slave in ancient Rome. At the start of the French Revolution, the *bonnet rouge* (red cap) was adopted by the "patriots," as the opponents of monarchy were called. ROBERT B. HOLTMAN

The Liberty Cap has long been a symbol of freedom.

LIBERTY FEDERATION is a conservative political organization in the United States. The group, originally called Moral Majority, tries to influence lawmakers on various issues. It also encourages religious conservatives to register to vote, run for public office, and support candidates who share the organization's views. The Liberty Federation believes that a number of decisions of the Supreme Court of the United States have helped bring about a decline of public decency in the country. The

The Historic Liberty Bell is a symbol of American independence. It was made in England in 1752 and was recast in 1753 in Philadelphia. The bell was rung each year until 1835, when it cracked while being rung during the funeral of Chief Justice John Marshall.

group especially objects to the rulings that banned organized prayer in public schools and those that legalized abortion. The Liberty Federation favors voluntary prayer in public schools. It supports abortion only in cases of rape or incest, or when the life of the mother is endangered. The federation also supports strong national defense policies and favors strict laws against pornography and drug abuse.

Jerry Falwell, a Baptist minister from Lynchburg, Va., founded the organization in 1979 as the Moral Majority. Falwell was joined by ministers, priests, rabbis, and others who shared his conservative ideas on moral and religious issues. The group became the Liberty Federation in 1986. Its leaders changed the name because they wanted to expand the organization's political activities. The federation then publicized its views on such matters as foreign policy and the federal budget.

The Liberty Federation has more than 4 million members. Its official name is Liberty Federation, Incorporated. It has headquarters at 305 Sixth Street, Lynchburg, VA 24504.   LEE THORNTON

LIBERTY HALL. See KENTUCKY (Places to Visit).

LIBERTY ISLAND is an island in Upper New York Bay on which the Statue of Liberty stands. The island, which lies southwest of Manhattan Island, covers 12 acres (5 hectares).

Before Liberty Island was officially renamed in 1956, it was called *Bedloe's Island*. It belongs to the U.S. government. The Statue of Liberty, given by France in 1884, was received in 1885 and dedicated in 1886. Fort Wood is the base on which the statue stands. The fort, built in the shape of an 11-point star, was completed in 1811 and named for an officer killed in the War of 1812. The area was a military post until 1937. Then the land was added to the Statue of Liberty National Monument. An American Museum of Immigration was dedicated there in 1972.   WILLIAM E. YOUNG

See also STATUE OF LIBERTY.

LIBERTY LEAGUE, also called the American Liberty League, was an organization that tried to rally public opinion against President Franklin D. Roosevelt's New Deal. Conservative Democrats who disapproved of Roosevelt's New Deal measures founded the group. Prominent members included John W. Davis and Alfred E. Smith, the Democratic presidential candidates in 1924 and 1928. In 1934, they combined with wealthy business executives, who provided most of the league's funds.

The league published pamphlets and sponsored radio programs, arguing that the New Deal was destroying personal liberty. However, the league failed to gain support in the 1934 and 1936 elections, and it soon disappeared.   DAVID A. SHANNON

LIBERTY LOAN. See SAVINGS BOND.

LIBERTY PARTY was the first political party in the United States to give most of its attention to the slavery question. The politician James G. Birney (1792-1857) and the poet John Greenleaf Whittier were the leading supporters of the group. From July, 1844, to March, 1845, Whittier edited the *Middlesex Standard*, a paper published in Lowell, Mass., by the Liberty Party. He was also chiefly responsible for editing the *Essex Transcript*, another of the Liberty Party's publications.

The Liberty Party nominated Birney for President in 1840, but he made a poor showing in the election.

Birney also headed the Liberty Party ticket in 1844 and polled 62,000 votes.

In 1848, the party met in Buffalo, N.Y., with other groups to form the Free Soil Party.   DONALD R. McCOY

See also ABOLITION MOVEMENT; FREE SOIL PARTY.

LIBIDO, *luh BEE doh*, is a psychoanalytic term referring primarily to instincts or urges that are satisfied pleasurably. Sigmund Freud was the first to use this term (see FREUD, SIGMUND).

Some psychoanalysts believe that the libido develops through certain stages. In the *oral* phase, the infant derives pleasure from such activities as sucking and biting. In the *anal* phase, the child obtains satisfaction and interest in bowel control. The *genital* phase includes early adolescence, with its problems of adjusting the sexual drives to fit the patterns of society.

Many psychiatrists believe that the libidinal development is a more continuous process, however, and that the phases are less distinct.   GEORGE A. ULETT

See also PSYCHOANALYSIS and its *Related Articles*.

LIBRA, *LEE bruh*, is the seventh sign of the zodiac. It is symbolized by a pair of weighing scales. Astrologers believe that Libra is ruled by the planet Venus, which is named for the ancient Roman goddess of love and beauty. Libra is an air sign.

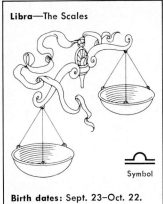

Libra—The Scales

Symbol

Birth dates: Sept. 23–Oct. 22.
Group: Air.
Characteristics: Companionable, diplomatic, friendly, intelligent, pleasant, thoughtful.

Signs of the Zodiac

Aries
Mar. 21–Apr. 19
Taurus
Apr. 20–May 20
Gemini
May 21–June 20
Cancer
June 21–July 22
Leo
July 23–Aug. 22
Virgo
Aug. 23–Sept. 22
Libra
Sept. 23–Oct. 22
Scorpio
Oct. 23–Nov. 21
Sagittarius
Nov. 22–Dec. 21
Capricorn
Dec. 22–Jan. 19
Aquarius
Jan. 20–Feb. 18
Pisces
Feb. 19–Mar. 20

WORLD BOOK illustration by Robert Keys

Astrologers consider people born under the sign of Libra, from September 23 to October 22, to have the characteristics of scales. Libras like balance and harmony in all things and dislike conflict, disagreement, and sudden changes. They are warm, friendly, and sociable. They also are intelligent and thoughtful and are good at patching up quarrels between other people. Libras often have trouble making up their minds because they are quick to listen to different viewpoints and reach a compromise.

Libras have a love of pleasing surroundings and an eye for beauty. They have a pleasant smile that comes naturally and frequently.   CHRISTOPHER McINTOSH

See also ASTROLOGY; HOROSCOPE; ZODIAC.

LIBRARIAN. See LIBRARY.

Libraries play an important role in the education, work, and recreation of millions of people. Many public libraries, such as the one above, offer a variety of materials and services in attractive surroundings. The people in the foreground are using computer catalogs to find books.

LIBRARY

LIBRARY. Libraries form a vital part of the world's systems of communication and education. They make available—through books, films, recordings, and other media—knowledge that has been accumulated through the ages. People in all walks of life—including students, teachers, business executives, government officials, scholars, and scientists—use library resources in their work. Large numbers of people also turn to libraries to satisfy a desire for knowledge or to obtain material for some kind of leisure-time activity. In addition, many people enjoy book discussions, film programs, lectures, story hours, and other activities that are provided by their local library.

The contributors of this article are Rebecca T. Bingham, Director of Library Media Services for the Jefferson County Public Schools, Louisville, Ky.; Pauline A. Cochrane, Professor at the School of Information Studies of Syracuse University; David Kaser, Professor at the School of Library and Information Science of Indiana University at Bloomington; Peggy A. Sullivan, Dean of the College of Professional Studies of Northern Illinois University; Roderick G. Swartz, State Librarian at the Washington State Library; and Robert Wedgeworth, Dean of the School of Library Service at Columbia University.

Libraries also play an important role in preserving a society's cultural heritage. For example, some libraries have special collections of such items as rare books, authors' original manuscripts, or works of local artists. In addition, the librarians in many libraries develop exhibits and offer programs to help people learn about their own community or about the culture of other civilizations. All in all, the library ranks as one of society's most useful service institutions.

The first section of this article, *The Library Today,* provides an overview of the varied contents and kinds of libraries, and discusses the many services these important institutions provide. It also deals with the challenges and problems faced by librarians and libraries. Other parts of the article describe in detail the different types of libraries that are designed to serve different poeple. The article discusses libraries in all parts of the world, the library profession, and the qualifications and training needed by librarians. The article also traces the history of libraries. For detailed information on how to use a library, see the section *A Student Guide to Better Writing, Speaking, and Research Skills* in the RESEARCH GUIDE/INDEX, Volume 22.

Today's libraries differ greatly from libraries of the past—not only in contents, kinds, and services, but even in physical layout and atmosphere. In turn, future libraries will differ from those of today. This is so because librarians constantly strive to find ways to expand and perfect the contributions that they and their institutions make to society.

Contents and Kinds of Libraries

Variety of Contents. The contents of libraries have changed so much through the years that the word *library* itself is, in a sense, inaccurate. The word comes from the Latin word *liber*, which means *book*. It is used because libraries traditionally were largely collections of books. Today's libraries house many books, of course. However, they also have a wide variety of other materials that communicate, educate, and entertain. These materials include magazines, newspapers, pamphlets, disk and tape recordings, films, photographs, microreproductions, computerized information, paintings, musical scores, and maps. In addition to regular books, a library may have large-type books and braille books. The inclusion of such materials in library collections reflects the efforts of librarians to keep pace with changing information formats and to serve people in as many ways as possible.

The expansion of library contents greatly increases the library's ability to communicate and educate. The following examples illustrate just a few of the countless advantages of today's multimedia libraries:

People interested in music can learn much by reading library books on the topic. They can add a great deal to their understanding and appreciation of music by listening to a library's musical recordings. Students of agriculture can learn from books about how crops are grown and can widen their understanding by watching a library film on the process. Many people use libraries to study current events. Library collections of magazines and newspapers provide the most up-to-date and detailed printed material in the field. A library that has only regular books is of no use to many partially sighted people and to all blind persons. But a library that owns recordings, braille books, and large-type magazines and newspapers can be an invaluable aid to those patrons and to others with various physical handicaps.

Variety of Kinds. In addition to expanding contents, librarians have developed many kinds of libraries to serve the needs of different people. The materials of each kind of library are selected to meet the needs of a specific group of patrons. College, university, and research libraries maintain large collections of detailed research materials for advanced students and scholars. School libraries have collections that provide the more basic information needed by elementary and high school students. Public libraries tailor their collections to a broad cross section of the public. Government library collections are geared chiefly toward serving the needs of government officials. Thousands of special libraries provide information for professional people, such as advertising specialists, bankers, editors, engineers, lawyers, physicians, and scientists. Each kind of library

mentioned in this paragraph is discussed in detail later in the article.

Library Services

Before the mid-1800's, most libraries were privately owned and were available chiefly to certain groups, such as scholars, university students, and the wealthy. Years of effort by librarians and other concerned citizens have radically changed this narrow role of libraries and have made the library the widespread, vital service institution that it is today. In many parts of the world, library materials are available to anyone who wants to

WORLD BOOK photo

School Libraries serve students by providing materials for a wide range of purposes and interests. The children in the library shown above are studying some of its collection of paintings and art books to help them with a school assignment.

Alphapress from Jeroboam, Inc.

The Bibliothèque Nationale in Paris is the national library of France and a world center of scholarship. This picture shows one of its reading rooms. The stacks in the background hold part of the famous library's collection of about 500,000 magazines.

use them. Librarians have extended library services far beyond making materials available. They offer many forms of assistance to library users. Librarians also work to interest people in library use, and they engage in a variety of activities that make the library an active force in society.

Providing Materials. Viewed historically, the library's role of making materials available ranks among the most important contributions ever made to human culture and technology. Libraries have long stored materials that enable ideas, knowledge, and experiences to be passed on from generation to generation. Without this line of communication, cultural and technological developments would be nowhere near as advanced as they are.

Viewed as a factor in day-to-day life, the library's materials serve as important resources in the education, work, and recreation of millions of people. To students, the library is a place where they can find materials that help them carry out school assignments. It is also a place where they can pursue knowledge beyond their classrooms, beyond their textbooks, and beyond their teachers.

Professional people in many fields rely on materials in special libraries for information they need in their work. Before going into court for a legal case, for example, a lawyer may spend hours in a law library studying cases to prepare arguments. Doctors use medical libraries to obtain information they need in order to treat unusual or complicated diseases. Many business executives find various library materials to be of great value in their work.

For many persons in all walks of life, the library is a place to get materials for leisure-time activities. Reading, viewing films, and listening to recordings rank among the most popular leisure-time activities, and libraries supply materials for all of them. Large numbers of people use a library to help them carry on a hobby. For example, stamp collectors can find books, pamphlets, and other materials to aid them. Amateur furniture makers can find instructions for building various pieces of furniture. Other people visit a library

frequently just to browse for something that will capture their interest and provide a few hours of relaxation and escape from the day-to-day world. A weary worker, for example, might find that the novels in a library offer a good way to unwind after a busy day.

The job of providing materials for library patrons is a challenging one. To do it well, a librarian must constantly stay aware of new publications and other materials. The librarian evaluates vast amounts of materials —either through personal inspection or by reading reviews—and decides which ones should be available in the library.

Since library budgets are limited, the amount of desirable material always exceeds the amount that can be afforded. Therefore, a librarian must have skill in money management, as well as good judgment and the ability to keep informed about publishing developments. After new materials are purchased, a librarian catalogs them and arranges them in the library so that users can locate them easily.

Assisting Patrons. The service provided by librarians goes far beyond getting and arranging library materials. Librarians help anyone who wants assistance in finding information. In all kinds of libraries this service involves teaching people how to use library resources, helping them find material to answer their questions, and supplying answers to their questions. If the library lacks some material a patron needs, the librarian may obtain it through the library's interlibrary loan system or try to direct the patron to a source where the material can be found.

Many libraries have a question-answering service called a *reference service* or *information service*. A reference librarian may be called on to answer any kind of question. These include basic reference questions, such as "Who was the first Vice-President of the United States?" and "How tall is the Statue of Liberty?" Other questions require more descriptive answers, such as telling how a hummingbird hovers or how wastepaper is recycled. Some libraries have librarians who receive and answer basic questions by telephone. This service saves much time for library patrons. Reference

WORLD BOOK photo

Music Lovers relax while listening to their favorite recordings in the audio section of a library. Many libraries have collections of tapes and phonograph records that patrons may use in the library or check out for use at home.

Music Helps Tell a Story during a library story hour, *above.* A skillful storyteller not only entertains young library patrons, but also can help encourage children to read on their own.

librarians deal increasingly with social issues as libraries increase their community-service activities. Librarians also often help organizations prepare programs on such social problems as drug abuse or environmental pollution.

Active Community Service. All libraries serve some kind of community—a town, city, state, nation, school, college, or business. A library serves by providing materials and assisting patrons. But librarians also devise many more ways of serving their communities.

Public libraries sponsor a variety of activities people can benefit from and enjoy. These include story hours for children and discussion programs for teenagers and adults. Many libraries feature displays or offer lecture programs on topics of interest to their community. Through such means as radio, television, and newspaper announcements, public librarians publicize the benefits and the pleasure to be derived from using library materials. As part of their efforts to make library materials available to everyone, many librarians take materials to people. They may operate a bookmobile service that carries library materials throughout cities, towns, and rural areas. They may establish branch libraries in many neighborhoods of the community. Through the efforts of librarians, library materials reach people in hospitals, prisons, outlying areas, and crowded inner-city areas that have a pressing need for greater informational and educational facilities. To meet the needs of inner-city areas, librarians may set up collections of materials in social service agencies, or even in stores or people's homes. Some libraries send out information by means of cable television.

School libraries supply materials that students and teachers need for learning and teaching, and the librarians teach students how to use a library—a skill that will benefit them throughout their lives. School librarians may also take part in curriculum development and changes and serve their schools in a variety of other ways. Government libraries supply government officials with materials they need in their work. But they also serve by distributing materials to other libraries in their state or nation and by working to coordinate the activities of all the libraries. See also the following sections of this article for discussions of library services: *Public Libraries; School Libraries; College, University, and Research Libraries; Government Libraries;* and *Special Libraries.*

Other Features

The contents, kinds, and services of libraries have all been improved through the years. But improvements extend even further. Librarians today realize that pleasant, comfortable surroundings aid patrons in their studies. Many libraries of the past would seem somewhat dark, dismal, and unattractive by today's standards. Modern libraries are planned so there is plenty of light from windows and artificial lighting systems. The arrangement of furniture and fixtures is both appealing and an aid to ease of use. The buildings of many modern libraries rank among the most attractive in their communities—both inside and out.

As previously mentioned, librarians try to provide easy access to library materials through such services as bookmobiles and neighborhood branch libraries. But librarians today also provide easier access to materials within their libraries than ever before. Many do so through the *open-stack* or *open-shelf* system. This system allows patrons to go through library materials themselves. Patrons can inspect the material firsthand and thus decide whether it will be useful to them. The system differs from the *closed-stack* or *closed-shelf* system, under which patrons must ask librarians to get material for them. The open-stack system is much more widespread today than it used to be.

Challenges and Problems

In spite of all their progress, libraries—like all institutions in today's complex world—face many challenges and problems. A major challenge for libraries is how to keep up with the rapid growth of information. Important problems include providing adequate finances to support library services, developing security measures to protect valuable library materials, and resolving difficulties related to the practice of photocopying and to the controversy over censorship. The following sections of this article deal with each of these issues.

The Growth of Information. Each year, more and more information becomes available about every subject that interests people. The volume of material published on almost every general topic doubles every 10 to 20 years.

The amount of material in what some sociologists call *The Information Society* poses challenges for librarians. It means that librarians must keep informed about more materials than ever before and be more selective in their purchases. As a library increases its purchases, the librarian's job of arranging and storing materials becomes harder. The amount of information also makes more difficult the job of locating materials for users.

Fortunately, the tools with which librarians work are improving. There are more and better guides, indexes, and catalogs than ever to help librarians locate what people want. Much cataloging is now done centrally or cooperatively, so that the task does not have to be repeated in each library.

Many of the tools that help librarians deal with problems caused by the growth of information result from technological advances. Microreproductions, of which microfilm and microfiche are the best known, make it possible to store information in less space and, sometimes, at lower cost than ever before. It is now possible to reproduce an entire book on a microfiche not much bigger than a playing card. If such a "book" could be sold in huge quantities, it would cost only a few cents.

Computers are another technological advance that help libraries. They are used to keep records involved in various jobs, such as ordering, cataloging, and circulating books. The Medlars system of the United States National Library of Medicine involves the use of computers for the creation of bibliographies (see the *United States Government Libraries* section of this article). Computer-based catalogs called *on-line public access catalogs* have replaced the card catalog in many libraries. Other advanced systems called *videotex* combine computers, television, and telephones and make it possible for libraries to offer various services in homes.

Participation in *library networks* and *library systems* also helps librarians deal with the growth of information. Library networks and systems enable a group of libraries to share information, materials, and services. For example, OCLC (Online Computer Library Center) in Dublin, Ohio, serves about 6,000 libraries. Such networks also can help participating libraries organize their collections and plan improved services. Some networks serve only a certain kind of library, such as an academic and research library. However, many networks and most systems are organized to serve a geographical area. Libraries throughout New England, for example, participate in the New England Library Information Network.

To be effective, the libraries in a network or system must be linked together by communications hookups. These hookups speed the sending of questions and answers about the availability of materials. Some systems own trucks that pick up and deliver materials from one library to another.

Online Computer Library Center

A Library Network helps librarians deal with the information boom. Computer terminals operated by the Online Computer Library Center in Dublin, Ohio, *left,* link over 6,000 libraries in the United States, Canada, Mexico, and Great Britain.

WORLD BOOK photo by Milt and Joan Mann

Storefront Libraries are one of the several ways that libraries have spread their services. Such libraries as the one at the left enable people to obtain library materials in their own neighborhoods.

Many library networks and systems already exist, and the trend toward them continues to grow. By means of reciprocal borrowing privileges among libraries and through use of microreproductions, computers, facsimile transmission, and other communication aids, a person in a future library may have quick access to much of the world's recorded information.

Finances. Libraries—like schools, hospitals, and other institutions—face financial problems. Public libraries and public school libraries get most of their funds from taxes. Local taxes are the traditional source of funds, although state and federal governments also have contributed to the development of these libraries. Other libraries are privately supported by the organizations that run them and by private donors. The funds available from both public and private sources are limited, and all libraries work within budgets. Rising costs for salaries, materials, and equipment, along with increased demands for library services, put a severe strain on library budgets. The librarian's job of choosing the best available material and the most useful services for a library thus becomes increasingly difficult. In addition, all libraries—whether their funds come from public or private sources—must compete with other institutions and other sectors of society for the available funds.

Security. Each year, libraries lose large amounts of valuable materials through theft. Librarians use various methods to fight this problem. Some libraries have adopted security systems. Under one such system, people leaving a library are required to pass through a turnstile at which a guard is stationed. The guard tries to detect anyone who is leaving the library with material that has not been checked out. Some libraries use electronic and magnetic devices to detect attempted theft. Materials sensitive to electric or magnetic impulses are put into library materials. If a person tries to leave the library with an item that has not been checked out, the substance sets off an alarm at the library exit. These security systems employ various methods to keep the substance from setting off the alarm when a person is removing a book that has been properly checked out.

Photocopying, or *photographic copying*, is the practice of making copies of parts of books, magazines, newspapers, and pamphlets for users. The practice is a valuable aid to the librarian's work and to the user. For example, people doing major research projects may need material from parts of dozens of books. They can get copies of the information they need from each book. Thus, they have permanent possession of the material they need, and they have it in a form much reduced from the bulk of dozens of books.

The copyright law regulates the reproduction of published material by photocopying. The law provides for some photocopying by libraries or users without permission from or payment to the holder of the copyright. The copyright rules forbid "systematic" copying in an attempt to avoid buying published materials. But the law does allow a limited exchange of photocopies among members of a library network or system, as long as such sharing does not deprive the publisher of sales. Some librarians believe that these restrictions hamper public use. Publishers respond that people may do any amount of photocopying they wish if they obtain permission and pay royalties to the holder of the copyright.

Censorship. The question of censorship is one of the most sensitive problems of librarians. Some people believe that certain material should not be published, and, if published, should not be available in a library. Such materials include many works dealing with religion or sex and works that promote such political or social views as Communism and revolution. Other people oppose all censorship. Librarians often receive bitter complaints from procensorship people for deciding to acquire certain works, and from anticensorship people for excluding certain works.

The **Children's Section** of a public library is designed especially for young patrons. Colorful posters, a gingerbread playhouse, and furniture made for children, *left,* may help attract youngsters to this department. Librarians use many methods to make public libraries appealing to all members of a community.

WORLD BOOK photo

Public libraries serve a far wider range of patrons than do all other kinds of libraries. These libraries aim to serve all members of a community—children, young adults, and adults from all walks of life. People use public libraries for schoolwork, their jobs, and for leisure-time activities. Public libraries must therefore store a variety of books and other materials and provide many services for members of the community. Many also must employ a variety of staff members who specialize in serving various age groups.

Kinds of Public Libraries. Public libraries range in size from huge big-city libraries with dozens of branches to small-town libraries that occupy only one room. There are about 14,700 public libraries in the United States. Of these, about 5,900 are branch libraries of a city, county, or regional library system. No matter what their size or where they are located, all public libraries have the same goal—to be of maximum service to their community.

To serve the needs of a large urban area, a big-city library must have a vast variety of books and other materials. It also needs branch libraries to serve people in their own neighborhoods. For example, the New York Public Library has about 9 million volumes and over 80 neighborhood branch libraries.

The materials in most large public libraries are organized into subject areas, such as history, science, and sports. These libraries also have special sections for children, adults, and, often, young adults. In addition, they may have specialized departments to serve the research needs of the industrial and scientific interests of the community. The Detroit Public Library, located in the world's chief automobile manufacturing center, has a large collection of materials devoted to automotive history.

Except in big cities, a public library does not have to be large to serve its community. A small library housed in a room or two can play an effective role if it has a good basic collection of reference books, subscribes to magazines of use to its patrons, and purchases enough new materials to keep up to date. But the essential element in any library is a librarian who makes it an active service institution and is interested in both library materials and the people who use them.

Services for Children. A good children's librarian makes a public library an exciting place. The librarian's friendly, understanding attitude can make the children's department fun and interesting. The librarian arranges the department so young patrons can use it easily. Desks, chairs, tables, shelves, and even water fountains are at convenient heights for children, and the room may have pictures and other decorations that make it warm and appealing.

The children's librarian may conduct story hours, book clubs, and other activities to help young patrons enjoy themselves and develop an interest in the library and its materials. The librarian may also work with child-oriented groups, including parent and community organizations and local schools, to establish programs for the education and recreation of children. Summer programs keep children interested in books and other materials during vacation.

Services for Young Adults. Librarians know that teen-agers need special attention because of their special needs and interests. Some large public libraries have separate departments for young adults. Here, the librarian helps teen-agers continue to develop reading interests that will carry over into adulthood.

Young-adult departments feature materials on careers, sports, travel, and other subjects of interest to teen-agers. Teen-agers as a group are especially interested in such social issues as citizenship, life styles, political change, pollution, and poverty. As a result, librarians try to obtain a wide variety of materials dealing with these subjects. Librarians in young-adult departments, as well as in children's departments, must be able to guide users to suitable books in the library's other departments when necessary.

Librarians for young adults, like those for children, conduct programs to encourage library use. Geared to the interests of young adults, such programs might involve discussions of books, films, popular music, and current social issues.

Services for Adults. The needs of adults, like those of children and young adults, change and expand constantly. Developments in every field of knowledge make it increasingly important that adults continue their education after leaving school. Public libraries can play an important role in adult education. In addition, many adults today have more leisure time than ever before. The public library is an important source of materials for leisure-time activity.

A public library maintains a wide selection of books for adults. The selection ranges from up-to-date reference works, such as almanacs, atlases, encyclopedias, and government publications, to nonfiction works that cover the whole broad range of peoples' interests, to fiction of the past and present.

Public librarians go beyond books to provide services to adults. They help patrons search the back issues of newspapers and magazines to find articles on specific subjects. They also lend films, recordings, scores of musical compositions, prints of great paintings, and other items. Public libraries have reference librarians who answer specific questions asked by patrons.

Services for Special Groups. Public libraries have always served the needs of special groups, such as handicapped persons. For example, many libraries distribute braille books to the blind. *Talking books* (recordings of books and articles) help individuals who cannot use regular books because of blindness, paralysis, or other handicaps.

Libraries are paying increasing attention to the needs of senior citizens. Many people nearing retirement turn to a library for help in planning the future. They seek information on such subjects as recreation, handling finances, health, and travel. Librarians prepare book lists for senior citizens and may hold meetings where older persons can discuss their interests and problems. Most public libraries make books in large print available to people with failing eyesight, a problem of many elderly people.

In addition to providing materials and services, some libraries help special groups in other ways. For example, a library may have a ramp at an entrance instead of stairs so that people confined to wheelchairs and anyone else who has difficulty using stairs can get in and out of the library easily.

Many public librarians make a special effort to help teachers by providing books and other materials for their use. Many also conduct film programs, group discussions, talks on library materials, and other activities

WORLD BOOK photo

A Reading Lounge in a public library has comfortable chairs for patrons who want to browse through a recently published book or catch up on the latest issue of their favorite magazine.

WORLD BOOK photo

Reference Librarians, such as the man shown above, are frequently called on to help patrons locate information. Some librarians conduct research to answer questions on various topics.

for various community groups. Organizations seeking help from public librarians in finding material on such subjects as managing money and raising children are provided with bibliographies. Many public libraries provide rooms where groups can meet. Business and industrial groups often use public libraries. For example, a public librarian might prepare a special list of books and other materials for use in a management-training conference. In communities with strong labor unions, public librarians frequently work with union leaders to further the education of workers. Some libraries provide books for factories or union halls. They also furnish books for adults who are learning to read. In effect, a good public library can be the main information source for the entire community.

A Bookmobile is a buslike motor vehicle used to bring library materials to people. Many public libraries operate these "libraries on wheels" as part of their effort to spread the service they provide.

WORLD BOOK photo

Spreading the Service. A major goal of public librarians is to make their services available to everyone. Bookmobiles and branch libraries help spread public library service. As another step toward this goal, libraries might participate in library networks or join together into library systems. The establishment of networks and systems, discussed in the section on *The Library Today*, has been a major factor in the greater distribution of library materials and services.

Much has been done toward bridging the gap between small-town and big-city libraries. Many county or regional libraries provide a wider range of services than small-town libraries can. Most county or regional libraries operate from a headquarters library, often in the county seat. The headquarters library places books in small-town libraries—and even in grocery stores and gasoline stations in areas that lack libraries. A headquarters library—and other public libraries as well—may even deliver books by mail or messenger.

Administering a Public Library is like running any complex organization. It requires skill, experience, and the ability to deal with people effectively. The staff of a public library is headed by the director. The director is responsible to the board of trustees, the group that sets policies for the library. In places that have no library board, the director may be responsible to the top government official of the community.

Most public libraries in the United States are administered by boards of trustees that consist of business executives, civic leaders, and other interested citizens. Most library boards are elected by the voters or are appointed by a local government official, such as the mayor.

The director has the responsibility of carrying out the policies set by the library board. In practice, the director often takes the lead in suggesting to the board the policies it should adopt. For this reason, the director and the members of the board must have confidence in one another. The director prepares the budget for the library, for approval by the board and the local government. After the budget has been established, the director makes sure the money is spent wisely and in accordance with the policies set by the board.

The director is responsible for the public relations of the library. He or she tries to interest the public in the library through newspaper articles, radio and television programs, and other forms of publicity. The director also guides the library staff in the selection of books and other library materials. A most important duty is keeping the library free from interference by groups that want to eliminate material which disagrees with their particular point of view. A good library collection must represent many different viewpoints.

A large public library may have separate departments for adult services; young-adult services; children's services; extension services, including branches and bookmobiles; technical processes, including ordering and cataloging library materials; public relations; personnel; maintenance; and business, including bookkeeping and other office functions. In a small public library, all these duties may be the responsibility of the director and a few assistants.

Supporting the Public Library. Public libraries, like all institutions, must have adequate funds to be able to serve the community. Public libraries in the United States spend an average of about $5 a year for each person in their communities. Some libraries spend much more, and some spend less.

Salaries for librarians and other personnel make up the largest part of a library's budget. A public library may spend about 60 per cent of its annual budget for salaries, 25 per cent for new materials, and 15 per cent for maintenance and miscellaneous expenses. However, rising salaries and other labor costs make these proportions difficult to maintain, and many libraries are finding that their budget for new materials must be cut down to meet labor costs.

Local taxes are the chief source of money for public libraries. Some municipalities set aside money for their library out of their general funds, and others collect special taxes for the library. A few public libraries have endowments from private sources.

Private citizens also aid public libraries in other ways. Many communities have a local group, usually called *Friends of the Library*, that helps raise money for the library and acts as a public relations channel for it. Such citizen groups work to publicize or supply library services and to remind the public of the importance of the library to the community.

Like other public institutions in a community, the public library must compete for funds with such important governmental agencies as the fire, police, and sanitation departments. Some communities do not have—or do not set aside—enough money to provide adequate library service.

The state and federal governments have taken steps to help libraries meet their increasing financial needs. Some states supplement local library budgets with state funds. The state may provide funds to a well-organized local library so that it can serve a larger number of communities in its area. In this way, smaller communities can have the advantages of services provided by large public libraries.

The U.S. government is becoming increasingly important in helping public libraries. In 1956, Congress passed the Library Services Act (later changed and renamed the Library Services and Construction Act) to improve library service in rural areas. The government agreed to provide as much as $7\frac{1}{2}$ million in annual grants to the states for five years on a matching basis. Major amendments to the Library Services and Construction Act in 1964, 1966, and 1970 provided aid to both urban and rural libraries. In the early 1980's, funds provided by the federal government under the act totaled about $70 million a year. Grants are made for the purchase of library materials and for the promotion of interlibrary cooperation through the development of library systems.

WORLD BOOK photo   Straub, Van Dine, Associates, Architects

Public Libraries of All Sizes and Designs can be seen throughout the United States. The traditional style of many libraries of the late 1800's and early 1900's is shown at the left. More modern libraries, such as the one at the right, have been built since the mid-1900's.

A Modern School Library is a multimedia center designed to complement classroom studies and offer a variety of educational materials to students and teachers. In the library shown above, natural light and comfortable furniture help provide pleasant surroundings for students working on assignments. Individual stalls called *carrels* offer privacy to students listening to recordings.

Every school needs a library, even if a good public library is nearby. Throughout the school day, teachers and students use library materials in the teaching and learning process. The quality of a school's instructional program depends, to a great extent, on quick access to library materials.

Today's school library serves as a center for a wide variety of educational media. These media include books, magazines, newspapers, and pamphlets; recordings; maps, films, photographs, and paintings; and, in some cases, *realia* (real objects). In addition, some school libraries have computer terminals with access to audio and visual materials from a main information storage center. The library also might provide such equipment as cameras, projectors, and tape recorders. Many libraries allow students to use this equipment in making their own films, slides, and tape recordings for classroom assignments. To reflect the expanded role of the school library in education, many schools call their libraries by other names. These names include *instructional materials center*, *learning resources center*, and *media center*.

School librarians are sometimes called *media specialists*. They work closely with teachers in helping students learn to use libraries and library materials and to develop good reading and study habits. School librarians should have a specialized education in librarianship. But because school librarians work closely with teachers, they—like teachers—must be skilled in subject matter and educational processes.

Many school systems provide services that help the individual school libraries and school librarians within the systems. For example, a school system may hire a school library supervisor to help plan media programs in the system's individual libraries. The supervisor might also coordinate the school system's media program with its total instructional program.

Elementary School Libraries provide boys and girls with some of their first experiences in using a library. Children go to their school library to hear stories; to browse through, read, view, or listen to library materials; to borrow materials; and to get information for classroom assignments. In the past, young children did little independent library research. Today, children begin independent use of the library as early as kindergarten and expand their independent study as their needs and abilities increase.

A good school library provides a wide range of material for use by students and teachers. If a fifth-grade class is studying Mexico, for example, the teacher can charge out books, magazines, and pictures about Mexican life and records or tapes on Mexican music for classroom use. Or the teacher might instruct the students to do independent research on Mexico at the school library, giving them an opportunity to explore, discover, and locate materials for themselves. In the library, the students may also work together in small groups, discussing research they have done or perhaps studying and listening to recordings. Some libraries have small, separate conference rooms for such activities, and many librarians believe there is a need for more of these facilities.

Middle School and Junior High School Libraries serve students who are growing out of childhood and into their teens. Students at this level have a wider range of interests, abilities, and needs than do most elementary school pupils. In addition, middle and junior high school teachers commonly assign more independent and small-group research projects than do teachers of lower grades. For these reasons, the materials provided by middle and junior high school libraries must cover a wider range of subjects than do those in elementary school libraries.

High School Libraries differ from elementary, middle, and junior high school libraries in two chief ways. Most of them are larger than other school libraries because most high schools have more students than do other schools. High school libraries also provide materials that cover a wider range of subjects and are more complex than those in libraries for lower grades. A library in a large high school might have separate departments—sometimes called *resource centers*—for languages, mathematics, science, and social studies.

In high school, students work on independent study projects even more than they do in elementary, middle, or junior high school. Independent study is a particularly important skill for students who are planning to go on to college. High school students continue the practice of sometimes working together in small groups in the library.

Many schools—on all grade levels—have library clubs. Members of these clubs may learn about library procedures and assist in the work required to run a library. A number of librarians first became interested in their field in this way.

School Library Standards. Many schools have good library facilities, but many others do not. About half the public elementary schools in the United States do not have even a central library. In these schools, library books are kept in the classrooms. Some schools have little or no library materials other than books. In many school libraries, the collection is too small or too out of date to serve the needs of the students. In other schools, students must rely on the public library or a visit by a bookmobile.

Librarians and other educators have long called for an upgrading of all inadequate school library facilities. They urge schools to meet certain standards in library service. These standards deal with such matters as the kinds and number of materials, audiovisual equipment, and personnel that school libraries should have. The American Library Association (ALA) and the Association for Educational Communications and Technology (AECT) have established standards for school libraries. These guidelines are set forth in detail in an ALA-AECT publication called *Media Programs: District and School*. The various states and the regional school accrediting associations also have established standards.

The U.S. government has given much financial aid for improvement of school libraries. Through such legislation as the National Defense Education Act (NDEA), the Elementary and Secondary Education Act of 1965, and the Higher Education Act, the government has helped provide funds for library resources and the education of librarians. The U.S. Department of Education employs specialists in the school library field.

WORLD BOOK photo

Books Written in Spanish are part of the collection of the library in a community that has a large Spanish-speaking population. Many school libraries have such foreign-language books and other special materials to help meet the needs of their patrons.

WORLD BOOK photo

Realia, or actual objects, are available for study in some school libraries. Such materials provide students with additional aid in their schoolwork. The boy shown above has checked out several birds' nests to examine while he reads a book on the subject.

A Rare Book Collection is an example of the vast and valuable holdings of university libraries. The collection shown at the left is part of the Beinecke Rare Book and Manuscript Library at Yale University. The six-story glass enclosure contains about 180,-000 rare volumes.

Ezra Stoller

College and University Libraries. The library is a major resource of any modern institution of higher education. College students study such a vast, fast-changing body of knowledge that few courses can be taught with one, two, or even a half a dozen textbooks. Research occupies a significant place in life at colleges —both two- and four-year schools—and at universities. The library has a vital role in this search for knowledge. It serves as a workshop for the entire college or university—students and faculty alike.

The United States has more than 4,000 college and university libraries. These libraries own more than 514 million books and other items, employ about 58,000 staff members, and spend about $1½ billion annually. Canada has about 350 college and university libraries. The world's largest university library, with about 10 million volumes, is at Harvard University.

A college or university library is a complex institution. It must have large quantities of books, magazines, documents, newspapers, films, recordings, photographs, and other materials to meet the demands of both students and faculty. Many university libraries have collections that are devoted to highly specialized subjects. For example, the libraries on the various campuses of the University of California have special research collections on astronomy, California history, citrus fruits, East Asia, early English literature, Latin America, oceanography, and many other topics.

A large university may have as many as 50 or more libraries in its various departments, schools, and branches. An entire library may be devoted to a single field of study, such as biology, education, music, or psychology. Such specialization gives students quick access to in-depth materials for major courses of study.

Since the 1960's, a trend in higher education has made too much compartmentalization a drawback. Teaching and research in colleges and universities have tended more and more to cross traditional lines of academic disciplines. The conventional divisions of knowledge—which are reflected in departmentalized libraries—work against the crossing of traditional lines. As a result, a new movement has emerged in the college and university library field. There is a trend in libraries toward organizing large collections of books that cover broad fields of knowledge, such as the sciences, the social sciences, and the fine arts. Such libraries are useful to students who want information on several subjects from a general point of view.

College and university libraries face problems that result from two major developments that began in the 1950's. These trends are the *information boom*, which is still going on, and the *explosion of students*, which peaked in the early 1980's.

Never before has society gained so much information so fast. Storing the results of this information boom places an ever-increasing burden on all libraries. Libraries used heavily for scholarly research—such as those of colleges and universities— are especially hard pressed. An enormous increase in college and university enrollments occurred along with the information boom. From 1948 to about 1980, the number of college and university students in the United States increased from about 2 ½ million to about 11½ million. Canada experienced a similar rate of growth, with an increase from about 68,000 students in 1951 to about 615,000 in 1979. Enrollments are expected to level off or decline slightly during the middle and late 1980's.

Colleges and universities have taken various steps to keep pace with the demands on libraries caused by these developments. Many schools have launched extensive library-building programs. Such schools are trying to plan their new libraries in ways that will serve all students with maximum efficiency. In the past, for example, many university libraries were more concerned with the needs of graduate students and faculty members than with the requirements of undergraduates. Concern for the library needs of undergraduates has increased, and many schools have even built separate libraries for these students. There is also a trend toward separate library buildings for rare books and for other highly specialized collections. Microreproductions and other aids—along with more library space—are helping college and university libraries solve the storage problem. Some libraries have begun using computers to help keep track of the vast amounts of information they are amassing.

Research Libraries. Many college and university libraries function as research libraries. But several other major types of libraries also serve researchers and scholars. These libraries are not directly connected with any educational institution. Some of the most famous ones are privately supported and controlled. The Pierpont Morgan Library in New York City specializes in the fine arts and in early printed books and manuscripts. The Folger Shakespeare Library in Washington, D.C., has one of the world's great collections dealing with the Elizabethan period of English history. Other famous private research libraries include the Newberry Library in Chicago, which specializes in history, literature, and the fine arts; the John Crerar Library in Chicago and the Linda Hall Library in Kansas City, Mo., specializing in science and technology; and the Henry E. Huntington Library in San Marino, Calif., which is rich in literature, early printing, and the fine arts.

Other kinds of libraries also have outstanding resources for research. Especially important are the Library of Congress and other libraries of the federal government, and the special libraries administered by associations, business organizations, and societies. These libraries are discussed in the sections *Government Libraries* and *Special Libraries*. Most public libraries are not mainly concerned with scholarly research. But many have collections that are useful to scholars, such as the Cleveland Public Library's collections on folklore and Oriental history.

The problem of providing adequate collections of materials for the people who use them is especially difficult for research libraries. Keeping up with the thousands of new books published each year throughout the world is a vast job in itself. But even more difficult is the job of keeping up with the thousands of scholarly and technical magazines published by academies, governments, societies, and other institutions. Throughout the world, for example, there are about 10,000 medical magazines and at least 50,000 magazines in other branches of science.

No one library can own all the material that researchers might request. Researchers often need rare, out-of-print books, and books published in foreign languages. To help solve this and other problems, many research libraries cooperate in buying, cataloging, and storing books and magazines. One of the chief means of cooperation is through "union" lists and catalogs of books and magazines. The Library of Congress maintains the *National Union Catalog*. This publication lists books, maps, pamphlets, periodicals, and other works in more than 1,000 libraries in the United States and Canada. The *Union List of Serials in the United States and Canada* gives the location of more than 100,000 magazines in libraries located in the United States and Canada. Many research libraries rely on computerized cataloging systems to locate materials in other libraries. Materials that appear on the lists and in the catalogs can often be borrowed through interlibrary loans or can be photocopied.

Libraries also cooperate in buying books from other countries. Under Public Law 480, the Library of Congress buys foreign books with money that the government receives from the sale of surplus agricultural goods. Such books have come from Egypt, India, Israel, Nepal, Pakistan, Sri Lanka, Yugoslavia, and elsewhere. The books are widely distributed to libraries in the United States, especially to those that specialize in the nations that supply the books. Under the National Program for Acquisitions and Cataloging (NPAC), the Library of Congress acquires books from nations not covered by Public Law 480. The Library of Congress keeps the books bought through the NPAC, but the program allows the Library of Congress to catalog the books promptly and to make the cataloging available to libraries that buy the books through commercial channels. Thus, the NPAC helps libraries reduce the high cost of cataloging.

Some libraries also cooperate in housing valuable, but seldom-used, books. For example, the Center for Research Libraries in Chicago serves as a storage center in the United States. This center also subscribes to thousands of seldom-used journals, which member libraries may borrow.

Normunds Berzins, Image Finders Photo Agency

The John P. Roberts Research Library at the University of Toronto is one of the largest academic library buildings in North America. It houses humanities and social sciences collections.

Government Libraries serve the reference needs of government officials. The National Agricultural Library also aids the agriculture industry of the United States and other users. Researchers in the library's telephone inquiry department, *left,* answer patrons' questions on agricultural topics.

United States Government Libraries. Every department and many agencies of the United States government maintain their own libraries to help their staffs. Three government libraries have such large and varied collections—and provide such wide-ranging services—that they are considered *national libraries*. These three national libraries, all located in or near Washington, D.C., are (1) the Library of Congress; (2) the National Agricultural Library of the Department of Agriculture; and (3) the National Library of Medicine, in the Public Health Service division of the Department of Health and Human Services. A fourth institution, the National Archives, can also be considered a national library. Valuable permanent records of the U.S. government are stored there. See NATIONAL ARCHIVES.

The Library of Congress is probably the largest library in the world. This enormous center of information contains more than 75 million items, including books, journals, music, films, photographs, and maps. Since 1870, the library has received two free copies of every book copyrighted in the United States. The U.S. Copyright Office is a department of the library. For more information, see the LIBRARY OF CONGRESS article.

The National Agricultural Library ranks second in size among U.S. government libraries. It was founded in 1862 to serve the Department of Agriculture. It now has a wide range of users, including other government agencies, the entire agricultural industry, chemical and drug companies, and universities. The library's huge collection of about $1\frac{1}{2}$ million items includes material on agricultural engineering, horticulture, soils, and other fields of agriculture. It also includes materials on biology, chemistry, home economics, and other subjects related to agriculture. The library prepares the monthly *Bibliography of Agriculture*, which lists articles in the library's books and related materials.

The National Library of Medicine collection includes over $2\frac{1}{2}$ million items in nearly all languages. The collection serves physicians, medical research scientists, medical schools, and libraries in many parts of the world.

The library's monthly publication, *Index Medicus*, lists by subject and author more than 200,000 items published each year in the field of medicine. Every year, this library makes copies of more than 2 million pages of articles and distributes them to the medical profession.

The National Library of Medicine has one of the most advanced mechanized information processing systems in the world. This system is called *Medlars*, a name that stands for *Med*ical *L*iterature *A*nalysis and *R*etrieval *S*ystem. Medlars enables the library to compile and publish bibliographies on medical subjects—including *Index Medicus*—electronically. Another mechanized feature of the National Library of Medicine is its *Medline* service. Medline stands for *Med*lars on-*line*. The service involves sending information from Medlars to medical libraries throughout the United States and Canada by way of direct computer lines.

Some large federal agencies operate library systems on a nationwide and worldwide scale. The largest of these systems are those of the Army, Navy, and Air Force. Each military organization supports libraries at its bases throughout the world for technical support and for educational and recreational purposes. The Navy also has libraries on its ships. The Veterans Administration has at least two kinds of libraries in each of its more than 175 hospitals. One library is run by a medical librarian and serves the medical staff. The second library is primarily for the use of the patients.

The United States Information Agency (USIA) operates libraries in about 80 countries. The libraries provide information about the United States. More than $2\frac{1}{2}$ million persons yearly visit USIA libraries to browse, attend cultural programs, or seek information.

There are more than 2,700 other important federal libraries. Each of the executive departments of government has an outstanding collection devoted to special fields related to the department's work. Other important libraries include those of the Bureau of Standards, the National Weather Service, the Office of Management and Budget, the Patent and Trademark Office, and the Environmental Protection Agency. The Smithsonian Institution has several libraries, which cover subjects ranging from air and space to the history of technology.

The Federal Library Committee, established in 1965, coordinates all federal library activities. It has its headquarters in the Library of Congress. Its membership includes representatives from the national libraries and the federal library community. The committee tries to make sure that the services provided in the U.S. government libraries meet the needs of the nation.

State Libraries. Most states have a state library. These libraries are agencies of the state governments, and their primary function is to make materials available to government officials. The libraries also provide materials to other libraries in their states. In addition, a state library plans—in cooperation with library leaders throughout the state—a statewide library program for the benefit of all the people. The amount of service provided by state libraries varies among the states, of course. This section gives a general description of more or less typical well-established state libraries.

Service to Government. A state library serves the state government in many ways. State officials use the library as a general library and information center. The state library agency may maintain a special law library, which serves as the state center for legal reference and research. The law library furnishes judges, legislators, and other officials with information on government, laws, and political science. A state library agency may maintain other special libraries in such fields as the humanities, medicine, the physical sciences, the social sciences, and technology. Special libraries of this kind are gaining increasing importance as governments take on a wider range of responsibilities. Today, government officials may need detailed information on almost any subject to help them reach decisions on many complex issues. The state library will provide research for state officials on any subject. This function is known as *legislative reference and research service.*

Service to Other Libraries. State libraries are sometimes called *librarians' libraries.* This term reflects the state library's role of serving other libraries in the state. A state library may function as the center of a state's interlibrary loan system. It may supply public, school, college, and university libraries with seldom-used and costly materials from the state collection. It may also offer technical and advisory assistance to these libraries, and gather statistics on libraries in the state.

State libraries work to provide quality library service for all citizens in their states. Since the 1960's, one of the chief ways by which state libraries have promoted good statewide library service has been through library cooperation. Programs include creating library systems, designating resource centers, and encouraging all types of libraries in the state to work together.

State libraries also serve as links between the state's public, school, and college libraries and the state and federal governments. They may propose legislation designed to benefit libraries, and they administer funds appropriated by the federal government under the Library Services and Construction Act. State libraries also administer funds that state governments provide for public libraries.

Other Services. State libraries work with other agencies for library improvement. These agencies include the American Library Association, the United States Department of Education, and the Council of State Governments. State libraries also coordinate the recruiting of librarians in their states and work with library educators in planning academic programs for the professional training of librarians. State libraries also conduct in-service training for librarians and library trustees in order to help keep them aware of new developments in librarianship.

State libraries collect and preserve official state records and documents and maintain collections of material on state history. They compile and distribute lists of state publications and distribute state documents to other libraries in and outside their states. Many state libraries receive braille and talking books from the Library of Congress and loan them to blind people in their states. In some states, the state library offers books and other library services to inmates of correctional and other institutions.

State libraries are also assuming a leadership role in the development of a national system of libraries. This role calls for the eventual coordination of the resources of all types of libraries throughout the United States.

Canadian Government Libraries. The Canadian government maintains the Library of Parliament, the National Library of Canada, the Canada Institute for Scientific and Technical Information, and about 250 other libraries that serve government departments and agencies. The main government libraries are in Ottawa, the national capital.

The Library of Parliament, like the Library of Congress, was established chiefly to serve the needs of its country's lawmakers. The library—which houses about 570,000 volumes—now serves many other needs, including those of scholars. The Library of Parliament has served Canada's government ever since the formation of the Dominion of Canada in 1867. The library evolved from the legislative libraries of Lower and Upper Canada, two political units that were created out of the old province of Quebec in 1791. After Lower and Upper Canada united in 1840, the two libraries became one. This library became the basis of the Library of Parliament.

The National Library of Canada began operations in 1953. It houses about 800,000 volumes, most of which deal with Canada. The National Library publishes *Canadiana,* a monthly and annual list of new books and pamphlets about Canada. Another service of the National Library is the *Canadian Union Catalogue,* which lists material in more than 300 Canadian government, public, university, and special libraries.

The Canada Institute for Scientific and Technical Information was founded in 1916 as the National Science Library. This library has 1 million volumes and houses the government's collections on science and technology. The institute also serves as the center of a national information network in science and in technology.

WORLD BOOK photo

WORLD BOOK photo

The Collection of a Special Library may feature items other than books. The map library shown above, for example, has thousands of maps for the use of its patrons.

A Special Library at the United Nations, *above,* provides delegates with materials on international law, economic and social affairs, and other subjects related to UN work.

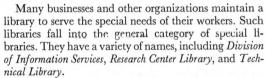

Many businesses and other organizations maintain a library to serve the special needs of their workers. Such libraries fall into the general category of special libraries. They have a variety of names, including *Division of Information Services, Research Center Library,* and *Technical Library.*

The library of a newspaper is a special library. So is the library of a bank, of an advertising agency, or of a company that makes guided missiles. THE WORLD BOOK ENCYCLOPEDIA maintains a special library for the use of its editors. Many of the research and government libraries discussed elsewhere in this article are special libraries. There are probably more than 12,000 special libraries in the United States and more than 1,200 in Canada.

The collection of a special library is tailored to the needs and goals of the organization that the library serves. For example, the materials in a chemical company's library deal chiefly with chemistry. In some fast-developing fields, special library collections may include relatively few books. To keep up with the latest developments, such libraries rely heavily on publications other than books. These publications include computer printouts, magazines and pamphlets, newspaper clippings, scientific papers, and research and government reports.

The special library is taking on increasing importance with the rapid developments in all fields of knowledge. Specialists in various fields must rely on information

to reach decisions. For this reason, they must be provided with the results of previous work and investigations before they start new programs. They depend on special libraries for the information they need.

The librarian of a special library must be able to provide the information required by the organization's staff. To do this job well, the librarian must (1) be thoroughly familiar with the operation and needs of the organization, (2) know the contents of the library in great detail, and (3) know where to turn for information if the library cannot provide needed information. Even the collections of the largest special libraries have limitations. Therefore, special librarians make extensive use of public, college, university, and research libraries; other special libraries; trade associations; government agencies; and other sources of information.

Many special librarians have training in both librarianship and a special subject. For example, the librarian of an art museum might have degrees in both art history and library science. Similarly, the librarian of a chemical company might be a chemist as well as a librarian.

Special librarians are organized into an association called the Special Libraries Association. This association has about 11,500 members in the United States, Canada, and other countries. It is divided into various divisions, such as Insurance, and Advertising and Marketing. The divisions enable people with similar interests to work together on common library problems.

Librarians draw on many fields of knowledge other than library science to help them in their work. One such field, called *information science*, deals with what information is and how people use it. Information science also involves the ways computers, microphotography, and other technological developments can help provide people with information. Librarians study information science to learn how to operate a library so that patrons can get information quickly and easily.

Information science brings together ideas from many other fields, including communications, computer technology, information theory, linguistics, management, mathematics, and psychology and other behavioral sciences. A few examples can help give an idea of how this wide variety of knowledge contributes to the operation of a library. Communications provides an understanding of the various media libraries can use to transmit information. Computer technology helps librarians design automated library procedures. Information theory, a branch of science and engineering, can be used to analyze the quality and characteristics of systems involving the transmission and use of information. Management supplies techniques for analyzing and improving library operations. Mathematics provides a means to formulate exact statements of library problems, and linguistics helps in the creation of indexes. Psychology and other behavioral sciences help librarians understand how the human mind reacts when faced with such problems as finding information in a library.

Information science has developed gradually during the 1900's. Today, most library schools recognize its importance and offer courses related to the field. Some schools offer doctoral programs in information transfer, and some have the words *information science* or *information studies* in their name. Others teach information science as part of engineering and other programs.

The American Society for Information Science (ASIS), a national organization, has many librarians among its members. The society provides useful information for persons interested in the field through a publication called the *Journal of the American Society for Information Science*. In addition, *Information Technology and Libraries* includes many articles that deal with the applications of information science to library work. This journal is published by the Library and Information Technology Association of the American Library Association.

Library work involving information science is well suited for people who are interested in computers and their applications and want to serve an important social institution. Many people who complete academic information science programs hold research positions on large public, school district, special, or college or university library staffs. Other information scientists may design or manage automated systems for the cataloging and retrieval of information in books, journals, and other media. Still others work in colleges or universities as information science teachers and researchers.

WORLD BOOK photo

Computers help librarians provide information. A computer system called *Medline* gives medical librarians access to a vast amount of data stored in a computer at the National Library of Medicine. A librarian uses a computer terminal, *above,* to obtain information from the system.

Novosti Press Agency, Moscow

Lenin State Library, in the heart of Moscow, is the largest library in the Soviet Union and one of the largest in the world. This ornately decorated library houses about 28 million items. It serves both as Moscow's main public library and as a center for Soviet scholarship.

Western Europe has many of the largest, oldest, and most important libraries in the world. The national libraries of Great Britain and France—the British Library in London and the Bibliothèque Nationale in Paris—are world centers of scholarship. The British Library owns about 14 million volumes, and the Bibliothèque Nationale owns about 9 million.

In addition to national libraries, Western Europe has dozens of world-famous university libraries, including those of Oxford University and Cambridge University in England, and of the University of Paris. There are also many important special libraries in Western Europe. Several of them are noted for collections of early manuscripts and books. Vatican Library in Vatican City, the central library of the Roman Catholic Church, is one such institution. Government libraries and libraries of industrial and research organizations operate throughout Western Europe.

Great Britain's public library system became well established during the late 1800's. But in most of the rest of Western Europe, public library systems did not develop until after the end of World War II in 1945. Today, there are good public library systems throughout the British Isles and Scandinavia. Many librarians consider Denmark's public library system a model for the

rest of the world. Much progress is being made toward improving the public library systems of France and other West European nations.

The development of library education in Western Europe has followed about the same pattern as the development of public libraries. Excellent library schools operate in France, West Germany, Great Britain, and the Scandinavian countries. All except the smallest Western European nations have library associations and publish library journals.

Eastern Europe and the Soviet Union. The countries of Eastern Europe have a long tradition of scholarly libraries. The libraries of Charles University in Prague, Czechoslovakia, and of Jagiellonian University in Kraków, Poland, rank among the oldest in Europe. Both date from the 1300's. Each country of Eastern Europe has a national library. The Czechoslovak State Library in Prague and the East German national library in East Berlin have about 5 million volumes each. The Hungarian national library in Budapest owns more than 2 million volumes.

The East European nations and the Soviet Union have Communist governments, and libraries play an important role in Communist education programs. The governments of these countries have set up public libraries and reading rooms in large cities, small towns, and rural villages. Trade unions and workers' councils in industry also maintain library systems. Public, trade union, and workers' libraries total about 25,000 in Poland, 20,000 in Czechoslovakia, 6,800 in Romania, 6,500 in Bulgaria, and 9,200 in Hungary.

The Soviet Union has about 360,000 libraries, far more than any other country. About 130,000 of them are public libraries. The Lenin State Library in Moscow is the Soviet Union's largest library and one of the largest in the world. Its collections of books, magazines, and newspapers include about 28 million items. The Library of the Academy of Sciences of the U.S.S.R. in Leningrad has about 13 million volumes. The M. E. Saltykov-Shchedrin State Public Library in that city houses more than 21 million volumes.

The Soviet Union and the countries of Eastern Europe have library associations, and journals and programs for the education of librarians.

The Middle East does not have many well-supported modern libraries. The largest library in the Middle East is the Jewish National and University Library in Jerusalem, Israel. Its collection totals more than 2 million volumes. Other relatively large libraries in the Middle East include the national libraries of Turkey and Lebanon, and the libraries of the American University in Beirut, Lebanon; the University of Teheran in Teheran, Iran; and the University of Ankara in Ankara, Turkey. Saudi Arabia has four university libraries. Egypt, which is part of both the Middle East and Africa, has large national and university libraries (see the *Africa* section of this article).

Public libraries are scarce throughout most of the Middle East. The most modern ones are in Jerusalem and Tel Aviv, Israel. Library education programs are offered at the Hebrew University, the University of Teheran, and the University of Ankara. Library associations have been established in Egypt, Iran, Iraq, Israel, Lebanon, and Turkey.

Africa. Millions of Africans have no public library service. In some African nations, the only important libraries are those connected with institutions of higher education. Some countries do not have any locally supported public libraries. The lack of library service is most serious in the more than 30 nations that became independent during the 1950's and 1960's. Some of these countries have made good beginnings, however. They include Ghana, Ivory Coast, Kenya, Nigeria, Sierra Leone, Tanzania, Tunisia, and Zaire.

Most of the largest and more important libraries are in far northern or southern Africa. The Egyptian National Library in Cairo has over $1\frac{1}{2}$ million volumes, and the Cairo University Library has more than a million. Algeria has a 600,000-volume university library and a large national library that was rebuilt after a fire in 1962. The National Library of Tunisia has more than 500,000 volumes. The Republic of South Africa has several large libraries. They include the Johannesburg Public Library, with about $1\frac{1}{2}$ million volumes; the Cape Town City Library, with about 1 million volumes; and the South African Library in Cape Town, with about 530,000 volumes. The libraries of the universities of Cape Town, Pretoria, and Witwatersrand house from 500,000 to 700,000 volumes each.

Biblioteca Vaticana

Vatican Library, in Vatican City, has one of the world's largest and most valuable collections of early manuscripts and books. Founded in the mid-1400's, it is the central library of the Roman Catholic Church. Scholars from all parts of the world are permitted to use the library.

Sven Doehner

The Library of the Museum of Anthropology in Mexico City, *above,* owns many ancient manuscripts. This student is studying a manuscript to learn about early Mexican Indian culture.

Africa has a few programs for educating librarians. These programs include those at the universities of Cape Town; Pretoria; Cairo; Ghana, in Accra, Ghana; Ibadan, in Ibadan, Nigeria; Ahmadu Bello, in Zaria, Nigeria; Dakar, in Dakar, Senegal; and Makerere, in Kampala, Uganda. Africa also has a number of library associations. Among them are the associations in Egypt, Ghana, Nigeria, South Africa, Tanzania, Togo, and Tunisia.

South and Southeast Asia. Most countries of South and Southeast Asia have national libraries, and one or more university libraries. Most of the libraries are small and poorly supported. The chief national libraries are those of the Philippines, Malaysia, India, Singapore, and Thailand. The largest and best-developed university libraries are at the University of the Philippines; the University of Singapore; and the Indian universities of Allahabad, Baroda, Bombay, Calcutta, and Delhi, and Banaras Hindu University. Most of the countries of South and Southeast Asia have scientific and commercial libraries, and many major government branches operate libraries.

Most of the free public libraries in South and Southeast Asia have been constructed since the end of World War II, but many countries in the region have made little progress. One of the largest libraries in South and Southeast Asia is the Delhi Public Library in India. It has about 630,000 volumes. This library was founded in 1951 with the assistance of the United Nations Educational, Scientific and Cultural Organization (UNESCO) to demonstrate what a modern public library should be like.

Training programs for librarians are offered in many parts of South and Southeast Asia. They include those of Chulalongkorn University in Bangkok, Thailand; the University of the Philippines in Quezon City; the universities of Delhi and Madras in India; and the University of Karachi in Pakistan. Library associations operate in many of the countries of South and Southeast Asia.

Australia and the Far East. The National Library of Australia, in Canberra, has more than $1\frac{1}{2}$ million volumes. The country's largest university library is that of the University of Sydney. It has more than 2 million volumes. Each state has a state library in its capital. The largest is the State Library of New South Wales in Sydney, with about $1\frac{1}{4}$ million volumes. Australia has many governmental libraries, and others that serve commercial, research, and industrial organizations. Almost every city and town has public and school libraries. Australia has a library association, a professional library journal, and several library schools.

Japan also has a well-developed library system. The National Diet Library in Tokyo owns more than 7 million volumes. It has about 30 branches. There are nearly 400 Japanese university libraries. The most important ones are the libraries of the universities of Tokyo and Kyoto, each of which has about 4 million volumes; Tohoku, Hokkaido, and Kyushu universities, each with over $1\frac{1}{4}$ million volumes; and Kobe and Waseda universities, each with about 900,000 volumes. Some public and school libraries operate in Japan. In some areas, bookmobiles provide library services to factories.

Many Japanese universities offer library education programs, including the Japan Library School at Keio University in Tokyo. Japan has several library associations and a professional library journal.

In spite of a trend toward increased contact between the United States and China in recent years, there is still a shortage of reliable information about the library system of China. The great National Library in Peking reportedly has more than 10 million volumes, and the Nan-ching Library owns about 4,700,000 volumes. Each province has at least one central library, with collections ranging from 100,000 to 3,500,000 volumes. Since 1949, when the Communists conquered China, dozens of universities, colleges, and technical institutes have been founded, all with libraries. The Communists have made efforts to bring books and libraries to the people through schools, factories, and some public libraries. The municipal library of Shanghai is reported to have several branches and about 6,900,000 volumes.

The other countries of the Far East have lagged behind in library development. The largest library of Taiwan is that of the National Taiwan University, which has about 1,200,000 volumes. South Korea has the 700,000-volume Central National Library, the million-volume Seoul National University Library, and the 400,000-volume Korea University Library, all in Seoul. Both Taiwan and South Korea have library schools and professional associations for librarians. The $1\frac{1}{2}$ million-volume State Central Library in Pyongyang is the largest library in North Korea.

Latin America. Libraries and librarianship have had a difficult time gaining recognition and support in most of Latin America. The major emphasis there has been on building national libraries and libraries for universities and other educational institutions. The most important national libraries of Latin America include those of Argentina, Brazil, Chile, Mexico, and Peru.

Each of these libraries has from 600,000 to 1,800,000 volumes. Large university library collections include those of the University of Buenos Aires and the University of Chile. Each collection has more than a million volumes, which are distributed among several branch libraries.

Large numbers of cities and towns in Latin America have no free public library service, but several countries are making important gains toward that goal. Brazil has developed some of the best public libraries in Latin America. The São Paulo Municipal Library is especially noteworthy. Other countries that have made advances in providing public library service are Argentina, Chile, Colombia, Panama, and Peru.

Most Latin-American countries have special schools to train librarians. These countries include Brazil, which has about 30 library schools, and Argentina, Chile, and Colombia. Almost all Latin-American countries have national library associations.

International Library Programs. Several international and national organizations work to improve libraries throughout the world, especially in developing countries. UNESCO and UNICEF—agencies of the United Nations—have done much to upgrade libraries in developing nations.

The many UNESCO library activities have included the establishment of model public libraries in developing countries, and of an inter-American library school in Colombia. UNICEF's many activities have included the provision of about 200 titles for each of 300 schools in parts of Nigeria that were devastated during a civil war in the 1960's.

The Agency for International Development (AID) of the United States government administers the non-military part of the U.S. foreign aid program. Part of the aid helps upgrade libraries in developing nations. Many other countries, including France, Germany, and Great Britain, have agencies that perform similar functions.

The American Library Association maintains an international relations program. The association has helped establish libraries and library schools in several countries and has coordinated many international library programs.

The International Federation of Library Associations and Institutions (IFLA) was founded in 1927 to promote international library cooperation. The IFLA has about 1,000 members and affiliates, representing about 110 countries. The IFLA meets annually and has done much to unify library procedures and standards and to promote understanding among the librarians of the world. The IFLA has headquarters in The Netherlands and publishes the quarterly *IFLA Journal*.

Several international associations promote cooperation among libraries that specialize in the same field. They include associations of law, music, and school libraries.

A number of private foundations help the international development of libraries. The American-sponsored Asia Foundation has worked to develop libraries in 17 Asian countries. The Ford Foundation has given financial support to develop libraries in Asia, Africa, and Latin America. Other foundations that give financial support to libraries of various nations include the China Medical Board of New York and the Gulbenkian Foundation.

Asia Foundation

Books for Asia, a library development program sponsored by the Asia Foundation, provides books and journals to a library in Papua New Guinea, *left.* The Asia Foundation has worked to develop public libraries in 17 Asian countries.

WORLD BOOK photo

A Librarian's Work often requires day-to-day contact with people—listening to them and answering their questions, *above.* Many librarians find such personal contact richly rewarding.

To be a librarian is to be part of an important and rapidly growing field. The importance of the library profession lies in bringing the knowledge of the past, the ideas that shape the future, and means of enjoyment to people of all ages.

Careers Within the Profession. The library profession offers a wide variety of careers because there are so many kinds of libraries and library services. A librarian can choose to follow a career in any one of several kinds of libraries—public, school, college or university, research, government, or special. Thus, a librarian's career may involve service to the general public, children, young adults, advanced students and scholars, public officials, or professional people.

Librarians also have a wide range of choice in the kind of work they do in a library. A person may want to work in a small library and handle a variety of library operations. In larger libraries, work is generally divided into several specialized functions. For example, some librarians work as *acquisitions librarians*, who purchase materials. Others are *catalogers*, who list, classify, and describe materials; and still others are *reference librarians*, who help patrons locate materials and answer their questions. A librarian in a large public library may operate the library's bookmobile service, or set up and operate an inner-city storefront library as part of the library's efforts to be of help to the urban poor. Other librarians deal with technical aspects of their profession, such as the adaptation of library procedures to computers or other technological devices. Some librarians

have abilities and interests that lead to work in administration, or in library publicity or public relations.

The Work of Librarians varies, of course, depending on what career they pursue within the profession. The work of some librarians—including reference librarians and those who bring materials and services to various parts of the community—involves direct dealings with library patrons. Other librarians—including catalogers and those involved in technical work—have little or no direct contact with patrons.

Even though the work of individual librarians varies widely, most library work is ultimately aimed at one of three goals: (1) collection development, (2) organization of materials, or (3) public service.

Collection Development may involve starting a new library or keeping up to date and otherwise improving the collection of an existing library. In either case, a librarian must determine the depth, scope, and types of material that the collection should include. These decisions must be made in relation to the purpose of the library, the patrons served, and the amount of money available. The librarian then decides what books, magazines, films, recordings, and other materials the library needs and can afford.

A librarian's professional skill helps in the difficult job of judging what to purchase from among the enormous mass of material produced each year. To choose wisely, librarians must be well informed about the subject fields for which they are responsible. They must be careful to choose materials most suitable for the people who use the library.

Keeping a collection up to date is a major and highly difficult part of collection development. For example, science materials may become out of date in only a few years. The librarian must be aware of such developments because the materials are no longer accurate and should be removed from the general collection.

Organization of Materials ranges from making simple physical arrangements to working with highly complex computers. The size and kind of library and its relations to other libraries or networks determine how the materials are organized.

When adding a new item to a collection, a librarian considers its subject matter and its relationship to other library materials. The librarian then classifies it. A book on economics, for example, will be classified—and arranged in the library—with other books on economics.

When classifying materials, the librarian usually gives them a call number. Author, title, and subject listings of the materials, with their call numbers, are prepared in card form, microreproduction, or *on-line*—that is, on the computer. These listings make up the catalog of materials in the library's collection. For more information on how librarians organize materials, see the section *A Student Guide to Better Writing, Speaking, and Research Skills* in the RESEARCH GUIDE/INDEX, Volume 22.

Public Service. This part of library work may take several forms. Often, a librarian simply helps a reader find information that answers a specific question, such as "What is the population of British Columbia?" For such requests, the librarian turns to readily available reference sources.

Library users often have broad questions, such as information on various Supreme Court decisions. In these cases, the librarian should find out exactly what kind of information the user needs and then provide that information.

A librarian is frequently asked just "to find a good book" for a person. The person's age, educational level, and background may determine what the librarian will recommend.

A librarian can best serve some people by giving them a brief explanation on how the library is organized and where various materials are located. Librarians serve others by helping them participate in group activities in the library, such as story hours, film programs, and book discussions.

Librarians also perform public service by sending information about the library—and sometimes part of the library itself—to people. Through advertising and public relations, a librarian informs people how they can benefit from using the library. A librarian may also bring library materials to hospitals, community centers, and prisons. *The Library Today* section of this article and the sections on the various kinds of libraries have more information on services performed by librarians.

Personality Requirements. The library profession attracts men and women of varying interests and personalities because of the wide variety of libraries and library services. The profession may appeal to a person who likes to help children learn, for example. Such a person may work in an elementary school library or in the children's section of a public library. The profession may attract someone who wants to be part of a scholarly research team. Such a person may work in a library that scientists or other specialists use in their work. The increased use of technological devices in libraries has attracted people interested in technology.

Yet most librarians share certain personality traits. One of the most important is a desire to serve their community. Some serve by doing behind-the-scenes work that makes the library a more effective institution. Others do work that involves contact with people.

Many librarians spend their working hours guiding and assisting others in reading and the use of other materials. They themselves must be readers and use other materials to do this job well. They must also know what is going on in their community, in their field of specialization, and in the world.

Educational Requirements. A person must have a master's degree in library science to qualify for most professional library positions in the United States. In their undergraduate work, future librarians may specialize in almost any subject because libraries need specialists in all fields. School librarians must take certain courses in education, as well as in library science, to meet the requirements of the various states. Children's librarians should take courses in child psychology and also have a knowledge of children's literature. Medical librarians need college courses in the biological sciences.

To obtain a master's degree in librarianship, students must attend a graduate library school. Most students must have a bachelor's degree to be admitted to a graduate school. There, they learn the principles, processes,

materials, and techniques of librarianship. They also have an opportunity to specialize in a particular field —in school, public, college, or special libraries; or in cataloging or reference work, for example.

There are about 60 graduate library education programs in the United States and Canada accredited by the American Library Association (see the table with this article). A number of other colleges and universities offer library science at the graduate or undergraduate level. Some of these programs meet requirements set by various states for school librarians. The programs also introduce librarianship to students who are unsure whether they wish to do graduate work.

Many libraries employ professional people from other fields. These people include experts in administration, audio-visual work, personnel, public relations, and systems analysis. They must meet the educational standards of their own profession.

Many persons who work for libraries have had training in information science. This field combines library science with knowledge from other fields. See the *Information Science* section of this article for details.

Most public, college, and university libraries hire students for part-time clerical work. In this way, a student can get some understanding of the library profession.

A high school student interested in librarianship should take a well-rounded high school program, including literature, science, social studies, and at least one foreign language. The student must also develop good reading skills. High school students can take part in student assistant programs and in library clubs.

Data Que (WORLD BOOK photo by Milt and Joan Mann)

A Library Consultant, such as the one above, helps clients obtain information from libraries. Librarians also serve the general public, students and teachers, and public officials.

The Need for Librarians. The importance of education has increased steadily throughout the 1900's. The extent of knowledge has also increased, and knowledge must be transmitted as quickly as possible. In addition, population and the number of high school and college graduates have grown. All these factors helped bring about a general increase in the need for librarians. Even so, the library profession—like all others—is affected by overall economic conditions. Costs began to soar in the United States during the 1960's, and libraries faced severe budget problems in the 1970's and early 1980's. One result of the financial problems has been a lessening of the number of library jobs available in relation to the number of people trained for library work.

Professional Associations. Librarians work together in a number of associations. The largest and oldest group is the American Library Association (ALA), which was founded in 1876. The ALA seeks to extend and improve library service and librarianship in the United States and throughout the world. It represents the interests of many kinds of libraries and types of library work. See AMERICAN LIBRARY ASSOCIATION.

The Canadian Library Association (CLA) is an association of Canadian librarians. Its aims, activities, and organization resemble those of the ALA. See CANADIAN LIBRARY ASSOCIATION.

Other library associations serve specialized interests of their members. These groups include the Special Libraries Association and the Catholic Library Association (see SPECIAL LIBRARIES ASSOCIATION; CATHOLIC LIBRARY ASSOCIATION). Other such associations are the American Association of Law Libraries, the American Society for Information Science, the Association of American Library Schools, the Association of Jewish Libraries, the Association of Research Libraries, the Bibliographical Society of America, the Library Public Relations Council, the Medical Library Association, the Music Library Association, and the Theatre Library Association. Many of these groups belong to the Council of National Library and Information Associations.

Accredited Library Schools

In the United States

Alabama, University of	University, Ala.	North Carolina, University of	Chapel Hill, N.C.
Arizona, University of	Tucson, Ariz.	North Carolina, University of	Greensboro, N.C.
Atlanta University	Atlanta, Ga.	North Carolina	
Brigham Young University	Provo, Utah	Central University	Durham, N.C.
California, University of	Berkeley, Calif.	North Texas State University	Denton, Tex.
California, University of	Los Angeles, Calif.	Northern Illinois University	De Kalb, Ill.
Catholic University		Oklahoma, University of	Norman, Okla.
of America	Washington, D.C.	Pittsburgh, University of	Pittsburgh, Pa.
Chicago, University of	Chicago, Ill.	Pratt Institute	New York, N.Y.
Clarion University	Clarion, Pa.	Rosary College	River Forest, Ill.
Columbia University	New York, N.Y.	Rutgers The State University	
Drexel University	Philadelphia, Pa.	of New Jersey	New Brunswick, N.J.
Emory University	Atlanta, Ga.	St. John's University	New York, N.Y.
Emporia State University	Emporia, Kans.	San Jose State University	San Jose, Calif.
Florida State University	Tallahassee, Fla.	Simmons College	Boston, Mass.
Hawaii, University of	Honolulu, Hawaii	South Carolina,	
Illinois, University of	Urbana-Champaign, Ill.	University of	Columbia, S.C.
Indiana University	Bloomington, Ind.	South Florida, University of	Tampa, Fla.
Iowa, University of	Iowa City, Iowa	Southern Connecticut	
Kent State University	Kent, Ohio	State University	New Haven, Conn.
Kentucky, University of	Lexington, Ky.	Southern Mississippi,	
Long Island University		University of	Hattiesburg, Miss.
(C. W. Post Campus)	Greenvale, N.Y.	Syracuse University	Syracuse, N.Y.
Louisiana State University	Baton Rouge, La.	Tennessee, University of,	
Maryland, University of	College Park, Md.	Knoxville	Knoxville, Tenn.
Michigan, University of	Ann Arbor, Mich.	Texas, University of	Austin, Tex.
Missouri, University of	Columbia, Mo.	Texas Woman's University	Denton, Tex.
New York, City University of		Vanderbilt University	Nashville, Tenn.
(Queens College)	New York, N.Y.	Washington, University of	Seattle, Wash.
New York, State		Wisconsin, University of,	
University of	Albany, N.Y.	—Madison	Madison, Wis.
New York, State		Wisconsin, University of,	
University of	Buffalo, N.Y.	—Milwaukee	Milwaukee, Wis.

In Canada

Alberta, University of	Edmonton, Alta.	Montreal, University of	Montreal, Que.
British Columbia, University of	Vancouver, B.C.	Toronto, University of	Toronto, Ont.
Dalhousie University	Halifax, N.S.	Western Ontario,	
McGill University	Montreal, Que.	University of	London, Ont.

Source: American Library Association, March 1986.

The history of libraries parallels the history of writing. For about 5,500 years, people have made written records of their ideas, their relations with others, and the world around them. They have kept their records on a variety of materials—bone, clay, metal, wax, wood, papyrus, silk, leather, parchment, paper, film, plastic, and magnetic tape. At almost every stage in the development of these materials, people have assembled collections of their records into libraries.

Libraries of Clay were established in ancient Mesopotamia, a region that now covers part of Iraq, Syria, and Turkey. The early peoples of Mesopotamia discovered that long-lasting records could be made by making marks on wet clay, which was then dried or baked. Thousands of these clay tablets still exist, but scholars have not yet learned the meaning of the markings on all of them.

Some of the oldest clay tablets discovered were made more than 3,000 years before the birth of Christ by the Sumerians, a people who lived in southern Mesopotamia. A library of 30,000 clay tablets has been found at the site of the ancient city of Nippur (see SUMER). Archaeologists have found other libraries of clay tablets in excavations of ancient cities in Syria and Turkey.

In 1850, British archaeologists discovered thousands of clay tablets at the site of Nineveh. Nineveh was the capital of ancient Assyria, which occupied northern Mesopotamia. The tablets formed part of a library in the palace of King Sennacherib of Assyria, who ruled from 704 to 681 B.C. In 1853, an even larger library was found nearby. This collection had been assembled by Sennacherib's grandson, Ashurbanipal. Ashurbanipal brought together a huge collection of records from earlier kingdoms and empires. See ASSYRIA (Language and Literature).

Libraries of Papyrus. During the period that the peoples of Mesopotamia were writing on clay, the Egyptians were using *papyrus*, a writing material made from the papyrus reed. This reed grew in the marshlands of the Nile River. The Egyptians cut its stems into strips, pressed the strips into sheets, and joined the sheets together to form scrolls. Some of the scrolls reached great length. One, called *Harris Papyrus 1*, is 133 feet (41 meters) long. This scroll is in the British Library.

Papyrus is extremely perishable. Even so, some ancient writings on papyrus have survived. The oldest ones date from about 2700 B.C. *Harris Papyrus 1* dates from the 1100's B.C.

Papyrus became the preferred writing material among peoples of the Mediterranean area about 500 B.C., and it remained so until about A.D. 300. The Egyptians used it until the 900's. See PAPYRUS; MANUSCRIPT (Papyrus Manuscripts).

The great libraries of ancient Egypt, Greece, and Rome all consisted of collections of papyrus scrolls. These libraries disappeared, and most of what we know about them is based on second-hand reports. For example, scholars have found references to Egyptian libraries at Amarna in the 1300's B.C., and at Thebes in the 1200's B.C. But the libraries themselves are gone.

Egypt. The most famous library of ancient times was the Alexandrian Library, a Greek institution of the Hel-

Bettmann Archive

Libraries of Clay were established in ancient times by peoples of Mesopotamia. The clay tablet above is from a Babylonian library. Text—written in cuneiform—appears below the illustration.

lenistic Age. It was located in Alexandria, Egypt. Alexander the Great founded Alexandria in the 330's B.C. His successors as ruler of Egypt, Ptolemy I and Ptolemy II, developed the Alexandrian Library into the greatest collection of scrolls in the ancient world. The Ptolemies borrowed books from libraries in Athens and other cities and had them copied. According to legend, Ptolemy II shut 70 Jewish scholars in cells on the island of Pharos until they produced the *Septuagint*, the first Greek translation of the Hebrew Old Testament.

The Alexandrian Library had a copy of every existing scroll known to the library's administrators. It owned more than 400,000 scrolls. A succession of famous scholars headed this library, which became renowned for the scholarly studies it supported as well as for its collection. Not a trace of the library remains today, and no one knows for certain what became of it.

Greece. The Greeks also used papyrus. Some historians credit Pisistratus, a ruler of Athens during the 500's B.C., with establishing that city's first government-owned library. Most people of ancient times could not read, and so "public" libraries—like that of Pisistratus—served only a small minority of the population.

Artist's conception of the Alexandrian Library (New York Public Library)

The Alexandrian Library In Alexandria, Egypt, was the most famous library of the ancient world.
It had a copy of every existing scroll known to the library's administrators.

The most famous library of ancient Greece was founded by the philosopher Aristotle at his school at the Lyceum. It served the same purpose as a university library today. The library no longer exists. According to one tradition, Aristotle's successors sold its collection to the Alexandrian Library. Another account says Lucius Cornelius Sulla, a Roman general who sacked Athens, took the collection to his palace in Rome.

Rome. The ancient Romans continued the library-founding tradition of the Egyptians and Greeks. The earliest Roman libraries were personal collections. Greek literature, which the Romans admired, formed the main part of these collections. The possession of a personal library became a status symbol in Rome, and satirical writers often mocked the practice.

The Roman soldier-statesman Julius Caesar made plans for a public library in Rome. The Octavian Library probably resulted from his plans. Emperor Augustus built this library on Rome's Palatine Hill in 37 B.C., seven years after Caesar's death. The Octavian Library may have been Rome's first public library. Many other public libraries were built soon after. A survey of important Rome buildings in A.D. 337 included 28 libraries. The best of these was the Ulpian Library,

built about A.D. 110 by Emperor Trajan. It had separate buildings for storing Greek and Latin books.

The Romans encouraged the establishment of libraries throughout their huge empire. Some of the buildings that resulted still stand. They include Hadrian's Library, which was built by Emperor Hadrian at the foot of the Acropolis in Athens about A.D. 125.

The great collections of the papyrus libraries of the Roman Empire disappeared, like those of ancient Egypt and Greece. But one collection, which belonged to a Roman nobleman named Lucius Calpurnius Piso, was recovered. Piso lived in Herculaneum, a town at the foot of Mount Vesuvius, a volcano. In A.D. 79, Vesuvius erupted, and Herculaneum and the nearby towns of Pompeii and Stabiae were buried. In the 1750's, excavators uncovered the library. The papyrus scrolls were still in place. The National Museum in Naples has about 1,800 of the scrolls.

Libraries of Animal Skins. Scholars of the ancient world wrote on leather—which is made from animal skins—when papyrus was not available. During the 1940's and early 1950's, hundreds of manuscripts, chiefly leather scrolls, were found in caves near the shore of the Dead Sea. These *Dead Sea Scrolls*, as they are called, probably belonged to the library of a Jewish religious group called the *Essenes*. The Essenes lived in the highlands near the Dead Sea at about the time of Christ. One of the main activities of the group's members was the copying of religious texts. The Dead Sea Scrolls include the oldest known manuscripts of the Bible. See DEAD SEA SCROLLS.

Parchment, made from thin layers of animal skin, was a great improvement over leather. According to legend, parchment came into wide use because of the rivalry between the library in Alexandria and the library of Pergamum, a city in what is now Turkey. When Pergamum's library threatened to become better than Alexandria's, the Egyptians cut off the supply of papyrus to Pergamum. So the people of Pergamum developed parchment. The word *parchment* comes from *Pergamum*.

Parchment sheets cannot be satisfactorily joined into rolls, as can sheets of papyrus. Therefore, scribes and librarians developed the practice of folding several sheets of parchment down the middle and sewing them together through the fold. This practice established the form that books have taken ever since. By the time the West Roman Empire ended in A.D. 476, parchment had largely replaced papyrus in Europe.

The Middle Ages. In A.D. 378, when the Roman Empire was declining, the historian Ammianus Marcellinus complained that "The libraries are closing forever, like tombs." His statement reflected part of a decline in all forms of education that was taking place in Europe.

In 476, the West Roman Empire ended and the period known as the *Middle Ages* began. This period lasted until the 1400's. During the first half of the Middle Ages—until about the late 900's—educational and artistic activity sank to a low level in Europe. Such activity took place in relatively few places in the Western world.

Chief among the places where education flourished was Constantinople (now Istanbul, Turkey), the capital of the Byzantine, or East Roman, Empire. The learning and cultural activity that continued there provided a link between ancient and modern European civilizations. During the 500's in Constantinople, for example, a group of legal scholars used library materials and other resources to produce the Justinian Code. This collection of Roman laws ranks among the most important legal documents of all time. It became the foundation for the legal systems of many countries today. Also in Constantinople, during the 900's, the encyclopedic work known as *Suidas* recorded much knowledge that would otherwise have been lost. The crusaders sacked Constantinople in 1205. After the Turks took over Constantinople in 1453, the city's libraries disappeared.

Christian monasteries made another major contribution to the preservation of libraries and learning during the early Middle Ages. The copying of manuscripts became a major activity of the monks who lived in monasteries throughout Europe and in parts of Asia and Africa. The monks worked in a room called a *scriptorium*. Most of the manuscripts they copied were from religious works, especially the Bible. But they also copied other works, including writings from ancient Greece and Rome. The monks sold some of the copies they made and kept others in the monastery libraries.

One of the oldest copies of the Bible was found in St. Catherine's monastery, on the Sinai Peninsula at the western tip of Asia. This manuscript, called *Codex Sinaiticus*, dates from the early 300's. It was found in 1844 and is now in the British Library. Other important texts were found in the libraries of Greek monasteries on Mount Athos and of Coptic monasteries in Egypt. In Bethlehem, from 386 to 420, St. Jerome produced a large body of sacred writings. These works included his famous Latin translation of the Bible, called the *Vulgate*, which is still in use.

About 540, Cassiodorus, a Roman nobleman, established a monastery on his estate in southern Italy. The monastery was devoted to the making of books, both religious and nonreligious. Cassiodorus has been called the *father of literary monasticism in the West*. Many other monasteries gained importance for their scriptoriums and libraries. Ireland contributed much to the movement. Irish monks produced many books and also founded monasteries in other parts of Europe.

The modern university began to develop in Europe during the 1100's. Instruction and discussion, rather than research, were the main features of the earliest universities. But research gained importance through the years, and the universities gradually amassed great library resources.

The growth of the universities reflected Europe's emergence from the Middle Ages and entry into the Renaissance, which began in Italy about 1300. Europeans acquired a great desire for art and learning and looked back to ancient Greece and Rome for inspiration. Scholars found and translated ancient writings, and writers created literatures of their own.

Bettmann Archive

A Monk in a Scriptorium copies a manuscript by hand. Such laborious work by medieval Christian monks helped preserve writings of ancient times for libraries of today.

The renewed interest in learning led many aristocrats to develop private libraries. One such private collection was begun by Cosimo de' Medici in Florence, Italy, during the 1400's. It formed the basis of the Laurentian Library, which ranks among the world's finest libraries today. The famous artist Michelangelo designed the library's building. In England, Humphrey, Duke of Gloucester, accumulated a large and valuable collection of writings. He gave it to Oxford University in the early 1400's. The university's library still has some of the writings. The Vatican Library also dates from the 1400's. This library of the Roman Catholic Church houses some of the world's most valuable literary treasures. See VATICAN LIBRARY.

The East. The Chinese developed a deep respect for scholars and scholarship far back in ancient times. Ancient Chinese libraries were established for use by scholars, royalty, and aristocrats. The libraries helped advance and preserve Chinese learning. This learning became a major influence in China and other countries of the East. The East did not experience a decline in learning during the Middle Ages, as did the West. But libraries and other educational tools were used only by scholars and the upper class until the 1900's.

Paper, Printing, and Libraries. The Chinese had invented paper by about A.D. 105. Paper is better suited for the manufacture of books than is any other material. The art of papermaking reached Baghdad (now in Iraq) by 800, Egypt by 900, and Europe by 1100. The use of paper grew rapidly in Europe, and, by 1500, paper had almost completely replaced parchment.

During the Renaissance in Europe, the spread of education and the increasing desire for knowledge created a demand for books which greatly exceeded the supply that could be created by hand copying. The problem was solved by the invention of printing from movable type, which had been known for centuries in Asia but was not discovered by Europeans until the 1400's. Johannes Gutenberg of Germany is credited with the invention of movable type in Europe. Gutenberg began printing books in the mid-1400's, and his technique spread rapidly. See GUTENBERG, JOHANNES.

Printing on paper revolutionized bookmaking. More and more books could be printed, and more and more persons could afford to buy them. The printed book also brought many changes in libraries. Books gradually replaced handwritten manuscripts. The books were put on open shelves, not in chests, as the manuscripts had been. By 1600, libraries had started to look like present-day libraries. Shelves of books lined the walls, and tables for readers stood in the middle of the room.

The 1600's and 1700's were a golden age for libraries. Many great libraries that still exist opened in Europe, a number of them in universities. The first state-supported libraries were also founded.

Great Britain. Duke Humphrey's library at Oxford was almost completely destroyed in the mid-1500's, when the government sought to wipe out all traces of Roman Catholicism. Sir Thomas Bodley, an English statesman, began to rebuild the library in the late 1500's. It was renamed the Bodleian Library. This library grew through the years, and today it ranks as Great Britain's second largest. See BODLEIAN LIBRARY.

In 1759, Great Britain opened the British Museum, which included a museum and a national library. The library, which became the British Library in 1973, is the nation's largest and contains many priceless treasures. See BRITISH LIBRARY.

The public library tradition in Great Britain has been strong since the late 1800's. But traces of it date back hundreds of years. The first known public library in the British Isles began in the Guildhall in London in 1425. The second began in Edinburgh, Scotland, in 1580. These libraries no longer exist. The first continuing library that was open to the public was founded in Manchester, England, in 1653. Parliament passed the Public Libraries Act in 1850, and public libraries gradually spread throughout Britain.

France. The national library of France, the Bibliothèque Nationale in Paris, began in 1367 as the Royal Library of King Charles V. During the French Revolution (1789-1799), the Royal Library became the Bibliothèque Nationale. The Bibliothèque Nationale ranks among the largest and most important libraries in the world. See BIBLIOTHÈQUE NATIONALE.

In 1643, Jules Cardinal Mazarin founded the great Mazarine Library in Paris. He collected books and manuscripts from all parts of Europe and opened the library to the public. The library is also famous for its influence on the methods of operating libraries. Cardinal Mazarin's librarian, Gabriel Naudé, wrote one of the first treatises on library management. Librarians consider much of what Naudé wrote as still valid today. The French government now owns the Mazarine Library.

Italy. The great libraries of Italy include the Laurentian Library in Florence, the Vatican Library in Vatican City, the Ambrosian Library in Milan, and the National Central Library in Florence. The Laurentian and Vatican libraries are described in *The Middle Ages* section of this article. The Ambrosian Library, founded in 1609, is noted for its collections of monastic, Oriental, and scientific manuscripts. The National Central Library collection is based on that of Antonio Magliabecchi, a famous book collector and bibliographer.

Germany. Before World War II began in 1939, the national library of Germany was in Berlin. It was founded in 1661 by Frederick William, ruler of the state of Brandenburg. The library became, in turn, the Royal Library, the Prussian State Library, and the German State Library. It suffered heavy damage during World War II. It now stands in East Berlin. The West German national library is in Marburg.

Soviet Union. The M. E. Saltykov-Shchedrin State Public Library in Leningrad has been one of the Soviet Union's chief libraries since it was founded in the late 1700's by Empress Catherine the Great. The largest Soviet library, the Lenin State Library in Moscow, dates from 1862.

Other European Libraries. The Royal Library of Denmark in Copenhagen was established in 1657. King Philip V founded the National Library of Spain in Madrid in 1711. In Portugal, the National Library in Lisbon dates from 1796. National libraries, as well as great university libraries, were founded in many other

European countries during the 1600's and the 1700's.

Libraries in Latin America. Spanish *conquistadors* (conquerors), priests, and colonists brought the first large collections of books to Latin America during the 1500's and 1600's. Latin America's oldest libraries are university libraries. The University of Santo Domingo in the Dominican Republic was founded in 1538. It is the oldest university in the Western Hemisphere. The National Autonomous University of Mexico in Mexico City and the University of San Marcos in Lima, Peru, were established in 1551. The libraries of these universities may date from the time the schools were founded.

Latin America's largest national libraries were established in the 1800's. Argentina's national library in Buenos Aires and Brazil's national library in Rio de Janeiro opened in 1810. The national library of Chile was established in Santiago in 1813. Mexico's national library dates from 1833.

Libraries in the United States. The first permanent English settlement in America was started at Jamestown in 1607. The Harvard University Library, the oldest U.S. library, was founded 31 years later. This library came as a result of a gift of money and about 400 books from John Harvard, a Massachusetts clergyman. The gift was so important that the school was promptly named for Harvard. Its location, Newtowne, was renamed Cambridge—for England's Cambridge University, the school Harvard had attended.

The first successful attempt to make books available for everyone was the establishment of subscription libraries. In 1731, Benjamin Franklin founded the first subscription library in America, the Library Company of Philadelphia. Members of the company paid dues, which were used to buy books. The members could then borrow the books free of charge. The company's original collection of books still exists. The success of the company led to the founding of many other subscription libraries in the American Colonies. See PHILADELPHIA (Libraries and Museums).

Many colonial leaders built up important personal libraries. Notable collections included those of William Byrd, Increase Mather, and Thomas Jefferson. In 1815, Congress bought Jefferson's collection for the Library of Congress, which had been burned during the War of 1812. The Library of Congress was redeveloped around Jefferson's books.

The American ideal of free public schooling for every child led naturally to a movement for free public libraries. One of the nation's first free tax-supported public libraries was established in Peterborough, N.H., in 1833. The idea spread rapidly. In 1846, the Smithsonian Institution, an institution devoted to research and learning, was founded in Washington, D.C. Some of its first projects reflected the keen interest in library establishment sweeping the country. The institution took a census of the nation's libraries. It attempted to develop a national union catalog and a procedure for printing catalogs. In 1853, the institution organized the first convention of librarians in the United States. It was held in New York City. All these activities were directed by Charles Coffin Jewett, the Smithsonian's first librarian.

Many important developments in library history occurred during the mid- and late 1800's. In 1847, John Edmands, a student-librarian at Yale University, prepared an index to periodicals to help his fellow students find debating material. Edmands' successor, William Frederick Poole, expanded and published the index in 1848. The index was widely praised. In 1876, the American Library Association suggested that a new edition of Poole's index be developed. Poole had become the first librarian of the Chicago Public Library. He and others produced *Poole's Index to Periodical Literature* (1882). This index ranks as a classic among reference books. It indexed periodical literature published between 1802 and 1881. Supplements carried the index up through 1906. A later work, *Readers' Guide to Periodical Literature*, brings the indexing service up to the present day.

Melvil Dewey became one of the major figures in the history of American libraries. Dewey had a part in three major library events that took place in 1876. He helped found the American Library Association that year. He also helped start the *Library Journal*, a magazine of library news and trends and of book reviews. In addition, Dewey published the Dewey Decimal Classification in 1876. See DEWEY, MELVIL.

In 1881, Andrew Carnegie gave the first of a series of gifts that made his name almost synonymous with public libraries. Carnegie had amassed a huge fortune in the steel industry. He used part of his wealth to help build more than 2,500 public libraries in the English-speaking world between 1881 and his death in 1919. About 1,700 of these libraries were built in the United States. See CARNEGIE, ANDREW.

During the 1900's, the United States has made great progress in the development of libraries and library services. The number of public libraries has multiplied

The Redwood Library in Newport, R.I., was built in 1750 and is still used as a library. Historians believe it was the first public library building in the American Colonies.

greatly, and more and more branches and bookmobile services have been established to serve more and more people. In 1900, only one library in the United States, the Library of Congress, had over a million items. But by the 1980's, about 150 libraries in the United States had collections of more than a million items. The 1900's also brought a rise in quantity and quality of school and special libraries.

The federal government has taken increasing interest in the nation's libraries during the 1900's. It has set up national libraries for agriculture and medicine and has supported a national library service for the blind. Today, the government makes grants to the states for library service and construction. It provides assistance to libraries in higher education and to medical libraries. In 1970, the government established the National Commission on Libraries and Information Science. This commission, a government advisory board, studies library programs and develops plans for coordinating library and other information programs in the United States.

Libraries in Canada. Library development in Canada has largely paralleled that in the United States. Canada's first college library was established in 1635 at the Jesuit College of Quebec. The Canadian Library Association was founded in 1946. In 1953, Canada established a national library in Ottawa. See the section on *Libraries* in each province article and the *Education* section in the article on CANADA.

REBECCA T. BINGHAM, PAULINE A. COCHRANE, DAVID KASER, PEGGY SULLIVAN, RODERICK G. SWARTZ, and ROBERT WEDGEWORTH

LIBRARY/*Study Aids*

Related Articles. See the section on *Libraries* in the articles on states, provinces, countries, and large cities. See also the following articles.

BIOGRAPHIES

Dewey, Melvil   MacLeish, Archibald

FAMOUS LIBRARIES

Alexandrian Library   Folger Shakespeare
Bibliothèque Nationale   Library
Bodleian Library   Library of Congress
British Library   Vatican Library

LIBRARY ASSOCIATIONS

American Library   Catholic Library
   Association   Association
Canadian Library   Special Libraries
   Association   Association

OTHER RELATED ARTICLES

Book   International Standard
Book Collecting   Book Number
Bookbinding   Library of Congress
Caldecott Medal   Classification
Carnegie Corporation of   Literature
   New York   Literature for Children
Censorship   (Careers)
Copyright   Manuscript
Communication   Microfilm
Dewey Decimal   Newbery Medal
   Classification   Obscenity and Pornography
Information Retrieval   Photographic Copying
Information Theory   Printing

Outline

I. The Library Today
   A. Contents and Kinds of Libraries
   B. Library Services
   C. Other Features
   D. Challenges and Problems
II. Public Libraries
   A. Kinds of Public Libraries
   B. Services for Children
   C. Services for Young Adults
   D. Services for Adults
   E. Services for Special Groups
   F. Spreading the Service
   G. Administering a Public Library
   H. Supporting the Public Library
III. School Libraries
   A. Elementary School Libraries
   B. Middle School and Junior
         High School Libraries
   C. High School Libraries
   D. School Library Standards
IV. College, University, and Research Libraries
   A. College and University Libraries
   B. Research Libraries
V. Government Libraries
   A. United States Government
         Libraries
   B. State Libraries
   C. Canadian Government
         Libraries
VI. Special Libraries
VII. Information Science
VIII. Libraries of the World
   A. Western Europe
   B. Eastern Europe and the Soviet Union
   C. The Middle East
   D. Africa
   E. South and Southeast Asia
   F. Australia and the Far East
   G. Latin America
   H. International Library Programs
IX. Careers in Library Work
   A. Careers Within the   D. Educational Require-
         Profession   ments
   B. The Work of   E. The Need for
         Librarians   Librarians
   C. Personality Re-   F. Professional
         quirements   Associations
X. History

Questions

What are some differences between today's libraries and those of the past?

What challenges and problems do libraries face?

Discuss the role of technology in today's libraries.

What services does a state library provide to the state government? To other libraries?

What role does the United States government play in the development of local public libraries?

Discuss and compare library development in various parts of the world.

What did Melvil Dewey and Andrew Carnegie contribute to the development of libraries?

What are some of the many careers available within the library profession?

How do school librarians serve their communities?

Why is the future development of libraries and librarianship so important?

Additional Resources

Level I

CLEARY, FLORENCE D. *Discovering Books and Libraries: A Handbook for Students in the Middle and Upper Grades.* 2nd ed. Wilson, 1977.

GORDON, CHARLOTTE. *How to Find What You Want in the Library*. Barron's, 1979.

Level II

ALA World Encyclopedia of Library and Information Services. Ed. by Robert Wedgeworth. American Library Assn., 1980.

The Bowker Annual of Library and Book Trade Information. Bowker. Published annually.

GATES, JEAN K. *Guide to the Use of Books and Libraries*. 5th ed. McGraw, 1983.

JOHNSON, ELMER D., and HARRIS, M. H. *History of Libraries in the Western World*. 3rd ed. Scarecrow, 1976.

KATZ, WILLIAM. *Your Library: A Reference Guide*. 2nd ed. Holt, 1984.

SULLIVAN, PEGGY A., and HEIM, K. M. *Opportunities in Library and Information Science*. Rev. ed. National Textbook, 1982.

LIBRARY OF CONGRESS, located just east of the United States Capitol, is one of the largest and most valuable research libraries in the world. The Library of Congress has about 77 million items in its collections, including over 18 million books and pamphlets, and millions of charts, engravings, manuscripts, maps, motion pictures, musical compositions, photographs, and recordings.

The library owns the largest collection of *incunabula* (books printed before 1501) in the Western Hemisphere. They represent the earliest products of the printing press, which was invented about 1450. This collection has about 5,600 books, including a perfect copy of the Gutenberg Bible, the first important book printed in the Western world. The library's 32-million-piece manuscript collection reflects all aspects of American life and culture. It is especially important for its U.S. history collection, which contains the papers of almost every President from George Washington to Calvin Coolidge. The library's collections of Chinese, Japanese, and Russian materials are the largest in the world outside the Far East and Russia.

The library's first responsibility is to provide research and reference assistance to the United States Congress. But it also serves as the national library, having extended its services over the years to government agencies, other libraries, scholars, and the general public. The Librarian of Congress administers the library. The Librarian is appointed by the President of the United States and must have the approval of the Senate.

The Library of Congress provides cataloging information to other libraries on printed cards, on magnetic tapes, and in book catalogs. Through a program called *Cataloging in Publication*, the library gives publishers cataloging data to be printed directly in books, usually on the back of the title page. The Library of Congress loans other libraries books that are unobtainable elsewhere and supplies photocopies of other materials. The library also provides books in braille and recorded books to blind and physically handicapped readers throughout the country. More than 160 cooperating libraries help distribute these materials.

One department of the library administers the copyright laws. Two copies of every publication for which an author requests copyright protection must be deposited in the library. The library selects items for its collections from these deposits.

Congress established the library in 1800. It appropriated $5,000 to buy books and furnish a room in the Capitol for the library. This first library was destroyed in 1814 when the British burned the Capitol.

Congress immediately began building up a new library in the Capitol. In 1815, it purchased the private library of Thomas Jefferson, which had about 6,000 books. The library continued to grow, although several fires—the most serious in 1851—damaged the collections. By 1897, the Library of Congress had grown so large that it could no longer be housed in the Capitol. The library moved to a new gray sandstone building east of the Capitol. In 1938, an annex of white Georgia marble was constructed on an adjoining site. In 1976, the annex was named the Library of Congress Thomas Jefferson Building. In 1980, Congress renamed the annex the John Adams Building and designated the 1897 structure as the Thomas Jefferson Building. The Library

Jack Novak, Photri

The Main Reading Room of the Library of Congress, *left,* is the center of the greatest research library in the United States. Scholars from all parts of the world come to study at the library.

LIBRARY OF CONGRESS CLASSIFICATION

of Congress James Madison Memorial Building was completed in 1981. Together, the three buildings have about 71 acres (29 hectares) of floor space.

Critically reviewed by the LIBRARY OF CONGRESS

See also LIBRARY; LIBRARY OF CONGRESS CLASSIFICATION; HAYES, RUTHERFORD B. (Congressman); MACLEISH, ARCHIBALD.

Additional Resources

GOODRUM, CHARLES A. *Treasures of the Library of Congress.* Abrams, 1980.

GOODRUM, CHARLES A., and DALRYMPLE, H. W. *The Library of Congress.* 2nd ed. Westview, 1982.

GURNEY, GENE, and APPLE, NICK. *The Library of Congress.* Rev. ed. Crown, 1981. A guidebook for the user.

LIBRARY OF CONGRESS CLASSIFICATION is a system for arranging materials in a library. Many large research and university libraries use this system. It provides greater precision in most fields and more room for expansion than the Dewey Decimal Classification (see DEWEY DECIMAL CLASSIFICATION).

Each Library of Congress classification is represented by a set of capital letters and numbers. The first letter in the set indicates one of 21 major areas of knowledge. These areas include: A-General Works; B-Philosophy, Psychology, and Religion; C to F-History; G-Geography, Anthropology, and Recreation; H-Social Sciences; J-Political Science; K-Law; L-Education; M-Music; N-Fine Arts; P-Language and Literature; Q-Science; R-Medicine; S-Agriculture; T-Technology; U-Military Science; V-Naval Science; and Z-Bibliography and Library Science. The second letter stands for a subclassification. The numbers represent a specific topic.

In the following example, the book *Familiar Trees of America*, by William C. Grimm, has the number QK 481. The Q stands for science, the K for botany, and the 481 for trees of North America.

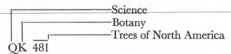

The Library of Congress developed its classification system in the early 1900's for its large collection of books. Specialists add or modify about 6,000 classification numbers yearly to account for current events and new knowledge. Critically reviewed by the LIBRARY OF CONGRESS

LIBRARY OF PARLIAMENT. See LIBRARY (Canadian Government Libraries).

LIBRARY SYSTEM. See LIBRARY (The Growth of Information).

LIBRETTO. See OPERA (The Libretto).

LIBREVILLE (pop. 130,000) is the capital and largest city of Gabon. Libreville lies in western Gabon on the Gulf of Guinea, an arm of the Atlantic Ocean, and is a major port. For location, see GABON (map).

The city is Gabon's center of commerce and culture. Factories in Libreville manufacture food products, furniture, lumber, and textiles. The city has a variety of educational and research institutions.

Libreville—the name means *free town*—was founded by French naval officers in 1849 as a refuge for freed slaves. In 1883, it became the capital of Gabon, a French colony at that time. It remained the capital

234

after Gabon became independent in 1960. Since the mid-1970's, a convention center and many other buildings have been erected in the city. L. H. GANN

LIBYA is an independent Arab country on the northern coast of Africa. It is bigger than any state in the United States, but has only about as many people as South Carolina. The Sahara covers over 90 per cent of Libya.

Until the 1960's, Libya was a poor country, largely because natural resources were scarce. But the discovery of oil in 1959 brought the country unexpected wealth. The government now receives a large income from oil and uses part of it to improve farmland and help the people in other ways.

Tripoli is Libya's capital and largest city. Libya's official language is Arabic. Its official name is the People's Socialist Libyan Arab Jamahiriya.

Government. Muammar Muhammad al-Qadhafi is Libya's most powerful government leader. His title is leader of the revolution. In 1969, Qadhafi led a military revolt that overthrew a monarchy that then ruled Libya. A General Secretariat and a General People's Congress assist Qadhafi in carrying out the operations of the government.

People. Among the influences that have determined the way of life in Libya are the country's large, dry area and the geographical and historical differences between eastern and western Libya. The discovery of oil has brought about changes in the way of life.

Libya

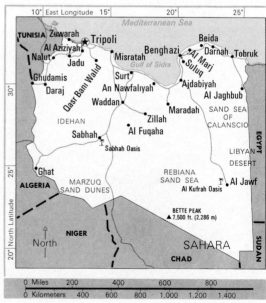

WORLD BOOK map

Most of the people speak Arabic and follow Islam. In eastern Libya, almost all the people are of Arab ancestry. In other areas, many people are of mixed Arab and Berber ancestry. About 4,000 Jews live in Libya.

Almost three-fourths of the people live in the northwest near the Mediterranean coast, and almost a fourth live near the northeast coast. Some Libyans live at desert oases. Others are nomads, moving with their sheep, goats, and camels in search of pasture.

About two-fifths of all Libyans live in rural areas, and about three-fifths live in cities and towns. Since the oil discoveries, people have begun to move to the cities, and their ways of life are changing. People who wore traditional Arab clothing when they lived in rural areas now wear European-style clothes.

About half the school-age children in Libya attend school. Over a third of the people can read and write. The University of Libya is the nation's only university.

Land. Libya's most fertile areas are the northwestern coastal plain and the northeastern highlands. Tripoli, the largest city of Libya, is on the northwest coast. Benghazi is the chief city of the northeast. The Sahara, with its vast seas of shifting sands, covers the rest of Libya. Fertile oases dot the Sahara in the southwest and the southeast. A huge underground lake at Al Kufrah in the southeast provides enough water to irrigate vast areas of land. Bette Peak, the highest point in Libya, rises 7,500 feet (2,286 meters) above sea level in the south.

Temperatures in the north vary widely. Winds from the sea bring mild temperatures, but hot winds from the south can raise the temperature as much as 40 Fahrenheit degrees (22 Celsius degrees) in a few hours. Northwestern and northeastern Libya may receive 20 inches (51 centimeters) of rain a year.

The rest of Libya has a desert climate. Days are extremely hot, nights are cool, and there is little rain. Summer temperatures reach 115° F. (46° C). Libya had the highest temperature ever recorded, 136° F. (58° C) at Al Aziziyah on Sept. 13, 1922. Winter temperatures range from 45° F. (7° C) to 86° F. (30° C).

Economy. Before oil was discovered in 1959, Libya's income per person was one of the lowest among the Arab countries. The government depended heavily on aid from Great Britain and the United States.

Today, income from oil makes up about 80 per cent of the government's revenue. The government uses the increased income from oil to pay for electric power works, irrigation systems, and other economic development projects. It also has enough extra income to provide loans to other countries and to import large quantities of military equipment and other goods. Libya is a member of the Organization of Petroleum Exporting Countries (OPEC).

Pipelines transport oil from the oil fields of north-central Libya to ports on the Mediterranean for export. Libyan and foreign companies operate the industry, which employs about 50,000 Libyans.

At least 80 per cent of Libya's working people make their living from the land. But only about 8 per cent of the land can be farmed. Most farmland is used for grazing livestock. Livestock, including cattle, sheep, and goats, is the single most important source of income for farmers. Libya's chief crops are barley, citrus fruits, dates, olives, peanuts, tomatoes, and wheat.

History. Greeks landed in Cyrenaica in what is now eastern Libya in the 600's B.C. About 700 B.C., Phoenicians settled in Tripolitania in what is now northwestern Libya. Tripolitania soon came under the control of Carthage, a powerful ancient city in what is now Tunisia. Later, Rome ruled Tripolitania and Cyrenaica for almost 500 years.

In the A.D. 400's and 500's, Vandals and Byzantines invaded Tripolitania and Cyrenaica, and left the country in ruins. Arabs ruled Tripolitania and Cyrenaica from the mid-600's to the 1500's, and eventually almost all Libyans came to speak Arabic and became Muslims.

From the 1500's to the 1900's, Libya was part of the Ottoman Empire, which was centered in Asia Minor (now Turkey). But its rulers had almost complete freedom during much of the period. This was the era of the Barbary pirates who preyed on European and U.S. shipping in the Mediterranean. The United States fought a war against the pirates during the early 1800's.

Italy gained control of Libya in 1912. It spent great

Facts in Brief

Form of Government: *Jamahiriya* (the Libyan government's name for a kind of republic).

Capital: Tripoli.

Official Language: Arabic.

Area: 679,362 sq. mi. (1,759,540 km²). *Greatest Distances*—north-south, 930 mi. (1,497 km); east-west, 1,050 mi. (1,690 km). *Coastline*—1,047 mi. (1,685 km).

Population: *Estimated 1987 Population*—4,030,000; distribution, 60 per cent urban, 40 per cent rural; density, 6 persons per sq. mi. (2 per km²). *1973 Census*—2,249,237. *Estimated 1992 Population*—5,168,000.

Chief Products: *Agriculture*—barley, citrus fruits, dates, livestock, olives, wheat. *Mining*—oil.

Flag: The flag of Libya is entirely green. Green is the traditional color of Islam, the religion of most Libyans. Adopted in 1977. See FLAG (picture: Flags of Africa).

Money: *Basic Unit*—dinar. See MONEY (table).

Shostal Associates

Tripoli is Libya's capital and the country's largest city. The picture above shows a street scene in the city, which lies along the Mediterranean Sea.

235

LIBYA

sums building roads, towns, and irrigation systems, and settled over 150,000 Italians there. But much of this was destroyed in World War II. Italy lost Libya after its defeat in the war. The United Nations declared Libya independent in 1951. Muhammad Idris al Mahdi as-Sanusi, leader of the Sanusi brotherhood, a Muslim religious and social reform group, became king.

Between 1951 and 1963, Libya was a monarchy made up of Fezzan, a province in the southwest, and the provinces of Tripolitania and Cyrenaica. The provinces had considerable authority to rule themselves, and they accurately reflected the geographical and historical differences in the country. But many leaders felt that this system blocked national unity. The provinces were abolished in 1963, and Libya became a monarchy controlled largely by the central government.

In late 1969, military officers overthrew King Idris and took control of the government. Colonel Muammar Muhammad al-Qadhafi, leader of the group, became the head of Libya's government. Under Qadhafi's rule, the government took control of many economic activities in Libya. Qadhafi has tried to form unions between Libya and several other Arab nations, but none of these attempts has been successful. Qadhafi has also sought to spread Libya's influence to other lands. For example, he sent troops and military equipment to Chad during a civil war there. For details, see CHAD (History). Qadhafi has provided financial aid to revolutionaries in many parts of the world. The leaders of many nations have denounced him for interfering in the affairs of other countries. President Ronald Reagan of the United States accused Qadhafi of aiding international terrorists. In 1986, Reagan ordered U.S. planes to bomb military installations in Libya. Terrorists were believed to be housed in the area. Reagan acted in response to evidence that linked Libya to the bombing of a West Berlin nightclub, in which an American serviceman was killed and many were injured.   LEON CARL BROWN

The Sahara Covers Most of Libya. Only a 50-mile (80-kilometer) coastal strip gets enough water for vegetation.

Authenticated News Int.

Related Articles in WORLD BOOK include:

Benghazi	Qadhafi, Muammar	World (picture: Making
Berbers	Muhammad al-	Barren Land
Idris I	Tripoli	Productive)

LIBYAN DESERT. See EGYPT (The Land).

LICE. See LOUSE.

LICENSE means *permission*. The word license is most often used to mean a permit granted by a public authority. Sometimes the granting authority is the federal government. Sometimes it is a state or city government.

A license may permit a person to carry on a business or to practice a profession. It implies that the person who receives the license can do the work without injuring the public. For example, a physician must receive a state license in order to practice medicine legally. The license means the state considers the physician qualified.

There are many other kinds of licenses. A person needs a license to legally hunt or fish. In many states and cities, owners must buy a license for their dogs.

Usually a person must pay a certain amount of money for a license. All states require the owner of an automobile to buy a vehicle license. This kind of license has two purposes. It brings funds into the state treasury, and it identifies the vehicle in case of an accident. Many cities also require vehicle licenses, usually in connection with a system of safety tests for automobiles.

License also is used in law to indicate a qualified right to do something. A *licensee* is a person who has a right, generally, to enter a building or to be on someone else's land. If a person rents a building and is allowed to park a car behind it, the person is a licensee.

An inventor may grant a license for the use of a patented invention. The license may be *exclusive* (restricted to one party) or *nonexclusive* (granted to more than one party).   JOHN ALAN APPLEMAN

See also HUNTING (Game Laws); MARRIAGE (Laws Concerning Marriage).

LICHEN, *LY kuhn,* is a flowerless plant that consists of two plants living together as a single unit. These plants are an alga and a fungus. The alga can make its own food, but it needs water to grow. The fungus absorbs water rapidly, but it cannot make its own food.

There are about 18,000 species of lichens. They can grow in soil, but, unlike most plants, they can also grow on such surfaces as rock and tree bark. Lichens live in many regions in which few other plants can survive. Some species live in the extreme cold of the Arctic. Others live in deserts or in the tropics.

Lichens have no leaves, roots, or stems. Most have an outer layer of green, brown, yellow, or gray fungal cells, which cover a layer of green or blue-green algal cells. Below the algal cells lies a whitish storage zone that contains food. This layer consists mainly of thread-like fungal structures called *hyphae.*

Botanists recognize three groups of lichens according to their general appearance. *Crustose lichens* are crust-like plants that lie flat on the *substratum* (surface on which they grow). *Foliose lichens* resemble leaves that stick up somewhat from the substratum. *Fruticose lichens* look like small shrubs growing on the substratum.

How Lichens Grow. Because lichens have no roots, they can grow only when moistened by dew or rain. When a moist lichen absorbs sunlight, the alga part produces food for the plant by the process of *photosynthesis* (see PHOTOSYNTHESIS). The food passes to the fungus and thus enables the entire plant to grow. Dry lichens do not grow. But they can survive in extreme temperatures that kill wet lichens. Most lichens add about 0.1 inch (3 millimeters) a year to their radius, but a few species grow about 10 times as fast. Many crustose lichens grow only .01 inch (0.3 millimeter) in radius yearly. Some are about 4,000 years old.

Lichens reproduce in one of three ways. In some lichens, the fungus releases *spores* into the air. A spore is a small body that can develop into a new organism. If a fungus spore lands next to a suitable alga, a new lichen may develop. Lichens also reproduce by means of cells called *soredia*. Soredia consist of several algal cells surrounded by a few strands of fungus. They grow on the surface of the lichen and are broken off and carried away by the wind or water. If soredia get trapped in a crack of a tree or rock, they begin to grow into new lichens. The third type of lichen reproduction occurs in species that have *isidia*. Isidia are tiny, peg-shaped growths on the lichen's surface. Like soredia, they are broken off and distributed by the wind and water.

The Importance of Lichens. People use lichens in many ways, and other animals and the environment also benefit from these plants. Some lichens produce acids that break down rocks into simple soil in which other plants can take root. However, scientists do not believe that the role of the lichens in soil formation is so important as was once thought. In the Arctic, lichens cover much of the ground surface. They keep the frozen ground from melting and thus prevent erosion. Many species, including *reindeer moss*, provide winter food for caribou and reindeer in the Arctic. In other regions, many insects, as well as snails and slugs, eat lichens.

In the Far East, people use lichens in making soups and salads that they consider a delicacy. In the Middle East, people use lichens in bread and stew.

One type of lichen is used in the manufacture of *litmus*, a substance used to determine if a solution is an acid or a base (see LITMUS). Another lichen is an important ingredient of perfumes and soaps made in Europe. It has a mossy fragrance and prevents scents from evaporating quickly. Dye manufacturers once obtained certain brown, purple, and yellow dyes from lichens. They now make these dyes from coal tar.

For more than 2,000 years, doctors have used drugs made from lichens to treat certain lung and skin diseases. Lichen drugs are still used in parts of Finland, Germany, and Russia. In other countries, antibiotics made from fungi have replaced lichen drugs.

Scientists also use lichens to determine the amount of sulfur dioxide pollution in the air. Sulfur dioxide, a poisonous gas, has many harmful effects on the environment. Lichens are extremely sensitive to this gas, and die when exposed to too much of it. Thus, scientists can estimate the amount of sulfur dioxide in an area by observing how many lichens are growing there.

Scientific Classification. Lichens are classified according to their fungal part. Most lichens belong to the phy-

Some Kinds of Lichens

C. P. Armstrong

Crustose Lichens, such as this script lichen, lie flat against the *substratum,* the surface on which they grow.

C. P. Armstrong

Foliose Lichens, including the parmelia lichen, shown above, resemble leaves that stick up from the substratum.

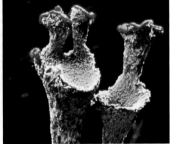

Kitty Kohout

Fruticose Lichens, such as this pyxie cup lichen, have only a little of their underside attached to the substratum.

Jana R. Jirak

Old Man's Beard, one of the most unusual lichens, hangs from tree branches. It grows up to 5 feet (1.5 meters) long.

C. P. Armstrong

Yellow Map Lichens rank among the oldest living things. Scientists believe some of them are thousands of years old.

C. P. Armstrong

Arctic Lichens cover much of the ground surface in the tundra. They provide winter food for caribou and reindeer.

lum *Eumycophyta*, class *Ascomycetes*. A few belong to the class *Basidiomycetes*. D. H. S. RICHARDSON

See also EARTH (How the Earth Changes [picture: Rocks Begin to Crumble]); SYMBIOSIS.

LICHTENSTEIN, *LIHK tuhn styn*, **ROY** (1923-), is an American painter and sculptor. He became one of the first and most popular artists of the American pop art movement of the 1960's.

Lichtenstein has created ceramics, graphic art, paintings, and sculptures. Most of his works show his interest in mass-produced commercial illustrations, especially comic strips. In many works, Lichtenstein creates images through the arrangement of large colored dots. This style reflects the influence of the Ben Day engraving process of reproducing illustrations for books and periodicals. Examples of Lichtenstein's comic-strip style appear in the WORLD BOOK articles on PAINTING and POP ART. As his style developed, Lichtenstein changed his subjects from comic-strip images to Greek temples, sunsets, and exaggerated views of strokes made by paintbrushes.

Lichtenstein has made sculptures of brass and mirrors. These works show the influence of geometric decorative art, which became popular during the 1930's. He was born in New York City. GREGORY BATTCOCK

LICK OBSERVATORY is an astronomical observatory on top of Mount Hamilton, 50 miles (80 kilometers) southeast of San Francisco. It is operated by the University of California.

The observatory includes several buildings that house one or more of its seven telescopes. Housing for scientists and other observatory personnel is also on the mountain, which rises about 4,200 feet (1,280 meters) above seal level. The largest telescope is a reflector with a mirror 120 inches (305 centimeters) in diameter. It is equipped with computers and photoelectric detectors.

The observatory includes a refracting telescope with a lens 36 inches (91 centimeters) in diameter and a tube 57 feet (17 meters) long. Edward Barnard, an American astronomer, used it to discover the fifth satellite of the planet Jupiter in 1892. A reflecting telescope 36 inches (91 centimeters) in diameter was donated to the observatory in 1895.

In 1929, Robert Trumpler of the observatory staff discovered the existence of dust clouds between stars. George Herbig later showed that stars form from the densest of these clouds. In 1969, Joseph Wampler and Joseph Miller used the observatory's 120-inch reflector to make the first photograph of the "flashes" of a *radio pulsar*. A radio pulsar is a small, rapidly rotating star that emits radio waves. Today, astronomers at the observatory use this reflecting telescope to conduct research into such subjects as exploding galaxies, the expansion of the universe, and the origin of the elements.

Critically reviewed by the LICK OBSERVATORY

See also COSMOLOGY; TELESCOPE.

LICORICE, *LIHK uhr ihs* or *LIHK rihsh*, is a perennial herb from which we get a valuable flavoring material. The licorice flavoring comes from the herb's long, sweet roots.

Licorice is a native of southern Europe and parts of Asia. A little is grown in the U.S., including a wild licorice with sweet-flavored roots. Over 40 million pounds (18 million kilograms) of dried licorice root are imported into the United States each year.

Licorice in medicine disguises the flavor of disagreeable drugs, and is contained in some cough medicines. It is used to flavor tobaccos, cigars, cigarettes, soft drinks, candy, and chewing gum.

N.Y. Bot. Garden
Licorice Leaves

The root fibers remaining after the licorice is extracted are valuable in making a fire-fighting foam, boxboard and insulation board, and other products. Commercial licorice is brownish. It is made by boiling the roots and evaporating extract. Substances are added to licorice-flavored candy to give it color. Black is the traditional color for such candy.

Scientific Classification. Licorice is a member of the pea family, Leguminosae. The licorice plant most valuable commercially is classified as genus *Glycyrrhiza*, species *G. glabra*. The wild licorice of North America is classified as *G. lepidota*. J. B. HANSON

LIDICE, *LIHD uh see*, was a village in Czechoslovakia that German military forces destroyed in an act of revenge during World War II (1939-1945). Lidice became a symbol of Nazi cruelty.

German troops occupied Czechoslovakia in 1939. In May 1942, Reinhard Heydrich, a Nazi who controlled much of the country, was fatally wounded. The Nazis claimed that residents of Lidice helped kill Heydrich. But no evidence was found to support this claim. On June 10, 1942, the Germans shot all of Lidice's approximately 180 men. The Nazis sent the rest of the villagers, about 200 women and 100 children, to concentration camps. There, about 50 of the women and nearly all the children were killed. The village was torn down. After the war, some of the survivors built a new village called Lidice near the original site. The original site now serves as a memorial to the sufferings of Czechoslovakia under German occupation. JAMES L. STOKESBURY

LIDO. See VENICE (The City).

LIDOCAINE, *LY duh kayn*, is a drug used to block pain sensation in a specific part of the body. Such drugs are called *local anesthetics*. Lidocaine is used in surgical and dental procedures for *regional nerve blocks*. That means it is injected around nerves that control sensation in particular areas of the body. Lidocaine also is used in prescription and nonprescription ointments and sprays, which produce anesthesia for minor injuries of the skin. In addition, lidocaine is used to treat certain types of abnormal heartbeats.

Pure lidocaine is a white, odorless powder with a slightly bitter taste. Its effects are similar to those of *procaine* (a local anesthetic with the brand name *Novocain*), but lidocaine lasts longer and is more potent. Lidocaine was first synthesized in 1946 and has since become the standard to which other local anesthetics are compared. Its brand name is *Xylocaine*. EDWIN S. MUNSON

See also ANESTHESIA (Local Anesthesia).

LIE, *lee*, **TRYGVE,** *TRIHG vuh* (1896-1968), a Norwegian statesman, served as the first secretary-general of the United Nations. He was elected for five years in 1946, and was continued in office for three years in 1950. He announced his resignation in 1952, and left office in April 1953. Russia opposed Lie because he supported the UN's action in South Korea. Lie resigned hoping to lessen international tensions.

Lie was born in Oslo, Norway. He brought experience and talent in handling political problems to his position in the United Nations. He had served as legal counsel to the Norwegian Federation of Labor. When the Labor Party came to power in 1935, Lie became minister of justice. From then until 1946, he held posts as minister of justice, of commerce, and of foreign affairs.

As minister of commerce during World War II, Lie helped manage supplies and shipping for the small Norwegian forces that fought Nazi Germany. In 1941, he became foreign minister and in 1945 he headed the Norwegian delegation to the UN Conference in San Francisco. There, he helped draw up the charter for the UN Security Council.   RAYMOND E. LINDGREN

See also UNITED NATIONS (picture).

LIE DETECTOR is a device that helps determine whether a person is telling the truth. A lie detector, also called a *polygraph*, records physical changes that occur in reaction to questions. Such changes include alterations in the blood pressure, pulse rate, and respiration that may occur when an individual lies. Lie detectors help police and other investigators question suspects about their possible involvement in a crime. The devices also help retail stores and other employers screen job applicants and investigate employee theft.

Polygraph experts and other supporters of lie detector testing believe that such tests are highly accurate. Some court cases are decided on the basis of lie detector tests, which can be used as evidence if all persons involved agree to their use. However, many legal experts believe that testimony obtained with the aid of lie detectors is not accurate enough to be used in court. These experts also say that such testimony may violate the Fifth Amendment to the U.S. Constitution, which protects people from testifying against themselves. The judges in most criminal cases do not permit testimony obtained with the help of lie detectors to be used as evidence.

No one can be required to take a lie detector test. A person who agrees to do so sits in a chair and answers a number of questions. The lie detector records the person's pulse rate, blood pressure, breathing, and perspiration. It makes a continuous record of these body functions by drawing lines on a moving graph.

Some of the questions asked during a lie detector test are related to the matter being investigated. Others are unrelated or only slightly related, but they are included to help improve the accuracy of the test.

Each question must be answered yes or no. If a person lies, the lie detector graph normally shows a change in one or more of the body functions being recorded. This change occurs because of the individual's emotional response to telling a lie. If the person tells the truth, little or no change normally occurs. After a test, a lie detector examiner interprets the results.

In 1921, John A. Larson, an American psychologist, developed one of the first lie detectors. In 1966, a number of lie detector organizations joined to form the American Polygraph Association. The association helps supervise the use of lie detectors and establishes qualifications for the examiners. In 1972, the American inventor Allen Bell developed a device called a *psychological stress evaluator*. This instrument detects slight tremblings in the voice. Such tremblings normally disappear when a person lies.   MARVIN E. WOLFGANG

LIEBIG, *LEE bick,* **BARON VON** (1803-1873), JUSTUS VON LIEBIG, helped found *organic chemistry*, the study of compounds that contain carbon. He made many discoveries in this field and improved the methods of organic analysis. His most important experiments involved the chemistry of the soil. He worked to develop fertilizers, and his book *Chemistry of Food* led to increased knowledge on how to prepare food. Liebig also was one of three discoverers of chloroform. The Liebig condenser, used in distilling liquids, was named for him. Liebig was born in Darmstadt, Germany, and studied chemistry in Paris.   K. L. KAUFMAN

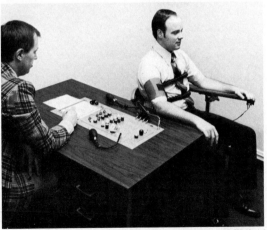

John E. Reid & Assoc. (WORLD BOOK photo)

A Lie Detector measures and records a person's physical reactions to questions. Such reactions include changes in various body functions that may occur when an individual lies.

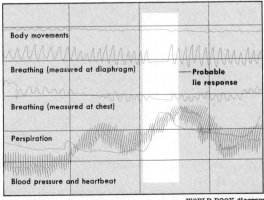

WORLD BOOK diagram

A Lie Detector Chart shows how certain body functions change when lying occurs. If the person being tested tells the truth, the chart normally reflects little or no change in the functions being recorded, as shown in the shaded area. If the person lies, the chart normally indicates a change in one or more of these functions, as shown in the unshaded area.

Liechtenstein

- ⭐ **Capital**
- • **Other City or Town**
- ---- **Road**
- ←→ **Rail Line**
- ▲ MOUNTAIN
- ⌇ *River*
- ⊔⊔ *Canal*

WORLD BOOK map

Ewing Galloway

Tiny Liechtenstein lies in a valley in the Alps between Austria and Switzerland. The Rhine River flows through the center of the valley, along Liechtenstein's western border.

LIECHTENSTEIN, *LIHK tuhn STYN,* is a tiny country in south-central Europe. It is one of the smallest countries in the world. The area of Liechtenstein is less than that of Washington, D.C. The country has only about 28,000 people.

Facts in Brief

Capital: Vaduz.

Official Language: German.

Form of Government: Principality.

Area: 62 sq. mi. (160 km²). *Greatest Length*—17.4 mi. (28 km). *Greatest Width*—7 mi. (11 km).

Elevation: *Highest*—8,527 ft. (2,599 m). *Lowest*—1,411 ft. (430 m).

Population: *Estimated 1987 Population*—28,000; distribution, 76 per cent rural, 24 per cent urban; density, 452 persons per sq. mi. (175 per km²). *1981 Census* —26,215. *Estimated 1992 Population*—30,000.

Chief Products: *Agriculture*—beef and dairy cattle. *Manufacturing*—handicrafts, precision instruments, cotton textiles.

Flag: Two stripes, the upper one blue (for the sky), the lower one red (for the glow of evening fires). The Liechtenstein coat of arms appears in the center, combining the shields of the branches of the ruling house. See FLAG (color picture: Flags of Europe).

Money: *Basic Unit*—Swiss franc. For its price in U.S. dollars, see MONEY (table: Exchange Rates [Switzerland]).

Liechtenstein lies between Switzerland and Austria, and has many close ties with the Swiss. The people speak a German dialect. Their customs are much like those of the Swiss. Liechtenstein uses Swiss money, and Switzerland operates its postal, telegraph, and telephone systems. Switzerland also represents Liechtenstein in diplomatic and trade relations.

Like Switzerland, Liechtenstein has maintained its neutrality through several wars. Liechtenstein has not fought in a war since 1866. It has been independent since 1806. Its official name in German, the official language, is Fürstentum Liechtenstein (Principality of Liechtenstein). Vaduz, a town of about 4,700 people, is the capital and largest town.

Government. Liechtenstein is ruled by a prince, but a prime minister actually directs the government. The prince is a member of the House of Liechtenstein. The throne usually passes to the prince's eldest son.

The people elect the 15 members of the *Landtag* (parliament) to four-year terms. The Landtag passes laws, prepares the national budget, and sets tax rates. Laws must be approved by the prince. The prince appoints the prime minister, and the Landtag appoints four government councilors to help the prime minister.

People. The people in Liechtenstein, like the Austrians and Swiss, are descended from a Germanic tribe that settled in the Alps during the A.D. 400's. They live quiet, simple lives, just like the people in rural areas of

240

Austria and Switzerland. Most Liechtensteiners live in small villages in the country. Until the 1930's, most people farmed for a living. Now, over half of them make a living as factory workers or craftworkers. Less than 10 per cent of the people still farm.

Almost all the people are Roman Catholics. Primary and secondary schooling is free, and children must attend school for eight years. Almost all of the people can read and write.

One of the world's finest private art collections is owned by the prince. It is housed in Vaduz, and includes works by Pieter Bruegel the Elder, Sandro Botticelli, Rembrandt, and Peter Paul Rubens.

Land. The Rhine River flows along the western border of Liechtenstein. A narrow strip of flat farmland lies next to the river. Most of the people live there. Snow-topped mountains cover most of the country's eastern and southern sections. The mountain slopes are covered with pine forests and fine grazing meadows.

Liechtenstein has a mild climate for a country surrounded by high mountains. Warm spring winds provide good weather for growing fruit. The average yearly temperature is 47° F. (8° C), and precipitation averages about 35 inches (89 centimeters) a year.

Economy. The people of Liechtenstein farm, make leather goods and pottery, or work in small factories that produce cotton textiles, heating appliances, pharmaceutical products, and precision instruments. Farmers raise beef and dairy cattle in upland meadows, grapes and other fruits on the upland slopes, or grow corn, potatoes, and other vegetables in the Rhine valley.

The government collects money by taxing foreign businesses that set up their headquarters in Liechtenstein. Liechtenstein offers low business and income taxes to such companies, and over 5,000 firms from other countries have established headquarters there. The government also makes money by selling postage stamps. Liechtenstein's stamps are prized by collectors throughout the world. Many of the stamps are reproductions of paintings in the prince's famous art collection.

Liechtenstein has two hydroelectric plants that produce electric power for the country. It also sells some power to Switzerland. Trains on the main railroad line from Switzerland to Austria go through Liechtenstein. But only a few trains stop in Liechtenstein. Buses link Liechtenstein with Austria and Switzerland.

History. Charlemagne, king of the Franks, controlled the area that is now Liechtenstein in the late A.D. 700's. The area was divided into Vaduz and Schellenberg after his death. Johann-Adam Liechtenstein, a prince from Vienna, bought Schellenberg in 1699 and Vaduz in 1712. His descendants still rule Liechtenstein.

Liechtenstein became part of the Holy Roman Empire in 1719. But Napoleon abolished this empire, and Liechtenstein became an independent country in 1806. In 1815, Liechtenstein joined the German Confederation, a league of German rulers, but kept its independence. The confederation was dissolved in 1866 at the end of the Seven Weeks' War. This was the last war in which Liechtenstein fought. It has remained neutral since then, and has had no army since 1868.

In 1852, Liechtenstein agreed on an economic union with Austria-Hungary. Liechtenstein ended its union with Austria after World War I. It signed a similar agreement with Switzerland in 1924.

Until 1984, only men were allowed to vote in Liechtenstein's elections. Women were given the right to vote that year. GEORGE KISH

LIEDER, *LEET uhr* or *LEE duhr,* is the German word for *songs.* The term refers particularly to art songs written by German composers during the romantic era of the late 1700's and the 1800's. Franz Schubert was probably the most important composer of lieder. Other major composers included Robert Schumann, Johannes Brahms, Hugo Wolf, and Gustav Mahler. Most lieder were written for voice and piano accompaniment. Most express a love of nature and were composed to words of great German romantic poets, including Goethe and Heinrich Heine.

LIÈGE, *lee AYZH* (pop. 207,496; met. area 410,160), lies on both banks of the Meuse River about 54 miles (87 kilometers) southeast of Brussels, Belgium. See BELGIUM (political map). It has many iron and steel factories and zinc smelters that work closely with nearby mines. Liège is famous for the manufacture of guns and glassware. Liège has a university that was founded in 1817. It is a leading cultural center of Belgium.

Opposing armies fought bitterly for control of Liège in World Wars I and II because of its strategic location and its products. DANIEL H. THOMAS

LIEN, *leen,* is a legal claim that one person has on the property of another as security for debt. The main types of liens are *common-law liens* and *statutory liens.* Common-law liens developed from judges' decisions in similar cases. Statutory liens are defined by laws passed by legislatures. A *mechanic's lien* is an example of a statutory lien. This lien gives building contractors assurance that they will be paid for their work and material (see MECHANIC'S LIEN).

Common-law liens may be either *specific* or *general.* A specific lien gives the holder the right to retain the property that is the basis for the debt that is owed. For example, a storage company owner may obtain a specific lien to hold goods stored by the company until the storage is paid for. A general lien gives the holder the right to property other than that which is the basis of the debt due. WILLIAM TUCKER DEAN

LIEUTENANT. See RANK, MILITARY.

LIEUTENANT GOVERNOR is a government official in the United States and Canada. In most states of the United States, the lieutenant governor ranks second to the governor. The lieutenant governor serves as governor if the governor dies, resigns, is impeached, or becomes unable to carry out the duties of the office. The official is elected at the same time as the governor, and for the same term. The lieutenant governor presides over the state senate in 37 of the 39 states that have lieutenant governors. In this position, the official's powers resemble those of the speaker in the lower house of the state legislature.

In Canada, each province has a lieutenant governor. The official is appointed by the governor general in council of Canada and represents Great Britain's head of state in the province. The position of the lieutenant governor, like that of the governor general, is largely ceremonial. DAVID FELLMAN

See also CANADA, GOVERNMENT OF (Provincial and Territorial Governments); GOVERNOR.

Manfred Kage from Peter Arnold

© Raymond A. Mendez, Earth Scenes   © Karl Weidmann, Animals Animals   Marvin Newman, Woodfin Camp, Inc.

The Earth's Incredible Variety of Living Things includes tiny one-celled organisms like the amebas, *upper left,* as well as huge animals like the elephant, *right.* The cactus, *lower left,* and the praying mantis, *center,* represent the two largest groups of living things—plants and insects.

LIFE

LIFE. Most people have little difficulty distinguishing living things from nonliving things. For example, they easily recognize that a butterfly, a horse, and a tree are alive but a bicycle, a house, and a stone are not. People call a thing living if it is capable of certain activities, such as growth and reproduction.

Biologists, however, find it hard to define life, though they have vast knowledge of living things. They have difficulty locating the dividing line between living and nonliving things. For example, a virus is a lifeless particle by itself, but it becomes active and multiplies rapidly when inside a living cell. Rather than trying to define life precisely, biologists concentrate on deepening their understanding of life by studying living things.

The earth has an enormous variety of living things— more than 2 million species. They range in size from microscopic bacteria to gigantic blue whales and towering sequoia trees. Living things can be found in all kinds of environments. Some organisms live in sun-scorched deserts. Others flourish in icy polar waters. Still others thrive in steamy jungles. Living things also vary widely in their behavior and food requirements. In spite of their differences, however, all living things

Harold J. Morowitz, the contributor of this article, is Professor of Biophysics and Biochemistry at Yale University. He is the author of Energy Flow in Biology *and other books on biology.*

consist of the same kinds of chemicals and carry out the same kinds of chemical reactions.

Scientists have long sought definite answers to two major questions about life: "How did life begin on the earth?" and "Does life exist elsewhere in the universe?" Research into these matters is underway both on the earth and in space. This research should help experts begin to formulate scientific theories that can be tested through experiments.

The Characteristics of Living Things

Nearly all living things share certain basic characteristics. These characteristics include (1) reproduction; (2) growth; (3) metabolism; (4) movement; (5) responsiveness; and (6) adaptation. Not every organism exhibits all these features, and even nonliving things may show some of them. However, these characteristics as a group outline the basic nature of living things.

Reproduction is the process by which living things create more of their own kind. There are two major types of reproduction—*asexual* and *sexual.* In asexual reproduction, a new organism develops from one existing organism. Some lower forms of animals and plants reproduce asexually. In sexual reproduction, a new organism develops from the union of two sex cells. In most cases, these cells come from two parents—one male and one female. Human beings and most higher animals and plants reproduce sexually. See REPRODUCTION.

Growth is the orderly increase in size that organisms undergo as they mature. Plants grow by taking in simple molecules, such as carbon dioxide and water, and chemically converting them into complex plant materials. Animals grow by eating food and converting it into animal tissue. Biological growth differs from the process of *accretion*. In this process, some nonliving things increase in size through the addition of new layers to their surfaces. For example, a salt crystal becomes larger through the accumulation of new layers of salt. See GROWTH.

Metabolism involves all the chemical processes by which an organism converts molecules and energy into forms that it can use. Metabolism supplies the molecular building blocks an organism needs for the growth of new tissues and the replacement of worn-out parts. These building blocks must either come from the breakdown of food material or be built up from simpler molecules within the organism.

Biological energy comes chiefly from sunlight. The energy is trapped by plants during the process of *photosynthesis* and stored in chemical compounds. All other biological activities in animals and plants depend on conversions of this energy into useful forms. Most such conversions occur in an organism through the combination of food with oxygen. This process, called *oxidation*, produces water, carbon dioxide, and many molecules of a high-energy compound called *adenosine triphosphate* (*ATP*). ATP molecules hold energy in its most biologically useful form and release the energy as it is needed. See METABOLISM.

Movement. Most living things move in some way. Plants have internal motions, such as the flow of sap. A plant may also bend toward the light, and its flowers may close at night. Movement is more obvious in most animals, which, unlike plants, must search about for food. Some animals, however, move only internally. For example, a sponge circulates water laden with food particles through its otherwise stationary body.

Responsiveness. Living things can sense and respond to changes in their surroundings. Changes that produce responses in organisms are called *stimuli*. Such factors as light and temperature can serve as stimuli. The responses of organisms take various forms, most of which involve some type of movement. For example, a turtle can contract into its shell, a plant can grow toward the sunlight, and a bacterium can swim away from concentrations of harmful substances.

Adaptation is the ability of living things to adjust to their environment. Both individual organisms and entire species must adapt to environmental changes to survive. An organism may adapt by adjusting its behavior or body chemistry. For example, when a person visits a foreign country, the body may have to adjust to a different altitude, climate, or diet. A species may gradually adapt to long-term changes in the environment. Such adaptation involves changes in the *genes* (units of heredity), which are passed on from generation to generation. For instance, changes in genes have made some species of insects resistant to certain insecticides. See ADAPTATION; NATURAL SELECTION.

Living Things and Their Environment

All animals and plants depend greatly on their physical surroundings and on other living things. An organism's environment must provide certain conditions for it to survive. For example, all living things require water and many other chemical substances. In addition,

life as we know it can exist only within a limited range of temperatures. Conditions capable of supporting life occur on and near the surface of the earth in a thin region called the *biosphere*.

The study of the relationships between living things and their environment forms the science of *ecology*. Such features as geological formations, climate, and soil make up an organism's *physical environment*. The other living things in the same area form the organism's *biological environment*. See ECOLOGY.

The Physical Environment determines which kinds of plants and animals can live in a given place. In general, areas with a warm climate and plenty of water have a great variety of living things. However, only specially adapted species can live in extreme environments. For example, the penguins of Antarctica have few neighbors in their bitter cold climate. Only a few kinds of algae and bacteria can live in hot springs, where temperatures may reach 185° F. (85° C).

The Biological Environment. All members of a given species living in a particular area form a *population*. All animal and plant populations that inhabit the area make up a *community*. The populations in a community relate to one another in many ways. In the most basic relationship, organisms obtain nutrients and energy by eating other organisms. Some kinds of animals eat plants, and others feed on animals. In addition, some types of bacteria and fungi get nutrients and energy from the decaying remains and waste matter of other organisms. Other relationships in a community include (1) competition; (2) parasitism; and (3) mutualism.

Competition occurs when two or more organisms require the same resource, such as food or nesting space.

© C. Haagner, Bruce Coleman Inc.

Penguins have become specially adapted for life in icy waters. Thick layers of fat keep them warm, and their wings have developed into flippers that enable them to swim but not to fly.

LIFE

The competition may take place between individuals from different populations or between organisms of the same population.

Parasitism occurs when one organism lives in or on another organism, called a *host*. The parasite takes its food from the tissues or digestive system of the host. For example, a tapeworm absorbs digested food from the intestines of its host.

Mutualism is an association between two organisms of different populations that benefits both organisms. For example, two simple plants—an alga and a fungus —may live together as a unit called a *lichen*. The alga can make its own food, but it must have water to grow. The fungus absorbs water well, but it cannot produce its own food.

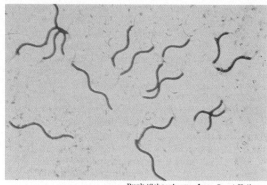

Runk/Schoenberger from Grant Heilman

The Simplest Living Things, such as the bacteria shown above, consist of a single cell that lacks a distinct nucleus.

The Structure of Living Things

All living things are made up of cells. The simplest organisms consist of only one cell, but such complex living things as dogs and human beings have many billions of cells.

The simplest organisms, including bacteria and many kinds of algae and protozoans, live their entire lives as individual cells. Some other types of algae and protozoans are *colonial* organisms. Such an organism consists of a loosely organized group of similar cells. Most species of animals and plants are *multicellular* organisms. They are made up of many kinds of cells, each having its own special functions.

The simplest multicellular animals include sponges and jellyfish. Sponges have some specialized cells but resemble colonial organisms. If the cells of a sponge are separated, they can readily rejoin and form a new individual. Jellyfish are somewhat more highly organized and have well-defined tissues. Higher animals have organs and organ systems.

Cells. A thin covering called the *plasma membrane* or *cell membrane* encloses every cell and separates it from its surroundings. All cells except those of bacteria and blue-green algae have two main parts—the *nucleus* and the *cytoplasm*. A *nuclear membrane* surrounds the nucleus and separates it from the cytoplasm. The nucleus contains the *chromosomes*, the hereditary material that carries the instructions for nearly all cellular activities. The cytoplasm contains many kinds of specialized structures called *organelles*. Each type of organelle has a specific task, such as manufacturing proteins or converting the energy of food molecules into usable forms.

Structural Units of Higher Organisms — Higher organisms have many specialized kinds of cells. Cells that are similar in structure and function make up a tissue. Tissues, in turn, are grouped together and form organs, which are the basic structural and functional units of higher plants and animals. The illustration below shows the main types of cells and tissues that make up the human heart.

WORLD BOOK diagram by Charles Wellek

Cells

Nerve Cell

Muscle Cell

Connective Tissue Cell

Tissues

Nerve Tissue

Muscle Tissue

Connective Tissue

Organ

Heart

Organelles and a well-defined nucleus are lacking only in the cells of bacteria and blue-green algae. Such cells are called *procaryotic*, which means *before the nucleus*. Biologists refer to all other cells as *eucaryotic*, which means *having a true nucleus*. For a detailed description of the structure of cells, see the article CELL (Inside a Living Cell).

Tissues, Organs, and Organ Systems. Higher organisms have many extremely specialized kinds of cells, which are grouped together and form larger, more complex structures. A *tissue* consists of a collection of cells that are similar in structure and function. Animal tissues include muscle tissue and nerve tissue. Plants also have several kinds of tissues. For example, tissue called *xylem* carries water and minerals from the roots to the rest of the plant.

The basic structural and functional units of higher organisms are *organs*. An organ consists of several types of tissues. The human heart, for example, consists of muscle tissue, nerve tissue, and connective tissue. Other animal organs include the brain, liver, and kidneys. The principal organs of flowering plants are the roots, stems, leaves, and flowers.

In higher animals, each important life function is carried out by a group of organs working together. Such a group is called an *organ system*. Major organ systems include the circulatory system, digestive system, and reproductive system.

The Chemical Basis of Life

All the chemical elements that make up living things are also present in nonliving matter. The most common elements in living things are carbon, hydrogen, nitrogen, oxygen, phosphorus, and sulfur. Living things also contain smaller amounts of other elements, including calcium, iron, magnesium, potassium, and sodium.

Water is the simplest chemical compound of importance to living things. Most organisms consist of 50 to 95 per cent water. Many properties of water make it essential to life processes. Its ability to dissolve a great variety of substances is vital because most chemical reactions within organisms can occur only in a water solution. In addition, water itself enters into many chemical reactions in living cells. Water also transports nutrients within organisms.

Except for water, all the principal compounds in living things contain carbon. Each carbon atom can form four chemical bonds of great stability with other atoms. Carbon atoms can also bond with one another and form chains of various lengths and shapes. These properties appear to be unique to carbon, and so it is hard to imagine life as we know it based on anything except carbon chemistry.

Carbon can form thousands of kinds of small molecules. However, almost all living material consists of about 50 kinds of carbon molecules and of the *macromolecules* (large, complex molecules) formed from them. There are four main types of these macromolecules. They are (1) carbohydrates; (2) lipids; (3) proteins; and (4) nucleic acids.

Carbohydrates consist of carbon, hydrogen, and oxygen. Carbohydrates contain these elements in the proportion of roughly 1 atom each of carbon and oxygen to every 2 atoms of hydrogen. The basic carbohydrate molecules are simple sugars called *monosaccharides*. Sugars provide energy to power all cellular processes.

The Importance of Carbon in Life

The ability of carbon atoms to form chains of various lengths and shapes is fundamental to the chemistry of life. The four main types of biological molecules—carbohydrates, lipids, proteins, and nucleic acids—are all made up of smaller carbon-containing molecules like the ones below. Sugars are found in carbohydrates, fatty acids in lipids, amino acids in proteins, and bases in nucleic acids.

WORLD BOOK diagram by Steven Liska

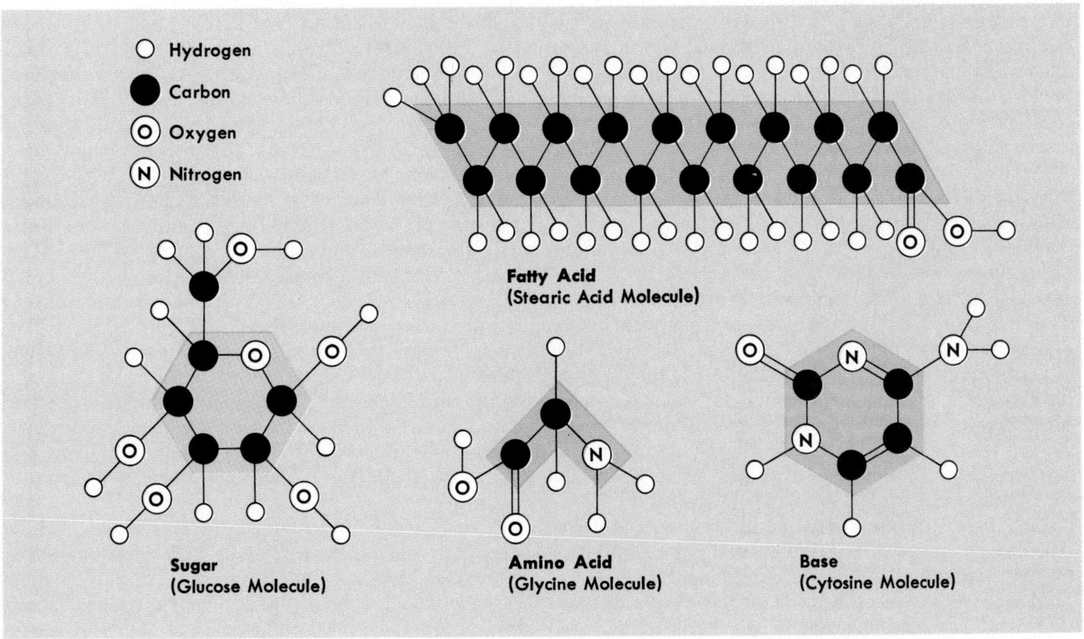

Hydrogen
Carbon
Oxygen
Nitrogen

Fatty Acid
(Stearic Acid Molecule)

Sugar
(Glucose Molecule)

Amino Acid
(Glycine Molecule)

Base
(Cytosine Molecule)

Living things combine simple sugars into long chains called *polysaccharides*. Some polysaccharides serve as a means of food storage. Starches are the main carbohydrate storage material in plants, and *glycogen* serves the same function in animals. Other polysaccharides provide structural support. The polysaccharide *cellulose* is the chief supporting material in green plants. Wood, for example, consists almost entirely of cellulose. See CARBOHYDRATE.

Lipids consist primarily of carbon and hydrogen, but they also contain a small proportion of oxygen. Some lipids contain nitrogen and phosphorus as well. The best-known lipids are animal fats and vegetable oils, which are rich sources of energy. Many kinds of organisms store food in the form of lipids.

Other important lipids, such as *phospholipids* and *steroids*, have more complicated structures than do fats and oils. Phospholipids contain phosphorus, and some also contain nitrogen. Layers of phospholipids form the basic structure of cell membranes. Steroids consist of four connected rings of carbon atoms with other atoms and molecules attached. Steroids include such substances as sex hormones, adrenal hormones, and cholesterol. See LIPID.

Proteins are far more complex molecules than carbohydrates or lipids. A protein is made up of one or more long chains called *polypeptides*. Polypeptides, in turn, consist of many small molecules called *amino acids*. All amino acids contain carbon, hydrogen, nitrogen, and oxygen. Some also contain sulfur. There are 20 kinds of amino acids in proteins, and each protein molecule may have from about 50 to more than 1,000 amino acid molecules.

Proteins are the most abundant macromolecules in living cells. The many kinds of amino acids and the large number of them in each protein molecule make possible an enormous variety of proteins. Each arrangement of amino acids has different chemical properties and different functions. Proteins can thus carry out a vast range of tasks. Some proteins, such as *keratin* in hair and *myosin* in muscle, form the major structural material in living things. Other proteins have chemical functions. Most such proteins are enzymes, which speed up chemical reactions within cells. Enzymes control cellular activity by determining which chemical reactions will take place in a cell. See PROTEIN; CELL (Producing Proteins); ENZYME.

Nucleic Acids store and transmit the information necessary for producing proteins. Nucleic acids consist of long chains of smaller molecules called *nucleotides*. The nucleotides are made of carbon, hydrogen, nitrogen, oxygen, and phosphorus. There are various types of nucleotides, which together compose a sort of code for expressing genetic messages. These messages completely control a cell's structure and activities by determining which proteins will be produced.

There are two main types of nucleic acids, *DNA* (deoxyribonucleic acid) and *RNA* (ribonucleic acid). DNA is the genetic substance in the chromosomes. DNA carries the hereditary information that an organism passes on to its offspring. DNA also determines the kinds of proteins a cell produces. RNA transmits DNA's instructions to the cytoplasm, where it serves as a pattern for building proteins. For a fuller discussion of nucleic acids, see CELL (The Code of Life); NUCLEIC ACID.

The Origin of Life

Religious Explanations. Nearly all religions have had *creation stories* to explain the origin of life. These stories tell how the world and living things were created. In the Western world, the best-known creation story comes from the Book of Genesis in the Bible. It tells how God created the earth and all living things.

Modern religious thinkers interpret the Biblical story of creation in various ways. Some believe that the creation occurred exactly as Genesis says it did. Others think that the story is a symbolic account of creation, which is a divine mystery that will never be fully understood. Still other religious scholars believe that God's method of creation is revealed through science and human understanding.

The Theory of Spontaneous Generation originated in ancient times and remained a common belief for thousands of years. The theory claimed that lower forms of life could arise from nonliving matter. For example, people believed that flies developed from decaying meat and that mice formed from piles of old rags.

During the mid-1600's, an Italian scientist named Francesco Redi conducted experiments which showed that meat protected from flies would not produce maggots. However, Redi's experiments did not end the dispute over spontaneous generation. A belief persisted that microscopic forms of life could arise spontaneously, and the argument raged for about 200 years.

The French chemist Louis Pasteur finally settled the controversy during the mid-1800's. He demonstrated that even the minutest bacteria do not arise spontaneously but always grow from other bacteria. After Pasteur's experiments, most biologists accepted the idea that all life comes from existing life. See SPONTANEOUS GENERATION.

Modern Theories. During the 1900's, biologists have developed scientific theories of the origin of life. Scientists think that life probably arose on the earth more than $3\frac{1}{2}$ billion years ago, and so they cannot base their understanding of that event on direct observation. As a result, their understanding of how life began is far less certain than their knowledge of such subjects as cell structure and biochemistry. Scientists construct explanations of the origin of life. They base their explanations on their knowledge of living things and on their understanding of the physical conditions on the earth during its early stages.

Scientists have proposed two major theories of the origin of life. They are (1) the theory of panspermia and (2) the theory of chemical evolution.

The Theory of Panspermia states that spores from some other part of the universe landed on the earth and began to develop. However, some scientists doubt that spores could survive a journey through the harsh conditions of outer space. Even if the theory is true, it explains only the origin of life on the earth and not how life arose in the universe.

The Theory of Chemical Evolution was developed independently during the 1920's by a Russian biochemist named Alexander I. Oparin and by J. B. S. Haldane, a British biologist. Most modern biologists now accept this theory. It claims that life developed through a series

Sigurgeir Jonasson

Lightning and Volcanoes may have played a role in the origin of life on the earth. According to one theory, energy from such sources as lightning, volcanoes, and sunlight powered reactions among the gases in the atmosphere of the early earth. The theory proposes that such reactions produced the first biological molecules.

of spontaneous chemical reactions in the atmosphere and oceans early in the earth's history. Pasteur showed that life cannot arise spontaneously under the chemical and physical conditions present on the earth today. Billions of years ago, however, the chemical and physical conditions on the earth were far different.

Scientific studies indicate that the atmosphere of the early earth contained little or no *free* (uncombined) oxygen. Because hydrogen is the most abundant element in the universe, many scientists have theorized that the earth's early atmosphere had large quantities of hydrogen. Under such conditions, the hydrogen-containing compounds ammonia, methane, and water would also have been abundant. The theory of chemical evolution proposes that energy from such sources as sunlight, lightning, and volcanoes powered reactions among these compounds that produced simple biological molecules. These molecules, such as sugars and amino acids, then combined and formed more complex molecules. Finally, the theory claims that these complex molecules became organized into the first organisms.

Two American chemists, Stanley L. Miller and Harold C. Urey, provided the first experimental evidence in support of the theory of chemical evolution in 1953. They subjected a mixture of ammonia, hydrogen, methane, and water to the energy of high-voltage sparks for one week. After that time, amino acids and other simple biochemical compounds had formed. Scientists have repeated this experiment under various conditions.

Some researchers have assumed that the early atmosphere contained little hydrogen but large quantities of carbon dioxide. They have substituted various hydrogen-poor "atmospheres" for the hydrogen-rich mixture of the Miller-Urey experiment. The hydrogen-poor mixtures also yielded biochemical compounds when exposed to high-voltage sparks. Such experiments have proved that a random process can produce most of the basic molecules of biochemistry. Many other experiments have combined simple biological molecules to form more complex ones.

Other scientific research also suggests that life arose through chemical evolution. The surface of the earth experiences a continuous flow of energy as it receives light from the sun and radiates heat into outer space. Physics research has demonstrated that such an energy flow increases molecular organization. Thus, the evolution of complex biochemical molecules may be viewed as part of this natural process. Other studies have shown that the basic structure of biological membranes will form spontaneously in a mixture of lipids and water. The mere presence of the right type of molecules seems to guarantee the formation of biological membranes.

Although scientists have experimental evidence to support parts of the theory of chemical evolution, many questions remain. For example, biologists are still searching for an explanation of how biological molecules could have first become organized into cell-like organisms. They are also trying to discover how nucleic acids and proteins became related in such a way that nucleic acids determine the kinds of proteins a cell produces. A complete theory of the origin of life will have to explain this relationship, which is a basic characteristic of life as we know it.

The Search for Life on Other Planets

The theory of chemical evolution suggests that life arises naturally under certain physical and chemical conditions. Astronomers believe that these conditions have probably existed in many places throughout the universe. Thus, many scientists conclude that life may have arisen on numerous other planets. The search for and study of life elsewhere in the universe make up the science of *exobiology*. See EXOBIOLOGY.

Exobiologists think that the chemistry of life anywhere in the universe would basically resemble that of life on the earth. However, the living things on another planet would have developed in response to the specific environmental conditions there. As a result, the life forms would almost certainly differ greatly in structure and appearance from those on the earth.

The development of space travel during the 1960's provided the opportunity to search for life on neighboring planets in our solar system. At that time, scientists thought that life might exist on two of those planets —Venus and Mars. The harsh environments on the other planets in our solar system make it highly unlikely that life could exist on any of them.

During the 1960's, the United States and Russia sent missions to Venus. These missions revealed that environmental conditions on the surface of Venus could not support life as we know it. However, some scientists believe that organisms could exist in the clouds that surround Venus.

In 1976, two United States space probes, *Viking I* and *Viking II*, landed on Mars and performed several experiments to test for life. These experiments indicated chemical activity in Martian soil, but a highly sensitive chemical detector failed to detect any organic compounds. Scientists thus concluded that the results of the experiments probably were due to high-energy chemicals in the soil. Some researchers, however, still believe that organisms may be present, and other missions have been recommended.

Exobiologists think that many stars beyond our solar system may have planets on which life could exist. However, enormous distances separate the earth from the stars. With our present technology, it is difficult even to detect the presence of other planets, much less to search for life on them. We can therefore learn of life on distant planets only if they are inhabited by intelligent beings capable of communicating across the vast reaches of space. Some scientists have begun using radio telescopes to listen for communication signals from distant civilizations.   HAROLD J. MOROWITZ

Related Articles in WORLD BOOK include:

Adaptation	Environment	Oparin, Alexander I.
Biogenesis	Evolution	Pasteur, Louis
Biology	Exobiology	Protoplasm
Botany	Growth	Reproduction
Cell	Life Cycle	Spontaneous
Death	Life Expectancy	Generation
Ecology	Metabolism	Zoology

Outline

I. **The Characteristics of Living Things**
  A. Reproduction
  B. Growth
  C. Metabolism
  D. Movement
  E. Responsiveness
  F. Adaptation
II. **Living Things and Their Environment**
  A. The Physical Environment
  B. The Biological Environment
III. **The Structure of Living Things**
  A. Cells   B. Tissues, Organs, and Organ Systems
IV. **The Chemical Basis of Life**
  A. Carbohydrates
  B. Lipids
  C. Proteins
  D. Nucleic Acids
V. **The Origin of Life**
  A. Religious Explanations
  B. The Theory of Spontaneous Generation
  C. Modern Theories
VI. **The Search for Life on Other Planets**

Questions

What are some basic characteristics of living things?
What features make up an organism's physical environment?
How do cells of bacteria and blue-green algae differ from all other cells?
What is the chief source of biological energy?
What experimental evidence do scientists have to support the theory of chemical evolution?
How many species of living things exist on the earth?
What are the two main ways in which living things adapt to changes in the environment?
Why is water essential to life processes?
What is *exobiology*?
In what ways do organisms use carbohydrates?

Additional Resources

Level I

ADLER, IRVING. *How Life Began.* Harper, 1977.
ASIMOV, ISAAC. *How Did We Find Out About the Beginning of Life?* Walker, 1982.
MARSHALL, KIM. *The Story of Life: From the Big Bang to You.* Holt, 1980.
OLLIVER, JANE, ed. *The Living World.* Watts, 1977.

Level II

FARAGO, PETER J., and LAGNADO, JOHN. *Life in Action: Biochemistry Explained.* Knopf, 1972.

GRIBBIN, JOHN R. *Genesis: The Origins of Man and the Universe.* Delacorte, 1981.
MARGULIS, LYNN. *Early Life.* Science Books Int., 1982.
MURCHIE, GUY. *The Seven Mysteries of Life: An Exploration in Science and Philosophy.* Houghton, 1978.

LIFE CYCLE is the sequence of forms and activities that a living thing passes through from a particular stage in one generation to the same stage in the next. Growth and reproduction always take place. The life cycle of mammals is relatively simple. They develop from a fertilized egg to an adult by growth. The adults produce *gametes* (sex cells). Fertilization of the egg begins development of a new individual. Many lower organisms have even simpler life cycles. But most plants and some animals go through complex life cycles, involving more than one kind of individual. In many, a generation of sexual reproduction follows one of asexual reproduction. The sequence of events in the life of an individual is called its *life history*.   NEAL D. BUFFALOE

Related Articles in WORLD BOOK include:

Alternation of	Life
Generations	Metamorphosis
Generation	Reproduction

LIFE EXPECTANCY is a statistical measure of the average number of years that a group of people of a certain age may expect to live. This measure is based on the death rates by age for a specific population at a specific time. It assumes that the death rates will not change in the future. If death rates decline, as has normally happened, life expectancy increases. Social scientists and health workers use life expectancy to summarize the effects of death rates on a population. Insurance companies use life expectancy to determine life insurance rates.

The table on the next page compares the life expectancies at birth for the male and female populations of various countries. Life expectancy varies from country to country because of differences in public health and standards of living. In general, the industrialized nations have the highest life expectancy, and the developing countries, especially those in Africa, have the lowest. With very few exceptions, females have a higher life expectancy than males.

Since 1900, three major changes have taken place in life expectancy in the United States. First, the average life expectancy at birth has increased by more than 26 years—from 47.3 years in 1900 to 74.6 years in 1983. Second, the gap in life expectancy between the sexes has widened. In 1900, newborn girls could be expected to live two years longer than newborn boys. In 1983, girls could be expected to live 7.1 years longer. Third, the difference in life expectancy between white Americans and Americans of other races has decreased. In 1900, whites could be expected to live 14.6 years longer than other Americans. By 1983, this difference had fallen to 4.1 years.   JEANNE CLARE RIDLEY

LIFE INSURANCE. See INSURANCE (Life Insurance).

LIFE JACKET is a device that is worn to keep afloat in water. Most life jackets are filled with light material, such as kapok, plastic foam, fiberglass, cork, or balsa wood. They are often brightly colored to make them easily visible. Most have no sleeves, so the wearer's arms can move freely. Some life jackets are also called *life preservers* or *life vests*.

Life jackets belong to a group of water-safety devices

Life Expectancy at Birth for Selected Countries

Country	Males	Females	Country	Males	Females	Country	Males	Females	Country	Males	Females
Africa			South Africa	49.8	53.2	Thailand	53.6	58.7	Switzerland	72.0	78.7
Algeria	58.5	61.4	Sudan	43.9	46.4	Vietnam	53.7	58.1	Yugoslavia	67.7	73.2
Angola	38.5	41.6	Togo	31.6	38.5	**Australia and**			**North America**		
Benin	39.0	42.1	Tunisia	57.6	58.6	**Pacific Islands**			Canada	71.9	78.9
Burkina Faso	32.1	31.1	Uganda	48.3	51.7	Australia	71.4	78.4	Costa Rica	66.3	70.5
Burundi	40.0	43.0	Zaire	46.4	49.7	New Zealand	70.7	76.9	Cuba	71.5	74.9
Cameroon	44.4	47.6	Zambia	47.7	51.0	Papua New			Dominican		
Central African			Zimbabwe	51.3	55.6	Guinea	50.5	50.0	Republic	57.2	58.6
Republic	33.0	36.0	**Asia**			**Europe**			El Salvador	56.6	60.4
Chad	29.0	35.0	Afghanistan	36.6	37.3	Albania	64.9	67.0	Guatemala	53.7	55.5
Congo	43.0	46.1	Bangladesh	55.3	54.4	Austria	69.2	76.6	Haiti	49.1	52.0
Egypt	51.6	53.8	Burma	51.0	54.1	Belgium	68.6	75.1	Honduras	59.9	55.5
Ethiopia	39.3	42.5	China	62.6	66.5	Bulgaria	68.7	73.9	Jamaica	62.7	66.6
Ghana	48.3	51.7	India	46.4	44.7	Czechoslovakia	67.0	74.3	Mexico	62.1	66.0
Guinea	36.7	39.8	Indonesia	47.5	47.5	Denmark	71.4	77.4	Nicaragua	55.3	57.3
Ivory Coast	43.4	46.6	Iran	57.6	57.4	Finland	69.5	77.8	Panama	68.4	71.9
Kenya	46.9	51.2	Iraq	57.2	60.9	France	70.4	78.5	Trinidad and		
Lesotho	45.7	49.0	Israel	72.5	75.8	Germany, East	69.1	75.1	Tobago	64.1	68.1
Liberia	45.8	44.0	Japan	74.2	79.7	Germany, West	70.2	76.9	United States	71.0	78.1
Libya	53.8	57.0	Jordan	52.6	52.0	Great Britain	67.8	73.8	**South America**		
Madagascar	37.5	38.3	Kampuchea	30.0	32.5	Greece	70.1	73.6	Argentina	65.4	72.1
Malawi	40.9	44.2	Korea, North	60.5	64.6	Hungary	66.6	73.8	Bolivia	46.5	50.9
Mali	46.9	49.7	Korea, South	62.7	69.1	Ireland	68.8	73.5	Brazil	57.6	61.0
Mauritania	40.4	43.6	Kuwait	66.4	71.5	Italy	69.7	75.9	Chile	61.3	67.6
Mauritius	60.7	65.3	Laos	46.1	49.0	The Netherlands	72.7	79.3	Colombia	60.0	64.5
Morocco	53.8	57.0	Mongolia	60.5	64.6	Norway	72.6	79.4	Ecuador	59.5	61.8
Mozambique	45.8	49.1	Nepal	44.6	43.1	Poland	67.2	75.2	Guyana	59.0	63.0
Niger	39.0	42.1	Pakistan	59.0	59.2	Portugal	65.1	72.9	Paraguay	61.9	66.4
Nigeria	37.2	36.7	Philippines	60.9	64.3	Romania	67.4	72.2	Peru	52.6	55.5
Rwanda	45.9	49.2	Saudi Arabia	51.5	54.6	Russia	64.0	74.0	Uruguay	65.7	72.4
Senegal	39.7	42.9	Singapore	68.9	74.2	Spain	70.4	76.2	Venezuela	64.9	70.7
Sierra Leone	30.6	33.5	Sri Lanka	64.8	66.9	Sweden	73.1	79.1			
Somalia	39.3	42.5	Syria	63.8	64.7						

Sources: *Demographic Yearbook, 1983*, UN; National Center for Health Statistics.

that float called *personal flotation devices* (PFD's). Other personal flotation devices include *buoyant cushions* (floating pillows) and doughnut-shaped *ring buoys*. Buoyant cushions and ring buoys can be thrown to a person in the water from a boat or from land. The person holds onto the cushion or buoy to keep afloat.

LIFE PRESERVER. See LIFE JACKET.

LIFE SPAN. See LIFE EXPECTANCY.

LIFEBOAT. See COAST GUARD, UNITED STATES (pictures).

Stearns Manufacturing Company

A Life Jacket keeps a person afloat in water. Everyone riding in an open boat should wear one at all times.

LIFESAVING. See SWIMMING (Water Safety); DROWNING; COAST GUARD, UNITED STATES (Protecting Life and Property); FIRST AID.

LIFT is the term used in Britain and other Commonwealth countries for an elevator. See ELEVATOR.

LIFT. See AERODYNAMICS (Lift).

LIFT PUMP. See PUMP.

LIGAMENT is fibrous tissue that holds organs of the body in place and fastens bones together. Ligaments are grouped together in cords, bands, or sheets. They are as strong as rope. A *sprain* occurs when ligaments covering a joint are torn or twisted. A sprained ankle is a partial tearing of the *talofibular* ligament that binds the bones of the lower leg to the bones of the foot. Ligaments heal slowly. They may never heal if they are completely torn apart. Physicians bind sprained body parts with tape or elastic bandage, or enclose them in plaster casts. This takes pressure off the joint, rests the joint, relieves pain, and helps ligaments to heal. See also SPRAIN; HUMAN BODY (picture: Ligaments and Tendons).   MARSHALL R. URIST

LIGATURE is a thread used in surgery to tie a bleeding blood vessel. Surgeons did not use ligatures extensively until germfree surgery developed in the mid-1800's. Before that time, ligatures almost always caused infection. The British surgeon Joseph Lister devised a sterile ligature, called *catgut*, from a sheep's bowel. The body absorbs this material without harm. Surgeons also use silk, cotton, linen, and nylon ligatures. These are not absorbed, but are not harmful.   MICHAEL L. MASON

LIGER. See LION.

LIGHT

FPG

Light from the Sun makes life on the earth possible. Plants need sunlight to grow, and animals eat plants or plant-eating animals.

LIGHT is so common that we often take it for granted. Yet the world would quickly change if suddenly there were no light. We could no longer see, because light that comes to our eyes makes seeing possible. Without light, we would have no food to eat or air to breathe. Green plants use the light from the sun to grow and to make food. All the food we eat comes from plants or animals that eat plants. As plants grow, they give off oxygen. This oxygen is a necessary part of the air we breathe.

Light gives us fuels. The energy in the sunlight that shone on the earth millions of years ago was stored by plants. After these plants died, they were changed into coal, natural gas, and oil. Today, we use the energy in these fuels to produce electricity and to run machines.

Light from the sun also heats the earth. Without the sun's light, the earth would soon become so cold that nothing could live on it. Even if we burned all our fuels, we could not keep the earth warm enough for life to exist. For more information on light and energy from the sun, see the WORLD BOOK articles on SOLAR ENERGY and SUN.

People have found ways of making and controlling light in order to see when there is no sunlight. At first, they produced light with campfires and torches. Later, they developed candles, oil lamps, gaslights, and electric lights.

People make and use light for many other purposes than to see by. For example, the pictures on a television screen consist of spots of light. Using scientific instruments, people can study light itself and learn much about the universe. For example, the light from distant stars can tell scientists what the stars are made of. It can also tell them if the stars are moving toward or away from the earth and how fast they are moving. See RED SHIFT.

What is light? This question has been a puzzle for centuries. People once thought light was something that traveled from a person's eyes to an object and then back again. If anything blocked the rays from the eyes, the object could not be seen. Since the 1600's, scientists have made many discoveries about light. They have learned that light is a form of energy that can travel freely through space. The energy of light is called *radiant energy*. There are many kinds of radiant energy, including infrared rays, radio waves, ultraviolet rays, and X rays. We can see only a tiny part of all the different kinds of radiant energy. This part is called *visible light* or simply *light*.

This article describes where light comes from, the nature of light, and how light behaves when it comes in contact with various materials. The article also tells how light is measured and discusses the important scientific discoveries about light. By building the Science Project included in this article, you can experiment with the behavior of light. For more information on how people use light for seeing, see LIGHTING.

Earle B. Brown, the contributor of this article, is a member of the technical staff of the Perkin-Elmer Corporation and the author of Modern Optics.

Light makes it possible for us to see. We see a few things—for example, the sun and lighted candles—because they give off their own light. Such things are called *sources* of light. But most things do not give off their own light. We see them because light from a source travels to them and then to our eyes.

Light sources can be classified as *natural* or *artificial*. Natural light comes from sources that people do not control. Such sources include the sun and the stars. Artificial light comes from sources that people control. These sources include candles and electric lamps. But all light—natural or artificial—comes from tiny particles of matter called *atoms*.

The atoms of all elements contain energy. The amount of energy in an atom can vary from the atom's normal *energy level*. If an atom absorbs additional energy, it moves to a higher energy level. Such an atom is called an *excited* atom. After absorbing the additional energy, the atom soon drops back to a lower energy level. When it drops back, the atom releases energy. An atom sometimes returns to its original level in two or more steps, releasing energy at each step. Atoms release and absorb energy in tiny bundles called *photons*. Light consists of streams of photons.

The higher the energy level an atom reaches before it drops back and releases a photon, the more energy that photon will have. Therefore, all photons do not have the same amount of energy. Photons with different amounts of energy make up light of different colors. The most energetic light photons make up blue light, and the least energetic ones form red light. Other colors of light have photons with energies between the energy of red and blue light. White light is a mixture of photons with energies that cover the whole range of visible light. Thus, white light consists of all the colors of light.

How Light Is Produced. Atoms can be excited in several ways to *emit* (give off) photons. One way is by being heated. For example, as a piece of iron is heated in a furnace until it is white-hot, the energy levels of the iron atoms rise. The atoms then drop to lower levels and emit photons of light. The iron emits white light be-cause the atoms release photons with energies covering the whole range of visible light. The furnace heat keeps raising the atoms back to higher energy levels, and so the iron continues to emit white light.

The piece of iron cools after it leaves the furnace. As a result, its atoms give off photons that are less energetic. More photons of red light are emitted than any others, and the iron appears red-hot.

Another way atoms can gain energy and emit photons is through a process called *phosphorescence*. In this process, atoms absorb light energy from one source and then give off their own light. See PHOSPHORESCENCE.

Natural Light. The sun is our most important source of light. The energy that excites atoms in the sun to emit photons comes from atomic reactions inside the sun that change matter into energy. Stars are another source of natural light. But stars are farther from the earth than is the sun, and so their light is fainter.

In addition to the sun and the stars, there are other sources of natural light. Some living things, including fireflies and certain bacteria, produce light by a process called *bioluminescence*. The energy that excites atoms in such animals and plants to emit photons comes from chemical reactions within these organisms. One of the most fascinating displays of natural light is the aurora borealis, or northern lights. These lights can sometimes be seen in the sky at night in the Northern Hemisphere. The aurora is produced when electrons from the sun excite atoms in the earth's upper atmosphere.

Artificial Light enables people to do many things they could not do if they had only natural light. For example, artificial light makes it possible for factories to run 24 hours a day and for automobiles, trains, and airplanes to travel at night. Artificial light comes from many different sources. The most widely used sources are electric lamps and fluorescent lamps.

During the late 1950's, scientists developed the *laser*. This device emits a narrow beam of photons, all of which have the same energy. The laser thus produces very pure light of a single color. Lasers have many uses in communication, industry, medicine, and scientific laboratories. See LASER.

Natural and Artificial Sources of Light

Natural light sources, such as fireflies and the northern lights, are not made by people. People make artificial light sources, such as candles and lasers.

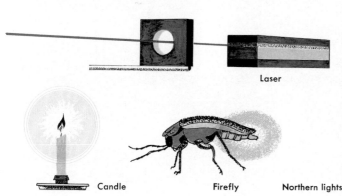

Laser

Candle   Firefly   Northern lights

In some ways, photons of light behave like streams of particles, such as bullets from a machine gun. In other ways, photons behave like waves, such as ripples on a pond. It is difficult to understand how a particle can act like a wave or how a wave can act like a particle. In fact, scientists argued for many years whether light consisted of particles or waves. They could not understand how it could be both. Yet they could not explain all they knew about light only in terms of either waves or particles.

In 1900, the German physicist Max Planck proposed a theory that helped explain how tiny particles, such as photons, behave like waves. His theory, which led to the *quantum theory*, helped scientists accept the idea that light behaves like both particles and waves. See QUANTUM MECHANICS.

Although light seems to be both a particle and a wave, it is easier sometimes to think of light as simply particles or simply waves. Most ideas about light can be described in terms of waves.

Scientists use various terms to describe the features of light waves and other kinds of waves. Imagine a group of waves coming from a rock tossed into a still pond. The height of the waves above—or their depth below—the level of the water when the pond is still is called the *amplitude* of the waves. The distance between any point on one wave and a comparable point on the next one is called the *wave length* of the waves. The number of waves that pass any point in one second is called the *frequency* of the waves.

Electromagnetic Waves. Photons of light are surrounded by an electric field and a magnetic field. For this reason, light is called *electromagnetic radiation* or *electromagnetic waves*. The electric and magnetic fields are always at right angles to each other and to the direction in which the wave is moving. In addition, the amplitudes of the two fields are always in proportion to each other at any point along the wave. For example, when the electric field reaches its greatest amplitude, the magnetic field will also be at its greatest amplitude. The amplitude of the two fields determines the *intensity* (brightness) of a light. If the fields have a large amplitude, the light will be bright.

Many kinds of waves need a material to travel through or on. For example, waves on a pond must travel on the water. But electromagnetic waves can travel freely through space. It is easier to think of light traveling through space as a stream of particles rather than as waves.

There are several kinds of electromagnetic waves besides light. Other electromagnetic waves differ from light in their frequencies and wave lengths. Some electromagnetic waves, such as microwaves and radio waves, have lower frequencies and longer wave lengths than light has. Others, including gamma rays and X rays, have higher frequencies and shorter wave lengths. A chart of all electromagnetic waves arranged according to their frequencies and wave lengths is called the *electromagnetic spectrum*. This spectrum extends in both directions from the tiny slice of it that is visible light. The whole electromagnetic spectrum extends from short gamma rays, which may have a wave length of $\frac{1}{2,500,000,000,000}$ inch (0.00000000001 millimeter) or less, to long radio waves, which have a wave length of many miles, or many kilometers. See ELECTROMAGNETIC WAVES.

The Visible Spectrum consists of all the electromagnetic waves that the eye can see. It appears as a band of colors because the eye sees the different wave lengths of light as different colors. These colors range from red —through orange, yellow, green, and blue—to violet. The longest waves are deep red, and the shortest are vio-

Electromagnetic Nature of Light

Light is one form of electromagnetic waves. These waves consist of an electric and a magnetic field. Both fields vibrate at right angles to each other and to the direction the wave is moving. The *amplitude* (strength) of the two fields is always the same at any point along the wave.

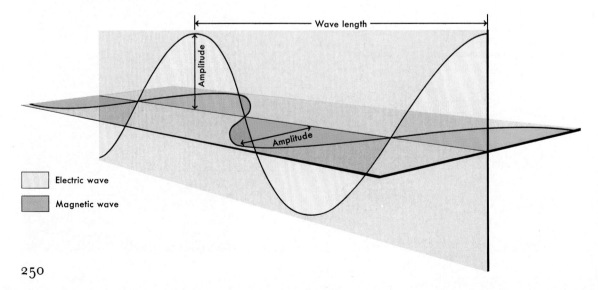

Wave length

Amplitude

Amplitude

☐ Electric wave

■ Magnetic wave

White Light and the Visible Spectrum

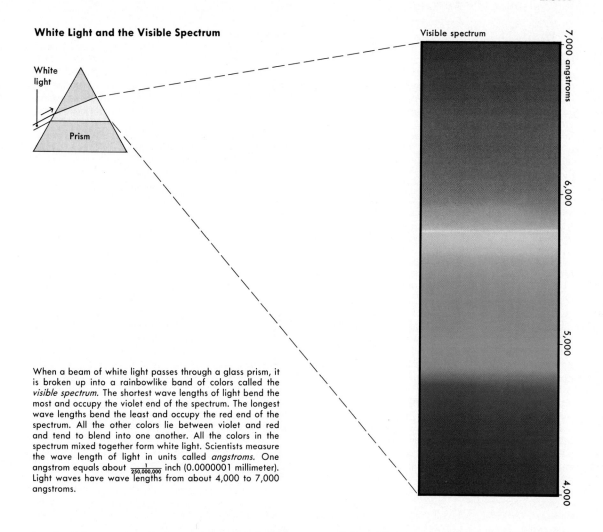

Visible spectrum

7,000 angstroms

6,000

5,000

4,000

When a beam of white light passes through a glass prism, it is broken up into a rainbowlike band of colors called the *visible spectrum*. The shortest wave lengths of light bend the most and occupy the violet end of the spectrum. The longest wave lengths bend the least and occupy the red end of the spectrum. All the other colors lie between violet and red and tend to blend into one another. All the colors in the spectrum mixed together form white light. Scientists measure the wave length of light in units called *angstroms*. One angstrom equals about $\frac{1}{250,000,000}$ inch (0.0000001 millimeter). Light waves have wave lengths from about 4,000 to 7,000 angstroms.

let. Sunlight contains all the wave lengths of visible light. When sunlight passes through a wedge-shaped glass object called a *prism*, these wave lengths spread out and form the visible spectrum. This spectrum is called a *continuous spectrum* because it has no gaps or missing colors.

Light from some sources does not contain all the wave lengths of the continuous spectrum. A spectrum from such a source has dark gaps. By studying the spectrum from any source, scientists can learn much about the source itself. This study is called *spectrum analysis*. Scientists analyze spectra with a *spectrometer*. In this device, light passes through a narrow slit and then spreads out so the various colors of the spectrum can be seen.

Spectrum analysis can reveal information about a light source because an excited atom emits photons at each of a number of exact wave lengths. A photon's wave length depends on the kind of atom that produced the photon and on how large a change in energy levels the electron that produced the photon made. In a spectrometer, light from the source forms a series of

spectral lines. The narrow slit inside the spectrometer creates these lines. Each element produces a pattern of lines that differs from the pattern produced by all other elements. These patterns can tell scientists what atoms are in a light source and what their energy levels are.

Atoms of gases produce clear spectral lines. But atoms that are tightly packed together in a solid or liquid produce blurred and overlapping lines. Molecules sometimes give off light. Molecules have more energy levels than do individual atoms, and the levels are closer together in molecules than in atoms. As a result, the light from molecules produces broad bands of light rather than clear lines of light when seen in a spectrometer.

Scientists have many uses for spectrum analysis. For example, they use it to identify the elements in stars and the sun. They also use spectrum analysis in chemical laboratories to find out what elements a piece of unknown material contains. The material is heated until it gives off light that can be analyzed. See Spectrometer.

The study of light is called *optics*. By learning how light acts when it meets different materials, scientists have been able to design microscopes, telescopes, and other optical instruments. These instruments have aided in the study of the universe. By learning about light's behavior, we can better understand such things as how photographic film records images and how artificial satellites receive electric power from sunlight.

Reflection, Refraction, and Absorption. When a ray of light falls on the surface of an object, one or a combination of the following three things happen: (1) The light may be *reflected* (thrown back). (2) It may be *refracted* (pass into the object). (3) It may be *absorbed* by the object. The way different materials reflect, refract, and absorb different wave lengths of light gives objects their individual appearance and color. If an object permits light to pass through it, as does a clear pane of glass, it is called *transparent*. If an object scatters the light that passes through it, as a frosted glass or a layer of milk does, it is called *translucent*. An object that does not permit light to pass through it is called *opaque*.

Light that is reflected bounces off an object much as a billiard ball bounces back from the edge of a billiard table. When a ray of light strikes a reflecting object, such as a mirror, it makes a certain angle with an imaginary line that is *normal* (at right angles) to the mirror. The angle is called the *angle of incidence*. The ray that is reflected from the mirror also makes an angle with the normal line. This angle is called the *angle of reflection*. According to the scientific law of reflection, the angle of incidence equals the angle of reflection.

Light reflected from a smooth surface, such as a mirror, bounces back without spreading out. But light reflected from a rough surface, such as a piece of paper, spreads out. A mirror thus forms a sharp image of the light it reflects, and paper forms no image at all. The law of reflection is true whether the light spreads out or not. See REFLECTION.

Refraction occurs when light passes into various substances, such as glass or water. Light slows down as it enters these substances. If light enters a substance at any angle except a right angle, the slowing down causes the light ray to bend at the surface of the substance. This bending is called refraction. A pencil placed at an angle in a glass of water appears to bend sharply at the surface because of refraction. The amount the light bends depends on the angle of incidence and the speed of the light in the material it enters. See REFRACTION.

When a material absorbs light, the light may raise the energy levels of the material's atoms, or it may be changed into heat. For example, light absorbed by a phosphorescent material raises the energy level of the atoms in the material. Later, the atoms release this energy as photons of light. Most objects placed in sunlight get warm from absorbing the light.

Scattering is similar to reflection. When light strikes small particles of matter, such as those found in the air, the particles scatter the light in all directions. The amount of light scattered and its distribution depend on the size of the particles and the wave length of the light.

Interference. When two light waves come together so that the peaks of one wave occur at the same points as the peaks of the other wave, the two waves are said to be *in phase* with each other. The waves combine and form one wave with an amplitude equal to the sum of the amplitudes of the two waves. But if the peaks of one wave come together with the low points of another wave, the two waves are *out of phase*. Two equal light waves that are exactly out of phase *interfere* with each other, cancel out, and leave darkness.

In 1801, the English physicist Thomas Young showed how interference occurs. Young passed light from a source through two narrow slits placed close together in an opaque material. The light fell on a screen as a pattern of bright and dark *fringes* (bands). At a point on the screen that was the same distance from both slits, the light coming through the slits was in phase. A bright fringe appeared there. But on either side of the band, the waves were not in phase because the distances to the two slits were unequal. At these points, the light waves interfered, and a dark fringe appeared.

Other points on the screen also had light and dark fringes, depending on the distance of the points from the slits. Bright fringes formed where the distance to one slit differed from the distance to the other slit by a full wave length. The light at these points was in phase. Dark fringes formed where the distance to each slit differed by half a wave length because the light there was out of phase. See INTERFERENCE.

Diffraction is the spreading of light waves around an opaque object. For example, when a light beam passes through a narrow slit, most of the light goes straight through. But at the edges of the slit, the light waves spread out in expanding circles—just as a stone dropped in a pond causes an expanding circle of ripples.

Light spreads out as it passes near the edges of the slit because of the way a beam of light travels. Every point along a beam of light consists of wavelets that could spread out in expanding circles. But in the beam, the wavelets combine and make the front of the beam straight. Thus, the light travels in a straight line. When most of the light beam is blocked by the slit, the wavelets that pass through have no wavelets on either side to combine with. Therefore, they begin to spread out in expanding circles.

Because of diffraction, the shadow cast by any object does not have perfectly sharp edges. Some diffracted light enters the shadow and blurs the edges. Diffracted light waves also interfere with each other and produce interference fringes near the edges of an object. Diffraction limits the ability of optical instruments to see fine details or objects that lie close together.

On the other hand, diffraction is essential to the study of the visible spectrum with a spectrometer. The spectrometer uses a *diffraction grating*, a plate with many thousands of closely spaced, parallel slits. The grating diffracts the light to be studied. The interference fringes caused by diffraction of the different wave lengths then fall at different points along a strip in the spectrometer. The location of a fringe along this strip indicates the position of the particular wave length of light in the visible spectrum. See DIFFRACTION.

THE BEHAVIOR OF LIGHT

In studying *optics* (the science of the behavior of light), physicists have discovered certain principles that describe how light behaves. The most important of these principles include (1) reflection, (2) refraction, (3) diffraction, and (4) interference.

Reflection

A beam of light will be reflected by a smooth surface. The beam coming toward the surface is called the *incident beam*. After the beam has been reflected, it is called the *reflected beam*. The angle the incident beam makes with an imaginary line *normal* (at right angles) to the surface equals the angle made by the reflected beam.

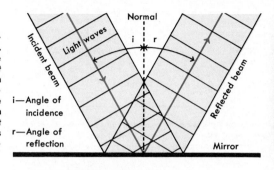

i—Angle of incidence

r—Angle of reflection

Refraction

Refraction causes a light beam to bend as the beam passes from one substance into another. The beam bends toward the normal if it slows down when entering a substance, as shown in the diagram. The *angle of refraction* then is less than the *angle of incidence*. If light travels faster in the substance, the beam bends away from the normal.

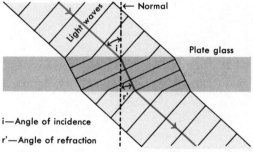

i—Angle of incidence

r′—Angle of refraction

From *PSSC Physics*, published by
D. C. Heath & Co.

Diffraction

Light and other waves usually travel in a straight line. But when waves pass through a slit about the same size as their own wave length, they no longer travel in a straight line. Instead, they *diffract* (spread out) into curving waves. The photograph shows water waves because light waves spread out so slightly that their diffraction is difficult to see.

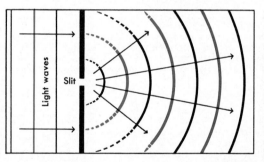

Interference

Light waves can interfere with each other in two ways. (1) Where the *crest* (peak) of one wave meets the crest of another wave—or where the *trough* (low point) of one wave meets the trough of another—the two waves combine and form a bright spot of light. (2) Where a crest meets a trough, the two waves cancel, leaving a dark spot. In the diagram, light waves diffracted through two slits provide two overlapping diffraction patterns. The two groups of waves interfere and produce a series of bright and dark *fringes* (bands) on a screen across from the slits.

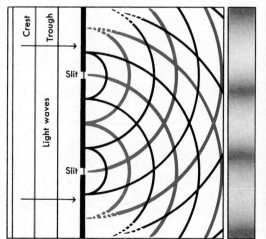

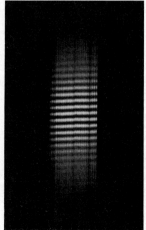

**A WORLD BOOK
SCIENCE PROJECT**

HOW LIGHT BEHAVES

The purpose of this project is to learn about the behavior of light by studying how light rays are reflected and refracted.

CAUTION: This project involves working with electricity, which can cause burns, shock, or fire. If you are not familiar with the precautions for working with electricity, you must have a knowledgeable person help you with this project.

A Projector for Studying Light, *left,* can be built of simple materials sold at local stores. The projector has cellophane filters, which create beams of colored light and so make it easy to trace the paths of the light rays. Put mirrors, glasses of water, and other materials on the viewing platform to see the reflection and refraction of light.

Reflection

You can find out how reflected light behaves by shining the beams of light from the projector on objects of various shapes as shown below. Use mirrors or highly polished pieces of metal as reflectors. Compare all the angles made by the three light beams as they are reflected from each piece. What conclusions can you draw from your observations of the behavior of reflected light?

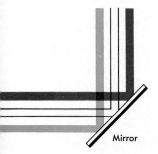
Mirror

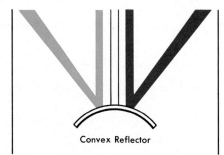
Convex Reflector

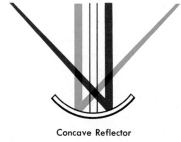
Concave Reflector

Refraction

You can show how refracted light behaves when it passes through the same kind of liquid in containers of different shapes. Fill each container with water. Then let the light from the projector shine through the container as shown below. Look at the beams of light as they pass through the water and out the opposite side. Note how the beams passing through the water glass cross at a point.

Bottle of Water

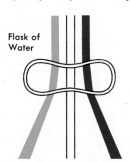
Flask of Water

Glass of Water

You can show how refracted light behaves when it passes through different kinds of liquids in containers of the same shape. Use three straight-sided glasses of the same size for this demonstration. Fill one glass with water, another with salad oil, and the third with alcohol. Shine the light through each glass. Note the *focal point,* where the three beams of light cross one another.

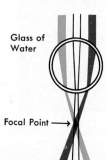
Glass of Water

Focal Point ⟶

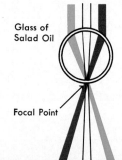
Glass of Salad Oil

Focal Point

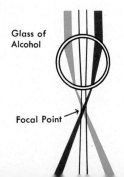
Glass of Alcohol

Focal Point ⟶

MATERIALS AND ASSEMBLY

Cut the projector housing from corrugated cardboard, following the dimensions shown at the right. Cut the other parts from noncorrugated cardboard. Paint the inside bottom of all glass containers white.

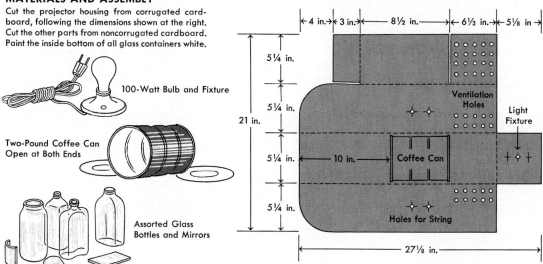

100-Watt Bulb and Fixture

Two-Pound Coffee Can Open at Both Ends

Assorted Glass Bottles and Mirrors

| 4 in. | 3 in. | 8½ in. | 6½ in. | 5⅛ in |

5¼ in.

5¼ in.

21 in.

5¼ in.

Ventilation Holes

Light Fixture

10 in.

Coffee Can

5¼ in.

Holes for String

27⅛ in.

To Make the Color Filters, cut a square of cardboard as shown at the left below and tape it to the front of the assembled projector. Cut a round piece as shown at the right below and tape it to the coffee can. Make three slides of cardboard as shown at the center below. The large pieces are the sides. Fasten the small pieces between the sides at top and bottom to form a narrow channel between the sides. On two slides, cover one end of the channel with colored cellophane. Leave the channel open in the third slide.

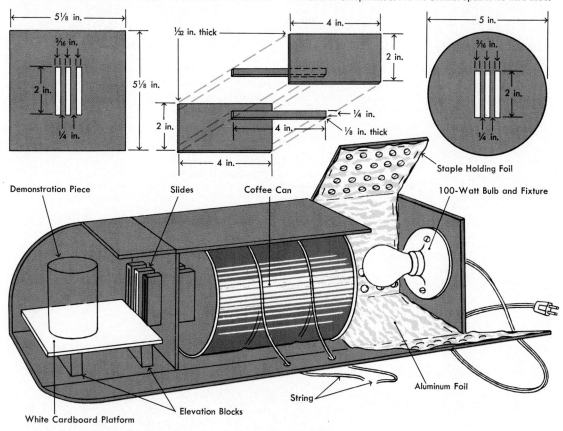

5⅛ in.

3/16 in.

2 in.

¼ in.

5⅛ in.

1/32 in. thick

4 in.

2 in.

2 in.

4 in.

¼ in.

⅛ in. thick

4 in.

5 in.

3/16 in.

2 in.

¼ in.

Staple Holding Foil

100-Watt Bulb and Fixture

Demonstration Piece

Slides

Coffee Can

Aluminum Foil

String

Elevation Blocks

White Cardboard Platform

To Assemble the Projector, put the coffee can in place. Staple aluminum foil to the sides behind the can. Insert the light fixture. Slip the slides through the slots in the front of the projector and into the coffee can. Use string to hold the can in place. Place the white cardboard platform on the elevation blocks in front of the slides. The platform holds the demonstration piece. To avoid overheating, turn off the projector when it is not in use. Do not let it run unattended.

Dispersion causes different wave lengths of light to spread apart. For example, when white light shines through a glass prism, the different wave lengths that make up the light disperse and form a visible spectrum. Dispersion occurs because different wave lengths have different speeds in such materials as glass and water. The angle at which a light wave is refracted as it passes into the material depends on the change in the speed of the wave. Therefore, different wave lengths are refracted at different angles, causing them to disperse.

Polarization of light occurs when the electric and magnetic fields of all the photons in a light beam line up in the same direction. Unpolarized light contains photons with fields in many directions.

Light can be polarized by passing it through a material called *Polaroid*. The Polaroid material allows only the photons with fields in one direction to pass through it. The material absorbs the other photons. When Polaroid is placed in a beam of light, only half the light passes through it. If a second piece of Polaroid is placed in the beam and rotated to various positions, there will be two positions in which all the polarized light will be transmitted and two other positions in which all the light will be blocked.

Light reflected at an angle from glass, water, or some rough materials is partially polarized. Polarized sunglasses reduce the glare from these surfaces by blocking the polarized portion of the light. See POLARIZED LIGHT.

Chemical Effects of Light. Photons of light cause chemical changes in many substances. For example, photons absorbed by photographic film chemically change some of the molecules in the film's coating. When the film is developed, these changed molecules produce a dark negative image where light struck the film. See PHOTOGRAPHY (Developing Film).

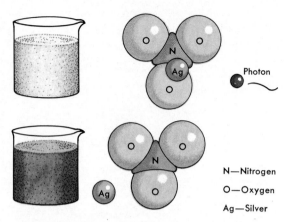

Light Causes Chemical Changes in some substances, such as silver nitrate. A photon, *top*, provides the energy needed to break up the molecule and turn the solution dark, *below*.

N—Nitrogen
O—Oxygen
Ag—Silver

Strong light can fade carpets, draperies, and other textile products because it chemically changes the dyes. *Photosynthesis*, the process by which green plants produce food, is a chemical reaction that requires light (see PHOTOSYNTHESIS).

Photoelectric and Photoconductive Effects. When photons of light are absorbed by certain materials, they release electrons from the atoms of those materials. The electrons can be made to flow along wires and form an electric current. Solar cells in satellites use the photoelectric effect of light to change the energy of sunlight into electricity. Electric eyes also operate by means of the photoelectric or photoconductive effects. See ELECTRIC EYE; PHOTOMULTIPLIER TUBE.

PHOTOELECTRIC EFFECT OF LIGHT

The energy of light photons creates an electric current in a solar cell. A photon releases an electron from an atom in the P-type layer and drives the electron across the P-N junction into the N-type layer. The electron then flows out of the cell, through a load, and back to the P-type layer.

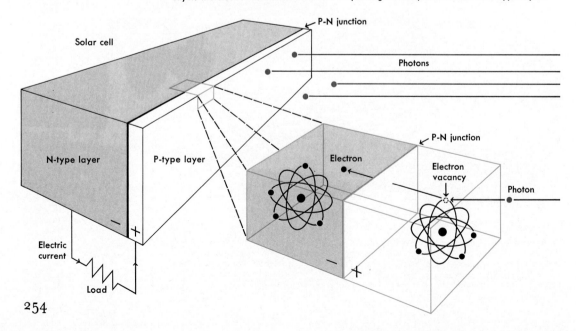

The wave lengths of light waves are measured in a unit called an *angstrom*, which equals 0.0000001 millimeter. About 250 million angstroms equal 1 inch. The shortest wave length of light measures about 4,000 angstroms. The longest measures about 7,000 angstroms.

The frequency of light waves is measured in units called *hertz*. One hertz equals one wave passing a point in one second. The shortest light waves have a frequency of about 750,000,000,000,000 hertz (750 terahertz), and the longest have a frequency of about 450,000,000,000,000 hertz (450 terahertz).

If the frequency and speed of a wave are known, the wave length can be calculated. The wave length equals the speed of the wave divided by its frequency. The speed of light in a vacuum is nearly 300,000 kilometers per second. Therefore, a light wave with a frequency of 600 terahertz has a wave length of 300,000 kilometers per second ÷ 600,000,000,000,000 hertz, which equals 0.0000000005 kilometer, or 5,000 angstroms.

The Brightness of Light. Scientists use various units to measure the brightness of a light source and the amount of energy in a beam of light coming from that source.

The amount of light produced by any light source is called the *luminous intensity* of that source. The standard unit used to measure luminous intensity is the *candela*. For many years, the luminous intensity of a certain size candle made from the wax of sperm whales served as the standard. The unit was called a *candle*. However, the sperm whale candle did not provide an easily used standard for light measurement. One candela is now defined as the intensity of the light given off by $\frac{1}{600,000}$ of a square meter of a perfectly radiating object heated to the temperature of freezing platinum (1772° C) under a pressure of 101,325 newtons per square meter.

The intensity of a light source in candelas does not indicate how bright the light will be when it reaches the surface of an object, such as a book or a desk. Before we can measure *illuminance* (the light falling on a surface), we must measure the light traveling through the space between the source and the object. Scientists measure a beam of light with a unit called the *lumen*. To see how the lumen is measured, imagine a light source placed at the center of a hollow sphere. On the inside surface of the sphere, an area is marked off equal to the square of the radius of the sphere. For example, if the radius is 1 foot, the area marked off is 1 square foot. If the light source has a luminous intensity of 1 candela, the marked area will receive a *luminous flux* (rate of light falling on it) of 1 lumen.

In the customary system of measurement, engineers measure illuminance in units called *foot-candles*. An illuminance of 1 foot-candle is produced by 1 lumen of light shining on an area of 1 square foot. The metric system uses a unit called the *lux*. An illuminance of 1 lux is produced by 1 lumen of light shining on an area of 1 square meter. See FOOT-CANDLE.

The intensity of light falling on a surface varies *inversely* (oppositely) with the square of the distance between the source and the surface. That is, if the distance increases, the illuminance decreases by the square of the distance. This relationship is called the *inverse square law*. If a surface that receives 1 lux of light at a distance of 1 meter from a source is moved 2 meters from the source, that surface will then receive $(\frac{1}{2})^2$, or $\frac{1}{4}$, lux of light. This happens because light spreads out from its source.

The Speed of Light. Although light seems to travel across a room the instant a window shade is raised, it actually takes some time to travel any distance. Scientists measuring the speed of light in a vacuum have found that it travels 186,282 miles (299,792 kilometers) per second.

Scientists call the speed of light a *fundamental constant* of nature. That is, its speed is the same whether the observers who measure it are moving or not. The German-born American physicist Albert Einstein, in his theory of relativity, described the speed of light as a fundamental constant (see RELATIVITY [Special Theory of Relativity]).

Basic Units of Light Measurement

A *1-candela* light source, *left,* inside a 1-foot-radius sphere illuminates every square foot of the sphere's surface with 1 *lumen* of light. One lumen falling on a 1-square-foot area, *right,* illuminates it with 1 *foot-candle.* Because light spreads as it travels, a surface 2 feet from the light source receives 1 lumen of light spread over 4 square feet, or $\frac{1}{4}$ foot-candle per square foot.

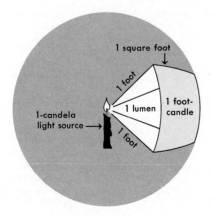

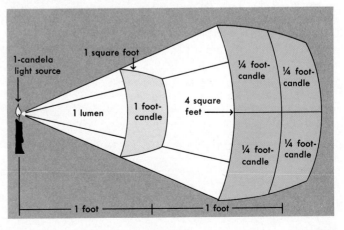

Throughout history, scientists have attempted to measure the speed of light. In the early 1600's, the Italian physicist Galileo devised an experiment to do so. He sent an assistant to a distant hill with instructions to open the shutter of a lantern when he saw Galileo on another hill open the shutter of his lantern. Galileo reasoned that because he knew the distance between the hills, he could find the velocity of light by measuring the time between opening his shutter and seeing the light of the second lantern. The experiment failed because the velocity of light is so great that Galileo could not measure the short time involved.

The Danish astronomer Olaus Roemer, in a paper published in 1675, announced the first real measurement of the speed of light. Roemer observed that the intervals between the disappearance of some of Jupiter's moons behind the planet varied with the distance between Jupiter and Earth. He realized that the velocity of light caused these differing intervals. Roemer's ob-servations indicated that light traveled at a speed of 226,000 kilometers per second. This figure was within 25 per cent of the actual velocity.

In 1926, the American physicist Albert A. Michelson made one of the first precise measurements of the velocity of light. He used a rapidly rotating mirror that reflected a beam of light to a distant reflector. The returning beam was then reflected back to the observer by the rotating mirror. Michelson adjusted the speed of the mirror until the mirror turned to the correct angle during the time the light traveled to the reflector and back. The speed of the mirror indicated the velocity of the light. Michelson actually used several mirrors on a drum so that the angle the drum had to turn while the light traveled out and back was small. He measured the speed of light at 299,796 kilometers per second. The measurement Michelson obtained in his experiment had a probable error of less than 4 kilometers per second.

LIGHT / People's Understanding of Light

Early Ideas About Light. People's understanding of light began during the 1600's. In 1666, the English scientist Sir Isaac Newton discovered that white light is made up of many colors. Using a prism, he found that each color in a beam of white light could be separated. Newton proposed the theory that light consists of tiny particles that travel in straight lines through space. He called these particles *corpuscles,* and his theory became known as the *corpuscular theory.*

About the same time that Newton proposed his theory of light, the Dutch physicist Christian Huygens suggested that light consists of waves. He proposed the *wave theory* to explain the behavior of light. The corpuscular and wave theories appear to be completely opposite, and scientists argued about them for about 100 years. Then, in 1801, the English physicist Thomas Young demonstrated the interference of light. He showed that two light beams cancel each other under certain conditions. Water waves also behave this way. Because it is hard to understand how interference could occur with particles, most scientists accepted Young's experiment as proof of the wave theory of light.

The Electromagnetic Theory. In 1864, the British physicist James Clerk Maxwell proposed the mathematical theory of electromagnetism. According to this theory, energy in the form of waves traveling through space should result from vibrating electric charges. Maxwell's theoretical waves had the exact mathematical properties that had been measured for light. The vibrating electric charges that produce light are the electric charges in the atom. Atomic physicists had already shown that these charges exist. Maxwell's work gave the wave theory of light a solid foundation.

Maxwell's electromagnetic theory also did away with an idea that had stood in the way of scientists' acceptance of the wave theory for more than a century. Scientists felt they had to find the *medium* (material) through which light waves travel. They reasoned that if light travels as waves, there must be something for them to vibrate and travel through, just as sound waves need air to vibrate and travel through. But for light, this something could not be matter, because light travels in a vacuum. To get around this difficulty, scientists suggested that the medium light traveled through was a substance called *luminiferous ether.*

All attempts to observe or measure the properties of ether failed. Scientists became increasingly convinced that ether did not exist. Maxwell's electromagnetic theory showed that the "medium" light waves vibrate is the electromagnetic field.

Quantum Mechanics. Scientists could easily see how electric charges spinning around the nucleus of an atom could give off electromagnetic radiation. But they found it difficult to explain why the atoms did not radiate all their energy rapidly and run down. Scientists working with radiant energy also found that the results of their experiments disagreed with the results predicted by their theories. In 1900, the German physicist Max Planck proposed a theory that agreed with the experiments in radiant energy. His theory led scientists to our present understanding of light.

Planck theorized that radiant energy comes in little packets, which he called *quanta.* Quanta were later named photons. Planck's theory was first called the quantum theory and later became known as *quantum mechanics.* His ideas about quanta made the results of experiments in radiant energy agree with the other theories about light. In time, scientists realized that changes in the energy levels of atoms produced the emission of photons. They could then explain why atoms do not radiate all the time, but only after they become excited with additional energy.

Planck's quanta pointed strongly to a particle nature for light, and the old controversy of whether light was a particle or a wave reappeared. But it was clear that both points of view were correct. Quantum mechanics assumes that both matter and radiation have particle and wave aspects.

EARLE B. BROWN

Sight, Light and Color. Simon & Schuster, 1984.

WHITE, JACK R. *The Invisible World of the Infrared*. Thomas Nelson, 1984. Discusses this form of light.

Related Articles in WORLD BOOK include:

BIOGRAPHIES

Einstein, Albert (The Papers of 1905)	Michelson, Albert A.
Foucault, Jean B. L.	Newton, Sir Isaac
Huygens, Christian	Planck, Max K. E. L.
Maxwell, James Clerk	Raman, Sir Chandrasekhara V.

OTHER RELATED ARTICLES

Aberration	Infrared Rays	Photosynthesis
Angstrom Unit	Interference	Polarized Light
Arc Light	Laser	Quantum
Aurora	Lens	Mechanics
Bioluminescence	Light Meter	Rainbow
Candela	Lighting	Reflection
Color	Luminescence	Refraction
Diffraction	Microscope	Shadow
Electric Eye	Mirage	Spectrometer
Electric Light	Newton's Rings	Sun
Electromagnetic	Optics	Telescope
Waves	Penumbra	Ultraviolet Rays
Ether (physics)	Phosphorescence	Waves
Fiber Optics	Photochemistry	Zeeman Effect
Fluorescence	Photomultiplier	
Foot-Candle	Tube	

Outline

I. Sources of Light
  A. How Light Is Produced
  B. Natural Light
  C. Artificial Light
II. The Nature of Light
  A. Electromagnetic Waves
  B. The Visible Spectrum
III. How Light Behaves
  A. Reflection, Refraction, and Absorption
  B. Scattering
  C. Interference
  D. Diffraction
  E. Dispersion
  F. Polarization
  G. Chemical Effects of Light
  H. Photoelectric and Photoconductive Effects
IV. Measuring Light
  A. The Brightness of Light
  B. The Speed of Light
V. People's Understanding of Light
  A. Early Ideas About Light
  B. The Electromagnetic Theory
  C. Quantum Mechanics

Questions

What color are the longest light waves? The shortest?

What are *photons*?

How do we use the sunlight that fell on the earth millions of years ago to produce electricity and run machines?

What property of a light source is measured in lumens?

What is *diffraction*? *Interference*? *Polarization*?

Why do very hot objects give off light?

Why did scientists propose the theory of luminiferous ether?

What is the *visible spectrum*?

Why does a slanting pencil sticking out of a glass of water appear to bend at the surface?

What theory about light did the English physicist James Clerk Maxwell propose?

Additional Resources

Level I

ADLER, IRVING. *The Story of Light*. Rev. ed. Harvey House, 1971.

Level II

LEVIN, EDITH M. *The Penetrating Beam: Reflections on Light*. Rosen Publishing, 1978.

SCIENTIFIC AMERICAN. *Light and Its Uses: Making and Using Lasers, Holograms, Interferometers, and Instruments of Dispersion*. W. H. Freeman, 1980.

WALDMAN, GARY. *Introduction to Light: The Physics of Light, Vision, and Color*. Simon & Schuster, 1983.

LIGHT, ELECTRIC. See ELECTRIC LIGHT.

LIGHT, INVISIBLE. See ULTRAVIOLET RAYS.

LIGHT BULB. See ELECTRIC LIGHT; EDISON, THOMAS.

LIGHT LISTS. See LIGHTHOUSE (Identifying Lighthouses).

LIGHT METER is an instrument used to measure the strength of light. Different light meters have been invented for use by astronomers, illumination experts, and photographers. Astronomers use them to measure light from stars. Illumination experts use a light meter called an *illuminometer, foot-candle meter*, or *luxmeter* to measure the lighting in homes, schools, and offices (see LIGHTING). Photographers use light meters, called *exposure meters*, to tell them how to set their cameras to expose film correctly. Some cameras have built-in exposure meters that automatically set the camera for the correct exposure (see PHOTOGRAPHY [Exposure Meters]).

Most light meters used today are *photoelectric light meters*. They use *photo cells* made of selenium, a substance which produces a weak electric current when light shines on it. As more light falls on the photo cell, more electric current flows. By measuring this current with a sensitive electric meter, the strength of the light is indicated. Other photoelectric light meters use a *cadmium sulfide* cell to control an electric current supplied by a battery. The amount of current the cell passes depends on how much light shines on it. This current then runs an electric meter.

Photoelectric light meters are replacing *photometers* and other light meters because they are easier to use. A photometer is a light meter that measures the strength of one light by comparing it with another light of known strength. Both lights illuminate separate parts of a viewing screen. Then the known light is dimmed by moving it away from the screen or with a wedge that absorbs light. When the illumination on both parts of the screen is equal, the strength of the unknown light can be found. A scale on the wedge, or the distance the known light was moved, will give the strength of the unknown light (see FOOT-CANDLE).

Light meter scales give readings in foot-candles, lumens, luxes, or a number that can be translated into other units. Photographers' meters give readings in camera settings for different light strengths.   GENE K. BEARE

See also CANDELA.

LIGHT SWITCH. See ELECTRIC SWITCH.

LIGHT-YEAR is the distance light travels in a year at a speed of 186,282 miles (299,792 kilometers) per second. This distance is 5.88 trillion miles (9.46 trillion kilometers).

See also ASTRONOMY (Stars); STAR (Stars in the Universe).

LIGHTHOUSE

U.S. Coast Guard

Thomas Point Shoal Light Station sits on a multilegged platform in the shallows of Chesapeake Bay, near Annapolis, Md. Its beacon beams alternate flashes of white and red light.

LIGHTHOUSE is a tower with an extremely strong light that serves as a navigational aid for mariners. Lighthouses help sailors determine their position, inform them that land is near, and warn them of dangerous rocks and reefs. Lighthouses are built at ports and harbors, on capes and peninsulas, and on isolated rocks. Some are built in the sea itself, with their foundations sunk into rock or coral beneath the water.

Lighthouses have been used as navigational aids for thousands of years. Since the 1940's, however, they have declined in importance because of the development and increased use of advanced electronic navigational aids (see NAVIGATION [Electronic Navigation]). As a result, the number of lighthouses operated in the United States has declined from about 1,500 in the early 1900's to about 340 today. In fact, there are only about 1,400 lighthouses currently in use worldwide.

The U.S. Coast Guard administers lighthouses in the United States. Canada's approximately 275 lighthouses are maintained by the Department of Transport.

Identifying Lighthouses. Every lighthouse emits a distinctive pattern of light known as its *characteristic*. There are five basic types of lighthouse signals: (1) fixed, (2) flashing, (3) occulting, (4) group flashing, and (5) group occulting. A fixed light is a steady beam. A flashing light has periods of darkness longer than periods of light. An occulting light's periods of light are longer than its periods of darkness. A group flashing light gives off two or more flashes at regular intervals, and a group occulting light consists of a fixed light with two or more periods of darkness at regular intervals. There are several variations of these basic patterns. For example, flashes of white light may alternate with flashes of red.

The characteristics and locations of lighthouses are recorded in publications called *light lists*. Mariners determine which lighthouse they are seeing and therefore their location by observing the characteristic of a lighthouse and consulting a light list.

In the daytime, lighthouses can be identified by their structure. Most lighthouses are simple towers made of stone, brick, wood, or steel. Some are metal skeletal towers, and others consist of houselike structures atop a multilegged platform. In areas where they are of similar construction, lighthouses are distinguished by their *day marker* pattern—a design of checks and stripes painted in vivid colors on lighthouse walls.

How Lighthouses Work. Lighthouses project their light through special lenses that increase the intensity of the light from their lamps. Many lighthouses are equipped with a *Fresnel*, or *classical, lens*, which is a huge compound lens that encircles the lamp. Each face of a Fresnel lens is surrounded by a ring of triangular prisms, which reflect and strengthen the light. Such a lens may project light more than 20 miles (32 kilometers). Some Fresnel lenses measure as much as 8 feet (2.4 meters) in height and 6 feet (1.8 meters) in diameter.

A Fresnel lens produces alternating intervals of light and darkness by flashing automatically. A flashing effect can also be produced by arranging the prisms of part of the lens so they prevent light from escaping, and then revolving the lens around the lamp. A series of flashes of different colors is obtained by covering sides of the lens with colored glass.

Some lighthouses produce their light through the use of *sealed-beam lamps*, which swing a beam across the horizon like a searchlight. The filament, reflector, and lens of such lamps are combined in a single unit. The number of times the light can be seen in a certain period depends on how fast the lamp is rotated.

The distance a lighthouse's signal can be seen depends on a number of factors, including the beam's

U.S. Coast Guard

West Quoddy Lighthouse in Lubec, Me., is noted for its striped pattern. This pattern serves as a *day marker,* enabling mariners to distinguish the lighthouse from others during the day.

strength and the height of the light. Haze, smoke, and bad weather—such as fog, rain, and snow—also affect visibility. As a result, many lighthouses have foghorns, bells, or other sound-making devices that are used to signal vessels under such conditions. Many lighthouses also are equipped with *radio beacons* that send out radio signals that can be picked up by shipboard radio direction finders.

History. The ancient Egyptians were probably the first people to use light to guide ships. They kindled fires on top of hills at night and later built lighthouses that also used fire as the light source. During the reign of Ptolemy II (283-246 B.C.), the Egyptians completed the Pharos of Alexandria, the tallest lighthouse ever constructed. The structure stood over 400 feet (122 meters) high. It guided ships for 1,500 years.

The Romans built lighthouses at a number of ports. About A.D. 43, for example, they constructed light towers on both sides of the English Channel, at Dover in Britain, and at Boulogne-sur-Mer in Gaul (now France). The light beam for these towers was probably produced by a system of multiple flames and mirrors.

The first lighthouse built on a wave-swept rock was Eddystone Rock Light, southwest of Plymouth, England. It had a base of huge blocks of stones. Completed in 1698, it was destroyed by a storm in 1703. Since then, three other lighthouses have occupied the site.

The first lighthouse in America was Boston Lighthouse, on Little Brewster Island in Boston Harbor. It was first lit in 1716. The British destroyed Boston Lighthouse in 1776, during the Revolutionary War in America. But another one was built on the site in 1783 and still stands. Kerosene, lard oil, and sperm-whale oil provided fuel for early American lighthouses.

In 1789, the U.S. government established the Federal Lighthouse Service to administer the nation's lighthouses. Lighthouses were operated by lighthouse keepers who lived with their families in or near the lighthouse. The lighthouse keeper's duties included lighting the wick, polishing the reflecting mirrors, cleaning soot off the tower windows, replacing the oil consumed by the light, rescuing shipwrecked sailors, and sometimes firing a warning cannon during periods of fog.

In 1822, Augustin Fresnel, a French physicist, invented the Fresnel lens. Initially, the Fresnel lens revolved around the lamp by means of a clocklike mechanism. But today, electric motors provide the power to revolve the lens and light the lamp. In addition, most lighthouses are now fully automated and do not need a keeper. Nevertheless, the U.S. Coast Guard, which became responsible for U.S. lighthouses in 1939, still employs people to care for lighthouses and their grounds, and to help prevent vandalism.   ROBERT L. SCHEINA

See also BEACON; NEW JERSEY (picture: Barnegat Lighthouse); SEVEN WONDERS OF THE ANCIENT WORLD; STEVENSON, ROBERT.

LIGHTING is a term that generally refers to artificial light—in most cases, electric light. We use artificial light both indoors and outdoors instead of—and in addition to—natural light from the sun. With lighting,

U.S. Coast Guard

Alligator Reef Light Station is located in the Florida Keys. Its metal stilts are screwed into the floor of the sea, and its metal skeletal tower can withstand winds of hurricane force.

U.S. Coast Guard

Boston Lighthouse, first lit in 1716, was the first lighthouse in America. The present structure was built in 1783, after the original was destroyed during the Revolutionary War.

Art Grossmann

WORLD BOOK photo

Lighting enables us to take part in activities we enjoy at any time we wish. Lights in sports stadiums allow fans to enjoy games at night. At home, lighting lets us read or study at any hour.

we can use windowless areas of homes, hospitals, offices, schools, stores, and other buildings 24 hours a day. Lighting also enables us to use outdoor sports areas, such as baseball and football fields and tennis courts, at night.

Lighting provides safety in a number of places. At home and at work, good lighting helps us see things clearly and avoid accidents. Street lights and automobile lights help us travel safely. Signal lights guide motorists, airplane pilots, railroad engineers, and ship captains.

Companies and stores use lighted signs to identify themselves and to advertise their products. Lighting also adds beauty to homes and other buildings and to parks.

Good lighting helps the eyes work easily. Reading or working in poor light cannot damage the eyes. But it may cause fatigue or eyestrain and lead to dizziness, headaches, or sleepiness.

How We Use Lighting

We use artificial lighting in four chief ways: (1) in the home; (2) in offices, stores, and factories; (3) on streets and highways; and (4) for outdoor events. Regardless of where lighting is used, we depend on it for general seeing and safety, for specific activities, and for decoration.

In the Home, electric lamps and lighting fixtures provide light and safety for people walking from room

to room or up and down stairs. Every room and passageway needs at least some general lighting so that things can be seen clearly enough to avoid accidents. Each area should have a light that can be turned on before entering.

Many activities require extra lighting in addition to general lighting. Bathrooms, for example, have special lighting that women use when putting on makeup and that men use for shaving. Bedrooms and living rooms have additional lighting for such activities as reading, studying, and sewing.

Interior decorators use lighting to create various moods and to bring out the colors of walls and fabrics in a home. Incandescent lamps and warm white fluorescent lamps emphasize reds, yellows, and oranges (see ELECTRIC LIGHT [Incandescent Lamps; Fluorescent Lamps]). Cool white fluorescent lamps bring out blues and greens. Many people arrange spotlights or tinted lights to create interesting shadow patterns. Others do so to draw attention to such things as pictures or vases.

In Offices, Stores, and Factories, proper lighting helps employees work efficiently and avoid costly accidents. Good lighting also provides a cheery atmosphere and reduces fatigue caused by eyestrain. In retail stores, proper lighting may help attract customers.

Most offices and stores provide a large amount of general illumination, with additional lighting for such detailed jobs as repairing watches or making maps. Many factory jobs require more difficult eye work than do office jobs. Thus, factories need good lighting for safe, efficient work. The Illuminating Engineering Society (IES), a professional association of lighting engineers, recommends lighting standards for various types of industrial work. Some manufacturers, after improving their lighting to meet IES standards, found that their production increased more than 15 per cent. They also reported that employee accidents decreased by 50 per cent.

Improvement of lighting can also improve the quality of a company's products because employees may avoid errors that they otherwise might have made. One manufacturer reported that his customers rejected 50 per cent fewer of his firm's products after he improved the lighting in his plant.

On Streets and Highways, lighting helps people travel safely. Several cities have reduced night traffic accidents by improving their street lighting. Night accidents in some cities dropped as much as 50 per cent after street lighting was improved. Freeway lights can reduce traffic deaths and injuries on these highways as much as 50 per cent.

Street lighting also helps to provide safety by discouraging criminals. Improved street lighting in Washington, D.C., helped lower the number of violent crimes there by 18 per cent. In some cities, relighting of streets reduced crime by more than 75 per cent. And if the crime rate in a community drops, the people become more willing to go out at night to shop or for entertainment.

Decorative lights on buildings may reduce the necessity for street lighting. In some cities, lighting designers plan light so that it accents the architecture as it illuminates the streets and sidewalks.

For Outdoor Events. Floodlights illuminate baseball and football fields, golf courses, race tracks, swimming pools, tennis courts, and many other facilities for sports competition at night. Some sports, such as golf and swimming, require relatively little light. Others, including baseball and football, need much more light because they use larger fields and attract larger crowds. Additional lighting is required to televise outdoor events.

Outdoor lighting also enables such events as county or state fairs and open-air theater performances to be held at night. Country clubs, resorts, and homes use decorative lighting for night parties on patios or in gardens.

What Is Good Lighting

Good lighting allows the eyes to function comfortably and efficiently. The eyes need different amounts and types of light for different activities. As a result, lighting that may be suitable for some activities may be inadequate for others.

Quantity of Light needed for various activities depends on three factors: (1) the size of the things we are looking at, (2) the length of time we have to look at them, and (3) the contrast between them and their background. A watchmaker, who works with tiny parts, requires more light than a plumber, who connects large pipes. A person needs more light to read a road sign while speeding past in a car than while walking by. A tailor needs more light to sew black thread on black cloth than to sew white thread on black cloth.

In the home, most people do not provide for the wide variety in the amount of light required for different activities. For example, a woman may use the same light for reading a newspaper and for hemming a black skirt with black thread. But her eyes need almost seven times as much light for this job as for reading.

Engineers use either the *foot-candle* or the *lux* to measure the amount of light that falls on a surface. The foot-candle is a unit in the customary system of measurement, and the lux is a metric unit. A sensitive instrument called a *light meter* records how much light a surface receives at that point. See FOOT-CANDLE; LIGHT METER; LIGHT (Measuring Light).

Three factors determine how much light reaches any object: (1) the *intensity* (strength) of the light, (2) the distance of the object from the light source, and (3) the light distribution.

Intensity. Scientists measure the intensity of light coming from any source in units called *lumens.* Until 1971, bulbs were marked only with their number of *watts.* Watts tell the amount of electricity used by a light bulb, not how much light the bulb produces. For example, two 50-watt bulbs supply fewer lumens than one 100-watt bulb. A 100-watt bulb may provide only a fourth as many lumens as a 100-watt fluorescent tube. In 1971, the United States Federal Trade Commission (FTC) issued a ruling requiring that bulb cartons be marked with both lumens and watts.

Distance. The amount of light an object receives depends on its distance from the source. An object placed 2 feet from a lamp receives only a fourth as much light as when it is placed 1 foot from the lamp.

Distribution. Dark colors absorb light, and so dark carpets, ceilings, curtains, furniture, or walls may limit the amount of light in rooms. But pale-colored walls and furnishings bounce light back into a room.

A lamp shade distributes the light from a bare bulb and shields the bulb from direct view. The shade directs light downward toward the seeing task and upward to help light the room. Opaque shades send all the light up and down, but translucent shades transmit some light to the room. Colored shades tend to color the light. For this reason, shades with white or near white linings should be used.

Lighting Problems may occur even if enough light has been provided for an activity. For example, a bright light that shines, or is reflected, directly into the eyes causes glare, which can cause discomfort. Severe glare, such as that caused by the headlights of some cars, may be temporarily blinding. Lamps and fixtures that *diffuse* (scatter) the light tend to produce more comfortable illumination.

An unshaded clear glass bulb gives off harsh, undiffused, glaring light. Lamps with frosted, or white, bulbs and tubes give some diffusion, but still should be shielded or positioned so they do not shine directly in a person's field of vision. A globe or diffusion bowl can be used to conceal the bulb and help scatter and soften the light.

LIGHTING

Examples of Good Lighting

These photographs show the use of proper lighting for different indoor activities. The diagrams to the right of each photograph show the light sources used and the areas they illuminate.

In an Office, fluorescent and incandescent lights recessed in the ceiling provide even desk light for efficient work. A table lamp helps furnish background light to soften the contrast between the desk area and the other parts of the room.

In a Large Area, such as a basketball court, factory, or warehouse, an even amount of light is needed over the entire floor. Incandescent lighting fixtures near the ceiling provide lighting for the floor and all the people or things on it.

Even if a light source does not cause glare directly, other surfaces may reflect it. They include glossy finishes on walls, furniture, and paper, which can produce reflected glare. Sharp color contrasts on work surfaces, such as white paper on a dark blotter, may also cause discomfort. At first, the color contrast helps the eyes see the objects. But in time it strains the eyes, which must refocus each time they move from a light to a dark surface.

Sharp contrasts in the brightness of lighting can also cause eyestrain. For this reason, a person should not watch television in a completely dark room or study by the light of a single intense lamp. To avoid harsh contrasts, the eyes need general lighting in addition to the light provided by the television screen or the lamp.

Lighting Devices

Many families use combinations of fluorescent and incandescent fixtures and portable lamps for attractive home lighting. Incandescent and fluorescent fixtures may be mounted on a wall or ceiling, recessed above the ceiling, or suspended from the ceiling. Suspended fixtures provide good general lighting for high-ceilinged halls or stairways. Recessed fixtures above sinks or other work areas furnish good lighting for various activities. Many kitchens and family rooms have *luminous ceilings*, in which fluorescent tubes are hung above the translucent ceiling. Such fixtures provide softly diffused general light. Many institutions, including hospitals, libraries, and schools, also have luminous ceilings.

Portable lamps give homes soft general lighting, and extra lighting for such activities as sewing or studying. The Better Light Better Sight Bureau (BLBS), a nonprofit educational organization, sets minimum standards for performance, quality, and safety of study lamps. The organization provides BLBS tags, which the manufacturer attaches to approved lamps.

In homes and small offices, lighting designers may conceal fluorescent tubes behind faceboards mounted at the edges of the walls or ceiling. Such *structural lighting* provides soft indirect light and draws attention to the walls and draperies. Structural lighting on two opposite walls of a square room makes the lighted walls seem farther apart than the unlighted ones. When mounted on a low ceiling, structural lights give the illusion of greater height in the room.

Most factories, large offices, schools, and stores use fluorescent fixtures for general lighting. Fluorescent lights produce as much as three times the light per watt of electricity as do incandescent lamps. Thus, for the same amount of light, fluorescent lamps cost less to burn. They also produce less heat. However, lighting

262

In a School, light from fluorescent fixtures in the ceiling supplements the natural light from the windows. The artificial light reduces the contrast between the areas near the windows and the darker corners of the room.

Architectural Camera Ltd.

In a Home, a combination of lamps provides good light for a study and hobby area. Overhead fluorescent lamps furnish background light. A movable spotlight and fluorescent lamp under the shelf give enough nonglare light for reading or for examining objects in detail.

General Electric Company

engineers sometimes prefer incandescent lamps because of their compact size, flexibility of use, or their more familiar warm color. Some stores use a combination of fluorescent fixtures for general lighting and incandescent lamps for decorative or accent lighting.

Mercury vapor lamps, mounted from 30 to 50 feet (9 to 15 meters) high on roadways and as high as 150 feet (46 meters) high on freeway interchanges, provide economical highway lighting. They last more than eight times as long as incandescent lamps and give a much higher light level per watt of electricity used. High-pressure sodium vapor lamps are the most efficient man-made light sources. They produce six to eight times as much light per watt as incandescent lamps. These sodium vapor lamps are finding wide use for street and highway lighting.   EDWARD A. CAMPBELL

Related Articles in WORLD BOOK include:

Beacon	Lamp
Candle	Lantern
Electric Light	Light
Fluorescent Lamp	Neon
Invention (Inventions That	Theater (Lighting)
Give People Light)	

LIGHTNING is a giant electrical spark in the sky. Most of the lightning people see takes place between a cloud and the ground. But lightning also occurs within a cloud, between a cloud and the air, and between two clouds. When lightning occurs in the atmosphere, its electrical energy scatters in the air. This energy may

damage airplanes traveling through it, but it does not cause harm on the ground. However, lightning that strikes the earth may kill people, destroy property, or cause fire.

Lightning that strikes the earth consists of one or more electrical discharges called *strokes*. The bright light that we see in a flash of lightning is called a *return stroke*. Return strokes travel at about the speed of light, which is 186,282 miles (299,792 kilometers) per second. They discharge about 100 million volts of electricity and heat the air in their paths to more than 60,000° F. (33,000° C). Air heated by return strokes expands quickly, producing a wave of pressure known as thunder. See THUNDER.

Flashes of lightning have different lengths. A flash between a cloud and the ground may be up to 9 miles (14 kilometers) long. Lightning that travels through many clouds side by side may reach lengths over 90 miles (140 kilometers).

Through the centuries, lightning has been one of the greatest mysteries of nature—and it is still not understood completely. The ancient Greeks and Romans thought lightning was a weapon of the gods. In some African societies, people and places hit by lightning were considered to be cursed. As late as the 1700's, some people in Europe and America believed lightning could be kept away by ringing church bells.

Serious study of lightning began in the 1700's. In 1752, Benjamin Franklin showed that lightning is electricity. He tied a metal key to the end of a kite string and

LIGHTNING

flew the kite in a thunderstorm. Cloud electricity raised the voltage of the kite string. The high voltage caused a spark to jump from the key to grounded objects, proving that the cloud was electrified. Franklin's experiment was dangerous, and some people who have flown kites in storms have been electrocuted by lightning. See Franklin, Benjamin (Experiments with Electricity).

How Lightning Occurs

Everything around us is made up of atoms. Although atoms are normally electrically neutral, they may become positive or negative if they lose or gain electrons. Positive and negative charges are attracted to one another. When they move through air toward one another, they form an electric current that causes a spark. Lightning is the spark that results from the rapid movement of electrically charged particles within a *cumulonimbus cloud* (thundercloud) or between such a cloud and the ground, the air, or another cloud.

Electrically Charged Clouds. Scientists are uncertain exactly how cumulonimbus clouds become electrically charged. Most believe, however, that the charge results from the collision of a cloud's light, rising water droplets and tiny pieces of ice against hail and other heavier, falling particles (see Cloud). When these bits of cloud collide, the heavier particles gain a negative charge and the lighter particles acquire a positive charge. The negatively charged particles fall to the bottom of the cloud, and most of the positively charged particles rise to the top. Lightning is produced when separated positive and negative charges flow toward one another—or toward opposite charges on the earth—thereby forming an electric spark.

The most common type of lightning, called *intracloud lightning*, is created when charges within a cloud form an electrical spark. Charges that flow between a cloud and the air cause *cloud-to-air lightning*, and an electrical current between two clouds produces *cloud-to-cloud lightning*. Lightning that results from the flow of charges between a cloud and the earth may be either *cloud-to-ground lightning*, or *ground-to-cloud lightning*, depending on the direction in which the charges first began to flow. Most of the lightning that people see is cloud-to-ground lightning.

Strokes. The first stroke of a flash of cloud-to-ground lightning is started by a *stepped leader*, which usually carries negative charges from a cloud toward the ground. No one knows for certain how a stepped leader begins. However, many scientists believe it is triggered by a spark between areas of positive and negative charges near the base of a thundercloud.

A stepped leader moves downward in a series of steps, each of which is about 50 yards (46 meters) long and lasts about 1 millionth of a second. It pauses between steps for about 50 millionths of a second. As the stepped leader nears the ground, positively charged upward-moving leaders travel up from such objects as trees and buildings to meet the negative charges. Usually, the upward-moving leader from the tallest object in the area is the first to meet the stepped leader and complete a route between the cloud and the earth. Negative charges then rush down to the ground along the path provided by the upward-moving leader. The negative charge nearest the ground moves downward first, followed by negative charges from higher and higher altitudes. This process of the upward motion of current is the return stroke. A return stroke produces the light people notice in a flash of lightning, but the current travels so quickly that its upward motion cannot be perceived.

A flash of lightning may end after one return stroke. But in most cases, *dart leaders*, which are similar to stepped leaders, carry more negative charges from the cloud down the main path of the previous stroke. Each dart leader is followed by a return stroke. The leader-stroke process commonly occurs 3 or 4 times in one flash, but may occur more than 20 times. People can

How Lightning Occurs

Lightning is caused by the movement of positive and negative electrical charges toward one another. During a storm, a thundercloud's particles collide and become electrically charged. The positively charged particles rise to the top of the cloud and the negatively charged particles fall to the cloud's base. When negative charges from the cloud's base move downward and meet with rising positive charges from the earth, *cloud-to-ground lightning* occurs. Lightning between charges within a cloud is called *intracloud lightning*. That which occurs between charges of different clouds is known as *cloud-to-cloud lightning*.

Before a Storm

Uncharged Particles Collide

Charged Particles Separate

Cloud-to-Ground Lightning

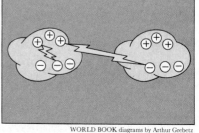

Intracloud and Cloud-to-Cloud Lightning

sometimes see the individual strokes of a flash. At such times, the lightning appears to flicker.

Forms of Lightning

Lightning occurs in a variety of forms. A single flash of lightning often varies in appearance, depending on the position of an observer in relation to it.

The major forms of lightning include *forked lightning, streak lightning, ribbon lightning,* and *bead,* or *chain, lightning.* Forked lightning refers to a flash in which multiple branches of a stroke are visible. Streak lightning is a flash that seems to illuminate a single jagged line. Ribbon lightning appears as parallel streaks of light. It is formed when wind separates the strokes of a flash. Bead, or chain, lightning is a flash that breaks up into a dotted line as it fades.

Some electrical flashes in the sky—such as *heat lightning* and *sheet lightning*—are not really separate forms of lightning, though they appear different in some ways. Heat lightning, often seen on summer nights, seems to occur without thunder. Actually, it is lightning that occurs too far away from an observer for its accompanying thunder to be heard. The people underneath what looks from a distance like heat lightning are experiencing a normal thunderstorm. Sheet lightning appears as an illumination of a portion of the sky. But it is lightning whose distinct flashes either are too far away to be seen or are hidden from view by clouds.

A form of lightning called *ball lightning* differs greatly from ordinary lightning. Ball lightning appears as a glowing, fiery ball that floats for several seconds before disappearing. It has reportedly been seen during thunderstorms, usually after ordinary lightning has occurred. It is described as a red, yellow, or orange ball that may be as large as a grapefruit. It has been reported floating along the ground and inside houses, barns, and airplanes. No one knows how or why ball lightning occurs, or what it consists of.

A glowing light called *St. Elmo's fire* may resemble ball lightning in some ways. St. Elmo's fire is caused by electrical discharges from a sharp object during a thunderstorm. It sometimes appears around airplanes, the masts of sailing ships, towers, and treetops. See SAINT ELMO'S FIRE.

Protection from Lightning

Lightning strikes the earth about 100 times each second. In the United States, about 100 people are killed by lightning each year. People can avoid being struck by lightning by following certain safety measures during thunderstorms.

Take shelter in a house or large building. It is safe to stay in an enclosed car or truck, but not in a convertible. Do not touch any metal inside the vehicle.

Use the telephone only in emergencies.

If you are caught in an open area sit or crouch down.

Do not stand under or near an individual tall tree or any similarly isolated object in an open area.

Do not rise above the landscape by standing on a hilltop, on a beach, or in an open field.

Stay out of and away from water.

Get away from open metal vehicles, such as bicycles, golf carts, farm equipment, and motorcycles.

If you are stranded in a forest, take cover beneath low shrubs or a group of trees of similar height.

© Leo Starz

Lightning is a giant electrical spark in the sky. It often strikes tall buildings, *above,* and may do little damage. But lightning can kill people, destroy property, or cause fire.

A person who has been struck by lightning should be treated with *cardiopulmonary resuscitation,* an artificial method of breathing and circulating blood. See FIRST AID (Heart Attack).

Metal poles called *lightning rods* help protect buildings from lightning. They are attached to building tops and must be well grounded. They attract lightning and direct its electricity through a wire or cable safely to the ground. See LIGHTNING ROD.   MARTIN A. UMAN

Additional Resources

KEEN, MARTIN L. *Lightning and Thunder.* Simon & Schuster, 1969. For younger readers. Includes a chapter on lightning safety.

SALANAVE, LEON E. *Lightning and Its Spectrum: An Atlas of Photographs.* Univ. of Arizona Press, 1980.

UMAN, MARTIN A. *Understanding Lightning.* Bek Technical, 1971.

LIGHTNING BUG. See FIREFLY.

LIGHTNING ROD is a device that protects homes and other buildings from damage by lightning. A common type has a metal rod installed on top of a building. A wire or cable leads from this rod to a *ground rod* buried 10 feet (3 meters) or more in the earth. The ground rod should be buried at least 2 feet (61 centimeters) from the building in moist earth. It should be as straight as possible. If a building has several metal supports, each should be connected to a lightning rod and there should be several ground connections.

Lightning rods are most often used in farming regions to protect homes, barns, and windmills. They are not often seen in cities, because there is so much metal used and the buildings stand close together. Other kinds of lightning protectors are used on power stations, telephone wires, and electric structures.   WALTER J. SAUCIER

LIGHTWEIGHT. See BOXING (Weight Classes).

LIGNIN, *LIHG nihn,* is a complex substance formed by certain plant cells. It is one of the chief substances in wood. Lignin, found in the cell walls of woody tissue, is closely associated with cellulose. It is made up of the same elements as cellulose, but its exact chemical composition is still unknown. Lignin, like cellulose, permits water and gases to pass through it. It turns yellow when treated with sulfuric acid and iodine, while cellulose turns blue. In the manufacture of paper, lignin is removed from wood by treating the wood fibers with sodium sulfite or sodium hydroxide.

Once regarded as a waste product in paper manufacturing, some lignin is now used as fuel in paper-pulp mills. It is also used in making plastics, fertilizer, artificial vanilla, cosmetics, building board, rubber, fire extinguishers, and other items.   ARTHUR W. GALSTON

LIGNITE, also called Brown Coal, is a coal of low quality. Lignite contains 20 to 60 per cent water when mined, much more than higher quality coal. In the United States, it is produced in Montana, North Dakota, and Texas, and is used locally. See also COAL (The Uses of Coal; How Coal Was Formed); NORTH DAKOTA (pictures).   CLARENCE KARR, JR.

LIGNUM VITAE, *LIHG nuhm VY tee,* is an extremely hard wood obtained from certain Latin-American trees. The trees grow in the West Indies, Mexico, Central America, and northern South America. They are sometimes called *guayacans.* The Latin words *lignum vitae* mean *wood of life.* The wood was so named because its resin was used to treat rheumatism, catarrh, and skin diseases.

The heartwood of lignum vitae is the most useful part of the tree. This wood is so heavy that it sinks in water. The wood is olive-brown, and contains an oily resin which acts as a lubricant when the wood is used for bearings. The grain of lignum vitae interlocks and makes it practically impossible for the wood to be split.

Lignum vitae is used for the stern propeller-shaft bearings in steamships, for the sheaves and blocks of pulleys, and for mallets, furniture casters, and band saw guides. A resin known as *guaiac* is extracted from the wood and used in the drug trade.

Scientific Classification. Lignum vitaes belong to the caltrop family, *Zygophyllaceae.* The two species are *Guaiacum officinale* and *Guaiacum sanctum.*   HARRY E. TROXELL

LIGUEST, PIERRE L. See SAINT LOUIS (History).

LIGUORI, SAINT ALPHONSUS. See ALPHONSUS LIGUORI, SAINT.

LIGURIAN SEA, *lih GYOO rih uhn,* is the broad portion of water between the Gulf of Genoa and the Mediterranean Sea. The Italian region of Liguria lies north along this sea beyond the gulf. The island of Corsica lies to the south. For location, see ITALY (physical map).

LIJ YASU. See ETHIOPIA (History).

LI'L ABNER. See CAPP, AL.

LILAC is a beautiful shrub that is loved throughout the world for its fragrant flowers. The *common lilac* from southeastern Europe grows to a height of 20 feet (6 meters) and has wide, spreading branches thick with flowers. Its green leaves are about 5 inches (13 centimeters)

Morton Arboretum

The Beautiful Lilac is popular throughout the world. The common lilac, *above,* grows wild in southeastern Europe. Nurseries have developed many varieties of this plant. In spring, lilacs blossom with clusters of fragrant flowers, *below.*

Grant Heilman

long. The white or purple flowers grow in clusters that may be 10 inches (25 centimeters) wide. Lilac bushes can be grown in almost any yard, and the plant needs little attention. It may be grown from seeds which are sown in early spring, or by cuttings from green lilac wood, ripe wood, or roots. Some kinds of lilac are grown by grafting or budding. In the northern states, most lilacs bloom in May. Nurseries have developed many different kinds which have larger and more colorful blossoms than the common lilac. Their colors vary from white to dark purple and deep red.

Lilacs can be made to bloom in the winter by keeping them under glass. The plants are put in pots in the spring and taken outdoors later in the summer. The plants bloom in three to five weeks if they are kept in a temperature from 60° to 80° F. (16° to 27° C).

A light purple color is called "lilac" after the lovely light purple flowers of some lilacs. Many poets have written about the beauty of lilacs. Perhaps the most beautiful of such poems is the ode Walt Whitman wrote on Lincoln's death, called "When Lilacs Last in the Dooryard Bloom'd."

Scientific Classification. Lilacs belong to the olive family, *Oleaceae*. The common lilac is classified as genus *Syringa*, species *S. vulgaris*. J. J. Levison

See also FLOWER (picture: Garden Perennials [Flowering Shrubs]); NEW HAMPSHIRE (picture).

LILIENTHAL, *LIHL ee uhn THAWL*, **DAVID ELI,** *EE ly* (1899-1981), was the first chairperson of the U.S. Atomic Energy Commission. He was appointed in 1946. He resigned in 1949 but continued to serve until February 1950, at the request of President Harry S. Truman. Lilienthal also was a director of the Tennessee Valley Authority (TVA) from 1933 to 1946. He served as chairperson of the TVA from 1941 to 1946. *The Journals of David E. Lilienthal*, his diaries, were published in 1965.

Lilienthal was born in Morton, Ill. He graduated from DePauw University and Harvard University Law School. In 1931, he became a member of the Wisconsin Public Service Commission. F. JAY TAYLOR

LILIENTHAL, OTTO. See GLIDER (History).

LILIUOKALANI, *lee LEE oo oh kah LAH nee*, **LYDIA KAMEKEHA,** *LIHD ee uh KAH meh KEH hah* (1838-1917), reigned as queen of Hawaii from 1891 to 1893. She became queen after the death of her brother, King David Kalakaua.

American settlers who controlled most of Hawaii's wealth revolted in 1893 when Liliuokalani tried to restore some of the monarchy's power. A republic was established in 1894, and the new government hoped the United States would annex Hawaii. But President Grover Cleveland tried in vain to restore Liliuokalani to her throne. Hawaii was annexed in 1898.

Liliuokalani made two trips to the United States after she lost her throne. She is perhaps best known today for her song, "Aloha Oe," which became the traditional farewell song of Hawaii. JOHN A. GARRATY

See also DOLE (Sanford Ballard); HAWAII (History).

LILLE, *leel* (pop. 168,424; met. area pop. 936,295), a French industrial city, lies 130 miles (209 kilometers) northeast of Paris (see FRANCE [political map]). The city is the center of the country's spinning and textile industries, producing vast quantities of cotton thread and cloth, and some of the world's finest woolen fabrics. Lille also has great printing houses, sugar and oil refineries,

and dye works. Its art museum has paintings by Rubens, Goya, Van Dyck, and others.

Lille was founded about 1030 by the Flemish. The government of Flanders gave it to France in 1312. Eugene, Prince of Savoy, captured the city in 1708, but the Peace of Utrecht in 1713 restored it to France. The armies of Germany captured and occupied Lille in World War I and again in World War II. EDWARD W. FOX

LILLIE, BEATRICE (1898-), LADY PEEL, an English actress, won fame as one of the brightest and most natural comediennes of her time. She appeared in more than 40 shows after her first professional appearance in 1914. She became especially known for her monologue called "Double Damask Dinner Napkins." Lillie was born in Toronto, Ont. As a girl, she sang with a Presbyterian church choir. But she was asked to resign because her comic antics interfered with the rehearsals of the church choir. RICHARD MOODY

Wide World
Beatrice Lillie

LILLO, GEORGE. See DRAMA (England).

LILLY ENDOWMENT is one of the largest and best-known foundations in the United States. It makes grants for charitable, educational, and religious purposes. The endowment was established in 1937 with gifts from members of the family that founded and directed the Eli Lilly and Company pharmaceutical firm. The foundation's headquarters are at 2801 N. Meridian Street, Indianapolis, Ind. 46208. For assets, see FOUNDATIONS (table). Critically reviewed by the LILLY ENDOWMENT, INC.

LILONGWE, *lih LAWNG way* (pop. 102,924) is the capital of Malawi, in southeast Africa. The city lies on the Lilongwe River in the heart of Malawi's agricultural area and is a marketing center for tobacco and other crops. For location, see MALAWI (map).

Lilongwe was settled in 1902. It became a city in 1966, when it was designated to replace Zomba as the Malawi capital. At that time, fewer than 20,000 persons lived in Lilongwe. The city's population climbed during the several years of an extensive government construction program that included factories, government buildings, and residential areas. Lilongwe officially became the capital in 1975. LEONARD M. THOMPSON

LILY is one of the largest and most important plant families. The name is used for many garden and hothouse flowers, such as the tiger lily, the Madonna lily, the white Easter lily, and the Chinese and Japanese lilies. The lily family also includes a number of plants that are important to agriculture, such as the asparagus, aloe, squill, and many others. A few flowers which do not have *lily* as part of their name, such as the hyacinth and the trillium, are also in the lily family. But the so-called calla lily and water lily are not members of the lily family.

There are more than 200 genera in the lily family, with about 4,000 species. Twelve species of true lilies are native to the United States. The *meadow lily* of the

Easter Lily	Lily of the	Solomon's-Seal
Flower	Valley	Squill
(pictures)	Mariposa Lily	Star-of-Bethlehem
Fritillary	Mosaic Disease	Tiger Lily
Greenbrier	Sego Lily	Trillium
Hyacinth	Soap Plant	Tulip

LILY, WATER. See WATER LILY.

LILY OF THE VALLEY is a fragrant garden flower. Each blossom is shaped like a tiny bell. It grows in North America, Europe, and northern Asia. Wild lily of the valley grows in the southern Allegheny regions of North America. The lily of the valley is called the *may bell* in Germany. It is one of the special flowers for the month of May.

The beautiful bell-shaped flowers are pure white. They hang down in a long cluster along a slender stem. The flower stalk rises from an underground stem. Each stalk usually has two wide, oblong leaves. The fruit is a red berry about $\frac{1}{4}$ inch (6 millimeters) in diameter. The plant grows well in slight shade and in deeply dug, rich soil containing leaf mold.

Lily of the valley is a perennial plant, flowering naturally in late spring. In hothouses it blooms during all seasons. Florists keep the plant frozen until they want it to flower. It also grows well outdoors, in the shade. It will grow for many years without needing to

WORLD BOOK illustration by Robert Hynes

Wood Lilies have bright, orange-red petals with purple spots. These flowers are found from the Midwestern States to New England. There are about 4,000 species of lilies.

southeast is reddish-orange with purple spots and grows about 5 feet (1.5 meters) tall. The *southern red lily* also grows along the southeastern coast. It is about 2 feet (61 centimeters) high with bright red and yellow flowers spotted with purple.

The tall *leopard lily* grows along the west coast from California to Oregon. It is about 8 feet (2.4 meters) high with reddish-orange flowers spotted purple. The *Sierra lily* of the same region is about 5 feet (1.5 meters) tall. It has red-orange flowers that are also purple-spotted.

The *wood lily* grows from Maine to Missouri. Its flowers are also orange-red with purple spots, and it grows to a height of 3 feet (91 centimeters).

Lily flowers grow from scaly bulbs. Most lilies have clusters of gay flowers on upright stems. The blossoms are trumpet-shaped, and made up of six parts.

Lilies grow best in deep, sandy loam that is kept well drained. They should be sheltered from strong winds and hot sun. Bulbs of most lilies are planted 6 inches (15 centimeters) or more under the soil in late fall. They are placed deep because many send out roots above the bulbs. As soon as the plants bloom, the seed pods should be removed. The *Madonna lily* is planted only in August and is set only 2 inches (5 centimeters) deep because it starts a growth of foliage in late summer.

The most serious disease that attacks lilies is called *mosaic*. It is carried from plant to plant by aphids and attacks every part of the plant except the seeds. When one of the plants becomes infected, it should be removed immediately and burned. Another disease, called *botrytis blight*, also attacks lilies. It can be controlled by spraying the flowers once a week with Bordeaux mixture, a solution of copper sulfate and hydrated lime in water.

Scientific Classification. True lilies belong to the lily family, Liliaceae. They are genus *Lilium.*   ALFRED C. HOTTES

Related Articles in WORLD BOOK include:

Aloe	Aspidistra	Crocus
Asparagus	Bulb	Day Lily
Asphodel	Colchicum	Dogtooth Violet

Derek Fell

The Lily of the Valley Has White, Bell-Shaped Blossoms.

be moved. In greenhouses, it should be kept at a temperature of about 65° F. (18° C) in order to bloom.

Lily of the valley is famous for its fragrance. A French toilet water called *eau d'or* is made from the flowers.

Scientific Classification. Lily of the valley is a member of the lily family, Liliaceae. It is *Convallaria majalis*. The wild lily of the valley is *C. montana*.   ALFRED C. HOTTES

See also FLOWER (picture: Garden Perennials).

LIMA, *LEE muh* (pop. 4,164,597; met. area pop. 4,608,010), is the capital and largest city of Peru. It is the nation's major commercial, cultural, and industrial center. Lima lies in western Peru, about 10 miles (16 kilometers) from the Pacific Ocean. For location,

The Plaza de Armas in Lima, Peru, marks the historic center of the city. Such major buildings as the cathedral shown above, the city hall, and the Government Palace face the square. The cathedral stands on the site of an earlier church built when Lima was founded in 1535.

see PERU (political map). The Lima metropolitan area extends west to the Pacific. The Andes Mountains rise east of the area.

The City. The Plaza San Martín lies in the center of Lima. The Colmena, Lima's main highway, runs east and west through the plaza. Hotels, office buildings, theaters, and private clubs surround the plaza. Farther south lies the Plaza de Armas, the original center of Lima. Several historic buildings face this square, including the Cathedral of Lima, the city hall, and the Government Palace.

Tall, modern buildings line the streets of the business district near the Plaza San Martín. Lima also has many mansions that were built when Peru was a colony of Spain—from the 1530's to the early 1800's. Many of these mansions are now government office buildings, museums, or restaurants.

Wealthy families live in some of the colonial mansions, and other residents of Lima occupy apartment buildings or luxurious suburban dwellings. But many of the city's people live in public housing or inner-city slums. About a third of the population lives in squatter communities called *young towns*, which surround the city. Many of the houses in these areas are little more than huts of bamboo, cardboard, straw, and tin.

Most of Lima's people are of Indian, Spanish, or mixed Indian and Spanish ancestry. They speak Spanish or Quechua, the language of the Inca Indians.

Attractions of Lima include the Museum of Peruvian Culture and the National Museum of Art. The ruins of Pachacamac, an ancient Indian city, are nearby. The National Library of Peru and the University of San Marcos, the oldest university in South America, are in Lima (see SAN MARCOS, UNIVERSITY OF). The city has a symphony orchestra and a national theater group. Motion pictures and soccer and other sports are favorite recreations among Lima's people.

Economy of Lima is based on the activities of the national government. The government is the largest employer of the city's people. Lima is also Peru's leading manufacturing center. Major products include beer, clothing, cotton and woolen fabrics, and fish meal. Museums and other cultural features in and near Lima help attract tourists. The nearby coastal city of Callao has a port and an airport that serve the capital.

History. Francisco Pizarro, a Spanish adventurer, conquered most of Peru in 1533 and founded Lima in 1535. During the 1600's and 1700's, Lima served as the center of Spanish government in South America.

Most of Lima's industrial growth has occurred during the 1900's. During the 1950's and 1960's, many people moved to the city from rural areas and small communities to search for jobs. Lima had a severe housing shortage by the 1970's, but its population continued to increase. The city also faced pollution problems during the 1970's because of its expanding industries and growing number of cars.   WILLIAM MANGIN

See also PERU (pictures).

LIMA, *LY muh,* Ohio (pop. 47,827; met. area pop. 154,795), is a trade and manufacturing center on the Ottawa River in the northwestern part of the state (see OHIO [political map]). Products manufactured in Lima include aircraft engine parts and electrical systems, automobile and truck engines, cigars, hearses, laundry deter-

269

gent, machine tools, and military tanks. Lima's oil fields, now mostly exhausted, were considered the world's largest in the late 1890's and early 1900's. The city now serves as an important pipeline and refining center. Lima also processes and markets farm products from the 10-county area it serves. The city is the home of a campus of Ohio State University.

Lima was organized as a town in 1842. It is the seat of Allen County and has a mayor-council form of government.   JAMES H. RODABAUGH

LIMA BEAN, *LY muh,* is the most nutritious member of the pea family. It is high in protein value, and rich in vitamin B. This wide, flat bean first grew in tropical America. It now grows in many warm lands, especially the United States.

Like other beans, Limas are seeds that grow in pods. The large Limas often grow 1 inch (25 millimeters) wide and $\frac{1}{4}$ inch (6 millimeters) thick. Some varieties have large seeds and others have small seeds. Lima beans may be green or white.

Some Limas grow on vines that can be trained on poles or trellises. The pole beans are usually planted in hills, 2 to 4 feet (61 to 122 centimeters) apart. Other kinds of Limas grow on bushes. Lima beans grow best in rich soil that does not have too much nitrogen. They need moist air and a long growing season. Limas rank as an important crop in California, where they are planted in May and ripen around September.

Scientific Classification. Lima beans are of the pea family, Leguminosae. They are classified as genus *Phaseolus,* species *P. limensis.*   ARTHUR J. PRATT

See also BEAN.

LIMBO, in Roman Catholic theology, is the home of souls who belong neither in heaven nor in hell. *Limbo* is a Latin word that means *on the border.* Souls in limbo enjoy perfect natural happiness but lack the supernatural joy of seeing God.

Roman Catholic theologians have developed two concepts of limbo. *Limbus patrum* (fathers' limbo) is the temporary place or state of the souls of holy people who died before Christian times. Many Christians believe that after Jesus Christ rose from the dead, He took these souls to heaven. *Limbus infantium* (infants' limbo) is the eternal place or state of infants who have died unbaptized. The idea of *limbus infantium* rests on the belief that baptism is needed to enter heaven but that unbaptized infants have not sinned and thus do not deserve hell. Many Roman Catholic theologians have taught the existence of *limbus infantium,* but it is not part of official church doctrine.   JILL RAITT

LIMBOURG, *LIHM burkh,* **POL DE,** *pahl duh* (? - 1416), was the best known of three brothers who were manuscript painters called *illuminators.* They worked in France during the 1400's for the Duc de Berry. Their most famous work is *Les Très Riches Heures* (*The Very Rich Hours*), one of the most beautiful manuscripts of the late Middle Ages. The book's illustrations show scenes of the life of the times, each associated with a month. The pictures are distinguished by brilliant coloring and fine command of space. Scenes from the book appear in the MIDDLE AGES and EUROPE articles. The Limbourg brothers were born sometime after 1385 in Nijmegen, the Netherlands.   JOSEPH C. SLOANE

LIME is a rounded fruit that is pointed at both ends. It is greener than the lemon, to which it is related. It grows on a small citrus tree. The lime tree comes from India. It now grows in the Mediterranean basin, the West Indies, Mexico, Florida, and southern California. Lime trees grow well in southern Florida, where most United States limes are produced.

The lime tree rarely grows higher than 10 to 12 feet (3

Calavo Growers of California

Zesty Limes grow in clusters. The photograph above shows clusters of mature fruit, *left,* and developing fruit, *right.* The juicy pulp, *below,* resembles that of a lemon, but is greener.

J. Horace McFarland

to 3.7 meters). The fruit is important as a source of lime juice and oil of lime, which are used to flavor beverages and food. A popular summer drink called *limeade* is prepared from limes in the same way that lemonade is prepared from lemons.

Scientific Classification. Lime trees belong to the rue family, Rutaceae. They are classified as genus *Citrus,* species *C. aurantifolia.*   WILLIAM GRIERSON

LIME is an important industrial chemical. The chemical name for lime is *calcium oxide,* and its chemical formula is CaO. The word *lime* is also used to refer to *calcium hydroxide.* Calcium hydroxide, which has a chemical formula of $Ca(OH)_2$, is formed by a reaction of calcium oxide with water. Calcium oxide is also known as *quicklime,* and calcium hydroxide is also called *slaked lime* and *hydrated lime.* Both substances are bases.

Slaked lime has a wide variety of uses. It serves as a *flux* in the production of steel (see FLUX). It also is used in the refining of aluminum, copper, and zinc. Lime "softens" water by removing certain minerals from it, and it plays a valuable role in the treatment of sewage as well. Many farmers spread lime on their fields to neutralize acid in soil, and homeowners often use it on their lawns to prevent the growth of moss. Lime also helps stabilize soil in the foundations of highways and airport runways. In the production of leather, tanneries use lime to remove hair from animal hides. The *mortar* that is layered between bricks or stones in the walls of buildings is composed of a mixture of lime, sand, and water. Lime is also a key ingredient in plaster and in a kind of cement called *portland cement*.

Most quicklime is made from small chunks of limestone. Limestone consists chiefly of calcium carbonate, which has the chemical formula $CaCO_3$. To produce quicklime, manufacturers place crushed limestone in a special oven, called a *kiln*, and heat it to a temperature of about 2000° F. (1204° C). This process releases carbon dioxide from the limestone, leaving a lump of powdery, grayish-white quicklime.

The production of slaked lime involves a further process called *slaking*. Water is added to a lump of cooled quicklime, resulting in a chemical reaction that produces heat and steam. As the steam evaporates, the lump of quicklime disintegrates into a fine, dry, white powder. This powder is slaked lime. If water is added in excess of the amount needed for slaked lime, a *slurry* (soupy mixture) of partially dissolved lime is created. This slurry is commonly known as *milk of lime*. When slaked lime is dissolved completely in water, the resulting product is a clear liquid called *limewater*. Limewater is used to detect the presence of carbon dioxide in a substance. If carbon dioxide is present, it turns the limewater milky-white.   ROBERT J. OUELLETTE

Related Articles in WORLD BOOK include:

Calcium	Glass (Soda-Lime Glass)
Calcium Carbonate	Leather (Preparing
Cement and Concrete	the Hides)
(How Cement Is Made)	Limestone

LIME-SODA PROCESS. See WATER SOFTENING.

LIME TREE. See LINDEN.

LIMERICK, *LIHM uhr ihk* (pop. 60,665), is the third largest city of the Republic of Ireland. Only Dublin and Cork are larger. Limerick lies in western Ireland, at the mouth of the River Shannon. For location, see IRELAND (map).

English Town, Limerick's oldest district, lies on an island in the Shannon. It and Irish Town, a district south of the river, have historic buildings and residential areas. Newtown-Pery, southwest of Irish Town, is Limerick's main business district and a residential area. Modern suburbs lie south of the city and north of the Shannon.

Limerick is one of Ireland's chief ports. Its varied industries include food processing and the production of appliances, cement, clothing, and steel cord.

Vikings founded Limerick about A.D. 900, when they settled on the island that later became English Town. The city gradually grew to include the Irish Town area. Newtown-Pery was created from a city plan during the 1700's. In 1939, Shannon Airport opened near Limerick. It has greatly increased tourism in the city. The airport and a large manufacturing center that was later built beside it have also provided many jobs for Limerick's people.   DESMOND A. GILLMOR

LIMERICK, *LIHM uhr ihk,* is a form of humorous verse. It takes its name from the city of Limerick, Ireland. No one knows how or where the form originated. The limerick is a poem of five lines, with strong beat and rough *anapestic* rhythm (*de-de-DUMM*). The first two lines (each with three such feet) rhyme with the fifth. The third and fourth lines (each with only two feet) also rhyme.

Limericks may cover a wide range of subjects. The first line often begins: "There was a . . ." and ends with the name of a person or place. The last line ends with an unusual or far-fetched rhyme. Edward Lear's *A Book of Nonsense* (1846) made the form popular. The following is a typical limerick by Lear:

> There was a young lady of Wilts,
> Who walked up to Scotland on stilts;
>   When they said it is shocking
>   To show so much stocking,
> She answered, "Then what about kilts?"
>
> CHARLES W. COOPER

LIMESTONE is a type of rock made up mostly of calcite, a mineral form of calcium carbonate. Most limestone is gray, but all colors of limestone from white to black have been found. Scientists test natural rock to see if it is limestone by pouring cold diluted hydrochloric or sulfuric acid on it. Limestone gives off bubbles of carbon dioxide.

Most fresh water and sea water contain dissolved calcium carbonate. All limestones are formed when the calcium carbonate crystallizes out of solution. It leaves the solution in many ways, and each way produces a different kind of limestone. All the different kinds can be divided into two groups.

The first group includes limestones that formed almost completely without the aid of organisms. This type of limestone is forced out of solution when the water evaporates. Such evaporation takes place in the hot lagoons of many coral reefs, and in most shallow tropical seas. In these places the high temperature causes the water on the surface to evaporate. A white "lime" mud is deposited on the bottom of the sea. This white mud slowly hardens into a light-colored limestone with a fine grain and even layers. Chalk is a limestone that remained soft.

When spring water evaporates on land, calcium carbonate forms a crust over moss, dead leaves, and the ground. It builds up a mound or terrace called *tufa*. Evaporation of water in limestone caverns forms another variety of limestone, called travertine, into stalactites and stalagmites (see STALACTITE; STALAGMITE).

Grant Heilman   Grant Heilman

Gray Limestone is the most common type. Limestone also occurs in many other colors.

Limestone Called Coquina, which occurs in Florida, is made up of coral and shells.

271

LIMEWATER

The second group of limestones forms by the work of organisms. Many animals and some water plants draw calcium carbonate out of the water and use it to make their shells and bones. The oysters, clams, snails, corals, and sea urchins do this. When the animals die, the shells and bones are broken up by waves into shell and coral sand and mud. Many of the beaches on Pacific islands are made of such coral mud and sand. Most of the limestone layers in all parts of the earth were once shell or coral sand and mud. A limestone called *coquina*, formed of shells and coral, occurs in Florida. It is used to make roads and in building.

Limestone makes an excellent building stone because it can be carved easily. Like sandstone, it can be cut any way without splitting. For this reason, both limestone and sandstone are often called *freestone*. Limestone is an especially good stone for foundations and walls where a high polish is not needed. Quarries in Indiana produce about half the building limestone in the United States.

Some factories use limestone to clean waste gases and water before releasing them into the environment. Limestone is also used to make lime and to smelt iron ore (see IRON AND STEEL [Raw Materials]).   ROBERT W. CHARLES

Related Articles in WORLD BOOK include:

Building Stone	Coral	Quarrying
Calcite	Dolomite	Rock (Sedimen-
Carbonate	Lime	tary Rock)
Cement and Concrete	Marble	Travertine
Chalk		

LIMEWATER. See LIME (chemical).
LIMITATION OF ARMAMENT. See DISARMAMENT.
LIMITATIONS, STATUTE OF. See STATUTE OF LIMITATIONS.

LIMITED COMPANY is a business organization in which each shareholder is responsible only for the shares he or she holds. A person owning stock worth $500 loses only that $500 investment if the company goes into debt. Creditors cannot sue the investor to recover money owed by the company. In British countries, the word *Limited* (*Ltd.*) after a company's name indicates a limited company.   L. T. FLATLEY

LIMNOLOGY, *lihm NAHL uh jee*, is the scientific study of lakes, streams, ponds, and other bodies of fresh water. Limnologists study the chemical and physical characteristics of these bodies of water. They also study the plants and animals that live in fresh water, and their relationship to each other and to their environment. Limnology is related to *ecology*, the study of the relations between organisms and their environments. Limnology has special importance in the management of fish for economic and recreational purposes.

See also ECOLOGY.

LIMÓN, *lee MAWN*, **JOSÉ**, *hoh SAY* (1908-1972), was an American dancer and *choreographer* (dance composer). Although he did not begin dancing until he was in his 20's, he achieved remarkable technical skill. Many of his ballets are based on literature. These include *The Moor's Pavane* (1949), a ballet of Shakespeare's *Othello*. Limón based several ballets on the Bible. *The Traitor* (1954) deals with Judas Iscariot's betrayal of Christ. *There Is a Time* (1956) is based on the Book of Ecclesiastes.

Limón was born in Culiacán, Mexico, and was brought to the United States when he was 7. He performed with the Humphrey-Weidman company from 1930 to 1940. He formed his own group in the late 1940's. Doris Humphrey, the group's artistic director, created many dance roles for him.   SELMA JEANNE COHEN

LIMONITE, *LY muh nyt*, is a yellowish or orange-brown to brownish-black mineral. It is a source of iron for industry and *ocher*, a yellow powder used in paints and pigments.

Limonite occurs where iron-bearing minerals break down. It is believed to be a mixture of several minerals, such as goethite and lepidocrocite, all basically made up of iron oxide and water.

Limonite may appear as a surface film on rocks, or as a slimy deposit on lakes and marshes. It also occurs in iron ore deposits called *bog iron ore*, which can be mined for iron. Small amounts of limonite are found in Sweden and Norway. In the United States, small amounts are found in Alabama, Colorado, Georgia, Minnesota, and Texas.   WILLIAM C. LUTH

LIMPET is a small sea animal with a protective shell. It lives along rocky coasts in all parts of the world. Most limpets are less than 3 inches (8 centimeters) long, but a west Mexican limpet may grow up to 8 inches (20 centimeters) in length. Limpets are easy to find at low tide. Their shells can be seen on exposed rocks, and resemble tiny, shallow bowls turned upside down. The shell completely covers each animal and protects it from hungry sea birds. Beneath the shell, the limpet's *foot* (a powerful, muscular organ) clamps its body firmly to the rock by suction. At high tide, the limpet moves over

Cy LaTour, Marineland of the Pacific

The Keyhole Limpet is distinguished from the true limpets by the small hole at the top of its shell.

rocks in search of seaweeds. It gathers food into its mouth with a *radula* (long ribbonlike tongue), which bears rows of teeth. Before the tide goes out, the limpet returns to its original resting place on the rock.

See also ANIMAL (color picture: Animals of the Oceans); MOLLUSK; SNAIL; SHELL (color picture).

Scientific Classification. Limpets are in the phylum *Mollusca*. The American limpet is a member of the limpet family, *Acmaeidae*. It is classified as genus *Acmaea*, species *A. testudinalis*.   R. TUCKER ABBOTT

LIMPOPO RIVER, *lihm POH poh*, is an important river that flows for about 1,000 miles (1,600 kilometers) in southeastern Africa (see SOUTH AFRICA [terrain map]). The Limpopo rises in the highlands and separates the Transvaal Province of South Africa from Botswana and Zimbabwe before it crosses Mozambique to the Indian Ocean. Rudyard Kipling described the river in his story, "The Elephant's Child," as "the great gray-green greasy Limpopo." It is also called the *Crocodile River*. The last 60 miles (97 kilometers) of the Limpopo are tidewater. Above this point, the river varies between a small trickle in the dry season and a roaring flood in the wet season. The Olifants River is the Limpopo's main tributary. HIBBERD V. B. KLINE, JR.

LIN BIAO, *leen bee ow* (1907-1971), also spelled *Lin Piao*, was defense minister of China from 1959 to 1971. In the late 1960's and early 1970's, Lin was officially designated to succeed Mao Zedong, chairman of the Chinese Communist Party. But in 1971, Lin disappeared from public view. In 1972, China reported that Lin had died in an airplane crash in Mongolia in 1971. The crash occurred while Lin was reportedly trying to flee China after failing in an attempt to kill Mao and overthrow the government.

Pictorial Parade

Lin Biao

As defense minister, Lin headed the People's Liberation Army. For a time, he also headed the Red Guards, a youth group formed in the 1960's to support Mao.

Lin was born in Hubei (or Hupeh) province. A top student under Chiang Kaishek at the Whampoa Military Academy, Lin joined Mao's Communist forces after graduation. In 1934 and 1935, he led advance troops on the 6,000-mile (9,700-kilometer) *Long March* to escape Chinese Nationalist forces. Lin won military victories over invading Japanese forces in the late 1930's and over Nationalist armies during China's civil war. DONALD W. KLEIN

LIN YUTANG, *lihn yoo tahng* (1895-1976), a Chinese scholar and writer, helped interpret Chinese culture to the West. Two of his writings in English, *My Country and My People* (1936) and *The Importance of Living* (1937), became best sellers in the United States. His novel, *Moment in Peking* (1939), dealing with changes in China since 1900, is still widely read because of its interesting plot and fluent style. His other works in English include *The Wisdom of Confucius* (1938), *A Leaf in the Storm* (1941), *The Vermilion Gate* (1953), and *The Pleasures of a Nonconformist* (1962).

Lin was interested in Chinese language reform, and played a major role in developing a romanized system of Chinese speech sounds known as *Gwoyeu Romatzyh*. This system of sounds simplified writing the Chinese language. Lin invented a Chinese typewriter in 1946.

Lin was born in Amoy. He received a master's degree from Harvard University in 1922 and a doctor's degree from Leipzig University in 1923. He taught at the National University of Peking for several years. After serving with the Nationalist government in 1927, Lin devoted himself to writing. SHAU WING CHAN

LINCOLN (pop. 75,617) is a city in east-central England. For location, see ENGLAND (political map). The city serves as the administrative, commercial, and industrial center for the surrounding region. Its many industries include engineering, food processing, and the manufacture of such products as cosmetics and plastics. Lincoln has a number of medieval buildings—including a castle and a magnificent Gothic cathedral—which attract many tourists to the city.

In A.D. 47, Roman soldiers established a settlement on the site of what is now Lincoln. During the Middle Ages, the community prospered as a center of the wool export trade. In the mid-1800's, the city began manufacturing agricultural and construction equipment. During the 1900's, a variety of light industries have been established in Lincoln. G. MALCOLM LEWIS

LINCOLN, Nebr. (pop. 171,932; met. area pop. 192,-884), became the capital of Nebraska in 1867, when Nebraska was admitted to the Union. It is the second largest city in the state and an important educational center. Lincoln was originally called Lancaster, but was renamed to honor Abraham Lincoln.

Lincoln lies 50 miles (80 kilometers) southwest of Omaha, the original capital (see NEBRASKA [political map]). It covers an area of about 24 square miles (62 square kilometers) on rolling prairie lands. The Capitol has a 400-foot (120-meter) central tower.

Lincoln is the home of two campuses of the University of Nebraska, Nebraska Wesleyan University, and Union College. It has about 1,300 acres (526 hectares) of wooded parks, two museums, and an art gallery.

Lincoln is an important business and industrial center served by passenger trains, five rail freight lines, two airlines, and numerous highways. It produces motor scooters, rubber belting, electrical and telephone appliances, railroad boxcars, dairy products, meat, and flour. The city dominates a large area in retailing and wholesaling, and is the home of several agencies of the federal and state governments.

Settlers were attracted to this area in 1856 by salt springs. The original townsite was established in 1859. A mayor-council form of government was adopted in 1937. JAMES C. OLSON

See also NEBRASKA (picture: Nebraska's Capitol).

University of Nebraska, Lincoln

University of Nebraska Students relax at a fountain next to the Nebraska Union building on the campus in Lincoln.

PIERCE
14th President
1853 — 1857

BUCHANAN
15th President
1857 — 1861

ABRAHAM LINCOLN

JOHNSON
17th President
1865 — 1869

GRANT
18th President
1869 — 1877

Mathew Brady, Library of Congress

16TH PRESIDENT OF THE UNITED STATES 1861-1865

LINCOLN, ABRAHAM (1809-1865), was one of the truly great men of all time. He preserved the American Union during the Civil War, and proved to the world that democracy can be a lasting form of government. Lincoln's Gettysburg Address, and many of his other speeches and writings, are classic statements of democratic beliefs and goals. In conducting a bitter war, Lincoln never became bitter himself. He showed a nobility of character which continues to grow in world-wide appeal. Lincoln, a Republican, was the first member of his party to become President. After his assassination, he was succeeded by Vice President Andrew Johnson.

The American people knew little about Lincoln when he became President. Nothing in his past experience indicated that he could meet successfully the greatest crisis in the nation's history. He received less than 40 per cent of the popular vote. As President, Lincoln was often a careless, inefficient administrator. At times, he gave way to political pressures which he might better have resisted.

But these failings mattered little when compared with Lincoln's great merits. His outstanding asset was insight. Lincoln realized at the beginning of the Civil War that the Union must be saved. The United States was the only important democracy in the world. Lincoln knew that self-government would be proved a failure if the nation could be destroyed by a minority of its own people. He determined that the nation, and democracy, would not be destroyed.

Lincoln's second great asset was his ability to express his convictions so clearly, and with such force, that millions of Americans made them their own. This he did in his first and second inaugural addresses, in his annual messages to Congress, in the Gettysburg Address, and in his letters. Lincoln would have been surprised that some of his speeches came to be honored as great literature. He sought only to be understood, and to convince.

Lincoln's third great source of strength was his iron will. The Civil War had to be carried on until the Union

was restored. At times, people in the North wavered in this purpose. Lincoln never doubted that in the end, right would make might, and the North would triumph. His unyielding faith in victory helped to win victory.

If the Union had not been preserved, the United States would have become two nations. Neither of these nations could have attained the prosperity and importance that the United States has today. Lincoln influenced the course of world history by his leadership of the North during the Civil War. His own life story has perhaps been just as important. He rose from humble origin to the nation's highest office. Millions of persons regard his career as proof that democracy offers all people the best hope of a full and free life.

Life in the United States during Lincoln's administration revolved almost entirely around the Civil War. To raise money to fight the war, Congress levied the first income tax in the history of the country. For the first time, federal officeholders had to take an oath of loyalty to the Union. Pioneers flocked to the western frontier, and mining towns sprang up overnight. The government gave free farms to settlers, and set aside land for colleges that later became state universities.

Soldiers and civilians alike sang "The Battle Hymn of the Republic" or "Dixie." Winslow Homer's painting *Prisoners from the Front* brought him his first fame. Patriotic literature included John Greenleaf Whittier's poem "Barbara Frietchie" and Edward Everett Hale's story "The Man Without a Country." Lincoln and thousands of other Americans chuckled at the humorous writings of Artemus Ward.

Early Life

Family Background. Soon after Lincoln was nominated for the presidency, he wrote an autobiography. It began: "Abraham Lincoln was born Feb. 12, 1809, then in Hardin, now in the more recently formed county of Larue, Kentucky. His father, Thomas, & grandfather Abraham, were born in Rockingham county Virginia, whither their ancestors had come from Berks county Pennsylvania. His lineage has been traced no farther back than this."

Since Lincoln's time, his ancestry has been traced to a weaver named Samuel Lincoln who emigrated from

◄ **Lincoln's Favorite Photograph** served as the model for this painting by Allen Tupper True. The portrait is in the Huntington Library and Art Gallery in San Marino, Calif.

275

─── IMPORTANT DATES IN LINCOLN'S LIFE ───

1809 (Feb. 12) Born near present-day Hodgenville, Ky.
1834 Elected to the Illinois General Assembly.
1842 (Nov. 4) Married Mary Todd.
1846 Elected to the U.S. House of Representatives.
1858 Debated slavery with Stephen A. Douglas.
1860 (Nov. 6) Elected President of the United States.
1864 (Nov. 8) Re-elected President.
1865 (April 14) Shot by John Wilkes Booth.
1865 (April 15) Died in Washington, D.C.

BOYHOOD YEARS

Brown Bros.

Lincoln's Birthplace, a log cabin near Hodgenville, Ky., may have been the cabin that now stands at the Abraham Lincoln Birthplace National Historic Site, *above.*

Travels of the Lincolns took them to Knob Creek, Ky., in 1811, then to Indiana in 1816, and to Illinois in 1830. Lincoln moved on his own to New Salem, Ill., in 1831.

Hingham, England, to Hingham, Mass., in 1637. This was only 17 years after the Pilgrims landed at Plymouth Rock. Samuel Lincoln founded the Lincoln family in America. The families of several of his children played important parts in Massachusetts history.

Descendants of Mordecai Lincoln, a son of Samuel, moved to New Jersey, Pennsylvania, and Virginia. One was a great-great-grandson named Abraham. This Abraham Lincoln was the grandfather of the future President. He owned a farm in the Shenandoah Valley of Virginia during the Revolutionary War. In 1782, he and his wife and five small children started over the long trail to the wilderness of Kentucky. An Indian killed him there in 1786.

One of his sons, Thomas Lincoln, became the father of the future President. In later years, the President said his father was "a wandering laboring boy, and grew up literally without education." Thomas Lincoln worked as a frontier farm hand during most of his youth. But he learned enough skill at woodworking to earn a living as a carpenter. In 1806, when he was 28 years old, he married Nancy Hanks. Nancy came from what her son described as an "undistinguished" Virginia family of humble, ordinary people. Historians know only that she was the daughter of a Lucy Hanks.

Thomas and Nancy Lincoln lived in Elizabethtown, Ky., for the first 18 months of their marriage. Their first child, Sarah, was born there in 1807. The next year, Thomas Lincoln bought a farm on the South Fork of the Nolin River, about 5 miles (8 kilometers) south of Elizabethtown. Abraham Lincoln was born on this farm.

Boyhood. The Lincolns lived for two years on the farm where Abraham was born. Then they moved to a farm on Knob Creek, 10 miles (16 kilometers) away. When Sarah and Abraham could be spared from their chores, they went to a log schoolhouse. There the children learned reading, writing, and arithmetic.

Many persons believe that because Lincoln began his life in a log cabin, he was born in poverty. But many families lived in log cabins during the early 1800's. The Lincolns were as comfortable as most of their neighbors, and Abraham and Sarah were well fed and well clothed for the times. A third child, Thomas, died in infancy.

Thomas Lincoln had trouble over property rights throughout his years in Kentucky. In 1816, he decided to move to Indiana, where a man could buy land directly from the government. Besides, Thomas Lincoln did not believe in slavery, and Indiana had no slavery.

The Lincolns loaded their possessions into a wagon. They traveled northward to the Ohio River and were ferried across. Then they traveled through the thick forests to Spencer County, in southwestern Indiana. There, Thomas Lincoln began the task of changing 160 acres (65 hectares) of forest land into a farm.

The Lincolns found life harder in Indiana than in Kentucky. They arrived early in winter, and needed shelter at once. Thomas and his son built a three-sided structure made of logs, called a "half-faced camp." A fire on the fourth side burned night and day. Soon after finishing this shelter, the boy and his father began to build a log cabin. The family moved into it in mid-February, 1817.

Bears and other wild animals roamed the forests of this remote region. Trees had to be cut and fields cleared so that a crop could be planted. Although Abraham was only 8, he was large for his age and had enough strength to swing an ax. For as long as he lived in Indiana, he was seldom without his ax. He later called it "that most useful instrument."

Slowly, life became happier on the farm. Then, in October, 1818, Nancy Lincoln died of what the pioneers called "milk sickness." This illness was probably caused by poison in the milk of cows that had eaten snakeroot. Thomas buried his wife among the trees on a hill near the cabin. The lack of a funeral service distressed 9-year-old Abraham. He was not content until a traveling preacher conducted a burial service over his mother's grave several months later.

The cabin became dull and cheerless after the death of Nancy Lincoln. Sarah, now 12, kept house as well as she could for more than a year. Then Thomas Lincoln returned to Kentucky for a visit. While there, on Dec. 2, 1819, he married Sarah Bush Johnston, a widow. He had known her before her first marriage. The new Mrs. Lincoln brought along her three children, aged 12, 8, and 5, and a wagonload of furniture and household goods. Her arrival at the cabin in Indiana ended the long months of loneliness. Years later, Abraham Lincoln remembered little about his own mother. He may have referred to his stepmother when he said: "God bless my mother; all that I am or ever hope to be I owe to her."

Education. Abraham Lincoln grew from a boy of 7 to a man of 21 on the wild Indiana frontier. His education can best be described in his own words:

"There were some schools, so called; but no qualification was ever required of a teacher, beyond '*readin, writin, and cipherin,*' to the Rule of Three. If a straggler

Abraham Helped Build a Cabin when the family moved to Indiana. Lincoln's mother died on this isolated frontier farm in 1818.

supposed to understand latin, happened to sojourn in the neighborhood, he was looked upon as a wizzard. There was absolutely nothing to excite ambition for education. Of course when I came of age I did not know much. Still somehow, I could read, write, and cipher to the Rule of Three; but that was all."

Lincoln's formal schooling totaled less than a year. Books could rarely be found on the frontier, and paper was almost as scarce. Like other boys and girls of his time, Lincoln made his own arithmetic textbook. Several pages of this book still exist. Abraham often worked his arithmetic problems on boards, then shaved the boards clean with a drawknife, and used them again and again. He would walk a great distance for a book. The few he could borrow were good ones. They included *Robinson Crusoe, Pilgrim's Progress, Aesop's Fables,* a history of the United States, and a schoolbook or two.

In 1823, when Abraham was 14, his parents joined the Pigeon Creek Baptist Church. There was bitter rivalry among Baptists, Methodists, Presbyterians, and members of other denominations. Young Lincoln disliked any display of bitterness among Christian people. This may explain why he never joined any church, and why he never attended church regularly. Yet he became a man of deep religious feelings. The Bible was probably the only book his parents ever owned. Abraham came to know it thoroughly. Biblical references and quotations enriched his later writings and speeches. As President, he kept a Bible on his desk and often opened it for comfort and guidance.

Another book also impressed the boy deeply, and led him to an understanding of the meaning of democracy. He told about it years later in a speech before the New Jersey Senate:

"May I be pardoned if, on this occasion, I mention that away back in my childhood, the earliest days of my being able to read, I got hold of a small book, such a one as few of the younger members have ever seen, Weems' *Life of Washington.* I remember all the accounts there given of the battle fields and struggles for the liberties of the country . . . and you all know, for you have all been boys, how these early impressions last longer than any others. I recollect thinking then, boy even though I was, that there must have been some-

Lincoln Studied by Firelight after working on the farm all day. This *diorama,* or three-dimensional scene, shows Lincoln and his parents in their log cabin on the Indiana frontier.

The Family Crossed into Illinois in 1830, and settled on a farm about 10 miles (16 kilometers) from Decatur. On the way, Abraham rescued a dog trapped in an icy stream.

Dioramas at the Chicago Historical Society

Diorama at the Chicago Historical Society

Lincoln's First Job after he moved to New Salem, Ill., in 1831 was as a clerk in the store of Denton Offutt. He lived in a room at the rear of the store. Lincoln later became postmaster of New Salem.

Militiamen of New Salem elected Lincoln captain of their company when they volunteered to serve in the Black Hawk War in 1832. Lincoln served in the army 90 days.

thing more than common that those men struggled for."

Youth on the Frontier. Abraham reached his full height of 6 feet 4 inches (193 centimeters) long before he was 20. He was thin and awkward, big-boned and strong. The young man developed great strength in his chest and legs, and especially in his arms. He had a homely face and dark skin. His hair was black and coarse, and stood on end.

Even as a boy, Lincoln showed ability as a speaker. He often amused himself and others by imitating some preacher or politician who had spoken in the area. People liked to gather at the general store in the crossroads village of Gentryville. Lincoln's gift for telling stories made him a favorite with the people there. In spite of his youth, he was well known in his neighborhood.

A boy of Lincoln's size and strength had no trouble finding hard work. People always needed great piles of cut wood for cooking and for warmth. He could split logs for fence rails. He could plow fields, cut and husk corn, and thresh wheat with a flail. Lincoln worked for a neighbor when his father could spare him.

The Ohio River, 15 miles (24 kilometers) away, attracted Lincoln strongly. The first money he earned was for rowing passengers to a steamboat in midstream. In 1828, he helped take a flatboat loaded with farm produce to New Orleans. The trip gave him his first view of the world beyond his own community. That same year, his sister died in childbirth.

In 1830, Thomas Lincoln decided to move again. The years in Indiana had not been successful. The dread milk sickness was again striking down settlers. Relatives in Illinois sent word of deep, rich, black soil on the treeless prairies. The Lincolns and several other families packed their belongings and started west. They reached their destination two weeks later, and settled 10 miles (16 kilometers) west of Decatur, on the north bank of the Sangamon River.

Lincoln was now 21, and free to strike out for himself. But he remained with his father one more year. He helped plant the first crop, and split rails for a cabin and fences. He worked for neighboring settlers during the winter. In the spring of 1831, when the streams were high, a trader named Denton Offutt hired Lincoln and two other young men to take a flatboat to New Orleans. This trip gave Offutt a good impression of his lanky boat hand. He hired Lincoln as a clerk in his new store in the village of New Salem, Ill., 20 miles (32 kilometers) northwest of Springfield. While Lincoln was away, his parents moved to Coles County, where they lived for the rest of their lives.

New Salem Years

Life on His Own began for Lincoln when he settled in New Salem. He lived there almost six years, from July, 1831, until the spring of 1837. The village consisted of log cabins clustered around a mill, a barrel-maker's shop, a wool-carding machine, and a few general stores.

The people of the village helped Lincoln in many ways. The older women mended his clothes, and often gave him meals. Jack Kelso, the village philosopher, introduced him to the writings of Shakespeare and Robert Burns. These works, and the Bible, became his favorite reading.

Lincoln arrived in New Salem, as he said, "a piece of floating driftwood." He earned little, and slept in a room at the rear of Offutt's store. Within a few months the business failed. Lincoln would have been out of a job if the Black Hawk War had not begun in 1832.

The Black Hawk War. In 1831, the federal government had moved the Sauk and Fox Indians from Illinois to Iowa. In the spring of 1832, Chief Black Hawk led a band of several hundred Indians back across the Mississippi River to try to regain their lands near Rock

Island (see BLACK HAWK). The governor called out the militia, and Lincoln volunteered for service.

Lincoln's company consisted of men from the New Salem area. The men promptly elected him captain. This was only nine months after he had settled in the village. Even after he had been nominated for President, Lincoln said this honor "gave me more pleasure than any I have had since." His comrades liked his friendliness, his honesty, and his skill at storytelling. They also admired his great strength and his sportsmanship in wrestling matches and other contests.

Lincoln's term of service ended after 30 days, but he re-enlisted, this time as a private. A month later, he enlisted again. He served a total of 90 days, but saw no fighting. He later recalled that he had "a good many bloody struggles with the mosquitoes."

Search for a Career. Before his military service, many of Lincoln's friends had encouraged him to become a candidate for the state legislature. Spurred by their faith, he announced his candidacy in March, 1832. The Black Hawk War prevented him from making much of a campaign. He arrived home in July, only two weeks before the election. Lincoln was defeated in the election, but the people in his own precinct gave him 277 of their 300 votes.

Lincoln faced the problem of making a living. He thought of studying law, but decided he could not succeed without a better education. Just then, he had a chance to buy a New Salem store on credit, in partnership with William F. Berry. Lincoln later recalled that the partnership "did nothing but get deeper and deeper in debt." The store failed after a few months.

In May, 1833, Lincoln was appointed postmaster of New Salem. Soon afterward, the county surveyor offered to make him a deputy. Lincoln knew nothing about surveying, but he prepared for the work by hard study. Odd jobs and fees from his two public offices earned him a living.

Berry died in 1835, leaving Lincoln liable for the debts of the partnership, about $1,100. It took Lincoln several years to pay these debts, but he finally did it. His integrity helped him earn the nickname "Honest Abe."

In New Salem, Lincoln knew a girl named Ann Rutledge. When she died in the summer of 1835, he grieved deeply. His sorrow gave rise to a belief that he and Ann had planned to be married. Careful study has reduced their supposed love affair to a myth. This conclusion is supported by the fact that Lincoln proposed marriage to a Kentucky girl, Mary Owens, less than 18 months later. He met her while she was visiting her sister in New Salem. The affair was not ardent on either side, and Miss Owens rejected him.

Success in Politics. In 1834, Lincoln again ran for the legislature. He had become better known by this time, and won election as a Whig (see WHIG). He served four successive two-year terms in the lower house of the Illinois General Assembly. During his first term, he met a young Democratic legislator, Stephen A. Douglas.

Lincoln quickly came to the front in the legislature. He was witty and ready in debate. His skill in party management enabled him to become the Whig floor leader at the beginning of his second term. He took a leading part in the adoption of a plan for a system of railroads and canals. This plan broke down after the

Panic of 1837. Lincoln also led a successful campaign for moving the state capital from Vandalia to Springfield.

While in the legislature, Lincoln made his first public statement on slavery. In 1837, the legislature passed resolutions condemning abolition societies. These societies urged freedom for slaves. Lincoln and another legislator, Dan Stone, filed a protest. They admitted that Congress had no power to interfere with slavery in the states where it existed. They believed that "the promulgation of abolition doctrines tend rather to increase than abate its evils." Their protest arose from the fact that the legislature failed to call slavery an evil practice. Lincoln and Stone declared that "the institution of slavery is founded on both injustice and bad policy." Slavery had become an even greater issue 23 years later, when Lincoln was nominated for President. He said then that his protest in the Illinois legislature still expressed his position on slavery.

Lincoln the Lawyer

Study. In 1834, during Lincoln's second campaign for the legislature, John T. Stuart had urged him to study law. Stuart was an attorney in Springfield and a member of the legislature. Lincoln overcame his doubts about his education. He borrowed law books from Stuart and studied them. He sometimes walked 20 miles (32 kilometers) from New Salem to Springfield for books. Henry E. Dummer, Stuart's law partner, recalled:

"Sometimes he walked, but generally rode. He was the most uncouth looking young man I ever saw. He seemed to have but little to say; seemed to feel timid, with a tinge of sadness visible in the countenance, but when he did talk all this disappeared for the time and he demonstrated that he was both strong and acute. He surprised us more and more at every visit."

On Sept. 9, 1836, Lincoln received his license to practice law, although his name was not entered on the roll of attorneys until March 1, 1837. The population of New Salem had dropped by that time, and Lincoln decided to move to the new state capital. Carrying all he owned in his saddlebags, he rode into Springfield on April 15, 1837. There he became the junior partner in the law firm of Stuart and Lincoln.

In Lincoln's time, there were few law schools. Most lawyers simply "read law" in the office of an attorney. Years later, in giving advice to a law student, Lincoln explained his method of study:

"If you are resolutely determined to make a lawyer of yourself, the thing is more than half done already. It is but a small matter whether you read *with* anybody or not. I did not read with anyone. Get the books, and read and study them till you understand them in their principal features; and that is the main thing. It is of no consequence to be in a large town while you are reading. I read at New Salem, which never had three hundred people living in it. The *books*, and your *capacity* for understanding them, are just the same in all places . . . Always bear in mind that your own resolution to succeed, is more important than any other one thing."

Early Practice. Lincoln's partnership with Stuart lasted until the spring of 1841. Then he became the junior partner of Stephen T. Logan, one of the greatest lawyers who ever practiced in Illinois. This partnership ended in the fall of 1844.

Lincoln then asked William H. Herndon to become his partner. Herndon, nine years younger than Lincoln, had just received his license to practice law. Lincoln called him "Billy," but Herndon always called his partner "Mr. Lincoln." The two men never formally dissolved their law firm. More than 16 years later, Lincoln visited his old office on his last day in Springfield before leaving for Washington to be inaugurated as President. He noticed the firm's signboard at the foot of the steps and said: "Let it hang there undisturbed. Give our clients to understand that the election of a President makes no change in the firm of Lincoln and Herndon."

The practice of law in Illinois was not specialized in Lincoln's time. He tried his first case in the circuit court of Sangamon County. He practiced in the Illinois federal courts within two years after his admission to the bar. A year later, he tried the first of many cases in the state supreme court. But all the while, he also handled cases before justices of the peace. He also gave advice and opinions on many matters for small fees.

Lincoln's Family. Soon after Lincoln moved to Springfield, he met Mary Todd (Dec. 13, 1818-July 16, 1882), a lively, dark-haired Kentucky girl who lived there with a married sister. They had a stormy courtship and at one time broke their engagement. They were married on Nov. 4, 1842, when Lincoln was 33 and his bride was 23.

Mary Todd Lincoln was high-strung and socially ambitious. Lincoln tended to be moody and absent-minded. Their contrasting personalities caused friction.

But their marriage was not so discordant as some writers have described it. See LINCOLN, MARY TODD.

Lincoln and his bride first lived in a Springfield boardinghouse, where they paid $4 a week. Eighteen months after his marriage, Lincoln bought the plain but comfortable frame house in which the family lived until he became President. By the time he bought the house, his first son, Robert Todd Lincoln, was 9 months old (see LINCOLN, ROBERT TODD). His second son, Edward Baker Lincoln, was born in 1846, but died four years later. William Wallace Lincoln, born in 1850, died in the White House at the age of 11. Their fourth son, Thomas Lincoln, became famous during his father's administration as "Tad." He became ill and died in 1871 at the age of 18.

The family lived modestly but comfortably. Lincoln was never the poverty-stricken failure of legend. He often cared for his own horse and milked the family cow, but so did most of his neighbors. The family usually had a servant to help with the housework.

Riding the Circuit. The state of Illinois was, and still is, divided into circuits for judicial purposes. Each circuit consisted of several counties where court was held in turn. The judge and many lawyers traveled from county to county. They tried such cases as came their way during each term.

Lincoln "traveled the circuit" for six months each year. He loved this kind of life. The small inns where the lawyers stayed had few comforts, but they offered many opportunities for meeting people. Lively talk and storytelling appealed to Lincoln. He also liked the long rides across the prairies. Lincoln's circuit at its largest included 15 counties, and covered about 8,000 square miles (21,000 square kilometers).

Lincoln developed traits as a lawyer that made him

LINCOLN THE LAWYER

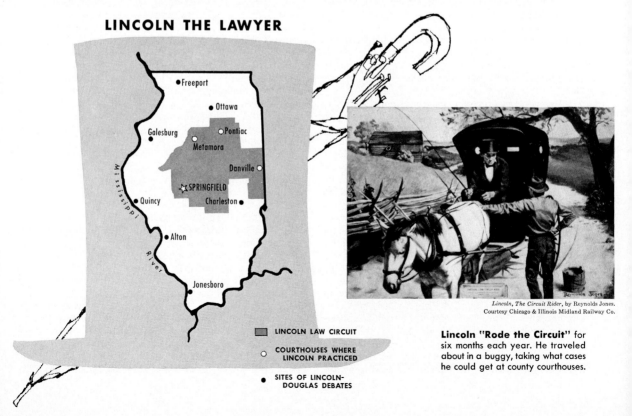

- Freeport
- Ottawa
- Galesburg
- Pontiac
- Metamora
- Danville
- SPRINGFIELD
- Quincy
- Charleston
- Alton
- Jonesboro

Mississippi River

▨ LINCOLN LAW CIRCUIT

○ COURTHOUSES WHERE LINCOLN PRACTICED

● SITES OF LINCOLN-DOUGLAS DEBATES

Lincoln, The Circuit Rider, by Reynolds Jones.
Courtesy Chicago & Illinois Midland Railway Co.

Lincoln "Rode the Circuit" for six months each year. He traveled about in a buggy, taking what cases he could get at county courthouses.

well known throughout Illinois. He could argue a case strongly when convinced that his client was right. If doubtful, he was much less powerful. He persuaded clients to settle their differences out of court whenever possible. This usually meant a smaller fee, or no fee at all, for him. In court, Lincoln could present a case so that 12 jurors, often poorly educated, could not fail to understand it. He could also argue a complicated case before a well-informed judge. He prepared his cases thoroughly, and was unfailingly honest.

National Politics

Search for Advancement. After four terms in the Illinois legislature, Lincoln wanted an office with greater prestige. He had served the Whig party well, and election to Congress became his goal.

In 1840, Lincoln made a speaking tour of the state for William Henry Harrison, the Whig candidate for President. He believed his service had earned him the nomination for Congress from his district. In 1843, and again in 1844, the nomination went to other men. Disappointed, but not bitter, Lincoln worked for the election of Henry Clay, the Whig presidential candidate in 1844. Two years later, Lincoln received his reward, and won the Whig nomination for the U.S. House of Representatives. His opponent in the election was Peter Cartwright, a well-known Methodist circuit rider. The Whigs held firm control of Lincoln's district, and he received 6,340 of the 11,418 votes cast.

Congressman. Lincoln took his seat in Congress on Dec. 6, 1847. By that time, the United States had won the Mexican War, although a peace treaty had not yet been signed. Lincoln joined his fellow Whigs in blaming President James K. Polk for the war. Lincoln voted to supply equipment to troops still in the field. But his stand against the President made him unpopular with the ardently patriotic people of his district.

Lincoln failed to make the reputation he had hoped for in Congress. He gave notice that he intended to introduce a bill to free the slaves in the District of Columbia, but he never did. He emphasized his position on slavery by supporting the Wilmot Proviso, which would have banned slavery in any territory acquired from Mexico (see WILMOT PROVISO).

Throughout his term, Lincoln supported the Whig policy of having the federal government pay for internal improvements. He made several speeches in support of this policy, and once reproved President Polk for vetoing a rivers and harbors appropriation bill. Lincoln worked for the nomination and election of Zachary Taylor, the Whig candidate for President in 1848.

Return to Law. Lincoln's term ended on March 4, 1849. He wanted another term, but knew he was too unpopular to win re-election. He tried unsuccessfully to get an appointment as Commissioner of the General Land Office. The administration offered to appoint him secretary, then governor, of Oregon Territory. Lincoln refused both offers.

Lincoln returned to Springfield, believing his political career had ended. He practiced law more earnestly than ever before. He continued to travel the circuit, but appeared more often in the higher courts. He also handled more important cases. Corporations and big businesses were becoming increasingly important in Illinois and neighboring states. Lincoln represented them frequently in lawsuits, and soon prospered. The largest fee he ever received, $5,000, was for his successful defense of the Illinois Central Railroad in an important tax case. After 1849, Lincoln's reputation grew steadily. In the 1850's, he was known as one of the leading lawyers of Illinois.

Re-Entry into Politics. A sudden change in national policy toward slavery brought Lincoln back into politics. The Missouri Compromise of 1820 had prohibited slavery in new territories north of an east-west line that was an extension of Missouri's southern boundary (see MISSOURI COMPROMISE). Early in 1854, Senator Stephen A. Douglas of Illinois introduced a bill to organize the territories of Kansas and Nebraska. As approved by Congress, this Kansas-Nebraska Act repealed the Missouri Compromise. It provided that the settlers of new territories should decide for themselves whether they wanted slavery. See KANSAS-NEBRASKA ACT.

Lincoln and many others had believed that slavery had been permanently limited. The new policy outraged them. The Founding Fathers had written a promise of freedom and equality into the Declaration of Independence. Lincoln believed they had intended to keep slavery from spreading so it would one day die.

Lincoln revered the Founding Fathers. He once said: "I have never had a thought politically which did not spring from the sentiments embodied in the Declaration of Independence." Henry Clay had been his political idol during his years as a Whig politician, but he looked to Thomas Jefferson for his political principles.

Lincoln always opposed slavery, but he never became an abolitionist. He believed that the bonds holding the nation together would be strained if Americans made a rapid break with the past. Lincoln granted that slavery should have the protection that the Constitution gave it. But he wanted the people to realize that slavery was evil, and should not spread.

Douglas refused to admit that slavery was wrong. He said he did not care whether slavery was morally right or wrong. Lincoln believed that the nation stood for freedom and equality. He felt it must not be indifferent to the unjust treatment of any person. To ignore moral values, he said, "deprives our republican example of its just influence in the world." It enabled the enemies of free institutions "to taunt us as hypocrites." Lincoln resolved to return to politics and do what he could to reverse the Kansas-Nebraska Act.

A Turning Point in Lincoln's life came with his return to politics. He had always been honest, able, and ambitious. But he had worked mainly in the interest of his party and for personal advancement. After passage of the Kansas-Nebraska Act, Lincoln's aims became broader. He worked to make the nation's ideals come true. His ambitions remained, but he directed them to a higher purpose. He had always been a clever and forceful speaker. Now, a new sincerity and deep conviction lent even greater power to his words.

Lincoln entered the congressional election campaign of 1854 to help a candidate who opposed the Kansas-Nebraska Act. But when Senator Douglas returned to Illinois to justify the new law, Lincoln opposed him wherever he could. At Springfield, Peoria, and Chicago, Lincoln delivered such powerful speeches that he became known as the leader of the Illinois forces opposing the Kansas-Nebraska Act. He was again elected to the Illinois legislature, but resigned in order to run for the United States Senate.

At that time, the legislature elected Senators. On the first ballot, Lincoln received 45 votes, which was 5 short of a majority. On each succeeding ballot, his vote dwindled. Finally, to keep a Douglas supporter from being elected, Lincoln persuaded his followers to vote for Lyman Trumbull, who had started with only 5 votes. Trumbull was elected.

The Whig party began falling apart during the 1850's because party members in various parts of the country could not agree on a solution to the slavery problem. In 1856, Lincoln joined the antislavery Republican party, then only two years old. During the presidential election campaign that year, he made more than a hundred speeches in behalf of John C. Frémont, the Republican candidate. Frémont lost the election to Democrat James Buchanan. But Lincoln had strengthened his own position in the party through his unselfish work.

The Debates with Douglas. In 1858, Lincoln was nominated to run against Douglas for the United States Senate. He accepted the honor with a speech that caused severe criticism. Many persons thought it stirred up conflict between the North and South. Lincoln said:

"A house divided against itself cannot stand. I believe this government cannot endure, permanently half *slave* and half *free*. I do not expect the Union to be *dissolved*—I do not expect the house to *fall*—but I *do* expect it will cease to be divided. It will become *all* one thing, or *all* the other. Either the *opponents* of slavery will arrest the further spread of it, and place it where the public mind shall rest in the belief that it is in the course of ultimate extinction; or its *advocates* will push it forward till it shall become alike lawful in *all* the States— *old* as well as *new*, *North* as well as *South*."

After a few speeches, Lincoln challenged Douglas to a series of debates. Douglas accepted, and named seven places for the meetings. The first debate was held at Ottawa, Ill., on Aug. 21, 1858. The last was at Alton, Ill., on October 15. Each candidate spoke for an hour and a half. Large crowds attended, except at Jonesboro, in the southernmost part of the state. Newspapers reported the debates, and the two men drew national attention.

The debates centered on the extension of slavery into free territory. Douglas defended the policy of the Kansas-Nebraska Act. He called this policy *popular sovereignty*. His opponents ridiculed it as *squatter sovereignty* (see POPULAR SOVEREIGNTY). Lincoln argued that the Supreme Court of the United States, in the Dred Scott decision, had opened the way for slavery to enter all the territories (see DRED SCOTT DECISION). In the debate held at Freeport, Ill., Douglas denied this argument. He contended that the people of any territory could keep slavery out of that territory simply by refusing to pass local laws protecting it. This position became known as the *Freeport Doctrine*. Lincoln emphasized the moral issue throughout the campaign. He insisted that there was a fundamental difference between Douglas and himself. Douglas ignored the moral question of slavery, but Lincoln regarded slavery "as a moral, social, and political evil."

In addition to the debates, both men spoke almost daily to meetings of their own. Each traveled far and wide. Before the exhausting campaign ended, Douglas' deep bass voice had become so husky that it was hard to understand him. Lincoln's high, penetrating voice still reached the limits of a large audience.

In the election, Lincoln candidates for the legislature received more votes than their opponents. But the state was divided into districts in such a way that Douglas men won a majority of the seats. As a result, Douglas was re-elected by a vote of 54 to 46.

The debates made Lincoln a national figure. Early in 1860, he delivered an address at Cooper Union in New York City. The speech ended with the famous plea: "Let us have faith that right makes might, and in that faith let us to the end dare to do our duty as we understand it." This address and others delivered later in New England made a strong impression on many influential eastern Republicans.

Election of 1860. The Republican national convention met in Chicago on May 16, 1860. Lincoln was by no means unknown to the delegates. The week before, at the Illinois state Republican convention, his supporters had nicknamed him "the Railsplitter." This nickname, recalling the days when Lincoln had split rails for fences, helped make him even better known to the delegates. But other party leaders had larger followings. Senator William H. Seward of New York had the strongest support, but he also had many enemies. Senator Salmon P. Chase of Ohio lacked the united support of even his own state. Lincoln had never held a prominent national office, and had no bitter enemies. He held moderate views on the slavery question. His humble

Diorama at the Chicago Historical Society

Lincoln-Douglas Debates were held in 1858 in seven Illinois cities. Lincoln was running against Stephen A. Douglas for the U.S. Senate. The two men debated the extension of slavery into free territory.

Painting by Herbert D. Stitt; Courtesy National Park Service

President-Elect Lincoln arrived in Washington, D.C., secretly. He had cut short a tour of Eastern cities because detective Alan Pinkerton, *left*, learned of an assassination plot.

for President. The Southern faction of the Democratic party chose Vice-President John C. Breckinridge. A fourth party, calling itself the Constitutional Union party, nominated former Senator John Bell of Tennessee.

Lincoln won election easily, receiving 180 electoral votes to 72 for Breckinridge, 39 for Bell, and 12 for Douglas. But more Americans voted against Lincoln than for him. The people gave him 1,865,593 votes, compared to a combined total of 2,823,975 for his opponents. All Lincoln's electoral votes, and nearly all his popular votes, came from the North.

Lincoln's Administration (1861-1865)

The South Secedes. Events moved swiftly in the South during the months before Lincoln's inauguration. Many Southern leaders had threatened to withdraw their states from the Union if Lincoln should win the election. On Dec. 20, 1860, South Carolina passed an Ordinance of Secession that declared the Union dissolved as far as that state was concerned. By the time Lincoln became President, six other Southern States had seceded. Four more followed later. The seceded states organized themselves into the Confederate States of America. See CONFEDERATE STATES OF AMERICA.

First Inauguration. Lincoln said farewell to his Springfield neighbors on Feb. 11, 1861. He parted with these words: "Here I have lived a quarter of a century, and have passed from a young to an old man. Here my children have been born, and one is buried. I now leave, not knowing when, or whether ever, I may return, with a task before me greater than that which rested upon Washington. Without the assistance of that Divine Being who ever attended him, I cannot succeed. With that assistance I cannot fail."

The long train trip to Washington, D.C., had been carefully planned to include stops at most large Eastern cities. This allowed many thousands of persons to see the man who would be their next President. In Philadelphia, Lincoln heard a report of an assassination plot. In Harrisburg, Pa., his advisers persuaded him to cut short his trip. Lincoln continued in secret to Washington, arriving early on the morning of February 23.

background could be counted on to arouse great enthusiasm among the voters.

On the first ballot, Seward received 173½ votes, Lincoln 102, and Chase 49. Lincoln gained the support of Pennsylvania and Indiana on the second ballot, and received 181 votes to 184½ for Seward. During the third ballot, Lincoln continued to gain strength. Before the result was announced, Ohio switched four votes from Chase to Lincoln. This gave Lincoln more than the 233 votes needed to win the nomination. The delegates nominated Senator Hannibal Hamlin of Maine for Vice-President.

Like other presidential candidates of his period, Lincoln felt it was undignified to campaign actively. He stayed quietly in Springfield during the election campaign. His followers more than made up for his inactivity. The Democratic party broke into two factions, which helped Lincoln immensely. Senator Douglas, the nation's leading Democrat, had angered the proslavery wing of his party. Northern Democrats nominated him

--------------- LINCOLN'S FIRST ELECTION ---------------

**Place of Nominating
    Convention**................Chicago

Ballot on Which Nominated...3rd

**Northern Democratic
    Opponent**................Stephen A. Douglas

**Southern Democratic
    Opponent**................John C. Breckinridge

**Constitutional Union
    Opponent**................John Bell

Electoral Vote...............180 (Lincoln) to:
                72 (Breckinridge)
                39 (Bell)
                12 (Douglas)

Popular Vote................1,865,593 (Lincoln) to:
                1,382,713 (Douglas)
                848,356 (Breckinridge)
                592,906 (Bell)

Age at Inauguration..........52

------- HIGHLIGHTS OF LINCOLN'S ADMINISTRATION -------

1861 (April 12) The Civil War began.
1861 (April 27) Lincoln proclaimed a blockade of Southern ports.
1861 (July 21) Confederate forces won the first Battle of Bull Run.
1862 (April 6-7) Union troops won the Battle of Shiloh.
1862 (April 16) Congress abolished slavery in the District of Columbia.
1862 (May 20) Congress approved the Homestead Act.
1862 (Sept. 17) Union forces won the Battle of Antietam.
1862 (Sept. 22) Lincoln issued a preliminary proclamation of emancipation.
1862 (Dec. 13) The Union suffered a terrible defeat at Fredericksburg.
1863 (Jan. 1) Lincoln issued the Emancipation Proclamation.
1863 (July 1-3) Union armies won the Battle of Gettysburg.
1863 (July 4) Vicksburg, Miss., fell to Union forces.
1863 (Nov. 19) Lincoln delivered the Gettysburg Address.
1864 (March 9) Grant took command of all Union armies.
1864 (Sept. 2) Sherman's army captured Atlanta, Ga.
1865 (April 9) The Civil War ended.

On March 4, 1861, Lincoln took the oath of office and became the 16th President of the United States. In his inaugural address, Lincoln denied that he had any intention of interfering with slavery in states where the Constitution protected it. He urged the preservation of the Union. Lincoln warned that he would use the full power of the nation to "hold, occupy, and possess" the "property and places" belonging to the federal government. By "property and places," he meant forts, arsenals, and customhouses. Lincoln's closing passage had great beauty and literary power. He appealed to "the mystic chords of memory, stretching from every battlefield and patriot grave to every living heart and hearthstone all over this broad land."

Lincoln announced his Cabinet the day after his inauguration. Two members, William H. Seward and Salmon P. Chase, had been his principal rivals for the presidential nomination. The Cabinet members represented many shades of opinion. Several of them administered their departments ably. But, as a group, they often gave Lincoln almost as much trouble as help.

Fort Sumter and War. As the Southern States seceded, they seized most of the federal forts within their boundaries. Lincoln had to decide whether the remaining forts should be strengthened. He also had to decide whether to try to retake the forts already in Southern hands.

Fort Sumter, in Charleston Harbor, became a symbol of an indivisible Union. Major Robert Anderson commanded the Union garrison there. If Lincoln withdrew the troops, a storm of protest would rise in the North. If he reinforced Fort Sumter, the South would consider it an act of war.

As a compromise, Lincoln decided to send only provisions to Anderson, whose supplies were running low. He informed South Carolina of his intention. Leaders of the state regarded the relief expedition as a hostile act, and demanded Anderson's surrender. Anderson refused, and on April 12, General Pierre G. T. Beauregard ordered Confederate artillery to fire on the fort. Anderson surrendered the next day. The Civil War began with the bombardment of Fort Sumter. See CIVIL WAR.

Lincoln met the crisis with energetic action. He called out the militia to suppress the "insurrection." He proclaimed a blockade of Southern ports, and expanded the army beyond the limit set by law. Southern sympathizers living in the North were obstructing the war effort. As a result, Lincoln gave the army the right to suspend the privilege of *habeas corpus* in areas where these Southern sympathizers were active (see HABEAS

VICE-PRESIDENTS AND CABINET

Vice-President	*Hannibal Hamlin
	*Andrew Johnson (1865)
Secretary of State	*William H. Seward
Secretary of the Treasury	*Salmon P. Chase
	*William P. Fessenden (1864)
	Hugh McCulloch (1865)
Secretary of War	Simon Cameron
	*Edwin M. Stanton (1862)
Attorney General	Edward Bates
	James Speed (1864)
Postmaster General	*Montgomery Blair
	William Dennison (1864)
Secretary of the Navy	*Gideon Welles
Secretary of the Interior	Caleb B. Smith
	John P. Usher (1863)

*Has a separate biography in WORLD BOOK

280

THE WORLD OF

★ ★ ★ ★ ★ ★ ★

UNITED STATES EVENTS

U.S. population was 32,351,000 in 1861. Eleven Southern States, with over 9,000,000 persons, seceded from the Union. West Virginia became a state in 1863, and Nevada in 1864. Congress created the Arizona and Idaho territories in 1863, and the Montana Territory in 1864.

The United States Flag had 33 stars and 13 stripes when Lincoln became President.

PRESIDENT LINCOLN

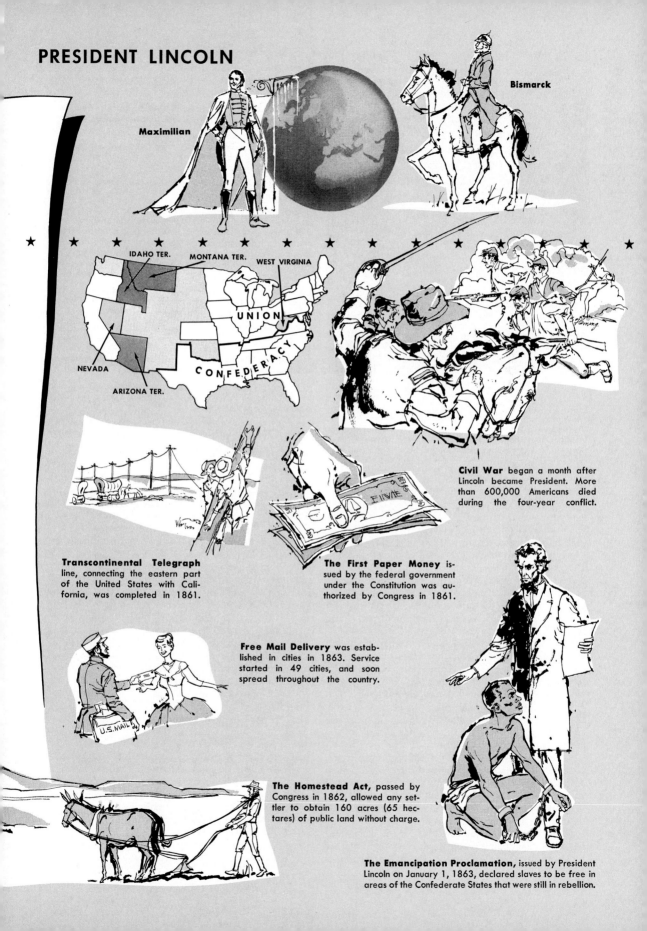

Maximilian

Bismarck

IDAHO TER. MONTANA TER. WEST VIRGINIA

UNION

NEVADA

ARIZONA TER.

CONFEDERACY

Civil War began a month after Lincoln became President. More than 600,000 Americans died during the four-year conflict.

Transcontinental Telegraph line, connecting the eastern part of the United States with California, was completed in 1861.

The First Paper Money issued by the federal government under the Constitution was authorized by Congress in 1861.

Free Mail Delivery was established in cities in 1863. Service started in 49 cities, and soon spread throughout the country.

U.S. MAIL

The Homestead Act, passed by Congress in 1862, allowed any settler to obtain 160 acres (65 hectares) of public land without charge.

The Emancipation Proclamation, issued by President Lincoln on January 1, 1863, declared slaves to be free in areas of the Confederate States that were still in rebellion.

America's Independent Electric Light and Power Companies

Statues of Lincoln stand in cities and towns throughout America. Sculptor Gutzon Borglum designed this striking monument, which stands in front of the county courthouse in Newark, N.J.

Some Famous Lincoln Quotations

Many of Lincoln's most famous quotations are included in the text of this article. Following are several additional quotations from speeches and letters.

Stand with anybody that stands right. Stand with him while he is right and part with him when he goes wrong.

The legitimate object of government, is to do for a community of people, whatever they need to have done, but cannot do, at all, or cannot so well do, for themselves—in their separate and individual capacities.

Nothing new here, except my marrying, which to me, is matter of profound wonder.

Property is the fruit of labor—property is desirable—is a positive good in the world. That some should be rich, shows that others may become rich, and hence is just encouragement to industry and enterprize. Let not him who is houseless pull down the house of another; but let him labor diligently and build one for himself, thus by example assuring that his own shall be safe from violence when built.

As I would not be a *slave*, so I would not be a *master*. This expresses my idea of democracy. Whatever differs from this, to the extent of the difference, is no democracy.

Fellow-citizens, we cannot escape history. We . . . will be remembered in spite of ourselves. No personal significance, or insignificance, can spare one or another of us. The fiery trial through which we pass, will light us down, in honor or dishonor, to the latest generation.

If we do not make common cause to save the good old ship of the Union on this voyage, nobody will have a chance to pilot her on another voyage.

The dogmas of the quiet past, are inadequate to the stormy present. The occasion is piled high with difficulty, and we must rise with the occasion. As our case is new, so we must think anew, and act anew.

CORPUS). He also ordered the spending of federal funds without waiting for congressional appropriations.

Lincoln believed all these actions to be within the war powers granted the President by the Constitution. He justified his acts when Congress met for the first time in his administration in July, 1861. The message Lincoln delivered to Congress ranks as one of his greatest state papers. Chief Justice Roger B. Taney had attacked Lincoln bitterly for suspending habeas corpus. In his message, Lincoln posed a question that no critic then or afterward ever answered: "Are all the laws *but one* to go unexecuted, and the government itself go to pieces lest that one be violated?"

Lincoln felt that the breakup of the American nation would be a tragedy. Not only Americans, but ultimately all mankind, would suffer. To him, the United States represented an experiment in the people's ability to govern themselves. If it failed, kings, dictators, and their supporters could say that people were not capable of ruling themselves, and that someone must rule them. Lincoln regarded the fate of world democracy as the central issue of the Civil War.

Building the Army. Two days after Fort Sumter fell, Lincoln called for 75,000 men for the army. The North offered far more volunteers than the government could equip. By July, 1861, an army had been assembled near Washington. An equal force of Confederates had taken position across the Potomac River in Virginia.

Many Northerners clamored for action. They believed the Union forces could end the war by defeating the Confederates in one battle. Newspaper headlines blazed with the cry "On to Richmond!" The administration yielded to these pressures. Lincoln ordered the Northern army forward under General Irvin McDowell. The result was the first Battle of Bull Run on July 21, in which Confederate forces decisively defeated the Union troops. People in the North now realized that the war would be a long one.

As commander in chief of the army, Lincoln had to select an officer capable of organizing green volunteers into armies and leading them to victory. General George B. McClellan turned out to be a fine organizer. But his Peninsular Campaign of 1862 ended in failure. This campaign had been aimed at capturing Richmond, Va., the Confederate capital. Lincoln relieved McClellan of much of his command. General John Pope was made commander of troops in Virginia. He was defeated in the second Battle of Bull Run, on August 29-30, 1862, and Lincoln called on McClellan to defend Washington. On September 17, "Little Mac" turned back the army of General Robert E. Lee in the Battle of Antietam. Then McClellan refused to move. In early November, Lincoln removed him for the second time, and put General Ambrose E. Burnside in command. Burnside met defeat in the Battle of Fredericksburg on December 13. His successor, General Joseph Hooker, lost the Battle of Chancellorsville on May 1-4, 1863.

Union forces made progress only in the valley of the Mississippi River. There, General Ulysses S. Grant was making a habit of victory. In 1862, Grant's troops won three battles: Fort Henry on February 6, Fort Donelson on February 16, and Shiloh on April 6-7.

REMINDERS OF ABRAHAM LINCOLN

Lincoln the "Railsplitter." He got this nickname in the campaign of 1860. Many paintings, such as this one by an unknown artist, showed him splitting fence rails.

Mementos of Lincoln's Assassination may be seen at Ford's Theatre in Washington, D.C. They are mounted on the door through which John Wilkes Booth entered the presidential box. The items include Mrs. Lincoln's opera-glass case, a playbill, the pistol that fired the fatal shot, a boot worn by Booth, and a poster offering a reward for the capture of the assassin.

Chicago Historical Society

By Arnold Newman. Reprinted by special permission from *Holiday*. © 1954 Curtis Publishing Co.

Wide World

Carl Sandburg, *left*, and many other outstanding historians and writers have honored Lincoln in their works.

Lincoln's Tomb stands in the Oak Ridge Cemetery at Springfield, Ill. Thousands of persons visit the tomb each year.

Herbert Georg Studio

Lincoln at Ford's Theatre. This diorama shows Lincoln in his box watching a play just before his assassination. John Wilkes Booth entered the box through the door behind Lincoln, *left*.

Diorama at the Chicago Historical Society

Strengthening the Home Front. Organization for military success was only one of Lincoln's tasks. Equally important, he had to arouse popular support for the Union armies. Different opinions among the people became plain after their first enthusiasm wore off. Many Northerners were willing to fight to preserve the Union, but not to destroy slavery. Other Northerners demanded that the destruction of slavery should be put above all other goals.

Lincoln realized that the border states would secede if the antislavery extremists had their way. This would mean the loss of Kentucky, Missouri, Delaware, and Maryland. The task of defeating the South would be much more difficult without the support of these states. Besides, the Constitution protected slavery in the states where it existed. Impulsive generals sometimes issued proclamations freeing slaves, but Lincoln overruled them. Time after time, he declared that the purpose of the war was to preserve the Union. His most famous statement was made in a letter to Horace Greeley, editor of the *New York Tribune*. In the letter, dated Aug. 22, 1862, Lincoln said: "My paramount object in this struggle is to save the Union, and is not either to save or to destroy slavery." By taking a moderate position, Lincoln kept all the border states in the Union.

Foreign Relations. While meeting his other challenges, Lincoln managed to keep a check on foreign policy. In 1861, Secretary of State Seward suggested that the United States could be unified by provoking several European nations to war. The President quietly ignored this proposal.

In November, 1861, Captain Charles Wilkes of the U.S. Navy stopped the British ship *Trent* and removed two Confederate commissioners, James M. Mason and John Slidell. The British angrily demanded the release of the two men, and prepared for war to support their demand. The United States formally apologized, and freed Mason and Slidell. By doing so, Lincoln avoided a war that would have been disastrous to the United States. See TRENT AFFAIR.

Life in the White House. To Lincoln, the presidency meant fulfillment of the highest ambition that an American citizen could have. The Civil War destroyed any hope he may have had for happiness in the White House. Aside from directing military affairs and stiffening the will of the North, he carried an enormous burden of administrative routine. His office staff was small. He wrote most of his own letters and all his speeches. He made decisions on thousands of political and military appointments. For hours each day, he saw everyone who chose to call. During all his years in office, Lincoln was away from the capital less than a month.

Lincoln found some relaxation in taking carriage drives, and he enjoyed the theater. He regarded White House receptions and dinners more as duties than as pleasures. Lincoln's frequent visits to army hospitals tore his gentle heart. Late at night, he sometimes found solace by reading Shakespeare or the Bible. But his official duties left little time for diversion.

To Mrs. Lincoln, life in the White House was a tragic disappointment. Her youngest brother, three half brothers, and the husbands of two half sisters were serving in the Confederate army, and she faced constant suspicion of disloyalty. The pressures of everyday life weighed heavily on her high-strung nature. Jealousy and outbursts of temper cost her many friendships.

Two of Lincoln's sons, William Wallace and Thomas, lived in the White House. For nearly a year, "Willie" and "Tad" enlivened the mansion with their laughter and pranks. Willie's death on Feb. 20, 1862, grieved the President deeply. Mrs. Lincoln could not be consoled. Robert Lincoln had been a student at Harvard when his father was elected. He remained in school until February, 1865, when he was appointed to General Grant's staff as a captain.

The Emancipation Proclamation. By late summer of 1862, Lincoln was convinced that the time had come for a change in policy toward slavery. Several foreign governments sympathized with the South. But they condemned slavery as evil, and thus did not dare support the Confederacy. Freed slaves could serve as Union soldiers. Besides, many Northerners who had been indifferent to slavery now believed that it had to be stamped out. Lincoln decided to issue a proclamation freeing the slaves. He did not ask the advice of his Cabinet, but he did tell the members what he intended to do. On Seward's advice, he withheld the proclamation until a Northern victory created favorable circumstances.

The Battle of Antietam, fought on Sept. 17, 1862, served Lincoln's purpose. He issued a preliminary proclamation five days later. Lincoln declared that all slaves in states, or parts of states, that were in rebellion on Jan. 1, 1863, would be free. He issued the final proclamation on January 1. Lincoln named the states and parts of states in rebellion, and declared that the slaves held there "are, and hence-forward shall be, free." See EMANCIPATION PROCLAMATION.

Actually, the proclamation freed no slaves. It applied only to Confederate territory, where federal officers could not enforce it. The proclamation did not affect slavery in the loyal border states. Lincoln repeatedly urged those states to free their slaves, and to pay the owners for their loss. He promised financial help from the federal government for this purpose. The failure of the states to follow his advice was one of his great disappointments.

The Emancipation Proclamation did have a great long-range effect. In the eyes of other nations, it gave a new character to the war. In the North, it paved the way for Amendment 13 to the Constitution. This amendment, adopted in December, 1865, ended slavery in all parts of the United States.

The Gettysburg Address. Union armies won two great victories in 1863. General George G. Meade's Union forces defeated the Confederates under Lee at Gettysburg, Pa., during the first three days of July. On July 4, Vicksburg, Miss., fell to Grant's troops. This city had been the last Confederate stronghold on the Mississippi River. "The Father of Waters again goes unvexed to the sea," Lincoln declared.

On Nov. 19, 1863, ceremonies were held to dedicate a cemetery on the Gettysburg battlefield. The principal speaker was Edward Everett, one of the greatest orators of his day. Everett spoke for two hours. Lincoln was asked to say a few words, and spoke for three minutes.

Many writers have said that Lincoln scribbled his speech while traveling on the train to Gettysburg. This is not true. He prepared the address carefully, well in advance of the ceremonies. Everett and many others knew at once that Lincoln's ringing declaration that "government of the people, by the people, for the people, shall not perish from the earth" would live as long as democracy itself. For the complete text of the speech, see GETTYSBURG ADDRESS.

The victories at Gettysburg and Vicksburg seemed to promise an early peace. But the war went on. In March, 1864, Lincoln put Grant in command of all the Union armies. The Army of the Potomac started to march toward Richmond two months later. At the same time, General William T. Sherman began his famous march from Tennessee to Atlanta, and then to the sea.

Election of 1864. Grant met skillful resistance in the South, and suffered thousands of casualties. Many people called him "the butcher," and condemned Lincoln for supporting the cigar-smoking commander. In 1864, Republicans and War Democrats—Democrats who supported Lincoln's military policies—formed the National Union Party. In June that year, the party nominated Lincoln for President. It selected former Senator Andrew Johnson of Tennessee, a leading War Democrat, for Vice President. The Democrats chose General George B. McClellan as their candidate for President, and Representative George H. Pendleton of Ohio for Vice President. A group called Radical Republicans persuaded General John C. Frémont to run for President, but he withdrew a month before the election.

Lincoln became less and less popular as the summer wore on. Late in August, he confessed privately that "it seems exceedingly probable that this administration will not be re-elected." Then the military trend changed. Rear Admiral David G. Farragut had won the Battle of Mobile Bay on August 5, and Sherman's hard-marching troops captured Atlanta on September 2. A series of Union victories cleared Confederate forces from the Shenandoah Valley of Virginia. Many discouraged Northerners took heart again.

The Union victories helped Lincoln win re-election. He defeated McClellan by an electoral vote of 212 to 21, and a popular majority of more than 400,000 votes.

Second Inauguration. The end of the war was clearly in sight when Lincoln took the oath of office a second time, on March 4, 1865. Grant had besieged Lee's weary troops at Petersburg, Va. The Southern armies were wasting away in Grant's bulldog grip. Sherman left a wide track of destruction as he marched through Georgia and the Carolinas.

For the first time, Lincoln could think of reuniting the nation. He never spoke words more truly characteristic, nor more beautiful, than in his second inaugural address. Instead of demanding vengeance on the South, he asked for "malice toward none" and "charity for all." He implored the people "to bind up the nation's wounds; to care for him who shall have borne the battle, and for his widow, and his orphan—to do all which may achieve and cherish a just and lasting peace . . . ."

Photographs taken of Lincoln shortly after his second inauguration show the effect of four years of war. His face had become gaunt and deeply lined. He slept little during crises in the fighting, and his eyes were ringed with black. Lincoln ate his meals irregularly, and had almost no relaxation.

In spite of his exhaustion, Lincoln continued to see widows and soldiers who called at the White House.

His delight in rough humor never deserted him. More than once, he shocked members of his Cabinet by reading to them from such humorists as Artemus Ward and Orpheus C. Kerr. Even so, the strain of melancholy that had appeared in him as a young man deepened.

As a youth, Lincoln's biting wit had once brought him a challenge to a duel from a man he had offended. After that, he made it a point not to hurt other people's feelings. Near the close of the war, he said: "So long as I have been here I have not willingly planted a thorn in any man's bosom."

Lincoln came to have a quiet confidence in his own judgment as he met the trials of war. Yet he had no false pride. He was a man of genuine humility. The war brought out his best qualities. He could rise to each new challenge. He was a master politician, and timed his actions to the people's moods. He led men by persuasion. Horace Greeley said: "He slowly won his way to eminence and fame by doing the work that lay next to him —doing it with all his growing might—doing it as well as he could, and learning by his failure, when failure was encountered, how to do it better."

End of the War. On April 9, 1865, Lee surrendered to Grant at Appomattox Court House in Virginia. Under authority from Lincoln, Grant extended generous terms to Lee and his army. A great wave of joy swept the North when the fighting ended.

Lincoln spoke soberly of the future to a crowd that serenaded him on the night of April 11. Louisiana had applied for readmission to the Union under Lincoln's plan of reconstruction. Many Northerners wanted to impose harsher terms. Some complained that Negroes would not receive the right to vote under Louisiana's new government. "I would myself prefer," said Lincoln, "that it [the vote] were now conferred on the very intelligent, and on those who serve our cause as soldiers."

Many persons insisted that Lincoln decide if "the seceded states, so called, are in the Union or out of it." No matter, said the President in his last public address on April 11, 1865, "finding themselves safely at home, it would be utterly immaterial whether they had ever been abroad." Lincoln admitted that the new government of Louisiana was imperfect. But, he asked, "Will it be wiser to take it as it is and help improve it, or to reject and disperse it?"

Assassination. On the evening of April 14, 1865, Lincoln attended a performance of *Our American Cousin* at Ford's Theatre in Washington. A few minutes after 10 o'clock, a shot rang through the crowded house. John Wilkes Booth, one of the best-known actors of the day, had shot the President in the head from the rear of the presidential box. In leaping to the stage, Booth caught his spur in a flag draped in front of the box. He

Lincoln's Second Election

Place of Nominating Convention	. .Baltimore
Ballot on Which Nominated	. . . . . . .1st
Democratic Opponent	. . . . .George B. McClellan
Electoral Vote	. . . . .212 (Lincoln) to 21 (McClellan)
Popular Vote	. . . . .2,206,938 (Lincoln) to 1,803,787 (McClellan)
Age at Inauguration	56

Library of Congress

Lincoln's Family. From left to right are Mrs. Mary Todd Lincoln and the Lincoln sons—William Wallace (Willie), Robert Todd, and Thomas (Tad).

fell and broke his leg. But he limped across the stage brandishing a dagger and crying: "Sic semper tyrannis" (Thus always to tyrants), the motto of Virginia.

Lincoln was carried unconscious to a neighboring house. His family and high government officials surrounded him. He died at 7:22 A.M. on April 15.

As President, Lincoln had been bitterly criticized. After his death, even his enemies praised his kindly spirit and selflessness. Millions of people had called him "Father Abraham." They grieved as they would have grieved at the loss of a father. The train carrying Lincoln's body started west from Washington. Mourners lined the tracks as it moved across the country. Thousands wept as they looked upon his face for the last time. On May 4, Lincoln was buried in Oak Ridge Cemetery in Springfield, Ill. The monument on his grave is a place of universal pilgrimage.

The Trial of the Conspirators. After shooting Lincoln, Booth fled to Maryland on horseback. A friend, David E. Herold, a former druggist's clerk, joined Booth there and helped him escape to Virginia. On April 26, 1865, federal troops searching for Booth trapped the two men in a barn near Port Royal, Va. Herold surrendered, but Booth was killed.

Several persons were believed to have been involved with Booth in both Lincoln's assassination and a plot to kill other government officials. Secretary of War Edwin M. Stanton ordered agents of his department to arrest them. Besides Herold, the accused conspirators included George Atzerodt, a carriage maker, for planning the murder of Vice President Andrew Johnson; Lewis Paine, a former Confederate soldier, for attempting to kill Secretary of State William H. Seward; and Mrs. Mary E. Surratt, the owner of a Washington boarding house, for helping the plotters. Booth and the others supposedly planned the crimes in Mrs. Surratt's house.

The Department of War also accused Samuel Arnold and Michael O'Laughlin, boyhood friends of Booth's,

of helping him plan the crimes. Samuel A. Mudd, a Maryland physician who had set Booth's broken leg after the assassination of Lincoln, was charged with aiding the plotters. Edward Spangler, a stagehand at Ford's Theatre, was charged with helping Booth escape.

A nine-man military commission tried the accused conspirators in Washington. The trial began on May 10, 1865, and lasted until June 30. The commission convicted all eight defendants and sentenced Atzerodt, Herold, Paine, and Mrs. Surratt to death. They were hanged on July 7. Arnold, Mudd, and O'Laughlin received sentences of life imprisonment, and Spangler received a six-year sentence. O'Laughlin died in prison of yellow fever in 1867. President Johnson pardoned Arnold, Mudd, and Spangler in 1869.   PAUL M. ANGLE

Related Articles in WORLD BOOK include:

Outline

Questions

How did Lincoln become involved in the debates with Douglas? How did the debates affect Lincoln's career? When did Lincoln first express himself on slavery?

Lincoln's Home in Springfield, Ill., is a national historic site. Lincoln bought this plain white frame house in 1844. He and his family lived there until he became President in 1861.

What was Lincoln's first political office?

How did Lincoln study for the bar?

What did Lincoln consider to be the main issue of the Civil War?

How did Lincoln get his early education?

What did Lincoln's second inaugural address show about his intentions toward the South?

What was "circuit riding"? Why did Lincoln enjoy it?

Why did repeal of the Missouri Compromise cause Lincoln to go back into politics?

Why did Lincoln at first deny that the Civil War centered on the issue of slavery? Why did he later change his stand?

Reading and Study Guide

See *Lincoln, Abraham*, in the RESEARCH GUIDE/INDEX, Volume 22, for a *Reading and Study Guide*.

Additional Resources

ANGLE, PAUL M., ed. *The Lincoln Reader*. Greenwood, 1981. Reprint of 1947 ed.

COOLIDGE, OLIVIA E. *The Apprenticeship of Abraham Lincoln*. Scribner, 1974. *The Statesmanship of Abraham Lincoln*. 1976. For younger readers.

CURRENT, RICHARD N. *The Lincoln Nobody Knows*. Greenwood, 1980. Reprint of 1958 ed.

FEHRENBACHER, DON E. *Prelude to Greatness: Lincoln in the 1850's*. Stanford, 1962. *The Leadership of Abraham Lincoln*. Wiley, 1970.

HANDLIN, OSCAR and LILIAN. *Abraham Lincoln and the Union*. Little, Brown, 1980.

NEELY, MARK E., JR. *The Abraham Lincoln Encyclopedia*. McGraw, 1981.

OATES, STEPHEN B. *With Malice Toward None: The Life of Abraham Lincoln*. Harper, 1977.

LINCOLN, MARY TODD (1818-1882), the wife of President Abraham Lincoln, was the daughter of Robert S. Todd, a banker of Lexington, Ky., and his wife Eliza Parker Todd. She was born on Dec. 13, 1818, and went to school in Lexington. In 1839, at the age of 21, she moved to Springfield, Ill., to live with a married sister. There she met Abraham Lincoln, a young lawyer. They were married on Nov. 4, 1842.

Mrs. Lincoln achieved her greatest ambition when her husband was elected President. But her four years as First Lady brought sorrow rather than happiness. Many persons unjustly suspected her of disloyalty to the Union because she came from the South. In addition, Mrs. Lincoln's haughty manner made her unpopular among the wives of government officials. The death of the

Lincolns' third son, William Wallace, in 1862 caused her deep grief. In 1865, the shock of the assassination of Lincoln left her a mental and physical wreck.

Years of travel failed to restore Mrs. Lincoln's health, which was further weakened in 1871 by the death of another son, Thomas. Her mental depression deepened until her oldest son, Robert, committed her to a private sanitarium in 1875. She was released the next year. Mrs. Lincoln died on July 16, 1882, in the Springfield home of her sister. She was buried in the Lincoln Tomb in Springfield.   PAUL M. ANGLE

See also LINCOLN, ABRAHAM (Lincoln's Family; Life in the White House; picture).

LINCOLN, NANCY HANKS. See LINCOLN, ABRAHAM (Early Life).

LINCOLN, ROBERT TODD (1843-1926), the oldest son of President Abraham Lincoln, became a well-known statesman and lawyer. In 1881, President James A. Garfield named him secretary of war. Lincoln held the same post under President Chester A. Arthur. From 1889 to 1893, he served as minister to Great Britain. He then became associated with the Pullman Company, and served as president of the firm from 1897 to 1911.

Robert T. Lincoln

Lincoln was born in Springfield, Ill., and studied at Harvard College and Harvard Law School. He served in the Union Army. After the Civil War, he practiced law.   RICHARD N. CURRENT

LINCOLN CENTER FOR THE PERFORMING ARTS is the home for some of New York City's most important cultural activities. The center's six buildings house the Metropolitan Opera, the New York Philharmonic, the Juilliard School, the New York City Ballet, the New York City Opera, the Film Society of Lincoln Center, the Chamber Music Society of Lincoln Center, and the New York Public Library at Lincoln Center. Avery Fisher Hall (formerly Philharmonic Hall) opened in 1962, the New York State Theater in 1964, the Library and Museum and Vivian Beaumont Theater in 1965, and the Metropolitan Opera House in 1966. The Juilliard School opened in 1969. Each of the center's constituent members is financially and artistically independent. Each is represented on the Lincoln Center Council.   Critically reviewed by the LINCOLN CENTER BOARD

See also NEW YORK CITY (Cultural Life and Recreation; picture).

LINCOLN HIGHWAY stretches 3,385 miles (5,448 kilometers) from New York City to San Francisco. It is sometimes called the *Main Street of the United States*. In 1912, Carl G. Fisher had the idea of a transcontinental highway to encourage better roads. The automotive industry raised money for it. President William Howard Taft felt the highway would help national unity. Fisher decided "Lincoln" would be a patriotic name for it. Construction began in 1914. The road is known as U.S. 30 for most of its length.   ARCHIBALD BLACK

IN THIS TEMPLE
AS IN THE HEARTS OF THE PEOPLE
FOR WHOM HE SAVED THE UNION
THE MEMORY OF ABRAHAM LINCOLN
IS ENSHRINED FOREVER

LINCOLN MEMORIAL is a beautiful monument in Washington, D.C., that honors Abraham Lincoln. It stands at the end of the Mall and ranks as one of the most handsome memorials of the 1900's.

The massive marble building is 189 feet (58 meters) long and 118⅔ feet (36.2 meters) wide. It has a great hall surrounded by 36 Doric columns, which stand for the 36 states in the Union at the time of Lincoln's death. The outside decorations show the names of the 48 states that existed when the building was dedicated, and the 36 states existing when Lincoln died. The hall has three sections. In the center section, which is open in front, sits a gigantic statue of Lincoln by Daniel Chester French. The side sections have tablets with the Gettysburg Address and the Second Inaugural Address, and two wall paintings by Jules Guerin. The paintings are titled *Emancipation* and *Reunion*.

The building stands on a high terrace that is reached by an imposing flight of steps. In front lies a long pool. The Potomac River can be seen from one side of the building. The other side presents a magnificent view up the Mall to the Washington Monument.

A national Lincoln memorial had been urged since 1867, but not until 1911 did Congress pass the law creating a Lincoln Memorial Commission. This commission chose the design by Henry Bacon and the site for the building. The cornerstone was laid on Feb. 12, 1915. The building was dedicated on May 30, 1922. Chief Justice William Howard Taft, as chairman of the commission, presented the memorial to President Warren G. Harding, who accepted it for the United States. Some criticized the design of the building. But it has been accepted as an expression of American ideals, and has inspired millions of visitors to Washington, D.C.

Critically reviewed by NATIONAL CAPITAL
REGION, NATIONAL PARK SERVICE

See also WASHINGTON, D.C. (color picture).

A Majestic Statue of Lincoln, *left,* dominates the interior of the Lincoln Memorial, *below,* in Washington, D.C. More than 2,500,000 persons visit the gleaming white memorial every year.
Louis C. Williams

The Lincoln Tunnel runs under the Hudson River and connects midtown New York City with Weehawken, N.J. At the lowest point, it dips 97 feet (30 meters) below the river's surface. The photograph above shows the New Jersey side of the tunnel.

LINCOLN PARK, Mich. (pop. 45,105), is a residential city in the southwestern part of the Detroit metropolitan area (see MICHIGAN [political map]). Most of its workers are employed in nearby auto and steel factories. The area is noted as the place where Chief Pontiac assembled his braves for the attack on Detroit in 1763. Incorporated in 1925, Lincoln Park has a mayor-council government.   WILLIS F. DUNBAR

LINCOLN TUNNEL is a tunnel for motor traffic under the Hudson River. It joins midtown New York City with Weehawken, N.J. The tunnel has three tubes, each with two traffic lanes. The 8,216-foot (2,504-meter) center tube, opened in 1937, carries vehicles in either or both directions, depending on traffic needs. Westbound vehicles travel in the 7,482-foot (2,281-meter) north tube, opened in 1945. The 8,006-foot (2,440-meter) south tube is for eastbound traffic. The completion of this tube in 1957 brought the total cost of the Lincoln Tunnel to about $190 million. About $30\frac{1}{2}$ million vehicles use the tunnel every year. See also HUDSON RIVER TUNNELS (The Lincoln Tunnel).

LINCOLN UNIVERSITY was the first institution in the United States chartered to provide higher education for blacks. It is in Lincoln University, Pa., about 45 miles (72 kilometers) southwest of Philadelphia. The school opened in 1854 as the Ashmun Institute. It was renamed Lincoln University in 1866 and has admitted students of all races since then.

Lincoln is coeducational and part of the state system of higher education. The university has divisions of humanities, natural sciences and mathematics, and social science. It grants bachelor's and master's degrees. For the university's enrollment, see UNIVERSITIES AND COLLEGES (table).   Critically reviewed by LINCOLN UNIVERSITY

LINCOLN'S BIRTHDAY is a legal holiday in about 30 states of the United States. It honors Abraham Lincoln, the 16th President, who was born on Feb. 12,

1809. Most of the states that celebrate Lincoln's birthday do so on February 12, but a few celebrate it on the first or third Monday of February.

The first observance of his birthday anniversary occurred in 1866, the year following his assassination. At that time, the President, his Cabinet, members of Congress, and representatives of the armed forces and the diplomatic corps met in his honor.

The Republican Club of New York City has held a dinner on February 12 each year since 1887. The corner-

Lincoln University's Campus, *above,* is in Lincoln University, Pa. The school, which opened in 1854, was the first institution in the United States to provide higher education for blacks.

stone of the Lincoln Memorial in Washington, D.C., was laid on Feb. 12, 1915. Congress established a Lincoln Sesquicentennial Commission that coordinated activities for the nationwide celebration of Lincoln's 150th birthday anniversary in 1959.   RAYMOND HOYT JAHN

See also LINCOLN, ABRAHAM.

LIND, JAMES. See NUTRITION (History).

LIND, JENNY (1820-1887), a Swedish soprano, became one of the most famous singers of the 1800's. She had a brilliant career in opera and on the concert stage. Her rich and warm coloratura voice and her remarkable vocal control were unique, and won for her the title the *Swedish Nightingale* from an adoring public.

Lind was born in Stockholm. She made her debut in 1838 as Agathe in *Der Freischütz*. Three years later she went to Paris to study, and then traveled to Dresden, Germany, to perfect her knowledge of the German language.

After 1849, Lind gave up her career as an opera singer. From 1850 to 1852, she toured the United States, part of the time under the management of showman P. T. Barnum (see BARNUM, P. T.).   SCOTT GOLDTHWAITE

LINDBERGH, ANNE MORROW (1906-   ), is an American poet and essayist. Her husband was the famous American aviator Charles A. Lindbergh. Their courtship in the late 1920's gained international attention. In the 1930's, the sensational press coverage of the kidnapping and murder of the couple's infant son resulted in their moving to Europe.

Anne Morrow Lindbergh is perhaps best known for two books. One is *Gift from the Sea* (1955), a collection of eight essays about the meaning of a woman's life. The other is *The Unicorn and Other Poems, 1935-1955* (1956). Some critics attacked this work as sentimental, but others defended it as sensitive and deeply felt.

Lindbergh was born in Englewood, N.J. Her father, Dwight W. Morrow, was a famous American diplomat. She became a licensed pilot and made many long flights with her husband. These trips furnished material for two of her books, *North to the Orient* (1935) and *Listen! The Wind* (1938). Lindbergh's other writings include *Dearly Beloved* (1962), a novel; and *Earth Shine* (1969), which consists of two essays. A selection of her diaries and letters from 1929 to 1932, *Hour of Gold, Hour of Lead*, was published in 1973.   EUGENE K. GARBER

See also LINDBERGH, CHARLES A.

LINDBERGH, CHARLES AUGUSTUS (1902-1974), an American aviator, made the first solo nonstop flight across the Atlantic Ocean on May 20-21, 1927. Other pilots had crossed the Atlantic before him. But Lindbergh was the first person to do it alone nonstop.

Lindbergh's feat gained him immediate, international fame. The press named him "Lucky Lindy" and the "Lone Eagle." Americans and Europeans idolized the shy, slim young man and showered him with honors.

Before Japan attacked Pearl Harbor in 1941, Lindbergh campaigned against voluntary American involvement in World War II. Many Americans criticized him for his noninvolvement beliefs. After the war, he avoided publicity until the late 1960's, when he spoke out for the conservation of natural resources. Lindbergh served as an adviser in the aviation industry from the days of wood and wire airplanes to supersonic jets.

Wide World

Charles A. Lindbergh and Anne Morrow Lindbergh flew throughout the world charting new routes for airlines. The famous aviator taught his wife to fly following their marriage in 1929.

Early Life. Charles Augustus Lindbergh was born on Feb. 4, 1902, in Detroit. He grew up on a farm near Little Falls, Minn. He was the son of Charles Augustus Lindbergh, Sr., a lawyer, and his wife, Evangeline Land Lodge. Lindbergh's father served as a U.S. congressman from Minnesota from 1907 to 1917.

In childhood, Lindbergh showed exceptional mechanical ability. At the age of 18 years, he entered the University of Wisconsin to study engineering. However, Lindbergh was more interested in the exciting, young field of aviation than he was in school. After two years, he left school to become a *barnstormer*, a pilot who performed daredevil stunts at fairs.

In 1924, Lindbergh enlisted in the United States Army so that he could be trained as an Army Air Service Reserve pilot. In 1925, he graduated from the Army's flight-training school at Brooks and Kelly fields, near San Antonio, as the best pilot in his class. After Lindbergh completed his Army training, the Robertson Aircraft Corporation of St. Louis hired him to fly the mail between St. Louis and Chicago. He gained a reputation as a cautious and capable pilot.

His Historic Flight. In 1919, a New York City hotel owner named Raymond Orteig offered $25,000 to the first aviator to fly nonstop from New York to Paris. Several pilots were killed or injured while competing for the Orteig prize. By 1927, it had still not been won. Lindbergh believed he could win it if he had the right airplane. He persuaded nine St. Louis businessmen to help him finance the cost of a plane. Lindbergh chose Ryan Aeronautical Company of San Diego to manufacture a special plane, which he helped design. He named the plane the *Spirit of St. Louis*. On May 10-11, 1927, Lindbergh tested the plane by flying from San Diego to New York City, with an overnight stop in St. Louis. The flight took 20 hours 21 minutes, a transcontinental record.

On May 20, Lindbergh took off in the *Spirit of St. Louis* from Roosevelt Field, near New York City, at

7:52 A.M. He landed at Le Bourget Field, near Paris, on May 21 at 10:21 P.M. Paris time (5:21 P.M. New York time). Thousands of cheering people had gathered to meet him. He had flown more than 3,600 miles (5,790 kilometers) in $33\frac{1}{2}$ hours.

Lindbergh's heroic flight thrilled people throughout the world. He was honored with awards, celebrations, and parades. President Calvin Coolidge gave Lindbergh the Congressional Medal of Honor and the first Distinguished Flying Cross in American history.

In 1927, Lindbergh published *We*, a book about his transatlantic flight. The title referred to Lindbergh and his plane. Lindbergh flew throughout the United States to encourage air-mindedness on behalf of the Daniel Guggenheim Fund for the Promotion of Aeronautics. Lindbergh learned about the pioneer rocket research of Robert H. Goddard, a Clark University physics professor. Lindbergh persuaded the Guggenheim family to support Goddard's experiments, which later led to the development of missiles, satellites, and space travel. Lindbergh also worked for several airlines as a technical adviser.

Good-Will Ambassador. At the request to the U.S. government, Lindbergh flew to various Latin-American countries in December 1927 as a symbol of American good will. While in Mexico, he met Anne Spencer Morrow, the daughter of Dwight W. Morrow, the American ambassador there. Lindbergh married Anne Morrow in 1929. He taught her to fly, and they went on many flying expeditions together throughout the world, charting new routes for various airlines. Anne Morrow Lindbergh also became famous for her poetry and other writings. See LINDBERGH, ANNE MORROW.

Lindbergh invented an "artificial heart" between 1931 and 1935. He developed it for Alexis Carrel, a French surgeon and biologist whose research included

experiments in keeping organs alive outside the body. Lindbergh's device could pump the substances necessary for life throughout the tissues of an organ.

The Lindbergh Kidnapping. On March 1, 1932, the Lindberghs' 20-month-old son, Charles Augustus, Jr., was kidnapped from the family home in New Jersey. About ten weeks later, his body was found. In 1934, police arrested a carpenter, Bruno Richard Hauptmann, and charged him with the murder. Hauptmann was convicted of the crime. He was executed in 1936.

The press sensationalized the tragedy. Reporters, photographers, and curious onlookers pestered the Lindberghs constantly. In 1935, after the Hauptmann trial, Lindbergh, his wife, and their 3-year-old son, Jon, moved to Europe in search of privacy and safety.

The Lindbergh kidnapping led Congress to pass the "Lindbergh law." This law makes kidnapping a federal offense if the victim is taken across state lines or if the mail service is used for ransom demands.

World War II. While in Europe, Lindbergh was invited by the governments of France and Germany to tour the aircraft industries of their countries. Lindbergh was especially impressed with the highly advanced aircraft industry of Nazi Germany. In 1938, Hermann Goering, a high Nazi official, presented Lindbergh with a German medal of honor. Lindbergh's acceptance of the medal caused an outcry in the United States among critics of Nazism.

Lindbergh and his family returned to the United States in 1939. In 1941, he joined the America First Committee, an organization that opposed voluntary American entry into World War II. Lindbergh became a leading spokesman for the committee. He criticized President Franklin D. Roosevelt's foreign policies. He

Culver

The "Lone Eagle," as Lindbergh was called, made the first solo nonstop flight across the Atlantic Ocean. His historic journey in 1927 in the *Spirit of St. Louis* took $33\frac{1}{2}$ hours and covered more than 3,600 miles (5,790 kilometers).

also charged that British, Jewish, and pro-Roosevelt groups were leading America into war. Lindbergh resigned his commission in the Army Air Corps after Roosevelt publicly denounced him. Some Americans accused Lindbergh of being a Nazi sympathizer because he refused to return the medal he had accepted.

After the Japanese attacked Pearl Harbor on Dec. 7, 1941, Lindbergh stopped his noninvolvement activity. He tried to reenlist, but his request was refused. He then served as a technical adviser and test pilot for the Ford Motor Company and United Aircraft Corporation (now United Technologies Corporation).

In April 1944, Lindbergh went to the Pacific war area as an adviser to the United States Army and Navy. Although he was a civilian, he flew about 50 combat missions. Lindbergh also developed cruise control techniques that increased the capabilities of American fighter planes.

After the War, Lindbergh withdrew from public attention. He worked as a consultant to the chief of staff of the U.S. Air Force. President Dwight D. Eisenhower restored Lindbergh's commission and appointed him a brigadier general in the Air Force in 1954. Pan American World Airways also hired Lindbergh as a consultant. He advised the airline on its purchase of jet transports and eventually helped design the Boeing 747 jet. In 1953, Lindbergh published *The Spirit of St. Louis,* an expanded account of his 1927 transatlantic flight. The book won a Pulitzer Prize in 1954.

Lindbergh traveled widely and developed an interest in the cultures of peoples in Africa and the Philippines. In the late 1960's, he ended his years of silence to speak out for the conservation movement. He especially campaigned for the protection of humpback and blue whales, two species of whales in danger of extinction. Lindbergh opposed the development of supersonic transport planes because he feared the effects the planes might have on the earth's atmosphere.

Lindbergh died of cancer on Aug. 26, 1974, in his home on the Hawaiian island of Maui. He was buried in a churchyard on the eastern edge of the island. The *Autobiography of Values,* a collection of Lindbergh's writings, was published in 1978.   RICHARD P. HALLION

Additional Resources

GILL, BRENDAN. *Lindbergh Alone.* Harcourt, 1977. His flight across the Atlantic Ocean.
LINDBERGH, CHARLES A. *Autobiography of Values.* Ed. by William Jovanovich. Harcourt, 1978.
ROSS, WALTER S. *The Last Hero: Charles A. Lindbergh.* Woodhill, 1979. First published in 1968.
STEIN, R. CONRAD. *The Story of the "Spirit of St. Louis."* Childrens Press, 1984. For younger readers.

LINDBERGH LAW. See KIDNAPPING.

LINDEN is any one of a group of graceful shade trees that grow in many parts of the world. The trees are also called *lime tree, linn,* and *basswood.* The *American linden* grows 120 feet (37 meters) high. It bears small fragrant white or yellow flowers. The light, soft wood of the American linden is used by wood carvers. The *European cut-leaf linden* and the *little-leaf linden* are widely planted as ornamentals.

Scientific Classification. Lindens belong to the family Tiliaceae. The American linden is *Tilia americana;* the

U.S. Forest Service

The American Linden, or Basswood, an attractive shade tree with dense foliage, is known for its symmetrical outline.

European cut-leaf is *T. platyphyllos,* variety *laciniata;* the little-leaf linden is *T. cordata.*   THEODORE W. BRETZ

LINDSAY, HOWARD (1889-1968), was an American playwright best known for the several plays he wrote with Russel Crouse. Lindsay and Crouse won the 1946 Pulitzer Prize for their political satire, *State of the Union* (1945). Their comedy *Life with Father* (1939) became the longest-running nonmusical play in American theater history. Lindsay starred in it with his wife, Dorothy Stickney. He was also a producer and director. He was born in Waterford, N.Y.   MARY VIRGINIA HEINLEIN

LINDSAY, JOHN VLIET (1921-   ), served as mayor of New York City from 1966 through 1973. In 1965, he scored an upset victory in the heavily Democratic city by defeating the Democratic and Conservative party candidates as the nominee of the Republican and Liberal parties. Lindsay's first term was marked by unrest and strikes in New York City's schools, transit system, and other public services. In 1969, Lindsay was defeated for renomination in the Republican primary election. However, he ran as the candidate of the Liberal and Independent parties, and he was reelected mayor.

Lindsay was born in

John V. Lindsay

New York City and graduated from Yale University and the Yale Law School. From 1955 to 1957, he served as executive assistant to the U.S. attorney general. In 1958, he won the first of four terms in the U.S. House of Representatives, where he strongly supported civil rights legislation. In 1964, he refused to support conservative Senator Barry M. Goldwater, the Republican presidential nominee. In 1967, President Lyndon B. Johnson appointed Lindsay vice chairman of the National Advisory Commission on Civil Disorders (Kerner Commission). The committee studied the causes of the riots in U.S. cities during the mid-1960's. In August 1971, Lindsay changed his party affiliation from Republican to Democrat. He was a candidate for the 1972 Democratic presidential nomination, but withdrew when he failed to gain support in the primaries.   DAVID S. BRODER

LINDSAY, VACHEL (1879-1931), was an American poet. He believed that poetry should be performed rather than simply read. Some of his poems, such as "The Congo" (1914), even include stage directions. Among his other effective stage pieces were "General William Booth Enters into Heaven" (1913) and "The Ghosts of the Buffaloes" (1917). Lindsay often took long walking tours through the countryside. He read aloud from his works in exchange for food and shelter.

Chicago Daily News
Vachel Lindsay

Lindsay's poems feature strong rhythms and vivid images. He often wrote about baseball players, circus performers, politicians, and movie stars. Much of his work shows his love of nature and democracy. But he also criticized the selfishness and emphasis on worldly things that he saw in America. His critical poems include "The Eagle That Is Forgotten" (1913) and "Abraham Lincoln Walks at Midnight" (1914). Lindsay was born Nicholas Vachel Lindsay in Springfield, Ill.   CLARK GRIFFITH

LINE. See FISHING (Lines).

LINE, in geometry, may be described as the track of a moving point. It has no breadth or thickness. Lines may be parallel, oblique, perpendicular, and they may be straight or curved. A straight line may be a *line segment* with two ends, a *ray* with one end, or an *endless line* with no ends.

See also GEOMETRY; SKEW LINE.

LINE ENGRAVING. See PHOTOENGRAVING AND PHOTOLITHOGRAPHY.

LINE ISLANDS, also called the Equatorial Islands, consist of 11 isolated, low coral islands in the central Pacific Ocean. The Line Islands lie on both sides of the equator. They have an area of 262 square miles (679 square kilometers) and a population of about 2,115. For location, see PACIFIC ISLANDS (map).

Three of the Line Islands—Jarvis, Kingman Reef, and Palmyra—are possessions of the United States. The eight other islands of the Line Island chain are part of the nation of Kiribati. They are Caroline, Christmas, Fanning, Flint, Malden, Starbuck, Vostok, and Washington. Kiribati is an island nation that also

includes the Gilbert Islands, the Phoenix Islands, and Ocean Island.   EDWIN H. BRYAN, JR.

See also CHRISTMAS ISLAND; KIRIBATI.

LINE OF DEMARCATION was an imaginary line drawn by Pope Alexander VI to settle land rights. The line was drawn in 1493, after Columbus returned from his first voyage to the Americas. The Pope hoped it would prevent disputes between Spain and Portugal over the right to explore and claim land in Asia and the Americas. The line ran from north to south about 350 miles (563 kilometers) west of the Azores and Cape Verde Islands. It barely touched the east coast of the South American mainland, which had not yet been discovered. Spain was permitted to claim land to the west of the line, and Portugal could claim land to the east of the line.

Neither nation found this settlement satisfactory. So the next year Spain and Portugal moved the line west to a point about 1,295 miles (2,084 kilometers) west of the Cape Verde Islands, by the Treaty of Tordesillas. This gave to Portugal territory that is now eastern Brazil. The line was never surveyed, so its exact location was not determined. Scholars think that it lay near the 48° west longitude line.

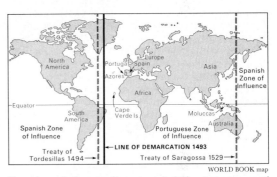
WORLD BOOK map

The Line of Demarcation separated the Portuguese and Spanish zones of influence in the Western Hemisphere. The Treaty of Saragossa did the same in the Eastern Hemisphere.

A continuation of the Line of Demarcation around the globe and into the Eastern Hemisphere gave Portugal the right to claim the Philippine Islands. Spain recognized this claim in the Treaty of Saragossa in 1529, which set the line 17° east of the Moluccas (Spice Islands). In later treaties with Spain, Portugal gave up its claim to the Philippines and won the rest of Brazil. But Portugal and Spain could not secure all the newly discovered lands, because France, England, and the Netherlands ignored the Line of Demarcation and claimed territory for themselves.   WALTER C. LANGSAM

LINE OF FORCE. See ELECTRIC GENERATOR (A Simple Generator).

LINEAR ACCELERATOR is a device that accelerates electrons, protons, and other electrically charged atomic particles to high energies. It is a type of *particle accelerator* that makes particles move along a straight line. The device is sometimes called a *linac*, a shortened form of *line*ar *ac*celerator.

Linear accelerators vary according to the way they speed up particles. In one type, the particles travel

LINEAR ELECTRIC MOTOR

down a cylindrical vacuum tank through a series of pipes called *drift tubes*, which are separated by gaps. As the particles pass across these gaps, electromagnetic waves of radio frequency, called *standing waves*, accelerate them in the direction of their travel. The waves provide an *electric field* that speeds up the particles by acting on their electric charges. The design and arrangement of the drift tubes enable the particles to coast from one accelerating gap to the next without losing speed.

Another type of linear device accelerates particles through one long pipe by means of an electromagnetic wave that travels with the particles. This high-frequency wave is called a *traveling wave*. An alternating electric field at the front of the wave is in the proper direction to accelerate the particles to increasingly higher energies. The particles continue to gain energy as long as the speed of the wave matches the speed of the particles.

Physicists use *standing-wave linear accelerators* chiefly to provide particles for other more powerful accelerators, such as proton synchrotrons. The largest linear devices of this type can accelerate particles to energies of up to 200 million electronvolts. *Traveling-wave linear accelerators* serve as important tools for scientific research into the forces that hold the nucleus of the atom together. They also are used as powerful X-ray machines in industry and medicine. The world's largest, most powerful traveling-wave linear accelerator, located at Stanford University, can speed up particles to 20 billion electronvolts. It is about 2 miles (3 kilometers) long.

The first linear accelerator was built in 1928 by the Norwegian physicist Rolf Wideröe. This type of particle accelerator became practical after the development of high-power radio frequency techniques in the early 1940's.　　　　　　　　　　　ERNEST D. COURANT

See also PARTICLE ACCELERATOR (with diagram); CANCER (Radiation Therapy; picture: Methods of Diagnosing and Treating Cancer); ELECTROMAGNETIC WAVES; X RAYS (How X Rays Are Produced).

LINEAR ELECTRIC MOTOR is a device used mainly to propel high-speed vehicles that do not run on wheels.

Such vehicles are supported by magnets or by a cushion of air (see AIR CUSHION VEHICLE).

The heart of a linear electric motor is a row of electromagnets that are turned on and off one after the other. This action produces a moving wave of magnetism that travels along the electromagnets just as a wave travels in water. This moving magnetic wave propels the vehicle.

There are two types of linear electric motors: (1) *linear induction*, and (2) *linear synchronous*.

In a linear induction motor, the row of electromagnets is located in the vehicle. The electromagnets face a strip of nonmagnetic metal, called a *reaction rail*, mounted in the center of the vehicle's track. The moving magnetic wave *induces* (creates) an electric current in the reaction rail. The induced current produces another magnetic field that pushes against the magnetic wave from the electromagnets. This push moves the vehicle.

In a linear synchronous motor, the electromagnets consist of electric wires that wind back and forth along the track. The wires create a moving magnetic wave that pushes against a powerful magnet mounted in the vehicle. The magnetic wave moves the vehicle just as an ocean wave pushes a surfboard. The motion of the magnetic wave and that of the vehicle must be *synchronous* (matched) for the motor to work.　　HENRY H. KOLM

LINEAR EQUATION. See ALGEBRA (Working with Equations).

LINEAR MEASURE. See WEIGHTS AND MEASURES (table: Length and Distance).

LINEN, *LIHN uhn*, refers to yarn and cloth made of fibers from the flax plant stalk. The fibers are from 6 to 40 inches (15 to 100 centimeters) long and are chiefly cellulose.

Linen Fabrics. Flax ranks among the strongest natural fibers known. It is used in products that require high strength, including sewing thread, fish nets, fire hose, and mattress covers. But new synthetic fibers, such as nylon and Dacron, are even stronger. They have replaced linen for some uses. Linen can be bleached white and has wide use in fine tablecloths, napkins, and handkerchiefs. It is also highly water absorbent and useful for towels.

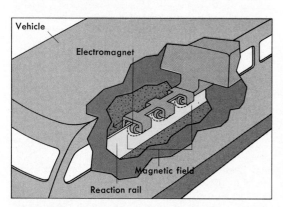

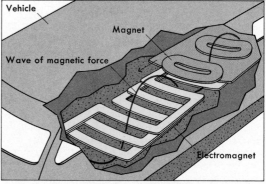

WORLD BOOK diagrams by Mas Nakagawa

A Linear Induction Motor has a row of electromagnets that face a strip of nonmagnetic metal, called a *reaction rail.* The electromagnets create a moving magnetic field that produces another magnetic field in the reaction rail. One magnetic field pushes against the other and thus moves the vehicle along.

A Linear Synchronous Motor has an electromagnet mounted beneath the track of the vehicle. The vehicle itself also carries strong magnets. The electromagnet creates a moving wave of magnetic force that pushes against the vehicle's magnets and moves the vehicle along just as an ocean wave propels a surfboard.

Preparing the Fibers. Flax harvested in late summer produces the best quality linen. The stalks are pulled, tied into bundles, and dried in the sun. Then they pass through a coarse comb that removes the seeds.

Next comes a process called *retting*, actually a form of rotting. In *dew retting*, the stalks are spread on grass and kept moist for several weeks. The combined action of bacteria and moisture decomposes the tissue surrounding the true flax fibers. The fibers can then be separated from the woody bark and straw of the stalk. In *water retting*, which is more common, the stalks are retted in slow-moving rivers or bogs for one to two weeks. In another method of water retting, the stems are soaked in large tanks of warm water for four to eight days. After retting, the flax is dried. Then a machine breaks the woody bark into small bits and separates out the fibers. Finally, the fiber is combed to produce long parallel fibers called *line*, and short fibers called *tow*.

Tow is spun into yarns by methods similar to those used for spinning cotton (see COTTON [Spinning; picture]; SPINNING). Special machinery spins the long linen fibers into fine yarns.

History. The ancient Egyptians grew flax along the Nile River about 7,000 years ago. They wrapped their mummies in linen before placing them in tombs. Egyptian and Hebrew priests wore linen cloth at religious ceremonies. The ancient Greeks wore linen clothing, and the Romans knew how to make linen paper as well as linen cloth.

Modern use of linen began in Europe in the 1600's. Skilled Flemish and French workers who left their countries to escape religious persecution helped develop linen spinning and weaving in England, the Netherlands, and Germany. Linen fabrics from France, Belgium, and Ireland have become internationally famous.

The first American settlers planted flaxseed so that they could make linen. But the invention of the cotton gin by Eli Whitney in 1793 made cotton yarn more economical than linen yarn. For this reason, the United States never produced large amounts of fiber flax. Today, fiber flax is not raised commercially anywhere in the United States. Most of the country's fiber flax must be imported from Europe.

Annual world fiber flax production amounts to about 655,000 short tons (594,000 metric tons). The Soviet Union accounts for more than half of the world's production of fiber flax. Other leading flax-producing countries include Czechoslovakia, France, Poland, and Romania.　　　　　　　　　　　ERNEST R. KASWELL

See also FLAX.

LINER. See SHIP.

LINGONBERRY is a small fruit related to the cranberry. It grows wild in northern sections of North America, Europe, and Asia. The lingonberry is known by many other names, including *bog cranberry, cowberry, foxberry, lengon, linberry, lingberry, lingenberry, mountain cranberry, rock cranberry,* and *partridgeberry.*

The fruit of the lingonberry is glossy and bright red. Raw lingonberries taste bitter, so the fruit usually is cooked for use in jellies and sauces. The cooked fruit has a spicy flavor. Lingonberry jellies and sauces are especially popular in eastern Canada and some Scandinavian regions.

Lingonberries grow on low evergreen shrubs. The plant's leaves are shiny and dark green on top and dark-

WORLD BOOK illustration by Susan Hillier
The Lingonberry Is Related to the Cranberry.

spotted on the underside. The plant grows best in a cool, mild climate. It is not widely cultivated.

Scientific Classification. The lingonberry belongs to the heather family, Ericaceae. Its scientific name is *Vaccinium vitisidaea.*　　　　　　　　　　　　　　GEORGE W. EATON

LINGUISTICS is the scientific study of language. Linguists try to answer questions about language, such as how languages change and why words mean what they mean. Linguists study both their own languages and languages they do not speak.

When linguists study a modern language, they analyze the speech of one or more native speakers of that language. They call such a person an *informant*. Many languages have no written form. Therefore, linguists must often use a set of symbols called a *phonetic alphabet* to write down the speech sounds of an informant. Linguists also study dead languages to trace the development of modern ones.

Linguists gather data, form theories and test them, and then establish facts about language. These experts believe they know extremely little about even the most familiar languages. They hope to record and study unfamiliar tongues before such languages become extinct. There are two chief fields of linguistics, *descriptive linguistics* and *comparative linguistics*.

Descriptive Linguistics

Descriptive linguistics studies the language of a single place and period. It is sometimes called *synchronic linguistics*. A linguist in this field tries to describe a language as it is acquired by the children of a community and used by the adults there. Such a study focuses on the ability of these people to speak and understand their language.

Linguists realize that people often make errors when they speak. For example, a linguist studying English might record several uses of the sentence *He did not go nowhere*. However, some of the informants would know that they should have said *He did not go anywhere*.

LINGUISTICS

Linguists use the term *linguistic performance* for what people actually say.

Constructing a Grammar. A descriptive linguist records the words and sentences of informants. From this record, the linguist constructs a *grammar*, a description of the ability of people to use their native language. This ability is called *linguistic competence*. The linguist often relies on the judgment of native speakers for help in constructing a grammar.

All languages have a creative aspect. It consists of the ability of native speakers to produce and understand sentences that they have never encountered before. The number of sentences in a language is infinite, and so no language could be described by listing these sentences. Instead, the linguist devises a grammar that tells, step by step, how to construct any sentence in the language.

The grammar performs its function by telling how to build new sentences out of old ones. For example, the sentence *The astronomer counted the stars* could be substituted for *it* in the sentence *The queen believed it*. This substitution would produce a new sentence, *The queen believed the astronomer counted the stars*.

A grammar may be used *prescriptively* as well as descriptively. Such a grammar attempts to tell people how they should use language. For example, the grammar might suggest using the sentence *I do not have any money* instead of *I do not have no money*. However, the rules of a particular grammar may not reflect the language as it is actually spoken. In addition, people often express their meaning well even if they follow different rules.

The Components of a Grammar. The grammar of a language has three components: (1) the phonological component, (2) the semantic component, and (3) the syntactic component.

The Phonological Component consists of rules that tell how to pronounce words and sentences. The *phonology* (sound system) of one language may differ greatly from that of another. For example, Spanish phonology does not distinguish the pronunciation of the two English vowels in the words *sheep* and *ship*. On the other hand, the Thai language distinguishes the sound of the *t*'s in *steam* and *team*, but English does not.

The Semantic Component tells what sentences mean. It tells whether one sentence means the same thing as another and whether one sentence implies another. For example, *The student managed to pass the test* implies *The student passed the test*. However, the sentence *The student tried to pass the test* does not imply *The student passed the test*.

The Syntactic Component shows the relationship between the meaning of a sentence and the arrangement of the words in the sentence. It may show that two or more arrangements of words have a single meaning. For example, the two sentences *The waitress gave the sandwich to the tallest girl* and *The waitress gave the tallest girl the sandwich* means the same thing. Linguists say that such sentences *paraphrase* each other.

The syntactic component may also show that a single arrangement of words has more than one meaning. For example, *The farmer thought the chicken was too hot to eat* has two possible meanings. Either the farmer thought his dinner was too warm, or he thought the chicken refused to eat because of the heat. A sentence that has more than one meaning is *ambiguous*.

Comparative Linguistics

Comparative linguistics is the study of language as it varies from place to place, from speaker to speaker, and from one period to another. This field is sometimes called *diachronic linguistics*.

Some comparative linguists attempt to formulate universally valid statements about language structure and language change. This area of study is called *linguistic typology*.

Comparative linguists would like to be able to state how language first developed and to describe the conditions that led to its invention. But written records are relatively recent because human beings have had systems of word writing for only about 5,000 years. People have used spoken languages far longer. As far as linguists can tell, all cultures of today have equally complex languages. For these reasons, almost nothing is known about the origin of language.

Comparative linguists use two chief procedures in their study of language. These procedures are called *internal reconstruction* and *comparative reconstruction*.

Internal Reconstruction involves using one stage in the development of a language to explain certain characteristics of an earlier stage. For example, a linguist may notice that the sound of *e* in the words *keep* and *kept* varies with the number of consonants that follow the vowel. The linguist may then hypothesize that the sound of *e* in the two words had been the same in earlier English. The linguist further hypothesizes that a sound change has altered the sound of the vowel in different ways, depending on the number of consonants that follow. Such a change is called a *sound shift*. The same relationship involving the sound of *e* occurs in many other words, including *sleep* and *slept* and *deep* and *depth*.

Comparative Reconstruction is a procedure in which a linguist uses several similar languages to reconstruct a hypothetical language called a *protolanguage*. The linguist assumes that the protolanguage was the ancestor of the languages from which it is reconstructed.

A linguist might note that some words which start with a certain letter in various languages start with a different letter in English. For example, the English word *feather* begins with an *f*. The Greek and Latin words for *feather*—*pteron* and *penna*—begin with a *p*. Likewise, the English word *thaw* begins with *th*, and the Greek and Latin versions of the word—*tekein* and *tabes*—begin with *t*. Similarly, the English word *hide* begins with an *h*. The Greek and Latin words for *hide* begin with a *k* or *k*-like sound—*kutos* and *cutis*.

The linguist could hypothesize that Greek and Latin contain the consonants of the protolanguage. As a result, the expert concludes that English underwent a sound shift that systematically replaced some consonants with others. This sound shift characterizes the Germanic languages, which include English, German, and Dutch.

Linguistics and Other Fields of Study

Many linguists study aspects of language that involve other fields. For example, *anthropological linguists* study the influences that language and other elements of culture exert on one another. *Sociolinguists* try to find out how language varies with differences in age, sex, and economic and social status. *Psycholinguists* seek regularities in the ways people acquire and use language. They also study diseases and injuries that affect the ability to use language. *Mathematical linguists* are interested in the relation between human languages and the artificial languages used in computer programming. Experts in *applied linguistics* attempt to use linguistic principles to improve the teaching of reading and foreign languages.

History

The Comparativists. Since ancient times, people have tried to answer many questions about language. The comparativists began their studies during the late 1700's. At that time, linguistics was called *comparative philology*, a term sometimes still used today. British people living in India noticed that Hindustani, a language of India, was similar to Latin and Greek. They concluded that Latin, Greek, and Sanskrit—the ancient form of Hindustani—all came from one earlier tongue.

Scholars then began studying and comparing the modern European languages. They discovered that almost all European languages, as well as the languages of Persia (now Iran), Afghanistan, and northern India, had developed from one parent tongue. Linguists named this protolanguage *Indo-European*. No record of Indo-European exists, but it may have been spoken in eastern Europe before 2000 B.C.

The leading early comparativist was a German scholar named Jakob Grimm, one of the two brothers known for their collection of fairy tales. Grimm showed that English, German, and other Germanic languages came from Indo-European, just as Greek, Latin, and Sanskrit did. He formulated *Grimm's Law*, which explains the relationships between the consonants of the Germanic languages and the consonants of other Indo-European languages.

Other comparativists included Franz Bopp and August Schleicher, both of Germany. Bopp compared Sanskrit with German and other languages, and Schleicher compiled a grammar of Indo-European itself.

During the 1870's, a group of linguists who called themselves *neogrammarians* developed from the comparativists. The neogrammarians declared that Grimm's Law and other linguistic laws were true without exception. They claimed that apparent irregularities in those laws resulted from the operation of still other laws.

Structuralism arose in the early 1900's. The structuralists viewed languages as systems composed of patterns of sounds and words. They studied these patterns to learn about the structure of a language. They believed each language has a distinct structure that cannot be compared with that of any other language. A Swiss linguist named Ferdinand de Saussure became the first leader of the structuralists. American structuralists included Leonard Bloomfield and Edward Sapir.

The Generative Theory of Language began during the 1950's with Noam Chomsky, an American linguist. Generative linguists believe a grammar of a language consists of certain rules for the construction of an infinite number of sentences. Generativists have shown that certain structuralist conceptions of grammar are inadequate for the description of languages.

LINNAEUS, CAROLUS

According to generative linguists, grammatical devices called *grammatical transformations* relate sentences to one another. These transformations are necessary for a complete description of many sentences. This kind of rule had no role in structuralist theory. During the late 1970's, there was much disagreement among generative linguists as they worked to discover basic and universal characteristics of human languages.   LARRY W. MARTIN

Related Articles in WORLD BOOK include:

Anthropology	Etymology	Phonetics
(Linguistic	Grammar	Sapir, Edward
Anthropology)	Grimm	Semantics
Bloomfield, Leonard	Language	Syntax
Chomsky, Noam		

Additional Resources

CRANE, L. BEN, and others. *An Introduction to Linguistics.* Little, Brown, 1981.
ROBINS, ROBERT H. *A Short History of Linguistics.* 2nd ed. Longman, 1979.
SAMPSON, GEOFFREY. *Schools of Linguistics.* Stanford, 1980. Describes and evaluates the major theories and interpretations.

LINIMENT, *LIHN uh muhnt,* is a liquid preparation that is used to treat certain aches and pains in the body. It is usually rubbed on the skin to produce reddening and heat. Liniments usually act by causing irritation or stimulation that increases the blood supply to the area. Liniments often contain stimulating agents such as ammonia and turpentine. Most liniments are poisonous when swallowed. They should not be used on sores and cuts unless a doctor advises it.   AUSTIN SMITH

LINK, EDWIN ALBERT (1904-   ), an American inventor and businessman, developed the *mechanical trainer,* a machine that simulates flying conditions on the ground. He built his first trainer in 1929, and received his first military order for six units in 1934. During World War II, thousands of Link trainers taught aviators to fly "blind." This ground training saved millions of dollars by reducing the flying time required to train a pilot. Link's company also produces elaborate trainers used by the crews of jet aircraft. He was born at Huntington, Ind.   ROBERT B. HOTZ

LINN. See LINDEN.

LINNAEA. See TWINFLOWER.

LINNAEUS, *lih NEE uhs,* **CAROLUS,** *KAR uh luhs* (1707-1778), a Swedish naturalist and botanist, established the modern scientific method of naming plants and animals. In this system, each living thing has a name with two parts. The first part is for the *genus* (group). The second part is for the *species* (kind). Linnaeus' book *Species Plantarum* (1753) forms the basis for plant classification. The 10th edition of his *Systema Naturae* (1758) covers animal classification. See CLASSIFICATION, SCIENTIFIC.

Linnaeus was born Karl von Linné in Råshult, near Kristianstad, Sweden. His father, the parish curate, wanted him to study for the ministry. But the boy

Ewing Galloway
Carolus Linnaeus

295

was so interested in plants that friends urged his parents to send him to medical school. While in medical school, Linnaeus supervised a small botanical garden and began an insect collection. He wrote careful descriptions of all the kinds of plants he knew, and these notes formed the basis for his books. He became famous as Carolus Linnaeus because he wrote his books in Latin.

With $50 given him by the Royal Society of Science, he spent five months in 1732 collecting plants in Lapland. During this trip, he walked nearly 1,000 miles (1,600 kilometers). Linnaeus then went to the Netherlands, where he received his medical degree. When he returned to Stockholm to practice medicine, the Swedish government gave him a position. In 1742, Linnaeus became a professor of botany at the University of Uppsala. LORUS J. MILNE and MARGERY MILNE

LINNET, *LIHN iht,* is a small bird in the finch family. Linnets live in Europe, northern Africa, and western Asia. They are light tan and brown with darker patches on the back and shoulders. In the spring and summer, the crown and breast of male linnets turn crimson. Like other finches, linnets have a sturdy bill that is well adapted to holding and cracking the seeds they eat.

Dennis Green, Bruce Coleman Ltd.

A Male Linnet feeds its hungry young.

These birds inhabit thickets, shrubs, and the edges of forests during the spring and summer, when they nest. They flock together in open country during the fall and winter. Some linnets migrate to warmer regions for the winter. Others stay in the same area all year.

Linnets build cuplike nests of stalks and grasses. They line the nests with feathers or fur. A nest usually is placed low in a shrub or tree growing in the open. Female linnets lay from 4 to 6 spotted, pale-bluish eggs. In North America, the distantly related house finch is sometimes called a linnet.

Scientific Classification. The linnet belongs to the subfamily Carduelinae of the finch family, Fringillidae. It is *Carduelis cannabina.* DAVID M. NILES

LINOLEUM, *luh NOH lee uhm,* is a smooth-surfaced floor covering made from linseed oil. It was the first smooth-surfaced floor covering to be manufactured on a large scale. Today, several kinds of flooring are made, and these new synthetic materials have replaced linoleum for most purposes. Such products are durable and easy to wash.

How Linoleum Is Made. A linoleum manufacturer first mixes purified linseed oil and oxygen in a tank. This process of *oxidation* changes the oil into a rubbery substance. Heat and certain gums are added to strengthen the mixture. The resulting *linoleum cement* is then stored for several days to give it even greater toughness. After the cement has reached the desired strength, it is put into a mixer. There, pigments and such filler materials as ground cork and wood flour are added.

A machine *calenders* (presses) the substance until it is glossy, and applies it to a *backing sheet* of burlap or felt. The backed linoleum is then dried and hardened in an oven. After this *stoving* process, the product gets a coating of lacquer or wax.

Kinds of Linoleum. There are two basic kinds of linoleum: (1) molded inlaid linoleum, made in designs of two or more colors; and (2) plain linoleum, made only in single colors.

Molded Inlaid Linoleum in elaborate designs accounts for most linoleum used today. A machine puts ingredients of different colors through a series of stencils onto a backing sheet. The colors are pressed onto the backing sheet. The material is then ready for stoving.

Plain Linoleum. Manufacturers make linoleum of a single color by adding a coloring pigment along with the filler. Plain linoleum is called *battleship linoleum* because it was once used extensively in warships. Today, it is used for linoleum-block printing (see BLOCK PRINTING). It may be black, brown, gray, or green.

History. Linoleum was invented about 1860 by Frederick Walton of England. He found that linseed oil, when exposed to air, became a rubber-like material that could be used as a floor covering. The oil comes from the flax plant, and so he called the product linoleum, from the Latin words *linum* (flax) and *oleum* (oil).

In the early 1900's, Walton invented a *straight-line inlay machine,* which produced linoleum in various patterns. Manufacturers still make linoleum by Walton's basic method, but the modern process is much faster.

The use of linoleum started to decline during the 1950's as floor coverings made of plastics replaced it in many homes and offices. These synthetic materials resist moisture and chemicals better than linoleum can. They also can be produced faster and in a greater variety of colors and patterns. Even newer kinds of flooring have special surfaces that shine without being waxed. See VINYL. RICHARD F. BLEWITT

LINOLEUM-BLOCK PRINTING. See BLOCK PRINTING.

LINOTYPE, *LY nuh typ,* is the brand name of a machine used to produce metal type for printing. It is the best-known brand of *linecaster,* a machine that forms a complete line of type at one time. Linotype typesetters were once used in the publication of nearly all newspapers and other printed material. However, *photocomposition* has almost entirely replaced the Linotype. Photocomposition is a form of typesetting that involves the production of images of type characters on photosensitive film or paper (see PRINTING [Typesetting]).

How the Linotype Works. The Linotype is operated by one person seated at a keyboard. Above the keyboard is a slotted metal tray called a *magazine.* The magazine holds hundreds of tiny brass molds that are in the shape of letters. These molds, which are called *mats* or *matrices,* fit into the slots of the magazine that correspond to keys on the keyboard. When the operator presses a letter key, the magazine releases the corresponding matrix, which drops into place in a line. At the end of each word, the operator presses another key to insert a *space band,* an expandable metal wedge. After reaching the end of the line, the operator *justifies* the line. Justification involves extending the line to fill its intended length and driving the space bands up between the words to create equal amounts of space between them.

When the line is completed, the operator presses a key

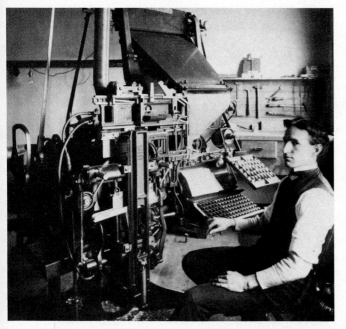

A Linotype, *left,* is a machine that produces metal type for printing. It casts the type in one-line units called *slugs, above.* Since the mid-1900's, the Linotype has been gradually replaced by photographic methods of typesetting.

to send the line to be cast. Molten metal, usually lead, is forced into the matrices. As the metal cools, it hardens into a line of type with raised letters. This *slug* then drops into a tray called a *galley,* while the empty matrices are carried back up to the magazine by a mechanical arm. The matrices are automatically sorted and returned to their proper slots to be used again. After printing, the slugs are melted down and the metal reused.

History. Ottmar Mergenthaler, a German-born inventor, demonstrated and patented the Linotype in 1884. The *New York Tribune* gave the Linotype its first major commercial use in 1886. In 1890, Mergenthaler introduced an improved machine, called the Simplex Linotype, which became a worldwide success. Before Mergenthaler's invention, galleys were assembled and taken apart by hand, one letter at a time. The Linotype improved typesetting speed and reduced its cost.

Linotype typesetters were used in nearly all typesetting work until the 1960's, when photocomposition began to replace metal composition. Today, most type produced in the United States is set through photocomposition. However, in many parts of Africa, Asia, and South America, Linotype typesetters still are commonly used. J. C. McCracken

See also Mergenthaler, Ottmar; Monotype; Printing; Teletypesetter.

LINSEED OIL is an oil derived from the seeds of the flax plant. It is a type of *drying oil*—that is, it takes in oxygen from the air to form a tough film that resists breaking, chipping, and changes in the weather. Linseed oil is used primarily in printing inks, paints, varnishes, linoleum, and other industrial products. In addition, it is sometimes used as a protective treatment for concrete.

Flax seeds are made up of about 40 per cent oil and 60 per cent water and solid material. To obtain linseed oil, workers grind the flax seeds into a meal and heat it. This meal is then either crushed by a hydraulic press or treated with chemicals called *solvents* to extract the oil. The oil is refined to remove impurities. Freshly extracted linseed oil is dark brown, but the refined product is light yellow. The remaining meal, which is high in protein, is used as feed for livestock.

Today, synthetic chemicals have replaced many of the uses of seed oil. As a result, world production of the oil is declining. Daniel R. Sullivan

See also Flax; Linoleum; Paint.

LINSEY-WOOLSEY is a rough cloth made of linen and wool. It is hand-woven and hand-spun with the linen threads running lengthwise, and the wool running crosswise. Linsey-woolsey was made by early American colonists and by pioneers of the American West until after the Civil War. They used linen threads because they did not have enough wool. Today, few people make linsey-woolsey. Kenneth R. Fox

LINT. See Cotton (Uses of Cotton; Classing).

LINTEL. See Architecture (table: Architectural Terms [Post and Lintel]).

LINTON, RALPH (1893-1953), was an American anthropologist. He developed the concepts of *status* and *role,* which are used by many social scientists.

According to Linton, a person's status consists of a "collection of rights and duties." Such status is either achieved by a person's own efforts, or given by society to an individual based on such traits as age, parentage, and sex. Linton believed a person's status shapes his or her role—that is, the way the person functions in society. Linton also showed how a person's role affects his or her personality. He helped develop the view that each culture produces a particular basic personality type.

Linton was born in Philadelphia. While earning a Ph.D. degree at Harvard University, he researched the archaeology of Polynesia. From 1925 to 1927, he lived in Madagascar and studied the culture there. He later taught at the University of Wisconsin and at Columbia and Yale universities. Linton's books include *The Study of Man* (1936) and *The Cultural Background of Personality* (1945). Igor Kopytoff

LION, in astrology. See Leo.

Norman Myers

A Pride of Lions Moves Across an Open, Grassy Plain in Africa.

LION is a big, powerful cat—probably the most famous member of the cat family. Man and most other animals fear these fierce animals. Men are frightened by the lion's thundering roar and impressed by its strength and royal appearance. The lion is called the "king of beasts," and is a well-known symbol of beauty and power.

Lions can live in cool climates and in the intense heat of semidesert areas. They do not like to live in thick forests. Most of them live in woodlands, grassy plains, and areas with thorny scrub trees. Lions live where they find a supply of food—deer, antelope, zebra, and other hoofed animals—and where they have a place to drink.

In ancient times, lions lived in Europe, the Middle East, India, and much of Africa. But man has killed thousands of lions as he settled in new areas. As a result, there are no more lions left in the Middle East and northern Africa. Only about 200 still live in Asia—all in the Gir Forest in India. Lions still live in east and central Africa. But most of these lions live in national parks and areas called *reserves*, where they are protected from hunters.

Thousands of lions also live in captivity in zoos

George B. Schaller, the contributor of this article, is a Research Associate with the New York Zoological Society and has studied lions in Tanzania, East Africa. He has written articles on lions and their behavior, and is author of The Deer and the Tiger.

throughout the world. And trained lions are popular performers in circuses.

The Body of a Lion

The lion and tiger are the largest members of the cat family. Lions are built for strength, not speed. A male lion usually weighs from 350 to 400 pounds (159 to 180 kilograms), but some weigh up to 500 pounds (230 kilograms). Most males are about 9 feet (3 meters) long from the nose to the end of the tail. They are about $3\frac{1}{2}$ feet (107 centimeters) tall at the shoulder. *Lionesses* (females) are smaller than males. They weigh only 250 to 300 pounds (113 to 140 kilograms) and are about 1 foot (30 centimeters) shorter.

Male lions are the only cats with *manes*. This collar of long, thick hair covers the head, except the face, and the neck down to the shoulders and chest. The mane makes the male look even bigger and stronger than he is. It also protects him during fights. The long, thick

——————————— **FACTS IN BRIEF** ———————————

Names: *Male,* lion; *female,* lioness; *young,* cub; *group,* pride.

Gestation Period: About $3\frac{1}{2}$ months.

Number in Litter: 1 to 6, usually 2 or 3.

Length of Life: 20 to 25 years, in captivity; in the wild, unknown.

Where Found: Africa south of the Sahara; the Gir Forest of India.

Scientific Classification: Lions belong to the class *Mammalia,* and the order *Carnivora.* They are in the cat family, *Felidae;* genus *Panthera,* species *P. leo.*

hair softens the blows of his foes. Young males have a little hair around their heads when they are about a year old. But the mane is not fully grown until the animal is about 5 years old. Manes may be blond, brown, or black. Most are a mixture of these colors. They become darker as the lion grows older.

The lion's coat is ideal for hiding. It is a brownish yellow, the same color as dead grass. Only the back of the ears and the tuft of hair at the end of the tail are black. *Cubs* (young lions) have spots on their coats, but the spots disappear by the time the cubs are a few months old.

The shoulders and forelegs of the lion are tremendously muscular. They give the lion the strength to clutch its prey and pull it to the ground. Each big, heavy paw is armed with curved claws that hook and

THE SKELETON OF A LION

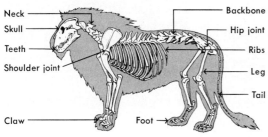

Neck — Backbone
Skull — Hip joint
Teeth — Ribs
Shoulder joint — Leg
— Tail
Claw — Foot

LION TRACKS

Front feet →
Hind feet ←

WORLD BOOK illustration by Tom Dolan

Norman Myers, Photo Researchers

A Lion's Long, Sharp Teeth and Huge Paws are fearsome weapons. He can disable or kill some prey with one swipe, then use his pointed teeth to tear it apart.

hold the prey. When not in use, each claw withdraws into a sheath in the paw so the claws stay sharp.

The lion has 30 teeth, and some of them have special duties. The four large *canine* (pointed) teeth are used to hold the prey, kill it, and to tear the meat. Four cheek teeth called the *carnassial* teeth are for cutting through tough skin and the *tendons* that join muscles to bone. There are no teeth suitable for chewing. The lion swallows food in chunks.

The Life of a Lion

The lion is the most companionable of all cats. A *pride* (group) may include from 10 to 20 lions, or as many as 35. Each pride has from one to three adult males, several lionesses, and cubs. The members of the pride may not always be together. Some of the lions may hunt in one place, a few in another. But when they are reunited, they greet each other by rubbing cheeks.

Life within the pride is peaceful. Lions usually spend about 20 hours a day sleeping or resting. Cubs chase each other and wrestle. A lioness sometimes twitches her tail while one of her cubs tries to catch the tuft of hair at the end of the tail. Hungry cubs nurse on any lioness that has milk, not just their own mothers.

Lions usually walk about 5 miles (8 kilometers) in a day. If they have had a big meal, they may rest for 24 hours. But if they are hungry, they may travel as far as 15 miles (24 kilometers) in search of food.

Habits. Each pride stays in a specific *territory* (area). The territory contains the food and water that lions need. Where prey is plentiful, territories may be about 15 square miles (39 square kilometers). Where prey is scarce, the territory may cover 100 square miles (260 square kilometers).

Lions do not allow strange animals to hunt in their territory. They warn intruders to stay away by roaring or by squirting a mixture of scent and urine on bushes. The strangers then know that the territory is occupied. If they ignore the warnings, they may be killed.

Pride members stay together like a family for years, but changes occur from time to time. All male cubs are chased from the territory by their fathers when they are between 2 and 3 years old. These young males then wander until they are fully grown. Then they may challenge some pride males. If they win, they can take over the territory and the lionesses it contains. Lions in captivity die of old age at about 20 to 25 years.

Cubs. A lioness becomes an adult and mates with the pride males when she is from 3 to 4 years old. About $3\frac{1}{2}$ months later, her cubs are born in a thicket. The cubs are blind and helpless at birth, and weigh about 3 pounds (1.4 kilograms) each. Lions do not have permanent dens. From time to time, the mother moves her cubs from one hiding place to another. She carries them in her mouth, one at a time. Hyenas, leopards, and even other lions may kill cubs while the mother is away hunting. Lions also have mated with tigers in captivity. Their offspring may be called a *tiglon*, a *tigon*, or a *liger*.

At first, the cubs live on milk. When they are about 2 months old, the mother leads them to an animal she has killed for their first meal of meat. The lioness usually does not have another litter until her cubs are

Marc & Evelyne Bernheim, Rapho Guillumette

Lions Like to Rest In a Cool, Shady Spot. The lionesses care for their cubs, *above.* Many male lions like to stretch out in the branches of a tree for a quiet nap, *right.* Females do most of the hunting. Males keep the pride's territory safe from intruders.

18 to 24 months old, old enough to hunt for themselves. Occasionally, a mother abandons her cubs. When food is scarce, the mother eats and lets the cubs starve. About half the cubs survive.

How a Lion Hunts

Lions have to kill to live. They prefer large prey—zebra, various kinds of antelope, buffalo, and warthog. But they will also eat fish, turtles, guinea fowl—anything they can catch. They eat animals that have died from disease, and even take prey from the cheetah.

The lion lives a life of feast or famine. It may not be able to catch an animal for perhaps a week. But it usually catches something to eat every three or four days. Then the lion stuffs itself. A male lion can eat 75

WHERE LIONS LIVE

The black areas in the map, *below,* show the parts of the world in which lions are found. Most lions live in the African plains.

pounds (34 kilograms) of meat in one meal. After killing an animal, the lion often drags it to a shady spot. One lion can drag a 600-pound (270-kilogram) zebra, something that six men would find difficult to do. All members of the pride eat together, with much growling and snarling as each animal tries to get the "lion's share" of the meat.

Catching a large animal is not easy for the lion. Most of the animals it likes to eat can run faster than the lion, which has a top speed of about 35 miles (56 kilometers) per hour. Therefore, the lion must surprise its prey by stalking. Moving slowly, its body close to the ground, the lion creeps closer. When it is about 50 feet (15 meters) away, it rushes forward, grabs the rump, side, or head of the animal, and pulls it down to the ground. Then it usually seizes the prey's throat in its mouth and strangles it.

Lions often hunt at night because they can surprise their prey more easily in the dark. Nature has equipped the lion well for this task. Its gold-colored eyes can see in the dark, and the lion has excellent senses of hearing and smell. Sometimes several lions hunt together. While several hide, others circle the prey and chase it toward the waiting lions that are crouched in the high grass. The male lions in the pride ordinarily let the lionesses do the hunting. But they kill for themselves when they find prey. Cubs learn to hunt by watching the adults.

Lions and Man

Hunting Lions. Whenever lions and man come into contact, the lion always loses. Man has killed the lions

Norman Myers   Richard Dranitzke, Photo Researchers

A Lioness Stalks Her Prey. Partially hidden in tall grass, *center foreground,* she creeps close to a herd of zebras. Then she suddenly leaps out, pulls her prey to the ground, and kills it. After making the kill, she drags the dead zebra to cover, *right,* where the whole pride will feast on it.

in most of Asia and much of Africa. Lions kill cows, goats, and other livestock for food. And on rare occasions they kill people. So people killed lions to protect themselves and their property.

For centuries people have also hunted lions as a way of showing courage. In about 1375 B.C., the Egyptian *pharaoh* (ruler) Amenhotep III hunted lions with bow and arrow from a chariot. He killed 102 in this manner. During the Seventh Crusade, Saint Louis and his followers chased lions on horseback and shot them with crossbows. Until recent times, the warriors of the Masai tribe in East Africa hunted lions on foot.

The Asiatic lion is an endangered species. The only Asiatic lions that remain in their natural surroundings live in India's Gir Forest sanctuary. But the people who live there have destroyed much of the lions' habitat by cutting down trees for fuel and timber. Deer and other natural prey are scarce, and so the lions have killed domestic animals, such as cattle, for food. This has made the lions unpopular with farmers in the area.

African lions have a much better chance for survival. Africa has many reserves where lions may not be shot. Hunters are still allowed to kill lions in certain areas, but they must have a special license. Most people would rather photograph lions than shoot them now.

The lion tries to avoid contacts with people. It rarely attacks people unless it is tormented or injured. For example, a person can be within 40 feet (12 meters) of lions in the Gir Forest without danger. People there seldom harm the lions. But when provoked, and particularly when wounded, the lion is a terrible foe.

Training Lions. Lions have been kept in captivity for centuries. Pharaoh Ramses II took a tame lion into battle as a mascot. The Roman Elagabalus rode in a chariot that was pulled by lions.

Trained lions have always been a favorite attraction in circuses and *menageries* (collections of wild animals). Lions can be trained to do tricks. The fact that lions look ferocious makes them spectacular show animals.

Training usually begins when a lion is about 2 years old. As long as the trainer is not careless, does not treat the lion cruelly, and remembers it is never completely tame, the trainer is safe. But lions always are liable to attack, and have mauled and even killed trainers.

In the past, lions were frequently caught in the wild and taken to zoos and circuses. They were trapped in nets or in pits dug in the ground. Sometimes cubs were taken from their mothers. Now, enough lions are born in captivity to fill zoo and circus needs. Some lionesses in zoos have as many as three litters in one year.

Lion cubs can be tamed easily. While they are small, they make delightful pets. Once they grow up, they are so big, strong, and potentially dangerous that they cannot be kept in the home.   GEORGE B. SCHALLER

See also ANIMAL (Animals of the Grasslands [color picture]).

Additional Resources

HANBY, JEANNETTE. *Lions Share: The Story of a Serengeti Pride.* Houghton, 1982.
JACKMAN, BRIAN, and SCOTT, JONATHAN. *The Marsh Lions: The Story of an African Pride.* Godine, 1983.
SCHALLER, GEORGE B. and KAY. *Wonders of Lions.* Dodd, 1977.

LION OF LUCERNE. See Swiss Guards.

LION OF THE NORTH. See Thirty Years' War (The Swedish Period).

LIONFISH. See Fish (color picture: The Beautiful Lionfish).

LIONS CLUBS, INTERNATIONAL ASSOCIATION OF, usually called *Lions International*, ranks as the world's largest service club organization. It has over 28,500 clubs and more than 1.1 million club members in about 150 countries and territories. Lions Clubs are associations of business and professional men who seek to recognize and meet the needs of their communities. Club activities include sight conservation and work for the blind; hearing conservation and work for the deaf; citizenship, educational, health, and social services; and work for international cooperation and understanding, including international youth camp and youth exchange programs. Some Lions Clubs sponsor Leo Clubs for young adults and Lioness Clubs for women. The Lions International Foundation raises funds to aid disaster victims.

Lions Clubs Emblem

The association was founded in Chicago in 1917. It publishes *The Lion Magazine* in English and 18 other languages. The organization holds an international convention each year. The International Association of Lions Clubs has headquarters at York and Cermak Roads, Oak Brook, Ill. 60521.

Critically reviewed by the International Association of Lions Clubs

LIP. See Mouth.

LIP READING is the technique by which one person understands the speech of another without hearing any sounds. A person does this by watching another person's mouth to see the shape it makes as each word is pronounced. Lip reading, also called *speech reading*, is used by persons who are deaf or hard-of-hearing.

Lip reading was used in the 1500's by the earliest teachers of the deaf. In 1778, Samuel Heinicke helped establish lip reading as a part of the German system of teaching the deaf. In 1843, the American educator, Horace Mann, observed methods of lip reading used in Germany, and urged that these techniques be adopted in the United States to provide a means of understanding the spoken word for the country's deaf and hard-of-hearing persons. Mann's proposals eventually led to the establishment of the first lip-reading school in the United States in 1867. Today, all schools for the deaf emphasize lip reading. Most cities offer lip-reading instruction. Many public-school systems provide training in lip reading for children who need it.

It is not easy to become a skilled lip reader. One of the difficulties is that the lips move rapidly, even during an ordinary conversation. Certain words, such as *nine* and *died*, cause confusion, because they appear as the same word on the lips. Other words, such as *under* and *easy*, cause trouble because they require little or no motion of the lips. If such difficulties are overcome, deaf and hard-of-hearing persons can communicate with others effectively, however, and without the use of sign language. Edmund Burke Boatner

LIPASE. See Enzyme (picture: Enzymes); Stomach (The Stomach's Work).

LIPCHITZ, *LIHP shihts*, **JACQUES,** *zhahk* (1891-1973), was a sculptor whose work represents many of the major movements in modern sculpture. He studied sculpture in Paris, and his early work shows the influence of French sculptor Auguste Rodin. Lipchitz met Pablo Picasso and, beginning in 1913, his sculpture reflects the style of cubism, with its overlapping, interacting planes. His forms gradually became more flexible, and he began creating what he called *transparent sculpture*. This style emphasized form distorted by movement and external and internal forces that seem to be pulling in opposite directions.

By the 1930's, Lipchitz had abandoned cubism. He turned to expressionism and surrealism, with its emphasis on the subconscious. More violent, sometimes mythological themes replaced his cubist symbols.

Lipchitz was born in what is now Lithuania. He studied and worked in Paris from 1909 to 1941, then moved to the United States to escape the Nazis. He became a U.S. citizen in 1957. Douglas George

See also Sculpture (Modern International).

Jacques Lipchitz' *Theseus* illustrates the sculptor's powerful and dramatic treatment of mythological and symbolic subjects.

Theseus (1942), a bronze sculpture by Jacques Lipchitz; Mrs. Vera List Collection (Marlborough-Gerson Gallery, New York City)

LIPID, *LIHP ihd* or *LY pihd*, is one of a large group of oily or fatty substances essential for good health. Lipids, carbohydrates, and proteins are the classes of compounds in all living things. Animal fats and plant oils are lipids. So are animal sex hormones and vitamins A, D, E, and K. Egg yolks, liver, and embryos of grains and other cereals are foods rich in lipids.

Importance of Lipids. Lipids are vital to animals and plants in many ways. They are a concentrated source of food energy, and yield about twice as many calories as an equal weight of protein or carbohydrate. Many kinds of organisms store food in lipid form. For example, the seeds of many plants contain lipids as food reserves for their embryos. The bone marrow, tissues beneath the skin and in the intestines, and tissue surrounding body organs in animals consist mostly of stored lipids.

Certain lipids form an essential part of the membranes that enclose and protect every living cell. Similar membranes surround all bodies within the cell, so that each cell body can do its job without unwanted interference from other cell bodies. Lipids are also valuable as *solvents* (dissolving substances) for vitamins A, D, E, and K, which do not dissolve in water.

Kinds of Lipids. Lipids are classified as *simple lipids* or *complex lipids*, according to their structure.

Simple Lipids contain only carbon, hydrogen, and oxygen. They consist of an alcohol in combination with certain organic acids containing a variable number of carbon atoms. A molecule of fat, the most common type of simple lipid, contains one molecule of an alcohol called *glycerol* and three molecules of *fatty acid* (a kind of organic acid). Fats include butter, lard (pig fat), tallow (beef or mutton fat), blubber (whale fat), castor oil, coconut oil, and olive oil. Waxes, another common group of simple lipids, contain an alcohol molecule that is larger than the glycerol molecule. For more details, see FAT; OIL (Fixed Oils); VEGETABLE OIL; WAX.

Complex Lipids have a more complicated structure than simple lipids. They include *phospholipids* (lipids that contain phosphorus), *steroids* (lipids made up of four rings of carbon atoms joined together), and other compounds such as *glycolipids* (lipids with one or more sugar molecules), *fat-soluble vitamins* (vitamins A, D, E, and K), and *terpenes* (yellow pigments like carotene).

Phospholipids are found in all bacteria, and in the cells of all plants and animals. They are most plentiful in sperm, eggs, embryos, and brain cells. A molecule of phospholipid contains a molecule of glycerol, a phosphate ion, and two molecules of fatty acid. Most phospholipids also contain a compound with nitrogen in it, and some contain the vitamin *inositol*.

Steroids make up an important part of living things. Many animal hormones, including the sex hormones and those produced by the *cortex* (outer part) of the adrenal glands, are steroids. Cholesterol, a substance found in the membranes of animal cells, is a steroid. Yeasts and other fungi and the seeds of higher plants also contain steroids.   D. RALPH STRENGTH

LIPIZZAN. See HORSE (Saddle Horses).

LIPOMA. See TUMOR.

LIPPERSHEY, HANS. See TELESCOPE.

LIPPI, *LEEP pee,* or *LIHP ee,* was the family name of two Italian painters of the Florentine school, father and son. They achieved popularity during the Renaissance.

Fra Filippo Lippi (1406?-1469), the father, first painted in the monumental style of Masaccio, an Italian painter. Lippi's later works are more gentle and intimate. His frescoes picturing scenes from the lives of John the Baptist and Saint Stephen are in the Cathedral of Prato, Italy.

Filippino Lippi (1457?-1504), reflects the line rhythms of Botticelli and the shadowy tones of Leonardo da Vinci in his work. His *Adoration of the Magi* is in the Uffizi Gallery in Florence.   CREIGHTON GILBERT

LIPPMANN, WALTER (1889-1974), was an American journalist who won worldwide fame as a political writer and philosopher. He became known for his clear, thoughtful writing.

In his writings, Lippmann expressed the view that civilized society could exist only if people govern their conduct by reason instead of impulse. He urged politicians to base their decisions on statesmanship rather than politics. Lippmann's opinions influenced political leaders throughout the world. Several United States

Presidents asked him for advice on various issues.

From 1931 to 1967, Lippmann wrote a column called "Today and Tomorrow" for the *New York Herald Tribune*. The column eventually was printed in more than 200 newspapers. Lippmann won the 1962 Pulitzer prize for international reporting and a special Pulitzer citation in 1958 for his commentary on national and international affairs.

Lippmann began his career in 1911 with *Everybody's Magazine*. In 1914, he helped found the *New Republic* magazine. Lippmann joined the staff of the *New York World* in 1921. He served as editor of the *World* from 1929 until the paper ceased publication in 1931.

Lippmann was born in New York City and graduated from Harvard University in 1910. After the United States entered World War I in 1917, he served in various government positions for about two years. He helped President Woodrow Wilson prepare the Fourteen Points that Wilson hoped would form the basis of a peace settlement (see FOURTEEN POINTS).

Lippmann wrote more than 20 books, including *A Preface to Politics* (1913), *Public Opinion* (1922), and *The Public Philosophy* (1955). *Walter Lippmann & the American Century* (1980) by Ronald Steel is an authoritative book about the journalist.   WILLIAM L. RIVERS

LIPPOLD, RICHARD (1915-   ), is an American sculptor. He creates complicated airy suspensions that seem to capture space and rays of light in thin gold wires that are sometimes enameled. An example of his

The Madonna and Child by Fra Filippo Lippi has a warm human quality for which the great Italian painter was famous. Lippi's son Filippino was also a celebrated artist.

Metropolitan Museum of Art

delicate abstract and geometric work is *Variation Number 7: Full Moon* It appears in the SCULPTURE article.

Lippold was born in Milwaukee and studied industrial design at the University of Chicago and the Art Institute of Chicago. Many of Lippold's sculptures have been created specifically for public buildings, including that of the foyer of Avery Fisher Hall in Lincoln Center in New York City.　　　　　　DOUGLAS GEORGE

LIPSTICK. See COSMETICS.

LIPTON, SIR THOMAS JOHNSTONE (1850-1931), a British tea merchant, became famous as a yachtsman. Between 1899 and 1930, he made five attempts to win the America's Cup, the highest award of international yachting. His sportsmanship in defeat endeared him to Americans.

Lipton began his career as a laborer and grocer's assistant in the United States from 1865 to 1869. On his twenty-first birthday, he opened in Glasgow, Scotland, the first of a chain of food stores, and in 1890 he entered the tea business. His successful advertising methods made his products widely known.

Lipton was born in Glasgow. He left his fortune to his native city for hospitals.　　　ROBERT H. BREMNER

LIQUEFACTION. See COAL (Coal Research).

LIQUEFIED PETROLEUM GAS. See GAS (Gas in the Home).

LIQUEUR. See ALCOHOLIC BEVERAGE (Liqueurs).

LIQUID, *LICK wid,* is one of the three states in which matter exists. The other two states are gaseous and solid. A liquid is similar to a gas because its molecules are not fixed to each other in any particular way, and a liquid can fit the shape of any container in which it is put. It is unlike a gas and similar to a solid because it has a definite volume, and its molecules are only slightly compressible. A liquid always seeks its own level. If a liquid is put in a container with several arms, it will rise to the same level in all the arms.

The surface of a liquid has a tension caused by molecular action, and acts like a skin. This is called *surface tension.* Because of surface tension, a greased needle will rest on the surface of water without sinking.

The molecules of a liquid often have a greater attraction for other substances than they have for each other. For this reason, they will rise in narrow tubes above their own level. This action is called *capillarity.* Plants draw water by capillary action.

If liquids are heated beyond a certain point, they change into gas. Water changes into steam. If liquids are cooled below a certain point, they change into solids. Water freezes into ice. Different liquids have different freezing and boiling points. Substances which are normally gases can be cooled and compressed into a liquid state. Some substances which are normally solid can be heated until they turn into a liquid. For added information on liquids, see the articles on the other two states of matter, GAS and SOLID, and the article on WATER.　　　　　　LOUIS MARICK

Related Articles in WORLD BOOK include:

Boiling Point	Freezing Point	Osmosis
Capillarity	Hydraulics	Siphon
Condensation	Liquid Air	Solution
Density	Matter	Surface Tension
Diffusion	Melting Point	Vapor
Distillation	Molecule	Viscosity

LIQUID AIR is a product made by greatly reducing the temperature of air until it turns into a fluid. Air becomes liquid at about −190° C. Liquid air is so cold that it boils when poured over ice, which is almost 200° C hotter. The liquid is bluish and looks like water. Liquid air, like the air we breathe, consists of about 78 per cent nitrogen, 21 per cent oxygen, and 1 per cent argon.

Scientists use liquid air in *cryogenics,* the study of temperatures −100° C and lower (see CRYOGENICS). Liquid air is considered a *cryogenic fluid* because of its extremely low temperature. It is a primary source of liquid forms of nitrogen, oxygen, and other gases. Scientists use liquid nitrogen in biology, chemistry, and physics research. It is also used in refrigerating and processing food. Liquid oxygen is used in compact, high-energy fuels for rocket engines that power spacecraft.

Properties. Liquid air affects different substances in a variety of ways. For example, liquid mercury becomes as hard as steel when liquid air is poured over it. A tennis ball that has been dipped in liquid air will shatter when bounced. A lead bell, which normally makes a dull sound, will temporarily produce a clear tone after being exposed to liquid air.

Scientists use liquid air to study the effects of extremely low temperatures on the strength of certain substances. Such materials as iron and plastics temporarily become brittle after being dipped into liquid air. However, copper and brass become tougher upon immersion in the fluid. Exposure to liquid air also makes metals better conductors of electricity and increases the strength of certain types of magnets.

Scientists measure the temperature of liquid air with special thermometers because mercury and alcohol thermometers cannot be used. The contents of such thermometers freeze at temperatures much higher than that of liquid air. The most accurate and widely used thermometer that measures the temperature of liquid air is the *platinum resistance thermometer.* This type of thermometer measures temperature by determining its effect on the electrical resistance of platinum. Platinum becomes a better or poorer conductor of electricity as its temperature changes. Another kind of special thermometer, the *constant-volume gas thermometer,* measures the effect of temperature on the pressure of a gas kept at a certain volume. Such gases as helium or neon are used to measure the temperature of liquid air because they turn into liquid at lower temperatures than air does.

Nitrogen and oxygen, the two major parts of air, can be separated and used in their liquid form by distilling liquid air. When liquid air is heated, the nitrogen turns into a gas before the oxygen does because the boiling point of nitrogen is lower. After the nitrogen has been removed, the remaining substance consists mostly of liquid oxygen. The high oxygen content of the undistilled liquid could cause an explosion if a flammable material came in contact with it.

Making Liquid Air. The process of making liquid air is based on the fact that compressed air becomes cooler when it expands. This cooling effect was described in detail in 1853 by two British physicists, James Prescott Joule and William Thomson, and it later became known as the *Joule-Thomson effect.* In 1877, Louis-Paul

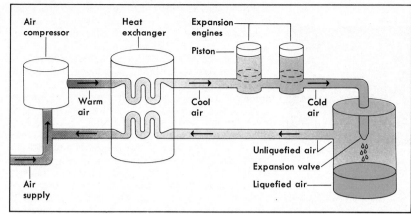

Most Liquid Air is manufactured by the Claude process. In this process, an *air compressor* increases the air pressure. The air, heated by compression, is cooled slightly in the *heat exchanger*. The air then enters *expansion engines*, which greatly reduce its temperature. Some of the air liquefies as it flows through the expansion valve.

Cailletet, a French physicist, liquefied air for the first time.

In 1895, the German chemist Carl von Linde invented a commercial process for liquid air production based on the Joule-Thomson effect. Linde's method is still used today but with many improvements. Compressors raise the air pressure in a chamber to about 3,000 pounds per square inch (210 kilograms per square centimeter). Compression heats the air, and so water jackets on the compressor, plus a device called a *heat exchanger*, are used to lower the compressed air's temperature before it is liquefied.

Air can be liquefied in one of two ways. In one method, called *Joule-Thomson expansion*, the compressed air flows through a series of throttling valves into increasingly larger chambers. The pressure and temperature of the air decreases in each chamber as the air expands. In the final chamber, some of the air has become cold enough to condense into liquid. The cold vapor from this chamber is circulated around the other chambers to help cool the air that is still going through the liquefying process.

In 1902, Georges Claude, a French engineer, developed the second method of liquefying air. This method resembles Joule-Thomson expansion but is more efficient because it makes use of work done by expanding air. In the Claude method, air enters a chamber and pushes a piston as it expands. As the piston moves, the volume of the chamber increases, which causes the air pressure and the temperature in the chamber to decrease. The air is sent through a series of these piston-equipped chambers, called *expansion engines*, until it becomes liquid.

Special containers called *Dewar flasks* protect liquid air from heat and evaporation. A Dewar flask is a bottle made of two layers of glass. There is space between the layers of glass to insulate the contents. The flask may be coated with silver to reflect heat. Large quantities of liquid air for industrial use are stored in huge insulated tanks.   JOHN B. BUTT

LIQUID CRYSTAL is a substance that flows like a liquid but has some properties of a solid within a certain temperature range. Many types of liquid crystals are brightly colored. Small changes in temperature cause their color to change. This property gives them practical medical and industrial uses. If a thin layer of liquid crystals is painted on a person's skin, the color changes will show the location of warm blood vessels and abnormal conditions, such as tumors. In industry, liquid crystals detect flaws in metal parts by showing temperature differences as changes in color on the parts' surfaces.

Liquid crystals behave differently from other substances because of the arrangement of their molecules. When an ordinary substance melts, its molecules move in all directions. When ice melts, for example, the molecules form water, with properties different from those of ice. But before a liquid-crystal substance melts completely, it forms a state between a solid and a liquid. Millions of its molecules line up side by side and form microscopic clusters that can slide past one another only in certain directions.   KENNETH SCHUG

See also WATCH (Electronic Display Watches).

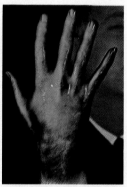

Liquid Crystals painted on a man's hand, *left*, show areas of different temperatures as different colors. Blue is the warmest area, green cooler, and red coolest. The color change to green, *right*, indicates that the temperature of the hand has dropped.

LIQUID FIRE. See FLAME THROWER.

LIQUID MEASURE. See WEIGHTS AND MEASURES; BARREL (pictures).

LIQUID OXYGEN. See OXYGEN (Other Uses).

LIQUIDATION. See STOCK, CAPITAL.

LIQUOR. See ALCOHOLIC BEVERAGE; DISTILLING.

LIQUOR LAWS. See PROHIBITION; LOCAL OPTION.

LIQUORICE. See LICORICE.

LIRA, *LIHR uh*, is a unit of money in Italy and Turkey. The word comes from the Latin term *libra*, mean-

The Five-Lira Italian Coin Is Shown Above.

ing *pound.* For the value of the lira, see MONEY (table: Exchange Rates).

LIRIPIPE. See CLOTHING (The Middle Ages).

LISA, MANUEL. See NEBRASKA (American Exploration and Settlement).

LISBOA, ANTÔNIO FRANCISCO. See LATIN AMERICA (Sculpture); BRAZIL (picture: Sculpture).

LISBON (pop. 817,627; met. area pop. 2,062,200) is the capital and largest city of Portugal. About a fifth of the nation's people live in the Lisbon area. The name of the city in Portuguese is LISBOA. Lisbon lies at the *estuary* (mouth) of the Tagus River. The estuary empties into the Atlantic Ocean about 10 miles (16 kilometers) west of the center of the city (see PORTUGAL [political map]). Lisbon is a major port and the political, economic, and cultural center of Portugal.

The City covers 32 square miles (84 square kilometers). It overlooks the Tagus estuary, one of Europe's most important natural harbors. The 25th of April Bridge, one of the longest suspension bridges in the world, extends 3,323 feet (1,013 meters) over the Tagus at Lisbon.

Downtown Lisbon is a low, flat district next to the harbor. It is called the *Baixa.* Most of Lisbon's finer shops are located in the Baixa. The rest of the city is hilly, with commercial, industrial, and residential districts.

Lisbon has many public squares, statues of Portuguese heroes, broad treelined avenues, and small parks with trees and flowers. Most of Lisbon's people live in pastel-colored houses and apartment buildings. Many tourists visit the São Carlos Opera House and the Castle of São Jorge, once the home of Portugal's kings. Another attraction is the Tower of Belém, built in the early 1500's to honor the Portuguese explorer Vasco da Gama. Lisbon has several universities, including the University of Lisbon and the Technical University. Portugal's national library is in the city.

Economy. Large shipments of Portuguese ceramics, cork, sardines, tomato paste, and wine are exported from Lisbon's harbor. One of Europe's chief shipyards is across the Tagus from Lisbon. Portugal's chief banks, insurance companies, and investment firms are in Lisbon. An international airport and major railroad lines serve the city. Public transportation in Lisbon includes buses, electric trains, streetcars, and a subway system.

History. In ancient times, the Greeks, Carthaginians, and Romans colonized Lisbon. The Visigoths captured Lisbon from the Romans during the A.D. 400's, and north African Muslims called *Moors* seized it during the 700's. In 1147, Christian forces led by Afonso I, the first king of Portugal, retook the city from the Moors.

Lisbon became the official capital of Portugal in the

Photri

Dom Pedro IV Square, popularly known as the Rossio, is a center of lively activity in Lisbon. A monument to Pedro IV, the first emperor of Brazil, stands in the middle of the square. The Rossio lies in an area of Lisbon called the *Bairro Alto,* which has many cafes, shops, and night clubs.

late 1200's. During the 1400's and 1500's, the city served as headquarters for the explorers and adventurers who established Portugal's empire in Africa, Asia, and South America. In 1755, an earthquake destroyed about two-thirds of Lisbon and killed more than 60,000 people. The Baixa was built as part of the reconstruction of the city.

During World War II (1939-1945), Lisbon became a center of international political activity because it was a neutral city. On April 25, 1974, a military revolt in Lisbon overthrew the dictatorship that had ruled Portugal since 1926. DOUGLAS L. WHEELER

See also PORTUGAL (pictures).

LISGAR, *LIHS gahr,* **BARON** (1807-1876), a British administrator, served as governor general of Canada from 1869 to 1872. He played an important advisory role in stopping the uprising known as the Red River Rebellion (1869-1870). While he was governor general, Manitoba and British Columbia became Canadian provinces. Plans were begun in 1871 to build a railway across the entire country. The Treaty of Washington, signed in 1871, ended quarrels between the United States and Great Britain about fishing rights in Canadian waters.

Lisgar was born in Bombay, India. His given and family name was John Young. He was elected to the British Parliament in 1831. Lisgar became chief secretary for Ireland in 1852, lord high commissioner of the Ionian Islands in 1855, and governor general of New South Wales in 1861. He was knighted in 1855 and became the first Baron Lisgar in 1870. JACQUES MONET

LISMER, ARTHUR. See GROUP OF SEVEN.

LISPING is a speech defect. Persons who lisp have difficulty pronouncing *sibilant* (hissing) sounds, such as *s* or *z*. They may substitute other sounds, or omit or distort these sounds. For example, in the sentence "I see my sister," a person who lisps may substitute *th* for the *s* sounds and say "I thee my thithter." Another person may omit the *s* altogether and say "I -ee my -i-ter." Still another may distort the *s* into a whistling sound instead of the normal hiss.

Many children lisp when they first begin to speak. During normal speech development, most children master the hissing sounds long before school age. But sometimes a child's speech development may be delayed. Various things can cause such delays. Among these may be loss of hearing and defects of mouth structures, particularly the tongue, teeth, and palate. Almost all children lisp when they lose their primary front teeth (see TEETH). Improper speech habits of parents may also delay a child's speech development.

When lisping results from mouth defects, the defects must be corrected before completely normal speech can be obtained. Speech therapists, who are specially trained to treat speech disorders, teach people who lisp to speak correctly. The therapist trains individuals to recognize their own speech errors and then to form the sounds properly. MARTIN F. PALMER

See also SPEECH THERAPY.

LIST SYSTEM. See PROPORTIONAL REPRESENTATION.

LISTER, SIR JOSEPH (1827-1912), founded antiseptic surgery. Before his time, people dreaded surgery. The most trivial operation was likely to be followed by infection, and death occurred in up to 50 per cent of all of the surgical cases.

After Louis Pasteur discovered that bacteria caused fermentation, Lister in 1865 realized that the formation of pus was also due to germs. At first, he used carbolic-acid sprays to kill germs in the air, but later he realized that germs were also carried by the surgeon's hands and instruments. He insisted on the use of antiseptics on hands, instruments, and dressings. He also introduced the use of catgut ligatures in 1880.

His application of antiseptics so revolutionized surgery that its whole history can be divided into two periods, pre-Listerian and post-Listerian. Mortalities fell to between 2 and 3 per cent of all patients operated on, and it became safe for doctors to open abdomens, chests, heads, and joints.

Lister was born at Upton, Essex, and studied medicine at University College, London. He served as professor of surgery at Glasgow University from 1860 to 1869, at Edinburgh University from 1869 to 1877, and at King's College, London, from 1877 to 1894. He was also surgeon to Queen Victoria. He was made a baronet in 1883. In 1897, he was elevated to the peerage, the first medical man so honored. His title was Baron Lister of Lyme Regis. HENRY J. L. MARRIOTT

See also ANTISEPTIC; SEMMELWEIS, IGNAZ P.

LISZT, *lihst,* **FRANZ,** *frahnts* (1811-1886), was a Hungarian pianist, composer, and teacher. He wrote many works for the piano and orchestra, and was the most celebrated pianist of the 1800's. He performed an invaluable service to the world of music as the teacher and sponsor of most of the brilliant musicians of his time.

His Life. Liszt was born in Raiding, Hungary. His father, a talented amateur musician, was his first piano teacher. The boy's musical talent appeared early. By the time he was 11, he had been presented in many parts of Europe as a child prodigy at the piano.

In 1823, Liszt went to Paris to study the piano systematically. The French recognized him as a brilliant performer with an almost uncanny ability to improvise on the key-

Bettmann Archive/BBC Hulton

Franz Liszt

board. He had once wanted to become a priest, but decided instead to follow a career in music. He was inspired by the success of Niccolò Paganini to become as much a master of the piano as Paganini was of the violin.

Liszt quickly became a favorite of the wealthy in France, not only because of his talent, but also because of his fascinating personality. His generosity, his fine family background, and his ability as a writer and critic added to his popularity.

In 1830, when Liszt was 19, he met Frédéric Chopin, Hector Berlioz, and Paganini. A few years later, he became interested in the Countess d'Agoult. He lived with her for about 10 years. He was also romantically involved with the woman writer, George Sand.

Liszt made triumphal tours throughout most of Europe as a concert pianist, and he achieved tremendous success. In 1848, he retired to the German Duchy of Weimar, where he had been appointed in 1842 as court music conductor. In Weimar, he began his brilliant career as a composer. He also conducted opera and concerts, and made Weimar the European headquarters for music. He sponsored the work of Richard Wagner and his new concept of musical theater (see WAGNER, RICHARD). While at Weimar, Liszt brought out Wagner's *Tannhäuser* and *Lohengrin*. He also produced *Benvenuto Cellini*, an opera by the French composer Hector Berlioz, as well as many other works.

The Princess Carolyne von Wittgenstein strongly influenced his career as a composer at Weimar. But in 1859, Liszt resigned his post there and went to Rome. In 1865, he joined the Franciscans, and was given the title of Abbé. From then on, he divided his time between Rome, Weimar, and Budapest, and began teaching piano and composition. Among his students were many who became great: Camille Saint-Saëns, Georges Bizet, Bedřich Smetana, and Rafael Joseffy.

In 1886, when he was 75 years old, Liszt made his last concert tour, playing at Paris, and at London for Queen Victoria. He died at Bayreuth, attending a Wagner festival. A statue at Weimar honors him.

His Works. Liszt's musical compositions have caused much controversy among critics. He had an obvious talent for melody and for colorful orchestration, and many have praised the brilliance of style evident in his piano music. But other critics have believed that he lacked great creative talent.

He is credited with developing the rhapsody as a form of serious music, although he was not the first to compose one. The *Hungarian Rhapsodies*, in which he used gypsy music and folk-dance themes, are among his best-loved compositions. He also made popular the symphonic poem. He developed the *leitmotif* (recurrent theme) used later by Wagner and Richard Strauss. His performances as a solo concert pianist set a style for such concerts which is still followed.

Liszt's works include two piano concertos; 14 symphonic poems, among which are *Les Préludes*, *Orpheus*, *Tasso*, and *Faust;* and the *Hungarian Fantasy* for piano and orchestra. Of his piano music, the best-known pieces are the *Sonata in B minor*, ballades in A minor and B minor, three "Liebesträume," and "Deux Légendes."

His transcriptions of the work of other composers include Johann Sebastian Bach's *Fantasia and Fugue in G minor* for organ, six of Bach's organ preludes and fugues, and "Grandes Études de Paganini," from Paganini's "Caprices." HANS ROSENWALD

LITANY, *LIHT uh nee*, is a form of prayer-dialogue in which the worshipers take responsive parts. The minister or priest recites its separate sentences, and the congregation "responds." A litany may be said at any religious service as a request for grace and mercy, or for deliverance from danger, pestilence, or sin. The three litanies most commonly said in the Roman Catholic Church are the *Litany of Saints*, the *Litany of the Holy Name of Jesus*, and the *Litany of the Blessed Virgin*. The Eastern Orthodox, the Anglican, the Episcopal, the Lutheran, the Reformed, and the Presbyterian are among other churches which include the litany in their worship services. MERVIN MONROE DEEMS and FULTON J. SHEEN

LITCHFIELD, Conn. (pop. 7,605), is a picturesque village in western Connecticut (see CONNECTICUT [political map]). It was settled in 1720. It has many well-preserved colonial homes, and broad, elm-lined streets.

In 1776, a lead statue of King George III was brought there from New York City and melted into more than 42,000 bullets for American soldiers in the Revolutionary War. In 1774, Tapping Reeve, a Litchfield judge, began teaching law in his home. In 1784, he built a law school next to his home. This school—founded as the Litchfield Law School and later called the Tapping Reeve Law School—was the first institution in the United States devoted entirely to teaching law. It operated until 1833. Its students included Aaron Burr and John C. Calhoun.

The Borough of Litchfield became the first Connecticut Historic District in 1959. ALBERT E. VAN DUSEN

LITCHI, *LEE chee*, is the name of an evergreen tree which is widely grown in southern China. Its name is

J. Horace McFarland
Litchi Fruits

also spelled *lychee* or *leechee*. It is occasionally grown in many other tropical and subtropical parts of the world. Commercial plantings of the litchi tree were begun in southern Florida, in the early 1940's. The tree has glossy light green leaves with several leaflets. It bears clusters of bright red fruits. The juicy white pulp surrounding the fruit's single seed has somewhat the flavor of a muscat grape. Dried litchis are sometimes referred to as litchi nuts.

Scientific Classification. Litchis are in the soapberry family, *Sapindaceae*. They are genus *Litchi*, species *L. chinensis*. JULIAN C. CRANE

LITER, *LEE tuhr*, is a commonly used measure of capacity and volume in the metric system. It is also spelled *litre*. The official unit for volume in the metric system is

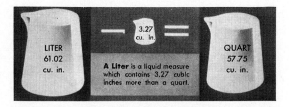

the cubic meter, but most people in countries using the metric system use the liter instead. In common usage, a liter equals a cubic decimeter, or 1,000 cubic centimeters. One liter contains 61.024 cubic inches and equals 1.0567 liquid quarts. See also WEIGHTS AND MEASURES; METRIC SYSTEM. E.G. STRAUS

LITERACY. See ILLITERACY; READING.

LITERACY TEST. See VOTING (Restrictions).

LITERARY AWARDS. See CALDECOTT MEDAL; GOVERNOR-GENERAL'S LITERARY AWARDS; NATIONAL BOOK AWARDS; NEWBERY MEDAL; NOBEL PRIZES; PULITZER PRIZES; REGINA MEDAL.

LITERARY CRITICISM. See CRITICISM.

LITERATURE, in its broadest sense, is everything that has ever been written. It includes comic books and pamphlets on potato bugs, as well as the novels of Mark Twain and the plays of William Shakespeare.

In a narrower sense, there are various kinds of "literatures." For example, we may read literature written in a certain language, such as *French literature*. We also study writings about a people—the *literature of the American Indian*. We often speak of the literature of a period, such as *literature of the 1800's*. We also refer to the literature of a subject, as in the *literature of gardening*.

But the word *literature*, in its strictest sense, means more than printed words. Literature is one of the fine arts. It refers to *belles-lettres*, a French phrase that means *beautiful writing*. We distinguish between literature and comic books much as we distinguish between a professional baseball game and a back yard game of catch. When we speak of a piece of writing as literature, we are praising it.

Literature has two main divisions: fiction and nonfiction. *Fiction* is writing that an author creates from the imagination. Authors may include facts about real persons or events, but they combine these facts with imaginary situations. Most fiction is narrative writing, such as novels and short stories. Fiction also includes drama and poetry. *Nonfiction* is factual writing about real-life situations. The chief forms of nonfiction include the essay, history, biography, autobiography, and diary.

Enjoying Literature

Why We Read Literature. We all read for a variety of reasons. These reasons change with our age, our interests, and the literature we read. Our basic reason for reading is probably pleasure. We read literature mostly because we enjoy it.

Reading for pleasure may take various forms. We may read just to pass the time. Or, we may want to escape the four walls that usually surround us. Reading serves as a jet airplane that speeds us away from ourselves into the worlds of other people.

We often read for information and knowledge. We find pleasure in learning about life in the Swiss Alps or on the Mississippi River. We find possible solutions to our problems when we meet people in books whose problems are like our own. Through literature, we sometimes understand situations we could not otherwise understand in real life.

We also read simply for the enjoyment we get from the arrangement of words. We can find pleasure even in nonsense syllables, just as children like the sound of "Ring Around the Rosie," although they may not know what the words mean.

How To Read Creatively. No work of literature has wisdom or beauty in itself. The greatest poem ever written is only a printed sheet of paper until a reader reacts to it. Writing, to become literature, requires a reader. The reader helps create literature by responding to the writer's thoughts, emotions, and beliefs.

A creative reader considers both *what* the writer wants to say and *how* it is said. Creative readers bring their own experiences of life and language to the experiences the writer presents on the printed page. They measure the honesty of the writer's approach by their own ideas of truth. Creative reading leads to the deepest enjoyment of literature.

Judging Literature. Reading is such a personal activity that there can be no final rules for judging a piece of writing. The taste and fashion of the times often enter into critical judgments. For example, a work considered a tragedy by one generation of readers may be regarded as a comedy by the next generation. Some books become best sellers overnight. But their popularity does not necessarily mean that they are great. Other works continue to be important for nonliterary reasons. Many students today read *Uncle Tom's Cabin* chiefly for its historical interest.

Yet, readers and critics do agree on certain writings that they consider *classics*, or literature of the highest rank. For example, thousands of stories have been published about young lovers whose parents disapproved of their romance. Most were soon forgotten. But for more than 300 years, Shakespeare's *Romeo and Juliet* has been considered a classic story of young love.

Shakespeare was a superb craftsman. In his play, he used words and phrases that are packed with meaning. But, perhaps more important, Shakespeare gave *Romeo and Juliet* broad human values. These values were not limited to one place or to one period of time. The characters of the play seem to be real persons who face real problems. They express feelings that people anywhere might have at any time. For the same reasons, the works of a novelist such as Jane Austen mean a great deal to creative readers of any generation. Her novels *Emma* and *Pride and Prejudice* express lasting truths and show the author's writing skill. They will probably appeal to readers during the 2000's just as they did in the 1800's.

Every reader is a critic. Even when we say we have no opinion of a book, we are making a judgment. But such a judgment is probably a poor one, based on little thought. Our ability to judge literature intelligently develops as our reading broadens. Our critical skills, like our muscles, develop with use.

The Elements of Literature

Almost every literary work includes four elements: (1) characters; (2) plot; (3) theme, or statement; and (4) style. A good writer tries to balance these elements in order to create a unified work of art.

Characters. Writers may want to describe actions or ideas. But they must also describe the characters—the persons or objects—affected by these actions and ideas. The characters make up the central interest of many dramas and novels, as well as biographies and autobiographies. Even a poem is concerned with characters. The speaker, or the poet, is often the main character of a poem. Writers must know their characters thoroughly and have a clear picture of each one's looks, speech, and thoughts.

Motivation means the reasons for a character's actions. Writers must be sure that the motives of their characters are clear and logical. In literature, as in life, character determines action. It would be difficult for Tom Sawyer and David Copperfield to change places. If Tom were in David's place, the novel *David Copperfield* would turn into a different kind of book.

Setting is the place in which a character's story occurs. Literary characters, like the persons who read about them, do not exist alone in space. They act and react with one another. They also respond to the world in which they live. Setting is another way of showing people. If Tom lived in England and David in Missouri, they would become different persons as they responded to and acted within their surroundings.

Plot tells what happens to the characters in a story. A plot is built around a series of events that take place within a definite period of time. No rules exist for the order in which the events are presented.

A unified plot has a beginning, a middle, and an end. That is, an author leads us from somewhere (a character with a problem), through somewhere (the character facing the problem), to somewhere (the character overcoming or being overcome by the problem). In literary terms, we speak of a story having an exposition, a rising action, a climax, and a denouement, or outcome. The *exposition* gives the background and situation of the story. The *rising action* builds upon the given material. It creates suspense, or a reader's desire to find out what happens next. The *climax* is the highest point of interest. The *denouement* ends the story.

Theme, or statement, is the basic idea expressed by a work of literature. It develops from the interplay of character and plot. A theme may warn the reader to lead a better life or a different kind of life. It may de-

clare that life is profitable or unprofitable, or that crime does or does not pay.

Serious writers strive to make their work an honest expression of *sentiment*, or true emotion. They avoid *sentimentality*, which means giving too much emphasis to emotion or pretending to feel an emotion. A writer of honest emotion does not have to tell the reader what to think about a story. A good story directs the reader to the author's conclusion.

Style is the way a writer uses words to create literature. It is one word following another, and one paragraph leading to the next. We can seldom enjoy a story's characters or plot without enjoying the author's style. The way writers write is part of what they have to say. From the first word to the last, a writer must solve problems of style by answering such questions as: "What kinds of words shall I use?" "How shall I present details?" "Should paragraphs be long or short?"

A writer's *point of view*, or the way a story is presented, is another part of style. A writer may tell a story in the first person (I) as though the narrator were a major or minor character in it. Or, the writer may use the third person (he or she) method, in which the narrator stands apart from the characters and describes the action. In the third person *limited* point of view, the narrator describes the events as a single character might see and hear them. In the third person *omniscient*, or all-

Literature Literary giants from the 1100's to the present include poets, dramatists, and novelists of many nations. The names of many of these writers are listed in chronological order. Great literature flourished long before the 1100's with such works as the epic poems of Homer in the 700's B.C.

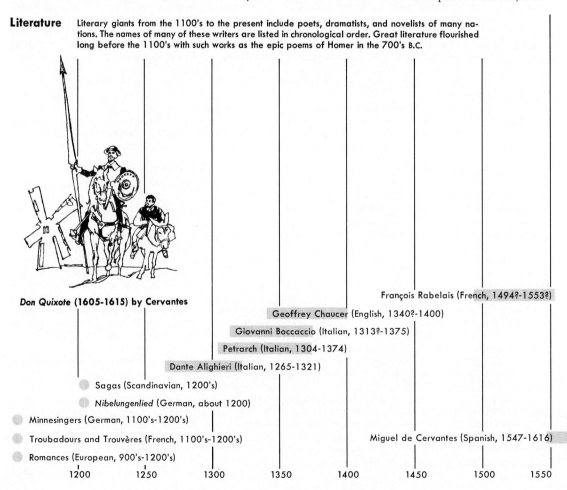

Don Quixote **(1605-1615) by Cervantes**

François Rabelais (French, 1494?-1553?)

Geoffrey Chaucer (English, 1340?-1400)

Giovanni Boccaccio (Italian, 1313?-1375)

Petrarch (Italian, 1304-1374)

Dante Alighieri (Italian, 1265-1321)

Sagas (Scandinavian, 1200's)

Nibelungenlied (German, about 1200)

Minnesingers (German, 1100's-1200's)

Miguel de Cervantes (Spanish, 1547-1616)

Troubadours and Trouvères (French, 1100's-1200's)

Romances (European, 900's-1200's)

| 1200 | 1250 | 1300 | 1350 | 1400 | 1450 | 1500 | 1550 |

knowing, point of view, the narrator reports on what several characters are thinking and feeling.

Kinds of Discourse

The word *discourse* refers to *communication*. In literature, it means the way writers tell their readers what they want them to know. A writer may use four kinds of discourse: (1) exposition, (2) argument, (3) description, and (4) narration. The writer's purpose determines which kind of discourse is used.

Exposition answers a real or an imaginary question. It is the writer's way of presenting facts or of explaining what a thing means, how it works, or why it is important. THE WORLD BOOK ENCYCLOPEDIA has many *expository* articles, including this one.

Argument tries to convince readers of an attitude, or to persuade them to share the writer's attitude. A writer may try to change the reader's mind by using argument that appeals to reason, to emotions, or to both.

Description is used to picture something that the writer wants the reader to see. Writers use description when they write about the appearance of a person, an apple, or a building. Through description, the writer appeals to the reader's sense of touch, taste, smell, or hearing. A writer has described skillfully when the reader senses the object described.

Narration gives an account of action or events. It tells the reader what is happening. If we think of description as a picture, narration may be considered as a motion picture.

A writer may use all four kinds of discourse in a single piece of literature. For example, "The Rime of the Ancient Mariner," by Samuel Taylor Coleridge, begins with *narration* when it tells how the Mariner stops a guest at a wedding feast:

> It is an ancient Mariner,
> And he stoppeth one of three.

The guest engages in *exposition* when he explains:

> The Bridegroom's doors are opened wide,
> And I am next of kin;
> The guests are met, the feast is set:

The Mariner makes use of *description* as he tells:

> And now came both mist and snow,
> And it grew wondrous cold:
> And ice, mast-high, came floating by,
> As green as emerald.

The author uses *argument* in the last section of the poem:

> He prayeth best, who loveth best
> All things both great and small;
> For the dear God who loveth us,
> He made and loveth all.

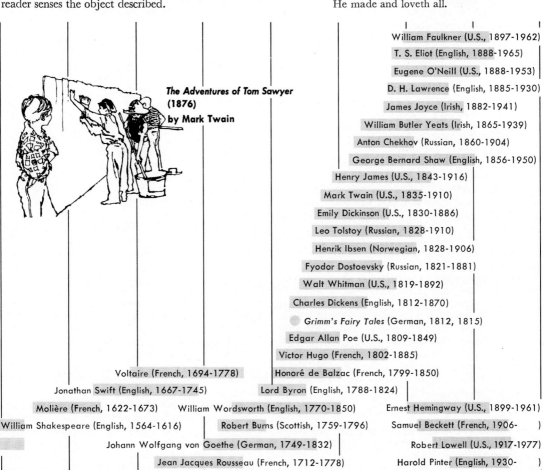

The Adventures of Tom Sawyer (1876) by Mark Twain

William Faulkner (U.S., 1897-1962)
T. S. Eliot (English, 1888-1965)
Eugene O'Neill (U.S., 1888-1953)
D. H. Lawrence (English, 1885-1930)
James Joyce (Irish, 1882-1941)
William Butler Yeats (Irish, 1865-1939)
Anton Chekhov (Russian, 1860-1904)
George Bernard Shaw (English, 1856-1950)
Henry James (U.S., 1843-1916)
Mark Twain (U.S., 1835-1910)
Emily Dickinson (U.S., 1830-1886)
Leo Tolstoy (Russian, 1828-1910)
Henrik Ibsen (Norwegian, 1828-1906)
Fyodor Dostoevsky (Russian, 1821-1881)
Walt Whitman (U.S., 1819-1892)
Charles Dickens (English, 1812-1870)
Grimm's Fairy Tales (German, 1812, 1815)
Edgar Allan Poe (U.S., 1809-1849)
Victor Hugo (French, 1802-1885)
Voltaire (French, 1694-1778)
Honoré de Balzac (French, 1799-1850)
Jonathan Swift (English, 1667-1745)
Lord Byron (English, 1788-1824)
Molière (French, 1622-1673)   William Wordsworth (English, 1770-1850)   Ernest Hemingway (U.S., 1899-1961)
William Shakespeare (English, 1564-1616)   Robert Burns (Scottish, 1759-1796)   Samuel Beckett (French, 1906-   )
Johann Wolfgang von Goethe (German, 1749-1832)   Robert Lowell (U.S., 1917-1977)
Jean Jacques Rousseau (French, 1712-1778)   Harold Pinter (English, 1930-   )

1600   1650   1700   1750   1800   1850   1900   1950   2000

LITERATURE

The World of the Writer

No literary work can be completely separated from the man or woman who created it. Authors must write from within their own experiences, both real and imagined. As readers, we can enlarge our literary understanding by looking into the world of the writer.

The Writer's Outer World. No author writes in a vacuum. The period and the society in which the author lives, and the works of other writers, all influence the author.

Many of the greatest contributions to literature have resulted from an author's reaction to social conditions. For example, the writings of Martin Luther and John Calvin influenced and were influenced by the Protestant Reformation in the 1500's. Percy Bysshe Shelley would probably have rebelled against any society he lived in. But the economic, political, and social situation in England during the early 1800's provided material for Shelley's rebellious nature.

The Writer's Inner World. The background, interests, and physical assets and handicaps of authors also affect their writing. Likewise, the personal relationships of writers to their homes, families, friends, and enemies all become the materials of their art. For example, Charles Lamb would probably have written differently if he had not stuttered, if he had not taken care of his sister Mary, and if he had not been a bachelor. The poetry of Elizabeth Barrett Browning and Emily Dickinson would have been different if the women could have exchanged lives.

Generally, the works of a writer have greater unity than do the writings of a particular period. For example, both the early and late works of John Donne show the poet's basic personality. This is true even though he was called "Mad Jack" in his youth and "Dr. Donne" as a mature man.

The Writer's Attitude. We cannot make a final generalization about the works of any author. Nor can we truthfully say that "Shakespeare is always like this," or "Ernest Hemingway is always like that." But we can identify a writer's attitude toward life. Perhaps the terms most often used in describing a writer's attitude are romantic and realistic.

Romantic writers admire the unusual, the picturesque, and the quaint in humanity and nature. They revolt against the traditional in thought and action, and emphasize the importance of the individual.

Realistic writers deal with the commonplace instead of the unusual. They try to record the world as they actually see it, even its most unpleasant aspects. They wish to present ideas as objective documents.

Critics often use the terms *romanticism* and *realism* for the literary movements that swept Europe during the 1800's. For a discussion of these movements, see the *History* section of this article.

Forms of Literature

The Novel is a long work of fiction that tells about events in the lives of real or imaginary persons. Most novels reflect the author's outlook on life. There are many kinds of novels, dealing with a great variety of subjects. For example, Eleanor H. Porter's sentimental novel *Pollyanna* describes the adventures of a young girl who always sees the good side of life. James Joyce's psychological novel *Finnegans Wake* explores the dream world of an Irish innkeeper.

A novel is a modern version of earlier forms of literature. Many of its features come from the *epic*, a serious narrative poem about a heroic figure (see EPIC). Others stem from the medieval *romance*, an adventure story of kings and knights (see ROMANCE). The Spanish *picaresque* story of the 1500's had an important influence on the growth of the novel. The picaresque story described disconnected events in the life of a *picaro*—a clever, dishonest hero. The novel also grew out of the *character* of the 1600's, which portrayed familiar types of people. See NOVEL.

The Short Story is a short work of fiction that usually centers around a single incident. Because of its shorter length, the characters and situations are fewer and less complicated than those of a novel. A short story may range in length from a *short short story* of 1,000 to 1,500 words to a *novelette*, or short novel, of 12,000 to 30,000 words. The short story has many qualities of the *ballad*, a story in verse form. It is also related to the *folk tale*, a story handed down by word of mouth from generation to generation. Many characteristics of the short story come from earlier literary forms that tried to teach a lesson. These forms include the *fable*, a story about animals, and the *parable*, a story with a religious lesson. See SHORT STORY; BALLAD; FABLE; PARABLE.

Drama is a story written to be presented by actors on a stage. It usually includes stage directions describing the appearances and actions of the characters. A drama takes the form of *dialogue*, or conversation, between two or more persons. The two major forms of drama are tragedy and comedy.

A *tragedy* is a serious drama that ends in disaster. Aristotle laid down the basic principles of tragedy in his *Poetics*. He wrote that the purpose of tragedy was to make the audience feel "pity and fear" for the characters. The hero of any ancient Greek tragedy was a great person who suffered because of a *tragic flaw*, or error in judgment. Later dramatists extended the meaning of tragedy to include the story of any person who faces misfortune.

A *comedy* is a light, amusing drama with a happy ending. The characters in a comedy entertain rather than disturb the audience by their actions. Comedy includes many forms. *Low comedy*, or *slapstick*, uses noisy, boisterous action and ridiculous situations. *High comedy* gets its humor from clever, witty dialogue. *Satire* pokes fun at the foolish things that people say and do. A *comedy of manners* ridicules the social habits of a period. A *tragicomedy* tells about a serious situation that ends happily. See DRAMA; COMEDY; SATIRE; TRAGEDY.

Poetry usually has meter and rhyme. Poets use *meter* when they arrange words in a pattern with a definite rhythm. They use *rhyme* when they repeat sounds within lines or at the ends of lines. A poem that does not have a regular metrical pattern or rhyme scheme is written in *free verse* (see FREE VERSE; METER; RHYME; RHYTHM). There are three main types of poetry: lyric, narrative, and dramatic.

Lyric Poems are short and songlike. They emphasize the thoughts and feelings of the poet or speaker. A lyric poem may be discussed in terms of either its subject matter or its form. When we call a poem an *elegy*, a lament for the dead, we are discussing subject matter. When we call a poem a *sonnet*, which is a 14-line poem with a definite rhyme scheme, we are discussing form.

Narrative Poems tell a story. An *epic* (heroic poem) describes the actions of a majestic hero, such as the Trojan warrior Aeneas. A *ballad* (short story in verse) has a more commonplace tone.

Dramatic Poems, like dramas, tell their stories through the speech of the characters. A poem in which only one character speaks is called a *dramatic monologue*. A *closet drama* is a play in verse form written to be read but not staged. See POETRY; BALLAD; ELEGY; EPIC; SONNET.

Nonfiction includes most of the writing we read in newspapers, magazines, and textbooks. Some nonfiction stands out as creative and imaginative literature.

The *essay* is the broadest form of nonfiction. It allows an author to record thoughts about any subject. *Informal*, or personal, essays reflect the author's personality. *Formal* essays, or articles, present their material in a more direct and impersonal way.

A *history* records the life of a people, a country, an institution, or a historic period.

A *biography* describes the life of a person. It is the most popular form of nonfiction today.

An *autobiography* is a person's own account of his or her life.

A *diary* is an autobiography written from day to day as the events in a person's life occur. See BIOGRAPHY; DIARY; ESSAY; HISTORY.

History

The Earliest Literature may have been written by the ancient Sumerians, who lived in present-day Iraq. Scholars estimate that the Sumerians kept simple records in writing as early as 5,000 years ago. By the end of the 3000's B.C., they were writing literature.

Other early peoples of the Middle East, such as the Assyrians, Babylonians, Egyptians, and Hebrews, also produced literature. Their writings include fables, epics, histories, hymns, love songs, myths, and philosophical essays. Scholars regard the Old Testament as the outstanding work of early literature (see OLD TESTAMENT).

The ancient Chinese, Indians, and Persians created many significant works of literature. Some of their writings influenced Western literature. For example, many of Aesop's fables come from Oriental sources. For information on Oriental literatures from early times to the present, see the Arts sections in the articles on various countries of Asia, such as IRAN (The Arts). See also the articles on JAPANESE LITERATURE and SANSKRIT LANGUAGE AND LITERATURE.

Ancient Literature. From 900 B.C. to 300 B.C., a civilization developed in ancient Greece that has seldom been equaled in history. The first major period of Greek literature, called the *Epic Age*, reached its height with the poems of Homer, who probably lived during the 700's B.C. Homer's long narrative poems, the *Iliad* and the *Odyssey*, show the poet's musical style and his skill at creating characters in action. See ILIAD; ODYSSEY.

Outstanding poets of the *Lyric Age* (about 800 B.C. to about 475 B.C.) included Sappho, who sang of love, and Pindar, whose *odes* (songs of praise) celebrated Greek victories.

Prose and poetic drama flourished during the *Attic*

Age (about 475 B.C. to about 300 B.C.). Drama achieved greatness with the tragedies of Aeschylus, Sophocles, and Euripides, and the comedies of Aristophanes. Herodotus, called the *Father of History*, wrote about the Persian Wars. Thucydides treated history as a science in his account of the Peloponnesian War. Plato and Aristotle were perhaps the most important Greek writers in their influence on Western civilization.

Theocritus created *pastoral* poetry that pictured country life. He probably contributed the most to the *Alexandrian Age* (about 300 B.C. to 146 B.C.). The *Greco-Roman Age* (146 B.C. to about A.D. 529) began after the Romans conquered Greece. It produced the *Lives* of Plutarch and several collections of poems called the *Greek Anthologies*.

The Roman conquerors copied Greek literary styles. Titus Maccius Plautus and Terence, the leading writers of Latin comedies, based their plays on Greek dramas. Virgil, the greatest Roman poet, modeled his national epic, the *Aeneid*, on Homer's *Iliad* and *Odyssey*. Ovid retold many Greek myths in his *Metamorphoses*, a collection of about 250 stories.

The speeches and writings of Marcus Tullius Cicero and Julius Caesar were composed from about the 60's B.C. to the 40's B.C. These works reflect Roman civilization more clearly than do many of the plays and poems of the time. Cicero is best known for his *Philippics*, a series of speeches attacking his political enemy Mark Antony. Caesar is particularly remembered as an author for his *Commentaries on the Gallic War*. See GREEK LITERATURE; LATIN LITERATURE.

The Middle Ages lasted from about the A.D. 400's to the 1400's. After Rome fell to the Goths in the 400's, most of the poems and plays of the Greeks and Romans were forgotten for many years. The ethnic groups that invaded the Roman Empire brought their own traditions. Epic poetry became an important form for recording legends that had been handed down by word of mouth for hundreds of years. The Anglo-Saxon epic *Beowulf* appeared about 700 (see BEOWULF). The French *The Song of Roland* was written about 1100, and the German *Nibelungenlied (Song of the Nibelungs)* appeared about 1200 (see ROLAND; NIBELUNGENLIED). Many Scandinavian *sagas* (long epic tales) were recorded during the 1200's (see SAGA).

Narrative stories of adventure, fantasy, and knightly love grew in importance from the 900's through the 1200's. These *romances* reflected the systems of feudalism and chivalry that dominated Europe (see KNIGHTS AND KNIGHTHOOD; ROMANCE). The Celtic tales of King Arthur and the Knights of the Round Table became popular in Great Britain (see ARTHUR, KING). Similar stories appeared in France, Germany, Spain, and Italy.

Lyric poetry grew in importance during the 1100's and 1200's. Wandering minstrels, called *troubadours* and *trouvères* in France and *Minnesingers* in Germany, composed songs of love to entertain noblemen and their ladies (see TROUBADOUR; TROUVÈRE; MINNESINGER).

In the 1300's, religious thought inspired Dante Alighieri's *Divine Comedy*, one of the great poems of all time. Dante broke away from the tradition that educated men must write only in Latin. He wrote his poem in Italian. The *Divine Comedy* is important not only for itself, but also because it was the first serious literary work written in a modern European language. See DIVINE COMEDY.

The genius of Geoffrey Chaucer dominated English literature during the late 1300's. Chaucer is often called the *Father of English Poetry*. In such works as the *Canterbury Tales* he helped fix the form of our present English language (see CANTERBURY TALES).

The Renaissance brought a rebirth of learning. It began in Italy about 1300 and spread throughout Europe during the 1400's and 1500's. Scholars rediscovered Greek and Roman classics. Philosophers became curious about the nature of human knowledge. Writers used new literary forms to express the vitality of the times.

The Italian writers Petrarch and Giovanni Boccaccio were among the first to study ancient literature. Petrarch mastered the *sonnet*, a poetic form that later became popular in all parts of Europe. Boccaccio's fame rests on his *Decameron*, a collection of a hundred short stories. In France, the new thirst for knowledge produced the *Essays* of Michel de Montaigne and the rollicking tales of François Rabelais.

The Renaissance did not reach England until the 1500's. But after it arrived, it led to some of the finest literature in the English language. Francis Bacon took "all knowledge" for his subjects. Christopher Marlowe expanded the use of *blank verse* (poetry written in unrhymed lines) in such plays as *The Tragical History of Doctor Faustus*. Ben Jonson wrote excellent poetry and comedies. William Shakespeare crowned the achievements of the age with his plays and sonnets.

Spanish literature enjoyed a golden age during the 1500's and 1600's. Miguel de Cervantes Saavedra, Spain's best-known writer, tried his hand at almost every form of literature. Many critics consider his masterful *Don Quixote*, written in the early 1600's, to be the world's greatest novel (see DON QUIXOTE).

The Age of Reason. The Greek and Roman classics gained new importance in the 1600's and 1700's. Artists, writers, and scholars modeled their works after those of the ancients. They tried to achieve the clarity, simplicity, and restraint of classical art.

The *neoclassicists*, or new classicists, rejected the authority of religious tradition that had governed society since the Middle Ages. They believed that obedience to *reason* (orderly thought) would hold society together. Such writers as Thomas Hobbes, John Locke, and Sir Isaac Newton expressed the spirit of the Age of Reason. They demonstrated the importance of logical thinking, and laid the foundation for modern science.

In England, the civil war that began in 1642 had an effect on literature. Both the Cavaliers, who defended the king, and the Puritans, who defended Parliament, produced prose and poetry reflecting their attitudes. The greatest poet of the Puritans was John Milton. But his work does not really represent the Age of Reason. He has properly been called the *last Renaissance man*. The writings of John Dryden, Jonathan Swift, Joseph Addison, and Alexander Pope are clearer expressions of the "reasonable man."

French classical literature of the 1600's reached its supreme expression in the field of drama. Outstanding works include the tragedies of Pierre Corneille and Jean Baptiste Racine, and the comedies of Molière. Voltaire wrote brilliant plays, poems, and stories.

Romanticism arose as a reaction against the Age of Reason. It dominated European literature from the second half of the 1700's through the mid-1800's. It also had important echoes in the United States. The romantics praised natural human instincts and wrote about their own emotions and sentiments.

Jean Jacques Rousseau of France, probably more than any other writer, represented the spirit of rebellion against the neoclassic world. Rousseau condemned the evils of civilization, and regarded the primitive human being as the "noble savage." He also emphasized the rights of the individual. Inspired by Rousseau and other political philosophers, writers and social leaders throughout Europe took up the cause of the common people. The Scottish poet Robert Burns became one of the most popular men in Edinburgh. He was loved not only because he wrote about the common people, but because he himself came from the lower classes.

The poetry of the romantics expressed new confidence in the unity, beauty, and goodness of the universe. The lyrics of Johann Wolfgang von Goethe of Germany, Alphonse de Lamartine of France, and William Wordsworth of England sang of the wonders of nature. In the United States, William Cullen Bryant wrote tender nature poems. A dark sense of melancholy often accompanied the romantic's glorification of the world. The poems of François de Chateaubriand and of Lord Byron are filled with dissatisfaction with the real world as compared to the world of the poet's dreams.

Many prose writers also composed important works during the romantic period. The novel flourished in the early 1800's with such writers as George Sand and Victor Hugo in France and Sir Walter Scott in Scotland. The Grimm brothers of Germany collected old stories and fables, and their *Grimm's Fairy Tales* became world-famous. The American author Edgar Allan Poe wrote haunting stories of horror. See ROMANTICISM.

Realism. The second half of the 1800's brought a reaction against romanticism. A new group of writers called *realists* turned against the exaggerated feelings stressed by the romantics. Truth and accuracy became the goals of the realists. The novel and the drama were their best means of expression.

The great novelists of realism include Stendhal, Honoré de Balzac, and Gustave Flaubert of France; and Ivan Turgenev, Fyodor Dostoevsky, and Leo Tolstoy of Russia. Realism was mixed with romanticism in the writings of the English author Charles Dickens. Émile Zola of France led the *naturalist* movement in literature. His writings emphasized the most sordid aspects of society. The naturalists and realists treated their characters as though they were specimens in a laboratory. Such playwrights as Henrik Ibsen in Norway, August Strindberg in Sweden, and George Bernard Shaw in England used much the same approach.

In the United States, Walt Whitman combined realism and romanticism in his poetry. William Dean Howells, long-time editor of *Harper's Magazine*, became a spokesman for realism, decency, and democracy in American literature. The novels of Mark Twain, Henry James, and Stephen Crane also reflected the realistic movement. See REALISM.

The 1900's. Fiction writers, dramatists, and poets broadened the terms *realism, naturalism, symbolism, impressionism,* and *romanticism* in the 1900's. Writers increasingly experimented with form and technique in novels, stories, plays, and poems.

During the early 1900's, literature often expressed the optimism and conservative ideals of the Victorian Age, the period from the early 1830's to 1900. Then many writers began to react against the conventions and restraints of Victorian society. The studies of the unconscious mind recorded by the Austrian physician Sigmund Freud contributed to this shift in attitude. Another reason was the destruction caused by World War I (1914-1918).

Authors of the 1920's wrote about disillusioned and rootless characters. These writers, often called the *Lost Generation,* included Ernest Hemingway and F. Scott Fitzgerald of the United States. The Great Depression of the 1930's led to literature that protested what the authors considered to be unjust social conditions. In the mid-1900's, works by modern Latin-American and Japanese authors first gained international acclaim.

Fiction. The works of such novelists as James Joyce of Ireland and D. H. Lawrence and Virginia Woolf of England reflect the literary currents of the early 1900's. Joyce's novel *Ulysses* revolutionized the technique of modern fiction. Henry Miller of the United States wrote frankly about sex in *Tropic of Cancer* and other works. The publication of his novels encouraged later writers to deal with controversial subjects.

The short story suffered a decline during the mid-1900's because many magazines devoted to publishing stories either went out of business or turned to printing nonfiction. A number of magazines sponsored by individuals or colleges and universities helped to keep the short story alive. Leading short-story writers of the second half of the 1900's include the Polish-born Isaac Bashevis Singer and Jorge Luis Borges of Argentina.

Drama. The Irish National Theatre, founded in 1902, produced the works of several outstanding playwrights, including Sean O'Casey, John Millington Synge, and William Butler Yeats. George Bernard Shaw was the most important figure in English drama during the early 1900's. Luigi Pirandello was the leading Italian dramatist of the period. Ibsen, Anton Chekhov of Russia, Gerhart Hauptmann of Germany, and Karel Čapek of Czechoslovakia all influenced modern drama.

In the United States, Eugene O'Neill's experiments in drama influenced such playwrights as Maxwell Anderson, Arthur Miller, and Tennessee Williams. The French theater enjoyed great popularity with the plays of Samuel Beckett, Jean Giraudoux, and Jean Anouilh. Today, the leading English-language playwrights include Harold Pinter, Tom Stoppard, David Storey, and Peter Shaffer of England and Edward Albee of the United States.

Poetry. Three poets of the 1800's had an enormous impact on poetry of this century. They were Gerard Manley Hopkins of Great Britain and Emily Dickinson and Walt Whitman of the United States. Hopkins' dense and concentrated language influenced many later poets. In deceptively simple lines and stanzas, Emily Dickinson examined the minute details of her isolated domestic existence. Whitman rejected formal verse styles in favor of an exuberant free-verse technique.

Whitman in particular influenced a number of modern poets, including William Carlos Williams, Allen Ginsberg, and Lawrence Ferlinghetti of the United States. Other important poets of the 1900's include T. S. Eliot and W. H. Auden of England, St. John Perse of France, and Theodore Roethke, Richard Wilbur, and Robert Lowell of the United States. Lowell served as a major influence on "confessional poets," who wrote in a frank, autobiographical style.   HOLLIS SUMMERS

Related Articles in WORLD BOOK. See *The Arts* section of the country articles, such as POLAND (The Arts). See also the following articles.

Outline

I. **Enjoying Literature**
    A. Why We Read Literature   C. Judging Literature
    B. How To Read Creatively
II. **The Elements of Literature**
    A. Characters   B. Plot   C. Theme   D. Style
III. **Kinds of Discourse**
    A. Exposition   C. Description
    B. Argument   D. Narration
IV. **The World of the Writer**
    A. The Writer's Outer World   C. The Writer's
    B. The Writer's Inner World   Attitude
V. **Forms of Literature**
VI. **History**

Questions

Do you enjoy reading literature? Why?

How does the reader help create literature?

How does environment influence a writer's work?

What are the four kinds of discourse? When does an author use each?

In what ways did the Renaissance influence the growth of literature?

What are two differences between a romantic and a realistic writer? Name one romantic and one realistic novel that you have read.

How does setting influence the characters in a story?

What are the three parts of a unified plot?

What were the aims of (1) the neoclassicists? (2) the naturalists? (3) the imagists?

What are the common forms of fiction?

Nacían con pelo, pero después los
depilaban untándoles ungüento de trementina. Los
criaban como animales domésticos y los hacían
engordar. Su carne se vendía en el tianguis. Los
españoles la consideraban tan sabrosa que
cambiaban piezas de res por esos animalitos. Así se
extinguieron.

Illustration by Felipe Dávalos from *Animales Mexicanos* by Rafael Martín del
Campo from *Colibrí*, Volume 1; edited by Dirección General de Publicaciones y
Bibliotecas, Secretaría de Educacíon Pública, México © CONAFE

Mexico

Illustration by the author from *The Hopeful Mouse*
by Johanna Jokipaltio; © Johanna Jokipaltio, 1981

Finland

Illustration by Meshack Asare from *My Name Is
Kofi*; by permission of Ghana Publishing Corp.
Publishing Division, Tema, Ghana

Ghana

Literature for Children opens a fascinating world of entertainment
and information to young people. The books illustrated on this and
the following page represent the rich variety of attractive and creative works that are available to young readers in many countries.

LITERATURE FOR CHILDREN

LITERATURE FOR CHILDREN consists of the huge
body of literature that has appeal for young readers—
individuals from the preschool ages through the teens.
Young readers today can choose from thousands of
works written and illustrated specially for them. These
works include biographies, novels, poems, collections of
folk literature, and books that provide information on
the arts, sciences, and social sciences. In addition, some
books written for adults have become extremely popular
among young readers. Examples of such books include
Daniel Defoe's *Robinson Crusoe*, Jonathan Swift's *Gulliver's Travels*, and the collection of folk tales known as
Grimm's Fairy Tales.

---

*Zena Sutherland, the contributor of this article, is Professor in the
Graduate Library School at the University of Chicago and the author
of* The Best in Children's Books.

There are many kinds of children's books. Some take
readers to imaginary lands of the future. Others describe
children whose experiences resemble those of the readers. Many children's books today discuss difficult problems that face individuals and society. For example,
many books examine such subjects as racial conflict, sex
education, drug abuse, children's rights, and the treatment of old people. Some children's books satisfy the
reader's curiosity about life in other lands, or about the
lives of famous men and women. Fine poetry is written
just for children. Children's literature also introduces
readers to the wonders of science and the beauty of art.

Illustrations are a special feature of children's literature. In general, children's books emphasize illustrations much more than adult books do. Books for young
children have more pictures than do books for older children. Illustrations often contribute as much to the reader's enjoyment as does the text.

Illustration by N. Parker from *The History of the Hoppers*
by B. Parker; David Ell Press, Sydney, Australia

Australia

Illustration by the author from *Hiroshima No Pika* by Toshi Maruki; © 1980 by Toshi Maruki.
By permission of Lothrop, Lee & Shepard Books (a Division of William Morrow & Co.)

Japan

Illustration by Niccola Bayley from *The Mouldy* by William Mayne; illustration
© 1983 by Niccola Bayley. Reprinted by permission of Alfred A. Knopf, Inc.

England

Illustration by the author from *Man and the Horse* by Pietro Ventura; © 1980 by
Arnoldo Mondadori Editore S.p.A. Reprinted by permission of G. P. Putnam's Sons

Italy

The history of children's literature in English dates back to the A.D. 600's. But for about 1,200 years, this branch of literature grew slowly. Before the 1800's, few authors wrote books intended for children. Almost none of those who did attempted to entertain their readers. Instead, most authors wrote to teach children what to believe and how to behave, or to teach school subjects—such as reading, history, and science.

In the 1800's, talented authors and illustrators began creating children's books intended to entertain rather than just instruct. From that time to the present, the number of books for children has grown steadily. This growth has made literature for children a major industry. Publishing houses now have staffs of editors that specialize in children's books and magazines. Public and school libraries provide large collections of books, records, and other materials for young people. In many countries, awards are made annually to authors and artists for outstanding achievements in children's literature.

The first section of this article deals with the various kinds of literature for children, and the second section traces its development. Both of these sections include and describe specific works of children's literature. The extensive bibliographies at the end of the article list and describe hundreds of additional children's works. The article also includes career information and some guides to selecting children's books. Reproductions of illustrations by important children's artists appear throughout the article.

Literature for children can be divided into five main categories: (1) poetry, (2) folk literature, (3) fiction, (4) biography, and (5) information books. Much folk literature, including ballads and epics, is written in verse. Folk literature in verse is discussed under *Folk Literature*, rather than under *Poetry*.

Poetry. Nursery rhymes provide many children with their first contact with literature. These short, simple

317

Illustration by the author from *Where the Wild Things Are* by Maurice Sendak; © 1963 Harper & Row, Publishers

Illustrations play an important part in most children's books. A menagerie of monsters in Maurice Sendak's *Where the Wild Things Are, above,* brings imaginary creatures to life.

poems are one of the oldest forms of children's literature. For hundreds of years, adults have entertained children and children have entertained themselves by reciting these rhymes.

Some nursery rhymes, including "Itisket, Itasket," were created long ago as parts of children's games. Others, including "Old King Cole" and "Little Jack Horner," may have been based on real people and events. (Details about the development of some nursery rhymes appear in the MOTHER GOOSE and NURSERY RHYME articles.) Most young persons today know little about the original meanings of nursery rhymes. Even so, the rhymes have many features that make them enjoyable. They are filled with humor, action, entertaining incidents, and—perhaps most importantly for very young children—musical language. Nursery rhymes can also help children learn the days of the week, the months of the year, the alphabet, and how to count.

Dozens of handsomely illustrated nursery rhyme books are available. They include *The Mother Goose Treasury* (1966), illustrated by Raymond Briggs; *The Mother Goose Book* (1976), illustrated by Alice and Martin Provensen; and *Gregory Griggs and Other Nursery Rhyme People* (1978), illustrated by Arnold Lobel.

Children who have outgrown nursery rhymes can find delight in many poems written especially for them. Much of this verse is humorous. One type of humorous children's poetry, called *nonsense verse*, appeals to children because it deals with illogical and silly characters and situations. Two English authors of the 1800's, Lewis Carroll and Edward Lear, were masters of nonsense verse. The American poets John Ciardi, David McCord, and Jack Prelutsky have written many popular collections of amusing poems as well as serious poetry.

Much of the best humorous poetry deals with children and animals. A. A. Milne of England wrote two such collections of verse—*When We Were Very Young* (1924) and *Now We Are Six* (1927). Many of the poems in these collections concern Christopher Robin, the author's young son. Milne also wrote about Christopher Robin and the boy's toy animals in his famous "Winnie-the-Pooh" prose stories.

Much nonhumorous children's poetry sensitively describes the feelings of children and how they see the world around them. For example, Robert Louis Stevenson of Scotland portrayed the world of children of the late 1800's in his classic collection of poems, *A Child's Garden of Verses* (1885). Gwendolyn Brooks of the United States dealt with the modern world of black American children in *Bronzeville Boys and Girls* (1956).

Poets like Myra Cohn Livingston and Aileen Fisher write with freshness and insight about the way the world looks from the viewpoints of children. Examples include Livingston's *Celebrations* (1985) and Fisher's *Rabbits, Rabbits* (1983).

Folk Literature includes fairy tales, folk tales, myths, epics, ballads, and fables. Folk literature has existed since prehistoric times. Early peoples handed down their folk literature orally, from generation to generation. Much of this literature was written down only after the invention of printing in the 1400's. As a result, the authorship of much folk literature is either unknown or uncertain.

Most folk literature was not created specially for children. However, much of this kind of literature is presented in a direct and simple style that appeals to the young. Also, young readers enjoy the action, colorful characters, and humor that is typical of folk literature. Folk literature can also inform. A work may tell the reader about the ethical and moral values of the people who produced it. Or, the reader may learn how a people explained natural occurrences such as floods, thunder, and death before there were scientific explanations for them.

Fairy Tales and Folk Tales are terms that are often used interchangeably. The terms refer to two different forms of literature, however. Folk tales deal with the legends, customs, superstitions, and beliefs of ordinary people. Fairy tales concern fairies, elves, pixies, and other imaginary beings with magical powers.

Readers can choose from collections of fairy and folk tales from nearly every major culture that has existed. For example, the *Arabian Nights*, which includes such stories as "Aladdin and the Wonderful Lamp" and

"The Seven Voyages of Sinbad the Sailor," is a collection of ancient fairy and folk tales from cultures in Asia and North Africa. Jakob and Wilhelm Grimm gathered a famous collection of German fairy and folk tales in the early 1800's. The best-known tales in this collection include "Rumpelstiltskin" and "Hansel and Gretel." Joel Chandler Harris ranks among the best-known American collectors of folk literature. He heard many folk tales of black people while living on a Southern plantation in the mid-1800's. Harris used these tales in his famous *Uncle Remus* stories. Other American folk tales include the stories about Paul Bunyan, John Henry, and Pecos Bill.

Some famous writers have been inspired by folk and fairy tale themes to create original stories based on them. The best-known of these writers is Hans Christian Andersen, a Danish author of the 1800's. Andersen wrote some of the most delightful children's classics of all time, including "The Ugly Duckling" and "The Emperor's New Clothes."

Myths. People long ago did not have explanations for such questions as: "What causes thunder and lightning?" "How does the sun rise and set?" and "How did the world begin?" To answer questions they could not explain, people developed stories of gods and heroes who controlled natural forces. These stories, called myths, were intended to answer basic questions about the world.

Many authors have adapted myths into stories for children. The stories are filled with fantastic adventures, and they provide insight into other cultures.

Epics are long stories about legendary heroes. The epic is a verse form of literature, but versions of epics for children are often adapted into prose. The best-known epics in Western literature, the *Iliad* and the *Odyssey*, have long been children's favorites. They are attributed

Illustration © 1981 by Alice and Martin Provensen. Reproduced from *A Visit to William Blake's Inn* by Nancy Willard by permission of Harcourt Brace Jovanovich, Inc.

A Collection of Poems describes the unusual group of travelers who arrive as guests at William Blake's inn.

to an ancient Greek poet named Homer. The *Iliad* tells about the last weeks of the Trojan War between Greece and Troy. The *Odyssey* describes the wanderings of the Greek king Odysseus (Ulysses in Latin) as he attempts to return home after the war.

The many epics about the English heroes King Arthur and the Knights of the Round Table also appeal to children. These epics include stories about King Arthur and his magic sword *Excalibur*, Sir Galahad, Sir Lancelot, and Merlin the magician.

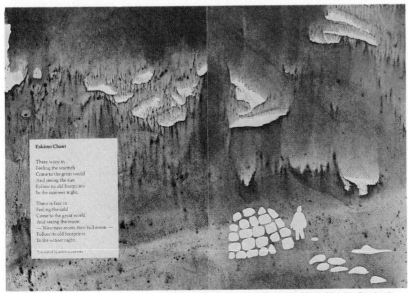

Eskimo Chant

There is joy in
Feeling the warmth
Come to the great world
And seeing the sun
Follow its old footprints
In the summer night.

There is fear in
Feeling the cold
Come to the great world
And seeing the moon
— Now new moon, now full moon —
Follow its old footprints
In the winter night.

Translated by Knud Rasmussen

An Eskimo Poem, called "Eskimo Chant," simply and vividly describes the summer and winter seasons in northern Canada. The illustration that accompanies the poem captures the feeling of the Canadian wilderness.

Illustration by Elizabeth Cleaver from *The Wind Has Wings* by Mary Alice Downie and Barbara Robertson; © 1968 Oxford University Press. Poem reprinted from *Beyond the High Hills: A Book of Eskimo Poems* by Knud Rasmussen; © 1961 The World Publishing Company

LITERATURE FOR CHILDREN

Ballads tell a dramatic story in verse. Like epics, they are often adapted into prose. Early ballads were sung or recited by wandering minstrels. Each generation of minstrels retained the basic outline of its ballads, but often changed the characters to include the popular heroes of the day.

Perhaps the most famous hero in ballads is Robin Hood. Robin lived in Sherwood Forest in England with his band of merry men. Robin Hood was an outlaw, but he was the friend of poor and oppressed people. Many ballads describe Robin's battles against the evil Sheriff of Nottingham. The character of Robin Hood first appeared in English ballads in the 1300's. Heroes of American ballads include the outlaw Jesse James, the railroad engineer Casey Jones, and "mighty" Casey, a baseball player.

Fables are brief stories that illustrate a moral lesson. Most of the characters are animals and objects that talk and act like human beings. These characters symbolize human traits, such as carelessness or wisdom. They act out episodes to prove such proverbs as "Don't count your chickens before they hatch." Many fables criticize human beings and their faults, and are intended for adults. But some fables became children's favorites because of their simple, clear examples of right and wrong and their animal characters.

The most famous collection of fables is *Aesop's Fables*, which is attributed to a Greek slave named Aesop who lived about 600 B.C. Jean de la Fontaine, a French author, wrote many delightful and graceful fables in the 1600's. He adapted some of his fables from earlier works. French schoolchildren have memorized La Fontaine's fables for generations.

Fiction makes up one of the largest categories of children's literature. There are many kinds of children's fiction, including: (1) fantasies, (2) adventure stories, (3) stories about animals, (4) stories that describe how people live in other countries, (5) historical fiction, (6) mystery and detective stories, (7) science fiction, and (8) stories that deal with social issues and personal problems. In most children's fiction of all types, the heroes are young people with whom the reader can identify.

Fantasies can be defined as stories that involve beings and events that could not exist in real life. These works may begin realistically, but soon turn into stories that could never really happen. The most famous fantasy in children's literature is Lewis Carroll's *Alice's Adventures in Wonderland* (1865). This masterpiece—which delights adults as well as children—describes the adventures of a girl named Alice, who reaches a magic land after she follows a white rabbit down a hole in the ground. Perhaps the most popular fantasy novel by an American children's author of the past is *The Wonderful Wizard of Oz* (1900) by L. Frank Baum. This book follows the adventures of a girl who was transported by a cyclone from Kansas to a magic land. A more recent classic, E. B. White's *Charlotte's Web* (1952), is a tender, humorous story of friendship among animals.

Adventure Stories are action-packed tales about daring heroes and cunning villains in larger-than-life situations. Robert Louis Stevenson's novel *Treasure Island* (1883) is an outstanding example of this popular form of children's literature. The story's hero is a boy named Jim Hawkins. In a search for buried treasure, Jim and his companions match wits with the pirate Long John Silver, one of the most memorable characters in children's literature.

Animal Stories, like real animals, fascinate many children. Some of the best animal stories stress the affection between animals and humans. For example, *The Incredible Journey* (1961) by Sheila Burnford, a Canadian author, describes how two dogs and a cat travel a great distance through the Canadian wilderness to reach the humans they love. Authors often use stories to give information about an animal, as in *The Cry of the Crow* (1980) by Jean Craighead George.

Stories of Other Countries help satisfy children's curiosity about the way people from other lands live. Such sto-

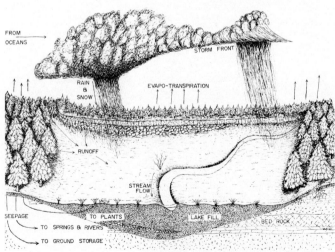

Illustration by Harold F. Heady from *High Meadow* by Eleanor B. Heady and Harold F. Heady; © 1970 Grosset & Dunlap, Inc.

An Information Book on Ecology describes how moisture rises from the earth, collects in the sky as clouds, and then falls back to earth as rain and snow.

Illustration (1900) by W. W. Denslow from *The Wizard of Oz* by L. Frank Baum; Henry Regnery Co.

Fantasies—Like *The Wizard of Oz*— are thrilling tales of imaginary lands.

Illustration by Leonard Everett Fisher from *America Moves Forward* by Gerald W. Johnson; © 1960 William Morrow and Company, Inc.

History Books bring to life the important events of the past. The U.S. history book above dramatically describes and illustrates American military victories during World War II.

ries help readers recognize the similarities as well as the differences among people. Young readers today can find novels about almost any place in the world. For example, John Nagenda's *Mukasa* (1973) is based on the author's memories of his childhood in Uganda. Peter Hartling's *Oma* (1977) tells about a boy in Germany who goes to live with his grandmother after his parents are killed in an accident.

Historical Fiction covers nearly every period of human existence. The best historical novels combine interesting stories with an accurate description of how people lived at a particular time. There are historical novels about all periods of American history. In *The Sign of the Beaver* (1983), Elizabeth Speare effectively shows the friendship between a settler and an Indian. *Johnny Tremain* (1943) by Esther Forbes is set in Boston at the time of the American Revolution. Laura Ingalls Wilder wrote a series of nine novels about pioneer life during the late

Illustration by the author from *West Coast Chinese Boy*
© 1979 by Sing Lim, published by Tundra Books

Books About Minorities, such as *West Coast Chinese Boy, above,* teach young readers about the customs and beliefs of other peoples.

1800's. For example, in *Little House on the Prairie* (1935), Wilder described life on the Kansas frontier during the 1870's.

Mystery and Detective Stories—one of the most popular forms of fiction with adult readers—are also enormously popular with young readers. Several outstanding authors have contributed mystery and detective stories to children's literature. In many such stories, young people are the chief characters. For example, in *The House of Dies Drear* (1968) by Virginia Hamilton, a 13-year-old black boy finds a buried treasure in a mysterious old house. Robert Newman's *The Case of the Frightened Friend* (1984) introduces enterprising young detectives who investigate the mystery of a classmate's family.

Science Fiction first gained great popularity among young readers during the mid-1900's. This imaginative form of literature describes adventures in such places as outer space, other planets, and the world of the future. The many exciting science fiction stories for children include Anne McCaffrey's series about the legendary land of Pern that begins with *Dragonsong* (1976). The time-shift story is a popular type of science fiction. In *Playing Beatie Bow* (1982), for example, Ruth Park wrote about a heroine who gains a better understanding of her own time after she returns from a visit to the past.

Social Issues and Personal Problems. Some modern children's fiction deals with serious problems and situations with a realism seldom attempted in earlier books. For example, the differences in attitudes among several generations of a Sioux family are described in *High Elk's Treasure* (1972) by Virginia Driving Hawk Sneve. John Donovan wrote *I'll Get There. It Better Be Worth the Trip* (1969). This realistic novel deals with the problems of a boy whose beloved grandmother has died and whose mother is an alcoholic. Jan Slepian's *The Alfred Summer* (1980) is a sensitive story about a friendship between two handicapped children.

Biography introduces young readers to the lives of important men and women. Through biographies, children can learn about people who have made great discoveries, changed the course of history, made contributions to the arts, or accomplished unusual deeds of courage or daring. A skillful biographer can make the life of a real person as exciting as the life of a fictional hero or heroine.

Most authors base their biographies on fact. However, they often invent incidents or even dialogue to make the stories more dramatic and lively, especially when they write for younger children. Jean Fritz included humor as well as accurate detail in a series of biographies set in the Revolutionary War period. James Haskins, in *Lena Horne* (1983), shows how lively a biography can be when it is possible to interview the subject.

Information Books are nonfiction works that introduce children to the world of learning. The wonders of science, the beauty of art, and the fascination of history unfold in the pages of information books written specially for children. Almost all subjects—from how Americans elect their Presidents, to why some animals hibernate, to how religions developed—are treated in these books.

Since the mid-1900's—for the first time—large numbers of information books that deal with modern problems have been published. For example, *What You Should Know About Drugs* (1970) by Charles W. Gorodetzky and Samuel T. Christian describes each class of drugs and how each can be abused. John Gabriel Navarra discusses environmental pollution in *The World You Inherit* (1970). Many information books deal with racial, religious, and social minorities. Ron Roy's *Move Over, Wheelchairs Coming Through!* (1985) deals with the disabled. Julia Singer describes the diversity among Puerto Rican children who move to the United States in *We All Come from Puerto Rico, Too* (1977).

LITERATURE FOR CHILDREN/*History*

Adults have told stories to children since prehistoric times. But children's literature written in English first appeared during the A.D. 600's. For hundreds of years, relatively few children's books were produced. Most children's books were lesson books, intended to educate rather than entertain.

During the 1800's, children's literature grew into a distinct branch of literature. In the early 1900's, the first modern biographies and information books for children were published. Today, young readers can choose from thousands of books, ranging from new editions of classics to serious discussions of social problems.

Early Children's Literature

The First Children's Books in England were textbooks written during the A.D. 600's. Saint Aldhelm, bishop of Sherborne, probably wrote the first of these books. He wrote in question and answer form and in verse. For almost 1,000 years, most English instruction books were written in this style.

John Amos Comenius, a Czech educator, was one of the first authors who believed that children's books should entertain as well as teach. His textbook *Orbis Sensualium Pictus* (*The World of Visible Objects in Pictures*, 1658) was the first children's book in which illustrations played a major part. Comenius stated that he wanted to attract the reader's attention "with pictures that amusingly teach the chief things of this world."

From the 1500's to the early 1800's, inexpensive little books were sold in England. The books contained shortened and often crude adaptations of ancient legends, medieval tales, and ballads. Educated adults considered these books trash, but children loved them.

The Puritans were English Protestants who became a powerful force in England and colonial New England. Puritan authors wrote children's books that reflected the ideals of their religion. In New England, the Puritan minister John Cotton wrote *Milk for Babes* (1646), a catechism memorized by generations of children. Another popular Puritan children's book in the colonies was *The New England Primer* (about 1690), compiled by Benjamin Harris, a Boston publisher. The book contained the alphabet, rules for behavior, and stories about Christian martyrs.

John Bunyan, an English Puritan, produced a major work of world literature that became popular with both adults and children. Bunyan's book, *The Pilgrim's Progress* (1678, 1684), is an allegory about a man's struggle to get to heaven. But adaptations for children emphasize the man's action-filled travels.

Mother Goose. The first classic of children's literature was *Stories and Tales of Past Times with Morals; or, Tales of Mother Goose.* Published in France in 1697, this book consisted of eight fairy tales collected by Charles Perrault. The tales included "Cinderella," "Little Red Riding Hood," and "The Sleeping Beauty." Beginning in the mid-1700's, editions contained nursery rhymes as well as songs and other material. The rhymes became so popular that the term *Mother Goose* became a general name for nearly all nursery rhymes.

The 1700's. During the 1700's in England, children's literature showed signs of developing as a separate branch of literature. Two masterpieces that became popular with both children and adults were published in England in the early part of the century. They were

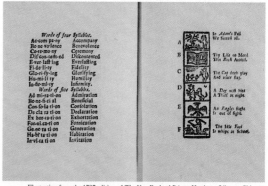

Illustration from the 1727 edition of *The New England Primer*; Newberry Library, Chicago

The New England Primer taught colonial American children the alphabet through crude illustrations and brief, simple rhymes.

Ring-a-ring-a-roses,
A pocket full of posies ;
Hush ! hush ! hush ! hush !
We're all tumbled down.

Illustration by Kate Greenaway from *Mother Goose* (1881);
Frederick Warne & Company, Inc.

Mother Goose fairy tales, rhymes, and songs have charmed
young children since the 1700's.

Robinson Crusoe (1719) by Daniel Defoe and *Gulliver's Travels* (1726) by Jonathan Swift.

Robinson Crusoe describes the adventures of a man shipwrecked on an island. The original story includes many philosophical reflections by the author. Children's editions omit these portions and emphasize the hero's ingenious battle for survival against the forces of nature.

Gulliver's Travels was the first great fantasy in children's literature. It describes four voyages to imaginary lands made by Lemuel Gulliver, a ship's doctor. Swift intended the book as a satire on the many follies he saw in the human race. But children enjoy the book—usually in adapted form—for its humor and imagination.

John Newbery of England made major contributions to the development of children's literature during the 1700's. Newbery was one of the first successful English publishers of children's books. In 1744, he published *A Little Pretty Pocket-Book*, "intended for the instruction and amusement" of boys and girls. The book included fables, games, rhymes, and songs. It was one of the first books in English that attempted exclusively to entertain rather than educate young readers. New-

bery also published *The History of Little Goody Two-Shoes* (1765), considered the first novel written specifically for children. The novel is attributed to the Irish author Oliver Goldsmith.

The 1800's

The 1800's marked the emergence of children's literature as a branch of literature. Many works of children's literature were written during the 1800's, and, for the first time, American authors contributed important books for young people. The first important illustrators of children's books lived during the 1800's.

Collections of Tales. Most of the best-known fairy and folk tales were collected and published during the 1800's. Jakob and Wilhelm Grimm of Germany compiled the first great collection. Their tales included "Hansel and Gretel." Peter Asbjørnsen and Jørgen Moe collected many Norwegian tales, including "The Three Billy Goats Gruff."

In Great Britain, Joseph Jacobs collected many English and Irish folk tales, including "The Story of the Three Little Pigs" and "Jack the Giant Killer." Andrew Lang, a Scottish scholar, compiled 12 books of fairy and folk tales from around the world, beginning with *The Blue Fairy Book* (1889).

Masterpieces of Fiction. Many of the classic novels in children's literature were published between 1865 and 1900. Lewis Carroll wrote perhaps the single most popular novel in all of children's literature—*Alice's Adventures in Wonderland* (1865). Carroll continued Alice's adventures in the novel *Through the Looking-Glass* (1871).

Mary Mapes Dodge wrote *Hans Brinker; or, the Silver Skates* (1865). This was the first important children's novel by an American that described how people lived in another country. The hero is Hans Brinker, a Dutch boy. The story contains much exciting action, but was written primarily to introduce readers to the history and customs of the Netherlands.

Louisa May Alcott wrote *Little Women* (1868-1869), the first major realistic children's novel about the life of an American family. The story takes place in a small New England community in the mid-1800's. The heroines are the four March sisters—Amy, Beth, Jo, and Meg. The author's realistic yet affectionate treatment of these characters has charmed children for generations.

Anna Sewell, an English author, wrote *Black Beauty* (1877), the first popular realistic novel about animals. The book describes the cruel treatment a horse receives from its masters. The author wrote the book partly as a plea for decent treatment of animals.

Robert Louis Stevenson and the French author Jules Verne produced some of the finest adventure novels in children's literature during the 1800's. Stevenson's *Treasure Island* (1883), *Kidnapped* (1886), and *David Balfour* (1893) all have boys as heroes. These novels show Stevenson's genius at creating colorful characters and breathtaking action and suspense. Verne was the first important author of science fiction. Young people enjoy the imaginative plots and exciting action of such Verne classics as *A Journey to the Center of the Earth* (1864).

Masterpieces of Poetry. The first important book of children's verse in the 1800's was *Original Poems for Infant Minds* (1804). The authors were two English sisters,

LITERATURE FOR CHILDREN

Illustration for "John Gilpin's Ride" from *R. Caldecott's Picture Book No. 1* (1879); Frederick Warne & Company, Inc.

Great Illustrators of the 1800's, including Randolph Caldecott, helped make pictures a major part of children's literature.

Ann and Jane Taylor. The best-known poem in their book is "Twinkle, Twinkle, Little Star." The American journalist and poet Eugene Field wrote some of the most popular children's poems, including "Little Boy Blue" and "Wynken, Blynken, and Nod." Edward Lear of England composed many books of delightful nonsense verse, beginning with *A Book of Nonsense* (1846). Lear's best-known nonsense poem is "The Owl and the Pussy-Cat" (1871). Lewis Carroll also wrote verse, much of which he included in his "Alice" books.

Two Americans composed popular children's ballads. Clement Clarke Moore is generally considered the author of "A Visit from Saint Nicholas" (1823). This poem, which begins " 'Twas the night before Christmas" remains a familiar part of the Christmas holiday season in America. "Casey at the Bat" (1888), a ballad by Ernest Lawrence Thayer, has become part of the folk literature of baseball. The ballad describes how "mighty" Casey struck out in the last inning, thus failing to win a baseball game for his Mudville team.

The Rise of Illustration. During the 1800's, illustrations became a major part of children's books. For the first time, illustrations were widely used to help young readers visualize the characters and the action of stories and poems.

Alice's Adventures in Wonderland and *Through the Looking-Glass* contain illustrations by Sir John Tenniel that are perhaps the most famous in all of children's literature. Tenniel's illustrations do much to heighten the humor and absurd situations in Carroll's works. See TENNIEL, SIR JOHN (picture).

By the mid-1800's, color illustrations were appearing widely in children's books. The use of color pictures was

partly due to the advances in color printing made by Edmund Evans, an English publisher and artist. Evans published the color illustrations of three of the major English children's artists of the 1800's—Randolph Caldecott, Walter Crane, and Kate Greenaway.

Caldecott is best known for his interpretations of scenes of humorous action. Perhaps his most famous illustrations are those published in an 1878 edition of "The Diverting History of John Gilpin" (1782), a ballad by the English poet William Cowper. The ballad describes how elderly John Gilpin tries to stay on a runaway horse. Caldecott's illustrations perfectly capture the frantic, hilarious action of the ballad.

Walter Crane's best illustrations were created for works intended for young children, notably his books of nursery rhymes including *Baby's Bouquet* and *Baby's Opera*. His illustrations are noted for their delicate colors and attention to details of clothing and objects.

Kate Greenaway illustrated her own children's poems, including the collection *Under the Window* (1878). Her illustrations portray charming, graceful scenes of happy children and peaceful landscapes.

English artists established children's book illustrations as a distinct art form. But American artists also made important contributions in the late 1800's. Arthur Frost gained fame for his clever and comic pen-and-ink illustrations for Joel Chandler Harris' *Nights with Uncle Remus* (1883). Howard Pyle captured the heroic and romantic spirit of the Robin Hood ballads in his vigorous illustrations.

The 1900's

More children's books have been published during the 1900's than in all the previous centuries combined. There are several reasons for this enormous growth. In-

Frederick Warne & Company, Inc.

The First Modern Picture Book was *The Tale of Peter Rabbit,* one of a series of animal stories written by Beatrix Potter. The author also illustrated the stories with delicate water colors.

324

fluential theories in education and psychology have stressed the importance of children's reading and urged parents to encourage young children to read. Improved printing techniques have allowed publishers to produce books that are carefully designed, printed, and illustrated. The range of subjects that interest children has grown. During the 1900's, there has been an increase in the number of school libraries and of public libraries with special departments serving children.

In the United States during the 1960's, the federal government provided funds to expand the facilities and services of school libraries. This stimulated the publishing of children's books. The expansion of publishing, in turn, led more authors and artists to concentrate primarily on children's literature. Children's artists in particular played an important role in children's books. The increased role of artists resulted partly from the enormous popularity and variety of heavily illustrated books called *picture books*.

Picture Books were the first important new development in children's literature in the 1900's. In picture books, illustrations are as important to the reader's enjoyment and understanding of a story as the text. The first modern picture book was *The Tale of Peter Rabbit* (1901) by the English author and artist Beatrix Potter. For the 1902 edition, Potter illustrated her simple animal story with beautiful water colors.

Today, thousands of picture books are available. Nearly all of the books are intended to be read aloud to preschool and kindergarten children. A few picture books are published for older readers.

Books for Beginning Readers became an important element in children's literature in the mid-1900's. These books are written for recreational reading rather than for school use. The books tell simple stories, often

Illustration by Ernest Shepard; © 1926, renewed 1954, E. P. Dutton & Co. and McClelland and Stewart Ltd.

Winnie-the-Pooh by A. A. Milne is a famous book about a boy and his adventures with his collection of stuffed toy animals.

through a carefully restricted vocabulary of words that are easy to read, and with concepts that are easy to understand. Writing under the name of Dr. Seuss, Theodor Seuss Geisel became one of the first authors to create such books. Teachers use many of his books in addition to, or in place of, basic readers to help young children learn to read.

Children's Nonfiction. From the 1800's to the 1920's, most of the important children's books were works of fiction or poetry. In 1921, the American historian Hendrik Van Loon published *The Story of Mankind*, the first significant modern information book. The work combines scholarship with a lively writing style then new to children's nonfiction. This book set the example for the interesting accurate presentation of knowledge that characterizes today's best information books.

Until the 1930's, most biographies for children were stuffy and filled with lifeless characters. Then authors began writing biographies that used descriptive detail and dialogue to provide a vivid feeling for the subject and the times in which he or she lived. *Babe Didrikson, Athlete of the Century* (1985) by Rozanne Knudson reflects the changing status of women. Gloria Kamen's *Fiorello: His Honor, the Little Flower* (1981) describes the life of a political hero.

Social and Personal Issues. Many modern children's books discuss subjects previously considered too mature for children. The many books about race relations or minority group problems in the United States include the novel *The Soul Brothers and Sister Lou* (1968) by Kristin Hunter. This book provides a realistic portrait of black children growing up in a big-city ghetto. Such stories attempt to reproduce the way the characters might speak in real life. Authors seldom used natural speech patterns and slang in children's literature before the mid-1900's. Authors write with a new frankness about topics rarely mentioned in earlier children's books. For example, Willo Davis Roberts deals realistically with child abuse in the novel *Don't Hurt Laurie!* (1977). Many works of fiction and nonfiction concern problems of modern life, such as pollution, the disposal of atomic waste, and the generation gap.

Since the establishment of school courses on family life and sex education, many books have been published on those and related topics. Some books advise adolescents on the many aspects of sexual change in their lives. *Are You There God? It's Me, Margaret* (1970) by

Illustration by Garth Williams; © 1952 Harper & Row, Publishers

Charlotte's Web is a modern children's classic by E. B. White about a farmyard friendship between a spider and a pig.

Illustration by N. C. Wyeth from *The Boy's King Arthur* edited by Sidney Lanier; © 1917, renewed 1945, Charles Scribner's Sons (collection of Jack Webb, WORLD BOOK photo by E. Cornachio)

Illustration by the author from *Fables* © 1980 by Arnold Lobel. Reprinted by permission of Harper & Row Publishers, Inc.

Great Illustrators of the 1900's include N. C. Wyeth and Arnold Lobel. Wyeth became known for his dramatic illustrations of children's classics, such as *The Boy's King Arthur, left.* Lobel gained popularity for his delightful pictures of animals in such books as *Fables, right.*

Judy Blume is a novel about a girl's curiosity about her developing body. In *Oh, Boy! Babies* (1980) by Alison Herzig and Jane Mali, a class of sixth grade boys learns to take care of babies.

Earlier in the 1900's, children's books portrayed adults, especially parents, in an idealized manner. Today, many books show adults as imperfect. One of the first examples was Louise Fitzhugh's novel *Harriet the Spy* (1964). The heroine portrays other characters, both young and adult, with biting frankness.

The Poetry Revival. During the early 1900's, publishers issued few books of poetry for children. Since the mid-1900's, however, many books of poetry for young people have been published.

Several children's poets, including David McCord, Karla Kuskin, and Eve Merriam, began to win popularity in the mid-1900's. McCord combines humor with imaginative wordplay in his collection *Far and Few: Rhymes of the Never Was and Always Is* (1952). Kuskin is the author of *Dogs and Dragons, Trees and Dreams* (1980). Merriam's books include *If Only I Could Tell You* (1983), a collection of poems about love.

Many young people have written poems that have been published in anthologies. For example, *I Heard a Scream in the Street* (1970), edited by Nancy Larrick, consists of verse by students from ages 9 through 18. The collection describes the reactions of young people growing up in cities throughout the United States.

Children's Magazines first appeared in the mid-1700's. Perhaps the most influential early children's

magazine in the United States was the *St. Nicholas* magazine, published from 1873 to 1943. Under the editorship of Mary Mapes Dodge from 1873 to 1905, the magazine helped upgrade the quality of children's literature in America. Contributors to *St. Nicholas* included many of the leading children's authors and illustrators of the day.

By the mid-1900's, children's magazines were extending children's literature into millions of classrooms and homes. Today, dozens of children's magazines provide young people with fiction, nonfiction, news about current events, games, and puzzles.

The oldest important magazines in the United States still being published are *Boy's Life*, started by the national Boy Scouts organization in 1911, and *American Girl*, begun by the Girl Scouts in 1917. The best-known children's magazine used in American schools is *My Weekly Reader*, founded in 1928. Separate editions of the magazine are published for kindergarten through the sixth grade. Some magazines contain material for preschool and kindergarten children. They include *Highlights for Children*, first published in 1946, *Humpty Dumpty's Magazine*, founded in 1952, and *Cricket*, founded in 1973.

Two well-known magazines for older students are *Junior Scholastic*, founded in 1937, and *Senior Scholastic*, founded in 1920. *Junior Scholastic* offers features on the social sciences, arts, and sciences for junior high school students. *Senior Scholastic* publishes articles on current events for senior high school students.

326

Awards. Many awards were established in the 1900's to provide recognition for outstanding achievements in children's literature. The awards also helped stimulate public interest in the field.

Frederick G. Melcher, an American publisher, established the two best-known awards in the United States —the Newbery Medal and the Caldecott Medal. Both awards are administered by the Association for Library Service to Children (ALSC) of the American Library Association. The Newbery Medal, established in 1921, is awarded to the author of the most distinguished contribution to American children's literature during the previous year. The Caldecott Medal, established in 1937, goes to the illustrator of the most distinguished American picture book for children during the previous year. See the articles NEWBERY MEDAL and CALDECOTT MEDAL for lists of winners of the medals.

The ALSC also administers the Laura Ingalls Wilder Award. The award, which was first presented in 1954, is given every three years to an author or illustrator for a body of work. Since 1959, the Catholic Library Associa-tion has awarded the Regina Medal to honor a person for a lifetime contribution to children's literature. In 1966, the ALSC established the Mildred Batchelder Award. It goes annually to the best translated children's book published by a U.S. firm. In 1975, the International Reading Association established a prize for the best first or second book by a new author. The National Council of Teachers of English founded a poetry award in 1977. In 1981, author Scott O'Dell established the Scott O'Dell Award for Historical Fiction. See WILDER, LAURA INGALLS; REGINA MEDAL.

The Canadian Association of Children's Librarians established the Book of the Year for Children Award in 1947. The award is given annually to children's books in both English and French.

Other countries award annual prizes, some open to authors and illustrators from any country. The Hans Christian Andersen Award, established in 1956, is given by the International Board on Books for Young People. It is awarded every two years to both an author and an illustrator for a lifetime of work.

LITERATURE FOR CHILDREN/*Careers*

Many rewarding careers are open to individuals who want to make children's literature their life's work. While some people devote themselves to writing or illustrating children's books, many others work as editors or librarians. Editors of children's books and children's librarians provide essential links between the creators of children's literature and the young reader. Such editors and librarians have done much to stimulate interest in reading among young people and to improve the quality and expand the scope of children's literature in the 1900's.

Children's Editors

In the early 1900's, some publishers began to issue beautifully illustrated editions of children's classics. Then, in 1919, the Macmillan Company publishing house took a giant step. It established a department devoted entirely to the production of new books for children. Louise Seaman Bechtel was the department's first editor. Other publishers established children's departments and, today, children's editors have become an important part of the staff of many publishing houses.

Children's editors work with artists and illustrators to produce books. Some of them have library experience and training. They understand the kinds of books needed to complement classroom instruction, and they have knowledge of the kinds of books children like and dislike. Other people who work in children's book publishing include art editors, translators, copy editors who check the authors' manuscripts, and promotion managers. Many of these people are former librarians.

The Children's Book Council promotes books and reading. The council consists of children's book editors and promotion managers. It cooperates with teachers, librarians, and parents to get publicity, sponsor book fairs, arrange book-related programs at conferences, and publish useful materials. The council also sponsors the annual Children's Book Week celebration throughout the United States.

Librarians

Librarians play many roles in their relations with young readers. Some librarians work with children from preschool through the elementary grades. Others work mainly with young people of junior and senior high school age.

Librarians discuss children's books with authorities and read reviews in professional periodicals. Librarians also read many of the children's books published each year and hear the reactions of children who have read the books. As a result, adults and children can use a librarian's experience and knowledge to help them select suitable books.

Children's Librarians. In the late 1800's, public libraries began to realize the importance of having a separate room for children. In the early 1900's, the Carnegie Library School in Pittsburgh offered the first training course for children's librarians. Other library schools quickly recognized the value of such training and offered similar courses. Trained children's librarians were better equipped to understand the development of literature for children and had well-defined standards for judging books. They had training in storytelling, and many also had a background in sociology that gave them understanding in working with the many groups in their communities. As these librarians worked with children, they gradually developed methods that had an important influence on the field of children's work in libraries.

At first, there were only a few librarians with training in children's literature. Today, however, there are thousands of library-school graduates working in school libraries and in children's rooms in public libraries. They work closely with teachers in supplying supplementary classroom materials, and they also take books and programs into their communities. They are interested in children as individuals and do all they can to help children discover interesting books. Children's librarians tell stories and they read aloud—often in intimate, informal groups. They also do outstanding work with discussion groups and with children who have hobbies. Through such activities, children's librarians provide an important stimulus to enjoyment and learning through reading.

Young People's Librarians. Public library services directed toward teen-agers have grown rapidly since the mid-1900's. Today, many librarians recognize that readers in junior and senior high school have a great need for special services. These readers often consider themselves too old for the children's department, but may not feel at home in the adult section. Young people's librarians help them bridge the gap.

Trained young people's librarians guide their readers in choosing books that will both satisfy their present interests and stimulate new ones. The librarians may organize group activities to encourage more and better reading. As one of their most important functions, the librarians provide educational and career information for teen-agers. They also cooperate with schools and local organizations in programs involving reading.

For more information about the duties of librarians, see the LIBRARY article.

LITERATURE FOR CHILDREN / *Selecting Children's Books*

There are thousands of children's books in print, and each year publishers issue hundreds of new titles. With such an enormous number of works available, people must find ways to determine whether a particular book is worth obtaining.

To provide guidance for parents and young people, evaluations of children's books appear in magazines, newspapers, professional periodicals, and such reference works as *Children and Books* (7th ed. 1986) by Zena Sutherland and May Hill Arbuthnot. Many organizations issue booklists devoted to recommending books for young readers. These sources evaluate the quality of text and pictures and provide information on the recommended age or grade level of a book.

In evaluating a book, experts seek answers to many questions. For example, if the book is fiction, do the events arise naturally out of a character's qualities or does the action seem forced? Is the plot interesting and well constructed? Whether fiction or nonfiction, is the book's subject within the child's comprehension? Is the style of writing distinctive and interesting, or commonplace and oversimplified? Is the book's format appropriate in terms of page size, type style, margins, and spacing? Do the illustrations complement the text in both design and subject matter?

Age and Grade Levels. A person selecting a book for a child should be sure the book generally matches the child's age or school grade. Some experts in children's literature prefer to rate books by grade. They believe that there is a more uniform reading-achievement level among children of a certain grade than among those of a certain age. Other experts prefer to rate children's books on the basis of age. They believe the age level best reflects a child's interests and emotional and social development.

Most book reviews and bibliographies include some recommendation on age or grade level. Usually, the age or grade rating covers a broad period. For example, an age recommendation might run from years 6 through 9, and a grade recommendation from kindergarten through third grade. All ratings should be considered only as a guide, not as a rigid limitation on the use of the book.

Several elements contribute to determining the age or grade level of a book. The most important include sentence length, difficulty of vocabulary, difficulty of concepts, amount of repetition, and the nature of the subject matter.

Book Reviews of children's literature appear in several leading general-circulation magazines and newspapers. Four major library periodicals also regularly review children's books. They are *The Booklist*, the *Bulletin of the Center for Children's Books*, *The Horn Book Magazine*, and the *School Library Journal*. *The Booklist* is published by the American Library Association. The *Bulletin* is sponsored by the University of Chicago Graduate Library School. Private publishers issue *Horn Book* and the *School Library Journal*.

Booklists are bibliographies of recommended children's books compiled by various authorities. Most lists are published monthly or annually in pamphlet form. A few are published in book form, and may be revised from time to time. Some lists provide only basic information about a book, including the author and publisher. In other booklists, authorities describe and evaluate the books. Up-to-date booklists of children's literature are available at many public and school libraries.

The Child Study Association annually compiles a booklist called *Children's Books of the Year*. Periodically, the Association for Childhood Education International publishes *Good & Inexpensive Books for Children*. Perhaps the best-known children's booklist is "Notable Children's Books," issued each year by the American Library Association. The ALA also publishes "Best Books for Young Adults," an annual list that includes both adult books and books published for adolescents.

Many books are intended to help parents aid children with their reading. One of the best is Betsy Hearne's *Choosing Books for Children: A Commonsense Guide* (1981). Another is *Let's Read Together* (1969), published by the ALA. Two selection guides are published primarily for teachers and librarians, but parents and young people also may find them useful. They are *The Best in Children's Books*, edited by Zena Sutherland, and *Children's Catalog*, published by the H. W. Wilson Company. Each is revised periodically and both provide annotations for each book listed.

Some booklists concentrate on titles dealing with members of minority groups. One such list is Barbara Pollock's *The Black Experience in Children's Books* (1974). Other lists may focus on a need, such as Joanne Bernstein's *Books to Help Children Cope with Separation and Loss* (1977). There are also specialized lists for science, social studies, individual countries, and particular age groups. Lists have been developed for people with reading problems. *Good Reading for the Disadvantaged Reader* (1975) by George Spache includes a list of books for minority-group children who have difficulty reading English. *Braille Book Review* has lists of books in braille for adults and children. *Talking Book Topics* lists books available on records and cassettes.   ZENA SUTHERLAND

LITERATURE FOR CHILDREN/*Books to Read*

This section contains bibliographies of recommended children's books. The first bibliography, *Beginning Books*, lists works best suited to be read to children of preschool and kindergarten age. The last bibliography, *Books About Children's Literature*, provides suggested reading for adults interested in learning more about children's literature. The other bibliographies cover various kinds of children's books. The books in these bibliographies are rated in one of three reading level categories: *young readers*, suitable for readers in grades 1 through 3; *intermediate readers*, suitable for readers in grades 4 through 6; and *older readers*, suitable for readers in grade 7 and up. A few books are rated *all ages* because they appeal to many readers at all grade levels.

The grade level rating of books in the bibliographies is intended merely as a general guide. The ratings should not be considered as a limitation on who should read a book. For example, a young student with a strong interest in astronomy may understand and enjoy a book on that topic even though it is rated far above the student's level.

The date given for each book is the year in which that particular edition was published. In some cases, the book originally was published much earlier.

This section covers books only. However, audiovisual materials adapted from children's books are also available. Some children's books have been adapted into filmstrips, motion pictures for classroom and home use, and recordings. Many children's libraries lend these materials or can provide information on how to get them.

Several abbreviations frequently appear in the booklists that follow. They are *ad.* for *adapter*, *comp.* for *compiler*, *ed.* for *edition* or *editor*, *illus.* for *illustrated*, *rev.* for *revised*, and *trans.* for *translated*.

Beginning Books

Anno, Mitsumasa. *Anno's Alphabet.* Illus. by the author. Crowell, 1975. Letters are shown as wood carvings. *Anno's Counting Book.* Illus. by the author. Crowell, 1977. An imaginative book on numbers.

Bemelmans, Ludwig. *Madeline.* Illus. by the author. Viking, 1962. The adventures of a precocious, independent girl attending a boarding school in Paris.

Brian Wildsmith's Mother Goose. Illus. by Brian Wildsmith. Watts, 1964. A collection of 86 traditional rhymes.

Brooke, L. Leslie. *Johnny Crow's Garden.* Illus. by the author. Warne, 1967. A famous picture book about Johnny Crow and the animals that visit his garden.

Brown, Marc and **Laurene.** *The Bionic Bunny Show.* Illus. by Marc Brown. Little, 1984. A funny behind-the-scenes look at a television show.

Browne, Anthony. *Gorilla.* Illus. by the author. Knopf, 1985. Dramatic handling of light and color in the pictures makes the story of a child's imaginary adventures beautiful as well as touching.

Brunhoff, Jean de. *The Story of Babar.* Trans. from the French by Merle S. Haas. Illus. by the author. Random House, 1960. The first of several books about an elephant who leaves the jungle to live in Paris.

Bunting, Eve. *The Man Who Could Call Down Owls.* Illus. by Charles Mikolaycak. Macmillan, 1984. Powerful pictures reflect the dramatic quality of a story of owls that take revenge on a man who murdered their friend.

R. Caldecott's Picture Book No. 1. Illus. by Randolph Caldecott. Warne, 1906. The first of four collections of poems illustrated by the famous English children's artist.

Caudill, Rebecca. *Did You Carry the Flag Today, Charley?* Illus. by Nancy Grossman. Holt, 1966. A story set in the Appalachian Mountains about a 4-year-old boy attending summer school.

Corey, Dorothy. *You Go Away.* Illus. by Lois Axeman. Whitman, 1976. A picture book that helps young children understand why a parent must sometimes leave them alone.

In the evening, after dinner, he tells the Old Lady's friends all about his life in the great forest.

Illustration by the author from *The Story of Babar* by Jean de Brunhoff; © 1933, renewed 1961, Random House, Inc.

The Story of Babar is a French children's classic about an elephant who runs away from the jungle to live in Paris.

LITERATURE FOR CHILDREN

Crews, Donald. *Parade*. Illus. by the author. Greenwillow, 1983. A bright, lively picture book about parades.

De Paola, Tomie. *Strega Nona*. Illus. by the author. Prentice-Hall, 1975. A picture-book version of a comic story about a greedy apprentice.

Gág, Wanda. *Millions of Cats*. Illus. by the author. Coward-McCann, 1928. An old man and an old woman want only one cat, but end up with millions of cats.

Hall, Donald. *Ox-Cart Man*. Illus. by Barbara Cooney. Viking, 1979. A picture story of rural life in New England in the early 1800's. Caldecott Medal winner.

Hoban, Russell. *The Great Gum Drop Robbery*. Illus. by Colin McNaughton. Philomel, 1982. A hilarious story about an imaginative children's game.

Hoban, Tana. *I Read Signs*. Photographs by the author. Greenwillow, 1983. An attractive book that helps to develop reading skills.

Hughes, Shirley. *Alfie Gets in First*. Illus. by the author. Lothrop, 1981. A realistic story about a small boy's predicament with a locked door.

Keats, Ezra Jack. *The Snowy Day*. Illus. by the author. Viking, 1963. A black boy named Peter plays in the first snowfall of the season. The first of a series. Caldecott Medal winner.

Kessler, Leonard. *Old Turtle's Winter Games*. Illus. by the author. Greenwillow, 1983. Animals enjoy winter sports in stories told with vitality and humor.

Kuskin, Karla. *The Philharmonic Gets Dressed*. Illus. by Marc Simont. Harper, 1982. A brisk, witty description of orchestra members preparing for a concert.

Leaf, Munro. *The Story of Ferdinand*. Illus. by Robert Lawson. Viking, 1936. A famous story about a bull who would rather smell fragrant flowers than fight.

Lobel, Arnold. *Frog and Toad Are Friends*. Illus. by the author. Harper, 1970. Five humorous adventures of a frog and his friend, a toad. *On Market Street*. Illus. by Anita Lobel. Greenwillow, 1981. An alphabetical series of figures made from such objects as apples, books, and clocks.

McCloskey, Robert. *Make Way for Ducklings*. Illus. by the author. Viking, 1963. A family of mallard ducks in Boston searches for a home. Caldecott Medal winner.

The Mother Goose Book. Illus. by Alice and Martin Provensen. Random House, 1976. A selection of nursery rhymes illustrated with softly colored pictures.

The Mother Goose Treasury. Illus. by Raymond Briggs.

Alphabet Books teach young children the alphabet by associating individual letters with pictures of familiar objects.

Coward, 1966. A noted British artist provides varied illustrations for this large collection of verses.

Oakley, Graham. *The Church Mice at Christmas*. Illus. by the author. Atheneum, 1980. Humorous pictures and lots of action in a story about the cat and mice who live in an English church.

Ormerod, Jan. *Sunshine*. Illus. by the author. Lothrop, 1981. A wordless picture book about a cozy family morning.

Oxenbury, Helen. *The Checkup*. Illus. by the author. Dial, 1983. Sunny pictures complement the humor of a visit to the doctor, which ends with the child happy and the doctor exhausted.

Potter, Beatrix. *The Tale of Peter Rabbit*. Illus. by the author. Warne, 1958. One of the best known of this author's many classic picture books about small field animals.

Scott, Ann Herbert. *Sam*. Illus. by Symeon Shimin. McGraw, 1967. A young black boy feels ignored by his family until the family finds the perfect job for him. *On Mother's Lap*. Illus. by Glo Coalson. McGraw, 1972. A small Eskimo boy learns that there is always room on Mother's lap, even when she is rocking the new baby.

Sendak, Maurice. *Where the Wild Things Are*. Illus. by the author. Harper, 1963. A boy—sent to his room for being too wild—imagines he is on an island where wild creatures crown him king. Caldecott Medal winner. *Outside*

One winter morning Peter woke up and looked out the window. Snow had fallen during the night. It covered everything as far as he could see.

The Snowy Day describes a boy's joy and wonder at seeing the season's first snowfall. Author-artist Ezra Jack Keats creatively combined collage and water colors in illustrating this picture book.

Illustration © 1976 by Lois Axeman from *You Go Away* by Dorothy Corey. Used with the permission of Albert Whitman & Co.

Illustration by the author from *The Cat in the Hat* by Dr. Seuss; © 1957 Random House, Inc.

You Go Away is a picture book that teaches young children not to be afraid if a parent leaves them alone for a short time.

The Cat in the Hat combines fanciful illustrations with simple, clever verse to describe the antics of a fantastic cat.

Over There. Illus. by the author. Harper, 1981. A romantic and beautifully illustrated fantasy about a girl's love for her baby sister.

Seuss, Dr. *The Cat in the Hat*. Illus. by the author. Random House, 1957. One of several books in verse about a fantastic cat who visits two children.

Steig, William. *Sylvester and the Magic Pebble*. Illus. by the author. Simon & Schuster, 1969. A young donkey finds a magic pebble and accidentally turns himself into a rock. Caldecott Medal winner.

Stevenson, James. *We Can't Sleep!* Illus. by the author. Greenwillow, 1982. The complaint of insomnia leads to a wildly improbable story from Grandpa.

Van Allsburg, Chris. *The Polar Express*. Illus. by the author. Houghton, 1985. Imaginative paintings illustrate a Christmas fantasy. Caldecott Medal winner.

Ward, Lynd K. *The Biggest Bear*. Illus. by the author. Houghton, 1952. A boy wants a bearskin but ends up with a live bear. Caldecott Medal winner.

Wells, Rosemary. *Hazel's Amazing Mother*. Illus. by the author. Dial, 1985. Mothers can do anything, even defeat bullies. *Max's First Word*. Illus. by the author. Dial, 1979. One of a series of humorous books.

Williams, Margery. *The Velveteen Rabbit*. Illus. by David Jorgensen. Knopf, 1985. A newly illustrated edition of a popular story about a toy brought to life by love.

Poetry

Adoff, Arnold, ed. *Celebrations: A New Anthology of Black American Poetry*. Follett, 1977. A selection from the works of 85 poets celebrating aspects of the black experience. Intermediate and older readers.

Alderson, Brian, comp. *Cakes and Custard*. Illus. by Helen Oxenbury. Morrow, 1975. A fine collection of traditional and modern nursery rhymes. Young readers.

Benét, Rosemary and **Stephen Vincent.** *A Book of Americans*. Illus. by Charles Child. Holt, 1961. Poems retelling stories and legends about famous people in American history. Intermediate readers.

Brooks, Gwendolyn. *Bronzeville Boys and Girls*. Illus. by Ronni Solbert. Harper, 1956. Simple poems about the experiences and feelings of black children in big cities. Intermediate readers.

Cendrars, Blaise. *Shadow*. Illus. and trans. from the French by Marcia Brown. Scribner, 1982. Collages and paintings illustrate a poem based on African folk tales. Caldecott Medal winner. All ages.

Ciardi, John. *Doodle Soup*. Illus. by Merle Nacht. Houghton, 1985. Light, skillful poems are often funny and sometimes stinging. Intermediate readers.

Coltman, Paul. *Tog the Ribber or Granny's Tale*. Illus. by Gillian McClure. Farrar, 1985. Bouncy pace and humor balance the spooky quality of a richly illustrated narrative poem. Intermediate readers.

Cullen, Countee. *The Lost Zoo*. Illus. by Joseph Low. Follett, 1969. Humorous verse stories about fantastic animals who were left off Noah's ark. Young readers.

Farjeon, Eleanor. *The Children's Bells*. Illus. by Peggy Fortnum. Walck, 1960. Poems on such subjects as magic, saints, and the seasons, selected from earlier books by this noted English author. Older readers.

Fisher, Aileen. *Rabbits, Rabbits*. Illus. by Gail Niemann. Harper, 1983. Brief, brisk poems about rabbits and nature. Young readers.

Greenfield, Eloise. *Daydreamers*. Illus. by Tom Feelings. Dial, 1981. Tender pictures of black children illustrate a gentle poem. Intermediate readers.

Kumin, Maxine. *The Microscope*. Illus. by Arnold Lobel. Harper, 1984. A merry poem, historically accurate, about a landmark invention in science history. Young readers.

Kuskin, Karla. *Something Sleeping in the Hall*. Illus. by the author. Harper, 1985. A breezy collection of humorous poems. Young readers.

Illustration of a grapevine by the author from *A Biblical Garden* by Carol Lerner; © 1982 by Carol Lerner. By permission of William Morrow & Co.

A Biblical Garden contains pictures and descriptions of 20 plants mentioned in the Hebrew Bible, or Old Testament.

Lear, Edward. *The Complete Nonsense Book.* Illus. by the author. Dodd, 1962. Limericks, nonsense poems, and humorous story poems by a famous English comic poet and artist of the 1800's. Intermediate readers.

Livingston, Myra Cohn. *Celebrations.* Illus. by Leonard Everett Fisher. Holiday, 1985. Handsome pictures and distinctive poems are nicely combined on oversized pages. Young readers.

Longfellow, Henry Wadsworth. *Hiawatha.* Illus. by Susan Jeffers. Dial, 1983. Romantic paintings complement the mood of a classic American poem. Young readers.

McCord, David. *The Star in the Pail.* Illus. by Marc Simont. Little, Brown, 1975. Witty, simple poems. Young readers.

Merriam, Eve. *If Only I Could Tell You.* Illus. by Donna Diamond. Knopf, 1983. A collection of brief and moving poems about love. Older readers.

Milne, A. A. *When We Were Very Young.* Dutton, 1952. *Now We Are Six.* Dutton, 1955. Both illus. by Ernest H. Shepard. Two classic collections of verse about children and their world. Young readers.

Prelutsky, Jack, ed. *The Random House Book of Poetry.* Illus. by Arnold Lobel. Random House, 1983. Heavily illustrated anthology includes almost every major children's poet. Intermediate readers.

Richards, Laura. *Tirra Lirra: Rhymes Old and New.* Illus. by Marguerite Davis. Little, Brown, 1955. Nonsense verses filled with humorous situations and made-up words. Intermediate readers.

Ryder, Joanne. *Inside Turtle's Shell and Other Poems of the Field.* Illus. by Susan Bonners. Macmillan, 1985. Gentle poems about the creatures who live in ponds and meadows. Young readers.

Stevenson, Robert Louis. *A Child's Garden of Verses.* Illus. by Alice and Martin Provensen. Golden Press, 1951. A classic collection of short poems about the everyday world. Young readers.

Folk Literature/Fairy Tales, Folk Tales, and Myths

Aardema, Verna. *Why Mosquitoes Buzz in People's Ears.* Illus. by Leo and Diane Dillon. Dial, 1975. *Half-a-Ball-of-Kenki.* Illus. by Diane Zuromskis. Warne, 1979. Two books based on African folk tales. First book a Caldecott Medal winner. Young readers.

Andersen, Hans Christian. *The Complete Fairy Tales and Stories.* Trans. from the Danish by Erik Christian Haugaard. Illus. Doubleday, 1974. A superb modern translation. Of the many editions of individual tales, the following are especially recommended: *The Emperor's New Clothes.* Adapted by Jean van Leeuwen. Illus. by Jack and Irene Delano. Random House, 1971. *The Nightingale.* Trans. by Eva Le Gallienne. Illus. by Nancy Burkert. Harper, 1965. *Thumbelina.* Trans. by R. P. Keigwin. Illus. by Adrienne Adams. Scribner, 1961. All books for all ages.

Asbjørnsen, Peter C., and **Moe, Jørgen.** *East of the Sun and West of the Moon and Other Tales.* Illus. by Tom Vroman. Macmillan, 1963. A famous collection of Norwegian fairy tales. Intermediate readers.

Baker, Olaf. *Where the Buffaloes Begin.* Illus. by Stephen Gammell. Warne, 1981. Distinctive drawings illustrate an American Indian myth that was first published in 1915 in *St. Nicholas Magazine.* Young readers.

Bierhorst, John, ed. *The Hungry Woman: Myths and Legends of the Aztecs.* Morrow, 1984. Aztec drawings of the 1500's illustrate an entertaining collection of folk tales and legends. Older readers.

Bierhorst, John, trans. *Spirit Child: A Story of the Nativity.* Illus. by Barbara Cooney. Morrow, 1984. An Aztec version of the Christmas story. Intermediate readers.

Calvino, Italo, comp. *Italian Folktales.* Trans. by George Martin. Harcourt, 1980. A rich resource for the storyteller as well as the reader. Intermediate readers.

Chase, Richard, ed. *The Jack Tales.* Houghton, 1943.

Jumanji is a fantasy about a jungle adventure game that two children play at home one afternoon after their parents go out.

Grandfather Tales. Houghton, 1948. Both illus. by Berkeley Williams, Jr. Two collections of folk tales from rural North Carolina and Virginia. Both books for intermediate readers.

Courlander, Harold. *The King's Drum, and Other African Tales.* Illus. by Enrico Arno. Harcourt, 1962. Folk tales from African lands south of the Sahara. Older readers.

D'Aulaire, Ingri and **Edgar Parin.** *Norse Gods and Giants.* Illus. by the authors. Doubleday, 1967. Stories about the great Norse gods and goddesses and a retelling of Norse myths about how the world began and how it will end. Intermediate readers.

El-Shamy, Hasan, comp. *Folktales of Egypt.* University of Chicago Press, 1980. A large and varied selection for children that should also interest students of folklore. Older readers.

Adaptations of Legends introduce young readers to the exciting adventures of heroes like the American Indian chief Hiawatha.

Evslin, Bernard. *The Green Hero*. Illus. by Barbara Bascove. Four Winds, 1975. A sophisticated and witty retelling of the early adventures of the Irish hero Finn McCool. Older readers.

Grimm, Jakob and **Wilhelm.** *The Complete Fairy Tales*. Illus. by Josef Scharl. Pantheon, 1974. A reissue of a standard edition. *The Juniper Tree and Other Tales from Grimm*. Lore Segal and Maurice Sendak, comp. Illus. by Maurice Sendak. Farrar, 1973. A new translation from the German that includes many less familiar tales. Both books for all ages. Of the many editions of single tales, the following are especially recommended: *Hans in Luck*. Illus. by Felix Hoffman. Atheneum, 1975. *The Shoemaker and the Elves*. Trans. by Wayne Andrews. Illus. by Adrienne Adams. Scribner, 1960. *The Sleeping Beauty*. Illus. by Trina Schart Hyman. Little, 1977. *Snow-White and the Seven Dwarfs*. Trans. by Randall Jarrell. Illus. by Nancy Ekholm Burkert. Farrar, 1972. All books for young and intermediate readers.

Hamilton, Virginia. *The People Could Fly: American Black Folktales*. Illus. by Leo and Diane Dillon. Knopf, 1985. Handsome pictures complement a major writer's retelling of traditional tales. Intermediate and older readers.

Harris, Christie. *Once Upon a Totem*. Illus. by John Frazer Mills. Atheneum, 1967. *Mouse-Woman and the Mischief-Makers*. Illus. by Douglas Tait. Atheneum, 1977. Folk tales from Indians of the Pacific Northwest. Both books for intermediate readers.

Hill, Kay. *More Glooscap Stories*. Illus. by John Hamberger. Dodd, 1970. Folk tales from the Abnaki Indians of northeastern Canada. Both books for intermediate readers.

Jacobs, Joseph, ed. *English Folk and Fairy Tales*. Putnam, 1904. *More English Folk and Fairy Tales*. Putnam, 1904. Both illus. by John D. Batten. Two famous collections of tales from England, Scotland, and Wales by a noted folklore scholar. *Tom Tit Tot*. Illus. by Evaline Ness. Scribner, 1965. A tale originally collected by Jacobs about a bragging countrywoman, her stupid daughter, and a greedy king. All books for intermediate readers.

Jagendorf, M. A. *Noodlehead Stories from Around the World*. Illus. by Shane Miller. Vanguard, 1957. Comic folk tales from many lands, all dealing with foolish people. Intermediate readers.

Lang, Andrew, ed. *The Blue Fairy Book*. Illus. by Ben

Illustration by Victor Ambrus from *Favorite Stories of the Ballet* by James Riordan; illustration © 1984 by Robert Mathias Publishing Workshop. By permission of Hodder & Stoughton.

Petrushka is a Russian folk tale about a puppet who comes to life. The puppet is the title character in a famous ballet.

Kutcher. McKay, 1948. One of a series of anthologies of fairy tales from around the world by a noted Scottish folklore scholar. Intermediate readers.

Lurie, Alison, ed. *Clever Gretchen and Other Forgotten Folktales*. Illus. by Margot Tomes. Crowell, 1980. A selection of tales about women. Intermediate readers.

McKinley, Robin. *Beauty: A Retelling of the Story of Beauty and the Beast*. Harper, 1978. A vigorous, imaginative retelling of the fairy tale. Older readers.

Minard, Rosemary, comp. *Womenfolk and Fairy Tales*.

Text © 1975 by Verna Aardema, pictures © 1975 by Leo and Diane Dillon. Published by The Dial Press

A West African Folk Tale called *Why Mosquitoes Buzz in People's Ears* explains why mosquitoes make a buzzing sound. The artists used elements of traditional African art in their illustrations.

Illus. by Suzanna Klein. Houghton, 1975. A collection of stories about women. Intermediate readers.

Perrault, Charles. *Perrault's Complete Fairy Tales.* Trans. from the French by A. E. Johnson and others. Illus. by W. Heath Robinson. Dodd, 1961. Original versions of 14 of the most famous fairy tales in literature, including "Cinderella" and "Little Red Riding Hood." Intermediate readers.

Sadler, Catherine, ad. *Treasure Mountain: Folktales from Southern China.* Illus. by Cheng Mung Yun. Atheneum, 1982. Fluent retelling of six tales. Intermediate readers.

Schwartz, Howard, ad. *Elijah's Violin & Other Jewish Fairy Tales.* Illus. by Linda Heller. Harper, 1983. Stories from Jewish oral folklore. Older readers.

Wilde, Oscar. *The Selfish Giant.* Illus. by Lisbeth Zwerger. Neugebauer Press, 1984. The mystic quality of a moral fairy tale is reflected in romantic pictures. Intermediate readers.

Folk Literature/Epics, Ballads, and Fables

Aesop. *Aesop's Fables.* Trans. by V. S. Vernon Jones. Illus. by Arthur Rackham. Watts, 1967. A famous collection of ancient fables. All ages. *More Fables of Aesop.* Retold and illus. by Jack Kent. Parents, 1974. Freely adapted from the Vernon Jones version. Young readers.

Barth, Edna, ad. *Cupid and Psyche: A Love Story.* Illus. by Ati Forberg. Seabury, 1976. A moving version of the love story about a Greek god and a mortal woman. Intermediate readers.

Bertol, Roland. *Sundiata: The Epic of the Lion King.* Illus. by Gregorio Prestopino. Crowell, 1970. An account of the triumphs of Sundiata, founder of the African empire of Mali. Intermediate readers.

Colum, Padraic. *The Children's Homer: The Adventures of Odysseus and the Tale of Troy.* Illus. by Willy Pogany. Macmillan, 1962. A retelling of Homer's ancient Greek epics, the *Iliad* and the *Odyssey.* Intermediate readers.

Illustration (1912) by Arthur Rackham; Franklin Watts, Inc.

Aesop's Fables is a collection of brief stories that illustrate morals. Most of the characters are animals. One fable tells how a tortoise—through perseverance—beats a hare in a race.

Illustration by Marcia Brown used with the permission of Charles Scribner's Sons. Illustration © 1982 Marcia Brown

Shadow is a West African folk tale about a spirit that was adapted and retold by the famous French poet Blaise Cendrars.

Evslin, Bernard. *Hercules.* Illus. by Jos. Smith. Morrow, 1984. A lively story about the mythical Greek hero. Older readers.

Gross, Gwen, ad. *Knights of the Round Table.* Illus. by Norman Green. Random House, 1985. Simplified stories of King Arthur and his knights. Younger readers.

Hastings, Selina, ad. *Sir Gawain and the Loathly Lady.* Illus. by Juan Wijngaard. Lothrop, 1985. Fine retelling of an Arthurian legend with paintings in medieval manuscript style. Intermediate readers.

Hazeltine, Alice, ed. *Hero Tales from Many Lands.* Illus. by Gordon Laite. Abingdon, 1961. Tales of real and legendary heroes of ballads and epics, from many countries, including England and Japan. Older readers.

Hodges, Margaret, ad. *Saint George and the Dragon.* Illus. by Trina Schart Hyman. Little, 1984. A retelling of the medieval legend. Caldecott Medal winner. Intermediate readers.

La Fontaine, Jean de. *Fables.* Trans. by Marianne Moore. Viking, 1954. All 241 fables written by the French author in an acclaimed translation by a noted modern American poet. All ages.

Malory, Sir Thomas. *The Boy's King Arthur.* Illus. by N. C. Wyeth. Scribner, 1952. Stories about King Arthur and his Knights of the Round Table. Adapted by the American poet Sidney Lanier. Intermediate readers.

Manniche, Lise, trans. *How Djadja-Em Ankh Saved the Day: A Tale from Ancient Egypt.* Illus. by the translator. Crowell, 1977. A 3,500-year-old tale of a magician printed in scroll form. Intermediate readers.

Nic Leodhas, Sorche. *By Loch and by Lin: Tales from Scottish Ballads.* Illus. by Vera Bock. Holt, 1969. A retelling of stories of adventure and romance adapted from traditional Scottish ballads. Intermediate readers.

Pitcher, Diana, ad. *Tokoloshi.* Illus. by Meg Rutherford. Celestial Arts, 1981. A retelling of 17 African folk tales from the Zulu people. Intermediate readers.

Plotz, Helen, comp. *As I Walked Out One Evening: A Book of Ballads.* Greenwillow, 1976. A broad selection of ballads. Intermediate readers.

Get on out of here, Philip Hall

by BETTE GREENE

Illustration by Charles Lilly from *Get On Out of Here, Philip Hall* © 1981 by Bette Greene. Used by permission of Dial Press.

Get On Out of Here, Philip Hall describes the experiences of a young black girl growing up in rural Arkansas.

Pyle, Howard. *The Merry Adventures of Robin Hood of Great Renown in Nottinghamshire.* Illus. by the author. Scribner, 1946. A classic adaptation of the ballads about the famous English outlaw-hero. Older readers.

Sutcliff, Rosemary. *The Light Beyond the Forest: The Quest for the Holy Grail.* Dutton, 1980. *The Sword and the Circle: King Arthur and the Knights of the Round Table.* Dutton, 1981. *The Road to Camlann.* Illus. by Shirley Felts. Dutton, 1982. Clear presentations of the major Arthurian tales. Intermediate and older readers.

Tehranchian, Hassan, ad. *Kalilah and Dimnah: Fables from the Middle East.* Illus. by Anatole Ur. Harmony, 1985. A collection of beast fables from a Persian manuscript. Intermediate readers.

Thompson, Brian. *The Story of Prince Rama.* Illus. by original paintings and by Jeroo Roy. Viking, 1985. An ancient Asian epic retold in a series of brief episodes. Intermediate readers.

Williams, Jay. *The Surprising Things Maui Did.* Illus. by Charles Mikolaycak. Four Winds, 1979. A collection of folk tales about the Hawaiian god Maui. Young readers.

Fiction/General Fiction*

Alcott, Louisa May. *Little Women.* Illus. by Jessie Wilcox Smith. Little, Brown, 1968. A classic novel about four sisters growing up in New England during the Civil War. Intermediate readers.

Alexander, Lloyd. *The Book of Three.* Holt, 1964. *The Black Cauldron.* Holt, 1965. *The Castle of Llyr.* Holt, 1966. *Taran Wanderer.* Holt, 1967. *The High King.* Holt, 1969. A series of five fantasies about an imaginary kingdom in Wales. *The High King* won the Newbery Medal. *The First Two Lives of Lukas-Kasha.* Dutton, 1978. The hero awakens to find himself in a strange land. Intermediate readers.

Babbit, Natalie. *Tuck Everlasting.* Farrar, 1975. A fascina-

*Including all kinds of fiction except historical, mystery and detective, and science fiction.

ting fantasy about a family who discover a spring that is a source of eternal youth. Intermediate readers.

Bailey, Carolyn Sherwin. *Miss Hickory.* Illus. by Ruth Gannett. Viking, 1946. The adventures of Miss Hickory, a wooden doll who spends a New Hampshire winter with forest and field animals. Newbery Medal winner. Intermediate readers.

Barrie, Sir James. *Peter Pan.* Edited by Josette Frank from *Peter Pan and Wendy.* Illus. by Marjorie Torrey. Random House, 1957. A classic fantasy about three children who fly to Never-Never Land with Peter Pan, a boy who refuses to grow up. Intermediate readers.

Baum, L. Frank. *The Wizard of Oz.* Illus. by W. W. Denslow. Reilly and Lee, 1956. A famous fantasy about Dorothy, a girl carried by a cyclone from a Kansas farm to a magical land. There she meets the cowardly lion, the tin woodsman, the scarecrow, and the wonderful Wizard of Oz. Intermediate readers.

Bawden, Nina. *The Finding.* Lothrop, 1985. A fast-paced English story about an adopted boy who runs away. Intermediate readers.

Belpré, Pura. *Santiago.* Illus. by Symeon Shimin. Warne, 1969. A Puerto Rican boy tries to adjust to his new home in New York City. Intermediate readers.

Blume, Judy. *Are You There God? It's Me, Margaret.* Bradbury, 1970. A realistic novel about an 11-year-old girl, her religious doubts, social problems, and her reactions to her maturing body. Intermediate readers.

Bond, Nancy. *A String in the Harp.* Atheneum, 1976. While spending a year in Wales, an American boy has visions of the past in which he finds the key to the harp of the legendary Welsh poet Taliesin. Intermediate readers.

Boston, Lucy M. *The Children of Green Knowe.* Harcourt,

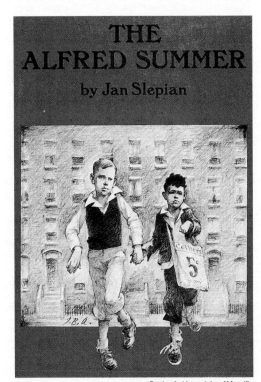

THE ALFRED SUMMER

by Jan Slepian

Reprinted with permission of Macmillan Publishing Co., Inc. from *The Alfred Summer* © 1980 by Jan Slepian

The Alfred Summer tells about four children, two of them handicapped, who build a boat to sail at New York City's Coney Island.

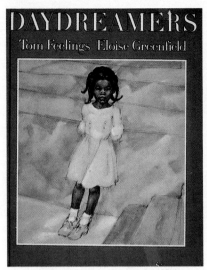

Illustration by Tom Feelings from *Daydreamers* by Eloise Greenfield; illustrations © 1981 by Tom Feelings. Reproduced by permission of the publisher, Dial Books for Young Readers

Daydreamers is a sensitively illustrated poem that explores the rich variety of moods of a number of black children in the act of daydreaming.

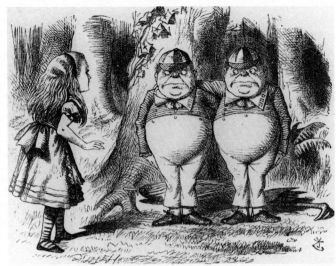

Illustration by Sir John Tenniel from the first edition (1872) of *Through the Looking Glass and What Alice Found There* by Lewis Carroll; Macmillan and Company (Newberry Library, Chicago)

Through the Looking Glass is a fantasy written by Lewis Carroll. It describes the adventures of a girl named Alice who was also the heroine of Carroll's *Alice in Wonderland*. In this picture, Alice meets Tweedle Dee and Tweedle Dum.

1955. *The Treasure of Green Knowe*. Harcourt, 1958. *The River at Green Knowe*. Harcourt, 1959. *The Stranger at Green Knowe*. Harcourt, 1961. *The Enemy at Green Knowe*. Harcourt, 1964. *The Stones of Green Knowe*. Atheneum, 1976. All illus. by Peter Boston. A series of fantasies about Green Knowe—an old English house—where children of today play with children of the past. All books for intermediate readers.

Burch, Robert. *Queenie Peavey*. Illus. by Jerry Lazare. Viking, 1966. A story set in rural Georgia about a girl whose father is in prison. Intermediate readers.

Burnford, Sheila. *The Incredible Journey*. Illus. by Carl Burger. Little, Brown, 1961. Two dogs and a cat struggle through the Canadian wilderness to reach the masters they love. Older readers.

Byars, Betsy. *The Summer of the Swans*. Illus. by Ted CoConis. Viking, 1970. A 14-year-old girl searches for her mentally retarded 10-year-old brother, who is missing. Newbery Medal winner. Intermediate readers.

Carlson, Natalie Savage. *The Empty Schoolhouse*. Illus. by John Kaufman. Harper, 1965. The experiences of a 10-year-old black girl in a recently desegregated parochial school in Louisiana. Intermediate readers.

Carroll, Lewis. *Alice in Wonderland and Through the Looking Glass*. Illus. by Sir John Tenniel. Grosset, 1963. Two classic fantasies about the adventures of a girl named Alice who, in an imaginary land, meets such unforgettable characters as the Mad Hatter and the Queen of Hearts. Intermediate readers.

Clark, Ann Nolan. *Little Navajo Bluebird*. Illus. by Paul Lantz. Viking, 1963. A story about Little Bluebird, a Navajo girl who refuses to abandon the customs of her people. Intermediate readers.

Cleary, Beverly. *Ramona and Her Father*. Illus. by Alan Tiegreen. Morrow, 1977. *Ramona Quimby, Age 8*. Illus. by Alan Tiegreen. Morrow, 1981. Two books in a warm and humorous series about a young girl. Young readers.

Collodi, Carlo. *The Adventures of Pinocchio*. Trans. from the Italian by Carol Della Chiesa. Illus. by Naiad Einsel. Macmillan, 1963. A wooden puppet has many adventures before he realizes his dream of becoming a real boy. Intermediate readers.

Cooper, Susan. *Over Sea, Under Stone*. Illus. by Margery Gill. Atheneum, 1966. *The Dark Is Rising*. Illus. by Alan E. Cober. Atheneum, 1973. *Greenwitch*. Illus. by Michael Heslop. Atheneum, 1974. *The Grey King*. Illus. by Michael Heslop. Atheneum, 1975. *Silver on the Tree*. Atheneum, 1977. A series of five fantasies about immortal beings who battle evil forces that threaten the world. *The Grey King* was a Newbery Medal winner. All books for intermediate readers.

Dallas-Smith, Peter. *Trouble for Trumpets*. Illus. by Peter Cross. Random House, 1984. An animal fantasy that contains humor and action. Young readers.

Defoe, Daniel. *Robinson Crusoe*. Illus. by N. C. Wyeth. Scribner, 1957. The adventures of the lone survivor of a shipwreck who uses his ingenuity to survive on an island. Older readers.

DeJong, Meindert. *The Wheel on the School*. Illus. by Maurice Sendak. Harper, 1954. Children try to lure storks—symbols of good luck—back to their village in the Netherlands. Newbery Medal winner. Intermediate readers.

Dickens, Charles. *A Christmas Carol*. Illus. by Arthur Rackham. Lippincott, 1966. A famous story about Ebenezer Scrooge, who changes from miser to warmhearted person after three ghosts show him his past, present, and future. Intermediate readers.

Donovan, John. *I'll Get There. It Better Be Worth the Trip*. Harper, 1969. A boy grows up with an alcoholic mother in a broken home. Older readers.

Enright, Elizabeth. *Thimble Summer*. Illus. by the author. Holt, 1966. A girl spends the summer on a Wisconsin farm. Newbery Medal winner. Intermediate readers.

Estes, Eleanor. *The Moffats*. Illus. by Louis Slobodkin. Harcourt, 1941. Affectionately told everyday adventures of the Moffat children. Intermediate readers.

Fitzhugh, Louise. *Harriet the Spy*. Illus. by the author. Harper, 1964. The story of an 11-year-old girl's questions about life and her reactions after she is ostracized by her friends for her bitter comments. Intermediate readers.

George, Jean Craighead. *Cry of the Crow*. Harper, 1980. A story set in the Florida Everglades about a girl's pet crow.

Intermediate readers. Another version, illustrated by Michael Hague, in a simpler format. Ariel/Holt, 1980. Intermediate readers.

Grahame, Kenneth. *The Wind in the Willows.* Illus. by Ernest H. Shepard. Scribner, 1961. A classic novel about animals in the English countryside who live and talk like humans. Older readers.

Greene, Bette. *Philip Hall Likes Me. I Reckon Maybe.* Illus. by Charles Lilly. Dial, 1974. *Get On Out of Here, Philip Hall.* Illus. by Charles Lilly. Dial, 1979. Two stories about a black girl in rural Arkansas. Intermediate readers.

Hall, Lynn. *The Boy in the Off-White Hat.* Scribner, 1984. A babysitter learns that her small charge is the terrified victim of sexual abuse. Intermediate readers.

Hamilton, Virginia. *M. C. Higgins, the Great.* Macmillan, 1974. A story about a black boy's protective love for his family. Newbery Medal winner. Older readers.

Henry, Marguerite. *King of the Wind.* Illus. by Wesley Dennis. Rand McNally, 1948. The adventures of a valuable Arabian horse on the journey from his native land to his new home in England. Newbery Medal winner. Intermediate readers.

Herzig, Alison, and **Mali, Jane.** *Thaddeus.* Illus. by Stephen Gammell. Little, 1984. An eccentric elderly relative arranges a series of birthday surprises. Young readers.

Hinton, S. E. *The Outsiders.* Viking, 1967. A novel written by a teen-aged girl about two teen-aged gangs of boys in Oklahoma. Older readers.

Houston, James. *Akavak: An Eskimo Journey.* Illus. by the author. Harcourt, 1968. An Eskimo boy and his grandfather undertake a dangerous journey across Baffin Island. *Long Claws: An Arctic Adventure.* Illus. by the author. Atheneum, 1981. In a time of hunger, a young Eskimo brother and sister brave a grizzly bear's attack to bring food back to their family. Both books for intermediate readers.

Howe, Deborah and **James.** *Teddy Bear's Scrapbook.* Illus. by David S. Rose. Atheneum, 1980. Teddy Bear brings out his fascinating scrapbook during a boring rainy afternoon. Intermediate readers.

Hunt, Irene. *Up a Road Slowly.* Follett, 1966. How Julie painfully matures over a 10-year period while living with her unsympathetic spinster aunt. Newbery Medal winner. Older readers.

Jukes, Mavis. *Like Jake and Me.* Illus. by Lloyd Bloom. Knopf, 1984. Love grows between a small boy and his stepfather. Young readers.

Konigsburg, Elaine. *Journey to an 800 Number.* Atheneum, 1982. As he tours conventions and fairs with his father,

snobbish Max meets some wonderful people. Intermediate readers.

Lawson, Robert. *Rabbit Hill.* Viking, 1944. *Tough Winter.* Viking, 1954. Both illus. by the author. Two stories about a family of rabbits living in the Connecticut countryside. *Rabbit Hill* won a Newbery Medal. Intermediate readers.

Le Grand. *How Baseball Began in Brooklyn.* Illus. by the author. Abingdon, 1958. A comic tall tale about how 10 Dutch boys and 9 Indian boys invented baseball in colonial New York. Intermediate readers.

Lenski, Lois. *Strawberry Girl.* Illus. by the author. Lippincott, 1945. A realistic novel with regional flavor about strawberry farmers in rural Florida in the early 1900's. Newbery Medal winner. Intermediate readers.

Lewis, C. S. *The Chronicles of Narnia.* Illus. by Pauline Baynes. Macmillan, 1950-1956. Seven fantasies about the adventures of four children in the magic land of Narnia. All for intermediate readers.

Little, Jean. *Home from Far.* Illus. by Jerry Lazare. Little, Brown, 1965. A realistic handling of how the death of a child affects the surviving members of a family, and especially the dead boy's twin brother. Older readers.

Lively, Penelope. *Uninvited Ghosts and Other Stories.* Illus. by John Lawrence. Dutton, 1985. Eight lively ghost stories with nonsensical plots. Intermediate readers.

Lowry, Lois. *Anastasia Krupnik.* Houghton, 1979. *Anastasia Again.* Illus. by Diane de Groat. Houghton, 1981. Two comic stories about the daily problems of a 10-year-old girl. Intermediate readers.

Mathis, Sharon Bell. *The Hundred Penny Box.* Illus. by Leo and Diane Dillon. Viking, 1975. A story about a small black child's love for a very old aunt. Intermediate readers.

McKinley, Robin. *The Hero and the Crown.* Greenwillow, 1984. A fantasy about a brave girl who slays a dragon. Newbery Medal winner. Older readers.

Milne, A. A. *Winnie-the-Pooh.* Dutton, 1954. *The House at Pooh Corner.* Dutton, 1956. Both illus. by Ernest H. Shepard. Two amusing books about Christopher Robin —the author's son—and the boy's adventures with his toy animals come-to-life. Intermediate readers.

Nordstrom, Ursula. *The Secret Language.* Illus. by Mary Chalmers. Harper, 1960. A girl at a boarding school overcomes her shyness after she and a new friend invent a secret language. Intermediate readers.

Paterson, Katherine. *Bridge to Terabithia.* Illus. by Don-

Illustration © 1975 by Leo and Diane Dillon from *The Hundred Penny Box* by Sharon Bell Mathis. Reprinted by permission of Viking Penguin Inc.

The Hundred Penny Box concerns an old woman who tells a boy about her life.

Illustration by the author from *The Checkup* by Helen Oxenbury. © 1983 by Helen Oxenbury. Reproduced by permission of the publisher, Dial Books for Young Readers

The Checkup is a humorous description of a child's visit to a doctor.

Illustration © 1984 by Stephen Gammell from *Thaddeus* © 1984 by Alison Cragin Herzig and Jane Lawrence Mali

Thaddeus tells of an eccentric elderly relative who arranges birthday surprises.

na Diamond. Crowell, 1977. A touching story of friendship suddenly ended by a death. Newbery Medal winner. *Come Sing, Jimmy Jo.* Lodestar, 1985. A novel about a young country music star. Both books for older readers.

Pearce, Philippa. *Tom's Midnight Garden.* Illus. by Susan Einzig. Lippincott, 1958. A boy wandering through a relative's home finds a Victorian garden and a playmate from an earlier era. Older readers.

Seredy, Kate. *The Good Master.* Illus. by the author. Viking, 1961. A tomboy from Budapest learns understanding after she lives with her sympathetic uncle on his farm in Hungary. Intermediate readers.

Singer, Isaac Bashevis. *The Fearsome Inn.* Illus. by Nonny Hogrogian. Trans. from Yiddish by the author and Elizabeth Shub. Scribner, 1967. A fantasy about three travelers in Poland who free three girls held as slaves by a witch in a remote inn. Intermediate readers.

Slepian, Jan. *The Alfred Summer.* Macmillan, 1980. A warm, sympathetic story about two handicapped children. Intermediate readers.

Sneve, Virginia Driving Hawk. *High Elk's Treasure.* Illus. by Oren Lyons. Holiday, 1972. A story about Joe High Elk and his Sioux Indian family. Intermediate readers.

Sperry, Armstrong. *Call It Courage.* Illus. by the author. Macmillan, 1940. The son of a Polynesian chief overcomes his fear of the sea and wins the respect of his people. Newbery Medal winner. Older readers.

Spyri, Johanna. *Heidi.* Trans. from the German by Helen B. Dole. Illus. by William Sharp. Grosset, 1945. A Swiss girl's love and wholesomeness bring happiness to those around her. Intermediate readers.

Sterling, Dorothy. *Mary Jane.* Illus. by Ernest Crichlow. Doubleday, 1959. A novel about the experiences of a black girl in the first integrated class in a junior high school. Intermediate readers.

Stevenson, Robert Louis. *Treasure Island.* Illus. by N. C. Wyeth. Scribner, 1939. A classic adventure novel in which young Jim Hawkins and his friends battle the villainous Long John Silver and his gang for possession of a buried treasure. Older readers.

Swift, Jonathan. *Gulliver's Travels.* Edited by Elaine Moss. Illus. by Hans Baltzer. Duell, 1961. A children's version of the famous fantasy about a ship's doctor who visits the imaginary lands of the tiny Lilliputians and the race of horses called Houyhnhnms. Older readers.

Tolkien, J. R. R. *The Hobbit.* Illus. by the author. Houghton, 1937. A famous fantasy about the adventures of a creature called a Hobbit who seeks a treasure guarded by a mighty dragon. Intermediate readers.

Travers, P. L. *Mary Poppins.* Illus. by Mary Shepard. Harcourt, 1962. The first of several fantasies about an English nursemaid with magical powers and her adventures with the Banks children. Intermediate readers.

Twain, Mark. *The Adventures of Tom Sawyer.* Illus. by Worth Brehm. Harper, 1938. *The Adventures of Huckle-*

berry Finn. Illus. by John Falter. Macmillan, 1962. Classics of American fiction about the adventures of two mischievous boys living near the Mississippi River in Missouri in the mid-1800's. Both books for older readers.

Van Allsburg, Chris. *Jumanji.* Illus. by the author. Houghton, 1981. An imaginatively illustrated fantasy about two children who find a jungle game and move into a magic world. Caldecott Medal winner. Young readers.

Walsh, Jill Paton. *Gaffer Samson's Luck.* Illus. by Brock Cole. Farrar, 1984. A touching story about the friendship between a young boy and an old man. Intermediate readers.

White, E. B. *Stuart Little.* Illus. by Garth Williams. Harper, 1945. A fantasy about a mouse born to human parents. *Charlotte's Web.* Illus. by Garth Williams. Harper, 1952. A friendship develops between a pig and a spider on a farm. *The Trumpet of the Swan.* Illus. by Edward Frascino. Harper, 1970. A Canadian swan born without a voice learns to communicate by playing the trumpet. All books for intermediate readers.

Fiction/Historical Fiction

Avi. *The Fighting Ground.* Lippincott, 1984. A powerful story of a boy's experiences during one intense day of the Revolutionary War. Older readers.

Benchley, Nathaniel. *Bright Candles.* Harper, 1974. Jens, a 16-year-old boy, becomes involved in the Danish resistance movement during the German occupation in World War II. Older readers.

Blos, Joan. *A Gathering of Days: A New England Girl's Journal, 1830-32.* Scribner, 1979. A girl helps a slave in spite of New Hampshire's slave laws. Newbery Medal winner. Older readers.

Clapp, Patricia. *Witches' Children: A Story of Salem.* Lothrop, 1982. Mary Warren gives a lively account of her role during the Salem witch hunt of the 1690's. Older readers.

Coatsworth, Elizabeth. *Away Goes Sally.* Illus. by Helen Sewell. Macmillan, 1934. A girl, in the early 1800's, moves by sled with her aunts from Massachusetts to Maine. Intermediate readers.

Collier, James and **Christopher.** *My Brother Sam Is Dead.* Four Winds, 1974. A story set during the Revolutionary War shows the anguish of a family divided between the American and British sides. Older readers.

Dalgliesh, Alice. *The Courage of Sarah Noble.* Illus. by Leonard Weisgard. Scribner, 1954. A girl accompanies her pioneer father in the Connecticut wilderness while he builds a house for his family. Intermediate readers.

Forbes, Esther. *Johnny Tremain.* Illus. by Lynd K. Ward. Houghton, 1943. A boy participates in events in Boston that lead to the outbreak of the Revolutionary War. Newbery Medal winner. Older readers.

Fox, Paula. *The Slave Dancer.* Illus. by Eros Keith. Bradbury, 1973. A boy witnesses the horrors of the slave trade while serving on a ship transporting slaves in 1840. Newbery Medal winner. Older readers.

Illustration © 1983 by the authors Alice and Martin Provensen. Reprinted by permission of Viking Penguin Inc.

The First Airplane Flight across the English Channel in 1909 is described in *The Glorious Flight: Across the Channel with Louis Blériot.* Blériot was a French aviation pioneer.

> Your humble servant, John Hancock. King George's Number One Enemy.
>
> "We'll show the king what we think of him!" they cried and amid a great round of laughter, they picked John Hancock up bodily and set him in the president's chair where, they voted unanimously, he should stay.

Illustration by Trina Schart Hyman reprinted by permission of Coward, McCann & Geohegan from *Will You Sign Here, John Hancock?* by Jean Fritz. Illustrations © 1976 by Trina Schart Hyman

A Biography of John Hancock tells the life story of one of the most famous signers of the Declaration of Independence.

Garner, Alan. *The Stone Book* and *Granny Reardon.* Illus. by Michael Foreman. World, 1978. *The Aimer Gate* and *Tom Fobble's Day.* Illus. by Michael Foreman. World, 1979. Four books that describe several generations of an English family. Young readers.

Kullman, Harry. *The Battle Horse.* Trans. by George Blecher and Lone Thygesen-Blecher. Bradbury, 1981. A powerful story about class conflict set in Sweden during the early 1900's. Older readers.

MacLachlan, Patricia. *Sarah, Plain and Tall.* Harper, 1985. Two children learn to love the mail-order stepmother who comes to their lonely frontier home. Newbery Medal winner. Intermediate readers.

Magorian, Michelle. *Good Night, Mr. Tom.* Harper, 1982. A moving story of the love between an old man and a small boy during World War II. Older readers.

O'Dell, Scott. *Island of the Blue Dolphins.* Houghton, 1960. An Indian girl is stranded for 18 years on a rocky island off the coast of California in the early 1800's. Newbery Medal winner. *Sarah Bishop.* Houghton, 1980. A tense story set during the Revolutionary War. Both books for older readers.

Sandin, Joan. *The Long Way to a New Land.* Illus. by the author. Harper, 1981. A crop failure in Sweden leads Carl Erik's family to emigrate to America. Young readers.

Speare, Elizabeth George. *The Witch of Blackbird Pond.* Houghton, 1958. A girl visiting Puritan Connecticut in the late 1600's becomes involved in witchcraft trials. Newbery Medal winner. Intermediate readers. *The Sign of the Beaver.* Houghton, 1983. A strong novel about interracial friendship in the colonial period. Older readers.

Stevenson, Robert Louis. *Kidnapped.* Illus. by C. B. Falls. World, 1947. A famous novel about a boy who becomes involved in a Scottish rebellion against England in the 1740's. Older readers.

Sutcliff, Rosemary. *Warrior Scarlet.* Illus. by Charles Keeping. Walck, 1958. A crippled boy living in Britain during the Bronze Age must kill a wolf to prove his manhood. *Song for a Dark Queen.* Crowell, 1979. A colorful story of the warrior-queen Boadicea who fought Roman invaders in her native Britain. Older readers.

Talbot, Charlene. *The Sodbuster Venture.* Atheneum, 1982. Two young women cope with the problems facing Kansas settlers in 1870. Intermediate readers.

Taylor, Mildred. *Roll of Thunder, Hear My Cry.* Illus. by Jerry Pinkney. Dial, 1976. A story of a black family during the Great Depression. Newbery Medal winner. Intermediate readers.

Vander Els, Betty. *The Bombers' Moon.* Farrar, 1985. An exciting story set in China during the Japanese invasion of 1942. Intermediate readers.

Westall, Robert. *The Machine Gunners.* Greenwillow, 1976. A story of English life during World War II, describing how a group of children build a fort to house a German machine gun they have found. Older readers.

Wilder, Laura Ingalls. *Little House in the Big Woods.* Illus. by Garth Williams. Harper, 1953. Pioneer family life in Wisconsin during the 1870's. Intermediate readers.

Yep, Laurence. *Dragonwings.* Harper, 1975. A boy travels to San Francisco about 1900 to join his father in the city's Chinese community. Intermediate readers.

Fiction/Mystery and Detective Stories

Adler, David. *The Fourth Floor Twins and the Fish Snitch Mystery.* Illus. by Irene Trivas. Viking, 1985. A group of children try to find out about the mysterious errands of an elderly couple. Young readers.

Babbitt, Natalie. *Goody Hall.* Illus. by the author. Farrar, 1971. A mystery-adventure tale with some comic touches set in mysterious Goody Hall in England. Intermediate readers.

Bawden, Nina. *Devil by the Sea.* Lippincott, 1976. A girl cannot get anyone to believe that she knows the identity of a child murderer. Intermediate readers.

Benchley, Nathaniel. *The Strange Disappearance of Arthur Cluck.* Illus. by Arnold Lobel. Harper, 1967. A wise old barn owl helps a worried hen search for her missing son. Young readers.

Bonham, Frank. *Mystery of the Fat Cat.* Illus. by Alvin Smith. Dutton, 1968. A mystery centering around a large inheritance, with a group of Puerto Rican and black youths as detectives. Intermediate readers.

Curry, Jane. *The Bassumtyte Treasure.* Atheneum, 1978. A long-lost treasure is discovered in time to save an old woman's estate. Intermediate readers.

Dickinson, Peter. *The Seventh Raven.* Dutton, 1981. A group of children join forces to prevent a kidnapping by terrorists. Older readers.

Hamilton, Virginia. *The House of Dies Drear.* Illus. by Eros Keith. Macmillan, 1968. A black boy helps uncover a treasure hidden in an old house by an abolitionist in the 1800's. Intermediate readers.

Hurd, Thacher. *Mystery on the Docks.* Illus. by the author. Harper, 1983. A restaurant worker comes to the rescue after his favorite opera star is kidnapped. Young readers.

Levy, Elizabeth. *Something Queer Is Going On.* Illus. by Mordecai Gerstein. Delacorte, 1973. Jill's mother helps Jill and Gwen search for a missing pet. *Something Queer on Vacation: A Mystery.* Illus. by Mordecai Gerstein. Delacorte, 1980. The girls solve a mystery at the beach. Both books for young readers.

Lewis, Thomas. *Mr. Sniff and the Motel Mystery.* Illus. by Beth Lee Weiner. Harper, 1984. A dog detective deals with baffling clues. Young readers.

Newman, Robert. *The Case of the Frightened Friend.* Atheneum, 1984. A well-plotted suspense story set in London during the 1800's. Older readers.

Prince, Alison. *Night Landings.* Illus. by Ellen Thompson. Morrow, 1983. Two children become involved in a mysterious smuggling operation. Intermediate readers.

Raskin, Ellen. *The Westing Game.* Dutton, 1978. A wealthy man leaves intricate clues for his potential heirs. Newbery Medal winner. Intermediate readers.

Singer, Marilyn. *A Clue in Code.* Illus. by Judy Glasser. Harper, 1985. Twin boys are the detectives in this lively story. Intermediate readers.

Sobol, Donald. *Encyclopedia Brown Saves the Day.* Illus. by Leonard Shortall. Nelson, 1970. A boy detective solves a number of mysteries. One of a long series. Intermediate readers.

Townsend, John Rowe. *Trouble in the Jungle.* Illus. by W. T. Mars. Lippincott, 1969. Children living in a slum in northern England uncover criminal activities. Intermediate readers.

Wells, Rosemary. *The Man in the Woods.* Dial, 1984. Nobody believes Helen is in danger even though she has witnessed a crime, so she turns detective. Older readers.

Winterfeld, Henry. *Mystery of the Roman Ransom.* Trans. from the German by Edith McCormick. Illus. by Fritz Biermann. Harcourt, 1971. A comic mystery story set in ancient Rome with a group of boys, their teacher, and a slave as detectives. Intermediate readers.

Fiction/Science Fiction

Christopher, John. *The White Mountains.* Macmillan, 1967. *The City of Gold and Lead.* Macmillan, 1967. *The Pool of Fire.* Macmillan, 1968. Three novels about three boys fighting against machinelike creatures who rule the world. All books for intermediate readers.

Dickinson, Peter. *The Weathermonger.* Little, Brown, 1969. *Heartsease.* Little, Brown, 1969. *The Devil's Children.* Little, Brown, 1970. Three stories set in an England of the future where rulers have banned all machines and technology. All books for older readers.

Hamilton, Virginia. *Justice and Her Brothers.* Greenwillow, 1978. Eleven-year-old Justice becomes aware that she has psychic powers. Older readers.

Hoban, Lillian and **Phoebe.** *The Laziest Robot in Zone One.* Illus. by Lillian Hoban. Harper, 1983. Robot children enjoy helping each other. Young readers.

Huddy, Delia. *The Humboldt Effect.* Greenwillow, 1982. A time-travel tale explores the origins of a Biblical story. Older readers.

Lawrence, Louise. *Children of the Dust.* Harper, 1985. A suspenseful science fantasy set in England after an atomic bomb attack. Older readers.

Le Guin, Ursula. *A Wizard of Earthsea.* Parnassus, 1968. *The Tombs of Atuan.* Atheneum, 1971. *The Farthest Shore.* Atheneum, 1972. A series of stories about the struggle between good and evil in the imaginary land of Earthsea. All books for older readers.

L'Engle, Madeleine. *A Wrinkle in Time.* Illus. Farrar, 1962. Meg and her brother and friend are taken to another part of the universe by three friendly witches and find Meg's father being held prisoner. Newbery Medal winner. Older readers.

MacGregor, Ellen. *Miss Pickerell Goes to Mars.* Illus. by Paul Galdone. McGraw, 1951. A comic story about an old lady who travels to Mars on a spaceship. Intermediate readers.

McCaffrey, Anne. *Dragonsong.* Atheneum, 1976. *Dragonsinger.* Atheneum, 1977. *Dragondrums.* Atheneum, 1979. A musically gifted 15-year-old girl leads a band of fire lizards in these related stories. Older readers.

Ormondroyd, Edward. *Time at the Top.* Illus. by Peggie Bach. Parnassus, 1963. A girl rides an elevator and gets off in a strange time and place. The story is continued in *All in Good Time.* Illus. by Ruth Robbins. Parnassus, 1975. Both books for intermediate readers.

Park, Ruth. *Playing Beatie Bow.* Atheneum, 1982. An Australian child goes back in time to the city of Sydney in the 1800's. Intermediate readers.

Pinkwater, Daniel. *Fat Men from Space.* Illus. by the author. Dodd, 1977. A comic story about aliens who rob the earth of all its junk food. Intermediate readers.

Slobodkin, Louis. *Space Ship Under the Apple Tree.* Illus. by the author. Macmillan, 1952. A Boy Scout finds a spaceship and a Martian boy his own age in his grandmother's apple orchard. Intermediate readers.

Snyder, Zilpha. *Below the Root.* Atheneum, 1975. *And All Between.* Atheneum, 1976. Both illus. by Alton Raible. Two stories about a split society of tree dwellers and "cast-outs" who live below ground. The two groups are united by the friendship and psychic powers of two girls, one from each group. Intermediate readers.

Voigt, Cynthia. *Building Blocks.* Atheneum, 1984. A boy travels back in time to experience his father's Great Depression era upbringing. Intermediate readers.

Westall, Robert. *The Wind Eye.* Greenwillow, 1977. Three children discover an old boat that takes them back to the Middle Ages. Intermediate readers.

Biographies and Autobiographies

Aliki. *A Weed Is a Flower: The Life of George Washington Carver.* Illus. by the author. Prentice-Hall, 1965. The life of a black American who was born a slave and became a great scientist. Young readers.

Bulla, Clyde R. *Squanto, Friend of the Pilgrims.* Illus. by Peter Burchard. Crowell, 1954. The life of an Indian who helped the Pilgrims after they first landed in the New World. Intermediate readers.

Clayton, Ed. *Martin Luther King: The Peaceful Warrior.* Illus. by David Hodges. Prentice-Hall, 1964. The life of the most famous black American civil rights leader. Intermediate readers.

Daugherty, James. *Daniel Boone.* Illus. by the author. Viking, 1939. The life of the famous American frontiersman who opened trails for pioneers moving westward. Newbery Medal winner. Intermediate readers.

Daugherty, Sonia. *Ten Brave Women.* Illus. by James Daugherty. Lippincott, 1953. Stories about the bravery and wisdom of 10 notable American women—Anne Hutchinson, Abigail Adams, Dolley Madison, Narcissa Whitman, Julia Ward Howe, Susan B. Anthony, Dorothea Dix, Mary Lyon, Ida M. Tarbell, and Eleanor Roosevelt. Older readers.

Eaton, Jeanette. *Trumpeter's Tale: The Story of Young Louis Armstrong.* Illus. by Elton Fax. Morrow, 1955. The early life of the jazz musician, describing his rise from poverty in New Orleans to international fame. Older readers.

Erlanger, Ellen. *Jane Fonda: More Than a Movie Star.* Lerner, 1984. A frank book about the famous actress. Intermediate readers.

Faber, Doris. *Oh Lizzie! The Life of Elizabeth Cady Stanton.* Lothrop, 1972. A biography of an early leader in the women's suffrage movement. Older readers.

Felton, Harold W. *Jim Beckwourth: Negro Mountain Man.*

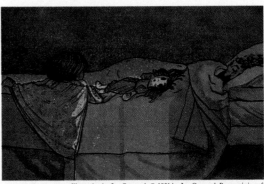

Illustration by Jan Ormerod. © 1981 by Jan Ormerod. By permission of Lothrop, Lee & Shepard Books (a division of William Morrow & Co.)

Sunshine is a story told entirely in pictures about the many morning activities of a little girl and her mother and father.

JEAN FRITZ

Where do you think you're going,
Christopher Columbus?

PICTURES BY MARGOT TOMES

Reprinted by permission of G. P. Putnam & Sons. *Where Do You Think You're Going, Christopher Columbus?* Text © 1980 by Jean Fritz. Illustration © 1980 by Margot Tomes

A Biography of Christopher Columbus describes the voyages he commanded that led to the discovery of the New World.

Illus. Dodd, 1966. The adventures of the black frontiersman who helped open many trails through the West. Intermediate readers.

Forbes, Esther, and **Ward, Lynd K.** *America's Paul Revere.* Illus. by Ward. Houghton, 1946. The life of the famous patriot set against a background of political unrest at the time of the American Revolution. Older readers.

Foster, Genevieve. *George Washington.* Illus. Scribner, 1949. The life and times of the first U.S. President. Intermediate readers.

Frank, Anne. *The Diary of a Young Girl.* Trans. from the Dutch by B. M. Mooyaart. Doubleday, 1967. A Jewish girl's autobiographical account of the suffering and heroism during the Nazi occupation of the Netherlands in World War II. Older readers.

Fritz, Jean. *Will You Sign Here, John Hancock?* Illus. by Trina Schart Hyman. Putnam, 1976. *Where Do You Think You're Going, Christopher Columbus?* Illus. by Margot Tomes. Putnam, 1980. Two well-researched books by a leading biographer for children. *Homesick: My Own Story.* Illus. by Margot Tomes. Putnam, 1982; and its sequel, *China Homecoming.* Putnam, 1985. Both books are autobiographical. All books for intermediate readers.

Goodsell, Jane. *Daniel Inouye.* Illus. by Haru Wells. Crowell, 1977. A good account of the life of the Hawaiian political leader. Intermediate readers.

Greenfield, Eloise. *Rosa Parks.* Illus. by Eric Marlow. Crowell, 1973. The story of the woman whose arrest started a civil rights bus strike in Montgomery, Ala., in 1955. Young readers.

Gunther, John. *Alexander the Great.* Illus. by Isa Barnett. Random House, 1953. The story of the greatest conqueror of ancient times. Intermediate readers.

Hamilton, Virginia. *Paul Robeson: The Life and Times of a Free Black Man.* Harper, 1974. A sympathetic biography of the actor and singer that also gives a picture of the social and political attitudes of his time. Older readers.

Haskins, James. *Pelé: A Biography.* Doubleday, 1976. An account of the life of the great Brazilian soccer player. *The Story of Stevie Wonder.* Lothrop, 1976. An objective and thoughtful biography of the blind musician and composer. *Lena Horne.* Coward, 1983. A biography of the entertainer that is both frank and sympathetic. All books for older readers.

Haskins, James, and **Benson, Kathleen.** *Space Challenger: The Story of Guion Bluford.* Carolrhoda, 1984. The informative and exciting story of the first black astronaut. Intermediate readers.

Highwater, Jamake. *Eyes of Darkness.* Lothrop, 1985. Touching and powerful biography of a Plains Indian who became a doctor illustrates the cultural conflict felt by many American Indians. Older readers.

Johnson, E. Harper. *Piankhy the Great.* Illus. by the author. Nelson, 1962. The life of a great African king who lived 2,500 years ago. Intermediate readers.

Judson, Clara Ingram. *City Neighbor: The Story of Jane Addams.* Illus. by Ralph Ray. Scribner, 1951. The life of the founder of Hull House, an organization in Chicago created to aid immigrants settling in the city. Intermediate readers.

Kamen, Gloria. *Fiorello: His Honor, the Little Flower.* Illus. by the author. Atheneum, 1981. A biography of Fiorello La Guardia, mayor of New York City from 1934 to 1945, written in a light style. Intermediate readers.

Kelly, Regina Z. *John F. Kennedy.* Illus. with photos. Follett, 1969. The life of the 35th U.S. President. Intermediate readers.

Knudson, Rozanne. *Babe Didrikson: Athlete of the Century.* Illus. by Ted Lewin. Viking, 1985. The even tone of the writing makes the subject's athletic skills seem even more dramatic. Intermediate readers.

Leighton, Margaret. *Cleopatra: Sister of the Moon.* Farrar, 1969. The life of the famous Egyptian queen and her encounters with the Roman leaders Julius Caesar and Mark Antony. Older readers.

McGovern, Ann. *The Secret Soldier: The Story of Deborah Sampson.* Illus. by Ann Grifalconi. Four Winds, 1975. A fictionalized biography of a woman who masqueraded as a man so that she could fight in the Revolutionary War. Intermediate readers.

Merriam, Eve. *The Story of Ben Franklin.* Illus. by Brinton Turkle. Four Winds, 1965. A simple introduction to the famous American's achievements. Young readers.

Miers, Earl Schenck. *Abraham Lincoln in Peace and War.* American Heritage, 1964. This story of the 16th President of the United States is told through paintings, photographs, and newspaper articles of his time. Intermediate readers.

Monjo, Ferdinand. *Letters to Horseface.* Illus. by Don and Elaine Bolognese. Viking, 1975. A vigorous, amusing account of the composer Mozart's travels in Italy as a boy. *Me and Willie and Pa.* Illus. by Douglas Gorsline. Simon and Schuster, 1973. The story of Abraham Lincoln's years in the White House as seen by his son Tad. Both books for intermediate readers.

Peare, Catherine Owens. *The Helen Keller Story.* Crowell, 1959. The story of a deaf and blind American girl who learned to communicate with others through the patient efforts of her teacher. Older readers.

Petry, Ann. *Harriet Tubman: Conductor on the Underground Railway.* Crowell, 1955. The story of a former slave who helped hundreds of slaves escape to freedom during the mid-1800's in America. Older readers.

Provensen, Alice and **Martin.** *Leonardo da Vinci: The Artist, Inventor, Scientist, in Three-Dimensional Movable Pictures.* Illus. by the authors. Viking, 1984. Crisp, balanced biography of the Renaissance genius. Intermediate readers.

Rosen, Sidney. *Galileo and the Magic Numbers.* Illus. by Harve Stein. Little, Brown, 1958. The life of the great Italian scientist and his struggles to gain acceptance for his methods and theories. Older readers.

Rudeen, Kenneth. *Wilt Chamberlain.* Illus. by Frank Mullins. Crowell, 1970. The life story of the greatest scorer in professional basketball history. Intermediate readers.

Shippen, Katherine B. *Mr. Bell Invents the Telephone.* Illus. by Richard Floethe. Random House, 1952. The life of Alexander Graham Bell and the difficulty he had gaining recognition for the telephone. Intermediate readers.

Tobias, Tobi. *Maria Tallchief.* Illus. by Michael Hampshire. Crowell, 1970. The daughter of an Osage Indian becomes a famous ballerina. Young readers.

Information Books/Science and Technology

Adler, Irving and **Ruth.** *Sets and Numbers for the Very Young.* Illus. by Peggy Adler. Day, 1969. Simple examples of cardinal and ordinal numbers, sets, and counting. Young readers.

Aliki. *Digging Up Dinosaurs.* Illus. by the author. Harper, 1980. An introduction to the excavation and study of fossilized dinosaur bones. Young readers.

Andrews, Roy Chapman. *In the Days of the Dinosaurs.* Illus. by Jean Zallinger. Random House, 1959. An introduction to the prehistoric world of dinosaurs written by a famous explorer. Young readers.

Asimov, Isaac. *Mars, the Red Planet.* Illus. by Giulio Maestro. Lothrop, 1977. A logically organized and clearly written study of Mars. Older Readers.

Bendick, Jeanne. *All Around You: A First Look at the World.* Illus. by the author. McGraw, 1960. A picture book that answers basic questions about nature. Young readers. *Electronics for Young People.* Illus. by the author. McGraw, 1960. A survey of electronics, including a discussion of automation, computers, nuclear energy, and radio telescopes. Intermediate readers.

Billings, Charlene. *Microchip: Small Wonder.* Dodd, 1984. Includes a good explanation of the binary system. Intermediate readers.

Branley, Franklyn. *Is There Life in Outer Space?* Illus. by Don Madden. Crowell, 1984. A simple, brief, and clear book by an astronomer. Young readers.

Cole, Joanna. *Large As Life Daytime Animals.* Illus. by Kenneth Lilly. Knopf, 1985. Carefully detailed, life-sized paintings accompany an informative text. Intermediate readers.

Dowden, Anne. *The Blossom on the Bough: A Book of Trees.* Illus. by the author. Crowell, 1975. Beautiful and accurate pictures illustrate a discussion of American trees that bear blossoms. Older readers.

Earle, Olive L. *Paws, Hoofs, and Flippers.* Illus. by the author. Morrow, 1954. A discussion of mammals with claws, hoofs, flippers, or nails. Intermediate readers.

Flanagan, Geraldine Lux. *Window into an Egg: Seeing Life Begin.* Illus. Young Scott, 1969. A description in text and photos of the development of a chicken in an egg from fertilization to hatching. Older readers.

George, Jean Craighead. *Spring Comes to the Ocean.* Illus. by John Wilson. Crowell, 1965. How plant and animal life in the sea responds to the increasing sunlight and warmth that comes with spring. Intermediate readers. *All Upon a Stone.* Illus. by Don Bolognese. Crowell, 1971. A description of the tiny creatures that have a rock for their home. Young readers.

Goudey, Alice E. *Here Come the Dolphins!* Illus. by Garry MacKenzie. Scribner, 1961. The story of a baby dolphin and a discussion of what science knows about the intelligence of dolphins. Young readers.

James, Elizabeth, and **Barkin, Carol.** *The Simple Facts of Simple Machines.* Photographs by Daniel Dorn, Jr. Lothrop, 1975. Diagrams and photographs help explain the balance between force and distance in six basic machines. Intermediate readers.

Johnson, Eric and **Corrine.** *Love and Sex and Growing Up.* Illus. Lippincott, 1970. A frank discussion of sexual functions and sexual behavior. Older readers.

Linn, Charles. *Probability.* Illus. by Wendy Watson. Crowell, 1972. One in a series of books for beginning mathematics students, this book describes the basic principles of probability. Young readers.

McKie, Robin. *Nuclear Power.* Gloucester Press, 1985. A clear discussion of the processes and the problems of nuclear energy. Intermediate readers.

Michel, Anna. *The Story of Nim: The Chimp Who Learned Language.* Knopf, 1980. A description of an experiment in which a baby chimp learned sign language. Intermediate readers.

Navarra, John Gabriel. *The World You Inherit: A Story of Pollution.* Illus. Natural History, 1970. The dangers of various forms of pollution and how pollution can be controlled. Both books for older readers.

Nilsson, Lennart. *How Was I Born? A Photographic Story of Reproduction and Birth for Children.* Delacorte/Seymour Lawrence, 1975. An explanation of reproduction that also stresses parental love. Intermediate readers.

Oxford Scientific Films. *Dragonflies.* Putnam, 1980. Fascinating photographs highlight this study of the beautiful water insect. All ages.

Patent, Dorothy. *Bacteria: How They Affect Other Living Things.* Holiday, 1980. A comprehensive and authoritative explanation. Older readers.

Provensen, Alice and **Martin.** *The Glorious Flight Across the Channel with Louis Blériot.* Illus. by the authors. Viking, 1983. Description of a landmark event in flight history. Caldecott Medal winner. Young and intermediate readers.

Schwartz, David. *How Much Is a Million?* Illus. by Steven Kellogg. Lothrop, 1985. An excellent book to help children understand the concept of large numbers. Young readers.

Scott, Jack. *Island of Wild Horses.* Putnam, 1978. Action photographs and simple text describe the small wild horses of Assateague Island off the coast of Maryland and Virginia. Intermediate readers.

Selsam, Millicent E. *Popcorn.* Photographs by Jerome Wexler. Morrow, 1976. A brief history of popcorn and a discussion of how and why the kernels "pop." Intermediate readers.

Showers, Paul. *A Drop of Blood.* Illus. by Don Madden. Crowell, 1967. What blood is, how it works in the body,

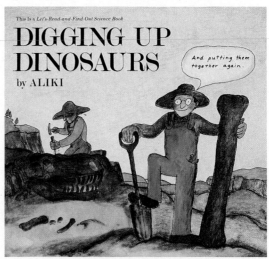

Jacket for *Digging Up Dinosaurs* by Aliki. © 1981 by Aliki Brandenberg. Reprinted by permission of Thomas Y. Crowell Co.

A Science Book describes various types of dinosaurs and how scientists dig up, preserve, and study fossilized dinosaur bones.

The History of Aviation is surveyed in *Flight: A Panorama of Aviation.* The book covers the history of flying from early theories to the present time.

Illustration © 1981 by Robert A. Parker from *Flight: A Panorama of Aviation* by Melvin B. Zisfein. Reprinted by permission of Pantheon Books, a division of Random House Inc.

how bleeding stops, and why the body never runs out of blood. Young readers.

Simon, Seymour. *How to Talk to Your Computer.* Illus. by Barbara and Ed Emberley. Crowell, 1985. A good introduction to the simplest kind of computer programming. Young readers.

Stolz, Mary. *Night of Ghosts and Hermits: Nocturnal Life on the Seashore.* Illus. by Susan Gallagher. Harcourt, 1985. Accurate information is provided within a fictional framework. Young readers.

Watson, Clyde. *Binary Numbers.* Illus. by Wendy Watson. Crowell, 1977. An excellent introduction to the binary system in mathematics. Young readers.

Weiss, Harvey. *Motors and Engines and How They Work.* Illus. Crowell, 1969. A discussion of many types of motors and engines and the mechanical principles by which each operates. The author covers water wheels, windmills, steam engines, solar engines, and rocket engines. He includes instructions on how to build model motors and engines. Older readers.

Zim, Herbert. *Quartz.* Morrow, 1981. An accurate and detailed description of the structure, special properties, and many uses of this mineral. Intermediate readers.

Reprinted by permission of G. P. Putnam & Sons. *Dragonflies* by Oxford Scientific Films. Text © 1980 by G. Whizzard Publications Ltd. Illustration © 1980 by Oxford Scientific Films

Dragonflies uses detailed photographs to describe the physical characteristics and habits of this beautiful water insect.

Zisfein, Melvin. *Flight: A Panorama of Aviation.* Illus. by Robert Andrew Parker. Pantheon, 1981. A comprehensive and heavily illustrated history of aviation from early theories to the present. Intermediate readers.

Information Books/Geography

Berger, Melvin. *Jigsaw Continents.* Illus. by Bob Totten. Coward, 1978. A good introduction to the theory of continental drift. Intermediate readers.

Bernheim, Marc and **Evelyne.** *In Africa.* Atheneum, 1973. An introduction to the geographic contrasts of this vast continent and a discussion of the various ways in which the peoples adapt to the region in which they live. Young readers.

Catchpole, Clive. *Mountains.* Illus. by Brian McIntyre. Dial, 1984. A comprehensive introduction to topography. Young readers.

Gans, Roma. *Caves.* Illus. by Giulio Maestro. Crowell, 1977. A description of the different kinds of caves and how they are formed. Young readers.

Gidal, Sonia. *My Village in Hungary.* Photos by the author. Pantheon, 1974. A Hungarian boy describes the physical features and economy of his country through an account of his own life. One of a series on life in villages throughout the world. Intermediate readers.

Goldner, Kathryn, and **Vogel, Carole.** *Why Mount St. Helens Blew Its Top.* Dillon, 1981. A dramatic account of the eruption of this volcano and its consequences. Intermediate readers.

Hine, Al, and **Alcorn, John.** *Where in the World Do You Live?* Illus. by Alcorn. Harcourt, 1962. An introduction to geography told in terms of the relationship between a child and the world around him. Young readers.

Hirsch, S. Carl. *The Globe for the Space Age.* Illus. by Burt Silverman. Viking, 1963. The history and significance of globes and maps from the early days of land and sea exploration to the modern space age. Intermediate readers.

Lauber, Patricia. *Tapping Earth's Heat.* Illus. by Edward Malsberg. Garrard, 1978. An introduction to the present and possible uses of the earth's internal heat. Intermediate readers.

Lye, Keith. *Take a Trip to Mexico.* Watts, 1982. A simple first book on the geography and the people of Mexico. Young readers.

Munro, Roxie. *The Inside-Outside Book of New York City.* Illus. by the author. Dodd, 1985. Paired pictures explore alternate views of various sites. Young readers.

Navarra, John. *Earthquake.* Chicago Museum of Science and Industry/Doubleday, 1980. A description of the causes, effects, and measuring of earthquakes. Intermediate readers.

Nixon, Hershell and **Joan.** *Glaciers: Nature's Frozen Rivers.*

Dodd, 1980. A discussion of the causes and effects of glaciers. Intermediate readers.

Peacock, Howard. *The Big Thicket of Texas: America's Ecological Wonder.* Little, 1984. A description of a national preserve that incorporates eight major ecosystems. Older readers.

Pringle, Laurence. *Estuaries: Where Rivers Meet the Sea.* Macmillan, 1973. A description of the ecology of an estuary and a discussion of its importance in the life chain. Intermediate readers.

Rollin, Sue. *The Illustrated Atlas of Archaeology.* Maps by Malcolm Porter. Watts, 1982. This useful reference source has material organized by large regions. Older readers.

Sasek, Miroslav. *This Is Ireland.* Macmillan, 1969. *This Is Washington, D.C.* Macmillan, 1973. Both illus. by the author. Two books in a series describing the buildings, monuments, and people of cities and countries throughout the world. All books for all ages.

Information Books/History

Asimov, Isaac. *The Birth of the United States: 1763-1816.* Houghton, 1974. *Our Federal Union: The United States from 1816 to 1865.* Houghton, 1975. Two detailed surveys of American history. Older readers.

Blumberg, Rhoda. *Commodore Perry in the Land of the Shogun.* Lothrop, 1985. Detailed, vigorous, and well-documented account of the missions of 1853 and 1854 that began trade relations between Japan and the United States. Older readers.

Boorstin, Daniel. *The Landmark History of the American People. From Plymouth to Appomattox.* Illus. Random House, 1968. *From Appomattox to the Moon.* Illus. Random House, 1970. American history from the landing of the first colonists in New England to the astronaut landings on the moon. Both for intermediate readers.

Brooks, Polly, and **Walworth, Nancy.** *When the World Was Rome.* Lippincott, 1972. A history of Rome from 753 B.C. to A.D. 476. Older readers.

Commager, Henry Steele. *The Great Declaration: A Book for Young Americans.* Illus. by Donald Bolognese. Bobbs, 1958. The story of how the Declaration of Independence was written and adopted. Older readers.

De Pauw, Linda. *Founding Mothers: Women of America in the Revolutionary Era.* Illus. by Michael McCurdy. Houghton, 1975. An examination of the roles played by women during the U.S. colonial period. Older readers.

Fisher, Leonard Everett. *The Hospitals.* Watts, 1980. *The Newspapers.* Holiday, 1981. Both illus. by the author. Both books provide historical background about their subjects. Intermediate readers.

Hoople, Cheryl, comp. *As I Saw It: Women Who Lived the American Adventure.* Dial, 1978. Letters and diaries give a vivid picture of the participation of women in U.S. history. Older readers.

Johnson, Gerald W. *America Is Born: A History for Peter.* Morrow, 1959. American history from the voyages of Columbus to the Constitutional Convention of 1787. *America Grows Up: A History for Peter.* Morrow, 1960. American history from the writing of the Constitution to World War I. *America Moves Forward: A History for Peter.* Morrow, 1960. American history from the end of World War I to the 1950's. All books illus. by Leonard Everett Fisher. All books for intermediate readers.

Lasker, Joe. *Merry Ever After.* Illus. by the author. Viking, 1976. Information about medieval life presented through a description of two arranged marriages, one of a wealthy couple and the other of two peasant children. Intermediate readers.

Lawson, Don. *The War in Vietnam.* Watts, 1981. An excellent summary of the conflict, but not coverage in depth. *The Eagle and the Dragon: The History of U.S.-China Relations.* Crowell, 1985. Carefully researched, objectively written, and comprehensive in coverage. Both books for older readers.

Lester, Julius. *To Be a Slave.* Illus. by Tom Feelings. Dial, 1968. A history of slavery in America from colonial times to the end of the Civil War, told in the actual words of the slaves themselves. Older readers.

McNeer, May. *The Canadian Story.* Illus. by Lynd K. Ward. Ariel, 1958. A broad survey of Canadian history from the early explorations by the Vikings to the building of the St. Lawrence Seaway. Older readers.

Meltzer, Milton. *In Their Own Words: A History of the American Negro, 1916-1966.* Crowell, 1967. One of a series of history books based on primary sources, such as letters, articles, and diaries. Older readers.

Morgan, Edmund S. *So What About History?* Illus. Atheneum, 1969. An explanation of why students should study history and what can be learned from the past. Intermediate readers.

Spier, Peter. *The Legend of New Amsterdam.* Illus. by the author. Doubleday, 1979. Detailed paintings complement the descriptive text about the early history of New York City. Young readers.

Sterling, Dorothy, ed. *The Trouble They Seen: Black People Tell the Story of Reconstruction.* Doubleday, 1976. The use of original materials gives this varied text vigor and immediacy. Older readers.

Information Books/Government and Politics

Blassingame, Wyatt. *The Look-It-Up Book of Presidents.* Random House, 1984. A useful and objective reference book. Intermediate readers.

Gray, Lee Learner. *How We Choose a President: The Election Year.* St. Martin's, 1976. A discussion of U.S. presidential elections, including the electoral college, campaign expenses, and the impact of television. Older readers.

Haines, Gail. *The Great Nuclear Power Debate.* Dodd Mead, 1985. An objective discussion of the issues. Older readers.

Johnson, Gerald W. *The Presidency.* Morrow, 1962. *The Supreme Court.* Morrow, 1962. *The Congress.* Morrow, 1963. *The Cabinet.* Morrow, 1966. All illus. by Leonard Everett Fisher. Descriptions of the history and functions of the major organs of U.S. government. All books for intermediate readers.

Liston, Robert. *The United States and the Soviet Union.* Parents, 1973. An objective assessment of the governments of these two nations, and their relations with each other. Older readers.

Pringle, Lawrence. *The Economic Growth Debate: Are There Limits to Growth?* Watts, 1978. A serious discussion of conflicts among various economic goals. Older readers.

Shapp, Martha and **Charles.** *Let's Find Out About the United Nations.* Illus. by Angela Conner. Watts, 1962. How the United Nations operates and how the organization tries to maintain world peace and to help people lead better lives. Young readers.

Switzer, Ellen. *How Democracy Failed.* Atheneum, 1975. An American citizen returns to Germany, a country she left as a teen-ager, and examines the Hitler regime and its aftermath. Older readers.

Walton, Richard J. *America and the Cold War.* Seabury, 1969. An analysis of the international tensions that developed between Russia and the United States after World War II. Older readers.

Information Books/Religion

Deedy, John. *The Vatican.* Illus. Watts, 1970. The history of the Vatican, an outline of how it governs the Roman Catholic Church, and a discussion of the role of the pope in the church. Intermediate readers.

Elgin, Kathleen. *The Quakers.* McKay, 1968. *Mormons: The Church of Jesus Christ of Latter-day Saints.* McKay, 1969. *The Episcopalians.* McKay, 1970. *The Unitarians.* McKay, 1971. All illus. by the author. Each book describes the beliefs, practices, customs, and history of a Christian church or group. Intermediate readers.

Fisher, Leonard Everett, ad. *The Seven Days of Creation.* Illus. by the adapter. Holiday, 1981. Striking paintings complement a simplified adaptation of the book of Genesis. All ages.

Greenfield, Howard. *Rosh Hashanah and Yom Kippur.* Holt,

Illustration by Barbara Cooney from *Ox-Cart Man* by Donald Hall; illustrations © 1979 by Barbara Cooney Porter. Reprinted by permission of Viking Penguin Inc.

Ox-Cart Man is a historical account of life in New England in the 1800's. The book describes the life of a farmer as he takes his produce to market by ox cart and returns to his farm.

1979. Explains beliefs, rituals, and symbols associated with the two holiest days in Judaism. Intermediate readers.

Haskins, James. *Religions*. Lippincott, 1973. A survey of Buddhism, Christianity, Hinduism, Islam, and Judaism. Older readers.

Lerner, Carol. *A Biblical Garden*. Illus. by the author. Morrow, 1982. Handsomely illustrated descriptions of plants mentioned in the Bible. Intermediate readers.

Meyer, Carolyn. *Amish People: Plain Living in a Complex World*. Atheneum, 1976. A fictional family is used to illustrate roles and relationships in an Amish family and community. Older readers.

Moskin, Marietta. *In the Name of God: Religion in Everyday Life*. Atheneum, 1980. A history of religious influences in the past and in today's world. Older readers.

Powell, Anton. *The Rise of Islam*. Warwick, 1980. A detailed account of Islamic culture to the 1500's. Intermediate readers.

Savage, Katharine. *The Story of World Religions*. Illus. Walck, 1966. The history of religion from the earliest religions through the creation of the major world faiths. Each religion is placed in its historical and cultural setting, and the beliefs of each are discussed. Older readers.

Smith, Betsy. *Breakthrough: Women in Religion*. Walker, 1978. An examination of the experiences and philosophies of five women who became modern religious leaders. Intermediate readers.

Smith, Ruth, ed. *The Tree of Life*. Illus. by Boris Artzybasheff. Viking, 1942. Selections from the sacred literatures of many religions. Older readers.

Spier, Peter. *Noah's Ark*. Doubleday, 1977. The Biblical story told almost entirely in pictures. Caldecott Medal winner. Young readers.

Weiss, Ann. *God and Government: The Separation of Church and State*. Houghton, 1982. An impartial and clear examination of a complex issue. Older readers.

Information Books/Minority Groups

Baker, Betty. *Settlers and Strangers: Native Americans of the Desert Southwest and History As They Saw It*. Macmillan, 1977. A dramatic and objective history of the Indians of the Southwest. Intermediate readers.

Bales, Carol Ann. *Chinatown Sunday: The Story of Lillian Derr*. Reilly and Lee, 1973. The life of a Chinese-American family in a Chicago suburb, based on taped interviews and photographs. Intermediate readers.

Blumenthal, Shirley. *Coming to America: Immigrants from Eastern Europe*. Delacorte, 1981. A carefully researched and sympathetically written study. Older readers.

Eiseman, Alberta. *Mañana Is Now: The Spanish-Speaking in the United States*. Atheneum, 1973. A discussion of Americans from Cuba, Mexico, and Puerto Rico and the discrimination they experience. Older readers.

Faber, Doris. *The Perfect Life: The Shakers in America*. Farrar, 1974. An examination of the beliefs and history of the Shaker sect and the hostility its members encountered in the United States. Older readers.

Garver, Susan, and **McGuire, Paula.** *Coming to America: From Mexico, Cuba, and Puerto Rico*. Delacorte, 1981. Frank, thorough, and carefully documented. Older readers.

Holbrook, Sabra. *Canada's Kids*. Atheneum, 1983. Describes ethnic groups and their integration into Canadian life. Older readers.

Hughes, Langston, and **Meltzer, Milton.** *A Pictorial History of the Negro in America*. Illus. Crown, 1963. Short accounts of the events and people that have played an important part in the black struggle for equal rights from colonial days to the present. Older readers.

Martin, Patricia Miles. *Chicanos: Mexicans in the United States*. Illus. by Robert Frankenberg. Parents' Magazine Press, 1971. The story of Chicanos—why they came to the United States, their way of life, and the problems they face. Young readers.

Meltzer, Milton. *Never to Forget: The Jews of the Holocaust*. Harper, 1976. A vivid documentary study. Older readers.

Nabokov, Peter, ed. *Native American Testimony: An Anthology of Indian and White Relations*. Crowell, 1978. A collection of statements by Indians over a 400-year period. Older readers.

Pascoe, Elaine. *Racial Prejudice: Issues in American History.* Watts, 1985. An excellent overview of minority groups and the prejudice they faced in the United States. Older readers.

Singer, Julia. *We All Come from Puerto Rico, Too.* Illus. by the author. Atheneum, 1977. Commentaries by children provide a rich and varied picture of Puerto Rican life in the United States. Intermediate readers.

Information Books/The Arts

De Mille, Agnes. *The Book of the Dance.* Illus. by N. M. Bodecker. Golden Press, 1963. A history of the dance with emphasis on ballet, written by a leading dancer and choreographer. Older readers.

Downer, Marion. *Discovering Design.* Illus. Lothrop, 1947. All ages. *The Story of Design.* Illus. Lothrop, 1963. Older readers. Two books that explore the rhythms and patterns of design in nature and as created by great artists and craftworkers.

Glubok, Shirley. *The Art of Egypt Under the Pharaohs.* Macmillan, 1980. Art forms are related to the culture of ancient Egypt. Intermediate readers.

Hodges, C. Walter. *Shakespeare's Theatre.* Illus. by the author. Coward-McCann, 1964. A survey of drama and theater design in Shakespeare's day. The author re-creates a performance of *Julius Caesar* as it might have looked to Elizabethan audiences. Older readers.

Hughes, Langston. *The First Book of Jazz.* Photos by Cliff Roberts. Watts, 1955. An analysis of what jazz is, and a history of the music from its origins to the mid-1900's. Older readers.

Janson, Horst and **Dora.** *The Story of Painting for Young People.* Illus. Abrams, 1962. A history of painting from prehistoric times to modern art. Older readers.

Kitchen, Bert. *Animal Alphabet.* Illus. by the author. Dial, 1984. Highly textured paintings and unusual composition make this an art book as well as an alphabet book. Intermediate readers.

Krementz, Jill. *A Very Young Dancer.* Knopf, 1976. *A Very Young Gymnast.* Knopf, 1978. Excellent photographs by the author add impact to these personal accounts. Intermediate readers.

Lomax, John A., and **Alan.** *Folk Song, U.S.A.* Duell, 1947. A selection of 111 American folk songs and ballads, with the history of each. Intermediate readers.

Luttrell, Guy. *The Instruments of Music.* Nelson, 1977. A discussion of the human voice, orchestral instruments, American folk instruments, and electronic instruments. Older readers.

Macaulay, David. *Cathedral: The Story of Its Construction.* Houghton, 1973. *Pyramid.* Houghton, 1975. *Castle.* Houghton, 1977. All illus. by the author. Descriptions of the planning and building of a cathedral, pyramid, and castle. Intermediate and older readers.

Manchel, Frank. *An Album of Great Science Fiction Films.* Illus. Watts, 1982. In addition to describing motion pictures, the author relates styles in filmmaking to popular taste and technological progress. Older readers.

Myrus, Donald. *Ballads, Blues, and the Big Beat.* Illus. Macmillan, 1966. A survey of folk music, protest songs, rock, and country music in America during the mid-1900's. Older readers.

Paine, Roberta M. *Looking at Sculpture.* Illus. Lothrop, 1968. An introduction to the appreciation of sculpture, with explanations of the sculptor's materials and methods and analyses of masterpieces. Older readers.

Riordan, James. *Favorite Stories of the Ballet.* Illus. by Victor Ambrus. Rand McNally, 1984. Notes on sources add to the usefulness of this good introduction to ballet stories. Intermediate readers.

Shaw, Arnold. *The Rock Revolution.* Crowell-Collier, 1969. A survey of the history of rock music since the 1950's, with discussions of such major performers as the Beatles, Bob Dylan, and Elvis Presley. Older readers.

Spilka, Arnold. *Paint All Kinds of Pictures.* Illus. Walck, 1963. A picture book that shows children how to create paintings by imaginatively using a brush, paint, and paper. Young readers.

Streatfeild, Noel. *A Young Person's Guide to Ballet.* Illus. by Georgette Bordier. Warne, 1975. The author describes ballet training and provides some ballet history through the story of two children attending ballet school. Intermediate readers.

Ventura, Piero. *Great Painters.* Illus. by the author. Putnam, 1984. A lively introduction to art history. Older readers.

Information Books/Hobbies and Sports

Aaseng, Nathan. *Baseball: You Are the Manager.* Lerner, 1983. The reader decides strategy in managerial problems of 10 real major league teams. Intermediate readers.

Adkins, Jan. *The Craft of Sail.* Illus. by the author. Walker, 1973. A description of sailing vessels and the techniques of sailing. Older readers.

Ashe, Arthur, and **Robinson, Louie.** *Getting Started in Tennis.* Atheneum, 1977. Advice on equipment, serving, and strategy. Intermediate readers.

Bunting, Glenn and **Eve.** *Skateboards: How to Make Them, How to Ride Them.* Harvey, 1977. Clearly written advice on construction and riding. Intermediate readers.

Cobb, Vicki. *Gobs of Goo.* Illus. by Brian Schatell. Lippincott, 1983. Home experiments that are interesting, simple, and safe. Young readers.

D'Ignazio, Fred. *Electronic Games.* Watts, 1982. A discussion of how games work and how best to play them. Older readers.

Eskenazi, Gerald. *Hockey.* Illus. with photographs. Grosset, 1973. A history of the sport and a discussion of the players and rules. Older readers.

Fisher, Leonard Everett. *The Sports.* Illus. by the author. Holiday, 1980. A fascinating look at sports in the United States in the 1800's. Intermediate readers.

Haddad, Helen. *Potato Printing.* Illus. by the author. Crowell, 1981. The author describes how to use an ordinary potato to print pictures, messages, and designs on fabric or paper. Intermediate readers.

Hobson, Burton. *Coins You Can Collect.* Illus. Hawthorn, 1967. For beginners who want to start a basic and inexpensive coin collection. Intermediate readers.

Horvath, Joan. *Filmmaking for Beginners.* Illus. Nelson, 1974. A discussion of every important aspect of filmmaking, including equipment and scriptwriting. Older readers.

Jackson, C. Paul. *How to Play Better Soccer.* Illus. by Don Madden. Crowell, 1978. A history of the game as well as rules and techniques. Intermediate readers.

Krementz, Jill. *The Fun of Cooking.* Photographs by the author. Knopf, 1985. Children give their favorite recipes in a handsome, useful cookbook. Intermediate and older readers.

Lasson, Robert. *If I Had a Hammer: Woodworking with Seven Basic Tools.* Illus. Dutton, 1974. General advice on woodworking as well as instructions for several projects. Intermediate readers.

Lipson, Shelley. *It's Basic: The ABC's of Computer Programming.* Holt, 1982. A detailed text on using the BASIC language to program a computer. Intermediate readers.

Paul, Aileen. *Kids Outdoor Gardening.* Illus. by John Delulio. Doubleday, 1978. A logically organized book for the beginning gardener. Intermediate readers.

Rockwell, Anne and **Harlow.** *The Toolbox.* Illus. by Harlow Rockwell. Macmillan, 1971. A description of the function of basic tools. Young readers.

Schiffer, Don. *The First Book of Basketball.* Illus. by Julio Granada. Watts, 1959. Information on how to play the game, suggestions for improving skills, and a discussion of basketball rules. Intermediate readers.

Siebert, Dick, and **Vogel, Otto.** *Baseball.* Illus. Sterling, 1968. The history and rules of baseball, including Little League baseball. The authors also discuss how to play each position, how to hit, and how to run bases. Intermediate readers.

Sullivan, George. *Better Softball for Boys and Girls.* Illus. Dodd, 1975. Explanations of individual and team play and information about clothing and equipment. Intermediate readers.

Weiss, Harvey. *Model Cars and Trucks and How to Build Them.* Illus. Crowell, 1974. Advice on general techniques and on specific projects for the beginner. Intermediate readers.

Zarchy, Harry. *The Stamp Collector's Guide.* Illus. by the author. Knopf, 1956. Explanations of different kinds of stamps, how to use a stamp catalog, and a dictionary of terms. Intermediate readers.

Information Books/General Nonfiction

Adler, David. *Prices Go Up, Prices Go Down: The Laws of Supply and Demand.* Illus. by Tom Huffman. Watts, 1984. A clear, simple introduction to a basic economic principle. Young readers.

Campbell, Patricia. *Passing the Hat: Street Performers in America.* Delacorte, 1981. Fascinating material arranged by the type of performance. Older readers.

Charlip, Remy, and others. *Handtalk: An ABC of Finger Spelling and Sign Language.* Illus. Parents, 1974. A picture book that describes the two major means of communication used by deaf people. Intermediate readers.

Cobb, Vickie. *The Secret Life of School Supplies.* Illus. by Bill Morrison. Lippincott, 1981. Facts about familiar objects are linked to scientific principles. Intermediate readers.

Curtis, Patricia. *Cindy: A Hearing Ear Dog.* Dutton, 1981. A description of a new training program for dogs that help the hearing-impaired. Intermediate readers.

Girard, Linda. *My Body Is Private.* Illus. by Rodney Pate. Whitman, 1984. The author uses a calm tone and a direct approach in a book that deals simply with child abuse. Young readers.

Herzig, Alison, and **Mali, Jane.** *Oh, Boy! Babies!* Little, 1980. A photodocumentary includes lively comments by sixth grade boys participating in a project to learn how to take care of babies. Intermediate readers.

Hyde, Margaret. *The Rights of the Victim.* Watts, 1983. An objective and informative book about the American system of justice. Older readers.

Krementz, Jill. *How It Feels When Parents Divorce.* Photographs by the author. Knopf, 1984. Frank interviews with children give a range of reactions. Intermediate readers.

Kujoth, Jean. *The Boys' and Girls' Book of Clubs and Organizations.* Prentice-Hall, 1975. A reference work that describes activities sponsored by various groups. Intermediate readers.

LeShan, Eda. *Grandparents: A Special Kind of Love.* Illus. by Tricia Taggart. Macmillan, 1984. A counselor discusses the pleasures and problems in relationships between children and grandparents. Intermediate readers.

Powledge, Fred. *So You're Adopted.* Scribner, 1982. A frank discussion of the feelings of adopted persons with an explanation of their legal rights. Older readers.

Rockwell, Harlow. *I Did It.* Illus. by the author. Macmillan, 1974. An assortment of projects, from easy to difficult ones, including making a mask from a grocery bag and baking bread. Young readers.

Roy, Ron. *Move Over, Wheelchairs Coming Through!* Houghton/Clarion, 1985. Seven stories of young people who are confined to wheelchairs. Older readers.

Sarnoff, Jane, and **Ruffins, Reynold.** *The Code and Cipher Book.* Illus. Scribner, 1975. A collection of codes, ciphers, and slang, and instructions for writing or deciphering cryptic language. Intermediate readers.

Sullivan, George. *How Does It Get There?* Westminster, 1973. A discussion of transportation techniques and developments. Intermediate readers.

Wandro, Mark, and **Blank, Joani.** *My Daddy Is a Nurse.* Illus. by Irene Trivas. Addison, 1981. A discussion of jobs now performed by men that were traditionally done by women. Intermediate readers.

Books About Children's Literature

Althouse, Rosemary. *The Young Child: Learning with Understanding.* Teachers College Press, 1981. A discussion of the characteristics and abilities of children.

Bader, Barbara. *American Picturebooks from "Noah's Ark" to "The Beast Within."* Illus. Macmillan, 1976. A historical survey, with pictures from the books discussed.

Carlsen, G. Robert. *Books and the Teen-Age Reader.* Rev. ed. Harper, 1980. A discussion of various kinds of books suitable for teen-agers, an analysis of teen-age reading patterns, and suggestions on how parents can help teen-agers improve their reading skills.

Cianciolo, Patricia. *Picture Books for Children.* American Library Association, 1981. Title suggestions and criteria for evaluation.

Egoff, Sheila. *The Republic of Childhood.* Oxford, 1967. A critical guide to Canadian children's literature in English.

Hazard, Paul. *Books, Children and Men.* Trans. from the French by Marguerite Mitchell. 4th ed. Horn Book, 1966. Essays by a noted scholar about the place of children's literature in different cultures.

Hearne, Betsy. *Choosing Books for Children: A Commonsense Guide.* Delacorte, 1981. An authoritative and sensible survey of children's needs and selection criteria.

Klemin, Diana. *The Art of Art for Children's Books.* Potter, 1966. A modern survey, including examples, of the works of 63 artists who specialize in illustrating children's literature.

Larrick, Nancy. *A Parent's Guide to Children's Reading.* Doubleday, 1975. How to buy books for children, the relation between television and reading, how reading is taught in schools today, and how parents can encourage their children to read.

McCann, Donnarae, and **Richard, Olga.** *The Child's First Books.* Illus. Wilson, 1973. A critical evaluation of the artistic and literary aspects of picture books.

Meigs, Cornelia, and others. *A Critical History of Children's Literature.* Illus. by Vera Bock. Rev. ed. Macmillan, 1969. A basic reference work describing children's literature from its origins to 1967.

The Oxford Companion to Children's Literature. Ed. by Humphrey Carpenter and Mari Prichard. Oxford, 1984. A thorough survey of all aspects of children's literature.

Rollock, Barbara, comp. *The Black Experience in Children's Books.* New York Public Library, 1984. A carefully selected annual bibliography.

Smith, Irene. *A History of the Newbery and Caldecott Medals.* Viking, 1957. This book tells how the awards were established, and how the winners were selected, and discusses many of the authors and artists who have won the medals.

Sutherland, Zena, and **Arbuthnot, May Hill.** *Children and Books.* 7th ed. Scott, Foresman, 1986. A survey of the major kinds of children's literature, an examination of the contributions of leading authors and illustrators, and extensive bibliographies.

LITERATURE FOR CHILDREN/ *Study Aids*

Related Articles in WORLD BOOK include:

AMERICAN AUTHORS

Alcott, Louisa May	Blume, Judy
Alexander, Lloyd	Bontemps, Arna
Alger, Horatio	Brink, Carol
Arbuthnot, May Hill	Brooks, Gwendolyn
Baum, L. Frank	Burgess, Thornton
Beard, Daniel	Burnett, Frances H.
Bemelmans, Ludwig	Byars, Betsy

Clark, Ann Nolan	Lofting, Hugh
Cleary, Beverly	London, Jack
Coatsworth, Elizabeth	Longfellow, Henry
Cooper, James Fenimore	Wadsworth
Cooper, Susan	McCord, David
Daugherty, James	Meigs, Cornelia
De Angeli, Marguerite	Moore, Clement Clarke
De Jong, Meindert	Norton, Andre
Dodge, Mary Mapes	O'Brien, Robert C.
Du Bois, William	O'Dell, Scott
Pène	O'Hara, Mary
Enright, Elizabeth	Paterson, Katherine
Field, Eugene	Raskin, Ellen
Field, Rachel	Richards, Laura
Finger, Charles	Sawyer, Ruth
Forbes, Esther	Selsam, Millicent E.
Fox, Paula	Seredy, Kate
George, Jean	Seton, Ernest Thompson
Craighead	Seuss, Dr.
Hamilton, Virginia	Singer, Isaac Bashevis
Hawthorne, Nathaniel	Sperry, Armstrong
Heinlein, Robert A.	Stockton, Frank
Henry, Marguerite	Stratemeyer, Edward
Hinton, S. E.	Tarkington, Booth
Irving, Washington	Taylor, Mildred
Konigsburg, Elaine	Twain, Mark
Krumgold, Joseph	White, E. B.
Lawson, Robert	Whittier, John Greenleaf
Le Guin, Ursula	Wiggin, Kate
L'Engle, Madeleine	Wilder, Laura Ingalls
Lenski, Lois	Yates, Elizabeth
Lobel, Arnold	Zim, Herbert

AMERICAN ILLUSTRATORS

Bemelmans, Ludwig	Lenski, Lois
Brown, Marcia	Lobel, Arnold
Burton, Virginia	McCloskey, Robert
Cooney, Barbara	Pyle, Howard
D'Aulaire (family)	Sendak, Maurice
Dillon (family)	Seuss, Dr.
Duvoisin, Roger	Slobodkin, Louis
Ets, Marie Hall	Ward, Lynd K.
Hogrogian, Nonny	Weisgard, Leonard
Keats, Ezra Jack	Wiese, Kurt
Lathrop, Dorothy	Zemach, Margot
Lawson, Robert	

BRITISH AUTHORS AND ILLUSTRATORS

Ardizzone, Edward	Jacobs, Joseph
Barrie, Sir James	Kipling, Rudyard
Belloc, Hilaire	Knight, Eric
Brooke, L. Leslie	Lamb, Charles (Mary Ann)
Bunyan, John	Lang, Andrew
Caldecott, Randolph	Lear, Edward
Carroll, Lewis	Lewis, C. S.
Crane, Walter	Milne, A. A.
Cruikshank, George	Newbery, John
Defoe, Daniel	Potter, Beatrix
De la Mare, Walter	Rackham, Arthur
Dickens, Charles	Scott, Sir Walter
Fleming, Ian	Sewell, Anna
Lancaster	Shepard, Ernest
Goble, Paul	Stevenson, Robert Louis
Grahame, Kenneth	Swift, Jonathan
Greenaway, Kate	Tenniel, Sir John
Hughes, Thomas	Tolkien, J. R. R.

OTHER AUTHORS AND ILLUSTRATORS

Andersen, Hans Christian	Perrault, Charles
Collodi, Carlo	Spyri, Johanna
Colum, Padraic	Travers, Pamela
Comenius, John Amos	Verne, Jules
Grimm (brothers)	Wyss, Johann R.
La Fontaine, Jean de	

CHARACTERS AND WORKS

Aesop's Fables	Mother Goose
Arabian Nights	Peter Pan
Arthur, King	Pied Piper of Hamelin
Bunyan, Paul	Robin Hood
Grimm's Fairy Tales	Robinson Crusoe
Gulliver's Travels	

OTHER RELATED ARTICLES

Ballad	Fairy	Newbery Medal
Book	Folklore	Nursery Rhyme
Caldecott Medal	Hornbook	Reading
Encyclopedia	Library	Regina Medal
Epic	Melcher, Frederic	Storytelling
Fable	Mythology	

Outline

I. Kinds
  A. Poetry   D. Biography
  B. Folk Literature   E. Information Books
  C. Fiction
II. History
III. Careers
  A. Children's Editors   B. Librarians
IV. Selecting Children's Books
  A. Age and Grade Levels
  B. Book Reviews
  C. Booklists
V. Books to Read

Questions

What is a booklist?
Who were Randolph Caldecott and Walter Crane?
What are some duties of a children's librarian?
What are fantasy novels?
What is the importance of the textbook, *Visible World?*
What are information books?
What was a chapbook?
Why was the *St. Nicholas* magazine significant?
Who was John Newbery?
What is the Regina medal?

LITHARGE, *LIHTH ahrj,* also called *lead monoxide,* (chemical formula, PbO), is a poisonous yellow or reddish-yellow solid, a compound of lead and oxygen. It is made by heating lead or certain of its compounds in air. Litharge is used in making lead glass, pottery glazes, and rubber.   HARRIET V. TAYLOR

LITHIUM, *LIHTH ee uhm,* is a soft, silvery-white metallic element, the lightest known metal. It is only half as heavy as an equal volume of water. Lithium reacts with water, as does sodium, to release hydrogen gas. But, unlike sodium, the reaction usually does not ignite the hydrogen.

Lithium is used to make certain types of batteries. Lithium compounds are used in the manufacture of various materials, including ceramic products, enamels, glass, and lubricants for use at high temperatures. They also are used in rubber products and in dyes for textiles. One compound, lithium carbonate, is used as a drug to treat *manic depression,* a kind of mental illness (see MENTAL ILLNESS [Affective Disorders]).

Lithium metal does not occur in nature because it combines easily with other elements. Chemists obtain the metal by passing electricity through *fused* (melted) lithium chloride.

The chemical symbol for lithium is Li. Its atomic number is 3, and its atomic weight is 6.941. Lithium melts at 180.54° C and boils at 1347° C. It was discovered in 1817 by Johann August Arfvedson, a Swedish chemist.   DUWARD F. SHRIVER

See also ALKALI; ELEMENT, CHEMICAL.

The Art Institute of Chicago, Glore Collection (WORLD BOOK photo)

A Color Lithograph by Henri de Toulouse-Lautrec, a French artist, decorated an 1893 magazine cover. The printer operates a lithographic press while his customer examines a proof.

LITHOGRAPHY is a printing process that has an important part in the fine arts and in commercial printing. Many artists have created lithographs that rank among the masterpieces of printmaking. Commercially, lithography is a leading method of printing books, magazines, newspapers, and other publications.

This article describes lithography in the fine arts. For information on commercial lithography, see the article on PRINTING (Printing by Offset Lithography).

How Lithography Works. Lithography is based on the principle that water does not mix with grease. The artist draws the picture on a level porous surface with a grease pencil, a crayon, or a greasy liquid drawing material called *tusche*. The most common surfaces are limestone or a plate made of a material such as aluminum, paper, or zinc with a specially prepared surface. The grain of the stone or plate enables the artist to create lithographs with a broad range of tones and textures.

After drawing the picture, the artist treats both the drawn and undrawn areas of the surface with solutions of nitric acid and gum arabic. The gum arabic surrounds the grease drawing and chemically prevents ink from sticking to the undrawn areas. The acid allows the grease and gum arabic to be more easily absorbed into the pores of the stone or plate. After applying the solutions, the artist uses turpentine to remove drawing

materials remaining on the surface of the stone or plate.

The artist then dampens the surface with water. The undrawn areas absorb water, but the greasy drawn areas reject it. The artist applies an oil-base ink to the surface with a roller. The ink sticks to the greasy areas but not to the wet ones.

Next, the artist places a sheet of paper on the printing surface and runs the paper and the stone or plate through a printing press under heavy pressure. The pressure transfers the inked design onto the paper. To make additional impressions of the picture, the artist redampens and reinks the surface.

Color Lithography. To make a lithograph in more than one color, the artist must prepare a separate surface for each color. For example, the picture may show green grass and a red house. On one surface, the artist draws the grass, which is printed with green ink. The house is drawn on a second stone or plate and then printed in red ink. The artist puts the paper through the press twice, once for each color of the total design. The artist must draw the grass and house so they appear in exactly the correct *registration* (relationship to each other) in the lithograph. Images printed on limestone or on zinc plates produce colored pictures having an especially luminous quality.

History. Alois Senefelder, a German, invented lithography in 1798. European painters soon began exploring the artistic possibilities of the new medium. They particularly liked the spontaneous effects they could achieve in their pictures by drawing directly on the printing surface.

The first masters of lithography included the French artists Eugène Delacroix and Honoré Daumier. During the late 1800's, the French painters Pierre Bonnard, Henri de Toulouse-Lautrec, and Edouard Vuillard raised color lithography to new heights of expression and refinement. Leading lithographers of the 1900's have included Marc Chagall, Edvard Munch, Emil Nolde, and Pablo Picasso in Europe; and Jasper Johns and Joseph Pennell in the United States.

Today, artists achieve unusual effects by combining lithography with other printmaking processes, such as silk-screen printing. Many artists have created lithographs by adapting new processes of commercial printing.   ANDREW J. STASIK, JR.

See also BELLOWS, GEORGE W.; CURRIER AND IVES; DAUMIER, HONORÉ; SENEFELDER, ALOIS.

LITHOSPHERE. See TECTONICS.

WORLD BOOK photos, courtesy Illinois Institute of Technology

Making a Lithograph. The artist draws on a lithographic stone with a greasy crayon, *left*. The artist dampens the stone and applies ink that sticks to the drawing but not to the rest of the stone, *center*. Then a sheet of paper is pressed against the inked stone to make a print, *right*.

Vilnius, the capital and largest city of Lithuania, is also a major cultural center. Gorki Street, *above,* was named after the Russian writer Maxim Gorki. The statue on the left honors Vincas Mickievicius-Kapsukas, a famous Lithuanian revolutionary leader.

Vance Henry, Taurus

LITHUANIA, *LIH thoo AY nee uh,* is a European land on the eastern shore of the Baltic Sea. Lithuania was an independent nation from 1918 to 1940, when the Soviet Union occupied it. It now makes up the Lithuanian Soviet Socialist Republic, one of the 15 republics of the Soviet Union. But the United States and some other countries still consider Lithuania a separate nation.

Lithuania covers 25,170 square miles (65,200 square kilometers) and has a population of about 3,539,000. Its area is slightly larger than that of West Virginia, but it has about twice as many people as that state. Most of Lithuania's people live in the central and southern parts of the republic. Vilnius is the capital and largest city.

People. About 80 per cent of the people of Lithuania are Lithuanians, a nationality group that has its own customs and language. About 9 per cent of the population are Russians, and a somewhat smaller number are Poles. Byelorussians make up about 2 per cent of the population, and Ukrainians make up about 1 per cent. Less than 1 per cent of the people of Lithuania are Jews, whom the Soviet government considers a separate nationality group. Before World War II (1939-1945), about 8 per cent of the population were Jews, but the Nazis killed most of them during the war.

About 90 per cent of the Lithuanians are Roman Catholics. Most of the rest of the Lithuanians belong to the Lutheran Church or another Protestant denomination. Lithuania's culture developed under Roman Catholic influence, and Catholic traditions remain part of the people's lives. However, the Russians have made the practice of many of the old Lithuanian customs very difficult. For example, Soviet laws forbid religious instruction, religious publications, and charity work. The Soviet government also discourages church attendance. For example, a person who attends church may be kept from good educational and job opportunities.

Lithuania was a rural society until the Russian conquest. About three-fourths of its people lived in rural villages. The Soviet government ended the traditional Lithuanian style of life by industrializing the country. The Russians took away private land and combined small farms into large state-owned farms. They built many factories, and large numbers of people moved from rural areas into cities to work in these factories. Today, about two-thirds of the people live in urban areas.

Many Russians moved to Lithuania after the Soviet take-over. They make up only a small minority of the population, but they hold many important management and policymaking positions.

Lithuanians wear clothing similar to that worn in the United States and Canada. But they cherish their decorative national costumes and wear them on festive occasions.

For recreation, Lithuanians especially enjoy singing and sports, particularly basketball, boxing, and rowing. Choral singing is highly developed in Lithuania, and thousands of people sing and dance in annual festivals. These festivals have become a Lithuanian tradition since the 1920's, and they attract huge crowds of spectators from throughout the republic. Many ancient Lithuanian songs, called *dainos,* and folk tales have been handed down in spoken form for generations. Lithuania has 11 theaters where ballet, drama, and opera are performed, and it also has a motion-picture industry.

Soviet law requires Lithuanian children to attend school from the age of 7 to 17. Lithuania has 12 universities and colleges. The V. Kapsukas State University in Vilnius was established in 1579 and is the oldest in the Soviet Union.

The Lithuanian people speak Lithuanian, but the Soviets have tried to increase the use of Russian. All schools must teach Russian, and most television programs are in Russian.

346

Land and Climate. Most of Lithuania consists of flat or gently sloping land. The highest elevations are in the southeast. The land dips down to central lowlands and rises slightly in the west. White sand dunes along the seacoast provide a popular resort area. The dunes are especially attractive on a long strip of land that separates a lagoon from the Baltic Sea.

The republic has about 3,000 small lakes and hundreds of rivers. The lakes cover about $1\frac{1}{2}$ per cent of Lithuania. The longest and largest river is the Neman (called Nemunas in Lithuanian). It begins in Byelorussia, which lies to the southeast, and drains most of Lithuania during its course to the Baltic.

Lithuania has no large, important mineral deposits. Its natural resources include clays and sands, gypsum, limestone, peat, a mineral called *dolomite*, and a hard, yellowish-brown substance called *amber* (see AMBER). Forests cover about a fourth of Lithuania's land. Small quantities of oil have been discovered in western Lithuania.

In January, the coldest month in Lithuania, the temperature averages from about 27° F. (−3° C) on the seacoast to 21° F. (−6° C) in the east. In July, the hottest month, temperatures average 61° F. (16° C) near the sea and 64° F. (18° C) in the east. The average annual precipitation ranges from 21 inches (53 centimeters) to 34 inches (86 centimeters).

Economy. The Soviet government has built many factories in Lithuania since taking control of the region. In 1940, Lithuania had little industry. Today, about two-thirds of the economic product is industrial. The government owns all of Lithuania's factories. The productivity and average income of the Lithuanians rank third, after those of the Estonians and Latvians, among all workers in the Soviet republics.

Lithuanian industry emphasizes chemical production, construction, electronics, food processing, machinery manufacture, and metal working. The republic produces a large number of metal-cutting lathes and more than half the electric motors used in Soviet appliances. Towns in southern and eastern Lithuania have many appliance factories. Most of Lithuania's food processing and chemical industries are in towns in the north. Kaunas, Memel (also called Klaipĕda), and Vilnius are Lithuania's major industrial centers. Memel has large shipyards.

Lithuanian agriculture specializes in dairy and meat production. Agriculture accounts for about a fourth of the republic's economic output. The state owns and administers all the farmland.

History. People lived in the region that is now Lithuania about 8000 B.C. Groups that were the ancestors of the Lithuanian people lived there at the time of Christ.

In the A.D. 100's, the Roman historian Tacitus made the first historical mention of the people who lived near the Baltic Sea. He reported that they sold amber to the Romans. Near the end of the 1100's, the Lithuanian peoples united into a single nation. The first great ruler of Lithuania was Mindaugas, who became king in 1251. Mindaugas was assassinated by nobles in 1263.

During the 1200's, the people fought a group of German crusaders called the Teutonic Knights, who tried to conquer Lithuania (see TEUTONIC KNIGHTS). Lithu-

WORLD BOOK map

Lithuania

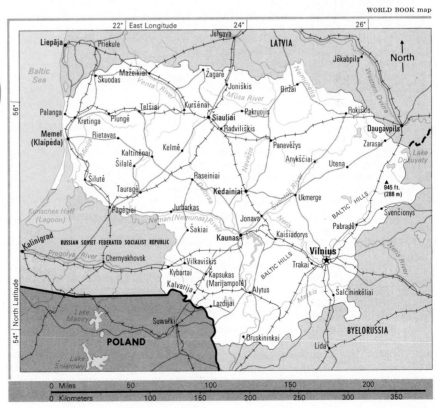

LITHUANIA

Novosti Press Agency

Traditional Folk Costumes brighten special Lithuanian celebrations, such as the ceremony shown above. But Lithuanians usually dress much as people in the United States and Canada do.

ania expanded its boundaries during the 1300's. In time, it extended nearly to Moscow in the east and to the Black Sea in the south.

In 1386, Grand Duke Jagiełło (Jogaila in Lithuanian) united Lithuania with Poland. At first, this union was a confederation of two separate states that were ruled mostly by the same king. The two were combined into a single state in 1569.

The Lithuanian-Polish government collapsed in the 1700's, and Lithuania came under the rule of the Russian czar in 1795. The people rebelled against Russian rule in 1831 and again in 1863 but failed to win independence. The czar tried to increase Russian influence in Lithuania. He prohibited books printed in Lithuanian and closed Lithuanian schools. But the people continued to educate their children and kept the national culture alive as well. Many Lithuanians emigrated to the United States during this period and also during later periods.

The movement for an independent Luthuania became organized in the 1880's. In 1905, a conference of elected representatives of Lithuania demanded self-government for their people within the Russian state. The Russians rejected this demand. During World War I (1914-1918), German troops occupied Lithuania. On Feb. 16, 1918, Lithuania became the first of the Baltic States to declare its independence from Russia and Germany (see BALTIC STATES). Lithuania established a democratic system of government in which the parliament had power over the president. A land-reform program broke up large estates and distributed land among the poor. The government also set up a school system, including colleges and a university.

Fighting continued in Lithuania after World War I ended. Russia attempted to take over the country. The Lithuanians defeated the Russians, and a peace treaty was signed in 1920. Poland occupied Vilnius in 1920, and held the city until 1939.

In 1926, a group of military officers and civilian politicians seized power in Lithuania. Antanas Sme-

tona became president. He gradually took over more and more of the authority that the president had shared with the parliament.

In March 1939, Germany seized part of Lithuania. A combination of Lithuanian political parties tried to restore democracy. But the parties failed to do so. Later in 1939, Germany and Russia reached agreements that gave Russia control of the Baltic region. The Russians then built some military bases in Lithuania.

In 1940, the Russians occupied all of Lithuania and made it a Soviet republic with a Communist government. After the Germans invaded Russia in 1941, the Lithuanians revolted against their Soviet rulers and established their own government. But the Germans conquered the country and occupied it until 1944, when the Russians again took over Lithuania.

From 1944 to 1952, Lithuanian guerrillas fought the Russians. Thousands of them were killed in the fighting. The Russians also sent about 350,000 Lithuanians to labor camps in Siberia for their political beliefs or as punishment for resisting Soviet rule.

The Soviet government has tried to eliminate the strong influence of the Roman Catholic Church in Lithuania. For example, the government does not allow enough men to become priests to replace those who die. However, the people have kept their religious beliefs.

In 1972, about 17,000 Lithuanians signed a petition to the United Nations (UN) asking for help in restoring religious freedom. That same year, many students and young workers demonstrated against the Soviet government, and several people burned themselves to death in protest. The desire for independence remains strong in Lithuania today.   V. STANLEY VARDYS

See also KAUNAS; KLAIPĖDA; VILNIUS.

LITMUS is a substance that is commonly used in chemistry to indicate whether a solution is an acid or a base. It can be prepared in an acidic form, which is red, and in a basic form, which is blue. An acidic solution will turn blue litmus red, but will not affect red litmus. A basic solution will turn red litmus blue, but will not affect blue litmus. A neutral solution, which is neither acidic nor basic, will not change the color of either blue or red litmus.

Litmus may be dissolved in water or alcohol to make an *indicating solution*. Because litmus is an intensely colored substance, only a few drops of litmus indicator need to be added to a solution to tell whether it is acidic or basic. Litmus indicator is also used when a solution is being neutralized. For example, litmus indicator will turn an acidic solution red. In order to neutralize the acid, base is slowly added. When the solution becomes neutral, the litmus indicator will change to purple. If more base is added, the solution will become basic, and the litmus will turn blue.

Litmus may also be added to absorbent paper to make *litmus paper*. Litmus paper is blue or red, depending on which form of litmus is present. When a drop of solution is placed on the paper, the color will indicate whether the solution is acidic, basic, or neutral.

Litmus is extracted from plants known as *lichens*. In the past, litmus was used as a blue or purple dye and in coloring beverages. Today, litmus is also used as a stain to make specimens easier to view under a microscope.

EMILY JANE ROSE

See also ACID; BASE; NEUTRALIZATION.

LITTLE AMERICA. See Antarctica (American Exploration).

LITTLE BEAR. See Big and Little Dippers.

LITTLE BIGHORN, BATTLE OF. See Crazy Horse; Custer, George A.; Gall; Reno, Marcus A.

LITTLE BOY BLUE. See Field, Eugene.

LITTLE CHIEF HARE. See Pika.

LITTLE CORPORAL. See Napoleon I.

LITTLE CROW. See Indian Wars (The Sioux Wars).

LITTLE DIPPER. See Big and Little Dippers.

LITTLE GIANT. See Douglas, Stephen Arnold.

LITTLE LEAGUE BASEBALL is an organization of baseball teams for players 8 to 12 years of age. Little Leagues use a diamond two-thirds the size of a regulation baseball diamond, and games last six innings instead of nine. The players wear rubber-cleated shoes and use bats no longer than 33 inches (84 centimeters). The ball weighs 5 to $5\frac{1}{4}$ ounces (142 to 149 grams). Batters and base runners must wear protective helmets.

A local league may have from 4 to 10 teams. Each team may include from 12 to 15 players. Teams play at least 15 games a season to determine the league champion. An all-star team selected from league teams competes in tournament play at the end of the regular season. Players on tournament teams must be 11 or 12 years of age. The tournaments are held to select eight regional winners—four from the United States, and one each from Canada, Europe, Latin America, and the Far East. The regional winners compete in the Little League World Series in Williamsport, Pa., in August.

The Little League Baseball organization was founded in 1939 in Williamsport. Today, more than 60,000 teams play in over 10,000 leagues throughout the world. More than two million players compete in Little League each summer. In 1974, girls were permitted for the first time to play on Little League Baseball teams.

Little League Baseball also conducts a Senior League Division for players 13 to 15 years of age and a Big League Division for players 16 to 18. The Senior League World Series is played in Gary, Ind., and the Big League World Series is held in Fort Lauderdale, Fla. In 1974, Little League Softball and Senior League Softball programs were begun. BEVERLY J. GRAY

LITTLE LORD FAUNTLEROY. See Burnett, Frances.

LITTLE NORWAY. See Wisconsin (Places to Visit).

LITTLE ROCK (pop. 158,915; met. area pop. 474,484) is the capital and largest city of Arkansas. It ranks as the state's chief trading and transportation center. For location see Arkansas (political map).

William Russell, a land speculator, established Little Rock in 1820. The site lay on the smaller of two rock bluffs that flank the Arkansas River. This bluff had been known as Little Rock for many years.

Description. Little Rock is the county seat of Pulaski County. It covers 91 square miles (236 square kilometers) on the south bank of the Arkansas River, including 4 square miles (10 square kilometers) of inland water. North Little Rock lies across the river. The metropolitan area covers 3,005 square miles (7,783 square kilometers) and consists of Faulkner, Lonoke, Pulaski, and Saline counties.

The central business district of Little Rock has an interesting mixture of historic and modern buildings. It includes the Arkansas Territorial Restoration, a city block that shows how Little Rock looked in the 1820's. The first State Capitol, built in the 1830's, also stands in downtown Little Rock. The present Capitol opened in 1911. It is about 10 blocks from the downtown area of the city.

Little Rock has about 40 public schools and about 50 private schools. In 1969, Little Rock University merged with the University of Arkansas to form the University of Arkansas at Little Rock. The city is also the home of Philander Smith College. The state operates schools for the deaf and the blind in Little Rock. The Arkansas Arts Center and the Museum of Science and History stand in MacArthur Park.

Little Rock is the home of the Arkansas Symphony Orchestra and the Community Theatre of Little Rock. War Memorial Park includes a 33-acre (13-hectare) zoo. The Arkansas State Fair and Livestock Exposition takes place in Little Rock in October.

Economy of Little Rock is based chiefly on manufacturing, wholesale and retail trade, and government. Each of these activities employs about a fifth of the city's work force. The Little Rock–North Little Rock metropolitan area has about 365 manufacturing plants. The manufacture of watches and cameras ranks as the area's chief industrial activity. Other products include bicycles, clothing, electric equipment, and processed foods. Little Rock is Arkansas's main center of trade and its principal market for cotton, rice, and soybeans. The city is also one of the state's chief ports. The Tactical Air Command's Little Rock Air Force Base contributes to the city's economy.

Railroads provide freight service for Little Rock. Airlines use Adams Field, located near the downtown section.

Government. Little Rock has a council-manager form of government. The voters elect the seven members of the council to four-year terms. The council members hire a city manager to carry out policies established by the group.

Vannucci Foto-Services from De Wys, Inc.

Champion Little League Teams from many countries compete in the Little League World Series at the end of each season.

LITTLE SISTERS OF THE POOR

History. The Quapaw Indians lived in what is now the Little Rock area before white explorers first arrived there. In 1820, the legislature of the Arkansas Territory chose Little Rock as the territorial capital. About 50 persons lived in the town at that time. The town began serving as the capital in 1821. Little Rock's location on the Arkansas River and its role as capital led to the town's growth as a trading center. By 1860, it had a population of 3,727. After the Civil War began in 1861, Confederate troops occupied the Army post at Little Rock and used the city as a supply center. Federal forces captured the city in 1863.

After the war ended in 1865, Little Rock prospered as a cotton and lumber market and as Arkansas's chief center of trade. By 1900, the city's population had grown to 38,039. Little Rock grew steadily during the first half of the 1900's, and its population reached 88,-129 by 1940. After the end of World War II in 1945, increased industrialization and government employment brought further growth. By 1960, Little Rock's population had grown to 107,813.

In 1957, Governor Orval E. Faubus attracted worldwide attention to Little Rock when he tried to prevent integration of the city's Central High School (see ARKANSAS [The Mid-1900's]). Completion of a federal navigation project on the Arkansas River in 1968 enabled barges to reach Little Rock. As a result, the city became an important port on the Arkansas River Navigation System. In 1973, Little Rock completed a large convention center overlooking the river. The city's population continued to grow during the 1960's and 1970's. By 1980, it had reached 158,915. WALTER L. BROWN

For the monthly weather in Little Rock, see ARKANSAS (Climate).

LITTLE SISTERS OF THE POOR is a religious congregation of the Roman Catholic Church. It is dedicated to providing the aged poor with affectionate care and attention until death. The congregation was founded in 1839 in St. Servan, France, by Jeanne Jugan. The Little Sisters of the Poor have almost 300 homes in 28 countries, including the United States and Canada. The mother house is at La Tour St. Joseph, St. Pern 35190 Tinteniac, France.

Critically reviewed by THE LITTLE SISTERS OF THE POOR

LITTLE TURTLE (1752-1812) was a Miami Indian chief in what is now Indiana and Ohio. He fought U.S. troops to protect the tribe's lands. His forces defeated General Josiah Harmar's troops in 1790, and drove back forces led by General Arthur St. Clair in 1791. Historians once believed Little Turtle was the Indian leader at the Battle of Fallen Timbers (1794). In the battle, Major General "Mad Anthony" Wayne's troops defeated nearly 2,000 Indians near what is now Toledo, Ohio. But recent research indicates that Little Turtle was not in command at the battle. In 1795, Little Turtle and other Indians signed a treaty that opened southern Ohio to settlement. He was born near the Eel River in what is now Indiana. See also INDIAN WARS (Other Midwestern Conflicts). PAUL E. MILLION, JR.

LITURGY, *LIHT uhr jee*, is a term that refers to acts of worship that are performed by the members of a religious group. A liturgy is also called a *rite* or a *ritual*. Most religions have their own liturgy. But within a religion, various churches and denominations may develop their own kinds of liturgy.

A liturgy may combine words, music, and gestures. It also may include religious objects, such as altars and special clothing; and symbolic acts, such as pouring or sprinkling water as part of the ceremony of baptism. Some liturgical services are held at certain times of the day, week, or year. They may take place on a fast day, festival, or Sabbath.

The principal liturgical service in Christianity is called the Eucharist, Holy Communion, or the Mass. The Eastern churches call the Eucharist the Divine Liturgy. The most important events of the Christian liturgical year are Christmas and Easter. The most important annual services in the Jewish liturgy are Rosh Ha-Shanah and Yom Kippur.

Christianity has many forms of liturgy. The most widespread ones are the Byzantine rite and the Latin, or Roman, rite. The Byzantine rite is used by the Greek Orthodox Church and several other Eastern churches. The Latin rite is used by the Roman Catholic Church.

Today, most Western Christian liturgies are undergoing reform in both style and text. The reforms include a stronger emphasis on the Bible and more involvement of the congregation. FREDERICK R. McMANUS

See also COMMUNION; EASTERN ORTHODOX CHURCHES (Services); MASS; ROMAN CATHOLIC CHURCH (Worship and Liturgy); SACRAMENT.

LIU PANG, *lyoo bahng*, also called Han Kao-tsu (248?-195 B.C.), was a Chinese emperor who founded the Han dynasty. He was the first commoner to become emperor. Liu reigned from 202 to 195 B.C. He revived feudalism in China by setting up regional kingdoms, with the rulers controlled by the central government. He was a skillful politician and made peace with tribes that were invading China from Mongolia. Although Liu was often cruel and ruthless, he eliminated many harsh laws. He was uneducated and scorned scholars. But by the end of his reign, he let a few scholars hold minor government positions.

Liu, a farmer's son, was born near Suchow. He became one of the generals who led revolutionary forces against the Ch'in dynasty from 207 to 206 B.C. The name Han Kao-tsu identifies Liu as "great ancestor" of the Han dynasty. EUGENE BOARDMAN

See also HAN DYNASTY.

LIU SHAOJI, *lyoo show jee* (1900?-1969?), also spelled *Liu Shao-chi*, succeeded Mao Zedong as chairman of the People's Republic of China in 1959. Liu was also regarded as the future successor to Mao as head of the Chinese Communist Party. But during the Cultural Revolution of the late 1960's, he was accused of opposing Mao. Liu was publicly criticized and humiliated. In 1968, the Chinese Communists stripped him of all his posts and expelled him from the party. In the 1970's, reports from China said Liu had died, but no details were given about his death. In 1980, a Chinese newspaper published a report indicating that Liu had died in prison in 1969. Also in 1980—four years after Mao's death—China's Communist leaders denounced the earlier criticism of Liu and held a special service to honor him.

Liu was born in Hunan province. Before the Communists won control of China in 1949, he worked as a labor organizer and underground agent. MARIUS B. JANSEN

U.S. Forest Service

U.S. Forest Service

William M. Harlow

The Beautiful Live Oak has wide-spreading branches, *above*. Its leaves, *above right,* are dark and glossy, and its thick bark, *right,* has a corklike texture.

LIVE-FOREVER. See Houseleek; Sedum.

LIVE OAK is a beautiful evergreen oak that grows along the southeastern coast of the United States. The tree grows about 50 feet (15 meters) high. Its horizontal limbs form a wide-spreading, dense head. The dark, glossy, oblong leaves may be 2 to 5 inches (5 to 13 centimeters) long. The live oak is a favorite tree for lawns and streets because it resists damage from storms, insects, and diseases. It is the state tree of Georgia.

Scientific Classification. The live oak is a member of the beech family, Fagaceae. It is classified as genus *Quercus*, species *Q. virginiana*. Louis Pyenson

See also Oak (Red Oaks; picture); Tree (Familiar Broadleaf and Needleleaf Trees [picture]).

LIVER is the largest gland in the human body and one of the most complex of all human organs. The liver serves as the body's main chemical factory and one of its major storehouses of food. The liver is a reddish-brown mass weighing about 3 pounds (1.4 kilograms). It lies in the upper right part of the abdomen, directly under the diaphragm and above the stomach and intestines.

The liver performs many essential functions. One of its most important tasks is to help the body digest food. The liver produces and discharges *bile,* a greenish-yellow digestive fluid. Bile travels from the liver to the small intestine, where it aids in the digestion of fats. Extra bile is stored in the *gall bladder,* a pear-shaped pouch that lies under the liver.

The liver also stores food. Digested food travels in the blood from the small intestine to the liver. The liver removes some of the digested food from the blood and stores it. When the body needs food, the liver releases it back into the blood. The liver also changes some digested food into compounds needed by the body's cells.

In addition, the liver filters poisons and wastes from the blood. Some substances produced by the liver help the body fight disease. Others enable the blood to clot.

Structure of the Liver

The liver consists of four sections, or *lobes.* There are two main lobes—the right lobe, which is by far the larger, and the left lobe. Two small lobes lie behind the right lobe.

Each lobe is made up of multisided units called *lobules.* Most livers have between 50,000 and 100,000 lobules. Each lobule consists of a central vein surrounded by tiny liver cells grouped in sheets or bundles. These cells perform the work of the liver. Cavities known as *sinusoids* separate the groups of cells within a lobule. The sinusoids give the liver a spongy texture and enable it to hold large amounts of blood.

The liver has an unusual blood supply system. Like other organs, the liver receives blood containing oxygen from the heart. This blood enters the liver through the *hepatic artery.* The liver also receives blood filled with *nutrients,* or digested food particles, from the small intestine. This blood enters the liver through the *portal vein.* In the liver, the hepatic artery and the portal vein branch into a network of tiny blood vessels that empty into the sinusoids.

The liver cells absorb nutrients and oxygen from the blood as it flows through the sinusoids. They also filter out wastes and poisons. At the same time, they secrete sugar, vitamins, minerals, and other substances into the blood. The sinusoids drain into the central veins, which join to form the *hepatic vein.* Blood leaves the liver through the hepatic vein.

Each lobule also contains *bile capillaries,* tiny tubes that carry the bile secreted by the liver cells. The bile capillaries join to form *bile ducts,* which carry bile out of the liver. Soon after leaving the liver, the bile ducts join together, forming the *hepatic duct.* The liver manufactures bile continuously, even if the small intestine is not digesting food. Excess bile flows into the gall bladder, where it is stored for later use. Bile from the liver and gall bladder flows into the small intestine through the *common bile duct.*

Functions of the Liver

The liver probably performs more separate tasks than any other organ in the body. Its chief functions are to help the body digest and use food and to help purify the blood of wastes and poisons.

Digestion and Use of Food. The secretion of bile ranks as one of the liver's most important digestive functions. Bile consists of bile salts and several other

351

LIVER

substances. The bile salts act on fats in the small intestine. They help break up globs of fat so enzymes in the intestine can convert fat molecules to fatty acids and glycerol.

The liver also regulates the amount of certain nutrients that the cells of the body receive. Digestive enzymes in the intestine break down proteins into amino acids, and carbohydrates into simple sugars, primarily glucose. The blood carries these nutrients, as well as vitamins, minerals, and fatty acids and glycerol, to the liver. The liver removes the excess glucose from the blood and stores it in the form of a starchlike compound called *glycogen*. Glucose serves as the chief fuel for the body's cells. When the body needs energy, the liver converts glycogen to glucose and releases it into the blood. The liver also converts fatty acids and amino acids into glucose when its store of glycogen is low. In this way, the liver helps ensure that the cells of the body receive a constant supply of fuel.

The liver also plays an essential role in the storage of certain vitamins. The liver stores vitamin A, as well as vitamins D, E, and K, and those of the B-complex group. It also stores iron and other minerals.

Purification of the Blood. Liver cells filter harmful substances from the blood. Such substances include insecticides, drugs, food additives, and industrial chemicals. Enzymes in the liver cells convert some of these substances into products that dissolve in water. The blood transports the substances to the kidneys, which discharge them in urine. Other harmful substances are excreted in the bile. The liver also filters many bacteria, viruses, and other microorganisms from the blood. Special liver cells surround these microorganisms and chemically digest them.

In addition, the liver filters out waste substances produced by the body. When red blood cells die, they release *hemoglobin*, the compound that enables them to carry oxygen. Cells in the liver and other organs break down hemoglobin into several substances, including iron and a reddish-yellow pigment called *bilirubin*. The liver discharges bilirubin in bile. It stores iron for use in producing new red blood cells. The liver also rids the body of *ammonia*, a poisonous waste formed when amino acids are changed to other compounds in the liver. The liver converts the ammonia to *urea*, which is eventually discharged in urine.

Other Functions. The liver manufactures various blood proteins, including *albumin*, *globulins*, and *fibrinogen*. Albumin helps to prevent *plasma* (the liquid portion of the blood) from seeping through the walls of the blood vessels. Globulins help the body fight infections. Fibrinogen enables the blood to seal broken blood vessels by forming a clot.

The liver also secretes *cholesterol*, a fatty substance. The body uses cholesterol to build cell membranes and to manufacture certain *hormones*, including the sex hormones. Hormones are chemicals that influence various body functions. Liver cells use cholesterol to manufacture bile salts.

Diseases of the Liver

Because the liver performs so many vital jobs, liver diseases can have serious consequences. Death occurs if the liver stops functioning. Fortunately, the liver has a remarkable ability to produce new cells to replace diseased or damaged cells.

Most liver diseases are painless in their early stages and therefore are difficult to detect. In many cases, one of the earliest signs of liver disease is *jaundice*. Jaundice occurs when the blood contains an excessive amount of bilirubin. This excess bilirubin causes a yellowish discoloration of the skin and the whites of the eyes. Jaundice may result if diseased liver cells fail to remove bilirubin from the blood. It also may occur if gallstones block the common bile duct, thus preventing the excretion of bilirubin in the bile (see GALLSTONE). Jaundice does not always signal a liver disorder. Some cases result from an increased breakdown of red blood cells.

The Liver The liver consists of two main sections—the right lobe and the left lobe—and two small lobes that lie behind the right lobe. Each lobe is made up of hexagonal-shaped units called *lobules*. The close-up section of the diagram below shows an enlarged view of a lobule.

WORLD BOOK diagram by Robert Demarest

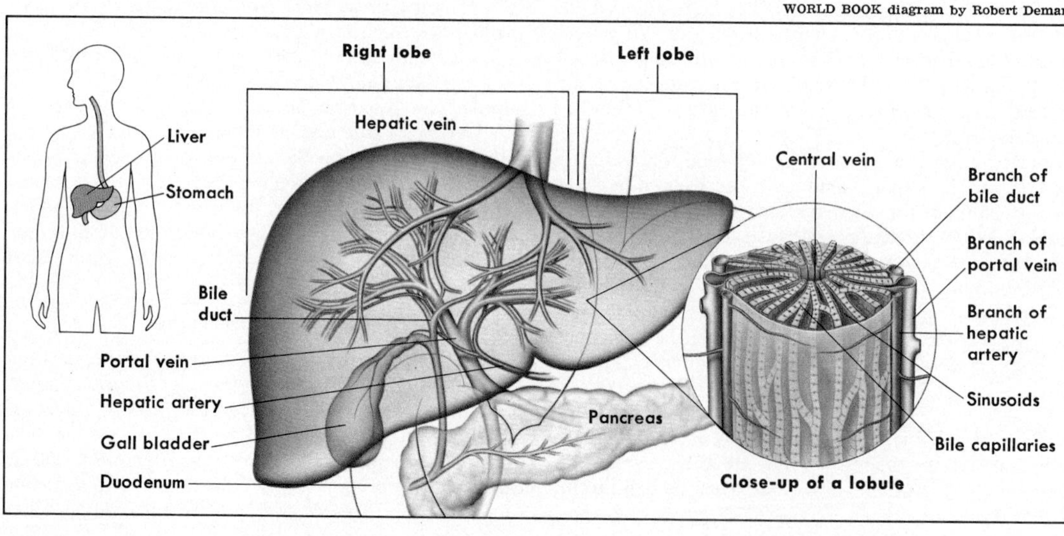

Right lobe · Left lobe · Hepatic vein · Central vein · Branch of bile duct · Branch of portal vein · Branch of hepatic artery · Sinusoids · Bile capillaries · Liver · Stomach · Bile duct · Portal vein · Hepatic artery · Gall bladder · Duodenum · Pancreas · Close-up of a lobule

Hepatitis is an inflammation of the liver. Hepatitis may be caused by viruses or by toxins. There are two main types of viral hepatitis: hepatitis A and hepatitis B. Hepatitis A usually spreads through food and water that have been contaminated by human or animal waste. Most cases do not result in serious illness. Hepatitis B is transmitted by contaminated blood, improperly sterilized medical instruments, and close contact with an infected person. Hepatitis B can lead to excessive bleeding, the failure of various functions of the liver, and coma. Physicians suspect that there may be a third type of viral hepatitis. The third type is called non-A, non-B hepatitis.

Toxic hepatitis results from exposure to various chemicals. Such substances include carbon tetrachloride and other cleaning fluids, industrial chemicals, and certain medications. See HEPATITIS.

Cirrhosis occurs when scar tissue replaces healthy liver cells. This process decreases the ability of the liver to perform its vital functions. Cirrhosis ranks as the sixth leading cause of death in the United States. However, not all cases of cirrhosis result in death. Alcoholism is the most common cause of cirrhosis. Hepatitis can also cause cirrhosis. See CIRRHOSIS.

Other Liver Diseases. Because the liver filters disease-causing microorganisms from the blood, it frequently becomes infected when diseases strike other parts of the body. Such diseases as tuberculosis, amebic dysentery, histoplasmosis, and syphilis—all of which begin elsewhere in the body—can eventually affect the liver. Cancers from other parts of the body also often spread to the liver. CHARLES S. LIEBER

Related Articles. See the Trans-Vision pictures with HUMAN BODY. See also the following articles:

Bile	Jaundice
Gall Bladder	Urea
Glycogen	

LIVERLEAF. See HEPATICA.

LIVERPOOL (pop. 503,722; met. area pop. 1,503,120) is a city in England, and a major port. The city has about 7 miles (11 kilometers) of docks along its waterfront. Liverpool lies on the River Mersey in western England, near where the river flows into the Irish Sea. For the location of Liverpool, see GREAT BRITAIN (political map).

The commercial center of Liverpool is one of the largest shopping districts in Great Britain. It borders the river and has several buildings that are landmarks of the city. They include the Royal Liver Building, which has twin towers. Each tower is topped by a sculpture of the *liver bird*, a mythical creature after which the city is said to have been named. Other famous buildings that stand in Liverpool's commercial center are the Town Hall, erected in the 1700's, and St. George's Hall, dating from the 1800's. St. George's Hall is a court building and public hall.

The inner city of Liverpool lies outside the commercial center. The inner city, which once made up a suburban area, has much old, run-down housing. However, this part of the city also includes Liverpool University, the Anglican Cathedral, and the Roman Catholic Metropolitan Cathedral. Suburbs are beyond the inner city. They have newer housing than the inner city. Many of Liverpool's people speak with an English accent called *Scouse*.

© Patrick Thurston

Liverpool is one of England's major ports. The Royal Liver Building, *left above*, a landmark of the city, stands on a bank of the River Mersey. The building is famous for its twin towers, each topped by a sculpture of the mythical liver bird.

Liverpool has a wide variety of cultural activities and sports events. The city's Walker Art Gallery owns one of the nation's finest collections of paintings outside London. Liverpool has an orchestra, several theaters, and two professional soccer teams.

Liverpool's port has declined somewhat in importance since the mid-1900's. But shipping and other industries connected with the docks are still the foundation of the city's economy. Major industrial facilities also include automobile manufacturing plants, flour mills, and sugar refineries.

Liverpool was founded in the early 1200's and began to flourish as a trade center in the 1700's. Ships based in Liverpool carried slaves from Africa to the West Indies and North America in exchange for various products. During the 1800's, manufacturing and trade activities in Liverpool increased sharply, and the city expanded rapidly.

Liverpool remained a busy port in the early 1900's. During World War II (1939-1945), German bombers heavily damaged the city and its docks. Since the war, the decline of the port, plus other factors, have contributed to a high rate of unemployment in the Liverpool community. ERIC MIDWINTER

See also MERSEY, RIVER.

LIVERWORT, *LIHV uhr wurt.* Liverworts are small green plants closely related to the mosses. They are found in all parts of the world, growing in damp shady places, on rocks and bark, and sometimes in water. The lower liverworts are shaped like minute leaves of seed plants with many lobes. The main body of the

LIVERWORT

plant, which looks like a leaf, is called the *thallus*. Liverworts get their name because the thallus is often shaped like the human liver. Superstitious persons once believed that they cured liver diseases.

L. W. Brownell

Each Liverwort Plant looks like a small leaf.

Tiny rootlets grow from the underside of the thallus. These structures are called *rhizoids*. They absorb water and the minerals that the liverwort needs for nourishment. The rootlets also hold the plant to the rocks and trees on which it grows.

Liverworts produce new plants in several different ways. One way involves two different *generations* (stages), and is called *alternation of generations*. The thallus is the *sexual* generation. It is called the *gametophyte*. Male and female sexual structures grow on the thallus. The male structures produce sex cells called *antherozoids*. The cells produced by the female structures are the *eggs*. Later the antherozoids swim through the moisture on the plant until they reach the eggs in the female structure. An egg is fertilized when the two cells join each other. The fertilized egg grows into a tiny new structure, the *sporophyte*.

The sporophyte is the *nonsexual* generation of the plant. It lives on the liverwort thallus, where it soon produces *spores*. Spores are tiny one-celled structures that grow into new organisms. The liverworts are among the lowest plants that have this two-stage type of reproduction.

Scientific Classification. Liverworts make up the liverwort class, *Hepaticae*. They are in the mosses and liverworts division, *Bryophyta*.   ROLLA M. TRYON

See also BRYOPHYTE; MOSS; PLANT (pictures: Liverworts and Mosses).

LIVESTOCK are domestic animals that are used to produce food and many other valuable products. The skins of some livestock provide such important materials as leather and wool. Various organs of livestock supply drugs used by countless people.

Farmers in developing nations use livestock to pull farm equipment. Some livestock in these countries also transport people and materials. Most livestock are raised on farms and ranches, but some people raise rabbits, chickens, or other small livestock in their backyards.

The chief kinds of livestock raised throughout the world are cattle, hogs, poultry, sheep, and horses. Other kinds of livestock include donkeys, goats, mules, and rabbits. In some countries, farmers raise such livestock as llamas, reindeer, water buffalo, and yaks. The science of raising, breeding, and caring for livestock is called *animal husbandry*.

At one time, people wandered from place to place hunting animals and gathering plants for food. Several thousand years ago, people began to domesticate and raise various kinds of livestock. The use of domesticated animals as a source of food and power made it possible for people to settle in one place and begin farming.

Throughout the centuries, farmers improved their livestock through various breeding methods. Today, many livestock raisers enter their animals in livestock shows, which are held in most parts of the world. Judges rate the livestock on such points as their size and their yield of meat.

This article provides general information on live-

Milt and Joan Mann

Grant Heilman

Modern Methods of Raising Livestock have increased production and efficiency. Many cattle receive special feed, *left*, that increases their growth rate. Some poultry houses, *right*, have equipment that automatically provides feed and water and collects eggs.

354

H. K. Bruske, Artstreet

Livestock Serve as Work Animals on farms in some countries. The Pakistani farmers shown above are using a team of oxen to pull a device to make the ground level.

stock. See also the separate WORLD BOOK articles on the animals discussed.

Uses of Livestock

In most parts of the world, livestock provide such food products as meat, butter, cheese, eggs, and milk. These foods contain large amounts of protein, which builds new tissue and maintains and repairs old tissue in the human body. Animal food products also supply minerals and vitamins that people need for good health.

Livestock also provide such valuable by-products as fur, hair, leather, and wool. These materials are used to produce blankets, brushes, clothing, shoes, and other goods. Manufacturers use the hoofs and horns of livestock to make such articles as buttons, combs, glue, and knives. Other livestock by-products are used in the preparation of livestock feed.

Some of the glands and organs of certain livestock are used to make such drugs as adrenalin, insulin, and pepsin. Processed animal fat, called *tallow*, can be made into livestock feed, shortening, and soap. Manufacturers use the feathers of ducks and geese in making bedding and insulated clothing.

Every year, livestock deposit tons of body wastes that fertilize the soil. This organic fertilizer increases the growth and food production of many plants.

Through the years, automated farm equipment has reduced the use of horses as work animals in most parts of the world. Today, people in developed nations use horses primarily for racing and other sports.

Care of Livestock

Feed. A domestic animal's daily food intake is called a *ration*. A balanced ration contains the nutrients that the animal needs for growth and good health. These nutrients include carbohydrates, fats, minerals, protein, and vitamins. Some livestock producers and animal feed companies use computers to determine the kind

and proportion of ingredients used in livestock rations.

Swine and poultry feed consists of various grains, minerals, vitamins, and concentrated plant and animal proteins. Cattle, sheep, and other *ruminants* (animals with more than one stomach compartment) eat the grasses of pastureland. They are also fed grain, hay, and the stalks of certain plants.

Many farmers raise cattle in fenced-in areas called *feed lots*. These animals receive special feed that increases their growth rate. The use of feed lots decreases the amount of land needed for grazing, but it also reduces the amount of animal wastes available for use as fertilizer. Some farmers move these wastes from the feed lots to the fields.

Livestock raisers feed additional cereal grains to some cattle to get a better quality of beef or a high level of milk production. When food shortages occurred in various countries during the mid-1970's, some farmers increased the amount of grass and hay fed to cattle. This feeding practice reduced the amount of grain used in animal feed and made more grain available for human consumption.

Drugs called *additives* are blended with some feeds to increase the animals' growth rate and reduce the chance of disease. These additives include antibiotics and synthetic hormones. The high cost of such drugs makes their use impossible in many countries. In the United States, the government controls the dosage and use of certain additives that might harm animal or human life. The governments of other nations where additives are included in animal feed are becoming increasingly concerned about controlling their use.

Farmers use automated equipment to transport livestock feed to barns, elevators, and silos, where it is stored. Other equipment measures and mixes the ingredients in the feed.

Shelter. Livestock require some protection from severe weather so they can maintain satisfactory growth and reproduction. At one time, these animals could live easily without shelter. Through the years, however, farmers have developed breeding methods designed to raise meat production. These methods produce less hardy types of livestock. Today, many livestock cannot withstand extreme cold or heat. Exposure to snow and wind can also harm the animals.

Livestock owners provide the most economical type of shelter that can best maintain the animals' levels of food production. Some livestock need only a windbreak or shade tree for shelter. Others are sheltered in climate-controlled buildings where the humidity, sound level, temperature, and ventilation are precisely regulated.

Livestock raised in climate-controlled buildings are placed in confined areas that range in size from 5 to 25 square feet (0.5 to 2.3 square meters). This type of shelter provides an efficient method of feeding the animals, but its waste control system eliminates valuable natural fertilizer. Some farmers have solved this problem by installing pumps that move animal wastes from the shelter to the fields.

Prevention of Disease ranks as a major concern of livestock raisers. Some diseases can kill large numbers of livestock or be transmitted to people. Sometimes,

355

to prevent an epidemic, farmers must destroy all live-stock that have come in contact with infected animals. Animals suffering from nutritional deficiencies produce less meat, milk, and eggs.

The chief causes of livestock diseases include bacteria, fungi, parasites, and viruses. Livestock also can become ill if they consume natural poisons or insecticides and other chemicals sprayed on grass and plants. Livestock inherit sensitivity to some diseases.

Many disease-carrying organisms that infect livestock are found in warm climates. Foot-and-mouth disease, tick fever, and other diseases severely limit livestock production in tropical countries.

Diseases spread extremely rapidly among hogs, poultry, and other livestock that are kept in confined areas. Young livestock also tend to become infected easily.

Scientists conduct many research programs to find new ways of combating livestock diseases. These experts work to identify and eliminate the organisms that spread such diseases as hog cholera and tuberculosis. Modern feeding methods have reduced the occurrence of some diseases.

Breeding Livestock

Livestock raisers select certain animals for reproduction. Such livestock may be chosen because they have a high rate of growth or produce large amounts of meat, eggs, or milk. This practice, called *selective breeding*, allows farmers to continually improve their livestock. Livestock raisers select only healthy and fertile animals for breeding purposes. Most of the offspring of such animals inherit the characteristics of their parents.

There are three chief methods of selective breeding: (1) random mating, (2) inbreeding, and (3) outbreeding.

Random mating is the simplest type of livestock breeding. Livestock producers place selected males and females of one species in the same area and allow them to mate at random.

Farmers practice inbreeding by mating animals that are closely related to each other. This method produces a pure breed of livestock. Livestock raisers select animals for inbreeding by studying their *pedigrees*, which list the traits of an animal's ancestors. Livestock that are closely related have similar genes, which are transmitted to their offspring. These offspring may have a high concentration of the parents' favorable genes. However, inferior genes, which were not apparent in the parents, may show up strongly in the young. Therefore, inbreeding may produce a small animal that lacks resistance to disease.

Outbreeding is the mating of unrelated animals. *Outcrossing* and *crossbreeding* are two methods of outbreeding often used by farmers. Outcrossing is the mating of unrelated animals of the same breed. Farmers use this method to introduce a desirable trait into a line of livestock. Crossbreeding is the mating of animals of different breeds. Most of the offspring have a higher performance level than the average performance level of the parents.

Many breeders use artificial insemination to improve the quality of their livestock. The reproductive organs of females are injected with *semen* (sperm-carrying fluid) from high-quality males. This technique increases the number of offspring that can be produced by superior male animals.

Marketing Livestock

Livestock prices are determined in the various markets where the animals are sold. There are three kinds of livestock markets: (1) auction markets, (2) terminal markets, and (3) direct markets.

Livestock buyers bid openly at auction markets. The auctioneer usually starts the bidding at a reasonable price. The animals are sold to the buyer who offers the highest price. If many buyers bid for a certain kind of livestock, the producer usually receives a high price for the stock. If few buyers bid, the price of livestock tends to be lower.

Most terminal markets are large and located near a big city. At one time, all trades made at terminals were private. Therefore, only the buyer and seller knew what price was paid for the livestock. Today, many terminal markets also operate auctions.

Professional market experts help livestock producers sell their animals at most auction and terminal markets. These agents receive a commission from the producer for each animal they sell.

Sales at direct markets are made between the producer and buyer without the help of a professional agent. Thus, the producer does not have to pay a commission to sell stock. Sometimes an inexperienced producer may not get a good price for livestock without professional help. Some meat packing companies have established buying stations throughout the United States that serve as direct markets.

The United States Department of Agriculture supervises the operations of markets that handle livestock shipped across state borders. The department regulates the fees charged by these markets and prevents unfair and fraudulent trade practices.

At one time, each type of livestock was brought to market during a certain season. Farmers regulated the rations of the animals to have them ready for sale at the proper time.

Today, many livestock are marketed throughout the year, but some animals continue to be sold chiefly during certain seasons. For example, more hogs are marketed during the fall and early winter than at any other time.

Farmers use trucks to transport their livestock to nearby markets. Semitrailers and freight trains carry the animals to distant markets.   DUANE ACKER

Related Articles in WORLD BOOK include:

CHIEF KINDS OF LIVESTOCK

Cattle	Poultry
Chicken	Rabbit
Duck	Sheep
Hog	Turkey
Horse	

OTHER RELATED ARTICLES

Agriculture	Environmental Pollution
Animal and Plant Health	(Economic Causes)
Inspection Service	Farm and Farming
Breeding	(with pictures)
Dairying (Dairy Farms)	Feed, Livestock
	Veterinary Medicine

LIVING STANDARD. See STANDARD OF LIVING.

LIVING THINGS. See BIOLOGY; CELL; LIFE.

LIVINGSTON, PHILIP (1716-1778), a signer of the Declaration of Independence, gave generously of his fortune to help the American cause in the Revolutionary War. As an importer in New York City, Livingston, like his brother William, took an active part in civic affairs. He served as a delegate to the Stamp Act Congress in 1765, to the Continental Congress from 1774 to 1778, and to the New York Provincial Congress. Livingston was born in Albany, N.Y., and was graduated from Yale University. ROBERT J. TAYLOR

LIVINGSTON, ROBERT R. (1746-1813), an American statesman, helped draw up the Declaration of Independence. He was a member of the New York convention that ratified the U.S. Constitution, and he helped draft the New York state constitution. Livingston ad-

Culver
Robert Livingston

ministered the oath of office to George Washington when he became the first President of the United States.

In 1775, Livingston served as a delegate to the Continental Congress. From 1777 to 1801, he was chancellor, or presiding judge, of the New York court of chancery. Livingston served as minister to France from 1801 to 1804. While in France, he negotiated the Louisiana Purchase, which added a vast new territory to the United States. Later, Livingston gave Robert Fulton help in building the steamboat *Clermont*. This ship was named for Livingston's home in New York. Livingston was born in New York City, and studied at King's College, now Columbia University. In 1875, the state of New York placed a statue of Livingston in the United States Capitol in Washington, D.C. IAN C. C. GRAHAM

See also JEFFERSON, THOMAS (The Louisiana Purchase).

LIVINGSTON, WILLIAM (1723-1790), was a New Jersey signer of the Constitution of the United States. He was the senior New Jersey delegate at the 1787 Constitutional Convention in Philadelphia and became known for his ability to help delegates work out compromises. Livingston served as chairman of the committee that created regulations for the slave trade and set up guidelines for direct taxation. He also led a committee that worked on such matters as the states' militia and federal payment of states' debts. Livingston later helped win swift and unanimous *ratification* (approval) of the Constitution by New Jersey.

Livingston was born in Albany, N.Y. He graduated from Yale College in 1741 and practiced law in New York City. In the 1760's, Livingston became a prominent opponent of British policy. He moved to New Jersey in 1772 and later represented the colony in the First and Second Continental Congresses. Livingston took command of the New Jersey militia in June 1776. Two months later, he was chosen the first governor of the state of New Jersey. He retained this position for the rest of his life. RICHARD D. BROWN

LIVINGSTONE, DAVID. See STANLEY AND LIVINGSTONE.

LIVORNO. See LEGHORN.

LIVY, *LIHV ee* (59 B.C.-A.D. 17), was one of the greatest Roman historians. His *Historiae ab Urbe Condita* (*History from the Founding of the City*) tells of Roman history from the founding of Rome until the death of Drusus in 9 B.C. He wrote this work in 142 books, but only 35 of them are still in existence.

Livy, whose real name was Titus Livius, lived in Rome during the reign of Augustus. The emperor was his friend and patron. Livy spent more than 40 years working on his history, which became famous during ancient times and was widely quoted. The lengthy work became known chiefly through short summaries or abridgments. Many of these summaries have survived.

Some scholars condemned Livy because he included legends and miraculous events that he found in his sources. But most historians regard his work as a valuable historical source. Livy was born at Padua in northern Italy. THOMAS A. BRADY

LIZARD is a reptile closely related to snakes. Like snakes, some lizards are legless. Others resemble snakes but have legs. Many large lizards look much like crocodiles. Lizards vary in size, shape, and color. They have many different ways of moving about and of defending themselves. Scientists have identified almost 3,000 different *species* (kinds) of lizards.

In the northeastern United States, many persons mistake lizards for salamanders. Few lizards live in this area, but there are many salamanders. The salamanders are commonly called "spring lizards" or "wood lizards." Salamanders and lizards look much alike, but they are not related. Both are *cold-blooded*, that is, they cannot keep their bodies much warmer or cooler than their surroundings. But lizards have dry, scaly skin and clawed toes. Salamanders are amphibians related to frogs, and have moist skin and no scales or claws. Lizards love to stay in the sun, and salamanders avoid sunlight. See COLD-BLOODED ANIMAL; SALAMANDER.

Where Lizards Live. Lizards lack the built-in body temperature control many other animals have. So, most lizards live in places where the ground never freezes. Those that live in areas with cold winters must hibernate underground. Lizards thrive in the tropics and warm parts of the temperate zones. They are the most common reptiles found in deserts and other dry regions. When the desert becomes too hot for comfort, lizards lie in the shade or under the sand to escape the sun's rays.

Sizes of Lizards. The smallest lizards are only a few inches or centimeters in length. The largest is the *Komodo dragon*. This huge East Indian lizard grows about 9 to 10 feet (2.7 to 3 meters) long and may weigh nearly 300 pounds (140 kilograms). The Komodo dragon belongs to a group of lizards known as *monitors*. Other monitors grow to be 6 to 7 feet (1.8 to 2.1 meters) long. These lizards live in Africa, India, and Australia.

How Lizards Move. The most remarkable thing about lizards is the variety of ways by which they move. More than 60 million years ago, huge lizards called *mosasaurs* swam in the sea. Even today, giant monitors sometimes swim from one island to another. No present-day lizard can fly, but a small group in Asia and the

The Nile Monitor of Africa grows more than 6 feet (1.8 meters) long. It digs, runs, and swims well, and can climb trees. This huge lizard spends much time in water and feeds on many kinds of smaller animals.

East Indies glide from tree to tree like flying squirrels. These lizards are the so-called *flying dragons*. They can spread out a fold of skin along either side of their body by moving several long ribs. This extended fold of skin forms a sort of sail that can be used to glide through the air.

Most lizards, however, live on the ground or in trees. Even on the ground, the lizards have many different ways of moving about. Many people in the United States know the swift little lizards that scamper over old fences and logs. Some *geckos*, lizards that spend much time in trees, have claws that they can draw in as a cat does. Some have slits on their toes that function like suction disks. The claws catch in rough surfaces such as bark, and the slits cling to smoother ones. A gecko can walk upside down across a plaster ceiling without trouble, and can even cling to a pane of glass. The Australian *fringed lizard* is one of several lizards that can run by raising the front of its body and running on its hind legs. It balances itself with its long tail.

Many lizards that live on the ground can get along without any legs. Some *skinks*, for example, have no legs. Other skinks have weak, nearly useless legs. The *glass snake* of the Eastern United States is really a lizard

The Six-Lined Race Runner of the Southeastern United States can run as fast as 18 miles (29 kilometers) per hour. It escapes its enemies by darting into a hole or under rocks.

without legs. It has well-developed eyelids and ear openings, both of which are absent in snakes.

Defenses. Lizards defend themselves in a great variety of ways. Like some snakes, many lizards bluff or play tricks. The glass snake has one of the most unusual methods of defense. This lizard's tail is twice as long as its body, and as brittle as an old twig. If an enemy seizes the lizard's tail, the animal pulls its body away from the tail and crawls to safety. Meanwhile, the tail keeps wriggling as though it were alive, fooling the enemy that struggles with it. The lizard does not seem to miss its tail, and in due time it grows a new one. Several other kinds of lizards, including skinks, can break off their tails and grow new ones to replace them.

Other common ways of bluffing include swelling up, hissing, and lashing the tail. The Australian *frilled lizard* ranks as one of the best bluffers. This lizard rears on its hind legs, spreads an enormous frill out on each side of its neck, opens its mouth, and hisses. These antics make the frilled lizard look several times as big and fierce as it really is. A large frilled lizard measures about 32 inches (81 centimeters) long.

Some lizards are not such harmless fighters. The monitors and their relatives use their large jaws for biting. They also use their tails as whips to strike a sharp blow. Unlike snakes, few lizards are poisonous. The only poisonous lizards are the *Gila monster* of the Southwestern United States and northern Mexico, and its close relative, the *beaded lizard* of Mexico.

The *horned toads* have an unusual trick. They can squirt a fine stream of blood from their eyes for a distance of 3 feet (91 centimeters). They will do this if a person or animal handles them roughly just after they have shed their old skin. A horned toad is not a real toad, but a lizard with a short tail. A number of sharp spines on its head and back give it added protection.

The *African chameleons* are famous for the way they can change color. Many other lizards have the same power. Many persons think that these changes help the animal to protect itself, but they are not always used

Karl H. Switak

The Collared Lizard is named for the black bands around its neck. It lives mainly in rocky areas of the Southwestern United States.

Warren Garst, Tom Stack & Assoc.

The Australian Frilled Lizard frightens enemies away by opening its mouth with a hiss and unfolding the large frill that encircles its head. The frill of an adult male may have a diameter of 9 inches (23 centimeters).

in this way. Sometimes, these lizards turn a darker color to absorb more heat from the sun's rays. Some lizards do rely on their colors for protection. Many desert lizards are light in hue, and those that dwell in the forest are darker. The different species have various combinations of green, red, gray, brown, white, and black.

Reproduction. Most lizards lay eggs. Some deposit them in simple nests. The female skink may coil around the eggs and drive away any intruders. If the eggs become scattered, she brings them back together.

Some lizards do not lay their eggs but give birth to living young after the eggs hatch inside the lizard's body. Still other lizards reproduce in somewhat the same way as mammals. These lizards also give birth to living young. Before birth, the developing lizard gets food from the mother lizard's body. Unlike female mammals, the female lizard does not nurse her young or care for them after birth.

Food. Lizards have less interesting eating habits than snakes. But, unlike snakes, some eat plants instead of animals. The *marine iguanas* of the Galapagos Islands feed on algae. They gather the plants off the rocks at low tide. Hundreds of species of lizards eat mostly insects and small animals. Most do not limit their diet to any one thing. A few lizards, such as African chameleons, have a tongue that they can shoot out beyond their snout. They capture insects on their tongue's mucus-coated tip. Other lizards seize their victims in their mouths. They swallow their prey as soon as it stops struggling.

Dangers to Lizards. Human activities threaten the survival of certain species of lizards. People hunt iguanas and other lizards for food in some countries. In many areas, the animal's habitats have been destroyed. In the past, some lizards were killed for their skins, which were used to make wallets, handbags, and other products. But many countries now have laws to protect lizards from being killed for this purpose.

Scientific Classification. Lizards belong to the class Reptilia. They are members of the order Squamata, along with snakes. Lizards alone make up the suborder Lacertilia (sometimes called Sauria).   CARL H. ERNST

Related Articles in WORLD BOOK include:

Animal (color picture: Animals of the Tropical Forests)	Flying Dragon	Monitor
	Gecko	Prehistoric
	Gila Monster	Animal
	Glass Snake	Reptile
Blindworm	Horned Toad	Swift
Chameleon	Iguana	Tegu
Chuckwalla	Komodo Dragon	

LJUBLJANA, *LYOO blyah nah* (pop. 173,853), is the capital and largest city of Slovenia, one of the six republics of Yugoslavia. For location, see YUGOSLAVIA (political map). Ljubljana is an important industrial center. Factories in the city produce electrical products, machinery, paper, textiles, and other manufactured goods. Ljubljana is also the cultural center of Slovenia. It has a university, several museums, and academies of art, drama, music, and science. The city was founded in 34 B.C.   ALVIN Z. RUBINSTEIN

LLAMA, *LAH muh,* is the largest member of the camel family that lives in South America. The llama, like its smaller relative, the *alpaca,* is a domesticated animal that was probably bred from the wild *guanaco.* The llama has no hump, and is about 4 feet (1.2 meters) tall at the shoulder. Its body is about 4 or 5 feet (1.2 to 1.5 meters) long. Its hair is thick and long. It may be colored brown, buff, gray, white, or black. Males over $3\frac{1}{2}$ years of age are used for pack animals. The females are used for breeding and furs. The female llama bears one kid at a time.

The llama is most useful as a pack animal. Llamas can carry about 100 pounds (45 kilograms) each, and are sure-footed on the mountain trails. They can travel from 15 to 20 miles (24 to 32 kilometers) a day with a full load. Sometimes hundreds or thousands of llamas are used on an engineering project. Llamas can be very

359

The Llama has thick hair and a long neck and looks somewhat like a small camel. But unlike camels, llamas have no hump.

Jerry Cooke, Animals Animals

stubborn animals. If a llama feels its pack is too heavy, or if it thinks it has worked hard enough, it will lie down, with its front legs under it, and refuse to move. When the llama is angry or under attack, it spits bad-smelling saliva in its enemy's face.

The llama is useful to the Indians of the South American Andes in many ways. The Indians use llamas to transport goods. They eat the meat of the young animals. They use the hair of the llama to make garments, and they use its hide to make sandals. The llama is inexpensive to keep. It is a hardy animal and lives on low shrubs, lichens, and other plants that grow on high mountains. It can live for weeks without drinking water. Instead, it gets its moisture from green plants.

Scientific Classification. Llamas are members of the camel family, *Camelidae*. They are genus *Lama*, species *L. glama*. DONALD F. HOFFMEISTER

See also ALPACA; CAMEL; GUANACO; RUMINANT.

LLANERO. See VENEZUELA (The Llanos).

LLANFAIRPWLLGWYNGYLLGOGERYCHWYRN-DROBWLLLLANTYSILIOGOGOGOCH is a village in Wales. It has the longest place name in Great Britain. The first 20 letters formed the name until the 1800's, when a cobbler invented the new name. The name means *Church of Saint Mary in a hollow of white hazel, near to a rapid whirlpool, and Saint Tysilio's Church of the red cave.* The church was dedicated first to St. Tysilio, and later to the Virgin Mary. The name of the village is often shortened to *Llanfair.* DAVID WILLIAMS

LLANO ESTACADO. See TEXAS (Land Regions).

LLANOS, *LAH nohz,* meaning *level lands,* is most often used to mean a great *savanna* (grassland) region in Venezuela and Colombia. This plain is known as the Orinoco Basin. The region covers about 300,000 square miles (780,000 square kilometers), an area larger than Texas. Heavy rains fall in the wet season, and the rivers flood the country. But after the rains, rich grasses grow to provide food for cattle, horses, and sheep. Hot winds scorch the grasses during part of the dry season, and the country becomes a desert. The animals then move

where water can be found. Similar plains in Argentina are called pampas. A high, level region in Texas and New Mexico is called the *Llano Estacado* (Staked Plain). See also PAMPA; SAVANNA. ERNEST L. THURSTON

LLEWELYN AP GRIFFITH. See WALES (Revolts Against England).

LLOYD, HAROLD CLAYTON (1894-1971), was a comedian who won fame in silent motion pictures. He created and acted the role of "Harold," a timid weakling who wins battles with fate through some lastminute turn of events. Lloyd made frequent use of the "sneak preview." He showed his films by surprise to audiences, and he later replaced any material that failed to get a laugh. His best silent comedies include *Grandma's Boy* (1922), *Safety Last* (1923), *The Freshman* (1925), and *Welcome Danger* (1929). Lloyd also made several sound comedies.

Pictorial Parade

Harold Lloyd

Lloyd was born in Burchard, Nebr. He began his screen acting career in 1916. After retiring, he remained active in Hollywood community affairs and in the Shriners and other organizations. RICHARD GRIFFITH

LLOYD, HENRY DEMAREST (1847-1903), an American writer, won fame for revealing unfair business practices in the United States in the late 1800's. He criticized the idea that what was good for business was also good for society, and preached that many corporations put their interests ahead of those of the worker, the public, and the government. Lloyd's exposures introduced a type of probing writing that became known as *muckraking* (see MUCKRAKERS).

Lloyd was born in New York City. In 1881, he wrote a magazine article accusing Standard Oil Company of receiving lower rates and *rebates* (returned money) from the railroads. He expanded his attack on big business in his best-known book, *Wealth Against Commonwealth* (1894). CHARLES B. FORCEY and LINDA R. FORCEY

LLOYD GEORGE, DAVID (1863-1945), a British Liberal Party leader, served as prime minister during the last half of World War I. He was also prominent in helping to draft the Versailles Peace Treaty. He led the British delegation at the conference which drew up the treaty that ended World War I. Lloyd George was active in British politics until his death.

Early Career. Lloyd George was born of Welsh parents in Manchester, England, on Jan. 17, 1863. His father died when he was a year old, and his mother then took him to Llanystumdwy in Caernarvonshire (now Gwynedd), Wales. There he grew up in the home of his uncle, Richard Lloyd, a shoemaker and Baptist minister. He was reared in an atmosphere of hostility to the landed aristocracy and to the Church of England. He was apprenticed to a law firm at 16, and began the practice of law at 21.

Lloyd George early associated himself with the Liberal Party. In 1890, on a platform of comprehensive social reform for Wales, he was elected to Parliament from the Caernarvon Boroughs. He represented this constituency continuously for 55 years. He soon established a reputation as a "radical," and became widely known through his attacks on the government's policy in South Africa before and during the Boer War.

When the Liberals returned to power in 1905, Lloyd George became president of the Board of Trade. From 1908 to 1915, he served as chancellor of the exchequer. He sponsored the Old Age Pension Act of 1908 and the National Insurance Act of 1911. His "People's Budget" of 1909 introduced a tax on "unearned income" and greatly increased land and inheritance taxes. The Conservative House of Lords rejected this budget. This caused a constitutional crisis with the House of Commons which ended in victory for Lloyd George and his party. The power to veto financial legislation was taken away from the House of Lords.

Prime Minister. The coming of war in 1914 changed Lloyd George from a pacifist to a staunch supporter of the war against Germany. As minister of munitions in 1915, he ended shortages in ammunition. In July, 1916, he succeeded Lord Horatio Kitchener as secretary of war, and in December, 1916, he replaced Herbert Asquith as prime minister of a coalition cabinet. Lloyd George is generally recognized as one of Britain's great war leaders. His leadership strengthened civilian morale. At the Paris Peace Conference in 1919, he mediated successfully between the idealism of President Woodrow Wilson and the severe peace terms sought by Premier Georges Clemenceau of France.

United Press Int.
David Lloyd George

An easy electoral victory in December, 1918, kept Lloyd George and his coalition government in office. But he did not achieve the economic reconstruction he had promised. His Irish policy led to the formation of the Irish Free State, but cost him Conservative support. His pro-Greek policy failed. He resigned in 1922. Though only 59 years old, he never again held office. The Liberal Party, divided in 1918 between his supporters and those of Lord Asquith, was reunited in 1923 but could not regain popular support. It soon became a weak third party.

Lloyd George tried unsuccessfully to make a comeback with an elaborate program of public works and agricultural reform. He visited Adolf Hitler at Berchtesgaden in 1936 and returned with praise for the German leader. But he soon became a severe critic of appeasement of Hitler. In 1945, shortly before his death, he was created Earl of Dwyfor.   ALFRED F. HAVIGHURST

LLOYD'S is an insurance society popularly known as LLOYD'S OF LONDON. It consists of individual members known as *Lloyd's underwriters*. The society is famous for insuring almost any risk. Lloyd's pioneered many forms of insurance that have since become commonplace, such as burglary, loss of profits, hurricane, and earthquake insurance. The society does not sell life insurance, except on a short-term basis.

By the mid-1970's, Lloyd's had about 7,500 underwriters grouped into about 270 *syndicates* (combinations).

Lloyd's
Lloyd's of London provides offices where thousands of brokers and underwriters insure almost any kind of risk or eventuality.

These syndicates vary in size from a few people to several hundred people. In 1968, Lloyd's admitted underwriters from countries other than Great Britain for the first time. Lloyd's provides its members with worldwide merchant shipping reports. This information is published daily in *Lloyd's List and Shipping Gazette*. Founded in 1734, this is the oldest newspaper in London.

Lloyd's originated in the coffee house of Edward Lloyd in about 1688. The coffee house was a favorite meeting place for ship owners and wealthy merchants who would *underwrite* (accept the risk of) a marine insurance policy. In the 1900's, Lloyd's partly or completely insured property lost in the San Francisco earthquake and fire in 1906, the sinking of the *Titanic* in 1912, the airship *Hindenburg*, which burned in 1937, and many hurricanes in the United States.

See also A 1; INSURANCE (History); UNDERWRITING.

LNG. See GAS (Storing Gas).

LOADSTONE, also spelled LODESTONE, is a hard black stone that exhibits magnetic properties. It is made up of magnetite, which is ferro-ferric oxide (Fe_3O_4).

According to a legend, the loadstone was discovered in Asia Minor by a shepherd who noticed that certain black stones stuck to the iron end of his staff. Large amounts of this stone were found in an ancient country of Asia Minor called *Magnesia*. The stones came to be called *magnes lapis*, which means *magnesian stone*.

About A.D. 1200, Europeans discovered that an oblong piece of this stone would point to the north and south if it were hung by a string. They called it a "leading stone," or *loadstone*. Loadstone made compasses possible, and sailors no longer had to steer by the stars. Today loadstones are mined in Siberia and the Island of Elba.   WILLIAM C. LUTH

See also MAGNET AND MAGNETISM (picture).

LOAM, *lohm,* is a soil that is between sandy soil and clay soil in texture. Loams are chiefly mixtures of sand, clay, and silt. They are among the most valuable soils in agriculture, and are easy to work. A typical loam soil feels smooth and is somewhat sticky. A piece of clay feels very smooth and sticky. Any soil between loam

LOAN

and clay in texture is called a *clay loam*. Soil between sand and loam is called *sandy loam*. *Silt loam* contains much silt. ERNEST E. WAHLSTROM

See also CLAY; HUMUS; SAND; SOIL.

LOAN. See BANK (Making Loans); BOND; INSURANCE (Life Insurance); LOAN COMPANY.

LOAN COMPANY is an organization that lends money to individuals. Some loan companies were organized chiefly to combat *loan sharks* (moneylenders who charge an illegal or high rate of interest). The personal finance company has been the most common type of successful small-loan company. It has taken much business away from the loan sharks.

The personal finance company is founded upon the Uniform Small Loan Law. This law was devised by the Russell Sage Foundation in 1916. It was adopted by Pennsylvania and New Jersey in 1916, and has since been adopted by many other states. The basic law entitled companies to lend money in small sums from $50 to $300, with or without security. It set interest rates at a maximum of $3\frac{1}{2}$ per cent per month, and made companies submit to licensing and supervision by state banking authorities. The law has been modified by some states to allow companies to make loans as high as $5,000 with lower maximum interest rates.

Many loan companies require only that the borrower's note be endorsed by two other acceptable parties. This is the method of the Morris Plan Bank. But the largest number of loans are usually made to families on the signature of both husband and wife. No comakers or endorsers are necessary. A chattel mortgage on the household goods or an assignment on wages is the most common security. Usually the loan is repaid in installments. This type of lending is similar to that formerly employed by the loan shark. But the borrower is protected by the state regulations under which the loan company operates. G. L. BACH

Related Articles in WORLD BOOK include:

Assignment	Interest	Savings and Loan
Credit	Mortgage	Association
Finance Company	Pawnbroker	Usury

LOAN-SHARKING. See CRIME (Organized Crime).

LOBBYING is an attempt to influence the decisions of government officials. A person who tries to persuade legislators to vote in a particular way is known as a *lobbyist*. The words refer to the lobby or anteroom outside the room where legislators vote on public bills. Lobbyists also frequently try to influence the decisions of officials in the executive branch. The lobbyist may be a member of a group interested in a particular law or a paid agent of a group that wants certain bills passed or defeated.

Properly used, lobbying can serve a useful purpose. It may be the best organized way in which groups can make their wishes known to legislators. Much government policymaking involves a two-way flow of information between private groups and public officials. But not all lobbying is conducted along these lines. Sometimes the lobbyist may try to persuade a legislator or other government official by offering favors or money. At this point, lobbying becomes bribery (see BRIBERY).

The U.S. Congress and about half of the states have laws to prevent corruption in lobbying. The basic idea of these laws is to make lobbying practices public so that corrupt influences will be uncovered. The Federal Regulation of Lobbying Act of 1946 requires individuals and groups trying to influence legislation to register and submit quarterly reports to Congress. They must report receipts and expenditures, and the bills in which they are interested.

Some constitutional questions may arise whenever laws limit or otherwise regulate lobbying. Such questions arise because the Constitution guarantees citizens the right of free speech and the right to petition legislators. CHARLES O. JONES

See also PROPAGANDA (Organizations).

Additional Resources

ALDERSON, GEORGE, and SENTMAN, EVERETT. *How You Can Influence Congress: The Complete Handbook for the Citizen Lobbyist.* Dutton, 1979.
CAPLAN, MARC. *Ralph Nader Presents a Citizens' Guide to Lobbying.* Dembner, 1983.
HOWE, RUSSELL W., and TROTT, S. H. *The Power Peddlers: How Lobbyists Mold America's Foreign Policy.* Doubleday, 1977.
The Washington Lobby. 4th. ed. Congressional Quarterly, 1982.

LOBEL, *LOH behl,* **ARNOLD** (1933-   ), is an American illustrator and writer of books for young children. He became known for his sensitive and humorous animal stories. Lobel won the 1981 Caldecott medal for his illustrations for *Fables* (1980), a book of animal tales he wrote. Lobel has written and illustrated a number of other books, including *Frog and Toad Are Friends* (1970), *Mouse Tales* (1972), and *Owl at Home* (1975).

Lobel has also illustrated about 40 books by other authors. Among these books are *The Comic Adventures of Old Mother Hubbard and Her Dog* (1968), *Sam the Minuteman* (1969), *Hildilid's Night* (1971), *The Clay Pot Boy* (1973), *As I Was Crossing Boston Common* (1973), and *Merry, Merry FIBruary* (1977).

Lobel was born in Los Angeles. His first book was *A Zoo for Mister Muster* (1962). MARILYN FAIN APSELOFF

See also LITERATURE FOR CHILDREN (picture: Great Illustrators of the 1900's).

LOBELIA, *loh BEEL yuh,* is the name of a group of flowers sometimes cultivated as ornamental plants. There are about 30 kinds in the United States. All lobelias produce a sharp, milky juice, and have flowers shaped like tubes flaring into two lips.

The *great lobelia* is a garden flower. It has many large blue flowers that bloom in midsummer. It grows well in moist soil. The *edging lobelia* is a low-growing annual often cultivated in window boxes. The *cardinal flower* is one of the best-known lobelias in the United States (see CARDINAL FLOWER). A lobelia called the *Indian tobacco* has blue flowers and thin leaves with toothed edges. It gets its name because North American Indians once used its dried leaves and blossoms in medicine.

Scientific Classification. Lobelias belong to the lobelia family, Lobeliaceae. The great lobelia is genus *Lobelia*, species *L. siphilitica;* the edging lobelia is *L. erinus;* the cardinal flower is *L. cardinalis;* and the Indian tobacco is *L. inflata.* MARCUS MAXON

LOBLOLLY. See PINE (Southeastern Pines; picture).

LOBSTER is a hard-shelled animal that lives on the bottom of the ocean near the shore. A stiff shell covers the lobster's entire body like a suit of armor. The animal

George H. Harrison, Bruce Coleman Inc.

An American Lobster, *above,* has thick legs and huge front claws. It uses its claws to kill and handle prey. Lobsters eat crabs, snails, small fish, and other lobsters.

has two large claws that reach out in front and are almost as long as its body. The lobster's tail spreads out behind like a fan. Most kinds of lobsters have dark green or dark blue shells with spots on them. The shells turn bright red when the lobsters are cooked.

The tasty meat of the lobster makes it a favorite seafood. Lobsters are found in both the Atlantic and Pacific oceans. But the best lobster meat comes from lobsters of the north Atlantic Ocean. In the United States and Canada, about 44,000 short tons (40,000 metric tons) of lobsters are caught annually.

Lobsters have no backbone. They belong to a group of animals called *crustaceans.* The word *crustacean* comes from a Latin word meaning *hard shell.* Other crustaceans include crabs, crayfish, and shrimp.

The Body of a Lobster

The common lobster of North America, usually called the American lobster, is 12 to 24 inches (30 to 61 centimeters) long and weighs 1 to 20 pounds (0.5 to 9 kilograms). Most European lobsters are smaller than American lobsters.

J. Laurens Barnard, the contributor of this article, is Curator of the Division of Crustacea at the National Museum of Natural History, Smithsonian Institution.

The lobster's body has 19 parts. The head has five parts, the *thorax* (center part) has eight, and the abdomen has six. Each part is covered by a section of the shell. The shell is thin and soft where the parts join, so the lobster can bend its body and move about. The lobster breathes through gills located beneath the shell on both sides of its thorax.

A lobster has two pairs of antennae on its head. The animal's eyes are on the ends of a pair of slender, jointed organs called *stalks.* Lobsters have *compound* eyes that consist of hundreds of lenses joined together. The lobster keeps its antennae and eye stalks moving constantly to search for food and to watch for enemies. The lobster's antennae, legs, and shell are covered with millions of tiny hairlike sensors that can detect chemicals. The sensors help the animal locate food.

A lobster has five pairs of jointed legs. Four pairs are thin, and the lobster uses them for walking. The fifth pair, which extend in front of the head, are thick and end in large claws. One of the claws is heavy and has thick teeth to crush prey. The other claw is smaller and has sharp teeth to tear food apart. All lobsters do not

Facts in Brief

Names: *Male,* cock; *female,* hen or chicken; *young,* none; *group,* none.
Gestation Period: 11 to 12 months.
Number of Newborn: 5,000 to 100,000 or more.
Length of Life: About 15 years.
Where Found: Atlantic Ocean, Pacific Ocean.
Scientific Classification: Lobsters belong to the class *Crustacea.* Common lobsters make up the genus *Homarus.* Spiny lobsters make up the genus *Panulirus.*

Alex Kerstitch, Black Star

A Spiny Lobster, *above,* has slender legs and claws. This kind of lobster was named for the sharp spines on its shell. It lives in coastal waters throughout much of the world.

LOBSTER

have the heavy claw on the same side. Some are "right-handed," and others are "left-handed." The front claws of the spiny lobster are long and slender. This lobster, named for the sharp spines on its shell, lives in coastal waters throughout much of the world.

The Life of a Lobster

Lobsters live on the bottom of the ocean near shore, and hide in holes or under rocks at depths of 6 to 120 feet (1.8 to 37 meters). A lobster sits in its burrow all day, waving its feelers outside the entrance. It holds its claws ready and pounces on any prey that comes near. Lobsters eat crabs, snails, small fish, and other lobsters. At night, the lobster walks along the ocean bottom looking for food. If an enemy such as a large fish or an octopus comes near, the lobster scoots back into its burrow with powerful flips of its tail.

Young. A female lobster usually lays eggs only once every two years. She may lay 5,000 to 100,000 or more eggs at a time. The number varies with her size and age. The female lobster carries the eggs under the curve of her tail for 11 to 12 months. When the eggs are ready to hatch, the lobster shakes the young out of the eggshells. Newborn lobsters are about $\frac{1}{3}$ inch (8 millimeters) long. They rise to the surface, and drift and swim about for three to five weeks. At this time, they are easy prey for sea birds, fish, and other enemies. Then the lobsters sink to the ocean bottom where they spend the rest of their lives. Lobsters live about 15 years.

Growth. Lobsters *molt* (cast off their shells) as they grow. The animal loses its first shell two days after

Roberta Deethmann, Artstreet

Lobster Pots are used to trap lobsters alive. Fishermen must empty the pots almost daily or the lobsters will attack each other.

hatching, and molts three more times during the first month. When molting, the lobster's body gives off a substance that softens the shell. Then, by expanding its muscles, the lobster splits the shell and steps out of it. This whole process takes about 15 minutes. The new shell, which had formed under the old one, is soft and gives the lobster no protection. The animal hides from its enemies until the new shell hardens.

Lobster Fishing

At one time, fishermen caught so many lobsters that the animals were in danger of dying out. Laws were passed to protect lobsters, and the animals were raised in areas where lobster fishing was forbidden.

Lobsters are caught in traps called *pots* (cages made of narrow pieces of wood or metal). A lobster can enter the pot, but cannot find the opening to get out.

A fisherman baits the trap with any kind of fish. He attaches rocks to weight the pot, and lowers it to the ocean floor. A float tied to a strong cord that is fastened to the trap shows the location of the pot. The fisherman must raise the trap and empty it every day or so. If two or more lobsters get in, they may fight and injure or kill one another. When the fisherman takes a lobster from a pot, he puts a wooden nail in the joint behind each claw to keep the claw from opening. The disarmed lobster can then be put in a container with others ready for market. J. LAURENS BARNARD

See also CRUSTACEAN; MAINE (pictures).

LOBWORM is a small sea worm with a soft body. It is also called *lugworm* or *lugbait*. Deep-sea fishermen often use this worm for bait. Lobworms are found along the Atlantic coasts of North America and Europe and around the Mediterranean Sea. They live under water, in burrows dug into the sand. During low tide, the burrows may be exposed. The lobworm's body is from 5 to 8 inches (13 to 20 centimeters) long, and is made up of rings or segments. The front end of the body is thicker than the hind end, and it is covered with bristles. The lobworm breathes with 13 pairs of tiny gills.

Scientific Classification. Lobworms are in the class *Polychaeta* and the phylum *Annelida*. JAMES A. MCLEOD

LOCAL ANESTHESIA. See ANESTHESIA.

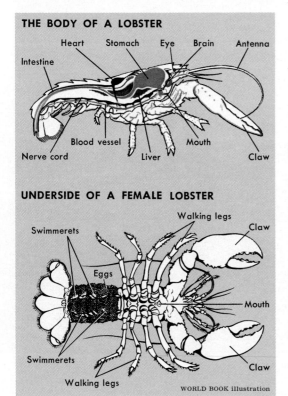

THE BODY OF A LOBSTER

Heart   Stomach   Eye   Brain   Antenna

Intestine

Blood vessel   Mouth

Nerve cord   Liver   Claw

UNDERSIDE OF A FEMALE LOBSTER

Walking legs

Swimmerets   Claw

Eggs

Mouth

Swimmerets

Claw

Walking legs

WORLD BOOK illustration

LOCAL GOVERNMENT generally refers to the government of an area smaller than a country, state, or province. Such areas include counties, cities, towns, and villages. Each unit of local government has some important responsibility for the welfare of its citizens and provides certain services. Most local governments are run by elected officials and have some power of taxation. In the United States, each state government creates and has legal control over all local governments in the state.

Traditionally, Americans have strongly supported the principle of local self-government. Some scholars argue that small local governments are more responsive to citizens' wishes than are large units of government. They also feel that local governments encourage people to become involved in the life of their community. Other scholars believe that local governments have certain weaknesses. One of the main weaknesses, they claim, is that an individual local unit often cannot deal effectively with such problems as transportation and pollution when they require the cooperation of other local units in the area.

This article deals mainly with local governments in the United States. The last section discusses local governments in other countries.

Units of Local Government

The United States has about 82,500 units of local government. There are five types of local governments: (1) *counties*, (2) *municipalities*, (3) *school districts*, (4) *special districts*, and (5) *townships*.

The county is the largest unit of local government in most states. The United States has more than 3,000 counties. In Louisiana, these units are called *parishes*.

There are about 19,000 municipalities in the United States, including cities, villages, and townlike units called *boroughs*. They lie within each county, or extend into two or more counties. Municipalities, often called *city governments*, are chartered by state governments to provide such services as police and fire protection.

School districts are responsible for running public school systems. There are about 15,000 school districts in the United States. Most school districts operate independently of city governments. The city governments of New York City and a few other communities in the Northeast operate their own public school systems.

Special districts are organized to provide one or more public services, such as mosquito control or transportation. There are about 29,000 special districts in the United States. The governing boards of these districts have authority to levy taxes and to spend public money.

The United States has about 17,000 towns and townships, most of which are subdivisions of a county. These governmental units perform few functions today. Most states have transferred town and township responsibilities to the county governments.

Functions of Local Government

Most of the activities of local government in the United States can be classified into three main groups: (1) health and safety functions, (2) welfare functions, and (3) housekeeping functions.

Health and Safety Functions of local government in the United States began with law enforcement by local police forces and through local courts. Today, most local governments also have responsibility for fighting fires, immunizing people against contagious diseases, and providing and maintaining hospital services, local roads, garbage collection, and safe drinking water. In addition, they conduct inspections and educational campaigns in the areas of health, housing, traffic safety, sanitation, and fire prevention. They are also concerned with reducing air pollution and water pollution.

Welfare Functions. Early in U.S. history, local governments began to provide public education. Today, they spend more money on education than on any other function. Local governments also provide libraries, museums, parks and other recreational and athletic facilities, and buses and subways for mass transportation. They cooperate with other levels of government in providing public housing for low-income families. Many local governments have zoning restrictions to protect and promote the beauty and land values in their area. Many also try to stimulate economic growth by attracting business and industry to their area.

Providing health, safety, and welfare services is an important part of the American political process. Such questions as how much to spend for schools or whether to allow a factory to be built in a certain part of the city often cause conflicts among citizens and groups. Such conflicts can be resolved only through the political process. In this process, individual citizens, organized groups, and influential leaders try to persuade and pressure government officials into making the decisions they want. But whatever decisions are made, usually some people will be pleased and others will be dissatisfied.

Housekeeping Functions are administrative activities. They are essential to the function of a governmental unit but are not part of its main activities. One housekeeping function is keeping official records of births, deaths, marriages, and property transfers and assessments. Local governments also collect taxes, hire public agency workers, and administer elections.

Relations with Higher Levels of Government

Government in the United States operates on three levels—national, state, and local. The U.S. Constitution grants certain powers to the federal and state governments, but it does not mention local governments. State legislatures, unless restricted by their state constitutions, may have complete control over local governments. The states may specify what activities local governments can undertake, as well as the kinds of taxes and tax rates they can levy. About half the states allow local governments to decide their own form of organization and to have considerable freedom in local matters. Such self-government is called *home rule*.

All three levels of government have increased their activities to deal with the growing problems of society. As a result, they share authority and responsibility in such matters as finance, education, and welfare. Many local governments receive a type of financial assistance called *grants-in-aid* from state governments to help pay for specific projects. Local governments—especially those of big cities—have also become increasingly dependent on federal aid. They receive federal grants directly or through payments transferred from their state government. In many cases, federal aid is provided only

LOCAL GOVERNMENT

if local governments agree to follow state or federal requirements. Other federal aid takes the form of *revenue sharing*. The federal government provides such funds without specifying how the money should be spent.

Issues Confronting Local Governments

Local governments face many problems in trying to provide services for their residents. Such problems as unemployment and inadequate community services have sometimes led to violent conflicts. During the 1960's, riots broke out in the black ghettos of such cities as Detroit, Los Angeles, and Cleveland. In 1980, a similar riot erupted in Miami. Blacks in the riot areas were disturbed about their few job opportunities, bad housing, and inferior schools. Several riots were also triggered by what blacks felt was unfair treatment by the police or courts. The most serious problems of local governments include population changes, financial problems, and conflicts in authority.

Population Changes. For the first 200 years of U.S. history, cities had to deal with the widespread movement of people from rural areas to the city. This development, called *urbanization*, strained local governments, which had to provide schools and other services for their increasing populations. Today, about three-fourths of the U.S. population live in metropolitan areas. Urbanization seems to be ending, and small towns and rural areas have begun to gain people.

During the 1900's, urbanization was especially strong among black Americans. In 1910, about 10 per cent of black Americans lived in urban areas. In 1980, about 60 per cent of blacks lived in urban areas. At the same time that blacks were moving to the city, many whites were leaving the city to settle in the suburbs. The migration of people to suburban areas, called *suburbanization*, created many problems for local governments. For example, the movement of businesses to the suburbs reduced job opportunities for inner-city residents.

The most recent population change affecting local governments is a regional shift involving the movement of people from the Northeast to the South and Southwest. For example, between 1950 and 1980, the population of Pittsburgh decreased by 37 per cent and that of Boston by 30 per cent. During the same period, the population of Houston grew by 167 per cent and that of Los Angeles by 51 per cent. Because of this shift, some local governments must deal with problems of growth while others suffer from a declining population and the loss of industries.

Financial Problems. Traditionally, the most important source of revenue for local governments has been property taxes. Local governments collect these taxes from homeowners, businesses, and other owners of taxable property. The amount of tax is based on the estimated value of the property. Many people object to property taxes. They point out that standards for *assessing* (determining the value of) property vary from city to city and from one assessor to another. Many people also believe that property ownership is a poor measure of the ability to pay taxes.

People in many parts of the United States have protested the taxes collected by local governments. For example, in 1978, California voters approved an amendment to the state constitution that reduced property taxes. This amendment was called *Proposition 13* because of its position on the ballot. As a result of its approval, many local governments in the state reduced services and laid off workers.

All municipalities have become more dependent on grants-in-aid and revenue sharing from the state and federal governments. Some local governments have financial troubles despite aid from the higher levels of government. A few cities, including Cleveland and New York City, have come close to bankruptcy. Such financial problems are more severe in Northern cities that have lost many people and businesses.

Conflicts in Authority. Almost every metropolitan area has a bewildering variety of local governments. The Philadelphia area has about 900 local governments. Chicago has more than 750, and Houston has more than 550. No one local government may have sufficient power to solve certain problems, and the different authorities with overlapping jurisdictions may find it difficult to work with one another.

Many experts on government believe that small, ineffective local units should be *consolidated* (combined) into larger, more efficient ones. At one time, cities solved part of this problem by *annexing* (adding) surrounding suburbs as the cities grew. But today, most large cities are surrounded by incorporated suburbs which the central city government could not annex if it wished to do so.

In some areas, citizens have tried to bring the central city and the suburbs under one government. This *metropolitan government* would be responsible for police protection, water supply, mass transportation, and other services that might be handled best by an areawide authority. The metropolitan areas of Miami and Jacksonville, Fla., and Nashville, Tenn., have metropolitan governments. However, most American voters have rejected such consolidation proposals because they fear higher taxes and because they believe that only small local governments can remain close to the people.

Although some citizens have worked for consolidation, others—especially those in large urban ghettos—have fought for more local control. Some blacks and members of other minority groups have demanded *decentralization* (splitting up) of authority to give neighborhood residents a greater say in controlling their own affairs and providing community services.

Local Government in Other Countries

Local government takes various forms in different countries. The degree of local authority and independence also varies from nation to nation. In some countries, governmental authority has been decentralized so that many important decisions are made at the local level. In other countries, authority is centralized in the national government. Most countries have either a *federal* or a *unitary* system of government.

Federal Systems divide the powers of government between the national government and the state or provincial governments. In most cases, the powers are set forth in a constitution. Although the state and provincial governments have legal control over local governments, they may give some authority to local units. Australia, Canada, Switzerland, the United States, and West Germany have federal systems of government. Local governments usually have more authority under federal systems than they have under unitary systems.

Unitary Systems give most of the chief powers to the central government. All local, state, and provincial governments are subject to control by the central government. They have only those powers that the central government gives them. Denmark, Great Britain, Norway, and Sweden have unitary systems of government. In these countries, local areas have considerable self-government, though they are under the central government's control. They have broad taxing powers and much authority for providing education, housing, and transportation.

In France, which also has a unitary system, the central government has strict and detailed control over local government units. However, local elected assemblies have some powers once held by a *prefect* (administrator) appointed by the central government. Italy and a few Latin-American countries still use prefects to supervise local governments. The prefects can veto actions of the local government. The people elect local councils in France and Italy. In France, the local council chooses a mayor from among its members. In Italy, the people elect the mayor.

Local Government in Communist Countries. In most Communist systems of government, decision making is highly centralized at the national level. Local governments operate almost completely according to the requirements of the central government. In the Soviet Union, for example, officials of the central government specify in great detail the activities of local governments and keep close watch over local administrators. The Soviet Union appears to have a federal system, but countries that allow only one political party or are under military rule actually have a unitary system. Yugoslavia and a few other Communist nations have taken some steps toward greater decentralization and local self-government.

Local Government in Developing Countries faces especially severe problems. Many developing nations have one or a few extremely large cities where rural families flock in search of jobs. In Lima, Peru, and other cities, many newcomers live on the fringes of the city. The population of such cities increases rapidly, severely straining many public services. Many local governments in these countries have little money to provide schools, sanitation systems, and other services to their residents. Local officials often must appeal to state or national governments for assistance.   ROBERT L. LINEBERRY

Related Articles. See CITY GOVERNMENT and its list of *Related Articles*. See also the following articles:

Canton	Home Rule	Sheriff
Constable	School (Public	Sunshine Laws
County	School Districts)	Township

Additional Resources

DANIELSON, MICHAEL N., and others. *One Nation, So Many Governments*. Lexington, 1977.

MARTIN, DAVID L. *Running City Hall: Municipal Administration in America*. Univ. of Alabama Press, 1982.

TINDALL, C. R. and S. N. *Local Government in Canada: An Introduction*. McGraw (Toronto), 1979.

LOCAL OPTION means *local choice*. The term refers particularly to the right of any political division to determine for itself the conditions under which intoxicating liquors shall be sold. The privilege temporarily lost its force during the period of national prohibition. A

township, city, county, or state may now again determine by vote whether or not liquor is to be sold. If liquor is to be sold, it can decide under what conditions. An act of legislature is required to give the right of local option to the people. Authority is then granted to the communities to determine the liquor and tavern question according to local opinion. The legislature names the smallest political district in which local option may be used. A majority vote by the eligible voters in the district determines the choice. In Canada, provincial government control of liquor prevails. An exception is the province of Quebec, where the license system is in force. See also PROHIBITION.   JOHN A. KROUT

LOCARNO CONFERENCE, *loh KAHR noh*, resulted in the Rhineland Security Pact and six other treaties. In October 1925, representatives of seven European countries met in Locarno, Switzerland, to discuss plans for building permanent peace in Europe. Delegates came from Belgium, Czechoslovakia, France, Germany, Great Britain, Italy, and Poland. The most important problem of the conference was to find a settlement between France and Germany. For the first time since World War I, the conference treated Germany as a friendly nation. When the conference ended on Oct. 16, 1925, the delegates had signed seven treaties.

The Rhineland Security Pact developed as the most important of these treaties. Belgium, France, Germany, Great Britain, and Italy signed the pact. Belgium, France, and Germany agreed never to fight each other again. Germany agreed to join the League of Nations. The treaty set up a neutral zone in the Rhineland, an area covering Belgian, French, and German soil. All signing powers vowed to guarantee the frontier between France and Germany and between Belgium and Germany. This meant that if Germany attacked France, the other nations would go to the aid of France.

The six other Locarno Conference treaties bound the participating nations to the peaceful settlement of international quarrels. Each country promised to discuss its problems before resorting to war.

In 1936, Germany denounced the Locarno treaties and sent its troops into the neutral Rhineland. The other Locarno powers did not act to prevent the aggressions that brought on World War II.   NORMAN D. PALMER

LOCH LOMOND, *lahk LOH muhnd*, is the largest and one of the most famous of the Scottish lakes. The lake

Loch Lomond

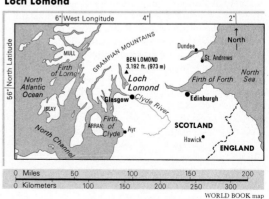

WORLD BOOK map

LOCH NESS MONSTER

lies about 20 miles (32 kilometers) northwest of Glasgow in the Scottish highlands. Loch Lomond is in a hilly region, and its waters have many islands. The lake is 23 miles (37 kilometers) long and 5 miles (8 kilometers) wide at its widest point. One of the most familiar Scottish folk songs is about Loch Lomond. In ancient days, Scottish clans gathered for meetings at the edge of this lake.   JOHN W. WEBB

LOCH NESS MONSTER, *lahk,* is a large animal that some people believe lives in Loch Ness, a lake in northern Scotland. If such a creature exists, it avoids people. But hundreds of persons have reported seeing the animal, which is nicknamed "Nessie." They describe it as measuring up to 30 feet (9 meters) long. The creature

Wide World

The Loch Ness Monster may be the dark form in this photograph, taken in 1934 by R. Kenneth Wilson, a British physician.

supposedly has flippers, one or two humps, and a long, slender neck. Some scientists think Nessie may be related to a dinosaurlike reptile or to a modern sea animal, such as the manatee or seal.

The earliest known description of a strange creature in Loch Ness dates from A.D. 565. Reported sightings increased during the 1930's, when a new highway made the lake more accessible to travelers.

In 1960, a British aircraft engineer named Tim Dinsdale made a short film of a dark shape moving through Loch Ness. Aerial photography experts from Great Britain's Royal Air Force reported that the film probably showed an "animate object"— that is, a living thing. Since then, several scientific expeditions have explored the waters of the lake. Investigations with *sonar,* a device that uses sound to detect underwater objects, have found large moving bodies in Loch Ness.

In 1972 and 1975, researchers from the Academy of Applied Science in Boston took underwater photographs of what they claimed was the Loch Ness monster. However, experts do not agree on exactly what the photographs show. The Loch Ness monster has been given the scientific name *Nessiteras rhombopteryx* so it can be protected by a British law that safeguards rare animals.   ROY P. MACKAL

Additional Resources

COSTELLO, PETER. *In Search of Lake Monsters.* Coward, 1974.

DINSDALE, TIM. *Loch Ness Monster.* 3rd ed. Routledge & Kegan, 1976.
MACKAL, ROY P. *The Monsters of Loch Ness: The First Complete Scientific Study and Its Startling Conclusions.* Swallow, 1976.

LOCHNER V. NEW YORK, *LAHK nuhr,* was a 1905 case in which the Supreme Court of the United States upheld the right of employer and employee to contract for hours and wages without government interference. The decision reflected the *laissez-faire* view that government should control business and industry as little as possible. A New York state law limited bakers to a 60-hour work week. By a 5-to-4 majority, the Supreme Court declared the law unconstitutional because it interfered with the "liberty of contract." This interpretation was a vague idea that some lawyers and judges derived from the 14th Amendment to the Constitution. Justice Oliver Wendell Holmes, in a dissenting opinion, said the ruling was based on "an economic theory which a large part of the country does not entertain." In 1908, the court modified its opinion, but it retained the same basic theory until 1937.   STANLEY I. KUTLER

LOCK, in canal construction. See CANAL (Canal Locks; pictures).

LOCK is a device that prevents a door or other objects from being opened or moved. People use locks to help protect themselves and to help guard their property against theft. For example, door locks provide protection for homes, and bicycle locks prevent the theft of bicycles.

There are many kinds of locks, and nearly all require a key to be opened. Types of locks that do not require a key include combination locks, time locks, chain locks, and some electronic door locks. Combination locks are opened by turning a dial to the correct combination of numbers. Time locks, a type of combination lock, can be opened only at a specific time at which the lock has been set. Chain locks have a metal chain that fastens to the inside surface of a door and to the doorframe. Electronic door locks open when a person inserts a coded plastic card into a slot beside the door.

Locks provide maximum security only when used on sturdy objects. A bicycle lock offers little protection against the theft of a bike if its chain can be easily cut or removed.

How Door Locks Work

All door locks have some type of *bolt* that prevents the door from being opened. In most door locks, the

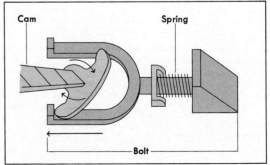

WORLD BOOK diagram by Zorica Dabich

The Bolt of a door lock slides back and forth. A long piece of metal called a *cam* controls the movement of the bolt.

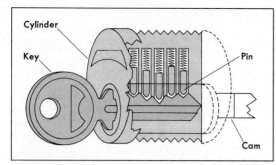

The Key is inserted into the cylinder-locking mechanism. The grooves of the key force the pins of the mechanism to align. This action frees the key to turn and thus activate the cam.

bolt slides into a metal plate in the doorframe. A long, narrow piece of metal called a *cam* controls the movement of the bolt. The cam is fastened to a *cylinder-locking mechanism* in the door.

People use a key to operate a door lock from the outside. They lock and unlock a door from the inside by turning a knob or a key. When a person inserts the proper key in a door lock, the grooves of the key force metal pins or plates called *tumblers* to align. When the tumblers are in line, the key is free to turn and activate the cam. The cam moves the bolt between the door and the doorframe.

The bolts used in most door locks are either *spring bolts* or *deadbolts*. Spring bolts are the most common type of bolt. They are convenient to use because they do not require a key to be locked. Spring bolts simply snap into the doorframe when the door closes and are held in place by a metal spring. However, locks with spring bolts do not provide good security because they can easily be opened without a key. Some spring bolts can be pried open by slipping a thin object between the door and the doorframe.

Deadbolts are the most secure type of bolt. Most of them are mounted into a steel frame on the inside surface of a door. These kinds of deadbolts lock with a key on the outside and by turning a small knob on the inside. Other deadbolts are set in the door and controlled by the cam. They are "dead" because they cannot be pried open.

Kinds of Locks

The most common locks are (1) mortise locks, (2) rim locks, (3) cylindrical locks, (4) tubular locks, (5) combination locks, and (6) padlocks. Each has its own shape and design, and each works differently.

Mortise Locks have the locking mechanism *mortised* (cut) into the door. The doorknobs screw into the locking mechanism. Mortise locks have either spring bolts, deadbolts, or both. A deadbolt measuring about 1 inch (2.5 centimeters) long provides the maximum amount of security. A key unlocks the door from the outside, and a small knob or a key unlocks it from the inside. Mortise locks are extremely strong when installed in a sturdy door.

Rim Locks provide additional security to doors already equipped with one or more other locks. They have a bolt mechanism mounted into a frame on the inside surface of the door.

Rim locks have a round cylinder that is set in the door. A connecting bar extends through the door and connects the cylinder with the deadbolt. Rim locks open with a key on the outside and by turning a knob or key inside.

Cylindrical Locks are the type most commonly found on household doors. These kinds of locks are often called *knob locks* because the cylinder-locking mechanism is part of the doorknob. Cylindrical locks have a keyhole in the doorknob.

Most cylindrical locks have a spring bolt. Some, called *pick-resistant locks*, have deadbolts. A key unlocks

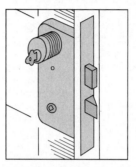

A Mortise Lock is cut into a door. The lock shown has a spring bolt and a deadbolt.

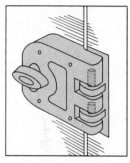

A Rim Lock has a bolt enclosed in a frame mounted on the inside surface of the door.

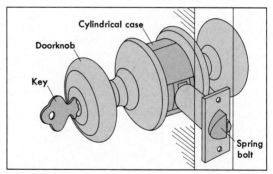

A Cylindrical, or Knob, Lock has a locking mechanism that is part of the doorknob. Most of these locks have a spring bolt.

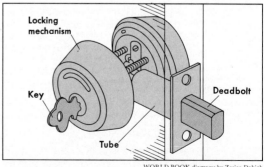

WORLD BOOK diagrams by Zorica Dabich

A Tubular Lock has a bolt encased in a tube that is attached to the locking mechanism. Most tubular locks have a deadbolt.

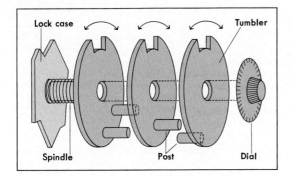

A Combination Lock has a dial that is connected to tumblers inside the lock case. As the dial is turned to the correct combination, the tumblers are aligned and the bolt is released.

WORLD BOOK diagrams by Zorica Dabich

A Padlock is a portable lock that has a steel case containing the locking mechanism. Padlocks require either a combination, *above*, or a key to release the *shackle* and open the lock.

the door from the outside, and a small knob or a key unlocks it from the inside.

Tubular Locks have a bolt—in most cases a deadbolt—that is enclosed in a tube attached to the locking mechanism. The deadbolt provides additional security for doors that also have a cylindrical lock.

Combination Locks have a movable dial with a series of numbers around it. To release the lock, a person must turn the dial left and right in a sequence of three or four numbers. The numbers, and the direction in which the dial is turned, make up the lock's *combination*. Most floor safes and wall safes are protected by combination locks.

A combination lock has disk-shaped tumblers. The tumblers are aligned with a bolt-release mechanism as the dial is turned to the correct combination. The bolt is released after the tumblers are aligned.

Thieves can easily *pick* (unlock) most inexpensive combination locks. They simply listen for the clicking noise of a tumbler being aligned with the bolt-release mechanism.

Padlocks are portable locks that require either a key or a combination to be opened. People use padlocks to fasten two objects together or to help protect such objects as bicycles, lockers, and trunks.

Padlocks have a steel case that contains the locking mechanism. A curved revolving bar called a *shackle* extends up from the case and fastens around the object. To activate the lock, a person pushes the bar through a hole in the case.

Other Kinds of Locks include *time locks* and *electrical switchlocks*. Time locks are a type of combination lock used mainly in bank vaults. Most time locks have automatic locking bolts that are activated by a timing device.

Electrical switchlocks generate electricity when the key is turned. As a person turns the key in the ignition lock of an automobile, for example, an electric current flows from the battery to the starter.

History

The first key-operated lock was invented in ancient Egypt about 2000 B.C. It consisted of a large wooden bolt that was fastened to the outside of a gate. Pegs called *pins* were inserted into holes in the bolt and pre-

vented it from being moved. A key raised the pins out of the holes so the bolt could be moved, thus opening the gate.

Later, locks were developed according to three basic locking principles: (1) the warded principle, (2) the lever principle, and (3) the pin-tumbler principle. The ancient Romans invented the warded principle. In padlocks and other warded locks, the mechanism contains a series of *wards* (obstacles) that the key must pass in order to unlock the bolt. Warded locks were the most common locks until the mid-1800's, and many are still used.

The lever principle was developed in the late 1700's. Lever locks have one or more levers in their mechanism. The levers must be raised to a specific height before the bolt can be removed. Only the correct key can raise the levers to precisely the height needed to remove the bolt.

The modern pin-tumbler lock was invented in 1865 by an American locksmith named Linus Yale, Jr. It was based on a principle similar to that of the ancient Egyptian lock. The pin-tumbler lock, used in most doors today, is one of the most secure key-operated locks ever invented. It also was the first lock to be mass-produced.   GLENN K. HARTMAN

See also TIME LOCK; YALE, LINUS, JR.

LOCK HAVEN UNIVERSITY. See UNIVERSITIES AND COLLEGES (table).

LOCKE, ALAIN LEROY (1886-1954), was an American educator and a writer on black culture. From 1912 to 1953, he taught philosophy at Howard University. His works include *The Negro in America* (1933), *The Negro and His Music* (1936), *Negro Art—Past and Present* (1937), and *When Peoples Meet* (1941). In 1942, he was selected in a poll as one of the most distinguished blacks of the year. Born in Philadelphia, Locke studied at Oxford, Berlin, and Harvard universities.   JOHN O. EIDSON

LOCKE, DAVID ROSS. See NASBY, PETROLEUM VESUVIUS.

LOCKE, JOHN (1632-1704), was an English philosopher. His writings have had great influence on political science as well as on philosophy. Locke's book *Two Treatises of Government* (1690) strongly influenced Thomas Jefferson in the writing of the Declaration of Independence.

His Life. Locke was born in Wrington in Somerset County. He attended Oxford University. In 1666, he met Anthony Ashley Cooper, who later became the first Earl of Shaftesbury. The two men became close friends. In 1679, the earl became involved in plots against the king, and suspicion also fell on Locke. The philosopher decided to leave England. In 1683, he moved to The Netherlands, where he met Prince William and Princess Mary of Orange. William and Mary became the rulers of England in 1689, and Locke returned to England as a court favorite. Until his death, he wrote widely on such subjects as educational reform, freedom of the press, and religious tolerance.

His Philosophy. Locke's major work was *An Essay Concerning Human Understanding* (1690). It describes his theory of how the mind functions in learning about the world. Locke argued against the doctrine of innate ideas, which stated that ideas were part of the mind at birth and not learned or acquired later from outside sources. Locke claimed that all ideas were placed in the mind by experience. He declared that there were two kinds of experience, outer and inner. Outer experience was acquired through the senses of sight, taste, hearing, smell, and touch, which provide information about the external world. Inner experience was acquired by thinking about the mental processes involved in sifting these data, which furnished information about the mind.

Locke believed that the universe contained three kinds of things—minds, various types of bodies, and God. Bodies had two kinds of properties. One kind was mathematically measurable, such as length and weight, and existed in the bodies themselves. The second kind was qualitative, such as sound and color. These properties were not in the bodies themselves but were simply powers that bodies had to produce ideas of colors and sounds in the mind.

According to Locke, a good life was a life of pleasure. Pleasure and pain were simple ideas that accompanied nearly all human experiences. Ethical action involved determining which act in a given situation would produce the greatest pleasure—and then performing that act. Locke also believed that God had established divine law. This law could be discovered by reason, and to disobey it was morally wrong. Locke thought that divine law and the pleasure principle were compatible.

Locke believed that people by nature had certain rights and duties. These rights included liberty, life, and ownership of property. By liberty, Locke meant political equality. The task of any state was to protect people's rights. States inconvenience people in various ways. Therefore, the justification for a state's existence had to be found in its ability to protect human rights better than individuals could on their own. Locke declared that if a government did not adequately protect the rights of its citizens, they had the right to find other rulers. He believed that the people should decide who governs them. STEPHEN A. ERICKSON

See also CIVIL RIGHTS (Natural Rights); DEMOCRACY (Democracy in England); EMPIRICISM; PHILOSOPHY (Modern Philosophy).

Additional Resources

AARON, RICHARD I. *John Locke.* 3rd ed. Oxford, 1971.
CRANSTON, MAURICE W. *John Locke: A Biography.* Arno, 1979. Reprint of 1957 ed.

VAUGHN, KAREN I. *John Locke: Economist and Social Scientist.* Univ. of Chicago Press, 1980.
YOLTON, JOHN W. *Locke and the Compass of Human Understanding.* Cambridge, 1970.

LOCKJAW. See TETANUS.

LOCKOUT occurs when an employer closes a plant in order to keep employees from working. The employer is using the economic weapon of a work and wage stoppage to get employees to agree to some particular condition of work or wages. The lockout is like the *strike* in that it is an economic weapon used in labor disputes. The lockout differs from the strike, however, because the strike is a work stoppage that the employees themselves start in order to compel the employer to meet certain demands.

Lockouts, like strikes, are usually caused by wage disputes. But the number of lockouts is far less than the number of strikes. Lockouts make up only about 3 to 4 per cent of the total number of work stoppages that occur. The reason the percentage is so low is that employers have more direct and effective means of placing economic pressure on workers, such as discharging workers involved in labor disputes. ROBERT D. PATTON

See also STRIKE (Kinds of Strikes).

LOCKWOOD, BELVA ANN BENNETT (1830-1917), was a reformer and woman-suffrage leader. She was one of the few women nominated for President of the United States. She taught school for many years, and became a lawyer in 1873. She worked for women's rights, and won equal pay for women government employees and a law allowing women to practice before the Supreme Court. She also success-

Brown Bros.

Belva Lockwood

fully defended land rights of the North Carolina Cherokee Indians. In 1884 and 1888, the Equal Rights party nominated her for President. She was born in Royalton, N. Y. LOUIS FILLER

LOCKWOOD, LORNA. See ARIZONA (The Mid-1900's).

LOCO-FOCOS was a nickname given in 1835 to the radical members of the New York Democratic party.

In October, 1835, New York Democrats held a meeting in Tammany Hall. The radical Democrats spoke against favoritism in banking laws. They wanted to form an organization to fight that kind of legislation. The conservative party members were not strong enough to stop the proposal. They turned out the lights and left the hall. Members of the radical faction used phosphorus friction matches, newly invented and called "loco-focos," to light candles, and continued the meeting. The Democratic press immediately named the reform Democrats "loco-focos." JOHN R. ALDEN

LOCOMOTION, in zoology, is the act of animals moving about. See ANIMAL (How Animals Move About); INSECT (The Bodies of Insects); MAMMAL (How Mammals Move).

Santa Fe Railway

Diesel Locomotives pull most freight and passenger trains and handle most yard-switching work. The diesel-electric, *above*, is the most widely used kind of diesel in the world.

Amtrak

Electric Locomotives run on power supplied by an electric power plant. These locomotives are especially useful for hauling high-speed passenger trains or fast, heavy freight trains.

LOCOMOTIVE is a machine that moves trains on railroad tracks. Early locomotives weighed from 3 to 6 short tons (2.7 to 5.4 metric tons) and could pull or push only a few light cars. A modern locomotive may weigh over 700 short tons (640 metric tons) and move more than 200 loaded freight cars at a time.

Locomotives designed to haul freight or passenger trains are called *road locomotives*. A *yard switcher locomotive* moves cars from track to track in railroad yards. A *general purpose locomotive* can be used to haul trains or for yard switching.

There are three main kinds of locomotives, depending on their source of power: (1) diesel, (2) electric, and (3) steam. A fourth kind, powered by machines called *gas turbines*, once hauled some freight in the United States. Railroads no longer use such locomotives, but gas turbines do power certain high-speed, lightweight passenger trains called *turbotrains*. Such turbines resemble those used in aircraft. Turbotrains do not have locomotives. Instead, their power units are built into one or more of the cars.

Steam locomotives once pulled most railroad trains,

and they are still used in some countries. But in the United States, diesel locomotives have replaced other kinds almost entirely. In the mid-1970's, U.S. railroads operated about 27,000 diesels and about 200 electric locomotives. About 100 steam locomotives remained in operation. They were used chiefly to pull tourist trains.

Kinds of Locomotives

Diesel Locomotives are actually traveling power plants. They have a diesel engine that works by compressing air in chambers called *cylinders*. When air is compressed, its temperature rises. The resulting heat ignites fuel that has been injected into the cylinder. The power produced during this process is then transmitted to the locomotive's driving wheels. For more detailed information on how a diesel engine works, see the WORLD BOOK article on DIESEL ENGINE.

Diesel locomotives have a number of advantages. They generate their own power and therefore can operate anywhere that there are rails. Diesel locomotives can also make long runs without refueling or servicing. They can be quickly stopped or started, and they speed

HISTORIC LOCOMOTIVES Many early locomotives contributed to the development of today's streamlined models.

The First Locomotive was a simple steam engine built by Richard Trevithick of England. It made its first run in 1804.

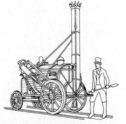

The *Rocket*, the first truly successful steam locomotive, was built by George Stephenson of England in 1829.

The *Stourbridge Lion*, a steam engine, in 1829 became the first full-sized locomotive to run on rails in North America.

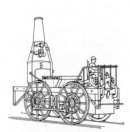

The *Best Friend of Charleston*, the first U.S. steam locomotive put in regular service, began operating in 1830.

Eric Wheater, Tom Stack & Associates

Steam Locomotives hauled nearly all trains before the invention of the diesel. Today, such steam engines as the one above still provide train service in some parts of the world.

up faster than steam engines. They also have a higher fuel efficiency than steam locomotives, require less servicing, and cost less to maintain.

A diesel locomotive may be a combination of one to four or more connecting units. These units are of two general types, called A and B. An *A unit* is designed and equipped for use by itself or as a lead unit when a number of units are combined. A *B unit* does not have the engineer's cab and controls needed to serve as a lead unit, and it is capable of only limited independent movement. A diesel locomotive may consist of a single A unit or of two, three, four, or more A and B units coupled together.

In the United States, railroads often use locomotives with six or even more units to pull heavy trains at high speeds or on mountain grades. Sometimes one or more *radio remote control units* are also used on extremely long trains. These units are placed near the middle of the train. The engineer controls them by radio signals from his cab, which is located in the lead unit at the front of the train.

Diesel locomotive units range from 400 to 6,600

horsepower (300 to 4,920 kilowatts) each. Most of those in freight and passenger train service run from 1,500 to 3,000 horsepower (1,120 to 2,200 kilowatts). Two 3,000-horsepower units coupled together make a 6,000-horsepower locomotive.

There are three types of diesel locomotives: (1) diesel-electric, (2) diesel-hydraulic, and (3) diesel-mechanical. Each transmits power from the engine to the driving wheels in a different way.

Diesel-Electric Locomotives are by far the most common type. Almost all locomotives in the United States are diesel-electrics. In these locomotives, the engine drives a machine called a *generator*, which produces an electric current. The current is then fed to *traction motors*, which drive gears that turn the locomotive's driving wheels.

Most diesel-electrics have generators that produce *direct current* (DC), a kind of current that flows in only one direction. Generators on some newer, large diesels produce *alternating current* (AC), which reverses direction many times every second. Most diesels have traction motors that operate on direct current. Therefore, locomotives with an AC generator must *rectify* (convert) the alternating current into direct current before it goes to the motors. Devices called *silicon rectifiers* perform this conversion.

Diesel-Hydraulic Locomotives. In this type of locomotive, the engine drives a *torque converter* instead of a generator. A torque converter is a device that uses fluids under hydraulic pressure to transmit and regulate power received from the engine. The converter includes a pump and a turbine. The turbine changes energy from the fluids into a force that can be used to perform work. The engine delivers oil to the converter and drives the pump. The pump forces the oil against the blades of the turbine. This action causes the turbine to rotate and to drive a system of gears and shafts that move the wheels.

Diesel-hydraulic locomotives are not used in the United States. However, they are widely used in some other countries, especially in Germany, where they first appeared.

Diesel-Mechanical Locomotives transmit power from the engine in much the same way that automobiles do—through a clutch and a system of gears and shafts. The clutch connects the engine to the transmission. The

The General, a Confederate steam locomotive, became famous after Union troops captured it in 1862, during the Civil War.

Engine 382 was the locomotive driven by the famous Casey Jones, who in 1900 gave his life to save his passengers.

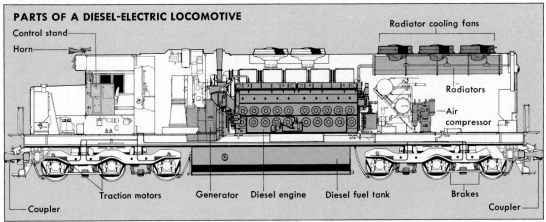

PARTS OF A DIESEL-ELECTRIC LOCOMOTIVE

Control stand
Horn
Radiator cooling fans
Radiators
Air compressor
Traction motors
Generator
Diesel engine
Diesel fuel tank
Brakes
Coupler
Coupler

Electro-Motive Division of General Motors Corporation (WORLD BOOK diagram)

Inside a Diesel-Electric Locomotive, a diesel engine turns a generator. Electricity produced by the generator runs traction motors that drive the wheels. An engineer regulates power and speed at the control stand, and the air compressor powers the brakes. The radiator equipment keeps the engine from overheating. Couplers connect the locomotive with other units.

gears and shafts fit together to transmit the power and drive the wheels. This mechanical drive delivers less power than do other systems, and so it works well only on small locomotives.

Electric Locomotives, unlike diesels, do not produce their own power. They use electric power supplied by a central power plant that may be miles away. Therefore, an electric locomotive needs special wires or rails from which it can get power.

Most electric locomotives in the United States use alternating current. They obtain the power from an overhead wire called a *catenary*. A hinged steel framework called a *pantograph*, which conducts electricity, connects this wire with the locomotive. Locomotives that operate on alternating current receive power at extremely high voltages. They have a device called a *transformer* that reduces the voltage to a level at which it can be used. The power is then fed into AC traction motors, or it is rectified and fed into DC traction motors.

Some locomotives that operate on direct current also obtain power by way of a catenary and pantograph. Other DC locomotives use an *electrical third rail*, which runs parallel to the regular rails. A metal device called a *contact shoe* is attached to these locomotives. The

shoe slides along the rail and picks up electricity from it.

An electrified rail network costs a tremendous sum to build because of the wires and other special equipment involved. However, electric locomotives can draw vast amounts of power from their central power plant. Diesels, on the other hand, are limited to the power they can produce themselves. Electric locomotives can be started instantly. They also are quiet and produce no smoke or exhaust gases. Therefore, they are sometimes used in heavily populated areas and on railroads that run underground or through long tunnels.

Like diesels, most electric locomotives can operate either singly or combined in groups of two or more units. However, electric locomotives can produce more power per unit than diesels can. Therefore, electric locomotives are especially useful for fast, heavy freight trains or high-speed passenger trains.

Many kinds of fuel can be used by a power plant to produce the electricity that runs an electric locomotive. For example, a power plant may use coal, gas, oil, water power, or atomic power. Diesel locomotives can run only on diesel oil, which someday may become scarce and costly. For this reason, some U.S. trans-

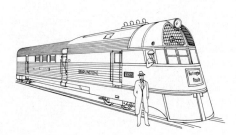

The Burlington *Zephyr* was the first streamlined passenger diesel in the United States. It went into operation in 1934.

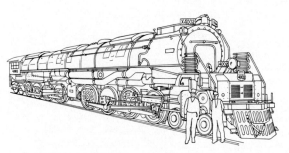

The *Big Boy,* a Union Pacific Railroad engine, was the largest steam locomotive in history. It was built in the early 1940's.

portation experts believe that electrification of the nation's railroads may in time become widespread.

Steam Locomotives produce heat by burning coal or fuel oil in a *firebox*. The heat turns the water in the locomotive's *boiler* into steam, which is fed into cylinders. There, the pressure produced by the steam drives steel rods called *pistons*. The pistons are connected to *piston rods*, *main rods*, and *side rods*, which move the driving wheels. A steam locomotive has an attached car called a *tender* that carries the fuel and water.

Steam locomotives have several disadvantages. For example, a steam locomotive needs frequent care, especially to keep the fire burning in the boiler. A long time is required to light the fire and to heat the boiler so that steam can be produced. In addition, steam locomotives cannot maintain the high average speeds of diesel or electric locomotives. They also have low fuel efficiency. A steam locomotive must burn large amounts of fuel to produce power, but little of the heat produced is used to run the locomotive. The rest is wasted.

History

Richard Trevithick of England invented the steam locomotive in 1804. In 1825, Colonel John Stevens built the first steam locomotive in the United States. This locomotive, an experimental model, ran on a circular track at Hoboken, N.J. These first locomotives had many failings. In 1829, George Stephenson, another Englishman, developed the first really successful locomotive. It ran on smooth rails and had direct drive between the cylinder pistons and the driving wheels. Also in 1829, a Pennsylvania canal company tested the first full-sized locomotive to be operated on a commercial railroad in the United States. The locomotive, the *Stourbridge Lion*, was built in England.

In 1830, a famous race was held between a horse and a steam locomotive, the *Tom Thumb*. Peter Cooper, a New York manufacturer and builder of the locomotive, wanted to convince officials of the Baltimore and Ohio Railroad to use locomotives rather than horses to pull their trains. The horse won the race after an engine belt slipped on the *Tom Thumb*. But this defeat was only a minor setback for the locomotive, which was sometimes called the "iron horse."

The first steam locomotive to be placed in regular passenger and freight service in the United States made its first run on Christmas Day in 1830. This locomotive, called the *Best Friend of Charleston*, was built by the West Point Foundry of New York for the South Carolina Canal and Rail Road Company. Steam railway transportation then developed rapidly.

The *General* was another famous steam locomotive of the 1800's. The *General* became legendary during the Civil War (1861-1865) after Union soldiers captured it from the Confederacy. The soldiers drove the locomotive northward from Georgia to Tennessee. After a long chase, Confederate troops in another engine caught up with the *General*.

The electric locomotive was introduced in the late 1800's. Many individuals contributed to the development of the electric locomotive. Thomas Edison tested his first model in 1880, and the first electric street railway began operating in Germany in 1881. In 1895, the first electric locomotives were placed in regular service by the Baltimore and Ohio Railroad in Baltimore.

Most American railroads continued to use steam locomotives until they began switching to diesels in the 1930's and 1940's. Huge, powerful steam locomotives called *Big Boys* were built from 1941 to 1944 to handle the freight traffic of World War II.

Diesel locomotives were introduced experimentally in 1923. In 1925, the first diesel placed in regular service by an American railroad began switching operations in a New York City freight yard. The first passenger diesel, the Burlington's *Zephyr*, went into operation in 1934. The first freight diesels went into service in 1940. Within a few years, diesel locomotives were hauling passenger trains in various parts of North America and taking over much of the freight and yard work. By 1960, diesels had replaced all the steam locomotives in regular service in the United States.

Today, research engineers are working to develop locomotives of higher horsepower and greater pulling power. They also are seeking ways to make locomotives easier to maintain and more reliable.   THOMAS C. SHEDD

Related Articles in WORLD BOOK include:

Baldwin, Matthias William	Railroad
Cooper, Peter	Rocket, The
Electric Railroad	Steam Engine
Free-Piston Engine	Stephenson
Jones, Casey	Tom Thumb

Additional Resources

NOCK, OSWALD S. *Great Steam Locomotives of All Time.* Arco, 1977.

WHITE, JOHN H. *A History of the American Locomotive: Its Development, 1830-1880.* Dover, 1979. Reprint of 1968 ed.

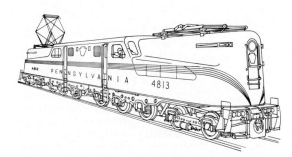

An Early Electric Locomotive, built in 1935, hauled passenger trains for the Pennsylvania Railroad for 32 years.

WORLD BOOK illustrations by Jackson-Zender

The First Gas-Turbine Electric Locomotive built and operated in the United States went into service in 1949.

LOCOMOTOR ATAXIA

LOCOMOTOR ATAXIA. See ATAXIA.

LOCOWEED is any one of several kinds of perennial herbs that grow in western North America. They have harmful effects when eaten by horses, cattle, or sheep. Locoweed gets its name from the Spanish word for *crazy*, because of the strange actions of animals poisoned by it.

There are about a hundred kinds of locoweeds, but many are not known to be poisonous. Three of the more common kinds are the *white*, *purple*, and *blue* locoweed. They are named for the color of their flowers, which resemble those of peas or beans. The plants have erect or spreading stems with many leaflets on each stem.

The effect of locoweeds on animals depends on the soil in which the plants grow. Scientists believe that the plants' poisonous effects result from their ability to absorb poisonous elements from the soil. Both the green and the dry plants are poisonous. The symptoms of poisoning vary somewhat in horses, cattle, and sheep. Horses become dull, drag their legs, eat infrequently, and lose muscle control. Soon they become thin and die. Cattle react in much the same way. But sometimes they run wildly about, bumping into objects in their path. Sheep react more mildly to the poison. Animals raised on a range usually do not eat locoweeds when other food is available. Ranchers destroy locoweeds by cutting the roots about 2 inches (5 centimeters) below the surface, or by spraying the plants with the herbicide 2,4-D.

Scientific Classification. Locoweeds belong to the pea family, *Leguminosae*. The white locoweed is genus *Oxytropis*, species *O. lambertii;* the purple is *Astragalus mollissimus;* and the blue is *A. diphysus.*   LOUIS PYENSON

LOCUST, *LOH kuhst,* is any one of about 20 plants native to North America. Four of these are shade trees with heavily scented flowers. The others are shrubs. The trees sometimes grow about 80 feet (24 meters) tall.

In the United States, the *black locust* is the best-known locust tree. This medium-sized tree grows widely throughout the eastern United States and southern

The Long Locust Pods are filled with wax-coated seeds.

Canada. Like most locusts, the black locust has spines. Its fragrant flowers hang in drooping clusters. They are white, and look much like pea blossoms. The fruit consists of a long, glossy brown pod with about a dozen wax-coated seeds. Black locusts have blue-green compound leaves. The bark and leaves of the black locust are poisonous.

Locusts grow rapidly on good soil. On poor soils, locust borers kill the trees while they are still young. Another insect enemy, the leaf miner, may cause the leaves to turn yellow and fall off before the first frost.

Locust wood is commercially important, because it is hard and lasts for a long time. It is valuable for insulator pins, because it swells only slightly when wet. Locust trees make good fence posts and mine timbers.

Scientific Classification. Locusts belong to the pea family, *Leguminosae*. The black locust is genus *Robinia*, species *R. pseudoacacia*. Other American species include the Kelsey, *R. kelseyi;* the New Mexican, *R. neomexicana*, and the clammy locust, *R. viscosa.*   T. EWALD MAKI

See also ACACIA; HONEY LOCUST; TREE (Familiar Broadleaf and Needleleaf Trees [picture]).

LOCUST is any short-horned grasshopper, or a grasshopper with short *antennae* (feelers). The long-horned grasshoppers and katydids belong to another family. A number of cicadas also are called locusts, but they, too, belong to a different family. Since ancient times, locusts have been known for destroying crops.

Most locusts are brownish and are about 2 inches (5 centimeters) long, with a large head, large eyes, and short antennae. They have long hind legs for jumping, and four wings which fold over their backs when they are not flying. Many locusts can make a sound by rubbing their ridged hind legs on their front wings. This causes the wings to vibrate and makes the noise.

Locust plagues occur in nearly all continents from time to time. Only extremely cold countries are free of these insects. Locusts travel in swarms and settle on green fields like a blanket. They eat green leaves and stalks. The female locust lays her eggs in the soil in a case that usually contains about 25 eggs. Swarms of locusts have ruined crops in many parts of the world. One swarm by the Red Sea was believed to cover an area of 2,000 square miles (5,200 square kilometers). The Rocky Mountain locust destroyed millions of dollars worth of crops in the Mississippi Valley between 1870 and 1880. Between 1930 and 1940, grasshoppers caused damage on the Pacific Coast, in the Southwest United States, and on the eastern side of the Rocky Mountains.

Swarms of migrating locusts are sometimes so large they shut out the sunlight. They interfere with railroad trains and make automobile travel dangerous. Millions of crushed locust bodies make rails and highways slippery. Swarms have been known to travel from Saskatchewan, Canada, to Texas. Others have been seen as much as 1,200 miles (1,930 kilometers) from land.

The Graceful Flowers of the Locust are very fragrant and resemble sweet peas. The leaves are blue-green in color.

The Locust has destroyed crops in many parts of the world since ancient times. A migrating swarm of locusts, *right,* clouds the sky on the Kenya-Uganda border in Africa.

L. W. Brownell; European

Scientists and farmers have found several ways to fight locusts. Harrowing and plowing the soil in the late fall destroys the eggs. A machine called a *hopperdozer* kills the adults. Pulled by a tractor, it spreads oil on the ground and makes the locusts jump, hit a canvas, and fall into the oil. The best control is to scatter *poison bran mash,* a mixture of bran and arsenic.

Scientific Classification. Locusts are in the order *Orthoptera,* and form the locust family, *Locustidae.*   URL LANHAM

See also GRASSHOPPER; PLANT (picture: Insects Damage Large Numbers of Plants).

LODESTONE. See LOADSTONE.

LODGE, HENRY CABOT (1850-1924), led Republican members of the Senate in a successful fight to keep the United States from joining the League of Nations after World War I. He opposed President Woodrow Wilson, the chief planner of the League. Lodge, who was chairman of the Senate Foreign Relations Committee, fought the League because he felt it would involve the United States too deeply in European affairs.

Lodge came from a wealthy Boston family. He graduated from Harvard University and served from 1873 to 1876 as an editor of an influential magazine, *North American Review.* He was a noted historian before being elected to the U.S. House of Representatives in 1886. As a Republican senator from 1893 until his death, he pioneered in civil service law and helped draft the Federal Food and Drugs Act of 1906.   WILLIAM J. EATON

LODGE, HENRY CABOT, JR. (1902-1985), served as a diplomat under four United States Presidents. In 1960, he was the vice presidential running mate of Richard M. Nixon on the Republican ticket.

Lodge was born in Nahant, Mass. He became a newspaperman following his graduation from Harvard University in 1924. He served in the Massachusetts legislature from 1933 to 1937 and won election to the U.S. Senate in 1936. He served there until 1944, when he resigned to enlist in the Army during World War II. He was reelected to the Senate in 1946.

In 1952, Lodge managed General Dwight D. Eisenhower's presidential campaign. Eisenhower won, but Lodge lost his Senate seat to a young Democrat,

John F. Kennedy. Under President Eisenhower, Lodge served as U.S. ambassador to the United Nations. Nixon and Lodge lost the 1960 presidential election to Kennedy and Lyndon B. Johnson. In 1963, President Kennedy appointed Lodge ambassador to South Vietnam. Lodge served 11 months. He held the same post from 1965 to 1967 under President Johnson. Lodge became ambassador to West Germany in 1968. He resigned in 1969 to become President Nixon's chief negotiator at the Vietnam peace talks in Paris. He served as U.S. envoy to the Vatican from 1970 until 1977. Lodge then retired from public office.   WILLIAM J. EATON

United Press Int.   Harris & Ewing
Henry Cabot Lodge, Jr.   **Sir Oliver Lodge**

LODGE, SIR OLIVER JOSEPH (1851-1940), an English physicist, investigated the nature of oscillations and electric waves in wires and in wireless telegraphy. His discoveries helped in developing the radio. His works include *Modern Views of Electricity* (1889), *Electrons* (1907), and *The Ether of Space* (1909). He served as professor of physics at University College, Liverpool. Later, he became deeply interested in spiritualism. Lodge was born in Penkhull, England.   CARL T. CHASE

ŁÓDŹ, *looj* or *lahdz* (pop. 825,200), is the second largest city in Poland. Only Warsaw is larger. Łódź is the capital of the province of Łódź in central Poland. For location, see POLAND (political map).

Łódź ranks as Poland's leading manufacturer of cotton cloth and other textiles. It also produces chemicals, electric appliances, machinery, and processed foods.

375

The city is the center of Poland's motion-picture industry and the home of the University of Łódź.

Łódź received a city charter in the early 1400's. It expanded rapidly when its textile industry developed during the 1800's. During World War II (1939-1945), German troops occupied Łódź, and it was severely damaged. The city was rebuilt after the war.　ADAM BROMKE

LOEB, *LOHB,* **JACQUES** (1859-1924), an American physiologist, made important studies of the chemistry underlying the activities of living organisms. He proved that eggs can be fertilized by artificial means. In his opinion, all aspects of life can be explained in terms of physical and chemical processes. His works include *The Dynamics of Living Matter* (1906), *The Mechanistic Conception of Life* (1912), *Artificial Parthenogenesis and Fertilization* (1913), and *Regeneration* (1924).

Loeb came to the United States from Germany in 1891. He taught at Bryn Mawr College and at the universities of Chicago and California. In 1910, he joined the Rockefeller Institute for Medical Research (now Rockefeller University). He was born in Mayen, Germany.　MORDECAI L. GABRIEL

LOESS, *LO ehs,* is a kind of silt that forms a fertile topsoil in some parts of the world. Loess consists of tiny mineral particles brought by wind to the places where they now lie. These mineral particles are finer than sand but coarser than dust or clay. Topsoils made up of loess are found in the central and northwestern parts of the United States, in central and eastern Europe, and in eastern China.

Two great sources have provided most of the world's loess. One source is the area once covered by the great ice sheets of the Ice Age (see ICE AGE). When the ice melted, it left vast plains of bare mud. When these plains dried, winds blew the mineral grains to the grasslands farther south. The other source of loess is the great deserts of central Asia. These deserts furnished the loess now in eastern China.　ERNEST E. WAHLSTROM

LOESSER, *LEH sehr,* **FRANK** (1910-1969), an American composer, wrote the music and lyrics for many musical comedies and films. He won the 1949 Academy Award for his song "Baby, It's Cold Outside." Loesser and playwright Abe Burrows shared the 1962 Pulitzer prize for drama for the musical comedy *How to Succeed in Business Without Really Trying* (1961).

Loesser, whose full name was Francis Henry Loesser, was born in New York City. In 1936, he moved to Hollywood, where he wrote lyrics for motion-picture musicals. Loesser wrote the lyrics for a number of hit songs, including "Two Sleepy People" and "I Don't Want to Walk Without You." In the early 1940's, he began to compose both music and lyrics. Loesser wrote such songs as "On a Slow Boat to China" and "Spring Will Be a Little Late This Year."

Loesser's first successful musical comedy was *Where's Charley?* (1948). His next show, *Guys and Dolls* (1950), ranks among the finest musicals in history. It includes the songs "If I Were a Bell," "I've Never Been in Love Before," and "I'll Know." Loesser wrote the story as well as the music and lyrics for *The Most Happy Fella* (1956).　THOMAS A. ERHARD

LÖFFLER, *LEF ler,* **FRIEDRICH** (1852-1915), a German bacteriologist, discovered the diphtheria bacillus

in 1884, with the help of Edwin Klebs. He then found a way to cultivate these organisms, and perfected a staining method so that they could be more easily observed under a microscope. He also developed a staining technique to demonstrate flagella, the whiplike structures used to propel some bacteria. In 1897, Löffler and Paul Frosch discovered the first known animal virus, the one that causes foot-and-mouth disease in cattle. Löffler was born in Frankfurt, in what is now East Germany.　STANLEY E. WEDBERG

LOFOTEN ISLANDS, *LOH foh t'n,* include several large islands and many islets off the northwest coast of Norway. They cover about 538 square miles (1,393 square kilometers) and have a population of about 26,000. The Vesterålen archipelago to the north is sometimes considered part of the Lofoten Islands. The Vesterålen group covers 580 square miles (1,502 square kilometers) and has about 34,000 people.

The Lofoten Islands are famous for their fisheries. The chief source of income is codfishing. The population of the islands doubles during the spring, when fishing enthusiasts come there to fish.

There are some industries on the islands. These include canning, quick-freezing, and processing of fish oil and fish meat. Svolvaer is the chief port of the islands. The famous whirlpool known as the Maelstrom is between the islands of Moskenesøya and Vaerøy.

During the German occupation of Norway in World War II, British and Norwegian commando forces carried out two daring and famous raids against the German garrison on the Lofoten Islands.　OSCAR SVARLIEN

LOFTING, HUGH (1886-1947), was the creator of Doctor Dolittle, a well-known character in children's fiction. Lofting first wrote about the doctor in letters to his children during World War I, when he served in the British Army. When *The Story of Doctor Dolittle* was published in 1920, it won such popular favor that Lofting was persuaded to continue the adventures of Doctor Dolittle and his animal friends in *The Voyages of Doctor Dolittle* (1922). He received the Newbery medal for this book in 1923. Lofting later wrote and illustrated a series of Doctor Dolittle books.

Lofting was born in Maidenhead, England, of Irish descent. He spent most of his life in the United States. He studied at the Massachusetts Institute of Technology and at the London Polytechnic, and traveled widely as a civil engineer.　JEAN THOMSON

Dr. Dolittle Is Puzzled by the *Pushmi-Pullyu,* a two-headed beast. Chee-Chee the monkey, Dab-Dab the duck, Gub-Gub the pig, and the dog Jip are amazed, too. The illustration was drawn by Hugh Lofting, who also wrote the book *The Story of Dr. Dolittle,* copyrighted in 1920 by the J. B. Lippincott Co.

LOG is an instrument that measures the speed of a ship. The most important kinds are (1) the chip, or common, log; (2) the taffrail log; (3) the harpoon log; (4) the ground log; (5) the Forbes log; and (6) the pitometer log.

The Chip Log is a piece of board about $\frac{1}{2}$ inch (13 millimeters) thick and shaped like a quarter of a circle, about 6 inches (15 centimeters) long on the two straight sides. The curved edge is weighted with lead so that the log floats upright with the curved edge down. A sailor throws the log into the water behind the ship, and a line attached to it unreels as the ship moves. By noting the amount of line that runs out in a given time, a sailor can determine the ship's speed.

The Taffrail Log works on the principle of the automobile speedometer. It consists of a rotator with spiral

rotation varies with the ship's speed. The rotator drives a *magneto*, or electric generator. The voltage generated is measured on voltmeters which are calibrated to read in knots. Thus the speed is read directly.

The Pitometer Log, like the Forbes log, records both speed and distance. But the pitometer log operates by the action of water pressure. The basic part of a pitometer log is a *Pitot tube*, which forms part of a *rod meter* that extends from 24 to 30 inches (61 to 76 centimeters) below the bottom of a ship. The Pitot tube has an opening on the side facing the bow of the vessel. Another tube surrounding the Pitot tube has an opening that faces toward one side of the ship.

When the ship is at rest, the water pressure at the

TWO KINDS OF LOGS

Taffrail Log
Records distance

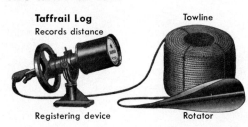

Registering device   Rotator

Towline

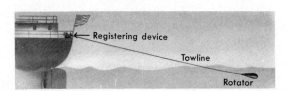

Registering device

Towline

Rotator

The Taffrail Log has a registering device fastened to the taffrail at the ship's stern. The log records distance traveled, but not speed. It may give inaccurate readings if an obstruction, such as seaweed, interferes with the free movement of its rotator.

Pitometer Log
Records speed and distance traveled

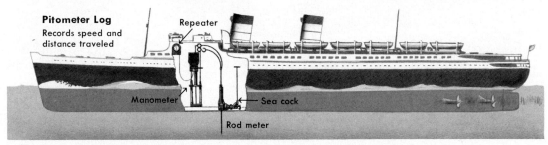

Repeater

Manometer

Sea cock

Rod meter

The Pitometer Log has a rod meter that extends into the water from the bottom of the ship. Different speeds change the water pressures in the meter. The pressures are measured by a manometer and are translated into speed and distance traveled. Repeaters give the speed and distance readings at various places on the ship.

fins that cause it to turn as a ship pulls it through the water. The rotator is connected by means of the towline to a recording device that looks like a clock. The recorder, attached to the stern of the ship, shows only the distance traveled. Because of this, a sailor must make two readings, with a known interval of time between them, to obtain the speed of the ship.

The Harpoon Log resembles the taffrail log, but its register is towed in the water with the rotator, and must be hauled in to be read.

The Ground Log is used in shallow water when a ship is moving slowly. It has a lead weight on the end of a lead line. A sailor throws the lead overboard and it sinks to the bottom. A known amount of line is paid out and the time noted, as in the case of the chip log. This method shows not only the speed of the ship, but the direction of the current.

The Forbes Log consists of a small rotator in a tube that projects through the ship's bottom. The speed of

opening of the Pitot tube and the surrounding tube is the same. This is known as *static* pressure. As the ship moves, the speed of the vessel increases the water pressure on the opening of the Pitot tube. This is known as *dynamic* pressure. The total pressure on the Pitot tube equals the sum of the static and dynamic pressures. But the opening in the outer tube receives only static pressure, whether the ship is at rest or in motion. Various devices inside the ship measure the differences in pressure between the two tubes and translate this into speed and distance.

Large, modern steamships measure speed by counting the revolutions of the ship's propeller. The accuracy of this method is affected by the weather, the shape of the ship, and the ship's bottom. If the sides and bottom are smooth, one revolution of the propeller can send the ship farther than it can if the sides are uneven or covered with barnacles or seaweed.   KENNETH M. SMITH

See also KNOT; LOGBOOK.

LOG CABIN

Fireplace Frame

Chinking Between Logs

Fitted Notches

Notching and Hewing

Splitting Log

American Pioneers Built Log Cabins entirely from the materials available in the wilderness. With their simple tools, they shaped, split, and notched logs to make these sturdy shelters. Log cabins served as both homes and fortresses on the frontier.

LOG CABIN. The first English colonists in North America did not know how to build houses of logs. They lived in shelters made of brush and bark until they could erect frame houses like those they had known in England. But colonists who had lived in the forests of Switzerland, Germany, and Scandinavia knew how to build log houses. Swedish settlers who came to Delaware in 1638 built the first log cabins in America. German pioneers who settled in Pennsylvania built the first log cabins there about 1710. But Scotch-Irish immigrants made the first wide use of logs when they moved to the "back country" of the Appalachian highlands after 1720. By the time of the American Revolutionary War, settlers along the whole western frontier were using log cabins.

The log cabin was not easy to build, although it required few tools. Builders used three types of logs: round, hewn on two sides, and squared. The logs had to be about the same size so that the cracks between them could be easily *chinked* (filled) with moss, clay, or mud. Builders had to be careful in cutting the notches where the logs fitted together. They usually covered the cabin roof with bark or thatch, and later with rough wooden shingles cut from logs. Most log cabins

did not have windows, because few people could afford glass panes. But settlers often covered openings with animal skins or greased paper. They made doors and floors from logs split lengthwise. The door was usually hung on leather hinges. Most log cabins had one story, with one or two rooms. Some had a loft for sleeping and storage, which people could reach with a ladder, or by steps cut into the cabin wall. Later, pioneers erected two-story log houses with several rooms.

Many noted Americans, including Abraham Lincoln, were born in log cabins. To rise from such humble beginnings to become President has long been part of the American dream of equality and opportunity. The log cabin came to symbolize the dream of being able to improve one's place in life.   WALKER D. WYMAN

See also PIONEER LIFE IN AMERICA (A Pioneer Home); COLONIAL LIFE IN AMERICA (Houses); BUCHANAN, JAMES (picture); KENTUCKY (picture: Lincoln Birthplace).

LOG-CABIN AND HARD-CIDER CAMPAIGN. See HARRISON, WILLIAM H. (Elections of 1836 and 1840).

LOGAN (1725?-1786?), a Cayuga Indian chief, won fame for a stirring speech in 1774. White settlers along the Ohio River had murdered some Indians, including several of Logan's relatives. In revenge, Logan waged war against the settlements. His speech explained his actions to John Gibson, a soldier who tried to persuade Logan to attend peace talks. Logan said that he had treated the white man as his brother, but the white man responded by murdering his relatives. This speech was praised by Thomas Jefferson. Logan's Indian name was Tachnechdorus. His father was Shickellamy, a famous mixed-blood Cayuga leader. Logan was born in the Indian settlement of Shamokin, Pa. WILLIAM T. HAGAN

LOGAN, JOHN ALEXANDER (1826-1886), gained fame as a Union general and political leader. After the Civil War, he helped organize the Grand Army of the Republic, a veterans' organization. Logan is also credited with naming May 30, 1868, as the first Memorial Day.

In 1862, Logan fought in all the Western campaigns under General Ulysses S. Grant. He later distinguished himself at the siege of Vicksburg, Miss., and served with General William T. Sherman on the march through Georgia. Logan became a major general of volunteers and a corps commander. His soldiers called him *Black Jack* because of his dark complexion, eyes, and hair.

Logan represented Illinois in the U.S. House of Representatives from 1859 to 1862 and from 1867 to 1871. He was a U.S. senator from Illinois from 1871 to 1877 and from 1879 until his death. He ran unsuccessfully for Vice President on the Republican ticket with James G. Blaine in 1884.

Logan was born in Jackson County, Illinois, on Feb. 9, 1826. After an interrupted education, he studied law at the University of Louisville and was admitted to the bar. He was a volunteer in the Mexican War, then served in the 1853 and 1857 sessions of the Illinois legislature. Early in the Civil War, he became colonel of an Illinois regiment. T. HARRY WILLIAMS

LOGAN, JOSHUA (1908-   ), is an American playwright, director, and producer. He won a Pulitzer Prize in 1950 as coauthor of the musical *South Pacific*. Logan shared the prize with Oscar Hammerstein II and Richard Rodgers. Logan coauthored and directed *Mister Roberts* in 1948. He directed such plays as *Annie Get Your Gun* (1946), *Picnic* (1953), *Fanny* (1954), and *The World of Suzie Wong* (1958). Logan also directed many films, including *Fanny* (1961) and *Camelot* (1967). He was born in Texarkana, Tex. GEORGE FREEDLEY

LOGAN, MOUNT. See MOUNT LOGAN.

LOGAN, STEPHEN TRIGG. See LINCOLN, ABRAHAM (Early Practice).

LOGAN, SIR WILLIAM EDMOND (1798-1875), a Canadian geologist, gained fame for his pioneer work on coal and on very ancient rocks. He was born in Montreal and educated in Scotland. After 23 years in business, he resigned to study coal deposits in Wales. He then returned to Canada and became the first director of the Geological Survey of Canada. His most important book was *A Report on the Geology of Canada* (1869). Logan also supervised Canada's geologic exhibits at several international fairs. CARROLL LANE FENTON

LOGAN ACT is a United States law that prohibits private citizens from opening negotiations with a foreign government on a dispute between that government and the United States. Congress passed the law in 1799 in reaction to the activities of George Logan, a Philadelphia Quaker. Logan had gone to Paris in 1798 to try to

end a naval dispute that had led to many battles between American and French sailors. Logan did no harm, but President John Adams warned Congress that Logan could have confused and harmed the negotiations that were then going on. Adams said that individuals should not interfere with official diplomatic relations between nations.

Punishment for violation of the Logan Act may include up to three years in prison and a fine of up to $5,000. A number of private citizens have held controversial meetings with foreign governments through the years, but there is no evidence that anyone has ever been convicted of violating the Logan Act. JERALD A. COMBS

LOGANBERRY is a small, reddish-purple fruit that grows on a trailing blackberry plant. Each loganberry consists of a cluster of tiny fruits called *drupelets*. The loganberry is probably a natural hybrid of a red raspberry and a type of blackberry called the *western dewberry*. Unlike other blackberries, which grow on erect bushes, loganberries and other dewberries develop on long, willowy *brambles* (see BRAMBLE). Loganberries usually are not eaten fresh because of their extremely tart flavor. Instead, they are canned or frozen, or are made into jam, jelly, juice, or wine.

Loganberries are grown commercially in sections of the Pacific Coast States and southwestern British Columbia. The plants grow best in fertile, well-drained, deep soil at temperatures above 14° F. (−10° C). They also need to be irrigated in order for their fruits and stems to develop properly.

Growers produce loganberry plants by burying sections of stems or roots in mounds of earth. As the plants grow, they are tied to stakes or wire frames. After the fruit is picked, growers remove the old stems in order to provide room for new stems to develop. Loganberry plants produce fruit annually until they are about 12 years old.

Scientific Classification. The loganberry plant belongs to the rose family, Rosaceae. Its scientific name is *Rubus loganobaccus*. GEORGE W. EATON

See also BLACKBERRY; DEWBERRY.

Lush, Purplish-Red Loganberries, *inset,* grow in clusters on trailing vines. The berries are a species of the blackberry.

USDA; Oregon State College

LOGARITHMS

LOGARITHMS, *LOG uh rith'mz*, are numbers, usually grouped in a table, used to reduce complicated multiplications and divisions to additions and subtractions, and to do other problems.

A logarithm is what is known in algebra as an exponent (see ALGEBRA [Terms Used in Algebra]). The equation $2^3 = 2 \times 2 \times 2 = 8$ expresses a relationship among the *number* 8, the *base* 2, and the *exponent* 3. This relationship can also be stated another way: 3 is the *logarithm* of the number 8 to the base 2. In general, if $b^x = p$, then by definition x is the logarithm of p to the base b. This can be written briefly as $x = \log_b p$.

The Laws of Logarithms

Because logarithms are exponents, the properties of exponents apply to them. The following equations show some of the important properties of exponents:

(1) $b^x \times b^y = b^{x+y}$ (3) $(b^x)^n = b^{nx}$
(2) $b^x \div b^y = b^{x-y}$ (4) $\sqrt[n]{b^x} = b^{x/n}$

These properties of exponents can be restated in the language of logarithms. To restate the first equation, let $b^x = p$, $b^y = q$, and $b^{x+y} = r$. Then, by the definition of a logarithm, $x = \log_b p$, $y = \log_b q$, and $x + y = \log_b r$. It follows then that $\log_b r = x + y = \log_b p + \log_b q$. But by the first property of exponents, $r = p \times q$. Thus we have $\log_b (p \times q) = \log_b p + \log_b q$ In words, *the logarithm, to the base b, of the product of two numbers is equal to the sum of the logarithms of the two numbers to the base b.*

To restate the second equation in logarithmic language, set $b^{x-y} = s$. Then, $\log_b s = x - y = \log_b p - \log_b q$. But by the second property of exponents, $s = \frac{p}{q}$. Thus, $\log_b (\frac{p}{q}) = \log_b p - \log_b q$. In words, *the logarithm, to the base b, of the quotient of two numbers is equal to the logarithm of the numerator to the base b minus the logarithm of the denominator to the base b.*

Next, set $b^{nx} = t$. Then $\log_b t = nx = n \log_b p$. But by the third property of exponents, $t = p^n$. Thus, $\log_b (p^n) = n \log_b p$. In words, *the logarithm, to the base b, of a power of a number is equal to the product of the exponent of the power and the logarithm of the number to the base b.*

Finally, set $b^{x/n} = u$. Then $\log_b u = \frac{x}{n} = \frac{1}{n} \log_b p$. But by the fourth property of exponents, $u = \sqrt[n]{p}$. Thus, $\log_b (\sqrt[n]{p}) = \frac{1}{n} \log_b p$. In words, *the logarithm, to the base b, of a root of a number is equal to the quotient of the logarithm of the number to the base b and the index of the root.*

Using Logarithms

Multiplication. To multiply two numbers using logarithms, look up the logarithms of the two numbers in a table. Add these logarithms to get the logarithm of the product of the two numbers. Then, using the table again, find the number whose logarithm is the logarithm of the product. This is the product of the two numbers.

Division. To divide one number by another, look up the logarithms of the two numbers in a table. Subtract the logarithm of the denominator from the logarithm of the numerator. Then, using the table again, find the number whose logarithm is the same as the logarithm found by subtraction. This number is the desired quotient.

Raising a Number to a Power. To raise a number to a power, look up the logarithm of the number in a table. Multiply this logarithm by the exponent of the power. Then, using the table, find the desired power of the given number.

Finding a Root. To find the root of a number, look up the logarithm of the number in a table, and divide this logarithm by the index of the root. Then, using the table again, find the number whose logarithm equals the number found by the preceding division. This is the root of the number. See ROOT; SQUARE ROOT.

Kinds of Logarithms

Common Logarithms. Any positive number, other than 1, can serve as a base for logarithms. However, 10 is the most convenient base because the most common number system is based on 10. Logarithms to the base 10 are called *common* logarithms.

The common logarithms of two numbers that have the same sequence of digits, such as 247 and 2.47, differ only by an *integer*, or whole number. For example, $247 = 100 \times 2.47 = 10^2 \times 2.47$. Therefore, $\log_{10} 247 = \log_{10} 10^2 + \log_{10} 2.47 = 2 + \log_{10} 2.47$. Thus, the common logarithms of 247 and 2.47 differ only by the whole number 2. In fact, to four decimal places, the common logarithm of 247 is 2.3927 and the common logarithm of 2.47 is 0.3927.

Because 247 lies between 100 and 1,000, that is between 10^2 and 10^3, $\log_{10} 247$ lies between $\log_{10} 10^2$ and $\log_{10} 10^3$. That is, the common logarithm of 247 lies somewhere between 2 and 3. Thus, the whole number part of $\log_{10} 247$, or of any other common logarithm, can be determined mentally.

In common logarithms, the whole number part is called the *characteristic*, and the decimal part is called the *mantissa*. For a given number, a shift in the position of the decimal point changes the characteristic, but does not change the mantissa. Because the characteristic can be determined mentally, logarithm tables only record mantissas. This is true only of common logarithms.

Natural Logarithms. Although common logarithms serve as the most convenient type for computation, mathematicians have found that natural logarithms are best for theoretical purposes. In the system of natural logarithms, the base is the number $e = 2 + \frac{1}{2} + \frac{1}{2 \times 3} + \frac{1}{2 \times 3 \times 4} + \ldots = 2.71828\ldots$ Natural logarithms are useful in theoretical mathematics because many important formulas in calculus take their simplest possible forms using them.

History

John Napier, a Scottish mathematician, prepared the first published discussion and table of logarithms in 1614 (see NAPIER, JOHN). Jobst Bürgi of Switzerland independently discovered logarithms at about the same time. In the early 1600's, Henry Briggs of England introduced the base 10 and began constructing a 14-place table of common logarithms. Adriaen Vlacq of The Netherlands completed Brigg's work.

About 1622, Edmund Gunter of England conceived the idea of marking equal logarithmic scales on strips and multiplying and dividing by sliding one strip along the other. This idea forms the basis for the slide rule (see SLIDE RULE).

The Briggs-Vlacq tables remained in use until 20-place common logarithm tables were calculated in Great Britain between 1924 and 1949.   HOWARD W. EVES

LOGBOOK is the written record of the events which take place during a ship's voyage. The log may be written up once a day by the captain of the ship, or it may be written by the officer in charge of each watch. It includes a record of the ship's course and speed, the weather, and any ships or lands sighted. It also includes any sickness, death, or crime on board ship, and any other unusual event. JOHN J. FLOHERTY

See also LOG.

LOGGERHEAD. See TURTLE (Sea Turtles).

LOGGING. See LUMBER (From Forest to Sawmill).

LOGIC is a branch of philosophy that deals with the rules of correct reasoning. Most work in the field of logic deals with a form of reasoning called an *argument*. An argument consists of a set of statements called *premises*, followed by another statement called the *conclusion*. If the premises support the conclusion, the argument is *valid* (correct). If the premises do not support the conclusion, the argument is *invalid* (incorrect).

Logic tells us whether an argument is valid or invalid. The validity of an argument depends on the form of the argument, not on the truth of its premises. As a result, an argument that depends on false premises could be valid, and an argument based on true premises could be invalid.

There are two types of arguments, *deductive* and *inductive*. In a valid deductive argument, the conclusion must be true if the premises are true. In a valid inductive argument, the conclusion is probably true on the basis of the premises. This article deals mainly with deductive reasoning. For more information on inductive reasoning, see INDUCTIVE METHOD.

The Categorical Syllogism is the most common form of argument in traditional deductive logic. The ancient Greek philosopher Aristotle was one of the first scholars to carry out a systematic study of the categorical syllogism.

A syllogism consists of two premises and a conclusion. A categorical syllogism is one in which every statement has one of the four forms: (1) All A are B. (2) No A are B. (3) Some A are B. (4) Some A are not B. The letters A and B, or any other letters that might be used, are terms that represent various classes of things, such as numbers, people, yellow objects, unpleasant sounds, or brown cows. The following argument is an example of a valid categorical syllogism: "All mammals are warm-blooded. All brown cows are mammals. Therefore, all brown cows are warm-blooded." The form of this syllogism is: "All A are B. All C are A. Therefore, all C are B."

The following categorical syllogism is invalid: "No stars are planets. Some satellites are not planets. Therefore, some satellites are not stars." This syllogism has the following form: "No A are B. Some C are not B. Therefore, some C are not A." We can determine that this syllogism is invalid by comparing it with another syllogism that has the same form and yields a false conclusion. Such a syllogism would be: "No precious stones are cheap things (true). Some diamonds are not cheap things (true). Therefore, some diamonds are not precious stones (false)." This syllogism fails to meet the requirement that the conclusion must be true if the premises are true. Therefore, the syllogism must be invalid.

The Rules of Syllogisms enable us to test a categorical syllogism without considering similar examples or examining the argument's structure in detail. These rules are based on certain features that occur in all valid syllogisms and distinguish them from invalid ones. For example, one rule states that no valid syllogism has two negative premises. There are two negative premises in this syllogism: "*No* stars are planets. Some satellites are *not* planets. Therefore, some satellites are not stars." As a result, we know immediately that this syllogism cannot be valid.

There are other rules for constructing valid syllogisms. (1) The syllogism must have exactly three terms. For example, consider this invalid syllogism: "All laws are made by Congress. $v = at$ is a law of falling bodies. Therefore, Congress made $v = at$." The term *law* is unclear. It can refer to a physical law, such as the law of falling bodies, or to legislative law. As a result, this syllogism has four terms instead of three—and is invalid. (2) Two positive premises must yield a positive conclusion. (3) A negative premise and a positive premise must yield a negative conclusion. (4) The term that occurs in both premises must be modified by the words *all* or *none* at least once. (5) A term that is modified by *all* or *none* in the conclusion must be modified by *all* or *none* in one of the premises.

Modern Logic extends far beyond the work of Aristotle. Modern *logicians* (scholars who study logic) have developed theories and techniques to deal with deductive arguments other than categorical syllogisms. Notable modern logicians include the British mathematicians George Boole and Alfred North Whitehead and the British philosopher Bertrand Russell. These logicians, unlike traditional ones, have used mathematical methods, as well as techniques that involve symbols.

Today, logic is used mainly to test the validity of arguments. However, it also has important uses in working with such devices as computers and electric switching circuits.

To test an argument, a logician first analyzes its statements and expresses them as symbols. In many cases, a letter or other character in an argument stands for a whole word or phrase. For example, logicians would write the sentence "Socrates is wise" as "Ws." The sentence "Every Greek is wise" would be written as a formula: "(x) (Gx → Wx)." The → means *if* _____, *then*_____.

Next, the logician uses *rules of derivation*, also called *inference rules*, to determine what new formulas may be derived from the original premises. For example, one rule enables the statement "Q" to be derived from the statements "P" and "(P → Q)." Thus, the statement "The picnic is canceled" may be derived from "It is raining" and "If it is raining, then the picnic is canceled." The logician continues to derive formulas until a conclusion has been reached.

Special Uses of Logic. Special branches of logic guide much reasoning in science, law, and certain other fields. Various branches of logic guide reasoning involved in obligations, promises, commands, questions, preferences, and beliefs.

Much of the reasoning that people do in everyday life is nondeductive—that is, it produces probable conclusions rather than definite ones. For example, physicians use nondeductive reasoning in diagnosing the probable

LOGISTICS

cause of a patient's symptoms. Legal scholars often use nondeductive methods to determine what law governs a particular case.   MORTON L. SCHAGRIN

Related Articles in WORLD BOOK include:

Aristotle	Science (How Scientists Work)
Deductive Method	Set Theory (In Logic)
Fallacy	Truth Table
Russell, Bertrand	Whitehead, Alfred North

Additional Resources

COPI, IRVING M. *Introduction to Logic*. 6th ed. Macmillan, 1982.

DEWEY, JOHN. *Logic: The Theory of Inquiry*. Irvington, 1981. Reprint of 1938 edition.

KNEALE, WILLIAM C. and MARTHA. *The Development of Logic*. Oxford, 1962. A history of logic.

QUINE, WILLARD VAN ORMAN. *Elementary Logic*. Rev. ed. Harvard, 1981. Symbolic and mathematical logic.

LOGISTICS, *loh JIHS tihks*, is the science of providing and maintaining soldiers, equipment, and supplies for military operations.

Modern armies armed with complex weapons and equipment require tremendous logistical effort to put them into battle and keep them there. For example, almost half of the total strength of the United States Army in World War II had to provide logistic support for the other half that came in direct contact with the enemy. One out of 4 men in a combat division performed duties related to logistics, such as supply and administration.

The extraordinary task of supplying an army can be imagined by comparing the amounts of artillery ammunition fired in World War I and in the American Civil War. During one average month of World War I, the British and French armies fired more than twice as much artillery ammunition as did the Union army during the entire four years of the Civil War.

Supply forms only one part of the task of logistics. Military forces must be moved from place to place. They must have lodging, food, and medical care. Records on the fighting forces must be kept.

On land and in the air, chemical, engineer, medical, ordnance, quartermaster, signal, and transportation units provide logistic support for combat units. At sea, cargo ships, hospital ships, icebreakers, minelayers, oilers, repair ships, transports, and tugs provide this support to warships.   CHARLES B. MACDONALD

LOGROLLING. See BIRLING.

LOGROLLING is the trading of votes as commonly practiced in legislative bodies. One party or group in a legislature may want to pass a bill in which it is vitally interested. Another party or group may want to pass a different bill. Each group may have little or no interest in the other's project. But each group, in turn, votes for the other's bill in order to obtain support for its own bill. A common case of logrolling arises in connection with approving appropriations for local improvements.   WILLIAM G. CARLETON

LOGWOOD comes from the hard, middle part of a tropical tree which belongs to the pea family. It is called logwood because it is shipped to market in logs weighing about 400 pounds (180 kilograms). The tree grows in Mexico, Central America, and some parts of the West Indies.

Logwood is heavy and firm-textured. Its natural color is blood-red. The coloring matter in the wood is used to

make many dyes. The blood-red color turns lighter when acids are added, and darker when alkalis are added. The dye from logwood is still used for coloring silk and woolen goods, but coal-tar dyes are taking its place. Logwood also is used in making ink.

Scientific Classification. Logwood belongs to the pea family, Leguminosae. It is genus *Haematoxylon*, species *H. campechianum*.   HAROLD NORMAN MOLDENKE

See also BELIZE CITY.

LOIRE RIVER, *lwahr*, is the longest river in France. It is about 650 miles (1,050 kilometers) long, and it drains about a fourth of the country. For location, see FRANCE (physical map). The Loire rises in the Velay Mountains, about 4,500 feet (1,370 meters) above sea level, and flows northward to Orléans. At Orléans, it turns westward and flows through the Loire Valley, which is known for its many *châteaux* (large country houses). It empties into the Bay of Biscay in western France. The river was an important navigable waterway in the past, but large, modern boats find it difficult to sail on the Loire because of occasional floods and many sandbanks. The wide mouth of the river at St.-Nazaire has been deepened by dredging from Nantes to the sea. Canals connect the Loire with the Saône, Rhône, and Seine rivers. The Loire's most important tributaries are the Allier, Cher, Indre, Maine, and Vienne rivers. The Romans called the Loire the *Liger*.   HUGH D. CLOUT

See also FRANCE (picture: The Loire River).

LOKI, *LOH kee*, was a god of Norse mythology who was known as a troublemaker and trickster. He was the son of a giant but lived among the gods, who were the enemies of the giants. Most stories of Loki portray him as evil, though some myths tell of occasions when he helped the gods. Loki could change his shape at will, and he often appeared in the form of an old woman or an animal.

The principal myth about Loki concerns his role in the murder of Balder, the handsome son of Odin, the chief god. Loki was jealous of Balder's beauty and popularity. Balder could be killed only by mistletoe, and so the gods made a sport of throwing things at him because he would not be hurt. One day, when the gods were amusing themselves in this way, Loki handed the blind god Hoder a sprig of mistletoe. Loki helped the unknowing Hoder aim the branch and throw it at Balder. The mistletoe pierced Balder's body and killed him.

When the gods learned what Loki had done, they sentenced him to be chained across three rocks, with a snake dripping poison onto his face. His devoted wife, Sigyn, caught the drops of poison in a bowl. But each time the bowl filled up and she left to empty it, the venom struck Loki and made him twist in agony.

According to legend, Loki will remain chained until the time of a battle called *Ragnarok*. He will then break free and lead the giants in an attack on the gods. The world will be destroyed in this battle, and all the gods and giants will die.   C. SCOTT LITTLETON

See also BALDER.

LOLLARDS were originally a religious group of the early 1300's in Holland. About 1387, the term began to be used as a name for the followers of the English religious reformer John Wycliffe. The Lollards preached obedience to God, reliance on the Bible as a guide to Christian living, and simplicity of worship. They rejected the richness of the Mass, most sacraments, and papal supremacy. They denied that an organized church was necessary for salvation. Most Lollards were poor priests or members of the laity. They wore long russet gowns, carried staffs, and lived on what they could beg. Henry IV, who became king in 1399, persecuted the Lollards because their views disagreed with religious law. By 1420, their movement had been practically stamped out.

The Lollards had little permanent effect on religious life in England, but they had great influence in Bohemia. There, John Hus was burned at the stake in 1415 for preaching Wycliffe's doctrines. One hundred years later, Martin Luther embraced some of Hus's ideas. In this way, the Lollards helped to pave the way for the Protestant Reformation.   WILLIAM H. MAEHL

See also WYCLIFFE, JOHN; HUS, JOHN.

LOMBARD, *LAHM bahrd,* **PETER** (1095?-1160), was a medieval theologian who wrote an important theological textbook, *The Four Books of Sentences*. It was completed by 1158, and served as a standard textbook in theological schools for 300 years.

In the *Sentences*, Lombard presented past and current opinions on theological problems in a systematic way. He compiled these opinions from a number of leading church authorities, especially Saint Augustine. Lombard also summarized the church's position and wrote his own views on the issues. For centuries, students of theology were required to comment on the *Sentences*. Some of these commentaries were the major works of leading medieval theologians and philosophers, including Saint Bonaventure, John Duns Scotus, and William of Ockham.

Lombard was born near Novara, Italy, and studied in Bologna. About 1134, he went to Paris and taught in the cathedral school of Notre Dame. Lombard quickly gained fame as a theologian and author. In 1159, he was appointed bishop of Paris.   WILLIAM J. COURTENAY

See also SCHOLASTICISM (The Scholastic Method).

LOMBARDI, *lahm BAHR dee,* **VINCE** (1913-1970), was one of the most successful coaches in professional football history. Lombardi was known for his demanding attitude toward his players and for his philosophy of hard work, dedication, and pride. He became identified with the motto, "Winning isn't everything: It's the only thing."

Lombardi had his greatest success coaching the Green Bay Packers of the National Football League (NFL) during the 1960's. He became head coach and general manager of Green Bay in 1959. In his nine years as head coach, the Packers won five NFL titles. They also won the first two Super Bowls, in 1967 and 1968.

Vincent Thomas Lombardi was born in New York City. He played football at Fordham University from 1934 to 1936. Lombardi was a coach at Fordham in 1947 and 1948 and at the U.S. Military Academy from 1949 to 1953. He served as offensive coach for the NFL's New York Giants from 1954 to 1959. Lombardi retired as Green Bay head

Vernon J. Biever

Vince Lombardi

coach in 1968. From 1969 until his death, he served as head coach, general manager, and part owner of the Washington Redskins.   RICHARD ROTTKOV

LOMBARDS, *LAHM bahrdz,* were members of a Germanic tribe that conquered much of Italy in the late A.D. 500's, and threatened the political power of the popes.

The Lombards probably came from Gotland Island in the Baltic Sea. They migrated to northern Germany along the lower Elbe River in the 100's B.C. In the A.D. 300's, they began to move southward. By about 490, they had settled in what is now Austria. The Lombards invaded Italy in 568 and seized control of much of the Italian peninsula. They settled in a part of northern Italy that is still called *Lombardy*.

The popes in Rome feared the Lombards would destroy their political power. In 754, Pope Stephen II asked the Franks for help. Pepin the Short, the Frankish king, invaded Italy and defeated the Lombards. Pepin gave part of central Italy to the pope in 756. In 774, Charlemagne, Pepin's son, crushed the Lombards. As a result of the Lombard defeat, the Franks won control of Italy and the popes' power remained secure.   WILLIAM G. SINNIGEN

LOMBARDY, *LAHM buhr dee,* is a region in northern Italy. It is named for the Lombards, a tribe that once lived there. Lombardy has a population of 8,898,653, and an area of 9,205 square miles (23,842 square kilometers). It includes the provinces of Bergamo, Brescia, Como, Cremona, Mantova, Milano, Pavia, Sondrio, and Varese. Lombardy, Italy's chief industrial region, produces much wine, silk, and cheese. Milan is the capital. See also LOMBARDS; MILAN.   BENJAMIN WEBB WHEELER

LOMÉ, *law MAY* (pop. 229,400), is the capital and chief seaport of Togo, a republic in West Africa. Railroads connect Lomé with Togo's inland cities. For location, see TOGO (map).

Most of the people of Lomé work for the government and for trading companies. Others are craftworkers, traders, and railroad and dock workers. Lomé has a natural harbor from which cocoa, coffee, palm oil, and other products are shipped.   IMMANUEL WALLERSTEIN

LOMOND, LOCH. See LOCH LOMOND.

LON NOL, *lahn nohl* (1913-1985), headed the government of Kampuchea (Cambodia) from 1970 to 1975. He and other Kampuchean leaders overthrew Prince Norodom Sihanouk because they opposed his friendly policy toward Communists in Vietnam. Lon Nol declared Kampuchea a republic later in 1970, but he soon began to rule as a dictator. He suffered a stroke in 1971 and gave up many of his duties. But in 1972, he set up a new government with himself as president.

Kampuchea became involved in the Vietnam War during the early 1970's. Kampuchean government troops fought Communist rebels. Lon Nol fled from Kampuchea to the United States in 1975, shortly before his government surrendered to the Communists. See KAMPUCHEA (History).

Lon Nol was born in Prey Veng Province in Kampuchea when the country was a French colony. He joined the army in 1952, and Kampuchea gained independence the next year. Lon Nol became a lieutenant general in 1961. He served as minister of defense from 1955 to 1966. He was prime minister from 1966 to 1967 and from 1969 to 1972.   DAVID P. CHANDLER

St. Paul's Cathedral, right, towers over London's oldest section, the City. The City began about A.D. 43 as a Roman trading post on the River Thames. It is now London's financial center.

Rick Strange

G. F. Allen, Bruce Coleman Inc.

The Landmarks of London include the statues of Trafalgar Square, *foreground,* and the famous Clock Tower of the Houses of Parliament, *background,* from which Big Ben booms out the hours.

Malcolm J. Gilson, Black Star

Colorful Ceremonies take place in London today just as they have for hundreds of years. These troops of the queen's Household Cavalry are changing the guard at Horse Guards Parade.

LONDON

LONDON is the capital of the United Kingdom of Great Britain and Northern Ireland. It ranks as one of the world's oldest and most historic cities. London traces its history back nearly 2,000 years. Over the years, it became the center of Britain's enormous overseas empire and the home of many of the world's greatest artists, poets, scientists, and statesmen.

Each year, millions of tourists visit London to see such historic sights as Buckingham Palace, Westminster Abbey, and the Tower of London. Buckingham Palace has long been the London home of Britain's monarchs, including the present queen, Elizabeth II. The nation's kings and queens are crowned in the beautiful church known as Westminster Abbey. Sir Walter Raleigh, Saint Thomas More, and many other famous persons were imprisoned in the Tower of London. Today, the tower serves as a museum and holds the fabulous crown jewels.

London is a large, lively city as well as a historic one. It is the 11th largest city in the world, with almost 7

Emrys Jones, the contributor of this article, is Professor of Geography at the University of London and the author of Atlas of London and the London Region.

million persons. London's banks, insurance companies, and shipping firms do business in almost every country. Few other cities have so many outstanding museums and art galleries or offer such a wide variety of plays and other entertainment.

London grew up around two old, historic cities—the City of London and the City of Westminster. The City of London started as a trading post of the Roman Empire about A.D. 43. The City of Westminster began as a residence for England's rulers about 1,000 years later. It stood about 2 miles (3 kilometers) southwest of London. A great stone wall surrounded the City of London. But as London grew, it spread far beyond its wall and took in the royal City of Westminster.

Today, the area where Roman London stood is still known as the City of London. It and the former City of Westminster lie at the center of modern London and make up much of its busy downtown section. Downtown London has tall office buildings, noisy traffic, and stores and sidewalks crowded with shoppers. But it also has beautiful parks and gardens nearby where people can escape the crowds and traffic. The rest of London extends 12 to 19 miles (19 to 31 kilometers) in every direction from this central section.

London was nearly destroyed twice, by fire in 1666 and by German air raids during World War II (1939-1945). Although each disaster wiped out much of London, many old landmarks were rebuilt.

J. Alex Langley, DPI

Piccadilly Circus, a downtown intersection, lies near the heart of London's fashionable *West End* section. The Piccadilly area is crowded with shops, department stores, theaters, and restaurants.

Carl Purcell

Hyde Park is one of five large parks near downtown London. The parks provide an escape from the noise and traffic of the City and West End, which make up most of the busy downtown area.

LONDON/*Greater London*

The old City of London and the communities surrounding it form one political unit, with definite boundaries and an overall government. This area is called *Greater London* or simply *London.*

London covers 610 square miles (1,580 square kilometers) near the southeast coast of England, one of the four countries that make up the United Kingdom. The River Thames (pronounced *tehmz*) flows generally eastward through the heart of London but curves north or south in some places. Near the river, the land ranges from low and flat to gently rolling. Away from the river, the land becomes hilly.

About 40 miles (64 kilometers) east of London, the Thames empties into the North Sea, an arm of the Atlantic Ocean. The river thus links London with shipping routes throughout the world.

London is divided into 32 *boroughs* (local units of government) plus the old City of London, often simply called *the City.* The City and each borough have their own governments.

This section gives a general description of London's central and outlying areas. The next three sections of this article describe these areas in more detail in discussing the people, cultural life, and economy of London.

Facts in Brief

Population: *Greater London*—6,608,598.

Area: *Greater London*—610 sq. mi. (1,580 km²).

Climate: *Average Temperature*—January, 39° F. (4° C); July, 63° F. (17° C). *Average Annual Precipitation* (rainfall, melted snow, and other forms of moisture)—24 in. (61 cm). For the monthly weather in London, see GREAT BRITAIN (Climate).

Government: Thirty-two borough governments, each consisting mainly of elected councils and headed by a mayor; and the City of London government made up of the lord mayor, 24 aldermen, and 137 common councilmen.

Founded: *City of London*—about A.D. 43. *Greater London* came into existence in 1965.

Central London covers about 10 square miles (26 square kilometers) on both sides of a great north-south bend in the River Thames. It includes the busiest and best-known parts of London.

Central London can be divided into three main sections: (1) the City, (2) the West End, and (3) the South Bank. The City and West End lie on the north side of the Thames. The South Bank lies across the river. A number of great bridges, including new London Bridge, Tower Bridge, and Westminster Bridge, link the South Bank with the City and West End.

The City forms London's famous financial district. It covers about 1 square mile (2.6 square kilometers) at the eastern edge of central London. Only about 6,000 people live in the City. But almost half a million office workers crowd its sidewalks each working day.

The City is London's oldest section. It stands where the walled City of London stood for hundreds of years. The City consists largely of modern bank and office buildings. But it also has some reminders of its colorful past. The tall dome of St. Paul's Cathedral, for example, still towers over other buildings in the area, just as it has for hundreds of years. Parts of the Guildhall date from the 1400's. This building has long served as the City's administrative center. Mansion House, the home of the City's lord mayor, dates from the mid-1700's. A 202-foot (62-meter) stone column called the Monument stands near the spot in the City where the Great Fire started in 1666.

The West End makes up the center of Britain's government and of London's retail trade and night life. It is also London's most fashionable residential area.

The West End covers about 7 square miles (18 square kilometers) just west of the City. Near the River Thames, a street called the Strand links the West End and the City. The Strand is one of London's oldest and busiest streets.

Britain's chief government buildings stand in the part of the West End that was formerly the City of Westminster. The Houses of Parliament, perhaps the best known of these buildings, tower dramatically along the Thames. From Parliament, the government buildings extend northward along a broad avenue called Whitehall. Number 10 Downing Street, the home of Britain's prime minister, stands just off Whitehall. Buckingham Palace lies a short distance to the southwest.

384a

London's main shopping and entertainment districts spread out from two huge West End intersections. One intersection, Trafalgar Square, is an area of open pavement with statues and fountains. Whitehall, the Strand, and streets from the upper West End meet at the square. At the other intersection, Piccadilly Circus, six busy downtown streets come together. Many of London's finest shops are in this area, along Bond, Oxford, and Regent streets. Piccadilly also forms the center of London's largest entertainment area. The area extends eastward to the Strand and northward into Soho, a district crowded with restaurants and nightclubs.

The South Bank is one of London's fastest-growing sections. It is the site of a large, modern cultural center which includes a number of theaters, concert halls, and art galleries.

The South Bank covers about 2 square miles (5 square kilometers) along the inside curve of the Thames. This area grew more slowly than the City and West End. But the cost of land in these sections has soared, forcing builders to look for cheaper locations across the river.

Outlying Areas. Crowded residential neighborhoods surround most of central London. Numerous small factories are mixed in with the houses in many of these communities, especially in the area known as the *East End*. The East End includes most of the borough of Tower Hamlets, just east of the City, and the southern part of the borough of Hackney. The heavily built-up neighborhoods around central London gradually give way to spacious, pleasant communities, which Londoners call *suburbs*.

A broad band of countryside, called the *Green Belt*, surrounds Greater London. City planners set aside this land to keep the built-up areas from spreading out endlessly. The planners also started communities called *new towns* just outside the Green Belt to ease overcrowding in London. Many thousands of Londoners have moved to the new towns since the mid-1940's.

London

London, one of the world's largest cities, lies on the River Thames in southeastern England. It is a world center of trade, finance, government, and the arts. Greater London, shown below, includes the old City of London at the center and the 32 London boroughs. Many familiar landmarks of historic interest appear on the large map of central London at the right.

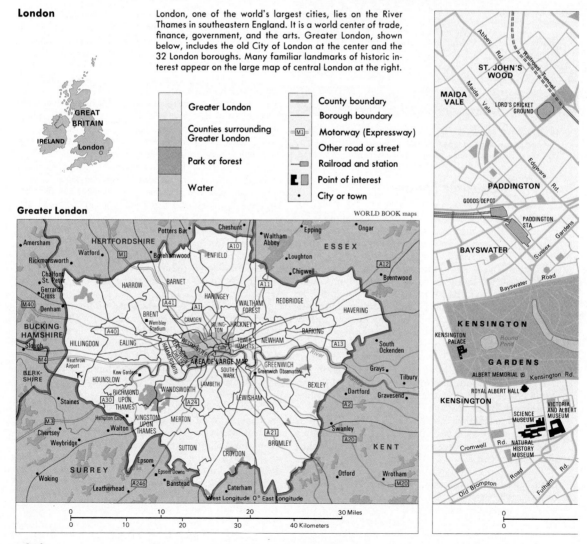

Greater London

WORLD BOOK maps

LONDON

Westminster, the oldest part of the West End, has been the center of Britain's government for more than 1,000 years. It includes the Houses of Parliament, the group of buildings along the Thames at the bottom center of this photograph. The stately church to the left of the Parliament buildings is Westminster Abbey. Other West End landmarks can be identified by comparing the photograph with the map below.

Aerofilms Limited

Julian Calder, Woodfin Camp, Inc.

London Lawyers called *barristers* attend court sessions in traditional wigs and robes.

Allan A. Philiba from Peter Arnold

A Crowd of Londoners reflects people of many nationalities. London has about a million immigrants, including many from India, Pakistan, and Britain's former West Indian colonies.

Ted Spiegel, Black Star

"Bobbies"—London police officers—are among the few unarmed police in the world.

London is so large that many Londoners think of themselves mainly as residents of a particular district, such as Chelsea, Soho, or Hampstead. The various districts were once separate communities, and many have kept their special character. Chelsea, for example, is known for its artists and entertainers, and Soho for its foreign grocery stores and restaurants.

Ancestry and Religion. According to tradition, the only "real" Londoners are *cockneys*. A cockney is anyone born within hearing distance of the bells of St. Mary-le-Bow, a historic church in the City. But cockneys are better known for their unusual English accent. This accent was made famous by Eliza Doolittle, the uneducated cockney girl in George Bernard Shaw's play *Pygmalion* and in the musical version of the play, *My Fair Lady*. London has few genuine cockneys today because few people are born in the City. But the cockney accent can still be heard in the poor districts just east and south of the City. See COCKNEY.

Most Londoners come from a long line of British-born ancestors. But over the years, London has attracted many new residents from outside Great Britain. Today, about a million Londoners are immigrants. Many others are the children or grandchildren of immigrants. Most immigrants have grouped together with people of the same nationality in and around central London. These districts therefore have a strong "foreign" character. Soho, for example, has many people of French and Italian ancestry. Areas bordering the West End have many immigrants from Australia, India, Pakistan, Poland, and Britain's former West Indian colonies. London has long had a large Jewish population, especially in the East End. But many wealthy Jews now live in the West End.

Most Londoners belong to the Church of England or to other Protestant churches. London's immigrants include many members of the Roman Catholic, Jewish, and Moslem faiths.

Residential Areas and Housing. Most Londoners live in suburban communities in the *outer boroughs*. These boroughs, such as Barnet, Croydon, Havering, and Hounslow, lie farthest from central London. The suburbs have their own stores, schools, churches, and places of recreation. Most of the residents live in com-

J. Allan Cash Ltd.

The Covent Garden Market, located in a building near the Strand, is a fashionable shopping attraction both for London residents and for tourists. The building, which was formerly the site of the Covent Garden wholesale produce market, now houses a number of elegant shops and fine restaurants.

fortable single-family houses, each with its own garden. Most suburban families own their homes.

London's oldest and most crowded residential areas lie in the *inner boroughs*. These boroughs, such as Hammersmith, Islington, Southwark, and Tower Hamlets, immediately surround the City and West End. Most of London's poor families and immigrants live in rented houses and apartments in these boroughs. The poorest sections include London's only slums.

The chief exceptions to low-class housing in the inner boroughs are in the borough of Westminster and the borough of Kensington and Chelsea. Westminster includes most of the West End. Many of London's richest families live in expensive apartment buildings in Westminster, especially in the fashionable Mayfair district. This prosperous section extends northwestward to the Hampstead district in the borough of Camden, which has many expensive houses. In Kensington and Chelsea, hundreds of large old homes have been turned into rooming houses or apartment buildings for single people who work in downtown London.

The City has few homes or apartments. But in the 1960's and 1970's, a large housing development, called the Barbican, was constructed along the City's northern edge. This development provides living quarters for about 6,500 persons.

Education. More than a million students attend about 2,300 elementary and 640 secondary schools in London. Most of the schools are publicly owned and operated. An agency called the Inner London Education Authority controls the schools in the inner boroughs and the City. Each outer borough runs its own school system.

London has several of Great Britain's famous *public schools* for boys. Although these schools are called public, they are actually private. London's public schools include Harrow, Westminster, and St. Paul's. All three trace their history back more than 400 years.

London has long been Britain's chief center for advanced study and research. The University of London, with about 40,000 full-time students, is the nation's largest university. In addition to its many colleges and medical schools, the university has 24 institutes of advanced study. A number of small colleges in London specialize in such fields as art or engineering.

Recreation. During the day, many Londoners enjoy going to colorful street markets, which sell everything from fresh fruits and vegetables to bargain jewelry and antiques. Popular street markets include the Petticoat Lane (Middlesex Street) market, at the eastern edge of the City; the Berwick Street market, in Soho; and the Portobello Road market, near Kensington Gardens.

Soccer, which the British call *football*, is the most popular sport in London. About 12 professional teams play on Saturdays from August through April. The annual championships are held in early May at Wembley Stadium, in the borough of Brent. The stadium, which seats about 100,000 spectators, also features other sports events throughout the year. See SOCCER.

Many amateur teams in London play Rugby, which resembles American football. The season lasts from September through April. International Rugby Union matches are held at the Twickenham Rugby ground in Richmond upon Thames. See RUGBY FOOTBALL.

Cricket, a game similar to American baseball, is a popular amateur sport played in spring and summer. Major matches take place at Lord's Cricket Ground, just west of Regent's Park, and at the Oval, a cricket ground in the borough of Lambeth. See CRICKET.

Londoners also enjoy such sports as golf, polo, horse racing, and tennis. The Crystal Palace National Sports Centre, in the borough of Bromley, has facilities for many sports. The annual Wimbledon Tournament, probably the most famous tennis tournament in the world, takes place in late June and early July at Wimbledon Park, in the borough of Merton. London has more than 2,300 licensed betting shops, where peo-

C. M. Dixon from Carl Östman

Houses with Gardens are common in London, even in this crowded neighborhood near the downtown area.

Adam Woolfitt, Woodfin Camp, Inc.

Town Houses, such as these in Chelsea, are among the fashionable types of housing in parts of central London.

Alan Band Associates

Typical Suburban Housing in London is comfortable and modern. These houses are in the borough of Hounslow.

London's Street Markets attract crowds of shoppers. The markets sell everything from fresh flowers and produce to bargain jewelry and antiques.

Kenneth Murray from Nancy Palmer

ple place bets on such sports as horse racing and football.

In the evening, many people enjoy watching television at home or a film at one of London's more than 200 *cinemas* (motion-picture theaters). Many people also like to spend the evening at their neighborhood *pub* (public house). London has about 5,600 pubs. They serve beer and other drinks, and many offer juke-box music and such games as billiards and darts. London also has many public and private nightclubs. The St. James's district in the West End is the home of London's famous all-male private clubs. Politicians and businessmen meet in these clubs for meals and conversation.

The *Cultural Life and Places to Visit* section of this article gives more information about recreation facilities in London.

Social Problems. Like most other large cities throughout the world, London has such problems as poverty, crime, and drug addiction. The problems are severest in the slum areas bordering central London.

Numerous slum families are large as well as poor. In many cases, a family of six or seven persons has to live in two or three rooms and share a bathroom and kitchen with neighbors. Many young people turn to shoplifting or more serious crimes. Some also begin to experiment with drugs.

London's housing authorities have moved thousands of slum families to the new towns outside the Green Belt. They have also replaced much slum housing with modern, low-rent apartments. But housing remains a serious problem in the inner boroughs.

Adam Woolfitt, Woodfin Camp, Inc.

Cricket, a game similar to baseball, is a traditional warm-weather sport in London. Two units of the Brigade of Guards are playing this match on the grounds of Chelsea Royal Hospital.

Maxwell Coplan, DPI

A Neighborhood Pub, one of about 5,600 in London, attracts nightly crowds. Friends gather to drink beer, talk, sing along to piano music, and play such games as billiards and darts.

The Arts. London ranks as one of the world's leading cultural centers. It has many professional theaters, whose programs range from musical comedies to the plays of the great English dramatist William Shakespeare. Britain's National Theatre Company presents plays by the world's finest playwrights. The company performs in three theaters in a cultural center on the South Bank. The Barbican Centre, a cultural complex located in the City, houses the Royal Shakespeare Company when it performs in London. This company also stages plays in Stratford-upon-Avon. It specializes in plays by Shakespeare and also presents works by other writers.

London has four world-famous symphony orchestras —the BBC (British Broadcasting Company) Symphony, London Philharmonic, London Symphony, and Royal Philharmonic. Most major concerts are held in the Royal Festival Hall or the Queen Elizabeth Hall, which are part of a South Bank cultural center, or in the Barbican Centre. The Royal Albert Hall, an older concert hall near Kensington Gardens, has a popular series of summer concerts. Britain's national ballet and opera companies perform at the Royal Opera House, at Covent Garden, near the Strand.

London's public art galleries include the National Gallery, on Trafalgar Square; the Tate Gallery, in south Westminster; and the Wallace Collection, housed in a mansion south of Regent's Park. Important visiting art exhibits are held at the Royal Academy of Arts, just west of Piccadilly Circus, and at the Hayward Gallery, a part of the South Bank cultural center.

Museums and Libraries. The British Museum, in the West End, is one of the world's most famous museums. It houses a priceless collection of objects from ancient civilizations as well as Britain's 15-million-volume national reference library. The library was formerly operated as part of the museum. But in 1973, it became part of the newly formed British Library. The reference collection will eventually be moved to a new building to be built in London. See BRITISH LIBRARY; BRITISH MUSEUM.

Other famous museums in London include the Victoria and Albert Museum, which has one of the world's largest collections of decorative art; the Natural History Museum; and the Science Museum. All three are just south of Kensington Gardens. The Museum of London houses the collections of the London Museum and Guildhall Museum. Both collections contain items related to London's history. London has over 400 public libraries, which are run by the City and borough governments.

Palaces. Over the centuries, Britain's rulers have lived in a number of splendid palaces in London. Few of these buildings survive in their original form, and most have been turned into museums or showplaces. For example, the superb royal dining hall called the Banqueting House is almost all that remains of Whitehall Palace. This magnificent palace, located in Whitehall, was a main residence of England's royal family from 1529 to 1698. The famous architect Inigo Jones completed the Banqueting House for King James I in 1622. Today, it is preserved as a showplace. For a picture of the Banqueting House, see JONES, INIGO.

St. James's Palace, between St. James's Park and Green Park in the West End, was the official royal residence from 1698 to 1837. It now provides office space for the lord chamberlain and various other royal officials as well as apartments for certain members of the royal family. Buckingham Palace has been the official royal residence since 1837. It was originally the home of John Sheffield, Duke of Buckingham, who lived there in the early 1700's. Other famous London palaces include Kensington Palace in Kensington Gardens and Hampton Court Palace in Richmond upon Thames.

The Houses of Parliament, in Westminster, serve as the meeting place of Great Britain's two legislative bodies, the House of Commons and the House of Lords. The buildings are officially called the New Palace of Westminster. They were constructed during the mid-1800's to replace the old palace buildings, which had burned to the ground in 1834. Big Ben, the huge bell in the Clock Tower, has boomed out the hours since 1859. During World War II, German bombs destroyed the House of Commons. It was rebuilt after the war. See PARLIAMENT (The British Parliament); BIG BEN.

The chief survivor of the 1834 fire was Westminster Hall, an assembly hall built in 1097 and remodeled during the late 1300's. It stands near the center of the Houses of Parliament. A terrorist bomb slightly damaged the hall in 1974.

Churches. St. Paul's Cathedral and Westminster Abbey are the most famous churches in London. St. Paul's serves as the center of the Church of England in London. The great English architect Sir Christopher Wren built the cathedral between 1675 and 1710 to

Photo Trends

Westminster Abbey is one of London's oldest and best-known churches. It dates from the 1000's and is the scene of coronations, royal weddings, and other important ceremonies.

replace the original St. Paul's, which was destroyed in the Great Fire of 1666. The church's huge dome towers 365 feet (111 meters) above the ground. Wren also rebuilt more than 50 other churches destroyed or damaged in the Great Fire.

The history of Westminster Abbey reaches back more than 900 years. In 1066, William the Conqueror was crowned king there. Since then, almost all the country's monarchs have been crowned in Westminster Abbey.

The church has been added to and remodeled over the centuries, but some of its present architecture dates from the 1200's. See WESTMINSTER ABBEY.

London also has many other famous churches. The oldest is the Chapel of St. John in the Tower of London. It dates from the late 1000's and still has some of its original architecture. Westminster Cathedral, a familiar landmark in the West End, is England's chief Roman Catholic church. Builders completed it in 1903.

PLACES TO VISIT IN LONDON

Each year, London attracts about 6 million tourists and other visitors from all parts of the world. The photographs in this section show some of London's most popular and most interesting tourist attractions. Other points of interest are pictured earlier in the article.

Julian Calder, Woodfin Camp, Inc.
The British Museum

J. Alex Langley, DPI
Changing the Guard at Buckingham Palace

Julian Calder, Woodfin Camp, Inc.
The National Gallery

Carl Purcell
Royal Festival Hall

Squares. Much of London's West End is laid out around a series of squares. The best-known square is Trafalgar. The huge Nelson Column towers 185 feet (56 meters) above the square. It consists of a tall granite column topped by a giant stone statue of the British naval hero Lord Horatio Nelson.

Other well-known West End squares include Bedford, Berkeley, Grosvenor, and Russell squares. Large, fashionable homes once lined these squares, and trees and gardens grew in the open space at the center of each square. The central landscaped areas remain. But most of the houses have been turned into hotels, schools, or business offices.

Parks. London's largest parks are the *royal parks*. These parks once formed part of royal estates but are now set aside for public use. Central London has five royal parks: St. James's Park, Green Park, Hyde Park, Kensington Gardens, and Regent's Park.

L. L. T. Rhodes from Nancy Palmer

The Tower of London

L. L. T. Rhodes from Nancy Palmer

Tower Bridge

Carl Purcell

No. 10 Downing Street

John Budde from Louis Mercier

St. Paul's Cathedral

Julian Calder, Woodfin Camp, Inc.

Royal Opera House, Covent Garden

Carl Purcell

Street Market on Portobello Road

St. James's Park and Green Park are noted for their shade trees and walking paths. A broad, tree-lined avenue called the Mall borders St. James's Park on the north and forms the chief route for royal parades. Hyde Park is famous for its great northeastern entranceway, the Marble Arch, and for Speakers' Corner, just south of the arch. Large crowds gather at Speakers' Corner to hear people express their opinions on everything from politics to religion. Kensington Gardens has beautiful formal gardens and a famous statue of Peter Pan. A man-made lake called the Serpentine separates Hyde Park and Kensington Gardens. Londoners use the lake for boating, fishing, and swimming. Regent's Park includes the huge London Zoo.

More than 80 other public parks lie in or near central London. Battersea Park, in the borough of Wandsworth, offers a variety of attractions, including a popular amusement park. Kew Gardens, also called the Royal Botanic Gardens, contain one of the world's largest collections of various species of trees and hothouse plants. The gardens are in Richmond upon Thames.

Other Places of Interest. The Tower of London, which borders the City in the borough of Tower Hamlets, is London's oldest landmark. It consists of a group of structures built around a central tower and surrounded by two stone walls. The central tower dates from the late 1000's. The Tower of London has served as a fortress, a palace, and a prison. Today, it is a national monument and museum. See TOWER OF LONDON.

The Inns of Court, Britain's center for the study and practice of law, consist of four groups of rambling buildings and courtyards just west of the City. Each group houses one of the Inns of Court, of which there are four: Gray's Inn, Lincoln's Inn, the Inner Temple, and the Middle Temple. Some of their architecture goes back hundreds of years. See INNS OF COURT.

Some places of interest lie outside central London. For example, the borough of Greenwich has a famous group of buildings designed by Wren for the Greenwich Hospital in the late 1600's. They now house the Royal Naval College. For a picture of the buildings, see the article WREN, SIR CHRISTOPHER.

Ceremonies. Guards, usually red-coated sentries of the Brigade of Guards, stand watch at Buckingham Palace. Each morning, the sentries hold their famous changing-of-the guard ceremony in the palace's front courtyard. The royal Household Cavalry also holds a daily changing of the guard at Horse Guards Parade, a parade ground next to the Horse Guards building in Whitehall. Another well-known ceremony takes place at the Tower of London, which is guarded by colorfully outfitted *yeomen warders*, or *beefeaters*. Each night at 10 o'clock, the chief warder locks the tower gates and presents the keys to the tower's governor. This custom is nearly 700 years old.

Two of London's most spectacular ceremonies are *Trooping the Colour* and the *Lord Mayor's Show*. Trooping the Colour forms part of the queen's official birthday celebration each June. Riding on horseback, the queen leads the Brigade of Guards and Household Cavalry past cheering crowds along the Mall to Horse Guards Parade. There, the queen inspects the troops, and the *colour* (ceremonial flag) is carried in review.

The Lord Mayor's Show takes place in the City on the second Saturday in November to celebrate the election of a new lord mayor. The new mayor, dressed in traditional robes and riding in a horse-drawn coach, leads a parade through the streets of the City. For more information about London ceremonies and a picture of Trooping the Colour, see ENGLAND (Traditions).

Rick Strange

Trafalgar Square, in downtown London, is famous for its many landmarks. This view shows the National Gallery, *left;* the church of St. Martin-in-the-Fields, *center;* and the South African embassy building, *right rear.* The huge monument in the foreground honors the British naval hero Lord Horatio Nelson.

London is Great Britain's chief economic center. Its industries and businesses employ nearly 4 million persons, about 20 per cent of the nation's workers.

Manufacturing. Factories in London employ more than 1¾ million workers. The leading industries include printing and publishing and the manufacture of clothing, food products, furniture, and precision instruments.

London's oldest industrial areas lie just north and east of the City. Hundreds of small factories and workshops are crowded among the houses in these areas. Many of the industries have long been associated with a particular district. For example, Whitechapel is the traditional center of the clothing industry. Another district, Clerkenwell, is the center for making watches and jewelry.

Another industrial area extends eastward along the Thames, from Greenwich to the limits of Greater London and beyond. This area specializes in such products as chemicals and paper. A similar industrial belt lies along the Lea River, which follows the eastern border of the boroughs of Enfield, Haringey, Hackney, and Tower Hamlets. London's newest industrial areas have developed in the western boroughs. The largest area is the Park Royal Industrial Estate in the borough of Brent. Factories there specialize in consumer goods, such as food products and household appliances.

Trade. London has long been a great world port and trading center. The Port of London Authority controls two huge docks and 43 miles (69 kilometers) of wharves along the Thames. In the past, the chief docks and wharves were just east of London Bridge and Tower Bridge. These facilities still handle some shipping. But the growth of *container shipping* during the 1960's required new facilities to handle *container ships*. These ships are designed to carry cargo packed in huge boxlike containers. The new container facilities were built at Tilbury, near the mouth of the Thames. Today, ocean ships load and unload thousands of containers at the Tilbury docks. Trains, trucks, and barges transport the containers between Tilbury and London.

London has more than 5,000 wholesale stores and warehouses and over 50,000 retail stores. The famous Covent Garden wholesale produce market handles more than 1 million short tons (910,000 metric tons) of fresh fruits and vegetables yearly. The market moved from its 300-year-old site near the Strand to the South Bank in 1974. Many of London's retail stores are small shops. These shops sell such items as clothing or furniture.

Finance and Business. Financial institutions and other businesses in London employ about 1 million workers. Great financial institutions in the City include the Bank of England, Britain's national bank; the London Stock Exchange, one of the world's busiest stock exchanges; and Lloyd's, the famous worldwide insurance company. Greater London has nearly 50,000 business offices. They house an enormous variety of companies, from shipping firms to advertising agencies. Many manufacturing industries in other parts of Britain have their home offices in London.

Transportation. Expressways and underground and surface railways carry more than 1 million commuters

Marvin E. Newman, Woodfin Camp, Inc.

The London Stock Exchange is one of the city's many important financial institutions. It ranks among the busiest stock exchanges in the world.

between the outlying areas and central London each workday. About 375,000 commuters travel by subway, more than 425,000 take surface trains, and about 145,000 go by bus. Nearly 90,000 persons drive their car to and from work. The London subway system, which Londoners call the *tube*, is the largest in the world. It includes over 100 miles (161 kilometers) of underground rail lines. London's famous red double-deck buses carry passengers throughout the central section.

The London Regional Transport Authority has overall responsibility for transportation in London, including operation of the subways and most of the buses. The British Railways Board runs surface commuter trains.

Heathrow Airport, in far western London, ranks as the world's busiest airport outside the United States. It handles about 29 million passengers yearly. Gatwick Airport, another airport used by Londoners, lies about 28 miles (45 kilometers) south of Greater London. It handles about 14 million passengers a year.

Communications. London is Great Britain's chief communications center. The country's 10 national morning newspapers and eight national Sunday papers are based in London, chiefly on or near Fleet Street in the City. London also has two evening newspapers. The British Broadcasting Corporation (BBC), the national radio and television service, has its main offices and studios in Broadcasting House, just south of Regent's Park. The Independent Broadcasting Authority is also based in London. This organization controls the operation of Great Britain's only commercial television service and the country's only commercial radio network.

Tourism. About 8 million tourists visit London each year. Providing goods and services for tourists is one of London's leading industries. London has about 75 hotels with 200 or more rooms, and over 2,000 restaurants. The largest hotels stand in the West End and in the western outlying areas near Heathrow Airport. The West End also has the most popular restaurants.

From 1965 to 1986, the government of the Greater London area consisted of the governments of the 32 boroughs, the City government, and the Greater London Council. The Greater London Council was a governing body that had authority over the governments of the boroughs and the City. It also had charge of such activities as overall city planning, road construction, traffic flow management, and fire department services.

The Greater London Council was abolished by an act of Parliament that went into effect in 1986. The council's responsibilities were taken over by the City and borough governments and other smaller agencies. Today, the Greater London area is governed chiefly by the governments of the 32 boroughs and the government of the City of London. Several other public agencies also provide a number of services to the people of London.

Borough Governments. Each London borough has its own government, which consists mainly of an elected council headed by a mayor. Borough residents elect new councils every four years. The size of the councils varies from borough to borough.

The borough councils are responsible for local health and welfare services, public libraries, and most public housing. Each outer borough also runs its own school system. The boroughs of London receive most of their income from *rates* (property taxes), rents, and grants from the national government.

The Government of the City of London is organized much as it was hundreds of years ago, when many thousands of people lived inside the City's walls. Today, the City has only about 5,000 residents, far fewer than even the smallest borough. But the City has such an important place in British history that it has equal standing with the boroughs.

An organization called the Corporation of the City of London governs the City. It acts through the Court of Common Council. The Court of Common Council consists of the lord mayor, 24 aldermen, and 137 common councilmen. The lord mayor is the City's chief administrator. Voters in the City elect the aldermen to life terms and the common councilmen to one-year terms. Each year, the aldermen and guild representatives elect the lord mayor.

Other Public Agencies. The London Regional Transport Authority provides several public transportation services. Its members are appointed by the British government. The national government also appoints the members of the Port of London Authority, which controls shipping activities.

Another agency of the national government is the Metropolitan Police Force. It provides police protection for all of Greater London except the City, and has its headquarters at New Scotland Yard. The City has its own police force.

The London Fire and Civil Defence Authority provides fire department services. Its membership consists of one elected councillor from each of the boroughs and the City. Members are appointed by the City or the boroughs that they represent. Schools in the inner boroughs and the City are run by the Inner London Education Authority. Its members are elected by the people of London.

London began about A.D. 43, when armies of the Roman Empire started to conquer Britain. The Romans built a seaport on the Thames near present-day London Bridge. They probably chose this site because the riverbanks east of this point were too marshy for settlement. The Romans called the port *Londinium*. The name *London* comes from this word.

By the early 200's, the Romans had built a wall around London, possibly to protect it from raiders. This wall, and the ones that later replaced it, formed London's boundaries for hundreds of years.

In 410, barbarian invaders attacked Rome. That same year, the Roman troops in Britain were called home to fight the invaders. This date thus marks the end of Roman control over Britain. The native Britons who had moved to London stayed there and kept the settlement alive as a trading center. Little of Roman London remains, except for parts of the original wall and the ruins of a few buildings.

The Middle Ages, the period of European history from the 400's to about 1500, began when the barbarian invaders broke Rome's hold over its huge empire. After the Romans left, seafaring Germanic tribes repeatedly attacked London. Beginning about 450, the two most powerful tribes, the Angles and Saxons, divided England into a number of separate kingdoms. After about 825, the Saxons, who controlled London, gradually united most of England into a single kingdom. But London grew little from the 400's to the 1000's.

In the mid-1000's, the Saxon king Edward the Confessor built a palace and rebuilt a church about 2 miles (3 kilometers) southwest of London. Before then, Saxon kings had lived mainly at Winchester, in south-central England. Edward's buildings became the start of the City of Westminster. The Palace of Westminster served as a chief residence of England's rulers until the 1520's. The church became Westminster Abbey.

In 1066, a French nobleman known as William the Conqueror seized control of England and was crowned king in Westminster Abbey. William granted Londoners self-government. But he built a castle, called the White Tower, just outside London to impress them with his authority and power. The White Tower today forms the central part of the Tower of London.

Other London landmarks also appeared during the Middle Ages. About 1100, work began on Old St. Paul's Cathedral to replace a church destroyed by fire. Builders finished it about 200 years later. In 1209, London Bridge became the first stone bridge across the Thames. It replaced a wooden bridge, often rebuilt, that had spanned the river since Roman times.

London's craft and trade guilds began to develop in the 1100's. Each guild represented certain craftsmen or

Long View of London (1616), an engraving by Claes Jansz Visscher; British Museum, London

London in the Early 1600's sprawled along both banks of the Thames and overflowed onto old London Bridge, *right*. The Great Fire of 1666 destroyed many of the houses and shops on the bridge and most of the buildings on the north bank, including Old St. Paul's Cathedral, *upper left*.

tradesmen, such as bakers, carpenters, goldsmiths, and grocers. The guilds were also called *livery companies* because each had its own *livery*—that is, official robes that members wore on special occasions. Each guild also had its own splendid meeting hall. A central Guildhall for all the guilds was completed in 1425.

Guild members elected London's first mayor in the 1190's. In 1215, King John confirmed London's right to govern itself. By the late 1400's, London had about 50,000 persons. Its mayor had become so important that he was now called the *lord mayor*.

Expansion Beyond the Walls. London grew rapidly during the 1500's and the first half of the 1600's. Under the reign of King Henry VIII, who ruled England from 1509 to 1547, noblemen built estates to the west, just outside London's walls. The West End thus began to develop. The king owned at least six palaces in the London area, including the Palace of Westminster. In 1547, the year Henry died, the Palace of Westminster became the meeting place of Parliament.

London developed into an important world trading center under Queen Elizabeth I, who reigned from 1558 to 1603. As the merchants grew increasingly rich, they built splendid homes, in which they conducted most of their business. But they also began to meet at the Royal Exchange building, which was completed in 1571 just north of London Bridge.

England's first public theaters opened in London's suburbs during Queen Elizabeth's reign. The theaters attracted such large, noisy crowds that they were prohibited inside London's walls. One of the most popular theaters was the Globe, across London Bridge in Southwark. William Shakespeare began to present his plays at the Globe about 1599. See SHAKESPEARE, WILLIAM (England of Shakespeare's Day).

By the mid-1600's, London had about half a million persons. Most Londoners now lived outside the walls in

such districts as Clerkenwell, St. Giles, and Whitechapel, which were rapidly becoming slums. The area inside the walls gradually came to be known as *the City*.

War, Plague, and Fire struck London in the mid-1600's. A struggle for power between King Charles I and Parliament resulted in civil war in 1642. London sided with Parliament, led by Oliver Cromwell and other Puritans. The Puritans were a religious and political group who opposed not only the king but also the established Church of England and the luxurious life of the nobility. The Puritans seized control of the government and beheaded the king in 1649.

London grew less prosperous under Puritan rule. The Puritans also made themselves unpopular by closing the theaters. When Parliament restored the monarchy in 1660, most Londoners welcomed the new king, Charles II.

The Great Plague—a terrible epidemic of *bubonic plague*—broke out in London in 1665. The disease was spread by fleas from infected rats, which swarmed through the slums surrounding the City. Before the epidemic died down in 1666, it had taken about 100,000 lives.

On Sept. 2, 1666, the Great Fire of London broke out in a baker's shop on Pudding Lane in the City. It was finally brought under control five days later. Most of the City, which was built largely of wood, lay in ashes. The losses included St. Paul's Cathedral and more than 80 other churches, the Royal Exchange, the halls of 44 craft and trade guilds, and about 13,000 houses. Amazingly, the fire caused no known deaths.

Rebuilding the City. Londoners rebuilt the City with brick and stone instead of timber. The great architect of the new City was Sir Christopher Wren, who rebuilt many structures lost in the fire, including St. Paul's Cathedral. But few people returned to live in the City. Many merchants moved to the West End, where at-

During World War II, German bombs destroyed much of London. Prime Minister Winston Churchill, *front,* inspects the ruins after a raid. The worst raids came in late 1940 and early 1941.

tractive residential squares were being laid out in such sections as Bloomsbury and Mayfair.

London's businesses soon recovered from losses suffered in the Great Fire. A new Royal Exchange opened about 1675. But the favorite places for doing business were the many coffee houses that sprang up in and near the City. Lloyd's insurance company started in the coffee house of Edward Lloyd in the 1680's. The London Stock Exchange began in the 1700's in a coffee house called Jonathan's. Coffee houses on or near Fleet Street were a chief source of news, and so London's newspaper industry grew up in this area during the 1700's.

The World's Greatest City. By 1800, London had about a million persons, more than any other city in the world. London remained the world's largest city throughout the 1800's.

One of the chief events of the 1800's was the spread of the Industrial Revolution, which had begun in Great Britain during the 1700's. The revolution resulted largely from the growth of factories, many of which sprang up in London. But London's main role in the revolution was to develop markets for the factory-produced goods. The City's merchants and bankers thus made enormous fortunes. Although wealthy Londoners made their money in the City, they spent it in the West End. By the mid-1800's, the West End had become famous for its fashionable social life.

The Industrial Revolution brought misery as well as prosperity to London. Factory, dock, and warehouse workers were desperately poor. They lived with their families in crowded, disease-ridden slums, chiefly in the East End (see CITY [picture: The Industrial Revolution]). During the last half of the 1800's, laws were passed to aid the working class. Conditions in London's slums then began to improve.

The Growth of the Suburbs. During the 1800's, more and more Londoners moved to the outlying areas. This

rapid suburban growth became possible largely because of improved transportation.

London Bridge had formed London's only link with the South Bank until 1750, when Westminster Bridge was completed. Engineers built other bridges after 1750. Horse-drawn vehicles provided the chief means of transportation throughout most of the 1800's. But railroad passenger service began to develop rapidly in London during the mid-1800's.

Starting in the 1840's, a ring of railroad stations went up around central London. The first station, Euston Station, opened in 1846. It was followed in the 1850's and 1860's by King's Cross, Paddington, Victoria, and St. Pancras stations. London's subway system, which was the first in the world, started in 1863. That same year, steam trains began to carry passengers underground between the railway stations that ringed central London.

The first major reform of London's government took place in 1888. The County of London was formed that year, and the London County Council was organized as its chief governing body. The county covered an area about a fifth the size of present-day Greater London. The City remained self-governing. In 1899, the county was divided into 28 boroughs.

By 1901, the City's population had dropped to about 27,000. Meanwhile, the population of the County of London had soared to about $4\frac{1}{2}$ million. This enormous suburban growth continued during the 1900's.

Destruction from the Air. German airships dropped a few bombs on London during World War I (1914-1918). But German bombers caused much worse damage during World War II (1939-1945).

In the summer of 1940, Germany began an all-out air attack on Britain. London became the chief target. The *London Blitz* lasted from September, 1940, to May, 1941. Night after night, German planes dropped tons of bombs on the built-up area. The City and the industrial East End were especially hard-hit. People took refuge in air-raid shelters and subway stations as fires raged through whole blocks of buildings.

The air attacks on London continued throughout the war but not so savagely as during the Blitz. When Germany surrendered on May 7, 1945, much of London lay in ruins. About 30,000 Londoners had been killed. Property losses included the Guildhall, the House of Commons, most of the Inns of Court, and many churches. Bombs had also destroyed or damaged about 80 per cent of London's houses.

Postwar Rebuilding. City planners had drawn up a new plan for London during the war. It called for a wide band of open country, a Green Belt, around London and for new towns to be built outside the belt. The plan also called for the rebuilding of heavily bombed areas and the development of the South Bank. Planners cleared part of the South Bank to provide exhibition space for the Festival of Britain in 1951. The festival celebrated Britain's recovery from the war.

In the 1960's, skyscrapers began to appear in central London, changing the skyline dramatically. The 26-story Shell Centre, the British headquarters of the Shell Oil Company, opened in 1962. In 1965, the 619-foot

J. Alex Langley, DPI

Modern Apartment Buildings like the one at the upper left have been built in and around central London. They have replaced many blocks of older houses like those in the foreground.

(189-meter) Post Office Tower became the tallest structure in Britain.

As London built upward, it also continued to spread outward. The London Government Act, passed by Parliament in 1963, replaced the County of London with Greater London. It also divided Greater London into 32 boroughs and created the Greater London Council. The act took effect on April 1, 1965.

Recent Developments. Since World War II, London has faced many of the same problems that trouble other cities. These problems include air pollution, housing shortages, and traffic jams. But London has had more success than most other cities in solving its problems.

Joint efforts by the central government and local authorities have helped clean up London's badly polluted air. London was long noted for its smogs, caused mainly by smoke from houses and industries. A terrible smog in 1952 killed about 4,000 Londoners. Parliament passed a Clean Air Act in 1956, which limited the use of smoke-producing fuels in London. By the 1970's, London was noted for its clean air.

The new towns outside the Green Belt have helped ease a housing shortage in London. By the 1970's, the London area had 11 new towns, with a total population of more than 750,000. In addition, housing projects in inner boroughs have cleared out many slums and provided low-cost housing for thousands of families.

Automobile traffic remains one of London's worst problems. The government has proposed building more expressways in central London. But many people oppose the plan because it requires moving hundreds of families from their homes.

The Local Government Act of 1985, passed by Parliament, abolished the Greater London Council. It transferred most of the council's responsibilities to the borough governments and the government of the City of London. It took effect on April 1, 1986.   EMRYS JONES

LONDON/Study Aids

Related Articles in WORLD BOOK include:

Outline

I. Greater London
  A. Central London   B. Outlying Areas
II. The People
  A. Ancestry and Religion   C. Education
  B. Residential Areas   D. Recreation
    and Housing   E. Social Problems
III. Cultural Life and Places to Visit
  A. The Arts   F. Squares
  B. Museums and Libraries   G. Parks
  C. Palaces   H. Other Places of
  D. The Houses of Parliament   Interest
  E. Churches   I. Ceremonies
IV. Economy
  A. Manufacturing   D. Transportation
  B. Trade   E. Communications
  C. Finance and Business   F. Tourism
V. Government
  A. Borough Governments
  B. The Government of the City of London
  C. Other Public Agencies
VI. History

Questions

What are some of London's famous landmarks?
What is Greater London?
How do people in London's outlying areas get to and from work in central London?
Into what three main sections can central London be divided?
What is the most popular sport in London?

Additional Resources

AUTOMOBILE ASSOCIATION, and BRITISH TOURIST AUTHORITY. *A-Z Visitors' London Atlas and Guide.* Merrimack, 1981.
Baedeker's City Guide: London. Merrimack, 1983.
DALZELL, W. R. *The Shell Guide to the History of London.* Norton, 1982.
MENEN, AUBREY. *The Great Cities: London.* Time Inc., 1976.
PRITCHETT, VICTOR S. *London Perceived.* Harcourt, 1966. Historical guide to places and people.

LONDON

LONDON, Ont. (pop. 254,280; met. area pop. 283,-668), is a distributing, financial, manufacturing, and transportation center in the southern part of the province. London lies on the Thames River, midway between Toronto and Detroit. For location, see ONTARIO (political map).

British settlers came to the area in 1826. They chose the site because of its riverside location and rich farmland. The settlers named the town for London, England. Years before, the river had been named for the River Thames, which flows through the English city.

Description. London, the county seat of Middlesex County, covers 69 square miles (178 square kilometers). It is the home of the University of Western Ontario.

City Hall and a concert and convention building called Centennial Hall stand in Civic Square. Springbank Park, the city's chief tourist attraction, lies along the Thames River. The park includes Storybook Gardens, a children's amusement center. Eldon House, a home built in the 1830's, also attracts visitors. A symphony orchestra called Orchestra London and a dramatic group called Theatre London perform in the city.

London has more than 300 manufacturing plants. The city's chief products include beverages, chemical and electrical products, diesel vehicles, foods, hosiery, and telephone equipment. Printing is also an important industry. London Airport lies just outside the city.

History. Iroquois Indians lived in what is now the London area before British settlers arrived in 1826. London became a trading center for the surrounding agricultural region. A fire destroyed most of London in 1845, but the people soon rebuilt their town. Railroads built in the 1850's linked London with other Canadian communities and helped bring industry to the area. London was incorporated as a city in 1855. It had a population of about 10,000 that year.

London served as an oil refining center during the 1860's and 1870's. But all the oil companies moved their headquarters to Petrolia, Ont., during the 1880's. In 1910, London became one of the first cities to receive power from hydroelectric plants at Niagara Falls. This power helped its industries grow.

The city's population increased steadily as a result of the industrial development. It reached 60,959 in 1921 and grew to 169,569 by 1961. By 1981, London had a population of 254,280.

A rebuilding program began in downtown London during the 1960's. Centennial Hall was completed in 1967, City Hall in 1971, and a new courthouse in 1974. London City Centre, a hotel and office complex, was completed in 1975. London has a mayor-council form of government.   D. M. L. FARR

LONDON, JACK (1876-1916), was an American author. His writings reflect his great interest in strong men who are driven by primitive emotions in the struggle for survival. London published about 50 volumes of short stories, novels, plays, and essays. He is one of the most frequently translated American writers.

London was born in San Francisco. He had to help support his family from the age of 14 and had little formal education. London entered high school at 19, and with hard study he passed the entrance examinations for the University of California the next year. He stayed at the university for one semester before going to work as a seaman and laborer.

During the gold rush of 1897, London spent a year in the Klondike region of the Yukon Territory in Canada. This was the most important period of his life because he found the material for the stories and novels that made him famous. London's first Klondike stories were collected in *The Son of the Wolf* (1900). These stories are vivid accounts of the struggle of men and dogs to survive in the frozen wastes of the north.

London's best-known work is *The Call of the Wild* (1903). This novel describes the adventures of Buck, a dog taken from California to the Yukon. Buck learns to be brutal in order to survive and then is befriended by a kind master. After his master is killed, Buck turns savage and eventually leads a wolfpack. In *White Fang* (1906), London reversed the story and portrayed a wolf being turned into a pet. These books were instant successes. London was portraying the instincts for freedom and power as opposed to the forces of social control and love.

London's interest in the survival of the fittest also appears in his novels about strong, brutal men who scorn social customs. In *The Sea-Wolf* (1904), he describes Wolf Larsen, a sea captain, as a superman so primitive that he could have been born "before the development of moral nature." The hero of *Martin Eden* (1909) is a brawling, primitive seaman whose thirst for knowledge and power leads him first to success as a writer, then to disgust with the human race, and finally to suicide. In these and many other novels and essays, London attacked capitalism. He is widely considered a spokesman for socialism. His understanding of and sympathy for the poor are strong elements in such works as the essays collected in *The People of the Abyss* (1903).   DEAN DONER

Brown Bros.

Jack London

Additional Resources

LABOR, EARLE. *Jack London.* Twayne, 1974.
LONDON, JOAN. *Jack London and His Times: An Unconventional Biography.* 2nd ed. Univ. of Washington Press, 1968. His daughter's story, told with letters and journals.
SINCLAIR, ANDREW. *Jack: A Biography of Jack London.* Harper, 1977.

LONDON, TOWER OF. See TOWER OF LONDON.

LONDON, TREATIES OF. Throughout history, many international treaties have been signed in London. Some of them are described on the following page.

The Treaty of 1913 was an attempt to end the first Balkan War. Delegates from Greece, Serbia, Bulgaria, and their enemy, Turkey, signed it on May 30, 1913. The defeated Turks were allowed to keep a small European foothold in eastern Thrace. Greece received Salonika, southern Macedonia, and Crete. Serbia gained central and northern Macedonia, and Bulgaria took western Thrace and the northern coast of the Aegean Sea. The treaty caused new conflicts. On June 29, 1913, Bulgaria attacked Greece and Serbia, and the second Balkan War began. See BALKANS.

The Treaty of 1915 was a secret treaty signed by Great Britain, France, Russia, and Italy. In return for entering World War I against Germany, Italy was promised the southern Tyrol, northern Dalmatia, Istria, and Gorizia. See WORLD WAR I (The Italian Front).

The Treaty of 1930 became known as the London Naval Treaty. On April 22, 1930, the United States, France, the British Empire, Italy, and Japan signed the pact to limit and reduce naval armaments. The treaty tried to place limitations on cruisers, destroyers, and submarines. It allowed the United States, Great Britain, and Japan to increase warship production if another power increased its naval production. France and Italy did not sign part of the treaty.

The Treaty of 1936 reaffirmed the naval treaty of 1930. The United States, France, and Great Britain signed it on March 25, 1936.   STEFAN T. POSSONY

LONDON, UNIVERSITY OF, is the largest university in Great Britain. It is made up of several institutions located in or near London. The university consists of 29 schools, each controlled by its own governing body, and 12 institutes established by the university government. These schools and institutes include the Courtauld Institute of Art, the London School of Economics and Political Science, St. Bartholomew's Hospital Medical College, the School of Oriental and African Studies, and University College. The university has about 40,000 full-time students. It was founded in 1836. In 1878, it became the first university in Great Britain to grant degrees to women.   P. A. McGINLEY

LONDON BRIDGE is one of 15 bridges in London that span the River Thames. Construction of the bridge began in 1967 and was completed in 1973. For location, see LONDON (color map).

The bridge replaced the famous London Bridge that was built between 1823 and 1831. Workers began dismantling the older bridge in 1967 because it was settling into the river and cracks were developing. The bridge was reconstructed in Lake Havasu City, Ariz. (see ARIZONA [Places to Visit]).

The London Bridge of the 1800's replaced a stone bridge completed in 1209, about 100 feet (30 meters)

Folger Shakespeare Library

Old London Bridge, shown in this engraving by Visscher, was the only bridge across the River Thames between 1209 and 1750.

downstream. The stone bridge stood on the site of an earlier wooden bridge. Houses lined both sides of the stone bridge, and the heads of executed traitors sometimes hung over the entrance. It was the only bridge over the Thames until 1750. Repairs kept the bridge in use until it was torn down about 1832.   JOHN W. WEBB

LONDON COMPANY was an association of "noblemen, gentlemen, and merchants" during the early days of the American colonies. It was part of a larger association, known as the Virginia Company. In 1606, King James I of England chartered the London Company to form a colony in North America. It founded the Jamestown colony in 1607.

The founders of the London Company believed that precious metals existed in the Americas. They spent about $10,000 to send settlers to Jamestown. Those who went to America and risked their lives were called *planters.* Those who stayed in England and invested their money in the company were called *adventurers.* Each planter and adventurer was to share in the company's profits. But the company failed to profit. The company reorganized under new charters in 1609, and again in 1612. But still there were no profits.

The House of Burgesses was formed in Jamestown in 1619. It was the first representative legislative body in the American colonies. The House passed measures designed to help the company prosper. But a serious Indian uprising in Jamestown in 1622 caused the adventurers to lose what little interest they had left.

In 1623, King James decided that the company was being managed poorly. He took over the association in 1624 and dissolved the company. It had never paid a cash dividend.   MARSHALL SMELSER

See also JAMESTOWN (Va.); VIRGINIA (History).

LONDON NAVAL TREATY. See LONDON, TREATIES OF (The Treaty of 1930).

LONDONDERRY, *LUHN duhn DEHR ee* (pop. 85,705), is Northern Ireland's second largest city. This seaport lies 64 miles (103 kilometers) northwest of Belfast. For location, see NORTHERN IRELAND (political map).

The city is on a hill overlooking the Foyle River. A wall, 1 mile (1.6 kilometers) long, was built in 1609. It helped in defending Londonderry against James II in 1689. Modern Londonderry, however, has spread far beyond the wall. The city's chief industries include brewing, tanning, and linen making. Londonderry has an excellent harbor, and is a center of sea trade with Great Britain and coastal cities of Northern Ireland.

Londonderry was the site of bloody fighting between Catholics and Protestants in the late 1960's and early 1970's. See NORTHERN IRELAND (The Civil Rights Movement).   JOHN W. WEBB

LONE STAR STATE. See TEXAS.

LONG is the name of the most powerful political family in Louisiana history. The Longs—all Democrats —have had great influence in both Louisiana and national politics since the late 1920's.

Huey Pierce Long (1893-1935) began the family's political rule. He had been a farm boy with little formal education beyond high school, but he became governor of Louisiana and a United States senator. Long, nicknamed the "Kingfish," gained high office by calling for social reforms to benefit poor farmers and workers. He adopted the slogan "Every Man a King."

Long was born near Winnfield, La., and passed the Louisiana bar examination after studying law briefly at Tulane University. He was elected governor in 1928. As governor, he built roads and hospitals, provided free schoolbooks, and established night schools to teach adults to read. In 1929, the Louisiana House of Representatives voted to impeach Long on the charge of misusing state funds. But the state Senate acquitted him.

Long was elected to the U.S. Senate in 1930. He refused to resign as governor until 1932, when his hand-picked successor was elected to the office and began to carry out Long's programs according to his orders. At first, Long supported President Franklin D. Roosevelt. But after Long failed in an attempt to make the New Deal more radical in its economic policies, he bitterly attacked Roosevelt. In 1934, Long organized the Share-the-Wealth Society, which promised homestead allowances and a minimum annual income for every American family. The plan gained him a national following, and in 1935 he became a candidate for President. His candidacy threatened to split the Democratic Party.

But Long was shot on Sept. 8, 1935, in the Louisiana State Capitol in Baton Rouge by Carl A. Weiss, a physician. Members of Weiss's family were political enemies of Long. Long's bodyguards killed Weiss immediately. Long died two days later. His widow, Rose McConnell Long, completed his term in the Senate. Long told of his rise to power in his autobiography, *Every Man a King* (1933). He represents Louisiana in Statuary Hall in the U.S. Capitol.

See also LOUISIANA (picture: Governor Huey P. Long).

Additional Resources

BRINKLEY, ALAN. *Voices of Protest: Huey Long, Father Coughlin, and The Great Depression.* Knopf, 1982.
Huey Long. Ed. by Hugh Davis Graham. Prentice-Hall, 1970. An assessment of Long from his own writings, friends, enemies, and historians.
MARTIN, THOMAS. *Dynasty: The Longs of Louisiana.* Putnam, 1960.
WILLIAMS, THOMAS HARRY. *Huey Long.* Knopf, 1969. A standard biography.

Russell Billiu Long (1918-   ), son of Huey Long, has been a member of the U.S. Senate since 1948. From 1966 to 1981, he served as chairman of the Senate Finance Committee. In that post, Long was a shrewd leader who greatly influenced the nation's taxes, social security, and welfare programs. He favored simplified tax returns, a heavier tax burden on the wealthy, and no change in the oil depletion allowance. Long also served as assistant majority leader of the Senate from 1965 to 1969. He was born in Shreveport, La.

Earl Kemp Long (1895-1960), younger brother of Huey Long, served three times as governor of Louisiana —from 1939 to 1940, from 1948 to 1952, and from 1956 to 1960. He was elected to the United States House of Representatives 10 days before he died. Earl and Huey became political foes in 1932 after Huey refused to name Earl as his organization's candidate for lieutenant governor. Earl Long was born near Winnfield, La., and studied law at Tulane and Loyola universities.

George Shannon Long (1883-1958), older brother of Huey Long, was the representative of a rural Louisiana district in the United States House of Representatives from 1953 until his death. He was born near Winnfield, La.   CHARLES BARTLETT

LONG, CRAWFORD WILLIAMSON (1815-1878), became, in 1842, the first doctor to use ether as an anesthetic for surgery. The anesthetic properties of ether had been demonstrated at "ether frolics," during which people took small amounts of ether to experience its strange effects. Long also had experimented with its effects on himself. On March 30, 1842, Long gave ether to James Venable and painlessly removed a tumor from Venable's neck. Long did not announce his experiment at the time and it received no professional or general publicity. Long himself remained unaware of the full value of anesthesia in surgery, although he continued to make occasional use of ether. Finally, in 1849, he published a description of his experiments with ether.

Meanwhile, in the mid-1840's, William T. G. Morton, a Boston dentist, used ether on a patient before extracting a tooth. This had been done at the suggestion of Charles T. Jackson, a professor of chemistry at Harvard University. Morton's use of ether became widely known in 1846, after he administered ether during a surgical operation at the Massachusetts General Hospital. Morton and Jackson each claimed sole credit for the discovery of ether anesthesia. Today, however, most historians give the credit to Long.

Long was born in Danielsville, Ga. He graduated from the Medical School of the University of Pennsylvania in 1839. The Crawford W. Long Medical Museum in Jefferson, Ga., exhibits some of his papers and early anesthesia equipment. A statue of Long represents Georgia in the U.S. Capitol.   EDWIN S. MUNSON

See also ANESTHESIA; ETHER; MORTON, WILLIAM T. G.

LONG, JANE (1798-1880), was called the *Mother of Texas* because of her spirited defense of her children during pioneer days. During the winter of 1821-1822, her husband, James, left their home to fight for Texas' independence. He assigned soldiers to guard his wife and baby, but the soldiers left when Long failed to return. Mrs. Long's only helper was a servant girl, who became ill. Mrs. Long and her family survived the winter, but she had to fight off Indians, hunt for food, and give birth to another baby. Her husband was murdered in Mexico, but she stayed in Texas. She was born in Charles County, Maryland.   H. BAILEY CARROLL

LONG, STEPHEN HARRIMAN (1784-1864), was an American explorer and railroad engineer. An Army officer, he had maps made for the government and gave it valuable information about the West. Between 1817 and 1823, he led Army expeditions to the upper Mississippi River area, the Rocky Mountains, the source of St. Peter's River in Minnesota, and the boundary of the United States in the Great Lakes region.

Long established Fort Smith, now an Arkansas city, in 1817. In 1820, he discovered the mountain near Denver now known as Longs Peak. From 1827 to 1830, Long helped select and survey the route of the Baltimore and Ohio Railroad. He served as chief engineer of the Atlantic and Great Western Railroad from 1837 to 1840. He also designed railroad bridges. Long was born in Hopkinton, N.H.   MONTE A. CALVERT

LONG BEACH, Calif. (pop. 361,355), is a major industrial center, seaport, and tourist area in the southern part of the state. Long Beach and Los Angeles form a metropolitan area with a population of 7,477,503. Long Beach lies along San Pedro Bay, 20 miles (32 kilometers) southeast of Los Angeles. For location, see CALIFORNIA (political map); LOS ANGELES (maps).

In 1784, a Spanish rancher named Manuel Nieto received a land grant that included what is now Long Beach. He became the first white settler in the area. In 1888, a group of land investors founded Long Beach, which they named for its 7 miles (11 kilometers) of beaches.

Description. Long Beach covers 64 square miles (166 square kilometers), including 14 square miles (36 square kilometers) of inland water. The city is the home of California State University, Long Beach. Long Beach City College ranks as one of the nation's largest junior colleges. Long Beach's Pacific Terrace is a concert and convention center. In 1967, Long Beach bought the ocean liner *Queen Mary*. The ship is docked in the city's harbor and attracts about 1½ million visitors to Long Beach annually.

Economy. Long Beach has rich oil deposits, including the Wilmington Oil Field. The Wilmington field produces about 188,000 barrels of oil daily and ranks as one of the most productive fields in the United States. The city's offshore oil wells provide income mostly to the state, but its inland oil deposits belong entirely to Long Beach.

Oil production ranks as the city's most important industry. Other leading industries produce aircraft, electrical machinery, and food products. The Port of Long Beach ranks among the busiest ports on the West Coast. It handles about 20 million short tons (18 million metric tons) of cargo annually.

History. Shoshoni Indians lived in what is now the Long Beach area before white settlers arrived there. The area consisted chiefly of ranchland until the mid-1880's, when railroads linked the Midwest and southern California. The railroads brought thousands of settlers there, and a group of land investors founded Long Beach in 1888. The town was incorporated as a city in 1897, when it had a population of about 1,700.

Long Beach developed as a resort city because of its beaches and warm climate. In 1921, oil was found in Signal Hill, now a small city surrounded by Long Beach. The discovery drew so many people that the population of Long Beach rose from 55,593 in 1920 to 142,032 in 1930. On March 10, 1933, an earthquake in the city killed 52 persons and caused property damage of more than $40 million.

The Wilmington Oil Field was discovered in 1936. The aircraft industry developed in Long Beach during World War II (1939-1945). The city's population increased from 164,271 in 1940 to 250,767 in 1950, largely because of industrial growth.

During the 1940's, areas of land near the Long Beach harbor began to sink because so much oil had been removed from the ground. In 1958, the city began to pump water into the ground. The resulting water pressure has prevented further sinkage.

Several building projects began in downtown Long Beach during the late 1960's. They included construction of a county building and a safety center. A Civic Center project completed in 1975 includes a new City Hall and a library. Oceangate, a commercial and financial center, was scheduled for completion in the 1980's.

Long Beach has a council-manager form of government.   LARRY ALLISON

LONG DIVISION. See DIVISION.

LONG HOUSE. See INDONESIA (Shelter; picture); INDIAN, AMERICAN (Shelter; picture).

LONG ISLAND (pop. 6,728,074), is an island that forms the southeastern part of New York. It has a greater population than that of 41 of the 50 states. The island consists of crowded urban areas, smaller residential towns, fishing villages, and resort centers. A section of western Long Island forms part of New York City.

Location and Size. Long Island extends eastward from the mouth of the Hudson River for about 120 miles (193 kilometers). For location, see NEW YORK (political map). It varies in width from 12 to 23 miles (19 to 37 kilometers), and covers 1,701 square miles (4,406 square kilometers). Long Island Sound separates the island from Connecticut on the north. The Atlantic Ocean lies to the east and south. On the west, Long Island is separated from Manhattan by the East River, from New Jersey by Upper New York Bay, and from Staten Island by the Narrows.

The Counties. Long Island consists of Kings, Queens, Nassau, and Suffolk counties. Kings County, or Brooklyn, and Queens County form part of New York City. Kings County, with 2,230,936 residents, has the largest population of any county in the state. Queens County has a population of 1,891,325. Nassau County, east of Kings and Queens, has a population of 1,321,582. Suffolk County, with a population of 1,284,231, occupies the eastern two-thirds of Long Island.

Nassau County once served largely as a residential area. It now has its own industries, including airplane plants, electronics factories, and plastics plants.

The population of Suffolk County increased by more than 1 million persons between 1950 and 1980. But farms and resorts still take up most of the county. The Brookhaven Laboratory in the county serves as a center for research in nuclear energy. Nassau and Suffolk counties offer sailing, fishing, and swimming.

History. The explorer Henry Hudson reached Long Island in 1609. He found Algonquian Indians living in small villages. During the 1600's, the Dutch settled the western end of the island, and New Englanders settled the eastern part. The original Dutch name for Long Island was *Lange Eylandt*. One of the most important battles of the Revolutionary War, the Battle of Long Island, took place in present-day Brooklyn on Aug. 27,

Location of Long Island

WORLD BOOK map

397

1776. The British defeated the Americans, but the colonial troops escaped capture. On the night of August 29, General George Washington took advantage of a heavy mist to retreat to Manhattan.   WILLIAM E. YOUNG

See also LONG ISLAND SOUND; NEW YORK CITY.

LONG ISLAND, BATTLE OF. See REVOLUTIONARY WAR IN AMERICA (table: Major Battles).

LONG ISLAND SOUND is a busy waterway that extends southwestward between Connecticut and Long Island. This arm of the Atlantic Ocean is nearly 110 miles (177 kilometers) long and about 20 miles (32 kilometers) wide at most points. The East River connects it with New York Bay. The Housatonic, Connecticut, and Thames rivers of Connecticut empty into Long Island Sound.   WILLIAM E. YOUNG

LONG ISLAND UNIVERSITY. See UNIVERSITIES AND COLLEGES (table).

LONG JUMP. See TRACK AND FIELD.

LONG PARLIAMENT refers to a session of the English Parliament that lasted without a break from 1640 to 1653. It was not formally dissolved until 1660. The Long Parliament opened with a direct conflict with King Charles I, met during the Civil War, ordered the king's execution, tried to rule in the uneasy years after the war, and was finally dissolved to make way for a new Parliament under King Charles II.

In its early sessions, the Long Parliament made many lasting political reforms. It abolished the hated court of the Star Chamber, where people were tortured for confessions and tried without a jury. It declared that the king could not collect money without its consent, or dissolve Parliament without its consent. It also brought about the execution of Charles's chief advisers, the Earl of Strafford and Archbishop William Laud.

On religious questions, the Long Parliament was seriously divided. Presbyterians opposed Puritans, and neither side would budge. Civil war began when the king's supporters withdrew from Parliament, and the House soon became divided into Presbyterians, who were moderate royalists, and Independents, who were republican in sympathy. The army, under Oliver Cromwell, supported the Independents. In 1648, a detachment under Colonel Thomas Pride kept the Presbyterian majority from entering the House. "Pride's Purge" resulted in what was called "the Rump Parliament," which had less than a fourth of the usual number of members. This remainder of the Long Parliament carried out the execution of Charles I and made England a commonwealth.

Cromwell, the real power in the commonwealth, found that the Rump Parliament was determined to hold onto its power. He suppressed it in 1653, leaving England without any representative legislature. But the people tired of Puritan dictatorship. The Long Parliament met again in 1660 and called elections. Charles II took the throne soon afterward.   W. M. SOUTHGATE

Related Articles in WORLD BOOK include:

Charles (I) of England	Rump Parliament
Cromwell, Oliver	Star Chamber
England (The Civil War)	

LONGBOW. See ARCHERY (History).

LONGEVITY, or LENGTH OF LIFE. See LIFE EXPECTANCY.

LONGFELLOW, HENRY WADSWORTH (1807-1882), was the most famous and most popular American poet of the 1800's. His reputation among critics declined sharply after his death, but many of his poems remain among the most familiar in American literature. His best-known works include the long poems *Evangeline*, *The Song of Hiawatha*, and *The Courtship of Miles Standish*, and shorter verses such as "The Village Blacksmith," "The Children's Hour," "Paul Revere's Ride," "The Wreck of the Hesperus," and "Excelsior."

Longfellow's Life

Childhood. Longfellow was born Feb. 27, 1807, in the seacoast town of Portland, Me. (then a part of Massachusetts). The Longfellows were a well-known Portland family. Longfellow's ancestors settled in New England about 1651. On his father's side, Longfellow descended from lawyers and legislators. His mother's father, Peleg Wadsworth, was an American general in the Revolutionary War.

Longfellow published his first poem when he was only 13. He entered Bowdoin College, in Brunswick, Me., at

J. Albert Robbins, the contributor of this article, is Professor of English at Indiana University at Bloomington.

the age of 15. A classmate, Nathaniel Hawthorne, also became a famous writer. By his senior year, Longfellow was determined to become a famous writer. "My whole soul burns most ardently for it," he wrote to his father.

Professor and Author. Longfellow loved learning and was a top student at Bowdoin. The college asked him to teach modern languages there after his graduation in 1825. But Longfellow first traveled in Europe for a little more than three years. He then

A sketch by Franquinet. The Longfellow House, Cambridge, Mass.

Longfellow in 1839 published his first collection of poems, *Voices of the Night*. He was then a young professor at Harvard.

returned to Bowdoin, where he taught French, Spanish, and Italian. He moved to Harvard College in 1836.

In addition to teaching, writing textbooks, and traveling to Europe to improve his ability to use other languages, Longfellow launched a separate career in literature. In 1835, he published *Outre-Mer*, a book of travel sketches. Longfellow's first volume of poems, *Voices of the Night*, appeared in 1839. The collection contained "Hymn to the Night" and "A Psalm of Life."

Longfellow resigned from Harvard in 1854. By that time he had published 12 books, not including textbooks. During these busy years, he wrote most of his better poems, completed a verse drama (*The Spanish Student*, 1843), and published *Evangeline* (1847).

Longfellow married Mary Potter in 1831. Mary died suddenly in 1835 while the couple was traveling in Europe. Trying to overcome his grief, Longfellow continued to travel and in 1836 in Switzerland he met a Boston family, the Appletons. He fell in love with one of the daughters, Frances, but she did not agree to marry him until 1843.

Longfellow's second marriage brought him six children and some 18 years of happy family life. His wife's father gave the couple Craigie House (now called Longfellow House), a handsome and historic mansion in Cambridge, Mass., a short walk from Harvard. It became a national historic site in 1972.

Author and World Celebrity. From his youth, Longfellow seemed destined for success. His first volume of verse sold well, and by 1854, his reputation as a writer was solidly established. In 1855, he published *The Song of Hiawatha*. According to one estimate, this work sold a million copies during Longfellow's lifetime, a remarkable record for any book, and especially remarkable

for poetry. Longfellow achieved further success in 1858 with *The Courtship of Miles Standish*. His verse was translated into many languages and he became known throughout the Western world.

In 1861, at the height of his success, fame, and happiness, Longfellow suffered a personal tragedy. His wife accidentally set her dress afire, probably with a burning match or hot sealing wax. By the time the poet could extinguish the flames, she was fatally burned. To make his grief bearable, Longfellow busied himself with translating Dante's epic poem, *The Divine Comedy*. Longfellow completed the translation in 1863. The truest testimony of Longfellow's sense of personal loss at his wife's death is the sonnet "The Cross of Snow." Found after his death, it is one of his most perfect and moving poems, ending with the lines:

> There is a mountain in the distant West
> That, sun-defying, in its deep ravines
> Displays a cross of snow upon its side.
> Such is the cross I wear upon my breast
> These eighteen years, through all the
> changing scenes
> And seasons, changeless since the day she died.

The remainder of Longfellow's life was lonely, though rewarding. During a trip to Europe in 1868 and 1869, he received honorary degrees from Oxford and Cambridge universities. Longfellow died in Craigie House on March 24, 1882. England paid tribute to him by placing a memorial bust in the Poet's Corner of Westminster Abbey. Longfellow is the only American so honored.

Longfellow's Works

Tastes and standards in poetry change, and what were considered Longfellow's best works in his day are not

A drawing by S. W. Rowse. The Longfellow House, Cambridge, Mass.

Longfellow in 1869, *right,* posed for this photograph with members of his family in Florence, Italy. His second wife, Frances Appleton, *above,* died in a fire in 1861. This great tragedy in Longfellow's life inspired perhaps his finest poem, "The Cross of Snow."

The Longfellow House, Cambridge, Mass.

Gendreau

Longfellow House, in Cambridge, Mass., was Longfellow's home from 1843 until his death in 1882. He wrote many of his works in the study, *right.* The mansion, once called Craigie House, was built in 1759. It served as a headquarters for George Washington during the Revolutionary War.

The Longfellow House, Cambridge, Mass.

always thought best today. During Longfellow's time, many readers treasured works that were sweetly sentimental and reassuring. Today, few mature writers or literary critics approve of these topics and attitudes. One of the poems considered important during Longfellow's time was "The Village Blacksmith." It is considered a minor work today, although a person might argue that it captures real values and convictions of an age now gone. On the other hand, "The Cross of Snow" is a timeless lyric—mature, profound, and imaginative.

Longfellow's best poems fall into three classes—narratives, lyrics, and translations. No poet of the 1800's could match Longfellow's variety of style and content. "The Children's Hour" shows his love of family life. "Mezzo Cammin" is a poem about an artist's concern for his career. "A Psalm of Life" has an instructive, moral purpose. Longfellow wrote poems on the simple life ("The Village Blacksmith"), patriotic historical poems ("Paul Revere's Ride"), tributes to nature ("Woods in Winter"), and ballads ("The Wreck of the Hesperus").

Longfellow also wrote poems—generally sonnets—about other writers, including Geoffrey Chaucer, William Shakespeare, and John Keats. He composed an excellent six-sonnet sequence on Dante's *Divine Comedy.* He also wrote antislavery poems and made fine translations of poems by European authors.

Narrative Poems. *Evangeline, A Tale of Acadie* was the first of Longfellow's four major narrative poems. It is a tale of injustice, describing the forced removal of French colonists from Nova Scotia during the French and Indian Wars of the 1700's. Even more, it is the pathetic story of two lovers separated during the move, Evangeline Bellefontaine and Gabriel Lajeunesse. Evangeline spends years searching for Gabriel. She finally settles in Philadelphia, where she becomes a nun. While nursing the sick during an epidemic, she recognizes a dying old man as Gabriel. She dies shortly after Gabriel, and they are buried side by side. Longfellow

wrote the poem in unrhymed *hexameters* (six feet in each line).

The Song of Hiawatha concerns a legendary Indian hero who is raised by a tribe on the shores of Lake Superior. The poem describes Hiawatha's many battles and contests, and his marriage to Minnehaha. Hiawatha prepares his people for the coming of white settlers and Christianity, and departs from the earth to become a god of the Northwest Wind.

The poem is an example of a romantic poet's tribute to the American Indian. Longfellow used folklore, myth, heroic characters, and natural grandeur to give a sense of Indian culture, ideals, and racial pride. The subject suited the author. It gave him the opportunity to use his scholarship, his resources as a student of other cultures, and his love of idealized narratives. *The Song of Hiawatha* is written in *trochaic tetrameters.* Each line consists of four measures, and each measure consists of an accented then unaccented syllable. See Song of Hiawatha.

The Courtship of Miles Standish is a romanticized story based on colonial New England legend and history. It is written in unrhymed hexameters. Miles Standish, being shy, asks his friend John Alden to propose marriage on his behalf to Priscilla Mullens. The task is difficult for Alden, because he also loves Priscilla. Alden finally proposes for Standish, at which point Priscilla asks the now famous question, "Why don't you speak for yourself, John?" Standish, believing his friend has betrayed him, goes off to fight the Indians. There is a false report of his death, but he returns in time to attend Alden's marriage to Priscilla, and the three are reunited in friendship.

Tales of a Wayside Inn is a series of 21 narrative poems published in three parts (1863, 1872, and 1874). The poems are told in turn by a group of friends at an inn in "Sudbury Town." The poems show Longfellow's scholarship and his interest in the life and history of other lands. Only three of the poems wholly

398b

concern American themes. Other poems tell stories about ancient Israel, Sicily, Italy, Norway, and Iceland. The most famous work in the collection is "Paul Revere's Ride," which opens with these familiar lines:

> Listen my children and you shall hear
> Of the midnight ride of Paul Revere.

Shorter Works. The longer narrative poems are considered major works because of their large and ambitious design. But many modern students of Longfellow bypass them in favor of several shorter poems of superior quality, including "Mezzo Cammin," "The Jewish Cemetery at Newport," "The Ropewalk," "Divina Commedia," "Keats," and "The Cross of Snow."

Prose Works. Longfellow wrote some prose, but none of it matches his poems in quality. His two romantic novels *Hyperion* (1839) and *Kavanagh* (1849) are seldom read today. Most interesting of his prose works is *Outre-Mer, A Pilgrimage Beyond the Sea* (1835), his first volume of creative writing. In this book, Longfellow imitated Washington Irving's *Sketch Book* but did not equal it in quality. But *Outre-Mer* has some charm, and it announces what was to occupy much of Longfellow's mind and talent—life beyond the sea.

Longfellow's Place in Literature

No one could hope for more fame and universal respect than Longfellow received during his lifetime. When famous literary visitors came to America and stopped in Boston, they always called at Craigie House to pay their respects to the famous poet.

Today, however, critics and scholars place considerably less value on Longfellow's works than they do on those of another poet of the 1800's, Walt Whitman. Whitman published the first edition of his *Leaves of Grass* in 1855, the year that Longfellow published *Hiawatha*. Whitman's experimental and original verse profoundly influenced poetry for many years. Longfellow's work has had no such lasting influence on later poetry.

As early as 1846, Margaret Fuller, an American critic and author, called Longfellow artificial and imitative. In the 1900's, the critic Walter Fuller Taylor said, Longfellow "is winsome, without being majestic." In *Longfellow, His Life and Work* (1963), scholar Newton Arvin tries to restore much of Longfellow's reputation. But Arvin feels obliged to say, "Let us agree, once and for all, that he is a minor writer."

Longfellow wrote poems to appeal to every taste except the most unusual or the most intellectual. He wrote on a wide range of subjects and placed no great burden of understanding upon his readers. This may account for his great popularity in his day. Some critics have commented that perhaps Longfellow's abilities as a poet were never fully tested because he led such an untroubled life. They note that he had some personal trouble, but perhaps not enough to sharpen his poetic powers or deepen his emotions. They point to "The Cross of Snow," a poem created out of personal grief, to show what the author could do when he was emotionally involved in his theme.

We can recognize Longfellow as a minor literary talent and still see him as a great American. He represented important areas of American life in his time: genteel values, scholarly interests, gracious living, the joys of family life, and intelligent responsiveness to European life. The English novelist Anthony Trollope said, "Of

all the poets of his day, [Longfellow] is the last that I should have guessed to be an American had I come across his works in ignorance of the fact." Yet Longfellow was thoroughly American. He simply demonstrated that Americans could be cosmopolitan, international citizens, and as versatile in literature as the best that the Old World could offer.   J. Albert Robbins

See also EVANGELINE; SONG OF HIAWATHA; MAINE (Places to Visit; picture: Wadsworth-Longfellow House).

Additional Resources

ARVIN, NEWTON. *Longfellow: His Life and Work.* Greenwood, 1977. Reprint of 1963 ed.

SMEATON, OLIPHANT. *Longfellow and His Poetry.* AMS, 1976. Reprint of 1913 ed.

WAGENKNECHT, EDWARD. *Henry Wadsworth Longfellow: A Full-Length Portrait.* Longman, 1955.

WILLIAMS, CECIL. *Henry Wadsworth Longfellow.* Twayne, 1964.

LONGHORN. See CATTLE (Beginning of Breeding; color picture).

LONGINUS, *lahn JY nuhs*, is the name given to the unknown author of *On the Sublime*, an ancient Greek *treatise* (long essay) on literary criticism. Many scholars rank it second in importance only to Aristotle's *Poetics* among ancient writings on literature. *On the Sublime* was probably written during the first 100 years after the birth of Jesus Christ.

The treatise identifies five sources of sublimity in literature. The author used *sublimity* as another term for *greatness*. The sources of sublimity are (1) the ability to conceive great thoughts, (2) intense emotion, (3) powerful figures of speech, (4) the choice of noble words, and (5) harmonious composition of sentences. *On the Sublime* compares the literary styles of the Greek orator Demosthenes and the Roman orator Cicero. It discusses the effect of tyranny on literature.   George Kennedy

LONGITUDE, *LAHN juh tood.* If one person travels directly north, and another person 50 miles (80 kilometers) west also travels directly north, their paths will meet at the North Pole. Each person will have traveled in the same direction along a *line of longitude.* Lines of longitude run north and south along the earth's surface. Map makers think of the earth as a huge globe divided into 360 equal parts. The lines between the parts on the outside of the globe are called *meridians.* These meridians are the principal lines of longitude on maps.

Longitude and Location. Most nations start counting longitude east and west from an imaginary line running through Greenwich, a borough of London, England. These countries have agreed that Greenwich lies at 0° longitude.

The earth is divided into two parts, or hemispheres, of east and west longitude. Each hemisphere has 180 degrees. Degrees of longitude are used to measure east and west distances on maps, and to locate certain points. For example, New York City lies at 74° west longitude. This means that if a person travels west from Greenwich to New York City and counts the imaginary meridians that are passed, New York City would lie on the 74th meridian west of Greenwich. Sailors and pilots use longitude to help determine the location of their ships and airplanes.

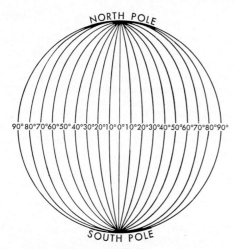

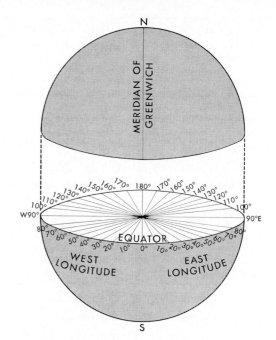

Meridians of Longitude are lines drawn from north to south on maps and globes to indicate distances and locate points. The prime meridian passes through Greenwich, England, *right*. All meridians of longitude meet at the North and South poles, *above*. The distance between meridians is greatest at the equator. It gradually decreases as the meridians near the poles.

The space between two meridians is greatest at the equator. This space narrows as the lines of longitude approach the North Pole and the South Pole. For example, a degree of longitude at New Orleans, La., is about 60 miles (97 kilometers) wide. At Winnipeg, Canada, which lies much nearer the North Pole, a degree of longitude is less than 45 miles (72 kilometers) wide. At Fairbanks, Alaska, which is closer to the pole than Winnipeg, it is even narrower.

Longitude and Time. Any point on the earth's surface passes through a whole circle—360 degrees—once every 24 hours. It does this because the earth turns once on its axis every 24 hours. All 360 degrees of the earth's circumference also pass beneath the sun once in 24 hours. In *one* hour, $\frac{1}{24}$ of 360 degrees, or 15 degrees, passes beneath the sun. Because it seems that the sun is moving instead of the earth, people say that one hour of time equals 15 degrees of longitude.

Each degree of longitude is divided into 60 parts called minutes. Each minute is divided into 60 seconds of longitude. One minute is written as 1′, and one second as 1″. These minutes and seconds of longitude measure distance, not time. But since an hour of time equals 15° of longitude, a minute or second of time equals a certain distance that can be expressed in minutes and seconds of longitude.

The following table gives the equivalent in distance for five units of time. These units range from a day to a second:

> 24 hours of time = 360° of longitude.
> 1 hour of time = 15° of longitude.
> 4 minutes of time = 1° of longitude.
> 1 minute of time = 15′ of longitude.
> 1 second of time = 15″ of longitude.

PAUL SOLLENBERGER

See also LATITUDE; MAP; MERIDIAN; TIME.

LONGS PEAK. See COLORADO (Land Regions; map); MOUNTAIN (table); ROCKY MOUNTAIN NATIONAL PARK (picture).

LONGSTREET, JAMES (1821-1904), was a Confederate general in the Civil War. His troops called him "Old Pete." As a lieutenant general, he commanded the First Corps of General Robert E. Lee's army, and he fought in most of the major battles in Virginia. Not aggressive in battle, Longstreet liked to take a strong position and hold it. This point of view made him the center of a great controversy after the Battle of Gettysburg. According to some students of the battle, Longstreet did not put his heart into Lee's plan of attack. Lee, however, continued to count on Longstreet throughout the Civil War. Longstreet was a dogged combat soldier and an able defensive commander.

Longstreet was born in Edgefield District, South Carolina. He graduated from the U.S. Military Academy in 1842, and later fought in the Mexican War.

In 1880, Longstreet, who had allied himself with the Republicans, was appointed minister to Turkey. He served as U.S. commissioner of railroads from 1898 until his death in 1904.   FRANK E. VANDIVER

LONGUEUIL, *lawng GAYL,* Quebec (pop. 124,320), is a suburb of Montreal on the southeast shore of the St. Lawrence River. A new city of Longueuil was created in April, 1969, when Longueuil merged with the city of Jacques-Cartier. In 1961, Longueuil had annexed Montreal-Sud, a small town. The Jacques-Cartier bridge links Longueuil and Montreal. For location, see QUEBEC (political map).

Longueuil produces airplane motors, bakery products, machine parts, and transportation equipment. The Charles Le Moyne Historical Museum, Jacques-Cartier Classical College, and the Louis Braille House for the Blind are in the city. Longueuil has a mayor-council form of government.

The first settlement at Longueuil was established in 1657 by Charles Le Moyne, Lord of Longueuil (see LE MOYNE, CHARLES). Longueuil received its city charter in 1874. Today, historic buildings stand close to such modern areas as Place Charles Le Moyne. Place

Charles Le Moyne includes a theater and a hotel completed in the early 1970's. HUBERT CHARBONNEAU

LOOKOUT MOUNTAIN. See COLORADO (Places to Visit [Buffalo Bill's Grave]); TENNESSEE (Places to Visit; color picture).

LOOKOUT MOUNTAIN, BATTLE OF. See CIVIL WAR (Chattanooga).

LOOM. See WEAVING; TEXTILE.

LOON is the name given to several water birds that dive underwater for fish. Loons are also called *divers*. Most of them are related to the grebes.

The *common loon*, or *great northern diver*, is found from the northern United States to the Arctic Circle. In summer, this bird lives in the small, lonely lakes in the interior of the country. The common loon is the state bird of Minnesota.

Loons are about 36 inches (91 centimeters) long. Their backs and wings are black, with white spots. The heads and necks are glossy black and green, and the neck has white streaks. The webbed feet are also black, and the tails are short. Loons look somewhat like ducks. Their loud screams can sometimes be heard echoing over the lakes at night. Loons feed chiefly on fish.

The *Pacific loon* has a purple-black throat. It is smaller than the great northern diver. The *red-throated diver* is about 25 inches (64 centimeters) long and has duller coloring than the common loon.

Scientific Classification. Loons belong to the loon family, Gaviidae. The common loon is *Gavia immer*. The Pacific loon is *G. arctica pacifica*. The red-throated is *G. stellata*.

JOSEPH J. HICKEY

See also BIRD (picture: Birds of Inland Waters).

LOOPER. See MEASURING WORM.

LOOSESTRIFE is any one of a group of more than 70 plants that belong to the primrose family. *Golden loosestrife*, native to Europe and Asia, is grown in the United States. It has sword-shaped leaves and yellow flowers. *Moneywort*, also called *creeping Charlie* and *creeping Jennie*, thrives in moist soils. It grows as a creeping vine and bears bright yellow blossoms.

Scientific Classification. Loosestrife is in the primrose family, Primulaceae. The golden is *Lysimachia vulgaris*. Moneywort is *L. nummularia*. DONALD WYMAN

LOPE DE VEGA. See VEGA, LOPE DE.

LÓPEZ ARELLANO, OSVALDO. See HONDURAS (Recent Developments).

LÓPEZ DE SANTA ANNA, ANTONIO. See SANTA ANNA, ANTONIO LÓPEZ DE.

LÓPEZ PORTILLO, *LOH pehz pawr TEE yoh,* **JOSÉ,** *hoh SAY* (1920-   ), served as president of Mexico from 1976 to 1982. López Portillo, a member of the Institutional Revolutionary Party, ran unopposed in the 1976 presidential election.

As president, López Portillo supported economic programs to encourage investment in private business in Mexico and to help the nation's poor people. Increased oil production at the start of his term helped improve Mexico's economy. But near the end of his term, severe economic problems developed in Mexico. See MEXICO (Mexico Today).

López Portillo was born in Mexico City. He received a law degree from the National Autonomous University of Mexico in 1946. He taught college courses in law, political science, and public administration from 1947 to 1959. In 1959, he became an adviser in the govern-

ment's Ministry of National Patrimony.

During the 1960's, López Portillo held increasingly important positions in the Mexican government. In 1970, he was named undersecretary of national patrimony. He was appointed director of the Federal Electricity Commission in Mexico in 1972. López Portillo held that office until 1973, when he became secretary of finance and public credit.

Organization of American States
José López Portillo

ROBERT E. QUIRK

LOQUAT, *LOH kwaht,* is an orange-yellow fruit that has the shape and size of an egg. A loquat is a *pome,* a type of fruit that has many seeds inside a papery core. It grows on the loquat tree, a small evergreen from 18 to 25 feet (5.5 to 7.6 meters) high. The loquat was brought to the United States from China and Japan in 1784. Loquats are grown commercially in California. They also grow along the Gulf Coast and in northern South America. The loquat has a mildly tart flavor. It is eaten fresh, cooked, and as a jelly.

Scientific Classification. Loquats belong to the rose family, Rosaceae. They are classified as *Eriobotrya japonica*. REID M. BROOKS

Loquats

LORAIN, *loh RAYN,* Ohio (pop. 75,416), is an industrial city on the shore of Lake Erie at the mouth of the Black River (see OHIO [political map]). With Elyria, Ohio, Lorain has a metropolitan area population of 274,909. The city is a leading Ohio iron and steel center and a shipping center. Its harbor accommodates freighters with iron ore from Lake Superior mines and coal from Ohio and other states. Lorain's products include bearings, clothing, electrical equipment, ingots and steel for castings, steel pipes and tubes, and ships.

Lorain was first settled in 1807. It has a mayor-council form of government. JAMES H. RODABAUGH

LORAN, *LAWR an,* stands for *long range navigation.* It is a system of radio navigation that helps ships and aircraft find their positions. Two stations, known as the *master* and the *slave* stations, continually send out radio signals. The ship or aircraft receives these signals with special equipment. The receiver equipment measures the time interval between the pulses it receives from the stations. The difference in time between receiving the signals from one pair of stations places the ship or aircraft at some point on a *loran line of position* on a chart. The chart is marked to show the position of the ship or aircraft according to the difference in time between the signals. In most cases, a single master station is paired with each of two slave stations. This allows the navigator to *intersect* (cross) two loran lines of position to fix a ship or aircraft's position.

In the United States and Canada, navigators use a system known as loran-C. Loran-C can transmit its signal more than 1,000 miles (1,600 kilometers) during the day. Under certain conditions, it has a range of more than 3,000 miles (4,800 kilometers) at night, when low-frequency radio waves travel farther. A position can be located within $\frac{1}{4}$ mile (1.4 kilometer).   G. D. DUNLAP

See also NAVIGATION (Loran); SHORAN.

LORCA, FEDERICO GARCÍA. See GARCÍA LORCA, FEDERICO.

LORD is a title added to a person's name or to his office. Great Britain's House of Lords includes the peers, called *Lords Temporal*, and dignitaries of the Church of England, called *Lords Spiritual*. The word *lord* is often used as a less formal title for a marquess, earl, or viscount, and always for a baron. The younger sons of dukes and marquesses have the title added to their names. It is used with the names of bishops (the Lord Bishop of London) and government offices (Lord Lieutenant of Ireland).   I. J. SANDERS

LORD HOWE ISLAND is a coral island 436 miles (702 kilometers) northeast of Sydney, Australia. For location, see PACIFIC ISLANDS (color map). This crescent-shaped island is about 7 miles (11 kilometers) long and 1 mile (1.6 kilometers) wide, and covers 7 square miles (17 square kilometers). Dense vegetation blankets it. The land is mountainous. Waves have cut many cliffs in the coral. The people engage in farming, fishing, and the tourist trade. About 245 persons live on the island, which was discovered in 1788. New South Wales governs Lord Howe Island.   C. M. H. CLARK

LORDS, HOUSE OF. See HOUSE OF LORDS.

LORD'S PRAYER is the most widely said Christian prayer. By tradition, it is one of the three basic statements of Christian faith. The other two are the Apostles' Creed and the Ten Commandments. For over 1,000 years, people who have been raised as Christians or have become Christians have memorized the Lord's Prayer.

The Lord's Prayer is also called the *pater noster*, two Latin words meaning *Our Father*, the first two words of the prayer. The prayer appears in two forms in the New Testament—in Matthew 6:9-13 and in Luke 11:2-4. Protestants and Roman Catholics now both use the longer form from Matthew.

The Lord's Prayer praises God, asks for food and forgiveness, and pleads for protection against evil. Both Gospels tell that Jesus taught the prayer to His followers as the best way to pray to God. Many scholars believe the prayer expresses the religion that Jesus taught His followers and wanted them to practice.

In the King James version of the prayer, the line "Forgive us our debts" is in Matthew, and "Forgive us our sins" is in Luke. A third version uses "Forgive us our trespasses." The words *debts*, *sins*, and *trespasses* all are translations from the same word used in the original Greek version. The Greek word means *to miss the mark*.

All Christian denominations say the Lord's Prayer, both in public worship and in private prayers. The prayer is also said by nonreligious groups, including athletic teams before or after games and organizations at meetings. Many composers have set the prayer to music. Albert H. Malotte, an American composer, wrote one of the best-known versions.   WILLIAM A. CLEBSCH

The words of the Lord's Prayer vary among the many translations of the New Testament. Four familiar versions from Matthew are:

The King James Version (Protestant):

Our Father which art in heaven, Hallowed be thy name. Thy kingdom come. Thy will be done in earth, as it is in heaven. Give us this day our daily bread. And forgive us our debts, as we forgive our debtors. And lead us not into temptation, but deliver us from evil: For thine is the kingdom, and the power, and the glory, for ever. Amen.

The New English Bible Version (Protestant):

Our Father in heaven, thy name be hallowed; thy kingdom come, thy will be done, on earth as in heaven. Give us today our daily bread. Forgive us the wrong we have done, as we have forgiven those who have wronged us. And do not bring us to the test, but save us from the evil one.

The Baltimore Catechism Version (Roman Catholic):

Our Father who art in heaven, hallowed be Thy name; Thy kingdom come; Thy will be done on earth as it is in heaven. Give us this day our daily bread; and forgive us our trespasses, as we forgive those who trespass against us; and lead us not into temptation, but deliver us from evil. Amen.

The New American Bible Version (Roman Catholic):

Our Father in heaven, hallowed be your name, your kingdom come, your will be done on earth as it is in heaven. Give us today our daily bread, and forgive us the wrong we have done as we forgive those who wrong us. Subject us not to the trial but deliver us from the evil one.

LORD'S SUPPER. See COMMUNION.

LORELEI, *LAWR uh ly*, is a high cliff that towers about 430 feet (131 meters) above the Rhine River between Mainz and Koblenz in Germany. At that point, the river is swift-flowing and dangerous. Legend says the echo heard at the cliff is the voice of a beautiful but wicked siren, or river nymph, luring boatmen to destruction. The German writer Clemens Brentano may have invented the myth in 1802. The Lorelei is the subject of a poem by Heinrich Heine and of an unfinished opera by Felix Mendelssohn. Others have also written about it. See also RHINE RIVER.   FRANK AHNERT

LORENTZ, *LOHR ehnts,* **HENDRIK ANTOON,** *AHN tohn* (1853-1928), was a Dutch physicist. He became famous for his electron theory of matter, and shared the 1902 Nobel prize for physics with Dutch physicist Pieter Zeeman for discovering the effects of magnetism on light (Zeeman effect).

Lorentz assumed that matter consists of electrically charged particles. His electron theory showed that moving bodies would appear to be shortened in the direction of motion. This was because forces between charged particles could be affected by motion, making the length of the bodies appear different when measured at rest. The change in length is too small to notice except in precise experiments carried on at high speeds.

The equations that show how bodies are deformed by motion are called the *Lorentz transformations*. Lorentz' theory predicted effects similar to those predicted by Einstein's theory of relativity (see RELATIVITY [picture]).

Lorentz was born at Arnhem, the Netherlands, and graduated from Leiden University.   CARL T. CHASE

LORENZ, *LOH rehnts,* **KONRAD ZACHARIAS,** *KOHN raht TSAH kah REE ahs* (1903-   ), an Austrian naturalist, was one of the founders of *ethology,* the study of animal behavior. Lorenz and two other ethologists—Karl von Frisch of Austria and Nikolaas Tinbergen, born in the Netherlands—received the 1973 Nobel Prize for physiology or medicine for their work on animal behavior.

Unlike psychologists, who had studied animal behavior in laboratories, Lorenz studied animals in their natural environments. He also raised wild creatures in his home. He observed that instinct plays a major role in animal behavior—a view that conflicted with the ideas of many psychologists. He described the instinctive process of *imprinting,* by which, for example, an animal may learn to identify its owner as its parent (see IN-STINCT [Imprinting]).

Lorenz was born in Vienna. He earned an M.D. degree in 1928 and a Ph.D. degree in 1933, both at the University of Vienna. In 1954, he became codirector of the Max Planck Institute for Physiology of Behavior in West Germany.

Lorenz wrote several books. *King Solomon's Ring* (1952) describes his experiences with animals. In *On Aggression* (1966), he compares aggressive behavior among animals to human actions.   JOHN A. WIENS

See also ETHOLOGY.

LORENZINI, CARLO. See COLLODI, CARLO.

LORENZO THE MAGNIFICENT. See MEDICI.

LORIS, *LAWR ihs,* is a slow-moving animal that lives in trees. Lorises are *primates,* members of the order of animals that includes monkeys and apes. The *slender loris*

© Tom McHugh, Photo Researchers

The Slow Loris, *above,* is found from India to Indonesia. Lorises live in trees and are active chiefly at night. These small, tailless animals use their hands and feet to grasp branches while climbing.

lives in India and Sri Lanka. The larger *slow loris* is found from India to Indonesia.

Most lorises are gray or brown, and grow 8 to 10 inches (20 to 25 centimeters) long. Their three-cornered faces and large eyes give them a weird appearance. They have no tails.

The loris lives alone. It sleeps in the daytime with its feet clasped around the limb of a tree, and its body rolled into a ball with the head tucked between the thighs. At night, the loris prowls around in search of food. The loris lives on fruit, insects, and bird eggs.

Scientific Classification. Lorises belong to the loris family, Lorisidae. The slender loris is classified as genus *Loris,* species *L. tardigradus.* The slow loris is *Nycticebus coucang.*   GEORGE SCHALLER

LORNE, *lawrn,* **MARQUESS OF,** *MAHR kwihs* (1845-1914), served as governor general of Canada from 1878 to 1883. In 1880, he helped establish an office in London called the office of high commissioner of Canada to improve communications between the Canadian and British governments. In 1882, he founded the Royal Society of Canada, which promotes the arts and sciences. Lorne also helped found the Royal Canadian Academy of Arts and the National Gallery of Canada.

Lorne was born in London. His given and family name was John Douglas Sutherland Campbell. In 1871, he married Princess Louise Caroline Alberta, a daughter of Queen Victoria.

Lorne was elected to the British Parliament in 1868. He served in the House of Commons as a member of the Liberal Party until 1878. He also served in the House of Commons as a Unionist from 1895 to 1900. Lorne became the ninth Duke of Argyll in 1900.   JACQUES MONET

LORRAIN, CLAUDE. See CLAUDE.

LORRAINE. See ALSACE-LORRAINE.

LORRY. See TRUCK.

LORY. See PARROT (Kinds).

LOS ALAMOS NATIONAL LABORATORY, in Los Alamos, N. Mex., is one of the world's leading research institutions. It is primarily involved in the application of science and technology to problems of United States national security. Activities at the laboratory include the development of nuclear warheads, the production and testing of nuclear materials, and the creation of designs for new weapons. The laboratory is also responsible for developing technology for use in verifying that other nations fulfill their arms control commitments. Other research at the laboratory focuses on such areas as nuclear physics, the U.S. energy supply, and the disposal of nuclear waste.

The University of California operates Los Alamos National Laboratory for the United States Department of Energy. The laboratory was established in 1943 as part of the World War II Manhattan Project to build the first nuclear weapons (see MANHATTAN PROJECT).

Today, more than 3,500 scientists, engineers, and other professionals work at the laboratory. It contains some of the largest and fastest computers in the world. Its Clinton P. Anderson Meson Physics Facility (LAMPF) houses a proton linear accelerator that is $\frac{1}{2}$ mile (0.8 kilometer) long. Many scientists consider LAMPF to be the most sophisticated nuclear science facility in the world.   ALVIN W. TRIVELPIECE

© Larry Lee, West Light

Downtown Los Angeles is ringed by high-speed freeways. The people of Los Angeles depend heavily on their automobiles to travel about their sprawling city. Los Angeles is the chief business, financial, and trade center of the Western United States.

LOS ANGELES

LOS ANGELES is a huge city in southern California. According to the 1980 census, it ranked as the third largest city in the United States, after New York and Chicago. But in 1982, U.S. Bureau of the Census estimates reported that Los Angeles had passed Chicago in population and had become the nation's second largest city. Few U.S. cities have grown as rapidly as Los Angeles. In 1850, when Los Angeles became a city, it had only 1,610 people. Today, it has about 3 million people.

Los Angeles is the seat of Los Angeles County, the nation's largest county in population. The county has about 7½ million people and includes 80 other cities besides Los Angeles. Los Angeles County makes up the city's metropolitan area. Los Angeles and other communities in the area run together and look much alike, making it difficult to tell where one community ends and another begins. For this reason, the area has been described as "a hundred suburbs in search of a city."

More than half the people of Los Angeles County moved there from other parts of the United States or from other countries. Many immigrants moved to Los Angeles seeking good jobs or to escape from political conflicts in their countries. Some people were attracted by the city's scenic location, pleasant climate, and outdoor way of life. Golden beaches line the Pacific Ocean to the west and south of the city, and tall, snow-capped mountains rise to the northeast. The ocean and the mountains help give Los Angeles a mild climate the year around. The climate makes it possible for people to enjoy most outdoor sports in any season. Most of the homes in Los Angeles have backyard patios, and many also have swimming pools.

Each year, millions of tourists visit the Los Angeles area. They come to enjoy the area's beaches, ski resorts, and other recreational facilities, as well as its many cultural and entertainment attractions.

Los Angeles is the business, financial, and trade center of the Western United States. It leads the nation in the production of aircraft and equipment for space exploration. The city's motion-picture and television industry is world famous. Banks and other financial institutions in Los Angeles rank among the largest in the country and have helped finance the area's rapid growth. The Port of Los Angeles is the busiest port on the West Coast. This port handles more trade with Japan and other Asian countries than any other port in the United States.

But along with all its glories, Los Angeles has serious problems. Many of these problems result from the rapid increase in population. The city has little open land left, and housing—especially low-cost housing—is in short supply. The people of Los Angeles depend mainly on automobiles for transportation, and they own more than 4 million cars. As a result, the area's freeway system is often jammed with traffic. Exhaust fumes from the great number of cars—as well as smoke from factories—have created a grave air pollution problem. To help reduce air pollution and traffic jams, Los Angeles has improved its public bus system since 1980.

Facts in Brief

Population: *City*—2,968,597. *Metropolitan Area*—7,477,503. *Consolidated Metropolitan Area*—11,497,568.

Area: *City*—465 sq. mi. (1,204 km²). *Metropolitan Area*—4,113 sq. mi. (10,653 km²). *Consolidated Metropolitan Area*—34,181 sq. mi. (88,528 km²).

Altitude: 275 ft. (84 m) above sea level.

Climate: *Average Temperature*—January, 55° F. (13° C); July, 73° F. (23° C). *Average Annual Precipitation* (rainfall, melted snow, and other forms of moisture)—15 in. (38 cm). For the monthly weather in Los Angeles, see CALIFORNIA (Climate).

Government: Mayor-council. *Terms*—4 years for the mayor and the 15 council members.

Founded: 1781. Incorporated as a city in 1850.

404

George Nelson, Artstreet

Los Angeles' Birthplace lies in a downtown area called the *Pueblo de Los Ángeles.* The city began here in 1781. The cross marks colorful Olvera Street, one of the Pueblo's oldest streets.

LOS ANGELES/*The City*

Los Angeles lies on the Pacific coast in southern California. It is about 350 miles (563 kilometers) southeast of San Francisco and about 130 miles (209 kilometers) northwest of San Diego and the Mexican border. Los Angeles covers 465 square miles (1,204 square kilometers), making it one of the nation's largest cities in area. It stretches about 50 miles (80 kilometers) from the San Fernando Valley in the north to Los Angeles Harbor at San Pedro Bay in the south. From east to west, the city extends about 30 miles (48 kilometers)—from the San Gabriel Mountains to the Pacific Ocean.

In the past, Los Angeles added to its area by annexing such nearby cities and towns as Hollywood, San Pedro, Van Nuys, and Westwood. These places are now districts of Los Angeles. Eighty independent communities lie outside the city in Los Angeles County. These cities include Burbank, Long Beach, Pasadena, and Santa Monica. Beverly Hills and San Fernando are independent communities surrounded by Los Angeles.

Los Angeles can be divided into eight main sections: (1) Downtown Los Angeles, (2) South-Central Los Angeles, (3) Central Los Angeles, (4) the San Fernando Valley, (5) West Los Angeles, (6) South Bay, (7) the Port of Los Angeles, and (8) East Los Angeles. These sections do not have definite boundaries and are not official government units. They are chiefly areas that have similar types of housing, people with similar backgrounds, or some other common features.

Downtown Los Angeles, the main business and shopping center, lies near the eastern edge of the city. Los Angeles residents do not depend on their downtown section so much as do the people of other cities. Los Angeles has many commercial and shopping districts because it spreads over such a large area and consists of several districts that were once separate communities.

Los Angeles' downtown area has changed greatly since 1957. That year, the city government repealed a law that prevented the construction of buildings higher than 150 feet (46 meters), or about 13 stories. The law was originally passed because of the threat of earthquakes. But by 1957, new engineering and construction methods made it possible to construct taller buildings that could withstand earthquakes. Today, several 40- and 50-story buildings rise in the downtown area. The city's tallest building—the United California Building—rises 62 stories, or 858 feet (262 meters), downtown.

City Hall, one of the best-known landmarks in Los Angeles, stands in the downtown area, near the major skyscrapers. For many years, this 26-story, or 454 foot (138 meter) structure, with its distinctive white tower, was the city's tallest building and the only exception to the 150-foot (46-meter) height limit. City Hall is part of a group of city, county, state, and federal buildings that make up the Civic Center.

At the west end of the Civic Center stands the Music Center for the Performing Arts. It consists of two theaters and a concert hall. A group of luxury apartment houses called Bunker Hill Towers and several tall office buildings form an impressive skyline in this area.

The downtown area also includes some of Los Angeles' oldest buildings. Northeast of the Civic Center lies an area called the *Pueblo de Los Ángeles* (Town of the Angels). A group of settlers from Mexico founded Los Angeles there more than 200 years ago. The area has been restored to resemble a village of old Mexico. The Pueblo includes the Old Plaza, a charming public square shaded by 100-year-old magnolia trees. Buildings dating back to the late 1800's surround the Plaza. Olvera Street, one of Los Angeles' oldest streets, begins at the Plaza and runs north. Colorful stalls selling Mexican handicrafts line the street. Adobe buildings from the early 1800's house Mexican craft shops and restaurants. Autos are not allowed on Olvera Street.

Three blocks southwest of City Hall lies a Latino—chiefly Mexican-American—shopping district. There, the sound of modern Mexican music pours from record shops and cafes and fills the streets. Newsstands sell

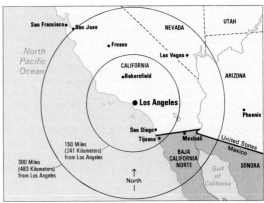

WORLD BOOK map

Los Angeles lies in southern California between San Francisco and the Mexican border. A number of well-known North American cities lie within 300 miles of Los Angeles.

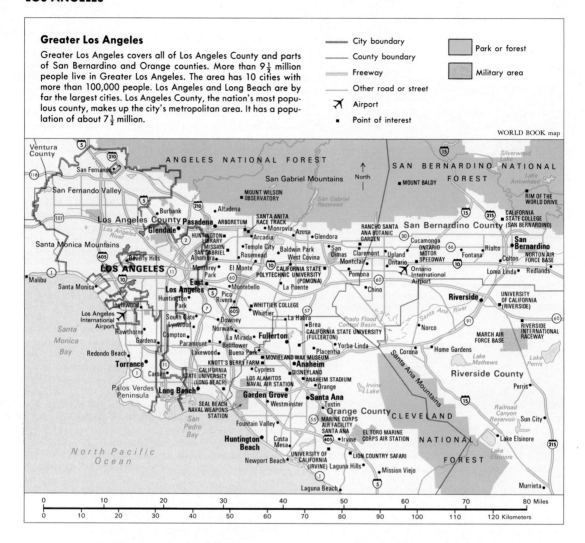

Greater Los Angeles

Greater Los Angeles covers all of Los Angeles County and parts of San Bernardino and Orange counties. More than 9½ million people live in Greater Los Angeles. The area has 10 cities with more than 100,000 people. Los Angeles and Long Beach are by far the largest cities. Los Angeles County, the nation's most populous county, makes up the city's metropolitan area. It has a population of about 7½ million.

City boundary
County boundary
Freeway
Other road or street
✈ Airport
■ Point of interest

Park or forest

Military area

WORLD BOOK map

Mexican magazines and newspapers, and Spanish is heard more often than English. Little Tokyo, a Japanese neighborhood, is two blocks southeast of City Hall. This area has many Japanese restaurants, shops that sell goods imported from Japan, art galleries, and food markets. Chinatown lies a few blocks north of Little Tokyo. There, many Chinese residents operate restaurants and shops that sell antiques, art objects, and souvenirs.

South-Central Los Angeles covers a huge region south of the downtown area. It is one of the largest black communities in the United States. During World War II (1939-1945), many blacks moved to South-Central Los Angeles to work in the area's war plants. After the war, the city's black population continued to increase. The black community spread south to include a district called Watts, about 10 miles (16 kilometers) from downtown. Watts has become the center of the black community in Los Angeles. The black population has also spread about 10 miles (16 kilometers) west to the border of the independent community of Inglewood. Some black neighborhoods of South-Central Los Angeles con-

sist of slum housing. But others have expensive, well-kept homes. In addition, thousands of blacks have moved to the suburbs. Latinos have moved into some formerly black areas of South-Central Los Angeles.

Central Los Angeles lies between the downtown area, on the east, and the independent community of Beverly Hills, on the west. Parts of this area contain a growing number of Asians. A large part of Central Los Angeles consists of Hollywood, a community famous for TV and motion-picture studios. Hollywood Boulevard, one of Los Angeles' best-known streets, runs through Hollywood's business district. The names of Hollywood celebrities are engraved on big stars set in the sidewalks along the boulevard and its side streets.

Sunset Boulevard, another famous Los Angeles street, is just south of Hollywood Boulevard. It begins in the downtown area and winds almost 25 miles (40 kilometers) through Central Los Angeles to the Pacific Ocean. The section that runs through the western part of Hollywood is called *Sunset Strip* or the *Strip*. It is lined with smart shops and expensive restaurants and cafes. It

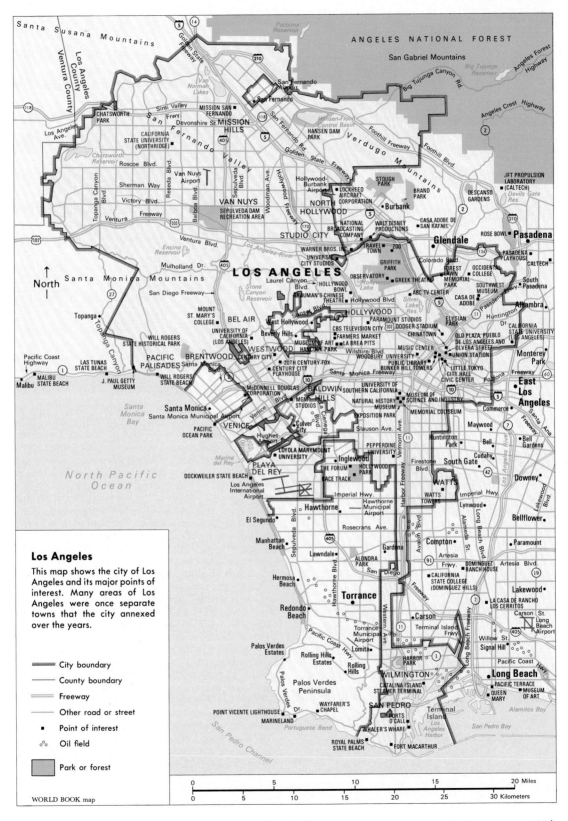

Los Angeles

This map shows the city of Los Angeles and its major points of interest. Many areas of Los Angeles were once separate towns that the city annexed over the years.

—— City boundary
—— County boundary
═══ Freeway
—— Other road or street
■ Point of interest
°° Oil field
▨ Park or forest

WORLD BOOK map

0   5   10   15   20 Miles
0   5   10   15   20   25   30 Kilometers

South-Central Los Angeles occupies a large region south of the downtown area. It includes one of the largest black communities in the United States. The Watts district, *above,* lies about 10 miles (16 kilometers) from downtown. It has become the center of Los Angeles' black community.

WORLD BOOK photo by J. R. Eyerman

WORLD BOOK photo by J. R. Eyerman

Elegant Wilshire Boulevard runs from the downtown area to the Pacific Ocean. Its most famous section, called the *Miracle Mile, above,* has many strikingly modern office buildings.

is also known for its nightclubs and coffeehouses.

Wilshire Boulevard, about $2\frac{1}{2}$ miles (4 kilometers) south of Sunset Boulevard, also runs from downtown through Central Los Angeles to the ocean. It is known for its tall office buildings and fine shops and department stores. A section of the street called the *Miracle Mile* is lined with handsome buildings of modern design.

The San Fernando Valley lies northwest of Hollywood across the Santa Monica Mountains. The Los Angeles section of the valley covers 234 square miles (606 square kilometers), which the city annexed in 1915. When Los Angeles annexed the section, it consisted of large open areas and several rural communities. Today, huge housing developments and shopping centers cover the San Fernando Valley. Over a million people, about a third of Los Angeles' residents, live in the valley. Most of them live in single-family houses with patios and barbecues in the backyard. Many homes include a backyard swimming pool. The area also has numerous small apartment buildings. The independent communities of Burbank and San Fernando also are in the valley.

West Los Angeles occupies the area from Beverly Hills to the city's western border. The Santa Monica Mountains cover much of West Los Angeles.

Century City, a planned community, borders Beverly Hills on the southwest. This "city within a city" was begun in 1961 and is scheduled for completion in the late 1980's. When completed, it will include 20 office buildings, 25 apartment houses, a 1,200-room hotel, a shopping center, many restaurants, and 3 theaters. Century City stands on land that was once part of the Twentieth Century-Fox motion-picture studio.

The community of Westwood and the University of California at Los Angeles (UCLA) lie west of Century City. Westwood began in the 1920's as a small village of Spanish-style buildings. It has grown with the UCLA campus and has become a lively college town and shopping area.

Three of the city's most fashionable communities—Bel Air, Brentwood, and Pacific Palisades—are in West Los Angeles at the foot of the Santa Monica Mountains. Bel Air is north of Westwood, and Brentwood and Pacific Palisades are west of it.

The community of Venice lies between the city of Santa Monica and Marina del Rey, a county harbor for small boats. Venice was designed in the early 1900's as a city of canals like Venice, Italy. Today, most of the canals have been filled in, and the area consists of aging beach homes and hotels.

South Bay lies along the Pacific Ocean from Marina del Rey south to the Palos Verdes Peninsula. It includes an area of the city of Los Angeles called Playa del Rey, as well as several independent communities. Playa del Rey, south of Marina del Rey, was once a pleasant beach community. Today, it is troubled by noise from Los Angeles International Airport.

The independent communities of El Segundo, Manhattan Beach, Hermosa Beach, and Redondo Beach stretch south along the ocean from Playa del Rey to the Palos Verdes Peninsula. Cities on the peninsula include Palos Verdes Estates and Rolling Hills Estates.

The Port of Los Angeles is on San Pedro Bay, about 20 miles (32 kilometers) south of the downtown area. It includes the communities of San Pedro and Wilmington. The port area is almost surrounded by independent cities and is connected to South-Central Los Angeles by a narrow strip of land annexed by the city in the early 1900's. The Port of Los Angeles has one of the world's largest artificial harbors. It covers about 7,000 acres (2,800 hectares). A breakwater, built between 1899 and 1914, protects both the Los Angeles Harbor and the Long Beach Harbor to the east. The breakwater is 9 miles (14 kilometers) long.

East Los Angeles lies east of the downtown section. Since the 1920's, many poor, unskilled immigrants to Los Angeles have settled in this area. East Los Angeles once had a large Jewish population. But since the 1940's, it has been made up almost entirely of Mexican Americans and other Latinos.

The people who live in East Los Angeles call the area the *barrio*, a Spanish word for *neighborhood*. Many of the people—especially younger Mexican Americans—call themselves *Chicanos. Chicano* is a short form of *Mexicano*, the Spanish word for Mexican. The barrio extends far beyond the Los Angeles city limits into parts of Los Angeles County that do not belong to any city. The entire area has more than 1½ million Mexican Americans and other Latinos, many of whom speak little English. Many of the houses in the barrio are run-down wood-frame cottages built in the 1920's.

Metropolitan Area. The Los Angeles metropolitan area, as defined by the federal government, covers all of

George Hall, Woodfin Camp Inc.

Hollywood Hills is a residential section of Hollywood, one of Los Angeles' most glamorous districts. Homes in Hollywood Hills extend far up the slopes of the Santa Monica Mountains.

Ron Church, Photography Unlimited

The Charming Community of Westwood lies near the campus of the University of California at Los Angeles (UCLA). It has grown with UCLA and become a lively college town.

Los Angeles County. The area is officially known as the *Los Angeles-Long Beach Metropolitan Statistical Area*. It has about 7½ million people and ranks as the nation's second largest metropolitan area, behind only the New York City metropolitan area.

An area commonly called *Greater Los Angeles* is even larger than the official metropolitan area. Greater Los Angeles takes in part of San Bernardino County, east of Los Angeles, and part of Orange County, which lies southeast. Many of the people who live in these counties work in Los Angeles. More than 9½ million people live in Greater Los Angeles. Only seven states—including California—have larger populations.

The communities in the Los Angeles metropolitan area blend together so that, in many cases, it is difficult to tell one from another. As a result, the entire metropolitan area is often referred to as simply Los Angeles. Many of the famous features and tourist attractions that people from other parts of the country think are in Los Angeles are actually outside the city.

The most important suburban communities north and east of Los Angeles include Burbank, Glendale, and Pasadena. The Walt Disney and Warner Brothers studios are in Burbank, and the National Broadcasting Company (NBC) has its West Coast headquarters in the city. Glendale includes famous Forest Lawn Memorial Park, an elaborately landscaped cemetery filled with statues and other works of art. Pasadena is known for its Tournament of Roses, held each New Year's Day. The tournament consists of a parade of flower-covered floats, followed by a football game in the Rose Bowl. Each year, the champions of the Big Ten and the Pacific Ten, two of the nation's top college conferences, compete in the Rose Bowl game.

Beverly Hills, which lies west of the Hollywood district, is almost completely surrounded by Los Angeles. It is a fashionable community of expensive homes, many of which belong to motion-picture and television stars. Santa Monica, an attractive residential and resort city, lies southwest of Beverly Hills along the Pacific Ocean. It is the site of McDonnell Douglas Corporation, one of the nation's largest aircraft manufacturers. Culver City, east of Santa Monica, has the Metro-Goldwyn-Mayer studios. The residential towns of Gardena and Torrance lie along the strip of land that connects the Port of Los Angeles with South-Central Los Angeles.

The Palos Verdes Peninsula makes up the southwest corner of Los Angeles County. It is the site of Marineland, a park that features performances by trained sea animals. The city of Long Beach is an important port. It borders the Port of Los Angeles on the east.

Many residential communities in Orange County lie in the Greater Los Angeles area. They include Anaheim, Buena Park, Garden Grove, and Santa Ana. Some of them have well-known tourist attractions. For example, Anaheim is the site of Disneyland, a world-famous amusement park. Knott's Berry Farm, which has a ghost town and an Indian village, is in Buena Park. The Los Angeles-Anaheim-Riverside Consolidated Metropolitan Area consists of four metropolitan areas. They are Los Angeles-Long Beach, Anaheim-Santa Ana, Oxnard-Ventura, and Riverside-San Bernardino.

Through the years, large numbers of people from other parts of the United States and the world have settled in Los Angeles. People of Latin-American, black, or Asian ancestry make up more than half of the city's population. Most of the rest of the people are of European ancestry. They include people of English, German, Irish, Italian, and Russian descent. Roman Catholics make up the city's largest religious group. Other large religious groups include Christian Scientists, Episcopalians, Jews, Lutherans, and Methodists.

Ethnic Groups. Latinos account for about 28 per cent of Los Angeles' population. People of Mexican ancestry make up the largest Latino group by far. Los Angeles has about 600,000 Mexican Americans, more than any other U.S. city. Most of them were born in the United States. But many others moved to the city from Mexico in search of higher-paying jobs and a better life. The city's Latino population also includes people from—and descendants of people from—Cuba, Puerto Rico, and the countries of Central America. Most of the city's Mexican Americans and other Latinos live in the overcrowded, run-down barrio of East Los Angeles. But there are also barrios in the San Fernando Valley and other sections of the city. Discrimination, a lack of education, and the inability to speak English prevent many Latinos from finding well-paying jobs and leaving the barrios.

Blacks make up about 17 per cent of the population of Los Angeles. The city has more than 500,000 blacks. Most of them live in South-Central Los Angeles. Many have been prevented from leaving this area by poverty, a lack of education, and discrimination in jobs and housing. But many other blacks live in integrated parts

WORLD BOOK photo by J. R. Eyerman

Mexican-American Stores in East Los Angeles cater to the area's thousands of people of Mexican ancestry. More Mexican Americans live in Los Angeles than in any other U.S. city.

of the city and its suburbs. In fact, more blacks live in suburban areas of Los Angeles than in those of any other U.S. city.

People of Asian ancestry make up about 7 per cent of the city's population. They include about 50,000 Japanese, 45,000 Chinese, 44,000 Filipinos, and 33,000 Koreans. Asians live in various parts of the city, and they have better opportunities for higher education and good jobs than Latinos and blacks do. But Asians once had much the same problems of poverty and discrimination that Latinos and blacks now face.

Housing. Before the 1960's, most of the housing in Los Angeles consisted of single-family bungalows, cottages, and ranch-style homes. Land in the area had been plentiful and inexpensive. Developers could buy large sections of land, build hundreds of houses at one time, and sell the homes at low prices. The construction of single-family housing developments reached its peak during the 1940's and 1950's. In such areas as the San Fernando Valley, many thousands of homes were built on land once covered by orange groves and farms.

By the 1960's, Los Angeles had little vacant land left—and that land was expensive. In addition, the cost of labor and materials had increased greatly. As a result, the majority of new single-family homes were more expensive than most families could afford. Builders then began to construct more apartment houses.

In 1962, for the first time in the city's history, more apartments were built than single-family houses. Since 1962, builders have continued to construct more apartments than houses. Many of these buildings—especially those that rent to single people only—have swimming pools, health clubs, and other luxury features.

Education. Los Angeles has the second largest public school system in the United States. Only New York City's system is larger. The Los Angeles Unified School District, as the public school system is officially called, extends beyond the city limits. It covers 710 square miles (1,840 square kilometers), an area about one and a half times as large as the city itself. The district includes more than 730 schools with about 670,000 students and about 30,000 teachers and administrators. Over 60,000 students attend about 225 private and church-supported schools in Los Angeles.

The Board of Education runs Los Angeles' public school system. The board consists of seven members elected by the voters to four-year terms. The board members appoint a superintendent to serve as chief administrator of the school system.

In the late 1960's, the Los Angeles school system began to have serious financial problems as enrollments and operating costs increased faster than the system's income. To save money, class sizes were increased, some teachers discharged, and class hours shortened. In 1970, about half the district's schoolteachers staged a month-long strike for higher wages and improved classroom conditions. The teachers accepted a pay raise, though many of them felt the money should be used for classroom improvements.

Before 1978, about 70 per cent of the school system's funds came from taxes on real estate and personal property of district residents. In 1978, California voters

J. R. Eyerman

The San Fernando Valley has over a third of Los Angeles' residents. Most of them live in single-family homes with a backyard patio and barbecue. Many homes also have a swimming pool.

Ron Church, Photography Unlimited

Institutions of Higher Education in Los Angeles rank among the nation's finest. Royce Hall, *above,* is the liberal arts building at the University of California at Los Angeles (UCLA).

passed an amendment to the state constitution cutting property taxes. As a result, the Los Angeles school system now depends on state aid for about 80 per cent of its expenses. About 20 per cent of its budget still comes from local real estate and personal property taxes.

Los Angeles has many institutions of higher education. The Los Angeles Community College District administers nine community colleges in and near the city. The colleges offer two-year programs in a variety of subjects. These colleges, formerly called junior colleges, also offer courses that can later be used for credit in senior colleges. About 120,000 students attend the district's community colleges.

The city's largest public university is the University of California at Los Angeles (UCLA), one of nine branches of the University of California. UCLA has about 34,000 students. Los Angeles also is the home of California State University at Los Angeles and California State University at Northridge.

The largest private university in Los Angeles is the University of Southern California (USC), which has about 27,000 students. Other private universities and colleges in the area include the California School of Professional Psychology, Loyola Marymount University, Mount St. Mary's College, Occidental College, Pepperdine University, and Woodbury University.

Social Problems. The chief social problems in Los Angeles, as in most other large U.S. cities, include poverty, and racial and ethnic conflicts. Los Angeles has one of the highest standards of living of any city in the nation. Yet many thousands of Los Angeles' residents do not share in the city's wealth. Most of these people are blacks who live in the ghettos of South-Central Los Angeles and Mexican Americans and other Latinos who live in the barrios of East Los Angeles and other parts of the city.

The people of the ghettos and barrios have similar problems. They live in run-down, overcrowded homes and have little education. Many have difficulty finding work, and others have low-paying jobs. Many students quit school, and crime is widespread. Many people in the barrios speak only Spanish. This limits their opportunities for jobs and education.

Conditions in the ghettos and barrios of Los Angeles have led to serious riots. In 1965, blacks in the Watts district of South-Central Los Angeles rioted for five days. The rioting resulted in 34 deaths and about $40 million in property damage. In 1970 and 1971, riots by Latinos in East Los Angeles caused 4 deaths and more than $1 million in damage.

The local, state, and federal governments have taken action to help blacks and Latinos in Los Angeles. Job-training courses have been set up to teach unskilled workers. Spanish-speaking teachers have been assigned to barrio schools, and black and Latino studies have been introduced in ghetto and barrio schools. Legal aid programs have been set up to help minority group members who feel they have been discriminated against in seeking a job or a place to live. But progress has been slow, partly because poor, unskilled people have continued to pour into the already overcrowded ghettos and barrios.

Los Angeles ranks as the most important center of industry, trade, and finance in the Western United States. The city's economy, like its population, has grown rapidly since World War II. Since the end of the war in 1945, the number of jobs in the Los Angeles area has increased greatly. During this period, a large number of new industries, financial institutions, and trading facilities moved into the Los Angeles area and existing ones expanded.

Industry. Los Angeles is the largest manufacturing center in the United States. The city's largest industry is the aerospace industry. This industry involves the manufacture of aircraft, spacecraft, and related parts and equipment. The Los Angeles area has almost 18,000 factories, and about 2,000 of them are engaged in aerospace production. The giant aerospace industry has attracted more engineers, mathematicians, scientists, and skilled technicians to Los Angeles than to any other city in the United States. The aerospace industry depends heavily on United States government contracts.

Los Angeles—especially the Hollywood district—has long been known as the motion-picture capital of the world. Filmmaking reached its peak in the Los Angeles area during the mid-1940's. By the late 1940's, television had begun to attract more and more moviegoers. The studios reduced the number of pictures they made and dismissed many of their employees. In time, the studios became increasingly involved in making films for television. In addition, separate network television facilities were built in the Los Angeles area. Today, most television films are made in Los Angeles and many other television comedies, dramas, and other shows originate there.

Los Angeles has rich deposits of petroleum, which is pumped from wells scattered throughout the area. The city's petroleum industry dates back to the late 1800's, when the first wells were drilled. In addition to producing petroleum, the city ranks as one of the nation's top oil-refining centers. It is also a major manufacturer of oil-field equipment.

Other important industries in Los Angeles produce a wide range of products. The city is a leading producer of automobiles, clothing, computers, furniture, rubber, and tires. Other manufactured products include chemicals, electric equipment, glassware and pottery, iron and steel, toys, and travel trailers. The construction industry and printing and publishing are also important. The Los Angeles area is also a major center of the music-recording industry and has more than 50 record companies.

The Port of Los Angeles is one of the nation's chief fishing ports and one of the largest fish-canning centers in the world. Every day, hundreds of fishing boats bring in huge catches of halibut, sea bass, tuna, and other fishes.

Trade. The Port of Los Angeles handles more cargo than any other U.S. port on the Pacific coast. This cargo includes foreign imports and exports, as well as goods going to or coming from other U.S. ports. Most of the trade between the United States and Japan flows through the Port of Los Angeles. The port also handles much of the nation's trade with Australia, Canada,

J. R. Eyerman, Black Star

The Port of Los Angeles, on San Pedro Bay, handles more foreign and domestic cargo than any other West Coast port. It is also one of the nation's leading fishing ports. In addition to berths for cargo and passenger ships and for fishing boats, the huge port has facilities for pleasure craft.

Mexico, South America, and Southeast Asia. Large amounts of domestic and international cargo are also handled at Los Angeles International Airport.

Los Angeles ranks after New York City and Chicago in retail trade. Each year, the city's retail stores sell more than $5 billion worth of goods. Many of the nation's largest retail chain stores have their headquarters in Los Angeles. The city also serves as the West Coast's chief wholesale distribution center. Wholesalers in the Los Angeles area sell about $21½ billion worth of goods yearly.

Finance. Los Angeles ranks as the leading financial center on the West Coast. Twenty-five major savings and loan associations and six major banks have their headquarters in the city. The banks operate more than 1,000 branches throughout the metropolitan area. About 70 insurance companies also have their headquarters in Los Angeles.

Tourism. Millions of tourists come to southern California every year. Most of them visit the Los Angeles area and contribute millions of dollars to the city's income. The tourist industry supports hotels, motels, and restaurants, as well as cultural and recreational facilities in the area.

Transportation. Los Angeles residents depend mainly on automobiles for transportation. The city has one of the world's most extensive *freeway* systems. This 650-mile (1,050-kilometer) network of high-speed expressways runs through Los Angeles, Orange, and Ventura counties. The system consists of a series of overpasses, underpasses, and interchanges. During morning and evening rush hours, slow-moving traffic jams the freeway system.

The Southern California Rapid Transit District, a public corporation, operates a bus system in Los Angeles. In the past, the system was extremely slow and did not provide adequate service throughout the sprawling Los Angeles area. However, bus service has improved. In addition, construction of an 18.6-mile (29.9 kilometer) subway system was scheduled to begin in Los Angeles in the mid-1980's. Funds from the federal government have been set aside for the subway, which was scheduled to be completed in the early 1990's.

Three major railroads—the Atchison, Topeka & Santa Fe; the Southern Pacific; and the Union Pacific—serve Los Angeles. Trains use the famous Los Angeles Union Station at the east edge of the downtown area. This huge terminal was built in the style of California's early Spanish missions, with a tiled roof and two patios.

Los Angeles International Airport, near Playa del Rey, is the world's third busiest airport. Only Chicago's O'Hare International Airport and Atlanta's Hartsfield International Airport handle more flights. Both domestic and foreign airlines use Los Angeles International.

Communication. Los Angeles has two general daily newspapers, the morning *Times* and the evening *Herald-Examiner*. The *Times* sells more than 1 million copies, daily, and the *Herald-Examiner* more than 260,000. About 40 daily community and foreign-language newspapers and more than 100 weekly and semiweekly community papers are also published in the Los Angeles area. In addition, Los Angeles has a number of *underground* newspapers, which deal with such matters as civil rights, pollution, and personal and sexual freedom.

Hundreds of magazines, technical publications, and trade journals are published in the Los Angeles area. They include *Los Angeles Magazine*, which features articles of general interest about the area. Many other magazines specialize in single subjects popular in the area, such as surfing, hot-rodding, and pottery making.

Ten television stations and more than 75 radio stations broadcast in the Los Angeles area. In addition, the nation's three largest television networks—the American Broadcasting Company (ABC), the Columbia Broadcasting System (CBS), and the National Broadcasting Company (NBC)—originate many programs from their studios in the area.

LOS ANGELES / Cultural Life and Recreation

Los Angeles has long been known for its outdoor way of life. The city's climate and its location along the ocean and near snow-covered mountains enable the people to enjoy most outdoor sports the year around. But over the years, the people of Los Angeles have also become increasingly interested in cultural matters. As a result, Los Angeles today ranks not only as one of the nation's top recreational centers, but also as one of the leading U.S. cultural centers.

The Arts. Los Angeles' handsome Music Center for the Performing Arts symbolizes the city's cultural leadership. The center, which was completed in 1967, is part of the Civic Center. It consists of the Dorothy Chandler Pavilion, which is a concert hall; and two theaters, the Ahmanson Theatre and the Mark Taper Forum. The Los Angeles Philharmonic Orchestra performs in the Pavilion from October to April. Other attractions at the Music Center for the Performing Arts include ballet, drama, folk dance, and opera.

Los Angeles has two famous open-air theaters. The Hollywood Bowl, which seats more than 20,000 people, is known for its summer concerts and Easter sunrise services. The Greek Theatre, in Griffith Park northeast of Hollywood, presents musical and dramatic programs. Other theaters and concert halls in Los Angeles include the Century City Playhouse, the Huntington Hartford Theatre, the Ivar Theatre, and the Shrine Auditorium, and the Shubert Theatre. The University of California at Los Angeles and the University of Southern California also present musical and dramatic programs in their campus theaters.

Thousands of actors, artists, musicians, and writers live in Los Angeles. Many of them have been attracted by the area's movie and TV studios and recording companies. In addition, Los Angeles has long offered creative people an atmosphere that encourages freedom of expression.

Architecture. Many styles of architecture can be seen in Los Angeles. The Spanish style, which features low stuccoed walls and tiled roofs, has long been especially popular. Thousands of small homes—as well as such large buildings as the Union Station and the main

WORLD BOOK photo by J. R. Eyerman

Los Angeles' Outdoor Way of Life attracts many visitors and new residents. Fine beaches like this one line the Pacific Ocean to the west and south of the city. Snow-capped mountains rise to the northeast. The city's pleasant climate makes it possible to enjoy outdoor living the year around.

WORLD BOOK photo by J. R. Eyerman

George Hall, Woodfin Camp Inc.

The Music Center for the Performing Arts consists of the Dorothy Chandler Pavilion, *above,* and two theaters. Attractions at the Music Center include ballet, concerts, drama, and opera.

The Los Angeles Zoo, in Griffith Park, includes an 80-acre (32-hectare) main zoo and a children's zoo. In the main zoo, all the animals native to a particular continent are grouped together.

branch of the Los Angeles Public Library—have been built in the Spanish style.

Los Angeles has been a center of modern architecture since the 1920's and 1930's. At that time, several of the nation's most imaginative architects, including Richard J. Neutra and Frank Lloyd Wright, designed a number of strikingly modern buildings in the area. Most large buildings constructed in Los Angeles since the 1950's have straight sides and glass walls.

Libraries. The Los Angeles Public Library, with about 4 million volumes, is the nation's third largest public library, after those of New York City and Chicago. The library has more than 60 branches and 5 bookmobiles. The main branch is a three-story, Spanish-style building. It stands among the modern high-rise buildings of the downtown area. Several museums in Los Angeles also have libraries.

Museums. The city's largest art museum is the Los Angeles County Museum of Art, located in Hancock Park just east of Beverly Hills. The museum has a large collection of works, ranging in time from those of ancient Egypt to those of the present. It also holds several special exhibits each year. There are several outstanding art museums in the Los Angeles area outside the city. One of the best known is the Henry E. Huntington Library and Art Gallery in San Marino. It houses some of the world's greatest paintings and an excellent research center on American and English history and literature. The J. Paul Getty Museum, in Malibu, has an outstanding collection of paintings and sculptures.

The Natural History Museum of Los Angeles County is in Exposition Park, southwest of the downtown area. Its exhibits include a collection of bones of prehistoric animals. Nearby stands the California Museum of

Science and Industry, which has displays on the state's agriculture, industry, and resources. It also features an outstanding exhibit on the space age.

Recreation. Los Angeles' location and climate make it possible to go surfing or swimming in the ocean in the morning and skiing at a mountain resort that afternoon. The Los Angeles area has about 75 miles (121 kilometers) of beaches along the Pacific, and many ski facilities are located in the Angeles National Forest, northeast of the city. Golf and boating are also popular all year.

Los Angeles has more than 210 parks, playgrounds, and other recreational facilities. Griffith Park is one of the largest city-owned parks in the world. It covers more than 4,000 acres (1,600 hectares). The park has about 50 miles (80 kilometers) of bridle paths and several baseball fields, golf courses, and tennis courts. The park also includes the Los Angeles Zoo and the Griffith Observatory and Planetarium.

The Greater Los Angeles area has seven major professional sports teams. The Los Angeles Dodgers of the National League play baseball in Dodger Stadium, north of the downtown area. The California Angels of the American League play baseball in Anaheim Stadium in Anaheim. The Los Angeles Rams of the National Football League play in Anaheim Stadium. The Los Angeles Raiders of the National Football League play in Memorial Coliseum. The Los Angeles Lakers of the National Basketball Association and the Los Angeles Kings of the National Hockey League play in the Forum, in suburban Inglewood. The Clippers of the National Basketball Association play in the Sports Arena. Other spectator sports in the area include auto racing and horse racing. Los Angeles hosted the Summer Olympic Games in 1932 and 1984.

La Brea Pits

J. R. Eyerman, Black Star

Farmers Market

Ian R. Gilbert, DPI

WORLD BOOK photo by J. R. Eyerman

Spanish Mission in the San Fernando Valley

Each year, millions of tourists and delegates to conventions and trade shows visit the Los Angeles area. To accommodate these visitors, the area has hundreds of hotels, motels, and rooming houses and thousands of restaurants. Following are descriptions of some of the many interesting places to visit in and near Los Angeles. Other places of interest in the area are discussed and pictured earlier in this article.

Beaches offer many opportunities for recreation and sightseeing. Well-known beaches in the Los Angeles area include Malibu, Redondo, Santa Monica, and Venice.

Farmers Market, in Hollywood, consists of more than 100 shops and stalls that sell everything from alfalfa juice to Hawaiian sportswear.

La Brea Pits, in Hancock Park east of Beverly Hills, contain the bones of thousands of animals trapped in layers of oil and tar during prehistoric times. Life-sized statues of the trapped animals are exhibited. The George C. Page Museum, on the site, exhibits bones dug up from the pits. See LA BREA PITS.

Marineland, at Palos Verdes Estates, is the world's largest oceanarium. It features trained dolphins, whales, and other sea animals.

Spanish Missions are located in the San Fernando Valley and in San Gabriel. They are among the 21 picturesque missions built in California by Franciscan friars during the late 1700's and early 1800's.

Universal Studios, in Universal City north of Hollywood, make up one of the largest movie-TV studios.

LOS ANGELES/*Government*

Los Angeles' government consists of a mayor, about 25 city commissions, and a 15-member City Council. The people elect the mayor to a four-year term. The mayor administers the government and appoints the members of the commissions. Each commission controls one or more departments and names the heads of the departments. For example, the police commission appoints the police chief, the harbor commission chooses the head of the harbor department, and the traffic commission selects the head of the traffic department.

The City Council makes the laws of Los Angeles and approves the budget, which the mayor prepares. One council member is elected from each of 15 districts in the city. Members of the City Council serve four-year terms. Much of the council's work is done by its 18 committees. These committees recommend legislation to the full council. The mayor can *veto* (reject) legislation passed by the council. However, the City Council can *override* (set aside) the mayor's veto with a two-thirds majority vote of the council members present when the vote is taken.

The city of Los Angeles has a budget of about $1.7 billion annually. Sources of the city's income include the property tax, a sales tax, license fees for businesses and professionals, and aid from the state government and the federal government.

A five-member County Board of Supervisors governs Los Angeles County. The members are elected to four-year terms in countywide elections. The county government administers certain programs, such as air pollution control and flood control, throughout the county. It also provides government services for areas of the county that do not belong to any city.

Other government units that operate within Los Angeles include the Board of Education, which supervises the Los Angeles Unified School District; the State Division of Highways, which controls the construction of freeways in the area; the California Highway Patrol, which polices the area's freeways; and the Southern California Rapid Transit District, which operates the area's bus system.

LOS ANGELES/*History*

American Indians were the first people to live in what is now the Los Angeles area. During the 1500's, a branch of the Shoshoni tribe lived in a village called Yang-na. The village lay along the Los Angeles River near what is now the downtown area.

Exploration. In 1542, Juan Rodríguez Cabrillo, a Portuguese explorer working for Spain, discovered Yang-na. Cabrillo noted the village on his map and then continued exploring the California coast.

No other explorers reported visiting the Los Angeles area until 1769. That year, Gaspar de Portolá, a Spanish Army captain, and Juan Crespi, a Franciscan priest, led an expedition from San Diego north to Monterey Bay. After the group reached Yang-na, Crespi wrote in his diary that the area was a "delightful place" and had all the features necessary for a large settlement. He and Portolá named the area *Nuestra Señora la Reina*

Robert Glaze, Artstreet

Los Angeles' City Hall stands in the heart of the downtown area. The 26-story landmark is one of a group of city, county, state, and federal buildings that make up the Civic Center.

Symbols of Los Angeles. The city's flag was adopted on Sept. 4, 1931, the 150th anniversary of the founding of Los Angeles. The city seal symbolizes Los Angeles' history under the governments of Spain, Mexico, the California Republic, and the United States.

de Los Ángeles de Porciúncula, meaning *Our Lady the Queen of the Angels of Porciúncula.* Porciúncula was a chapel in Italy associated with Saint Francis of Assisi, founder of the Franciscan order of the Roman Catholic Church.

Settlement. Soon after the Portolá party left the site of Los Angeles, Spain began its efforts to colonize the area. The first step was to establish a mission there. In 1771, Franciscan priests built Mission San Gabriel Arcángel, just east of the future city of Los Angeles. The mission was one of 21 that the Franciscans built on and near the California coast. San Gabriel, like the other missions, became an important agricultural, cultural, and religious center.

After San Gabriel was built, Felipe de Neve, the Spanish governor of California, selected Crespi's "delightful place" as the site for a new *pueblo* (town). De

Neve sent soldiers into northern Mexico to offer free land, animals, tools, and money to anyone willing to move to the new settlement.

In February 1781, a group of pioneers gathered at Guaymas, Mexico, to begin the long journey to Los Angeles. They arrived on Sept. 4, 1781, and officially founded the Pueblo of Los Angeles. The settlers totaled 44 people—11 men, 11 women, and 22 children. The group consisted of Indians, blacks, Spaniards, and people of mixed white and Indian ancestry and mixed white and black ancestry.

Mexican Rule. Los Angeles grew quickly, and by 1800 it had 315 residents. The town began as a farming community, but it soon became a cattle-raising center. Much of the land in the area was divided into huge ranches on which thousands of longhorns were raised. In 1821, Mexico gained its independence from Spain and took control of Los Angeles and the rest of California.

Under Mexican rule, Los Angeles and Monterey alternated as the capital of California. In 1826, Jedediah Smith, an American fur trapper, became the first white person to reach Los Angeles by land from the east. In 1841, the first group of overland settlers from the United States arrived in the area. Other groups soon followed. But Mexicans and Spaniards continued to make up most of Los Angeles' population.

War broke out between Mexico and the United States in May 1846. In August, U.S. troops captured Los Angeles. But the people rebelled, and the Americans were forced to withdraw from the city in October. The United States recaptured Los Angeles in January 1847. Mexico lost the war and signed the Treaty of Guadalupe Hidalgo in 1848. Under the terms of the treaty, Mexico gave the entire California region to the United States.

Development and Growth. On April 4, 1850, Los Angeles was incorporated as a city. Five months later, California became a state of the United States. Los Angeles had a population of 1,610 in 1850. The city grew rather slowly during the next 20 years. It had 4,385 people in 1860 and 5,728 in 1870. But with the coming of the railroads, Los Angeles' population soared.

In 1876, the Southern Pacific Railroad was completed between Los Angeles and San Francisco. It provided the city with a rail link to the rest of the United States through San Francisco. In 1885, the Santa Fe Railroad provided a direct connection between the Los Angeles area and the Midwest. Competition between the Southern Pacific and the Santa Fe led to lower and lower fares, which brought more and more people to Los Angeles. In the spring of 1886, the fare from the Midwest to Los Angeles dropped to $1. Trainloads of people from the East and Midwest came to Los Angeles. The Los Angeles area, in turn, shipped trainloads of oranges and other farm products to the Midwest and East. By 1890, the city's population had climbed to more than 50,000. By 1900, it had soared to more than 100,000.

In 1899, Los Angeles began to build a huge artificial harbor at San Pedro. The harbor was completed in 1914, the same year the Panama Canal was completed. Los Angeles quickly became a major seaport.

By the 1920's, tourism had become a big business in

Century City, a planned community in West Los Angeles, covers 180 acres (73 hectares). When completed in the late 1980's, this "city within a city" will include 20 office buildings, 25 apartment houses, a large hotel, a shopping center, many restaurants, and 3 theaters.

Los Angeles. Many tourists liked the climate so much they decided to become residents. The area's new motion-picture industry was booming. The oil industry, which had begun in the 1890's, was spurred by the discovery of rich new fields. Also during the 1920's, new aircraft plants opened in the city, and factories began to make furniture, pottery, tires, and other products.

The Mid-1900's. Los Angeles' economy slumped during the Great Depression of the 1930's. But its population continued to grow as thousands of jobless and homeless people drifted into the area, hoping their luck would change. The city's economy recovered and reached new heights following the outbreak of World War II in 1939. Hundreds of thousands of new residents flocked to the city to work in aircraft factories, shipyards, and other war plants. By the war's end in 1945, Los Angeles had more than 1½ million people.

Los Angeles' spectacular population growth continued after World War II. Thousands of new homes were built and quickly covered the city's open spaces. By 1960, the population of Los Angeles had risen to nearly 2½ million.

Recent Developments. Los Angeles today is a huge, thriving urban center. But like other large cities, it faces many problems. Unemployment is high among blacks and Latinos, and the city has been troubled by racial and ethnic conflicts. See the *Social Problems* section of this article.

Air pollution has been a serious problem in Los Angeles since the 1950's. On calm days, smoke from factories and exhaust fumes from automobiles collect near the ground and form a thick yellow haze called *smog*. Smog irritates the eyes and lungs and can kill plant life. When the smog level gets too high—which happens about seven days a year on the average—the county's Air Pollution Control District issues a smog alert. During an alert, factories are asked to stop burning fuel oil, and people are requested to drive their cars only if necessary.

Los Angeles receives little rain. The area's long, dry summers turn the brush and grass in the hills around the city dry and brown, creating a severe fire hazard in the early fall. In 1970, brush fires swept from the San Fernando Valley to Malibu on the Pacific coast, killing 11 people and destroying about 400 homes. Since the early 1900's, Los Angeles has had to obtain huge amounts of water from distant places by way of aqueducts to satisfy the city's growing requirements. In 1973, the California Aqueduct was completed. This aqueduct brings water to Los Angeles from California's Central Valley, 685 miles (1,102 kilometers) to the north.

The Los Angeles area lies in a region of earthquake activity. Most of the earthquakes cause little damage. But in 1971, an earthquake centered in San Fernando, just north of the Los Angeles city limits, caused 64 deaths and more than $500 million in damage.

In 1973, Thomas Bradley, a member of the City Council, was elected mayor of Los Angeles. He became the city's first black mayor. Bradley was reelected in 1977 and 1981.

KENNETH REICH

LOS ANGELES/*Study Aids*

Related Articles in WORLD BOOK include:

METROPOLITAN LOS ANGELES

Beverly Hills
Burbank

Long Beach
Pasadena

GREATER LOS ANGELES

Anaheim
San Bernardino

San Juan Capistrano

OTHER RELATED ARTICLES

Aqueduct (Present-Day
  Aqueducts)
Bradley, Thomas
California (pictures)
Hollywood

La Brea Pits
Latinos
Mexican Americans
  (picture)
Motion Picture

Outline

I. The City
  A. Downtown Los Angeles
  B. South-Central Los Angeles
  C. Central Los Angeles
  D. The San Fernando Valley
  E. West Los Angeles
  F. South Bay
  G. The Port of Los Angeles
  H. East Los Angeles
  I. Metropolitan Area
II. People
  A. Ethnic Groups
  B. Housing
  C. Education
  D. Social Problems

III. Economy
  A. Industry
  B. Trade
  C. Finance
  D. Tourism
  E. Transportation
  F. Communication
IV. Cultural Life and Recreation
  A. The Arts   C. Libraries   E. Recreation
  B. Architecture D. Museums
V. A Visitor's Guide
VI. Government
VII. History

Questions

What are some reasons for Los Angeles' great population growth?

When did the railroad fare from the Midwest to Los Angeles cost $1? Why did it cost so little?

What is the role of the City Council's committees?

Why did Los Angeles have only one high-rise building before 1957?

What are some of Los Angeles' major problems?

Why has the Los Angeles metropolitan area been described as "a hundred suburbs in search of a city"?

What is Los Angeles' largest industry?

How did Father Juan Crespi describe the future site of Los Angeles in 1769?

What are Los Angeles' major ethnic groups?

What is the Hollywood Bowl? Marineland? The Miracle Mile?

LOS ANGELES

LOS ANGELES, an airship. See AIRSHIP (picture: The Uses of Airships).

LOS ANGELES INTERNATIONAL AIRPORT. See LOS ANGELES (Transportation; map); AIRPORT (table: World's 25 Busiest Airports).

LOS ANGELES ZOO. See LOS ANGELES (Recreation; picture: The Los Angeles Zoo).

LOS NEGROS ISLAND. See ADMIRALTY ISLANDS.

LOST COLONY is the name given to an early settlement on Roanoke Island, off the shore of what is now the state of North Carolina. The colony is called *lost* because no one has ever discovered what happened to it. In 1948, an announcement was made that archaeological surveys by the National Park Service had located the outlines of the fort that had been built by the lost colonists.

A little band of 108 men sailed from England on April 9, 1585. They were sent by Sir Walter Raleigh to settle in the new region that was then known as Virginia. This region was a great territory in North America that stretched from the present state of Pennsylvania to what is now South Carolina. Raleigh probably wished to establish a base for raiding the Spanish empire in America.

The band of colonists had hard times on Roanoke Island. Within a year, the men sailed back to England on the ships of Sir Francis Drake. More colonists and needed supplies arrived from England a few days after the men had left. Most of the second group of colonists also returned to England, but 15 adventurers from this group remained in America.

In 1587, Raleigh sent a group of 117 settlers—91 men, 17 women, and 9 children—to the colony in Virginia. John White, who led the group, was instructed to settle the shores of Chesapeake Bay. But the sailors refused to carry the colonists farther than Roanoke Island. The group of colonists was forced to land on the island on July 22, 1587. Not one of the 15 men who had remained on Roanoke Island the year before was found alive.

On August 18, just 27 days after the colonists landed, a baby girl was born. The infant was John White's grandchild, and the first English child to be born on the continent. She was christened Virginia Dare.

The colonists expected to live on English supplies. White returned to England for greatly needed provisions. But because of the Spanish war, he was not able to come back to America until 1590. When he landed at the site of the English colony on Roanoke Island, the only traces of the colonists he found were the letters *CRO* carved on one tree and the word *Croatoan* carved on another.

Some believed the colonists may have gone with friendly Indians in search of food, or that they may have been captured by hostile Indians. It is possible that the colonists were carried off by passing Spaniards, who had already laid claim to the region. But no Spanish record of the colony is known to exist.

The colonists were never found, and nobody knows what happened to them. Among the few facts that make up the record of the Lost Colony are the arrival of the colonists in Virginia, the birth and baptism of Virginia Dare, the return of John White, and the carved word *Croatoan.*

The Main Clue to the Lost Colony was the word *Croatoan* carved on a tree. John White left the Roanoke colonists and sailed back to England for badly needed supplies. When he returned in 1590, the colonists had completely disappeared. Although there is no proof, some persons believe the colonists may have married into an Indian tribe and been forgotten.

Culver

A group of Indians formerly known as the Croatan, now called the Lumbee, live in and near Robeson County in southeastern North Carolina. Most of the Indians have English names. Some historians believe the Lumbee are descendants of the lost colonists and Indians who lived nearby.   MARSHALL SMELSER

See also LUMBEE INDIANS.

Additional Resources

DURANT, DAVID N. *Raleigh's Lost Colony.* Atheneum, 1981.
LACY, DAN M. *The Lost Colony.* Watts, 1972. For younger readers.
QUINN, DAVID B., ed. *The Roanoke Voyages, 1584-1590: Documents to Illustrate the English Voyages to North America Under the Patent Granted to Walter Raleigh in 1584.* 2 vols. Hakluyt, 1955.

LOST GENERATION. See AMERICAN LITERATURE (The "Lost Generation"); LITERATURE (The 1900's).

LOT was Abraham's nephew. His story is told in the Old Testament. Lot lived in the city of Sodom (see SODOM AND GOMORRAH). When Sodom and Gomorrah were destroyed by the angels of Jehovah because they were wicked cities, Lot fled from Sodom with his wife and two daughters. His wife, in defiance of the command they had been given, turned back to look at the fiery destruction of the cities, and was changed immediately into a pillar of salt as punishment for her curiosity and disobedience (Gen. 19: 26). See also ABRAHAM.

LOTHARINGIA. See VERDUN, TREATY OF.

LÖTSCHBERG TUNNEL is a railroad tunnel that cuts through the Bernese Alps of south-central Switzerland near the Jungfrau (see SWITZERLAND [map]). The tunnel, which opened in 1913, is 9.1 miles (14.6 kilometers) long. It is part of the Swiss Lötschberg Railway, which is 46 miles (74 kilometers) long and connects Spiez and Brigue. Before the railroad reaches Kandersteg, the tunnel's northern entrance, it crosses many bridges and viaducts and passes through 38 tunnels. At Göppenstein, the tunnel's southern end, the railroad descends into the Rhône Valley, where it connects with the Simplon Tunnel leading into northern Italy.   FRANKLIN CARL ERICKSON

LOTTERY is perhaps the most widespread form of gambling. In most lotteries, the gamblers buy numbered tickets. Duplicate numbered tickets kept by the seller are drawn at random, and the persons holding the matching tickets win prizes. Sweepstakes, pools, and raffles are forms of lotteries. Lotteries have also been used to determine the order in which men are drafted into a nation's armed forces (see DRAFT, MILITARY).

Draw-prize drawings, another form of lottery, were entertainment features at dinner parties given by many Roman emperors. Nero let his guests draw for such prizes as slaves and country estates. Emperor Elagabalus added a touch of humor by mixing such odd and worthless prizes as dead insects or other animals among the valuable prizes. Augustus Caesar sponsored the first known public lottery. This lottery was designed to raise funds to repair Rome.

An English lottery in 1612 supported the English settlement in Jamestown, Va. Lotteries also financed various state and local governmental activities in the United States. Some churches and school buildings were built with funds from lotteries. In the 1830's, many people began to oppose lotteries. State after state prohibited them. By 1894, Congress had closed interstate and foreign commerce to lottery materials, and

legal lotteries were no longer held in the United States. In 1963, New Hampshire revived the tradition by adopting a state-operated lottery. Since then, many other states have established lotteries. National lotteries are still held in many countries.   JOHN SCARNE

See also GAMBLING; IRELAND (Recreation).

LOTUS is a name given to many different kinds of plants. The lotus known in most places is the Egyptian water lily. The American lotus is also well known.

The Egyptian water lily is a familiar sight along the Nile River and neighboring streams. This plant has white or rose-purple flowers that may be 1 foot (30 centimeters) across. They grow on a weak stalk, 4 to 8 feet (1.2 to 2.4 meters) long, and rise only a little above the water. The leaves spread out on the water's surface.

The lotus was a sacred flower to the people of Egypt, India, and China. The plant is also the national flower of India. A species of the lotus appears in ancient Egyptian art.

The American lotus is a close relative of the East-Indian lotus. It also is known as the *water chinquapin* and *yellow water lily.* Its yellow flowers and leaves are on stout stalks that stand 2 to 3 feet (61 to 91 centimeters) above the water. There is a large lotus bed in Grass Lake, about 50 miles (80 kilometers) northwest of Chicago. These plants cover about 600 acres (240 hectares), and make a wonderful sight in August. Other lotus beds are found near New York City, in Monroe, Mich., in southern California, and in the valleys of the Missouri and Mississippi rivers.

The botanical name *Lotus* belongs to a genus of the pea family. There are about 80 species. The flowers are

The Big Waxy Flowers of the Hindu Lotus make this water lily one of the most unusual blossoms of the streams and ponds.

J. Horace McFarland

white, yellow, red, or purple, and have a shape and size resembling pea flowers.

Scientific Classification. The Egyptian, East Indian, and American lotuses belong to the water lily family, Nymphaeaceae. The Egyptian is genus *Nymphaea*, species *N. lotus*. The East Indian is *Nelumbo nucifera*. The American is *Nelumbo lutea*. The genus *Lotus* is classified as a member of the pea family, Leguminosae.   GEORGE H. M. LAWRENCE

See also FLOWER (picture: Flowers of the Tropics and Subtropics; table: National Flowers); TREFOIL.

LOTUS-EATER belonged to a race of people who were thought to live in North Africa. In ancient Greek mythology, lotus-eaters were called Lotophagi (pronounced *loh TAHF uh jy*). It was said that their only food was the fruit and blossoms of the lotus, or jujube tree. People who ate of this magical tree forgot their homeland and the ties of friendship and family. The Greek epic poem the *Odyssey* describes an encounter between the lotus-eaters and the Greek hero Odysseus (Ulysses in Latin). Lord Tennyson's poem "The Lotos-Eaters" is based upon this story (see ODYSSEY). Today, people who continually daydream or think of impractical ideas are sometimes called lotus-eaters.   VAN JOHNSON

LOTZE, *LOHT suh,* **RUDOLF HERMANN** (1817-1881), was a German philosopher. He attempted to reconcile apparent conflicts between science and religion. Lotze influenced many thinkers of the 1800's, notably the American philosopher Josiah Royce.

Lotze supported the mechanical interpretation of nature as the indispensable method of scientific research. This interpretation explains nature in terms of mechanical causes. Lotze denied that any separate nonmechanical principle accounted for organic existence. However, he insisted that this interpretation has limits and that people's moral values force them to think beyond scientific evidence. He formulated a theory in which nature acts according to a purpose and natural things have a spiritual character. Lotze believed the highest spiritual nature is a personal God, in whom all things exist. Lotze stated that God exercises His will through mechanical causes and the laws of nature.

Lotze was born in Bautzen, in what is now East Germany. He taught philosophy at the University of Göttingen. Lotze wrote many books, including *Metaphysics* (1841), *Logic* (1843), *Microcosmus* (1856-1864), and *System of Philosophy* (1874-1879).   W. W. BARTLEY III

LOU GEHRIG'S DISEASE. See AMYOTROPHIC LATERAL SCLEROSIS.

LOUANGPHRABANG, *LWAHNG prah BAHNG* (pop. 44,244), is a city in Laos. Its name is also spelled *Luang Prabang*. Until 1975, both Louangphrabang and Vientiane were considered capitals of Laos. Louangphrabang was called the *royal capital* because it was the site of the king's palace. In 1975, Communists took control of Laos and abolished the Laotian monarchy. Vientiane then became the country's only capital. See also LAOS (map; History).   DAVID P. CHANDLER

LOUD, JOHN. See PEN (History).

LOUDSPEAKER. See INTERCOM; SPEAKER.

LOUGH NEAGH, *lahk NAY,* in Northern Ireland, is the largest lake in the British Isles. It is about 18 miles (29 kilometers) long and about 11 miles (18 kilometers) wide. It covers about 153 square miles (396 square kilo-

Northern Ireland Tourist Board

Lough Neagh, in Northern Ireland, is the largest lake in the British Isles. Its marine life includes eels, salmon, and trout. The lake is a popular place for fishing.

meters). For location, see NORTHERN IRELAND (political map).

Ten rivers flow into Lough Neagh, but only one river—the Lower Bann—flows out. The Lower Bann empties into the Atlantic Ocean, north of Lough Neagh. Lough Neagh has a flat bed that averages about 45 feet (14 meters) in depth. Lough Neagh attracts many wild fowl, including the rare whooper swan. The lake's many eels, salmon, and trout attract large numbers of fishing enthusiasts.   ADRIAN ROBINSON

LOUIS, *LOO ee, LOO ihs,* or *lwee,* is the name of many famous French kings. The name means *famous warrior,* a characteristic most of the early kings of France possessed. Their efforts to build up an absolute monarchy

Ewing Galloway

Louis IX Dispensed Justice under an oak tree in a forest near Paris. His French subjects loved him for his fairness to everyone. The Roman Catholic Church canonized Louis in 1297.

Louis XIV built the magnificent palace at Versailles.

Louis XV plunged his country deeply into debt.

Louis XVI was executed during the Revolution.

Louis XVIII ruled France after Napoleon's defeat in 1814.

reached a climax under Louis XIV. Later reigns were marked by a growing dissatisfaction among the common people.

Louis I (778-840), called "the Pious," was king of the Franks and emperor of the Romans. In 814, he succeeded his father Charlemagne. In 817, he arranged for the succession after his death by dividing the empire among his three sons. After his first wife died, Louis married again, and a fourth son, Charles, was born in 823. Louis redivided his empire in 829 in order to give Charles a share. The older sons resented the new division and revolted. Louis was removed from the throne in 833, but was restored the next year. The bitter struggle between his sons continued until Louis died in 840.

Between that time and the accession of Louis IX in 1226, the seven kings of France who bore this name generally ruled only a few years, often in hectic circumstances. Exceptions were Louis VI, the Fat, who held the throne from 1108 to 1137 and Louis VII, who reigned from 1137 to 1180.

Louis IX (1214-1270), or **Saint Louis**, the leader of two crusades, was the son of Louis VIII and Blanche of Castile (1187?-1252). He came to the throne when he was 12, with his mother as regent. Under her training, he became a pious, unselfish ruler. He fought a war with Henry III of England, who at that time ruled part of France. This war ended in 1259 when the two kings signed the Treaty of Paris. Louis increased royal power at the expense of the nobles, but he won their respect by being fair and just.

In 1248, Louis led a crusade to the Holy Land. He was defeated in Egypt and taken prisoner. The Muslims released him after he agreed to pay a large ransom. Louis led another crusade in 1270, but died in northern Africa when a plague broke out in his army. He was considered an ideal ruler. Even his enemies admired him for his fairness. Louis was *canonized* (made a saint) by Pope Boniface VIII in 1297. See CRUSADES.

Louis XI (1423-1483), the son of Charles VII, was known as the *terrible king*. While he was still *dauphin* (crown prince), he plotted against his father. Once he was exiled, and once he had to flee for his life. When he came to the throne in 1461, he set out to break the power of the nobles, who were almost independent of royal control. Charles the Bold, Duke of Burgundy, led the nobles. After the duke was killed in battle in 1477, Louis seized most of his territory. Later, the king added Provence, Maine, and Anjou to the royal domain.

Louis used cruel methods to keep his power. He made and broke laws and levied taxes at will. But he strengthened the government, encouraged art and learning, promoted industry and agriculture, opened roads and canals, and helped the poor obtain justice.

Louis XII (1462-1515), called "the Father of his People," was the son of Charles, Duke of Orléans. He came to the throne in 1498, succeeding Charles VIII, his distant cousin. He married Charles' widow, Anne of Brittany. France prospered under Louis XII, even though he carried on many wars. The king invaded Italy because he claimed Milan, but he was driven out in 1512. The next year, Henry VIII of England defeated Louis in the Battle of the Spurs.

Louis XIII (1601-1643) came to the throne in 1610 after the assassination of his father, Henry IV. His mother, Marie de Médicis, acted as regent until 1617. Cardinal Richelieu served as the chief minister and real ruler of France from 1624 until he died in 1642. He destroyed the political power of the Protestant Huguenots, centralized authority in the hands of the king, and made France an absolute monarchy (see RICHELIEU, CARDINAL). During this period, France fought in the Thirty Years' War (see THIRTY YEARS' WAR).

Louis XIV (1638-1715), called "the Grand Monarch" or "Louis the Great," was four years old when he succeeded his father, Louis XIII. His 72-year reign was the longest in modern European history. He was an outstanding example of the absolute monarch. He is said to have boasted, "*L'état c'est moi*" ("I am the State"). These words express the spirit of a reign in which the king held all political authority (see DIVINE RIGHT OF KINGS). Louis chose the sun as his royal emblem, and was often called *Le roi-soleil* (The Sun King).

The king's mother, Anne of Austria, acted as regent until 1661. Cardinal Mazarin served as her chief minister. In 1648, the Thirty Years' War came to an end. This war strengthened France and weakened Austria and the Habsburgs. But Mazarin was unpopular in France, and his policies led to several years of civil war in a revolt called the *Fronde* (see MAZARIN, JULES CARDINAL). Twice Mazarin had to flee from Paris, but finally in 1653 he put down the rebellion. The failure of the revolt strengthened the king's authority over the nobles.

When Mazarin died in 1661, Louis declared that he would be his own chief minister. His education had been neglected, but he was shrewd in choosing wise counselors. The greatest of his ministers was Jean Colbert, who reorganized French finance and promoted economy and industry (see COLBERT, JEAN BAPTISTE).

Louis encouraged writers and artists, and played a part in the development of French literature. Historians often call the 1600's in France "the Century of Louis XIV."

Louis fought four major wars. His great aim was to make himself supreme in Europe. As a start, he hoped to conquer all the land west of the Rhine River. He gained several important territories, but was always checked by the alliances that other countries formed against him. In the War of the Spanish Succession, England took an important part in defeating him. This war, which ended in 1714, left France exhausted and weakened.

Louis married Marie Thérèse of Spain in 1660. But his mistresses influenced him more than she did. The most important of these was Madame de Maintenon (see MAINTENON, MARQUISE DE). He secretly married her after Marie Thérèse died in 1683. Madame de Maintenon was probably partly responsible for Louis' harsh treatment of the French Protestants, who were called *Huguenots*. For nearly 100 years, they had enjoyed religious toleration and civil rights under the Edict of Nantes. In 1685, Louis revoked this edict (see HUGUENOTS; NANTES, EDICT OF). The government persecuted the Huguenots savagely in an effort to compel them to change their religion. Perhaps 200,000 Huguenots fled from the country. France suffered when the Huguenots left, because among them were many of the most prosperous and industrious persons in the country.

After 1685, Louis' reign was less glorious than it had been in the early years. After Colbert died, the country was plunged into debt by wars. Louis built a magnificent palace in Versailles. He and his court lived there in luxury, while many of the people lived in poverty. The extravagance of court life added to France's financial problems. Louis made the nobles live at Versailles instead of on their provincial estates. France became a nation of absentee landlords who had no contact with their tenants. This condition was one of the causes of the French Revolution. Yet, under Louis, France ranked above all other nations in art, in literature, in war, and in statesmanship. After Louis died, French political influence in Europe declined. See DANCING (The 1600's and 1700's; picture: Magnificent Court Balls).

Additional Resources

GOUBERT, PIERRE. *Louis XIV and Twenty Million Frenchmen.* Pantheon, 1970. Contrasts the life of the court with the life of the people.
HATTON, RAGNHILD. *Louis XIV and His World.* Putnam, 1972.
LEWIS, W. H. *The Splendid Century: Life in the France of Louis XIV.* Morrow, 1953.
WOLF, JOHN B. *Louis XIV of France.* Norton, 1968. The standard biography.

Louis XV (1710-1774), the great-grandson of Louis XIV, came to the throne at the age of five. Philippe, Duke of Orléans, a relative of the king, served as regent. Louis was declared of age in 1723. Soon after, the Duke of Orléans died, and the Duke of Bourbon became the chief minister. In 1726, the king's tutor, André Hercule Cardinal de Fleury, became the real ruler. Under his government, financial conditions improved greatly, and France showed signs of economic recovery.

When Fleury died in 1743, the king announced that he would rule without a minister, as Louis XIV had done. But he was weak and pleasure loving. A series of mistresses and court favorites dominated him. For 20 years, Madame de Pompadour dictated policies and appointed ministers (see POMPADOUR, MARQUISE DE). She was followed by Madame du Barry (see DU BARRY, MADAME). The king's favorites and mistresses looted the treasury, and France's financial disorder grew worse.

In 1725, Louis married Maria Leszczyńska, daughter of Stanislas I, the exiled king of Poland. France fought the War of the Polish Succession in a vain attempt to restore Stanislas to his throne. France won Lorraine in this war, but gained nothing in the War of the Austrian Succession (see SUCCESSION WARS). In the Seven Years' War, which ended in 1763, France lost its colonies in Canada and India to Great Britain. In North America, this conflict was called the French and Indian War (see FRENCH AND INDIAN WARS; SEVEN YEARS' WAR). The French hated Louis for his costly and disastrous wars and for the scandals of his personal life. His reign did much to bring on the French Revolution. Louis could see the coming disaster, but cared little. He is best remembered for his cynical remark, "After me, the deluge!"

Louis XVI (1754-1793), the grandson of Louis XV, came to the throne in 1774. He was a man of personal virtue and good intentions, but was a weak ruler. He was more interested in hunting than in public affairs. In 1770, he married the beautiful Marie Antoinette of Austria. Louis often relied on the advice of his wife. But she was unpopular because of her frivolity and her extravagance.

The young king made Robert Turgot minister of finance, and promised to support him in dealing with the public debt. Turgot met opposition when he tried to abolish some of the privileges of the nobles and higher clergy, and Louis dismissed him in 1776. The king then turned to Jacques Necker and promised to support him. The new minister also ran into opposition when he tried to make reforms, and was forced to resign in 1781. By this time, the king had lost the sympathy of his people. During this period, France helped the United States gain its independence in the Revolutionary War against Great Britain. The war with Great Britain increased France's national debt.

Louis was forced to recall Necker in 1788. Necker asked the king to call the States-General, or national assembly, which had not met since 1614. The meeting of the States-General in 1789 marked the beginning of the French Revolution. Louis pretended to sympathize with the Revolution. But actually, influenced by the advice of his wife, he opposed it. He and his family were forced to move from Versailles and live under guard in the Tuileries palace in Paris (see TUILERIES).

In 1791, Louis and his family tried to flee from France, but were arrested. Radicals then seized control of the Revolutionary government. Rioters invaded the Tuileries in August, 1792, and murdered the Swiss Guard. The National Convention deposed the king and declared France a republic. Louis was tried for treason. He defended himself with dignity, but was found guilty. He was guillotined on Jan. 21, 1793. Later, Marie

Antoinette met the same fate. See FRENCH REVOLUTION; MARIE ANTOINETTE.

Louis XVII (1785-1795) was king in name only, for two years after his father, Louis XVI, was guillotined in 1793. The young *dauphin* (prince) was taken from his mother in 1793 and kept in prison. He died on June 8, 1795, from abuse and neglect. He became known as "the lost dauphin" because there were many stories that he was not dead. Some of these stories said that the young Louis XVII had been rescued and placed in hiding.

Louis XVIII (1755-1824), a brother of Louis XVI, became "the Restoration King" of France after the French Revolution. As the Count of Provence, he fled from France in 1791. He set up a court in Koblenz, in Germany, and issued proclamations against the Revolution. His actions enraged the French people against Louis XVI, and hastened his execution. When Louis XVII died in 1795, the Count assumed the title of king. During the period when Napoleon Bonaparte was in power, he lived in several countries in Europe. But Louis XVIII spent the later years of his exile living in England.

In 1814, after Napoleon was defeated, the allied powers gave Louis the throne. He promised to rule as a constitutional monarch. In 1815, during the "Hundred Days" of Napoleon's return, Louis was driven from his throne. But he was restored after the Battle of Waterloo. Louis proclaimed a liberal constitution, and followed moderate policies in his rule. He tried to follow a middle course between the liberals and the reactionaries, who wanted to wipe out all the changes made by the French Revolution. RICHARD M. BRACE

See also BOURBON; DAUPHIN; FURNITURE (Louis XIV Furniture; French Styles); VERSAILLES.

LOUIS, *LOO ihs*, **JOE** (1914-1981), held the world heavyweight boxing championship longer than any other man. He turned professional in 1934, and won the title in June, 1937, by knocking out James J. Braddock in the eighth round. Louis successfully defended his title 25 times, scoring 20 knockouts. He retired in March, 1949, and later failed in two comeback attempts. Louis combined a steady forward movement with a swift, two-fisted attack. Joe Louis Barrow was born in Lafayette, Ala., and moved to Detroit as a child. LYALL SMITH

See also BOXING (picture).

Additional Resources

ASTOR, GERALD. *And A Credit To His Race: The Hard Life and Times of Joseph Louis Barrow, a.k.a. Joe Louis.* Saturday Review Press, 1974.
LIBBY, BILL. *Joe Louis: The Brown Bomber.* Morrow, 1980. For younger readers.
LOUIS, JOE, and others. *Joe Louis: My Life.* Harcourt, 1978.

LOUIS NAPOLEON. See NAPOLEON III.

LOUIS PHILIPPE, *LOO ee fuh LEEP* (1773-1850), was king of France from 1830 to 1848. He is often called *The Citizen King.* He was born in Paris, the eldest son of Philippe Égalité, Duke of Orléans. He sympathized with the democratic ideas of the French Revolution, and joined the national guard at the beginning of the revolt. He became a lieutenant general and took part in the battles of Valmy, Jemappes, and Neerwinden. But he later became involved in a plot against the republic and had to leave France.

In 1814, Louis Philippe returned to France and re-

gained his large estates. He was proclaimed "Citizen King" of France after Charles X was forced to give up the throne in the revolution of 1830. A week later Louis Philippe was made king. During his 18-year reign, he was unpopular with all classes of the French people. The *legitimists* opposed him because they were loyal to the descendants of Charles X. The Republicans disliked his autocratic ways. His reign was prosperous but uneventful. "France is bored" became a common saying.

The Revolution of 1848 broke out partly because he refused to reform the election laws. He was forced to give up his throne, and escaped to England. ANDRÉ MAUROIS

See also JULY REVOLUTION; NAPOLEON III.

LOUISBOURG, *LOO ihs BURG,* Nova Scotia (pop. 1,410), lies on the east coast of Cape Breton Island. It lies 20 miles (32 kilometers) southeast of Sydney. For location, see NOVA SCOTIA (political map). The French established it as a fortress in the 1700's. The old town exists today only as ruins. The present town is a winter port, and serves as an important fishing center. Louisbourg also has a large fish-processing and cold-storage industry.

The French founded Louisbourg in 1713, and named it for King Louis XIV. They built the fortress to guard the entrance to the Saint Lawrence River. It cost so much to build it that King Louis asked if its streets were paved with gold. The Canadian government restored some of the ruins, and built a museum to house relics in 1935-1936. It established the Fortress of Louisbourg as a national park in 1940.

First Battle of Louisbourg. The fortress became a constant threat to the British colonies. The French used it as a base from which to attack Canso in 1744. British colonists from Massachusetts then equipped a force to attack Louisbourg. Nearly 4,000 men, commanded by Colonel William Pepperell, sailed from Boston, Mass., in a fleet of 100 ships. Ten British ships-of-war, under the command of Commodore Peter Warren, arrived from the West Indies to join them. The combined forces attacked on April 30, 1745. On June 17, the fortress surrendered. In 1748, the Treaty of Aix-la-Chapelle returned Louisbourg to the French.

Second Battle of Louisbourg. The French held and strengthened Louisbourg for 10 years. In 1758, during the last French and Indian War, another battle occurred at Louisbourg. British troops led by Major General Jeffery Amherst again took the base, and destroyed most of the fortifications. THOMAS H. RADDALL

LOUISBOURG, FORTRESS OF. See CANADA (table: National Historic Parks and Sites).

LOUISE, LAKE. See LAKE LOUISE.

LOUISE OF MECKLENBURG-STRELITZ, *MEHK luhn burk SHTRAY lihts* (1776-1810) ruled Prussia, with her husband Frederick William III, from 1797 to 1810. Her beauty, generosity, and courage in the face of trouble made her popular with her people. She reigned during the time of Napoleon's attacks on Prussia, and urged her timid husband to resist the French. After Prussian defeats at the Battle of Jena, she appealed to Napoleon to spare her country, but was unsuccessful. Louise was born in Hanover, Germany. She was the daughter of Duke Charles of Mecklenburg-Strelitz. She married in 1793. CHARLES W. INGRAO

WORLD BOOK photo by W. R. Wilson

Mississippi River Delta

The contributors of this article are George A. Stokes, Vice President for University Affairs, Northwestern State University of Louisiana; Joseph G. Tregle, Jr., Professor Emeritus of History, University of New Orleans; and Edmund J. Tunstall, Assistant to the Publisher of the Times-Picayune Publishing Corporation.

LOUISIANA

Facts in Brief

Capital: Baton Rouge.

Government: *Congress*—U.S. senators, 2; U.S. representatives, 8. *Electoral Votes*—10. *State Legislature*—senators, 39; representatives, 105. *Parishes* (counties)—64.

Area: 47,752 sq. mi. (123,677 km²), including 3,230 sq. mi. (8,366 km²) of inland water but excluding 1,016 sq. mi. (2,631 km²) of Gulf of Mexico coastal water; 31st in size among the states. *Greatest Distances*—north-south, 237 mi. (381 km); east-west, 236.5 mi. (380.6 km). *Coastline*—397 mi. (639 km).

Elevation: *Highest*—Driskill Mountain, 535 ft. (163 m) above sea level. *Lowest*—5 ft. (1.5 m) below sea level at New Orleans.

Population: *1980 Census*—4,206,098; 19th among the states; density, 88 persons per sq. mi. (34 persons per km²); distribution, 69 per cent urban, 31 per cent rural. *1970 Census*—3,644,637.

Chief Products: *Agriculture*—soybeans, beef cattle, rice, cotton, milk, sugar cane. *Fishing Industry*—shrimp, menhaden. *Fur Industry*—nutria, muskrat. *Manufacturing*—chemicals, petroleum and coal products, food products, paper products, transportation equipment, electric machinery and equipment, fabricated metal products. *Mining*—natural gas, petroleum, natural gas liquids, sulfur, salt, sand and gravel, stone.

Statehood: April 30, 1812, the 18th state.

State Abbreviations: La. (traditional); LA (postal).

State Motto: *Union, Justice, and Confidence.*

State Songs: "Give Me Louisiana." Words and music by Doralice Fontane. "You Are My Sunshine." Words and music by Jimmy H. Davis and Charles Mitchell.

Louisiana (blue) ranks 31st in size among all the states, and sixth in size among the Southern States (gray).

Louisiana Dept. of Commerce and Industry

Muskrat Trapper on a Bayou

Gulf Shrimp Fisherman

WORLD BOOK photo

THE PELICAN STATE

LOUISIANA lies where the mighty Mississippi River empties into the Gulf of Mexico. This important location has made Louisiana one of the country's busiest commercial areas. Water routes link the state with both the heart of America and lands across the sea.

The Mississippi tells the story of Louisiana's progress. In colonial days, traders and fur trappers traveled the river in canoes, hollowed-out logs, or flatboats. During the 1800's, colorful paddle-wheel steamboats brought cotton to New Orleans and Baton Rouge for shipment throughout the world. Today, tugboats push chains of river barges more than 1,000 feet (300 meters) long. New Orleans, Louisiana's largest city, ranks among the world's busiest ports. Ocean ships can travel about 250 miles (402 kilometers) up the river to Baton Rouge, the state capital.

White-columned mansions, built before the Civil War, symbolize Louisiana's past glory as a leader of the Old South. Oil and natural-gas wells are a vital part of the new Louisiana scene. They represent Louisiana's greatest source of wealth. Rapid industrial growth based on these minerals began during World War II and is still going on. In the 1960's, Louisiana became a major space age industrial center.

The life of Louisiana is based on a mixture of many peoples, cultures, and customs. The influence of the early French and Spanish settlers can be seen throughout the state, especially in the south. There live the *Creoles*, the descendants of the original settlers, and the *Cajuns*, some of whose French ancestors came from Canada.

Millions of tourists come to Louisiana each year. People from all parts of the United States visit New Orleans for the city's festive carnival season and famous Mardi Gras. The visitors enjoy seeing the old French and Spanish section, where delicious food is served in world-famous restaurants. Tourists also listen to New Orleans-style jazz, in the area known as the *Cradle of Jazz*. The plentiful wildlife of Louisiana lures many hunters to the state.

Louisiana was named by the French explorer Robert Cavelier, Sieur de la Salle. He traveled down the Mississippi River in 1682, and claimed the entire Mississippi River Valley for France. La Salle named the region Louisiana in honor of the French king, Louis XIV. A nickname for Louisiana is the *Pelican State*, because of the brown pelicans that live along the coast of the state. Louisiana is also known as the *Bayou State*, because of its many *bayous* (slow-moving inlets or outlets of lakes and rivers).

419

Constitution. The present Constitution of Louisiana —the 11th in the state's history—was adopted in 1974. It replaced a Constitution that had been *amended* (changed) more than 535 times. The old Constitution, adopted in 1921, included more than 250,000 words and ranked as the longest state constitution. The 1974 Constitution has about 35,000 words.

An amendment to the Constitution may be proposed by the Legislature or by a constitutional convention. The Legislature, by a two-thirds vote of each house, may call a constitutional convention. An amendment proposed in the state Senate or House of Representatives must be approved by two-thirds of the members of both houses. An amendment proposed by the Legislature or a constitutional convention must be approved by a majority in a statewide election.

Executive. The governor of Louisiana holds office for a four-year term. The governor is limited to two terms in a row, but can serve an unlimited number of terms. The governor receives a yearly salary of $73,440. The governor has the power to veto any bill passed by the state Legislature. But the Legislature can override the veto by a two-thirds vote in each house.

The Constitution of Louisiana requires that the state government be organized into no more than 20 departments. The governor appoints the heads of many of these departments. All appointments must be approved by the state Senate. For a list of all the governors of Louisiana, see the *History* section of this article.

The voters also elect other chief state officials to four-year terms. These include the lieutenant governor, secretary of state, attorney general, treasurer, commissioner of agriculture, and superintendent of education.

Legislature consists of a Senate of 39 members and a House of Representatives of 105 members. Louisiana has 39 senatorial districts and 105 representative districts. Voters in each senatorial district elect one senator. Voters in each representative district elect one representative. The senators and representatives serve four-year terms.

Both houses of the Legislature meet every year. Regular sessions begin on the third Monday of April. They last for 60 legislative days. Special sessions may run only 30 days.

Courts. Louisiana is the only state in which judges do not decide cases chiefly on the basis of *common law*. Under the common-law system, rulings are determined by previous court decisions and the customs of the people. In Louisiana, judges decide civil cases on the basis of a *code* (set of rules). They can disregard the decisions of other judges in similar cases. Louisiana's civil code is based largely on the Napoleonic code of France. See CODE NAPOLÉON; COMMON LAW.

Louisiana's highest court is the Supreme Court, which hears both civil and criminal cases. It has a chief justice and six associate justices, all elected to 10-year terms. The associate justice with the longest service becomes the chief justice. The court system in Louisiana also includes 5 courts of appeal and 40 district courts.

Local Government. Louisiana is the only state that calls its counties *parishes*. The parishes arose as administrative units of the Roman Catholic Church during Spanish rule of the area. Under the Constitution of 1845, Louisiana dropped its county organization, and the parishes took over the counties' functions. Louisiana now has 64 parishes. Most of them have a central governing body called the *police jury*, which resembles a county board of commissioners. The members of each jury elect one of their number as president. Most police jurors and other parish officials are elected to four-year terms. Louisiana has about 300 incorporated cities, towns, and villages. Almost all of them have a mayor-council form of government.

Revenue. Taxation provides about three-fourths of the state government's *general revenue* (income). Almost all the rest comes from federal grants and other U.S. government programs. Louisiana taxes, in order of revenue, include a tax on mineral production, a sales tax, and a gasoline tax. The state also taxes personal and corporation incomes.

The Governor's Mansion stands on landscaped grounds east of the Louisiana Capitol. It is near the Mississippi River. The two-story building was completed in 1962. Towering white pillars accent the Southern colonial architecture.

Louisiana Tourist Development Comm.

Capitol Steps bear the names of the states in the order of their admission to the Union. Each of the first 48 steps has a single state and date. On the 49th step, the names and dates for Alaska and Hawaii flank the inscription "E Pluribus Unum."

WORLD BOOK photo by W. R. Wilson

The State Seal

Symbols of Louisiana, the state seal and flag, bear a mother pelican feeding and protecting her brood. This design shows the state's role as the protector of its people and resources. Both the seal, adopted in 1902, and the flag, adopted in 1912, show the state motto: *Union, Justice, and Confidence.*

Flag, flower, and bird illustrations, courtesy of Eli Lilly and Company

The State Flag

Politics. The Democratic Party has controlled Louisiana politics throughout most of the state's history. But the Republican Party began to gain strength in the state during the 1950's. For a discussion of this change, see *The Mid-1900's* in the *History* section of this article.

Democratic candidates carried the state in all presidential elections from 1880 through 1944. Since then, Louisiana has given its electoral votes to Republican presidential candidates in half of the elections. For the state's electoral votes and voting record in presidential elections, see ELECTORAL COLLEGE (table).

In 1979, David C. Treen became the first Republican to be elected governor of the state since 1877, when federal control ended after the Civil War. In 1972, Treen had become the first Republican to be elected to the U.S. House of Representatives from Louisiana since the late 1880's.

The State Bird
Brown Pelican

The State Capitol, in Baton Rouge, rises 450 feet (137 meters). Baton Rouge has been Louisiana's capital since 1882. Former capitals were New Orleans (1812-1830), Donaldsonville (1830-1831), New Orleans (1831-1849), Baton Rouge (1849-1862), New Orleans (Union, 1862-1882), Opelousas (Confederate, 1862-1863), and Shreveport (Confederate, 1863-1865).

Alpha Photo Associates

The State Flower
Magnolia

The State Tree
Bald Cypress

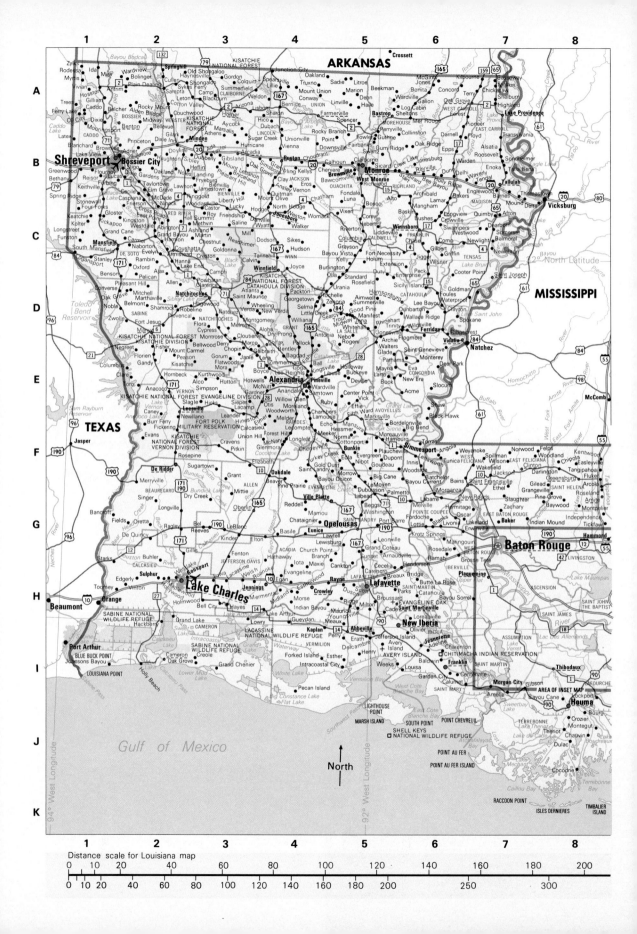

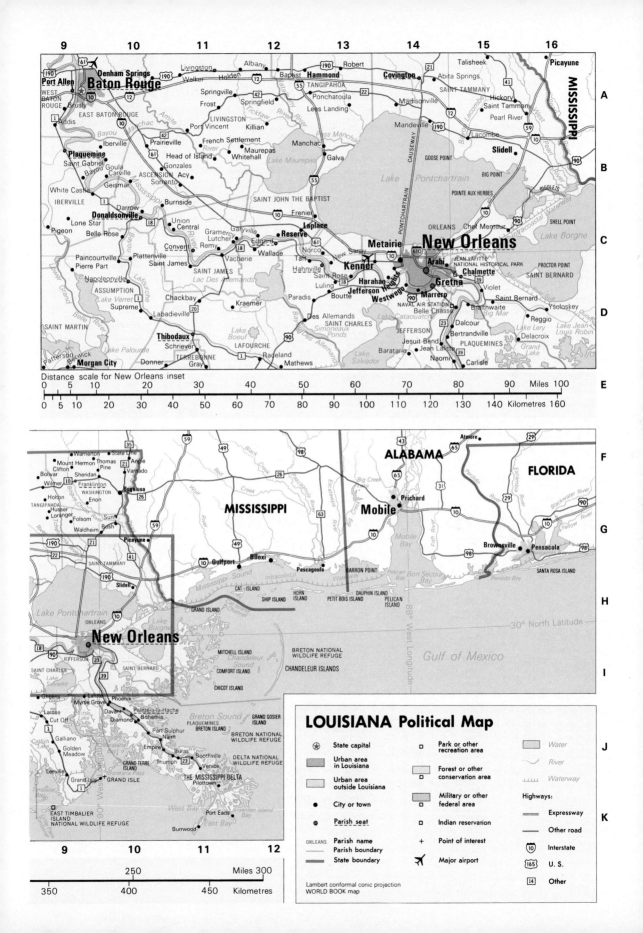

LOUISIANA Political Map

State capital

Urban area in Louisiana

Urban area outside Louisiana

• City or town

◉ Parish seat

ORLEANS Parish name

Parish boundary

State boundary

□ Park or other recreation area

Forest or other conservation area

Military or other federal area

□ Indian reservation

+ Point of interest

✈ Major airport

Water

River

Waterway

Highways:

Expressway

Other road

10 Interstate

165 U.S.

14 Other

Lambert conformal conic projection
WORLD BOOK map

Louisiana Map Index

Population

Population		Year
4,206,098	Census	1980
3,644,637	"	1970
3,257,022	"	1960
2,683,516	"	1950
2,363,880	"	1940
2,101,593	"	1930
1,798,509	"	1920
1,656,388	"	1910
1,381,625	"	1900
1,118,588	"	1890
939,946	"	1880
726,915	"	1870
708,002	"	1860
517,762	"	1850
352,411	"	1840
215,739	"	1830
153,407	"	1820
76,556	"	1810

Metropolitan Areas

Alexandria	135,282
Baton Rouge	494,151
Houma-Thibodaux	176,876
Lafayette	190,231
Lake Charles	167,223
Monroe	139,241
New Orleans	1,256,256
Shreveport	333,079

Parishes (Counties)

Acadia	56,427	G	4
Allen	21,390	G	3
Ascension	50,068	H	7
Assumption	22,084	I	7
Avoyelles	41,393	F	5
Beauregard	29,692	G	2
Bienville	16,387	B	3
Bossier	80,721	A	2
Caddo	252,437	B	1
Calcasieu	167,223	H	2
Caldwell	10,761	C	5
Cameron	9,336	I	3
Catahoula	12,287	D	6
Claiborne	17,095	A	3
Concordia	22,981	E	6
De Soto	25,727	C	2
East Baton Rouge	366,191	G	7
East Carroll	11,772	B	7
East Feliciana	19,015	F	7
Evangeline	33,343	G	4
Franklin	24,141	C	6
Grant	16,703	D	4
Iberia	63,752	I	6
Iberville	32,159	H	6
Jackson	17,321	B	4
Jefferson	454,592	I	9
Jefferson Davis	32,168	H	3
Lafayette	150,017	H	5
Lafourche	82,483	I	8
La Salle	17,004	D	5
Lincoln	39,763	B	4
Livingston	58,806	H	8
Madison	15,682	C	7
Morehouse	34,803	A	5
Natchitoches	39,863	D	3
Orleans	557,927	H	9
Ouachita	139,241	B	5
Plaquemines	26,049	J	11
Pointe Coupee	24,045	G	6
Rapides	135,282	F	4
Red River	10,433	C	2
Richland	22,187	B	5
Sabine	25,280	D	2
St. Bernard	64,097	I	10
St. Charles	37,259	I	9
St. Helena	9,827	G	8
St. James	21,495	H	8
St. John the Baptist	31,924	H	8
St. Landry	84,128	G	5
St. Martin	40,214	H	6
St. Mary	64,253	I	6
St. Tammany	110,869	H	9
Tangipahoa	80,698	G	9
Tensas	8,525	C	7
Terrebonne	94,393	J	7
Union	21,167	A	4
Vermilion	48,458	I	4
Vernon	53,475	E	2
Washington	44,207	G	9
Webster	43,631	A	2
West Baton Rouge	19,086	G	7
West Carroll	12,922	A	6
West Feliciana	12,186	F	6
Winn	17,253	C	4

Cities, Towns, and Villages

Abbeville	12,391	°I	5
Abita Springs	1,072	A	14
Acme		E	6
Ada		B	3
Addis	1,320	A	9
Adner		B	2
Afton		C	7
Aimwell		D	5
Ajax		D	2
Albany	857	A	12
Alco		E	3
Alden Bridge		A	2
Alexandria	51,565	°E	4
Allen		D	2
Aloha		D	3
Alsatia		B	7
Alto		B	5
Amelia	3,617	I	7
Amite	4,301	°G	8
Anacoco	90	E	2
Anandale		E	4
Angie	311	F	10
Angola		F	6
Ansley		B	4
Antonia		D	4
Antrim		A	2
Arabi	10,248	C	15
Arcadia	3,403	°B	3
Archibald		B	6
Archie		D	5
Arcola		F	8
Arizona		A	3
Armistead		C	2
Arnaudville	1,679	G	5
Ashland	307	C	3
Athens	419	B	3
Atlanta	127	D	4
Avery Island		I	5
Avondale*	6,699	I	9
Aycock		A	3
Bagdad		E	4
Bains		F	6
Baker	12,865	G	7
Baldwin	2,644	I	6
Ball	3,405	E	4
Bancroft		G	1
Baptist		A	12
Barataria	1,123	E	14
Basile	2,635	G	4
Baskin	286	C	6
Bastrop	15,527	°A	5
Batchelor		F	6
Baton Rouge	219,844	°G	7
Bawcomville, see Brownsville [-Bawcomville]			
Bayou Blue*	2,729	H	5
Bayou Cane	15,723	I	8
Bayou Chicot		F	4
Bayou Current		F	6
Bayou Goula		B	9
Bayou Sorrel		H	7
Bayou Vista*	5,805	I	7
Baywood		G	8
Beaver		F	4
Bee Bayou		B	6
Beekman		A	5
Beggs		G	5
Bel		G	3
Belcher	436	A	1
Bell City		H	3
Belle Chasse	5,412	D	15
Belle Rose		C	10
Bellevue		B	2
Bellwood		D	2
Belmont		D	2
Benson		D	1
Bentley		E	4
Benton	1,864	°A	1
Bernice	1,956	A	4
Bertrandville		D	14
Berwick	4,466	E	9
Bethany		B	1
Bienville	249	B	3
Big Bend		F	6
Big Cane		F	5
Blackburn		A	3
Black Hawk		F	6
Blanchard	1,128	B	1
Blanks		G	6
Bogalusa	16,976	F	10
Bohemia		J	10
Bolinger		A	2
Bolivar		F	9
Bonita	503	A	6
Book		E	5
Boothville		J	11
Bordelonville		F	5
Bosco		C	5
Bossier City	50,817	B	2
Bourg	2,073	J	8
Boutte		D	13
Boyce	1,198	E	4
Braithwaite		D	15
Branch		G	4
Breaux Bridge	5,922	H	5
Broadmoor*	7,051	H	5
Broussard	2,923	H	5
Brownlee		B	1
Brownsville [-Bawcomville]	7,252	B	5
Brownville		B	5
Brusly	1,762	A	9
Bryceland	94	B	3
Buckeye		E	5
Buhler		H	2
Bunkie	5,364	F	5
Buras [-Triumph]	4,137	J	11
Burr Ferry		F	2
Burrwood		K	11
Bush		G	10
Bushes		C	6
Caddo		A	1
Cade		H	5
Calcasieu		F	4
Calhoun		B	4
Calumet		I	6
Calvin	263	C	3
Cameron	1,736	°I	2
Camp		A	3
Campti	1,069	D	3
Caney		E	2
Cankton	303	H	5
Carencro	3,712	H	5
Carlisle		E	15
Carlyss*	1,806	H	2
Carmel		C	2
Carville	1,037	B	10
Caspiana		B	2
Castor	195	C	3
Catahoula		H	6
Cecile		B	2
Cecelia		H	5
Center Point		E	5
Centerville		I	6
Central		C	11
Chackbay		D	11
Chalmette	33,847	°D	15
Chambers		E	4
Charenton		I	6
Chase		C	6
Chataignier	431	G	4
Chatham	714	B	4
Chauvin	3,338	J	8
Chef Menteur		C	15
Cheneyville	865	F	4
Cheniere		B	5
Chestnut		C	3
Chickasaw		A	7
Chipola		F	8
Chopin		E	3
Choudrant	809	B	4
Church Point	4,599	G	5
Claiborne	6,278	B	5
Clare		E	2
Clarence	612	D	3
Clarks*	931	C	5
Clay		B	4
Clayton	1,204	D	6
Clifton		F	9
Clinton	1,919	°F	7
Cloutierville		D	3
Cocodrie		J	8
Colfax	1,680	°D	4
Collinston	439	B	6
Colquitt		A	3
Columbia	687	°C	5
Columbus		E	2
Como		C	6
Concord		A	6
Convent		°C	11
Converse	449	D	1
Conway		A	4
Cooter Point		C	6
Corey		C	5
Cotton Valley	1,445	A	2
Cottonport	1,911	F	5
Couchwood		A	2
Coushatta	2,084	°C	2
Covington	7,892	°A	14
Cravens		F	3
Creole		I	3
Creston		C	3
Crew Lake		B	5
Cross Roads		C	2
Crowley	16,036	°H	4
Crowville		C	6
Crozier	1,150	J	8
Cullen	1,869	A	2
Cut Off	5,049	J	9
Cypress		D	3
Dalcour		D	15
Danville		C	3
Darlington		F	8
Darnell		B	6
Darrow		C	10
Davant		I	10
Dean		A	5
Deer Park		E	6
Delacroix		D	16
Delcambre	2,216	I	5
Delhi	3,290	B	6
Delta	295	C	7
Denham Springs	8,563	A	10
De Quincy	3,966	G	2
De Ridder	11,057	°F	2
Derry		D	3
Des Allemands	2,920	D	12
Destrehan*	2,382	I	9
Deville		E	5
Diamond		J	10
Dixie		A	1
Dixie Gardens		B	2
Dixie Inn	453	B	2
Dodson	469	C	4
Donaldsonville	7,901	°C	10
Donner		E	10
Downsville	213	B	4
Doyline	801	B	2
Dry Creek		G	3
Dry Prong	526	D	4
Dubach	1,161	B	4
Dubberly	421	B	3
Dubuisson		F	5
Dulac		J	8
Dunbarton		D	6
Dunn		B	6
Dupont		F	5
Duson	1,253	H	5
Easleyville		F	8
East Hammond*	1,937	G	9
East Hodge*	439	C	4
East Point		C	2
Echo		F	5
Edgard		°C	12
Edgefield*	312	C	2
Edgerly		H	2
Effie		E	5
Egan		H	4
Elizabeth	454	F	3
Elm Grove		B	2
Elmer		E	4
Elton	1,450	G	4
Empire		J	10
Englewood		B	7
Enoka		B	7
Enterprise		D	5
Eola		F	5
Epps	672	B	6
Erath	2,259	I	5
Eros	158	B	4
Erwinville		G	6
Estelle*	12,724	H	9
Esther		I	5
Estherwood	691	H	4
Ethel		F	7
Eunice	12,479	G	4
Eva		E	6
Evangeline		H	4
Evans		F	2
Evelyn		C	2
Evergreen	272	F	5
Extension		C	6
Fairbanks		B	5
Farmerville	3,768	°A	4
Fenton	491	G	3
Ferriday	4,472	D	6
Ferry Lake		A	1
Fields		G	2
Fifth Ward		F	5
Fillmore		B	2
Fisher	325	E	2
Fishville		E	4
Flatwoods		E	3
Flora		D	3
Florien	964	E	2
Flournoy		B	1
Floyd		B	7
Fluker		F	8
Folsom	319	G	9
Fondale		B	5
Forbing		B	1
Fordoche	676	G	6
Forest	299	A	6
Forest Hill	494	F	4
Forked Island		I	4
Fort Jesup		D	2
Fort Necessity		C	6
Fort Polk North*	1,644	F	3
Fort Polk South*	12,498	F	3
Foules		D	6
Four Forks		C	1
Fowler		B	5
Franklin	9,584	°I	6
Franklinton	4,119	°F	9
French Settlement	761	B	11
Frenier		C	13
Friendship		C	3
Frierson		C	2
Frogmore		D	6
Frost		A	11
Fryeburg		B	3
Funston		C	1
Galbraith		E	3
Galion		A	6
Galliano	5,159	J	9
Galva		B	13
Gardner		E	4
Gardner City		I	6
Garyville	2,856	C	12
Gassoway		A	7
Geismar		B	10
Georgetown	381	D	4
Gheens		I	9
Gibsland	1,354	B	3
Gibson		I	7
Gilark		B	2
Gilbert	800	C	6
Gilead		F	8
Gilliam	244	A	1
Gillis		G	2
Girard		B	6
Glade		E	5
Glenmora	1,479	F	4
Gloster		C	1
Gold Dust		F	5
Golden Meadow	2,282	J	9
Goldman		D	7
Goldonna	526	C	3
Gonzales	7,287	B	10
Good Pine, see Trout [-Good Pine]			
Goosport		H	2
Gordon		A	3
Gorum		E	3
Goudeau		F	5
Grambling	4,226	B	4
Gramercy	3,211	C	11
Grand Bayou		C	2
Grand Cane	252	C	1
Grand Chenier		I	3
Grand Coteau	1,165	G	5
Grand Isle	1,982	J	10
Grand Lake		H	2
Grangeville		G	8
Grant		F	3
Gray		E	11
Grayson	564	C	5
Greensburg	662	°F	8
Greenwood	1,043	B	1
Gretna	20,615	°D	14
Griffin		C	6
Grosse Tete	749	G	6
Gueydan	1,695	H	4
Gum Ridge		B	6
Guthrie		B	5
Hackberry		H	2
Hagewood		D	3
Hahnville	2,947	°C	13
Haile		A	5
Hall Summit	276	C	2
Hamburg		F	5
Hammond	15,043	G	8
Hanna		C	2
Harahan	11,384	C	14
Harmon		C	2
Harrisonburg	610	°D	6
Harvey*	22,709	I	9
Hathaway		G	4
Haughton	1,510	B	2
Hayes		H	3
Haynesville	3,454	A	3
Head of Island		B	11
Hebert		C	5
Heflin	279	B	3
Henderson	1,560	H	6
Henry		I	5
Hermitage		G	7
Hessmer	743	F	5
Hickory		A	15
Hicks		E	3
Hico		A	4
Highland		A	7
Hineston		E	3
Hodge	708	C	4
Holden		A	12
Holloway		E	5
Holly Beach		I	2
Holly Ridge		B	6
Hollywood		H	2
Holmwood		H	3
Holton		G	9
Holum		C	5
Homer	4,307	°A	3
Hornbeck	470	E	2
Hosston	480	A	1
Hotwells		E	4
Houma	32,602	°J	8
Hudson		C	4
Hurricane		B	3
Husser		G	9
Hutton		E	3
Iberville		B	10
Ida	306	A	1
Independence	1,684	G	8
Indian Bayou		H	4
Indian Mound		G	7
Innis		F	6
Intracoastal City		I	5
Iota	1,326	H	4
Iowa	2,437	H	3
Jackson	3,878	F	7
Jamestown	131	B	3
Janie		E	3
Jean Lafitte	541	D	14
Jeanerette	6,511	I	6
Jefferson*	15,550	I	9
Jefferson Heights		C	14
Jefferson Island		I	5
Jena	4,375	°D	5
Jennings	12,401	°H	4
Jesuit Bend		D	14
Jigger		C	6
Johnsons Bayou		I	1
Jones		A	6
Jonesboro	5,061	°C	4
Jonesburg		B	6
Jonesville	2,828	D	6
Joyce		C	4
Junction City	727	A	4
Kaplan	5,016	H	4
Keatchie	342	C	1
Keithville		B	1
Kelly		C	5
Kellys		B	4
Kenner	66,382	C	13
Kentwood	2,667	F	8
Kickapoo		C	1
Kilbourne	286	A	7
Killian	611	A	12
Kinder	2,603	G	3
Kingston		C	2
Kingsville		E	4
Kisatchie		E	3
Kolter		C	1
Kraemer		D	11
Krotz Springs	1,374	G	6
Kurthwood		E	3
Labadieville	2,138	D	10
Labarre		G	6
Lacamp		E	3
Lacassine		H	3
Lacombe	5,146	B	15
Lafayette	81,961	°H	5

Lafitte .... 1,312..I 9
Lake Arthur ... 3,615..H 4
Lake Charles . 75,226.°H 2
Lake End ....C 2
Lake
  Providence .. 6,361.°A 7
Lake View ....B 1
Lakeland ....G 6
Lamar ....B 4
Lamourie ....F 4
Laplace .... 16,112.°C 12
Larose .... 5,234..J 9
Larto ....E 5
Latex ....B 1
Lawhon ....B 3
Lawtell ..... 1,014..G 5
Leander ....E 3
Lebeau ....G 5
LeBlanc ....G 3
Lecompte .... 1,661..F 4
Lee Bayou ....D 6
Lee Heights ....E 4
Lee Landing ....A 13
Leesville .... 9,054.°F 2
Leeville ....J 9
LeMoyen ....F 5
Lena ....E 3
Leonville .... 1,143..G 5
Leton ....A 3
Lettsworth ....F 6
Lewisburg ....G 5
Liberty Hill ....C 3
Libuse ....E 4
Liddieville ....C 6
Lillie .... 172..A 4
Linville ....A 3
Lisbon .... 138..A 3
Litroe ....A 5
Little Creek ....D 4
Livingston .. 1,260.°A 11
Livonia ...... 980..G 6
Lockport .... 2,424..I 8
Log Cabin ....D 4
Logansport .. 1,565..C 1
Lone Star .... 1,593..C 2
Longleaf ....F 4
Longstreet .... 281..C 1
Longview ....C 6
Longville ....G 2
Loranger ....G 9
Loreauville .. 860..H 6
Lottie ....G 6
Louisa ....I 6
Lower
  Vacherie* .. 3,189..H 8
Lucas ....B 2
Lucky .... 370..C 3
Luling ...... 4,006..D 13
Luna ....B 5
Lutcher ..... 4,730..C 11
Madisonville .. 799..A 14
Mamou ...... 3,194..G 4
Manchac ....B 13
Mandeville .. 6,076..A 14
Mangham .... 867..C 6
Manifest ....D 5
Mansfield ... 6,485.°C 1
Mansura .... 2,074..F 5
Many .... 3,988.°D 2
Maplewood ....H 2
Marco ....D 4
Maringouin .. 1,291..G 6
Marion ...... 989..A 5
Marksville ... 5,113.°F 5
Marrero .... 36,548..D 14
Marsalis ....B 3
Marthaville ....C 3
Martin ...... 584..C 3
Mathews ....E 12
Maurepas ....B 12
Maurice ..... 478..H 5
Maxie ....H 4
Mayna ....E 5
McDade ....B 2
McGinty ....A 6

McNary .... 240..F 4
McNutt ....E 4
Meaux ....H 5
Melder ....F 4
Melrose ....E 6
Melville .... 1,764..G 6
Mer Rouge .... 802..A 6
Mermentau .... 771..H 4
Merryville ... 1,286..F 2
Metairie ... 164,160..C 14
Methvin ....C 2
Midland ....H 4
Midway ....A 2
Midway ....D 5
Mill ....C 3
Millikin ....H 5
Milton ....H 5
Mimosa Park* . 3,737..I 9
Minden ..... 15,084.°B 2
Mira ....A 1
Mitchell ....D 2
Mittie ....G 3
Monroe .... 57,597.°B 6
Monterey ....D 5
Montgomery ... 843..D 3
Montpelier ... 219..G 8
Montrose ....D 3
Mooringsport .. 911..A 1
Mora ....E 3
Moreauville .. 853..F 5
Moreland ....E 4
Morgan City . 16,114..I 7
Morganza .... 846..G 6
Morrow ....F 5
Morse .... 835..H 4
Moss Bluff* .. 7,004..H 2
Mound .... 40..B 7
Mount Carmel ....E 2
Mount Hermon ....F 9
Mount Lebanon . 105..B 3
Mount Olive ....B 3
Mount Union ....A 4
Myrtle Grove ....J 10
Naborton ....C 2
Nairn ....J 10
Naomi ....E 15
Napoleonville . 829.°D 10
Natchez ...... 527..D 3
Natchitoches . 16,664.°D 3
Nebo ....D 4
Negreet ....E 2
New Era ....E 6
New Iberia .. 32,766.°H 5
New
  Orleans ..557,927.°I 9
New Roads ... 3,924.°G 6
New Sarpy ... 2,249..C 13
New Verda ....D 3
Newellton ... 1,726..C 7
Newlight ....C 7
Newllano ... 2,213..F 2
Ninock ....C 1
Noble .... 194..D 1
Norco ...... 4,416..C 13
Norma ....F 5
North Hodge .. 573..C 4
Norwood ..... 421..F 7
Oak Grove ....D 2
Oak Grove ....B 3
Oak Grove ... 2,214.°A 7
Oak Grove ....I 3
Oak Ridge .... 257..B 6
Oakdale .... 7,155..F 4
Oakland ....B 2
Oakland ....A 3
Oberlin .... 1,764.°G 3
Oil City .... 1,323..A 1
Old Shongaloo ......A 2
Olivier ....H 6
Olla .... 1,603..D 5
Opelousas .. 18,903.°G 5
Oretta ....G 2
Oscar ....G 6
Otis ....E 4
Oxford ....D 2

Packton ....D 4
Paincourtville . 2,004..C 10
Palmetto ..... 327..G 5
Paradis ....D 13
Parhams ....E 6
Parks .... 545..H 5
Patterson .. 4,693..E 9
Pearl River . 1,693..A 16
Peason ....E 2
Pecan Island ....I 4
Peck ....C 6
Pelican ....D 2
Perry ....I 5
Perryville ....B 5
Phoenix ....I 10
Pickering ....F 2
Pierre Part . 3,153..C 9
Pigeon ....H 7
Pilottown ....K 11
Pine ....F 9
Pine Grove ....G 8
Pine Prairie .. 734..F 4
Pineville ... 12,034..E 4
Pioneer ..... 221..A 6
Pitkin ....F 3
Plain Dealing . 1,213..A 2
Plaquemine .. 7,521.°H 7
Plaquemine
  Southwest* . 1,467..H 7
Plattenville ....C 10
Plauchevile .. 196..F 5
Pleasant Hill . 776..D 2
Point ....B 5
Pointe-a-la-Hache ..°J 10
Pollock ..... 399..E 4
Ponchatoula . 5,469..A 13
Port Allen .. 6,114.°A 9
Port Barre .. 2,625..G 5
Port Eads ....K 11
Port Sulphur . 3,318..J 10
Port Vincent . 450..A 11
Powhatan .... 279..D 3
Poydras* .... 5,722..I 10
Prairieville ....B 10
Princeton ....B 2
Provencal .... 695..D 3
Quimby ....C 7
Quitman ..... 231..B 4
Raceland ... 6,302..E 12
Ragley ....G 2
Ramah ....G 6
Rambin ....C 2
Rayne ...... 9,066..H 5
Rayville .... 4,610.°B 6
Readhimer ....C 3
Reddell ....F 4
Reeves ...... 199..G 3
Reggio ....D 16
Reisor ....B 1
Remy ....C 12
Reserve .... 7,288..C 12
Rhinehart ....D 5
Richmond* .... 505..C 7
Richwood ... 1,223..B 5
Ridge ....H 5
Ridgecrest ... 895..D 5
Ringgold ... 1,655..B 2
River Ridge* . 17,146..I 9
Riverton ....B 6
Roanoke ....H 3
Robeline ..... 238..D 2
Robert ....A 13
Rocky Branch ....B 5
Rocky Mount ....A 2
Rodessa ..... 337..A 1
Rogers ....D 5
Roosevelt ....D 5
Rosedale ..... 658..G 6
Rosefield ....D 5
Roseland ... 1,346..G 8
Rosepine .... 953..F 2
Roy ....C 3
Ruby ....D 5
Ruston .... 20,585.°B 4
Sadie ....A 5

St. Bernard ....D 15
St.
  Francisville . 1,471.°F 6
St. Gabriel ....B 10
St. James ....C 11
St. Joseph .. 1,687.°D 7
St. Landry ....F 5
St. Martinville . 7,965.°H 5
St. Maurice ....D 3
St. Rose ....C 13
St. Tammany ....A 15
Saline ...... 293..C 3
Samtown ....E 4
Sarepta ..... 831..A 2
Schriever ....E 11
Scotland-
  ville* ..... 15,113..G 7
Scott ...... 2,239..H 5
Searcy ....D 5
Selma ....D 2
Seymourville* . 2,891..H 7
Shamrock ....D 2
Sharon ....A 4
Shaw ....A 6
Shelburn ....A 7
Sheltons ....A 5
Sheridan ....A 4
Shongaloo .... 163..A 2
Shreveport . 205,820.°B 1
Sibley ..... 1,211..B 2
Sicard ....B 5
Sicily Island . 691..D 6
Sieper ....A 4
Sikes ...... 226..C 4
Simmesport .. 2,293..F 6
Simpson ..... 534..E 3
Simsboro .... 553..B 4
Singer ....G 2
Slagle ....E 3
Slaughter .... 729..G 7
Slidell .... 26,718..H 10
Sligo ....B 2
Sondheimer ....B 7
Sorrento ... 1,197..B 11
South Mansfield 1,463..C 1
Spearsville .. 181..A 4
Spencer ....A 5
Spillman ....B 7
Spokane ....D 6
Spring Ridge ....B 1
Springfield .. 424..A 12
Springhill .. 6,516..A 2
Springville ....A 11
Standard ....B 6
Stanley ..... 151..C 1
Starks ....H 1
Start ....B 6
State Line ....A 5
Sterlington* . 1,400..B 5
Stonewall ... 1,175..B 1
Sugartown ....F 3
Sulphur .... 19,709..H 2
Summerfield ....A 3
Summerville ....D 5
Sun .... 338..G 10
Sunset .... 2,300..G 5
Supreme ....D 10
Swampers ....C 6
Swartz ....B 5
Taft ....C 12
Talisheek ....A 15
Talla Bena ....B 7
Tallulah ... 11,341.°B 7
Tangipahoa ... 493..F 8
Tannehill ....C 4
Taylor ....B 3
Taylortown ....B 2
Tendal ....B 7
Terry ....D 5
Terrytown* .. 23,548..I 9
Theriot ....I 8
Thibodaux .. 15,810.°I 9
Thomastown ....C 4
Tickfaw ..... 571..G 8
Timberlane* . 11,579..I 9

Tioga ....E 4
Toomey ....H 1
Toro ....E 2
Torras ....F 6
Transylvania ....B 7
Trees ....A 1
Trinity ....D 6
Triumph, see Buras
  [-Triumph]
Trout [-Good
  Pine] ..... 1,033..D 5
Truxno ....A 4
Tullos ...... 772..D 4
Tunica ....F 6
Turkey Creek .. 366..F 4
Union ....C 11
Union Hill ....F 4
Unionville ....A 5
Urania ...... 849..D 5
Vacherie .... 2,169..C 11
Varnado ..... 249..F 10
Venice ....I 11
Verda ....D 4
Vernon ....B 4
Vick ....E 5
Vidalia .... 5,936.°D 6
Vienna ...... 519..B 4
Ville Platte . 9,201.°G 4
Vinton ..... 3,631..H 2
Violet .... 11,678..D 15
Vivian ..... 4,225..A 1
Vixen ....C 5
Waggaman* .. 9,004..I 9
Wakefield ....F 7
Waldheim ....G 10
Walker .... 2,957..A 11
Walker ....C 4
Wallace ....C 12
Wallace Ridge ......D 6
Walters ....D 5
Warden ....B 6
Wardview ....A 2
Wardville ....A 5
Warnerton ....F 9
Washington .. 1,266..G 5
Waterproof .. 1,339..D 6
Waverly ....B 6
Weeks ....I 5
Weldon ....A 4
Welsh ..... 3,515..H 3
West
  Ferriday* .. 1,399..D 6
West Monroe . 14,993..B 5
Westdale ....C 2
Westlake ... 5,246..H 2
Weston ....C 4
Westwego .. 12,663..D 14
Westwood ....C 7
Weyanoke ....F 6
Wheeling ....D 3
White Castle . 2,160..B 9
Whitehall ....B 11
Whitehall ....D 5
Wildsville ....D 6
Williana ....D 4
Willow Glen ....E 4
Wilmer ....F 9
Wilson ...... 656..F 7
Winnfield .. 7,311.°C 4
Winnsboro .. 5,921.°C 6
Wisner .... 1,424..C 6
Womack ....C 4
Woodardville ....C 2
Woodland ....F 7
Woodside ....F 6
Woodworth ... 412..E 4
Wyatt ....C 3
Youngsville . 1,053..H 5
Yscloskey ....D 16
Zachary .... 7,297..G 7
Zenoria ....D 4
Zimmerman ....A 4
Zwolle ..... 2,602..D 2
Zylks ....A 1

°Parish seat.
*Does not appear on map; key shows general location.
Source: 1980 census. Places without population figures are unincorporated areas.

Shreveport Chamber of Commerce

Shreveport, the state's third largest city, lies on the Red River, in the northwest corner of Louisiana. Shreveport is a leading center of Louisiana industry and trade.

The 1980 United States census reported that Louisiana had 4,206,098 persons. The state's population had increased about 15 per cent over the 1970 census figure of 3,644,637.

More than two-thirds of the people of Louisiana live in urban areas. About half live in the metropolitan areas of New Orleans, Baton Rouge, and Shreveport. In all, Louisiana has eight metropolitan areas (see METROPOLITAN AREA). For the population of these areas, see the *Louisiana Map Index.*

The state has 14 cities with populations of more than 20,000. New Orleans is the largest city in Louisiana. Other large cities, in order of population, include Baton Rouge, Shreveport, Lafayette, Lake Charles, and Kenner. Large unincorporated areas in Louisiana include Metairie, Marrero, and Chalmette. See the separate articles on Louisiana cities listed in the *Related Articles* at the end of this article.

Louisianians often think of their state as having two parts—a French, Roman Catholic south and an Anglo-Saxon, Protestant north. Many of the people of southern Louisiana are descendants of the original French and Spanish settlers. These people are called *Creoles.* Others, called *Cajuns,* are descendants of French settlers from the Acadia region of eastern Canada. Most of the people of northern Louisiana are of Anglo-Saxon descent. Their ancestors were pioneers who came from neighboring states. Blacks make up about 30 per cent of the population of Louisiana. See ACADIA; CREOLE.

The culture of the early French and Spanish settlers still has an important influence in southern Louisiana. Many of the people there speak both French and English. Until the early 1900's, state laws and official notices appeared in both languages. Some blacks

Population Density

About two-thirds of Louisiana's residents live in an urban area, primarily in the southern half of the state. About 30 per cent of the state's population live in metropolitan New Orleans.

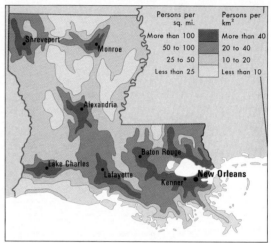

Persons per sq. mi.		Persons per km²
More than 100		More than 40
50 to 100		20 to 40
25 to 50		10 to 20
Less than 25		Less than 10

WORLD BOOK map; based on U.S. Bureau of the Census data.

speak a *dialect* (variation) of French called *Gumbo* or *Gombo.* Southern Louisiana has a reputation for fine cooking. Some famous dishes are *huitres en coquille à la Rockefeller* (oysters baked on rock salt with spinach sauce) and *pompano en papillote* (pompano fish baked with shellfish sauce in a paper bag). Soups made with fish include *bisque* and *bouillabaisse.* Many Louisianians flavor their strong, black coffee with chicory.

The French and Spanish brought the Roman Catholic religion to the Louisiana region. Today, about a third of the people belong to the Roman Catholic Church. Other large religious groups in Louisiana include Baptists, Episcopalians, Methodists, and Presbyterians.

Russell A. Thompson, Taurus

The French Quarter of New Orleans attracts many visitors. It was so named because French colonists settled the area. The area features Spanish architecture and many historic sites.

Louisiana Office of Tourism

Pirogue, or Wood Canoe, Racers compete in the World Championship Pirogue Races in Lafitte. These races, which are held in June, are a popular annual event in Louisiana.

Schools. Louisiana's first schools were established in New Orleans during the early French rule of the area. Capuchin friars founded the first school about 1725. In 1727, Ursuline nuns started a girls' school that still exists. The Spanish colonial government opened the first public school in 1772. However, the wealthier colonists preferred to send their children to private schools. Some sent their sons to colleges in Europe or the northern colonies. Many girls attended the Ursuline nuns' school or other local private schools.

Little progress in public education was made until the Constitution of 1845 created the office of state superintendent of education. Alexander Dimitry, the first superintendent, set up a statewide public school system. He became known as the *father of Louisiana elementary education.* The state Constitution of 1898 provided the first effective financial support of the school system. The Constitution gave parish school districts the power to issue bonds to obtain educational funds.

A state board of elementary and secondary education controls public elementary and high schools in Louisiana. It consists of eight elected members and three members appointed by the governor with the approval of the state Senate. All board members serve four-year terms. A state superintendent of education, elected to a four-year term, administers the board's policies.

Louisiana has 66 local school districts. These districts consist of the 64 parishes plus two cities that operate their own school systems—Bogalusa and Monroe. The voters of each district elect a school board, which appoints a superintendent. Louisiana law requires children 7 through 15 years of age to attend school. For information on the number of students and teachers in Louisiana, see EDUCATION (table).

Libraries. A public subscription library was established in New Orleans in 1805. By 1920, there were only five free public libraries in the state. In 1925, the Louisiana State Library in Baton Rouge began organizing parish-wide public library systems, which now serve all 64 parishes. Louisiana has many academic and specialized libraries.

Museums. The Louisiana State Museum, founded in 1906, is the state's oldest and largest museum. It is

WORLD BOOK photo by W. R. Wilson

The New Orleans Museum of Art has one of Louisiana's largest collections of fine arts. It is particularly noted for its Italian Renaissance paintings. The museum, established in 1910, was given to the city by Isaac Delgado, a wealthy industrialist.

Louisiana State University in Baton Rouge is one of the largest universities in the South. The campus spreads for about 2 miles (3.2 kilometers) along the east bank of the Mississippi River. The Memorial Tower, which honors Louisiana's World War I dead, rises 175 feet (53 meters) above the grounds. Its base houses an art museum.

Louisiana State University

housed in eight historic structures in the New Orleans French Quarter. It contains large collections of historic paintings, decorative arts, photographs, and items related to jazz. The New Orleans Museum of Art has one of the state's largest art collections. Paintings by Louisiana artists hang in the Louisiana State Exhibit Museum in Shreveport. The Louisiana Historical Association's Confederate Museum in New Orleans has Civil War exhibits.

Universities and Colleges

Louisiana has 20 universities and colleges accredited by the Southern Association of Colleges and Schools. For enrollments and further information, see UNIVERSITIES AND COLLEGES (table).

Name	Location	Founded	Name	Location	Founded
Centenary College of Louisiana	Shreveport	1825	Northwestern State University of Louisiana	Natchitoches	1884
Dillard University	New Orleans	1869	Notre Dame Seminary Graduate School of Theology	New Orleans	1923
Grambling State University	Grambling	1901	Our Lady of Holy Cross College	New Orleans	1922
Louisiana College	Pineville	1906	St. Joseph Seminary College	St. Benedict	1891
Louisiana State University	*	*	Southeastern Louisiana University	Hammond	1925
Louisiana Tech University	Ruston	1894	Southern University	*	*
Loyola University	New Orleans	1912	Southwestern Louisiana, University of	Lafayette	1898
McNeese State University	Lake Charles	1938	Tulane University of Louisiana	New Orleans	1834
New Orleans Baptist Theological Seminary	New Orleans	1917	Xavier University of Louisiana	New Orleans	1915
Nicholls State University	Thibodaux	1948			
Northeast Louisiana University	Monroe	1931			

*For campuses and founding dates, see UNIVERSITIES AND COLLEGES (table).

Art Show in Jackson Square in New Orleans

WORLD BOOK photo by W. R. Wilson

Louisiana Tourist Development Comm.

Fishing in the Gulf of Mexico

LOUISIANA / *A Visitor's Guide*

Millions of tourists visit Louisiana every year. New Orleans, with its famous French Quarter, or *Vieux Carré* (Old Square), is the chief tourist attraction. The state's many other attractions include Acadiana, the homeland of the Cajuns, and magnificent old plantation homes. Louisiana has abundant wildlife, rolling hills, and marshy lowlands to delight hunters and photographers. Fishing enthusiasts catch fresh-water fish in lakes and rivers, and charter boats take them along the Gulf Coast in search of salt-water fish.

Places to Visit

Following are brief descriptions of some of Louisiana's most interesting places to visit.

Acadiana, a region in the south-central part of the state, is known for the Cajuns and their unique food, music, and dialect. The Cajuns are descendants of the French people who settled in the region after leaving Acadia (now Nova Scotia) in 1755. Acadiana was made famous by Henry Wadsworth Longfellow's poem *Evangeline* (see EVANGELINE). A monument commemorating the poem stands in St. Martinville.

Avery Island lies among sea marshes and swampy thickets near New Iberia. This wooded island covers a huge salt deposit. Plants from all parts of the world can be seen in the island's Jungle Gardens, which also contain an egret sanctuary.

Feliciana Country includes the parishes of East and West Feliciana. John J. Audubon, the famous naturalist and painter of birds, made many sketches among the wooded hills of the region. The area has many old plantation homes, several of which are open to the public.

Grand Isle lies south of New Orleans at the entrance to Barataria Bay. A few descendants of the pirate crew of Jean Laffite live in the village on this island (see LAFFITE, JEAN). Grand Isle is a fishing center.

Jean Lafitte National Historical Park and Preserve includes an area where part of the Battle of New Orleans was fought during the War of 1812. A marble monument stands near the spot where General Andrew Jackson directed the American forces.

Natchitoches Country, in west-central Louisiana, includes the oldest town in the Louisiana Territory. Natchitoches, on the banks of the Cane River, was established in 1714 by a French trader. The area still has much of its early French character.

New Orleans, famous for its Old World charm, is often called *America's Most Interesting City*. Its chief attractions include the old French and Spanish section, fine restaurants, and the Mardi Gras. See NEW ORLEANS.

Chris L. Sarrat, Sr., Photri

Jean Lafitte Park and Preserve near Chalmette

Bernie Donahue, Publix

Audubon State Commemorative Area near St. Francisville

428

Jazz Band in Preservation Hall in New Orleans

Mardi Gras Parade in New Orleans

Shreveport, in northwestern Louisiana, is the site of many interesting attractions. These attractions include the gardens of the American Rose Society, the Louisiana Downs thoroughbred racetrack, and the Meadows Museum of Indochinese Art at Centenary College. The R. W. Norton Art Gallery has a noted collection of paintings that portray life in the West. See SHREVEPORT.

National Parks and Forests. Jean Lafitte National Historical Park and Preserve is the only national park in Louisiana. Kisatchie National Forest is located in the central part of the state. It is primarily a conservation area, and has facilities for boating, camping, fishing, and swimming. The national forest was established in 1930.

State Parks. Louisiana has 33 state parks, state commemorative areas, and state preservation areas. For information on these areas, write to the Office of State Parks, P.O. Drawer 1111, Baton Rouge, LA 70821.

Evangeline Monument in St. Martinville

Annual Events

Visitors from all parts of the country come to New Orleans for its famous carnival season and Mardi Gras. The merrymaking begins on Twelfth Night—January 6 —and includes many dances and parties throughout the following weeks. Colorful daily parades start about two weeks before Shrove Tuesday, the day before Lent begins. Many people in masks and showy costumes take part in these parades. The Mardi Gras, held on Shrove Tuesday, climaxes the carnival season. This celebration features grand parades of beautiful floats and marching bands, followed by several fancy-dress balls. See MARDI GRAS.

Other annual events in Louisiana include:

January-March: Sugar Bowl football game in New Orleans (New Year's Day); Mardi Gras celebrations in numerous locations, including Madisonville and Slidell (before Mardi Gras Day), and Covington, Houma, and New Roads (Mardi Gras Day); Louisiana Redbud Festival in Vivian (March); Audubon Pilgrimage in St. Francisville (March).

April-June: New Orleans Spring Fiesta (April); Holiday in Dixie in Shreveport (April); New Orleans Jazz and Heritage Festival (April-May); Contraband Days in Lake Charles (May); Tomato Festival in Chalmette (May); Bayou Lacombe Crab Festival in Lacombe (June); World Champion Pirogue Races in Lafitte (June).

July-September: Tarpon Rodeo in Grand Isle (July); Bayou Lafourche Antiques Show and Sale in Thibodaux (September); Louisiana Shrimp and Petroleum Festival and Fair in Morgan City (September); Festivals Acadiens in Lafayette (September); Frog Festival in Rayne (September).

October-December: French Food Festival in Larose (October); International Rice Festival in Crowley (October); Louisiana Cotton Festival in Ville Platte (October); Louisiana State Fair in Shreveport (October); Christmas Festival in Natchitoches (December); Bonfires on the Mississippi River Levee (Christmas Eve).

429

Map Index

LOUISIANA/*The Land*

Most of what is now Louisiana was once part of an ancient bay of the Gulf of Mexico. The Mississippi and other rivers flowing from the north brought huge amounts of *silt* (particles of earth) to the bay. This action over thousands of years built up the land area to its present size.

Land Regions. Louisiana has three main land regions. All are part of the fertile lowland that lies along the Gulf Coast of the United States. These regions are (1) the East Gulf Coastal Plain, (2) the Mississippi Alluvial Plain, and (3) the West Gulf Coastal Plain.

The East Gulf Coastal Plain in Louisiana covers the area east of the Mississippi River and north of Lake Pontchartrain. It rises gradually from marshes in the west and south to low, rolling hills in the north. The British and the Spanish once claimed most of this region as part of the territory of West Florida. The parishes in the area are still called the *Florida parishes*.

The Mississippi Alluvial Plain lies along the lower Mississippi River. In Louisiana, it reaches from the Arkansas state line to the Gulf of Mexico. Broad, low ridges and hollows parallel the river as it winds down the plain. Louisianians call the high fields atop the ridges *frontlands*. The frontlands slope away from the river to *backlands*, which are great stretches of clay and silt. The backlands have several ancient channels of the Mississippi, far from its present course.

The great Mississippi Delta was formed of silt brought down to the river's mouth. It covers about 13,000 square miles (33,700 square kilometers)—about a fourth of Louisiana's total area. The delta has the most fertile soil in the state.

The West Gulf Coastal Plain includes all Louisiana west of the Mississippi Alluvial Plain. At the southern end of the plain, low sand ridges called *barrier beaches* lie along the Gulf of Mexico. Behind these beaches, marshes stretch inland for about 20 miles (32 kilometers). Throughout the marshes are large underground formations called *salt domes*. These domes cap great deposits of salt. Pools of natural gas and petroleum are trapped along the sides of the salt deposits. Sulfur is sometimes found in the top of the domes between the salt and the upper crust.

North of the marshlands, the gently rolling Louisiana prairies—about 60 miles (97 kilometers) wide—reach westward across the plain to Texas. North of the prairies, the land rises gradually as it stretches toward Arkansas. The highest point in Louisiana is 535-foot

Land Regions of Louisiana

(163-meter) Driskill Mountain, about 40 miles (64 kilometers) from the Arkansas line.

Coastline. Louisiana has a general coastline of 397 miles (639 kilometers) along the Gulf. But the marshy coast has been made extremely uneven by silt deposits. As a result, Louisiana's tidal shoreline—including bays, offshore islands, and river mouths—is 7,721 miles (12,-426 kilometers) long. Among the states, only Alaska and Florida have tidal shorelines that are greater in length.

Rivers, Bayous, and Lakes. The waters of all the rivers in Louisiana find their way to the Gulf of Mexico. The Mississippi, of course, is Louisiana's most important river (see MISSISSIPPI RIVER). Other important rivers in the state include the Atchafalaya, Black, Calcasieu, Ouachita, Pearl, Red, and Sabine.

The huge amounts of silt carried by Louisiana's rivers have raised the level of the riverbeds. This action has made the Mississippi and other rivers higher than the nearby backlands. As a result, water from major floods on the Mississippi could cover about a third of Louisiana.

The chief natural drains of overflow water are the *bayous* (slow-moving inlets or outlets of lakes and rivers). Louisiana has many bayous, especially in the Mississippi Delta. See BAYOU.

Since colonial times, people have built walls called *levees* along Louisiana's rivers to help control the flood-

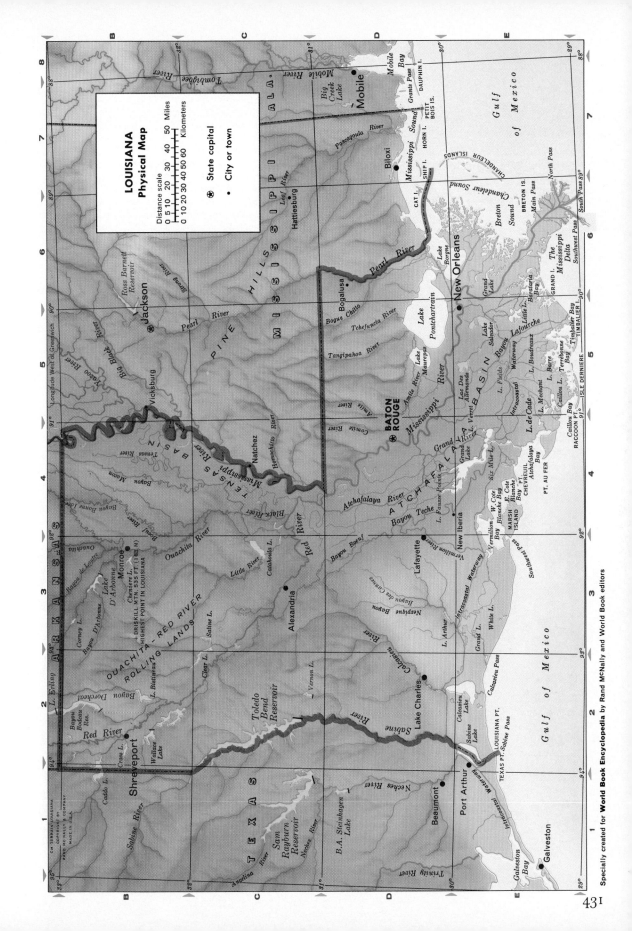

LOUISIANA
Physical Map

Distance scale

State capital
City or town

Specially created for **World Book Encyclopedia** by Rand McNally and World Book editors

431

Fertile Lands form broad belts along each side of the Mississippi River and make up the Mississippi Alluvial Plain. This view of Port Sulphur shows the flatlands of the delta.

WORLD BOOK photo by W. R. Wilson

waters. Levees now stretch along about 1,650 miles (2,655 kilometers) of the rivers. The Bonnet Carré Spillway on the Mississippi and floodways built along the Atchafalaya River provide further flood control. They can be opened to carry off high water when it threatens to flow over the levees. See LEVEE.

Louisiana has about 3,400 square miles (8,810 square kilometers) of inland water. The largest lake, Lake Pontchartrain, is a 625-square-mile (1,619-square-kilo-meter) *brackish* (part saltwater) lake. There are many saltwater lakes in the state. These were once extensions of the sea that became cut off by ridges of sand or deposits of silt. Louisiana's many freshwater lakes include *oxbow lakes*. These half-moon-shaped lakes used to be curves of rivers that became cut off from the main streams. Many of them lie along the western side of the Mississippi River north of Baton Rouge.

Plant and Animal Life. Forests cover about half of Louisiana. The state's trees include magnolias, oaks, longleaf pines, and shortleaf pines. Spanish moss hangs from cypress and oak trees. Flowers that bloom in Louisiana include azaleas, camellias, honeysuckle, jasmine, lilies, and orchids.

Wildlife thrives in Louisiana. Rabbits are plentiful and the northwestern hills have large numbers of gray foxes and beavers. White-tailed deer and wildcats roam wooded swamps. Minks, muskrats, opossums, raccoons, skunks, and wild hogs live in many wooded lowlands in the state. Some alligators and beaverlike rodents called *nutrias* live in the coastal bayous and marshes. Louisiana has about 900,000 acres (364,200 hectares) of wildlife-refuge areas.

Birds in the state include doves, egrets, quails, and wild turkeys. Almost half the wild ducks and geese in North America spend the winter in the state's coastal marshes. The brown pelican, Louisiana's state bird, also lives there.

Louisiana's freshwater fish include bass, catfish, gaspergou (also called freshwater drumfish), and sunfish. Giant rays, menhaden, pompanos, and tarpons are found in the Gulf of Mexico. Great numbers of shrimp and oysters thrive along the coast.

Cypress Swamps similar to this one near Lake Charles cover the land in parts of Louisiana's West Gulf Coastal Plain region.

Alpha Photo Associates

Fontainebleau Park Forest in St. Tammany Parish is part of Louisiana's East Gulf Coastal Plain region.

Louisiana Tourist Development Comm.

LOUISIANA/*Climate*

Most of Louisiana has a hot, humid, subtropical climate. It is one of the wettest states, with a yearly average of 56 inches (142 centimeters) of precipitation.

Southern Louisiana has an average January temperature of 55° F. (13° C), and a July average of 82° F. (28° C). The northern part of the state has an average January reading of 49° F. (9° C), and a July average of 82.5° F. (28° C). Louisiana's lowest recorded temperature, −16° F. (−27° C), was at Minden on Feb. 13, 1899. The highest temperature on record was 114° F. (46° C), at Plain Dealing on Aug. 10, 1936.

Hurricanes sometimes strike the coastal areas of Louisiana, causing loss of life and property. Since 1875, about 30 hurricanes and 55 lesser tropical storms have struck. About half the hurricanes occur in September.

Hurricanes such as this one in New Orleans, *left,* whip the Louisiana coast. The rampaging storms cause heavy damage.

Wide World

Seasonal Temperatures

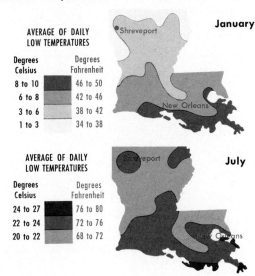

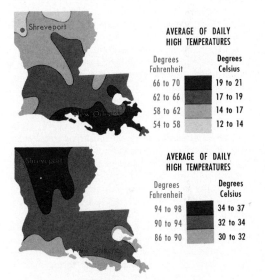

Average Yearly Precipitation

(Rain, Melted Snow, and Other Moisture)

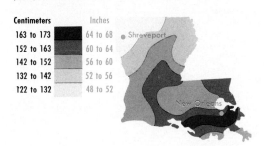

Centimeters	Inches
163 to 173	64 to 68
152 to 163	60 to 64
142 to 152	56 to 60
132 to 142	52 to 56
122 to 132	48 to 52

WORLD BOOK maps

Average Monthly Weather

	NEW ORLEANS					SHREVEPORT				
	Temperatures F°		Temperatures C°		Days of Rain or Snow		Temperatures F°		Temperatures C°		Days of Rain or Snow
	High	Low	High	Low			High	Low	High	Low	
JAN.	64	48	18	9	10	JAN.	56	40	13	4	10
FEB.	67	50	19	10	9	FEB.	60	43	16	6	7
MAR.	71	55	22	13	9	MAR.	68	49	20	9	9
APR.	78	62	26	17	7	APR.	77	57	25	14	10
MAY	84	68	29	20	9	MAY	83	64	28	18	9
JUNE	89	74	32	23	13	JUNE	91	71	33	22	6
JULY	90	76	32	24	15	JULY	93	74	34	23	7
AUG.	91	76	33	24	14	AUG.	95	74	35	23	7
SEPT.	87	73	31	23	10	SEPT.	89	69	32	21	4
OCT.	80	65	27	18	6	OCT.	80	57	27	14	5
NOV.	70	55	21	13	8	NOV.	66	47	19	8	9
DEC.	65	50	18	10	10	DEC.	58	41	14	5	7

Mining is the single most important economic activity in Louisiana. It accounts for nearly a fifth of the *gross state product*—the total value of all goods and services produced in a state in a year. Service industries taken together make up over half of the gross state product.

Natural Resources. Rich *alluvial soil* (soil deposited by rivers) covers about a third of Louisiana. Silt from the Mississippi River forms a rich, dark soil. The Red River deposits reddish-brown soil along its banks. Peat and muck soils are found in the coastal marshes. The prairies in southwestern Louisiana have clay and clay loam.

Louisiana is a leader among the states in known reserves of natural gas and petroleum. Much of these reserves lie in a narrow belt across southern Louisiana that is part of an underground region called the *Tuscaloosa Trend*. This region also extends beneath portions of Texas, Mississippi, and the Gulf of Mexico. Rich petroleum deposits lie under nearly every one of Louisiana's 64 parishes, and extend into the gulf. The best-developed deposits are in southern Louisiana and the gulf. Most of the state's gas fields lie in the southern section. This region has huge deposits of salt and sulfur.

Forests cover about half the state. One of the country's largest forest-experimentation stations is in New Orleans. It is operated by the U.S. Forest Service. More than 150 kinds of trees grow in Louisiana. They include magnolias, oaks, longleaf pines, and shortleaf pines.

Service Industries account for 60 per cent of the gross state product of Louisiana. Most of the state's service industries are concentrated in the eight metropolitan areas.

Wholesale and retail trade is the most valuable service industry in Louisiana. It accounts for 15 per cent of the gross state product and employs more people than any other industry in the state. New Orleans, a major world seaport, handles much international trade. It is also one of the South's main centers of retail and wholesale trade. Baton Rouge is a regional center of agricultural trade.

Community, social, and personal services make up 12 per cent of the gross state product. These services include education and health care; advertising and data processing; and the operation of beauty shops, funeral homes, and cleaning establishments.

Three service industries each account for 11 percent of the gross state product. These industries are government; transportation, communication and utilities; and finance, insurance, and real estate. Government is Louisiana's second largest employer. State government offices in Baton Rouge, the state capital, employ many Louisianians.

Mining. Louisiana ranks second only to Texas among the states in value of mineral production. Mining accounts for 18 per cent of Louisiana's gross state product. Mineral products provide a yearly income of about $14½ billion. The chief minerals are petroleum and natural gas. The petroleum industry operates about 24,800 wells, mainly in the southern marshlands and the Shreveport area. Some offshore oil wells have been sunk from platforms resting on tall supports in the Gulf of Mexico and from floating rigs. The annual production of petroleum totals about 515 million barrels. Most of the natural gas is near the southern oil fields. About 6

trillion cubic feet (174 billion cubic meters) of gas are produced annually.

Louisiana leads the states in the production of salt. Most of the salt mines are in the coastal marshes. Annual production totals about 14 million short tons (12.7 million metric tons). Louisiana ranks second only to Texas in U.S. sulfur production. The state produces about 2 million short tons (1.8 million metric tons) of sulfur a year. Louisiana also produces natural gas liquids, sand, gravel, and stone.

Manufacturing accounts for 13 per cent of the gross state product of Louisiana. Products manufactured in the state have a *value added by manufacture* of about $11¾ billion. This figure represents the increase in value of raw materials after they become finished products. Louisiana has about 2,900 manufacturing firms.

The manufacture of chemicals ranks as Louisiana's leading industry. It has an annual value added of about $3 billion. Baton Rouge, Lake Charles, Monroe, New Orleans, and Shreveport are the chief production centers. The state's chemical products include drugs, fertilizers, paint, plastics, and soap.

Louisiana's Gross State Product

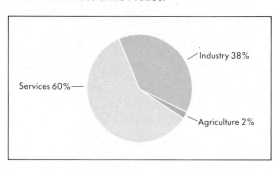

Services 60%—
Industry 38%
Agriculture 2%

The gross state product (GSP) is the total value of goods and services produced in a state in a year. The GSP measures a state's total economic performance and can also be used to compare the economic output and growth of states. Louisiana's GSP was $57,775,000,000 in 1982.

Production and Workers by Economic Activities

Economic Activities	Per Cent of GSP Produced	Employed Workers Number of Persons	Employed Workers Per Cent of Total
Mining	18	80,500	5
Wholesale & Retail Trade	15	368,100	23
Manufacturing	13	179,800	11
Community, Social, & Personal Services	12	304,500	19
Finance, Insurance, & Real Estate	11	82,600	5
Government	11	316,600	20
Transportation, Communication, & Utilities	11	117,900	7
Construction	7	114,300	7
Agriculture	2	41,000	3
Total	100	1,605,300	100

Sources: College of Administration and Business, Louisiana Tech University; *Employment and Earnings*, May 1984, Bureau of Labor Statistics; *Farm Labor*, August 1984, USDA.

The manufacture of petroleum and coal products is the second most important industry, with an annual value added of about $2½ billion. Baton Rouge, Lake Charles, and Norco have huge petroleum refineries.

Food processing is Louisiana's third-ranking industry. About 15 mills process rice in southwestern Louisiana. Many of the rice mills are near Crowley, the *Rice Center of America*. The U.S. Department of Agriculture has a Rice Experiment Station in the town. Six sugar refineries operate near New Orleans.

Louisiana's forests include about 15 million acres (6.1 million hectares) of commercial timber. Sawmills there cut about 1 billion board feet (2.4 million cubic meters) of lumber a year. Pines of northern Louisiana supply wood for building materials and paper. Other important industries in the state manufacture fabricated metal products and transportation equipment.

Agriculture in Louisiana accounts for two per cent of the gross state product. Farm products provide a yearly income of nearly $2 billion. The state has about 36,500 farms, plantations, and ranches. They cover about 10 million acres (4 million hectares). The farms average 277 acres (112 hectares). Hired workers, sharecroppers, and tenant farmers raise the crops on plantations.

Soybeans are the most valuable farm product in Louisiana. This crop earns about a fourth of the state's cash farm income. Soybean production totals about 68 million bushels a year. About 20 per cent of all the sugar cane grown in the United States is raised in Louisiana. About 6 million short tons (5.4 million metric tons) of

Shreveport Chamber of Commerce

Gas Storage Tanks, manufactured in Shreveport, are loaded on trucks for shipping. Dealers will fill the tanks with propane gas.

sugar cane are produced in Louisiana each year, providing about 603,000 short tons (547,000 metric tons) of raw sugar. Louisiana also is a leader in the production of cotton and rice.

Louisiana ranks second only to North Carolina among the states in sweet potato production. In the mid-1970's, Louisiana's farmers produced a yearly harvest of about 2½ million hundred-pound bags (113 million kilograms) of sweet potatoes, called *Louisiana yams* locally. Farmers grow clover and other kinds of hay for cattle feed. They also grow corn to feed to livestock, but sell some for the manufacture of cereals and cornmeal. Farmers also raise some Irish, or white, potatoes, which can be harvested within a hundred days. Farmers can then plant other crops in the fields.

The sale of beef cattle and calves earns about 10 per cent of Louisiana's cash farm income. Other leading livestock products include eggs, *broilers* (chickens between 9 and 12 weeks old), and hogs. Most of the large cattle ranches are in the southwestern part of the state, and along the Red and Ouachita rivers. Dairy farms operate near the larger cities.

Truck farms in southern Louisiana produce beans, cabbage, peppers, tomatoes, and other vegetables. During the winter and spring, Louisiana helps supply vegetables to the northern and eastern states. Louisiana is a leader in strawberry production. The state also produces many pecans and tung nuts.

Farm, Mineral, and Forest Products

This map shows where the state's leading farm, mineral, and forest products are produced. The major urban areas (shown on the map in red) are the state's important manufacturing centers.

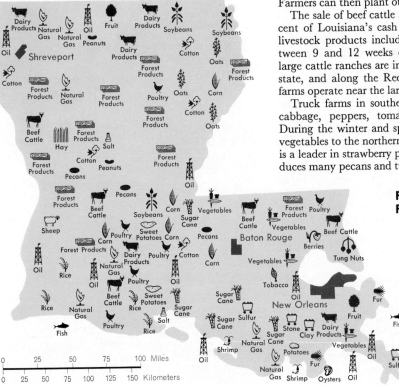

WORLD BOOK map

432c

LOUISIANA

St. James Parish is the world's only source of a kind of tobacco called *perique*. Tobacco companies buy the dark, strong perique leaves to blend with other tobaccos.

Fishing and Fur Industries. Louisiana is a leader among the states in commercial fishing. It has a yearly catch valued at about $240 million. The chief products are menhaden and shrimp. Each year, Louisiana fishing crews bring in about 2 billion pounds (900 million kilograms) of shrimp, menhaden, and other fish.

Louisiana is a leading state in the production of fur from animals. The state's fur industry has a value of about $10 million annually. Trappers sell about 450,000 muskrat pelts a year. In 1930, breeders brought a few nutrias from Argentina. Today, about 1 million of their pelts go to fur markets annually. See NUTRIA.

Electric Power. Widespread electrification began in Louisiana around 1940. All of Louisiana's electric power is generated by plants that burn oil, gas, or coal.

Transportation. The Mississippi and other rivers of Louisiana have been both an aid and a barrier to transportation in the state. During the early years, riverboats provided the chief means for moving people and products. But the Mississippi and other rivers were also major obstacles to the construction of highways and railroads.

To solve this problem, the state increased the number of bridges over the smaller rivers during the 1930's. But until 1935, ferryboats were Louisiana's only means of getting automobiles and trains across the wide Mississippi. The Huey P. Long Bridge, which opened in 1935 near New Orleans, was the first bridge entirely within the state to cross the Mississippi. Bridges also cross the river at Baton Rouge, Donaldsonville, and Vidalia. The state opened the world's longest bridge, the Lake Pontchartrain Causeway, in 1956. The bridge has a total length of about 29 miles (47 kilometers). It crosses 24 miles (39 kilometers) of water, and connects New Orleans with St. Tammany Parish to the north. The Greater New Orleans Bridge links the heart of New Orleans with the river's west bank. It was completed in 1958. It has a span of 1,575 feet (480 meters)—one of the longest spans of any cantilever bridge in the nation.

Aviation. Over 15 major airlines serve Louisiana. Flights connect Louisiana with all parts of the United States and with many Central and South American and European cities. The state has about 290 airports.

Railroads. The Pontchartrain Railroad was the first railroad west of the Allegheny Mountains. It began operating in 1829, between New Orleans and Lake Pontchartrain. Today, about 30 freight railroads operate on about 4,000 miles (6,400 kilometers) of track in Louisiana. Passenger trains serve seven cities.

Roads and Highways. Louisiana has about 55,000 miles (88,500 kilometers) of highways, roads, and streets. Most of them are surfaced.

Shipping. Most port activities are centered in New Orleans, Baton Rouge, and Lake Charles. About 5,000 ships dock at New Orleans annually. The city handles more cargo than any other port in the United States. Based on total tonnage, it is one of the largest ports in the world. Baton Rouge is the most inland deepwater port on the Mississippi River. It lies about 235 miles (378 kilometers) from the Gulf of Mexico, but oceangoing ships can travel up the river and dock.

Waterways. Louisiana has about 5,000 miles (8,000 kilometers) of navigable rivers and other waterways. The Mississippi River-Gulf Outlet, a canal 76 miles (122 kilometers) long, provides a direct route between New Orleans and the Gulf of Mexico. The Gulf Intracoastal Waterway provides a sheltered east-west route across the coastal marshes.

Communication. The first newspaper in Louisiana was established at New Orleans in 1794 by Louis Duclot. This French-language journal, *Le Moniteur de la Louisiane* (*The Louisiana Monitor*), was the only newspaper in the region until 1803. That year, Louisiana's first English-language newspaper, the *New Orleans Union*, was started. Louisiana has about 25 daily newspapers and about 85 weeklies. *The Times-Picayune/States-Item* of New Orleans leads in circulation. Other important papers include the *Shreveport Times* and the *Baton Rouge Advocate*.

Louisiana's first radio stations, WWL in New Orleans and KEEL in Shreveport, started broadcasting in 1922. The first television station, WDSU-TV in New Orleans, was started in 1948. The state has about 20 television stations and about 170 radio stations.

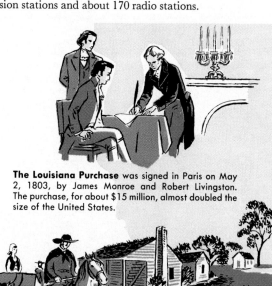

The Louisiana Purchase was signed in Paris on May 2, 1803, by James Monroe and Robert Livingston. The purchase, for about $15 million, almost doubled the size of the United States.

Acadians from Nova Scotia settled in Louisiana between the 1760's and 1790. Henry Wadsworth Longfellow described their journey in his poem *Evangeline*.

The Pirates of Jean Laffite terrorized the entire Louisiana coast in the early 1800's.

Indian Days. When the first Europeans arrived, about 12,000 Indians lived in what is now the state of Louisiana. They belonged to about 30 tribes, including the Atakapa, Caddo, Chitimacha, and Tunica. The Indians lived mainly in villages on the banks of rivers and bayous. They built huts of poles, thatched with leaves and sometimes plastered with mud. The women worked in the fields, and the men hunted and fished.

Exploration and Early Settlement. In 1541, Hernando de Soto led a group of Spanish explorers into the lower Mississippi River area in a useless search for gold. The Spaniards made no further exploration of the lower Mississippi River region after De Soto died there in 1542.

In 1682, the French explorer Robert Cavelier, Sieur de la Salle, led about 50 Frenchmen and Indians into the area. They came down the Mississippi River from the Great Lakes region. On April 9, 1682, La Salle claimed the entire Mississippi Valley for France. He erected a cross and a column bearing the French coat of arms near the mouth of the river. La Salle named the region Louisiana, in honor of Louis XIV, the king of France.

Louisiana became a French *royal colony* (a colony controlled by a king) in 1699. Pierre le Moyne, Sieur d'Iberville, founded a French settlement at what is now Ocean Springs, Miss. This settlement at Ocean Springs was the capital of Louisiana until 1702. That year, the capital was moved to Fort Louis de la Mobile, near the site of present-day Mobile, Ala. Iberville was governor of the royal colony until his death in 1706, although he was absent from Louisiana after 1702 while fighting in the War of Spanish Succession.

In 1712, France gave exclusive trading rights in Louisiana to Antoine Crozat, a merchant. This transfer of control made the area a *proprietary colony*. Louis Juchereau de St. Denis, a trader, established Natchitoches on the banks of the Red River in 1714. This settlement became the first permanent town in Louisiana. In 1717, Crozat's trading rights were transferred to John

HISTORIC LOUISIANA

The Name *Louisiana* was given to the region by Sieur de la Salle when he claimed the entire Mississippi Valley area in 1682. He named it in honor of Louis XIV of France.

The Steamboat *New Orleans* completed the first steam-powered trip down the Mississippi in 1812, from Pittsburgh to New Orleans. By 1846, nearly 1,200 steamboats chugged up and down the river on regular schedules.

The Sugar Industry started in Louisiana in 1795, when Étienne de Boré found a new way to granulate sugar.

★ BATON ROUGE

Mandeville ●

Lake Pontchartrain

● New Orleans

The World's Longest Bridge, the Lake Pontchartrain Causeway, opened in 1956. It extends about 29 miles (47 kilometers) and speeds motor traffic between New Orleans and Mandeville, La.

Andrew Jackson defeated the British in the Battle of New Orleans on Jan. 8, 1815, with a small army of frontiersmen and pirates. The battle took place after the peace treaty of the War of 1812 had been signed. News of the treaty had not been received.

The French Opera House, built in 1859, was the center of cultural and musical life in New Orleans. The building was completely destroyed by fire in 1919.

MISSISSIPPI R.

The Steamboat *Richmond,* which was built in 1867, traveled the Mississippi River between New Orleans and St. Louis. This painting by Boyd Cruise shows the *Richmond* in the Port of New Orleans.

Law, a Scottish financial promoter in Paris. Law started an investment scheme to colonize Louisiana.

In 1718, the governor of Louisiana began building New Orleans. He was Jean Baptiste le Moyne, Sieur de Bienville, a brother of Iberville. New Orleans became the capital in 1722.

Spanish Rule. John Law's scheme to colonize Louisiana finally failed in 1720. Louisiana again became a royal colony of France in 1731. But the French were disappointed with the small income produced in the colony. In 1762, France secretly ceded to Spain the *Isle of Orleans,* which included New Orleans, and the area of Louisiana west of the Mississippi River. French colonists learned of the transfer in 1764 and became angry. In 1768, a band of Frenchmen drove out the Spanish governor. But Spain took firm control of its new possession in 1769.

Between the 1760's and 1790, about 4,000 French settlers from Canada arrived in Louisiana. British troops had driven them from their homes in Acadia, in eastern Canada. The Acadians settled chiefly along the Teche, Lafourche, and Vermilion bayous. Their descendants came to be known as *Cajuns.* See ACADIA.

During the American Revolutionary War (1775-1783), Spain allowed agents of the Continental Congress to use New Orleans as a base. These agents shipped supplies up the Mississippi and Ohio rivers to the struggling American colonies.

Louisiana prospered under Spanish rule. The government was stable, and encouraged business and commerce. The Louisiana sugar industry began in 1795, when Étienne de Boré developed a method of processing sugar on a large scale. Louisiana planters began growing sugar cane as a major crop. In 1800, France secretly persuaded Spain to return Louisiana to France. However, Spain kept the region until November, 1803.

Territorial Days. France sold Louisiana, which included the Mississippi Valley region, to the United States for about $15 million. The United States took possession on Dec. 20, 1803. See LOUISIANA PURCHASE.

In 1804, Congress divided the huge territory to make it easier to govern. One part became the Territory of Orleans. It covered about the same area as the present state of Louisiana. William C. C. Claiborne became the first and, as it developed, the only governor of the territory. The other part, beyond the present northern

boundary of the state, became the District of Louisiana. This area became the Territory of Louisiana in 1805. In 1812, it was renamed the Territory of Missouri.

A period of commercial expansion began in 1812, when the steamboat *New Orleans* completed the first trip down the Ohio and Mississippi rivers from Pittsburgh, Pa. The Mississippi River soon became the chief ship-

Important Dates in Louisiana

1541 Hernando de Soto led a Spanish expedition into the lower Mississippi River area.

1682 Robert Cavelier, Sieur de la Salle, reached the mouth of the Mississippi River and claimed the river valley for France.

1699 The royal French colony of Louisiana was founded.

1714 Louis Juchereau de St. Denis founded Natchitoches, the first permanent town in Louisiana.

1718 Jean Baptiste le Moyne, Sieur de Bienville, founded New Orleans.

1762 France ceded Louisiana to Spain.

1795 Étienne de Boré developed a large-scale method for granulating sugar.

1800 Spain ceded Louisiana back to France.

1803 The United States purchased Louisiana from France.

1812 Louisiana entered the Union as the 18th state on April 30.

1815 Andrew Jackson defeated the British in the Battle of New Orleans.

1861 Louisiana seceded from the Union and joined the Confederacy.

1862 Union troops captured New Orleans.

1868 Louisiana was readmitted to the Union.

1879 James B. Eads deepened the mouth of the Mississippi River so that large ocean ships could reach New Orleans.

1901 Oil was discovered near Jennings and White Castle.

1916 The Monroe natural gas field was opened.

1928 Huey P. Long became governor.

1935 Long was assassinated.

1961 The National Aeronautics and Space Administration selected the Michoud Ordnance Plant (now Michoud Assembly Facility) in New Orleans to produce Saturn rocket boosters.

1963 The 76-mile (122-kilometer) Mississippi River-Gulf Outlet, a short cut for shippers between New Orleans and the sea, opened.

1964 Two Republicans were elected to the Louisiana legislature, the first ones since Reconstruction.

1975 A new state constitution went into effect.

ping waterway of the inland area of the United States.

In September 1810, American settlers in the Spanish possession of West Florida revolted against Spain. They organized the Republic of West Florida, which included part of what is now eastern Louisiana. U.S. troops occupied part of the republic in October 1810. President James Madison declared that the region belonged to the United States as part of the Louisiana Purchase.

Statehood. On April 30, 1812, the Territory of Orleans was renamed Louisiana, and became the 18th state of the Union. It had about 76,000 persons. William C. C. Claiborne was the first governor of the state, and New Orleans was the first capital.

The War of 1812 (1812-1815) began soon after Louisiana became a state. In December 1814, and January 1815, the British tried to capture New Orleans. General Andrew Jackson and his little army of frontiersmen and pirates defeated the British. The final clash of the Battle of New Orleans took place on Jan. 8, 1815. Unknown to both sides, a treaty of peace had already been signed in Ghent, Belgium, two weeks earlier. See JACKSON, ANDREW (Glory at New Orleans).

Thousands of new settlers arrived in Louisiana between 1815 and 1860. Trade expanded during the 1830's after Henry M. Shreve, a steamboat builder and operator, cleared out the Red River for navigation. Alexandria, Natchitoches, and Shreveport (named for Shreve) became trade centers as river traffic developed.

The state capital was moved to Donaldsonville in 1830, but moved back to New Orleans the next year. The state legislature moved the capital to Baton Rouge in 1850, where it remained until 1862.

The Civil War and Reconstruction. On Jan. 26, 1861, Louisiana *seceded* (withdrew) from the Union and prepared for war. The state joined the Confederacy on March 21. The Civil War (1861-1865) did not touch Louisiana until 1862. That year, a Union naval squadron under David G. Farragut bombarded the Mississippi River forts guarding New Orleans. Union soldiers under General Benjamin F. Butler occupied the city on May 1, 1862, without a battle.

The Union forces maintained a capital in New Orleans throughout the war. The Confederate state government established its capital at Opelousas in 1862, and moved to Shreveport in 1863. Union troops gradually extended their control. There was little fighting, but great property destruction.

When the war ended, Louisiana was bankrupt. Only Georgia, South Carolina, and Virginia had suffered more casualties and destruction. Louisiana was readmitted to the Union on June 25, 1868. That year, Henry C. Warmoth took office as governor. He won an election under a new constitution that allowed blacks to vote and took away voting rights from some whites, including those who had held political office under the Confederacy for more than a year. The state government increased taxes to help pay for new public services. Louisiana's taxes had been relatively low before the Civil War, and so the higher taxes angered many people. A group from New Orleans tried unsuccessfully to seize control of the government in a battle on Sept. 14, 1874.

President Rutherford B. Hayes withdrew the federal troops from Louisiana in 1877, and ended Reconstruction there. The troops had remained in Louisiana later

than in any other Southern state. During the next 10 years, Louisianians built new railroads and schools, and improved their waterways. Commerce revived after 1879, when engineers deepened the mouth of the Mississippi River. The dredging allowed large ocean-going ships to dock at New Orleans. The legislature adopted a new constitution in 1879. Baton Rouge replaced New Orleans as the capital in 1882.

Growth of Commerce and Industry. Railroads expanded rapidly in Louisiana as New Orleans increased in importance as a port. By 1883, New Orleans had rail connections with all the major cities in the United States. Foreign commerce in the city increased even more after the Panama Canal was completed in 1914.

The discovery of great mineral resources in the early 1900's led to industrial expansion and many local improvements. Oil was first discovered near Jennings and White Castle in 1901. In 1916, natural gas was found near Monroe. Great fields of natural gas, petroleum, and sulfur attracted many new industries. Trunkline railroads spread into every section of the state. Road builders began to lift Louisiana out of the mud of its dirt roads. Parishes improved their school buildings and educational programs.

Leon Trice, Publix

Governor Huey P. Long, *center,* and other officials celebrated adoption of the Mississippi Valley Flood Control Act in 1928. The bill provided $325,000,000 in federal funds to build spillways to control river water run-off during flood stages.

A disastrous flood on the Mississippi River struck northern and south-central Louisiana in 1927. As a result, the federal government joined with Louisiana to start building vast flood-control projects.

Huey P. Long built a powerful political organization in Louisiana during the late 1920's. The people elected him governor in 1928. Long became practically a dictator, but his vigorous program of public works and social welfare helped develop the state. During Long's administration, Louisiana extended its highway and bridge systems, enlarged the state university, and built a new capitol in Baton Rouge. The state also began giving free textbooks to schoolchildren. Long was elected a U.S. Senator in 1930. He was shot to death at the state Capitol in 1935. In 1939, the federal government convicted many leaders of the Long group for fraud and other crimes. A reform group took control of the state government in 1940. But the Long organization quickly revived, and has remained a strong force in Louisiana.

The Mid-1900's. During World War II (1939-1945), many new industries, including shipbuilding and petrochemical production, began in Louisiana. The oil and gas industries expanded rapidly, and shipping through the Port of New Orleans increased sharply. Louisiana industry continued to grow throughout the 1940's and 1950's, when the number of factories rose about 60 per cent. Thousands of Louisianians moved from rural areas to cities so they could work in the new factories.

The Governors of Louisiana

	Party	Term
W. C. C. Claiborne	*Jeff. Rep.	1812-1816
Jacques Villeré	*Jeff. Rep.	1816-1820
Thomas B. Robertson	*Jeff. Rep.	1820-1824
Henry S. Thibodaux	*Jeff. Rep.	1824
Henry Johnson	*Jeff. Rep.	1824-1828
Pierre Derbigny	*Jeff. Rep.	1828-1829
Armand Beauvais	*Jeff. Rep.	1829-1830
Jacques Dupré	*Jeff. Rep.	1830-1831
Andre B. Roman	Whig	1831-1835
Edward D. White	Whig	1835-1839
Andre B. Roman	Whig	1839-1843
Alexandre Mouton	Democratic	1843-1846
Isaac Johnson	Democratic	1846-1850
Joseph Walker	Democratic	1850-1853
Paul O. Hebert	Democratic	1853-1856
Robert C. Wickliffe	Democratic	1856-1860
Thomas O. Moore	Democratic	1860-1864
	Federal Military Rule	1862-1864
Henry W. Allen	Democratic	1864-1865
Michael Hahn	Republican	1864-1865
James M. Wells	Republican	1865-1867
Benjamin Flanders	Republican	1867-1868
Joshua Baker	Republican	1868
Henry C. Warmoth	Republican	1868-1872
P. B. S. Pinchback	Republican	1872-1873
John McEnery	Democratic	1873
William P. Kellogg	Republican	1873-1877
Francis T. Nicholls	Democratic	1877-1880
Louis A. Wiltz	Democratic	1880-1881
Samuel D. McEnery	Democratic	1881-1888
Francis T. Nicholls	Democratic	1888-1892
Murphy J. Foster	Democratic	1892-1900
William W. Heard	Democratic	1900-1904
Newton C. Blanchard	Democratic	1904-1908
Jared Y. Sanders	Democratic	1908-1912
Luther E. Hall	Democratic	1912-1916
Ruffin G. Pleasant	Democratic	1916-1920
John M. Parker	Democratic	1920-1924
Henry L. Fuqua	Democratic	1924-1926
Oramel H. Simpson	Democratic	1926-1928
Huey P. Long	Democratic	1928-1932
Alvin O. King	Democratic	1932
Oscar K. Allen	Democratic	1932-1936
James A. Noe	Democratic	1936
Richard W. Leche	Democratic	1936-1939
Earl K. Long	Democratic	1939-1940
Sam H. Jones	Democratic	1940-1944
James H. Davis	Democratic	1944-1948
Earl K. Long	Democratic	1948-1952
Robert F. Kennon	Democratic	1952-1956
Earl K. Long	Democratic	1956-1960
James H. Davis	Democratic	1960-1964
John J. McKeithen	Democratic	1964-1972
Edwin W. Edwards	Democratic	1972-1980
David C. Treen	Republican	1980-1984
Edwin W. Edwards	Democratic	1984-

*Jeffersonian Republican, sometimes called Democratic-Republican

Louisiana started to play a major role in the U.S. space program in 1961. That year, the National Aeronautics and Space Administration (NASA) selected the old Michoud Ordnance Plant in New Orleans to produce the Saturn rocket. This plant, renamed the Michoud Assembly Facility, produced its first rocket in 1963. Michoud's Saturn V rocket launched the Apollo 11 astronauts to the moon in 1969.

New Orleans helped increase its foreign trade by opening International House in 1944 and the International Trade Mart in 1948. These facilities provided information on world trade, as well as space for offices and trade exhibits. In 1963, the Mississippi River-Gulf Outlet opened. This 76-mile (122-kilometer) canal gave shippers a 44-mile (71-kilometer) short cut between New Orleans and the Gulf of Mexico. Also in 1963, workers completed a project in order to keep the Mississippi River from changing its course into the Atchafalaya River, away from New Orleans. The Army Corps of Engineers built a dam, floodway, and levees as part of this project.

Like many northern and southern states, Louisiana faced serious racial problems in the 1950's and 1960's. The graduate school at Louisiana State University in Baton Rouge became integrated in 1950. This integration took place under an order by the United States Circuit Court of Appeals. In 1954, the Supreme Court of the United States ruled that compulsory segregation in public schools was unconstitutional. In Louisiana, the first black pupils entered all-white public elementary schools in 1960, in New Orleans. In addition, Louisiana's libraries and restaurants became integrated in the 1960's.

The Republican Party gained strength in Democratic Louisiana during the 1950's and 1960's. In 1956, Dwight D. Eisenhower became the first Republican to win Louisiana's electoral votes in a presidential election since 1876. In 1964, two Republicans became the first members of their party since the 1800's to be elected to the Louisiana House of Representatives.

In 1968, Ernest N. Dutch Morial of New Orleans became the first black since Reconstruction to win election to the Louisiana House of Representatives. In 1977, Morial was elected as the first black mayor of New Orleans. In 1979, David C. Treen became the first Republican to win election as governor of Louisiana since the 1870's.

Louisiana Today is still enjoying rapid industrial growth. Agriculture remains important to the state's economy, but more Louisianians now work in factories than on farms. About two-thirds of the people live in urban areas. The state's problems include finding new sources of income to pay for the rising costs of education, highways, and welfare. Louisiana's *per capita* (per person) income ranks among the lowest in the United States.

In 1974, Louisiana voters approved a new state Constitution. The Constitution went into effect in 1975. Later in 1975, the Louisiana Superdome, a domed sports complex, opened in New Orleans. In the 1970's, the Michoud Assembly Facility participated in a project to produce fuel tanks for NASA space shuttles. These shuttles, reusable space vehicles attached to rockets, began traveling in space in the early 1980's.

GEORGE A. STOKES, JOSEPH G. TREGLE, JR., and EDMUND J. TUNSTALL

LOUISIANA/*Study Aids*

Related Articles in WORLD BOOK include:

BIOGRAPHIES

Armstrong, Louis
Audubon, John J.
Beauregard, Pierre G. T.
Bienville, Sieur de
Bontemps, Arna
Butler, Benjamin F.
Cable, George W.
Capote, Truman
Cliburn, Van
Fiske, Minnie M.
Hellman, Lillian
Laffite, Jean

La Salle, Sieur de
Law, John
Long (family)
Mason and Slidell
 (John Slidell)
Pinchback, P. B. S.
Polk, Leonidas
Richardson, Henry H.
Taylor, Zachary
White, Edward D.

CITIES

Baton Rouge
Lake Charles

New Orleans

Shreveport

HISTORY

Acadia
Cajuns
Civil War
Code Napoléon
Confederate States of America

Creole
Louisiana Purchase
New France
Reconstruction
War of 1812

PHYSICAL FEATURES

Bayou
Gulf of Mexico
Jetty
Lake Pontchartrain

Levee
Mississippi River
Red River

OTHER RELATED ARTICLES

Jazz

Mardi Gras

Outline

I. Government
  A. Constitution
  B. Executive
  C. Legislature
  D. Courts
  E. Local Government
  F. Revenue
  G. Politics

II. People
III. Education
  A. Schools
  B. Libraries
  C. Museums
IV. A Visitor's Guide
  A. Places to Visit
  B. Annual Events
V. The Land
  A. Land Regions
  B. Coastline
  C. Rivers, Bayous, and Lakes
  D. Plant and Animal Life
VI. Climate
VII. Economy
  A. Natural Resources
  B. Service Industries
  C. Mining
  D. Manufacturing
  E. Agriculture
  F. Fishing and Fur Industries
  G. Electric Power
  H. Transportation
  I. Communication
VIII. History

Questions

How does the legal system of Louisiana differ from those of all the other states?

How were the many salt-water lakes in Louisiana formed?

What are counties called in Louisiana?

What is Louisiana's part in the U.S. space program?

Who are the *Cajuns* and the *Creoles*?

In what way is the Lake Pontchartrain Causeway notable?

How did Louisiana become a part of the United States?

What is the most popular annual event held in the state?

What was the Mississippi River's part in forming the richest farmlands of Louisiana?

What is the single most important economic activity in Louisiana?

Additional Resources

Level I

CARPENTER, ALLAN. *Louisiana.* Rev. ed. Childrens Press, 1978.

DAVIS, EDWIN A. *Louisiana: The Pelican State.* 4th ed. Louisiana State Univ. Press, 1975.

FRADIN, DENNIS B. *Louisiana in Words and Pictures.* Childrens Press, 1981.

HALL-QUEST, OLGA. *Old New Orleans, the Creole City: Its Role in American History, 1718-1803.* Dutton, 1968.

KNIFFEN, FRED B. *Indians of Louisiana.* Pelican, 1976. Reprint of 1945 ed.

Level II

CONRAD, GLENN R., ed. *Readings in Louisiana History.* Louisiana Historical Assn., 1978.

FEIBLEMAN, PETER S. *The Bayous.* Time Inc., 1973.

HUBER, LEONARD V. *Louisiana: A Pictorial History.* Scribner, 1975.

KNIFFEN, FRED B. *Louisiana: Its Land and People.* Louisiana State Univ. Press, 1968.

Louisiana: A Guide to the State. Hastings, 1971. A rev. ed. in the Amer. Guide Series.

RUSHTON, WILLIAM F. *The Cajuns: From Acadia to Louisiana.* Farrar, 1979.

TAYLOR, JOE GRAY. *Louisiana Reconstructed, 1863-1877.* Louisiana State Univ. Press, 1974. *Louisiana: A Bicentennial History.* Norton, 1976.

WINTERS, JOHN D. *The Civil War in Louisiana.* Louisiana State Univ. Press, 1979. Reprint of 1963 ed.

National Aeronautics and Space Administration

Michoud Assembly Facility is located in New Orleans. The plant is involved in the U.S. space shuttle program.

LOUISIANA PURCHASE

LOUISIANA PURCHASE was the most important event of President Thomas Jefferson's first administration. In this transaction, the United States bought 827,-987 square miles (2,144,476 square kilometers) of land from France for about $15 million. This vast area lay between the Mississippi River and the Rocky Mountains, stretching from the Gulf of Mexico to the Canadian border. The purchase of this land greatly increased the economic resources of the United States, and cemented the union of the Middle West and the East. Eventually all or parts of 15 states were formed out of the region.

Reasons for the Purchase. When Jefferson became President in March 1801, the Mississippi River formed the western boundary of the United States. The southern boundary extended to the 31st parallel north latitude. The Floridas (with West Florida extending to the Mississippi and including New Orleans) lay to the south, and the Louisiana Territory to the west. Spain owned both these territories.

Farmers who lived west of the Appalachian Mountains shipped all their surplus produce by boat down rivers that flowed into the Gulf of Mexico, especially the Mississippi. In a treaty of 1795, Spain agreed to give Americans the "right of deposit" at New Orleans. This right allowed Americans to store in New Orleans, duty-free, goods shipped for export. Arks and flatboats transported a great variety of products, including flour, tobacco, pork, bacon, lard, feathers, cider, butter, cheese, hemp, potatoes, apples, salt, whisky, beeswax, and bear and deer skins.

In New Orleans, the merchants exchanged the goods for Spanish currency. They then returned to their homes by keelboat or on horseback by way of Natchez. This arrangement was acceptable to western farmers, because Spain was a weak nation. If at any time Spain had closed the Mississippi to American ships, the port of New Orleans could have been seized.

Trouble Begins. In the same month that Jefferson became President, the United States minister to England, Rufus King, heard that Spain planned to give part of its American colonies to France. Jefferson feared that an ambitious nation such as France might interfere with the trade of the western territories. He believed that Spain would cede the Floridas to France, and quickly directed his diplomats to prevent this transfer. Secretary of State James Madison warned the French chargé d'affaires, Louis Pichon, that the United States expected to have an outlet to the sea. Robert Livingston, who was the newly appointed minister to France, sailed for that country in September 1801. He received instructions to inform the French government that the United States was not willing to see the American colonies of Spain transferred to any country except the United States.

In November 1801, King sent Madison a copy of the treaty in which Spain ceded Louisiana to France. But Jefferson still did not know just how much territory this included. He instructed Livingston to prevent the cession if possible. If it had already taken place, Livingston was to persuade France to transfer the Floridas, especially West Florida, to the United States. New Orleans lay on the east side of the river, so it would become a possession of the United States. Napoleon spurned Livingston's proposals.

Events of 1802 brought little change in the situation. Napoleon planned to subdue a rebellion in France's West Indian colony, Santo Domingo. He also planned to send troops to take possession of Louisiana. But the French army in Santo Domingo was almost annihilated, and the transfer of Louisiana did not take place. Jefferson arranged for his friend, Pierre du Pont de Nemours, to carry dispatches to Livingston and to help him influence the French government against acquiring the American colonies. Du Pont's instructions read as follows: ". . . you may be able to impress on the government of France the inevitable consequences of their taking possession of Louisiana . . . This measure will

The Louisiana Purchase almost doubled the area of the United States. This 1803 treaty with France extended the western U.S. boundary from the Mississippi River to the Rocky Mountains. Part or all of 15 states were later formed from the region.

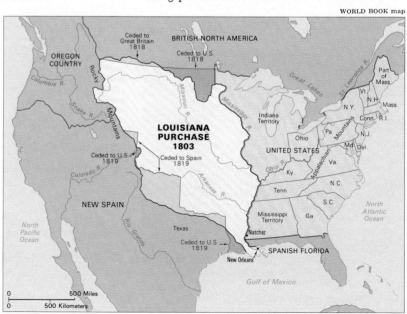

cost, and perhaps not very long hence, a war which will annihilate her on the ocean . . ." Du Pont was to warn France that if it annexed Louisiana, the United States would form an alliance with England against France. Du Pont felt that this ultimatum might make Napoleon even more determined to acquire the desired territory. Being a businessman, he suggested that the United States offer to buy the Floridas, paying as much as $6 million for them. This seems to be the first suggestion of buying the territory.

New Orleans Closed to Americans. Meanwhile, Jefferson's worst fears seemed to be confirmed when, on Oct. 18, 1802, the Spanish intendant (governor) of New Orleans suspended the right of deposit. He was following orders received from Spain, probably dictated by Napoleon, but the action was made to appear as his own decision. The governor of the Mississippi Territory warned Madison: "The late act of the Spanish Government at New Orleans has excited considerable agitation in Natchez and its vicinity:—It has inflicted a severe wound upon the Agricultural and Commercial interests of this Territory, and must prove no less injurious to all the Western Country." Madison protested to the Spanish government and also warned Napoleon through Pichon that Americans were people of action and were aroused by a war fever.

Napoleon would not abandon his hopes of building an empire in America. The news of his army's defeat in Santo Domingo did not stop him, and he ordered 15,000 troops to that island. Livingston was discouraged. Jefferson decided to send James Monroe to France to support Livingston in his negotiations with the French government. Congress voted $2 million which the two envoys could use in trying to purchase the east bank of the Mississippi. Jefferson privately advised them to offer as much as $9,375,000 for the Floridas and New Orleans. If France rejected their offer, they were to try to obtain at least the right of deposit at New Orleans.

Napoleon's Decision. Napoleon knew that war with Great Britain would soon break out again. Pichon warned him that the Americans might seize Louisiana as soon as France became engaged in a European war, and that the British navy might seize the territory. Napoleon also feared the possibility of an Anglo-American alliance. Pichon had warned that the United States was considering sending 50,000 troops to take New Orleans by force. American newspapers describing the war ferment seemed to substantiate this warning.

On April 10, 1803, Napoleon notified his finance minister, François de Barbé-Marbois, that he was considering ceding all the Louisiana Territory to the United States. Monroe arrived in Paris just after Marbois had offered Livingston the whole of Louisiana. Jefferson had instructed the two envoys to purchase only the Floridas, but they felt confident that the United States would accept this larger offer. They agreed to Marbois' price of 60 million francs plus the assumption of American claims against France (a total of about $15 million). The treaty, dated April 30, was signed May 2. It reached Washington on July 14, 1803.

Ratifying the Treaty. Jefferson was uncertain about the course he should follow. The Federalists objected to the possible creation of a fringe of states that would differ in background and nationality from the original states. But Jefferson believed Americans would inhabit any states thus formed in the course of expansion.

The Constitution did not authorize the acquisition of land, but it did provide for the making of treaties, so that Jefferson felt the acquisition of new territory was constitutional. He admitted that he had "stretched the constitution until it cracked." But he thought of himself as a guardian who made an investment of funds entrusted to his care. In a message to Congress on Oct. 17, 1803, Jefferson said: "Whilst the property and sovereignty of the Mississippi and its waters secure an independent outlet for the produce of the Western States and an uncontrolled navigation through their whole course, . . . the fertility of the country, its climate and extent, promise in due season important aids to our Treasury, an ample provision for our posterity, and a wide spread for the blessings of freedom and equal laws." The U.S. Senate ratified the treaty on October 20. Congress passed laws to provide for borrowing the money from English and Dutch bankers, payable in 15 years. The United States took possession of the territory on Dec. 20, 1803. See Louisiana (History).

Boundary Disputes arose over the Louisiana Territory, because the treaty did not state specific boundaries. The United States and Great Britain agreed in 1818 to establish the northern boundary at the 49th parallel. In the south, the United States claimed West Florida and part of Texas. Jefferson pointed out that as early as 1696 France had actual possession of the Gulf Coast from Mobile westward, and that in 1755 maps published by the French government showed the Perdido River as the eastern boundary of France's possessions. This, Jefferson claimed, was part of the land that Spain gave back to France in 1800, and therefore part of the purchase. In the Adams-Onís Treaty of 1819 with Spain, the United States acquired Florida, and surrendered its claim to Texas. Spain in return gave up its claim to West Florida. INA WOESTEMEYER VAN NOPPEN

Additional Resources

CHIDSEY, DONALD B. *Louisiana Purchase.* Crown, 1972.
DE CONDE, ALEXANDER. *This Affair of Louisiana.* Scribner, 1976.

LOUISIANA STATE UNIVERSITY (LSU) is a coeducational state-supported university system. The main campus in Baton Rouge has colleges of agriculture, arts and sciences, business administration, chemistry and physics, education, and engineering; professional schools of environmental design, law, library science, music, social welfare, and veterinary medicine. It also has an extension division and a graduate school. Other divisions include Louisiana State University in Shreveport; the University of New Orleans; and two-year campuses in Alexandria and Eunice. The school also has a medical center with two campuses in New Orleans and one in Shreveport. LSU has an agricultural extension service and 17 agricultural research centers.

LSU was founded in Pineville in 1855 as the Louisiana State Seminary of Learning and Military Academy. The name was changed to Louisiana State University in 1870, and LSU merged with the Agricultural and Mechanical College in 1877. For enrollment, see UNIVERSITIES AND COLLEGES (table).

Critically reviewed by LOUISIANA STATE UNIVERSITY

John Nation   Jim Reed, *Louisville Magazine*

Louisville, the largest city in Kentucky, lies on the Ohio River. The downtown Riverfront Plaza, *right,* includes a pool with stepping stones that help provide an attractive setting.

LOUISVILLE, *LOO ee VIHL* or *LOO ih VUHL*, is the largest city in Kentucky and a major industrial center of the Southeast. Louisville serves as an important transportation link between the North and the South. The city lies on the Ohio River along the northern boundary of Kentucky. Louisville grew up beside the falls of the river, and it is sometimes called the *Falls City*. About a fifth of Kentucky's people live in the Louisville metropolitan area.

The Kentucky Derby, one of the world's most famous horse races, is held at Churchill Downs in Louisville on the first Saturday in May. The race draws more than 100,000 spectators each year.

In 1778, a group of pioneers led by the American explorer George Rogers Clark established a settlement on the site of what is now Louisville. The next year, Clark named the town for King Louis XVI of France. He did so in gratitude for France's help to the American Colonies during the Revolutionary War (1775-1783).

River trade accounted for much of Louisville's early development. Since World War II (1939-1945), its industry has expanded rapidly.

The City covers 65 square miles (168 square kilometers)—including about 5 square miles (13 square kilometers) of inland water—in Jefferson County. It is the seat of Jefferson County. The Louisville metropolitan area spreads over 2,293 square miles (5,939 square kilometers). It covers all of Jefferson, Bullitt, Oldham, and Shelby counties and extends over all of Clark,

Floyd, and Harrison counties in Indiana. Low, rolling hills rise to the south and to the east of the city.

Downtown Louisville consists mainly of an area 1 mile (1.6 kilometers) square, bordered by the Ohio River, First Street, Tenth Street, and Broadway. Most of the city's large banks, hotels, and stores are within this area. The downtown section also includes city, county, and federal government buildings. Founders Square, an information center, is at Fifth and Walnut streets. Next to the square stands Louisville Gardens, a convention center that can hold more than 6,800 people. A statue of George Rogers Clark and a stained-glass window with scenes of Louisville's history are features of the Belvedere

Facts in Brief

Population: *City*—298,694. *Metropolitan Area*—956,756.

Area: 65 sq. mi. (168 km²). *Metropolitan Area*—2,293 sq. mi. (5,939 km²).

Altitude: 450 ft. (137 m) above sea level.

Climate: *Average Temperature*—January, 35° F. (2° C); July, 78° F. (26° C). *Average Annual Precipitation* (rainfall, melted snow, and other forms of moisture)—42 in. (107 cm). For the monthly weather in Louisville, see KENTUCKY (Climate).

Government: Mayor-council. *Terms*—4 years for the mayor and 2 years for the 12 council members (aldermen).

Founded: 1778. Incorporated as a city in 1828.

Riverfront Plaza, located on the Ohio River between Fourth and Sixth streets.

Four bridges across the Ohio River link Louisville with the Indiana cities of Clarksville, Jeffersonville, and New Albany. Freeways connect downtown Louisville with the city's suburbs. The United States government keeps its gold reserve in huge vaults at Fort Knox, an Army base 30 miles (48 kilometers) south of Louisville.

The People. More than 98 per cent of Louisville's people were born in the United States. The city's population includes large groups of people of English, German, and Irish descent. Blacks make up more than a fourth of the population of Louisville. Most of the blacks live in the West End district and in the central city. Slums and unemployment are problems in both of these areas.

About half the people of Louisville are Protestants, of whom Baptists, Methodists, and Presbyterians make up the largest denominations. More than 40 per cent of the people are Roman Catholics.

Economy. The Louisville metropolitan area has about 1,100 factories. They produce about $15 billion worth of goods annually. Louisville is one of the largest tobacco-manufacturing centers in the United States. It is also one of the country's largest producers of gin and whiskey. Other major products of the city include chemicals, electric appliances, paint, plumbing fixtures, and sporting goods. Lumber milling, meat packing, and printing are also important industries. The American Printing House for the Blind, the world's largest publisher of braille products, is located in Louisville.

Louisville, a major river port, is linked by towboats and barges with other communities on the Ohio and Mississippi rivers. Freight railroads and more than 130 truck lines also serve the Louisville area. Most commercial airliners use Standiford Field, and Bowman Field serves smaller planes.

Louisville has two daily newspapers, *The Courier-Journal* and *The Louisville Times.* Twenty-four radio stations and four television stations broadcast from the city.

Louisville's economy has grown since the late 1940's, but the city still faces economic problems. During the early 1980's, the city experienced a decline in manufacturing. But an increase in service industry activities—such as health care, finance, and tourism—took place during the same period.

Reduced employment in Louisville's tobacco industry has also been a problem. A decline in cigarette sales began during the 1960's and forced tobacco companies to lay off many employees. Industrial development led to increased air pollution in the Louisville area. Local governments passed pollution control laws to reduce this problem.

Education. The Jefferson County Public School District includes all the public elementary and high schools in Louisville and most of the rest of Jefferson County. It has a total enrollment of about 93,000 students. Blacks make up about 30 per cent of the enrollment. In 1975, a busing program designed to desegregate Louisville area schools began in the district. Under the program, several thousand black children are bused from the city to suburban schools, and several thousand white children ride buses to schools in Louisville. More than 22,000 stu-

dents attend about 85 parochial and private schools in Jefferson County.

Louisville has several colleges and universities. More than 19,000 students attend the University of Louisville, founded in 1798. It was the first city-owned university in the United States. Other institutions of higher learning include Bellarmine College, Jefferson Community College, Louisville Presbyterian Theological Seminary, Southern Baptist Theological Seminary, and Spalding University. The Kentucky School for the Blind is also in Louisville.

Louisville's public school system, like that of other cities, faces financial problems. Some colleges in the Louisville area have also had financial troubles. Kentucky Southern College closed in 1969 because of a shortage of funds. The University of Louisville was under municipal control until 1970. But, faced with rising costs, the university became a state-supported school that year.

The Louisville Free Public Library, founded in 1816,

City of Louisville

Louisville, the largest city in Kentucky, is a major port on the Ohio River. The map shows important points of interest in and around Louisville.

☐ City of Louisville

▨ Area outside Louisville

═ Main road

─ Other road

┼┼ Rail line

● Point of interest

was one of the nation's first public library systems. It has about 20 branches.

Cultural Life. The Kentucky Opera Association, the Louisville Ballet Company, and the Louisville Orchestra perform at the Kentucky Center for the Arts downtown. The Actors Theatre of Louisville is the home of the city's professional resident theater company. The Memorial Auditorium presents dance productions, plays, and concerts. The Playhouse, which is on the University of Louisville campus, offers plays and other stage productions. Central Park presents a series of Shakespearean plays each summer. Louisville Gardens is used for such events as concerts, circuses, and sports contests.

The J. B. Speed Art Museum, on the University of Louisville campus, features traveling art shows in addition to its own collection. The Museum of History and Science offers a variety of exhibits. The Kentucky Railway Museum has a collection of steam locomotives and trolley and railroad cars from the 1800's. The Kentucky Derby Museum at Churchill Downs features displays and information about horse racing. The Filson Club has exhibits of Kentucky history.

Recreation. Jefferson County has about 11,000 acres (4,450 hectares) of parks and playgrounds. Iroquois Park includes a large amphitheater for summer musicals. The 396-acre (160.3-hectare) Kentucky Fair and Exposition Center is one of the largest exhibition centers and fairgrounds in the United States. The center's coliseum seats about 20,000 people for conventions and other events. The Louisville Zoological Garden features a MetaZoo, an indoor exhibit that includes a re-creation of a Kentucky pond.

Horse racing is one of the city's most popular sports. Races are held in the spring and fall at Churchill Downs. Louisville Downs features harness racing.

Louisville has many historical attractions. Locust Grove, the home of George Rogers Clark, and Farmington, a house designed by Thomas Jefferson, draw many tourists. Other historic places include the Cave Hill Cemetery, where Clark is buried, and the Zachary Taylor National Cemetery.

Government. Louisville has a mayor-council form of government. The voters elect the mayor to a four-year term. They elect the 12 members of the city council—called the Board of Aldermen—to two-year terms. City property taxes provide the government's main source of income.

The chief problem of the Louisville city government, like that of many other city governments, is its lack of *home rule* (self-government). Louisville must have the approval of the state legislature to act on many local matters. Legislators from rural areas often oppose measures that would benefit Louisville and other cities. Some city officials favor the establishment of a government for the Louisville metropolitan area. They feel that such a government could cut costs that result from overlapping city and suburban services. Suburban voters have opposed a metropolitan government, declaring that such a government would raise taxes.

History. In 1778, the explorer George Rogers Clark led a group of pioneers from Pennsylvania down the Ohio River. After a brief stay on an island in the river, the pioneers established a settlement on the shore of the Ohio. The town was named Louisville in 1779. By 1800, about 350 people lived there.

Louisville's location helped make the town an important river port and frontier community. The first ocean-going ship to reach Louisville arrived in 1800. In 1811, the *New Orleans* became the first steamship to dock there. Louisville received a city charter in 1828. The Portland Canal, completed in 1830, enabled ships to bypass the falls of the river.

During the 1830's and 1840's, many people moved to Louisville from the Eastern United States and from Europe. They were attracted by the city's economic opportunities, and they contributed greatly to Louisville's political and cultural development.

Kentucky became a major tobacco-producing state during the 1830's, and much tobacco processing took place in Louisville. By the 1840's, the city ranked as one of the top tobacco centers in the world. By 1850, the population of Louisville had risen to more than 43,000. The growth of railroads during the 1850's led to further growth for Louisville. By 1859, train service had begun between Louisville and Nashville, Tenn.

During the Civil War (1861-1865), both Northern and Southern sympathizers lived in the city. But Kentucky remained in the Union, and Louisville became a supply depot for Northern troops. All trade was cut off with the South. A period of prosperity followed the war. Louisville business people regained their Southern markets, and railroads connected Louisville with Atlanta, New Orleans, and other Southern cities. By 1870, more than 100,000 people lived in Louisville.

Since the opening of Louisville's first race track in 1830, horse racing has been a leading sport in the city. Many of the horses have been raised in Kentucky's famous bluegrass pastures. In 1874, a group of sportsmen founded the Louisville Jockey Club. Each of the 320 original members contributed $100. Colonel M. Lewis Clark, a horse breeder, used this money to build Churchill Downs. The first Kentucky Derby was held there in 1875. By 1900, Louisville's population had reached about 205,000.

In 1937, the Ohio River overflowed its banks and swept through the city. The flood caused over $52 million in damage. A floodwall now protects the city.

During World War II, the United States government built three large ammunition plants in the Louisville area. Workers flocked to the city from rural communities to take factory jobs. The Army trained fliers at Bowman Field and infantrymen at Fort Knox. The increased defense activities helped raise the population to about 370,000 by 1950.

Racial progress took place in Louisville during the 1950's and 1960's. Peaceful desegregation of the public schools began in 1954, and all public accommodations were integrated in 1960.

The 1950's, 1960's, and 1970's also brought rapid growth to the Louisville area. A number of expressways and high-rise buildings were built. The city also began a major beautifying program for downtown Louisville, including construction of public greens and fountains. In one project, the city built the Fourth Avenue Mall on three blocks of centrally located Fourth Street.

During the early 1970's, downtown redevelopment led to construction of new office buildings and a second large convention center. The University of Louisville opened a modern medical center with a large hospital. Private developers built a hotel and bank buildings along the waterfront, and the city opened a giant parking garage there.

Between 1970 and 1980, Louisville's population declined by more than 60,000. During the same period, however, the population of the city's suburbs continued to grow. The economic recession of the early 1980's led to the loss of thousands of manufacturing jobs in the Louisville area. At the same time, the downtown redevelopment continued. It included the construction of the $144-million Galleria, which features many shops and two office towers.   JOHN EDWARD PEARCE

See also KENTUCKY (pictures); KENTUCKY DERBY.

LOUISVILLE, *LOO ee VIHL,* **UNIVERSITY OF,** is a state-supported coeducational institution in Louisville, Ky. It has a college of arts and sciences, and schools of business, dentistry, education, engineering, law, medicine, music, police administration, and social work. It also has a graduate school. Courses at the university lead to bachelor's, master's, and doctor's degrees.

The University of Louisville was founded in 1798. It was under municipal control until 1970, when it became a state school. For enrollment, see UNIVERSITIES AND COLLEGES (table).   WOODROW M. STRICKLER

LOURDES, *loord* or *loordz* (pop. 17,425), is a town in southwestern France near the Pyrenees foothills (see FRANCE [political map]). It is famous as a shrine for Roman Catholic pilgrims, for it is believed that here, in 1858, the Virgin Mary appeared to a peasant girl, Bernadette Soubirous. A beautiful church, called the Rosary, and a statue of the Virgin stand at the grotto where the vision occurred.

Thousands of people visit these shrines every year, leaving gifts. Some leave their crutches as evidence of cure. Others bathe in the sacred waters of the grotto spring, in hope that a miracle will restore them to health. The visitors come all year long. Many French Roman Catholics make a pilgrimage to Lourdes for

The Shrine at Lourdes marks the spot where many persons believe the Virgin Mary appeared to Bernadette Soubirous in 1858.

ceremonies on August 20 of each year. The shrine at Lourdes attracts about 2 million pilgrims a year. The shrine ranks as one of the greatest pilgrimage centers in the world. The underground Basilica of St. Pius X in Lourdes, opened in 1958, is the second largest Roman Catholic church in the world. Only St. Peter's in Rome can accommodate more people.   ROBERT E. DICKINSON

See also BERNADETTE, SAINT.

LOURENÇO MARQUES. See MAPUTO.

LOUSE, is a small insect that sucks the sap of plants or the blood of animals. Lice are animal and plant parasites.

The American Museum of Natural History

A Body Louse feeds by piercing its victim's skin and drawing blood through its beaklike sucker mouth. The front view, *above left,* shows the crablike legs and hooked claws of the louse. The top view, *above right,* shows the tiny hairs that cover its body.

Three kinds of lice prey on man—*head, body,* and *crab* lice. Body lice are the chief spreaders of typhus fever. They are the "cooties" that bother soldiers. Crab lice attack the pelvic region, armpits, and chest.

Lice that prey on humans are small, wingless creatures, with flattened, almost transparent bodies. They have hooked feet fitted for holding to hairs. The mouth part is a sucking organ like a beak. It is soft, but can pierce the skin so the animal can draw blood.

The lice eggs are called *nits.* Head lice attach the eggs to hairs with a gummy substance. The nits hatch in six days, and the louse is full grown 18 days later.

It is easy for one person to catch lice from another. The best way to discourage both head and body lice is to keep the body clean. Body lice lay their eggs in the seams of clothing or bedding. It is necessary to steam or boil these articles in order to rid them of the pests. Physicians prescribe medicated shampoos, creams, and lotions to kill lice.

A group of lice called *chewing lice,* or *biting lice,* eat feathers and bits of loose skin from birds. They also attack horses, raccoons, and other animals.

Plant lice are called *aphids.* Some kinds of aphids are harmful to crops and garden plants. See APHID.

Scientific Classification. Lice make up two chief orders. Chewing lice, or bird lice, make up the order Mallophaga. True lice and sucking lice make up the order Anoplura. This order includes the lice that attack human beings. The human louse, or body louse, is in the body louse family, Pediculidae. It is classified as *Pediculus humanus.* Plant lice are in the order Homoptera.   H. H. ROSS

LOUSEWORT. See FIGWORT FAMILY.

The Louvre Today covers more than 40 acres (16 hectares) and houses one of the world's largest and most important art collections. The building complex took its present form in the 1850's.

L'OUVERTURE, TOUSSAINT. See TOUSSAINT L'OU-VERTURE.

LOUVRE, *LOO vruh*, is one of the largest and most famous art museums in the world. The Louvre covers more than 40 acres (16 hectares) on the north bank of the Seine River in Paris. The Louvre was built as a residence for the kings of France, but today it exhibits some of the world's greatest art treasures.

The Louvre has about 8 miles (13 kilometers) of galleries and contains more than a million works of art. Many paintings are exhibited in the Grand Gallery, which is more than 1,300 feet (400 meters) long. The Louvre has especially fine collections of Egyptian,

The First Louvre was built as a fortress by King Philip II about 1200. It became the royal residence in the 1300's.

Greek, Oriental, and Roman art. It also has an outstanding collection of paintings and sculptures of the 1800's as well as decorative art. The most famous works in the Louvre include the Greek sculptures *Venus de Milo* and *Winged Victory* and the *Mona Lisa* by the Italian painter Leonardo da Vinci. The Louvre also houses the French Ministry of Finance.

King Phillip II originally built the Louvre as a fortress in about 1200. King Charles V had the building remodeled into a fortified country house during the early 1300's. The Louvre began to take on its present appearance in the mid-1500's. In 1546, King Francis I decided to transform the building into a palace that would rival the greatest structures of Renaissance Italy. Francis

hired the French architect Pierre Lescot to direct construction. Jean Goujon, a French sculptor, decorated the palace and its grounds with statues based on Greek models. Later kings added large courts and long wings to the original building.

The period of expansion ended in 1670 with the completion of the Louvre's east front designed by Claude Perrault. A few years later, the royal court moved to a new palace at Versailles, near Paris. In 1793, during the French Revolution, the revolutionary government opened the Louvre as a public museum to display works from the captured royal collection. Construction resumed under Napoleon I in the early 1800's, and the Louvre gained its modern form in the mid-1800's with the completion of two wings. A major expansion and modernization project began in 1984 and was scheduled to be completed in the late 1980's.   WILLIAM J. HENNESSEY

See also EUROPE (picture: Masterpieces of Art); PARIS (picture: The Venus de Milo).

LOVE. See EMOTION; SEX.

LOVE, NAT (1854-1921), was a black American cowboy of the Old West. Love worked in cattle drives for about 20 years, traveling across the Western United States and Mexico. He became known on the open range for his expert horsemanship and ability to identify cattle brands.

Love was born a slave in Davidson County, Tennessee. He left home when he was 15 years old and went to work as a cowboy near Dodge City, Kans. He worked in cattle drives until 1889. He became a railroad porter in 1890.

Nat Love

Love was nicknamed "Deadwood Dick" after he won a riding, roping, and shooting contest in Deadwood, S. Dak., in 1876. His autobiography, *The Life and Adventures of Nat Love, Better Known in the Cattle Country as Deadwood Dick* (1907), has many cowboy stories. It includes tales about such famous Western characters as Bat Masterson, Billy the Kid, Buffalo Bill, and Jesse James. But, like many other legends of the

Old West, Love's stories are greatly exaggerated, and his true adventures are difficult to distinguish from the "tall tales." RAYMOND W. SMOCK

LOVE APPLE. See TOMATO (History).

LOVE CANAL. See NEW YORK (New York Today).

LOVEBIRD is any one of several kinds of small parrots. They are called *lovebirds* because the mating birds show great affection, caressing each other with their

All-Pets Magazine

Lovebirds Are Popular Pets. They are famous for their affectionate manner. Many lovebirds have brilliantly colored feathers.

bills and remaining in closely knit pairs. True lovebirds live in Africa, but a similar group inhabits the tropical regions of South America. Some African species have a remarkable way of carrying grass and straw to their nests. They tuck these materials under the feathers at the base of the tail. Then they fly to their nests with the grasses and straws streaming behind. Lovebirds in captivity often tear strips of paper or pick up pieces of string to tuck beneath their feathers. Lovebirds have curved beaks and short tails that are typical of the parrot family. They are popular cage birds.

Scientific Classification. Lovebirds belong to the parrot family, *Psittacidae*. They are members of the genus *Agapornis* and of the genus *Psittacula*. HERBERT FRIEDMANN

LOVEJOY is the family name of two American brothers who were *abolitionist* (antislavery) leaders during the early 1800's.

Elijah Parish Lovejoy (1802-1837), a clergyman and editor, attacked slavery as editor of a religious newspaper, the *St. Louis Observer*. Although threatened, Lovejoy refused to stop backing the abolition of slavery in the nation. He moved across the Mississippi River to Alton, Ill., in 1837. Here he published the *Alton Observer* and helped organize the Illinois Anti-Slavery Society. Two of his presses were wrecked, and, in November 1837, a mob gathered to destroy his newest press. Lovejoy was killed trying to stop them. Many Northerners became abolitionists after his death. Lovejoy was born in Albion, Me. He attended Waterville (now Colby) College and the Theological Seminary in Princeton, N.J.

Owen Lovejoy (1811-1864), a clergyman and statesman, served as a pastor in Princeton, Ill., for 17 years. He helped organize the Illinois abolitionist movement, but also helped persuade the Republican Party to accept Abraham Lincoln's more cautious leadership. As a

member of the U.S. House of Representatives from 1857 to 1864, he denounced slavery while supporting Lincoln against extreme abolitionists. He was born in Albion, Me., and attended Bowdoin College. LOUIS FILLER

See also ABOLITIONIST; PHILLIPS, WENDELL.

LOVELACE, RICHARD (1618-1657), was a member of a group of English lyric poets called the *Cavalier* poets. These poets emphasized ideals of love, beauty, and honor. Lovelace is known chiefly for a few famous lines. "Stone walls do not a prison make, / Nor iron bars a cage" comes from the poem "To Althea, from Prison" (1642). "I could not love thee, dear, so much, / Loved I not honor more" appears in the poem "To Lucasta, Going to the Wars" (1648).

Lovelace was born either in Woolwich or in the Netherlands. He was educated at Oxford University and lived for a time at his wealthy family's country estate. Lovelace served as a soldier in the army of King Charles I. He was imprisoned twice during the civil war that broke out in 1642. He wrote his two famous poems in prison. Lovelace lost his estate while he was serving the king, and he died in poverty. THOMAS H. FUJIMURA

LOVELL, *LUHV uhl,* **SIR BERNARD** (1913-), an English astronomer, built the world's first completely steerable radio telescope. This telescope can be pointed in any direction. Lovell became famous for tracking the first artificial satellite, Russia's *Sputnik I*, with the telescope in October 1957. The telescope has a reflector 250 feet (76.2 meters) wide that focuses radio waves on an antenna in the center of the reflector. It is called the Jodrell Bank telescope after its site near Manchester, England.

Lovell was born in Gloucestershire and studied physics at Bristol University. During World War II (1939-1945), he worked with radar and became interested in radio astronomy. Radio astronomers study radio waves produced by stars and other celestial objects.

Lovell built the Jodrell Bank telescope because he wanted an instrument that could receive radio waves from most of the visible sky. Queen Elizabeth II knighted Lovell in 1961. ROGER H. STUEWER

See also JODRELL BANK OBSERVATORY.

LOVELL, *LUHV uhl,* **JAMES ARTHUR, JR.** (1928-), a United States astronaut, commanded the Apollo 13 space flight that was to have landed on the moon in April 1970. About 56 hours after the flight began, an oxygen tank exploded, forcing cancellation of the landing and endangering the lives of Lovell and astronauts Fred W. Haise, Jr., and John L. Swigert, Jr. The three men piloted their crippled spacecraft to a safe landing in the Pacific Ocean about $3\frac{1}{2}$ days later.

In December 1965, Lovell and Frank Borman established a space endurance record by spending 14 days in earth orbit aboard the Gemini 7 spacecraft. During this mission they achieved the first *rendezvous* (close approach) in space with the Gemini 6 spacecraft piloted by Walter M. Schirra, Jr., and Thomas P. Stafford. In November 1966, Lovell commanded the Gemini 12 flight. In December 1968, he served as command module pilot aboard Apollo 8, and on Christmas Eve he, Frank Borman, and William A. Anders became the first persons to circle the moon.

Lovell was born in Cleveland. He attended the Uni-

LOW, JULIETTE GORDON

versity of Wisconsin from 1946 to 1948, and graduated from the U.S. Naval Academy in 1952. He served as a test pilot and flight instructor before becoming an astronaut in 1962. Lovell resigned from the astronaut program in 1971 to become a deputy director of the National Aeronautics and Space Administration. He entered private business in 1973. WILLIAM J. CROMIE

LOW, JULIETTE GORDON (1860-1927), founded the Girl Scouts in America. Among her close friends were Sir Robert and Lady Baden-Powell, the founders of Scouting. Mrs. Low organized a troop of Girl Guides on her estate at Glenlyon, Scotland. On her return to the United States, she began a patrol in Savannah, Ga., in 1912. In 1913, the organization changed its name to Girl Scouts (see GIRL SCOUTS). It was incorporated in 1915, and set up national headquarters in Washington, D.C. Mrs. Low served as president of the Girl Scouts until 1920, when she received the title of *Founder*.

Girl Scouts

Juliette Gordon Low

She was born in Savannah, Ga., the daughter of a general. She married a wealthy Englishman, William M. Low, and lived in England, Scotland, and the United States. Mrs. Low was a talented sculptor. She was deaf, and had poor health. ALAN KEITH-LUCAS

LOW CHURCH. See ANGLICANS.

LOW COUNTRIES are coastal regions between France and Germany. The Low Countries were once known as *the Netherlands*, but were later divided into Belgium, Luxembourg, and the Netherlands. Each of these countries has a separate article in WORLD BOOK.

LOWELL, *LOH uhl*, Mass. (pop. 92,418; met. area pop. 235,052), is a city in northeastern Massachusetts. It lies along the Merrimack River. For location, see MASSACHUSETTS (political map). Lowell is best known as the first planned industrial community in the United States. The city was founded in the early 1800's by textile manufacturers. In 1978, the part of Lowell where early textile manufacturing was centered became a national historical park.

Historic sites in Lowell include the restored Francis Gatehouse and Merrimack Gatehouse. The gatehouses formerly served as locks that controlled the water level in the city's canal system. The canals provided water power to run the textile mills. Lowell's Textile Museum has fabric exhibits and exhibits of looms and other machinery used in the textile mills. The birthplace of the painter James Abbott McNeill Whistler is in Lowell, and is preserved as a museum.

Textile manufacturing is still important in Lowell. The city's other industries include printing and publishing and the production of computers and food products.

Lowell was incorporated as a town in 1826, and as a city in 1836. It was named for the American textile manufacturer Francis Cabot Lowell. Lowell has a council-manager government. Lowell and Cambridge are the seats of Middlesex County. KENDALL M. WALLACE

See also LOWELL, FRANCIS CABOT.

LOWELL, *LOH uhl*, **AMY** (1874-1925), was an American poet, critic, and biographer. Like a number of other poets of her day, Lowell was strongly influenced by the American poet Ezra Pound. She was particularly influenced by Pound's belief that many poetic conventions of the past were worn out and restricted the poet's creativity. With Pound and other poets, Lowell became a leader of a movement called *imagism*. The imagists emphasized the clear, objective, and precise treatment of images, objects, and events. They wrote in a style known as *free verse* (see FREE VERSE).

Lowell experimented with her own version of free verse, beginning with her second volume of poems, *Sword Blades and Poppy Seed* (1914). She called her style *polyphonic*, which means *many-voiced*, because it used all the "voices" of poetry, including assonance, alliteration, meter, and rhythm. Her poems "Patterns" and "Lilacs" were experimental works that came to represent what was considered "modern" in poetry. "Patterns" was published in her collection *Men, Women, and Ghosts* (1916). "Lilacs" was published in *What's O'Clock* (1925), a collection that won the Pulitzer Prize for poetry in 1926, after the author's death.

Lowell wrote several critical works on the poetry of her day. They include *Six French Poets* (1915), *Tendencies in Modern American Poetry* (1917), and *A Critical Fable* (1922). She also wrote *John Keats* (1925), a long biography of the English poet.

Amy Lawrence Lowell was born in Brookline, Mass., into an old and distinguished New England family. She was educated at private schools and traveled widely, carefully preparing herself for a career in the arts. Lowell had a colorful personality and became known for her unconventional lifestyle. Her *Complete Poetical Works* was published in 1955. ELMER W. BORKLUND

LOWELL, *LOH uhl*, **FRANCIS CABOT** (1775-1817), an American textile manufacturer, founded the first mill that carried through the entire cotton-manufacturing process from raw material to finished cloth. In 1810, Lowell was allowed to inspect the Lancashire cotton mills in England. On his return, he and Paul Moody designed spinning and weaving machinery superior to the best English models. Lowell installed these machines in a mill at Waltham, Mass., which he and others had established in 1814. He also planned good living conditions for his workers. After his death, his associates put this plan into effect in the industrial city of Lowell, Mass., which was named for him.

Lowell was born in Newburyport, Mass. He graduated from Harvard University. KENNETH WIGGINS PORTER

LOWELL, *LOH uhl*, **JAMES RUSSELL** (1819-1891), was an American author who played an important part in the cultural life of the United States during the 1800's. In his own day, Lowell became best known as a poet, but he was also a noted editor, literary critic, lecturer, teacher, scholar, reformer, and diplomat.

Early Career. Lowell, a member of a noted New England family, was born in Cambridge, Mass. He graduated from Harvard University in 1838 as class poet.

Lowell earned a law degree at Harvard in 1840 and practiced law briefly before he decided to devote himself entirely to literature. Beginning about 1840, he

wrote poetry and prose for
many magazines and news-
papers. In 1843, Lowell
and a friend, Robert Car-
ter, founded *The Pioneer*, a
literary magazine. They
published works by such
noted authors as Elizabeth
Barrett Browning, Nathan-
iel Hawthorne, Edgar Al-
lan Poe, John Greenleaf
Whittier, and Lowell him-
self. The *Pioneer* showed
promise of growing into a
major cultural periodical.

Brown Bros.

James R. Lowell

But after Lowell became ill, it failed financially and
ceased publication after three issues.

Soon after leaving Harvard, Lowell became active in
the abolitionist movement. In 1844, he married Maria
White. She also had strong abolitionist convictions and
joined him in support of that cause. During the late
1840's, Lowell contributed to several abolitionist publications, including the *National Anti-Slavery Standard*,
which he helped edit, and the *Pennsylvania Freeman*.

Literary Success. Lowell reached the peak of his
literary achievement in 1848. Three of his best-known
poetic works—*A Fable for Critics*, *The Biglow Papers*,
and *The Vision of Sir Launfal*—were published then.

The author's sense of humor dominates *A Fable for
Critics* and *The Biglow Papers*. His humor and critical
insight combine to make *A Fable for Critics* a good-
natured verse satire on writers of his day, including
Lowell himself. In *The Biglow Papers*, Lowell used
humor for social criticism. This work consists of poems
and prose notes that show Lowell's opposition to U.S.
involvement in the Mexican War (1846-1848). Hosea
Biglow, the chief character, is an uneducated but prac-
tical-minded New England farmer who speaks in a
rural New England dialect. Lowell's comic treatment of
this dialect earned him a lasting place among leading
American humorists.

Lowell based *The Vision of Sir Launfal* on the legendary search for the Holy Grail, the cup that Jesus used
at the Last Supper. The poem has a moral and Christian
theme. It represents Lowell's early idealism but it is
not an example of his best poetry. The hero is Sir
Launfal, a mythical British knight (see LAUNFAL, SIR).
For quotations from the poem, see JUNE.

Teacher and Editor. Tragedy struck Lowell during
the years that he became known as a leading poet. Between 1847 and 1852, three of his four children died
and his wife, Maria, died in 1853. Although Lowell's
outlook remained optimistic, he suffered periods of
despondency that continued even after his marriage to
Frances Dunlap in 1857. For several years, Lowell's
grief over the deaths in his family hampered his ability
to write. To earn a stable income, he took teaching and
editing jobs. All these developments drew him away
from his dedication to poetry.

In 1855, Lowell succeeded the famous poet Henry
Wadsworth Longfellow as professor of modern languages at Harvard. He taught there from 1855 to 1872
and again from 1874 to 1876. During most of those
years, Lowell also held important editing positions.
From 1857 to 1861, he served as the first editor of the

Atlantic Monthly. From late 1863 to 1872, he was co-
editor of the *North American Review*. Under Lowell's
leadership, both magazines achieved major literary and
intellectual importance.

Lowell continued to write poetry, but his most important literary work after about 1860 was increasingly
in prose. His essays on such famous authors as Dante,
Shakespeare, and William Wordsworth showed his
sharp critical judgment and literary taste. Lowell also
wrote outspoken articles on social issues, including the
guarantee of full rights of citizenship to blacks.

During the 1860's, Lowell wrote some significant
poetry, including a second series of *The Biglow Papers*
for the *Atlantic Monthly*. This series reflected his antislavery position and his support of the North during
the Civil War (1861-1865). He also wrote two impressive long poems, the *Commemoration Ode* (1865) and
The Cathedral (1869).

Political Activities. After the Civil War, Lowell
became increasingly active in politics. He served as
a delegate to the Republican National Convention in
1876 but declined an opportunity to run for Congress
that year. Lowell supported the Republican presidential candidate, Rutherford B. Hayes. After Hayes became President, he appointed Lowell United States
minister to Spain. Lowell held this post from 1877 to
1880 and then served as minister to England until 1885.
During his years in Spain and England, Lowell became
a popular figure in European society and a spokesman
for American ideals of democracy.

In 1885, Lowell retired to Elmwood, the family home
where he had been born. He lived quietly for the rest
of his life but spoke at a number of public events.

Many volumes of Lowell's writings appeared during
his lifetime. But with the exception of *A Fable for
Critics*, the two series of *The Biglow Papers*, and a few
shorter poems, his work has been largely forgotten.
In most of his poetry, Lowell failed to achieve excellence. He was, however, a man who followed his conscience on humanitarian and social issues and served
his country and the world of learning well in a variety
of capacities.   SARGENT BUSH, JR.

Additional Resources

DUBERMAN, MARTIN. *James Russell Lowell*. Houghton, 1966.
HEYMANN, C. DAVID. *American Aristocracy: The Lives and Times
of James Russell, Amy, and Robert Lowell*. Dodd, 1980.
LOWELL, JAMES RUSSELL. *The Poetical Works of James Russell
Lowell*. Ed. by Marjorie R. Kaufman. Rev. ed. Houghton,
1978.
WAGENKNECHT, EDWARD. *James Russell Lowell: Portrait of a
Many-Sided Man*. Oxford, 1971.

LOWELL, PERCIVAL (1855-1916), an American astronomer, became best known for his belief in the possibility of life on Mars and in the existence of canals there.
He began his career as a businessman. Soon, however,
his interests turned to astronomy. In 1894, he completed the Lowell Observatory in Flagstaff, Ariz. He
wrote several books, which had wider popular appeal
than scientific value. In 1905, his studies led him to predict the discovery of the planet Pluto (see PLUTO).
Lowell was born in Boston.   HELEN WRIGHT

LOWELL, ROBERT (1917-1977), was a leading American poet. His poems often use mental illness as a symbol

for the sickness of society. His poetry dramatizes the pain and tenderness of personal relationships, and his belief that society has been distorted by its overemphasis on worldly things. Lowell received the 1947 Pulitzer prize for poetry for *Lord Weary's Castle* (1946) and the 1974 Pulitzer prize for poetry for *The Dolphin* (1973).

Lowell's early poems dealt with the failures and strengths of religious and historical tradition. They were brilliant, complex, and very formal. *The Mills of the Kavanaughs* (1951) gave more personal expression to his themes by using the dramatic monologue. He adopted an offhand and autobiographical style in such works as *Life Studies* (1959), *For the Union Dead* (1964), and *Day by Day* (1977). *Life Studies* won the 1960 National Book Award for poetry. Lowell was also a distinguished translator and wrote three plays about early United States history. These plays were published as *The Old Glory* (1965).

Robert Traill Spence Lowell, Jr., was born in Boston. He was related to the poets James Russell Lowell and Amy Lowell. He was a conscientious objector during World War II and was active in antiwar movements during the 1960's.   MONA VAN DUYN

See also AMERICAN LITERATURE (Personal and Confessional Poetry; picture).

LOWLANDS. See SCOTLAND (The Land).

LOWRY, *LOWR ee,* **MALCOLM,** *MAL cuhm* (1909-1957), was an English author best known for his novel *Under the Volcano* (1947). In that novel, Lowry created a complex psychological and symbolic study of a disturbed mind. The story takes place on the last day in the life of Geoffrey Firmin, a former British diplomat living in Mexico, who has become a hopeless alcoholic.

Clarence Malcolm Lowry was born in New Brighton, near Birkenhead, England, and graduated from Cambridge University in 1932. Lowry wrote *Ultramarine* (1933), a fictional account of a sea voyage he took as a young man. He did much of his writing from 1939 to 1954 while living in Canada, near Vancouver, B.C. Lowry left considerable unpublished material when he died. Some of it was published after his death, including a book of poems, a collection of letters, and several works of fiction.   CLAUDE T. BISSELL

LOYAL ORDER OF MOOSE. See MOOSE, LOYAL ORDER OF.

LOYALISTS. See REVOLUTIONARY WAR IN AMERICA; UNITED EMPIRE LOYALISTS.

LOYOLA, *loy OH luh,* **SAINT IGNATIUS,** *ihg NAY shuhs* (1491 or 1495-1556), was a Roman Catholic religious leader who founded the Society of Jesus. Members of this religious order of men are known as Jesuits.

Ignatius was born into an aristocratic Basque family near Azpeitia, Spain. His real name was Iñigo de Loyola. In 1516, Ignatius became a soldier in the army of the Duke of Nájera. While fighting the French at Pamplona in 1521, Ignatius suffered severe wounds. During his long period of recovery, he read a book about the life of Jesus and stories about the saints. These books convinced him that he should abandon his life of ambition and pleasure. After his recovery, he went to the Benedictine monastery of Montserrat, near Barcelona. There, he hung up his sword at the altar of the Virgin Mary and dedicated himself to a spiritual life.

During much of 1522 and 1523, Ignatius lived in a cave near Manresá, where he prayed and subjected himself to many physical discomforts. During this time, he underwent mystical experiences. Ignatius drew on these experiences when he wrote *Spiritual Exercises* (1522-1541), a manual of self-discipline and prayer.

To prepare for the priesthood, Ignatius studied humanities and theology in Paris from 1528 to 1535. In 1534, he and six other men formed the Society of Jesus. They took vows of poverty and chastity.

Ignatius was ordained a priest in 1537. He and the other Jesuits then went to Rome to offer their services to the pope. On the way, Ignatius had a vision at the shrine of La Storta, near Rome. In the vision, God told Jesus, "I desire you to take this man for your servant." Then Jesus said to Ignatius, "I will be favorable to you in Rome." Pope Paul III approved the Society of Jesus in 1540. Ignatius became its first *superior general* (head). He also wrote the order's constitutions, which established the Jesuits' organization and way of life.

Under the leadership of Ignatius, the Jesuits helped reform the church during a self-renewal movement called the Counter Reformation (see ROMAN CATHOLIC CHURCH [The Counter Reformation]). The Jesuits also promoted religious education in schools and colleges and preached the Gospel in Asia and the New World. Ignatius regarded himself as divinely chosen to lay the foundation for all these undertakings.

Ignatius was *cannonized* (declared a saint) in 1622. His feast day is July 31.   JOHN A. HARDON

See also JESUITS; XAVIER, SAINT FRANCIS.

LP-GAS. See BUTANE AND PROPANE; GAS (Gas in the Home).

LSD is an extremely powerful drug that causes distortions in thinking and feeling. These distortions include *hallucinations*, during which a person sees, hears, smells, or feels things that do not really exist. A dose of only 100 to 200 millionths of a gram of LSD can produce a mental and emotional experience called a *trip* that lasts from 8 to 12 hours. Most scientists believe that people who use LSD do not become physically dependent on the drug.

The letters *LSD* stand for *lysergic acid diethylamide.* LSD is made from *ergot*, a fungus that grows on rye and wheat. Two Swiss chemists, Arthur Stoll and Albert Hofmann, first made LSD in 1938. In 1943, Hofmann accidentally swallowed a small amount of LSD and discovered the drug's hallucinatory effects.

The effects of LSD can seem either pleasant or frightening. The drug may give users the feeling that they are gaining new insights into their personality and past experiences. LSD also makes individuals anxious, confused, or terrified. The user may panic and require medication to overcome the effects of LSD. Some scientists believe the drug can cause birth defects in the babies of women who take LSD during pregnancy.

A person who takes LSD may see shifting patterns of light and "hear" colors. The sensory reactions become exaggerated and moods may alter rapidly from intense happiness to deep depression.

A user of LSD may experience a *flashback* when not under the influence of the drug. During a flashback, a person relives a frightening trip that occurred weeks or months before. The person may also become anxious or depressed and fear losing his or her mind.

The U.S. government prohibits the possession, distribution, or sale of LSD except for research approved by the Department of Justice. Different states have various laws covering control of the drug. DONALD J. WOLK

See also HALLUCINOGENIC DRUG.

LUANDA, *loo AHN duh* (pop. 600,000), is the capital and largest city of Angola, and the country's chief industrial center and port. It lies on the west coast of Africa, along the Atlantic Ocean (see ANGOLA [map]).

Industrial facilities include foundries; sawmills; textile mills; and cement, printing, and food processing plants. An airport and a railroad serve the city.

The Portuguese ruled Angola as a colony for about 400 years until the country gained independence in 1975. They founded Luanda in 1576, and the city became the main center of Portuguese settlement in Angola. The Portuguese built many impressive European-style structures in Luanda, including a fortress; churches; libraries; houses; and business, government, and university buildings. Run-down areas called *shantytowns* lie outside the city.

Civil war broke out after Angola became independent, and almost all the Portuguese left. Today, most of Luanda's people are black Africans. L. H. GANN

LUANG PRABANG. See LOUANGPHRABANG.

LUBA, *LOO buh*, are an important ethnic group in the African country of Zaire. Approximately 3 million Luba live in Zaire. Most of them live in the grasslands of the central and southeastern parts of the country. The Luba consist of two main groups—the Luba-Kasai and the Luba-Shaba.

Most of the Luba-Kasai live in cities and towns. They are familiar with Western culture, and many hold high posts in government, industry, and trade. Most of the Luba-Shaba live in small rural villages and work as farmers. They grow cassava, corn, millet, and other crops. Luba farmers prepare the land for planting by burning away the grasses and using the ash as fertilizer.

The Luba speak a language called Tshiluba, which belongs to the Bantu family of African languages. The traditional Luba religion recognizes a supreme being as well as lesser gods and the spirits of ancestors. Luba woodcarvers are world famous for beautiful masks and statues that honor the memory of their ancestors.

The Luba descended from Bantu-speaking peoples who probably came to central Africa about 2,000 years ago. By 1700, a number of Luba-Shaba groups had united to form the Luba Empire. They developed a powerful army that conquered many neighboring peoples. The Luba also established a prosperous trade in such goods as copper, iron tools, and salt. The empire collapsed in the late 1800's after it was invaded by African, Arab, and Portuguese slave traders.

During the early 1900's, large numbers of Luba-Kasai began to move from rural to urban areas and to adopt numerous aspects of Western culture. Many others took jobs in copper mines in the southern part of the country. During the early 1960's, the competition for jobs and for political influence led to outbreaks of violence in several cities between the Luba-Kasai and other ethnic groups. THOMAS Q. REEFE

LUBBOCK, *LUHB uhk*, Tex. (pop. 173,979; met. area pop. 211,651), is the world's leading manufacturer of cottonseed products. The city ranks as a major United States cotton market and as an industrial center of Texas. It is a trade and transportation center of the High Plains, a thriving, irrigated farm region of northwest Texas. Lubbock is often called the *Hub of the High Plains.* For location, see TEXAS (political map).

Description. Lubbock, the county seat of Lubbock County, covers about 92 square miles (238 square kilometers). The Lubbock metropolitan area occupies about 901 square miles (2,334 square kilometers).

Cotton markets in Lubbock handle about 1 billion pounds (450 million kilograms) of cotton annually. The city also has about 260 manufacturing plants. Lubbock produces about $1\frac{1}{2}$ billion pounds (680 million kilograms) of cottonseed oil yearly. Other industries include meat packing and the manufacture of farm equipment and other nonelectrical machinery. Lubbock also ranks as an important cattle-feeding center. Two railroad freight lines and seven major highways serve the city. Lubbock International Airport lies outside Lubbock.

Lubbock is the home of Lubbock Christian College and Texas Tech University. The Texas Tech Museum in the city features an exhibit of historic ranch buildings. The Lubbock Symphony Orchestra performs in the Lubbock Memorial Civic Center.

History. Comanche Indians lived in what is now the Lubbock area when whites first arrived there. During the 1880's, settlers established cattle ranches in the area. In 1890, land developers founded two villages near what is now Lubbock. The next year, the developers moved the buildings of both villages to a single site where two small rivers meet. They named the resulting town Lubbock in honor of Lieutenant Colonel Thomas S. Lubbock of the Confederate Army. Lubbock was incorporated in 1909.

During the 1920's, landowners in the area converted many ranches to cotton farms. As a result, Lubbock became a center of cotton marketing. After Texas Tech University opened in 1925, the city became an educational center. The 1950's brought rapid industrial growth to the area.

In 1970, a tornado struck Lubbock and killed 26 people. By the mid-1970's, most of the damaged buildings in the city had been repaired or replaced. In the mid-1970's, a ruined area of downtown Lubbock became the site of an urban renewal project called the Lubbock Memorial Civic Center. The project included an amphitheater, a convention hall, and an exhibition hall. Lubbock has a council-manager form of government. R. M. SANDERS

LÜBECK, *LOO behk* (pop. 224,790), is a shipping and manufacturing center in West Germany. It lies on the Trave River, near the Baltic Sea (see GERMANY [political map]). A natural harbor made the city an important trading point almost from the time it was founded in the mid-1100's. Lübeck became a free city in the early 1200's (see FREE CITY).

During the Middle Ages, Lübeck was the recognized leader of a union of German cities known as the Hanseatic League. The league dissolved when new trade routes were opened to America, and Lübeck lost much of its importance. JAMES K. POLLOCK

See also HANSEATIC LEAGUE.

LUBITSCH, *LOO bihch,* **ERNST** (1892-1947), a German-born film director and producer, became famous for his comedies and farces. His films are characterized

445

by clever filming devices and an ironic insight into human nature—especially the battle between the sexes.

Lubitsch was born in Berlin. He gained fame as the director of *Gypsy Blood* (1918), *Passion* (1919), and other historical spectacles. He arrived in Hollywood in 1923 and surprised everyone by turning to sophisticated light comedy which became known for "the Lubitsch touch." His major comedies include *Trouble in Paradise* (1932) and *Ninotchka* (1939), starring Greta Garbo. Lubitsch also directed serious films and musicals. His early musicals *The Love Parade* (1929) and *The Smiling Lieutenant* (1931) contributed to the technical development of sound films. RICHARD GRIFFITH

LUBRICANT is a substance that reduces friction between moving parts of a machine or other device. Lubricants form a thin film between the parts and prevent them from rubbing against each other. Many lubricants also help to cool the parts and to protect them from rust and wear. There are four types of lubricants: (1) oils, (2) greases, (3) solids, and (4) gases.

Oils. Most lubricating oils are refined from crude petroleum. These mineral oils include oils for automobile engines, gear lubricants, and transmission fluids. Some lubricating oils come from organic materials other than petroleum. Esters, silicones, polyglycols, and similar synthetic oils are made to perform under higher or lower temperatures, or to last longer, than mineral oils.

Various chemicals are added to most lubricating oils to improve their performance. For example, *viscosity index improvers* are often included in oils used in automobile engines and other devices that operate over a wide range of temperatures. Viscosity is the property of a fluid that causes it to resist flowing. Variations in temperature affect an oil's viscosity and therefore its ability to reduce friction. Viscosity index improvers help to keep an oil's viscosity constant despite changes in temperature. See VISCOSITY.

Greases. A lubricating grease is a solid or semifluid mixture of a lubricating oil and a thickening agent. Thickening agents used in greases include clay and silica, and the fatty acid soaps of aluminum, calcium, lithium, and sodium. Many greases also include a number of additives. Lubricating greases remain on surfaces where lubricating oils would drain away. They also act as a seal against dirt and moisture. Greases are used primarily to lubricate bearings.

Solids. Solid lubricants include graphite, molybdenum disulfide, and talc. They are used when the temperature, pressure, or speed of machinery is too high for oils or greases to be effective.

Gases. Air, steam, and other gases provide lubrication for a number of precision scientific instruments, including gyroscopes and ultracentrifuges. They are also used in such industrial machinery as gas turbines and compressors. GEOFFREY E. DOLBEAR

See also FRICTION; GRAPHITE; OIL; SILICONE.

LUCAS, GEORGE (1944-), is an American motion-picture producer, director, and writer. He wrote and directed the science-fiction fantasy *Star Wars* (1977), one of the most popular films in movie history. The film became an international success because of its creative special effects, appealing characters, and suspenseful story of good versus evil. Lucas produced two

later films in the *Star Wars* series, *The Empire Strikes Back* (1980) and *Return of the Jedi* (1983).

Lucas produced the popular movies *Raiders of the Lost Ark* (1981) and *Indiana Jones and the Temple of Doom* (1984). Both were directed by his friend Steven Spielberg. The films reflect the love both men feel for the action-packed adventure movies of their youth.

Lucas was born in Modesto, Calif. He won a national student film competition in 1967 for his short film *Electronic Labyrinth: THX 1138-4EB*. He was coauthor of a feature-length version of the work, *THX 1138* (1971). Lucas also served as coauthor and director of *American Graffiti* (1973). This film about teen-agers in the early 1960's reflects his own high school years and his love for cars. CHARLES CHAMPLIN

LUCE, *loos,* **CLARE BOOTHE** (1903-), became famous for her activities in American politics and government. She was also a noted playwright. Luce served in the U.S. House of Representatives from 1943 to 1947 as a Republican from Connecticut. She served as U.S. ambassador to Italy from 1953 to 1956. Luce became one of the first women to represent the United States in a major diplomatic post. She was appointed ambassador to Brazil in 1959, but resigned the post a few days after winning Senate approval because several senators questioned her ability.

Luce's plays are noted for their sharp dialogue and sarcastic characterizations. Her most successful play, *The Women* (1936), satirizes rich, idle American women. Luce's other plays include *Abide with Me* (1935), *Kiss the Boys Good-bye* (1938), and *Margin for Error* (1939).

Clare Boothe was born in New York City. She worked as a magazine editor and journalist from 1929 to 1934. In 1935, she married Henry R. Luce, the founder of *Time* and *Life* magazines. After converting to Roman Catholicism in 1946, she wrote several articles on religious subjects. JOHN B. VICKERY

United Press Int.   Time Inc.

Clare Boothe Luce   **Henry R. Luce**

LUCE, *loos,* **HENRY ROBINSON** (1898-1967), was a noted American publisher and editor. *Time*, his weekly news magazine, added new words and introduced writing twists to the American language. *Life*, a pictorial magazine begun by Luce, had many imitators.

Luce and his friend Briton Hadden founded *Time* magazine in 1923, and in 1930 Luce started *Fortune*, a periodical for business people. His radio program *March of Time* began in 1931, and a series of the same name began as newsreels in 1935. Both were abandoned in 1953. Luce purchased *Architectural Forum* in 1932 and began publishing *Life* as a weekly in 1936. He launched another periodical, *House and Home*, in 1952. In 1964, the publishing rights to *Architectural Forum* were given away and *House and Home* was sold. *Life* ceased publication in 1972, but resumed in 1978 as a monthly. The first issue of Luce's magazine *Sports Illustrated* appeared in 1954.

Luce was born in Tengchow (now Penglai), China. His parents were Presbyterian missionaries. Luce was graduated from Yale University. His wife, Clare Boothe Luce, gained fame as a politician, diplomat, and playwright.   KENNETH N. STEWART

See also LUCE, CLARE BOOTHE.

Additional Resources

ELSON, R. T. *Time, Inc.: The Intimate History of a Publishing Enterprise* 2 vols. Atheneum, 1968-1973.
KOBLER, JOHN. *Luce: His Time, Life, and Fortune.* Doubleday, 1968.
SWANBERG, W. A. *Luce and His Empire.* Scribner, 1973.

LUCERNE, *loo SURN* (pop. 63,700; met. area pop. 156,500), is a tourist center and historic city in central Switzerland. The German name of the city is *Luzern.* Lucerne lies on the western shore of the Lake of Lucerne and on the banks of the Reuss River. For location, see SWITZERLAND (map).

Lucerne is the capital of the *canton* (state) of Lucerne. The city's location along the lake and near magnificent mountains attracts thousands of visitors annually. Its other attractions include medieval houses, the covered Chapel Bridge, an annual music festival, and the Swiss Transport Museum and other museums. The famous *Lion of Lucerne* monument in the city honors Swiss soldiers who were killed while serving the king of France during the French Revolution.

Lucerne dates from the early 700's. In 1332, it became the first town to enter into an alliance with the peasants of central Switzerland. This action was an important step in the unification of Switzerland.   HEINZ K. MEIER

LUCERNE. See ALFALFA.

LUCERNE, LAKE OF. See LAKE OF LUCERNE.

LUCIFER, *LOO suh fuhr*, is a name for the Devil. This usage comes from the Bible sentence, "How art thou fallen from heaven, O Lucifer, son of the morning!" (Is. 14: 12). Early Bible interpreters thought the verse referred to the archangel who was hurled from heaven for his wickedness and revolt against God. Later translators substituted *daystar* for *Lucifer.* They believed the verse referred to a king of Babylon. *Lucifer* in Latin means *light-bearing.* In John Milton's *Paradise Lost*, Lucifer represents the Devil. The word may also mean the planet Venus as the morning star.

LUCKNOW (pop. 895,947; met. area pop. 1,060,000) is a city in north-central India. It serves as the capital of the state of Uttar Pradesh. For location, see INDIA (political map).

Lucknow stands along the Gomati River. The city's minarets and gilded cupolas present a striking appearance from a distance. An old commercial district lies in the northwest part of Lucknow. The old district has many silversmith shops and the stores of other handicraft workers. Modern offices and shops lie southeast of the old commercial district. Lucknow's products include silver, gold, and brass wares; embroidery; and cotton fabrics. Mangoes and melons are grown in rural areas that surround the city.

Muslims built a fort on the site of what is now Luck-

now during the 1200's. The Lucknow area became part of the British Empire in 1856. In 1857, during the Sepoy Rebellion, Indian soldiers seized Lucknow. But British forces recaptured the city in 1858 (see SEPOY REBELLION). In 1947, Lucknow and the rest of India gained independence from Britain.   P. P. KARAN

LUCRETIUS, *loo KREE shih uhs* or *loo KREE shuhs* (99?-55? B.C.), was a Roman poet and philosopher. His only surviving work is a philosophical and scientific poem called *De rerum natura* (*On the Nature of Things*). Lucretius wrote the poem to free humanity from religious superstition and the fear of death. The poem's emotional power and vivid language help to make it a masterpiece of Latin literature.

Lucretius was inspired by the teachings of the Greek philosopher Epicurus in writing *De rerum natura.* The poem reflects the Epicurean ideals of a tranquil mind and freedom from irrational fear. It argues that people need not fear a life after death, because the soul—like everything else—is a cluster of atoms and therefore disperses after death. The poem also argues that people should not fear the gods, because the gods remain aloof from human affairs. The poem gives rational explanations for earthquakes, thunder, and other phenomena that might be feared as supernatural events.

Lucretius' full name was Titus Lucretius Carus. According to one story, Lucretius went mad after taking a love potion. He wrote poetry during brief periods of sanity, and eventually killed himself. Scholars cannot verify this story, but Lucretius' poem does bitterly denounce the passions of love.   W. W. BARTLEY III

See also ATOMISM; EPICURUS.

LUDDITES. See INDUSTRIAL REVOLUTION (The Working Class); RIOT (Causes of Riots).

LUDENDORFF, *LOO duhn dawrf*, **ERICH FRIEDRICH WILHELM,** *AY rihkh FREE drihkh VIHL hehlm* (1865-1937), a German general, served as chief of staff to Paul von Hindenburg during World War I. Ludendorff's help in organization and planning resulted, historians believe, in many victories for Germany.

During World War I, Ludendorff rose from the rank of chief quartermaster of the Second Army to chief of staff of the entire German Army. After the collapse of the German Army in 1918, Ludendorff fled to Sweden. He returned in 1919 to enter politics, and aligned himself with the Nazis.

He took part in the unsuccessful *Beer Hall Putsch* (revolution), organized by Adolf Hitler, in Munich in 1923. Ludendorff went to trial along with Hitler, but was freed because of his war record. Later, he broke with Hitler. He became a believer in a pagan religion which worshiped the old German god Wotan. Ludendorff was born near Posen, Germany (now Poznań, Poland). He received a military education. GABRIEL A. ALMOND

LUDINGTON, SYBIL (1761-1839), was a heroine of the Revolutionary War in America (1775-1783). At the age of 16, she made a courageous ride on horseback to assemble American troops for a fight against the British at Danbury, Conn.

Sybil Ludington was born and raised in Putnam County, N.Y. Her father, Colonel Henry Ludington, commanded a military regiment there. On April 26, 1777, a messenger brought news that the British were attacking nearby Danbury, where the local patriots stored their military supplies. The messenger had arrived exhausted, and so Sybil volunteered to round up her father's regiment. She rode through the night and covered nearly 40 miles (64 kilometers). The British looted and burned Danbury. However, they later suffered about 200 casualties in a battle that included the troops Sybil had gathered.   WILLIAM M. FOWLER, JR.

LUFFA. See GOURD.

LUFTWAFFE, *LUFT* VAHF *uh*, has been the name of the German Air Force since 1935. The word means *air weapon* or *air arm*. Reich Marshal Hermann Goering commanded the Luftwaffe during World War II. He succeeded in making it a separate force with a status equal to that of the German army and navy. The Luftwaffe effectively supported German ground forces in Poland, Norway, France, Crete, and Russia. But it failed to win the critical Battle of Britain. See also AIR FORCE (Famous Air Battles); GOERING, HERMANN WILHELM.   CHARLES B. MACDONALD

LUGWORM, or LUGBAIT. See LOBWORM.

LUISETTI, HANK (1916-   ), an American basketball player, revolutionized the game with his one-handed push shot. Previously, players had used a two-handed set shot. Luisetti learned the new shot from Tommy DeNike, his high school basketball coach, and perfected it while playing at Stanford University. In 1936, Luisetti introduced the shot to Eastern fans in a famous Stanford victory that ended a 43-game winning streak of Long Island University. His shot increased the scoring and action in basketball, and countless players adopted it.

Angelo Enrico Luisetti was born in San Francisco. At Stanford, the 6-foot 2-inch (188-centimeter) forward broke the national college four-year scoring record with 1,596 points. In 1938, he scored 50 points against Duquesne University. He was the first basketball player to score that many points in one game.   NICK CURRAN

LUKE, SAINT, is generally considered the author of the third Gospel of the New Testament and its continuation, the Acts of the Apostles, in the Bible. These books describe a number of the events that took place in the lifetime of Jesus Christ, Peter, Paul, and Luke himself.

According to tradition, Luke was the "beloved physician" mentioned by Paul. Scholars believe Luke accompanied Paul on two of his missionary journeys, and that he kept a diary of their travels. Luke was already a believer in Christ when he met Paul. He joined Paul at Troas and went with him to Macedonia. From that time on, Luke was Paul's companion. Luke's knowledge of medicine may have been helpful to him.

Luke was probably born in Antioch, in ancient Syria (now in Turkey), of a non-Jewish family. He received a good education, studying great books as well as medicine.

See also ACTS OF THE APOSTLES; GOSPELS.

LUKS, GEORGE BENJAMIN (1866-1933), was an American painter and illustrator. He became a member of the group of realistic painters called *The Eight* (later called the *Ashcan School).* Luks' lusty paintings of life in the streets reflect the spontaneous, honest approach to painting that characterizes the spirit of

The Eight. For more information on the group, see HENRI, ROBERT.

Luks was born in Williamsport, Pa. He studied painting in Philadelphia and Europe, and began his career as a newspaper illustrator and cartoonist in Philadelphia. From 1896 to 1902, he drew Sunday newspaper comics for *The* (New York) *World*. After 1902, he turned to painting chiefly in New York City. Luks soon joined The Eight, and was one of the original members who exhibited together in 1908.   E. MAURICE BLOCH

LULLY, *loo LEE,* **JEAN BAPTISTE,** *zhahn bah TEEST* (1632-1687), an Italian-born composer, wrote the first significant French operas. Lully's emphasis on a sense of motion in his music, whether slow or lively, was typical of the baroque style (see BAROQUE). He established a slow-fast-slow tempo sequence for the musical form called *French overture*. He thus set up a contrast with the fast-slow-fast pattern of the *Italian overture*. The melodies of Lully's *arias* (solos) are filled with emotion.

Lully was born in Florence and was brought to France as a child. He became a clever and unscrupulous courtier in the court of Louis XIV. In his operas, Lully adapted ancient myths to heighten the glory of the king, who became his patron. Lully's best-known operas include *Cadmus and Hermione* (1673), *Amadis de Gaule* (1684), *Roland* (1685), and *Armide et Renaud* (1686). He also composed music for many ballets. Lully influenced the works of Jean Philippe Rameau in France and of Johann Sebastian Bach and George Frideric Handel in Germany.   JAMES SYKES

LUMBEE INDIANS are the largest Indian tribe in the United States east of the Mississippi River. More than 40,000 Lumbee live in and near Robeson County in southeastern North Carolina.

Most historians agree that the Lumbee are a mixture of peoples, but scholars have several theories about their exact origin. According to one theory, the Lumbee are descendants of the Hatteras tribe and of English colonists who settled on Roanoke Island in 1587. This island lies off the coast of North Carolina. The settlement there came to be called the *Lost Colony* because it disappeared mysteriously, but the people may simply have joined the Indians. Many Lumbee have the same last names as the missing colonists (see LOST COLONY). Other theories trace the Lumbee ancestry to the Cherokee, the Tuscarora, or an eastern band of the Sioux.

During the 1800's, the Lumbee were called the *Croatan*. Early records tell that they looked like Indians but lived like white settlers. The federal government classified them as different from the Indians on reservations. In the 1880's, North Carolina gave the Croatan separate legal status, including the right to have their own schools. They opened their first school, the Croatan Normal School, in Pembroke, N.C., in 1887. This school is now Pembroke State University.

In 1953, the North Carolina legislature voted that the Indians in and near Robeson County be known as the Lumbee Indians. The name comes from the Lumber River, formerly called the Lumbee, which flows through the county. In 1956, Congress declared the Lumbee a tribe but did not make the people eligible for government Indian benefits.

Today, the Lumbee are the nation's largest group of Indians without a reservation. Many of them farm the land for a living.   ADOLPH L. DIAL

LUMBER includes boards and larger pieces of wood that have been sawed from logs. Almost every house uses at least some lumber in its construction. Lumber furnishes material for flooring, siding, woodwork, doors, and other building parts. Nearly three-fourths of the lumber in the United States is used by the construction industry. The rest goes from sawmills to factories that make boxes, crates, furniture, farm tools, toys, railroad cars, boats, and hundreds of other products.

Every time a piece of wood is cut at a sawmill, sawdust and small pieces of wood fall to the floor. These leftover bits of wood can be made into many valuable products. Often, mills send both logs and wood scraps through a chipper. Pulp mills treat the chips with chemicals that change them into wood pulp. Manufacturers use pulp to make paper, plastics, rayon, and other products. Sawdust is used for fuel, insulation, and packing. Small pieces of wood ground into *wood flour* can be formed into bowling balls. For a description of the products obtained from trees, see FOREST PRODUCTS.

The giant lumber industry employs thousands of persons to cut down trees, transport logs to mills, saw logs into boards, and then sell the boards. The United States uses almost 45 billion board feet (106 million cubic meters) of lumber every year, more than any other country. Russia and the United States lead the world in lumber production. Other important lumber-producing countries include Brazil, Canada, China, Finland, France, Japan, Sweden, and West Germany.

Kinds of Lumber

Lumber experts divide lumber into two main classes: *softwood* and *hardwood*. These classes are not based on the softness or hardness of the wood. They refer to the kind of tree from which the lumber came. Some softwood lumber is harder to cut or saw through than most hardwood. Also, lumber from certain hardwood trees is softer than lumber from most softwoods.

Lumber is also classed by its condition. *Rough lumber* has straight sides and edges, but is rough and splintery. *Dressed lumber* comes in smooth, evenly cut boards.

Worked lumber is dressed lumber that has a design cut in it for decoration or to make boards fit together.

Softwood Lumber comes from trees called *conifers*. The word refers to the cones in which the seeds of most softwood trees develop (see CONE-BEARING PLANT). Common conifers include pines and firs. These trees have thin, waxy, needle-shaped or scale-like leaves. They are also called *evergreens*. Pines, Douglas fir, Western true firs, hemlock, and redwood produce most softwood lumber. Their wood is used for doors, frames, panels, other building materials, and boxes.

Softwood lumber can be classified according to its use. Carpenters use *yard lumber* to build houses. *Structural lumber* can stand heavy strain. It is used for posts, planks, joists, and beams. Sawmills usually sell *factory and shop lumber* directly to factories for making boxes, toys, and other products.

Hardwood Lumber is sawed from broad-leaved trees. These trees are usually *deciduous*, which means they lose their leaves in autumn (see DECIDUOUS TREE). Hardwoods used for lumber include oak, maple, yellow poplar, sweet gum, birch, tupelo, cottonwood, aspen, and beech. Tropical hardwoods, such as mahogany, ebony, teak, and rosewood, are used in fine furniture. Hardwoods are also used for paneling, flooring, baseball bats, tool handles, and many other items.

Much hardwood lumber is sawed into small pieces called *hardwood dimension parts*. This cuts out defects and provides greater usefulness. Manufacturers use it to make chair arms, piano legs, and other furniture parts. When furniture or tool factories want plain blocks of hardwood, they order *rough hardwood dimension*. If they need trimmed, molded, or sanded wood, they order *surfaced hardwood dimension*. If manufacturers want to buy parts of a chair, such as legs, arms, or seats, that are ready to be assembled, they order *finished market products*.

From Forest to Sawmill

Since the early days of colonial life in North America, lumbering has been an important and exciting industry. Forests echoed with the long-drawn warning cry of "Timbe..e..err" as great trees came crashing to earth. *Lumberjacks*, who cut down trees and delivered logs to the mills, became famous as strong, hearty, courageous workers. Many legends sprang up about their exploits as they cleared forests and took logs to the mill by ox team, by raft, or by guiding them down rushing streams after spring thaws. Some of the stories about early loggers are true. Others, such as the tales of the legendary giant Paul Bunyan, are humorous exaggerations (see BUNYAN, PAUL).

The Life of a Logger. Lumberjacks must have strength, courage, and be highly skilled in their work. Large-scale lumbering operations require special mechanical equipment and technical knowledge.

The life that loggers lead today differs greatly from their life before the 1900's. Years ago, loggers lived in large bunkhouses in logging camps where there were few comforts. They spent most of their time either working or sleeping. Today, most loggers live in their own homes. They drive to work in the morning just as people with other jobs do. Some loggers ride to where the trees are being cut in company trucks or buses. They live in a logging camp only if the logging site lies in a hard-to-reach place, such as in a rugged mountain area. Only a few logging camps still exist in the United States today. But modernized camps are still being used in the forests of Canada. The modern camp, unlike the camp of long ago, has comfortable facilities for eating, sleeping, and recreation. Some camps have private houses for families.

Cutting Down Trees. Before the loggers go into the woods, a *forester* decides which trees they should cut.

LUMBER TERMS

Board Foot is a piece of lumber 1 foot (30 centimeters) long, 1 foot wide, and 1 inch (2.5 centimeters) thick. It equals 0.083 cubic foot (0.0024 cubic meter).

Flooring is lumber used in floors. It is usually hardwood, 1 inch (2.5 centimeters) thick and 2 to 4 inches (5 to 10 centimeters) wide.

Landing is a central place in the forest where logs are brought before being taken to a sawmill.

Log Rule is a table that shows about how much lumber can be sawed from logs of different sizes.

Lumberjack, or Logger, is a worker who cuts down trees, saws them into logs, and brings them to the mill.

Millwork is material made of finished wood in millwork plants or planing mills. It includes doors, blinds, frames, cornices, columns, mantels, and panelwork.

Paneling is lumber made into panels, especially for the insides of buildings.

Plank is a piece of lumber 2 to 4 inches (5 to 10 centimeters) thick and 4 or more inches wide.

Plywood is a panel made of thin layers of wood glued together under heavy pressure.

Sawmill is a plant that saws logs into lumber.

Sawtimber means trees large enough to be cut for lumber.

Siding is lumber used to cover the outsides of buildings.

Skid Road is a road or trail leading from a cutting area to the skidway or landing.

Skidding means hauling or dragging logs from the cutting area to the landing.

Slabs are the outside pieces of a log removed in sawing lumber.

Stumpage is timber that stands uncut in a forest.

The forester is a scientist trained in growing crops of trees so that they will yield the greatest possible amount of lumber. He or she also knows how to protect forests from fire, insects, disease, and grazing animals.

Loggers called *fallers* come to work carrying their own power saws. They *fell*, or cut down, trees that the forester has marked for cutting. The power saw that the fallers use may weigh as much as 40 pounds (18 kilograms). With its small gasoline motor and whirling chain saw, it can slice through a tree trunk in a few seconds.

In felling a tree, the faller first makes an *undercut*. A wedge-shaped piece is cut out of the tree trunk with an ax or power saw. The faller makes the undercut on the side of the tree that is to fall toward the ground. The cut is made close to the ground to avoid wasting valuable wood by leaving a high stump. After the saw has cut through the tree trunk, the undercut makes the tree lose its balance and fall toward that side. Expert fallers can drop a tree exactly where they want it. They can avoid striking other trees, or hitting stumps that might break or damage the trunk of the falling tree.

Some tree trunks may measure 200 feet (61 meters) or more in length. Workers called *buckers* cut the trunks into shorter lengths, so that they can take them out of the forest more easily. Buckers use axes or power saws to lop off the limbs. Then they saw the trunks into logs from 8 to 40 feet (2.4 to 12 meters) long.

Since the mid-1900's, large modern machines have simplified the work of loggers. For example, hydraulic *tree shears* quickly cut through a tree like giant scissors. They are built into tractors that move from tree to tree (see FORESTRY [picture: Harvesting and Planting Trees Mechanically]). Other machines do more than one job. Some *tree harvesters* fell a tree, remove its branches, cut it into logs, and sort the logs in bunches.

Transporting Logs from the woods to the sawmill is the second step in logging. It consists of two operations. First, the loggers *skid* (drag or haul) the logs to the *landing* (a central place in the woods). Then they transport the logs from the landing to the sawmill.

Workers use horses, tractors, or long cables called *draglines* to skid the logs to the landing. Usually, the logs are hauled over the ground. But sometimes workers transport them in special carriers. In the Northern Forest, for example, loggers use big sleds to carry logs over icy roads in winter.

A system called *high-lead* (pronounced *leed*) *logging* uses pulleys and steel cables to drag logs up steep slopes or to swing them across ravines. The pulleys and cables are supported by portable towers and are powered by giant diesel, steam, or electric winches. The cables pick up only one end of the log. The other end may drag along the ground. High-lead logging can bring logs to a landing as far away as 800 to 1,500 feet (240 to 457 meters). Other cable-logging systems can carry logs 2,500 feet (762 meters) or more. Such systems use cables called *skylines*. Skylines pick up the entire log instead of dragging one end over the ground. Logging with skylines does less damage to the forest floor than high-lead logging.

After skidding, the logs are piled at the landing until they can be moved to the mill. If the landing lies near a road, trucks carry the logs to the mill. If it is on a railroad line, flatcars transport the logs. If the landing is on the bank of a stream or river, workers use chains to bind the logs into rafts that float to the mill. Sometimes barges carry logs. Trucks transport the largest number of logs to sawmills.

From Sawmill to Lumberyard

The United States has about 30,000 sawmills. Most lumber comes from small sawmills, each of which produces less than 10 million board feet (24,000 cubic meters) of lumber a year. Some mills are so small that the *headrig*, or sawing machinery, can be loaded on a truck trailer and hauled into the woods.

Many large softwood mills stand beside a pool of water. This pool is the *log pond*, in which the logs are kept until they go into the mill. The water protects them from insects, fungi, stain, and fire. Large trucks carrying logs to the mill dump their loads into the log pond. *Boom men* wearing spiked boots walk about on the wet logs in the pond. They use long poles to sort the logs. They make sure that all the logs of one kind or size go into the mill together. A growing number of softwood mills store their logs on dry land and handle them with modern loading devices. Hardwood mills also store their logs on dry land because heavy hardwood logs may sink in water.

Sawing Logs. A moving conveyor chain carries the logs up a wooden chute into the mill. Jets of water forced through overhead pipes give the logs a stinging bath. By the time the logs enter the mill, no sand, dirt, or small bits of metal remain on them that might dull the sharp saw blade.

In many mills, a *log debarker* removes the bark before the log reaches the first saw, called a *headsaw*. One kind of debarker consists of metal bars or knives that rub off or chip off the bark. Another type of debarker tears off the bark by the force of water shot onto the log under great pressure.

As a log enters the sawmill, machinery moves it onto a platform called a *carriage*. The carriage looks somewhat like a small railroad flatcar. It carries the logs into the teeth of the headsaw. The saw makes a screaming sound as it tears into the wood. Each time the carriage goes past the saw, the saw slices off a board until the log has become a pile of boards.

Moving belts then carry the newly made boards, called *green lumber*, to the *edger*, a set of smaller saws. These saws trim the rough edges from each board and make the sides straight and even. Next, the edged boards go to the *trimmer*. This set of saws makes the ends of the boards square, and cuts the boards to the exact lengths ordered by lumber dealers. The trimmer also cuts off weak or bad spots.

Gang saws are used in most lumber mills in Europe and in some mills in the United States. In these mills, after the outer slabs of the logs are removed, the edged log moves into a set of several straight-bladed saws. These saws are spaced to cut the "squared-up" log into boards of the desired thickness in one operation.

Grading Lumber. The green boards, now called *rough lumber*, ride slowly on the *green chain*, a moving belt. Workers called *graders* walk along the green chain, examining each board carefully and deciding its grade. They sort the boards according to size, quality, and kind of wood. Each grader carries two long sticks. One stick has a hook, which the grader uses to flip boards over. The other stick has a crayon on the end, with which the grader marks the grade on each board.

There are eight grades used by the National Hardwood Lumber Association to classify hardwood. The grades are, from highest to lowest: (1) *firsts*, (2) *seconds*, (3) *selects*, (4) *No. 1 common*, (5) *No. 2 common*, (6) *sound wormy*, (7) *No. 3A common*, and (8) *No. 3B common*.

The grades of hardwood factory lumber and rough hardwood dimension parts are based on the proportion of the wood that can be used to manufacture various products. If a large proportion can be used, the lumber receives a high grade. Hardwood finished market products, such as flooring and stair treads, are graded for their particular use. A high-grade piece of such lumber goes through little or no manufacturing.

Softwood-lumber associations use various grades for their lumber. Yard-lumber grades include *selects*, or *finish*, in grades A (highest quality) through D; *common boards*, numbered 1 through 5; and *common dimensions*, numbered 1 through 4. The lower numbers designate lumber of higher quality. Softwood factory lumber and shop lumber are graded for appearance. Softwood structural lumber is graded according to the load it can carry when used as beams, frames, joists, or planks.

Seasoning Lumber means removing excess moisture from the wood. More than half the weight of green lumber may come from moisture in the wood. After seasoning, less than a tenth of the weight of the lumber may come from moisture. Mills also ship lumber without seasoning. But for most uses the moisture must be removed so the wood will not warp. In the process, the wood shrinks in size.

Mills sometimes season lumber by *air drying*. Workers

Leading Lumber-Producing States and Provinces

British Columbia	11,954,000,000 bd. ft. (28,207,900 m³)
Oregon	5,859,000,000 bd. ft. (13,825,500 m³)
California	4,085,000,000 bd. ft. (9,639,400 m³)
Quebec	3,415,000,000 bd. ft. (8,058,400 m³)
Washington	3,171,000,000 bd. ft. (7,482,600 m³)

Sources: U.S. Bureau of the Census; Statistics Canada. Figures are for 1980.

Leading Lumber-Producing Countries

Russia	41,615,500,000 bd. ft. (98,200,000 m³)
United States	29,716,900,000 bd. ft. (70,123,000 m³)
Canada	16,508,900,000 bd. ft. (38,956,000 m³)
Japan	15,646,000,000 bd. ft. (36,920,000 m³)
China	7,395,900,000 bd. ft. (17,452,000 m³)

Source: FAO. Figures are for 1981.

How a Sawmill Saws Large Logs into Lumber

A Circular Saw cuts large logs into shorter lengths in a process called *bucking*. Before the logs reach the saw, a mechanical debarker strips them of their bark.

A Headsaw slices each log into boards or other pieces of lumber. The headsaw shown in the diagram is a *band saw*, an endless steel belt that runs on two pulleys. The teeth of the saw are on an edge of the belt.

A Resaw cuts lumber to its proper width and thickness. The lumber then goes through *side edgers*. These devices remove the rough edges and make the sides straight and even.

A Trimmer Saw cuts lumber to standard lengths and makes the ends square. Next, workers called *graders* sort the lumber according to size, quality, and kind of wood. The lumber is then stacked outdoors to dry.

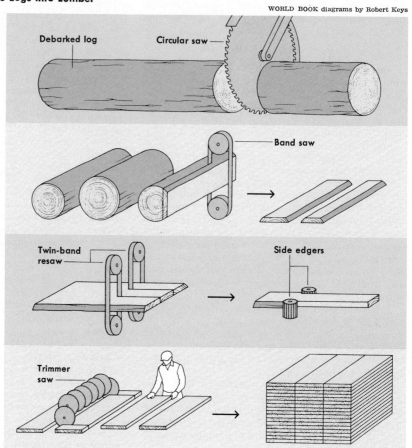

How a Sawmill Saws Small Logs into Lumber

A Chipper-Canter, *right,* saws small logs. This machine has rotating *heads* (knives) that chip wood from the top, bottom, and sides of logs. A set of circular saws cuts each log into rectangular pieces called *cants*. Devices called *splitters* then separate the cants.

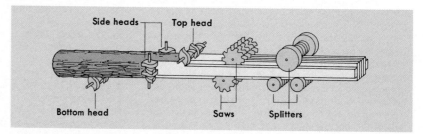

Patterns for Sawing Large and Small Logs

Log-Sawing Patterns vary, depending on the size of the log. Mills manufacture as much lumber as possible from each log. The diagram shows several patterns that may be used to saw large and small logs.

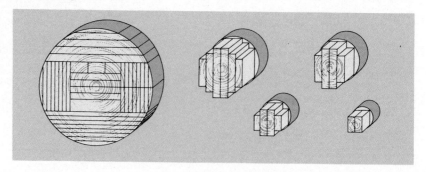

stack the wood outdoors to let the sun and wind dry it. A quicker way of seasoning lumber is to put green lumber in *dry kilns*, or special heated buildings in which instruments control the temperature and moisture of the air. The instruments tell how much moisture remains in the wood. Some mills use both drying methods.

Planing. A small amount of rough lumber is used in construction. It is shipped to lumber dealers throughout the United States or in other countries. But the rest of the lumber must pass through a *planing mill* before it goes to market. This mill may be near the sawmill or in another city. In a planing mill, lumber passes through machines that have sharp knife blades in them. These knives shave and smooth the rough boards. Lumber also receives further treatment to make it into dressed lumber or worked lumber.

Shipping. Most mills ship lumber to wholesale dealers in the United States. The wholesalers sell to retail lumberyards, to factories that make wooden articles, and to construction companies. From forest to mill to retailer, lumber may travel by truck, by rail, or by ship. Most long-distance hauling is by rail. But ships bring large amounts of lumber from the West through the Panama Canal to markets on the East Coast. Trucks make most of the short lumber-carrying trips in all parts of the country.

Buying Lumber

When selecting lumber, buyers should keep in mind the work they want it to do and the effect they wish to achieve. Lumber for decorative use should be chosen for its color, grain, knots, and texture. For construction purposes, strong and durable lumber should be used. Different kinds of wood are used for various types of construction. For example, Douglas fir and pine are used for home building. Oak and maple are popular for flooring, and redwood and red cedar make fine siding.

In the United States and Canada, the width and thickness of lumber are expressed in inches, and the length in feet. For example, a 2 by 4 by 12 board is 2 inches thick, 4 inches wide, and 12 feet long. Lumber is measured before it is seasoned and planed, and so the finished pieces are actually smaller than the *nominal* (named) size. Lumber with a 4-inch nominal thickness is actually only $3\frac{1}{2}$ inches thick.

Standard nominal sizes of lumber vary depending on the type of wood or piece. Mills cut hardwood lumber into a variety of widths and into lengths that can be divided evenly into 1-foot sections. Softwood structural lumber is cut into lengths that can be divided evenly into 2-foot sections. Its nominal widths range from 2 to 16 inches. The nominal thickness of any lumber classifies it as a *board*, a *dimension*, or a *timber*. Boards have a nominal thickness of less than 2 inches; dimensions range from 2 inches to, but not including, 5 inches; and timbers measure 5 or more inches thick.

Lumber prices generally refer to 1,000 board feet (2.4 cubic meters). Lumber priced at $200 for 1,000 board feet would sell at 20 cents per board foot.

History

For thousands of years, forests have contributed to human progress. Primitive people built homes out of branches or logs. They used wood as handles for their tools and weapons. Cross sections cut from logs served

A Mechanical Conveyor moves logs to a saw for cutting. The worker operates the conveyor from a booth above the mill floor. Television monitors provide different views of the operation.

as crude wheels for early carts. Logs fastened together formed rafts for transportation. Wood used as fuel for fires provided warmth and a means of cooking.

The pioneers of North America began to clear vast forests. Lumbering was the first industry in the colonies. The colonists traded with Europe, sending sassafras bark, white pine logs, clapboards, wainscoting, and naval stores (see NAVAL STORES).

Plenty of raw material was available in those days. Heavy, dark forests covered the eastern half of what is now the United States, and most of Canada. Trees had to be cut down to make way for roads and farms.

The first boards manufactured in the colonies were sawed over pits. One person stood beneath and another above the log, at the ends of a two-person saw. Sawmills probably first appeared in the United States in Maine and Virginia between 1608 and 1620. The earliest sawmills were crude, water-powered mills. Steam power replaced water power in the mills about 1830.

In the 1860's, the lumber industry centered in Pennsylvania. As settlers cut down forests and cleared land, the industry gradually moved toward the West and South. By 1870, it had moved into Michigan. By 1909,

A Sealed "Treating" Cylinder applies chemicals to lumber before it is shipped from the sawmill to wholesale dealers. The chemicals protect the lumber from fungi, insects, and moisture.

Standard Lumber Sizes in the United States and Canada

The thickness and width of lumber are expressed in inches. For example, a 1 x 2 board—called a "1 by 2"—is 1 inch thick and 2 inches wide. The actual size is smaller than the *nominal* (named) size because lumber is measured before being planed.

| **Boards** | | **Dimensions** | |
Nominal Size in inches	Actual Size in inches	Nominal Size in inches	Actual Size in inches
1 x 2	¾ x 1½	2 x 2	1½ x 1½
1 x 4	¾ x 3½	2 x 2½	1½ x 2
1 x 5	¾ x 4½	2 x 3	1½ x 2½
1 x 6	¾ x 5½	2 x 4	1½ x 3½
1 x 7	¾ x 6½	2 x 6	1½ x 5½
1 x 8	¾ x 7¼	2 x 10	1½ x 9¼
1 x 9	¾ x 8¼	2 x 12	1½ x 11¼
1 x 10	¾ x 9¼	2½ x 3	2 x 2½
1 x 11	¾ x 10¼	2½ x 4	2 x 3½
1 x 12	¾ x 11¼	2½ x 6	2 x 5½
1½ x 2	1¼ x 1½	2½ x 10	2 x 9¼
1½ x 4	1¼ x 3½	2½ x 12	2 x 11¼
1½ x 5	1¼ x 4½	3 x 3	2½ x 2½
1½ x 6	1¼ x 5½	3 x 4	2½ x 3½
1½ x 7	1¼ x 6½	3 x 6	2½ x 5½
1½ x 8	1¼ x 7¼	3 x 10	2½ x 9¼
1½ x 9	1¼ x 8¼	3 x 12	2½ x 11¼
1½ x 10	1¼ x 9¼	4 x 4	3½ x 3½
1½ x 11	1¼ x 10¼	4 x 6	3½ x 5½
1½ x 12	1¼ x 11¼	4 x 10	3½ x 9¼
		4 x 12	3½ x 11¼

Timbers (5 or more inches thick): The nominal size of any timber is ½ inch more than its actual size.

---

the pine forests of the South led in lumber production. Since 1920, the center of the lumber industry has been in the Pacific Northwest, with the South running a close second.

The lumber industry in Canada became important during the 1800's. Canada exported timber to Great Britain, and to the United States after the mid-1800's. Most of the lumber in the early 1800's came from eastern Canada. By 1900, British Columbia had become an important source. British Columbia is the chief source of Canada's lumber today.

Today, as in the past, houses, furniture, ships, and many other necessary items are made of wood. Some products of colonial times have been replaced, including Conestoga wagons and covered bridges. But wood is even more essential today than in colonial times. Scientists have developed many important new products made from wood, including cellophane, plastics, and rayon.   HARRY E. TROXELL

Related Articles in WORLD BOOK include:

Carpentry	Oregon	Washington (pic-
Colonial Life in	(pictures)	ture: Sawmills)
America (Lumbering	Plywood	Weyerhaeuser,
and Shipbuilding)	Rot	Frederick
Forest Products	Tree	Wood
House	Veneer	Woodworking

Outline

I. Kinds of Lumber
 A. Softwood Lumber   B. Hardwood Lumber
II. From Forest to Sawmill
 A. The Life of a Logger
 B. Cutting Down Trees   C. Transporting Logs
III. From Sawmill to Lumberyard
 A. Sawing Logs   B. Grading Lumber

IV. Buying Lumber
V. History

C. Seasoning Lumber   D. Planing   E. Shipping

Questions

What is the most important use of lumber?
How do fallers aim a tree?
What is high-lead logging?
What do boom men do?
Why must logs be washed before they are sawed?
How may lumber be seasoned?
How was lumber sawed in colonial times?
What is a *board foot*?
How does softwood differ from hardwood?
What two kinds of wood are the most important in home building?

LUMEN. See CANDELA; LIGHT (Measuring Light).

LUMIÈRE BROTHERS, *loo MYAIR,* were two French brothers who became noted scientists. Auguste (1862-1954) and Louis Jean (1864-1948) became known for their work in photochemistry. In 1895, they invented the *Cinematographe,* a combination motion-picture camera, printer, and projector. Some of the first motion pictures were produced and shown to audiences with this apparatus. In 1904, the Lumière brothers patented the *autochrome plate,* the first popular direct-color photographic process. The Lumière brothers were born in Besançon, France.   RICHARD RUDISILL

LUMINESCENCE, *LOO muh NEHS uhns,* is the emission of light by means other than heat. For example, fireflies give off a visible glow often called *cold light.* Certain substances glow at low temperatures when they are exposed to cathode rays or X rays. Thus, nonluminous radiation, such as X rays, can produce luminous radiation.

Luminescence that continues only as long as the radiation is applied is called *fluorescence.* In a fluorescent lamp, invisible ultraviolet rays bombard a phosphor coating to produce light.

Luminescence that lasts after the radiation is removed is called *phosphorescence.* Many minerals are phosphorescent. The light given off by fireflies and certain fungi is called *bioluminescence.*   CLARENCE E. BENNETT

See also BIOLUMINESCENCE; FLUORESCENCE; PHOSPHORESCENCE.

LUMPFISH, also called *lumpsucker,* is a fish that lives near the shore in the cold ocean waters of the north. Its body and head are thick and short. Its back is arched. The lumpfish has a sucking disk that enables it to cling to rocks. It has wartlike *tubercles* (lumps) instead of

John G. Shedd Aquarium
The Bulky Shape of the Lumpfish Gives It Its Name.

scales. Lumpfishes have no commercial use. In Great Britain, they are also known as *cockpaddles*.

Scientific Classification. The lumpfish is in the lumpsucker family, Cyclopteridae. The North Atlantic lumpfish is genus *Cyclopterus*, species *C. lumpus*. The lumpfish in Puget Sound is *Lethotremus vinolentus*. LEONARD P. SCHULTZ

LUMPY JAW. See ACTINOMYCOSIS.

LUMUMBA, PATRICE. See ZAIRE (History).

LUNA. See SPACE TRAVEL (Space Probes).

LUNA, *LOO nuh*, was the goddess of the moon in Roman mythology. She closely resembled Selene, the Greek moon goddess. The Romans associated Luna with recurrent diseases. Many people believed that the goddess would drive people insane if they offended her. The word *lunatic*, which means *moonstruck* in Latin, comes from her name. See also MONDAY; SELENE.

LUNAR DAY. See MOON (The Orbit of the Moon).

LUNAR ECLIPSE. See ECLIPSE (with picture); MOON (Eclipses).

LUNAR MODULE. See SPACE TRAVEL (pictures).

LUNAR MONTH. See CALENDAR.

LUNAR ROVER. See MOON (picture); SPACE TRAVEL (Exploring the Moon; picture).

LUNCH, SCHOOL. See SCHOOL LUNCH.

LUNDA, *LOON duh* or *LOON dah*, are a people who live in Zaire, Angola, and Zambia. They ruled several central African kingdoms from the 1600's to the 1800's.

Most Lunda live in small rural villages and farm the land for a living. They grow a root crop called cassava and several grains, including corn, millet, and sorghum. They also fish and sell their catch to towns in the rich copper-mining areas of Zaire and Zambia. Since about 1960, large numbers of Lunda have moved from rural areas to towns and cities. The people speak a language that belongs to the Bantu group of African languages (see BANTU). Many Lunda are Christians.

During the early 1600's, the Lunda formed a powerful kingdom under a series of rulers called the *mwaant yaar* (king). The Lunda kingdom became one of central Africa's largest empires. It covered large parts of what are now Zaire, Angola, and Zambia. During the 1700's, several groups broke away and established their own kingdoms. One of these kingdoms—Kazembe in northeastern Zambia—became a major center of commerce in the 1800's. Kazembe carried on long-distance trade with people on the east and west coasts of Africa.

During the 1900's, the Lunda played a major role in African political developments. The Lunda in Zambia helped drive out the nation's British colonial rulers in 1964. The Lunda in Zaire's Katanga Province (now the Shaba Region) participated in a movement to make the province independent. The independence struggle resulted in a series of armed revolts during the 1960's and 1970's. Also during the 1970's, the Lunda took part in a civil war in Angola between rival groups that wanted to rule the country. ROBERT H. BATES

LUNDY, BENJAMIN (1789-1839), an American abolitionist and editor, prepared the way for the national antislavery movement. In 1815, Lundy organized the Abolitionist Union Humane Society, in St. Clairsville, Ohio. He organized other antislavery groups, and published *The Genius of Universal Emancipation*, the *National Enquirer*, and other periodicals. Lundy lectured and traveled widely, seeking places for free blacks. He influenced John Quincy Adams' efforts to prevent the expansion of slavery, when Adams was a congressman. Lundy was born in Sussex County, New Jersey. See also GARRISON, WILLIAM LLOYD. LOUIS FILLER

LUNDY'S LANE, BATTLE OF. See WAR OF 1812 (Lundy's Lane; map).

LUNG is the chief breathing organ of mammals, birds, reptiles, and most adult amphibians. The main job of the lungs is to exchange gases. As blood flows through the lungs, it picks up oxygen from the air and releases carbon dioxide. The body needs oxygen to burn food for energy, and it produces carbon dioxide as a waste product. This article discusses the human lungs, but the lungs of other animals function in a similar way.

Parts of the Lungs. Human beings have two lungs—a left lung and a right lung—which fill up most of the chest cavity. A lung has a spongy texture and may be thought of as an elastic bag filled with millions of tiny air chambers, or sacs. If the walls of the air sacs could be spread out flat, they would cover about half a tennis court. The somewhat bullet-shaped lungs are suspended within the ribcage. They extend from just above the first rib down to the *diaphragm*, a muscular sheet that separates the chest cavity from the abdomen. A thin, tough membrane called the *visceral pleura* covers the outer surface of the lungs. The heart, large blood vessels, and *esophagus* (the tube connecting the mouth and stomach) lie between the two lungs.

The lungs are designed to receive air, which enters the body through the mouth or nose. The air passes through the *pharynx* (back of the nose and mouth) and the *larynx* (voice box) and enters the *airways*—a system of tubes that leads into the lungs. The largest of these tubes is the *trachea* (windpipe), which divides into two smaller tubes called *bronchi*. Each bronchus enters one lung, about a third of the way from the top to the bottom of the lung. Within the lung, the bronchus divides into smaller and smaller tubes, much as a tree limb divides into branches and twigs. The final "twigs" are tiny tubes called *bronchioles*. The smallest bronchioles, called *terminal bronchioles*, lead to the *respiratory units* of the lung. The respiratory units are made up of many *alveolar sacs*. Each alveolar sac contains about 20 tiny air spaces called *alveoli*. The walls of each alveolus contain networks of extremely small blood vessels called *pulmonary capillaries*. It is here that gas exchange takes place.

Three to five terminal bronchioles and the alveoli that they supply with air form a *lobule*. Many lobules unite to form the major subdivisions of the lung, called *lobes*. The left lung has two lobes, and the right lung has three. Each lobe has its own branches of bronchi and blood vessels, so a diseased lobe may be removed without sacrificing the usefulness of the other lobes.

Blood reaches the lung through two routes. Almost all of the blood comes through the *pulmonary circulation*. This blood has already circulated through the body tissues, where it has given up its oxygen and picked up carbon dioxide. A small amount of blood reaches the lungs through the *bronchial circulation*. This blood is rich in the oxygen and nutrients that the airway tissues—like all other body tissues—need.

Gas Exchange in the Lungs. In order to supply oxygen to the blood and remove carbon dioxide from it, the lungs must draw in fresh air and expel stale air. Fresh air

Parts of a Human Lung

The lungs consist of lobes—three in the right lung and two in the left. Air enters each lung through a tube called a *bronchus*. The bronchus divides into smaller tubes called *bronchioles*. Each bronchiole leads to a *respiratory unit* with many *alveolar sacs*.

WORLD BOOK illustrations by Charles Wellek

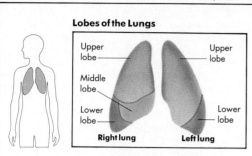

Lobes of the Lungs

Upper lobe

Upper lobe

Middle lobe

Lower lobe

Lower lobe

Right lung　　**Left lung**

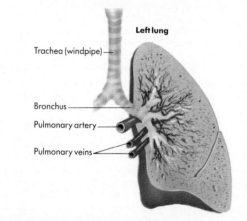

Left lung

Trachea (windpipe)

Bronchus

Pulmonary artery

Pulmonary veins

Enlarged Section of a Lung

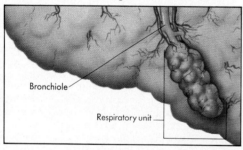

Bronchiole

Respiratory unit

Cross Section of an Alveolar Sac

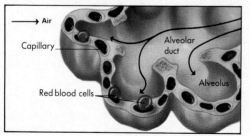

Air

Capillary

Alveolar duct

Red blood cells

Alveolus

An Alveolar Sac consists of an alveolar duct and about 20 alveoli. Blood picks up oxygen and releases carbon dioxide as it passes through capillaries in the alveolar walls.

is drawn in when the diaphragm and the muscles between the ribs contract. This action—called *inspiration* or *inhalation*—makes the chest volume larger and causes the lungs to expand. The expansion creates a slight vacuum in the lungs, and air from the atmosphere flows in. When the muscles relax, the lungs return to a smaller volume, and gas flows out into the atmosphere. This action is called *expiration* or *exhalation*.

Blood entering the lungs through the pulmonary circulation is dark-colored, low in oxygen, and high in carbon dioxide. It is pumped by the right side of the heart into the *pulmonary arteries*, which lead to the lungs. The pulmonary arteries divide into smaller and smaller blood vessels, ending with pulmonary capillaries in the walls of the alveoli. The alveolar walls are so thin that oxygen and carbon dioxide move through them easily. Oxygen passes from the alveoli to the blood in the capillaries. At the same time, carbon dioxide leaves the blood and enters the alveoli. Once this exchange is completed, the blood becomes bright red and enters the *pulmonary venous system*. In this system, small vessels join to form larger vessels. The largest vessels, the *pulmonary veins*, carry blood to the left side of the heart. The oxygen-rich blood is then pumped by the left side of the heart back to the body tissues.

Other Jobs of the Lungs. Because the lungs must inhale the air from the environment, they are exposed to bacteria, viruses, dust, and pollutants. A sticky fluid called *mucus* lines the airways and traps most of these foreign substances. Tiny, hairlike structures called *cilia* move together in a wavelike manner that pushes the mucus upwards into the throat. There, the mucus and its trapped "invaders" are coughed up or harmlessly swallowed. Some foreign substances do not get caught in the mucus and thus make their way into the alveoli. There, special cells called *alveolar macrophages* engulf the particles and carry them to the mucus or destroy them.

The lungs also help clean the blood of certain harmful substances. Blood flowing through the capillaries of the lung is filtered so that particles such as blood clots and fat globules are removed. Macrophages and other specialized cells then break up and remove the trapped material.

Another function of the lungs can be compared to the operations of a chemical processing plant. Some cells make a fatty substance called *surfactant*, which coats the alveoli and allows them to expand easily. Other cells add, remove, or change materials in the blood that affect the function of the lungs or other organs.

Finally, the air exhaled by the lungs is used to make the vocal cords in the larynx vibrate. This action creates the sound necessary for speech.

Diseases of the Lungs occur despite the defenses provided by the mucus and macrophages. Sometimes, the number of harmful particles reaching the alveoli is so great that the macrophages cannot remove them all. In other cases, the particles can resist or destroy the macrophages.

Because lung diseases can result from many different causes, they are usually grouped by how they affect lung functions. *Obstructive lung diseases,* such as emphysema, asthma, and chronic bronchitis, cause the airways to become partly blocked or narrower, making it more difficult for air to move through them. Cigarette smoking and air pollution are major causes of these diseases. *Re-*

strictive lung diseases make it harder for the respiratory system to expand. They can cause a stiffening of the lung or chest wall or make the respiratory muscles unable to respond to nerve signals. Breathing in substances such as asbestos, silica, and coal dust can cause some types of restrictive disease. *Pulmonary vascular diseases* affect the circulation of blood in the lungs. For example, in pulmonary hypertension, the small blood vessels of the lung become narrower, making it difficult for the right side of the heart to pump blood.

Some diseases are difficult to categorize because they can harm the lungs in a number of ways. Some pollutants—particularly cigarette smoke—affect the cilia, causing the upward movement of mucus to slow or stop. Smoking cigarettes is also a major cause of lung cancer. Infectious lung diseases, such as tuberculosis and pneumonia, are caused by bacteria, viruses, or other infectious organisms. These diseases are major killers in developing countries.   HAROLD I. MODELL and JACK HILDEBRANDT

Related Articles. See the Trans-Vision three-dimensional color picture with HUMAN BODY. See also:

Asthma	Human Body (picture:	Pharynx
Black Lung	Carbon Dioxide)	Pleura
Bronchitis	Hyaline Membrane	Pleurisy
Brown Lung	Disease	Pneumonia
Chest	Iron Lung	Pneumothorax
Diaphragm	Larynx	Respiration
Drowning	Legionnaires'	Sarcoidosis
Emphysema	Disease	Tuberculosis
Histoplasmosis	Nose	Windpipe

LUNG CANCER. See CANCER; LUNG (Diseases).

LUNGFISH is a type of fish that can breathe out of water. It breathes air by means of a lunglike organ called a *swim bladder* or *gas bladder*. The lungfish is one of the oldest known kinds of fish. Scientists have found fossils of lungfish that date from about 400 million years ago. Many scientists believe that land-dwelling *vertebrates* (animals with a backbone) developed from the lungfish.

There are six species of lungfish. They live in freshwater marshes, swamps, and rivers. Four species are found in Africa, one in Australia, and one in South America. African lungfish are the largest kinds. Some grow up to 7 feet (2 meters) long.

The Australian lungfish is the most primitive of the six species. It breathes chiefly with its gills. It gulps air at the water's surface only when the water contains little oxygen. This lungfish has a long, broad body and two pairs of flipperlike fins.

African and South American lungfish are eel-shaped with two pairs of long, threadlike fins. These lungfish

WORLD BOOK illustration by Colin Neuman, Linden Artists Ltd.
The South American Lungfish has an eel-shaped body with threadlike fins. It gets most of its oxygen by breathing air.

have poorly developed gills and breathe almost entirely with their "lung." If held underwater, they will drown. African and South American lungfish can survive hot, dry periods when the water in which they live dries up. At such times, they tunnel into the mud and remain there inactive until the rains return. This behavior is called *estivation.* During estivation, lungfish live off protein stored in their muscle tissues. African lungfish estivate inside a cocoon made of mud and a slimy substance given off by their body. This cocoon can be easily dug from the ground and the fish removed for food.

Lungfish eat mainly small fish and other water animals, such as frogs and snails. Female lungfish lay eggs. Among African and South American lungfish, the males fiercely protect the eggs and young.

Scientific Classification. Lungfish make up the order Dipteriforms in the class of bony fish, Osteichthyes. African lungfish are in the family Protopteridae. South American lungfish make up the family Lepidosirenidae. Australian lungfish make up the family Ceratodontidae.   JOHN E. MCCOSKER

LUNGWORT is the name of several perennial plants of the borage family. The most common is also called *Virginia cowslip* and *Virginia bluebell.* It grows from southern Canada to South Carolina, and west to Kansas. Farther west, the *lanceleaf* lungwort replaces it. These plants have smooth stems and large leaves. The bell-shaped flowers appear pink at first, but turn blue.

Another plant of the same name grows in Europe. It has small blue flowers and white-spotted leaves. These leaves were supposed to resemble a diseased lung. The plant was once a popular remedy for lung diseases, and was called *lungwort.* An olive-green lichen found on tree trunks in mountainous regions of North America and Europe is also called lungwort.

Scientific Classification. Lungworts are in the borage family, Boraginaceae. The Virginia cowslip is *Mertensia virginica;* the lanceleaf is *M. lanceolata;* the blue lungwort, or Jerusalem sage, is *Pulmonaria officinalis.* The lichen is in the family Parmeliaceae. It is *Sticta pulmonaria.*   EARL L. CORE

LUNT, ALFRED (1892-1977), an American actor, and his wife, Lynn Fontanne, became the most famous couple in the American theater. See FONTANNE, LYNN.

Lunt began his stage career with a Boston theater company, and toured with Margaret Anglin, an American star. Lunt's first real fame came in 1919 as the star in *Clarence.*

In 1924, Lunt and his wife joined the Theatre Guild. They starred together for the first time in the *Guardsman.* Other successes include *Reunion in Vienna, The Taming of the Shrew, Idiot's Delight, Amphitryon 38,* and *I Know My Love.* In England, the Lunts played in *There Shall Be No Night, Love in Idleness,* and other plays. Lunt and Fontanne won fame for their brilliant acting and perfect technique. They toured Europe during World War II (1939-1945) to perform before Allied troops. Lunt starred alone in *Marco Millions* and *Volpone.* He was born in Milwaukee, Wis.   MARY VIRGINIA HEINLEIN

LUPERCALIA, *LOO puhr KAY lee uh,* was an important religious festival in ancient Rome. It was celebrated on February 15. During the festival, priests sacrificed a dog and several goats in the Lupercal, a cave in the Palatine Hill. Priests made whips from the hides of the sacrificed goats. Two young men ran around the Palatine Hill, striking women with the whips. The Romans believed that women struck by the whips would become fertile. According to Roman mythology, a wolf in the Lupercal had nursed the infant twins Romulus and Remus, the legendary founders of Rome.　CAROL BAIN

LUPINE, *LOO puhn,* is the name of a group of plants in the pea family. Lupines have wandlike clusters of showy blue, yellow, white, or red flowers that resemble sweet peas. The leaves have several narrow leaflets, all attached at the same point. About a hundred kinds of lupines grow in North America. Some contain poisonous alkaloids, but the seeds of others can be eaten.

Scientific Classification. The lupines are classified as members of the pea family, Leguminosae. They make up the genus *Lupinus.*　ARTHUR CRONQUIST

See also BLUEBONNET; FLOWER (pictures: Garden Perennials; Flowers of the Arctic Tundra).

LUPUS, *LOO puhs,* is the name of any of a group of diseases that affect the skin. The word generally refers to the disease *lupus erythematosus.* However, it may also refer to *lupus vulgaris,* a tuberculosis of the skin of the face. This article discusses lupus erythematosus.

The most serious form of lupus erythematosus is *systemic lupus erythematosus* (SLE), which attacks many internal organs as well as the skin. People with SLE have such symptoms as fever, painful and swollen joints, and a butterfly-shaped rash across the nose and cheekbones. They also may suffer sores in the mouth and nose, lose their hair, and be sensitive to sunlight. Most victims are women from 15 to 35 years old. SLE occurs about four times as frequently in blacks as in whites.

The basic cause of SLE is unknown. However, researchers believe the disease involves a breakdown of the body's *immune system.* Normally, this system protects the body from infection by producing substances called *antibodies,* which attack harmful bacteria and viruses. In SLE, the immune system apparently produces antibodies that attack healthy tissue instead.

Mild cases of SLE require no treatment. Physicians treat more severe cases with such drugs as aspirin and cortisone, which reduce inflammation in internal organs. Severe cases of SLE can be fatal, especially if the kidneys are damaged. SLE cannot be cured completely, but most patients under treatment for the disease have no symptoms for long periods of time.

Another form of lupus, *discoid lupus erythematosus* (DLE), affects only the skin. In rare cases, DLE may leave scars or develop into SLE.　MICHAEL D. LOCKSHIN

LURAY CAVERNS, *LOO ray* or *lu RAY,* are a group of underground caves near the town of Luray, Va. The caverns lie in a limestone belt of the Shenandoah Valley on the west side of the Blue Ridge Mountains. The caves have many large rooms. Some of them are more than 140 feet (43 meters) high. Some of the many-colored hanging rocks called *stalactites* are over 50 feet (15 meters) long. The caverns were discovered by Andrew J. Campbell and his companions in August 1878. See also STALACTITE (picture).　ELDRED D. WILSON

LURE. See DOG RACING; FISHING (Bait); FISHING INDUSTRY (Hooks).

LUSAKA, *loo SAH kuh* (pop. 520,000), is the capital and largest city of Zambia. The city lies on a high plateau in south central Zambia. It is near the midpoint of a railroad and at the junction of two main roads. For location, see ZAMBIA (map).

Lusaka has many large buildings, including the parliament buildings and the University of Zambia. Most of the city's commercial and government buildings stand along wide, shaded streets. Lusaka is a city of contrasts, with upper-class areas and slums. The city has several scenic parks. The main shopping district is famous for open-air bazaars that sell handmade items.

Lusaka is an important trade center and a major market for farm products raised in rural areas of Zambia. Industries in Lusaka make cement, furniture, shoes, textiles, and other products, and process beverages, food, and tobacco. The Zambian government employs many of the city's people.

European settlers established Lusaka about 1905 as a small trading post. It was originally called *Lusaakas.* The city came under British rule in the early 1900's. In 1935, Great Britain made Lusaka the capital of its colony of Northern Rhodesia. The colony became the independent nation of Zambia in 1964.　L. H. GANN

See also ZAMBIA (picture).

LUSITANIA, *LOO sih TAY nee uh,* was a British passenger ship that sank near Ireland after the German submarine *U-20* torpedoed it on May 7, 1915, during World War I. A total of 1,198 people died, including 128 Americans. Many people considered the sinking an act of barbarism. Afterward, Germany stopped attacking

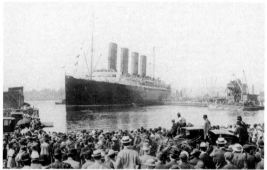

Bettmann Archive

The *Lusitania* was a British passenger ship that was sunk by a torpedo from a German submarine in 1915, during World War I. The ship, shown departing on its last voyage, sank near Ireland.

neutral and passenger ships around Great Britain for nearly two years.

The German government had claimed the *Lusitania* was a legal target because it was armed and carried war materials. An official British inquiry denied that the ship was armed, but confirmed that it had a supply of ammunition. As a result of the sinking, support for Britain increased in the United States. The United States entered the war in 1917, and "Remember the *Lusitania!*" became a common slogan.　JAMES L. STOKESBURY

LUTE is an ancient stringed musical instrument. A lute has a pear-shaped body, a neck with a *fretted* (ridged) fingerbox, and a *pegbox* that is attached to the neck at a sharp angle. The pegs are turned to tune the 11 strings, which run along the neck to a low *bridge* near the bottom of the body. The player plucks the strings with the thumb and fingers of the right hand. The fingers of

The Lute Is a Very Old Musical Instrument. The body and neck resemble those of a large mandolin, but the angle at which the head is set into the neck gives it a distinctive appearance.

NBC

the left hand press down on the strings along the neck to set the pitch.　　　　　　　　　　　　　ABRAM LOFT

LUTETIUM, *loo TEE shee uhm* (chemical symbol, Lu), is one of the rare-earth metals. It has an atomic number of 71 and an atomic weight of 174.967. The name comes from *Lutetia*, the ancient name for Paris. The French scientist Georges Urbain discovered lutetium in 1907. He developed a process for separating the original element ytterbium into two elements, lutetium and ytterbium, or neoytterbium. Lutetium is found with ytterbium in the minerals gadolinite, xenotime, and other minerals that bear rare earths. It is best separated from the other rare earths by ion-exchange processes. The metal has a silver color. It has a melting point of 1656° C (3013° F.) and a boiling point of 3315° C (5999° F.). It is the heaviest of the rare-earth elements. See also ELEMENT, CHEMICAL; RARE EARTH; YTTERBIUM.　　　　　　　　　　FRANK H. SPEDDING

LUTHER, MARTIN (1483-1546), was the leader of the Reformation, a religious movement that led to the birth of Protestantism. His influence has reached beyond Protestantism and even beyond Christianity. For example, Luther's translation of the Bible into German is a literary masterpiece. It did more than any other single force to create the modern German language.

Next to the Bible translation, Luther's most influential literary work was his *Small Catechism of 1529*. It became known as the *layman's Bible*. In clear, simple language, it summarized what Christians should believe and how

Detail of an oil portrait on wood (1526) by Lucas Cranach; Nationalmuseum, Stockholm

Martin Luther

they should live. Millions of people have learned the fundamentals of Christianity from Luther's catechism or from one of its adaptations.

Luther's role in the history of music is almost as significant as his contributions to German literature and the German language. His hymns opened a new era in music. Luther's best-known hymn was "A Mighty Fortress Is Our God."

Early Life. Luther was born in Eisleben in Saxony on Nov. 10, 1483. He entered the University of Erfurt in 1501 and decided to become a lawyer. But in 1505 he entered a monastery, shortly after undergoing an intense religious experience during a thunderstorm.

Luther was ordained a priest in 1507 and taught briefly at the University of Wittenberg in 1508. In 1512, he received a doctor's degree in theology and was appointed a professor of theology at Wittenberg. He held that position for the rest of his life.

Justification by Faith. There is no evidence that Luther as a young man considered himself anything but a faithful son of the Roman Catholic Church. Yet he was already puzzling over questions that later led to the Reformation. These questions did not deal with the external structure of the church or its moral values, all of which Luther considered important but not vital. Luther concerned himself with the meaning of the Christian Gospel: How does an individual find favor with God? To Luther, this was not a problem to be settled by discussion of human merit in relation to divine grace. It was an intensely personal problem that affected, first of all, Luther himself.

For Luther, the life of the church, especially the ordered life of a monastery, provided remedies for those who were troubled by their relation to the judgment of an angry God. Individuals could say more prayers, fast more strictly, and whip themselves more mercilessly. Finally, they would achieve the certain knowledge that God regarded them favorably. Luther tried all these methods, but none worked for him. The harder he tried to please God, the more he realized that he was depending not on God, but on his own efforts.

The answer came to Luther in 1508 or 1509 while he was studying the Book of Psalms and the Epistles of Paul. Luther concluded that God's favor is not a prize to be won, but a gift. Only when individuals stop trying to achieve God's favor by their own abilities and accomplishments can they understand the grace of God. God *justifies* individuals—that is, makes them righteous before Him—not through their moral goodness or faithfulness to duty, but because of His kindness. God's kindness, Luther believed, was given to the world in the life, death, and Resurrection of Jesus Christ. This was the meaning of justification solely by faith in God's grace, the doctrine for which Luther became famous.

At first, Luther did not regard justification by faith as anything new. He blamed himself for not having discovered sooner what he felt all the great theologians had known and taught. The doctrine involved Luther in controversy for the rest of his life.

The Ninety-Five Theses. The first controversy in which Luther became involved concerned *indulgences*. The church had developed indulgences as a means of pardoning sinners from part of the penalty for their sins.

459

Woodcut (about 1550) from the workshop of Lucas Cranach the Elder;
Staatliche Lutherhalle, Wittenberg, East Germany

Martin Luther gives Communion to Duke John of Saxony, *left*.
The dukes of Saxony were Luther's protectors during the Reformation. The artist also showed the Protestant reformer John Hus giving Communion to Duke Frederick the Wise of Saxony, *right*. But
Hus actually had died before Luther was born.

For example, individuals could be ordered to go on a *pilgrimage* (journey to a sacred place) to make up for their
sins and to prove they were sincere about repenting. An
indulgence permitted them to contribute a certain
amount of money to a worthy cause instead.

The practice of selling indulgences was sometimes
abused as a means of raising money. In addition, Luther believed that indulgences degraded the forgiving
grace of God and weakened the church itself.

On Oct. 31, 1517, Luther posted his famous Ninety-
Five Theses on the door of the Castle church in Wittenberg. The theses included statements challenging indulgences. Luther acted in response to a sale of indulgences
near Wittenberg by Johann Tetzel, a Dominican monk.
The theses drew Luther into direct conflict with the
church as none of his other statements had done, though
many of them were more radical. These radical statements dealt with such issues as the authority of the Bible
and the doctrine of God's grace.

Reformation Leader. In 1518, Luther met the German scholar Philipp Melanchthon, who became his
chief associate during the Reformation. In 1519,
Luther had a famous debate in Leipzig with Johann
Eck, a Roman Catholic theologian. During this debate,
Luther denied the supremacy of the pope and declared
that church councils could make mistakes.

In 1521, Luther was excommunicated by Pope
Leo X. Charles V, emperor of the Holy Roman Empire, then ordered Luther to appear before a *diet* (meeting) of princes, nobles, and clergymen in Worms, Germany, in April of that year. The diet demanded that
Luther retract his teachings, but he refused to do so.

Luther stood before Charles and declared: "Unless I am
convinced by the testimony of the Scriptures or by clear
reason (for I do not trust either in the pope or in councils
alone, since it is well known that they have often erred
and contradicted themselves), I am bound by the Scriptures I have quoted and my conscience is captive to the
Word of God. I cannot and I will not retract anything,
since it is neither safe nor right to go against conscience.
I cannot do otherwise."

For most of his public career, Luther did not belong
to any of the various opposing groups of the Reformation. For example, he revised the worship of the church.
But the new liturgy he created in the language of the
common people was too Protestant for the Catholics and
too Catholic for the Protestants. Luther also insisted
that individual Christians must do their own believing,
just as they must do their own dying. But after some
Protestants concluded that infants—who cannot believe
for themselves—should not be baptized, Luther vigorously defended the tradition of infant baptism.

During the Reformation, Luther discovered to his
surprise and disappointment that he had founded a
new church. Luther complained that he did not want
to give his name to a community that should take its
name only from Christ. But Lutheranism remains the
name of the doctrines and beliefs that he originated.

Theological Writings. In spite of his active public life,
Luther was primarily a university scholar. In 1520, he
wrote many works, including two that had far-reaching
effects. *The Babylonian Captivity of the Church* attacked
church sacraments. *The Freedom of the Christian Man* declared that a Christian was a free person, subject to no
one, yet at the same time a willing servant, freely subject
to everyone. Luther considered *The Bondage of the Will*
(1525) his most significant writing. It attacked the
Dutch humanist Desiderius Erasmus and tried to prove
that people cannot do anything to contribute to their
salvation. They must receive it from God as a gift.

The majority of Luther's writings were discussions
about books of the Bible. Most of them were delivered
as classroom lectures and then published. The most
important of these works, *Lectures on Galatians* (1535),
summarized many of Luther's chief ideas.

Luther's Place in History. By the time of his death
in Eisleben on Feb. 18, 1546, Luther was recognized as
a major figure in the history of Christianity and the
world. He symbolizes the split within Christianity between Protestants and Roman Catholics. This split has
affected the political and cultural development of every
nation in Europe and North and South America. Luther
also continues to be the source of some of the most
powerful ideas in Christian thought. Many of the reforms adopted by the Roman Catholic Church during
the 1960's recall points that Luther made more than 400
years earlier. One such point involved using the language of the people, rather than Latin, for worship.

Luther has been called the most influential German
who ever lived. Knowledge of his life and work is necessary to understand the history of Scandinavia, England,
and the Americas. Luther has been extravagantly
praised and extravagantly condemned. As a result, it is
difficult to discover the real Luther behind the myths of
his disciples and enemies. Every aspect of Luther's life
has been examined by both friends and foes. During the
1900's, the excessively one-sided views have been soft-

ened by historical research, and something like general agreement has begun to emerge.   JAROSLAV PELIKAN

Related Articles in WORLD BOOK include:

Augsburg Confession
Bible (Early English Translations)
Eck, Johann
German Language (Development)
Indulgence
Leo (Leo X)

Lutherans
Melanchthon, Philipp
Peasants' War
Protestantism
Reformation
Tetzel, Johann

See also *Luther, Martin*, in the RESEARCH GUIDE/INDEX, Volume 22, for a *Reading and Study Guide*.

Additional Resources

BAINTON, ROLAND H. *Here I Stand: A Life of Martin Luther*. Abingdon, 1950.

EDWARDS, MARK, and TAVARD, GEORGE. *Luther: A Reformer for the Churches: An Ecumenical Study Guide*. Fortress, 1983.

MANNS, PETER. *Martin Luther: An Illustrated Biography*. Crossroad, 1982.

PELIKAN, JAROSLAV, and LEHMANN, HELMUT. *Luther's Works: The American Edition*. Fortress, 1955-.

LUTHERAN CHURCH IN AMERICA is the largest Lutheran church body in the United States. It was formed in 1962 by the union of four churches—the American Evangelical Lutheran Church, the Augustana Evangelical Lutheran Church, the Finnish Evangelical Lutheran Church, and the United Lutheran Church in America. The four uniting churches drew up a new *confessional statement* (expression of beliefs) that retained the confessions and creeds of Lutheranism. In 1982, the Lutheran Church in America voted to merge with the American Lutheran Church and the Association of Evangelical Lutheran Churches. The merger was scheduled to be completed by 1988.

The Lutheran Church in America has 33 regional jurisdictional units called *synods*. There are 29 in the United States, 3 in Canada, and 1 in Puerto Rico and the Virgin Islands. Overseas ministries are conducted in more than 30 countries in Africa, East Asia, South Asia, and South America. The church operates 9 theological seminaries, 19 colleges, and 113 social service institutions. The church has about 3 million members. Headquarters are at 231 Madison Avenue, New York, NY 10016.   Critically reviewed by the LUTHERAN CHURCH IN AMERICA

See also LUTHERANS.

LUTHERAN CHURCH—MISSOURI SYNOD is one of the largest Lutheran church bodies in the United States. It was organized in 1847 by German immigrants. The standards of faith of the church are based on the Bible and described in detail in the Book of Concord (1580). This book contains the *confessional writings* (expression of beliefs) of Lutheranism.

The church has more than $2\frac{1}{2}$ million members and more than 6,100 congregations. The church operates 4 seminaries and 13 colleges in the United States and Canada. In addition, its congregations operate about 1,600 elementary schools and 60 high schools. The church has sponsored religious broadcasts since the 1920's, and also sponsors television shows seen worldwide. The church began missionary work in the 1890's, and today has missions in more than 30 countries. Headquarters are at 1333 South Kirkwood Road, St. Louis, MO 63122.

Critically reviewed by the LUTHERAN CHURCH—MISSOURI SYNOD

See also LUTHERANS.

LUTHERANS make up the largest Protestant church in the world. The Lutheran church was founded in the early 1500's on doctrines and beliefs voiced by the Refor-

mation religious leader Martin Luther. Yet the church claims descent from the authentic Christian tradition in the centuries before the Reformation.

Lutherans do not have any single form of organization that distinguishes them from other Christian groups. Some Lutheran groups have bishops, while some insist on the sovereignty of the local congregation. Other Lutheran groups fall between these two extremes.

Lutherans have no uniform way of worship. Some Lutheran *liturgies* (services) are as formal as the Roman Catholic Mass. Other Lutheran services seem very close to the severe simplicity of Puritan worship.

Doctrine. What sets the Lutherans apart from other Christian churches are the teachings of Luther's Reformation. The best-known statements of Luther's teachings appear in two catechisms he wrote in 1529 and in the Augsburg Confession of 1530. These three statements provide the basis for the Lutheran belief that people can be saved only by faith—rather than through their own moral efforts or good works. Instead, people are freed from sin by God through God's gift of grace through Jesus Christ on the cross. Once set free from sin by the grace of God, people become new creatures, able and willing to serve God and their neighbor. Lutherans see this message of God's forgiving love as uniquely set forth in the Bible. Lutherans believe the Bible has authority over all teaching in the church.

Lutherans have two sacraments, baptism and the Lord's Supper. The Lord's Supper is also called the Eucharist or Sacrament of the Altar.

Lutheran beliefs and attitudes have also been formed by the social history of the church. Many Lutherans live in the Scandinavian countries, where Lutheranism is the state religion, and in Germany. Lutherans living outside Europe are usually descended from these North Europeans. Many of the qualities associated with North European cultures are closely related to the Lutheran heritage. For example, the strong sense of personal duty identified with a kind of German Lutheranism is a characteristic of Germany as well as of Lutheranism.

Lutherans have tended to be relatively conservative on political and social issues. This attitude can be traced partly to the church's association with North European cultures and with the ruling classes within them. Luther helped set the pattern for this conservatism. He stressed the virtue of obedience and feared anarchy more than injustice. But in some historical instances—for example, Hungary in the 1800's—Lutheranism has been more revolutionary than other Christian churches.

Lutheranism in America. Lutherans were among the earliest settlers in the American Colonies. Many Lutherans arrived in the 1700's, settling largely in Pennsylvania and New York. But most Lutherans arrived in the United States in the 1800's. They came from Norway, Sweden, and Germany, and most of them settled in the Midwest and upper Midwest. Today, Lutherans are the fourth largest Christian group in the United States.

Lutheran immigrants usually formed their own church bodies, but the trend in the 1900's has been toward unification. Most Lutherans today belong to one of three major *synods:* the Lutheran Church in America; the American Lutheran Church; or the Lutheran Church—Missouri Synod. In 1982, the Lutheran

Church in America, the American Lutheran Church, and the Association of Evangelical Lutheran Churches voted to combine into a single church body. The merger was scheduled to be completed by 1987.   JAROSLAV PELIKAN

Related Articles in WORLD BOOK include:

American Lutheran Church	Lutheran Church in America	Reformation Sweden
Augsburg Confession	Lutheran Church— Missouri Synod	(Religion)
Luther, Martin		

Additional Resources

GRITSCH, ERIC W., and JENSON, R. W. *Lutheranism: The Theological Movement and Its Confessional Writings.* Fortress, 1976.

PIEPKORN, ARTHUR C. *Profiles in Belief: The Religious Bodies of the United States and Canada. Vol. 2: Protestant Denominations.* Harper, 1978. Pages 3-132 discuss Lutheran churches.

LUTHULI, *loo TOO lee,* **ALBERT JOHN** (1898-1967), won the 1960 Nobel Peace Prize for his peaceful efforts to end racial segregation in South Africa. Luthuli, a former Zulu chief, led the African National Congress until the government banned it in 1960. In 1959, the government prohibited him from making speeches and from leaving his home village of Groutville, near Durban. However, he was allowed to go to Norway for his prize.

LUTYENS, *LUHCH uhnz* or *LUHT yuhnz,* **SIR EDWIN LANDSEER** (1869-1944), was one of the most important English architects of the early 1900's. His designs show the influence of Palladian Revival and other English architectural styles of the 1700's (see ARCHITECTURE [The Palladian Revival]).

Lutyens first became prominent for country houses he designed with the English landscape architect Gertrude Jekyll. Their best-known country houses included Munstead Wood (1896) near Godalming, Surrey, and Deanery Garden (1901) in Sonning, Berkshire. Later in his career, Lutyens turned to town planning. Two of his most important projects were the village center in Hampstead Garden Suburb, London, and the layout for the city of New Delhi, India. Lutyens' other works include the Cenotaph war memorial (1920) in London and the British Embassy in Washington, D.C. (1930). Lutyens was born in London.   LELAND M. ROTH

LUXEMBOURG, *LUHK suhm burg,* is one of Europe's oldest and smallest independent countries. It lies in northwestern Europe where West Germany, France, and Belgium meet. Luxembourg covers only 998 square miles (2,586 square kilometers) and has only about 368,000 people.

Luxembourg has scenic areas of rolling hills and dense forests. The whitewashed houses of the country's small towns and villages cluster around medieval castles and churches. Luxembourg is one of the world's most industrialized countries. Most of its industries are located in the southwest corner of the country.

Luxembourg was established as an independent state in 963. Its official name is Grand-Duché de Luxembourg in French and Grossherzogtum Luxemburg in German (Grand Duchy of Luxembourg). The city of Luxembourg is the country's capital and largest city.

Government. Luxembourg is a constitutional monarchy. The grand duke (or duchess) of the House of Nassau serves as monarch and the country's chief executive. The monarchy is a *hereditary* office. It passes to the oldest son or daughter of the monarch. A 64-member parliament called the Chamber of Deputies makes Luxembourg's laws. The people elect the members to five-year terms. The monarch appoints a prime minister and 10 other Cabinet ministers to carry out the operations of the government. The Cabinet members must have the support of a majority of the members of parliament. The monarch also appoints for life a 21-member advisory body called the Council of State.

For purposes of local government, Luxembourg is divided into three districts, each headed by a commissioner appointed by the national government. The districts are divided into 12 cantons, and the cantons are divided into communes. Elected officials head the cantons and communes.

People. Luxembourgers have close cultural ties with neighboring Belgium, France, and West Germany. But they maintain an independent spirit, as expressed in words of their national anthem, "*Mir welle bleiwe wat mir sin*" ("We want to remain what we are"). Most Luxembourgers enjoy a high standard of living. They have better food and housing than many other Europeans have. The country has extensive government-sponsored systems of social security and health care benefits.

Ham and freshwater fish, especially trout, are favorite Luxembourg foods. Beer and wine are popular beverages. Many people live in charming villages where buildings constructed in the 1900's stand beside those

Luxembourg

⊛ Capital
• Other City or Town
— Road
+—+ Rail Line
▲ MOUNTAIN

WORLD BOOK map

Cameramann International Ltd. from Marilyn Gartner

The City of Luxembourg is the capital and largest city of Luxembourg. The city lies on steep cliffs overlooking the Alzette and Petrusse rivers.

dating from the 1100's, 1300's, and 1700's. The cities have many modern office and apartment buildings.

Luxembourg has three official languages: French, German, and Letzeburgesch. Letzeburgesch, a *dialect* (local form) of German, is a widely used everyday language. German is used in most of the elementary schools, and French in most high schools. The country's newspapers are printed in German. French is used in the courts and parliament. More than 95 per cent of Luxembourg's people are Roman Catholics.

The law requires children between the ages of 6 and 15 to attend school. Luxembourg has an International University of Comparative Science and several technical and vocational schools. Almost all adult Luxembourgers can read and write.

Land. Luxembourg has two distinct land regions, the Ardennes and the Bon Pays (Good Land). The Ardennes cover the northern third of Luxembourg, and the

Facts in Brief

Capital: Luxembourg.

Languages: *Official*—French, German, Letzeburgesch.

Form of Government: Constitutional monarchy.

Area: 998 sq. mi. (2,586 km²). *Greatest Distances*—north-south, 55 mi. (89 km); east-west, 35 mi. (56 km).

Elevation: *Highest*—Buurgplaatz, 1,835 ft. (559 m) above sea level, in the Ardennes Mountains. *Lowest*—435 ft. (133 m) above sea level on the Moselle River.

Population: *Estimated 1987 Population*—368,000; distribution, 82 per cent urban, 18 per cent rural; density, 369 persons per sq. mi. (142 per km²). *1981 Census*—364,602. *Estimated 1992 Population*—370,000.

Chief Products: *Agriculture*—grapes, oats, potatoes, wheat, livestock. *Mining*—iron ore. *Manufacturing*—steel, chemicals, plastics, tires, wine.

National Anthem: "Ons Hemecht" ("Our Homeland").

Flag: The flag has horizontal red, white, and blue stripes (top to bottom). The colors come from the coat of arms of Luxembourg. Adopted 1845. See FLAG (picture: Flags of Europe).

Money: *Basic Unit*—franc. See MONEY (table).

Bon Pays makes up the rest of the country. The Ardennes are part of a mountain system that extends from West Germany's Rhineland into Belgium and Luxembourg. River valleys cut deeply through the region's low hills. Buurgplaatz (1,835 feet, or 559 meters), a hill in the Ardennes, is Luxembourg's highest point.

Most of the Bon Pays is a hilly or rolling plateau with level areas along its rivers. The Attert, Alzette, Moselle, and Sûre rivers flow through the region. The Bon Pays is an important farming region.

Most of Luxembourg has a cool, moist climate. The average temperature in the city of Luxembourg is about 32° F. (0° C) in January and about 63° F. (17° C) in July. Rainfall varies from about 40 inches (100 centimeters) a year in southwestern Luxembourg to from 12 to 16 inches (30 to 41 centimeters) a year in the southeast. Most snowfalls occur high in the Ardennes.

Economy. Luxembourg's most valuable resource is iron ore, which is mined and made into steel. Luxembourg ranks as one of Europe's leading steel producers. Although the country remains a major steel producer, the number of iron ore mines has decreased greatly since World War II (1939-1945). Since the war, the government of Luxembourg has worked to add variety to the economy. Luxembourg now has a number of high technology industries. These industries produce such goods as computers and other electronic equipment. Many foreign companies have opened factories that make such products as chemicals, plastics, and tires.

Luxembourg is an international financial center. Many foreign banks have offices in the country. Tourism is also a major industry.

Farmers in the Bon Pays region raise oats, potatoes, and wheat. They raise pigs and poultry and have fairly large herds of cattle and sheep. Grapes grown on terraces along the Moselle River produce good wine. Although about half of the total land is farmed, only 6 per cent of Luxembourg's workers are farmers.

Luxembourg is a member of the European Community, and trades chiefly with other members. Iron ore and steel products make up about half of the country's exports. The chief imports are food and machinery.

Luxembourg has about 3,200 miles (5,100 kilometers) of roads. Its 170 miles (270 kilometers) of railroads connect eastern France with Belgium. A major international airport is located just outside the capital.

History. Luxembourg was established as an independent state in 963, when Siegfried, count of Ardennes, gained control of the area and built a castle on the site of the present-day city of Luxembourg. In 1308, Henry VII, count of Luxembourg, became emperor of the Holy Roman Empire. His grandson, Charles IV, created the Duchy of Luxembourg in 1354. A period of prosperity began. Philip the Good of Burgundy conquered Luxembourg in 1443. In 1684, France took control of Luxembourg. Luxembourg became part of Spain in 1697. Austria gained control of it in 1714. In 1795, Luxembourg again became part of France.

In 1815, after the defeat of Emperor Napoleon I of France, the Congress of Vienna made Luxembourg a grand duchy that was technically ruled by the Netherlands. The king of the Netherlands was also the grand duke of Luxembourg. However, Luxembourg was largely self-governing. In 1890, Wilhelmina became queen of the Netherlands. Luxembourg then broke away from the Netherlands and named its own monarch, because the grand duchy's laws did not allow a woman to rule. In 1912, the laws were changed to allow Marie Adélaïde of Nassau to become the ruling grand duchess. Her sister Charlotte succeeded her as grand duchess in 1919. In 1964, Charlotte abdicated to allow her son, Prince Jean, to become grand duke.

Germany occupied Luxembourg during parts of World War I (1914-1918) and World War II (1939-1945). In the winter of 1944 and 1945, part of the Battle of the Bulge was fought in northern Luxembourg. Thousands of Americans killed in that battle are buried in Hamm. In 1945, Luxembourg became a member of the United Nations (UN). It joined an economic union called Benelux in 1948, and became a member of the North Atlantic Treaty Organization (NATO) in 1949. In the 1950's, Luxembourg joined five other nations in forming the European Coal and Steel Community, the European Economic Community, and Euratom. These groups form the basis of the European Community.

Today, Luxembourg plays an important role in European matters. The city of Luxembourg serves as the headquarters of several international agencies, including the European Coal and Steel Community and the European Court of Justice.   JANET L. POLASKY

Related Articles in WORLD BOOK include:

Benelux	European Community
Christmas (In the Netherlands,	European Monetary
Belgium, and Luxembourg)	Agreement
Europe, Council of	Luxembourg (city)

LUXEMBOURG (pop. 78,400) is the capital and largest city of the country of Luxembourg. For location, see the map with the LUXEMBOURG (country) article. A picturesque city, Luxembourg stands on a plateau high above gorges formed by the Alzette and Petrusse rivers. Its landmarks include the Grand Ducal Palace, built in the 1500's; the Gothic Cathedral of Notre Dame, which dates from the early 1600's; and the town hall, built in the early 1800's. The Grand Ducal Palace is the residence of the country's monarch.

Luxembourg serves as the headquarters of several European international agencies, including the European Coal and Steel Community and the European Court of Justice. The city is also an international financial center. Many foreign banks have offices there.

Roman soldiers began constructing a fort at what is now Luxembourg in the A.D. 300's. In 963, Siegfried, count of Ardennes, built a castle there, and a walled town grew up around the castle. Through the years, the walls were strengthened for defense against attacks. Gradually, much of the castle was destroyed. The walls were largely dismantled in the mid-1800's. But some parts still stand.   JANET L. POLASKY

See also LUXEMBOURG (country [picture]).

LUXEMBURG, *LUHK suhm BURG,* **ROSA** (1871-1919), was a German socialist writer and revolutionary. She was a follower of Karl Marx, the founder of revolutionary Communism.

Luxemburg was born in Zamość, Poland, and became acquainted with Marx's writings after graduating from high school. At the age of 18, she fled to Switzer-

land to avoid arrest for political activities. Luxemburg received a doctorate in economics from the University of Zurich in 1898. That same year, she moved to Germany and joined the German Social Democratic Party. She became known as a brilliant writer and speaker.

Luxemburg spent most of the period of World War I (1914-1918) in prison for antiwar activities. She was released briefly in 1916. During this period, Luxemburg helped establish the Spartacus Party, a more revolutionary wing of the Social Democratic Party. The Spartacus Party was named after the leader of a slave uprising in ancient Rome. In 1918, Luxemburg helped found the German Communist Party and its newspaper, *Rote Fahne (Red Flag)*. She was killed in Berlin during a workers' revolt against the government.   JUNE SOCHEN

LUXOR. See EGYPT, ANCIENT (map); OBELISK.

LUZERN. See LUCERNE.

LUZON. See PHILIPPINES (The Main Islands).

LVOV, *luh VAWF* (pop. 728,000), is a major city of the Ukraine, in the southwest Soviet Union. It serves as the capital and administrative center of a region called Lvov Oblast. Lvov is an industrial and commercial center. Located at major highway and railroad junctions, it is also an important transportation center. For location, see RUSSIA (political map).

Lvov's major products include agricultural machinery, automobiles and buses, processed foods, refined petroleum, and textiles. Lvov's Ivan Franko University is one of the oldest and most famous in the Soviet Union. Lvov also has a branch of the Ukrainian Academy of Sciences, and many museums and libraries.

Lvov was founded in the 1200's in the kingdom of Galicia (see GALICIA). The city was captured by Poland in the 1340's. It became part of Austria in 1772. Poland retook the city after World War I ended in 1918. The Soviet Union formally took control of Lvov in 1945, after World War II.

LYCANTHROPY. See WEREWOLF.

LYCÉE. See FRANCE (Education).

LYCEUM, *ly SEE uhm,* is an organization that sponsors lectures, concerts, and other adult educational programs. The name comes from the school of Aristotle in Athens (see ARISTOTLE). Josiah Holbrook started the American lyceum movement in 1826 in Millbury, Mass.

The main purpose of the early lyceum movement was to improve the schools, bring about better teacher training, and establish libraries. The Chautauqua movement and universities took over most of the lyceum's work in the late 1800's (see CHAUTAUQUA).   R. FREEMAN BUTTS

LYCEUM, *ly SEE uhm,* was a gymnasium where boys and young men of ancient Athens received physical training and listened to the lectures of famous teachers. It stood outside the walls of Athens along the Ilissus River. It was near the grove sacred to the god Apollo Lykeios, for whom it was named. Aristotle established a famous school there about 335 B.C.   WILLIAM P. DONOVAN

LYCHEE. See LITCHI.

LYCOPODIUM. See CLUB MOSS.

LYCURGUS, *ly KUR guhs,* was a Spartan legislator. He is supposed to have set up the government that made Sparta the great military power of the Greek states. His birth and death dates and his exact achievements are uncertain.

Lycurgus probably lived during the 800's B.C., and was a member of one of the two Spartan royal families.

The stories about him say he traveled to other parts of Greece, and to Asia and Egypt, to study their laws. On his return, he was asked to develop a new form of government for Sparta.

The system he devised was designed to eliminate weaklings. Strict supervision from birth enforced discipline and military training. Lycurgus made his fellow Spartans promise not to change the system of government until he returned from another trip. Then he went into exile, and so forced the Spartans to keep the government he had planned. DONALD KAGAN

See also SPARTA.

LYDDITE, *LIHD yt,* is an explosive mixture of picric acid and collodion. In the Boer War, the British used lyddite to fill shells. The explosive known as TNT later proved more effective. See also TNT.

LYDIA, *LIHD ee uh,* was an ancient country in Asia Minor. It was famous for its fertile soil and its rich mineral deposits, especially the gold of the River Pactolus. In the early 500's B.C., Lydia was an independent and

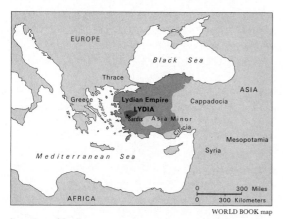

Location of Lydia

WORLD BOOK map

prosperous kingdom. In 546 B.C., the Persians conquered Croesus, the last king of the Lydians. Later, Lydia fell to the Macedonians and the Romans. Because Lydia lay at the western end of the great road connecting Mesopotamia and the East with the Aegean Sea and Greece, it was a great commercial center. Lydia was one of the first countries to cast coins. In 1958, a group of archaeologists began to excavate Sardis, the capital city of Lydia. See also CROESUS; PHRYGIA; CYRUS THE GREAT; MONEY (The First Coins). JACOB J. FINKELSTEIN

LYE, also called *caustic soda,* is an important industrial chemical. It serves as the main ingredient in many commercial drain cleaners and oven cleaners. It is also used in the manufacture of soap and paper.

Lye is a solid, white material that readily absorbs moisture. It produces extremely corrosive solutions. Lye, both as a solid and in solution, can severely damage skin if it comes into contact with it. If splashed into eyes, lye solution can cause blindness in just a few seconds. For these reasons, special care should be taken when handling products that contain lye.

Lye is produced from brine by *electrolysis* (see ELECTROLYSIS). The chemical name for lye is *sodium hydroxide.* Its chemical formula is NaOH. ROBERT J. OUELLETTE

See also ALKALI; CAUSTIC; FIRST AID (table).

LYELL, *LY uhl,* **SIR CHARLES** (1797-1875), a British scientist, is often called the founder of modern geology. Between 1830 and 1833, he published the three volumes of his *Principles of Geology,* which organized existing information about that science. Lyell showed in his book that the earth has changed slowly and gradually through the ages by means of processes that are still going on. Until then, many persons believed that changes in the earth occurred in sudden worldwide upheavals.

The book was so successful that Lyell spent much of his life preparing new editions and keeping them up to date. He was among the first scientists to accept modern theories about the Ice Age and evolution. His book *The Antiquity of Man* (1863) concerned prehistoric people in Europe. He also wrote *Travels in North America* (1845). Lyell was born in Kinnordy, Scotland, and studied at Oxford University. CARROLL LANE FENTON

See also GEOLOGY (Experimental Geology).

LYLY, *LIHL ee,* **JOHN** (1554?-1606), was an English writer. He was important in the history of prose style and the development of Elizabethan popular comedy of high literary quality. Lyly was born in Canterbury. He established his literary reputation with *Euphues: The Anatomy of Wit* (1578), a fashionable book combining essay and fiction. The book's artificial style, called *euphuism,* was meant to set a new pattern for sophisticated English prose.

Lyly turned to playwriting as part of an effort, ultimately unsuccessful, to further his advancement at court. His comedies treat idealized love and flatteringly reflect attitudes of the Elizabethan courtier. Written to be performed by troupes of boy actors, they emphasize style, song, and witty dialogue. *Campaspe* (1584) and *Endymion* (1588) are typical of Lyly's plays. Shakespeare's romantic comedies show the influence of Lyly's work. LAWRENCE J. ROSS

LYMPHATIC SYSTEM, *lihm FAT ihk,* is a network of small vessels that resemble blood vessels. The lymphatic system returns fluid from body tissues to the blood stream. This process is necessary because fluid pressure in the body continuously causes water, proteins, and other materials to seep out of tiny blood vessels called *capillaries.* The fluid that has leaked out, called *interstitial fluid,* bathes and nourishes body tissues.

If there were no way for excess interstitial fluid to return to the blood, the tissues would become swollen. Most of the extra fluid seeps into capillaries that have low fluid pressure. The rest returns by way of the lymphatic system and is called *lymph.* Some scientists consider the lymphatic system to be part of the circulatory system because lymph comes from the blood and returns to the blood.

The lymphatic system also serves as one of the body's defenses against infection. Harmful particles and bacteria that have entered the body are filtered out by small masses of tissue along the lymphatic vessels. These bean-shaped accumulations are called *lymph nodes.*

Parts of the Lymphatic System

Lymphatic Vessels, like blood vessels, are found throughout the body. Lymph flows from tiny vessels with many branches into larger vessels. Eventually,

LYMPHATIC SYSTEM

lymph from all but the upper right quarter of the body reaches the *thoracic duct*, the largest lymphatic vessel. The thoracic duct lies along the front of the spine. Lymph flows upward through this duct into a blood vessel near the junction of the neck and the left shoulder. Lymph from the upper right quarter of the body flows into the *right lymphatic ducts* in the right half of the chest. The lymph then drains from these ducts into the bloodstream near the junction of the neck and right shoulder.

Lymph is chemically much like plasma, the liquid part of the blood. But lymph contains only about half as much protein as plasma, because large protein molecules do not seep through blood vessel walls so easily as do some other substances. Lymph is transparent and straw-colored.

Lymph Nodes may be found at many places along the lymphatic vessels. They look like bumps and have diameters from $\frac{1}{25}$ to 1 inch (1 to 25 millimeters). The term *node* comes from the Latin word *nodus*, meaning *knot*, and lymph nodes resemble knots in a "string" of lymphatic vessels. The nodes are bunched together in certain areas, especially in the neck and armpits, above the groin, and near various organs and large blood vessels. Lymph nodes contain large cells called *macrophages* that absorb harmful matter and dead tissue.

Lymphocytes are a kind of white blood cell produced in the lymph nodes. They defend the body against infection. When abnormal cells or materials from outside the body pass into the lymph nodes, lymphocytes in the nodes produce substances called *antibodies*. The antibodies either destroy the abnormal or foreign matter or make it harmless. See IMMUNITY.

Large numbers of lymphocytes are found in the lymph nodes and in lymph itself. They outnumber all other kinds of cells in lymph.

Lymphoid Tissue resembles the tissue of the lymph nodes. It is found in some parts of the body that are not generally considered part of the lymphatic system. For example, the adenoids and tonsils, the spleen, and the thymus consist of lymphoid tissue. This tissue produces and contains lymphocytes, and it aids in the body's defense against infection.

Work of the Lymphatic System

Return of Interstitial Fluid. Interstitial fluid is produced continuously by seepage from the capillaries. For this reason, some of the fluid must constantly be returned from body tissues to the bloodstream. If the lymphatic vessels are blocked, fluid gathers in nearby tissues and causes swelling called *edema*.

The flow of lymph, after it reaches the larger lymphatic vessels, always takes place in the same direction —toward the thoracic duct. Much of the flow, including that within the thoracic duct, is upward. Yet lymph has no pump—as the blood has the heart—to keep it moving forward. The flow is caused by pressure from muscular movement, breathing, and the pulse beat in nearby blood vessels. Valves in the larger lymphatic vessels prevent the lymph from flowing backward. These valves resemble those in the veins.

Fighting Infection. Lymphocytes and macrophages both play vital roles in fighting infection—lymphocytes

466

The Lymphatic System

The lymphatic system consists of a network of vessels throughout the body. Clusters of lymph nodes occur in the groin, neck, and armpits and near certain internal organs and blood vessels.

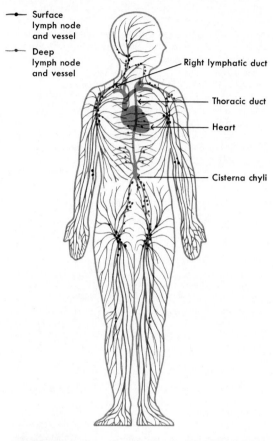

- Surface lymph node and vessel
- Deep lymph node and vessel

Right lymphatic duct
Thoracic duct
Heart
Cisterna chyli

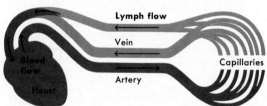

Lymph flow
Vein
Blood flow
Capillaries
Artery
Heart

Fluid Seeps Out of the Capillaries and collects in the lymphatic vessels. The collected fluid, called lymph, flows in the lymphatic vessels and drains into blood veins near the heart.

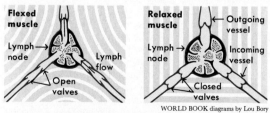

Flexed muscle
Lymph node
Lymph flow
Open valves

Relaxed muscle
Outgoing vessel
Lymph node
Incoming vessel
Closed valves

WORLD BOOK diagrams by Lou Bory

Flexing and Relaxing of Muscles near the lymphatic vessels produces a squeezing action that pushes lymph along its course. Valves in the vessels prevent lymph from flowing back.

by producing antibodies and macrophages by swallowing up foreign particles. During an infection, the lymph nodes that drain an infected area may swell and become painful. The swelling indicates that the lymphocytes and macrophages in the lymph nodes are fighting the infection and working to stop it from spreading. Such swellings are often called "swollen glands," though lymph nodes—not glands—are swollen.

Lymphocytes also flow into the bloodstream and circulate throughout the body combating infection. Many lymphocytes find their way to areas just under the skin. There they produce antibodies against bacteria and various substances that cause allergies.

Absorption of Fats. Lymphatic vessels in the wall of the intestine have an important part in the absorption of fats by the body. These vessels are called *lacteals*. In the intestine, digested fats combine with certain proteins. The resulting particles enter the lacteals and give the lymph there a milky-white color. This milky-white lymph is called *chyle*. The chyle passes through the lacteals to the *cisterna chyli*, an enlarged area in the lower part of the thoracic duct. Then the chyle and other lymph fluids flow through the thoracic duct into the bloodstream. Absorption of fats thus differs from that of carbohydrates and proteins, which blood vessels absorb and transport to the liver.

Rejection of Transplanted Tissue. Lymphocytes also take part in the body's rejection of tissue that has been transplanted from one person to another. They react against transplanted tissue in the same way that they do against other foreign material—by producing antibodies. After a person has received a transplanted organ, doctors reduce antibody production by destroying lymphocytes. However, this destruction reduces the patient's ability to fight infection.   STANLEY YACHNIN

See also BLOOD; ELEPHANTIASIS; HODGKIN'S DISEASE.

LYMPHOCYTE. See BLOOD (White Blood Cells); LYMPHATIC SYSTEM.

LYNCH, THOMAS, JR. (1749-1779), was a South Carolina signer of the Declaration of Independence. He served in South Carolina's first general assembly and in the Second Continental Congress. Lynch was born near Georgetown, S.C. He was graduated from Cambridge University and then studied law in London. In 1775, while he was serving in the Revolutionary War, a severe illness left him a semi-invalid.   RICHARD B. MORRIS

LYNCHING usually means the killing, generally by hanging, of a person by a mob in defiance of law and order. Victims of a lynching do not have a chance to defend themselves. The mob simply assumes its victims are guilty, whether or not the victims have had a trial. Lynch mobs not only promote disrespect for law, order, and basic human rights, but they also encourage mass brutality.

Most states have attempted to stop lynchings by laws. Some states prosecute under the laws against homicide, riot, and assault. Other states have specific lynch laws. But legal controls have not succeeded in preventing lynchings. One of the problems is the difficulty in picking out the leaders of the mob. Another problem is the lack of jury convictions, even with evidence. The decline in lynching in the United States is due primarily to increased public opinion against mob violence.

The term *lynching* probably originated with Charles Lynch, a planter who lived in Virginia during the 1700's. Lynch and his neighbors took the law into their own hands and punished *Tories* (British sympathizers) and others who plundered their property. The term came to be applied to physical punishment such as whipping and tarring and feathering.

In pioneer communities on the far western frontier, many lynch mobs punished persons for horse stealing, highway robbery, or murder. Lynchings began to take the form of hangings. During this period, people took the law into their own hands because there was no duly established legal authority. With the establishment of law and order throughout the United States, lynch mobs began to act in opposition to the law, instead of supporting it.

Before 1890, most lynching victims were white. Since then, most lynchings have occurred in the South, and the victims have usually been blacks. About 4,752 lynchings occurred between 1882 and 1968, including 1,307 whites and 3,445 blacks. The peak year for these killings was 1892, with 230 victims. From 1957 to 1968, there were seven lynchings. No recorded lynchings have taken place since 1968. New England is the only section of the United States in which no lynchings have ever occurred.   MARVIN E. WOLFGANG

See also WELLS-BARNETT, IDA BELL.

LYNDON B. JOHNSON LIBRARY. See TEXAS (Places to Visit); AUSTIN (picture).

LYNDON B. JOHNSON SPACE CENTER. See JOHNSON SPACE CENTER.

LYNEN, FEODOR (1911-1979), a German chemist, carried out experiments that revealed the chemical changes performed by enzymes upon fatty acids. For this work, Lynen shared the 1964 Nobel Prize for physiology or medicine with an American biochemist, Konrad Bloch. Their findings showed how the body makes and uses cholesterol and fatty acids. This was considered an important step in controlling certain circulatory diseases. Lynen was born in Munich.

LYNN, JAMES THOMAS (1927-   ), served as U.S. secretary of housing and urban development from 1973 to 1975. From 1975 to 1977, he served as director of the Office of Management and Budget under President Gerald R. Ford.

Lynn was born in Cleveland. He graduated from Western Reserve (now Case Western Reserve) University in 1948 and from the Harvard University Law School in 1951. He then joined Cleveland's largest law firm. In 1969, Lynn was named general counsel of the U.S. Department of Commerce. He was appointed undersecretary of commerce in 1971.   CHARLES BARTLETT

LYNX, *lihngks*, is a wild animal that belongs to the cat family. Lynxes are considerably smaller than such other wild cats as leopards and mountain lions. Most lynxes weigh from 15 to 25 pounds (6 to 11 kilograms), though some lynxes weigh as much as 45 pounds (20 kilograms).

Lynxes live in parts of Africa, Asia, Europe, and North America. The *Canada lynx* ranges across the Northern States, Canada, and Alaska. The *European lynx* was once common in Europe and northern Asia, but it is now scarce. The African lynx is called the *caracal*.

The Siberian Lynx, like the other lynxes, is a large and powerfully built wild cat with tufted ears.

Holisher

The lynx's fur grows long all over its body. The fur is light gray or grayish brown and long and silky. It is spotted and striped with a darker shade. The fur is valuable for scarves and ladies' jackets. Lynxes have stubby tails and long tufts of hair on their pointed ears.

Lynxes live in forests or in rocky, brush-covered places. They hunt mainly at night and feed primarily on snowshoe rabbits and other small animals. Lynxes kill great numbers of harmful rodents and rabbits and so are helpful to people. When their usual prey is scarce, hungry lynxes will kill foxes and even deer, as well as some domestic animals. In winter, the huge feet of the lynx serve as snowshoes and enable the animal to run swiftly over the snow.

Lynxes sleep in caves or hollow trees. They like to climb trees and lie stretched out on a limb. Young lynxes look like domestic kittens. The mother lynx fights viciously anything that comes near her young. She bears from one to five babies in a litter.

Scientific Classification. Lynxes belong to the cat family, Felidae. The Canada lynx is genus *Lynx*, species *L. canadensis*.   ERNEST S. BOOTH

See also BOBCAT; CARACAL; WILDCAT.

LYON, *lyawn* (pop. 413,095; met. area pop. 1,220,-844), is the third largest city in France. Only Paris and Marseille have more people. Lyon lies in southeastern France (see FRANCE [political map]). The city serves as the capital of the Rhône *department* (administrative district) and the Rhône-Alpes region.

The Rhône and Saône rivers meet at Lyon, dividing the city into three parts. Busy docks and warehouses line the riverfront. Lyon's main commercial and entertainment district lies on a peninsula between the rivers. On the west bank of the Saône is the city's oldest section, which has narrow streets and towering houses.

The newest area of Lyon is on the east bank of the Rhône. It includes factories, a large university, and many attractive residences. Among Lyon's major landmarks are the Church of St. Martin d'Ainey and the Cathedral of St. Jean, both of which date from the 1100's.

Lyon is famous for the manufacture of textiles, especially silk and rayon. The city has many spinning, weaving, and dyeing plants. Other industries in Lyon produce automobiles, chemicals, metal goods, and such agricultural products as wine and cheese.

In 43 B.C., Roman soldiers established a colony on the site of what is now Lyon. During the 1400's, Lyon became a prosperous trading center. The introduction of silk manufacturing from Italy during the 1500's brought greater, and long-lasting, prosperity. Lyon was a center of French resistance to German occupation forces during World War II (1939-1945).   MARK KESSELMAN

LYON, *LY uhn,* **MARY** (1797-1849), pioneered in providing higher education for women. She founded Mount Holyoke College, which opened as Mount Holyoke Seminary in 1837, and served as president of the school until her death. She aimed, through educational opportunities, to help young women develop their

Gérard Amsellem

Lyon's Modern Buildings include the Maurice Ravel Auditorium, *left.* Named for the famous French composer, the striking building is a concert hall that seats 2,000 people. It lies in Lyon's main commercial and entertainment district.

abilities and talents and to use them in service to others. Miss Lyon became a teacher at the age of 17. With her savings, she later attended school in Amherst. She was born in Buckland, Mass. CLAUDE A. EGGERTSEN

LYRA, *LY ruh,* also called the Harp, is a small constellation of stars located west of the Northern Cross. It contains Vega, the fifth brightest star visible, excluding the sun, and the third brightest star in the northern celestial hemisphere. Because of the precession of the equinoxes, Vega will be considered the North Star in approximately 12,000 years.

Lyra has several double stars. One of them, *Epsilon Lyrae,* is visible to the keen eye as a pair of stars. Through a telescope, each of these stars is seen to be double. The Ring, or Annular Nebula, is another beautiful sight in Lyra. It is one of a class of objects that astronomers believe originated when central stars threw off great waves of gaseous material. I. M. LEVITT

See also BINARY STAR.

LYRE, *lyr,* is an ancient stringed musical instrument that resembles a small harp. It has a bowl- or box-shaped frame with two arms extending upward. A crossbar is attached to the top of the arms. The instrument has 4 to 10 strings, which extend from the crossbar to the base of the frame. The player plucks the strings with the

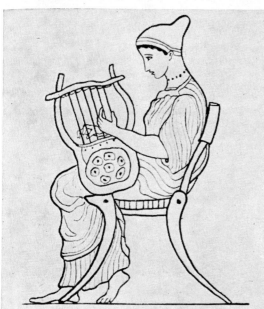

Woman Playing a Greek Lyre. This picture was painted on a vase about 350 B.C. Apollo, the Greek god of music and poetry, was usually painted holding a lyre.

fingers of one hand or with a *plectrum* (pick). The fingers of the other hand press down on the strings to set the required pitch. In Europe, some types of lyres are played with a bow instead of by plucking the strings. The sound of a lyre is amplified by a piece of cattle skin stretched tightly across the open side of the frame.

The lyre was especially popular among the ancient Greeks. It was the symbol of Apollo, the Greek god of music and poetry. The Greeks used the lyre to accompa-

ny songs and recitations. The words *lyric* and *lyrical* come from this use of the instrument. ABRAM LOFT

LYREBIRD, *LYR burd,* is one of the most unusual Australian birds. The tail of the male lyrebird has large and spreading feathers which are arranged like the ancient lyre. Two broad feathers curve upward with slender feathers in between. Normally, the tail is carried low. When the tail is raised and arched, it is about 2 feet (61 centimeters) long. The lyrebird itself is only about the size of a chicken. The tail does not reach full growth until the bird is 7 or 8 years old.

The lyrebird has brown plumage. These birds have a strong, melodious song, and they can imitate the songs of other birds. The lyrebird can fly. But it uses its wings chiefly when running and leaping. The lyrebird makes its nest on the ground, and the female lays one egg in it.

American Museum of Natural History

The Male Lyrebird proudly displays its handsome tail and sings a sweet song to attract females during the mating season.

Scientific Classification. Lyrebirds belong to the lyrebird family, Menuridae. There are two species, *Menura superba* and *M. alberti.*

RODOLPHE MEYER DE SCHAUENSEE

See also BIRD (picture: Birds of Australia and the Pacific Islands).

LYRIC POETRY. See POETRY (Lyric Poetry); GREEK LITERATURE (Lyric Poetry).

LYSANDER, *ly SAN duhr* (? -395 B.C.), was a statesman and general of the ancient Greek state of Sparta. He took command of Spartan military forces in the Aegean and the Hellespont late in the Peloponnesian War between Sparta and Athens. Through his friendship with Cyrus, son of the king of Persia, he got Persia to help build and support a fleet. In 405 B.C., Lysander commanded the final battle of the war at Aegospotami. In this famous sea battle, the new Spartan fleet destroyed the superior Athenian navy.

In charge of Sparta's foreign policy, Lysander established the government of Thirty Tyrants to rule Athens after the war. He also helped set up the government of *decarchies.* Decarchies were boards of 10 that governed in Greek states Sparta had freed from Athenian rule. Lysander was killed in battle in Boeotia in the Corinthian War. DONALD KAGAN

LYSENKO, *lih SEHNG koh,* **TROFIM DENISOVICH,** *trah FEEM deh NEE sah vihch* (1898-1976), was the most important biologist in Russia from the mid-1930's to the late 1950's. Russian dictator Joseph Stalin supported Lysenko's theories for improving farm production because they promised quick success. But the theories proved faulty, and later Russian leaders blamed them for slowing the growth of the country's agri-

469

culture. Lysenko held back Russian research in *genetics* (the science of heredity) for more than 20 years.

Lysenko believed that new species of crops could be created from the old species by altering the crops' *environment* (surroundings) and affecting the phases of their life cycles. The resulting changes would be passed to the next generation, and create improved breeds, better adjusted to the conditions of their environment. Lysenko said, in effect, that organisms could be "trained" to change. He rejected the idea that units called *genes* determine heredity. His ideas have been rejected by present-day biologists.

Lysenko was born in Karlovka, a village near Poltava. His parents were farmers.   JOHN A. BARBOUR

LYSERGIC ACID DIETHYLAMIDE. See LSD.

LYSIAS, *LIHS ee uhs* (459?-380? B.C.), was a great orator of ancient Greece. He wrote more than 200 speeches and helped establish the study of oratory.

Lysias was born in the Greek colony of Syracuse in Sicily. His father was a wealthy shield manufacturer. Lysias moved to Athens in Greece and became a strong supporter of that city's democratic government.

Nearby Sparta conquered Athens in the Peloponnesian War (431-404 B.C.). The Spartans installed a powerful group of men, known as the *Thirty Tyrants*, to govern Athens. Lysias was arrested by the government because of his wealth and democratic beliefs, but he escaped into exile.

Lysias returned to Athens when democracy was restored in 403 B.C. That year, he attacked the cruelty and corruption of the Thirty Tyrants in one of his most famous speeches, "Against Eratosthenes."   DONALD KAGAN

LYSINE. See NUTRITION (International Concern).

LYSIPPUS, *ly SIHP uhs*, was a famous Greek sculptor of the 300's B.C. He produced bronze statues ranging in size from small figurines to colossal works such as the *Zeus* of Tarentum, which stood 60 feet (18 meters) high. He changed the rules of sculpture for the proportions of the human body, making the heads smaller and the bodies slenderer. He won praise for the extreme delicacy of his work in even the smallest details.

An ancient story tells that Lysippus put a gold coin in a box each time he sold a statue. When the box was opened after his death, it supposedly contained more than 1,500 coins. However, until 1964 it was thought that none of his statues had survived. In that year, Italian fishermen caught an ancient Greek bronze statue in their nets. An Italian scholar identified the work as a statue of an athlete made by Lysippus. The statue is now in the J. Paul Getty Museum in Malibu, California.   H. L. STOW

LYSOSOME. See CELL (The Cytoplasm; diagram: The Structures of a Cell).

LYSOZYME. See FLEMING, SIR ALEXANDER.

LYTE, HENRY FRANCIS (1793-1847), a British clergyman, is best remembered for the hymns he wrote, including "Abide with Me" and "Jesus, I My Cross Have Taken." For 25 years, he served as clergyman in the small fishing village of Lower Brixham on the Devonshire coast. In this village, Lyte developed a Sunday school of 800 students and trained more than 70 teachers. Lyte worked constantly, preaching and visiting the members of his parish. He is said to have written "hymns for his little ones, hymns for fishermen, and hymns for sufferers."

Lyte was born in Ednam, Scotland, near Kelso. He attended Trinity College in Dublin and was ordained as a minister in the Anglican Church when he was 21 years old.   LEONARD W. VAN CAMP

LYTTON, BARON. See BULWER-LYTTON, EDWARD GEORGE EARLE LYTTON.

LZ-1. See AIRSHIP (The Zeppelins).